ALEXANDRIA CITY

AND

ARLINGTON COUNTY, VIRGINIA

RECORDS INDEX

Volume 1

WESLEY E. PIPPENGER

HERITAGE BOOKS
2020

HERITAGE BOOKS
AN IMPRINT OF HERITAGE BOOKS, INC.

Books, CDs, and more—Worldwide

For our listing of thousands of titles see our website
at
www.HeritageBooks.com

Published 2020 by
HERITAGE BOOKS, INC.
Publishing Division
5810 Ruatan Street
Berwyn Heights, Md. 20740

International Standard Book Numbers
Paperbound: 978-1-58549-718-8
Clothbound: 978-0-7884-8999-0

INTRODUCTION

The purpose of this index is to assist researchers in locating records of individuals within the masses of paperwork created by the various courts of the City of Alexandria and Alexandria County, Virginia. Individual records are not themselves indexed, rather this index identifies separate records within larger groups. For example, a bond book may contain bonds for the appointment of officials, ministers, estate administrators and estate executors, or for issuing a merchant or tavern license. This index will list each of the bonds in the book by citing the person bonded (or the subject of the bond), but will not list each of the names listed on each bond (witnesses, sureties). Additional records will be added as volumes in this series as they are consulted. This first volume includes over 25,000 entries.

People who created records were not always of the highest education or did not have the nicest handwriting (spelling in some records is very bad). Although we may know different based on other sources, the record's spelling is preserved here as it is interpreted by the compiler. Researchers should search for alternate spellings, even for the simplest names. A helpful explanation of this is found under comments for the 1800 Census.

The location column will show both "Alexandria" and "Arlington." The intent here is to differentiate in two ways, geographically and by library classification. First, we presently have a courthouse in the City of Alexandria, and one on Ft. Meyer heights in Arlington County. Second, we have differing catalogue descriptions of original records and microfilm within the collections of the Library of Virginia in Richmond. For the latter, the Library maintains the majority of these records, both original and on microfilm, under the category "Arlington County." This is primarily because the original records were transferred to that institution from the Arlington County courthouse throughout the 1950's through 1980's. This classification of "Arlington County," oftentimes has little or no bearing on whether the records cover the City of Alexandria, or the former Alexandria County, and thus should all be consulted.

Wesley E. Pippenger
Arlington, Virginia
Summer 2001

RECORDS FEATURED

Given below is descriptive information of the reference codes used in this work. If microfilm of the original records was used or is available, the microfilm number is given in brackets. All microfilm is available from the Library of Virginia, and is generally catalogued as "Arlington County" records, unless otherwise noted.

TAX LISTS. There are several series of tax lists: land, land and personal property, and personal property. The Personal Property Tax lists for 1791, 1792, 1793, 1794, 1797 are not known to have survived in the format below. For those we do have, the age of white male as tithable shifts from over 21 years to over 16 years. The final column often notes whether the taxed person possessed a chariot or carriage. The originals records are at the Library of Virginia. The original for the 1791 land tax list, showing rents due, has not been located, but a copy is at the Alexandria Library.

Code	Records Featured
Tax L 1787	Land Tax Book (Auditor's Copy). The earliest of this series, and was prepared by James Hendricks, Commissioner for the district of Alexandria. Column headings are below. The original is in rough alphabetical order and has small page numbers at the bottom of each page. Owners often have houses and/or lots at multiple locations. [Reel 348]: Owners names of houses & lots By whom occupied Where situated Rents: rents in fee, annual rents Total amount of rents Other similar records of this type will be included in additional volumes of this compiler's series.
Tax L 1790	More than one copy exists for what appears to be the 1790 Land Tax list. The state Auditor's copy, dated 1790, is part of the regular microfilm series of land tax lists [LVA Reel 348]. It is inscribed: "I Peter Wagener, Clerk of the Court of Hustings, for the Town of Alexandria, do hereby certify that the Foregoing List of Taxable Property is a true copy, taken from the Original, examined by the Vouchers returned by the Commissioner. Given under my hand this 29th day of October 1790. [signed] P. Wagener, Cl." The record is 13 pages. Another is dated 1791, with precisely the same information, has better spelling. It is dated 28 February 1791. Column headings are ""Owners Names of Houses & Lots," "By Whom Occupied," "On What Streets Situated," "Rents," "Amount Rents." The record is 13 pages, which are numbered by this compiler. Entries are roughly alphabetical by initial letter. The final page of the 1791 copy is noted "Alexandria. I do hereby Certifie that the foregoing List or return, of Tax on Houses and Lots, in the Town of Alexandria, is a true Copy, Exd. By the Vouchers retd. By the Com., this 28 February 1791. Test. G. Deneale." The 1791 copy appears to be a transcript, and perhaps a minor revision, of the 1790 copy.

Code	Records Featured
	Names of owners and occupants are given in this index. The 1790 record reflects a total of £6,265.5.0 in rents due, while the math of the 1791 record reflects a total of £6,264.4.4.0 in rents due.
	This data was previously published in different form as the "Alexandria City Directory, 1791," by Marjorie D. Tallichet of the Alexandria Library's former Lloyd House. This data is **not** a city directory, but a land tax list, evidenced by it's form of listing rents due for the year. The purpose of taking the list was to determine taxes due. A photocopy of the original 1791 list is filed with Tallichet's backup at the Alexandria Library. The original of the 1790 record is at the Library of Virginia, while the original of the 1791 record has not been located by this compiler.
Tax L 1795	The 1795 Land Tax list, copy of the Auditor of Public Accounts. Column headings are "Names of owners of houses," "By whom occupied," "On which street situate," "Rents," "Amount of rents," and "Tax." The record is 34 pages, which are numbered by this compiler. Entries are roughly alphabetical by initial letter. [LVA Reel 348; Alexandria Library Reel 26]
Tax PP 1795	The 1795 Personal Property Tax list, was taken by William Halley, Fairfax. The following column headings are used [LVA Reel 349; LDS Reel 1905755]: Persons Names Chargeable with the Tax No. of white males over 16 No. of Blacks above 12 & under 16 No. of Blacks above 16 No. or Horses, Mares, Colts & Mules No. of Coaches & Chariots No. of Phaetons & Stage Waggons No. of Two Wheeled Riding Chairs No. of Ordinary Licenses No. of Billiard Tables
Tax PP 1796	The 1796 Personal Property Tax list, taken by Hugh West, has the following headings [LVA Reel 349; LDS Reel 1905755]: Date of receiving lists from individual Persons Names chargeable with the Tax White Males above 16 years old Blacks above 12 years old Blacks above 16 years old Horses, Mares, Colts & Mules Ordinary Licenses Billiard Tables Stud Horses Rates of Covering Coaches, Chariots & Post Chaises Other Riding, 4-wheel Carriages Riding Carriages with 2 Wheels

Code	Records Featured
Tax LP 1796	The 1796 Land and Personal Property Book was recorded by William Halley, and finalized April 1, 1796. The list is roughly alphabetical, without page numbers. This compiler has assigned page numbers. Column headings are [LVA Reel 349]: Proprietors names Houses & lots Assessed value Male tithables Billiard tables Tavern licenses Horses Dogs Carts Waggons Drays Riding chairs Four-wheeled carriages Total amount of tax Other similar records of this type will be included in additional volumes of this compiler's series.
Tax PP 1798	Columns for the 1798 Personal Property Tax list are the same as 1796. List taken by Hugh West. Following the 1798 personal property tax list is found a "Return of Licenses for wholesale & retail Merchants within the District of Hugh West, Commissioner of Alexandria, State of Virginia." The list contains four columns [LVA Reel 349; LDS Reel 1905755]: Name Place [not labeled, entries are "Alexa."] Dollars per license [most entries are "15"] [Blank] A final column is used for company licenses, although not labeled, sometimes contains a value of "40".
Tax PP 1799	The Personal Property Tax list for 1799 is taken by Wm. Lanphier, Jr., Commissioner of Revenue, and is signed October 25, 1799. Column headings are modified from the previous year, and are as below. The list totals 1,001 white males above 16 years old, 95 blacks above 12 and under 16 years, 12 chariots, 64 phaetons, and 62 2-wheeled riding chairs. [LVA Reel 349; LDS Reel 1905755]: Date of Receipt of Lists &c. Persons names chargeable with the tax White males above 16 years old Blacks above 12 & under 16 Blacks above 16 years old Horses, Mares, Colts & Mules Ordinary License Coaches, Chariots &c. Other riding 4-wheel carriages

Code	Records Featured

Riding carriages with 2 wheels

Following the 1799 personal property tax list is a list of merchant licenses in the town of Alexandria granted on the accounts of Mr. Lewis Summers, deputy to John Moss the Sheriff of Fairfax County in the year 1799. The inside cover reads, *List of Licenses granted on the Receipts of Lewis Summers, Collector of the Revenue, for John Moss, Sheriff of Fairfax, to Merchants in the Town of Alexandria, by William Lanphier, Commissioner, for the year 1799.* The columns separate a $15 fee for retail licenses (r), a $40 fee for wholesale licenses (w), and a total fee. These designations follow the page number reference.

Tax PP 1800 — The 1800 Personal Property Tax list, within the district of Wm. Lanphier, Commissioner in the Town of Alexandria, has column headings as below. The 31-page list totals 465 slaves above age 16 years, 14 ordinary licenses, 52 coaches and riding chairs, 28 phaetons and stage waggons, and 58 2-wheeled riding chairs. Of the white people enumerated, 879 were white male above 16. [LVA Reel 349; LDS Reel 1905755]:

Date of receiving lists
Persons names chargeable with the tax
White [male] above 16
Slaves above 16
Slaves between 12 & 16
Horses, mares, mules &c.
Ordinary licenses
Coaches, chariots &c.
Phaetons & stage waggons
Two-wheeled riding chairs

Following the 1800 tax list, is found a list of licenses granted to merchants in the town of Alexandria in the year 1800, to the 15th of September, according to the receipts of the office of Deneale's deputies. The list is similar to that found for 1799. The columns separate a $15 fee for retail licenses (r), a $40 fee for wholesale licenses (w), and a total fee. These designations follow the page number reference which begin with 54(10).

CENSUS RECORDS

Code	Records Featured

1795 — Special Census of 1795, Fourth Ward. Two versions exist. Both are in the file with Mrs. Tallichet's work on the 1791 tax list (or "directory" as she styled it). The versions are different, and both are difficult to read because or either poor or small handwriting. Version one, with the most accurate spelling, contains 9 pages. The final page notes "Census taken by George Coryell & William Bushby, Wardens of the 4th or South District of Alexandria." This is used as the base source, and compared to the other. Version two, with poor spelling and elementary handwriting, contains 11 pages. Entries from version two are as

Code Records Featured

noted here as "1795(4a)." The two versions are *not* in the same order. The column headings are ["Name,"] "Occupation," "Whites Above 16," "Whites Under 16," Blacks Above 16," Blacks Under 16," and "Total." The original records have not been located by this compiler. Both copies are filed at the Alexandria Library with Mrs. Tallichet's backup to her work she styled the "1791 Directory" (see comments above under the 1790 Land Tax list).

1796 Special Census of 1796, Third Ward. Taken by Aaron Hewes and John Korn, with a total of 1,841 persons listed. Column headings are "Householders & Heads of Family," "White Persons in Each Family," "Trade or Occupation," "Numbers of Blacks," and "Total." The first column notes whether a wife and children are included. This compiler has considered that data, as well as occupation, into a single entry, with the wife as "w" and number of children in parenthesis ( ), followed by the number of blacks. For example, Ephraim Evans, w (5)1, chairmaker, means the head of household had a wife and five children, one black, and was occupied as a chairmaker. The seven pages are not numbered in the original. Spelling is not particularly good in the record, and it is presumed that the multiple use of "backer" means baker. [Alexandria Library Reel 552]

1799 Special Census of 1799, Second Ward. Original at the Library of Virginia, inscribed *A Census of the Inhabitants of the second Ward of the Town of Alexandria being that part which lies to the South of King Street & from the River Potowmak* [sic] *to its Western limits.* Column headings are "Names of Housekeepers," "Occupation," "No. of Children," "Names of Boarders," "Occupation" [of Boarder], "No. of Apprentices," "House Servants," "Slaves Above 16," "Slaves Under 16," "Total Slaves," and "Total." Although the original 20 pages are not numbered, this compiler has assigned numbers with "A" and "B" for the record's left and right page faces. Inscribed on the last page: *This within is a correct list of the Inhabitants of the second Ward of the Town of Alexandria according to which it appears that the whole number of inhabitants of said Ward amounts to Three thousand & seventy.* Signed Wm. Milnor, Warden, Alexa., May 1st 1799. In addition, there were 366 slaves. [Alexandria City Reel 51; LDS Reel 1887711]

1800 Special Census of 1800, Fourth Ward. Original at the Library of Virginia. Inscribed *Robert Abercrombie's Ward Book, beginning in the senter of duke street all that part of the town being south of the street as above Mentioned is cald the fourth Ward, Runing east & West from the River potomak to the boundrie line of the corporation.* Note that Mr. Abercrombie's spelling is poor.

Unfortunately, *very* poor spelling continues with the names listed throughout. Familiar names like Smoot are "Smute," or Muir as "Mure" or "Muyr," Lloyd as "Lawyed," Samuel as "Samul," Maffit as "Morfit," or Dalton as "Dolton," Cartwright as "Carterite," etc. Occupations are also poorly spelled, and we find clerk as "clarke," merchant as "murchant," seaman as "seemen," semptress [seamstress] as "sumpster," mariner as "marrener," ship carpenter as "shiperpenter," laborer as "labourrer," schoolmaster as "scoolmaster," and the like.

Pages are left and right face per number. Although the original are not numbered, this compiler has assigned numbers "A" and "B" for the record's 16 sets of left and right page faces. The record begins with a right face with different column headings from the others, indicating that it may have been for another ward. Column headings for the remaining pages are: "Heads of Families," "Profession or Trade," "Boarders and Hirelings," Trade or Occupation," Children," Names of Servants & Apprentices,"Persons of Colour Not Slaves," "Slaves," "Free Persons Above 16 Years of Age," and "Total in Each Family." For those people listed in the "Free Persons Above 16 Years of Age" column, this compiler identifies them in this record as "Resident." [Alexandria City Reel 51; LDS Reel 1887711]

1808 Special Census of 1808, submitted March 23, 1808, by John Mandeville, Superintendent of Police, for the town of Alexandria, Wards 1, 2, 3 and 4. The original record, at the Library of Virginia, contains 31 pages in tabular form. Column headings are "Names of House Keepers," "Occupations," "White Males Above the Age of 16," "All Other White Persons," "Free Males of Colour Above the Age of 16," "All Other Free Persons of Colour," "Slaves," "Total," "No. of Stories," "No. of Bucket(t)s," and "Remarks." Each page number includes a left and right face. Summary statistics show enumeration as: 1st Ward (1,921), 2nd Ward (1,661), 3rd Ward (1,523), and 4th Ward (1,438), for a total of 6,543 persons. Of this number, 677 free people of colour, 1,270 slaves, and 4,596 white persons. Recapitulation of previous enumerations (the original records of which are not known to have survived) shows 6,377 persons in 1805; 5,915 in 1806; and 6,208 in 1807. For a complete transcript of the 1808 Census see Wesley E. Pippenger, Alexandria, Virginia 1808 Census (Wards One, Two, Three and Four) (Westminster, Md.: Willow Bend Books, 2000). Reference gives year (ward):page, i.e. 1808(4):10A. [Alexandria City Reel 51; LDS Reel 1887711]

1810 Special Census of 1810, for the town of Alexandria, Wards 1, 2, 3 and 4. Column headings are "Names," "Occupations," "White Males Over 16," "White Males Under 16," "White Females Over 16," "White Females Under 16," "Coloured Males Over 16," "Coloured Males Under 16," "Coloured Females Over 16," "Coloured Females Under 16," "Coloured Male Slaves Over 16," "Coloured Male Slaves Under 16," "Coloured Female Slaves Over 16," and "Coloured Female Slaves Under 16." Pages are left and right face per number. The original pages are numbered on the left face and in sets for each ward. Each ward is followed by summary statistics, with grand totals at the end of the fourth ward. Statistics show a total of 4,968 white inhabitants, 868 free people of color, and 2,251 slaves. Unlike earlier census records, this one lists only the name of head of household. Reference gives year (ward):page, i.e. 1810(4):09A. [Alexandria City Reel 51; LDS Reel 1887711]

ESTATE ACCOUNTS. Originals are at the Library of Virginia.

Code Records Featured

AB1 Account Book No. 1, 1810-1814 (Guardians Accounts, Etc.), unpaged index, 355 pages. [Reel 26]

Code	Records Featured
AB2	Account Book No. 2, 1814-1817 (Guardians Accounts, Etc.), unpaged index, 429 pages. [Reel 26]
AB3	Account Book No. 3, 1817-1819 (Guardians Accounts, Etc.), unpaged index, 406 pages. [Reel 26]
AB4	Account Book No. 4, 1819-1821 (Guardians Accounts, Etc.), unpaged index, 352 pages. [Reel 26]
AB5	Account Book No. 5, 1821-1825 (Guardians Accounts, Etc.), unpaged index, 424 pages. [Reel 27]
AB6	Account Book No. 6, 1825-1830 (Guardians Accounts, Etc.), unpaged index, pages 1-294 and 395-526. [Reel 27]
AB7	Account Book No. 7, 1830-1839 (Guardians Accounts, Etc.), unpaged index, 373 pages. [Reel 28]
AB8	Account Book No. 8, 1839-1844 (Guardians Accounts, Etc.), unpaged index, 506 pages [Reel 28]
AB9	Account Book No. 9, 1844-1850 (Guardians Accounts, Etc.), unpaged index, 324 pages. [Reel 28]

ORDINARY BONDS AND LICENSES. The individual documents in the books called Ordinary Bonds and Licenses show original signatures of the licensed ordinary keeper as well as witnesses and sureties. Applicants are licensed to keep an ordinary at Alexandria, in the District of Columbia (or the County of Alexandria), unless otherwise noted. It is not always clear if the ordinary was still located within the town limits which is sometimes considered to also be within the boundaries of the county. In most instances the location in the original record is given as "Town of Alexandria," but not always.

OBL1	Ordinary Bond and License Book, 1802-1806, unpaged [Reel 49; County Reel 2008]
OBL2	Ordinary Bond and License Book, 1806-1811, unpaged [Reel 49; County Reel 2008]
OBL3	Ordinary Bond and License Book, 1820-1824, unpaged [Reel 50; County Reel 2009A]
OBL4	Ordinary Bond and License Book, 1825-1832, unpaged [Reel 50; County Reel 2009A]
OBL5	Ordinary Bond and License Book, 1833-1839, unpaged [Reel 50; County Reel 2009A]
OBL6	Ordinary Bond and License Book, 1841-1850, unpaged [Reel 50; County Reel 2009A]

OTHER

Code	Records Featured
ABB	County Court Administrator's Bond Book, 1847-1850, unpaged. Original at the Library of Virginia, Bar Code 1100294. [Reel 49; County Reel 2008]
ACO	Admiralty Court Orders, 1801-1827, 275 pages, index. Pages 110-111 are not on the film. [Reel 54; County Reel 2013]
ACR	Admiralty Court Records, 1806-1830, 91 pages, no index [Reel 54; County Reel 2013]
BB	County Court General Bond Book, 1850-1855, unpaged. Original at the Library of Virginia, Bar Code 1100261. [Reel 49; County Reel 2008]
CF	Chancery File. At the time of this work, bundled chancery papers from both the City of Alexandria and Arlington County are being flat-folded under separate grants of the Virginia Circuit Court Records Preservation Program of the Library of Virginia. Chancery files from 1847 forward are at the Arlington County Courthouse. Previous ones, are mixed with other court papers of Alexandria County and the town of Alexandria, and catalogued at the Library of Virginia as "judgments." Chancery files for the City of Alexandria begin in 1870, and are located in the Circuit Clerk's office on King Street.
CLOB	Common Law Order Books, series at Arlington Courthouse [Volume:page]

Complete Records Series. Originals are at the Library of Virginia.

CRA	Complete Records (Wills, Bonds, Inventories, Etc.) A, 1786-1800 [Hustings Court, Town of Alexandria], unpaged index, 363 pages [Reel 7]
CRB	Complete Records, Vol. B, 1801, 358 pages [Reel 7]
CRC	Complete Records, Vol. C, 1801-1802, 310 pages [Reel 7a]
CRD	Complete Records, Vol. D, 1801-1803, 216 pages [Reel 7a]
CRE	Complete Records, Vol. E, 1805-1808, 355 pages [Reel 7a]
CRF	Complete Records, Vol. F, 1804-1811, 349 pages [Reel 7b]
CRG	Complete Records, Vol. G, 1808-1809, 440 pages [Reel 7b]
CRH	Complete Records, Vol. H, 1810-1811, 571 pages [Reel 7c]
CRI	Complete Records, Vol. I, 1811-1814, 431 pages [Reel 7c]
CRK	Complete Records, Vol. K, 1814-1819, 504 pages [Reel 7d]
CRL	Complete Records, Vol. L, 1817-1822, 604 pages [Reel 7d]

Code	Records Featured
DB	Deed Books, series at Arlington Courthouse or City of Alexandria Circuit Court Clerk's office. Originals for Alexandria County are located at the Arlington Courthouse. Originals for the City of Alexandria have been cut apart for digital filming, and are not accessible to researchers. [Volume:page]
E	Exemplifications and Plats, Frederick County, 1747-c.1850's. Original at the Library of Virginia, Bar Code 1016870.
EBB	County Court Executor's Bond Book, 1847-1850, unpaged. Original at the Library of Virginia, Bar Code 1100293. [Reel 49; County Reel 2008]
FBB	Fiduciary Bond Book, 1851-1877, 43 pages [Reel 49; County Reel 2008]
File#	Loose Original Wills, Arlington Courthouse; jacket number
GBB	County Court Guardian's Bond Book, 1848-1850, unpaged. Original at the Library of Virginia, Bar Code 1100302. [Reel 49; County Reel 2008]
ID	Insolvent Debtors, 1826-1833, 422 pages, index. Records typically detail proceedings of the insolvent debtor, list property, and copy an indenture of the property in trust. [Reel 52; County Reel 2011]
ID1	Insolvent Debtors, 1833-1846, 283 pages, index. Records typically detail proceedings of the insolvent debtor, list property, and copy an indenture of the property in trust. [Reel 52; County Reel 201]
ID2	Schedule of Insolvent Debtors, Volume A, 1810-1819, 495 pages, index. Page numbering skips from 229 to 330 in error. [Reels 224 and 225; County Reel 2018]
ID3	Insolvent Debtors, 1803-1810, pages 1-273 (partial), index [Reel 50; County Reel 2009]
LSA	Alexandria County, Virginia Land Suits A, 1834-1843, 167 pages. Original at the Library of Virginia. [Reel 25]
OCR1801	Orphans Court Records Minute Book, 1801-1805, unpaged index, 324 pages [Reel 29]
OCR1811	Orphans Court Records Minute Book, 1811-1817, unpaged index, 356 pages. Contains numerous apprenticeship indentures. [Reel 29]
OCR1822	Orphans Court Records Minute Book, 1822-1830, unpaged index, 173 pages [Reel 29]
OCR1842	Orphans Court Records Minute Book, 1842-1847, unpaged index, 224 pages [Reel 48; County Reels 2007 and 2008]
OT	Court of Oyer and Terminer, Town of Alexandria, Opinions, 1794-1800, unpaged, date order (DD/MM/YY). Many of the entries deal either with persons who are presently in the jail [gaol] and must post funds to be set free,

Code	Records Featured
	or persons who admit they are indebted to "his Excellency" [Henry Lee]. In the latter case, a sum is levied of their respective goods and chattles, lands and tenements, upon condition that they make personal appearance before the court to give evidence against [a person] to be indicted for a crime. The record appears to be in the handwriting of Amos Alexander, whose signature appears at the end. Library of Virginia Bar Code 1100021. Also see Examination of Criminals, Volume 3, 1794-1800, pages 1-26. [Reel 53]
PA	Circuit Court of the District of Columbia and Alexandria County, Record of Pleas, Liber A, 1801-1802, 357 pages, index [Reels 54 and 55]
RA	Reports of Aliens, 1801-1832. Page heading is inscribed, *Abstract of Reports of Aliens made to the Clerk of the Circuit Court of the District of Columbia for the County of Alexandria, who have arrived at the said Town of Alexandria in the District aforesaid, with an Intention of residing within the United States and under the Jurisdiction of the same from the Twenty fourth day of June 1801, Eighteen Hundred & one.* Column headings are: "Dates of Report," "Names of Persons Reported," "Sex," "Place of Birth," "Age," "Nation," "Place of Allegiance or Citizenship," "Condition or Occupation," "Place of Actual or Intended Residence," and "By Whom Report Made." Date given is date of report (DD/MM/YY), i.e. RA:06/07/01, is July 6th 1801. [Reel 52; County Reel 2011]

WILL BOOKS. The naming of will books is similar amongst the will books for the town's early Hustings Court, Corporation Court, and Circuit Court, as well as Alexandria (now Arlington) County's Circuit Court and County Court. Because of this, it is often necessary to match both the book coding and the dates. Original wills for Alexandria (now Arlington) County, from 1800 to the present, and the City of Alexandria, from 1800 to 1870, are at the Arlington County Courthouse. These are filed chronologically and have a file jacket number. Original wills for the City of Alexandria after 1870 are filed with the Clerk of the Circuit Court in Alexandria. Data from additional Corporation Court and Circuit Court will books from the City of Alexandria will be presented in a future volume.

Code	Records Featured
WBA	Orphans Court Will Book A, 1800-1804, unpaged index, 336 pages. Original at the City of Alexandria. [Alexandria Reel 38]
WBB	Orphans Court Will Book B, 1804-1807, unpaged index, 548 pages. Original at the City of Alexandria. [Alexandria Reel 38]
WBC	Orphans Court Will Book C, 1807-1810, unpaged index, 542 pages. Original at the City of Alexandria. [Alexandria Reel 38]
WB1	Orphans Court Will Book 1, 1810-1815, unpaged index, 345 pages. Original at the City of Alexandria. [Alexandria Reel 39]

Code	Records Featured
WB1	Corporation Court Will Book 1, 1870-1892, 602 pages. Original at the City of Alexandria.
WB2	Orphans Court Will Book 2, 1815-1821, unpaged index, 432 pages. Original at the City of Alexandria. [Alexandria Reel 39]
WB2	Corporation Court Will Book 2, 1891-1905, 600 pages. To 1900 only, using pages 1-409. Original at the City of Alexandria.
WB3	Orphans Court Will Book 3, 1821-1831, unpaged index, 393 pages. Original at the City of Alexandria. [Alexandria Reel 39]
WB4	Orphans Court Will Book 4, 1831-1846, unpaged index, 432 pages. Original at the City of Alexandria. [Alexandria Reel 40]
WB5	County Court Will Book 5, 1847-1851, unpaged index, 341 pages. Original at the City of Alexandria. [Alexandria Reel 40]
WB6	County Court Will Book 6, 1851 [1849]-1855, 463 pages. Original at the City of Alexandria. [Alexandria Reel 40]
WB7	County Court Will Book 7, 1855-1860, 568 pages. Original at the City of Alexandria. [Alexandria Reel 41]
WB8	County Court Will Book 8, 1860-1867, 576 pages. Original at the City of Alexandria. [Alexandria Reel 41]
WB9	Will Book 9, 1858[67]-1878, 522 pages, index. Original at Arlington Courthouse. [Arlington Reel 6]
WB10	Will Book 10, 1879-1901, 472 pages, index. Original at Arlington Courthouse.

LOOSE PAPERS AT THE LIBRARY OF VIRGINIA. A number of original records series at the Library of Virginia, Records Center, have been consulted. Where the original loose record was found, the Location volume includes "LVA-LP." In some cases an original record was found where a corresponding book entry was not readily identified. Because a complete location, including series description, box and folder location, is lengthy, the burden is left with users of this guide to determine in which series the record is maintained. The key Record Center identifier to each box is a bar code which is given here in brackets, i.e. *BC1100294*. A description of the LVA-LP series consulted is below.

Estate Accounts (and Wills), 1801-1897, 24 cu. ft. [Bar Codes 1043674 to 1043678, 1043680 to 1043687, 1043689, and 1043691]

Estate Accounts and Wills, Alexander-Zimmerman, 1786-1897, 2 cu. ft. [Bar Codes 1043696 and 1043697]

Estate Accounts, Petitions, Guardian Accounts, Power of Attorney, 1832-1850, 2 cu. ft. [Bar Code 1043688] Boxes numbered 213 and 214.

Various Estate Accounts, 1828-1841, 2 cu. ft., boxes numbered 215 and 216.

Inventories and Appraisements, 1795-1848, 3 cu. ft. [Bar Codes 1043698, 1043699 and 1043701]

Petitions, 1832-1846, ca. .2 cu. ft. [inside Bar Code 1043688]

Wills, 1803-1804, ca. .1 cu. ft.

Wills, Accounts, etc., 1847-1897, 5 cu. ft. [Bar Codes 1043690, and 1043692 to 1043793]

ABBREVIATIONS

Account	Estate account
Account B.	An estate account that is related to a business, or a business account
Account F.	Final account or settlement by an administrator or executor
Admin.	Administrator Bond, or proceedings on administering an estate
Appraisal	Estate appraisal, often combined with inventory
Appraisal S.	Appraisement of slaves
Apprentice	Apprenticeship record
b/o	Brother of
Bond	May be a number of bonds, for appointment of official, minister, administrator's bond or executor's bond
Bond M.	Bond for a minister to perform the rites of matrimony
(C)	Colored
c/o	Child of
Debts	List of debts due the estate, or list of debts owed by deceased
Deed	Land conveyance record
def.	Defendant in court proceedings
Deposition	Response to court proceedings
Division	Proceedings to divide real or personal property
Division S.	Division of slaves
Dower	Proceedings regarding the widow's 1/3 estate
Exhibits	Additional items used in support of court proceedings
Fid. Bond	Fiduciary Bond
gc/o	Grandchild of
Guard.	Guardianship Bond
Guard. Acct.	Guardianship Account
Indenture D.	An indenture to convey in trust a list of property of the grantor as relief of an insolvent debtor
Letter(s)	Correspondence that is part of another record
LVA-LP	Loose papers at the Records Center of the Library of Virginia, Richmond. See previous discussion under "Records Featured."
Mer. License	Merchant License
n/o	Nephew of
ni/o	Niece of
P. of Atty.	Power of Attorney
Petition	Petition to the court for remedy
plt.	Plaintiff in court proceedings
Renounce	Person, often a widow, relinquishes their right to administer an estate
Rev.	Reverend
s/o	Son of
Sale	Inventory of sales from an estate
Sale S.	Sale of slaves
Settlement	Or final account, presented by an administrator or executor
sl/o	Son-in-law of
Suit	Person listed is party to a court suit
Tax Charge	Person listed is charged with personal property tax on the list cited
Tithable	Person listed is on the personal property tax for the year cited; age category is given as found on the tax list.
wid/o	Widow of
Will	Text of the last will and testament of a deceased person

Will (N)	Nuncupative will; often oral
Will P.	Proceedings to probate a will; will was first presented in court

NAME OR SUBJECT	LOCATION	TYPE	YEAR	REFERENCE(S)
A				
A. & W. Ramsay	Alexandria	Mer. License	1800	Tax PP 1800:54(19)w
Abbott, Ephraim	Arlington	Claim	1812	ACO:124
Abbott, James	Arlington	Defendant	1808	ACO:080, 081, 084
Abbott, James	Arlington	Defendant	1808	ACO:086
Abbott, James	Arlington	Defendant	1809	ACO:107
Abbott, James, Master	Arlington	Respondent	1806	ACO:053, 056, 063
Abbott, James, Master	Arlington	Respondent	1806	ACO:065
Abbott, James, Master	Arlington	Deposition	1806	ACR:007, 017
Abbott, James, Master	Arlington	Defendant	1806	ACR:001
Abbott, John	Arlington	Apprentice	1846	OCR1842:195
Abercrombie, Eliz. Smallwood, c/o Robt.	Arlington	Guard.	1811	WB1:019
Abercrombie, Martha	Arlington	Guard. Acct.	1827	AB6:439
Abercrombie, Martha Alice, c/o Susan	Arlington	Guard.	1823	OCR1822:050a
Abercrombie, Martha, c/o Robert	Arlington	Guard.	1823	WB3:108
Abercrombie, Robert	Alexandria	Tax Charge	1799	Tax PP 1799:01
Abercrombie, Robert	Alexandria	Tax Charge	1800	Tax PP 1800:01
Abercrombie, Robert	Arlington	Admin.	1810	WBC:473
Abercrombie, Robert	Arlington	Inventory	1810	WBC:474
Abercrombie, Robert	Arlington	Account	1811	AB1:121; LVA-LP
Abercrombie, Robert	Arlington	Sale	1811	AB1:120
Abercrombie, Robert	Arlington	Account	1812	AB1:269; LVA-LP
Abercrombie, Robert	Arlington	Guard. Acct.	1814	AB2:026; LVA-LP
Abercrombie, Robert	Arlington	Inventory	1822	AB5:119; LVA-LP
Abercrombie, Robert	Arlington	Sale	1822	AB5:121
Abercrombie, Robert	Arlington	Will P.	1822	OCR1822:024a
Abercrombie, Robert	Arlington	Will	1822	WB3:069; File #210A
Abercrombie, Robert	Arlington	Bond	1822	WB3:069
Abercrombie, Robert	Arlington	Account	1823	AB5:197; LVA-LP
Abercrombie, Robert	Arlington	Account	1824	AB5:361; LVA-LP
Abercrombie, Robert	Arlington	Account	1825	AB6:127; LVA-LP
Abercrombie, Robert	Arlington	Account	1827	AB6:439; LVA-LP
Abercrombie, Robert	Arlington	Account	1833	AB7:071; LVA-LP
Abercrombie, Robert & wife Martha	Alexandria	Resident	1800	1800(4):16B
Abercrombie, Robert, c/o Martha	Arlington	Apprentice	1811	OCR1811:045
Abercrombie, Robert, c/o Robert	Arlington	Guard.	1811	WB1:019
Abercrombie, Robert, cooper	Alexandria	Head	1800	1800(4):16A
Abercrombie, Robert, grantee	Arlington	Indenture D.	1806	ID3:163
Abercrombie, Robt. & wife, cooper	Alexandria	Housekeeper	1799	1799(2):04A
Abercrombie, Robt., constable	Alexandria	Head	1810	1810(3):02A
Abercromby, Elizabeth S.	Arlington	Guard. Acct.	1812	AB1:227
Abernathy, James	Alexandria	Tithable +21	1787	Tax PP 1787:09
Abernathy, James	Alexandria	Tithable +16	1788	Tax PP 1788:10
Abert, Jno.	Alexandria	Tax Charge	1798	Tax PP 1798:01
Abert, Jno., Fairfax St.	Alexandria	Occupant	1795	Tax L 1795:13
Abert, John	Alexandria	Tax Charge	1795	Tax PP 1795:01
Abert, John	Alexandria	Tax Charge	1796	Tax LP 1796:01
Abert, John	Alexandria	Tax Charge	1796	Tax PP 1796:01
Abram, Charles	Alexandria	Tithable +16	1789	Tax PP 1789:08
Abrams, Charles	Alexandria	Tax Charge	1796	Tax PP 1796:01
Abrams, Charles	Alexandria	Tax Charge	1800	Tax PP 1800:01
Abrams, Chas.	Alexandria	Tax Charge	1798	Tax PP 1798:01
Abrams, Chas.	Alexandria	Tax Charge	1799	Tax PP 1799:01
Acheson, Wm., shoemaker	Alexandria	Head	1810	1810(1):11A
Ackley, Francis	Alexandria	Tax Charge	1788	Tax PP 1788:01
Ackley, Francis	Alexandria	Tax Charge	1789	Tax PP 1789:01
Act for Erecting Town at Hunting Creek	Alexandria	Act	1748	CRI:357
Adam, Elizabeth	Alexandria	Tax Charge	1787	Tax PP 1787:01
Adam, Elizabeth	Alexandria	Tax Charge	1788	Tax PP 1788:01
Adam, Francis	Alexandria	Tithable +16	1788	Tax PP 1788:11
Adam, Francis	Alexandria	Tithable +16	1789	Tax PP 1789:12

NAME OR SUBJECT	LOCATION	TYPE	YEAR	REFERENCE(S)
Adam, James	Arlington	Admin.	1816	WB2:146
Adam, Jane	Alexandria	Boarder	1800	1800(4):07A
Adam, John	Arlington	Exor. Bond	1848	EBB(np)
Adam, John	Arlington	Will	1848	WB5:079; File #444A
Adam, John	Arlington	Account	1859	WB7:436; LVA-LP
Adam, Mary	Arlington	Will	1857	WB7:197; File #540A
Adam, Robert	Alexandria	Owner	1787	Tax L 1787:01
Adam, Robert	Alexandria	Tithable +16	1789	Tax PP 1789:08
Adam, Robert	Alexandria	Tithable +16	1790	Tax PP 1790:06
Adam, Robert	Alexandria	Tithable +16	1790	Tax PP 1790:14
Adam, Robert, Admr. of, plt.	Alexandria	Suit	1801	CRB:045
Adam, Robert, Estate, btw. Union/Water	Alexandria	Owner	1795	Tax L 1795:01
Adam, Robert, Estate, Cameron St.	Alexandria	Owner	1790	Tax L 1790:01
Adam, Robert, Estate, Fairfax St.	Alexandria	Owner	1790	Tax L 1790:01(3)
Adam, Robert, Estate, Fairfax St.	Alexandria	Owner	1795	Tax L 1795:01(3)
Adam, Robert, Estate, King St.	Alexandria	Owner	1790	Tax L 1790:01
Adam, Robert, Estate, nr. Princess St.	Alexandria	Owner	1790	Tax L 1790:01
Adam, Robert, Estate, on the wharf	Alexandria	Owner	1790	Tax L 1790:01(2)
Adam, Robert, Estate, Queen St.	Alexandria	Owner	1790	Tax L 1790:01(3)
Adam, Robert, Estate, Queen St.	Alexandria	Owner	1795	Tax L 1795:01
Adam, Robert, Estate, Union St.	Alexandria	Owner	1795	Tax L 1795:01
Adam, Robert, Estate, Water St.	Alexandria	Owner	1795	Tax L 1795:01(2)
Adam, Robert, Estate, Water St.	Alexandria	Owner	1795	Tax L 1795:01
Adam, Robert, Estate, wharf & warehse.	Alexandria	Owner	1795	Tax L 1795:01
Adam, Robert, Fairfax St.	Alexandria	Occupant	1787	Tax L 1787:01
Adam, Robert, Princess St.	Alexandria	Occupant	1787	Tax L 1787:01
Adam, Robt.	Alexandria	Boarder	1800	1800(4):07A
Adam, Robt., Jr.	Alexandria	Tithable +16	1788	Tax PP 1788:07
Adam, William Wallace	Alexandria	Will	1877	WB1:220; LP
Adams, Abednego	Alexandria	Tax Charge	1800	Tax PP 1800:01
Adams, Abednego, bricklayer	Alexandria	Head	1810	1810(3):08A
Adams, Abednego, Jr.	Alexandria	Tax Charge	1798	Tax PP 1798:01
Adams, Abednego, Jr.	Alexandria	Tax Charge	1799	Tax PP 1799:01
Adams, Abednego, mason	Alexandria	Housekeeper	1808	1808(1):06A
Adams, Abednigo, brick mason	Alexandria	Head	1800	1800(4):08A
Adams, Abednigo & wife Clarissa	Alexandria	Resident	1800	1800(4):08B
Adams, Abijah	Arlington	Defendant	1823	ACO:211, 212
Adams, Ada C.	Arlington	Will	1890	WB10:158; File #744A
Adams, Adam	Alexandria	Tax Charge	1796	Tax PP 1796:01
Adams, Adam (C)	Alexandria	Tax Charge	1795	Tax PP 1795:01
Adams, Austin L.	Arlington	Complainant	1841	LSA:075
Adams, Eliza, Queen St.	Alexandria	Occupant	1787	Tax L 1787:01
Adams, Francis	Alexandria	Tax Charge	1790	Tax PP 1790:01
Adams, George Martin C., s/o Robert	Arlington	Apprentice	1814	OCR1811:214
Adams, Grase, laundress	Alexandria	Head	1800	1800(4):06A
Adams, James	Alexandria	Serv./Appr.	1800	1800(4):09B
Adams, James, brick mason	Alexandria	Boarder	1800	1800(4):08A
Adams, Jane	Alexandria	Resident	1800	1800(4):06B
Adams, Jeremiah	Arlington	Will	1809	WBC:167; File #045A
Adams, Jno.	Alexandria	Tax Charge	1798	Tax PP 1798:01
Adams, Jno., back building	Alexandria	Occupant	1795	Tax L 1795:03
Adams, John	Alexandria	Tax Charge	1795	Tax PP 1795:01
Adams, John	Alexandria	Deed	1797	CRH:341
Adams, John	Alexandria	Tax Charge	1799	Tax PP 1799:01
Adams, John	Alexandria	Tax Charge	1800	Tax PP 1800:01
Adams, John, shopkeeper & silversmith	Alexandria	Housekeeper	1808	1808(4):25A
Adams, John, silversmith	Alexandria	Head	1810	1810(4):04A
Adams, Leonard	Alexandria	Tax Charge	1795	Tax PP 1795:01
Adams, Leonard	Arlington	Ordinary	1803	OBL1(np)
Adams, Leonard	Arlington	Ordinary	1804	OBL1(np)
Adams, Leonard	Arlington	Ordinary	1821	OBL3(np)

NAME OR SUBJECT	LOCATION	TYPE	YEAR	REFERENCE(S)
Adams, Leonard, at his house	Arlington	Ordinary	1832	OBL4(np)
Adams, Leonard, drayman	Alexandria	Housekeeper	1808	1808(4):28A
Adams, Leonard, drayman	Alexandria	Head	1810	1810(4):05A
Adams, Leonard, grantor	Arlington	Indenture D.	1813	ID2:342
Adams, Leonard, in jail bounds	Arlington	Insolvent	1814	ID2:337
Adams, Mary Ann	Arlington	Will	1893	WB10:255; File #758A
Adams, Mary R.	Arlington	Will	1825	WB3:207; File #241A
Adams, Mary R.	Arlington	Bond	1825	WB3:208
Adams, Nancy (Somers), heirs of	Arlington	Defendants	1841	LSA:075
Adams, Robert	Alexandria	Tithable +16	1789	Tax PP 1789:17
Adams, Robert, Estate	Alexandria	Tax Charge	1796	Tax LP 1796:01
Adams, Saml. & wife, merchant	Alexandria	Housekeeper	1799	1799(2):17A
Adams, Samuel	Alexandria	Mer. License	1798	Tax PP 1798:20-1
Adams, Samuel	Alexandria	Tax Charge	1799	Tax PP 1799:01
Adams, Samuel	Alexandria	Mer. License	1800	Tax PP 1800:54(10)r
Adams, Samuel	Arlington	Defendant	1802	PA:280
Adams, Sarah	Arlington	Apprentice	1843	OCR1842:027
Adams, Shedrick (C)	Arlington	Apprentice	1812	OCR1811:136
Adams, Susan	Arlington	Defendant	1841	LSA:075
Adams, Susanna	Arlington	Apprentice	1843	OCR1842:027
Adams, Thomas	Alexandria	Tax Charge	1799	Tax PP 1799:01
Adams, Thos.	Alexandria	Tax Charge	1798	Tax PP 1798:01
Adams, Thos., turner	Alexandria	Housekeeper	1799	1799(2):09A
Adams, Wesley	Alexandria	Deed	1797	CRH:341
Adams, William G.	Arlington	Inventory	1821	AB4:224, 236; LVA-LP
Adams, William G.	Arlington	Account	1822	AB5:093; LVA-LP
Adams, William G.	Arlington	Account	1824	AB5:415; LVA-LP
Adams, William G.	Arlington	Account	1825	AB5:415
Adams, William Godfrey	Arlington	Bond	1821	WB2:418
Adams, William Godfrey	Arlington	Will	1821	WB2:417; File #190A
Adams, [blank], taylor	Alexandria	Boarder	1799	1799(2):03A
Adamson, Benjamin, cabinet maker	Alexandria	Head	1810	1810(2):03A
Adamson, Benjn., cabinet maker	Alexandria	Housekeeper	1808	1808(2):13A
Adamson, Polly	Alexandria	Boarder	1799	1799(2):04A
Addams, Samuel	Alexandria	Tax Charge	1800	Tax PP 1800:01
Adderton, Jeremiah	Alexandria	Tax Charge	1795	Tax PP 1795:01
Addison, Andrew, drayman	Alexandria	Head	1810	1810(2):04A
Addison, Andw. (C)	Alexandria	Boarder	1808	1808(4):25B
Addison, Augustus E., of Baltimore MD	Alexandria	Will	1881	WB1:338; LP
Addison, Walter D., of Baltimore MD	Alexandria	Will	1898	WBC1:075; LP
Adkins, William	Arlington	Apprentice	1815	OCR1811:259
Adkins, William, c/o Sarah Moreland	Arlington	Apprentice	1813	OCR1811:174
Adlersterren, D.W.	Alexandria	Tax Charge	1799	Tax PP 1799:01
Adlersterren, G.W., physician	Alexandria	Boarder	1799	1799(2):01A
Adrain, Hugh	Alexandria	Tax Charge	1800	Tax PP 1800:01
Adrain, Robt.	Alexandria	Boarder	1808	1808(2):13A
Affty, Abram (C)	Alexandria	Housekeeper	1808	1808(4):24A
Afty, Abraham, gardner	Alexandria	Head	1810	1810(4):09A
Agen, William	Arlington	Crime	1797	OT:16/01/1797
Agnew, John P.	Alexandria	Will	1892	WB2:030; LP
Aikens, Wm.	Alexandria	Tax Charge	1796	Tax PP 1796:01
Aires, William	Alexandria	Tithable +16	1788	Tax PP 1788:03
Aitkins, Nathanl.	Alexandria	Tax Charge	1799	Tax PP 1799:01
Albrand, Elizabeth	Alexandria	Will	1890	WB1:574; LP
Aldridge & McLean	Alexandria	Mer. License	1798	Tax PP 1798:20-1
Aldridge, Ann	Alexandria	Boarder	1799	1799(2):08A
Alexander, Alexr.	Alexandria	Tax Charge	1796	Tax LP 1796:01
Alexander, Alexr.	Alexandria	Tax Charge	1798	Tax PP 1798:01
Alexander, Amos	Alexandria	Tax Charge	1798	Tax PP 1798:01
Alexander, Amos	Alexandria	Tax Charge	1799	Tax PP 1799:01
Alexander, Amos	Alexandria	Account B.	1800	CRC:081

NAME OR SUBJECT	LOCATION	TYPE	YEAR	REFERENCE(S)
Alexander, Amos	Alexandria	Tax Charge	1800	Tax PP 1800:01
Alexander, Amos	Arlington	Defendant	1802	PA:284
Alexander, Amos	Arlington	Defendant	1805	ACO:045
Alexander, Amos	Alexandria	Deposition	1805	CRE:264
Alexander, Amos	Arlington	Defendant	1823	ACO:220, 221, 223
Alexander, Amos	Arlington	Defendant	1824	ACO:241, 243, 247
Alexander, Amos	Arlington	Defendant	1825	ACO:252, 257
Alexander, Amos	Arlington	Defendant	1826	ACO:260, 263
Alexander, Amos	Arlington	Defendant	1827	ACO:267
Alexander, Amos & Mark	Alexandria	Mer. License	1798	Tax PP 1798:20-1
Alexander, Amos & wife, merchant	Alexandria	Housekeeper	1799	1799(2):06A
Alexander, Amos, assignees of	Arlington	Plaintiffs	1823	ACO:220
Alexander, Amos, at Caton's Tavern	Alexandria	Deposition	1808	CRH:121
Alexander, Amos, death	Arlington	Suit Abates	1827	ACO:270
Alexander, Amos, def.	Alexandria	Suit	1801	CRB:020
Alexander, Amos, def.	Alexandria	Suit	1801	CRB:250
Alexander, Amos, def.	Alexandria	Suit	1801	CRC:078
Alexander, Amos, def.	Alexandria	Suit	1802	CRD:169
Alexander, Amos, def.	Alexandria	Suit	1803	CRD:078
Alexander, Amos, def.	Alexandria	Suit	1819	CRK:501
Alexander, Amos, inspector	Alexandria	Head	1810	1810(4):01A
Alexander, Amos, plt.	Alexandria	Suit	1801	CRC:147
Alexander, Amos, plt.	Alexandria	Suit	1804	CRF:001
Alexander, Amos, plt.	Alexandria	Suit	1820	CRL:213
Alexander, Amos, trustee, grantee	Arlington	Indenture D.	1812	ID2:081
Alexander, Amos, [flour] inspector	Alexandria	Housekeeper	1808	1808(4):27A
Alexander, Augustine	Arlington	Appraisal	1831	LVA-LP
Alexander, Augustine	Arlington	Admin.	1831	WB4:035
Alexander, Augustine	Arlington	Account	1833	AB7:102
Alexander, Catharine F.	Arlington	Bond	1855	BB(np)
Alexander, Catharine F.	Arlington	Appraisal	1857	WB7:228; LVA-LP
Alexander, Catherine F.	Arlington	Will	1855	WB6:423; File #521A
Alexander, Catherine, w/o Walter S.	Arlington	Defendant	1840	LSA:048
Alexander, Charles	Alexandria	Owner	1787	Tax L 1787:01
Alexander, Charles	Alexandria	Deed	1805	CRI:360
Alexander, Charles	Arlington	Will (N)	1806	WBB:278; File #375A
Alexander, Charles	Arlington	Admin.	1806	WBB:307
Alexander, Charles	Arlington	Inventory	1807	WBB:432; LVA-LP
Alexander, Charles	Alexandria	Deposition	1808	CRH:114
Alexander, Charles	Arlington	Inventory	1814	AB2:075; LVA-LP
Alexander, Charles	Arlington	Will	1814	WB1:299; File #121A
Alexander, Charles	Arlington	Bond	1814	WB1:307
Alexander, Charles	Arlington	Account	1816	AB2:305
Alexander, Charles	Arlington	Account	1817	AB3:099; LVA-LP
Alexander, Charles	Arlington	Sale	1819	AB3:393; LVA-LP
Alexander, Charles	Arlington	Rents	1819	AB3:393; LVA-LP
Alexander, Charles	Arlington	Admin.	1819	WB2:339
Alexander, Charles	Arlington	Account	1822	AB5:113; LVA-LP
Alexander, Charles Armistead	Arlington	Complainant	1835	LSA:005
Alexander, Charles Armistead	Arlington	Will (NR)	1870	CLOB3:171; File #669A
Alexander, Charles, def.	Alexandria	Ejectment	(nd)	CRI:282
Alexander, Charles, def.	Alexandria	Suit	1801	CRE:078
Alexander, Charles, for trodden grass	Arlington	Defendant	1802	PA:263
Alexander, Charles, gs/o Robert	Alexandria	Deed	1776	CRI:212
Alexander, Charles, heirs of, def.	Alexandria	Suit	1811	CRI:176
Alexander, Charles, heirs of	Alexandria	Plat	1820	CRL:181
Alexander, Charles, Jr.	Alexandria	Tax Charge	1800	Tax PP 1800:01
Alexander, Charles, Jr.	Arlington	Sale	1817	AB3:092
Alexander, Charles, Jr.	Arlington	Account	1825	AB6:148; LVA-LP
Alexander, Charles, orphans of	Arlington	Guard. Acct.	1819	AB3:388; LVA-LP
Alexander, Charles, orphans of	Arlington	Farm Acct.	1819	AB3:391; LVA-LP

NAME OR SUBJECT	LOCATION	TYPE	YEAR	REFERENCE(S)
Alexander, Charles, plt.	Alexandria	Suit	1801	CRB:118
Alexander, Charles, plt.	Alexandria	Suit	1801	CRB:150
Alexander, Charles, plt.	Alexandria	Suit	1802	CRC:238
Alexander, Charles, plt.	Alexandria	Suit	1802	CRC:213
Alexander, Charles, plt.	Alexandria	Suit	1802	CRC:175
Alexander, Charles, plt.	Alexandria	Suit	1813	CRI:158
Alexander, Charles, Sr.	Alexandria	Lease	1798	CRB:154
Alexander, Charles, Sr., plt.	Alexandria	Suit	1802	CRC:266
Alexander, Chas. Armistead, c/o Chas.	Arlington	Guard.	1817	WB2:210
Alexander, Chas., Jr.	Alexandria	Tax Charge	1799	Tax PP 1799:01
Alexander, Columbus	Arlington	Will	1905	WB11:035; File #026
Alexander, Frances	Arlington	Will	1823	WB3:216; File #243A
Alexander, Frances	Arlington	Inventory	1824	AB5:254; LVA-LP
Alexander, Frances	Arlington	Slaves	1824	AB5:257
Alexander, Frances	Arlington	Admin.	1824	OCR1822:063
Alexander, Frances	Arlington	Bond	1824	WB3:118
Alexander, Frances	Arlington	Account	1825	AB5:408
Alexander, Frances	Arlington	Account	1826	LVA-LP
Alexander, Frances	Arlington	Account	1839	AB7:342
Alexander, Frances, def.	Alexandria	Suit	1811	CRI:176
Alexander, Frances, Mrs.	Alexandria	Deposition	1808	CRH:113
Alexander, Frances, relict of Charles	Alexandria	Suit	1820	CRL:175
Alexander, Francis, wid/o Charles	Alexandria	Suit	1811	CRI:176
Alexander, George Dent	Arlington	Will Proc.	1840	WB4:336
Alexander, George Dent	Arlington	Will P.	1842	OCR1842:015, 017
Alexander, George Dent	Arlington	Will P.	1845	OCR1842:126
Alexander, Gerard	Arlington	Guard.	1819	WB2:339
Alexander, Gerard	Arlington	Inventory	1821	AB4:194
Alexander, Gerard	Arlington	Admin.	1821	WB2:414
Alexander, Gerrard	Arlington	Account	1822	AB5:071
Alexander, Gustavus B., plt.	Alexandria	Suit	1820	CRL:175
Alexander, Gustavus Brown, c/o Chas.	Arlington	Guard.	1806	WBB:369
Alexander, Gustavus, def.	Alexandria	Suit	1811	CRI:176
Alexander, John, Estate	Alexandria	Owner	1787	Tax L 1787:03
Alexander, John, Estate	Alexandria	Owner	1787	Tax L 1787:04
Alexander, John, s/o Robert	Alexandria	Boarder	1808	1808(3):19A
Alexander, Laura, c/o Chas.	Arlington	Guard.	1817	WB2:210
Alexander, Lee M.	Arlington	Account	1836	AB7:225; LVA-LP
Alexander, Lee Massey	Arlington	Inventory	1834	LVA-LP
Alexander, Lee Massey	Arlington	Will	1834	WB4:072; File #327A
Alexander, Lee Massey	Arlington	Bond	1834	WB4:074
Alexander, Lee Massey	Arlington	Account	1839	LVA-LP
Alexander, Lee Massey, c/o Chas.	Arlington	Guard.	1806	WBB:368
Alexander, Lee Massey, def.	Alexandria	Suit	1811	CRI:176
Alexander, Lee Massey, plt.	Alexandria	Suit	1820	CRL:175
Alexander, Louisa Elizabeth, c/o Chas.	Arlington	Guard.	1817	WB2:210
Alexander, Mark	Alexandria	Tax Charge	1799	Tax PP 1799:01
Alexander, Mark	Alexandria	Tax Charge	1800	Tax PP 1800:01
Alexander, Mark	Arlington	Admin.	1802	WBA:088
Alexander, Mark	Arlington	Account	1802	WBA:100
Alexander, Mark	Arlington	Inventory	1802	WBA:095
Alexander, Mark	Arlington	Account	1803	WBA:159
Alexander, Mark	Arlington	Account	1805	WBB:154, 510; LVA-LP
Alexander, Mark	Arlington	Account	1807	LVA-LP
Alexander, Mark & wife, merchant	Alexandria	Housekeeper	1799	1799(2):18A
Alexander, Mark, Estate, def.	Alexandria	Suit	1803	CRD:166
Alexander, Mark, merchant	Alexandria	Head	1800	1800(4):11A
Alexander, Marke & wife Elizebeth	Alexandria	Resident	1800	1800(4):11B
Alexander, Mary Ann Frances, c/o Chas.	Arlington	Guard.	1817	WB2:210
Alexander, Mary B.	Arlington	Renounce	1814	WB1:307
Alexander, Mrs. Chas.	Alexandria	Head	1810	1810(3):09A

NAME OR SUBJECT	LOCATION	TYPE	YEAR	REFERENCE(S)
Alexander, Philip	Arlington	Ordinary	1803	OBL1(np)
Alexander, Richard B., def.	Alexandria	Suit	1811	CRI:176
Alexander, Richard B., Dr.	Arlington	Sale	1857	WB7:178; LVA-LP
Alexander, Richard B., Dr.	Arlington	Inventory	1857	WB7:168; LVA-LP
Alexander, Richard B., plt.	Alexandria	Suit	1820	CRL:175
Alexander, Richard, c/o Chas.	Arlington	Guard.	1806	WBB:368
Alexander, Robert	Arlington	Defendant	1802	PA:317, 320
Alexander, Robert	Arlington	Defendant	1802	PA:336
Alexander, Robert	Arlington	Will	1803	WBA:220
Alexander, Robert	Arlington	Bond	1803	WBA:223
Alexander, Robert	Arlington	Will	1859	WB7:445; File #569A
Alexander, Robert	Arlington	Inventory	1860	WB7:493; LVA-LP
Alexander, Robert, def.	Alexandria	Suit	1802	CRB:273
Alexander, Robert, def.	Alexandria	Suit	1802	CRB:324
Alexander, Robert, Estate	Alexandria	Property	1810	CRH:150
Alexander, Robert, Estate	Alexandria	Plat	1810	CRH:153
Alexander, Robert, Fairfax Parish	Alexandria	Deed	1793	CRH:080
Alexander, Robert, heirs of	Frederick	Plat	1800	E
Alexander, Robert, of Fairfax Co.	Alexandria	Will	1793	CRH:095
Alexander, Robert, of Pr. William Co.	Alexandria	Plat	1741	CRI:211
Alexander, Robert, of Stafford Co.	Alexandria	Will	1736	CRI:208
Alexander, Robt., shoemaker	Alexandria	Housekeeper	1808	1808(3):19A
Alexander, Robt., shoemaker	Alexandria	Head	1810	1810(3):06A
Alexander Smith & Son	Alexandria	Mer. License	1799	Tax PP 1799:52-10r
Alexander v. Wise	Arlington	Suit	1843	OCR1842:041, 050
Alexander v. Wise	Arlington	Suit	1843	OCR1842:030, 035-6
Alexander, Walter S.	Arlington	Juryman	1804	ACO:026
Alexander, Walter S.	Arlington	Plat	1840	LSA:053
Alexander, Walter S.	Arlington	Defendant	1840	LSA:048
Alexander, Walter S., plt.	Alexandria	Suit	1809	CRH:046
Alexander, Walter Stoddert	Arlington	Guard.	1802	WBA:070
Alexander, Walter Stoddert	Arlington	Guard. Acct.	1803	WBA:227
Alexander, William B.	Arlington	Defendant	1824	ACO:242, 248
Alexander, William B.	Arlington	Defendant	1825	ACO:253, 258
Alexander, William B.	Arlington	Defendant	1826	ACO:261, 264
Alexander, William B.	Arlington	Defendant	1827	ACO:267, 274
Alexander, William B., def.	Alexandria	Suit	1811	CRI:176
Alexander, William Brown, c/o Chas.	Arlington	Guard.	1806	WBB:367
Alexander, William F.	Arlington	Defendant	1835	LSA:005
Alexander, William Fontaine	Arlington	Guard.	1825	WB3:209
Alexander, William Fontaine, c/o Chas.	Arlington	Guard.	1817	WB2:210
Alexander, William, plt.	Alexandria	Suit	1820	CRL:175
Alexander, William T.	Alexandria	Tax Charge	1796	Tax LP 1796:01
Alexander, William Thornton, plt.	Alexandria	Suit	1802	CRD:059
Alexandria & Washington Railroad	Arlington	Trustee Rep.	1862	WB8:115
Alexandria Canal Co., plaintiff	Arlington	Suit	1842	LSA:149
Alexandria Common Council, plt.	Alexandria	Suit	1811	CRI:104
Alexandria Common Council, plt.	Alexandria	Suit	1818	CRL:035
Alexandria Flour Mill Co.	Arlington	Trustees	1863	WB8:178
Alexandria lots at Potomac River	Alexandria	Plat	1779	CRI:359
Alexandria Mayor & Commonalty, plt.	Alexandria	Suit	1801	CRE:078
Alexandria Mayor & Commonalty, plt.	Alexandria	Suit	1806	CRE:065
Alexandria Poor House	Arlington	Reference	1839	LSA:041, 092, 165
Alford, John L., grantor	Arlington	Indenture D.	1828	ID:196
Alford, John L., in jail	Arlington	Insolvent	1828	ID:191
AllBriden, John, carter	Alexandria	Boarder	1800	1800(4):09A
Allbriten, John	Alexandria	Resident	1800	1800(4):09B
Alldridge, Wm. Joseph	Alexandria	Tax Charge	1798	Tax PP 1798:01
Allen, Capt.	Alexandria	Tax Charge	1800	Tax PP 1800:01
Allen, Dennis	Alexandria	Deposition	1822	CRL:536
Allen, Dennis	Arlington	Appraisal	1830	LVA-LP

NAME OR SUBJECT	LOCATION	TYPE	YEAR	REFERENCE(S)
Allen, Dennis	Arlington	Admin.	1830	WB3:382
Allen, Elizabeth, seamstress	Alexandria	Head	1810	1810(2):04A
Allen, George Hood	Arlington	Will	1817	WB2:184; File #139A
Allen, George Hood	Arlington	Admin.	1817	WB2:185
Allen, Helen M., c/o Ignatius	Arlington	Apprentice	1844	OCR1842:072
Allen, Henry William	Arlington	Apprentice	1826	OCR1822:116a
Allen, Ignatius	Arlington	Inventory	1843	AB8:406; LVA-LP
Allen, Ignatius	Arlington	Appraisal	1843	AB8:423; LVA-LP
Allen, Ignatius	Arlington	Admin.	1843	WB4:372
Allen, Ignatius	Arlington	Account	1844	AB9:020; LVA-LP
Allen, Ignatius	Arlington	Debts Due	1844	AB8:423; LVA-LP
Allen, Ignatius	Arlington	Petition	1844	LVA-LP (Box 214)
Allen, Ignatius	Arlington	Petition	1844	OCR1842:070
Allen, Ignatius, Capt.	Arlington	Sale	1844	AB8:423
Allen, Ignatius [Clouisa Catharine]	Arlington	Bond	1843	OCR1842:051
Allen, James	Alexandria	Tax Charge	1787	Tax PP 1787:01
Allen, James	Arlington	Inventory	1840	AB8:100; LVA-LP
Allen, James	Arlington	Admin.	1840	WB4:239
Allen, James, in Alexandria Co.	Arlington	Ordinary	1838	OBL5(np)
Allen, James, at Alexandria	Arlington	Ordinary	1833	OBL5(np)
Allen, James, at his house	Arlington	Ordinary	1831	OBL4(np)
Allen, James, at his house	Arlington	Ordinary	1832	OBL4(np)
Allen, James, at his house	Arlington	Ordinary	1834	OBL5(np)
Allen, James, at his house	Arlington	Ordinary	1835	OBL5(np)
Allen, James, at his house	Arlington	Ordinary	1836	OBL5(np)
Allen, James, c/o Ignatius	Arlington	Apprentice	1844	OCR1842:072
Allen, John	Alexandria	Tax Charge	1787	Tax PP 1787:01
Allen, John	Alexandria	Tax Charge	1790	Tax PP 1790:01
Allen, John	Arlington	Apprentice	1827	OCR1822:141a
Allen, John	Arlington	Admin.	1837	WB4:153
Allen, John, Capt.	Arlington	Account	1837	AB7:262; LVA-LP
Allen, John, Fairfax St.	Alexandria	Occupant	1787	Tax L 1787:07
Allen, Mitchel, joiner	Alexandria	Head	1810	1810(1):11A
Allen, Nancy	Alexandria	Will	1874	WB1:088; LP
Allen, Philip, retailer	Alexandria	Housekeeper	1808	1808(3):19A
Allen, Salathan & wife Mary	Alexandria	Resident	1800	1800(4):12B
Allen, Salathan, marrener	Alexandria	Head	1800	1800(4):12A
Allen, Salathiel	Arlington	Plaintiff	1801	PA:195
Allen, Sambo, labourer	Alexandria	Head	1810	1810(1):10A
Allen, Saml.	Alexandria	Boarder	1799	1799(2):17A
Allen, Samuel	Arlington	Inventory	1806	WBB:328, 533
Allen, Samuel	Arlington	Admin.	1806	WBB:322
Allen, Samuel	Arlington	Sale	1806	WBB:330
Allen, Samuel	Arlington	Account	1807	WBC:161; LVA-LP
Allen, Samuel	Arlington	Account	1807	WBC:005; LVA-LP
Allen, Samuel	Arlington	Account	1812	AB1:195; LVA-LP
Allen, Samuel	Arlington	Guard.	1822	WB3:048
Allen, Samuel	Arlington	Apprentice	1823	OCR1822:051a
Allen, Samuel (C)	Arlington	Apprentice	1822	OCR1822:002a
Allen, Samuel, age 21	Alexandria	Deposition	1821	CRL:589
Allen, Thos., shoemaker	Alexandria	Head	1810	1810(3):07A
Allen, Thos., shoemaker	Alexandria	Head	1810	1810(3):04A
Allen, Thos., shopkeeper & shoemaker	Alexandria	Housekeeper	1808	1808(3):22A
Allen, Tippett and George Carter	Arlington	Estray	1876	WB9:384
Allen, William	Arlington	Inventory	1808	WBC:082; LP
Allen, William	Arlington	Admin.	1808	WBC:041
Allen, William Edward	Alexandria	Will	1892	WB1:602; LP
Alley, Amos	Alexandria	Tax Charge	1798	Tax PP 1798:01
Alley, Stephen	Alexandria	Tax Charge	1796	Tax LP 1796:01
Alley, Stephen	Alexandria	Tax Charge	1796	Tax PP 1796:01
Alleys & Boone	Alexandria	Tax Charge	1796	Tax PP 1796:01

NAME OR SUBJECT	LOCATION	TYPE	YEAR	REFERENCE(S)
Allison, Amos	Alexandria	Tax Charge	1798	Tax PP 1798:01
Allison, Amos	Alexandria	Tax Charge	1799	Tax PP 1799:01
Allison, Amos	Alexandria	Mer. License	1800	Tax PP 1800:54(10)r
Allison, Amos	Alexandria	Tax Charge	1800	Tax PP 1800:01
Allison, Amos	Arlington	Plaintiff	1802	PA:268
Allison, Amos & Co.	Alexandria	Mer. License	1798	Tax PP 1798:20-1
Allison, Amos, plt.	Alexandria	Suit	1802	CRC:103
Allison, Ann, gentlewoman	Alexandria	Housekeeper	1808	1808(1):01A
Allison, Ann, seamstress	Alexandria	Head	1810	1810(1):07A
Allison, David, [?] baker	Alexandria	Housekeeper	1808	1808(2):17A
Allison, Eliza., nr. Fairfax St.	Alexandria	Occupant	1790	Tax L 1790:02
Allison, James	Arlington	Inventory	1822	AB5:131; LVA-LP
Allison, James	Arlington	Sale	1822	AB5:133
Allison, James	Arlington	Admin.	1822	OCR1822:028a
Allison, James	Arlington	Admin.	1822	WB3:073
Allison, James	Arlington	Account	1823	AB5:207; LVA-LP
Allison, James	Arlington	Inventory	1823	LVA-LP
Allison, James	Arlington	Account	1824	AB5:261; LVA-LP
Allison, James	Arlington	Account	1826	AB6:162; LVA-LP
Allison, James	Arlington	Account	1827	AB6:410
Allison, James & wife, carpenter	Alexandria	Housekeeper	1799	1799(2):19A
Allison, James, merchant	Alexandria	Head	1810	1810(3):01A
Allison, Jno.	Alexandria	Boarder	1808	1808(1):01A
Allison, John	Alexandria	Owner	1787	Tax L 1787:01
Allison, John	Alexandria	Tax Charge	1787	Tax PP 1787:01
Allison, John	Alexandria	Tax Charge	1788	Tax PP 1788:01
Allison, John	Alexandria	Tax Charge	1789	Tax PP 1789:01
Allison, John	Alexandria	Tax Charge	1790	Tax PP 1790:01
Allison, John	Arlington	Guard.	1823	OCR1822:041a
Allison, John, c/o James	Arlington	Guard.	1823	WB3:089
Allison, John, Fairfax St.	Alexandria	Occupant	1787	Tax L 1787:01
Allison, John, King St.	Alexandria	Occupant	1787	Tax L 1787:08
Allison, John, King St.	Alexandria	Occupant	1790	Tax L 1790:02
Allison, John T., c/o Harrison	Arlington	Guard.	1851	BB(np)
Allison, Nancy	Arlington	Admin.	1821	WB2:427
Allison, Patrick	Alexandria	Owner	1787	Tax L 1787:01
Allison, Patrick, Cameron St.	Alexandria	Owner	1790	Tax L 1790:01
Allison, Patrick, King St.	Alexandria	Owner	1790	Tax L 1790:01
Allison, Robert	Alexandria	Owner	1787	Tax L 1787:01
Allison, Robert	Alexandria	Tax Charge	1787	Tax PP 1787:01
Allison, Robert	Alexandria	Tax Charge	1788	Tax PP 1788:01
Allison, Robert	Alexandria	Tax Charge	1795	Tax PP 1795:01
Allison, Robert	Alexandria	Tax Charge	1796	Tax LP 1796:01
Allison, Robert	Alexandria	Tax Charge	1796	Tax PP 1796:01
Allison, Robert	Arlington	Apprentice	1801	OCR1801:001
Allison, Robert, King St.	Alexandria	Occupant	1787	Tax L 1787:01
Allison, Robert, King St.	Alexandria	Owner	1790	Tax L 1790:01
Allison, Robt., King St.	Alexandria	Occupant	1795	Tax L 1795:24
Allison, Robt., Union St.	Alexandria	Occupant	1795	Tax L 1795:21
Allison, Sarah	Alexandria	Housekeeper	1799	1799(2):05A
Allison, Sarah	Alexandria	Resident	1800	1800(4):11B
Allison, Sarah, sempstress	Alexandria	Housekeeper	1808	1808(1):01A
Allison, Sarah, sumpster	Alexandria	Head	1800	1800(4):11A
Allison, Thompson, of Fairfax Co.	Arlington	Will	1835	LVA-LP
Allison, William	Alexandria	Tax Charge	1787	Tax PP 1787:01
Allison, William	Alexandria	Tax Charge	1788	Tax PP 1788:01
Allison, William	Alexandria	Tax Charge	1789	Tax PP 1789:01
Allison, William	Alexandria	Tax Charge	1790	Tax PP 1790:01
Allison, William	Alexandria	Tax Charge	1796	Tax LP 1796:01
Allison, William	Alexandria	Mer. License	1798	Tax PP 1798:20-1
Allison, William	Arlington	Account	1806	WBB:273; LVA-LP

NAME OR SUBJECT	LOCATION	TYPE	YEAR	REFERENCE(S)
Allison, William	Arlington	Inventory	1806	WBB:272; LVA-LP
Allison, William	Arlington	Guard.	1823	OCR1822:041a
Allison, William, b. Tyrone	Arlington	Alien Entry	1812	RA:15/07/12
Allison, William, c/o James	Arlington	Guard.	1823	WB3:089
Allison, William, plt.	Alexandria	Suit	1803	CRD:158
Allison, Wm.	Alexandria	Tax Charge	1795	Tax PP 1795:01
Allison, Wm.	Alexandria	Tax Charge	1796	Tax PP 1796:01
Allison, Wm.	Alexandria	Tax Charge	1798	Tax PP 1798:01
Allison, Wm., merchant	Alexandria	Boarder	1799	1799(2):02A
Alliston, Amos	Alexandria	Mer. License	1799	Tax PP 1799:52-01r
Alliston, Jas., shopkeeper	Alexandria	Housekeeper	1808	1808(3):22A
Alliston, Wm., shopkeeper	Alexandria	Housekeeper	1808	1808(3):22A
Allman, Mary & Ebe Magin	Alexandria	Housekeeper	1799	1799(2):14A
Allmond, Mary	Alexandria	Resident	1800	1800(4):10B
Allmond, Mary, sumpster	Alexandria	Head	1800	1800(4):10A
Alls, Mary	Alexandria	Resident	1800	1800(4):14B
Alls, Mary, sumpster	Alexandria	Boarder	1800	1800(4):14A
Alman, Mary	Alexandria	Tax Charge	1787	Tax PP 1787:01
Alman, Mrs., Princess St.	Alexandria	Occupant	1787	Tax L 1787:09
Alricks, Ann	Alexandria	Boarder	1799	1799(2):06A
Altefritt, Peter, brickmaker	Alexandria	Housekeeper	1808	1808(4):24A
Alter, John	Alexandria	Tax Charge	1800	Tax PP 1800:01
Alton, John	Alexandria	Tax Charge	1787	Tax PP 1787:01
Alton, John	Alexandria	Tax Charge	1795	Tax PP 1795:01
Alton, John	Alexandria	Tax Charge	1796	Tax PP 1796:01
Ambler, John, plt.	Alexandria	Suit	1803	CRD:099
Ambrose, Doctr.	Alexandria	Tax Charge	1796	Tax LP 1796:01
Ambrose, Jno., Royal St.	Alexandria	Occupant	1795	Tax L 1795:20
Ambrose, John, Union St.	Alexandria	Occupant	1795	Tax L 1795:05
Amerger, Daphney	Arlington	Guard.	1819	WB2:284
Ames, Okes, of Bristol Co. MA	Arlington	Will	1887	WB10:097; File #728A
Amos, Charles Henry	Arlington	Admin.	1822	WB4:052
Amos, Charles Henry	Arlington	Admin.	1832	LVA-LP (Accounts)
Amos, Charles Henry	Arlington	Account	1834	AB7:127; LVA-LP
Amos, Jno. & wife, hatter	Alexandria	Housekeeper	1799	1799(2):14A
Amos, John	Alexandria	Tax Charge	1800	Tax PP 1800:01
And, James, c/o William	Alexandria	Apprentice	1812	OCR1811:133
Anderson & Jameson, Lyle's alley	Alexandria	Occupant	1787	Tax L 1787:19
Anderson & Jamieson, Royal St.	Alexandria	Occupant	1790	Tax L 1790:07
Anderson, Amelia	Arlington	Guard.	1824	WB3:127
Anderson, Betsey, washerwoman	Alexandria	Head	1810	1810(2):05A
Anderson, Caleb	Alexandria	Tax Charge	1795	Tax PP 1795:01
Anderson, Eliza., King St.	Alexandria	Occupant	1790	Tax L 1790:01
Anderson, George	Alexandria	Tax Charge	1787	Tax PP 1787:01
Anderson, George	Arlington	Inventory	1818	AB3:131; LVA-LP
Anderson, George	Arlington	Admin.	1818	WB2:227
Anderson, J.	Alexandria	Reference	1808	1808(3):18B
Anderson, James	Alexandria	Tax Charge	1800	Tax PP 1800:01
Anderson, James	Arlington	Defendant	1823	ACO:209
Anderson, James	Arlington	Admin.	1823	OCR1822:056
Anderson, James	Arlington	Admin.	1823	WB3:117
Anderson, James & Co., merchants	Alexandria	Housekeeper	1808	1808(3):21A
Anderson, James, def.	Alexandria	Suit	1808	CRG:147
Anderson, James, for playing Faro	Arlington	Defendant	1801	PA:107
Anderson, James, merchant	Alexandria	Head	1810	1810(3):02A
Anderson, Jane	Arlington	Apprentice	1843	OCR1842:027
Anderson, Jas.	Alexandria	Reference	1808	1808(4):24B
Anderson, John	Alexandria	Tax Charge	1796	Tax LP 1796:01
Anderson, John	Arlington	Admin.	1806	WBB:230
Anderson, John	Arlington	Account	1809	WBC:298; LVA-LP
Anderson, John	Arlington	Account	1812	AB1:249; LVA-LP

NAME OR SUBJECT	LOCATION	TYPE	YEAR	REFERENCE(S)
Anderson, John & Brandey, 2, baker	Alexandria	Head	1795	1796(3):7
Anderson, John, & Co.	Alexandria	Tax Charge	1796	Tax PP 1796:01
Anderson, John, shopkeeper	Alexandria	Housekeeper	1808	1808(3):20A
Anderson, John, *Towlston* from Fairfax	Alexandria	Lease	(nd)	CRH:553
Anderson, Joseph	Alexandria	Boarder	1808	1808(3):21A
Anderson, Joseph, Comptroller	Arlington	Letter	1829	ACR:088
Anderson, Levi, labourer	Alexandria	Head	1810	1810(1):09A
Anderson, Ninian	Alexandria	Tithable +16	1789	Tax PP 1789:10
Anderson, Ninian	Alexandria	Tax Charge	1790	Tax PP 1790:01
Anderson, Ninien	Alexandria	Tax Charge	1788	Tax PP 1788:01
Anderson, Ninion	Alexandria	Tithable +21	1787	Tax PP 1787:08
Anderson, Robert	Alexandria	Tithable +16	1790	Tax PP 1790:01
Anderson, Robert	Alexandria	Tax Charge	1796	Tax LP 1796:01
Anderson, Robert	Alexandria	Tax Charge	1796	Tax PP 1796:01
Anderson, Robert	Arlington	Juryman	1808	ACO:081
Anderson, Robert	Arlington	Defendant	1809	ACO:108
Anderson, Robert	Arlington	Defendant	1812	ACO:126
Anderson, Robert	Arlington	Defendant	1817	ACO:149
Anderson, Robert	Arlington	Appraisal	1833	LVA-LP
Anderson, Robert	Arlington	Will	1833	WB4:060; File #322B
Anderson, Robert	Arlington	Bond	1833	WB4:062
Anderson, Robert	Arlington	Account	1834	AB7:116; LVA-LP
Anderson, Robert, def.	Alexandria	Suit	1812	CRK:002
Anderson, Robt.	Alexandria	Tithable +16	1789	Tax PP 1789:10
Anderson, Robt.	Alexandria	Tax Charge	1795	Tax PP 1795:01
Anderson, Robt.	Alexandria	Tax Charge	1798	Tax PP 1798:01
Anderson, Robt., b. baker	Alexandria	Housekeeper	1808	1808(2):16A
Anderson, Robt., merchant	Alexandria	Head	1810	1810(2):05A
Anderson, Thomas	Arlington	Apprentice	1844	OCR1842:068
Anderson, William	Alexandria	Tax Charge	1787	Tax PP 1787:01
Anderson, Wm.	Alexandria	Tax Charge	1788	Tax PP 1788:01
Anderson, Wm., Fairfax St.	Alexandria	Occupant	1787	Tax L 1787:07
Anderson, Wm., heirs of, King St.	Alexandria	Owner	1790	Tax L 1790:01
Anderson, Wm., King St.	Alexandria	Occupant	1787	Tax L 1787:11
Andrew Jamison & Co.	Alexandria	Tax Charge	1787	Tax PP 1787:08
Andrew, Martin	Alexandria	Tax Charge	1788	Tax PP 1788:01
Andrew, Martin	Alexandria	Tithable +16	1789	Tax PP 1789:06
Andrew, Martin	Alexandria	Tax Charge	1790	Tax PP 1790:01
Andrew, Richard, w(1)2, sadler	Alexandria	Head	1796	1796(3):5
Andrew, Richd.	Alexandria	Tax Charge	1798	Tax PP 1798:01
Andrews, Benjamin, w, carpenter	Alexandria	Head	1796	1796(3):1
Andrews, Benjn.	Alexandria	Tax Charge	1796	Tax LP 1796:01
Andrews, Edward	Arlington	Apprentice	1811	OCR1811:023
Andrews, Edward	Arlington	Guard.	1811	WB1:046
Andrews, Edward, ward of John Throop	Arlington	Apprentice	1811	OCR1811:004
Andrews, Jacob	Arlington	Ordinary	1805	OBL1(np)
Andrews, Jacob	Arlington	Ordinary	1806	OBL2(np)
Andrews, Jacob, shopkeeper	Alexandria	Housekeeper	1808	1808(2):13A
Andrews, Jacob, taylor	Alexandria	Head	1810	1810(2):02A
Andrews, Robert Pitts	Arlington	Will	1851	WB6:021; File #473A
Andrews, Robert Pitts	Arlington	Account	1853	WB6:183; LVA-LP
Andrews, Robert Pitts	Arlington	Account	1856	WB7:117; LVA-LP
Andrews, Shubel	Arlington	Bond	1818	WB2:245
Andrews, Shubel	Arlington	Sale	1819	AB3:351
Andrews, Shubell	Arlington	Account	1819	AB3:352; LVA-LP
Andrews, Subell	Arlington	Inventory	1818	AB3:166; LVA-LP
Angel, Barny, seaman	Alexandria	Head	1810	1810(1):05A
Angel, William, c/o Barnaby C.	Arlington	Apprentice	1813	OCR1811:164
Ansberry, Mary	Alexandria	Head	1810	1810(3):04A
Antonia, Cross	Arlington	Ordinary	1809	OBL2(np)
Anthony, Lewis	Arlington	Libellant	1811	ACO:119

NAME OR SUBJECT	LOCATION	TYPE	YEAR	REFERENCE(S)
Appich, Daivd, in Alexandria Co.	Arlington	Ordinary	1849	OBL6(np)
Appich, David	Alexandria	Will	1887	LP
Appich, David, at his house	Arlington	Ordinary	1848	OBL6(np)
Appich, David, in Alexandria Co.	Arlington	Ordinary	1847	OBL6(np)
Appich, Dorothea	Alexandria	Will	1898	WB2:300; LP
Appich, Gottlieb	Arlington	Will	1866	WB8:443
Appich, Louis	Alexandria	Will	1878	WB1:244; LP
Appleby, George	Alexandria	Tax Charge	1800	Tax PP 1800:01
Appleby, Robert	Alexandria	Tax Charge	1795	Tax PP 1795:01
Archer, Ann	Alexandria	Boarder	1799	1799(2):17A
Ardery, John, shopkeeper & tavern lic.	Alexandria	Housekeeper	1808	1808(1):03A
Ardey, Alexander	Arlington	Admin.	1831	WB4:035
Ardrey, Alexander	Arlington	Appraisal	1831	LVA-LP
Ardrey, Alexander	Arlington	Account	1836	AB7:220; LVA-LP
Ardrey, John	Arlington	Ordinary	1806	OBL2(np)
Arell, Catherine, infant under 21, plt.	Alexandria	Suit	1801	CRC:115
Arell, David	Alexandria	Owner	1787	Tax L 1787:06
Arell, David	Alexandria	Owner	1787	Tax L 1787:05
Arell, David	Alexandria	Tax Charge	1788	Tax PP 1788:01
Arell, David	Alexandria	Tax Charge	1789	Tax PP 1789:01
Arell, David	Alexandria	Tax Charge	1790	Tax PP 1790:01
Arell, David, Fairfax St.	Alexandria	Occupant	1787	Tax L 1787:27
Arell, David, Wilkes St.	Alexandria	Owner	1790	Tax L 1790:01
Arell, David, Wilkes St.	Alexandria	Occupant	1790	Tax L 1790:01
Arell, Mrs.	Alexandria	Head	1795	1795(4):08
Arell, Richard	Alexandria	Owner	1787	Tax L 1787:02
Arell, Richard	Alexandria	Tax Charge	1788	Tax PP 1788:01
Arell, Richard	Alexandria	Tax Charge	1789	Tax PP 1789:01
Arell, Richard	Alexandria	Tax Charge	1790	Tax PP 1790:01
Arell, Richard	Arlington	Guard.	1805	WBB:194
Arell, Richard	Arlington	Guard. Acct.	1808	WBC:043; LVA-LP
Arell, Richard	Arlington	Guard.	1808	WBC:042
Arell, Richard	Arlington	Defendant	1824	ACO:249
Arell, Richard, Duke St.	Alexandria	Occupant	1787	Tax L 1787:02
Arell, Richard, Duke St.	Alexandria	Occupant	1790	Tax L 1790:01
Arell, Richard, Duke St.	Alexandria	Owner	1790	Tax L 1790:01
Arell, Richard, Estate	Alexandria	Tax Charge	1796	Tax LP 1796:01
Arell, Richard, Estate, Duke St.	Alexandria	Owner	1795	Tax L 1795:01(2)
Arell, Richard, Estate, Fairfax St.	Alexandria	Owner	1795	Tax L 1795:01(2)
Arell, Richard, Estate, King St.	Alexandria	Owner	1795	Tax L 1795:02
Arell, Richard, Estate, Royal St.	Alexandria	Owner	1795	Tax L 1795:01(3)
Arell, Richard, Estate, Union St.	Alexandria	Owner	1795	Tax L 1795:02
Arell, Richard, Fairfax St.	Alexandria	Owner	1790	Tax L 1790:01(3)
Arell, Richard, infant under 21, plt.	Alexandria	Suit	1801	CRC:115
Arell, Richard, Jr.	Alexandria	Tithable +16	1788	Tax PP 1788:01
Arell, Richard, King St.	Alexandria	Owner	1790	Tax L 1790:01
Arell, Richard, Royal St.	Alexandria	Occupant	1787	Tax L 1787:02
Arell, Richard, Royal St.	Alexandria	Owner	1790	Tax L 1790:01(3)
Arell, Richard, Union St.	Alexandria	Owner	1795	Tax L 1795:01(4)
Arell, Richd., Duke St.	Alexandria	Occupant	1795	Tax L 1795:01
Arell, Samuel	Alexandria	Owner	1787	Tax L 1787:05
Arell, Samuel, Duke St.	Alexandria	Owner	1790	Tax L 1790:01(2)
Arlington Customs House	Arlington	Bond	1811	ACO:116
Armistead, George	Alexandria	Tax Charge	1796	Tax PP 1796:01
Armistead, Lucy, def.	Alexandria	Suit	1801	CRB:214
Armistead, Richardetta (DeButts)	Arlington	Guard. Acct.	1836	AB7:239
Armistead, Richardetta (DeButts)	Arlington	Guard. Acct.	1839	AB8:132; LVA-LP
Armistead, Richardetta (DeButts)	Arlington	Guard. Acct.	1840	AB8:132
Armistead, Wm.	Alexandria	Tithable +16	1789	Tax PP 1789:09
Armitage, James	Alexandria	Tax Charge	1799	Tax PP 1799:01
Armitage, Jas. & wife, plaisterer	Alexandria	Housekeeper	1799	1799(2):14A

NAME OR SUBJECT	LOCATION	TYPE	YEAR	REFERENCE(S)
Armitage, Sarah	Arlington	Apprentice	1823	OCR1822:033
Armitage, Wm., laborer	Alexandria	Housekeeper	1808	1808(1):09A
Armitage, Wm., seaman	Alexandria	Head	1810	1810(1):07A
Armstead, Willm.	Alexandria	Tax Charge	1795	Tax PP 1795:01
Armstead, Wm.	Alexandria	Tithable +16	1788	Tax PP 1788:07
Armstead, Wm.	Alexandria	Tax Charge	1796	Tax LP 1796:01
Armstead, Wm., King St.	Alexandria	Occupant	1795	Tax L 1795:06
Armstead, [blank], Water St.	Alexandria	Occupant	1795	Tax L 1795:33
Armstrong, Elizabeth	Alexandria	Head	1795	1795(4a):10
Armstrong, Franklin, c/o William	Arlington	Guard.	1837	WB4:155
Armstrong, James	Arlington	Apprentice	1804	OCR1801:207
Armstrong, James	Arlington	Apprentice	1804	OCR1801:145
Armstrong, Jas.	Alexandria	Boarder	1808	1808(1):04A
Armstrong, John, c/o Elizabeth Wheatly	Arlington	Apprentice	1804	OCR1801:146
Armstrong, John D.	Arlington	Admin.	1828	WB3:338
Armstrong, John W., c/o William	Arlington	Guard.	1837	WB4:155
Armstrong, Saml., cooper	Alexandria	Housekeeper	1808	1808(2):16A
Armstrong, Samuel, cooper	Alexandria	Head	1810	1810(2):04A
Armstrong, Tibby, weaver	Alexandria	Housekeeper	1808	1808(4):28A
Armstrong, Venorando, c/o William	Arlington	Guard.	1837	WB4:155
Armstrong, William, cooper	Alexandria	Head	1810	1810(2):04A
Armstrong, Wm., cooper	Alexandria	Housekeeper	1808	1808(4):27A
Arnadell, Andrew, grantor	Arlington	Indenture D.	1828	ID:164
Arnadell, Andrew, in jail	Arlington	Insolvent	1828	ID:162
Arnold, Ada, c/o Alexander	Arlington	Guard.	1864	FBB(np)
Arnold, Alexander	Arlington	Appraisal	1860	WB7:545; LVA-LP
Arnold, Alexander [Jane]	Arlington	Renounce	1860	WB7:502; LVA-LP
Arnold, Ann E.	Alexandria	Will	1878	WB1:231; LP
Arnold, Bill	Alexandria	Boarder	1808	1808(3):21A
Arnold, Edmond, seaman	Alexandria	Head	1810	1810(4):07A
Arnold, Edwd. [or Edmond], waterman	Alexandria	Housekeeper	1808	1808(4):29A
Arnold, Gerard	Arlington	Admin.	1827	OCR1822:146a
Arnold, Gerard	Arlington	Account	1828	LVA-LP
Arnold, Gerrard	Arlington	Inventory	1827	LVA-LP
Arnold, Janet, shoemaker	Alexandria	Housekeeper	1808	1808(4):24A
Arnold, Julian, c/o Alexander	Arlington	Guard.	1864	FBB(np)
Arnold, Mary E., c/o Alexander	Arlington	Guard.	1864	FBB(np)
Arnold, Sarah Jane	Arlington	Suit	1860	LVA-LP
Arnold, Sarah Jane, of Baltimore MD	Arlington	Will	1865	WB8:252; File #629A
Arnold, William, of Baltimore MD	Alexandria	Will	1900	WB2:358; LP
Arrell, David	Alexandria	Tax Charge	1787	Tax PP 1787:01
Arrell, David, Estate	Alexandria	Tax Charge	1796	Tax LP 1796:01
Arrell, Richard	Alexandria	Tax Charge	1787	Tax PP 1787:01
Arrell, Richard, Jr.	Alexandria	Tithable +21	1787	Tax PP 1787:01
Arrell, Saml., Estate	Alexandria	Tax Charge	1796	Tax LP 1796:01
Arrington, Nancy, bc/o Daniel Whalen	Arlington	Bond	1853	BB(np)
Arthur, Robert	Alexandria	Tithable +16	1788	Tax PP 1788:17
Arthur, Samuel, b. Cornwall	Arlington	Alien Entry	1817	RA:22/12/17
Arwin, William	Alexandria	Tax Charge	1800	Tax PP 1800:01
Ary, Lucy	Alexandria	Head	1810	1810(4):06A
Ash, Michael, ropemaker	Alexandria	Head	1795	1795(4a):05
Ashby & Wharton	Arlington	Trustee Acct.	1867	WB8:455
Ashford, Henry, c/o Judith	Arlington	Apprentice	1822	OCR1822:002a
Ashton, Charles	Alexandria	Tithable +16	1788	Tax PP 1788:08
Ashton, R.W. & Co., Water St.	Alexandria	Occupant	1787	Tax L 1787:14
Ashton, Richard W.	Alexandria	Tax Charge	1787	Tax PP 1787:01
Ashton, Richard W.	Alexandria	Tax Charge	1788	Tax PP 1788:01
Ashton, Richard W., Water St.	Alexandria	Owner	1790	Tax L 1790:01
Askins, Catharine (alias Nancy)	Arlington	Apprentice	1816	OCR1811:340
Askins, Nancy	Arlington	Apprentice	1824	OCR1822:064
Aston [Easton], David	Alexandria	Tax Charge	1800	Tax PP 1800:01

NAME OR SUBJECT	LOCATION	TYPE	YEAR	REFERENCE(S)
Athy, Benjamin Walker, c/o Ann Bozwell	Arlington	Apprentice	1816	OCR1811:335
Atkins, Micah	Arlington	Admin.	1803	WBA:129
Atkins, [blank] & wife, bricklayer	Alexandria	Housekeeper	1799	1799(2):19A
Atkinson, Alice M.	Alexandria	Will	1872	WB1:046; LP
Atkinson, Charles Calvert	Arlington	Apprentice	1815	OCR1811:247
Atkinson, Ellen, c/o Thomas	Arlington	Guard. Acct.	1866	WB8:392
Atkinson, Guy	Alexandria	Tithable +16	1790	Tax PP 1790:04
Atkinson, Guy	Alexandria	Tax Charge	1796	Tax LP 1796:01
Atkinson, Guy	Alexandria	Tax Charge	1796	Tax PP 1796:01
Atkinson, Guy	Alexandria	Mer. License	1798	Tax PP 1798:20-1
Atkinson, Guy	Alexandria	Tax Charge	1798	Tax PP 1798:01
Atkinson, Guy	Alexandria	Mer. License	1799	Tax PP 1799:52-01r
Atkinson, Guy	Alexandria	Tax Charge	1799	Tax PP 1799:01
Atkinson, Guy	Alexandria	Mer. License	1800	Tax PP 1800:54(10)r
Atkinson, Guy	Alexandria	Tax Charge	1800	Tax PP 1800:01
Atkinson, Guy	Arlington	Juryman	1824	ACO:237
Atkinson, Guy	Arlington	Bond	1835	WB4:094
Atkinson, Guy	Arlington	Will	1835	WB4:092; File #336A
Atkinson, Guy	Arlington	Account	1836	AB7:230; LVA-LP
Atkinson, Guy	Arlington	Inventory	1836	LVA-LP (Accounts)
Atkinson, Guy	Arlington	Suit	1837	LVA-LP (Judgments)
Atkinson, Guy	Arlington	Account	1838	AB7:310; LVA-LP
Atkinson, Guy	Arlington	Account	1839	AB7:310
Atkinson, Guy, def.	Alexandria	Suit	1801	CRB:283, 287, 290
Atkinson, Guy, def.	Alexandria	Suit	1801	CRB:294
Atkinson, Guy, def.	Alexandria	Suit	1808	CRG:337
Atkinson, Guy, Fairfax St.	Alexandria	Occupant	1795	Tax L 1795:16
Atkinson, Guy, merchant	Alexandria	Head	1810	1810(2):02A
Atkinson, Guy, plt.	Alexandria	Suit	1801	CRB:048
Atkinson, Guy, plt.	Alexandria	Suit	1801	CRD:023
Atkinson, Guy, plt.	Alexandria	Suit	1802	CRC:107
Atkinson, Guy, retailer	Alexandria	Housekeeper	1808	1808(2):12A
Atkinson [Akinson], Guy	Alexandria	Tax Charge	1795	Tax PP 1795:01
Atkinson, James	Arlington	Admin. Bond	1849	ABB(np)
Atkinson, James	Arlington	Inventory	1849	WB5:177; LVA-LP
Atkinson, James, b. Nottinghamshire	Arlington	Alien Entry	1817	RA:22/12/17
Atkinson, Thomas C.	Arlington	Admin.	1859	WB8:023
Atkinson, Thomas C.	Arlington	Account	1860	WB8:140; LVA-LP
Atkinson, Thomas C.	Arlington	Account	1860	WB8:023; LVA-LP
Atkinson, Thomas C.	Arlington	Inventory	1860	WB7:532; LVA-LP
Atkinson, Thomas C.	Arlington	Appraisal	1860	WB7:532; LVA-LP
Atkinson, Thomas C.	Arlington	Account	1860	WB8:361
Atkinson, Thos.	Alexandria	Tax Charge	1789	Tax PP 1789:01
Atkinson, William	Alexandria	Tithable +16	1790	Tax PP 1790:04
Atklins, Miah	Arlington	Account	1803	LVA-LP
Attwell, John	Alexandria	Tax Charge	1796	Tax PP 1796:01
Attwell, John	Alexandria	Tax Charge	1798	Tax PP 1798:01
Attwell, John	Alexandria	Tax Charge	1799	Tax PP 1799:01
Attwell, John, grantor	Arlington	Indenture D.	1828	ID:151
Attwell, John, in prison bounds	Arlington	Insolvent	1828	ID:150
Atwell, Catharine S.	Alexandria	Will	1884	WB1:398; LP
Atwell, John	Alexandria	Tax Charge	1796	Tax LP 1796:01
Atwell, John	Alexandria	Tax Charge	1800	Tax PP 1800:01
Atwell, John, c/o John	Arlington	Apprentice	1815	OCR1811:329
Atwell, John, drayman	Alexandria	Housekeeper	1808	1808(3):22A
Atwell, John, drayman	Alexandria	Head	1810	1810(3):08A
Atwell, Richard	Arlington	Admin.	1828	OCR1822:157a
Atwell, Richard	Arlington	Admin.	1828	WB3:337
Atwell, William	Arlington	Apprentice	1823	OCR1822:058
Atwell, William	Arlington	Apprentice	1824	OCR1822:079
Atwood, [blank]	Alexandria	Boarder	1808	1808(3):22A

NAME OR SUBJECT	LOCATION	TYPE	YEAR	REFERENCE(S)
Aubrey, John, waggoner	Alexandria	Head	1810	1810(3):09A
Aubrey, William	Arlington	Bond	1822	WB3:054
Aubrey, William	Arlington	Will (N)	1822	WB3:053; File #206A
Aud [And], James, natural c/o William	Arlington	Apprentice	1812	OCR1811:133
Audley, Thomas, at his house	Arlington	Ordinary	1826	OBL4(np)
Audly, John, c/o Mary Goins	Arlington	Apprentice	1804	OCR1801:160
Auld, Colin	Alexandria	Letter	1800	CRE:327
Auld, Colin	Alexandria	Reference	1808	1808(2):14B
Auld, Colin	Alexandria	Boarder	1808	1808(3):21A
Auld, Colin	Arlington	Inventory	1840	AB8:159; LVA-LP
Auld, Colin	Arlington	Bond	1840	WB4:244
Auld, Colin	Arlington	Will	1840	WB4:243; File #375A
Auld, Colin	Arlington	Account	1841	AB8:228; LVA-LP
Auld, Colin	Arlington	Release	1845	AB9:090
Auld, Colin	Arlington	Bond	1845	OCR1842:101
Auld, Colin, def.	Alexandria	Suit	1801	CRC:282
Auld, Colin, def.	Alexandria	Suit	1806	CRE:171
Auld, Colin, def.	Alexandria	Suit	1808	CRG:001
Auld, Colin, def.	Alexandria	Suit	1819	CRK:438
Auld, Colin, in Glasgow	Alexandria	Deed	1800	CRC:299
Auld, Colin, late of Glasgow	Alexandria	Deed	1800	CRE:332
Auld, Colin, late of Glasgow	Alexandria	Deed	1800	CRE:221
Auld, Colin, plt.	Alexandria	Suit	1805	CRE:001
Auld, Collin	Alexandria	Tax Charge	1800	Tax PP 1800:01
Auld, Collin, grantee	Arlington	Indenture D.	1806	ID3:245
Auld, Collin, master in chy.	Alexandria	Head	1810	1810(2):04A
Auld, James, grantee	Arlington	Indenture D.	1827	ID:087
Austin, Edward	Arlington	Apprentice	1802	OCR1801:041
Austin, Edward	Alexandria	Boarder	1808	1808(2):11A
Austin, John, grantor	Arlington	Indenture D.	1812	ID2:173
Austin, John, in jail bounds	Arlington	Insolvent	1812	ID2:171
Austin, John, taylor	Alexandria	Housekeeper	1808	1808(3):22A
Austin, John, taylor	Alexandria	Head	1810	1810(3):06A
Austin, Priscilla, c/o Mary	Arlington	Apprentice	1801	OCR1801:009
Austin, Thomas	Alexandria	Tithable +16	1789	Tax PP 1789:12
Austin, Thomas	Alexandria	Tax Charge	1790	Tax PP 1790:01
Austin, Thos.	Alexandria	Tithable +16	1788	Tax PP 1788:11
Avery, James	Arlington	Apprentice	1822	OCR1822:029a
Avery, James, cartman	Alexandria	Housekeeper	1808	1808(3):22A
Avery, James, drayman	Alexandria	Head	1810	1810(3):08A
Avery, John, grantee	Arlington	Indenture D.	1826	ID:018
Avery, John, waggonman	Alexandria	Housekeeper	1808	1808(3):18A
Avery, Richard W.	Alexandria	Will	1899	WB2:324; LP
Avery, Westley, c/o Ann	Arlington	Apprentice	1829	OCR1822:167a
Avery, Westley, c/o Ann	Arlington	Apprentice	1829	OCR1822:169
Awbrey, Francis, age 54	Alexandria	Deposition	1767	CRI:243
Ayres, Jas.	Alexandria	Housekeeper	1808	1808(2):10A

NAME OR SUBJECT	LOCATION	TYPE	YEAR	REFERENCE(S)
B				
B. & Watts	Alexandria	Tax Charge	1798	Tax PP 1798:02
Bacchius, John	Alexandria	Tax Charge	1799	Tax PP 1799:03
Backer, Walther, w(2), brickmaker	Alexandria	Head	1796	1796(3):2
Bacon, Ebenezer	Arlington	Will	1867	WB9:007; File #657A
Bacon, James	Alexandria	Mer. License	1799	Tax PP 1799:52-01r
Bacon, James	Alexandria	Tax Charge	1799	Tax PP 1799:03
Bacon, James	Alexandria	Letters	1805	CRG:232-234
Bacon, James	Arlington	Juryman	1808	ACO:081
Bacon, James	Arlington	Inventory	1810	WBC:363
Bacon, James	Arlington	Admin.	1810	WBC:350, 351
Bacon, James	Arlington	Sale	1810	WBC:391
Bacon, James	Arlington	Account	1811	AB1:083; LVA-LP
Bacon, James	Arlington	Account	1813	AB1:295
Bacon, James, def.	Alexandria	Suit	1801	CRB:283, 287, 290
Bacon, James, def.	Alexandria	Suit	1801	CRB:294
Bacon, James, def.	Alexandria	Suit	1807	CRG:211
Bacon, Jas.	Alexandria	License Due	1800	Tax PP 1800:54(24)
Badden, Tobias, taylor	Alexandria	Head	1810	1810(2):08A
Baden, Benjamin	Alexandria	Tax Charge	1800	Tax PP 1800:02
Baden, Benjamin	Arlington	Appraisal	1830	LVA-LP
Baden, Benjamin	Arlington	Will	1830	WB3:360; File #286A
Baden, Benjamin	Arlington	Bond	1830	WB3:361
Baden, Benjamin	Arlington	Account	1831	AB7:005
Baden, Benjamin, brickmaker	Alexandria	Head	1810	1810(3):03A
Baden, Benjn., brickmaker	Alexandria	Housekeeper	1808	1808(3):19A
Baden, John, Prince St.	Alexandria	Occupant	1795	Tax L 1795:05
Baden, Nehemiah	Alexandria	Boarder	1808	1808(3):19A
Baden, Toby, taylor	Alexandria	Housekeeper	1808	1808(4):28A
Bader, Samuel R.	Alexandria	Tax Charge	1796	Tax PP 1796:02
Badin, Benj.	Alexandria	Tax Charge	1799	Tax PP 1799:04
Badin, Benja. & wife, carter	Alexandria	Housekeeper	1799	1799(2):09A
Badin, John	Alexandria	Tax Charge	1795	Tax PP 1795:03
Badin, John	Alexandria	Tax Charge	1796	Tax LP 1796:03
Badin, John	Alexandria	Tax Charge	1796	Tax PP 1796:01
Badin, John Baptist, w(2), shopkeeper	Alexandria	Head	1796	1796(3):2
Bador, Saml.	Alexandria	Tax Charge	1796	Tax LP 1796:02
Baggenel, Wm.	Alexandria	Tax Charge	1795	Tax PP 1795:02
Bagget, Alexander	Alexandria	Tax Charge	1799	Tax PP 1799:03
Bagget, Nancey	Alexandria	Resident	1800	1800(4):10B
Bagget, Nancey	Alexandria	Head	1800	1800(4):10A
Bagget, Samuel	Alexandria	Tax Charge	1799	Tax PP 1799:03
Baggett, Alexander	Arlington	Inventory	1822	AB5:053; LVA-LP
Baggett, Alexander	Arlington	Admin.	1822	OCR1822:001a, 003a
Baggett, Alexander	Arlington	Admin.	1822	WB3:46, 131
Baggett, Alexander	Arlington	Admin.	1823	OCR1822:058a
Baggett, Alexander	Arlington	Account	1824	AB5:280; LVA-LP
Baggett, Alexander	Arlington	Account	1824	AB5:304; LVA-LP
Baggett, Alexander	Arlington	Account	1825	AB5:407
Baggett, Alexander, orphans of	Arlington	Guard.	1823	OCR1822:043a
Baggett, Alexander, orphans of	Arlington	Guard.	1823	WB3:102
Baggett, Alexr.	Alexandria	Tax Charge	1798	Tax PP 1798:01
Baggett, Alexr., carpenter	Alexandria	Housekeeper	1808	1808(3):18A
Baggett, Aloysius	Arlington	Apprentice	1824	OCR1822:064
Baggett, Anna, c/o Ignatius	Arlington	Guard.	1850	BB(np)
Baggett, Chas.	Alexandria	Boarder	1808	1808(3):18A
Baggett, John	Arlington	Apprentice	1828	OCR1822:158a
Baggett, John, c/o Mary	Arlington	Apprentice	1804	OCR1801:180
Baggett, John, shoemaker	Alexandria	Housekeeper	1808	1808(1):02A
Baggett, John, shoemaker	Alexandria	Head	1810	1810(1):02A
Baggett, Josephine, c/o Ignatius	Arlington	Guard.	1850	BB(np)

NAME OR SUBJECT	LOCATION	TYPE	YEAR	REFERENCE(S)
Baggett, Polly	Arlington	Bond	1851	BB(np)
Baggett, Saml., laborer	Alexandria	Housekeeper	1808	1808(3):18A
Baggett, Samuel	Arlington	Apprentice	1826	OCR1822:108a
Baggett, Samuel	Arlington	Appraisal	1828	LVA-LP
Baggett, Samuel	Arlington	Will	1828	WB3:327; File #278A
Baggett, Samuel	Arlington	Bond	1828	WB3:328
Baggett, Townsend	Alexandria	Will	1887	WB1:466; LP
Baggett, Townsend	Arlington	Will	1887	WB10:129; File #731A
Baggett, William	Arlington	Apprentice	1828	OCR1822:157a
Baggot, Alexander	Alexandria	Tax Charge	1800	Tax PP 1800:03
Baggot, Chas., house joiner	Alexandria	Head	1810	1810(3):06A
Baggot, Ignatius	Alexandria	Tax Charge	1800	Tax PP 1800:02
Baggott, Alexander, def.	Alexandria	Suit	1821	CRL:369
Baggott, Alexr., house joiner	Alexandria	Head	1810	1810(3):09A
Baggott, Elizabeth	Arlington	Guard.	1804	WBA:252
Baggott, Harvey, c/o John	Arlington	Apprentice	1844	OCR1842:068
Baggott, John T.	Arlington	Will	1868	WB9:063; File #663A
Baggott, Samuel	Arlington	Admin.	1803	WBA:104
Bagnell, Wm.	Alexandria	Tax Charge	1796	Tax PP 1796:02
Bagnell, Wm., Water St.	Alexandria	Occupant	1795	Tax L 1795:01
Bagner, Richard	Alexandria	Tax Charge	1796	Tax LP 1796:02
Bagot, Saml. & wife, labourer	Alexandria	Housekeeper	1799	1799(2):14A
Bailey, Elisha	Alexandria	Tax Charge	1796	Tax LP 1796:02
Bailey, Elisha T.	Alexandria	Tax Charge	1798	Tax PP 1798:01
Bailey, Elizabeth, formerly Bailey	Arlington	P. of Atty.	1828	LVA-LP (Accounts)
Bailey, Geo. Wm.	Alexandria	Tax Charge	1798	Tax PP 1798:01
Bailey, George	Alexandria	Tax Charge	1796	Tax PP 1796:01
Bailey, George W.	Alexandria	Tax Charge	1796	Tax LP 1796:02
Bailey, George Wm.	Alexandria	Tax Charge	1799	Tax PP 1799:04
Bailey, Robt.	Alexandria	Boarder	1808	1808(2):14A
Bailey, Thomas	Alexandria	Tax Charge	1795	Tax PP 1795:03
Bailey, William	Alexandria	Tax Charge	1799	Tax PP 1799:03
Bailey, Wm.	Alexandria	Tax Charge	1798	Tax PP 1798:02
Bailiss, Thomas L.P., grantee	Arlington	Indenture D.	1827	ID:102
Bailiss, William, grantor	Arlington	Indenture D.	1813	ID2:204
Bailiss, Wm., in jail bounds	Arlington	Insolvent	1813	ID2:201
Baily, Ann, seamstress	Alexandria	Head	1810	1810(2):03A
Baily, Elisha, w(3)1, carpenter	Alexandria	Head	1796	1796(3):3
Baily, Elizabeth, seamstress	Alexandria	Head	1810	1810(1):07A
Baily, Venice, washer woman	Alexandria	Head	1810	1810(1):01A
Baily, Wm., w, bricklayer	Alexandria	Head	1796	1796(3):3
Baine, Timothy, of Washington DC	Arlington	Apprentice	1805	OCR1801:311
Baird, Thomas E., grantee	Arlington	Indenture D.	1826	ID:049
Baker, B.W.	Alexandria	Tax Charge	1796	Tax LP 1796:02
Baker, Barton	Alexandria	Tax Charge	1796	Tax PP 1796:01
Baker, Francis	Alexandria	Tax Charge	1800	Tax PP 1800:02
Baker, Frederick	Alexandria	Will	1897	WB2:237; LP
Baker, James	Arlington	Apprentice	1802	OCR1801:053
Baker, John, Queen St.	Alexandria	Occupant	1787	Tax L 1787:01
Baker, Martin	Alexandria	Tax Charge	1787	Tax PP 1787:02
Baker, Mary	Arlington	Apprentice	1803	OCR1801:087
Baker, William	Alexandria	Tax Charge	1787	Tax PP 1787:02
Baker, William	Arlington	Trustee Acct.	1857	LVA-LP
Baker, William, as Marshal	Arlington	Letter Patent	1801	ACO:003
Baker, William, def.	Alexandria	Suit	1801	CRB:155
Baker, William, Fairfax St.	Alexandria	Owner	1790	Tax L 1790:02
Baker, Wm. & Co., Fairfax & Duke sts.	Alexandria	Occupant	1787	Tax L 1787:13
Balch, John R.	Alexandria	Tithable +16	1790	Tax PP 1790:07
Balderston v. Scholfield's Exor.	Arlington	Suit	1845	LVA-LP (Box 214)
Baldridge, Mattw.	Alexandria	Tax Charge	1795	Tax PP 1795:02
Baldwin, Edward Francis, c/o James	Arlington	Guard.	1854	BB(np)

NAME OR SUBJECT	LOCATION	TYPE	YEAR	REFERENCE(S)
Baldwin, Jonah	Arlington	Guard.	1854	BB(np)
Baldwin, Jonah, c/o James	Arlington	Guard.	1853	BB(np)
Baldwin, Jonah, c/o James	Arlington	Guard.	1854	BB(np)
Baldwin, Thomas F.	Arlington	Guard.	1854	BB(np)
Baldwin, Thomas F., c/o James	Arlington	Guard.	1853	BB(np)
Balfour, James	Alexandria	Tax Charge	1788	Tax PP 1788:02
Balfour, James	Alexandria	Tax Charge	1789	Tax PP 1789:02
Balfour, James	Alexandria	Tax Charge	1790	Tax PP 1790:01
Balfour, James, King St.	Alexandria	Occupant	1790	Tax L 1790:10
Balfour [Belfour], James	Alexandria	Tax Charge	1787	Tax PP 1787:02
Ball, Ann Eliza	Arlington	Guard. Acct.	1840	AB8:095
Ball, Ann Eliza, c/o Stephen	Arlington	Guard.	1837	WB4:154
Ball, Eliza, c/o Stephen	Arlington	Guard.	1831	WB4:040
Ball, Erasmus	Alexandria	Tax Charge	1796	Tax PP 1796:02
Ball, Horatio	Alexandria	Deposition	1822	CRL:535
Ball, Horatio	Alexandria	Deposition	1822	CRL:472
Ball, Horatio	Arlington	Will	1873	WB9:351; File #687A
Ball, James, Capt.	Frederick	Indenture	1768	E
Ball, James T., Alexandria Co.	Arlington	Ordinary	1834	OBL5(np)
Ball, James T., Alexandria Co.	Arlington	Ordinary	1836	OBL5(np)
Ball, James T., at his house	Arlington	Ordinary	1835	OBL5(np)
Ball, John	Arlington	Admin.	1814	WB1:319
Ball, John	Arlington	Sale	1815	AB2:096
Ball, John	Arlington	Account	1815	AB2:222; LVA-LP
Ball, John	Arlington	Inventory	1823	AB5:190; LVA-LP
Ball, John	Arlington	Admin.	1823	OCR1822:038a
Ball, John	Arlington	Will P.	1823	OCR1822:036, 037a
Ball, John	Arlington	Admin.	1823	WB3:090
Ball, John	Arlington	Account	1824	AB5:342; LVA-LP
Ball, John	Arlington	Will	1858	WB7:366; File #560A
Ball, John & J.T., on Union St.	Arlington	Ordinary	1847	OBL6(np)
Ball, John & Son, on Union St.	Arlington	Ordinary	1845	OBL6(np)
Ball, John, at his house	Arlington	Ordinary	1829	OBL4(np)
Ball, John, bricklayer	Alexandria	Housekeeper	1808	1808(1):07A
Ball, John, bricklayer	Alexandria	Head	1810	1810(4):09A
Ball, John, c/o Stephen	Arlington	Guard.	1831	WB4:040
Ball, John, Sr.	Arlington	Inventory	1815	AB2:082; LVA-LP
Ball, John T., at his house	Arlington	Ordinary	1849	OBL6(np)
Ball, John T., in Alexandria Co.	Arlington	Ordinary	1850	OBL6(np)
Ball, John T., on Union St.	Arlington	Ordinary	1846	OBL6(np)
Ball, Lewis, c/o Stephen	Arlington	Guard.	1831	WB4:040
Ball, Lewis, c/o Stephen	Arlington	Guard.	1837	WB4:154
Ball, Lewis D.	Arlington	Guard. Acct.	1840	AB8:096
Ball, Louisa	Arlington	Guard. Acct.	1842	AB8:309
Ball, Louisa	Arlington	Guard. Acct.	1844	AB8:436; LVA-LP
Ball, Louisa, c/o Stephen	Arlington	Guard.	1831	WB4:040
Ball, Louisa, c/o Stephen	Arlington	Guard.	1837	WB4:154
Ball, Louisa, c/o Stephen	Arlington	Guard. Acct.	1846	AB9:175; LVA-LP
Ball, Louisa H.	Arlington	Guard. Acct.	1840	AB8:097
Ball, Louisa H.	Arlington	Guard. Acct.	1844	AB8:469, 471
Ball, Louisa H., c/o Stephen	Arlington	Guard. Acct.	1841	AB8:192
Ball, Louisa H., c/o Stephen	Arlington	Guard. Acct.	1843	AB8:360; LVA-LP
Ball, Louisa H., c/o Stephen	Arlington	Guard. Acct.	1843	OCR1842:036, 052
Ball, Louisa H., c/o Stephen	Arlington	Guard.	1843	WB4:317
Ball, Moses, age about 50	Alexandria	Deposition	1767	CRI:258
Ball, Phil.	Alexandria	Tax Charge	1795	Tax PP 1795:02
Ball, Robert	Arlington	Admin.	1823	OCR1822:042
Ball, Robert, in Alexandria Co.	Arlington	Ordinary	1833	OBL5(np)
Ball, Robert, at his house	Arlington	Ordinary	1831	OBL4(np)
Ball, Robert, at his house	Arlington	Ordinary	1832	OBL4(np)
Ball, Robert, near the Cross Roads	Arlington	Ordinary	1830	OBL4(np)

NAME OR SUBJECT	LOCATION	TYPE	YEAR	REFERENCE(S)
Ball, Robert, Sr.	Arlington	Will	1863	WB8:177; File #607A
Ball, Stephen	Arlington	Guard. Acct.	1842	AB8:309
Ball, Stephen	Arlington	Guard. Acct.	1843	AB8:360; LVA-LP
Ball, Stephen	Arlington	Guard. Acct.	1844	AB8:436; LVA-LP
Ball, Stephen	Arlington	Guard. Acct.	1844	AB8:470
Ball, Stephen	Arlington	Account	1844	LVA-LP
Ball, Stephen, c/o Stephen	Arlington	Guard.	1831	WB4:040
Ball, Stephen, c/o Stephen	Arlington	Guard.	1837	WB4:154
Ball, Stephen, c/o Stephen	Arlington	Guard. Acct.	1840	AB8:098
Ball, Stephen, c/o Stephen	Arlington	Guard. Acct.	1841	AB8:193
Ball, Stephen, c/o Stephen	Arlington	Guard. Acct.	1843	AB8:360
Ball, Stephen, c/o Stephen	Arlington	Guard. Acct.	1843	OCR1842:036, 052
Ball, Stephen, c/o Stephen	Arlington	Guard.	1843	WB4:318
Ball, Stephen, c/o Stephen	Arlington	Guard. Acct.	1846	AB9:176; LVA-LP
Ball, Stephen, children of	Arlington	Petition	1843	OCR1842:021, 024
Ball, Stephen, children of	Arlington	Guard.	1844	LVA-LP
Ball, Stephen, children of	Arlington	Guard.	1844	OCR1842:074
Ball, Stephen, children of	Arlington	Petition	1844	OCR1842:078; LVA-LP
Ball, Thomas, clerk	Alexandria	Boarder	1800	1800(4):08A
Ball, Thos., bricklayer	Alexandria	Head	1810	1810(3):07A
Ball, William R.	Arlington	Appraisal	1857	WB7:180; LVA-LP
Ballard, Edward	Arlington	Apprentice	1827	OCR1822:143a
Ballard, William	Alexandria	Tax Charge	1799	Tax PP 1799:03
Ballard, William, house joiner	Alexandria	Head	1810	1810(3):09A
Ballard, William, in jail	Arlington	Insolvent	1812	ID2:141
Ballard, William, plt.	Alexandria	Suit	1801	CRB:128
Ballard, Wm., carpenter	Alexandria	Housekeeper	1808	1808(3):18A
Ballenger, Francis, age 50	Alexandria	Deposition	1767	CRI:250
Ballenger, John T., at his house	Arlington	Ordinary	1848	OBL6(np)
Ballenger, Vallentine, labourer	Alexandria	Head	1810	1810(2):06A
Ballinger, Val.	Alexandria	Boarder	1808	1808(2):17A
Baltimore, Lewis	Alexandria	Will	1881	WBC1:037; LP
Baltzel, Jacob	Alexandria	Tax Charge	1800	Tax PP 1800:02
Bane, Henry	Alexandria	Mer. License	1799	Tax PP 1799:52-01r
Bane, Henry	Alexandria	Tax Charge	1800	Tax PP 1800:02
Bangs, William	Arlington	Guard.	1812	WB1:206
Bank of Alexandria	Alexandria	Tax Charge	1796	Tax LP 1796:02
Bank of Alexandria, Cameron St.	Alexandria	Occupant	1795	Tax L 1795:03
Bank of Alexandria, Cameron St.	Alexandria	Owner	1795	Tax L 1795:03
Bank of Alexandria, def.	Alexandria	Suit	1812	CRH:492
Bank of Alexandria, plt.	Alexandria	Suit	1807	CRE:145, 149
Bank of Alexandria, plt.	Alexandria	Suit	1808	CRG:117
Bank of Alexandria, plt.	Alexandria	Suit	1819	CRK:497
Bank of Alexandria, plt.	Alexandria	Suit	1819	CRL:024
Bank of Alexandria, plt.	Alexandria	Suit	1821	CRL:159
Bank of Alexandria, plt.	Alexandria	Suit	1821	CRL:089
Bank of Columbia, plt.	Alexandria	Suit	1817	CRK:301
Bank of the United States	Alexandria	Deed	1811	CRK:045
Bank of the United States, plt.	Alexandria	Suit	1822	CRL:600
Bank of the United States, plt.	Alexandria	Suit	1822	CRL:576
Banks, Ann, washerwoman	Alexandria	Head	1810	1810(1):07A
Banks, Henry, at Richmond	Alexandria	Deposition	1817	CRK:369
Banks, John	Arlington	Guard.	1820	WB2:374
Banks, Nancy (C), washwoman	Alexandria	Housekeeper	1808	1808(1):09A
Barber, Sarah, huckster	Alexandria	Housekeeper	1799	1799(2):01A
Barber, Weadon	Alexandria	Will	1895	WB2:129; LP
Barbine [Berbine], Charles	Arlington	Admin.	1812	WB1:190
Barbour, John	Alexandria	Tax Charge	1796	Tax PP 1796:02
Barbour, John S.	Alexandria	Will	1892	WB2:014; LP
Barbour, Susan Sewall, of DC	Alexandria	Will	1887	WB1:447; LP
Barclay, Francis, Rev.	Alexandria	Head	1810	1810(3):06A

NAME OR SUBJECT	LOCATION	TYPE	YEAR	REFERENCE(S)
Barclay, Thomas	Alexandria	Owner	1787	Tax L 1787:08
Barclay, Thomas	Alexandria	Tax Charge	1787	Tax PP 1787:02
Barclay, Thomas, Prince St.	Alexandria	Occupant	1787	Tax L 1787:08
Barclay, Thomas, Prince St.	Alexandria	Occupant	1787	Tax L 1787:14
Barcroft, John W.	Arlington	Will	1895	WB10:267; File #762A
Barcroft [Bearcroft], Domini	Arlington	Receipt	1830	LVA-LP
Barecraft, Domini (C)	Alexandria	Tax Charge	1800	Tax PP 1800:03
Barecroft, Domini, shopkeeper	Alexandria	Head	1810	1810(2):07A
Barecroft, Dominick	Arlington	Ordinary	1805	OBL1(np)
Barker, Catharine	Arlington	Inventory	1856	WB7:087; LVA-LP
Barker, John	Arlington	Deposition	1806	ACR:030
Barker, John	Alexandria	Boarder	1808	1808(3):21A
Barker, Nathaniel	Arlington	Witness	1794	OT:03/07/1794
Barker, Presley	Alexandria	Boarder	1808	1808(3):19A
Barker, Washington (C)	Arlington	Apprentice	1828	OCR1822:164a
Barker, Washington (C)	Arlington	Apprentice	1829	OCR1822:173a
Barlow, George	Arlington	Admin.	1818	WB2:263
Barlow, George	Arlington	Sale	1819	AB3:285
Barlow, George	Arlington	Inventory	1819	AB3:284; LVA-LP
Barnaby, Davis	Alexandria	Tax Charge	1799	Tax PP 1799:04
Barnes, Elizabeth	Arlington	Admin.	1816	WB2:129
Barnes, Hannah	Alexandria	Will	1888	WBC1:053; LP
Barnes, Jacob, grantor	Arlington	Indenture D.	1806	ID3:191
Barnes, Jacob, in jail	Arlington	Insolvent	1806	ID3:188
Barnes, Jesse, carpenter	Alexandria	Boarder	1799	1799(2):09A
Barnes, John	Alexandria	Account B.	1801	CRD:166
Barnes, John	Arlington	Admin.	1811	WB1:116
Barnes, John, plt.	Alexandria	Suit	1802	CRD:163
Barnes, John [Nancy]	Arlington	Letter	1812	LVA-LP
Barnes, Joseph	Arlington	Inventory	1811	AB1:133; LVA-LP
Barnes, Joseph	Arlington	Account	1812	AB1:191; LVA-LP
Barnes, Samuel	Alexandria	Will	1870	WB1:008; LP
Barnes, Susan, seamstress	Alexandria	Head	1810	1810(4):10A
Barnes, Victoria	Arlington	Sale	1818	AB3:143
Barnes, Victoria	Arlington	Admin	1818	WB2:229
Barnes, Victoria, seamstress	Alexandria	Head	1810	1810(2):06A
Barnes, Victoria, sempstress	Alexandria	Housekeeper	1808	1808(2):17A
Barnett, Mary	Alexandria	Tax Charge	1790	Tax PP 1790:02
Barnett, Michael	Alexandria	Tax Charge	1788	Tax PP 1788:02
Barnett, Michael	Alexandria	Tax Charge	1796	Tax PP 1796:02
Barnhill, John	Alexandria	Tax Charge	1790	Tax PP 1790:02
Barnicoat, John	Arlington	Defendant	1808	ACO:105
Barnicoat, John	Arlington	Defendant	1808	ACO:093
Barnicoat, John	Arlington	Defendant	1810	ACO:113
Barnicoat, John, master	Arlington	Respondent	1806	ACO:070
Barque Henry	Arlington	Suit	1803	ACO:013
Barr, Elizabeth	Alexandria	Boarder	1799	1799(2):05A
Barr, Hugh	Alexandria	Tax Charge	1788	Tax PP 1788:01
Barr, Hugh	Alexandria	Tax Charge	1795	Tax PP 1795:02
Barr, Hugh	Alexandria	Tax Charge	1796	Tax PP 1796:01
Barr, Hugh	Alexandria	Mer. License	1798	Tax PP 1798:20-1
Barr, Hugh	Alexandria	Tax Charge	1798	Tax PP 1798:01
Barr, Hugh	Alexandria	Tax Charge	1799	Tax PP 1799:04
Barr, Hugh	Alexandria	Mer. License	1799	Tax PP 1799:52-01r
Barr, Hugh	Alexandria	Mer. License	1800	Tax PP 1800:54(11)r
Barr, Hugh	Alexandria	Tax Charge	1800	Tax PP 1800:02
Barr, Hugh & wife, grocer	Alexandria	Housekeeper	1799	1799(2):05A
Barr, Hugh, King St.	Alexandria	Occupant	1795	Tax L 1795:07
Barr, Hugh, shopkeeper	Alexandria	Housekeeper	1808	1808(3):23A
Barr, Hugh, shopkeeper	Alexandria	Housekeeper	1808	1808(4):27A
Barr, Hugh, shopkeeper	Alexandria	Head	1810	1810(4):01A

NAME OR SUBJECT	LOCATION	TYPE	YEAR	REFERENCE(S)
Barr, Hugh, w(1), shopkeeper	Alexandria	Head	1796	1796(3):2
Barrel of Hats, etc.	Arlington	Suit	1820	ACO:179
Barrel of Hats, etc.	Arlington	Suit	1821	ACO:187, 190
Barrel of Hats, etc.	Arlington	Suit	1819	ACO:157, 160-163
Barrels of Brown Sugar	Arlington	Suit	1827	ACO:269, 270, 274
Barrett, Jno. & wife, comb maker	Alexandria	Housekeeper	1799	1799(2):07A
Barrett, John	Alexandria	Tax Charge	1799	Tax PP 1799:04
Barrett, John C.	Alexandria	Will	1884	WBC1:046; LP
Barrett, Oliver	Arlington	Plaintiff	1815	ACO:143
Barron, James	Arlington	Deposition	1806	ACR:026, 028
Barrow, Thomas	Arlington	Admin.	1805	WBB:223
Barry, Eliza, of Georgetown DC	Arlington	Will	1880	WB10:005; File #701A
Barry, James	Alexandria	Tax Charge	1790	Tax PP 1790:01
Barry, James C., grantor	Arlington	Indenture D.	1829	ID:233
Barry, James C., in jail bounds	Arlington	Insolvent	1829	ID:231
Barry, Mary	Alexandria	Boarder	1800	1800(4):07A
Barry, Mary	Alexandria	Resident	1800	1800(4):07B
Barry, Mary	Arlington	Sale	1825	AB6:133
Barry, Mary	Arlington	Inventory	1825	AB6:128; LVA-LP
Barry, Mary	Arlington	Admin.	1825	OCR1822:101
Barry, Mary	Arlington	Admin.	1825	WB3:195
Barry, Mary	Arlington	Account	1828	AB6:449; LVA-LP
Barry, Mary & 1 child	Alexandria	Boarder	1799	1799(2):17A
Barry, Mary, schoolmistress	Alexandria	Head	1810	1810(3):03A
Barry, Mary, tutoress	Alexandria	Housekeeper	1808	1808(3):19A
Barry, Peter	Alexandria	Tax Charge	1799	Tax PP 1799:03
Barry, Peter	Alexandria	Tax Charge	1800	Tax PP 1800:02
Barry, Robert, grantor	Arlington	Indenture D.	1832	ID:377
Barry, Robert, in jail bounds	Arlington	Insolvent	1832	ID:374
Barry, Samuel, b. Waterford, Ire.	Arlington	Alien Entry	1826	RA:20/05/26
Barry, Tholomiah, mariner	Alexandria	Head	1810	1810(1):08A
Barry, Thomas	Alexandria	Tax Charge	1796	Tax PP 1796:02
Bartell, Andw., retailer & tavern lic.	Alexandria	Housekeeper	1808	1808(1):03A
Bartell, Saml.	Alexandria	Boarder	1808	1808(1):03A
Bartle, Andrew	Arlington	Ordinary	1804	OBL1(np)
Bartle, Andrew	Arlington	Ordinary	1805	OBL1(np)
Bartle, Andrew	Arlington	Ordinary	1806	OBL2(np)
Bartle, Andrew	Arlington	Ordinary	1807	OBL2(np)
Bartle, Andrew	Arlington	Ordinary	1808	OBL2(np)
Bartle, Andrew	Arlington	Ordinary	1810	OBL2(np)
Bartle, Andrew	Alexandria	Account B.	1814	CRL:353
Bartle, Andrew, def.	Alexandria	Suit	1817	CRL:350
Bartle, Andrew, def.	Alexandria	Suit	1817	CRK:268
Bartle, Andrew, house joiner	Alexandria	Head	1810	1810(2):04A
Bartle, Samuel	Arlington	Will	1863	WB8:159; File #599A
Bartle, Samuel, def.	Alexandria	Suit	1818	CRK:315
Bartle, Samuel, grantee	Arlington	Indenture D.	1829	ID:238
Bartle, Susannah	Arlington	Inventory	1867	WB8:447
Bartle, Susannah	Arlington	Account	1867	WB9:005
Bartle, Susannah	Arlington	Account C.	1870	WB9:248
Bartleman, Margaret, w/o William	Arlington	Will	1861	WB8:081; File #588A
Bartleman, Rebecca J.	Alexandria	Will	1880	WB1:307; LP
Bartleman, William	Alexandria	Tithable +16	1788	Tax PP 1788:11
Bartleman, William	Alexandria	Tithable +16	1789	Tax PP 1789:12
Bartleman, William	Alexandria	Tithable +16	1790	Tax PP 1790:10
Bartleman, William	Alexandria	Mer. License	1799	Tax PP 1799:52-01r
Bartleman, William	Alexandria	Tax Charge	1799	Tax PP 1799:04
Bartleman, William	Alexandria	Tax Charge	1800	Tax PP 1800:02
Bartleman, William	Alexandria	Mer. License	1800	Tax PP 1800:54(11)r
Bartleman, William	Arlington	Juryman	1804	ACO:026
Bartleman, William	Arlington	Inventory	1843	AB8:353; LVA-LP

NAME OR SUBJECT	LOCATION	TYPE	YEAR	REFERENCE(S)
Bartleman, William	Arlington	Will	1843	WB4:312; File #391A
Bartleman, Wm., merchant	Alexandria	Boarder	1799	1799(2):02A
Bartleman, Wm., merchant	Alexandria	Head	1810	1810(1):07A
Bartleman, Wm., retailer	Alexandria	Housekeeper	1808	1808(2):11A
Bartlett, Margaret	Arlington	Guard.	1805	WBB:190
Bartlett, Susannah	Arlington	Account	1868	WB9:135
Barton, Benjamin	Arlington	Inventory	1816	AB2:303; LVA-LP
Barton, Benjamin	Arlington	Admin.	1816	WB2:119
Barton, Benjamin, clockmaker	Alexandria	Head	1810	1810(2):04A
Barton, Benjn., watchmaker	Alexandria	Housekeeper	1808	1808(2):14A
Barton, George W.	Arlington	Apprentice	1822	OCR1822:021a
Barton, Mary	Arlington	Account	1859	WB7:417; LVA-LP
Barton, Richard C.	Arlington	Will	1869	WB9:149; File #668A
Basford, Thomas	Alexandria	Boarder	1808	1808(3):21A
Bates, Isaac	Arlington	Libellant	1821	ACO:198
Bates, Isaac	Arlington	Libellant	1822	ACO:205
Bates, Isaac	Arlington	Libellant	1823	ACO:211
Bates, Thomas	Alexandria	Tax Charge	1799	Tax PP 1799:04
Bates, Thos.	Alexandria	Tax Charge	1800	Tax PP 1800:02
Bathurst, Ann (aka Nancy Batters)	Arlington	Will	1821	WB3:003; File #195A
Batman, William	Arlington	Plaintiff	1802	PA:271
Batters, Nancy (aka Ann Bathurst)	Arlington	Bond	1821	WB3:021
Batters, Nancy (aka Ann Bathurst)	Arlington	Will	1821	WB3:003; File #195A
Bauer, George	Alexandria	Will	1892	WB2:017; LP
Baugh, Jacob	Alexandria	Boarder	1808	1808(4):27A
Baumgarner, John P.	Alexandria	Tithable +21	1787	Tax PP 1787:02
Bayard, William, of New York	Alexandria	Deed	1811	CRK:048
Bayless, Johannah	Arlington	Will	1822	WB3:071; File #211A
Bayley, Elisha & wife, carpenter	Alexandria	Housekeeper	1799	1799(2):10A
Bayley, Elisha Thomas	Alexandria	Tax Charge	1799	Tax PP 1799:04
Bayley, Geo. W. & wife, bricklayer	Alexandria	Housekeeper	1799	1799(2):10A
Bayley, Thomas	Alexandria	Tithable +16	1790	Tax PP 1790:13
Bayley, Wm. & wife, coppersmith	Alexandria	Housekeeper	1799	1799(2):05A
Baylis, Elizabeth, weaver	Alexandria	Head	1810	1810(4):06A
Baylis, William, labourer	Alexandria	Head	1810	1810(3):09A
Bayliss, Johannah	Arlington	Will P.	1822	OCR1822:026
Baylor, Louis	Alexandria	Boarder	1808	1808(2):10A
Bayly, Thomas Elisha	Alexandria	Tithable +16	1789	Tax PP 1789:17
Bayne & Cartwright	Arlington	Ordinary	1803	OBL1(np)
Bayne & Cartwright	Arlington	Division	1815	AB2:136
Bayne, Charity, seamstress	Alexandria	Head	1810	1810(4):08A
Bayne, George H.	Arlington	Will	1858	WB7:318; File #556A
Bayne, George H.	Arlington	Appraisal	1858	WB7:362; LVA-LP
Bayne, George H.	Arlington	Sale S.	1860	WB8:087; LVA-LP
Bayne, George H.	Arlington	Account	1861	WB8:082, 464; LVA-LP
Bayne, George H.	Arlington	Trustee Acct.	1861	WB8:088, 476; LVA-LP
Bayne, Henry	Alexandria	Tax Charge	1799	Tax PP 1799:04
Bayne, Henry	Alexandria	Mer. License	1800	Tax PP 1800:54(11)r
Bayne, Henry	Arlington	Ordinary	1802	OBL1(np)
Bayne, Henry	Arlington	Division	1815	AB2:136
Bayne, Henry	Arlington	Inventory	1826	AB6:166
Bayne, Henry	Arlington	Admin.	1826	OCR1822:109a
Bayne, Henry	Arlington	Will	1826	WB3:220; File #245A
Bayne, Henry	Arlington	Bond	1826	WB3:221
Bayne, Henry, c/o Samuel	Arlington	Apprentice	1815	OCR1811:348
Bayne, Henry, merchant	Alexandria	Head	1810	1810(4):07A
Bayne, John, grantee	Arlington	Indenture D.	1827	ID:099
Bayson, Andrew	Alexandria	Tax Charge	1800	Tax PP 1800:02
Beach, Ebenezer, w, shoemaker	Alexandria	Head	1796	1796(3):7
Beach, Elisha, laborer	Alexandria	Housekeeper	1808	1808(3):18A
Beach, Nath., in market square	Arlington	Ordinary	1846	OBL6(np)

NAME OR SUBJECT	LOCATION	TYPE	YEAR	REFERENCE(S)
Beach, Nathaniel, in market square	Arlington	Ordinary	1845	OBL6(np)
Beach, Nathaniel, in market square	Arlington	Ordinary	1847	OBL6(np)
Beach, Nathaniel, near market square	Arlington	Ordinary	1842	OBL6(np)
Beach, Nathaniel, on Sharpshinn Alley	Arlington	Ordinary	1843	OBL6(np)
Beach, Nathl., his house near market	Arlington	Ordinary	1841	OBL6(np)
Beach, S. Ferguson	Alexandria	Will	1893	WBC1:065; LP
Beach, S. Ferguson	Alexandria	Trustee Acct.	1871	WB1:014
Beach, Samuel F., Notary Public	Arlington	Appointment	1853	BB(np)
Beach, Samuel F., Notary Public	Arlington	Appointment	1854	BB(np)
Beach, Silas, at his house	Arlington	Ordinary	1834	OBL5(np)
Beach, Silas, at his house	Arlington	Ordinary	1835	OBL5(np)
Beach, Silas, at his house	Arlington	Ordinary	1836	OBL5(np)
Beach, Silas, at his house	Arlington	Ordinary	1837	OBL5(np)
Beach, Silas, his house near market	Arlington	Ordinary	1838	OBL5(np)
Beach, Varnell	Alexandria	Boarder	1808	1808(3):18A
Beacon, James	Alexandria	Tax Charge	1800	Tax PP 1800:03
Beadel, Thos.	Alexandria	Tax Charge	1800	Tax PP 1800:02
Beagle, Alfred	Arlington	Apprentice	1826	OCR1822:110a
Beak, David, seaman	Alexandria	Head	1810	1810(2):06A
Beale, Jno., King St.	Alexandria	Occupant	1795	Tax L 1795:19
Beale, John	Alexandria	Tithable +21	1787	Tax PP 1787:07
Beale, John	Alexandria	Tax Charge	1790	Tax PP 1790:01
Beale, John	Alexandria	Tax Charge	1795	Tax PP 1795:02
Beale, John	Alexandria	Tax Charge	1796	Tax LP 1796:02
Beale, John	Alexandria	Tax Charge	1796	Tax PP 1796:02
Beale, John, King St.	Alexandria	Occupant	1790	Tax L 1790:08
Beale, Peter	Alexandria	Tax Charge	1796	Tax PP 1796:01
Beale, Thos. K., house joiner	Alexandria	Head	1810	1810(4):07A
Beall, John	Alexandria	Tithable +16	1788	Tax PP 1788:07
Beall, John, c/o Hellender Wilson	Arlington	Apprentice	1803	OCR1801:075
Beall, Thomas, def.	Alexandria	Suit	1801	CRD:111
Beall, William	Arlington	Apprentice	1805	OCR1801:297
Bean, [blank]	Alexandria	Boarder	1808	1808(2):12A
Beane, Jane	Arlington	Inventory	1819	AB3:295; LVA-LP
Beane, Jane	Arlington	Will	1819	WB2:275; File #158A
Beane, Jane	Arlington	Bond	1819	WB2:276
Beane, Jane	Arlington	Account	1820	AB4:125; LVA-LP
Beane, Jane	Arlington	Sale	1820	AB4:125
Bearcraft, Dominick	Arlington	Ordinary	1806	OBL2(np)
Bearcraft, Dominick	Arlington	Ordinary	1807	OBL2(np)
Bearcroft, Domini	Arlington	Ordinary	1803	OBL1(np)
Bearcroft, Domini	Arlington	Ordinary	1821	OBL3(np)
Bearcroft, Domini	Arlington	Ordinary	1823	OBL3(np)
Bearcroft, Domini	Arlington	Appraisal	1830	LVA-LP
Bearcroft, Domini	Arlington	Bond	1830	WB3:362
Bearcroft, Domini	Arlington	Will	1830	WB3:361; File #287A
Bearcroft, Domini	Arlington	Guard. Acct.	1834	LVA-LP
Bearcroft, Domini	Arlington	Account	1835	AB7:170; LVA-LP
Bearcroft, Domini	Arlington	Account	1835	AB7:166; LVA-LP
Bearcroft, Domini	Arlington	Account	1839	AB7:324
Bearcroft, Domini, at his house	Arlington	Ordinary	1826	OBL4(np)
Bearcroft, Domini, at his house	Arlington	Ordinary	1828	OBL4(np)
Bearcroft, Domini, at his house	Arlington	Ordinary	1829	OBL4(np)
Bearcroft, Domini, at his house	Arlington	Ordinary	1830	OBL4(np)
Bearcroft, Domini, children of	Arlington	Guard. Acct.	1839	AB7:324
Bearcroft, Domini, in Alexandria Co.	Arlington	Ordinary	1822	OBL3(np)
Bearcroft, Domini, in Alexandria Co.	Arlington	Ordinary	1824	OBL3(np)
Bearcroft, Domini, in Alexandria Co.	Arlington	Ordinary	1825	OBL4(np)
Bearcroft, Domini, in Alexandria Co.	Arlington	Ordinary	1827	OBL4(np)
Bearcroft, Domini, orphans of	Arlington	Guard. Acct.	1833	LVA-LP
Bearcroft, Dominic	Arlington	Ordinary	1808	OBL2(np)

NAME OR SUBJECT	LOCATION	TYPE	YEAR	REFERENCE(S)
Bearcroft, Dominic, orphans of	Arlington	Guard.	1832	WB4:054, 55
Bearcroft, Dominick	Arlington	Ordinary	1809	OBL2(np)
Bearcroft, Dominy, shopkeeper & T.L.	Alexandria	Housekeeper	1808	1808(2):17A
Bearcroft, Ephraim	Arlington	Guard.	1832	WB4:053
Bearcroft, Ephraim	Arlington	Account	1834	AB8:328; LVA-LP
Bearcroft, Ephraim	Arlington	Guard. Acct.	1835	AB7:164
Bearcroft, Ephraim	Arlington	Guard. Acct.	1836	AB7:164; LVA-LP
Bearcroft, Ephraim	Arlington	Guard. Acct.	1837	AB7:341; LVA-LP
Bearcroft [Barcroft], Ephraim	Arlington	Guard. Acct.	1838	AB7:341; LVA-LP
Bearcroft, Ephraim	Arlington	Guard. Acct.	1839	AB7:327, 341
Bearcroft, Ephraim	Arlington	Guard. Acct.	1843	AB8:359; LVA-LP
Bearcroft, Ephraim, orphans of	Arlington	Guard. Acct.	1833	LVA-LP
Bearcroft, Sally, her house Cameron St.	Arlington	Ordinary	1831	OBL4(np)
Bearcroft, William H.	Arlington	Guard.	1832	WB4:054
Bearcroft, William H.	Arlington	Guard. Acct.	1833	AB7:085; LVA-LP
Bearcroft, William H.	Arlington	Guard. Acct.	1834	AB7:130; LVA-LP
Bearcroft, William H.	Arlington	Guard. Acct.	1835	AB7:159; LVA-LP
Beard, Jno.	Alexandria	Tax Charge	1795	Tax PP 1795:02
Bears, Peter	Alexandria	Tax Charge	1800	Tax PP 1800:03
Beatis, John	Alexandria	Tax Charge	1790	Tax PP 1790:02
Beatis, John, St. Asaph St.	Alexandria	Occupant	1790	Tax L 1790:09
Beattis, John	Alexandria	Tax Charge	1795	Tax PP 1795:02
Beatty & Walker, Royal St.	Alexandria	Occupant	1795	Tax L 1795:19
Beatty, James	Alexandria	Deposition	1808	CRI:425, 434
Beatty, John	Alexandria	Tax Charge	1795	Tax PP 1795:02
Beatty, John, King St.	Alexandria	Occupant	1795	Tax L 1795:21
Beatty, Zaccheus	Alexandria	Tax Charge	1795	Tax PP 1795:02
Beaty, John, c/o William	Arlington	Apprentice	1805	OCR1801:272
Beckley, Archibald, grantee	Arlington	Indenture D.	1832	ID:395
Beckley, Edgar R., c/o John A.	Arlington	Guard.	1854	BB(np)
Beckley, Jesse, grantor	Arlington	Indenture D.	1830	ID:268
Beckley, Jesse, grantor	Arlington	Indenture D.	1832	ID:395
Beckley, Jesse, in jail	Arlington	Insolvent	1830	ID:266
Beckley, Jesse, in jail bounds	Arlington	Insolvent	1832	ID:394
Beckley, John A.	Arlington	Appraisal	1854	WB6:391; LVA-LP
Beckley, John A.	Arlington	Account	1854	WB6:411; LVA-LP
Beckley, Mary Elizabeth, c/o John A.	Arlington	Guard.	1854	BB(np)
Beckwith, Rezin	Alexandria	Tax Charge	1795	Tax PP 1795:02
Beckwith, Rezin	Alexandria	Tax Charge	1796	Tax PP 1796:02
Beddinger, Jacob	Alexandria	Tax Charge	1789	Tax PP 1789:02
Bedinger, Katharine H.	Arlington	Inventory	1866	WB8:443
Bedinger, Katharine H.	Arlington	Will	1866	WB8:417; File #649A
Beech, Charles, in Alexandria Co.	Arlington	Ordinary	1821	OBL3(np)
Beedle, Henry, c/o Mary	Arlington	Apprentice	1814	OCR1811:239
Beedle, Thomas	Alexandria	Tax Charge	1798	Tax PP 1798:01
Beedle, Thomas	Alexandria	Tax Charge	1799	Tax PP 1799:03
Beedle, Thomas	Arlington	Inventory	1803	WBA:199; LVA-LP
Beedle, Thomas	Arlington	Admin.	1803	WBA:183
Beedle, Thomas	Arlington	Sale	1804	WBA:269
Beedle, Thomas	Arlington	Account	1804	WBB:100; LVA-LP
Beek, David, taylor	Alexandria	Head	1810	1810(1):07A
Beeler, Benja.	Alexandria	Tax Charge	1796	Tax LP 1796:03
Beeler, Lewis, confectioner	Alexandria	Head	1810	1810(2):02A
Beeler, Lewis, def.	Alexandria	Suit	1822	CRL:232
Beeler, Lewis, def.	Alexandria	Suit	1822	CRL:232
Beeler, Louis, at his house	Arlington	Ordinary	1825	OBL4(np)
Beeler, Louis, at his house	Arlington	Ordinary	1826	OBL4(np)
Beeler, Louis, at his house	Arlington	Ordinary	1828	OBL4(np)
Beeler, Louis, at his house	Arlington	Ordinary	1830	OBL4(np)
Beeler, Louis, in Alexandria Co.	Arlington	Ordinary	1824	OBL3(np)
Beeler, Louis, in Alexandria Co.	Arlington	Ordinary	1827	OBL4(np)

NAME OR SUBJECT	LOCATION	TYPE	YEAR	REFERENCE(S)
Beeler, Louis, on King St.	Arlington	Ordinary	1823	OBL3(np)
Beery, Jacob	Alexandria	Tax Charge	1799	Tax PP 1799:03
Belflower, Jno.	Alexandria	Boarder	1808	1808(2):12A
Belford, James	Alexandria	Tax Charge	1796	Tax PP 1796:02
Belfore, James	Alexandria	Tax Charge	1795	Tax PP 1795:02
Belfore, James	Alexandria	Tax Charge	1796	Tax LP 1796:03
Belfore, James, w, brewer	Alexandria	Head	1796	1796(3):6
Belfore, Jas., Water St.	Alexandria	Occupant	1795	Tax L 1795:23
Belfour, James	Alexandria	Tax Charge	1799	Tax PP 1799:04
Belfour, James & wife, brewer	Alexandria	Head	1795	1795(4):01
Belfour, Jas.	Alexandria	Tax Charge	1798	Tax PP 1798:02
Bell, Betty, alias Mullican, def.	Alexandria	Suit	1802	CRC:220
Bell, Boaz	Arlington	Respondent	1808	ACO:082
Bell, Boaz, Master	Arlington	Respondent	1806	ACO:052, 071
Bell, Boaz, Owner	Arlington	Respondent	1807	ACO:074, 080
Bell, Boaz, sea captain	Alexandria	Housekeeper	1808	1808(4):26A
Bell, Boaz, seaman	Alexandria	Head	1810	1810(4):04A
Bell, Charles, Queen St.	Alexandria	Occupant	1790	Tax L 1790:05
Bell, Dolly	Arlington	Account	1818	AB3:245; LVA-LP
Bell, Dolly	Arlington	Trustee Acct.	1819	AB3:383; LVA-LP
Bell, Dolly	Arlington	Account	1819	AB3:309; LVA-LP
Bell, Dolly	Arlington	Account	1821	AB4:308; LVA-LP
Bell, Dolly	Arlington	Guard. Acct.	1822	AB5:137; LVA-LP
Bell, Dolly, children of	Arlington	Guard. Acct.	1824	AB5:273; LVA-LP
Bell, Dolly, children of	Arlington	Guard. Acct.	1826	AB6:235; LVA-LP
Bell, Elias (C)	Arlington	Apprentice	1826	OCR1822:118a
Bell, Forrester (C), laborer	Alexandria	Housekeeper	1808	1808(2):14A
Bell, Foster, labourer	Alexandria	Head	1810	1810(1):06A
Bell, Harry (C)	Alexandria	Boarder	1808	1808(1):05B
Bell, Henry (C), c/o Judy	Arlington	Apprentice	1815	OCR1811:268
Bell, James	Alexandria	Tithable +21	1787	Tax PP 1787:13
Bell, James	Alexandria	Tithable +16	1788	Tax PP 1788:14
Bell, James, def.	Alexandria	Suit	1803	CRD:074
Bell, John Anderson, sl/o George Page	Arlington	Apprentice	1815	OCR1811:307
Bell, Judy, washerwoman	Alexandria	Head	1810	1810(3):07A
Bell, Mary	Alexandria	Will	1894	WB2:080; LP
Bell, Monnaca, washerwoman	Alexandria	Head	1810	1810(1):10A
Bell, Robert	Arlington	Libellant	1813	ACO:137
Bell, Robert	Alexandria	Will	1894	WB2:079; LP
Bell, Robert (C)	Arlington	Apprentice	1815	OCR1811:301
Bell, Robert (C)	Arlington	Apprentice	1826	OCR1822:115
Bell, Sally (C), washer woman	Alexandria	Housekeeper	1799	1799(2):19A
Bell, Sarah	Alexandria	Resident	1800	1800(4):09B
Bell, Sarah (C)	Alexandria	Head	1795	1795(4a):09
Bell, Sarah, sempster	Alexandria	Head	1800	1800(4):09A
Bell, William, in prison rules	Arlington	Insolvent	1806	ID3:195
Bell, Wm., sea captain	Alexandria	Housekeeper	1808	1808(1):08A
Belmain, Andrew, def.	Alexandria	Suit	1802	CRC:270
Belt, Walter S., of Colchester	Alexandria	Mer. License	1800	Tax PP 1800:54(11)r
Bence, A., Thorn alley	Alexandria	Occupant	1787	Tax L 1787:25
Bence, Adam	Alexandria	Tax Charge	1787	Tax PP 1787:02
Bence, Adam	Alexandria	Tax Charge	1788	Tax PP 1788:02
Bence, Adam	Alexandria	Tax Charge	1789	Tax PP 1789:02
Bence, Adam	Alexandria	Tax Charge	1790	Tax PP 1790:01
Bence, Adam, nr. Gibbons St.	Alexandria	Occupant	1790	Tax L 1790:02
Bence, Adam, nr. Gibbons St.	Alexandria	Owner	1790	Tax L 1790:02
Benham, Alexander	Alexandria	Tithable +16	1788	Tax PP 1788:08
Benkert, John D.	Arlington	Inventory	1821	AB4:327; LVA-LP
Benkert, John D.	Arlington	Admin.	1821	WB3:026
Bennet & Watts	Alexandria	Mer. License	1799	Tax PP 1799:52-01w
Bennet, Ann, seamstress	Alexandria	Head	1810	1810(3):09A

NAME OR SUBJECT	LOCATION	TYPE	YEAR	REFERENCE(S)
Bennet, Chas.	Alexandria	Tax Charge	1795	Tax PP 1795:03
Bennet, Jona., merchant	Alexandria	Boarder	1799	1799(2):02A
Bennet, Mary, washer	Alexandria	Head	1795	1795(4):05
Bennet, Richard	Alexandria	Tax Charge	1800	Tax PP 1800:03
Bennet, Richard & wife Sarah	Alexandria	Resident	1800	1800(4):03B
Bennet, Richard, shopkeeper	Alexandria	Head	1800	1800(4):03A
Bennet, William	Alexandria	Tax Charge	1799	Tax PP 1799:03
Bennet, William, labourer	Alexandria	Head	1810	1810(4):09A
Bennet, Wm. & wife (C), labourer	Alexandria	Housekeeper	1799	1799(2):14A
Bennett & Watts	Alexandria	Tax Charge	1796	Tax LP 1796:02
Bennett & Watts	Alexandria	Tax Charge	1796	Tax PP 1796:01
Bennett & Watts	Alexandria	Mer. License	1798	Tax PP 1798:20-1
Bennett & Watts	Alexandria	Tax Charge	1799	Tax PP 1799:03
Bennett & Watts	Alexandria	Mer. License	1800	Tax PP 1800:54(11)w
Bennett & Watts	Alexandria	Tax Charge	1800	Tax PP 1800:02
Bennett & Watts, King St.	Alexandria	Occupant	1795	Tax L 1795:27
Bennett & Watts, plt.	Alexandria	Suit	1801	CRB:105
Bennett & Watts, plt.	Alexandria	Suit	1801	CRB:063
Bennett & Watts, plt.	Alexandria	Suit	1801	CRB:252
Bennett & Watts, plt.	Alexandria	Suit	1801	CRB:275
Bennett & Watts, plt.	Alexandria	Suit	1801	CRB:155
Bennett & Watts, plt.	Alexandria	Suit	1802	CRB:324
Bennett, Barbara	Alexandria	Will	1877	WB1:213; LP
Bennett, Bill, drayman	Alexandria	Housekeeper	1808	1808(4):24A
Bennett, Charles	Alexandria	Tithable +16	1789	Tax PP 1789:08
Bennett, Charles	Alexandria	Tithable +16	1790	Tax PP 1790:07
Bennett, Charles	Arlington	Plaintiff	1802	PA:065
Bennett, Charles	Arlington	Claim	1812	ACO:124
Bennett, Charles	Arlington	Debts	1839	AB8:006; LVA-LP
Bennett, Charles	Arlington	Inventory	1839	AB8:001; LVA-LP
Bennett, Charles	Arlington	Will	1839	WB4:191; File #363A
Bennett, Charles	Arlington	Account	1840	AB8:140a; LVA-LP
Bennett, Charles	Arlington	Account	1841	AB8:176
Bennett, Charles	Arlington	Account	1841	AB8:253; LVA-LP
Bennett, Charles	Arlington	Account	1842	AB8:259; LVA-LP
Bennett, Charles	Arlington	Receipt	1842	AB8:294
Bennett, Charles	Arlington	Release	1842	AB8:294
Bennett, Charles	Arlington	Account	1842	AB8:318; LVA-LP
Bennett, Charles	Arlington	Account	1842	OCR1842:003, 006
Bennett, Charles	Arlington	Account	1843	AB8:362; LVA-LP
Bennett, Charles	Arlington	Account	1844	AB8:456; LVA-LP
Bennett, Charles	Arlington	Petition	1844	LVA-LP (Box 214)
Bennett, Charles	Arlington	Will P.	1844	OCR1842:063
Bennett, Charles	Arlington	Account	1845	AB9:046; LVA-LP
Bennett, Charles	Arlington	Account	1846	AB9:269; LVA-LP
Bennett, Charles	Arlington	Account	1847	AB9:318
Bennett, Charles	Arlington	Account	1847	AB9:269
Bennett, Charles	Arlington	Account	1849	WB5:136; LVA-LP
Bennett, Charles	Arlington	Account C.	1850	WB5:244; LVA-LP
Bennett, Charles	Arlington	Account	1852	WB6:072; LVA-LP
Bennett, Charles, plt.	Alexandria	Suit	1801	CRB:063
Bennett, Charles, plt.	Alexandria	Suit	1802	CRC:274
Bennett, Chas., merchant	Alexandria	Housekeeper	1808	1808(2):11A
Bennett, Chas., merchant	Alexandria	Head	1810	1810(2):02A
Bennett, Daniel (C)	Arlington	Apprentice	1845	OCR1842:154
Bennett, Joseph T.	Arlington	Ordinary	1803	OBL1(np)
Bent, Leml.	Alexandria	Tax Charge	1796	Tax LP 1796:02
Bent, Lemuel	Alexandria	Tax Charge	1795	Tax PP 1795:03
Bent, Lemuel	Alexandria	Tax Charge	1796	Tax PP 1796:02
Bent, Lemuel	Alexandria	Tax Charge	1798	Tax PP 1798:02
Bent, Lemuel & wife, merchant	Alexandria	Head	1795	1795(4):01

NAME OR SUBJECT	LOCATION	TYPE	YEAR	REFERENCE(S)
Bent, Lemuel, Estate, alley btw. Union	Alexandria	Owner	1795	Tax L 1795:02
Bent, Nathl.	Alexandria	Tax Charge	1796	Tax LP 1796:02
Benter, Harriet Virginia, c/o Wesley	Arlington	Guard.	1847	OCR1842:198
Benter, John W., grantor	Arlington	Indenture D.	1830	ID:263
Benter, John W., in jail bounds	Arlington	Insolvent	1830	ID:260
Benter, William, grantor	Arlington	Indenture D.	1826	ID:018
Benter, William, in prison rules	Arlington	Insolvent	1826	ID:016
Benter, William, shopkeeper	Alexandria	Head	1810	1810(2):02A
Benton, Saml., cooper	Alexandria	Housekeeper	1808	1808(4):26A
Benton, Saml., cooper	Alexandria	Head	1810	1810(4):02A
Benton, Samuel	Arlington	Guard.	1805	WBB:165
Bentz, Adam, Water St.	Alexandria	Occupant	1787	Tax L 1787:05
Berbeck, Michael	Alexandria	Tithable +21	1787	Tax PP 1787:12
Berbine [Barbine], Charles	Arlington	Account	1812	AB1:255; LVA-LP
Berbine [Barbine], Charles	Arlington	Inventory	1812	AB1:254; LVA-LP
Berkley, Jane	Alexandria	Resident	1800	1800(4):03B
Berkley, Jane, labourer	Alexandria	Boarder	1800	1800(4):03A
Berkley, Peggy, washer	Alexandria	Head	1795	1795(4):03
Berkley, William	Arlington	Apprentice	1803	OCR1801:089
Berkley, William N.	Alexandria	Will	1897	WB2:231; LP
Bernard, John F.	Alexandria	Tithable +16	1788	Tax PP 1788:09
Bernard, Michael	Alexandria	Tax Charge	1789	Tax PP 1789:02
Bernard, Michael	Alexandria	Tax Charge	1790	Tax PP 1790:02
Berry, Benjamin, grantor	Arlington	Indenture D.	1817	ID2:415
Berry, Benjamin Harrison, Clerk	Arlington	Appointment	1852	BB(np)
Berry, Benjamin, in jail	Arlington	Insolvent	1817	ID2:413
Berry, Elizabety, seamstress	Alexandria	Head	1810	1810(3):05A
Berry, George, at his house	Arlington	Ordinary	1848	OBL6(np)
Berry, George, at his house	Arlington	Ordinary	1849	OBL6(np)
Berry, George, in Alexandria Co.	Arlington	Ordinary	1847	OBL6(np)
Berry, Henry	Arlington	Appraisal	1855	WB6:428; LVA-LP
Berry, Henry	Arlington	Will	1855	WB6:425; File #517A
Berry, James (C)	Arlington	Apprentice	1828	OCR1822:152
Berry, Jane, sempstress	Alexandria	Housekeeper	1808	1808(1):08A
Berry, Laura, of King George Co.	Alexandria	Will	1899	WBC1:082
Berry, Samuel, c/o Joanna	Arlington	Apprentice	1801	OCR1801:006
Berry, Tholemiah, seaman	Alexandria	Housekeeper	1808	1808(1):06A
Berry, Tholomiah	Arlington	Respondent	1813	ACO:137
Berry, Wm., waterman	Alexandria	Housekeeper	1808	1808(4):24A
Betsold, Dorothea, b. Kinebeau	Arlington	Alien Entry	1819	RA:20/05/19
Bevan, Samuel, of Baltimore MD	Arlington	Will	1892	WB10:194; File #753A
Beverley, Munford	Arlington	Respondent	1803	ACO:022
Beverley, Peter R.	Arlington	Appointment	1854	BB(np)
Beverley, Peter R., def.	Alexandria	Suit	1820	CRL:070
Beverley, William B., of Essex Co.	Alexandria	Will	1898	WB2:260; LP
Beverly, Munford	Arlington	Respondent	1804	ACO:029, 031
Beverly, Munford	Arlington	Respondent	1804	ACO:024
Beverly, Peter R., plt.	Alexandria	Suit	1822	CRL:232
Beverly, Robert, plt.	Alexandria	Suit	1811	CRI:131
Beverly, Robert, plt.	Alexandria	Suit	1814	CRI:440
Bibby, Jim	Alexandria	Boarder	1808	1808(1):03A
Bickerton, Alexander, grantor	Arlington	Indenture D.	1806	ID3:211
Bickerton, Alexander, in jail	Arlington	Insolvent	1806	ID3:205
Bickerton, Alexr., seaman	Alexandria	Head	1810	1810(1):09A
Bickley & Buckner	Alexandria	Mer. License	1798	Tax PP 1798:20-1
Bicksbey, Daniel, merchant	Alexandria	Head	1810	1810(3):04A
Bicksler, John, weaver	Alexandria	Head	1810	1810(3):03A
Bickster, John, shopkeeper & distiller	Alexandria	Housekeeper	1808	1808(4):26A
Biggerton, Alexr., waterman	Alexandria	Housekeeper	1808	1808(1):07A
Bigginton, Alexr. & wife, musician	Alexandria	Housekeeper	1799	1799(2):15A
Biggs, James	Arlington	Apprentice	1826	OCR1822:111

NAME OR SUBJECT	LOCATION	TYPE	YEAR	REFERENCE(S)
Billie, Peter & wife Mary Ann	Alexandria	Resident	1800	1800(4):11B
Billie, Peter, Scotsman	Alexandria	Head	1800	1800(4):11A
Billington, William	Alexandria	Tax Charge	1799	Tax PP 1799:03
Billington, William	Alexandria	Tax Charge	1800	Tax PP 1800:03
Billington, William	Arlington	Defendant	1802	PA:144
Billington, William	Alexandria	Deposition	1804	CRE:340
Billington, Wm.	Alexandria	Tax Charge	1798	Tax PP 1798:01
Billington, Wm. & wife, grocer	Alexandria	Housekeeper	1799	1799(2):05A
Billmyers, Thos. & wife, butcher	Alexandria	Housekeeper	1799	1799(2):15A
Billmyers, Thos., butcher	Alexandria	Housekeeper	1808	1808(1):08A
Billy, Peter & wife	Alexandria	Housekeeper	1799	1799(2):20A
Billy, Peter, gardener	Alexandria	Housekeeper	1808	1808(1):10A
Billy, Peter, gardner	Alexandria	Head	1810	1810(1):11A
Bilmier, Thomas & wife Sarah	Alexandria	Resident	1800	1800(4):03B
Bilmier, Thomas, butcher	Alexandria	Head	1800	1800(4):03A
Bilmire, Thomas	Alexandria	Tax Charge	1796	Tax PP 1796:01
Bilmire, Thos.	Alexandria	Tax Charge	1798	Tax PP 1798:02
Bilmire, Thos.	Alexandria	Tax Charge	1799	Tax PP 1799:04
Bilmire, Thos.	Alexandria	Tax Charge	1800	Tax PP 1800:02
Binney, Horace, of Philadelphia	Alexandria	Deed	1811	CRK:048
Birch, Caleb, c/o Jacob	Arlington	Guard.	1823	WB3:082
Birch, Caleb L.	Arlington	Will	1886	WB10:075; File #723A
Birch, Isaac	Arlington	Guard.	1815	WB2:070
Birch, Jacob	Arlington	Guard.	1816	WB2:146
Birch, Jacob	Arlington	Guard.	1819	WB2:338
Birch, Jacob	Arlington	Admin.	1823	WB3:081
Birch, Jacob	Arlington	Guard. Acct.	1824	AB5:275; LVA-LP
Birch, Jacob, c/o John	Arlington	Guard.	1857	WB7:301; LVA-LP
Birch, James	Arlington	Plaintiff	1802	PA:263
Birch, James	Alexandria	Deposition	1822	CRL:474
Birch, James	Alexandria	Deposition	1822	CRL:537
Birch, James	Arlington	Inventory	1854	WB6:307; LVA-LP
Birch, James	Arlington	Account	1855	WB6:462; LVA-LP
Birch, James, at the Cross Roads	Arlington	Ordinary	1822	OBL3(np)
Birch, James, def.	Alexandria	Suit	1801	CRB:150
Birch, James, drayman	Alexandria	Head	1810	1810(3):08A
Birch, James, in Alexandria Co.	Arlington	Ordinary	1822	OBL3(np)
Birch, James, in Alexandria Co.	Arlington	Ordinary	1825	OBL4(np)
Birch, James, Jr.	Arlington	Insolvent	1826	ID:034
Birch, James, Jr., grantor	Arlington	Indenture D.	1826	ID:035
Birch, Jesse	Arlington	Admin.	1816	WB2:135
Birch, John	Arlington	Will	1855	WB6:422; File #516A
Birch, John	Arlington	Sale	1856	WB7:090; LVA-LP
Birch, John	Arlington	Appraisal	1856	WB7:089; LVA-LP
Birch, John	Arlington	Account	1856	WB7:096; LVA-LP
Birch, John	Arlington	Account	1858	WB7:327; LVA-LP
Birch, John	Arlington	Account	1858	WB7:483; LVA-LP
Birch, John	Arlington	Account C.	1860	WB8:047; LVA-LP
Birch, John T.	Arlington	Will	1900	WB10:416; File #794A
Birch, Joseph	Arlington	Sale	1815	AB2:224
Birch, Joseph	Arlington	Inventory	1815	AB2:160; LVA-LP
Birch, Joseph	Arlington	Admin.	1815	WB2:054
Birch, Joseph	Arlington	Account	1816	AB2:392
Birch, Joseph	Arlington	Admin.	1830	WB3:383
Birch, Joseph, c/o Jacob	Arlington	Guard.	1823	WB3:082
Birch, Joseph, c/o Joseph	Arlington	Guard.	1831	WB4:005
Birch, Lucy, c/o John	Arlington	Guard.	1857	WB7:300; LVA-LP
Birch, Samuel	Arlington	Appraisal	1874	WB9:366
Birch, Sarah Jane	Arlington	Will	1891	WB10:190; File #751A
Birch, Theoddorus	Alexandria	Boarder	1808	1808(3):18A
Birch, William	Arlington	Will	1870	WB9:277; File #682A

NAME OR SUBJECT	LOCATION	TYPE	YEAR	REFERENCE(S)
Birch, William, c/o Jacob	Arlington	Guard.	1823	WB3:082
Birch, William Henry, c/o Joseph	Arlington	Guard.	1831	WB4:005
Bird, John	Arlington	Will	1820	WB2:345; File #171A
Bird, John [Rebecca F.]	Arlington	Receipt	1821	AB4:227
Bird, Thomas	Arlington	Ordinary	1821	OBL3(np)
Bird, Thomas, in Alexandria Co.	Arlington	Ordinary	1822	OBL3(np)
Bird, William	Alexandria	Owner	1787	Tax L 1787:07
Bird, William, Fairfax St.	Alexandria	Owner	1790	Tax L 1790:02(2)
Bird, Wm., St. Asaph St.	Alexandria	Occupant	1787	Tax L 1787:07
Bishop, Ann	Alexandria	Head	1810	1810(3):01A
Bishop, Bishop	Arlington	Plaintiff	1802	PA:300
Bishop, Daniel	Alexandria	Tax Charge	1798	Tax PP 1798:02
Bishop, Daniel	Alexandria	Tax Charge	1799	Tax PP 1799:03
Bishop, Joshua, c/o Ann	Arlington	Apprentice	1812	OCR1811:049
Bishop, Joshua, c/o Ann	Arlington	Apprentice	1812	OCR1811:086
Bishop, Mrs., w/o Wm., sempstress	Alexandria	Housekeeper	1808	1808(3):20A
Bishop, Samuel	Alexandria	Mer. License	1798	Tax PP 1798:20-1
Bishop, Samuel	Alexandria	Tax Charge	1800	Tax PP 1800:02
Bishop, Sarah, seamstress	Alexandria	Head	1810	1810(3):03A
Bixio, Joseph, M.G.	Arlington	Ordination	1852	BB(np)
Bixler, John	Alexandria	Tax Charge	1800	Tax PP 1800:02
Black, Alexr., Estate	Alexandria	Owner	1787	Tax L 1787:06
Black, Andrew	Alexandria	Tithable +16	1788	Tax PP 1788:01
Black, Benja.	Alexandria	Tithable +16	1788	Tax PP 1788:17
Black, Benjamin	Alexandria	Tithable +21	1787	Tax PP 1787:16
Black, Benjamin	Alexandria	Tithable +16	1789	Tax PP 1789:20
Black, Capt. D., seaman	Alexandria	Head	1810	1810(3):01A
Black, Charles	Alexandria	Tax Charge	1799	Tax PP 1799:03
Black Charles (C)	Alexandria	Tax Charge	1788	Tax PP 1788:04
Black, David	Arlington	Admin.	1836	WB4:106
Black, David & wife & 1 child	Alexandria	Boarder	1799	1799(2):17A
Black, David & wife Eliza	Alexandria	Resident	1800	1800(4):13B
Black, David, def.	Alexandria	Suit	1809	CRH:423
Black, David M., grantee	Arlington	Indenture D.	1826	ID:035
Black, David, marriener	Alexandria	Head	1800	1800(4):13A
Black, David, retailer	Alexandria	Housekeeper	1808	1808(1):03A
Black, David, storekeeper	Alexandria	Housekeeper	1808	1808(4):24A
Black, Eliza	Arlington	Will	1850	WB5:224; File #458A
Black, James, grantor	Arlington	Indenture D.	1832	ID:381
Black, James, in confinement	Arlington	Insolvent	1832	ID:379
Black, Jas., Queen St.	Alexandria	Owner	1795	Tax L 1795:03
Black, Jeremiah S., of York Co. PA	Arlington	Will	1883	WB10:046; File #715A
Black, Nancy, washerwoman	Alexandria	Head	1810	1810(2):04A
Black, Robert	Alexandria	Tax Charge	1799	Tax PP 1799:04
Black, Robert, M.D.	Alexandria	Tax Charge	1800	Tax PP 1800:02
Black's Estate	Alexandria	Tax Charge	1796	Tax LP 1796:03
Blackably, Griegg	Arlington	Ordinary	1810	OBL2(np)
Blackaby, Cath. Thos., washwoman	Alexandria	Housekeeper	1808	1808(1):05A
Blackbee, Catherine, segar maker	Alexandria	Head	1810	1810(1):05A
Blackburn, Christian	Arlington	Inventory	1816	AB2:242; LVA-LP
Blackburn, Christian [Mrs.]	Arlington	Will	1815	WB1:337
Blackburn, Christian [Mrs.]	Arlington	Bond	1815	WB1:340
Blackburn, Sarah Ann Eleanor	Alexandria	Will	1898	WB2:290; LP
Blackburrn, Christian	Arlington	Account	1816	AB2:314
Blackerby, Grigg, blacksmith	Alexandria	Head	1810	1810(1):05A
Blacklock, Ann McCarty	Alexandria	Will	1873	WB1:085; LP
Blacklock, George R.	Arlington	Trustee Acct.	1858	LVA-LP
Blacklock, Nicholas F.	Arlington	Inventory	1818	AB3:265; LVA-LP
Blacklock, Nicholas F., grantee	Arlington	Indenture D.	1817	ID2:403
Blacklock, Nicholas Frederick	Arlington	Bond	1818	WB2:259
Blacklock, Nicholas Frederick	Arlington	Will	1818	WB2:256; File #154A

NAME OR SUBJECT	LOCATION	TYPE	YEAR	REFERENCE(S)
Blacklock, Robert S., grantor	Arlington	Indenture D.	1827	ID:118
Blacklock, Robert S., in jail	Arlington	Insolvent	1827	ID:115
Blackwell, Joseph A.	Arlington	Guard.	1834	WB4:099
Bladen, Alfred, c/o Thomas	Arlington	Apprentice	1812	OCR1811:085
Bladen, John B.	Arlington	Will	1857	WB7:209; File #543A
Bladen, Thos., cartman	Alexandria	Housekeeper	1808	1808(3):22A
Bladen, Thos., drayman	Alexandria	Head	1810	1810(3):08A
Bladin, Thos.	Alexandria	Boarder	1808	1808(3):18A
Blagrove, Henry B.	Arlington	Inventory	1854	WB6:316; LVA-LP
Blaik, Andrew	Alexandria	Tithable +21	1787	Tax PP 1787:08
Blake, Jas. H., physician	Alexandria	Housekeeper	1808	1808(4):26A
Blakeney, Abel	Alexandria	Tax Charge	1795	Tax PP 1795:02
Blakeney, Abel	Alexandria	Tax Charge	1796	Tax PP 1796:02
Blakeney, Abel	Alexandria	Tax Charge	1798	Tax PP 1798:02
Blakeney, Abel	Alexandria	Tax Charge	1799	Tax PP 1799:03
Blakeney, Abel	Alexandria	Deposition	1802	CRI:076
Blakeney, Abel	Arlington	Defendant	1802	PA:294
Blakeney, Abel & wife, carpenter	Alexandria	Housekeeper	1799	1799(2):06A
Blakeney, Abel, carpenter	Alexandria	Housekeeper	1808	1808(3):20A
Blakeney, Abel, grantor	Arlington	Indenture D.	1812	ID2:074
Blakeney, Abel, in jail bounds, carpenter	Arlington	Insolvent	1811	ID2:070
Blakeney, Abel, King St.	Alexandria	Owner	1795	Tax L 1795:03
Blakeney, Abel, King St.	Alexandria	Occupant	1795	Tax L 1795:03
Blakeney, Jane, seamstress	Alexandria	Head	1810	1810(1):12A
Blakeny, Abel	Alexandria	Tax Charge	1796	Tax LP 1796:03
Blakeny, Abel	Alexandria	Tax Charge	1800	Tax PP 1800:02
Blakeny, Abel, house joiner	Alexandria	Head	1810	1810(3):01A
Blakeny, John	Alexandria	Tax Charge	1800	Tax PP 1800:02
Bland, Elizabeth, c/o Samuel	Arlington	Guard.	1819	WB2:331
Bland, Martha, c/o Samuel	Arlington	Guard.	1819	WB2:331
Bland, Mary, c/o Samuel	Arlington	Guard.	1819	WB2:331
Bland, Samuel	Arlington	Inventory	1819	AB3:281; LVA-LP
Bland, Samuel	Arlington	Sale	1819	AB3:303
Bland, Samuel	Arlington	Account	1819	AB3:399; LVA-LP
Bland, Samuel	Arlington	Admin	1819	WB2:271
Bland, William, c/o Samuel	Arlington	Guard.	1819	WB2:331
Blanford, Francis	Alexandria	Boarder	1799	1799(2):19A
Blanford, Francis	Alexandria	Tax Charge	1800	Tax PP 1800:02
Bleckley, Abel, w1, cabinet maker	Alexandria	Head	1796	1796(3):2
Blincoe, Charles W.	Arlington	Account C.	1858	WB7:344; LVA-LP
Blincoe, Charles W.	Arlington	Appraisal	1859	WB7:415; LVA-LP
Blincoe, Charles W.	Arlington	Account	1860	WB7:534; LVA-LP
Blincoe, Charles W., Heirs of	Arlington	Account	1860	WB7:536; LVA-LP
Blincoe, William F., Constable	Arlington	Appointment	1853	BB(np)
Blodgett, Charles F., of S.C.	Alexandria	Deposition	1810	CRK:176
Blondelet, Michael	Alexandria	Tax Charge	1787	Tax PP 1787:01
Blondelett, M., King St.	Alexandria	Occupant	1787	Tax L 1787:07
Blondelett, Michael	Alexandria	Owner	1787	Tax L 1787:07
Blood, Jack	Alexandria	Tithable +21	1787	Tax PP 1787:01
Bloss, Adam	Alexandria	Tithable +16	1788	Tax PP 1788:01
Bloss, Adam	Alexandria	Tax Charge	1789	Tax PP 1789:01
Bloss, Adam	Alexandria	Tax Charge	1790	Tax PP 1790:01
Bloss, Adam, Fairfax St.	Alexandria	Occupant	1790	Tax L 1790:01
Bloss, Adam, Queen St.	Alexandria	Occupant	1790	Tax L 1790:01
Blount (also see Blunt)				
Blount, Joseph	Alexandria	Boarder	1808	1808(1):05A
Blount, Sarah, sempstress	Alexandria	Housekeeper	1808	1808(1):05A
Blount, Washer	Alexandria	Tax Charge	1788	Tax PP 1788:02
Blount, Washer	Alexandria	Tax Charge	1789	Tax PP 1789:02
Blount, Washer	Alexandria	Tax Charge	1795	Tax PP 1795:03
Blount, Washer, Prince St.	Alexandria	Owner	1795	Tax L 1795:04

NAME OR SUBJECT	LOCATION	TYPE	YEAR	REFERENCE(S)
Blount, Washer, Prince St.	Alexandria	Occupant	1795	Tax L 1795:04
Blount, Washer, Water St.	Alexandria	Occupant	1795	Tax L 1795:13
Blouse, Sefer	Alexandria	Will	1897	WB2:243; LP
Blow, William C.	Arlington	Guard. Acct.	1866	WB8:363, 574
Blow, William D.	Arlington	Guard.	1860	WB7:565; LVA-LP
Blow, William D.	Arlington	Guard. Acct.	1869	WB9:145
Bloxam, Elizabeth, seamstress	Alexandria	Head	1810	1810(3):09A
Bloxham, Elizabeth	Arlington	Account	1816	AB2:332
Bloxham, Elizabeth, sempstress	Alexandria	Housekeeper	1808	1808(3):22A
Bloxham, John T.	Arlington	Apprentice	1815	OCR1811:246
Bloxham, Mrs.	Arlington	Sale	1816	AB2:323
Blue, Jerre (C), laborer	Alexandria	Housekeeper	1808	1808(1):09A
Blue, John, chairmaker	Alexandria	Housekeeper	1808	1808(4):26A
Blue, John, chairmaker	Alexandria	Head	1810	1810(4):05A
Blueford, Jeremiah, seaman	Alexandria	Head	1810	1810(1):07A
Blunt (also see Blount)				
Blunt, Sarah	Alexandria	Head	1810	1810(1):10A
Blunt, Washer	Alexandria	Owner	1787	Tax L 1787:06
Blunt, Washer	Alexandria	Tax Charge	1787	Tax PP 1787:01
Blunt, Washer	Alexandria	Tax Charge	1790	Tax PP 1790:01
Blunt, Washer	Alexandria	Tax Charge	1796	Tax LP 1796:03
Blunt, Washer	Alexandria	Tax Charge	1796	Tax PP 1796:02
Blunt, Washer	Alexandria	Tax Charge	1798	Tax PP 1798:02
Blunt, Washer	Alexandria	Tax Charge	1799	Tax PP 1799:04
Blunt, Washer	Alexandria	Tax Charge	1800	Tax PP 1800:02
Blunt, Washer & wife, block maker	Alexandria	Head	1795	1795(4):04
Blunt, Washer & wife, block maker	Alexandria	Housekeeper	1799	1799(2):17A
Blunt, Washer & wife Sarrah	Alexandria	Resident	1800	1800(4):04B
Blunt, Washer, nr. Prince St.	Alexandria	Owner	1790	Tax L 1790:02
Blunt, Washer, nr. Prince St.	Alexandria	Occupant	1790	Tax L 1790:02
Blunt, Washer, Prince St.	Alexandria	Occupant	1787	Tax L 1787:06
Blunt, Washer, pump maker	Alexandria	Head	1800	1800(4):04A
Blunt, Washer, Thorn alley	Alexandria	Occupant	1787	Tax L 1787:25
Blunt, Washer, Water St.	Alexandria	Occupant	1790	Tax L 1790:06
Boa, Cavan	Alexandria	Tax Charge	1795	Tax PP 1795:02
Boa, Cavan	Alexandria	Tax Charge	1796	Tax LP 1796:02
Boa, Cavan	Alexandria	Tax Charge	1796	Tax PP 1796:02
Boa, Cavan	Alexandria	Mer. License	1798	Tax PP 1798:20-1
Boa, Cavan	Alexandria	Tax Charge	1798	Tax PP 1798:02
Boa, Cavan	Arlington	Account	1804	WBA:242; LVA-LP
Boa, Cavan, Union St.	Alexandria	Occupant	1795	Tax L 1795:21
Boa, Cavan, w3, shopkeeper	Alexandria	Head	1795	1796(3):7
Boa, Wm. & wife, cooper	Alexandria	Head	1795	1795(4a):02
Boan, John	Alexandria	Tax Charge	1800	Tax PP 1800:02
Boardley, Hy.	Alexandria	Tax Charge	1798	Tax PP 1798:01
Boarman, Bennet	Alexandria	Resident	1800	1800(4):05B
Boarman, Bennett	Alexandria	Serv./Appr.	1800	1800(4):05B
Bodkin, Washington L.	Arlington	Bond	1855	BB(np)
Bodkin, Washington L.	Arlington	Appraisal	1855	WB6:427; LVA-LP
Bogan, John	Arlington	Ordinary	1808	OBL2(np)
Bogan, John	Arlington	Ordinary	1809	OBL2(np)
Bogan, John	Arlington	Ordinary	1810	OBL2(np)
Bogan, John	Arlington	Apprentice	1815	OCR1811:257
Bogan, John, grantee	Arlington	Indenture D.	1812	ID2:133
Bogan, John, shopkeeper & tavern lic.	Alexandria	Housekeeper	1808	1808(2):15A
Bogan, John, tavern keeper	Alexandria	Head	1810	1810(2):05A
Bogan, Samuel Janney	Arlington	Apprentice	1815	OCR1811:305
Bogan, Thomas V.	Arlington	Guard.	1822	WB3:064
Boggess, Robert, age 61	Alexandria	Deposition	1767	CRI:235
Boggess, Robert, def.	Alexandria	Suit	1801	CRB:183
Boggess, Sarah Ann	Alexandria	Housekeeper	1799	1799(2):13A

NAME OR SUBJECT	LOCATION	TYPE	YEAR	REFERENCE(S)
Bogle, Robert, plt.	Alexandria	Suit	1802	CRB:168
Bogue, John	Alexandria	Tax Charge	1796	Tax PP 1796:02
Bogue, John	Alexandria	Tax Charge	1798	Tax PP 1798:02
Bogue, John	Alexandria	Tax Charge	1799	Tax PP 1799:04
Bogue, John, plt.	Alexandria	Suit	1801	CRB:163, 166
Bohraus, Jacob	Alexandria	Will	1888	WB1:505; LP
Bohrer, Molly, plt.	Alexandria	Suit	1802	CRD:054
Bohrer, Molly, plt.	Alexandria	Suit	1803	CRD:068
Bohrer, Peter	Alexandria	Tax Charge	1787	Tax PP 1787:02
Bohrer, Peter, Estate, plt.	Alexandria	Suit	1802	CRD:054
Bolling, John	Alexandria	Tax Charge	1798	Tax PP 1798:02
Bolt & Folke	Alexandria	Mer. License	1799	Tax PP 1799:52-01w
Bolt, Jacob	Alexandria	Tax Charge	1795	Tax PP 1795:03
Bolte & Focke	Alexandria	Tax Charge	1799	Tax PP 1799:04
Bolte, [blank], merchant	Alexandria	Boarder	1799	1799(2):02A
Bonce, Davis, tavern keeper	Alexandria	Head	1810	1810(2):03A
Bond, Mrs., Wilks St.	Alexandria	Occupant	1795	Tax L 1795:04
Bond, Richard	Alexandria	Tithable +16	1788	Tax PP 1788:06
Bond, Richard	Alexandria	Tithable +16	1789	Tax PP 1789:07
Bond, Richard, Fairfax St.	Alexandria	Owner	1790	Tax L 1790:02
Bond, Richd.	Alexandria	Tax Charge	1796	Tax LP 1796:02
Bond, Richd., Fairfax St.	Alexandria	Owner	1795	Tax L 1795:03
Bond, Tobias	Alexandria	Tax Charge	1790	Tax PP 1790:01
Bond, Tobias	Alexandria	Tax Charge	1799	Tax PP 1799:03
Bond, Tobias	Alexandria	Tax Charge	1800	Tax PP 1800:02
Bond, Tobies	Alexandria	Resident	1800	1800(4):16B
Bond, William	Arlington	Admin.	1819	WB2:321
Bond, William, seaman	Alexandria	Head	1810	1810(1):03A
Bond, Wm., sailor & shopkeeper	Alexandria	Housekeeper	1808	1808(1):01A
Bonde, Tobies, printer	Alexandria	Boarder	1800	1800(4):16A
Bonfier, Mathew & wife, plasterer	Alexandria	Head	1795	1795(4a):09
Bonham, Mary	Alexandria	Housekeeper	1799	1799(2):10A
Bonham, Mary, seamstress	Alexandria	Head	1810	1810(1):12A
Bonham, Mary, sempstress	Alexandria	Housekeeper	1808	1808(4):28A
Bonnett, Wm., back building	Alexandria	Occupant	1795	Tax L 1795:02
Bonon, Elizabeth	Alexandria	Resident	1800	1800(4):09B
Bonon, Elizabeth, labourrer	Alexandria	Boarder	1800	1800(4):09A
Bonsal, Ed.	Alexandria	Boarder	1799	1799(2):05A
Bonsal, Edward, hatter	Alexandria	Head	1810	1810(3):03A
Bonsal, Jane	Alexandria	Boarder	1799	1799(2):05A
Bonsal, Jno.	Alexandria	Boarder	1799	1799(2):05A
Bonsal, Jno.	Alexandria	Boarder	1808	1808(4):27A
Bonsal, John	Alexandria	Deposition	1808	CRG:364
Bonsale, Jane	Arlington	Will	1821	WB3:004; File #196A
Bonsel, John	Alexandria	Tax Charge	1800	Tax PP 1800:03
Bontz, Henry	Arlington	Will	1901	WB10:471; File #806A
Bontz, Jacob	Alexandria	Deposition	1814	CRI:506
Bontz, Jacob & Co., Water & Duke sts.	Alexandria	Occupant	1787	Tax L 1787:08
Bontz, John	Arlington	Complainant	1841	LSA:070
Bontz, Valentine	Alexandria	Tax Charge	1788	Tax PP 1788:02
Bontz, Valentine	Alexandria	Tax Charge	1789	Tax PP 1789:02
Bontz, Valentine	Arlington	Inventory	1820	AB4:116; LVA-LP
Bontz, Valentine	Arlington	Will	1820	WB2:347
Bontz, Valentine	Arlington	Bond	1820	WB2:348
Bontz, Valentine, Jr.	Alexandria	Tithable +16	1788	Tax PP 1788:02
Bontz, Valentine, Jr.	Alexandria	Tithable +16	1789	Tax PP 1789:02
Bonus, William	Alexandria	Tithable +16	1790	Tax PP 1790:06
Bonwe, Wm., w(3)1, taylor	Alexandria	Head	1796	1796(3):5
Boody, Andw.	Alexandria	Boarder	1808	1808(2):15A
Boon, Casius, 1, merchant	Alexandria	Head	1796	1796(3):5
Boone, A. & J.	Alexandria	Tax Charge	1796	Tax LP 1796:03

NAME OR SUBJECT	LOCATION	TYPE	YEAR	REFERENCE(S)
Boontz, Valentine, grantee	Arlington	Indenture D.	1814	ID2:373
Booth, Jeremiah	Arlington	Ordinary	1810	OBL2(np)
Boothe, Jeremiah	Arlington	Sale	1821	AB4:328
Boothe, Jeremiah	Arlington	Account	1821	AB5:015; LVA-LP
Boothe, Jeremiah	Arlington	Debts Due	1821	AB4:329
Boothe, Jeremiah	Arlington	Inventory	1821	AB4:326, 333; LVA-LP
Boothe, Jeremiah	Arlington	Admin.	1821	WB3:023, 34
Boothe, Jeremiah	Arlington	Account	1822	OCR1822:002
Boothe, William J.	Alexandria	Will	1894	WB2:089; LP
Borer, John, Water St.	Alexandria	Owner	1790	Tax L 1790:02
Borer, Peter	Alexandria	Tax Charge	1796	Tax LP 1796:02
Boress, William	Alexandria	Tithable +16	1789	Tax PP 1789:08
Borgoss, Sarah Ann	Alexandria	Head	1800	1800(4):05A
Borrer, Jno., Water St.	Alexandria	Owner	1795	Tax L 1795:04
Borrowdale, Capt.	Arlington	Sale	1817	AB3:046
Borrowdale, John	Alexandria	Boarder	1808	1808(2):15A
Borrowdale, John	Arlington	Inventory	1816	AB2:288; LVA-LP
Borrowdale, John	Arlington	Admin.	1816	WB2:119
Borrowdale, John	Arlington	Account	1817	AB3:054
Borus, Michael (C)	Arlington	Apprentice	1813	OCR1811:208
Bose, James	Alexandria	Tax Charge	1796	Tax PP 1796:02
Bosley, Sarah	Alexandria	Resident	1800	1800(4):09B
Bosley, Sarah, spinster	Alexandria	Head	1800	1800(4):09A
Bossart, George A., of Fairfax Co.	Alexandria	Will	1879	WBC1:029; LP
Bossel, Benjamin, w(3)1, drayman	Alexandria	Head	1796	1796(3):5
Bostock, John, b. Manchester, Eng.	Arlington	Alien Entry	1801	RA:29/07/01
Boston, Mat.	Alexandria	Boarder	1808	1808(3):21A
Boswell, Benj., Prince St.	Alexandria	Occupant	1795	Tax L 1795:33
Boswell, Benja.	Alexandria	Tax Charge	1796	Tax LP 1796:03
Boswell, Benja. & wife, drayman	Alexandria	Housekeeper	1799	1799(2):04A
Boswell, Benjamin	Alexandria	Tax Charge	1789	Tax PP 1789:02
Boswell, Benjamin	Alexandria	Tax Charge	1790	Tax PP 1790:01
Boswell, Benjamin	Alexandria	Tax Charge	1795	Tax PP 1795:03
Boswell, Benjamin	Alexandria	Tax Charge	1796	Tax PP 1796:01
Boswell, Benjamin	Alexandria	Tax Charge	1798	Tax PP 1798:02
Boswell, Garrison, c/o Sarah	Arlington	Apprentice	1803	OCR1801:081
Boswell, Hanson	Alexandria	Tithable +16	1790	Tax PP 1790:16
Boswell, James	Alexandria	Tithable +16	1788	Tax PP 1788:12
Boswell, Robt. & wife, labourer	Alexandria	Housekeeper	1799	1799(2):18A
Botner, Elias, sadler	Alexandria	Housekeeper	1808	1808(3):21A
Botner, Elias, sadler	Alexandria	Head	1810	1810(3):01A
Bott, Jacob, Duke St.	Alexandria	Occupant	1795	Tax L 1795:04
Bott, Jacob, Duke St.	Alexandria	Owner	1795	Tax L 1795:04
Bottomley, Joseph	Alexandria	Tax Charge	1790	Tax PP 1790:02
Bottomly, Joseph	Alexandria	Tax Charge	1789	Tax PP 1789:02
Boucher, Charles	Alexandria	Tax Charge	1789	Tax PP 1789:01
Boucher, Charles	Alexandria	Tax Charge	1796	Tax LP 1796:02
Boucher, Charles	Alexandria	Tax Charge	1799	Tax PP 1799:03
Boucher, Charles	Alexandria	Tax Charge	1800	Tax PP 1800:02
Boucher, Charles & wife, carpenter	Alexandria	Housekeeper	1799	1799(2):18A
Boucher, Chas.	Alexandria	Tax Charge	1795	Tax PP 1795:02
Boucher, Chas.	Alexandria	Tax Charge	1798	Tax PP 1798:02
Boucher, Chas., carpenter	Alexandria	Housekeeper	1808	1808(4):24A
Boucher, Chas., house joiner	Alexandria	Head	1810	1810(4):09A
Boucher, Chas., Queen St.	Alexandria	Occupant	1795	Tax L 1795:12
Boucher, Jonothan	Alexandria	Boarder	1800	1800(4):13A
Boucher, Theobd.	Alexandria	Tax Charge	1795	Tax PP 1795:02
Boudet, Dominic W., grantor	Arlington	Indenture D.	1812	ID2:110
Boudet, Dominic W., in prison rules	Arlington	Insolvent	1811	ID2:107
Boudinot, Elias, of N.J.	Alexandria	Deed	1811	CRK:048
Bouge, John	Alexandria	Tax Charge	1796	Tax LP 1796:02

NAME OR SUBJECT	LOCATION	TYPE	YEAR	REFERENCE(S)
Bouger, Charles & wife Eve	Alexandria	Resident	1800	1800(4):13B
Bouger, Charles, carpenter	Alexandria	Head	1800	1800(4):13A
Bouldon, Jos.	Alexandria	Boarder	1808	1808(2):15A
Bouling, Keziah, seamstress	Alexandria	Head	1810	1810(4):05A
Bouquet, Henry Le	Alexandria	Tax Charge	1787	Tax PP 1787:02
Bousch, Samuel C.	Arlington	Admin.	1838	WB4:159
Boush, Nathaniel	Alexandria	Will	1873	WB1:065; LP
Boush, Samuel	Arlington	Account	1837	AB7:263
Boush, Samuel C.	Arlington	Account	1838	AB7:263; LVA-LP
Bouy, Monsieur, schoolmaster	Alexandria	Head	1810	1810(4):04A
Bowden, Alexander	Arlington	Inventory	1865	WB8:214
Bowden, Alexander	Arlington	Account	1868	WB9:045
Bowden, Joseph	Alexandria	Deposition	1808	CRG:367
Bowden, Patrick	Alexandria	Tax Charge	1788	Tax PP 1788:01
Bowdin, Jos., clerk	Alexandria	Boarder	1799	1799(2):02A
Bowen, Danl., ship carpenter	Alexandria	Housekeeper	1808	1808(1):07A
Bowen, Obadiah	Alexandria	Tithable +16	1788	Tax PP 1788:11
Bowie & Kurtz	Alexandria	Suit	1818	CRK:458
Bowie, Alice A.M.	Arlington	Guard.	1825	WB3:191
Bowie, Davis	Arlington	Ordinary	1808	OBL2(np)(2)
Bowie, Davis	Arlington	Ordinary	1809	OBL2(np)
Bowie, Davis	Arlington	Ordinary	1810	OBL2(np)
Bowie, Davis	Arlington	Suit	1814	ID2:372
Bowie, Davis, grantee	Arlington	Indenture D.	1813	ID2:228
Bowie, Davis, grantee	Arlington	Indenture D.	1831	ID:364
Bowie, Davis, grantor	Arlington	Indenture D.	1814	ID2:373
Bowie, Davis, in jail	Arlington	Insolvent	1814	ID2:369
Bowie, Davis, taylor	Alexandria	Housekeeper	1808	1808(2):12A
Bowie, Elizabeth	Alexandria	Head	1810	1810(4):07A
Bowie, George	Alexandria	Tithable +21	1787	Tax PP 1787:10
Bowie, George	Alexandria	Tithable +16	1788	Tax PP 1788:11
Bowie, James P.	Arlington	Ordinary	1808	OBL2(np)
Bowie, James P.	Arlington	Ordinary	1808	OBL2(np)(2)
Bowie, James P.	Arlington	Ordinary	1809	OBL2(np)
Bowie, James P.	Arlington	Ordinary	1810	OBL2(np)
Bowie, James P.	Arlington	Account	1811	AB1:125, LVA LP
Bowie, James P., shopkeeper	Alexandria	Head	1810	1810(4):07A
Bowie, James Peel, retailer	Alexandria	Housekeeper	1808	1808(4):29A
Bowie, John F., Jr.	Alexandria	Account B.	1800	CRB:201
Bowie, John F., Jr., def.	Alexandria	Suit	1801	CRB:197
Bowie, Maria	Arlington	Guard.	1819	WB2:290
Bowie, Theophilus	Arlington	Ordinary	1806	OBL2(np)(2)
Bowie, Theophilus	Arlington	Ordinary	1808	OBL2(np)
Bowie, Theophilus, grantee	Arlington	Indenture D.	1806	ID3:211
Bowie, Theophilus, seaman	Alexandria	Head	1810	1810(3):08A
Bowie, Theophilus, shopkeeper	Alexandria	Housekeeper	1808	1808(2):13A
Bowie, Theophilus, waterman	Alexandria	Housekeeper	1808	1808(4):28A
Bowie, Washington	Arlington	Defendant	1810	ACO:114
Bowie, Washington, complt.	Alexandria	Suit	1819	CRK:438
Bowie, Washington, of George Town	Alexandria	Letter	1809	CRI:144(2)
Bowie, Washington, of George Town	Alexandria	Letter	1809	CRI:141
Bowie, Washington, plt.	Alexandria	Suit	1802	CRD:169
Bowie, Washington, plt.	Alexandria	Suit	1818	CRK:458
Bowie, William	Alexandria	Tax Charge	1795	Tax PP 1795:02
Bowie, William	Alexandria	Tax Charge	1796	Tax PP 1796:02
Bowie, William	Alexandria	Tax Charge	1798	Tax PP 1798:01
Bowie, William	Alexandria	Tax Charge	1799	Tax PP 1799:03
Bowie, William	Alexandria	Tax Charge	1800	Tax PP 1800:02
Bowie, William	Arlington	Guard.	1825	OCR1822:096
Bowie, William, c/o Davis	Arlington	Apprentice	1811	OCR1811:078
Bowie, Wm.	Alexandria	Tax Charge	1796	Tax LP 1796:02

NAME OR SUBJECT	LOCATION	TYPE	YEAR	REFERENCE(S)
Bowie, Wm., Fairfax St.	Alexandria	Occupant	1795	Tax L 1795:31
Bowlan, Green	Alexandria	Boarder	1808	1808(3):20A
Bowles, Aaron	Alexandria	Will	1891	WB1:595; LP
Bowles, Henry, c/o Thomas & Betsy	Arlington	Apprentice	1805	OCR1801:248
Bowles, John (C)	Arlington	Apprentice	1826	OCR1822:113
Bowles, Richard	Arlington	Admin.	1841	WB4:281
Bowles, Richard	Arlington	Inventory	1842	AB8:287; LVA-LP
Bowles, Thomas, c/o Thomas & Betsy	Arlington	Apprentice	1805	OCR1801:250
Bowling, Ambrose, rope maker	Alexandria	Head	1810	1810(3):07A
Bowling, Ann	Alexandria	Serv./Appt.	1800	1800(4):15B
Bowling, Ann, laundress	Alexandria	Head	1800	1800(4):15A
Bowling, Ann, seamstress	Alexandria	Head	1810	1810(4):05A
Bowling, Ann, washwoman	Alexandria	Housekeeper	1808	1808(4):27A
Bowling, Eliza Maria, c/o Samuel	Arlington	Guard.	1813	WB1:257
Bowling, Elizabeth	Arlington	Guard.	1810	WBC:448
Bowling, Garret	Arlington	Apprentice	1804	OCR1801:196
Bowling, Garret	Arlington	Guard.	1805	WBB:134
Bowling, Geo.	Alexandria	Head	1810	1810(4):08A
Bowling, George	Arlington	Guard.	1807	WBB:483
Bowling, George	Arlington	Admin.	1818	WB2:231
Bowling, George	Arlington	Guard. Acct.	1819	AB3:379; LVA-LP
Bowling, Gerard	Alexandria	Boarder	1808	1808(2):17A
Bowling, Jno.	Alexandria	Boarder	1808	1808(4):25A
Bowling, Jno. & wife, carpenter	Alexandria	Housekeeper	1799	1799(2):10A
Bowling, John	Alexandria	Tax Charge	1796	Tax LP 1796:02
Bowling, John	Alexandria	Tax Charge	1796	Tax PP 1796:02
Bowling, John	Alexandria	Tax Charge	1799	Tax PP 1799:03
Bowling, John	Alexandria	Tax Charge	1800	Tax PP 1800:02
Bowling, John	Arlington	Will	1805	WBB:202; File #002A
Bowling, John	Arlington	Bond	1805	WBB:203
Bowling, John	Arlington	Inventory	1806	WBB:241; LVA-LP
Bowling, John	Arlington	Account	1806	WBB:326; LVA-LP
Bowling, John	Arlington	Sale	1806	WBB:243
Bowling, John	Arlington	Guard.	1807	WBB:483
Bowling, John	Arlington	Settlement	1808	WBC:105; LVA-LP
Bowling, John	Arlington	Guard. Acct.	1827	AB6:432; LVA-LP
Bowling, John, c/o Patsy	Arlington	Apprentice	1812	OCR1811:127
Bowling, John, St. Asaph St.	Alexandria	Occupant	1787	Tax L 1787:08
Bowling, John, w(4), carpenter	Alexandria	Head	1796	1796(3):1
Bowling, Joseph, house joiner	Alexandria	Head	1810	1810(3):10A
Bowling, Josiah & wife, brickmaker	Alexandria	Housekeeper	1799	1799(2):12A
Bowling, Josias	Alexandria	Tax Charge	1799	Tax PP 1799:03
Bowling, Robert	Arlington	Guard.	1810	WBC:470
Bowling, Samuel, c/o Ann	Arlington	Apprentice	1815	OCR1811:243
Bowling, Sarah	Arlington	Guard.	1817	WB2:194
Bowling, Simon	Arlington	Guard.	1805	WBB:134
Bowling, Thomas	Alexandria	Tax Charge	1799	Tax PP 1799:04
Bowling, Thos. & wife, labourer	Alexandria	Housekeeper	1799	1799(2):12A
Bowling, William	Alexandria	Tithable +16	1788	Tax PP 1788:07
Bowling, William	Arlington	Admin.	1805	WBB:123
Bowling, William	Arlington	Sale	1805	WBB:170
Bowling, William	Arlington	Inventory	1805	WBB:124
Bowling, William	Arlington	Account	1806	WBB:323; LVA-LP
Bowling, William	Arlington	Guard.	1807	WBB:483
Bowling, William	Arlington	Account	1807	WBB:529; LVA-LP
Bowling, William	Arlington	Guard. Acct.	1822	AB5:037; LVA-LP
Bowling, William	Arlington	Apprentice	1822	OCR1822:029
Bowling, Wm., stage driver	Alexandria	Housekeeper	1808	1808(2):14A
Bowman & Forrest, plt.	Alexandria	Suit	1803	CRD:182
Bowne & Hamilton	Alexandria	Tax Charge	1796	Tax PP 1796:02
Bowne, Hamilton & Co.	Alexandria	Tax Charge	1796	Tax LP 1796:09

NAME OR SUBJECT	LOCATION	TYPE	YEAR	REFERENCE(S)
Bowne, M.F. & Co., Union St.	Alexandria	Occupant	1795	Tax L 1795:33
Bownes, Wm.	Alexandria	Tax Charge	1795	Tax PP 1795:03
Bowser, Isaac	Arlington	Libellant	1804	ACO:029
Bowser, Isaac	Arlington	Libellant	1805	ACO:035
Boyd, James	Arlington	Inventory	1824	AB5:373; LVA-LP
Boyd, James	Arlington	Admin.	1824	WB3:148
Boyd, James P.	Arlington	Apprentice	1825	OCR1822:096a
Boyd, James P.	Arlington	Apprentice	1827	OCR1822:151
Boyd, James, shoemaker	Alexandria	Housekeeper	1808	1808(4):29A
Boyd, James, shoemaker	Alexandria	Head	1810	1810(3):04A
Boyd, John, grantee	Arlington	Indenture D.	1814	ID2:380
Boyd, John, seaman	Alexandria	Head	1810	1810(1):12A
Boyd, Lucy, sempstress	Alexandria	Housekeeper	1808	1808(1):06A
Boyd, Rebecca	Arlington	Guard.	1812	WB1:196
Boyd, Washington, marshal	Arlington	Payment	1808	ACO:095
Boye, John	Alexandria	Mer. License	1798	Tax PP 1798:20-1
Boyer, Adam, c/o Eve	Arlington	Apprentice	1805	OCR1801:296
Boyer, Elizabeth	Arlington	Guard.	1804	WBB:091, 360
Boyer, Erwin	Alexandria	Boarder	1808	1808(2):11A
Boyer, Eve, gentlewoman	Alexandria	Housekeeper	1808	1808(2):11A
Boyer, Henry	Alexandria	Tax Charge	1787	Tax PP 1787:02
Boyer, Henry	Alexandria	Tax Charge	1788	Tax PP 1788:02
Boyer, Henry	Alexandria	Tax Charge	1789	Tax PP 1789:02
Boyer, Henry	Alexandria	Tax Charge	1790	Tax PP 1790:01
Boyer, Henry	Alexandria	Tax Charge	1795	Tax PP 1795:03
Boyer, Henry	Alexandria	Tax Charge	1796	Tax LP 1796:03
Boyer, Henry	Alexandria	Tax Charge	1796	Tax PP 1796:02
Boyer, Henry	Alexandria	Tax Charge	1798	Tax PP 1798:02
Boyer, Henry, w(3), carpenter	Alexandria	Head	1795	1796(3):7
Boyer, Jno., Union St.	Alexandria	Occupant	1795	Tax L 1795:03
Boyer, Jno., Union St.	Alexandria	Owner	1795	Tax L 1795:03
Boyer, John	Alexandria	Tax Charge	1787	Tax PP 1787:01
Boyer, John	Alexandria	Tax Charge	1788	Tax PP 1788:02
Boyer, John	Alexandria	Tax Charge	1789	Tax PP 1789:02
Boyer, John	Alexandria	Tax Charge	1790	Tax PP 1790:01
Boyer, John	Alexandria	Tax Charge	1795	Tax PP 1795:02
Boyer, John	Alexandria	Tax Charge	1796	Tax LP 1796:02
Boyer, John	Alexandria	Tax Charge	1798	Tax PP 1798:02
Boyer, John	Alexandria	Tax Charge	1799	Tax PP 1799:04
Boyer, John	Alexandria	Tax Charge	1800	Tax PP 1800:03
Boyer, John	Arlington	Apprentice	1802	OCR1801:049
Boyer, John	Arlington	Admin.	1802	WBA:103
Boyer, John	Arlington	Inventory	1803	WBA:107; LVA-LP
Boyer, John	Arlington	Account	1805	WBB:222; LVA-LP
Boyer, John	Alexandria	Boarder	1808	1808(2):11A
Boyer, John	Arlington	Will	1820	WB2:351; File #172A
Boyer, John & wife, cooper	Alexandria	Housekeeper	1799	1799(2):01A
Boyer, John, Union St.	Alexandria	Owner	1790	Tax L 1790:02
Boyer, John, Water St.	Alexandria	Occupant	1795	Tax L 1795:22
Boyer, Margaret, cookshop	Alexandria	Housekeeper	1799	1799(2):07A
Boyle, Peter, Water St.	Alexandria	Occupant	1787	Tax L 1787:05
Bozwell, Benjamin	Arlington	Witness	1794	OT:03/07/1794
Bozwell, George, b/o Henrietta	Arlington	Apprentice	1814	OCR1811:223
Bozwell, Lewis, c/o Martha Swallow	Arlington	Apprentice	1803	OCR1801:134
Bozwell, [blank], Fairfax St.	Alexandria	Occupant	1790	Tax L 1790:12
Bradan, Thomas, def.	Alexandria	Suit	1802	CRD:048
Braddock, Robert	Alexandria	Tax Charge	1788	Tax PP 1788:02
Braddock, Robert	Alexandria	Tax Charge	1799	Tax PP 1799:04
Braddock, Robert	Alexandria	Tax Charge	1800	Tax PP 1800:02
Braddock, Robert	Arlington	Inventory	1812	AB1:275; LVA-LP
Braddock, Robert	Arlington	Will	1812	WB1:206; File #106A

NAME OR SUBJECT	LOCATION	TYPE	YEAR	REFERENCE(S)
Braddock, Robert	Arlington	Bond	1812	WB1:208
Braddock, Robert	Arlington	Account	1814	AB2:029; LVA-LP
Braddock, Robert (C)	Alexandria	Tax Charge	1787	Tax PP 1787:01
Braddock, Robt.	Alexandria	Tax Charge	1789	Tax PP 1789:02
Braddock, Robt. (C), carpenter	Alexandria	Housekeeper	1808	1808(3):23A
Braddock, Robt., house joiner	Alexandria	Head	1810	1810(3):07A
Braddock, Thomas	Arlington	Will P.	1829	OCR1822:173a
Braddock, Thomas	Arlington	Bond	1829	WB3:345
Braddock, Thomas	Arlington	Will	1829	WB3:342; File #280A
Braddock, Thomas	Arlington	Account	1835	AB7:182; LVA-LP
Braddock, Thomas	Arlington	Account	1836	AB7:182
Braddock, Thos., s/o Robt.	Alexandria	Boarder	1808	1808(3):23B
Bradferd, Capt., seaman	Alexandria	Head	1810	1810(4):08A
Bradford, Chas., sea captain	Alexandria	Housekeeper	1808	1808(4):24A
Bradley, Gabriel	Arlington	Apprentice	1814	OCR1811:240
Bradley, Gabriel, c/o Martha	Arlington	Apprentice	1813	OCR1811:154
Bradley, Hannah, seamstress	Alexandria	Head	1810	1810(1):01A
Bradley, Harrison	Alexandria	Will	1872	WB1:050; LP
Bradley, John, c/o Daniel, Fairfax Co.	Arlington	Apprentice	1813	OCR1811:150
Bradley, John, grantor	Arlington	Indenture D.	1832	ID:368
Bradley, John, in jail	Arlington	Insolvent	1832	ID:366
Bradley, Nancy, c/o Daniel	Arlington	Apprentice	1804	OCR1801:191
Bradley, William	Alexandria	Tax Charge	1798	Tax PP 1798:01
Bradley, William	Alexandria	Tax Charge	1799	Tax PP 1799:04
Bradley, William, w(2), shopkeeper	Alexandria	Head	1795	1796(3):7
Bradley, Wm. & wife, grocer	Alexandria	Housekeeper	1799	1799(2):07A
Bradock, T.	Alexandria	Boarder	1808	1808(2):14A
Bradstock, Grastang, plt.	Alexandria	Suit	1802	CRC:280
Brady, Benjamin	Alexandria	Mer. License	1798	Tax PP 1799:52-11r
Brady, Benjamin	Alexandria	Mer. License	1799	Tax PP 1799:52-01r
Brady, Benjamin	Alexandria	Tax Charge	1800	Tax PP 1800:02
Brady, Benjamin	Alexandria	Mer. License	1800	Tax PP 1800:54(11)r
Brady, Benjamin	Arlington	Bond	1812	WB1:282
Brady, Benjamin	Arlington	Inventory	1814	AB2:015; LVA-LP
Brady, Benjamin	Arlington	Will	1814	WB1:282; File #116A
Brady, Benjamin	Arlington	Account	1815	AB2:090; LVA-LP
Brady, Benjamin	Arlington	Sale	1815	AB2:089
Brady, Benjamin, for retailing liquors	Arlington	Defendant	1802	PA:032
Brady, Benjamin, shopkeeper	Alexandria	Head	1810	1810(2):08A
Brady, Benjn., retailer	Alexandria	Housekeeper	1808	1808(2):16A
Brady, Caleb	Alexandria	Deposition	1822	CRL:468
Brady, Caleb	Arlington	Will P.	1823	OCR1822:054
Brady, Caleb	Arlington	Will	1823	WB3:110; File #219A
Brady, Caleb	Arlington	Bond	1823	WB3:111
Brady, Caleb	Arlington	Sale	1824	AB5:369; LVA-LP
Brady, Caleb	Arlington	Inventory	1824	AB5:368; LVA-LP
Brady, Caleb	Arlington	Account	1824	AB5:371; LVA-LP
Brady, Julia Ann	Arlington	Guard.	1824	WB3:143
Brandes, James	Alexandria	Tax Charge	1800	Tax PP 1800:02
Brandon, James	Alexandria	Tax Charge	1799	Tax PP 1799:04
Brandon, Jas., flour inspector	Alexandria	Boarder	1799	1799(2):15A
Brandt, Clement Brook, c/o Richard	Arlington	Apprentice	1802	OCR1801:055
Brandt, Logan	Arlington	Guard. Acct.	1833	AB7:103
Brandt, Logan	Arlington	Guard. Acct.	1834	AB7:129; LVA-LP
Brandt, Logan	Arlington	Guard. Acct.	1835	AB7:160
Brandt, Logan	Arlington	Guard. Acct.	1837	AB7:270; LVA-LP
Brandt, Logan	Arlington	Guard. Acct.	1838	AB7:270
Brandt, Logan	Arlington	Guard. Acct.	1839	AB8:080; LVA-LP
Brandt, Logan	Arlington	Guard. Acct.	1840	AB8:099; LVA-LP
Brandt, Logan	Arlington	Guard. Acct.	1840	AB8:079
Brandt, Logan	Arlington	Guard. Acct.	1841	AB8:195

NAME OR SUBJECT	LOCATION	TYPE	YEAR	REFERENCE(S)
Brandt, Logan	Arlington	Guard. Acct.	1842	AB8:262
Brandt, Logan	Arlington	Guard. Acct.	1843	AB8:356; LVA-LP
Brandt, Logan	Arlington	Guard. Acct.	1844	AB8:425; LVA-LP
Brandt, Logan	Arlington	Guard. Acct.	1845	AB9:024; LVA-LP
Brandt, Logan	Arlington	Guard. Acct.	1846	AB9:147
Brandt, Logan	Arlington	Guard. Acct.	1847	AB9:266
Brandt, Logan	Arlington	Guard. Acct.	1850	LVA-LP (Box 214)
Brandt, Logan	Arlington	Guard. Acct.	1850	WB5:261
Brandt, Logan	Arlington	Guard. Acct.	1851	LVA-LP
Brandt, Logan, c/o Richard B.	Arlington	Guard.	1831	WB4:006
Brandt, Logan, c/o Richard H.	Arlington	Guard. Acct.	1844	OCR1842:060
Brandt, Notley, n/o Richard	Arlington	Apprentice	1804	OCR1801:225
Brandt, Richard	Arlington	Apprentice	1815	OCR1811:317
Brandt, Richard B.	Arlington	Inventory	1815	AB2:116
Brandt, Richard B., Capt.	Arlington	Account	1816	AB2:284; LVA-LP
Brandt, Richard Brooke	Arlington	Bond	1815	WB2:013
Brandt, Richard Brooke	Arlington	Will	1815	WB2:012
Brandt, Richard Brooke, Capt.	Arlington	Sale	1815	AB2:182
Brandt, Richard C.	Arlington	Account	1835	AB7:153
Brandt, Richard H.	Arlington	Bond	1831	WB4:010
Brandt, Richard H.	Arlington	Will	1831	WB4:010; File #301A
Brandt, Richard H.	Arlington	Account	1834	AB7:131; LVA-LP
Brannon, James	Alexandria	Resident	1800	1800(4):04B
Branon, James, inspector	Alexandria	Boarder	1800	1800(4):04A
Branson, Benja.	Alexandria	Tax Charge	1796	Tax LP 1796:02
Branson, Vincent	Alexandria	Tax Charge	1796	Tax PP 1796:02
Brashall, Nancy	Alexandria	Boarder	1808	1808(3):18A
Brashear, Dennis F.	Alexandria	Will	1881	WB1:336; LP
Brashears, Benedict	Alexandria	Boarder	1808	1808(1):04A
Brashears, Saml.	Alexandria	Boarder	1808	1808(2):11A
Brashears, Trueman	Alexandria	Boarder	1808	1808(1):04A
Brashears, Trueman, merchant	Alexandria	Housekeeper	1808	1808(4):27A
Brastow, George M.	Arlington	Admin.	1809	WBC:305
Brastow, George M.	Arlington	Inventory	1809	WBC:306; LVA-LP
Brastow, George M.	Arlington	Account	1810	AB1:009
Brawner, Basil	Alexandria	Will	1893	WB2:051; LP
Brawner, Henry	Alexandria	Boarder	1808	1808(2):14A
Braxton, Geo. M.	Alexandria	Boarder	1808	1808(2):16A
Bray, Elizabeth	Alexandria	Tax Charge	1787	Tax PP 1787:02
Bray, Joseph	Alexandria	Tithable +16	1789	Tax PP 1789:10
Bray, Mrs., Princess St.	Alexandria	Occupant	1787	Tax L 1787:26
Bray, William	Alexandria	Tax Charge	1799	Tax PP 1799:03
Bray, William	Alexandria	Tax Charge	1800	Tax PP 1800:02
Bray, Wm.	Alexandria	Tax Charge	1798	Tax PP 1798:01
Bready, Benjamin	Alexandria	Tax Charge	1799	Tax PP 1799:04
Breast, George Alonza	Arlington	Apprentice	1827	OCR1822:134
Breckenridge, James, of Monroe Co.	Alexandria	Deposition	1804	CRE:249
Breilatt, Tho.	Alexandria	Tax Charge	1798	Tax PP 1798:01
Breilatt, Thomas	Alexandria	Tax Charge	1796	Tax PP 1796:01
Brelaitt, Thomas	Alexandria	Tax Charge	1796	Tax LP 1796:02
Bremont, Lawrence	Arlington	Apprentice	1815	OCR1811:355
Bremont, Lawrence	Arlington	Guard.	1815	WB2:089
Bremont, Mary	Arlington	Apprentice	1825	OCR1822:098
Brent, Christopher Neale	Arlington	Schedule	1825	AB6:105; LVA-LP
Brent, Christopher Neale	Arlington	Will	1825	WB3:192; File #238A
Brent, Christopher Neale	Arlington	Bond	1825	WB3:193
Brent, Daniel Carroll, as Marshal	Arlington	Bill	1807	ACO:076
Brent, Daniel Carroll, def.	Alexandria	Suit	1808	CRG:155
Brent, Daniel Carroll, def.	Alexandria	Suit	1808	CRG:005
Brent, George	Arlington	Will P.	1845	OCR1842:113
Brent, George	Arlington	Will	1845	WB4:393; File #422A

NAME OR SUBJECT	LOCATION	TYPE	YEAR	REFERENCE(S)
Brent, George	Arlington	Account	1846	AB9:238; LVA-LP
Brent, George	Arlington	Debts Due	1846	AB9:172
Brent, George	Arlington	Inventory	1846	AB9:171; LVA-LP
Brent, George William	Alexandria	Will	1872	WB1:044; LP
Brent, Henry, grantee	Arlington	Indenture D.	1831	ID:290
Brent, John	Alexandria	Tax Charge	1787	Tax PP 1787:02
Brent, John	Alexandria	Tax Charge	1788	Tax PP 1788:02
Brent, John & Co., Fairfax St.	Alexandria	Occupant	1787	Tax L 1787:15
Brent, John H.	Alexandria	Will	1882	WB1:370; LP
Brent, Martin	Alexandria	Boarder	1808	1808(2):11A
Brent, William	Arlington	Admin. Bond	1849	ABB(np)
Brest, Clement, c/o Clement	Arlington	Apprentice	1813	OCR1811:206
Brest, Clement, hatter	Alexandria	Housekeeper	1808	1808(2):14A
Brest, Clement, hatter	Alexandria	Head	1810	1810(2):06A
Brest, Mary, infant d/o Clement, plt.	Alexandria	Suit	1801	CRD:056
Brewer, John W., Constable	Arlington	Appointment	1851	BB(np)
Brewis, A.	Alexandria	Inventory	1871	WB1:030
Brice, Benja., & wife (C)	Alexandria	Housekeeper	1799	1799(2):05A
Brice, Hannah	Alexandria	Owner	1787	Tax L 1787:06
Brice, Hannah, washerwoman	Alexandria	Head	1810	1810(1):03A
Brice, J., Estate, Prince St.	Alexandria	Occupant	1787	Tax L 1787:16
Brice, Robert	Alexandria	Owner	1787	Tax L 1787:06
Brice, Robert	Alexandria	Tax Charge	1796	Tax PP 1796:02
Brice, Robert	Alexandria	Tax Charge	1800	Tax PP 1800:03
Brice, Robert, Fairfax St.	Alexandria	Occupant	1787	Tax L 1787:02
Brice, Robt.	Alexandria	Tax Charge	1795	Tax PP 1795:02
Brice, Robt.	Alexandria	Tax Charge	1798	Tax PP 1798:02
Brice, William	Alexandria	Tax Charge	1790	Tax PP 1790:01
Brickey, Mary, sempster	Alexandria	Boarder	1800	1800(4):08A
Bricklay, Helen B.C.	Arlington	Admin.	1810	WBC:486
Bride Kirk, tract called	Arlington	Suit	1840	LSA:055
Brig *Benefactor*	Arlington	Suit	1818	ACO:152
Brig *Cumberland*	Arlington	Suit	1821	ACO:195, 196
Brig *Cumberland*	Arlington	Suit	1827	ACO:275
Brig *Hunter*, Condemed Contents	Alexandria	Sale	1818	CRL:594
Brig *John*	Arlington	Suit	1812	ACO:122
Brig *John*	Arlington	Suit	1815	ACO:143
Brig *Nancy Ann*	Arlington	Suit	1811	ACO:119
Brig *Union*	Arlington	Suit	1805	ACO:042
Brig *Union*	Arlington	Suit	1805	ACO:046
Brig *Union*	Arlington	Suit	1806	ACO:051
Brig *Winifred*	Arlington	Suit	1823	ACO:232
Brig *Winifred*	Arlington	Suit	1823	ACO:218
Brig *Winifred*	Arlington	Suit	1823	ACO:206, 208, 209
Brigantine *Cumberland*	Arlington	Suit	1820	ACO:174, 176, 179
Brigantine *Cumberland*	Arlington	Suit	1821	ACO:199
Bright, Charles	Alexandria	Tax Charge	1795	Tax PP 1795:03
Bright, Elizabeth	Alexandria	Owner	1787	Tax L 1787:07
Bright, Elizabeth, Fairfax St.	Alexandria	Occupant	1787	Tax L 1787:07
Bright, Elizabeth, midwife	Alexandria	Housekeeper	1799	1799(2):09A
Bright, Henry, grantor	Arlington	Indenture D.	1828	ID:160
Bright, Henry, in jail	Arlington	Insolvent	1828	ID:158
Bright, John	Alexandria	Tax Charge	1787	Tax PP 1787:02
Bright, John	Alexandria	Tax Charge	1788	Tax PP 1788:02
Bright, John	Alexandria	Tax Charge	1789	Tax PP 1789:01
Bright, John	Alexandria	Tax Charge	1790	Tax PP 1790:01
Bright, John, Fairfax St.	Alexandria	Occupant	1790	Tax L 1790:01
Bright, John, Fairfax St.	Alexandria	Owner	1790	Tax L 1790:01
Bright, John, Fairfax St.	Alexandria	Owner	1795	Tax L 1795:03
Bright, John, grantee	Arlington	Indenture D.	1828	ID:160
Brill, Louis, Sr.	Alexandria	Will	1890	WB1:558; LP

NAME OR SUBJECT	LOCATION	TYPE	YEAR	REFERENCE(S)
Brise, Robert	Alexandria	Resident	1800	1800(4):16B
Brise, Robt., brick maker	Alexandria	Head	1800	1800(4):16A
Britingham, Ann, sempstress	Alexandria	Housekeeper	1808	1808(4):26A
Britingham, Jas., taylor	Alexandria	Housekeeper	1808	1808(1):07A
Brittain, [blank], King St.	Alexandria	Owner	1795	Tax L 1795:03
Brittenham, Dixon	Alexandria	Mer. License	1798	Tax PP 1798:20-1
Brittenham, Dixon	Alexandria	Tax Charge	1798	Tax PP 1798:01
Brittenham, Dixon	Alexandria	Tax Charge	1799	Tax PP 1799:03
Brittenham, Dixon	Alexandria	Tax Charge	1800	Tax PP 1800:03
Brittenham, James, taylor	Alexandria	Head	1810	1810(1):12A
Brittingham, Ann, seamstress	Alexandria	Head	1810	1810(4):06A
Brittingham, Dixon & wife	Alexandria	Housekeeper	1799	1799(2):18A
Brittingham, Dixon & wife Ma__y	Alexandria	Resident	1800	1800(4):09B
Brittingham, Dixon, taylor	Alexandria	Head	1800	1800(4):09A
Brittingham, Nancy	Alexandria	Boarder	1799	1799(2):18A
Broad, Michael	Arlington	Inventory	1813	AB1:324; LVA-LP
Broad, Michael	Arlington	Admin.	1813	WB1:226
Broad, Thomas	Alexandria	Tithable +16	1790	Tax PP 1790:08
Broadwater, Guy	Arlington	Deposition	1806	ACR:029
Broadwater, Henry, age 90	Alexandria	Deposition	1767	CRI:241
Broadwell, Simon, plt.	Alexandria	Suit	1801	CRC:066
Brocchus, Amelia, shopkeeper	Alexandria	Housekeeper	1808	1808(4):25A
Brocchus, Peter	Arlington	Apprentice	1812	OCR1811:076
Brocchus, Thomas	Arlington	Defendant	1824	ACO:241, 247
Brocchus, Thomas	Arlington	Defendant	1825	ACO:257
Brocchus, Thomas	Arlington	Defendant	1825	ACO:252
Brocchus, Thomas	Arlington	Defendant	1826	ACO:260, 263
Brocchus, Thomas	Arlington	Defendant	1827	ACO:266, 273
Brocchus, Thomas	Arlington	Inventory	1833	LVA-LP
Brocchus, Thomas	Arlington	Admin.	1833	WB4:070
Brocchus, Thomas, assignee	Arlington	Plaintiff	1823	ACO:222
Brocchus, Thos., taylor	Alexandria	Housekeeper	1808	1808(2):11A
Brochus, Milly, seamstress	Alexandria	Head	1810	1810(4):04A
Brochus, Thos.	Alexandria	Tax Charge	1800	Tax PP 1800:03
Brochus, Thos., taylor	Alexandria	Head	1810	1810(3):08A
Brock, Adam & Henry Schnyder, lab.	Alexandria	Housekeeper	1799	1799(2):18A
Brockass, [blank]	Alexandria	Tax Charge	1796	Tax PP 1796:01
Brockers, Tho.	Alexandria	Tax Charge	1795	Tax PP 1795:02
Brocket, Elizabeth	Arlington	Admin.	1828	WB3:346
Brocket, Milly & child	Alexandria	Boarder	1799	1799(2):09A
Brocket, Robert	Arlington	Admin.	1829	OCR1822:169a
Brocket, Robert, def.	Alexandria	Suit	1801	CRB:118
Brocket, Robert, def.	Alexandria	Suit	1802	CRC:266
Brocket, Robert, def.	Alexandria	Suit	1803	CRD:084
Brocket, Robert, Washington St.	Alexandria	Occupant	1790	Tax L 1790:01
Brocket, Robert, Washington St.	Alexandria	Owner	1790	Tax L 1790:01
Brocket, Walter Ann	Arlington	Guard. Acct.	1835	LVA-LP
Brockett, A.	Alexandria	Reference	1808	1808(3):18B
Brockett, Robert	Alexandria	Tax Charge	1787	Tax PP 1787:02
Brockett, Robert	Alexandria	Tax Charge	1788	Tax PP 1788:01
Brockett, Robert	Alexandria	Tax Charge	1789	Tax PP 1789:02
Brockett, Robert	Alexandria	Tax Charge	1790	Tax PP 1790:01
Brockett, Robert	Alexandria	Tax Charge	1796	Tax LP 1796:02
Brockett, Robert	Alexandria	Tax Charge	1796	Tax PP 1796:02
Brockett, Robert	Alexandria	Tax Charge	1800	Tax PP 1800:03
Brockett, Robert	Alexandria	Deposition	1808	CRH:117
Brockett, Robert	Arlington	Account	1833	AB7:077
Brockett, Robert	Arlington	Account F.	1834	AB7:114; LVA-LP
Brockett, Robert	Arlington	Inventory	1839	AB7:325; LVA-LP
Brockett, Robert	Arlington	Sale	1839	AB7:326
Brockett, Robert	Arlington	Will	1867	WB8:549

NAME OR SUBJECT	LOCATION	TYPE	YEAR	REFERENCE(S)
Brockett, Robert, bricklayer	Alexandria	Head	1810	1810(3):10A
Brockett, Robert, btw. Union	Alexandria	Owner	1795	Tax L 1795:03
Brockett, Robert, def.	Alexandria	Suit	1802	CRC:238
Brockett, Robert, Washington St.	Alexandria	Owner	1795	Tax L 1795:03
Brockett, Robt.	Alexandria	Tax Charge	1795	Tax PP 1795:02
Brockett, Robt.	Alexandria	Tax Charge	1798	Tax PP 1798:02
Brockett, Robt.	Alexandria	Tax Charge	1799	Tax PP 1799:04
Brockett, Robt., bricklayer	Alexandria	Housekeeper	1808	1808(3):18A
Brockett, Robt., bricklayer	Alexandria	Head	1810	1810(3):08A
Brockett, Robt., Washington St.	Alexandria	Occupant	1795	Tax L 1795:03
Brockett, Walter	Alexandria	Boarder	1808	1808(3):18A
Brockett, Walter	Arlington	Admin.	1818	WB2:222
Brockett, Walter	Arlington	Guard.	1834	WB4:098
Broders, Joseph	Alexandria	Owner	1787	Tax L 1787:06
Broders, Joseph	Alexandria	Tax Charge	1787	Tax PP 1787:02
Broders, Joseph	Alexandria	Will	1900	WB2:377; LP
Broders, Joseph, grantee	Arlington	Indenture D.	1826	ID:032
Broders, Joseph, grantee	Arlington	Indenture D.	1826	ID:022
Broders, Joseph, Queen St.	Alexandria	Occupant	1787	Tax L 1787:06
Brodus, Melinda (Monroe)	Alexandria	Will	1893	WB2:053; LP
Brogden, Geo., labourer	Alexandria	Head	1810	1810(4):03A
Brokett, John	Alexandria	Tax Charge	1787	Tax PP 1787:02
Bromley, William	Alexandria	Tax Charge	1787	Tax PP 1787:02
Bromley, William	Alexandria	Tax Charge	1788	Tax PP 1788:02
Bromley, William	Alexandria	Tax Charge	1789	Tax PP 1789:02
Bromley, William	Alexandria	Tax Charge	1790	Tax PP 1790:02
Bromley, William, nr. Fairfax St.	Alexandria	Owner	1790	Tax L 1790:02
Bromley, Wm., Fairfax St.	Alexandria	Occupant	1787	Tax L 1787:05
Bromley, Wm., nr. Fairfax St.	Alexandria	Occupant	1790	Tax L 1790:02
Bronaugh, Carey	Alexandria	Boarder	1808	1808(4):27A
Bronaugh, John	Alexandria	Owner	1787	Tax L 1787:06
Bronaugh, John	Alexandria	Tax Charge	1787	Tax PP 1787:02
Bronaugh, John, Royal St.	Alexandria	Occupant	1787	Tax L 1787:06
Bronaugh, John W.	Arlington	Admin.	1834	WB4:101
Bronaugh, Sarah	Arlington	Admin.	1808	WBC:038
Bronough, Sarah	Alexandria	Death	1795	CRE:202
Brook, George, grantor	Arlington	Indenture D.	1812	ID2:081
Brook, George, in jail	Arlington	Insolvent	1812	ID2:077
Brook, Richard	Alexandria	Tax Charge	1800	Tax PP 1800:02
Brook, Richd., profits taker	Alexandria	Housekeeper	1808	1808(3):21A
Brook, Thos. F.	Alexandria	Tithable +16	1788	Tax PP 1788:03
Brook, William	Alexandria	Tax Charge	1800	Tax PP 1800:02
Brooke, Ann	Arlington	Dower	1823	AB5:213; LVA-LP
Brooke, Ann	Arlington	Inventory	1823	AB5:212; LVA-LP
Brooke, Ann	Arlington	Division S.	1823	OCR1822:056a
Brooke, Ann	Arlington	Admin.	1823	OCR1822:054
Brooke, Ann	Arlington	Admin.	1823	WB3:115
Brooke, Commodore [Ann]	Arlington	Division S.	1823	AB5:213; LVA-LP
Brooke, Henrietta T.	Arlington	Guard. Acct.	1858	WB7:316; LVA-LP
Brooke, Henrietta T., c/o John H.	Arlington	Guard.	1853	BB(np)
Brooke, Jno. T., sea captain	Alexandria	Boarder	1799	1799(2):17A
Brooke, John	Alexandria	Tax Charge	1796	Tax PP 1796:02
Brooke, John H.	Arlington	Apprentice	1824	OCR1822:069
Brooke, Milly, washerwoman	Alexandria	Head	1810	1810(1):09A
Brooke, Walter Baker	Arlington	Apprentice	1813	OCR1811:165
Brookes, Esther Jane	Alexandria	Will	1881	WB1:332; LP
Brookes, William	Arlington	Apprentice	1844	OCR1842:089
Brooks, Capt.	Alexandria	Tax Charge	1796	Tax LP 1796:02
Brooks, David, grantor	Arlington	Indenture D.	1832	ID:372
Brooks, David, in jail	Arlington	Insolvent	1832	ID:370
Brooks, Henry	Arlington	Admin.	1832	WB4:056; LVA-LP

NAME OR SUBJECT	LOCATION	TYPE	YEAR	REFERENCE(S)
Brooks, James	Arlington	Ordinary	1809	OBL2(np)
Brooks, James	Arlington	Ordinary	1810	OBL2(np)
Brooks, James, tavern keeper	Alexandria	Head	1810	1810(2):03A
Brooks, Jno.	Alexandria	Boarder	1808	1808(1):07A
Brooks, Joe (C)	Alexandria	Boarder	1808	1808(1):01B
Brooks, John	Alexandria	Resident	1800	1800(4):12B
Brooks, John, marriener	Alexandria	Boarder	1800	1800(4):12A
Brooks, John T.	Alexandria	Tax Charge	1799	Tax PP 1799:04
Brooks, John T.	Alexandria	Tax Charge	1800	Tax PP 1800:03
Brooks, John T.	Arlington	Inventory	1821	AB4:229; LVA-LP
Brooks, John T.	Arlington	Account	1822	AB5:095; LVA-LP
Brooks, John T., def.	Alexandria	Suit	1811	CRI:131
Brooks, John T., def.	Alexandria	Suit	1814	CRI:440
Brooks, John T., of St. Mary's	Alexandria	Letter	1809	CRI:146
Brooks, John Turnpin	Arlington	Will	1821	WB2:410; File #188A
Brooks, John Turnpin	Arlington	Bond	1821	WB2:413
Brooks, Joseph, a slave of R. Mease	Arlington	Crime	1797	OT:01/08/1797
Brooks, Thomas	Alexandria	Tax Charge	1789	Tax PP 1789:02
Brooks, Widow	Alexandria	Reference	1808	1808(1):07A
Brooks, Wm. & wife Mary	Alexandria	Resident	1800	1800(4):08B
Brooks, Wm., marriner	Alexandria	Head	1800	1800(4):08A
Brooks, [Blank]	Alexandria	Tithable +16	1790	Tax PP 1790:04
Brown & Long	Alexandria	Tax Charge	1798	Tax PP 1798:01
Brown & Long	Alexandria	Tax Charge	1799	Tax PP 1799:03
Brown & Long	Alexandria	Tax Charge	1800	Tax PP 1800:02
Brown, Aaron	Alexandria	Resident	1800	1800(4):16B
Brown, Adam	Alexandria	Tithable +21	1787	Tax PP 1787:15
Brown, Ann	Arlington	Admin.	1810	WBC:487
Brown, Aquila	Alexandria	Tithable +16	1788	Tax PP 1788:03
Brown, Aquila	Alexandria	Tithable +16	1789	Tax PP 1789:09
Brown, Aquilla	Alexandria	Tithable +16	1790	Tax PP 1790:06
Brown, Aron, coopper	Alexandria	Boarder	1800	1800(4):16A
Brown, Bedford	Alexandria	Will	1897	WB2:238; LP
Brown, Ben, laborer	Alexandria	Housekeeper	1808	1808(4):28A
Brown, Ben, ship carpenter	Alexandria	Head	1810	1810(4):03A
Brown, Benj.	Alexandria	Tax Charge	1795	Tax PP 1795:02
Brown, Benjamin	Arlington	Account	1808	WBC:073
Brown, Benjamin	Arlington	Inventory	1816	AB2:342; LVA-LP
Brown, Benjamin	Arlington	Bond	1816	WB2:141
Brown, Benjamin	Arlington	Will	1816	WB2:132; File #134A
Brown, Benjamin	Arlington	Account	1817	AB3:033; LVA-LP
Brown, Benjn., millstone maker	Alexandria	Housekeeper	1808	1808(3):20A
Brown, Betty	Alexandria	Head	1795	1795(4):07
Brown, Catharine	Arlington	Appraisal	1804	DBI:009
Brown, Catharine	Arlington	Account	1806	WBB:356; LVA-LP
Brown, Catharine	Arlington	Guard.	1817	WB2:200
Brown, Catherine	Arlington	Will	1803	WBA:176
Brown, Catherine	Arlington	Bond	1803	WBA:184
Brown, Catherine	Arlington	Inventory	1804	WBA:262; LVA-LP
Brown, Celia	Alexandria	Will	1878	WB1:250; LP
Brown, Daniel	Alexandria	Tax Charge	1787	Tax PP 1787:02
Brown, Daniel	Arlington	Account	1803	WBA:158; LVA-LP
Brown, Darkey	Alexandria	Boarder	1808	1808(4):25A
Brown, David	Alexandria	Tax Charge	1800	Tax PP 1800:03
Brown, Eliza, c/o Henry	Arlington	Apprentice	1811	OCR1811:024
Brown, Eliza, c/o Henry	Arlington	Apprentice	1812	OCR1811:077
Brown, Elizabeth	Arlington	Guard.	1817	WB2:200
Brown, Elizabeth	Arlington	Inventory	1825	AB6:105; LVA-LP
Brown, Elizabeth	Arlington	Bond	1825	WB3:197
Brown, Elizabeth	Arlington	Will	1825	WB3:196; File #240A
Brown, Ellen D.	Alexandria	Will	1873	WB1:079; LP

NAME OR SUBJECT	LOCATION	TYPE	YEAR	REFERENCE(S)
Brown, George	Alexandria	Tithable +16	1790	Tax PP 1790:03
Brown, Gustavus A., M.D., def.	Alexandria	Suit	1822	CRL:574
Brown, Hannah	Arlington	Guard.	1807	WBB:449
Brown, Harry	Alexandria	Tax Charge	1799	Tax PP 1799:03
Brown, Henry	Alexandria	Head	1810	1810(4):08A
Brown, Henry	Arlington	Will	1849	WB5:140; File #449A
Brown, Henry	Arlington	Will	1857	WB7:201; File #541A
Brown, Henry	Arlington	Inventory	1857	WB7:220
Brown, Henry (C), shopkeeper	Alexandria	Housekeeper	1808	1808(1):02A
Brown, Henry & wife (C), labourer	Alexandria	Housekeeper	1799	1799(2):14A
Brown, James	Alexandria	Tax Charge	1796	Tax PP 1796:02
Brown, James	Alexandria	Tax Charge	1799	Tax PP 1799:04
Brown, James	Alexandria	Tax Charge	1799	Tax PP 1799:03
Brown, James	Alexandria	Tax Charge	1800	Tax PP 1800:03
Brown, James (C)	Arlington	Apprentice	1844	OCR1842:091
Brown, James & wife, boarding house	Alexandria	Housekeeper	1799	1799(2):01A
Brown, James, w(3), boarding house	Alexandria	Head	1796	1796(3):6
Brown, Jas.	Alexandria	Tax Charge	1798	Tax PP 1798:02
Brown, Jno. D.	Alexandria	Boarder	1808	1808(4):27A
Brown, John	Alexandria	Boarder	1808	1808(3):21A
Brown, John	Arlington	Libellant	1812	ACO:127-128, 132-135
Brown, John	Arlington	Petition	1812	ACR:050
Brown, John	Arlington	Libellant	1813	ACO:137
Brown, John, b. Flinsburg, Den.	Arlington	Alien Entry	1823	RA:04/08/23
Brown, John, s/o Benjn.	Alexandria	Boarder	1808	1808(3):20A
Brown, Julia A.	Arlington	Will	1899	WB10:397; File #789A
Brown, Margaret	Arlington	Guard.	1817	WB2:200
Brown, Martha	Alexandria	Head	1795	1795(4a):07
Brown, Mary	Alexandria	Boarder	1799	1799(2):01A
Brown, Mary	Arlington	Guard.	1807	WBB:497
Brown, Mary	Arlington	Apprentice	1825	OCR1822:105a
Brown, Mary Eliza	Arlington	Guard.	1834	WB4:090
Brown, Mary G.	Arlington	Bond	1854	BB(np)
Brown, Mary G.	Arlington	Will	1854	WB6:308; File #504A
Brown, Mary Julia Ann	Arlington	Will	1838	WB4:185; File #360A
Brown, Mathew, Estate	Alexandria	Owner	1787	Tax L 1787:08
Brown, Matthew, plt.	Alexandria	Suit	1801	CRB:313
Brown, Matthew, plt.	Alexandria	Suit	1801	CRB:329
Brown, Polly, seamstress	Alexandria	Head	1810	1810(3):09A
Brown, Richard	Alexandria	Tithable +16	1788	Tax PP 1788:16
Brown, Robert	Alexandria	Tax Charge	1799	Tax PP 1799:04
Brown, Robert	Alexandria	Tax Charge	1800	Tax PP 1800:03
Brown, Robert	Arlington	Inventory	1805	WBB:157
Brown, Robert	Arlington	Sale	1805	WBB:164
Brown, Robert	Arlington	Admin.	1805	WBB:153
Brown, Robert	Arlington	Account	1806	WBB:287, 451
Brown, Robert H., c/o Sarah	Arlington	Apprentice	1822	OCR1822:015
Brown, Robt. & wife, cooper	Alexandria	Housekeeper	1799	1799(2):11A
Brown, S.M., Fairfax St.	Alexandria	Occupant	1787	Tax L 1787:15
Brown, S.W.	Alexandria	Mer. License	1798	Tax PP 1798:20-1
Brown, Saml.	Alexandria	Boarder	1808	1808(1):06A
Brown, Saml. M.	Alexandria	Tax Charge	1788	Tax PP 1788:01
Brown, Saml. M.	Alexandria	Tax Charge	1788	Tax PP 1788:02
Brown, Samuel	Arlington	Appraisal	1831	LVA-LP
Brown, Samuel M.	Alexandria	Tax Charge	1787	Tax PP 1787:02
Brown, Samuel M.	Alexandria	Tax Charge	1790	Tax PP 1790:02
Brown, Samuel W.	Alexandria	Tax Charge	1799	Tax PP 1799:03
Brown, Sanford	Alexandria	Will	1879	WB1:257; LP
Brown, Sarah Ann	Arlington	Will	1851	WB5:242; File #459A
Brown, Sophia, c/o Henry	Arlington	Apprentice	1812	OCR1811:093
Brown, Steven	Alexandria	Serv./Appr.	1800	1800(4):08B

NAME OR SUBJECT	LOCATION	TYPE	YEAR	REFERENCE(S)
Brown, Thomas	Alexandria	Tax Charge	1798	Tax PP 1798:01
Brown, Thos. (C)	Alexandria	Boarder	1808	1808(1):07B
Brown, William	Alexandria	Owner	1787	Tax L 1787:06
Brown, William	Alexandria	Tax Charge	1787	Tax PP 1787:02
Brown, William	Alexandria	Tax Charge	1789	Tax PP 1789:02
Brown, William	Arlington	Crime	1800	OT:08/11/1800
Brown, William	Arlington	Guard.	1807	WBB:448
Brown, William	Arlington	Witness	1812	ACR:057
Brown, William	Arlington	Apprentice	1823	OCR1822:031
Brown, William (C)	Arlington	Apprentice	1843	OCR1842:052
Brown, William, Cameron St.	Alexandria	Occupant	1787	Tax L 1787:06
Brown, William, Dr.	Alexandria	Tax Charge	1788	Tax PP 1788:02
Brown, William, Dr.	Alexandria	Tax Charge	1789	Tax PP 1789:02
Brown, William, Dr.	Alexandria	Tax Charge	1790	Tax PP 1790:02
Brown, William, Fairfax St.	Alexandria	Occupant	1787	Tax L 1787:06
Brown, William, Fairfax St.	Alexandria	Occupant	1790	Tax L 1790:02
Brown, William, Fairfax St.	Alexandria	Owner	1790	Tax L 1790:02
Brown, William H., merchant	Alexandria	Head	1810	1810(3):03A
Brown, William, M.D.	Alexandria	Tax Charge	1787	Tax PP 1787:02
Brown, William N.	Alexandria	Will	1890	WB1:561; LP
Brown, Winny, washerwoman	Alexandria	Head	1810	1810(2):06A
Brown, Wm., Dr., Estate, Fairfax St.	Alexandria	Owner	1795	Tax L 1795:04
Brown, Wm., Dr., Estate, Cameron St.	Alexandria	Owner	1795	Tax L 1795:03
Brown, Wm., Estate	Alexandria	Tax Charge	1796	Tax LP 1796:02
Brown, [blank], Water St.	Alexandria	Occupant	1790	Tax L 1790:07
Brownell, John, rigger	Alexandria	Housekeeper	1808	1808(2):17A
Browning, Josiah, labourer	Alexandria	Head	1810	1810(1):13A
Bruce, Dinah, b. Bermuda	Arlington	Alien Entry	1801	RA:24/06/01
Bruce, James, ward of Fanny Thomas	Arlington	Apprentice	1811	OCR1811:020
Bruce, Samuel, b. Africa	Arlington	Alien Entry	1801	RA:24/06/01
Bruffield, Sarah	Alexandria	Head	1795	1795(4):02
Bruffield, Sarah, Duke St.	Alexandria	Occupant	1795	Tax L 1795:04
Brumer, Isaac, c/o Barbara Thompson	Arlington	Apprentice	1812	OCR1811:116
Brumley, [blank], Fairfax St.	Alexandria	Occupant	1795	Tax L 1795:08
Bruneau, Benja.	Alexandria	Tithable +16	1788	Tax PP 1788:12
Bruner, Jno. & wife, currier	Alexandria	Housekeeper	1799	1799(2):11A
Bruner, Jno., Water St.	Alexandria	Occupant	1795	Tax L 1795:08
Bruner, John	Alexandria	Tax Charge	1795	Tax PP 1795:03
Bruner, John	Alexandria	Tax Charge	1796	Tax LP 1796:03
Bruner, John	Alexandria	Tax Charge	1796	Tax PP 1796:02
Bruner, John	Alexandria	Tax Charge	1798	Tax PP 1798:01
Bruner, John	Alexandria	Tax Charge	1799	Tax PP 1799:04
Bruner, John	Alexandria	Tax Charge	1800	Tax PP 1800:02
Brunet, John B., on King St.	Arlington	Ordinary	1823	OBL3(np)
Brunoe, George, Barbara	Arlington	Apprentice	1804	OCR1801:186
Bruster, Charles	Arlington	Crime	1795	OT:22/06/1795
Bryan & Adams	Arlington	Trustee Acct.	1867	WB8:495, 568
Bryan & Adams Trustees	Arlington	Account	1868	WB9:124
Bryan, Barney	Alexandria	Tax Charge	1796	Tax LP 1796:02
Bryan, Berd.	Alexandria	Tax Charge	1798	Tax PP 1798:02
Bryan, Bernard	Alexandria	Tax Charge	1795	Tax PP 1795:02
Bryan, Bernard	Alexandria	Tax Charge	1796	Tax PP 1796:02
Bryan, Bernard	Alexandria	Tax Charge	1799	Tax PP 1799:03
Bryan, Bernard	Alexandria	Tax Charge	1800	Tax PP 1800:03
Bryan, Bernard	Arlington	Will	1841	WB4:289; File #384A
Bryan, Bernard, shoemaker	Alexandria	Housekeeper	1808	1808(2):12A
Bryan, Bernard, shoemaker	Alexandria	Head	1810	1810(2):02A
Bryan, Charles	Alexandria	Owner	1787	Tax L 1787:08
Bryan, Charles	Alexandria	Tax Charge	1787	Tax PP 1787:01
Bryan, Charles	Alexandria	Tax Charge	1788	Tax PP 1788:01
Bryan, Charles	Alexandria	Tax Charge	1789	Tax PP 1789:02

NAME OR SUBJECT	LOCATION	TYPE	YEAR	REFERENCE(S)
Bryan, Charles	Alexandria	Tax Charge	1790	Tax PP 1790:02
Bryan, Charles, King St.	Alexandria	Occupant	1787	Tax L 1787:18
Bryan, Charles, King St.	Alexandria	Owner	1790	Tax L 1790:02
Bryan, Jno. & wife, sadler	Alexandria	Housekeeper	1799	1799(2):05A
Bryan, John	Alexandria	Tax Charge	1795	Tax PP 1795:02
Bryan, John	Alexandria	Tax Charge	1796	Tax LP 1796:02
Bryan, John	Alexandria	Tax Charge	1796	Tax PP 1796:01
Bryan, John	Alexandria	Mer. License	1798	Tax PP 1798:20-1
Bryan, John	Alexandria	Tax Charge	1798	Tax PP 1798:01
Bryan, John	Alexandria	Tax Charge	1799	Tax PP 1799:03
Bryan, John	Alexandria	Tax Charge	1800	Tax PP 1800:02
Bryan, John	Arlington	Admin.	1823	WB3:107
Bryan, John	Arlington	Account	1854	LVA-LP
Bryan, John A.	Arlington	Apprentice	1826	OCR1822:109a
Bryan, John, King St.	Alexandria	Occupant	1795	Tax L 1795:17
Bryan, John, King St.	Alexandria	Occupant	1795	Tax L 1795:07
Bryan, Saml., sadler	Alexandria	Housekeeper	1808	1808(3):21A
Bryan, Samuel, sadler	Alexandria	Head	1810	1810(3):01A
Bryan, Susanna W.	Arlington	Will P.	1843	OCR1842:023
Bryan, Susanna W.	Arlington	Will	1843	WB4:313; File #392A
Bryan, William, labourer	Alexandria	Head	1810	1810(1):02A
Bryant, Emma	Alexandria	Will	1875	WB1:123; LP
Bryant, George W.	Alexandria	Will	1887	WB1:477; LP
Bryce, Hannah, Prince St.	Alexandria	Owner	1790	Tax L 1790:02
Bryce, William, Union St.	Alexandria	Occupant	1790	Tax L 1790:07
Brymer, Alexr.	Alexandria	Tax Charge	1798	Tax PP 1798:01
Bryon, John, w(2)2, sadler	Alexandria	Head	1796	1796(3):4
Bryson, Andrew	Alexandria	Tax Charge	1799	Tax PP 1799:03
Bryson, Andrew, clerk	Alexandria	Boarder	1799	1799(2):03A
Buchan, Alexander	Alexandria	Tithable +21	1787	Tax PP 1787:08
Buchan, Jno.	Alexandria	Tax Charge	1798	Tax PP 1798:01
Buchan, Wm.	Alexandria	Tax Charge	1796	Tax PP 1796:01
Buchannan, Robert	Arlington	Apprentice	1826	OCR1822:116a
Buchur, Jonothan	Alexandria	Resident	1800	1800(4):13B
Bucker, Larry	Alexandria	Tithable +21	1787	Tax PP 1787:05
Buckingham, Isaac	Arlington	Will	1864	WB8:194; File #613A
Buckingham, James	Arlington	Guard.	1837	WB4:153
Buckingham, Sarah Ellen Garner, of MD	Arlington	Will	1862	WB8:107
Buckingham, William	Arlington	Appraisal	1870	WB9:226
Buckious, John	Alexandria	Tax Charge	1800	Tax PP 1800:02
Buckland & Muir	Alexandria	Tax Charge	1796	Tax PP 1796:02
Buckland & Muir, Fairfax St.	Alexandria	Occupant	1795	Tax L 1795:04
Buckland, Ann	Alexandria	Housekeeper	1799	1799(2):05A
Buckland, Ann	Arlington	Will	1834	WB4:076; File #329A
Buckland, Ann, gentlewoman	Alexandria	Housekeeper	1808	1808(3):21A
Buckland, Ann	Alexandria	Head	1810	1810(3):01A
Buckland, Mary	Arlington	Guard.	1816	WB2:155
Buckland, Wm.	Alexandria	Tax Charge	1795	Tax PP 1795:03
Buckland, Wm.	Alexandria	Tax Charge	1796	Tax LP 1796:02
Buckland, Wm.	Alexandria	Tax Charge	1798	Tax PP 1798:01
Buckley, Mary	Alexandria	Housekeeper	1799	1799(2):16A
Buckley, Mary	Alexandria	Resident	1800	1800(4):08B
Buckner, Bickley	Alexandria	Tax Charge	1798	Tax PP 1798:01
Buckner, Richard	Alexandria	Tax Charge	1799	Tax PP 1799:03
Buckner, Winny, washer woman	Alexandria	Boarder	1799	1799(2):01A
Budd, Henry	Alexandria	Tax Charge	1787	Tax PP 1787:02
Budd, Henry	Alexandria	Tax Charge	1788	Tax PP 1788:02
Budd, Henry	Alexandria	Tax Charge	1789	Tax PP 1789:02
Budd, Henry	Alexandria	Tax Charge	1790	Tax PP 1790:01
Budd, Henry	Alexandria	Tax Charge	1796	Tax LP 1796:23
Budd, Henry, Prince St.	Alexandria	Occupant	1790	Tax L 1790:05

NAME OR SUBJECT	LOCATION	TYPE	YEAR	REFERENCE(S)
Budd, Jacob	Alexandria	Tax Charge	1787	Tax PP 1787:02
Budd, John	Alexandria	Tithable +21	1787	Tax PP 1787:02
Budd, R., Royal St.	Alexandria	Occupant	1787	Tax L 1787:23
Buddicom, William, plt.	Alexandria	Suit	1801	CRD:206
Buddicomb, W., Cameron St.	Alexandria	Occupant	1787	Tax L 1787:15
Bull, Sarah, washer	Alexandria	Head	1795	1795(4):07
Bullen, Roger H., to *Ship Potomac*	Arlington	Apprentice	1815	OCR1811:265
Bullock, James, seaman	Alexandria	Head	1810	1810(3):08A
Bumford, Benjamin	Arlington	Libellant	1803	ACO:007
Bundy, Cristiana	Alexandria	Boarder	1799	1799(2):03A
Bunker, Thomas, of Nantucket, Mass.	Alexandria	Deposition	1818	CRK:479
Bunn, Rev. Mr.	Alexandria	Head	1810	1810(4):01A
Burch, Hilary	Arlington	Trustee Acct.	1857	R:003; LVA-LP
Burch, Jas., shopkeeper & drayman	Alexandria	Housekeeper	1808	1808(3):22A
Burch, Joseph, c/o Joseph	Arlington	Guard. Acct.	1835	LVA-LP
Burch, William Henry, c/o Joseph	Arlington	Guard. Acct.	1835	LVA-LP
Burchell, Edward	Arlington	Will	1866	WB8:386; File #645A
Burchell, Edward	Arlington	Appraisal	1866	WB8:407
Burchell, Edward	Arlington	Inventory	1866	WB8:407
Burchell, Edward	Arlington	Account	1867	WB8:572
Burd, Henry	Alexandria	Head	1795	1795(4a):09
Burford, Hannah	Arlington	Will	1812	WB1:205; File #105A
Burford, Hannah	Arlington	Bond	1812	WB1:204
Burford, Hannah	Arlington	Account	1816	AB2:344
Burford, Henry & wife Rositter	Alexandria	Resident	1800	1800(4):14B
Burford, Henry, murchant	Alexandria	Head	1800	1800(4):14A
Burford, John A.	Alexandria	Housekeeper	1808	1808(2):13A
Burford, John A., retailer	Alexandria	Housekeeper	1808	1808(1):02A
Burford v. Crandell's Admor.	Arlington	Suit	1816	LVA-LP
Burgen, Mary, sempstress	Alexandria	Housekeeper	1808	1808(1):09A
Burgess, William, cabinett maker	Alexandria	Head	1810	1810(4):07A
Burgess, William H.	Alexandria	Will	1894	WB2:073; LP
Burgis, Wm.	Alexandria	Boarder	1799	1799(2):16A
Burke, William	Arlington	Apprentice	1815	OCR1811:312
Burke, William H.	Alexandria	Will	1883	WB1:381; LP
Burley, James	Arlington	Appraisal	1864	WB8:196
Burley, Jno., sadler	Alexandria	Boarder	1799	1799(2):09A
Burley, John	Alexandria	Tax Charge	1799	Tax PP 1799:04
Burman, Richard	Alexandria	Tax Charge	1796	Tax PP 1796:01
Burman, Richd.	Alexandria	Tax Charge	1795	Tax PP 1795:02
Burman, Richd., Union St.	Alexandria	Occupant	1795	Tax L 1795:26
Burmelen, Jacob	Arlington	Libellant	1811	ACO:119
Burnes, Henry	Alexandria	Serv./Appr.	1800	1800(4):09B
Burnet, Molly	Alexandria	Owner	1787	Tax L 1787:07
Burnet, Molly, Love alley	Alexandria	Occupant	1787	Tax L 1787:07
Burnett, Mary, Love Alley	Alexandria	Owner	1790	Tax L 1790:02
Burnett, Molly, Love alley	Alexandria	Occupant	1787	Tax L 1787:02
Burnett, Richard	Alexandria	Tax Charge	1796	Tax PP 1796:01
Burnett, Richd.	Alexandria	Tax Charge	1798	Tax PP 1798:02
Burnett, Richd., cook	Alexandria	Housekeeper	1808	1808(3):22A
Burns, Isabella	Alexandria	Will	1899	WB2:327; LP
Burns, John	Alexandria	Tax Charge	1787	Tax PP 1787:02
Burns, John	Alexandria	Tax Charge	1788	Tax PP 1788:02
Burns, John	Alexandria	Tax Charge	1789	Tax PP 1789:01
Burns, John	Alexandria	Tax Charge	1790	Tax PP 1790:01
Burns, John, Fairfax St.	Alexandria	Occupant	1790	Tax L 1790:02
Burns, John, Fairfax St.	Alexandria	Owner	1790	Tax L 1790:02
Burns [Byrne], John	Arlington	Account	1823	AB5:216; LVA-LP
Burns, Patrick	Alexandria	Tax Charge	1789	Tax PP 1789:01
Burns, Patrick	Alexandria	Tax Charge	1790	Tax PP 1790:01
Burns, Patrick	Alexandria	Tax Charge	1795	Tax PP 1795:03

NAME OR SUBJECT	LOCATION	TYPE	YEAR	REFERENCE(S)
Burns, Patrick	Alexandria	Tax Charge	1796	Tax LP 1796:03
Burns, Patrick	Arlington	Ordinary	1802	OBL1(np)
Burns, Patrick	Arlington	Ordinary	1803	OBL1(np)
Burns, Patrick, Prince St.	Alexandria	Occupant	1790	Tax L 1790:08
Burns, Patrick, Prince St.	Alexandria	Occupant	1795	Tax L 1795:04
Burns, Patrick, Prince St.	Alexandria	Owner	1795	Tax L 1795:04
Burot, Alexander	Arlington	Admin.	1814	WB1:283
Burrel, Ellen (C)	Arlington	Apprentice	1826	OCR1822:120
Burroughs, John H.	Alexandria	Will	1887	WB1:471; LP
Burroughs, Margaret	Alexandria	Boarder	1799	1799(2):10A
Burrows, Samuel	Arlington	Admin.	1829	WB3:377
Burset, Henry & wife, merchant	Alexandria	Housekeeper	1799	1799(2):17A
Burton, Nicholas F.	Arlington	Inventory	1820	AB4:102; LVA-LP
Burton, Robert & wife, laborer	Alexandria	Head	1795	1795(4):05
Bush, Mark, c/o John (Norwich, Eng.)	Arlington	Apprentice	1805	OCR1801:237
Bush, Samuel C.	Arlington	Admin.	1838	WB4:159
Bush, Thomas (C)	Arlington	Apprentice	1812	OCR1811:048
Bush, Thomas (C), c/o Henrietta	Arlington	Apprentice	1811	OCR1811:035
Bush, Thomas (C), c/o Henrietta	Arlington	Apprentice	1812	OCR1811:135
Bushby, Joseph	Alexandria	Tax Charge	1787	Tax PP 1787:02
Bushby, Joseph	Alexandria	Tax Charge	1788	Tax PP 1788:02
Bushby, Joseph	Alexandria	Tax Charge	1789	Tax PP 1789:02
Bushby, Joseph, def.	Alexandria	Suit	1821	CRL:369
Bushby, Joseph, Duke St.	Alexandria	Occupant	1787	Tax L 1787:07
Bushby, Joseph, Fairfax St.	Alexandria	Occupant	1790	Tax L 1790:02
Bushby, Mary, of Washington D.C.	Alexandria	Deed	1817	CRL:382
Bushby, William	Alexandria	Owner	1787	Tax L 1787:07
Bushby, William	Alexandria	Tax Charge	1787	Tax PP 1787:02
Bushby, William	Alexandria	Tax Charge	1788	Tax PP 1788:02
Bushby, William & wife, painter	Alexandria	Head	1795	1795(4):05
Bushby, William, def.	Alexandria	Suit	1821	CRL:369
Bushby, William, Fairfax St.	Alexandria	Owner	1790	Tax L 1790:02(3)
Bushby, William, Fairfax St.	Alexandria	Owner	1790	Tax L 1790:02
Bushby, William, nr. Duke St.	Alexandria	Owner	1790	Tax L 1790:02
Bushby, William, nr. Fairfax St.	Alexandria	Owner	1790	Tax L 1790:02
Bushby, William, nr. Fairfax St.	Alexandria	Owner	1790	Tax L 1790:02(2)
Bushby, William, of Fairfax Co.	Alexandria	Deed	1796	CRL:383
Bushby, William, of Washington D.C.	Alexandria	Will	1810	CRL:379
Bushby, Willm.	Alexandria	Tax Charge	1795	Tax PP 1795:03
Bushby, Wm.	Alexandria	Tax Charge	1796	Tax LP 1796:03
Bushby, Wm.	Alexandria	Tax Charge	1796	Tax PP 1796:01
Bushby, Wm. & Co., Fairfax St.	Alexandria	Occupant	1787	Tax L 1787:07
Bushby, Wm., cor. Duke & F.	Alexandria	Occupant	1795	Tax L 1795:02
Bushby, Wm., Estate, back building	Alexandria	Owner	1795	Tax L 1795:02(3)
Bushby, Wm., Estate, back building	Alexandria	Owner	1795	Tax L 1795:03(5)
Bushby, Wm., Estate, cor. Duke & F.	Alexandria	Owner	1795	Tax L 1795:02
Bushby, Wm., Estate, cor. Duke & F.	Alexandria	Owner	1795	Tax L 1795:02
Bushby, Wm., Estate, Duke St.	Alexandria	Owner	1795	Tax L 1795:02(2)
Bushby, Wm., Estate, Fairfax St.	Alexandria	Owner	1795	Tax L 1795:02(4)
Bushby, Wm., Estate, Royal St.	Alexandria	Owner	1795	Tax L 1795:02(2)
Bustlefagan, Saml.	Alexandria	Tithable +16	1790	Tax PP 1790:05
Bustlefagan, Samuel	Alexandria	Tithable +16	1788	Tax PP 1788:06
Butcher & Paton, King St.	Alexandria	Occupant	1790	Tax L 1790:01
Butcher, Aaron	Alexandria	Tithable +16	1788	Tax PP 1788:15
Butcher, Ann	Arlington	Inventory	1826	AB6:184
Butcher, Ann	Arlington	Will	1826	WB3:224; File #497A
Butcher, Ann	Arlington	Will	1826	WB3:224
Butcher, Ann	Arlington	Bond	1826	WB3:228
Butcher, Ann	Arlington	Account	1827	AB6:441
Butcher, Ann	Arlington	Account	1828	LVA-LP
Butcher, Ann	Arlington	Account	1832	AB7:045; LVA-LP

NAME OR SUBJECT	LOCATION	TYPE	YEAR	REFERENCE(S)
Butcher, Ann	Arlington	Account	1832	AB7:043; LVA-LP
Butcher, Ann	Arlington	Account	1834	AB7:108; LVA-LP
Butcher, Ann	Arlington	Account	1834	AB7:152; LVA-LP
Butcher, Ann	Arlington	Account	1835	AB7:152
Butcher, Geo., Duke St.	Alexandria	Occupant	1787	Tax L 1787:07
Butcher, Jno. & wife, merchant	Alexandria	Housekeeper	1799	1799(2):13A
Butcher, Jno., King St.	Alexandria	Owner	1795	Tax L 1795:03
Butcher, Jno., Wolf St.	Alexandria	Occupant	1795	Tax L 1795:03
Butcher, Jno., Wolf St.	Alexandria	Owner	1795	Tax L 1795:03
Butcher, John	Alexandria	Owner	1787	Tax L 1787:07
Butcher, John	Alexandria	Tax Charge	1787	Tax PP 1787:02
Butcher, John	Alexandria	Tax Charge	1788	Tax PP 1788:02
Butcher, John	Alexandria	Tax Charge	1789	Tax PP 1789:02
Butcher, John	Alexandria	Tax Charge	1790	Tax PP 1790:01
Butcher, John	Alexandria	Tax Charge	1795	Tax PP 1795:03
Butcher, John	Alexandria	Tax Charge	1796	Tax LP 1796:02
Butcher, John	Alexandria	Tax Charge	1796	Tax PP 1796:01
Butcher, John	Alexandria	Tax Charge	1799	Tax PP 1799:03
Butcher, John	Alexandria	Tax Charge	1800	Tax PP 1800:03
Butcher, John	Arlington	Bond	1811	WB1:123
Butcher, John	Arlington	Will	1811	WB1:120; File #097A
Butcher, John	Arlington	Account	1812	AB1:258; LVA-LP
Butcher, John	Arlington	Inventory	1812	AB1:198; LVA-LP
Butcher, John	Arlington	Account	1827	AB6:435; LVA-LP
Butcher, John & wife, merchant	Alexandria	Head	1795	1795(4):09
Butcher, John & wife Ann	Alexandria	Resident	1800	1800(4):13B
Butcher, John, King St.	Alexandria	Occupant	1787	Tax L 1787:02
Butcher, John, merchant	Alexandria	Head	1800	1800(4):13A
Butcher, John, merchant	Alexandria	Housekeeper	1808	1808(1):06A
Butcher, John, merchant	Alexandria	Head	1810	1810(1):08A
Butcher, John, merchant	Alexandria	Head	1810	1810(4):09A
Butcher, John, Pitt St.	Alexandria	Occupant	1787	Tax L 1787:07
Butcher, John, Wolf St.	Alexandria	Owner	1790	Tax L 1790:01
Butcher, John, Wolf St.	Alexandria	Occupant	1790	Tax L 1790:01
Butcher, Jona., retailer	Alexandria	Housekeeper	1808	1808(4):24A
Butcher, Jonathan	Alexandria	Tax Charge	1799	Tax PP 1799:03
Butcher, Jonathan	Alexandria	Tax Charge	1800	Tax PP 1800:03
Butcher, Jonathan	Arlington	Juryman	1824	ACO:237
Butcher, Jonathan, clerk	Alexandria	Boarder	1799	1799(2):13A
Butler, Ann	Arlington	Guard.	1812	WB1:181
Butler, Ann (M), c/o Elizabeth	Arlington	Apprentice	1804	OCR1801:159
Butler, Ann, ward of Mary Butler	Arlington	Apprentice	1812	OCR1811:098
Butler, Betsy, sempstress	Alexandria	Housekeeper	1808	1808(2):15A
Butler, Betsy, washwoman	Alexandria	Housekeeper	1808	1808(2):16A
Butler, Charles	Arlington	Inventory	1818	AB3:272; LVA-LP
Butler, Charles	Arlington	Guard.	1818	WB2:239
Butler, David (C)	Arlington	Apprentice	1845	OCR1842:117
Butler, David, c/o Elizabeth	Arlington	Apprentice	1823	OCR1822:036a
Butler, Edward	Arlington	Apprentice	1803	OCR1801:095
Butler, Edward, c/o Ann	Arlington	Apprentice	1801	OCR1801:007
Butler, Elizabeth (M), c/o Elizabeth	Arlington	Apprentice	1804	OCR1801:162
Butler, Elizabeth, seamstress	Alexandria	Head	1810	1810(2):06A
Butler, Ferdinand	Arlington	Apprentice	1823	OCR1822:036a
Butler, Ignatius	Arlington	Guard.	1811	WB1:065
Butler, Ignatius & wife (C), labourer	Alexandria	Housekeeper	1799	1799(2):14A
Butler, Ignatius, c/o Mary	Arlington	Apprentice	1811	OCR1811:016
Butler, Isaac	Arlington	Plaintiff	1802	PA:047
Butler, Isaac, plt.	Alexandria	Suit	1801	CRB:186
Butler, Jacob (C)	Arlington	Apprentice	1803	OCR1801:108
Butler, James	Arlington	Apprentice	1802	OCR1801:033
Butler, James	Arlington	Apprentice	1825	OCR1822:100

NAME OR SUBJECT	LOCATION	TYPE	YEAR	REFERENCE(S)
Butler, Joe (C)	Alexandria	Boarder	1808	1808(2):15B
Butler, John	Alexandria	Tithable +16	1789	Tax PP 1789:05
Butler, John	Alexandria	Tithable +16	1790	Tax PP 1790:03
Butler, John B. (C), carpenter	Alexandria	Housekeeper	1808	1808(1):06A
Butler, John, c/o Mary Ann (C)	Arlington	Apprentice	1812	OCR1811:054
Butler, John, taylor & shopkeeper	Alexandria	Housekeeper	1808	1808(2):15A
Butler, Kitty (C)	Arlington	Apprentice	1828	OCR1822:165a
Butler, Lydia (C)	Arlington	Apprentice	1813	OCR1811:195
Butler, Mary Ann (C)	Arlington	Agreement	1812	OCR1811:054
Butler, Nace, trunk maker	Alexandria	Head	1810	1810(1):09A
Butler, Nan (C)	Alexandria	Boarder	1808	1808(2):13B
Butler, Peter	Alexandria	Boarder	1808	1808(2):16A
Butler, Silas	Alexandria	Boarder	1808	1808(1):04A
Butler, Susan	Arlington	Guard.	1813	WB1:223
Butler, Susan, c/o Mary Ann	Arlington	Apprentice	1812	OCR1811:146
Butler, Timo.	Alexandria	Boarder	1808	1808(2):13A
Butler, William (C)	Arlington	Apprentice	1822	OCR1822:009a
Butler, William, c/o Betsy	Arlington	Apprentice	1815	OCR1811:274
Butler, Wm. (C), drayman	Alexandria	Housekeeper	1808	1808(1):09A
Butler, Wm., labourer	Alexandria	Head	1810	1810(1):07A
Butt, A., Prince St.	Alexandria	Occupant	1787	Tax L 1787:16
Butt, Adam	Alexandria	Tax Charge	1787	Tax PP 1787:01
Butt, Adam	Alexandria	Tax Charge	1789	Tax PP 1789:02
Butt, Adam	Alexandria	Tax Charge	1790	Tax PP 1790:01
Butt, Adam, Jr.	Alexandria	Tax Charge	1788	Tax PP 1788:02
Butt, Adam, Prince St.	Alexandria	Occupant	1790	Tax L 1790:06
Butt, Adam, Water St.	Alexandria	Occupant	1787	Tax L 1787:05
Butt, Jacob	Alexandria	Tax Charge	1788	Tax PP 1788:02
Butt, Jacob	Alexandria	Tax Charge	1789	Tax PP 1789:02
Butt, Jacob	Alexandria	Tax Charge	1790	Tax PP 1790:01
Butt, Jacob	Arlington	Guard.	1802	WBA:089
Butt, Jacob	Arlington	Inventory	1803	WBA:146
Butt, Jacob	Arlington	Account	1803	WBA:146; LVA-LP
Butt, Jacob	Arlington	Apprentice	1804	OCR1801:201
Butt, Jacob	Arlington	Guard.	1806	WBB:228
Butt, John	Alexandria	Tithable +16	1788	Tax PP 1788:02
Butt, John	Alexandria	Tithable +16	1789	Tax PP 1789:02
Buttimore, Dennis	Alexandria	Will	1897	WB2:225; LP
Butts, Augustine	Arlington	Admin.	1828	WB3:334; LVA-LP
Butts, Augustine	Arlington	Account	1830	AB6:507, 510
Butts, Augustus	Arlington	Account	1829	AB6:507; LVA-LP
Butts, Augustus	Arlington	Account	1829	AB6:510; LVA-LP
Butts, Augustus, tobacconist	Alexandria	Housekeeper	1808	1808(1):05A
Butts, Jacob	Arlington	Guard. Acct.	1807	WBB:400; LVA-LP
Butts, Jacob	Arlington	Guard. Acct.	1807	WBC:023; LVA-LP
Butts, Jacob	Alexandria	Boarder	1808	1808(2):15A
Butts, Jacob	Arlington	Guard. Acct.	1808	WBC:160; LVA-LP
Butts, Jacob	Arlington	Guard. Acct.	1812	LVA-LP
Butts, Jacob, baker	Alexandria	Head	1810	1810(2):01A
Butts, Jacob, Duke St.	Alexandria	Owner	1790	Tax L 1790:02
Butts, Jacob, Duke St.	Alexandria	Occupant	1790	Tax L 1790:02
Butts, Mark	Alexandria	Tax Charge	1799	Tax PP 1799:04
Butts, Mark	Alexandria	Tax Charge	1800	Tax PP 1800:03
Butts, Mark	Arlington	Admin.	1843	OCR1842:050
Butts, Mark	Arlington	Admin.	1843	WB4:372
Butts, Mark	Arlington	Inventory	1844	AB8:460; LVA-LP
Butts, Mark & wife, sea captain	Alexandria	Housekeeper	1799	1799(2):12A
Butts, Mark, Capt.	Arlington	Account	1845	AB9:028; LVA-LP
Butts, Mark, def.	Alexandria	Suit	1802	CRD:193
Butts, Mark, merchant	Alexandria	Head	1810	1810(3):05A
Butts, Mark, [?] merchant	Alexandria	Housekeeper	1808	1808(3):19A

NAME OR SUBJECT	LOCATION	TYPE	YEAR	REFERENCE(S)
Butts, Napoleon Augustus, c/o Augustus	Arlington	Apprentice	1844	OCR1842:079
Butts, William D., grantee	Arlington	Indenture D.	1832	ID:384
Butts, William P., grantor	Arlington	Indenture D.	1832	ID:384
Butts, William P., in jail bounds	Arlington	Insolvent	1832	ID:383
Byers, James, at Steamboat Hotel	Arlington	Ordinary	1842	OBL6(np)
Byers, Jos. & wife, carpenter	Alexandria	Housekeeper	1799	1799(2):15A
Byrne, John	Arlington	Account	1823	AB5:216; LVA-LP
Byrne, John	Arlington	Admin.	1823	OCR1822:049a
Byrne, Patk.	Alexandria	Tax Charge	1798	Tax PP 1798:02
Byrne, Patric	Alexandria	Tax Charge	1800	Tax PP 1800:03
Byrne, Patrick	Alexandria	Tax Charge	1788	Tax PP 1788:02
Byrne, Patrick	Alexandria	Tax Charge	1796	Tax PP 1796:02
Byrne, Patrick	Alexandria	Mer. License	1798	Tax PP 1798:20-1
Byrne, Patrick	Alexandria	Tax Charge	1799	Tax PP 1799:03
Byrne, Patrick	Arlington	Ordinary	1804	OBL1(np)
Byrne, Patrick, shopkeeper	Alexandria	Housekeeper	1808	1808(2):12A
Byrne, Patrick, w(3), shopkeeper	Alexandria	Head	1796	1796(3):6

NAME OR SUBJECT	LOCATION	TYPE	YEAR	REFERENCE(S)
C				
Caddus, Mary, washwoman	Alexandria	Housekeeper	1808	1808(1):10A
Caden, James, b. Monagham, Ire.	Arlington	Alien Entry	1822	RA:14/06/22
Cades, Mary	Alexandria	Head	1810	1810(3):02A
Cadogan, Philip, waiter	Alexandria	Head	1810	1810(1):06A
Caffery, Thomas	Alexandria	Tax Charge	1796	Tax LP 1796:04
Cain & Slaid	Alexandria	Mer. License	1799	Tax PP 1799:52-02r
Cain, John	Alexandria	Tax Charge	1788	Tax PP 1788:03
Cain, John	Alexandria	Tax Charge	1788	Tax PP 1788:02
Cain, John	Alexandria	Tax Charge	1789	Tax PP 1789:04
Cain, John	Alexandria	Tax Charge	1789	Tax PP 1789:03
Caine & Slade	Alexandria	Tax Charge	1798	Tax PP 1798:03
Cairn, Barbara Anna Horwell, c/o Jacob	Arlington	Apprentice	1844	OCR1842:073
Cairn, Catharine	Arlington	Apprentice	1844	OCR1842:083
Caldwell, Elias B., Attorney	Arlington	Proof	1804	ACO:024
Caldwell, Maria H., of Washington DC	Alexandria	Will	1887	WBC1:048; LP
Caleb Shreve & Co.	Alexandria	Tax Charge	1799	Tax PP 1799:37
Caleb Shreve & Co., plt.	Alexandria	Suit	1801	CRB:255
Calhoun, Jonathan C.	Arlington	Will	1900	WB10:411; File #792A
Callender, Barthhw.	Alexandria	Boarder	1808	1808(3):18A
Callender, Margaret	Arlington	Will	1868	WB9:035
Callow, Thomas	Alexandria	Tax Charge	1789	Tax PP 1789:03
Callwell, Conn	Alexandria	Tax Charge	1798	Tax PP 1798:02
Calvin, John	Alexandria	Tax Charge	1798	Tax PP 1798:06
Calvo, John, b. Lyons	Arlington	Alien Entry	1820	RA:10/06/20
Cambell, J., Prince St.	Alexandria	Occupant	1787	Tax L 1787:06
Cameck, Jas., King St.	Alexandria	Occupant	1795	Tax L 1795:13
Cammock, James	Alexandria	Tax Charge	1796	Tax LP 1796:05
Camock, Jas.	Alexandria	Tax Charge	1795	Tax PP 1795:04
Campbell, Chas., laborer	Alexandria	Housekeeper	1808	1808(2):17A
Campbell, Chas., labourer	Alexandria	Head	1810	1810(2):06A
Campbell, Daniel, taylor	Alexandria	Head	1810	1810(2):03A
Campbell, Daniel, taylor & retailer	Alexandria	Housekeeper	1808	1808(2):12A
Campbell, Danl., clerk	Alexandria	Boarder	1799	1799(2):07A
Campbell, Geo.	Alexandria	License Due	1800	Tax PP 1800:54(24)
Campbell, Geo., merchant	Alexandria	Boarder	1799	1799(2):02A
Campbell, George	Alexandria	Resident	1800	1800(4):08B
Campbell, George	Arlington	Plaintiff	1802	PA:064
Campbell, George, b. Scotland	Arlington	Alien Entry	1801	RA:07/07/01
Campbell, George, clerk	Alexandria	Boarder	1800	1800(4):08A
Campbell, Jacob, Fairfax St.	Alexandria	Occupant	1795	Tax L 1795:11
Campbell, James	Alexandria	Tithable +21	1787	Tax PP 1787:13
Campbell, James	Alexandria	Tax Charge	1788	Tax PP 1788:03
Campbell, James	Alexandria	Tax Charge	1790	Tax PP 1790:02
Campbell, James	Alexandria	Tax Charge	1796	Tax LP 1796:05
Campbell, James	Alexandria	Tax Charge	1796	Tax PP 1796:03
Campbell, James	Alexandria	Tax Charge	1798	Tax PP 1798:03
Campbell, James	Alexandria	Tax Charge	1799	Tax PP 1799:07
Campbell, James	Alexandria	Tax Charge	1800	Tax PP 1800:04
Campbell, James	Arlington	Inventory	1821	AB4:237a; LVA-LP
Campbell, James	Arlington	Will	1821	WB3:001; File #194A
Campbell, James	Arlington	Inventory	1831	LVA-LP
Campbell, James	Arlington	Admin.	1831	WB4:038
Campbell, James	Arlington	Account	1834	AB7:112; LVA-LP
Campbell, James & wife, mariner	Alexandria	Head	1795	1795(4a):05
Campbell, James, c/o Jane	Arlington	Apprentice	1805	OCR1801:261
Campbell, James, Cryer	Arlington	Appointment	1801	ACO:001, 005
Campbell, James, Fairfax St.	Alexandria	Occupant	1790	Tax L 1790:10
Campbell, James, grantee	Arlington	Indenture D.	1804	ID3:031
Campbell, James, grantee	Arlington	Indenture D.	1805	ID3:106
Campbell, James, grantee	Arlington	Indenture D.	1805	ID3:172

NAME OR SUBJECT	LOCATION	TYPE	YEAR	REFERENCE(S)
Campbell, James, grantee	Arlington	Indenture D.	1805	ID3:116
Campbell, James, grantee	Arlington	Indenture D.	1806	ID3:269
Campbell, James, jailor	Alexandria	Housekeeper	1808	1808(2):12A
Campbell, James W.	Arlington	Apprentice	1826	OCR1822:107a
Campbell, Jas.	Alexandria	Reference	1808	1808(4):29B
Campbell, Jas., jailor	Alexandria	Head	1810	1810(2):08A
Campbell, John	Alexandria	Tax Charge	1787	Tax PP 1787:03
Campbell, John	Alexandria	Tax Charge	1788	Tax PP 1788:04
Campbell, John	Alexandria	Tax Charge	1789	Tax PP 1789:03
Campbell, John	Alexandria	Tax Charge	1790	Tax PP 1790:03
Campbell, London	Arlington	Account	1838	AB8:182; LVA-LP
Campbell, Louden	Arlington	Account	1840	AB8:081; LVA-LP
Campbell, Louden	Arlington	Distribution	1840	AB8:083
Campbell, Louden, house joiner	Alexandria	Head	1810	1810(3):04A
Campbell, Loudon	Arlington	Account	1839	AB8:083; LVA-LP
Campbell, Loudon, carpenter	Alexandria	Housekeeper	1808	1808(3):21A
Campbell, Loudoun	Alexandria	Tax Charge	1800	Tax PP 1800:04
Campbell, Loudoun	Arlington	Appraisal	1837	LVA-LP
Campbell, Loudoun	Arlington	Will	1837	WB4:132; File #347A
Campbell, Nicholas	Alexandria	Head	1810	1810(4):08A
Campbell, Sally (C), washwoman	Alexandria	Housekeeper	1808	1808(1):06A
Campbell, William	Arlington	Appraisal	1858	WB7:310; LVA-LP
Campbell, William W., on Union St.	Arlington	Ordinary	1841	OBL6(np)
Campbell, Wm., carpenter	Alexandria	Housekeeper	1808	1808(1):09A
Campbell, Wm., carptenter	Alexandria	Head	1810	1810(1):06A
Campell, Daniel	Alexandria	Tax Charge	1799	Tax PP 1799:06
Cane, John	Arlington	Crime	1796	OT:12/07/1796
Cann, Christopher	Alexandria	Tax Charge	1789	Tax PP 1789:03
Cannavan, William	Alexandria	Tax Charge	1790	Tax PP 1790:03
Canniford, Henry	Alexandria	Tax Charge	1799	Tax PP 1799:06
Canniford, Henry & wife, carptner	Alexandria	Housekeeper	1799	1799(2):16A
Canniford, Hy.	Alexandria	Tax Charge	1798	Tax PP 1798:02
Cannon, Jno.	Alexandria	Tax Charge	1799	Tax PP 1799:07
Cannon, Margaret W.	Arlington	Guard.	1817	WB2:208
Cannon, Mary	Arlington	Guard.	1806	WBB:321
Cannon, Susan, washwoman	Alexandria	Housekeeper	1808	1808(1):03A
Cannon, Susanna, teacher	Alexandria	Head	1810	1810(1):07A
Cannon, Ward	Alexandria	Boarder	1808	1808(1):04A
Card, James	Alexandria	Tax Charge	1796	Tax LP 1796:05
Card, James	Alexandria	Tax Charge	1800	Tax PP 1800:04
Card, Jas.	Alexandria	Tax Charge	1798	Tax PP 1798:02
Card, [blank], boarding house	Alexandria	Housekeeper	1799	1799(2):01A
Carday, Ann	Alexandria	Serv./Appr.	1800	1800(4):05B
Care, John, master	Arlington	Respondent	1804	ACO:025
Carey & Williams, Royal St.	Alexandria	Owner	1795	Tax L 1795:31
Carey, Caleb	Alexandria	Boarder	1808	1808(1):02A
Carey, Catharine & child	Alexandria	Boarder	1799	1799(2):04A
Carey, John, Washington St.	Alexandria	Occupant	1787	Tax L 1787:04
Carey, Jos.	Alexandria	Tax Charge	1795	Tax PP 1795:05
Carey, Jos. & wife, merchant	Alexandria	Housekeeper	1799	1799(2):15A
Carey, Joseph	Alexandria	Tithable +16	1788	Tax PP 1788:17
Carey, Joseph	Alexandria	Tax Charge	1796	Tax PP 1796:04
Cargo of Captured Ship Sold	Alexandria	List	1804	CRG:070
Carlin, Andrew W.F.	Arlington	Will	1885	WB10:070; File #720A
Carlin, Ann E.A.	Arlington	Will	1892	WB10:227; File #730A
Carlin, G.W., schoolmaster	Alexandria	Head	1810	1810(4):03A
Carlin, George W.	Arlington	Inventory	1843	AB8:379; LVA-LP
Carlin, George W.	Arlington	Will P.	1843	OCR1842:043
Carlin, George W.	Arlington	Bond	1843	WB4:364
Carlin, George W.	Arlington	Will	1843	WB4:363; File #406A
Carlin, George W.	Arlington	Citation	1844	OCR1842:084

NAME OR SUBJECT	LOCATION	TYPE	YEAR	REFERENCE(S)
Carlin, George W.	Arlington	Account	1845	AB9:029; LVA-LP
Carlin, Hugh, carpenter	Alexandria	Housekeeper	1808	1808(2):16A
Carlin, Hugh, house joiner	Alexandria	Head	1810	1810(2):04A
Carlin, James F.	Alexandria	Will	1882	WBC1:039; LP
Carlin, James, of Alexandria	Rappahannock	Will	1882	CF1903-004
Carlin, Nancy	Arlington	Apprentice	1804	OCR1801:169
Carlin, Wesley	Arlington	Will	1875	WB9:380; File #693A
Carlin, Wesley	Arlington	Inventory	1877	WB9:465
Carlin, William	Arlington	Inventory	1820	AB4:167; LVA-LP
Carlin, William	Arlington	Will	1820	WB2:378; File #179A
Carlin, William	Arlington	Account	1821	AB5:013; LVA-LP
Carlin, William	Arlington	Account	1849	WB5:152; LVA-LP
Carlin, Wm., Fairfax St.	Alexandria	Owner	1795	Tax L 1795:05
Carling, Geo. W., schoolmaster	Alexandria	Head	1810	1810(3):02A
Carlisle, [blank]	Alexandria	Boarder	1808	1808(2):12A
Carlyle, David	Alexandria	Tithable +16	1789	Tax PP 1789:17
Carlyle, Gardiner	Alexandria	Tax Charge	1799	Tax PP 1799:06
Carman, Richd.	Alexandria	Tax Charge	1795	Tax PP 1795:04
Carne & Slade	Alexandria	Mer. License	1800	Tax PP 1800:54(11)r
Carne & Slade, Fairfax St.	Alexandria	Occupant	1795	Tax L 1795:09
Carne, Jane	Arlington	Guard. Acct.	1818	LVA-LP
Carne, Jane, c/o William	Arlington	Guard.	1812	WB1:149
Carne, Richard	Arlington	Guard. Acct.	1818	LVA-LP
Carne, Richard L.	Arlington	Guard. Acct.	1814	AB2:028, 131; LVA-LP
Carne, Richard L.	Arlington	Account	1815	AB2:131; LVA-LP
Carne, Richard Libbey	Arlington	Guard. Acct.	1816	AB2:279
Carne, Richard Libby, c/o William	Arlington	Guard.	1812	WB1:149
Carne, Susan	Arlington	Guard. Acct.	1814	AB2:028, 131; LVA-LP
Carne, Susan, c/o William	Arlington	Guard.	1812	WB1:149
Carne, Susan L.	Arlington	Guard. Acct.	1818	LVA-LP
Carne, William	Arlington	Bond	1811	WB1:144
Carne, William	Arlington	Inventory	1812	AB1:161; LVA-LP
Carne, William	Arlington	Will	1812	WB1:142; File #098A
Carne, William	Arlington	Account	1813	AB1:285; LVA-LP
Carne, William	Arlington	Guard. Acct.	1813	AB1:286
Carne, William	Arlington	Guard. Acct.	1814	AB2:028, 131; LVA-LP
Carne, William	Arlington	Guard. Acct.	1816	AB2:279; LVA-LP
Carne, William, c/o William	Arlington	Guard.	1812	WB1:149
Carne, William H., grantor	Arlington	Indenture D.	1832	ID:391a
Carne, William H., in confinement	Arlington	Insolvent	1832	ID:390
Carne, William, w(3)1, merchant	Alexandria	Head	1796	1796(3):5
Carne [Carna], Wm.	Alexandria	Tax Charge	1795	Tax PP 1795:04
Carne, Wm.	Alexandria	Tax Charge	1796	Tax PP 1796:03
Carne, Wm. & wife, ironmonger	Alexandria	Housekeeper	1799	1799(2):08A
Carne, Wm., merchant	Alexandria	Housekeeper	1808	1808(1):04A
Carne, Wm., merchant	Alexandria	Head	1810	1810(1):11A
Carolin, Hugh & Jas.	Alexandria	Tax Charge	1798	Tax PP 1798:03
Carolin, James	Arlington	Sale	1808	WBC:078
Carolin, James	Arlington	Inventory	1808	WBC:077; LP
Carolin, James	Arlington	Admin.	1808	WBC:073
Carolin, James	Arlington	Account	1810	WBC:428; LVA-LP
Carolin, James	Arlington	Account	1811	AB1:117; LVA-LP
Carolin, Jas. & H.	Alexandria	Tax Charge	1800	Tax PP 1800:04
Carolin, Jas. & Hugh	Alexandria	Tax Charge	1799	Tax PP 1799:06
Carpenter, Charles	Alexandria	Tax Charge	1796	Tax LP 1796:04
Carpenter, Charles (C)	Alexandria	Tax Charge	1788	Tax PP 1788:03
Carpenter, Chas. (C)	Alexandria	Tax Charge	1795	Tax PP 1795:04
Carpenter, Jack (C)	Alexandria	Boarder	1808	1808(4):24B
Carpenter, Randall (C)	Alexandria	Boarder	1808	1808(4):24B
Carr & Lowe, Prince St.	Alexandria	Occupant	1787	Tax L 1787:06
Carr, Dabney	Arlington	Apprentice	1815	OCR1811:313

NAME OR SUBJECT	LOCATION	TYPE	YEAR	REFERENCE(S)
Carr, David	Arlington	Ordinary	1821	OBL3(np)
Carr, David, b. Donegaugh, Ire.	Arlington	Alien Entry	1819	RA:27/12/19
Carr, David, in Alexandria Co.	Arlington	Ordinary	1822	OBL3(np)
Carr, John	Alexandria	Tithable +21	1787	Tax PP 1787:09
Carr, John	Arlington	Apprentice	1828	OCR1822:152
Carr, Julia, school mistress	Alexandria	Head	1810	1810(4):03A
Carrel, Wm.	Alexandria	Tax Charge	1795	Tax PP 1795:04
Carrol, Charles	Alexandria	Tax Charge	1790	Tax PP 1790:02
Carroll, Charles	Alexandria	Tax Charge	1788	Tax PP 1788:03
Carroll, Charles	Alexandria	Tax Charge	1789	Tax PP 1789:03
Carroll, Daniel, of *Dudington*	Arlington	Defendant	1824	ACO:239
Carroll, Elizabeth, washwoman	Alexandria	Housekeeper	1808	1808(2):12A
Carroll, James	Arlington	Apprentice	1822	OCR1822:029a
Carroll, James, c/o Elizabeth	Arlington	Apprentice	1813	OCR1811:168
Carroll, Mary	Arlington	Guard.	1816	WB2:145
Carry, Joseph, murchant	Alexandria	Head	1800	1800(4):06A
Carson, Andrew	Arlington	Ordinary	1806	OBL2(np)
Carson, Andrew	Arlington	Ordinary	1807	OBL2(np)
Carson, Andrew, mariner	Alexandria	Head	1810	1810(1):12A
Carson, Andw., shopkeeper & tavern lic.	Alexandria	Housekeeper	1808	1808(1):03A
Carson, Geo.	Alexandria	Boarder	1808	1808(3):19A
Carson, James, grantee	Arlington	Indenture D.	1805	ID3:101
Carson, James, merchant	Alexandria	Head	1810	1810(3):03A
Carson, James plt.	Alexandria	Suit	1812	CRK:002
Carson, James, retailer	Alexandria	Housekeeper	1808	1808(3):19A
Carson, Jno.	Alexandria	Boarder	1808	1808(2):13A
Carson, Jno. M.	Alexandria	Tithable +21	1787	Tax PP 1787:16
Carson, Jno. M.	Alexandria	Tithable +16	1788	Tax PP 1788:17
Carson, John B.	Arlington	Appraisal	1861	WB8:073; LVA-LP
Carson, John, Fairfax St.	Alexandria	Occupant	1790	Tax L 1790:05
Carson, John M.	Alexandria	Tax Charge	1789	Tax PP 1789:03
Carson, John Millar	Alexandria	Tax Charge	1790	Tax PP 1790:02
Carson, John, shoemaker	Alexandria	Head	1810	1810(1):05A
Carson, Joseph	Arlington	Bond	1854	BB(np) (2)
Carson, Joseph	Arlington	Account	1856	WB7:059; LVA-LP
Carson, Joseph, at his house	Arlington	Ordinary	1848	OBL6(np)
Carson, Joseph, at his house	Arlington	Ordinary	1849	OBL6(np)
Carson, Joseph C., on Cameron St.	Arlington	Ordinary	1846	OBL6(np)
Carson, Nehemiah, merchant	Alexandria	Housekeeper	1808	1808(2):13A
Carson, Nehemiah, merchant	Alexandria	Head	1810	1810(2):04A
Carson, Richard	Arlington	Admin.	1805	WBB:187
Carson, Richard, Jr., plt.	Alexandria	Suit	1806	CRE:063
Carson, Samuel	Arlington	Account	1831	LVA-LP
Carson, Samuel	Arlington	Bond	1831	WB4:006
Carson, Samuel	Arlington	Will	1831	WB4:004; File #298A
Carson, Samuel	Arlington	Citation	1845	OCR1842:098
Carter & Wife v. Dulany & DeButts	Arlington	Suit	1839	LVA-LP (Accounts)
Carter, Henry (C)	Arlington	Apprentice	1828	OCR1822:155
Carter, James	Arlington	Apprentice	1803	OCR1801:113
Carter, James	Arlington	Admin.	1813	WB2:096
Carter, James	Arlington	Apprentice	1828	OCR1822:161a
Carter, James Landon	Arlington	Will	1867	WB8:548; File #654A
Carter, James, shopkeeper & fidler	Alexandria	Housekeeper	1808	1808(3):20A
Carter, James, waiter	Alexandria	Head	1810	1810(2):04A
Carter, Jesse	Alexandria	Tax Charge	1799	Tax PP 1799:06
Carter, John, c/o James	Arlington	Apprentice	1815	OCR1811:297
Carter, Mary Burwell	Arlington	Inventory	1846	AB9:231; LVA-LP
Carter, Mary Burwell	Arlington	Will P.	1846	OCR1842:175
Carter, Mary Burwell	Arlington	Will	1846	WB4:421; File #317A
Carter, Mary W.	Arlington	Guard. Acct.	1837	AB7:251
Carter, Richardetta, late DeButts	Arlington	Guard. Acct.	1835	AB7:149

NAME OR SUBJECT	LOCATION	TYPE	YEAR	REFERENCE(S)
Carter, Robert	Arlington	Apprentice	1803	OCR1801:114
Carter, Robert	Arlington	Apprentice	1828	OCR1822:161a
Carter, Sally	Arlington	Will	1809	WBC:324, 477, 504
Carter, Sally	Arlington	Statement	1811	WB1:074, 092, 107
Carter, Sally	Arlington	Statement	1812	WB1:047, 054, 070
Carter, Sally	Arlington	Exhibits	1813	LVA-LP
Carter, Sally	Arlington	Bond	1813	WB1:229
Carter, Sally, gentlewoman	Alexandria	Housekeeper	1808	1808(3):22A
Carter, Sally, Heirs of, plt.	Alexandria	Suit	1813	CRH:507
Carter, Sarah	Alexandria	Head	1810	1810(3):09A
Carter, Thomas C.	Alexandria	Will	1890	WB1:580; LP
Carterite, Seth & wife Mary	Alexandria	Serv./Appt.	1800	1800(4):15B
Carterite, Seth, marriner	Alexandria	Head	1800	1800(4):15A
Carter's Heirs, plt.	Alexandria	Suit	1811	CRI:106
Carthington, John & wife Prisiler	Alexandria	Resident	1800	1800(4):14B
Carthington, John, labourrer	Alexandria	Head	1800	1800(4):14A
Cartledge, Charles, Prince St.	Alexandria	Owner	1795	Tax L 1795:05
Cartledge, Chs.	Alexandria	Tax Charge	1796	Tax LP 1796:04
Cartlet & Meeks	Alexandria	Mer. License	1799	Tax PP 1799:52-02r
Cartwright, Alice, c/o Seth	Arlington	Guard.	1812	WB1:172
Cartwright, Capt. & wife, mariner	Alexandria	Head	1795	1795(4):09
Cartwright, Capt., St. Asaph St.	Alexandria	Occupant	1795	Tax L 1795:09
Cartwright, Elizabeth, c/o Seth	Arlington	Guard.	1812	WB1:172
Cartwright, James, c/o Seth	Arlington	Guard.	1812	WB1:172
Cartwright, Jonathan	Arlington	Will	1848	WB5:105; File #446A
Cartwright, Jonathan, c/o Seth	Arlington	Guard.	1812	WB1:172
Cartwright, Rachael, Bladensburg MD	Arlington	Will	1869	WB9:185; File #672A
Cartwright, Septimus, c/o Seth	Arlington	Guard.	1812	WB1:172
Cartwright, Septimus, c/o Seth	Arlington	Guard.	1824	OCR1822:069
Cartwright, Septimus, c/o Seth	Arlington	Guard.	1824	WB3:180
Cartwright, Seth	Alexandria	Tax Charge	1796	Tax LP 1796:04
Cartwright, Seth	Alexandria	Tax Charge	1796	Tax PP 1796:03
Cartwright, Seth	Alexandria	Tax Charge	1798	Tax PP 1798:03
Cartwright, Seth	Alexandria	Tax Charge	1799	Tax PP 1799:07
Cartwright, Seth	Alexandria	Tax Charge	1800	Tax PP 1800:05
Cartwright, Seth	Arlington	Ordinary	1805	OBL1(np)
Cartwright, Seth	Arlington	Will	1811	WB1:031; File #091A
Cartwright, Seth	Arlington	Bond	1811	WB1:034
Cartwright, Seth	Arlington	Account	1812	AB1:203; LVA-LP
Cartwright, Seth	Arlington	Account	1813	AB1:324; LVA-LP
Cartwright, Seth	Arlington	Guard. Acct.	1813	AB1:325
Cartwright, Seth	Arlington	Division	1815	AB2:136
Cartwright, Seth	Arlington	Guard. Acct.	1818	AB3:167; LVA-LP
Cartwright, Seth	Arlington	Guard. Acct.	1819	AB3:337; LVA-LP
Cartwright, Seth	Arlington	Guard. Acct.	1820	AB4:182; LVA-LP
Cartwright, Seth	Arlington	Guard. Acct.	1821	AB4:271
Cartwright, Seth	Arlington	Guard. Acct.	1822	AB5:091; LVA-LP
Cartwright, Seth	Arlington	Guard. Acct.	1823	AB5:179; LVA-LP
Cartwright, Seth	Arlington	Guard. Acct.	1824	AB5:253; LVA-LP
Cartwright, Seth	Arlington	Guard. Acct.	1825	AB6:096; LVA-LP
Cartwright, Seth	Arlington	Guard. Acct.	1826	AB6:217; LVA-LP
Cartwright, Seth	Arlington	Guard. Acct.	1827	AB6:438
Cartwright, Seth	Arlington	Guard. Acct.	1829	AB6:479; LVA-LP
Cartwright, Seth & wife, mariner	Alexandria	Head	1795	1795(4a):11
Cartwright, Seth & wife, sea captain	Alexandria	Housekeeper	1799	1799(2):12A
Cartwright, Seth, c/o Seth	Arlington	Guard.	1812	WB1:172
Cartwright, Seth, Capt.	Arlington	Inventory	1811	AB1:084; LVA-LP
Cartwright, Seth, Capt.	Arlington	Account	1812	AB1:194; LVA-LP
Cartwright, Seth, Capt.	Arlington	Account	1821	AB4:271
Cartwright, Seth, retailer	Alexandria	Housekeeper	1808	1808(4):27A
Cartwright, Seth, seaman	Alexandria	Head	1810	1810(4):08A

NAME OR SUBJECT	LOCATION	TYPE	YEAR	REFERENCE(S)
Cartwright, Thomas, c/o Seth	Arlington	Guard.	1812	WB1:172
Cartwright, Thomas, c/o Seth	Arlington	Receipt	1830	AB7:118
Cartwright, Thomas, n/o Jas. Lawracon	Arlington	Apprentice	1811	OCR1811:040
Cartwright, Thomas, n/o Jas. Lawrason	Arlington	Apprentice	1811	OCR1811:060
Carveille, Peter	Alexandria	Tax Charge	1788	Tax PP 1788:03
Carveille, Peter	Alexandria	Tax Charge	1789	Tax PP 1789:03
Carver, Jno. & wife, shoemaker	Alexandria	Housekeeper	1799	1799(2):05A
Carver, John	Alexandria	Tax Charge	1798	Tax PP 1798:03
Carver, William	Alexandria	Tax Charge	1799	Tax PP 1799:06
Carver, William, silversmith	Alexandria	Head	1810	1810(4):07A
Carver, Wm. & wife Mary Ann	Alexandria	Resident	1800	1800(4):10B
Carver, Wm., smith	Alexandria	Head	1800	1800(4):10A
Carville, P., Thorn alley	Alexandria	Occupant	1787	Tax L 1787:24
Carville, Peter	Alexandria	Owner	1787	Tax L 1787:08
Carville, Peter	Alexandria	Tax Charge	1787	Tax PP 1787:03
Carville, Peter	Alexandria	Tax Charge	1790	Tax PP 1790:02
Carville, Peter, Fairfax St.	Alexandria	Occupant	1790	Tax L 1790:07
Carville, Peter, Union St.	Alexandria	Occupant	1787	Tax L 1787:08
Cary, Joseph	Alexandria	Tithable +21	1787	Tax PP 1787:16
Cary, Joseph	Alexandria	Tithable +16	1789	Tax PP 1789:19
Cary, Joseph	Alexandria	Mer. License	1798	Tax PP 1798:20-2
Cary, Joseph	Alexandria	Tax Charge	1798	Tax PP 1798:02
Cary, Joseph	Alexandria	Tax Charge	1799	Tax PP 1799:07
Cary, Joseph	Alexandria	Tax Charge	1800	Tax PP 1800:05
Cary, Joseph	Arlington	Will	1803	WBA:167
Cary, Joseph & wife Mary	Alexandria	Resident	1800	1800(4):06B
Cary, Joseph, assignee, plt.	Alexandria	Suit	1801	CRC:199
Cary, Joseph, def.	Alexandria	Suit	1802	CRC:047
Cary, Joseph, plt.	Alexandria	Suit	1802	CRB:273
Cary, William	Alexandria	Tax Charge	1790	Tax PP 1790:02
Casanove, Anthony & Co.	Alexandria	Mer. License	1798	Tax PP 1798:20-2
Casenove, A.C.	Alexandria	Mer. License	1799	Tax PP 1799:52-02r
Casey, Daniel	Alexandria	Tithable +16	1788	Tax PP 1788:10
Casey, Daniel	Alexandria	Tithable +16	1789	Tax PP 1789:11
Casey, Daniel	Alexandria	Tithable +16	1790	Tax PP 1790:08
Casey, John	Arlington	Apprentice	1803	OCR1801:102
Casey, Milly	Alexandria	Boarder	1799	1799(2):09A
Casey, Robt., clerk	Alexandria	Boarder	1799	1799(2):04A
Casey, Thos., clerk	Alexandria	Boarder	1799	1799(2):03A
Cash, Jos. & wife, grocer	Alexandria	Housekeeper	1799	1799(2):11A
Cash, Joseph, Estate	Alexandria	Tax Charge	1799	Tax PP 1799:07
Cash, Susannah	Arlington	Guard.	1817	WB2:215
Cash, William	Alexandria	Tax Charge	1796	Tax LP 1796:05
Cash, William	Alexandria	Mer. License	1799	Tax PP 1799:52-02r
Cash, William	Alexandria	Tax Charge	1799	Tax PP 1799:07
Cash, William	Alexandria	Tax Charge	1800	Tax PP 1800:04
Cash, William, Jr.	Alexandria	Mer. License	1798	Tax PP 1798:20-2
Cash, Wm.	Alexandria	Tax Charge	1796	Tax PP 1796:04
Casine, Barton, shoemaker	Alexandria	Housekeeper	1808	1808(2):15A
Caske, Peter	Alexandria	Boarder	1808	1808(2):11A
Casody, Solomon	Alexandria	Tax Charge	1800	Tax PP 1800:04
Cassady, Solomon	Arlington	Inventory	1816	AB2:301; LVA-LP
Cassady, Solomon	Arlington	Account	1824	AB5:324; LVA-LP
Cassanave, Peter, King St.	Alexandria	Owner	1790	Tax L 1790:03
Cassidy, Solomon	Arlington	Sale	1816	AB2:304
Cassidy, Solomon	Arlington	Will	1816	WB2:121; File #131A
Cassidy, Solomon	Arlington	Account	1817	AB3:043; LVA-LP
Cassidy, Solomon, grantor	Arlington	Indenture D.	1813	ID2:221
Cassidy, Solomon, in jail	Arlington	Insolvent	1813	ID2:216
Cassin, James, native of Dublin	Arlington	Citizenship	1808	ACO:079
Castburn, Jos.	Alexandria	Tax Charge	1795	Tax PP 1795:06

NAME OR SUBJECT	LOCATION	TYPE	YEAR	REFERENCE(S)
Castor Oil, on Ship *William & John*	Arlington	Suit	1811	ACO:116, 118
Casy, Daniel	Alexandria	Tithable +21	1787	Tax PP 1787:13
Catlet, Peter	Alexandria	Tax Charge	1800	Tax PP 1800:04
Catlet, Peter & wife Susanah	Alexandria	Resident	1800	1800(4):16B
Catlet, Peter, murchant	Alexandria	Head	1800	1800(4):16A
Catlett & Meeks	Alexandria	Mer. License	1800	Tax PP 1800:54(11)r
Catlett, Charles J. & wife Ann, plt.	Alexandria	Suit	1813	CRH:512
Catlett, Charles J. & wife Anne, complt.	Alexandria	Suit	1815	CRK:127
Catlett, Charles J., plt.	Alexandria	Suit	1822	CRL:232
Catlett, Chas. J., merchant	Alexandria	Housekeeper	1808	1808(2):11A
Catlett, Chas. J., merchant	Alexandria	Head	1810	1810(3):06A
Catlett, Erskine, of NY	Arlington	Will	1856	WB7:097; File #529A
Catlett, John	Arlington	Admin.	1809	WBC:257
Catlett, John	Arlington	Admin.	1811	WB1:083
Cato, Thos., Water St.	Alexandria	Occupant	1795	Tax L 1795:01
Caton, James	Alexandria	Tithable +16	1788	Tax PP 1788:11
Caton, James	Alexandria	Tithable +16	1789	Tax PP 1789:11
Caton, James	Alexandria	Tithable +16	1790	Tax PP 1790:09
Caton, James	Alexandria	Tax Charge	1796	Tax LP 1796:16
Caton, James, bricklayer	Alexandria	Head	1810	1810(4):05A
Caton, John	Alexandria	Tithable +16	1789	Tax PP 1789:03
Caton, Mary, Royal St.	Alexandria	Occupant	1790	Tax L 1790:10
Caton, Mary, Royal St.	Alexandria	Occupant	1795	Tax L 1795:25
Caton, Mary, seamstress	Alexandria	Head	1810	1810(2):05A
Caton, Mary, washwoman	Alexandria	Housekeeper	1808	1808(2):15A
Caton, Michael	Alexandria	Tithable +21	1787	Tax PP 1787:06
Caton, Michael	Alexandria	Tithable +16	1789	Tax PP 1789:08
Caton, William	Arlington	Ordinary	1809	OBL2(np)
Caton, William	Arlington	Apprentice	1829	OCR1822:172a
Cator, Thomas	Alexandria	Tax Charge	1796	Tax LP 1796:04
Catterton, Diln	Alexandria	Boarder	1808	1808(1):09A
Catterton, Dilos	Alexandria	Serv./Appr.	1800	1800(4):10B
Catterton, Jno.	Alexandria	Tax Charge	1798	Tax PP 1798:03
Catterton, John	Alexandria	Tax Charge	1799	Tax PP 1799:06
Catterton, John	Alexandria	Tax Charge	1800	Tax PP 1800:04
Catterton, Michel	Alexandria	Serv./Appr.	1800	1800(4):10B
Catteton, John & wife, labourer	Alexandria	Housekeeper	1799	1799(2):07A
Cattlett, John, plt.	Alexandria	Suit	1809	CRG:234
Catts, Samuel	Arlington	Ordinary	1820	OBL3(np)
Caulfield, Barnard, b. Newry, Ire.	Arlington	Alien Entry	1823	RA:12/11/23
Caulson, Joseph, stage driver	Alexandria	Head	1810	1810(4):02A
Cavan, James	Alexandria	Tithable +16	1789	Tax PP 1789:13
Cavan, James	Alexandria	Tax Charge	1796	Tax LP 1796:04
Cavan, James	Alexandria	Tax Charge	1796	Tax PP 1796:04
Cavan, James	Alexandria	Tax Charge	1798	Tax PP 1798:03
Cavan, William	Arlington	Apprentice	1805	OCR1801:322
Cavans, James	Alexandria	Tax Charge	1795	Tax PP 1795:05
Cave, Philip	Arlington	Juryman	1804	ACO:024, 027
Cavens, James	Alexandria	Tithable +16	1790	Tax PP 1790:04
Caverley, Joseph	Alexandria	Occupant	1795	Tax L 1795:17
Caverly, Joseph	Alexandria	Tax Charge	1787	Tax PP 1787:03
Caverly, Joseph	Alexandria	Tax Charge	1788	Tax PP 1788:03
Caverly, Joseph	Alexandria	Tax Charge	1789	Tax PP 1789:03
Caverly, Joseph	Alexandria	Tax Charge	1790	Tax PP 1790:03
Caverly, Joseph, Washington St.	Alexandria	Occupant	1787	Tax L 1787:04
Caverly, Joseph, Washington St.	Alexandria	Occupant	1790	Tax L 1790:03
Caverly, Joseph, Washington St.	Alexandria	Owner	1790	Tax L 1790:03
Caverly, Joseph, Wolf St.	Alexandria	Occupant	1790	Tax L 1790:03
Caverly, Peter	Alexandria	Tithable +16	1788	Tax PP 1788:07
Caverly, Peter	Alexandria	Tithable +16	1789	Tax PP 1789:03
Caverly, Peter	Alexandria	Tithable +16	1790	Tax PP 1790:03

NAME OR SUBJECT	LOCATION	TYPE	YEAR	REFERENCE(S)
Caverly, Peter, guardian	Alexandria	Suit	1801	CRC:115
Caverly, Peter, Union St.	Alexandria	Owner	1790	Tax L 1790:03
Caverly, Peter, Union St.	Alexandria	Occupant	1790	Tax L 1790:03
Caving, Joseph, schoolmaster	Alexandria	Head	1810	1810(3):06A
Cavins, James, 2, merchant	Alexandria	Head	1795	1796(3):7
Cavins, William	Alexandria	Tax Charge	1787	Tax PP 1787:03
Cawood, Daniel, grantor	Arlington	Indenture D.	1817	ID2:403
Cawood, Daniel, in jail	Arlington	Insolvent	1817	ID2:400
Cawood, Moses O.B., grantee	Arlington	Indenture D.	1832	ID:368
Cawood, Thos., St. Asaph St.	Alexandria	Occupant	1795	Tax L 1795:32
Caws, Richard (C)	Arlington	Apprentice	1801	OCR1801:003
Caywood, Grafton	Alexandria	Boarder	1808	1808(3):21A
Cazenove, A.C.	Alexandria	Tax Charge	1798	Tax PP 1798:03
Cazenove, A.C.	Alexandria	Mer. License	1800	Tax PP 1800:54(11)r
Cazenove, A.C.	Alexandria	Tax Charge	1800	Tax PP 1800:04
Cazenove, Anthony C.	Alexandria	Tax Charge	1799	Tax PP 1799:06
Cazenove, Anthony C. & wife, merchant	Alexandria	Housekeeper	1799	1799(2):08A
Cazenove, Anthony C., merchant	Alexandria	Housekeeper	1808	1808(2):14A
Cazenove, Anthony C., merchant	Alexandria	Head	1810	1810(2):04A
Cazenove, Anthony Charles	Arlington	Will	1852	WB6:157; File #488A
Cazenove, Anthony Charles	Arlington	Sale	1853	WB6:222; LVA-LP
Cazenove, Anthony Charles	Arlington	Account	1853	WB6:276; LVA-LP
Cazenove, Anthony Charles	Arlington	Inventory	1853	WB6:209; LVA-LP
Cazenove, Anthony Charles	Arlington	Account	1853	WB6:375; LVA-LP
Cazenove, Anthony Charles	Arlington	Account	1855	WB7:032; LVA-LP
Cazenove, Anthony Charles	Arlington	Account	1855	WB7:163, 319; LVA-LP
Cazenove, Anthony Charles	Arlington	Account	1859	WB7:391; LVA-LP
Cazenove, Anthony Charles	Alexandria	Will	1897	WB2:197; LP
Cazenove, Anthony Charles plt.	Alexandria	Suit	1812	CRK:002
Cazenove, Charles C.S.	Arlington	Guard. Acct.	1853	WB6:287, 391
Cazenove, Charles C.S.	Arlington	Guard. Acct.	1855	WB7:038
Cazenove, Charlotte L.	Arlington	Guard. Acct.	1855	WB7:037; LVA-LP
Cazenove, Charlotte L.	Arlington	Guard. Acct.	1855	WB7:191, 323
Cazenove, Charlotte L.	Arlington	Guard. Acct.	1859	WB7:401, 519
Cazenove, Charlotte L., c/o Louis A.	Arlington	Guard. Acct.	1861	WB8:097, 375; LVA-LP
Cazenove, Charlotte Louisa	Arlington	Guard. Acct.	1853	WB6:286, 390
Cazenove, Children	Arlington	Account	1868	WB9:033
Cazenove, Frances A.	Arlington	Guard. Acct.	1853	WB6:285, 389
Cazenove, Frances A.	Arlington	Guard. Acct.	1855	WB7:039, 192, 322
Cazenove, Frances A.	Arlington	Guard. Acct.	1859	WB7:402, 520
Cazenove, Frances A., c/o Louis A.	Arlington	Guard. Acct.	1861	WB8:100, 369
Cazenove, Louis A.	Arlington	Bond	1852	BB(np)
Cazenove, Louis A.	Arlington	Inventory	1852	WB6:120; LVA-LP
Cazenove, Louis A.	Arlington	Account	1853	WB6:408; LVA-LP
Cazenove, Louis A.	Arlington	Account	1853	WB6:289; LVA-LP
Cazenove, Louis A.	Arlington	Account	1856	WB7:094, 194, 324
Cazenove, Louis A.	Arlington	Guard. Acct.	1870	WB9:214
Cazenove, Louis A.	Arlington	Guard. Acct.	1871	WB9:328
Cazenove, Louis A., children of	Arlington	Guard. Acct.	1859	WB7:403, 518
Cazenove, Louis A., children of	Arlington	Guard. Acct.	1861	WB8:101, 367, 516
Cazenove, Louis A., infants of	Arlington	Guard. Acct.	1853	WB6:388; LVA-LP
Cazenove, Louis A., infants of	Arlington	Guard. Acct.	1853	WB6:284; LVA-LP
Cazenove, Louis A., infants of	Arlington	Guard. Acct.	1855	WB7:040, 189; LVA-LP
Cazenove, Louis A., infants of	Arlington	Guard. Acct.	1856	WB7:321; LVA-LP
Cazenove, Louis A., Jr.	Arlington	Guard. Acct.	1859	WB7:400, 517; LVA-LP
Cazenove, Louis A., Jr., c/o Louis A.	Arlington	Guard. Acct.	1861	WB8:099, 372, 518
Cazenove, Louis A. [Harriott]	Arlington	Dower	1853	WB6:189; LVA-LP
Cazenove, Octavius A.	Arlington	Will	1841	WB4:299; File #388A
Cazenove, William G.	Alexandria	Will	1877	WB1:215; LP
Ceely, Elias, of Nantucket, Mass.	Alexandria	Deposition	1818	CRK:472
Celley, Elizebeth	Alexandria	Resident	1800	1800(4):16B

NAME OR SUBJECT	LOCATION	TYPE	YEAR	REFERENCE(S)
Celley, Elizebeth, nurs [sic]	Alexandria	Boarder	1800	1800(4):16A
Celley, Nancey	Alexandria	Resident	1800	1800(4):14B
Celly, Nancey, tanner	Alexandria	Boarder	1800	1800(4):14A
Chace, Gorton	Alexandria	Tax Charge	1790	Tax PP 1790:02
Chace, Sukey, washerwoman	Alexandria	Head	1810	1810(4):03A
Chacon, Paul, Sp. Consul	Alexandria	Housekeeper	1808	1808(4):26A
Chacon, Paul, spanish consul	Alexandria	Head	1810	1810(4):01A
Chacon, Raymond, Sp. Consul	Alexandria	Housekeeper	1808	1808(4):26A
Chadwick, James	Alexandria	Tithable +16	1788	Tax PP 1788:10
Chaise, Gurtin	Alexandria	Tax Charge	1789	Tax PP 1789:03
Chalmbey, Jonathan	Alexandria	Head	1810	1810(4):05A
Chambard, J.B.	Alexandria	Boarder	1808	1808(1):08A
Chamberlain, Charles, c/o Lincoln	Arlington	Guard.	1834	WB4:097
Chamberlain, Charles, c/o Lincoln	Arlington	Guard.	1837	WB4:149
Chamberlain, Charles, c/o Lincoln	Arlington	Guard. Acct.	1846	AB9:157; LVA-LP
Chamberlain, George, c/o Lincoln	Arlington	Guard.	1837	WB4:147
Chamberlain, George, c/o Lincoln	Arlington	Guard. Acct.	1846	AB9:157; LVA-LP
Chamberlain, George W.	Arlington	Guard.	1834	WB4:098
Chamberlain, Jacob	Arlington	Bond	1831	WB4:021
Chamberlain, Jacob	Arlington	Will	1831	WB4:021; File #308A
Chamberlain, Jacob	Arlington	Account	1836	AB7:206; LVA-LP
Chamberlain, Joseph, c/o Lincoln	Arlington	Guard.	1834	WB4:097
Chamberlain, Joseph, c/o Lincoln	Arlington	Guard.	1837	WB4:146
Chamberlain, Joseph, c/o Lincoln	Arlington	Guard. Acct.	1846	AB9:156; LVA-LP
Chamberlain, Lincoln	Arlington	Inventory	1834	LVA-LP
Chamberlain, Lincoln	Arlington	Admin.	1834	WB4:097, 147
Chamberlain, Lincoln	Arlington	Account	1835	LVA-LP (Accounts 2nd)
Chamberlain, Lincoln	Arlington	Account	1839	AB7:315
Chamberlain, Lincoln	Arlington	Account	1848	WB5:050; LVA-LP
Chamberlain, Lincoln, children of	Arlington	Guard.	1842	OCR1842:009
Chamberlain, Lincoln, children of	Arlington	Guard.	1843	OCR1842:043, 059
Chamberlain, Lincoln, children of	Arlington	Guard. Acct.	1844	AB8:434; LVA-LP
Chamberlain, Lincoln, children of	Arlington	Births	1844	AB8:435; LVA-LP
Chamberlain, Lincoln, children of	Arlington	Guard.	1844	OCR1842:070
Chamberlain, Lincoln, heirs of	Arlington	Guard. Acct.	1846	AB9:155; LVA-LP
Chamberlain, Lincoln, heirs of	Arlington	Guard. Acct.	1848	WB5:048; LVA-LP
Chamberlain, Luther	Arlington	Inventory	1828	LVA-LP
Chamberlain, Luther	Arlington	Will	1828	WB3:320; File #274A
Chamberlain, Luther	Arlington	Account	1830	AB6:494; LVA-LP
Chamberlain, Luther	Arlington	Guard.	1837	WB4:148
Chamberlain, Luther, c/o Lincoln	Arlington	Guard.	1834	WB4:097
Chamberlain, Luther, c/o Lincoln	Arlington	Guard. Acct.	1846	AB9:156; LVA-LP
Chamberlain, Mary, c/o Lincoln	Arlington	Guard.	1834	WB4:098
Chamberlain, Mary, c/o Lincoln	Arlington	Guard.	1837	WB4:149
Chamberlain, Mary, c/o Lincoln	Arlington	Guard. Acct.	1846	AB9:156
Chamberlaine, George	Arlington	Apprentice	1844	OCR1842:070
Chamberlin, Hannah, Duke St.	Alexandria	Occupant	1790	Tax L 1790:01
Champ, Walker	Alexandria	Will	1876	WB1:188; LP
Chancey, Catharine, c/o John	Arlington	Guard.	1852	BB(np)
Chancey, Joseph, c/o John	Arlington	Guard.	1852	BB(np)
Chandler, William, taylor	Alexandria	Head	1810	1810(3):10A
Chapin & Ashton, Fairfax St.	Alexandria	Occupant	1787	Tax L 1787:09
Chapin, Charles, c/o Gurden	Arlington	Guard.	1812	WB1:161
Chapin, G.	Alexandria	Reference	1808	1808(4):25B
Chapin, Gurd.	Alexandria	Tax Charge	1795	Tax PP 1795:05
Chapin, Gurden	Alexandria	Tax Charge	1787	Tax PP 1787:03
Chapin, Gurden	Alexandria	Tax Charge	1788	Tax PP 1788:03
Chapin, Gurden	Alexandria	Tax Charge	1789	Tax PP 1789:03
Chapin, Gurden	Alexandria	Tax Charge	1790	Tax PP 1790:02
Chapin, Gurden	Alexandria	Tax Charge	1796	Tax PP 1796:03
Chapin, Gurden	Alexandria	Tax Charge	1798	Tax PP 1798:03

NAME OR SUBJECT	LOCATION	TYPE	YEAR	REFERENCE(S)
Chapin, Gurden	Alexandria	Tax Charge	1799	Tax PP 1799:06
Chapin, Gurden	Alexandria	Tax Charge	1800	Tax PP 1800:05
Chapin, Gurden	Arlington	Inventory	1811	AB1:113; LVA-LP
Chapin, Gurden	Arlington	Admin.	1811	WB1:074
Chapin, Gurden	Arlington	Account	1812	AB1:207
Chapin, Gurden	Arlington	Sale	1812	AB1:204
Chapin, Gurden	Arlington	Account	1813	AB1:328; LVA-LP
Chapin, Gurden, c/o Gurden	Arlington	Guard.	1812	WB1:161
Chapin, Gurden, cashier A. Bank	Alexandria	Housekeeper	1808	1808(2):12A
Chapin, Gurden, King St.	Alexandria	Occupant	1790	Tax L 1790:06
Chapin, Gurden, Pitt St.	Alexandria	Occupant	1795	Tax L 1795:06
Chapin, Gurden, Pitt St.	Alexandria	Owner	1795	Tax L 1795:06
Chapin, Gurdin	Alexandria	Tax Charge	1796	Tax LP 1796:04
Chapin, Gurdin & wife, cashier of bank	Alexandria	Housekeeper	1799	1799(2):09A
Chapin, Gurdin, cashier	Alexandria	Head	1810	1810(2):02A
Chapin, Gurdin, King St.	Alexandria	Occupant	1787	Tax L 1787:13
Chapin, Gurdy, w(1)3, bank officer	Alexandria	Head	1796	1796(3):2
Chapin, Hiram	Alexandria	Tax Charge	1787	Tax PP 1787:03
Chapin, Hiram	Alexandria	Tax Charge	1790	Tax PP 1790:02
Chapin, Julianna, c/o Gurden	Arlington	Guard.	1812	WB1:161
Chapin, Margaret	Alexandria	Owner	1787	Tax L 1787:09
Chapin, Margaret	Alexandria	Tax Charge	1787	Tax PP 1787:03
Chapin, Margaret	Alexandria	Tax Charge	1788	Tax PP 1788:03
Chapin, Margaret, Fairfax St.	Alexandria	Owner	1790	Tax L 1790:03
Chapin, Margaret R.	Arlington	Will	1843	WB4:374; File #410A
Chapin, Margaret R.	Arlington	Account	1844	AB9:008; LVA-LP
Chapin, Margaret R.	Arlington	Will P.	1844	OCR1842:059
Chapin, Margaret R.	Arlington	Admin.	1844	OCR1842:062
Chapin, Margaret R.	Arlington	Inventory	1845	AB9:110; LVA-LP
Chapin, Margarett	Alexandria	Tax Charge	1790	Tax PP 1790:02
Chapin, Margt., Fairfax St.	Alexandria	Occupant	1790	Tax L 1790:03
Chapin, Nancy R.	Arlington	Guard.	1819	WB2:294
Chapin, Nancy Reeder, c/o Gurden	Arlington	Guard.	1812	WB1:161
Chapman, Allen M., clerk	Alexandria	Boarder	1799	1799(2):03A
Chapman, Charles T., Dep. Collector	Arlington	Deposition	1806	ACR:021
Chapman, Chas., clerk	Alexandria	Head	1810	1810(4):01A
Chapman, Chas., clerk newspaper ofc.	Alexandria	Housekeeper	1808	1808(1):06A
Chapman, David	Arlington	Ordinary	1805	OBL1(np)
Chapman, Elizabeth	Arlington	Ordinary	1806	OBL2(np)
Chapman, Emily Louisa, c/o John B.	Arlington	Guard.	1839	LVA-LP
Chapman, Geo. & wife, farmer	Alexandria	Housekeeper	1799	1799(2):09A
Chapman, George	Alexandria	Owner	1787	Tax L 1787:08
Chapman, George	Alexandria	Tax Charge	1796	Tax LP 1796:04
Chapman, George	Arlington	Plaintiff	1802	PA:142
Chapman, George	Arlington	Inventory	1815	AB2:105; LVA-LP
Chapman, George	Arlington	Bond	1815	WB1:334
Chapman, George	Arlington	Will	1815	WB1:333; File #675A
Chapman, George, Duke St.	Alexandria	Owner	1790	Tax L 1790:03
Chapman, George, Duke St.	Alexandria	Owner	1795	Tax L 1795:04
Chapman, George H.	Arlington	Defendant	1802	PA:304
Chapman, George H., def.	Alexandria	Suit	1802	CRC:274
Chapman, George, Jr., & wife Susannah	Alexandria	Suit	1811	CRI:176
Chapman, George, Jr. & wife Susannah	Alexandria	Suit	1820	CRL:175
Chapman, George, Jr., plt.	Alexandria	Suit	1808	CRG:005
Chapman, George, of *Thoroughfare*	Arlington	Will	1869	WB9:202; File #675A
Chapman, James	Alexandria	Tax Charge	1788	Tax PP 1788:04
Chapman, John	Arlington	Admin.	1812	WB1:174
Chapman, John G.	Arlington	Guard.	1828	WB3:335
Chapman, John S.	Alexandria	Will	1880	WBC1:034; LP
Chapman, Mary Gabriella, c/o John B.	Arlington	Guard.	1839	LVA-LP
Chapman, Matilda L.H., Charles Co. MD	Alexandria	Will	1875	WB1:143; LP

NAME OR SUBJECT	LOCATION	TYPE	YEAR	REFERENCE(S)
Chapman, Nathaniel	Arlington	Admin.	1807	WBB:522
Chapman, Nathaniel	Arlington	Admin.	1813	WB1:188
Chapman, Susan P.	Arlington	Will	1856	WB7:157; File #532A
Chapman, Susan P.	Arlington	Appraisal	1857	WB7:226; LVA-LP
Chapman, Susan P.	Arlington	Account	1859	WB7:429; LVA-LP
Chapman, Wil., Capn.	Alexandria	Tax Charge	1800	Tax PP 1800:05
Chapman, William	Arlington	Admin.	1800	CRA:335
Chapman, William	Arlington	Account	1800	WBA:167
Chapman, William	Arlington	Inventory	1800	WBA:137
Chapman, William	Arlington	Sale	1803	WBA:139
Chapman, William	Arlington	Account	1808	LVA-LP
Chard, James	Alexandria	Tax Charge	1796	Tax PP 1796:03
Charles, Duncan	Alexandria	Tax Charge	1796	Tax PP 1796:03
Charles, Duncan	Alexandria	Tax Charge	1798	Tax PP 1798:02
Charles, Duncan	Alexandria	Tax Charge	1799	Tax PP 1799:06
Charles, Duncan & wife, baker	Alexandria	Housekeeper	1799	1799(2):16A
Charles, Dunkin, w, baker	Alexandria	Head	1796	1796(3):7
Charles, Margret	Alexandria	Resident	1800	1800(4):02B
Charters, John	Alexandria	Resident	1800	1800(4):14B
Charters, John, tanner	Alexandria	Boarder	1800	1800(4):14A
Chartres, Jno., tanner	Alexandria	Boarder	1799	1799(2):12A
Chase, Sarah	Arlington	Apprentice	1824	OCR1822:073a
Chatham, Henry	Arlington	Will	1866	WB8:299; File #640A
Chatham, Henry	Arlington	Appraisal	1866	WB8:382
Chatham, Henry, blacksmith	Alexandria	Head	1810	1810(3):03A
Chatham, James	Alexandria	Tax Charge	1788	Tax PP 1788:03
Chatham, James	Alexandria	Tax Charge	1789	Tax PP 1789:03
Chatham, James	Alexandria	Tax Charge	1790	Tax PP 1790:03
Chatham, James	Alexandria	Tax Charge	1796	Tax LP 1796:04
Chatham, James	Alexandria	Tax Charge	1796	Tax PP 1796:03
Chatham, James	Alexandria	Tax Charge	1800	Tax PP 1800:04
Chatham, James	Alexandria	Will	1885	WB1:419; LP
Chatham, James & wife, blacksmith	Alexandria	Head	1795	1795(4):03
Chatham, James, Duke St.	Alexandria	Occupant	1790	Tax L 1790:01
Chatham, Jas.	Alexandria	Tax Charge	1795	Tax PP 1795:05
Chatham, Jas.	Alexandria	Tax Charge	1798	Tax PP 1798:03
Chatham, Jas. & wife, blacksmith	Alexandria	Housekeeper	1799	1799(2):15A
Chatham, Jas., Duke St.	Alexandria	Occupant	1795	Tax L 1795:08
Chatham, John	Alexandria	Tax Charge	1787	Tax PP 1787:03
Chatham, Martha, formerly Lunt	Alexandria	Will	1889	WB1:539; LP
Chatom, James	Alexandria	Tax Charge	1799	Tax PP 1799:06
Chattam, Ann	Alexandria	Resident	1800	1800(4):05B
Chattam, Ann, sempster	Alexandria	Boarder	1800	1800(4):05A
Chattam, Henry	Alexandria	Resident	1800	1800(4):05B
Chattam, Henry, smith	Alexandria	Boarder	1800	1800(4):05A
Chattam, James & wife Dianer	Alexandria	Resident	1800	1800(4):05B
Chattam, James, smith	Alexandria	Head	1800	1800(4):05A
Chattam, Jas., blacksmith	Alexandria	Housekeeper	1808	1808(1):08A
Chattham, Henry	Alexandria	Boarder	1808	1808(1):08A
Chauncey, William	Alexandria	Will	1900	WB2:372; LP
Chealier, Mazey, Fairfax St.	Alexandria	Occupant	1795	Tax L 1795:30
Cheeks, William	Alexandria	Tax Charge	1787	Tax PP 1787:04
Chenault, Elijah	Arlington	Inventory	1823	AB5:189; LVA-LP
Chenault, Elijah	Arlington	Admin.	1823	WB3:120
Chenault, Elijah, constable	Alexandria	Head	1810	1810(3):04A
Chenault, Elijah, grantee	Arlington	Indenture D.	1811	ID2:067
Chenault, Elijah [Sarah]	Arlington	Admin.	1823	OCR1822:049, 062a
Chenault, Eliza	Arlington	Account	1825	AB6:101; LVA-LP
Chenowith, Edwd.	Alexandria	Boarder	1808	1808(1):05A
Cherni, Paul A.	Alexandria	Tax Charge	1796	Tax PP 1796:03
Cherui, P.A., Wolf St.	Alexandria	Occupant	1795	Tax L 1795:11

NAME OR SUBJECT	LOCATION	TYPE	YEAR	REFERENCE(S)
Chesser, Ephraim, at his house	Arlington	Ordinary	1847	OBL6(np)
Chesser, Ephraim, in Alexandria Co.	Arlington	Ordinary	1849	OBL6(np)
Chevalier, Barber, Fairfax St.	Alexandria	Occupant	1787	Tax L 1787:06
Chevalier, Mrs., Love Alley	Alexandria	Occupant	1790	Tax L 1790:02
Chew, John	Alexandria	Owner	1787	Tax L 1787:08
Chew, John	Alexandria	Tax Charge	1787	Tax PP 1787:03
Chew, John	Alexandria	Tax Charge	1788	Tax PP 1788:03
Chew, John	Alexandria	Tax Charge	1789	Tax PP 1789:04
Chew, John, St. Asaph St.	Alexandria	Occupant	1787	Tax L 1787:08
Chew, Roger	Alexandria	Owner	1787	Tax L 1787:09
Chew, Roger	Alexandria	Tax Charge	1787	Tax PP 1787:03
Chew, Roger	Alexandria	Tax Charge	1788	Tax PP 1788:03
Chew, Roger	Alexandria	Tax Charge	1789	Tax PP 1789:03
Chew, Roger	Alexandria	Tax Charge	1790	Tax PP 1790:02
Chew, Roger, Estate	Alexandria	Tax Charge	1796	Tax LP 1796:04
Chew, Roger, Estate, Fairfax St.	Alexandria	Owner	1795	Tax L 1795:30(3)
Chew, Roger, Fairfax St.	Alexandria	Occupant	1787	Tax L 1787:08
Chew, Roger, Fairfax St.	Alexandria	Occupant	1787	Tax L 1787:09
Chew, Roger, Fairfax St.	Alexandria	Occupant	1790	Tax L 1790:02
Chew, Roger, Fairfax St.	Alexandria	Owner	1790	Tax L 1790:02(3)
Cheys, Ann Eliza	Arlington	Guard.	1828	WB3:335
Childs, Ann Eliza, Sumter Dist. SC	Alexandria	Will	1876	WB1:170; LP
Childs, Cassandra, Fairfax St.	Alexandria	Occupant	1795	Tax L 1795:06
Childs, Cassandra, teacher	Alexandria	Head	1795	1795(4):04
Childs, David, carpenter	Alexandria	Housekeeper	1808	1808(3):18A
Childs, Frederick L.	Alexandria	Will	1894	WB2:098; LP
Childs, John	Arlington	Apprentice	1827	OCR1822:131
Childs, John	Arlington	Apprentice	1829	OCR1822:172a
Childs, John	Arlington	Will	1829	WB3:319; File #273A
Childs, John	Arlington	Bond	1829	WB3:320
Childs, John	Arlington	Account	1836	AB7:349; LVA-LP
Childs, John	Arlington	Account	1839	AB7:349
Childs, Thomas	Arlington	Bond	1854	BB(np)
Childs, Thomas	Arlington	Inventory	1855	WB6:456; LVA-LP
Childs, Thomas	Arlington	Account	1855	WB6:461; LVA-LP
Childs, Thomas	Arlington	Account	1858	WB7:296; LVA-LP
Childs, Thomas	Arlington	Account	1858	WB7:346, 447; LVA-LP
Childs, Thomas	Arlington	Appraisal	1866	WB8:380
Childs, Thomas, Gen.	Arlington	Account	1860	WB8:025; LVA-LP
Childs, Thomas, U.S.A.	Arlington	Will	1854	WB6:311; File #505A
Chin, William	Alexandria	Head	1810	1810(4):08A
Chinault, Elisha, brickmaker	Alexandria	Housekeeper	1808	1808(4):24A
Ching, Thomas	Arlington	Will	1838	WB4:179; File #358A
Ching, Thomas	Arlington	Bond	1838	WB4:180
Ching, Thomas	Arlington	Account	1840	AB8:091; LVA-LP
Ching, Thomas, b. Slapton, Devon.	Arlington	Alien Entry	1826	RA:05/05/26
Chinn, Bill (C), slave of Rd. Hewitt	Alexandria	Housekeeper	1808	1808(4):24A
Chinn, Charles	Arlington	Apprentice	1842	OCR1842:017
Chinn, John	Alexandria	Tithable +16	1788	Tax PP 1788:15
Chipley, Samuel N., Constable	Arlington	Appointment	1852	BB(np)
Chipley, Samuel N., Constable	Arlington	Appointment	1854	BB(np)
Chisholm, Jas.	Alexandria	Boarder	1808	1808(1):04A
Chisley, Male Child	Arlington	Apprentice	1827	OCR1822:146
Chism, Geo., seaman	Alexandria	Head	1810	1810(4):02A
Chisolm, Geo., seaman	Alexandria	Housekeeper	1808	1808(3):23A
Choate, Jacob, Master Ship *Gov. Strong*	Arlington	Bond	1801	ACO:006
Chorue, Paul A., French counsul	Alexandria	Head	1795	1795(4):08
Christ, [blank], sadler	Alexandria	Head	1810	1810(3):08A
Christie, Jno.	Alexandria	Boarder	1808	1808(2):17A
Christopher Raborg & Son, plt.	Alexandria	Suit	1816	CRK:156
Chun, Robert	Alexandria	Mer. License	1798	Tax PP 1798:20-2

NAME OR SUBJECT	LOCATION	TYPE	YEAR	REFERENCE(S)
Chun, Robt.	Alexandria	Tax Charge	1796	Tax PP 1796:03
Chunn, Robert	Alexandria	Tax Charge	1796	Tax LP 1796:04
Church, Gilbert, seaman	Alexandria	Housekeeper	1808	1808(1):01A
Church, Gilbert, seaman	Alexandria	Head	1810	1810(3):02A
Church, Samuel	Arlington	Apprentice	1815	OCR1811:254
Church Wardens of Christ Church	Alexandria	Suit	1822	CRL:389
Church Wardens of the Episcopal Ch.	Alexandria	Suit	1813	CRI:158
Church Wardens of the Episcopal Ch.	Alexandria	Suit	1813	CRL:438
Church, William	Arlington	Apprentice	1827	OCR1822:141a
Churchman, Elizabeth	Arlington	Inventory	1829	LVA-LP
Churchman, Elizabeth	Arlington	Admin.	1829	WB3:354
Churchman, Frederick	Arlington	Inventory	1821	AB4:228; LVA-LP
Churchman, Frederick	Arlington	Will	1821	WB2:419; File #191A
Churchman, Frederick	Arlington	Account	1823	AB5:195; LVA-LP
Churchman, Frederick	Arlington	Appraisal	1829	LVA-LP
Churchman, Frederick	Arlington	Distribution	1830	AB6:514; LVA-LP
Churchman, Frederick & wife, taylor	Alexandria	Housekeeper	1799	1799(2):11A
Churchman, Frederick, baker	Alexandria	Head	1810	1810(4):02A
Churchman, John	Arlington	Will	1865	WB8:246; File #624A
Churchman, Mary	Arlington	Distribution	1830	AB6:515; LVA-LP
Churchwll, Albert Nelson (C)	Alexandria	Will	1883	WB1:388; LP
Chutz, Conrod A.	Arlington	Account	1818	AB3:179
Claget, Horatio, at his house	Arlington	Ordinary	1829	OBL4(np)
Clagett, Ann	Arlington	Account	1864	WB8:222
Clagett, Catherine M., Charles Co. MD	Arlington	Will	1865	WB8:233; File #622A
Clagett, Elizabeth A.	Arlington	Guard.	1828	WB3:336
Clagett, George	Alexandria	Tithable +21	1787	Tax PP 1787:03
Clagett, Horatio	Arlington	Ordinary	1820	OBL3(np)
Clagett, Horatio	Arlington	Inventory	1844	AB9:001; LVA-LP
Clagett, Horatio	Arlington	Admin.	1844	OCR1842:066
Clagett, Horatio	Arlington	Account	1845	AB9:117
Clagett, Horatio	Arlington	Account	1847	AB9:322
Clagett, Horatio, at his house	Arlington	Ordinary	1823	OBL3(np)
Clagett, Horatio, at his house	Arlington	Ordinary	1826	OBL4(np)
Clagett, Horatio, at his house	Arlington	Ordinary	1828	OBL4(np)
Clagett, Horatio, at his house	Arlington	Ordinary	1831	OBL4(np)
Clagett, Horatio, at his house	Arlington	Ordinary	1832	OBL4(np)
Clagett, Horatio, def.	Alexandria	Suit	1822	CRL:389
Clagett, Horatio, in Alexandria Co.	Arlington	Ordinary	1822	OBL3(np)
Clagett, Horatio, in Alexandria Co.	Arlington	Ordinary	1822	OBL3(np)
Clagett, Horatio, in Alexandria Co.	Arlington	Ordinary	1824	OBL3(np)
Clagett, Horatio, in Alexandria Co.	Arlington	Ordinary	1825	OBL4(np)
Clagett, Horatio, in Alexandria Co.	Arlington	Ordinary	1830	OBL4(np)
Claggett, Thos., gentleman	Alexandria	Head	1810	1810(3):02A
Clairfatt, Peter P. cor. Duke & F.	Alexandria	Occupant	1795	Tax L 1795:02
Clamosel, Bernard	Arlington	Libellant	1819	ACO:165, 167-172
Clamosel, Bernard	Arlington	Libellant	1820	ACO:177
Clapdore, Jacob	Arlington	Inventory	1831	LVA-LP
Clapdore, Jacob	Arlington	Admin.	1832	WB4:049
Clapdore, Jacob, grantee	Arlington	Indenture D.	1829	ID:247
Claptor, Philip C. & wife, labourer	Alexandria	Housekeeper	1799	1799(2):18A
Clare, Christiana	Arlington	Guard.	1806	WBB:231
Clark, Catharine	Arlington	Defendant	(nd)	LSA:124
Clark, Elizabeth	Arlington	Apprentice	1803	OCR1801:139
Clark, Elizth., Fairfax St.	Alexandria	Occupant	1795	Tax L 1795:02
Clark, Henry, Alexandria Co.	Arlington	Ordinary	1837	OBL5(np)
Clark, Henry, at his house	Arlington	Ordinary	1838	OBL5(np)
Clark, James	Arlington	Apprentice	1802	OCR1801:063
Clark, James	Arlington	Apprentice	1804	OCR1801:206
Clark, James	Arlington	Admin.	1816	WB2:102
Clark, John	Arlington	Inventory	1818	AB3:132; LVA-LP

NAME OR SUBJECT	LOCATION	TYPE	YEAR	REFERENCE(S)
Clark, John	Arlington	Admin.	1818	WB2:230
Clark, John, labourer	Alexandria	Head	1810	1810(4):07A
Clark, Leo	Arlington	Apprentice	1826	OCR1822:120
Clark, Lucy	Alexandria	Head	1810	1810(4):09A
Clark, Michael	Alexandria	Tax Charge	1788	Tax PP 1788:04
Clark, Nancy	Alexandria	Boarder	1799	1799(2):17A
Clark, Richard	Alexandria	Tax Charge	1787	Tax PP 1787:03
Clark, Richard	Alexandria	Tax Charge	1788	Tax PP 1788:03
Clark, Richard, Water St.	Alexandria	Occupant	1787	Tax L 1787:05
Clark, Robert	Alexandria	Mer. License	1798	Tax PP 1798:20-2
Clark, Robert	Alexandria	Tax Charge	1799	Tax PP 1799:06
Clark, Rose	Arlington	Will	1810	WBC:381; File #054A
Clark, Rose	Arlington	Bond	1810	WBC:382
Clark, Sarah	Alexandria	Resident	1800	1800(4):10B
Clark, Sarah & Eliza., mantua makers	Alexandria	Head	1795	1795(4):05
Clark, Sarah Ann, on Peyton St.	Arlington	Ordinary	1844	OBL6(np)
Clark, Sarah, washerwoman	Alexandria	Head	1810	1810(1):09A
Clark, Sarah, widow	Alexandria	Tax Charge	1799	Tax PP 1799:06
Clark, Septimeus, clerk	Alexandria	Boarder	1799	1799(2):13A
Clark, Thomas	Alexandria	Tax Charge	1796	Tax PP 1796:03
Clark, Thomas	Alexandria	Tax Charge	1799	Tax PP 1799:06
Clark, Thoms.	Alexandria	Tax Charge	1796	Tax LP 1796:05
Clark, Thos.	Alexandria	Tax Charge	1795	Tax PP 1795:05
Clark, Thos.	Alexandria	Tax Charge	1798	Tax PP 1798:03
Clark, Thos.	Alexandria	Tax Charge	1800	Tax PP 1800:04
Clark, Thos. & mother, block maker	Alexandria	Housekeeper	1799	1799(2):18A
Clark, Walter	Alexandria	Tax Charge	1790	Tax PP 1790:03
Clark, William M.	Arlington	Ordinary	1810	OBL2(np)
Clark, William, seaman	Alexandria	Head	1810	1810(2):01A
Clarke, Anastaia, c/o Henry	Arlington	Guard. Acct.	1841	AB8:240; LVA-LP
Clarke, Anastatia, c/o Henry	Arlington	Guard.	1840	WB4:241
Clarke, Bailey E., def.	Alexandria	Suit	1801	CRB:023
Clarke, Catharine	Arlington	Account	1836	AB7:259; LVA-LP
Clarke, Catharine	Arlington	Account	1837	AB7:259
Clarke, Catharine	Arlington	Guard.	1852	BB(np)
Clarke, Catherine	Arlington	Admin.	1835	WB4:089
Clarke, Edward, c/o Elizabeth	Arlington	Apprentice	1822	OCR1822:008a
Clarke, Henry	Arlington	Inventory	1840	AB8:101; LVA-LP
Clarke, Henry	Arlington	Admin.	1840	WB4:240
Clarke, Henry	Arlington	Account	1841	AB8:239
Clarke, Henry, at his house	Arlington	Ordinary	1834	OBL5(np)
Clarke, Henry, at his house	Arlington	Ordinary	1835	OBL5(np)
Clarke, Henry, b. Cumberland, Eng.	Arlington	Alien Entry	1817	RA:22/12/17
Clarke, Henry L., c/o Henry	Arlington	Guard.	1840	WB4:241
Clarke, Horatio D.	Arlington	Admin.	1835	WB4:088
Clarke, John Y.	Arlington	Guard.	1852	BB(np)
Clarke, Joseph H., c/o Henry	Arlington	Guard.	1840	WB4:241
Clarke, Joseph H., c/o Henry	Arlington	Guard. Acct.	1841	AB8:240; LVA-LP
Clarke, Mary E.	Arlington	Guard.	1852	BB(np)
Clarke, Mary L., c/o Henry	Arlington	Guard. Acct.	1841	AB8:240; LVA-LP
Clarke, Michael	Alexandria	Tax Charge	1789	Tax PP 1789:04
Clarke, Peyton	Arlington	Apprentice	1825	OCR1822:097a
Clarke, Pierson, b. Cumberland, Eng.	Arlington	Alien Entry	1817	RA:22/12/17
Clarke, Richard	Alexandria	Tax Charge	1789	Tax PP 1789:04
Clarke, Richard, Water St.	Alexandria	Occupant	1790	Tax L 1790:04
Clarke, Richd.	Alexandria	Boarder	1808	1808(3):21A
Clarke, Samuel	Arlington	Apprentice	1804	OCR1801:199
Clarke, Sarah Ann	Arlington	Ordinary	1841	OBL6(np)
Clarke, Sarah Ann, Alexandria Co.	Arlington	Ordinary	1842	OBL6(np)
Clarke, Sarah Ann, Alexandria Co.	Arlington	Ordinary	1843	OBL6(np)
Clarke, Sarah Ann, at her house	Arlington	Ordinary	1839	OBL5(np)

NAME OR SUBJECT	LOCATION	TYPE	YEAR	REFERENCE(S)
Clarke, Sarah Ann, on Peyton St.	Arlington	Ordinary	1845	OBL6(np)
Clarke, Thomas	Arlington	Admin.	1806	WBB:365
Clarke, Thornton	Arlington	Slave	1853	BB(np)
Clarke, Thos., Sr.	Alexandria	Tax Charge	1800	Tax PP 1800:04
Clarke, William, c/o Elizabeth	Arlington	Apprentice	1822	OCR1822:012
Clarke, Wm., seaman	Alexandria	Head	1810	1810(1):08A
Clarke [Clake], Sarah, sumpster	Alexandria	Boarder	1800	1800(4):10A
Clarkson, Edward	Arlington	Apprentice	1822	OCR1822:009a
Clarkson, Richard Fendall	Arlington	Apprentice	1815	OCR1811:330
Clarkson, Virginia E.	Alexandria	Will	1888	WB1:492; LP
Clarry, John, b. Wexford	Arlington	Alien Entry	1819	RA:14/07/19
Clarvoe, John H., at his house	Arlington	Ordinary	1831	OBL4(np)
Clarvoe, John H., at his house	Arlington	Ordinary	1832	OBL4(np)
Clarvoe, John H., at his house	Arlington	Ordinary	1833	OBL5(np)
Clary, Michael	Arlington	Ordinary	1805	OBL1(np)
Clary, Michael	Alexandria	Deposition	1810	CRG:411
Clary, Michel	Alexandria	Serv./Appt.	1800	1800(4):15B
Clary, Michl., clerk	Alexandria	Head	1810	1810(1):03A
Claughton, P.C., cor. Cameron/Royal	Arlington	Ordinary	1845	OBL6(np)
Claughton, Peter C., Comr. of Revenue	Arlington	Appointment	1852	BB(np)
Claughton, Peter C., Comr. of Revenue	Arlington	Appointment	1854	BB(np)
Claughton, Peter C., on Cameron St.	Arlington	Ordinary	1847	OBL6(np)
Clay, James, painter	Alexandria	Housekeeper	1808	1808(1):04A
Cleary, Michael	Arlington	Ordinary	1805	OBL1(np)
Cleary, Michael, clerk	Alexandria	Boarder	1799	1799(2):13A
Cleary, Michael, clerk & shopkeeper	Alexandria	Housekeeper	1808	1808(1):04A
Cleary v. Douglas	Arlington	Suit	1838	LVA-LP (Accounts)
Cleaver, John	Alexandria	Tax Charge	1798	Tax PP 1798:03
Cleaver, John	Alexandria	Tax Charge	1799	Tax PP 1799:06
Cleaver, John	Alexandria	Tax Charge	1800	Tax PP 1800:04
Cleaver, John	Arlington	Ordinary	1802	OBL1(np)
Cleaver, John	Arlington	Ordinary	1803	OBL1(np)
Cleaver, John	Arlington	Ordinary	1805	OBL1(np)
Cleaver, John	Arlington	Ordinary	1807	OBL2(np)
Cleaver, John	Arlington	Ordinary	1808	OBL2(np)
Cleaver, John & wife, huckster	Alexandria	Housekeeper	1799	1799(2):01A
Cleaver, John, ret. liquor w/o license	Arlington	Defendant	1802	PA:331
Cleaver, John, retailer & tavern lic.	Alexandria	Housekeeper	1808	1808(1):03A
Cleaver, John, shopkeeper	Alexandria	Head	1810	1810(1):13A
Cleavor, John	Arlington	Ordinary	1804	OBL1(np)
Clegg, Jno. & wife, shoe store	Alexandria	Housekeeper	1799	1799(2):01A
Clegg, John	Alexandria	Tax Charge	1798	Tax PP 1798:03
Clegg, John	Alexandria	Tax Charge	1799	Tax PP 1799:06
Clegg, John	Alexandria	Tax Charge	1800	Tax PP 1800:04
Clegg, John, and wife Mary	Arlington	Victim	1802	PA:044
Clegg, John, w(3), clerk	Alexandria	Head	1796	1796(3):6
Clegg, Mary	Arlington	Plaintiff	1802	PA:057
Clemenson, George	Alexandria	Mer. License	1799	Tax PP 1799:52-02w
Clements, Bede	Alexandria	Tithable +16	1790	Tax PP 1790:06
Clements, Bede	Arlington	Inventory	1814	AB2:048a; LVA-LP
Clements, Bede	Arlington	Will	1814	WB1:290; File #119A
Clements, Bede	Arlington	Bond	1814	WB1:290
Clements, Bede	Arlington	Account	1815	AB2:180; LVA-LP
Clements, Bede	Arlington	Account F.	1816	AB2:292
Clements, Bede, Capt.	Arlington	Sale	1814	AB2:061
Clements, Bede, mariner	Alexandria	Head	1810	1810(1):11A
Clements, Charles	Arlington	Apprentice	1805	OCR1801:253
Clements, Geo.	Alexandria	Tithable +16	1789	Tax PP 1789:18
Clements, George	Alexandria	Tithable +21	1787	Tax PP 1787:01
Clements, George	Alexandria	Tithable +16	1788	Tax PP 1788:16
Clements, George	Alexandria	Tax Charge	1790	Tax PP 1790:02

NAME OR SUBJECT	LOCATION	TYPE	YEAR	REFERENCE(S)
Clements, John W., in Alexandria Co.	Arlington	Ordinary	1848	OBL6(np)
Clements, Robert H.	Arlington	Defendant	1823	ACO:210
Clementson, Andrew	Alexandria	Deposition	1806	CRE:137
Clementson, Geo.	Alexandria	Tithable +16	1789	Tax PP 1789:08
Clementson, Geo.	Alexandria	Tax Charge	1795	Tax PP 1795:05
Clementson, Geo.	Alexandria	Tax Charge	1798	Tax PP 1798:03
Clementson, Geo. & wife, merchant	Alexandria	Housekeeper	1799	1799(2):13A
Clementson, Geo., merchant	Alexandria	Housekeeper	1808	1808(3):21A
Clementson, Geo., murchant	Alexandria	Head	1800	1800(4):15A
Clementson, Geo., St. Asaph St.	Alexandria	Occupant	1795	Tax L 1795:04
Clementson, George	Alexandria	Tithable +16	1788	Tax PP 1788:14
Clementson, George	Alexandria	Tithable +16	1790	Tax PP 1790:06
Clementson, George	Alexandria	Tax Charge	1796	Tax PP 1796:03
Clementson, George	Alexandria	Mer. License	1798	Tax PP 1798:20-2
Clementson, George	Alexandria	Tax Charge	1799	Tax PP 1799:07
Clementson, George & wife, merchant	Alexandria	Head	1795	1795(4):09
Clementson, George & wife Jane	Alexandria	Serv./Appt.	1800	1800(4):15B
Clementson, George, def.	Alexandria	Suit	1803	CRD:095
Clementson, George, St. Asaph St.	Alexandria	Owner	1795	Tax L 1795:04
Cleminson, George	Alexandria	Tax Charge	1796	Tax LP 1796:04
Clemmenson, George	Alexandria	Tax Charge	1800	Tax PP 1800:05
Clemmenston, Geo.	Alexandria	License Due	1800	Tax PP 1800:54(24)
Clifferd, Abedier & wife Betsy	Alexandria	Resident	1800	1800(4):08B
Clifford, Jeremiah	Alexandria	Tax Charge	1787	Tax PP 1787:03
Clifford, Jeremiah	Alexandria	Tax Charge	1788	Tax PP 1788:03
Clifford, Jeremiah	Alexandria	Tax Charge	1789	Tax PP 1789:02
Clifford, Jeremiah	Alexandria	Tax Charge	1790	Tax PP 1790:02
Clifford, Jeremiah, Princess St.	Alexandria	Occupant	1790	Tax L 1790:03
Clifford, Jeremiah, Princess St.	Alexandria	Owner	1790	Tax L 1790:03
Clifford, Jeremih.	Alexandria	Tax Charge	1795	Tax PP 1795:04
Clifford, John	Arlington	Will	1858	WB7:303; File #555A
Clifford, Monica	Alexandria	Tax Charge	1787	Tax PP 1787:03
Clifford, Nehemiah	Alexandria	Tithable +21	1787	Tax PP 1787:03
Clifford, Nehemiah	Alexandria	Tithable +16	1789	Tax PP 1789:02
Clifford, Nehemiah	Alexandria	Tax Charge	1790	Tax PP 1790:02
Clifford, Nehemiah	Alexandria	Tax Charge	1798	Tax PP 1798:02
Clifford, Nehemiah	Alexandria	Tax Charge	1799	Tax PP 1799:06
Clifford, Nehemiah	Alexandria	Tax Charge	1800	Tax PP 1800:04
Clifford, Nehemiah, drayman	Alexandria	Head	1810	1810(3):06A
Clifford, Nehemiah, Princess St.	Alexandria	Owner	1790	Tax L 1790:03
Clifford, Nehemiah, shopkeeper	Alexandria	Housekeeper	1808	1808(3):18A
Clifford, Obadiah	Alexandria	Boarder	1799	1799(2):02A
Clifford, Obedier, murchant's clerk	Alexandria	Head	1800	1800(4):08A
Clifford, Washington	Arlington	Apprentice	1822	OCR1822:012a
Clingman, Jacob	Alexandria	Tax Charge	1796	Tax PP 1796:03
Close, James T.	Arlington	Debts	1870	WB9:230
Close, James T.	Arlington	Appraisal	1870	WB9:222
Close, James T.	Arlington	Account	1871	WB9:297
Clowe, Nicholas	Alexandria	Tithable +16	1788	Tax PP 1788:02
Coad, John	Arlington	Inventory	1818	AB3:259; LVA-LP
Coad, John	Arlington	Will	1818	WB2:240; File #152A
Coad, John	Arlington	Account	1819	AB3:375; LVA-LP
Coad, John	Arlington	Account	1824	AB5:320; LVA-LP
Coad [Cook] John	Arlington	Guard.	1825	OCR1822:096
Coakley, James W., of Fairfax Co.	Arlington	Will	1832	LVA-LP
Coale, James, tanner	Alexandria	Head	1810	1810(4):09A
Coale, Susanah, washerwoman	Alexandria	Head	1810	1810(2):05A
Coale, Toby, drayman	Alexandria	Head	1810	1810(2):08A
Coates, Samuel, of Philadelphia	Alexandria	Deed	1811	CRK:048
Coates, Sarah, seamstress	Alexandria	Head	1810	1810(1):05A
Coats, Daniel	Arlington	Will	1831	WB4:008; File #299A

NAME OR SUBJECT	LOCATION	TYPE	YEAR	REFERENCE(S)
Coats, Daniel	Arlington	Bond	1831	WB4:009
Coats, Daniel	Arlington	Account	1834	AB7:104; LVA-LP
Coats, Lucy, washwoman	Alexandria	Housekeeper	1808	1808(4):24A
Coats, Nancy	Alexandria	Boarder	1799	1799(2):10A
Coats, [blank], King St.	Alexandria	Occupant	1795	Tax L 1795:32
Cobb, Elkannah	Arlington	Plaintiff	1815	ACO:143
Cobbins, Collen	Alexandria	Serv./Appr.	1800	1800(4):11B
Cobbs, Thomas	Alexandria	Deed	1793	CRD:145
Cobert, Colin (C)	Arlington	Apprentice	1803	OCR1801:086a
Coburn, Primus	Alexandria	Tax Charge	1788	Tax PP 1788:03
Cochoran, George	Arlington	Apprentice	1812	OCR1811:045
Cochran, James	Alexandria	Tax Charge	1789	Tax PP 1789:02
Cochran, James	Alexandria	Tax Charge	1790	Tax PP 1790:02
Cochran, Jas.	Alexandria	Boarder	1808	1808(2):13A
Cochran, John	Alexandria	Tax Charge	1790	Tax PP 1790:02
Cocke, Benja., clerk	Alexandria	Boarder	1799	1799(2):03A
Cocke, Benjamin, for playing Faro	Arlington	Defendant	1801	PA:097
Cockerell, George Henry	Arlington	Apprentice	1827	OCR1822:139a
Cockerill, William, c/o Catharine	Arlington	Apprentice	1823	OCR1822:047
Cockran, James	Alexandria	Tax Charge	1787	Tax PP 1787:04
Cockran, James	Alexandria	Tax Charge	1788	Tax PP 1788:03
Cockrell, Ellen	Alexandria	Will	1888	WB1:504; LP
Cockrell, Hiram, of Fairfax Co.	Alexandria	Will	1886	WB1:435; LP
Cockren, Jennet	Alexandria	Serv./Appr.	1800	1800(4):12B
Code, John	Alexandria	Resident	1800	1800(4):05B
Code, John	Alexandria	Serv./Appr.	1800	1800(4):05B
Codogan, Charles	Alexandria	Tax Charge	1800	Tax PP 1800:04
Coe, Richd., inspector	Alexandria	Head	1810	1810(2):07A
Coe, Richd., tobacco inspector	Alexandria	Housekeeper	1808	1808(2):16A
Coffee, one bag of	Arlington	Suit	1821	ACO:184, 188, 193
Coffee, sugar and logwood	Arlington	Suit	1806	ACO:053, 056, 063
Coffee, sugar and logwood	Arlington	Suit	1806	ACO:065
Coffer, John, c/o Mary	Arlington	Apprentice	1812	OCR1811:113
Coffer, John, c/o John	Arlington	Guard.	1813	WB1:209
Coffer, Mary	Alexandria	Head	1810	1810(4):02A
Coffer, Mary, c/o John	Arlington	Guard.	1813	WB1:237
Coffey, Chas. H. & Co.	Alexandria	Mer. License	1798	Tax PP 1798:20-2
Coffin, Daniel, seaman	Alexandria	Housekeeper	1808	1808(1):04A
Coffin, Isaac, of Nantucket, Mass.	Alexandria	Deposition	1818	CRK:470
Coffin, Owen	Alexandria	Tax Charge	1788	Tax PP 1788:03
Coghill, Smallwood, clerk	Alexandria	Boarder	1799	1799(2):03A
Cogswell, Susan M., of Plainfield NJ	Arlington	Will	1892	WB10:242; File #776A
Cohagan, Jno.	Alexandria	Tax Charge	1799	Tax PP 1799:07
Cohagan, Jno.	Alexandria	Reference	1808	1808(4):29B
Cohagan, John	Alexandria	Tax Charge	1800	Tax PP 1800:04
Cohagan, John	Arlington	Juryman	1824	ACO:237
Cohagan, John	Arlington	Will	1865	WB8:262; File #632A
Cohagan, John	Arlington	Account	1868	WB9:137
Cohagan, John & wife Ann	Alexandria	Resident	1800	1800(4):04B
Cohagan, John, bricklayer	Alexandria	Housekeeper	1808	1808(4):29A
Cohagan, John, Capt. & wife	Arlington	Inventory	1862	WB8:110
Cohagan, John, mason	Alexandria	Head	1800	1800(4):04A
Cohagan, John, plt.	Alexandria	Suit	1801	CRB:318
Cohagan, Mrs.	Arlington	Sale	1862	WB8:112; LVA-LP
Cohagan, W.W.	Arlington	Admin.	1825	WB3:183
Cohagen, John, bricklayer	Alexandria	Head	1810	1810(4):06A
Cohen, Sophia	Alexandria	Will	1875	WB1:152; LP
Cohen, William	Alexandria	Tax Charge	1799	Tax PP 1799:06
Cohen, William	Alexandria	Tax Charge	1800	Tax PP 1800:04
Cohen, Wm.	Alexandria	Tax Charge	1798	Tax PP 1798:03
Cohen, Wm., silversmith	Alexandria	Housekeeper	1799	1799(2):12A

NAME OR SUBJECT	LOCATION	TYPE	YEAR	REFERENCE(S)
Cohen, Wm., silversmith	Alexandria	Housekeeper	1808	1808(4):30A
Colbert, John	Alexandria	Head	1810	1810(4):08A
Colbert, John (C), carpenter	Alexandria	Housekeeper	1808	1808(4):24A
Colbert, Mary Ann, of Rappa. Co. VA	Arlington	Will	1887	WB10:132; File #732A
Colbert, Saml., labourer	Alexandria	Head	1810	1810(1):10A
Cole, Betty & 4 children (C)	Alexandria	Boarder	1799	1799(2):12A
Cole, Betty, washwoman	Alexandria	Housekeeper	1808	1808(3):18A
Cole, Charlotte	Arlington	Will P.	1844	OCR1842:081, 082
Cole, Charlotte	Arlington	Will	1844	WB4:384; File #416A
Cole, Charlotte	Arlington	Account	1845	AB9:134; LVA-LP
Cole, Charlotte	Arlington	Inventory	1845	AB9:093; LVA-LP
Cole, Charlotte	Arlington	Petition	1845	LVA-LP (Box 214)
Cole, Charlotte	Arlington	Account	1846	AB9:236; LVA-LP
Cole, Charlotte	Arlington	Account	1848	WB5:088; LVA-LP
Cole, Charlotte	Arlington	Account	1852	WB6:105
Cole, Charlotte (C)	Alexandria	Housekeeper	1799	1799(2):12A
Cole, Charlotte, heirs of	Arlington	Guard.	1845	OCR1842:108, 109
Cole, George, c/o Mary	Arlington	Apprentice	1805	OCR1801:310
Cole, Isaac (M)	Alexandria	Tax Charge	1789	Tax PP 1789:04
Cole, Jack, labourer	Alexandria	Head	1810	1810(1):07A
Cole, James	Alexandria	Tax Charge	1796	Tax LP 1796:05
Cole, James	Alexandria	Serv./Appr.	1800	1800(4):14B
Cole, James	Arlington	Apprentice	1825	OCR1822:095
Cole, James, tanner	Alexandria	Housekeeper	1808	1808(4):24A
Cole, Jas. (C)	Alexandria	Tax Charge	1795	Tax PP 1795:04
Cole, Jas., Queen St.	Alexandria	Occupant	1795	Tax L 1795:09
Cole, John	Alexandria	Tax Charge	1796	Tax PP 1796:03
Cole, May	Arlington	Apprentice	1804	OCR1801:216
Cole, Philis	Arlington	Crime	1795	OT:09/01/1794
Cole, Solleman, labourrer	Alexandria	Head	1800	1800(4):10A
Cole, Solloman & wife Nancey	Alexandria	Resident	1800	1800(4):10B
Cole, Solomon	Arlington	Crime	1795	OT:05/06/1795
Cole, Solomon	Alexandria	Tax Charge	1799	Tax PP 1799:06
Cole, Solomon (C)	Alexandria	Tax Charge	1800	Tax PP 1800:04
Cole, Sukey, gentlewoman	Alexandria	Housekeeper	1808	1808(1):08A
Cole, Thomas	Alexandria	Tax Charge	1795	Tax PP 1795:04
Cole, Thomas	Arlington	Defendant	1809	ACO:107
Cole, Thomas	Arlington	Inventory	1814	AB2:042; LVA-LP
Cole, Thomas	Arlington	Will	1814	WB1:286; File #117A
Cole, Thomas	Arlington	Bond	1814	WB1:286
Cole, Thomas	Arlington	Guard.	1816	WB2:132
Cole, Thomas, Capt.	Arlington	Sale	1814	AB2:040
Cole, Thomas, mariner	Alexandria	Head	1810	1810(1):10A
Cole, Thos. & Jno. Gordon, butchers	Alexandria	Housekeeper	1799	1799(2):18A
Cole, Thos., sea captain	Alexandria	Housekeeper	1808	1808(1):07A
Cole, Toby & Jack, laborers	Alexandria	Housekeeper	1808	1808(2):14A
Cole, William	Alexandria	Tax Charge	1795	Tax PP 1795:04
Cole, William	Alexandria	Tax Charge	1798	Tax PP 1798:03
Cole, William	Alexandria	Tax Charge	1799	Tax PP 1799:06
Cole, William	Alexandria	Tax Charge	1800	Tax PP 1800:05
Cole, William (C)	Arlington	Apprentice	1828	OCR1822:166
Cole, Wm. & wife, labourer	Alexandria	Housekeeper	1799	1799(2):12A
Cole, Wm. & wife Filles	Alexandria	Resident	1800	1800(4):14B
Cole, Wm., labourrer	Alexandria	Head	1800	1800(4):14A
Coleby, Daniel	Arlington	Defendant	1820	ACO:183
Coleby, Daniel, failed to appear as	Arlington	Witness	1820	ACO:175
Coleby, Daniel, mate	Arlington	Defendant	1821	ACO:195, 196
Colegate, Edward, at his house	Arlington	Ordinary	1831	OBL4(np)
Colegate, Edward, at his house	Arlington	Ordinary	1832	OBL4(np)
Coleman, Alice	Arlington	Will P.	1828	OCR1822:157
Coleman, Alice	Arlington	Admin.	1828	OCR1822:157

NAME OR SUBJECT	LOCATION	TYPE	YEAR	REFERENCE(S)
Coleman, Alice	Arlington	Bond	1828	WB3:323
Coleman, Alice	Arlington	Will	1828	WB3:313; File #271A
Coleman, Alice	Arlington	Inventory	1830	LVA-LP
Coleman, Elice, shopkeeper	Alexandria	Head	1810	1810(1):12A
Coleman, Geo., sea captain	Alexandria	Housekeeper	1808	1808(3):21A
Coleman, Geo., seaman	Alexandria	Head	1810	1810(3):01A
Coleman, George	Arlington	Admin.	1829	OCR1822:171
Coleman, George	Arlington	Admin.	1829	WB3:351
Coleman, George	Arlington	Account	1830	AB7:021; LVA-LP
Coleman, George	Arlington	Account	1831	AB7:025; LVA-LP
Coleman, George	Arlington	Account	1833	AB7:081; LVA-LP
Coleman, George	Arlington	Account	1836	AB7:221; LVA-LP
Coleman, George	Arlington	Account F.	1846	AB9:190; LVA-LP
Coleman, George, plt.	Alexandria	Suit	1817	CRL:350
Coleman, George, plt.	Alexandria	Suit	1817	CRK:268
Coleman, George, plt.	Alexandria	Suit	1818	CRK:315
Coleman, James	Alexandria	Tax Charge	1790	Tax PP 1790:03
Coleman, James, Fairfax St.	Alexandria	Occupant	1790	Tax L 1790:06
Coleman, James, Union St.	Alexandria	Owner	1790	Tax L 1790:03
Coleman, James, Union St.	Alexandria	Occupant	1790	Tax L 1790:03
Coleman, Jos. & wife, cooper	Alexandria	Housekeeper	1799	1799(2):17A
Coleman, Joseph	Alexandria	Tax Charge	1789	Tax PP 1789:03
Coleman, Joseph	Alexandria	Tax Charge	1789	Tax PP 1789:03
Coleman, Joseph	Alexandria	Tax Charge	1795	Tax PP 1795:06
Coleman, Joseph	Alexandria	Tax Charge	1796	Tax LP 1796:04
Coleman, Joseph	Alexandria	Tax Charge	1796	Tax PP 1796:03
Coleman, Joseph	Alexandria	Tax Charge	1798	Tax PP 1798:02
Coleman, Joseph	Alexandria	Tax Charge	1799	Tax PP 1799:06
Coleman, Joseph	Alexandria	Tax Charge	1800	Tax PP 1800:04
Coleman, Joseph	Alexandria	Boarder	1808	1808(1):07A
Coleman, Joseph	Arlington	Will	1810	WBC:344; File #053A
Coleman, Joseph	Arlington	Inventory	1810	WBC:352
Coleman, Joseph	Arlington	Bond	1810	WBC:349
Coleman, Joseph	Arlington	Account	1812	AB1:155; LVA-LP
Coleman, Joseph & wife, cooper	Alexandria	Head	1795	1795(4):06
Coleman, Joseph & wife Alice	Alexandria	Resident	1800	1800(4):10B
Coleman, Joseph, cooper	Alexandria	Housekeeper	1808	1808(1):07A
Coleman, Joseph, Fairfax St.	Alexandria	Occupant	1795	Tax L 1795:07
Coleman, Margaret Mary, c/o George	Arlington	Guard.	1830	WB3:381
Coleman, Thomas R., c/o George	Arlington	Guard.	1830	WB3:381
Coleman, [blank]	Alexandria	Boarder	1808	1808(2):13A
Collard, George	Alexandria	Tithable +16	1788	Tax PP 1788:08
Collard, George	Alexandria	Tithable +16	1789	Tax PP 1789:09
Collard, George, plt.	Alexandria	Suit	1802	CRB:227
Collard, Saml.	Alexandria	Tax Charge	1796	Tax PP 1796:04
Collard, Saml.	Alexandria	Tax Charge	1798	Tax PP 1798:03
Collard, Samuel	Alexandria	Tithable +16	1789	Tax PP 1789:09
Collen, Samul & wife Elizebeth	Alexandria	Resident	1800	1800(4):08B
Collen, Samul, labourrer	Alexandria	Head	1800	1800(4):08A
Collier, Jas.	Alexandria	Tithable +16	1788	Tax PP 1788:12
Collier, Thomas	Alexandria	Tax Charge	1789	Tax PP 1789:04
Collier, Thomas	Alexandria	Tax Charge	1790	Tax PP 1790:02
Collings, Richard	Alexandria	Resident	1800	1800(4):14B
Collings, Richard, tanner	Alexandria	Boarder	1800	1800(4):14A
Collins, John	Alexandria	Tax Charge	1787	Tax PP 1787:03
Collins, Maria	Alexandria	Will	1900	WB2:387; LP
Collins, Robt., plaisterer	Alexandria	Housekeeper	1808	1808(1):03A
Collins, Spindeloe	Alexandria	Will	1875	WB1:139; LP
Collins, Sukey	Alexandria	Head	1810	1810(2):05A
Collins, Sukey, washwoman	Alexandria	Housekeeper	1808	1808(2):17A
Collock, [blank] (C)	Alexandria	Tax Charge	1800	Tax PP 1800:05

NAME OR SUBJECT	LOCATION	TYPE	YEAR	REFERENCE(S)
Colman, Joseph, cooper	Alexandria	Head	1800	1800(4):10A
Colson, Joseph	Alexandria	Housekeeper	1808	1808(1):07A
Colston, Betsy (C), washwoman	Alexandria	Housekeeper	1808	1808(1):09A
Colston, Lucy	Alexandria	Head	1810	1810(1):09A
Colston, Lucy, gentlewoman	Alexandria	Housekeeper	1808	1808(4):25A
Colston, Mump., coppersmith	Alexandria	Head	1810	1810(1):09A
Colston, Rawleigh	Alexandria	Account B.	1800	CRK:105
Colston, Rawleigh	Alexandria	Account B.	1800	CRL:124
Colston, Rawleigh, Berkeley Co.	Alexandria	Agreement	1811	CRK:112
Coltart, Roger	Alexandria	Tax Charge	1788	Tax PP 1788:03
Coltart, Roger	Alexandria	Tithable +16	1789	Tax PP 1789:14
Colter, Docy, seamstress	Alexandria	Head	1810	1810(1):06A
Columbia Insurance Co.	Alexandria	Suit	1822	CRL:232
Columbian Insurance Co., def.	Alexandria	Suit	1822	CRL:578
Colvin, Cornelius	Alexandria	Tax Charge	1799	Tax PP 1799:06
Colwell, James, shopkeeper	Alexandria	Head	1796	1796(3):4
Combe, Griffith	Arlington	Plaintiff	1820	ACO:173, 178, 180
Combe, Griffith	Arlington	Plaintiff	1820	ACO:182
Combs, Fielding, plt.	Alexandria	Suit	1803	CRD:074
Combs, J.J., Fairfax St.	Alexandria	Occupant	1787	Tax L 1787:07
Combs, John	Alexandria	Tax Charge	1788	Tax PP 1788:03
Comes, Elisebeth	Alexandria	Resident	1800	1800(4):03B
Compton, Ann	Arlington	Will	1825	WB3:210; File #242A
Compton, Henry T.	Arlington	Inventory	1821	AB5:018; LVA-LP
Compton, Henry T.	Arlington	Admin.	1821	WB3:002
Compton, Henry T., grantor	Arlington	Indenture D.	1812	ID2:128
Compton, Henry T., in jail bounds	Arlington	Insolvent	1812	ID2:122
Compton, Jas.	Alexandria	Boarder	1808	1808(2):15A
Compton, Josiah	Alexandria	Tax Charge	1800	Tax PP 1800:04
Compton, Martha V., c/o Adeline B.	Arlington	Guard.	1853	BB(np)
Compton, Rosia A., c/o Adeline B.	Arlington	Guard.	1853	BB(np)
Compton, Virginia F., c/o Adeline B.	Arlington	Guard.	1853	BB(np)
Compton, Wilson	Alexandria	Tithable +16	1788	Tax PP 1788:02
Conard, Priscilla	Arlington	Will	1815	WB2:055
Condon, David	Alexandria	Tax Charge	1795	Tax PP 1795:05
Condon, David & wife, laborer	Alexandria	Head	1795	1795(4):02
Conely, John, w(2), ship carpenter	Alexandria	Head	1796	1796(3):3
Conn, Cassina	Arlington	Inventory	1805	WBB:193
Conn, Cassina	Arlington	Admin.	1805	WBB:191
Conn, Cassina	Arlington	Account	1810	AB1:001
Conn, P. & Co., Pitt St.	Alexandria	Occupant	1787	Tax L 1787:25
Conn, Phil.	Alexandria	Tax Charge	1795	Tax PP 1795:05
Conn, Phil.	Alexandria	Tax Charge	1798	Tax PP 1798:03
Conn, Phil., Pitt St.	Alexandria	Occupant	1795	Tax L 1795:05
Conn, Philip	Alexandria	Owner	1787	Tax L 1787:08
Conn, Philip	Alexandria	Tax Charge	1787	Tax PP 1787:03
Conn, Philip	Alexandria	Tax Charge	1788	Tax PP 1788:02
Conn, Philip	Alexandria	Tax Charge	1789	Tax PP 1789:03
Conn, Philip	Alexandria	Tax Charge	1790	Tax PP 1790:02
Conn, Philip	Alexandria	Tax Charge	1796	Tax LP 1796:05
Conn, Philip	Alexandria	Tax Charge	1796	Tax PP 1796:03
Conn, Philip	Arlington	Defendant	1802	PA:271
Conn, Philip, carpenter	Alexandria	Housekeeper	1808	1808(4):27A
Conn, Philip, Fairfax St.	Alexandria	Owner	1790	Tax L 1790:03
Conn, Philip, Pitt St.	Alexandria	Occupant	1787	Tax L 1787:08
Conn, Philip, Pitt St.	Alexandria	Occupant	1790	Tax L 1790:03
Conn, Philip, Pitt St.	Alexandria	Owner	1795	Tax L 1795:05(2)
Conn, Philip, w(1), shopkeeper	Alexandria	Head	1796	1796(3):3
Conn, Phillip, house joiner	Alexandria	Head	1810	1810(4):01A
Conn, Thomas	Alexandria	Owner	1787	Tax L 1787:08
Conn, Thomas	Alexandria	Tax Charge	1787	Tax PP 1787:02

NAME OR SUBJECT	LOCATION	TYPE	YEAR	REFERENCE(S)
Conn, Thomas	Alexandria	Tax Charge	1788	Tax PP 1788:03
Conn, Thomas	Alexandria	Tax Charge	1795	Tax PP 1795:04
Conn, Thomas	Alexandria	Tax Charge	1796	Tax LP 1796:05
Conn, Thomas	Alexandria	Tax Charge	1798	Tax PP 1798:02
Conn, Thomas	Alexandria	Tax Charge	1799	Tax PP 1799:06
Conn, Thomas	Alexandria	Tax Charge	1800	Tax PP 1800:04
Conn, Thomas, King St.	Alexandria	Occupant	1787	Tax L 1787:08
Conn, Thos., Royal St.	Alexandria	Occupant	1795	Tax L 1795:05
Conn, Thos., Royal St.	Alexandria	Owner	1795	Tax L 1795:05
Connell, James	Alexandria	Tax Charge	1790	Tax PP 1790:03
Connelly, Patrick	Arlington	Admin.	1828	WB3:339
Conner, Charlotte	Arlington	Apprentice	1803	OCR1801:091
Conner, Dennis	Alexandria	Boarder	1808	1808(4):24A
Conner, John	Alexandria	Tax Charge	1798	Tax PP 1798:03
Conner, William	Arlington	Apprentice	1828	OCR1822:165a
Connor, Hannah, c/o Ann	Arlington	Apprentice	1804	OCR1801:233
Connor, John Wash., c/o Susannah	Arlington	Apprentice	1815	OCR1811:318
Conrad & McMunn, def.	Alexandria	Account B.	1801	CRC:110
Conrad, Louise	Arlington	Will	1863	WB8:168; File #602A
Conrad, Priscilla	Alexandria	Boarder	1799	1799(2):09A
Conrad, [blank], def.	Alexandria	Suit	1802	CRC:107
Constable, Mary C.	Arlington	Guard. Acct.	1857	WB7:222; LVA-LP
Constable, Mary C.	Arlington	Guard. Acct.	1859	WB7:463; LVA-LP
Constable, Mary C.	Arlington	Guard. Acct.	1869	WB9:176
Constable, Mary D.	Arlington	Will	1860	WB7:525; File #573A
Contee, Alexander, plt.	Alexandria	Suit	1801	CRC:190
Contee, Jane	Arlington	Inventory	1820	AB4:168; LVA-LP
Contee, Jane	Arlington	Will	1820	WB2:371; File #178A
Contee, Jane	Arlington	Account	1823	AB5:184; LVA-LP
Conway, Harriet N., c/o Joseph	Arlington	Guard.	1815	WB2:098
Conway, Joseph	Arlington	Renounce	1806	WBB:387
Conway, Joseph	Arlington	Admin.	1815	WB2:099
Conway, Joseph	Arlington	Account	1818	AB3:252; LVA-LP
Conway, Richard	Alexandria	Owner	1787	Tax L 1787:08
Conway, Richard	Alexandria	Tax Charge	1787	Tax PP 1787:03
Conway, Richard	Alexandria	Tax Charge	1788	Tax PP 1788:04
Conway, Richard	Alexandria	Tax Charge	1789	Tax PP 1789:04
Conway, Richard	Alexandria	Tax Charge	1790	Tax PP 1790:02
Conway, Richard	Alexandria	Tax Charge	1795	Tax PP 1795:04
Conway, Richard	Alexandria	Tax Charge	1796	Tax PP 1796:04
Conway, Richard	Alexandria	Tax Charge	1798	Tax PP 1798:03
Conway, Richard	Alexandria	Tax Charge	1799	Tax PP 1799:07
Conway, Richard	Alexandria	Tax Charge	1800	Tax PP 1800:05
Conway, Richard	Arlington	Will	1806	WBB:370; File #025A
Conway, Richard	Arlington	Bond	1806	WBB:379
Conway, Richard	Arlington	Inventory	1807	WBB:451; LVA-LP
Conway, Richard	Arlington	Account	1807	WBB:460
Conway, Richard	Arlington	Account	1807	WBC:071; LVA-LP
Conway, Richard	Arlington	Stock Sale	1807	WBC:004
Conway, Richard	Arlington	Account	1812	AB1:228
Conway, Richard	Arlington	Account	1814	AB2:047; LVA-LP
Conway, Richard	Arlington	Account	1816	AB2:394; LVA-LP
Conway, Richard	Arlington	Account	1828	LVA-LP
Conway, Richard, Capt.	Arlington	Account	1807	WBC:001; LVA-LP
Conway, Richard, Estate	Alexandria	Sale	1807	CRH:123
Conway, Richard, Estate, def.	Alexandria	Suit	1809	CRH:046
Conway, Richard, for wharfage	Arlington	Payment	1805	ACO:037
Conway, Richard, Oronoka St.	Alexandria	Occupant	1787	Tax L 1787:08
Conway, Richard, Oronoka St.	Alexandria	Owner	1790	Tax L 1790:02
Conway, Richard, Oronoka St.	Alexandria	Occupant	1790	Tax L 1790:02
Conway, Richard, plt.	Alexandria	Suit	1802	CRC:277

NAME OR SUBJECT	LOCATION	TYPE	YEAR	REFERENCE(S)
Conway, Richard, Union St.	Alexandria	Occupant	1787	Tax L 1787:08
Conway, Richard, Water St.	Alexandria	Owner	1790	Tax L 1790:02
Conway, Richard, wharf	Alexandria	Owner	1790	Tax L 1790:02(2)
Conway, Richd.	Alexandria	Tax Charge	1796	Tax LP 1796:04
Conway, Richd., Oronoko St.	Alexandria	Owner	1795	Tax L 1795:05
Conway, Richd., Oronoko St.	Alexandria	Occupant	1795	Tax L 1795:05
Conway, Richd., Union St.	Alexandria	Owner	1795	Tax L 1795:05(2)
Conway, Richd., Water St.	Alexandria	Owner	1795	Tax L 1795:05
Conway, Robert	Arlington	Guard. Acct.	1807	WBC:023; LVA-LP
Conway, Robert	Arlington	Guard. Acct.	1808	WBC:179; LVA-LP
Conway, Robert	Arlington	Guard. Acct.	1810	WBC:379; LVA-LP
Conway, Robert	Arlington	Guard. Acct.	1811	AB1:111
Conway, Robert, c/o Robert	Arlington	Guard.	1806	WBB:378
Conway, Robert, gentleman	Alexandria	Head	1810	1810(2):06A
Conway, Robt.	Alexandria	Boarder	1808	1808(2):11A
Conway, Thomas	Arlington	Guard. Acct.	1808	WBC:163; LVA-LP
Conway, Thomas, c/o Robert	Arlington	Guard.	1806	WBB:386
Conway, [blank], King St.	Alexandria	Occupant	1790	Tax L 1790:04
Conway's Devisees v. Conways's Exors.	Arlington	Suit	1835	LVA-LP (Judgments)
Coock, Lewis, w(2), stone mason	Alexandria	Head	1796	1796(3):1
Cook, David, clerk	Alexandria	Boarder	1799	1799(2):03A
Cook, Eleanor (C), washwoman	Alexandria	Housekeeper	1808	1808(2):17A
Cook, Elenor, seamstress	Alexandria	Head	1810	1810(3):04A
Cook, Eliza	Alexandria	Boarder	1799	1799(2):08A
Cook, Fields	Alexandria	Will	1896	WB2:185; LP
Cook, George	Arlington	Bond	1831	WB4:031
Cook, George	Arlington	Will	1831	WB4:030; File #313A
Cook, Henry	Arlington	Appraisal	1869	WB9:171
Cook, Henry	Arlington	Account	1870	WB9:245
Cook, Henry	Arlington	Account	1877	WB9:470
Cook, Henry, grantee	Arlington	Indenture D.	1831	ID:317
Cook, Hortensia H.	Alexandria	Will	1881	WB1:326; LP
Cook, John	Alexandria	Tax Charge	1795	Tax PP 1795:04
Cook, John & wife, shoemaker/laborer	Alexandria	Head	1795	1795(4a):05
Cook, John W.	Arlington	Admin.	1830	WB3:380
Cook, John W.	Arlington	Account	1839	AB8:087; LVA LP
Cook, John W.	Arlington	Account F.	1840	AB8:087
Cook, Joseph, c/o Enealor	Arlington	Apprentice	1805	OCR1801:317
Cook, Leonard	Alexandria	Tax Charge	1799	Tax PP 1799:07
Cook, Leonard	Arlington	Apprentice	1822	OCR1822:008
Cook, Leonard	Arlington	Apprentice	1824	OCR1822:069
Cook, Leonard & Thomas, def.	Alexandria	Suit	1809	CRG:234
Cook, Leonard, grantor	Arlington	Indenture D.	1826	ID:060
Cook, Leonard, in jail	Arlington	Insolvent	1826	ID:051
Cook, Leonard, merchant	Alexandria	Housekeeper	1808	1808(4):27A
Cook, Leonard, merchant	Alexandria	Head	1810	1810(4):09A
Cook, Leond.	Alexandria	Tax Charge	1798	Tax PP 1798:02
Cook, Lewis	Alexandria	Owner	1787	Tax L 1787:09
Cook, Lewis	Alexandria	Tax Charge	1787	Tax PP 1787:03
Cook, Lewis	Alexandria	Tax Charge	1788	Tax PP 1788:02
Cook, Lewis	Alexandria	Tax Charge	1789	Tax PP 1789:03
Cook, Lewis	Alexandria	Tax Charge	1790	Tax PP 1790:02
Cook, Lewis	Alexandria	Tax Charge	1795	Tax PP 1795:05
Cook, Lewis	Alexandria	Tax Charge	1796	Tax PP 1796:03
Cook, Lewis	Alexandria	Tax Charge	1798	Tax PP 1798:02
Cook, Lewis	Alexandria	Tax Charge	1799	Tax PP 1799:07
Cook, Lewis	Alexandria	Tax Charge	1800	Tax PP 1800:04
Cook, Lewis & wife, bricklayer	Alexandria	Head	1795	1795(4):08
Cook, Lewis & wife, bricklayer	Alexandria	Housekeeper	1799	1799(2):10A
Cook, Lewis, Fairfax St.	Alexandria	Owner	1790	Tax L 1790:03
Cook, Lewis, Pitt St.	Alexandria	Occupant	1787	Tax L 1787:09

NAME OR SUBJECT	LOCATION	TYPE	YEAR	REFERENCE(S)
Cook, Lewis, Pitt St.	Alexandria	Occupant	1790	Tax L 1790:03
Cook, Mary	Alexandria	Resident	1800	1800(4):02B
Cook, Mary, laundress	Alexandria	Head	1800	1800(4):02A
Cook, Paty, washwoman	Alexandria	Housekeeper	1808	1808(1):08A
Cook, Rebecca	Arlington	Will	1867	WB8:444; File #651A
Cook, Stephen	Alexandria	Tax Charge	1796	Tax LP 1796:04
Cook, Stephen & wife, physician	Alexandria	Housekeeper	1799	1799(2):08A
Cook, Stephen, def.	Alexandria	Suit	1802	CRC:009
Cook, Stephen, w(6)3, doctor	Alexandria	Head	1796	1796(3):5
Cook, Thomas	Alexandria	Deposition	1805	CRE:306
Cook, Thomas	Arlington	Inventory	1818	AB3:139; LVA-LP
Cook, Thomas	Arlington	Will	1818	WB2:236; File #151A
Cook, Thomas	Arlington	Account	1819	AB3:377; LVA-LP
Cook, Thos., merchant	Alexandria	Head	1810	1810(4):09A
Cook, Whiting	Arlington	Admin.	1829	WB3:349
Cook, William	Alexandria	Will	1881	WB1:323; LP
Cook, Wm.	Alexandria	Boarder	1808	1808(4):24A
Cooke & Whann, plt.	Alexandria	Suit	1801	CRD:178
Cooke, George	Arlington	Account	1833	AB7:068; LVA-LP
Cooke, James, c/o Eleanor	Arlington	Apprentice	1805	OCR1801:308
Cooke, John W., grantee	Arlington	Indenture D.	1826	ID:064
Cooke, Leonard, plt.	Alexandria	Suit	1807	CRF:131
Cooke, Lewis	Arlington	Crime	1795	OT:15/07/1795
Cooke, Lewis, def.	Alexandria	Suit	1802	CRB:168
Cooke, Rezin, grantor	Arlington	Indenture D.	1814	ID2:334
Cooke, Rezin, in jail bounds	Arlington	Insolvent	1814	ID2:331
Cooke, Stephen	Alexandria	Occupant	1795	Tax L 1795:31
Cooke, Stephen	Alexandria	Tax Charge	1795	Tax PP 1795:05
Cooke, Stephen	Alexandria	Tax Charge	1798	Tax PP 1798:03
Cooke, Stephen	Alexandria	Tax Charge	1799	Tax PP 1799:07
Cooke, Stephen	Alexandria	Tax Charge	1800	Tax PP 1800:04
Cooke, Stephen, def.	Alexandria	Suit	1802	CRC:170
Cooke, Stephen, Fairfax St.	Alexandria	Owner	1795	Tax L 1795:06
Cooke, Stephen, King St.	Alexandria	Owner	1795	Tax L 1795:05
Cooke, Stephen, King St.	Alexandria	Owner	1795	Tax L 1795:06(3)
Cooke, Stephen, plt.	Alexandria	Suit	1801	CRB:259
Cooke, Stephen, plt.	Alexandria	Suit	1802	CRB:220
Cooke, Thomas	Alexandria	Deposition	1801	CRE:252
Cooke, Thomas	Alexandria	Deposition	1801	CRE:285
Cooke, Thomas	Arlington	Apprentice	1822	OCR1822:008a
Cooke, Thomas, plt.	Alexandria	Suit	1801	CRD:178
Cooke, Thomas, plt.	Alexandria	Suit	1807	CRF:131
Cooke, Thos., merchant	Alexandria	Housekeeper	1808	1808(4):27A
Cookes & Spilman, plt.	Alexandria	Suit	1807	CRF:131
Coombs, John	Alexandria	Tax Charge	1790	Tax PP 1790:03
Coombs, Joseph	Arlington	Defendant	1802	PA:268
Coombs, Levi	Alexandria	Tithable +16	1788	Tax PP 1788:18
Coombs, Levi	Alexandria	Tithable +16	1789	Tax PP 1789:21
Cooney, John	Alexandria	Will	1878	WB1:236; LP
Cooney, Joseph	Arlington	Apprentice	1842	OCR1842:013
Cooney, Joseph	Alexandria	Will	1876	WB1:189; LP
Coons, Mary	Arlington	Guard.	1804	WBA:314
Coons, Peggey	Alexandria	Resident	1800	1800(4):03B
Coons, Peggy	Alexandria	Boarder	1800	1800(4):03A
Cooper, Alexander	Alexandria	Tax Charge	1787	Tax PP 1787:03
Cooper, Alexander	Alexandria	Tax Charge	1788	Tax PP 1788:02
Cooper, Alexr., Water St.	Alexandria	Occupant	1787	Tax L 1787:01
Cooper, David	Alexandria	Tax Charge	1796	Tax LP 1796:05
Cooper, David, seaman	Alexandria	Head	1810	1810(2):04A
Cooper, Edwd.	Alexandria	Tax Charge	1795	Tax PP 1795:05
Cooper, Edwd. (C), sailor	Alexandria	Housekeeper	1808	1808(1):05A

NAME OR SUBJECT	LOCATION	TYPE	YEAR	REFERENCE(S)
Cooper, Eliza., Cameron St.	Alexandria	Owner	1790	Tax L 1790:03
Cooper, George	Alexandria	Tax Charge	1788	Tax PP 1788:03
Cooper, George	Alexandria	Tax Charge	1789	Tax PP 1789:04
Cooper, George	Alexandria	Tax Charge	1790	Tax PP 1790:02
Cooper, George, Queen St.	Alexandria	Occupant	1790	Tax L 1790:09
Cooper, Jacob	Alexandria	Will	1891	WB1:587; LP
Cooper, Jno., Royal St.	Alexandria	Owner	1795	Tax L 1795:05
Cooper, Jno., Royal St.	Alexandria	Occupant	1795	Tax L 1795:05
Cooper, Joel, Estate	Alexandria	Owner	1787	Tax L 1787:08
Cooper, Joel, Estate	Alexandria	Tax Charge	1796	Tax LP 1796:04
Cooper, Joel, Estate, Fairfax St.	Alexandria	Owner	1790	Tax L 1790:02
Cooper, Joseph	Arlington	Ordinary	1807	OBL2(np)
Cooper, Joseph	Arlington	Ordinary	1809	OBL2(np)
Cooper, Joseph	Arlington	Ordinary	1810	OBL2(np)
Cooper, Joseph, at Ramsay's wharf	Arlington	Ordinary	1822	OBL3(np)
Cooper, Joseph, retailer	Alexandria	Housekeeper	1808	1808(2):12A
Cooper, Joseph, tavern keeper	Alexandria	Head	1810	1810(2):08A
Cooper, Julia (C)	Arlington	Apprentice	1826	OCR1822:107a
Cooper, Mrs., Fairfax St.	Alexandria	Occupant	1787	Tax L 1787:08
Cooper, Ned (C)	Alexandria	Tax Charge	1795	Tax PP 1795:04
Cooper, Saml.	Alexandria	Tax Charge	1798	Tax PP 1798:03
Cooper, Saml.	Alexandria	License Due	1800	Tax PP 1800:54(24)
Cooper, Saml., l. bread baker	Alexandria	Housekeeper	1808	1808(1):09A
Cooper, Samuel	Alexandria	Tax Charge	1799	Tax PP 1799:06
Cooper, Samuel	Alexandria	Tax Charge	1800	Tax PP 1800:04
Cooper, Samuel	Alexandria	Deposition	1802	CRI:077
Cooper, Samuel	Arlington	Defendant	1802	PA:284
Cooper, Samuel	Alexandria	Deposition	1808	CRI:088
Cooper, Samuel	Arlington	Admin.	1840	WB4:262
Cooper, Samuel, baker	Alexandria	Head	1810	1810(3):02A
Cooper, Samuel, def.	Alexandria	Suit	1803	CRD:078
Cooper, Samuel, grantor	Arlington	Indenture D.	1804	ID3:056
Cooper, Samuel, in jail bounds	Arlington	Insolvent	1804	ID3:049
Cooper, Spencer	Arlington	Ordinary	1805	OBL1(np)
Cooper, Thomas, c/o John	Arlington	Apprentice	1805	OCR1801:304
Cooper, William	Arlington	Sale	1819	AB3:365
Cooper, William	Arlington	Inventory	1819	AB3:363; LVA-LP
Cooper, William	Arlington	Will (N)	1819	WB2:319
Cooper, William	Arlington	Account	1820	AB4:176; LVA-LP
Cooper, William	Arlington	Sale	1826	AB6:186; LVA-LP
Coote v. Cole's Exor.	Arlington	Suit	1845	LVA-LP (Box 214)
Copper, Cyrus	Arlington	Admin.	1803	WBA:135
Copper, Cyrus, Estate	Alexandria	Owner	1787	Tax L 1787:08
Copper, Cyrus, Estate	Alexandria	Tax Charge	1796	Tax LP 1796:04
Copper, Cyrus, Estate, market	Alexandria	Owner	1795	Tax L 1795:04
Copper, Cyrus, Estate, Oronoko St.	Alexandria	Owner	1795	Tax L 1795:04
Copper, Cyrus, Estate, Union St.	Alexandria	Owner	1795	Tax L 1795:04
Copper, Tho.	Alexandria	Tax Charge	1795	Tax PP 1795:05
Copper, Thomas	Alexandria	Tax Charge	1787	Tax PP 1787:03
Copper, Thomas	Alexandria	Tax Charge	1788	Tax PP 1788:03
Copper, Thomas	Alexandria	Tax Charge	1789	Tax PP 1789:03
Copper, Thomas	Alexandria	Tax Charge	1796	Tax PP 1796:03
Copper, Thomas	Alexandria	Tax Charge	1799	Tax PP 1799:07
Copper, Thomas	Alexandria	Tax Charge	1800	Tax PP 1800:04
Copper, Thomas & wife, mariner	Alexandria	Head	1795	1795(4):01
Copper, Thomas, Union St.	Alexandria	Occupant	1790	Tax L 1790:04
Corbett, Frank E.	Alexandria	Will	1897	WB2:212; LP
Corbett, Frank E.	Arlington	Will	1899	WB10:380; File #788A
Corbett, Isaiah	Alexandria	Tithable +16	1788	Tax PP 1788:04
Corbett, Jane A.	Arlington	Will	1883	WB10:033; File #709A
Corbett, Lawrence W.	Alexandria	Will	1897	WB2:179; LP

NAME OR SUBJECT	LOCATION	TYPE	YEAR	REFERENCE(S)
Corbett, Virgil P.	Arlington	Appraisal	1875	WB9:375
Corbett, Zach.	Alexandria	Tax Charge	1795	Tax PP 1795:05
Corbett, Zachariah	Alexandria	Tithable +16	1789	Tax PP 1789:05
Corbett, Zachariah	Alexandria	Tithable +16	1790	Tax PP 1790:03
Corell, George, house carpenter	Alexandria	Head	1800	1800(4):05A
Cornwall, Conn	Alexandria	Tax Charge	1795	Tax PP 1795:04
Cornwall, William	Alexandria	Tax Charge	1788	Tax PP 1788:03
Cornwell, William	Alexandria	Tax Charge	1790	Tax PP 1790:03
Correll, George & wife Nancey	Alexandria	Resident	1800	1800(4):05B
Correll, Mary	Alexandria	Resident	1800	1800(4):05B
Correll, Mary, seamster	Alexandria	Boarder	1800	1800(4):05A
Corryell, George	Alexandria	Tax Charge	1800	Tax PP 1800:04
Corryton, Joseph	Alexandria	Tax Charge	1795	Tax PP 1795:05
Corryton, Josiah	Alexandria	Tax Charge	1796	Tax LP 1796:04
Corryton, Josiah	Alexandria	Tax Charge	1796	Tax PP 1796:03
Corse, Elizabeth, w/o Montgomery D.	Alexandria	Will	1895	WB2:108; LP
Corse, Jno.	Alexandria	Boarder	1808	1808(4):25A
Corse, John	Arlington	Will P.	1845	OCR1842:155
Corse, John	Arlington	Will	1845	WB4:412; File #432A
Corse, John	Arlington	Account	1846	AB9:274; LVA-LP
Corse, John	Arlington	Debts Due	1846	AB9:164
Corse, John	Arlington	Inventory	1846	AB9:162; LVA-LP
Corse, John	Arlington	Account	1847	AB9:274
Corse, John	Arlington	Petition	1847	LVA-LP (Box 214)
Corse, John	Arlington	Will P.	1847	OCR1842:200
Corse, John, grantee	Arlington	Indenture D.	1827	ID:144
Corse, John, grantee	Arlington	Indenture D.	1831	ID:321
Coryel, George	Alexandria	Tax Charge	1796	Tax PP 1796:04
Coryell, Geo.	Alexandria	Tax Charge	1795	Tax PP 1795:05
Coryell, Geo.	Alexandria	Tax Charge	1798	Tax PP 1798:02
Coryell, Geo. & wife	Alexandria	Housekeeper	1799	1799(2):15A
Coryell, Geo., assessor	Alexandria	Housekeeper	1808	1808(1):08A
Coryell, Geo., Duke St.	Alexandria	Occupant	1787	Tax L 1787:08
Coryell, Geo., Duke St.	Alexandria	Occupant	1790	Tax L 1790:03
Coryell, Geo., Duke St.	Alexandria	Occupant	1795	Tax L 1795:04
Coryell, Geo., Duke St.	Alexandria	Occupant	1795	Tax L 1795:01
Coryell, Geo., King St.	Alexandria	Owner	1795	Tax L 1795:05(2)
Coryell, Geo., Union St.	Alexandria	Owner	1795	Tax L 1795:05
Coryell, George	Alexandria	Owner	1787	Tax L 1787:08
Coryell, George	Alexandria	Tax Charge	1787	Tax PP 1787:03
Coryell, George	Alexandria	Tax Charge	1796	Tax LP 1796:04
Coryell, George	Arlington	Bond	1851	BB(np)
Coryell, George	Arlington	Will	1851	WB5:297; File #463A
Coryell, George & wife, merchant	Alexandria	Head	1795	1795(4):03
Coryell, George, Assessor	Alexandria	Head	1810	1810(1):07A
Coryell, George, def.	Alexandria	Suit	1801	CRB:259
Coryell, George, Duke St.	Alexandria	Occupant	1787	Tax L 1787:05
Coryell, George, Duke St.	Alexandria	Owner	1790	Tax L 1790:03
Coryell, George, Duke St.	Alexandria	Owner	1795	Tax L 1795:04
Coryell, George, plt.	Alexandria	Suit	1801	CRB:088
Coryell, Mary	Alexandria	Boarder	1795	1795(4a):03
Coryell, Mary	Alexandria	Boarder	1799	1799(2):15A
Coryton, Ann Eliza, c/o Josiah	Arlington	Guard.	1810	WB1:002
Coryton, Josiah	Alexandria	Tax Charge	1798	Tax PP 1798:03
Coryton, Josiah	Alexandria	Tax Charge	1799	Tax PP 1799:06
Coryton, Josiah & wife, watchmaker	Alexandria	Housekeeper	1799	1799(2):05A
Coryton, Josiah, c/o Josiah	Arlington	Guard.	1810	WB1:002
Coseen, John	Arlington	Will	1837	WB4:138; File #350A
Cosgrove, James, seaman	Alexandria	Head	1810	1810(1):09A
Cosgrove, Jas., retailer	Alexandria	Housekeeper	1808	1808(1):07A
Cosgrove, Lawrence	Alexandria	Tax Charge	1790	Tax PP 1790:03

NAME OR SUBJECT	LOCATION	TYPE	YEAR	REFERENCE(S)
Cotter, Mathew, w(1)1, plasterer	Alexandria	Head	1796	1796(3):1
Cottingham, William	Alexandria	Tax Charge	1788	Tax PP 1788:04
Cottman, Lazarus	Arlington	Apprentice	1805	OCR1801:259
Cottom & Steuart	Alexandria	Tax Charge	1798	Tax PP 1798:03
Cottom & Stewart	Alexandria	Mer. License	1799	Tax PP 1799:52-02r
Cottom & Stewart	Alexandria	Tax Charge	1799	Tax PP 1799:06
Cottom & Stewart	Alexandria	License Due	1800	Tax PP 1800:54(24)
Cottom, Peter	Alexandria	Tax Charge	1800	Tax PP 1800:04
Cottom, Peter, for playing Faro	Arlington	Defendant	1801	PA:078
Couchman, Jacb.	Alexandria	Tax Charge	1795	Tax PP 1795:06
Couchman, Jacob	Alexandria	Tithable +16	1789	Tax PP 1789:03
Couchman, Jacob	Alexandria	Tax Charge	1790	Tax PP 1790:03
Couchman, Jacob	Alexandria	Tax Charge	1799	Tax PP 1799:06
Couchman, Jacob, Prince St.	Alexandria	Occupant	1795	Tax L 1795:11
Couchman, Letitia, washwoman	Alexandria	Housekeeper	1808	1808(1):09A
Couchman, M., spinstress	Alexandria	Head	1810	1810(1):06A
Coudre, Jeremiah	Alexandria	Tax Charge	1788	Tax PP 1788:03
Coulter, Thomas, age 65	Alexandria	Deposition	1767	CRI:255
Coupar, Henry, def.	Alexandria	Suit	1821	CRL:347
Coupar, Robert	Alexandria	Tax Charge	1788	Tax PP 1788:03
Coupar, Robert	Alexandria	Tax Charge	1789	Tax PP 1789:03
Coupar, Robert	Alexandria	Tax Charge	1790	Tax PP 1790:02
Coupar, Robert	Alexandria	Tithable +16	1790	Tax PP 1790:04
Couper, Robert	Alexandria	Tax Charge	1787	Tax PP 1787:03
Couper, Robert, Fairfax St.	Alexandria	Occupant	1790	Tax L 1790:10
Couper, Robert, King St.	Alexandria	Occupant	1787	Tax L 1787:01
Courtney, Jno.	Alexandria	Boarder	1799	1799(2):01A
Courtney, Mary	Alexandria	Boarder	1799	1799(2):01A
Couse, Ann Eliza	Arlington	Guard.	1827	WB3:283
Coutney, Sarah	Arlington	Fid. Bond	1853	FBB(np)
Coutsman, Jacob	Alexandria	Tithable +16	1788	Tax PP 1788:03
Covert, Eli	Arlington	Apprentice	1825	OCR1822:097a
Cowing, Joseph, schoolmaster	Alexandria	Housekeeper	1808	1808(3):20A
Cowing, William, b. New Castle, Eng.	Arlington	Alien Entry	1823	RA:08/07/23
Cowling, Richard	Alexandria	Will	1893	WB2:056; LP
Cowman, Andrew E.	Arlington	Suit	1860	LVA-LP
Cowper, Samuel	Alexandria	Tax Charge	1796	Tax PP 1796:03
Cox, Capt., Prince St.	Alexandria	Occupant	1787	Tax L 1787:25
Cox, Caroline	Alexandria	Will	1891	WB1:596; LP
Cox, Elisha	Alexandria	Tithable +16	1790	Tax PP 1790:13
Cox, George	Alexandria	Tithable +16	1788	Tax PP 1788:04
Cox, George	Alexandria	Tax Charge	1789	Tax PP 1789:03
Cox, George	Alexandria	Tithable +16	1790	Tax PP 1790:03
Cox, Jacob	Alexandria	Owner	1787	Tax L 1787:09
Cox, Jacob	Alexandria	Tax Charge	1787	Tax PP 1787:04
Cox, Jacob	Alexandria	Tax Charge	1788	Tax PP 1788:04
Cox, Jacob	Alexandria	Tax Charge	1789	Tax PP 1789:03
Cox, Jacob	Alexandria	Tax Charge	1790	Tax PP 1790:03
Cox, Jacob	Alexandria	Tax Charge	1795	Tax PP 1795:06
Cox, Jacob	Alexandria	Tax Charge	1796	Tax LP 1796:04
Cox, Jacob	Alexandria	Tax Charge	1796	Tax PP 1796:03
Cox, Jacob	Alexandria	Resident	1800	1800(4):16B
Cox, Jacob & Co., Wilks St.	Alexandria	Occupant	1787	Tax L 1787:03
Cox, Jacob, Fairfax St.	Alexandria	Owner	1795	Tax L 1795:04
Cox, Jacob, gentleman	Alexandria	Head	1795	1795(4a):06
Cox, Jacob, tobacconist	Alexandria	Head	1795	1795(4):04
Cox, Jacob, tobacness	Alexandria	Head	1800	1800(4):16A
Cox, Jacob, Water St.	Alexandria	Owner	1795	Tax L 1795:04
Cox, Jacob, Wilkes St.	Alexandria	Owner	1790	Tax L 1790:03
Cox, Jacob, Wilkes St.	Alexandria	Occupant	1790	Tax L 1790:03
Cox, Jacob, Wilks St.	Alexandria	Occupant	1787	Tax L 1787:09

NAME OR SUBJECT	LOCATION	TYPE	YEAR	REFERENCE(S)
Cox, Jacob, Wilks St.	Alexandria	Occupant	1795	Tax L 1795:04
Cox, Jacob, Wilks St.	Alexandria	Owner	1795	Tax L 1795:04(2)
Cox, James S., of Philadelphia	Alexandria	Deed	1811	CRK:045, 048
Cox, Jesse	Alexandria	Tax Charge	1799	Tax PP 1799:06
Cox, Jesse	Alexandria	Tax Charge	1800	Tax PP 1800:05
Cox, Jessey & wife Nancey	Alexandria	Resident	1800	1800(4):11B
Cox, Jessey, marrener	Alexandria	Head	1800	1800(4):11A
Cox, Samuel	Arlington	Admin.	1827	OCR1822:134
Cox, Samuel	Arlington	Admin.	1827	WB3:282
Cox, Samuel	Arlington	Account	1832	AB7:141; LVA-LP
Cox, Samuel	Arlington	Account	1835	AB7:141
Cox, Thomas	Alexandria	Tithable +16	1789	Tax PP 1789:03
Cox, Walter	Alexandria	Boarder	1808	1808(2):10A
Cox, William	Alexandria	Tithable +16	1788	Tax PP 1788:06
Cox, William	Alexandria	Tithable +16	1789	Tax PP 1789:17
Coxall, Charles Henry	Arlington	Apprentice	1812	OCR1811:104
Coxe, Willm. & wife, mariner	Alexandria	Housekeeper	1799	1799(2):20A
Coynton, Catharine	Arlington	Appraisal	1866	WB8:381
Crab, Charles & wife & 2 children (C)	Alexandria	Boarder	1799	1799(2):20A
Cracroft, Elizabeth, gentlewoman	Alexandria	Housekeeper	1808	1808(1):04A
Craddock, Edmond	Arlington	Admin.	1820	WB2:389
Craddock, Edmund	Alexandria	Tax Charge	1789	Tax PP 1789:03
Craddock, Edmund	Alexandria	Tax Charge	1790	Tax PP 1790:03
Crafford, Thos., Princess St.	Alexandria	Occupant	1795	Tax L 1795:12
Crager, Lawrence & wife	Alexandria	Boarder	1799	1799(2):04A
Craig, Catharine	Arlington	Sale	1829	LVA-LP
Craig, Edward, c/o Charles	Arlington	Payment	(nd)	LVA-LP
Craig, George, c/o Charles	Arlington	Payment	(nd)	LVA-LP
Craig, Henry, c/o Charles	Arlington	Payment	(nd)	LVA-LP
Craig, James, M.D.	Alexandria	Tax Charge	1800	Tax PP 1800:05
Craig, James, w(2)3, doctor	Alexandria	Head	1796	1796(3):6
Craig, John	Alexandria	Tax Charge	1796	Tax PP 1796:03
Craig, John	Alexandria	Boarder	1808	1808(1):08A
Craig, John H.	Arlington	Apprentice	1827	OCR1822:146a
Craig, John H., c/o Charles	Arlington	Payment	(nd)	LVA-LP
Craig, Robert, Fairfax St.	Alexandria	Occupant	1787	Tax L 1787:05
Craig, Sam., Fairfax St.	Alexandria	Occupant	1795	Tax L 1795:16
Craig, Saml.	Alexandria	Tax Charge	1795	Tax PP 1795:04
Craig, Saml.	Alexandria	Tax Charge	1796	Tax LP 1796:05
Craig, Saml.	Alexandria	Tax Charge	1796	Tax LP 1796:04
Craig, Saml.	Alexandria	Tax Charge	1796	Tax PP 1796:03
Craig, Saml.	Alexandria	Tax Charge	1798	Tax PP 1798:03
Craig, Saml. & wife, merchant	Alexandria	Housekeeper	1799	1799(2):04A
Craig, Saml., merchant	Alexandria	Housekeeper	1808	1808(1):08A
Craig, Saml., Prince St.	Alexandria	Owner	1795	Tax L 1795:06
Craig, Samuel	Alexandria	Tithable +16	1788	Tax PP 1788:04
Craig, Samuel	Alexandria	Mer. License	1798	Tax PP 1798:20-2
Craig, Samuel	Alexandria	Tax Charge	1799	Tax PP 1799:07
Craig, Samuel	Alexandria	Mer. License	1799	Tax PP 1799:52-02w
Craig, Samuel	Alexandria	Mer. License	1800	Tax PP 1800:54(11)w
Craig, Samuel	Alexandria	Tax Charge	1800	Tax PP 1800:04
Craig, Samuel	Arlington	Inventory	1808	LP
Craig, Samuel	Arlington	Inventory	1808	WBC:051
Craig, Samuel	Arlington	Will	1808	WBC:032; File #037A
Craig, Samuel	Arlington	Bond	1808	WBC:040
Craig, Samuel	Arlington	Sale	1809	WBC:168
Craig, Samuel	Arlington	Account	1809	WBC:214; LVA-LP
Craig, Samuel	Arlington	Debts	1809	WBC:171
Craig, Samuel	Arlington	Account	1812	AB1:222; LVA-LP
Craig, Samuel	Arlington	Account	1814	AB2:033; LVA-LP
Craig, Samuel	Arlington	Account	1818	AB3:205; LVA-LP

NAME OR SUBJECT	LOCATION	TYPE	YEAR	REFERENCE(S)
Craig, Samuel	Arlington	Account	1819	AB3:387; LVA-LP
Craig, Samuel	Arlington	Account	1828	AB6:458; LVA-LP
Craig, Samuel, Estate, def.	Alexandria	Suit	1809	CRG:121, 128
Craig, Samuel, plt.	Alexandria	Suit	1801	CRB:056
Craig, Samuel, Prince St.	Alexandria	Occupant	1795	Tax L 1795:06
Craig, Samuel, w2, merchant	Alexandria	Head	1796	1796(3):4
Craigg, Samuel	Alexandria	Tax Charge	1789	Tax PP 1789:04
Craik, Charles	Alexandria	Tithable +16	1788	Tax PP 1788:18
Craik, Doctr. & Co., Fairfax St.	Alexandria	Occupant	1787	Tax L 1787:17
Craik, Geo. W., postmaster	Alexandria	Housekeeper	1808	1808(4):27A
Craik, Geo. Washington	Alexandria	Boarder	1800	1800(4):05A
Craik, George Washington	Alexandria	Resident	1800	1800(4):05B
Craik, George Washington	Arlington	Inventory	1809	LVA-LP
Craik, George Washington	Arlington	Appraisal	1809	WBC:209
Craik, George Washington	Arlington	Will	1809	WBC:175; File #042A
Craik, George Washington	Arlington	Bond	1809	WBC:176
Craik, George Washington	Arlington	Account	1810	WBC:434; LVA-LP
Craik, J., Fairfax St.	Alexandria	Occupant	1787	Tax L 1787:22
Craik, James	Alexandria	Tax Charge	1787	Tax PP 1787:03
Craik, James	Alexandria	Tax Charge	1788	Tax PP 1788:03
Craik, James	Alexandria	Tax Charge	1796	Tax LP 1796:04
Craik, James	Alexandria	Tax Charge	1799	Tax PP 1799:06
Craik, James	Arlington	Account	1803	LVA-LP
Craik, James	Arlington	Account	1809	LVA-LP
Craik, James & wife Mariamne	Alexandria	Resident	1800	1800(4):05B
Craik, James, doctor	Alexandria	Head	1800	1800(4):05A
Craik, James, Dr.	Alexandria	Tax Charge	1789	Tax PP 1789:03
Craik, James, Jr.	Alexandria	Tax Charge	1787	Tax PP 1787:03
Craik, James, Jr.	Alexandria	Tax Charge	1788	Tax PP 1788:03
Craik, James, Jr.	Alexandria	Tithable +16	1789	Tax PP 1789:03
Craik, James, Jr.	Arlington	Settlement	1803	WBA:128
Craik, James, M.D.	Alexandria	Tax Charge	1796	Tax PP 1796:04
Craik, James, physician	Alexandria	Housekeeper	1808	1808(1):08A
Craik, James, Prince St.	Alexandria	Occupant	1790	Tax L 1790:06
Craik, James, Sr., Dr.	Alexandria	Tax Charge	1790	Tax PP 1790:02
Craik, Jas.	Alexandria	Tax Charge	1795	Tax PP 1795:05
Craik, Jas.	Alexandria	Tax Charge	1798	Tax PP 1798:03
Craik, Jas. & wife, physician	Alexandria	Housekeeper	1799	1799(2):15A
Craik, Jas., Prince St.	Alexandria	Occupant	1795	Tax L 1795:15
Craik, Marianne	Arlington	Will	1815	WB2:056
Craik, Samuel	Alexandria	Tax Charge	1790	Tax PP 1790:02
Craik, Sarah, Water St.	Alexandria	Owner	1795	Tax L 1795:05(4)
Craik, Widow	Alexandria	Tax Charge	1796	Tax LP 1796:05
Craik, William	Arlington	Bond	1807	WBB:478
Craik, William	Arlington	Will	1807	WBB:418; File #28A
Craik, William	Arlington	Inventory	1807	WBB:480; LVA-LP
Craik, William	Arlington	Account	1811	AB1:064
Craik, William	Arlington	Sale	1811	AB1:071
Craik, William	Arlington	Account	1812	AB1:235; LVA-LP
Craik, William	Arlington	Account	1813	AB1:335; LVA-LP
Craik, William, def.	Alexandria	Suit	1801	CRB:239
Craik, William, def.	Alexandria	Suit	1801	CRB:243
Cram, Samuel, grantor	Arlington	Indenture D.	1812	ID2:148
Cram, Samuel, in jail bounds	Arlington	Insolvent	1812	ID2:147
Crammond, William, def.	Alexandria	Suit	1804	CRF:001
Cranch, Richard	Arlington	Admin.	1826	OCR1822:113
Cranch, Richard	Arlington	Admin.	1826	WB3:229
Cranch, William, Chief Judge	Arlington	Letter Patent	1806	ACO:048
Cranch, William, Hon.	Arlington	Letter	1810	ACO:113
Cranch, William, Hon., of ill health	Arlington	Letter	1808	ACO:102
Crandall, Catharine (McKnight), w/o P.	Arlington	Defendant	1842	LSA:082

NAME OR SUBJECT	LOCATION	TYPE	YEAR	REFERENCE(S)
Crandall, Philip	Arlington	Defendant	1842	LSA:082
Crandall, Samuel	Alexandria	Tax Charge	1799	Tax PP 1799:07
Crandall, Thomas	Alexandria	Tax Charge	1799	Tax PP 1799:06
Crandall, Thos.	Alexandria	Tax Charge	1796	Tax PP 1796:03
Crandel, Saml.	Alexandria	Tax Charge	1795	Tax PP 1795:04
Crandel, Samuel	Alexandria	Tax Charge	1800	Tax PP 1800:04
Crandel, Thomas, Union St.	Alexandria	Occupant	1790	Tax L 1790:02
Crandel, Thos.	Alexandria	Tax Charge	1800	Tax PP 1800:04
Crandell, Elizabeth	Arlington	Guard.	1809	WBC:235
Crandell, Elizabeth	Arlington	Guard. Acct.	1812	AB1:273; LVA-LP
Crandell, John	Alexandria	Tax Charge	1790	Tax PP 1790:03
Crandell, Joseph	Arlington	Inventory	1813	AB1:333; LVA-LP
Crandell, Joseph	Arlington	Will	1813	WB1:253; File #112A
Crandell, Joseph	Arlington	Bond	1813	WB1:254
Crandell, Joseph	Arlington	Account	1814	AB2:050; LVA-LP
Crandell, Joseph	Arlington	Account	1814	AB2:073; LVA-LP
Crandell, Joseph	Arlington	Account	1814	AB2:073; LVA-LP
Crandell, Joseph, c/o Thomas	Arlington	Apprentice	1801	OCR1801:001b
Crandell, Joseph, grantee	Arlington	Indenture D.	1812	ID2:139
Crandell, Lemuel	Arlington	Guard.	1810	WBC:423
Crandell, Lemuel	Arlington	Apprentice	1811	OCR1811:038
Crandell, Philip	Arlington	Guard.	1809	WBC:235
Crandell, Philip	Arlington	Guard. Acct.	1812	AB1:271; LVA-LP
Crandell, Saml.	Alexandria	Boarder	1808	1808(1):03A
Crandell, Saml., baker	Alexandria	Boarder	1799	1799(2):01A
Crandell, Saml., Fairfax St.	Alexandria	Occupant	1795	Tax L 1795:03
Crandell, Samuel	Alexandria	Tithable +16	1789	Tax PP 1789:03
Crandell, Sarah, gentlewoman	Alexandria	Housekeeper	1808	1808(1):03A
Crandell, Susan	Arlington	Guard. Acct.	1812	AB1:273; LVA-LP
Crandell, Susannah	Arlington	Guard.	1809	WBC:236
Crandell, Thomas	Alexandria	Tax Charge	1788	Tax PP 1788:03
Crandell, Thomas	Alexandria	Tax Charge	1789	Tax PP 1789:03
Crandell, Thomas	Alexandria	Tax Charge	1790	Tax PP 1790:02
Crandell, Thomas	Alexandria	Tax Charge	1796	Tax LP 1796:04
Crandell, Thomas	Arlington	Sale	1806	WBB:359
Crandell, Thomas	Arlington	Inventory	1806	WBB:336, 358; LVA-LP
Crandell, Thomas	Arlington	Admin.	1806	WBB:332
Crandell, Thomas	Arlington	Account	1807	WBB:512; LVA-LP
Crandell, Thomas	Arlington	Account	1811	AB1:040; LVA-LP
Crandell, Thomas, Union St.	Alexandria	Occupant	1790	Tax L 1790:11
Crandell, Thos.	Alexandria	Tax Charge	1795	Tax PP 1795:04
Crandell, Thos.	Alexandria	Mer. License	1798	Tax PP 1798:20-2
Crandell, Thos.	Alexandria	Tax Charge	1798	Tax PP 1798:02
Crandell, Thos. & wife, baker	Alexandria	Housekeeper	1799	1799(2):01A
Crandell, Thos., cooper	Alexandria	Head	1810	1810(2):01A
Crandell, Thos., on the wharf	Alexandria	Occupant	1790	Tax L 1790:01
Crandell, Thos., Union St.	Alexandria	Occupant	1795	Tax L 1795:05
Crandell, Thos., Union St.	Alexandria	Owner	1795	Tax L 1795:05
Cranden, Jno., Oronoko St.	Alexandria	Occupant	1795	Tax L 1795:06
Crandle, Joseph	Arlington	Inventory	1814	AB2:050
Crandle, Thomas, w(7)4, baker	Alexandria	Head	1795	1796(3):7
Crandle, Thomas [Susan]	Arlington	Account	1828	LVA-LP
Crane, Thomas	Alexandria	Tax Charge	1790	Tax PP 1790:02
Cranford, Ign.	Alexandria	Tax Charge	1800	Tax PP 1800:04
Cranford, Jas.	Alexandria	Boarder	1808	1808(2):16A
Cranstill, John	Alexandria	Tithable +16	1789	Tax PP 1789:03
Cranston, Jno.	Alexandria	Tax Charge	1798	Tax PP 1798:03
Cranston, John	Alexandria	Tithable +16	1788	Tax PP 1788:03
Cranston, John	Alexandria	Tax Charge	1799	Tax PP 1799:06
Cranston, John	Alexandria	Tax Charge	1800	Tax PP 1800:04
Cranston, John, baker	Alexandria	Head	1810	1810(2):07A

NAME OR SUBJECT	LOCATION	TYPE	YEAR	REFERENCE(S)
Cranston, John, grantee	Arlington	Indenture D.	1817	ID2:415
Cranston, John, l.b. baker	Alexandria	Housekeeper	1808	1808(2):17A
Craser, A.	Alexandria	Tax Charge	1796	Tax PP 1796:03
Craven, Maris, retailer	Alexandria	Housekeeper	1808	1808(2):10A
Craven, Wiliam, labourer	Alexandria	Head	1810	1810(2):06A
Crawford, Ann, c/o Martha	Arlington	Apprentice	1812	OCR1811:118
Crawford, Ignatius	Alexandria	Tax Charge	1798	Tax PP 1798:03
Crawford, Ignats. (C)	Alexandria	Tax Charge	1795	Tax PP 1795:05
Crawford, James, c/o Ann Moxley	Arlington	Apprentice	1803	OCR1801:124
Crawford, James, in Alexandria Co.	Arlington	Ordinary	1823	OBL3(np)
Crawford, James, plt.	Alexandria	Suit	1804	CRF:067
Crawford, Jno. & wife, hairdresser	Alexandria	Housekeeper	1799	1799(2):01A
Crawford, John, barber	Alexandria	Housekeeper	1808	1808(2):14A
Crawford, John, barber	Alexandria	Head	1810	1810(2):05A
Crawford, Samuel	Alexandria	Tax Charge	1798	Tax PP 1798:02
Crawford, Samuel	Alexandria	Tax Charge	1799	Tax PP 1799:06
Crawford, Sarah, plt.	Alexandria	Suit	1821	CRL:172
Crawford, Thomas, age 64	Alexandria	Deposition	1767	CRI:220
Crawford, Thos.	Alexandria	Tax Charge	1796	Tax LP 1796:05
Crawford, William	Arlington	Apprentice	1815	OCR1811:308
Crawford, William, Estate, plt.	Alexandria	Suit	1821	CRL:172
Crawford, William H.	Arlington	Certificate	1830	ACR:090
Crawford, [blank], shoemaker	Alexandria	Boarder	1799	1799(2):04A
Crawly, Timothy	Alexandria	Tax Charge	1800	Tax PP 1800:04
Craycroft, Ann R.	Arlington	Guard.	1816	WB2:124
Craycroft, Elizabeth	Arlington	Appraisal	1831	LVA-LP
Craycroft, Elizabeth	Arlington	Bond	1831	WB4:032
Craycroft, Elizabeth, boarding house	Alexandria	Head	1810	1810(1):04A
Craycroft, Elizabeth Oland	Arlington	Will	1831	WB4:031; File #314A
Craycroft, Francis	Alexandria	Tax Charge	1798	Tax PP 1798:03
Craycroft, Francis	Arlington	Admin.	1804	WBA:273
Craycroft, Francis	Arlington	Inventory	1804	WBA:322; LVA-LP
Craycroft, Harriet	Arlington	Guard.	1819	WB2:285
Crease & Mandeville	Arlington	Debts Due	1814	AB2:014
Crease, Anthony	Arlington	Inventory	1820	AB4:178; LVA-LP
Crease, Anthony	Arlington	Will	1820	WB2:383; File #100A
Crease, Anthony	Arlington	Sale	1821	AB5:017
Crease, Anthony	Arlington	Account	1821	AB5:020; LVA-LP
Crease, Anthony	Arlington	Defendant	1821	ACO:197
Crease, Anthony	Arlington	Account	1823	AB5:193; LVA-LP
Crease, Anthony	Arlington	Accounts	1824	LVA-LP
Crease, Anthony	Arlington	Account	1825	AB6:106; LVA-LP
Crease, Anthony	Arlington	Account	1827	AB6:426; LVA-LP
Crease, Anthony	Arlington	Account	1836	LVA-LP
Crease, Anthony	Arlington	Admin.	1838	WB4:164, 273; LVA-LP
Crease, Anthony	Arlington	Admin. Bond	1849	ABB(np)
Crease, Anthony	Arlington	Exor. Bond	1849	EBB(np)
Crease, Anthony, b. Falmouth	Arlington	Alien Entry	1809	RA:20/04/09
Crease, Anthony, clerk	Alexandria	Boarder	1799	1799(2):02A
Crease, Anthony, Jr.	Arlington	Libellant	1812	ACO:122
Crease, Anthony, Jr.	Arlington	Inventory	1815	AB2:100; LVA-LP
Crease, Anthony, Jr.	Arlington	Sale	1815	AB2:138
Crease, Anthony, Jr.	Arlington	Libellant	1815	ACO:143
Crease, Anthony, Jr.	Arlington	Account	1816	AB2:286
Creese, Anthony, Jr., merchant	Alexandria	Head	1810	1810(3):07A
Creese, John	Alexandria	Boarder	1808	1808(4):25A
Creighton & Bodkin	Arlington	Sale	1851	WB6:021; LVA-LP
Creighton & Bodkin	Arlington	Account	1853	LVA-LP
Creighton, John, grantee	Arlington	Indenture D.	1827	ID:125
Creighton, Mary	Alexandria	Will	1895	WB2:109; LP
Creighton, Thomas B.	Arlington	Trustee Acct.	1853	WB6:291; LVA-LP

NAME OR SUBJECT	LOCATION	TYPE	YEAR	REFERENCE(S)
Creighton, Vernon, master	Arlington	Suit	1803	ACO:022
Cressey, Anthony	Alexandria	Boarder	1808	1808(3):20A
Crevel, John, shopkeeper	Alexandria	Housekeeper	1808	1808(1):03A
Crew, Jane, c/o Solomon (9)	Arlington	Alien Entry	1818	RA:30/11/18
Crivel, John, rigger	Alexandria	Head	1810	1810(1):06A
Croachman, Jacob & wife, blacksmith	Alexandria	Housekeeper	1799	1799(2):09A
Crocker, Ellen H.	Arlington	Will	1898	WB10:347; File #779A
Crocker, Francis Platt	Arlington	Will	1873	WB9:351; File #686A
Crocker, Francis Platt	Arlington	Inventory	1873	WB9:354
Crocker, Lott W.	Arlington	Will	1876	WB9:386; File #695A
Crofford, John	Alexandria	Tax Charge	1800	Tax PP 1800:04
Croggen, Tho.	Alexandria	Tax Charge	1795	Tax PP 1795:04
Croggon, Charles S., c/o Thomas (16)	Arlington	Alien Entry	1817	RA:27/12/17
Croggon, Isaac N., c/o Thomas (8)	Arlington	Alien Entry	1817	RA:27/12/17
Croggon, John, b. Cornwall	Arlington	Alien Entry	1817	RA:22/12/17
Croggon, Samuel, c/o Thomas (11)	Arlington	Alien Entry	1817	RA:27/12/17
Croggon, Thomas, b. Cornwall	Arlington	Alien Entry	1817	RA:27/12/17
Croggon, Thomas, c/o Thomas (17)	Arlington	Alien Entry	1817	RA:27/12/17
Croggon, William, c/o Thomas (20)	Arlington	Alien Entry	1817	RA:27/12/17
Crohan, Matthew	Alexandria	Tax Charge	1787	Tax PP 1787:03
Cromwell, Jesse	Arlington	Ordinary	1820	OBL3(np)
Cromwell, Troy	Alexandria	Will	1887	WB1:462; LP
Crook, Bernard	Alexandria	Tax Charge	1799	Tax PP 1799:06
Crook, Bernard	Alexandria	Tax Charge	1800	Tax PP 1800:04
Crook, Bernard	Arlington	Inventory	1819	AB3:366; LVA-LP
Crook, Bernard	Arlington	Will	1819	WB2:324; File #167A
Crook, Bernard	Arlington	Account	1821	AB4:196
Crook, Bernard	Arlington	Admin.	1840	WB4:276
Crook, Bernard	Arlington	Inventory	1841	AB8:183; LVA-LP
Crook, Bernard	Arlington	Account	1842	LVA-LP
Crook, Bernard, c/o Bernard	Arlington	Guard.	1820	WB2:399
Crook, Bernard C.	Arlington	Defendant	1841	LSA:062
Crook, Bernard, children of	Arlington	Defendants	1841	LSA:062
Crook, Bernard, stone cutter	Alexandria	Head	1810	1810(4):01A
Crook, Bernard, stonecutter	Alexandria	Housekeeper	1808	1808(4):26A
Crook, Charles	Arlington	Defendant	1841	LSA:062
Crook, Elizabeth, c/o Bernard	Arlington	Guard.	1820	WB2:399
Crook, Ellen	Arlington	Defendant	1841	LSA:062
Crook, George, heirs of	Arlington	Defendants	1841	LSA:062
Crook, Joseph	Arlington	Defendant	1841	LSA:062
Crook, Joseph, c/o Bernard	Arlington	Guard.	1820	WB2:399
Crook, Priscilla, c/o Bernard	Arlington	Guard.	1820	WB2:399
Crook, Robt.	Alexandria	Tax Charge	1798	Tax PP 1798:03
Crook, William, shoemaker	Alexandria	Head	1810	1810(4):07A
Crook, Wm.	Alexandria	Boarder	1808	1808(1):01A
Crooke, Robert	Arlington	Admin.	1815	WB2:084
Crookes, Robert	Arlington	Inventory	1815	LVA-LP
Crosbey, Winey	Alexandria	Serv./Appt.	1800	1800(4):15B
Crosbey, Winney, laundress	Alexandria	Head	1800	1800(4):15A
Crosby, Andrew D.	Arlington	Admin.	1847	OCR1842:200
Crosby, Jesse	Arlington	Will	1804	WBB:102; LVA-LP
Crosby, Laurence	Alexandria	Tithable +16	1789	Tax PP 1789:07
Crosby, Lawrence	Alexandria	Tithable +16	1788	Tax PP 1788:06
Crosby, Winny (C)	Alexandria	Housekeeper	1799	1799(2):19A
Cross, Antonia	Arlington	Ordinary	1809	OBL2(np)
Cross, Reid	Arlington	Bond	1851	BB(np)
Cross, Reid	Arlington	Inventory	1851	WB5:309; LVA-LP
Cross, Reid	Arlington	Will	1851	WB5:304; File #465A
Cross, Reid	Arlington	Account	1852	WB6:092; LVA-LP
Cross, Reid	Arlington	Account	1856	WB7:071; LVA-LP
Cross, Richard Y.	Arlington	Will	1860	WB8:020; File #577A

NAME OR SUBJECT	LOCATION	TYPE	YEAR	REFERENCE(S)
Cross, Richard Y.	Arlington	Account	1862	WB8:125
Cross, Richard Y.	Arlington	Account	1868	WB9:140
Cross, Samuel, in jail	Arlington	Insolvent	1806	ID3:273
Cross, Sarah W.	Arlington	Will	1865	WB8:273; File #633A
Cross, Sarah W.	Arlington	Account	1870	WB9:287
Cross, William	Arlington	Apprentice	1822	OCR1822:006a
Crossby, Jesse	Alexandria	Boarder	1799	1799(2):05A
Crossly, William, seaman	Alexandria	Head	1810	1810(2):08A
Crossman, Isaac	Arlington	Will; Plat	1900	WB10:462; File #805A
Crouder, John Thomas	Arlington	Apprentice	1826	OCR1822:115a
Crout, William	Alexandria	Tax Charge	1799	Tax PP 1799:06
Crout, Wm. & wife	Alexandria	Housekeeper	1799	1799(2):14A
Crow, Lanty	Alexandria	Tax Charge	1796	Tax LP 1796:05
Crow, Lanty	Alexandria	Tax Charge	1800	Tax PP 1800:04
Crowdhill, James	Arlington	Sale	1820	AB4:117
Crowdhill, James	Arlington	Inventory	1820	AB4:114, 119; LVA-LP
Crowdhill, James	Arlington	Account	1821	AB4:210
Crowdhill, James	Arlington	Admin.	1833	WB4:084
Crowdhill, Jas., sea captain	Alexandria	Boarder	1799	1799(2):02A
Crowdhill, John	Arlington	Account	1827	AB6:433; LVA-LP
Crowdill, James, Capt.	Arlington	Will	1820	WB2:396; File #182A
Crowdill [Croudhill], James, Capt.	Arlington	Will	1819	WB2:322
Crowe, Lanty	Alexandria	Tithable +16	1788	Tax PP 1788:11
Crowe, Lanty	Alexandria	Tax Charge	1789	Tax PP 1789:03
Crowe, Lanty	Alexandria	Tax Charge	1790	Tax PP 1790:02
Crowe, Lanty	Alexandria	Tax Charge	1795	Tax PP 1795:04
Crowe, Lanty	Alexandria	Tax Charge	1796	Tax PP 1796:03
Crowe, Lanty	Alexandria	Tax Charge	1798	Tax PP 1798:03
Crowe, Lanty	Alexandria	Tax Charge	1799	Tax PP 1799:07
Crowe, Lanty, Fairfax St.	Alexandria	Occupant	1790	Tax L 1790:02
Crowe, Lanty S.	Alexandria	Tithable +21	1787	Tax PP 1787:10
Crowley, David	Alexandria	Tax Charge	1790	Tax PP 1790:03
Crowley, John, c/o Timothy	Arlington	Apprentice	1803	OCR1801:103
Crowley, Tim.	Alexandria	Tax Charge	1798	Tax PP 1798:03
Crowley, Timothy	Alexandria	Tax Charge	1796	Tax PP 1796:03
Crowley, Timothy	Alexandria	Tax Charge	1799	Tax PP 1799:06
Crowley, Timothy & wife, ship builder	Alexandria	Head	1795	1795(4a):06
Crowley, Timothy & wife Mary	Alexandria	Resident	1800	1800(4):02B
Crowley, Timothy, ship carpenter	Alexandria	Head	1800	1800(4):02A
Crowly, Timothy & wife, mariner	Alexandria	Head	1795	1795(4):04
Crowly, Timothy & wife, ship builder	Alexandria	Housekeeper	1799	1799(2):16A
Crowner, Arthur, tanner	Alexandria	Boarder	1799	1799(2):12A
Crowse, John	Alexandria	Tax Charge	1800	Tax PP 1800:04
Croxall, Mary	Alexandria	Housekeeper	1799	1799(2):08A
Cruit, Robert, of Washington DC	Arlington	Will	1862	WB8:103; File #590A
Crump, Ann E., w/o James T.	Arlington	Will	1865	WB8:251; File #628A
Cruse, Anthony	Alexandria	Boarder	1808	1808(3):19A
Cruse, Geo., tanner	Alexandria	Head	1810	1810(4):08A
Cruse, Thomas	Alexandria	Mer. License	1799	Tax PP 1799:52-02r
Cruse, Thomas	Arlington	Will (NR)	1832	File #316A
Cruse, Thomas, def.	Alexandria	Suit	1801	CRC:082
Cruse, Thos.	Alexandria	Tax Charge	1800	Tax PP 1800:04
Cruse, Thos.	Alexandria	License Due	1800	Tax PP 1800:54(24)
Cruse, Thos., brewer & storekeeper	Alexandria	Housekeeper	1808	1808(2):15A
Cruse, Thos., merchant	Alexandria	Head	1810	1810(2):04A
Cryer, Ben	Alexandria	Head	1810	1810(4):09A
Cryse, Fredk.	Alexandria	Boarder	1808	1808(3):21A
Cryss, Frederick, grantee	Arlington	Indenture D.	1814	ID2:348
Culean, Barthewmey, servant	Alexandria	Boarder	1800	1800(4):08A
Cullen, Barthewmey	Alexandria	Resident	1800	1800(4):08B
Cullin, Daniel, b. Wexford	Arlington	Alien Entry	1819	RA:02/07/19

NAME OR SUBJECT	LOCATION	TYPE	YEAR	REFERENCE(S)
Cullinane, Patrick	Arlington	Will	1885	WB10:064; File #717A
Cummings, Richard	Arlington	Sale	1814	AB2:035
Cummings, Richard	Alexandria	Will	1814	CRI:460
Cummings, Richard	Arlington	Admin.	1814	WB1:280
Cummings, Richard	Arlington	Bond	1814	WB1:287
Cummings, Richard	Arlington	Will	1814	WB2:019; File #127A
Cummings, Richard	Arlington	Account	1816	AB2:308; LVA-LP
Cummings, Richard	Arlington	Account	1817	AB2:410; LVA-LP
Cummings, Richard	Arlington	Account F.	1818	AB3:159; LVA-LP
Cummings, Richard, applt.	Alexandria	Suit	1814	CRK:001
Cummings, Richard, Estate, def.	Alexandria	Suit	1814	CRI:459
Cummings, Richd., shopkeeper	Alexandria	Housekeeper	1808	1808(3):20A
Cummins, Richard, shop keeper	Alexandria	Head	1810	1810(3):02A
Cummins, Wm.	Alexandria	Tax Charge	1795	Tax PP 1795:04
Cunnigan, Silvey (C), laundress	Alexandria	Head	1800	1800(4):11A
Cunningham, Bogle & Findlay, plt.	Alexandria	Suit	1802	CRB:168
Cunningham, Henry	Alexandria	Tithable +21	1787	Tax PP 1787:03
Cunningham, Robert G.	Arlington	Will	1895	WB10:298; File #764A
Cunningham, Thos.	Alexandria	Boarder	1808	1808(2):16A
Cunningham, William, plt.	Alexandria	Suit	1802	CRB:168
Cunningham, Wm.	Alexandria	Tax Charge	1787	Tax PP 1787:04
Currell, George	Alexandria	Tax Charge	1788	Tax PP 1788:04
Currell, George	Alexandria	Tax Charge	1789	Tax PP 1789:03
Currey, Mathias, c/o Jane	Arlington	Apprentice	1816	OCR1811:339
Currey, Thomas Reid, c/o Patrick	Arlington	Apprentice	1812	OCR1811:095
Currie, Patrick, carpenter	Alexandria	Housekeeper	1808	1808(3):22A
Curry, Anthony, seaman	Alexandria	Head	1810	1810(3):09A
Curry, James	Alexandria	Tax Charge	1800	Tax PP 1800:04
Curry, James, coppersmith	Alexandria	Head	1810	1810(2):08A
Curry, Jas.	Alexandria	Boarder	1808	1808(2):11A
Curry, Jas., tinman	Alexandria	Housekeeper	1808	1808(2):15A
Curry, Patrick	Alexandria	Tax Charge	1795	Tax PP 1795:04
Curry, Patrick	Alexandria	Tax Charge	1796	Tax LP 1796:05
Curry, Patrick	Alexandria	Tax Charge	1796	Tax PP 1796:03
Curry, Patrick	Alexandria	Tax Charge	1798	Tax PP 1798:02
Curry, Patrick	Alexandria	Tax Charge	1799	Tax PP 1799:07
Curry, Patrick, house joiner	Alexandria	Head	1810	1810(3):08A
Curson, Peter, clerk	Alexandria	Boarder	1799	1799(2):18A
Curtain, Daniel	Alexandria	Tax Charge	1795	Tax PP 1795:05
Curtain, Daniel	Alexandria	Tax Charge	1796	Tax PP 1796:03
Curtain, Daniel	Arlington	Account	1812	AB1:169; LVA-LP
Curtain, Daniel	Arlington	Account	1813	AB1:301; LVA-LP
Curten, Daniel	Alexandria	Tax Charge	1798	Tax PP 1798:02
Curten, Daniel	Alexandria	Tax Charge	1799	Tax PP 1799:06
Curtin, Daniel	Arlington	Will	1800	CRA:312
Curtin, Daniel	Arlington	Sale	1800	WBA:041
Curtin, Daniel	Arlington	Inventory	1800	WBA:039
Curtin, Daniel	Arlington	Account	1800	WBA:044; LVA-LP
Curtin, Daniel	Arlington	Settlement	1801	WBA:063
Curtin, Daniel	Arlington	Account	1805	WBB:212; LVA-LP
Curtin, Daniel	Arlington	Sale	1806	WBB:364; LVA-LP
Curtin, Daniel	Arlington	Account	1807	WBB:510; LVA-LP
Curtin, Daniel	Arlington	Account	1809	WBC:184, 214; LVA-LP
Curtin, Daniel	Arlington	Account	1809	WBC:280; LVA-LP
Curtin, Daniel	Arlington	Account	1818	AB3:191; LVA-LP
Curtin, Daniel & wife, cooper	Alexandria	Head	1795	1795(4):01
Curtin, Daniel & wife, cooper	Alexandria	Housekeeper	1799	1799(2):16A
Curtin, Danl.	Alexandria	Tax Charge	1796	Tax LP 1796:04
Curtis, Elizabeth, w/o Jacob	Arlington	Defendant	(nd)	LSA:124
Curtis, Harry	Alexandria	Head	1810	1810(4):05A
Curtis, Henry, cooper	Alexandria	Housekeeper	1808	1808(3):20A

NAME OR SUBJECT	LOCATION	TYPE	YEAR	REFERENCE(S)
Curtis, Jacob	Arlington	Defendant	(nd)	LSA:124
Curtis, Jacob	Arlington	Bond	1852	BB(np)
Curtis, Jacob	Arlington	Will	1852	WB6:010; File #471A
Curtis, Jacob	Arlington	Account	1852	WB6:319; LVA-LP
Curtis, Jacob	Arlington	Account	1852	WB6:170; LVA-LP
Curtis, Jacob, seaman	Alexandria	Head	1810	1810(3):05A
Curtis, Jacob, seaman & shopkeeper	Alexandria	Housekeeper	1808	1808(3):19A
Curtis, Jane	Alexandria	Resident	1800	1800(4):05B
Curtis, Jane	Alexandria	Boarder	1800	1800(4):05A
Curtis, Joseph	Alexandria	Tax Charge	1796	Tax LP 1796:05
Curtis, Joseph	Alexandria	Tax Charge	1796	Tax PP 1796:03
Curtis, Josiah	Alexandria	Boarder	1808	1808(1):05A
Curtis, Virginia W.	Arlington	Guard.	1819	WB2:309
Curtis, William	Arlington	Guard.	1813	WB1:224
Curtis, William (C)	Arlington	Apprentice	1813	OCR1811:148
Curtis, William (C), c/o Jane	Arlington	Apprentice	1805	OCR1801:240
Curtis, William Wallace	Arlington	Will	1888	WB10:148; File #740A
Cusine, John	Arlington	Ordinary	1805	OBL1(np)
Custis, George W.P.	Arlington	Report	1860	LVA-LP
Custis, George W.P., at *Arlington*	Arlington	Slaves	1858	LVA-LP
Custis, George W.P., at *Romanoke*	Arlington	Inventory	1858	LVA-LP
Custis, George W.P., def.	Alexandria	Suit	1809	CRG:187
Custis, George Washington Parke	Arlington	Appraisal	1857	WB7:279
Custis, George Washington Parke	Arlington	Will	1857	WB7:267; Vault
Custis, George Washington Parke	Arlington	Inventory	1858	WB7:369; LVA-LP
Custis, George Washington Parke	Arlington	Account	1860	WB7:485
Custis, George Washington Parke	Arlington	Account	1861	WB8:092; LVA-LP
Cutler, Edward	Alexandria	Serv./Appr.	1800	1800(4):05B
Cutting, John B. & wife Sally Carter, def.	Alexandria	Suit	1813	CRH:507
Cutting, John B., gentleman	Alexandria	Housekeeper	1808	1808(3):20A
Cutting, John Brown	Arlington	Defendant	1824	ACO:246
Cutting, John Brown	Arlington	Defendant	1825	ACO:256
Cutting, John Brown & wife Sally, def.	Alexandria	Suit	1811	CRI:106
Cutts, Richard	Arlington	Deposition	1830	ACR:076

D

NAME OR SUBJECT	LOCATION	TYPE	YEAR	REFERENCE(S)
Dabney, Jas. B.	Alexandria	Tithable +16	1788	Tax PP 1788:14
Dabney, Jno. B.	Alexandria	Tax Charge	1795	Tax PP 1795:07
Dabney, Jno. B., Fairfax St.	Alexandria	Occupant	1795	Tax L 1795:14
Dabney, Jno. B., Wolf St.	Alexandria	Occupant	1795	Tax L 1795:17
Dabney, John B.	Alexandria	Tithable +16	1789	Tax PP 1789:16
Dabney, John B.	Alexandria	Tithable +16	1790	Tax PP 1790:12
Dabney, John B. & wife, merchant	Alexandria	Head	1795	1795(4):01
Dacy, Hezekiah	Alexandria	Boarder	1808	1808(1):05A
Dade, B., St. Asaph St.	Alexandria	Occupant	1787	Tax L 1787:22
Dade, Baldwin	Alexandria	Tax Charge	1788	Tax PP 1788:05
Dade, Baldwin	Alexandria	Tax Charge	1789	Tax PP 1789:05
Dade, Baldwin	Alexandria	Deed	1797	CRI:320
Dade, Baldwin	Alexandria	Deposition	1807	CRE:293
Dade, Baldwin & wife Catherine	Alexandria	Deed	1801	CRI:324
Dade, Baldwin & wife Catharine	Alexandria	Deed	1801	CRI:330
Dade, Baldwin & wife Catherine	Alexandria	Deed	1803	CRI:347
Dade, Baldwin, def.	Alexandria	Suit	1801	CRC:001
Dade, Baldwin, def.	Alexandria	Suit	1802	CRC:207
Dade, Baldwin, gentleman	Alexandria	Housekeeper	1808	1808(4):24A
Dade, Baldwin, plt.	Alexandria	Suit	1801	CRB:079
Dade, Beheathland	Arlington	Will	1806	WBB:241; File #018A
Dade, Beheathland	Arlington	Bond	1806	WBB:251
Dade, Behethland	Alexandria	Deed	1778	CRI:285, 290
Dade, Catherine	Alexandria	Deed	1778	CRI:285, 290
Dade, Catherine	Alexandria	Head	1810	1810(1):10A
Dade, Charles, mariner	Alexandria	Head	1810	1810(1):11A
Dade, Charles S.	Arlington	Inventory	1812	AB1:241; LVA-LP
Dade, Charles S.	Arlington	Will	1812	WB1:182; File #103A
Dade, Charles S.	Arlington	Bond	1812	WB1:184
Dade, Charles S.	Arlington	Account	1813	AB1:331; LVA-LP
Dade, Eliza	Arlington	Admin.	1828	OCR1822:166
Dade, Eliza L.	Arlington	Will	1844	WB4:386; File #417A
Dade, Elizabeth	Alexandria	Deed	1778	CRI:285, 290
Dade, Frances T.	Arlington	Will	1838	WB4:176; File #357A
Dade, Hetty, Miss	Alexandria	Tax Charge	1800	Tax PP 1800:06
Dade, Jane	Alexandria	Will	1873	WB1:055; LP
Dade, Langhorn, c/o Catharine	Arlington	Apprentice	1811	OCR1811:037
Dade, Margaret	Alexandria	Deed	1778	CRI:285, 290
Dade, Margaret	Arlington	Bond	1806	WBB:250
Dade, Margaret	Arlington	Will	1806	WBB:248; File #019A
Dade, Mary T.	Arlington	Will	1866	CLOB2:402; File #184A
Dade, Parthenia	Alexandria	Deed	1778	CRI:285, 290
Dade, Parthenia, w/o Townshend	Alexandria	Deed	1776	CRI:212
Dade, Townshend, Jr., churchwarden	Alexandria	Deed	1770	CRI:172
Dade, Walter S.	Alexandria	Boarder	1808	1808(4):24A
Dades, Miss	Alexandria	Tax Charge	1796	Tax PP 1796:05
Dades, Miss	Alexandria	Tax Charge	1798	Tax PP 1798:04
Dades, Miss	Alexandria	Tax Charge	1799	Tax PP 1799:09
Daff [Duff], John	Arlington	Apprentice	1805	OCR1801:293
Dagen, Geo., baker	Alexandria	Head	1810	1810(3):05A
Dagen, Henry B., baker	Alexandria	Head	1810	1810(3):05A
Dagg, John	Alexandria	Tithable +21	1787	Tax PP 1787:12
Dagg, Robert	Alexandria	Tithable +16	1788	Tax PP 1788:13
Dailey, Edward	Alexandria	Tax Charge	1799	Tax PP 1799:09
Dailey, Edwd., carpenter	Alexandria	Housekeeper	1808	1808(4):29A
Dailey, Elizabeth A., at her house	Arlington	Ordinary	1832	OBL4(np)
Dailey, Elizabeth, her house King St.	Arlington	Ordinary	1833	OBL5(np)
Dailey, Isabella Virginia, c/o Richard B.	Arlington	Guard.	1833	WB4:068
Dailey, John Richard, c/o Richard B.	Arlington	Guard.	1833	WB4:068; WB8:052
Dailey, Moses	Alexandria	Tax Charge	1796	Tax PP 1796:05

NAME OR SUBJECT	LOCATION	TYPE	YEAR	REFERENCE(S)
Dailey, Ursella, c/o Richard B.	Arlington	Guard.	1861	WB8:052
Dailey, Ursula Elizabeth, c/o Richard B.	Arlington	Guard.	1833	WB4:068; WB8:052
Dailey, Virginia, c/o Richard B.	Arlington	Guard.	1861	WB8:052
Daily, Edward	Alexandria	Tax Charge	1800	Tax PP 1800:07
Daily, Edward, house joiner	Alexandria	Head	1810	1810(4):03A
Daily, Richard B., at his house	Arlington	Ordinary	1827	OBL4(np)
Daily, Richard B., at his house	Arlington	Ordinary	1830	OBL4(np)
Daily, Richard B., at his house	Arlington	Ordinary	1831	OBL4(np)
Daily, Richard R., at his house	Arlington	Ordinary	1828	OBL4(np)
Daingerfield, B.	Arlington	Respondent	1811	ACO:118
Daingerfield, Bathurst	Arlington	Inventory	1827	AB6:406; LVA-LP
Daingerfield, Bathurst	Arlington	Will	1827	WB3:275; File #256A
Daingerfield, Bathurst	Arlington	Bond	1827	WB3:279
Daingerfield, Edward	Arlington	Account C.	1840	LVA-LP
Daingerfield, Eliza	Arlington	Renounce	1845	OCR1842:143
Daingerfield, Eliza	Arlington	Will P.	1845	OCR1842:135
Daingerfield, Eliza	Arlington	Will	1845	WB4:407; File #428A
Daingerfield, Eliza L.	Alexandria	Will	1880	WB1:304; LP
Daingerfield, Eliza R., w/o Henry, Sr.	Alexandria	Will	1898	WBC1:071; LP
Daingerfield, Henry	Arlington	Plat	1839	LSA:047
Daingerfield, Henry	Arlington	Appraisal	1866	WB8:408
Daingerfield, Henry	Arlington	Account	1867	WB8:458
Daingerfield, Henry	Arlington	Guard. Acct.	1867	WB9:004
Daingerfield, Henry	Arlington	Guard. Acct.	1868	WB9:105
Daingerfield, Henry	Arlington	Account	1868	WB9:019
Daingerfield, Henry	Arlington	Account	1869	WB9:209
Daingerfield, Henry	Arlington	Guard. Acct.	1869	WB9:197
Daingerfield, Henry, physician	Alexandria	Head	1810	1810(1):04A
Daingerfield, John	Arlington	Respondent	1811	ACO:118
Daingerfield, John B.	Alexandria	Will	1886	WB1:425; LP
Daingerfield, Margaret B., w/o Edward	Alexandria	Will	1887	WB1:482; LP
Daingerfield, Margaret B., w/o Edward	Arlington	Will	1887	WB10:134; File #734A
Daingerfield, Maria H.	Arlington	Complainant	1837	LSA:017
Daingerfield, Reverdy J.	Arlington	Guard. Acct.	1868	WB9:107
Daingerfield, Reverdy Johnson	Arlington	Guard. Acct.	1867	WB9:003
Daingerfield, Reverdy Johnson	Arlington	Guard. Acct.	1869	WB9:199
Daingerfield, Reverdy Johnson	Arlington	Guard. Acct.	1870	WB9:272
Daingerfield, Reverdy Johnson	Arlington	Guard. Acct.	1871	WB9:324
Dalby, Philip	Alexandria	Tax Charge	1787	Tax PP 1787:04
Dalby, Philip, King St.	Alexandria	Occupant	1787	Tax L 1787:23
Dale, George, b. Co. Antrim	Arlington	Alien Entry	1816	RA:29/07/16
Dalton, Ann	Alexandria	Housekeeper	1799	1799(2):13A
Dalton, Catharine	Arlington	Inventory	1845	AB9:115; LVA-LP
Dalton, Daniel, turner	Alexandria	Boarder	1800	1800(4):11A
Dalton, Daniel, turner	Alexandria	Housekeeper	1808	1808(3):21A
Dalton, Danl., turner	Alexandria	Head	1810	1810(1):05A
Dalton, J. & S. Groons, Fairfax St.	Alexandria	Occupant	1795	Tax L 1795:02
Dalton, Jno.	Alexandria	Tax Charge	1795	Tax PP 1795:08
Dalton, Jno.	Alexandria	Boarder	1808	1808(1):07A
Dalton, John & mother, carpenter	Alexandria	Head	1795	1795(4):05
Dalton, Katharine	Arlington	Will P.	1845	OCR1842:120, 123
Dalton, Katharine	Arlington	Account F.	1846	AB9:233; LVA-LP
Dalton, Katherine	Arlington	Will	1845	WB4:398; File #426A
Dalton, Tristam, gentleman	Alexandria	Housekeeper	1808	1808(3):21A
Dalton, Tristram, gentleman	Alexandria	Head	1810	1810(3):04A
Damutt, Peter	Alexandria	Tax Charge	1798	Tax PP 1798:04
Dandridge, Bartholomew	Arlington	Translate	1803	WBA:210
Dandridge, Bartholomew	Arlington	Will	1804	WBA:206
Dandridge, Bartholomew	Arlington	Bond	1804	WBA:292
Dandridge, Bartholomew	Arlington	Inventory	1804	WBA:306
Dandridge, Bartholomew	Arlington	Sale	1804	WBB:067

NAME OR SUBJECT	LOCATION	TYPE	YEAR	REFERENCE(S)
Dandridge, Bartholomew	Arlington	Account	1805	WBB:183; LVA-LP
Dangerfield, Bathurst, sea captain	Alexandria	Housekeeper	1808	1808(3):18A
Dangerfield, Capt., seaman	Alexandria	Head	1810	1810(3):04A
Dangerfield, Doctr.	Alexandria	Head	1810	1810(3):05A
Dangerfield, Wm., physician	Alexandria	Housekeeper	1808	1808(3):19A
Daniel, Francis	Arlington	Inventory	1804	WBB:097; LVA-LP
Daniel, Francis	Arlington	Admin.	1804	WBB:062
Daniels, Edy, washwoman	Alexandria	Housekeeper	1808	1808(3):19A
Darby, John	Alexandria	Tax Charge	1798	Tax PP 1798:05
Darle, Michael	Alexandria	Tithable +16	1788	Tax PP 1788:04
Darley, Caroline	Alexandria	Head	1810	1810(4):06A
Darley, Caroline	Arlington	Sale	1811	AB1:063
Darley, Caroline	Arlington	Inventory	1811	AB1:039; LVA-LP
Darley, Caroline	Arlington	Admin.	1811	WB1:025
Darley, Caroline	Arlington	Account	1812	AB1:167; LVA-LP
Darley, Caroline, sempstress	Alexandria	Housekeeper	1808	1808(4):29A
Darley, George	Alexandria	Will	1900	WB2:376; LP
Darley, John	Arlington	Collection	1820	WB2:429
Darley, John, c/o Michael	Arlington	Apprentice	1802	OCR1801:056
Darley, Michael	Alexandria	Tax Charge	1796	Tax PP 1796:04
Darley, Michael	Alexandria	Tax Charge	1799	Tax PP 1799:09
Darley, Michael	Arlington	Inventory	1805	WBB:226
Darley, Michael	Arlington	Will	1805	WBB:198; File #003A
Darley, Michael	Arlington	Bond	1805	WBB:199
Darley, Michael & wife, grocer	Alexandria	Housekeeper	1799	1799(2):07A
Darley, Michl.	Alexandria	Tax Charge	1795	Tax PP 1795:07
Darley, Michl.	Alexandria	Tax Charge	1796	Tax LP 1796:07
Darley, Michl.	Alexandria	Mer. License	1798	Tax PP 1798:20-2
Darley, Michl.	Alexandria	Tax Charge	1798	Tax PP 1798:04
Darley, Michl., Union St.	Alexandria	Occupant	1795	Tax L 1795:01
Darley, Michl., w(1), cooper	Alexandria	Head	1795	1796(3):7
Darley, Thomas, c/o Michael	Arlington	Apprentice	1802	OCR1801:068
Darley, Thos., cooper	Alexandria	Housekeeper	1808	1808(4):27A
Darley, Thos., cooper	Alexandria	Head	1810	1810(4):02A
Darlin, Joseph	Alexandria	Tithable +16	1788	Tax PP 1788:08
Darling & Earp, King St.	Alexandria	Occupant	1790	Tax L 1790:03
Darling, Ann, w/o Robert	Arlington	P. of Atty.	1819	LVA-LP
Darling, Elinor	Alexandria	Head	1795	1795(4):07
Darling, Geo.	Alexandria	Tax Charge	1795	Tax PP 1795:07
Darling, Geo.	Alexandria	Tax Charge	1798	Tax PP 1798:04
Darling, Geo.	Alexandria	Mer. License	1798	Tax PP 1798:20-2
Darling, Geo.	Alexandria	Mer. License	1800	Tax PP 1800:54(12)r
Darling, Geo., retailer	Alexandria	Housekeeper	1808	1808(2):10A
Darling, Geo., shopkeeper	Alexandria	Head	1810	1810(2):02A
Darling, George	Alexandria	Tithable +21	1787	Tax PP 1787:06
Darling, George	Alexandria	Tithable +16	1788	Tax PP 1788:07
Darling, George	Alexandria	Tax Charge	1789	Tax PP 1789:05
Darling, George	Alexandria	Tax Charge	1790	Tax PP 1790:03
Darling, George	Alexandria	Tax Charge	1796	Tax LP 1796:06
Darling, George	Alexandria	Tax Charge	1796	Tax PP 1796:04
Darling, George	Alexandria	Tax Charge	1799	Tax PP 1799:09
Darling, George	Alexandria	Mer. License	1799	Tax PP 1799:52-02r
Darling, George	Alexandria	Tax Charge	1800	Tax PP 1800:06
Darling, George	Arlington	Admin.	1803	WB1:260
Darling, George	Arlington	Inventory	1813	AB1:336; LVA-LP
Darling, George	Arlington	Account	1814	AB1:151; LVA-LP
Darling, George	Arlington	Account	1814	AB2:151; LVA-LP
Darling, Joseph	Alexandria	Tithable +16	1789	Tax PP 1789:09
Darling, Joseph	Alexandria	Tax Charge	1790	Tax PP 1790:04
Darling, Robert [Ann]	Arlington	Letter	1819	LVA-LP
Darling, Sellwood	Alexandria	Will	1890	WB1:570; LP

NAME OR SUBJECT	LOCATION	TYPE	YEAR	REFERENCE(S)
Darly, Michl.	Alexandria	Tax Charge	1800	Tax PP 1800:06
Darne, Belinda	Arlington	Sale	1825	AB5:410
Darne, Belinda	Arlington	Inventory	1825	AB5:401; LVA-LP
Darne, Belinda	Arlington	Admin.	1825	OCR1822:082a
Darne, Belinda	Arlington	Admin.	1825	WB3:152
Darne, George	Arlington	Apprentice	1815	OCR1811:351
Darne, George, c/o Thomas	Arlington	Guard.	1815	WB2:014
Darne, Janet, c/o Thomas	Arlington	Guard.	1815	WB2:014
Darne, Margaret, c/o Thomas	Arlington	Guard.	1815	WB2:014
Darne, Simon	Arlington	Admin.	1825	WB3:160
Darne, Thomas	Arlington	Sale	1814	AB2:077
Darne, Thomas	Arlington	Inventory	1814	AB2:071; LVA-LP
Darne, Thomas	Arlington	Admin.	1814	WB1:306
Darne, Thomas	Arlington	Division	1815	AB2:164
Darne, Thomas	Arlington	Account	1816	AB2:312; LVA-LP
Darne, Thomas	Arlington	Account	1825	AB6:032
Darne, Thomas	Arlington	Admin.	1825	OCR1822:084a
Darnell, Henry	Arlington	Will	1852	WBO:054; File #475A
Darnell, Henry, drayman	Alexandria	Head	1810	1810(4):03A
Darnell, John	Alexandria	Will	1880	WB1:295; LP
Darragh, Wm., wheelwright	Alexandria	Boarder	1799	1799(2):04A
Darrel, Cloe, washer	Alexandria	Head	1795	1795(4):05
Darrell, Sampson, sheriff, age 55	Alexandria	Deposition	1767	CRI:271
Darrell, William S., grantee	Arlington	Indenture D.	1814	ID2:334
Dary, John, plaisterer	Alexandria	Head	1810	1810(1):08A
Dasher, Charles	Alexandria	Tax Charge	1796	Tax LP 1796:11
Datcher, Charles	Alexandria	Tax Charge	1799	Tax PP 1799:10
Datcher, Chas., barber	Alexandria	Head	1810	1810(3):02A
Datcher, Chas., oysterman	Alexandria	Housekeeper	1808	1808(2):13A
Datcher, Leonard (C), laborer	Alexandria	Housekeeper	1808	1808(4):28A
Datcher, Leonard, millstone maker	Alexandria	Head	1810	1810(4):03A
Dateshorne, John	Alexandria	Boarder	1808	1808(2):16A
Daugherty, Robert	Alexandria	Tax Charge	1790	Tax PP 1790:03
Daughety, Robert	Alexandria	Tax Charge	1789	Tax PP 1789:05
Daughterty, D.L., comb maker	Alexandria	Housekeeper	1808	1808(3):22A
Dausser, George	Alexandria	Tax Charge	1788	Tax PP 1788:04
Davenport, James	Alexandria	Tax Charge	1799	Tax PP 1799:09
Davenport, Jas. & wife, farmer	Alexandria	Housekeeper	1799	1799(2):08A
Davey, Davey	Alexandria	Deed	1795	CRI:046
Davey, Davey	Arlington	Ordinary	1803	OBL1(np)
Davey, Davey	Arlington	Ordinary	1804	OBL1(np)
Davey, Davey	Arlington	Claims	1812	LVA-LP
Davey, Davey, Estate, def.	Alexandria	Suit	1809	CRI:001
Davey, David	Alexandria	Sale	(nd)	CRI:065
Davey, David	Alexandria	Account B.	1796	CRI:059
Davey, David	Alexandria	Deed	1796	CRI:055
Davey, David	Alexandria	Tax Charge	1796	Tax PP 1796:04
Davey, David	Alexandria	Account B.	1797	CRI:084
Davey, David	Alexandria	Tax Charge	1798	Tax PP 1798:04
Davey, David	Alexandria	Tax Charge	1799	Tax PP 1799:09
Davey, David	Alexandria	Mer. License	1799	Tax PP 1799:52-02r
Davey, David	Alexandria	Mer. License	1800	Tax PP 1800:54(12)r
Davey, David	Arlington	Ordinary	1806	OBL2(np)
Davey, David	Arlington	Bond	1807	WBB:404
Davey, David	Arlington	Will	1807	WBB:403; File #017A
Davey, David	Arlington	Inventory	1807	WBB:423; LVA-LP
Davey, David	Arlington	Sale	1807	WBB:427
Davey, David	Arlington	Sale	1809	WBC:183
Davey, David	Arlington	Account	1809	WBC:182, 493; LVA-LP
Davey, David	Arlington	Account	1818	LVA-LP
Davey, David, insolvent debtor	Alexandria	Sale	1798	CRC:074

NAME OR SUBJECT	LOCATION	TYPE	YEAR	REFERENCE(S)
Davey, David, King St.	Alexandria	Occupant	1795	Tax L 1795:22
Davey, David, plt.	Alexandria	Suit	1801	CRC:072
Davey, David, plt.	Alexandria	Suit	1801	CRB:298
Davey, Elizabeth, shopkeeper	Alexandria	Housekeeper	1808	1808(3):19A
Davey, Thomas	Alexandria	Will	1877	WB1:204; LP
Davey, Thomas, b. Cornwall, Eng.	Arlington	Alien Entry	1825	RA:14/02/25
David, David	Alexandria	Tax Charge	1795	Tax PP 1795:07
David, David, w1, shopkeeper	Alexandria	Head	1796	1796(3):1
Davidson, Basil, sea captain	Alexandria	Housekeeper	1808	1808(1):08A
Davidson, Bazil H.	Alexandria	Deposition	1820	CRL:596
Davidson, Charles, plt.	Alexandria	Suit	1801	CRC:098
Davidson, Francis	Arlington	Apprentice	1825	OCR1822:095a
Davidson, Francis K.	Alexandria	Will	1888	WB1:507; LP
Davidson, Isaac	Alexandria	Boarder	1808	1808(2):11A
Davidson, James	Arlington	Ordinary	1802	OBL1(np)
Davidson, James	Arlington	Ordinary	1803	OBL1(np)
Davidson, James	Arlington	Ordinary	1804	OBL1(np)
Davidson, James	Arlington	Ordinary	1805	OBL1(np)
Davidson, James R.	Alexandria	Tax Charge	1800	Tax PP 1800:06
Davidson, Jas.	Alexandria	Tax Charge	1798	Tax PP 1798:04
Davidson, Jas. R.	Alexandria	Tax Charge	1799	Tax PP 1799:09
Davie, David	Alexandria	Tithable +16	1789	Tax PP 1789:14
Davies, Allen, Jr.	Alexandria	Tax Charge	1798	Tax PP 1798:05
Davies, Ann	Arlington	Account	1840	AB8:113
Davies, Ann, c/o Benjamin	Arlington	Guard.	1811	WB1:029
Davies, Benj.	Alexandria	Mer. License	1798	Tax PP 1798:20-2
Davies, Benj.	Alexandria	Tax Charge	1798	Tax PP 1798:04
Davies, Benjamin	Alexandria	Tax Charge	1799	Tax PP 1799:09
Davies, Benjamin	Arlington	Ordinary	1803	OBL1(np)
Davies, Benjamin	Arlington	Ordinary	1807	OBL2(np)(2)
Davies, Benjamin	Arlington	Ordinary	1808	OBL2(np)
Davies, Benjamin	Arlington	Bond	1810	WBC:503
Davies, Benjamin	Arlington	Inventory	1810	WBC:540
Davies, Benjamin	Arlington	Will	1810	WBC:500; File #056A
Davies, Benjamin	Arlington	Account	1811	AB1:107; LVA-LP
Davies, Benjamin	Arlington	Admin.	1837	WB4:152
Davies, Benjamin	Arlington	Account	1840	AB8:113
Davies, Cathren, labourer	Alexandria	Boarder	1800	1800(4):02A
Davies, Edward	Arlington	Apprentice	1814	OCR1811:218
Davies, Edward, c/o Ann	Arlington	Apprentice	1814	OCR1811:218
Davies, Jno., Sr.	Alexandria	Tax Charge	1798	Tax PP 1798:04
Davies, John, Jr.	Alexandria	Tax Charge	1798	Tax PP 1798:04
Davies, John, Sr.	Alexandria	Tax Charge	1799	Tax PP 1799:10
Davis, Aletha	Arlington	Apprentice	1828	OCR1822:155
Davis, Allen	Alexandria	Tax Charge	1795	Tax PP 1795:06
Davis, Allen	Alexandria	Tax Charge	1796	Tax PP 1796:05
Davis, Allen	Alexandria	Tax Charge	1798	Tax PP 1798:04
Davis, Allen	Alexandria	Tax Charge	1799	Tax PP 1799:09
Davis, Allen	Alexandria	Tax Charge	1800	Tax PP 1800:07
Davis, Allen & wife, drayman	Alexandria	Housekeeper	1799	1799(2):19A
Davis, Allen, cartman	Alexandria	Housekeeper	1808	1808(1):07A
Davis, Allen, drayman	Alexandria	Head	1810	1810(1):10A
Davis, Allen, plt.	Alexandria	Suit	1803	CRD:081
Davis, Ann	Arlington	Admin.	1838	WB4:182
Davis, Augustus	Arlington	Will	1888	WB10:136; File #735A
Davis, Barnaby & wife, carpenter	Alexandria	Housekeeper	1799	1799(2):01A
Davis, Bameby	Alexandria	Mer. License	1799	Tax PP 1799:52-03r
Davis, Bazil H., mariner	Alexandria	Head	1810	1810(1):09A
Davis, Ben.	Alexandria	Reference	1808	1808(3):18B
Davis, Benjamin	Alexandria	Tax Charge	1800	Tax PP 1800:06
Davis, Benjamin	Arlington	Ordinary	1804	OBL1(np)

NAME OR SUBJECT	LOCATION	TYPE	YEAR	REFERENCE(S)
Davis, Benjamin	Arlington	Ordinary	1805	OBL1(np)
Davis, Benjamin	Arlington	Ordinary	1809	OBL2(np)
Davis, Benjamin	Arlington	Ordinary	1810	OBL2(np)
Davis, Benjamin	Arlington	Apprentice	1815	OCR1811:321
Davis, Benjamin	Arlington	Apprentice	1822	OCR1822:011a
Davis, Benjamin, tavern keeper	Alexandria	Head	1810	1810(2):05A
Davis, Benjn.	Alexandria	Boarder	1808	1808(2):14A
Davis, Benjn., shopkeeper & tavern lic.	Alexandria	Housekeeper	1808	1808(2):14A
Davis, Catherine	Arlington	Apprentice	1803	OCR1801:131
Davis, Charles	Alexandria	Tax Charge	1798	Tax PP 1798:04
Davis, Charles B.	Alexandria	Tax Charge	1799	Tax PP 1799:09
Davis, Charles B.	Alexandria	Tax Charge	1800	Tax PP 1800:06
Davis, Charlotte V.	Alexandria	Will	1897	WB2:187; LP
Davis, Conny, c/o Thomas	Arlington	Apprentice	1812	OCR1811:087
Davis, Cornelius, grantor	Arlington	Indenture D.	1817	ID2:427
Davis, Cornelius, in jail	Arlington	Insolvent	1817	ID2:424
Davis, Daniel, labourer	Alexandria	Head	1810	1810(3):07A
Davis, Edward	Alexandria	Tax Charge	1795	Tax PP 1795:06
Davis, Elijah	Alexandria	Tax Charge	1799	Tax PP 1799:09
Davis, Elijah, hatter	Alexandria	Boarder	1799	1799(2):03A
Davis, Francis	Alexandria	Tax Charge	1796	Tax PP 1796:05
Davis, Hanson	Alexandria	Tax Charge	1795	Tax PP 1795:06
Davis, Hanson	Alexandria	Tax Charge	1796	Tax PP 1796:05
Davis, Hanson	Alexandria	Tax Charge	1798	Tax PP 1798:04
Davis, Hanson	Alexandria	Tax Charge	1800	Tax PP 1800:06
Davis, Hanson, Water St.	Alexandria	Occupant	1795	Tax L 1795:05
Davis, Harry, seaman	Alexandria	Head	1810	1810(1):10A
Davis, Henry	Alexandria	Tax Charge	1796	Tax LP 1796:06
Davis, Henry & wife, drayman	Alexandria	Head	1795	1795(4a):10
Davis, Henry, cartman	Alexandria	Housekeeper	1808	1808(1):09A
Davis, Henry, watchman	Alexandria	Head	1810	1810(1):06A
Davis, James	Arlington	Apprentice	1823	OCR1822:042
Davis, Jno. & wife, drayman	Alexandria	Housekeeper	1799	1799(2):10A
Davis, Jno. & wife, ironmonger	Alexandria	Housekeeper	1799	1799(2):08A
Davis, Jno., King St.	Alexandria	Occupant	1795	Tax L 1795:05
Davis, John	Alexandria	Tax Charge	1796	Tax LP 1796:06
Davis, John	Arlington	Witness	1794	OT:07/11/1794
Davis, John	Alexandria	Tax Charge	1796	Tax PP 1796:04
Davis, John	Alexandria	Tax Charge	1798	Tax PP 1798:04
Davis, John	Alexandria	Tax Charge	1799	Tax PP 1799:09
Davis, John	Alexandria	Tax Charge	1800	Tax PP 1800:06
Davis, John	Alexandria	Boarder	1808	1808(2):11A
Davis, John (dray)	Alexandria	Tax Charge	1800	Tax PP 1800:06
Davis, John, c/o William	Arlington	Apprentice	1814	OCR1811:229
Davis, John, grantee	Arlington	Indenture D.	1817	ID2:410
Davis, John, plaisterer	Alexandria	Housekeeper	1808	1808(1):05A
Davis, John, Sr.	Alexandria	Tax Charge	1800	Tax PP 1800:06
Davis, John, w(3)1, drayman	Alexandria	Head	1796	1796(3):1
Davis, Josiah	Alexandria	Boarder	1808	1808(1):08A
Davis, Josiah H.	Arlington	Will	1864	WB8:211; File #617A
Davis, Lucy (C), washwoman	Alexandria	Housekeeper	1808	1808(1):06A
Davis, Mary	Alexandria	Housekeeper	1799	1799(2):17A
Davis, Mary	Alexandria	Resident	1800	1800(4):10B
Davis, Mary	Arlington	Apprentice	1804	OCR1801:144
Davis, Mary	Arlington	Bond	1825	WB3:194
Davis, Mary	Arlington	Will	1825	WB3:194; File #239A
Davis, Mary, boarding house	Alexandria	Head	1810	1810(1):08A
Davis, Mary E.	Alexandria	Will	1900	WB2:402; LP
Davis, Mary, gentlewoman	Alexandria	Housekeeper	1808	1808(1):08A
Davis, Mary, murchant	Alexandria	Head	1800	1800(4):07A
Davis, Monachy	Alexandria	Housekeeper	1799	1799(2):14A

NAME OR SUBJECT	LOCATION	TYPE	YEAR	REFERENCE(S)
Davis, Penelopy	Alexandria	Head	1810	1810(2):07A
Davis, Penny	Alexandria	Housekeeper	1808	1808(2):17A
Davis, Priscilla	Alexandria	Lease	1800	CRB:154
Davis, Sally, seamstress	Alexandria	Head	1810	1810(2):07A
Davis, Sam.	Alexandria	Tax Charge	1795	Tax PP 1795:07
Davis, Saml.	Alexandria	Tax Charge	1796	Tax LP 1796:07
Davis, Saml., Fairfax St.	Alexandria	Owner	1795	Tax L 1795:06
Davis, Saml., Fairfax St.	Alexandria	Occupant	1795	Tax L 1795:28
Davis, Saml., nr. Fairfax St.	Alexandria	Occupant	1790	Tax L 1790:03
Davis, Samuel	Alexandria	Tax Charge	1796	Tax PP 1796:04
Davis, Samuel	Arlington	Settlement	1807	WBB:470; LVA-LP
Davis, Samuel & wife, shipmaster	Alexandria	Head	1795	1795(4):04
Davis, Samuel, Estate	Alexandria	Tax Charge	1799	Tax PP 1799:09
Davis, Samuel, nr. Fairfax St.	Alexandria	Owner	1790	Tax L 1790:03
Davis, Theodore E., of DC	Alexandria	Will	1900	WB2:373; LP
Davis, Thomas	Alexandria	Tax Charge	1796	Tax LP 1796:06
Davis, Thomas	Alexandria	Tax Charge	1799	Tax PP 1799:09
Davis, Thomas	Arlington	Apprentice	1822	OCR1822:017a
Davis, Thomas Jefferson	Arlington	Apprentice	1822	OCR1822:029
Davis, Thomas Jefferson	Arlington	Apprentice	1825	OCR1822:089a
Davis, Thomas M.	Arlington	Ordinary	1821	OBL3(np)
Davis, Thomas M., at his house	Arlington	Ordinary	1828	OBL4(np)
Davis, Thomas M., at his house	Arlington	Ordinary	1830	OBL4(np)
Davis, Thomas M., in Alexandria Co.	Arlington	Ordinary	1826	OBL4(np)
Davis, Thomas M., in Alexandria Co.	Arlington	Ordinary	1827	OBL4(np)
Davis, Thomas M., on Prince St.	Arlington	Ordinary	1822	OBL3(np)
Davis, Thomas, plt.	Alexandria	Suit	1801	CRC:183
Davis, Thomas, shoemaker	Alexandria	Head	1810	1810(1):02A
Davis, Thornton	Arlington	Will	1898	WB10:357; File #782A
Davis, Thos.	Alexandria	Tax Charge	1795	Tax PP 1795:07
Davis, Thos.	Alexandria	Tax Charge	1798	Tax PP 1798:04
Davis, Thos.	Alexandria	Tax Charge	1800	Tax PP 1800:06
Davis, Thos. & wife, carpenter	Alexandria	Housekeeper	1799	1799(2):11A
Davis, Thos., D.D.	Alexandria	Tax Charge	1796	Tax PP 1796:04
Davis, Thos., D.D.	Alexandria	Tax Charge	1798	Tax PP 1798:05
Davis, Thos., labourer	Alexandria	Head	1810	1810(3):02A
Davis, Thos. M., shoemaker	Alexandria	Housekeeper	1808	1808(1):01A
Davis, Thos., shoemaker	Alexandria	Housekeeper	1808	1808(2):11A
Davis, Wesley	Arlington	Guard.	1838	WB4:174
Davis, William, c/o Thomas	Arlington	Apprentice	1812	OCR1811:057
Davis, William, drayman	Alexandria	Head	1810	1810(4):05A
Davis, William M.	Alexandria	Will	1896	WB2:153; LP
Davis, Wm., drayman	Alexandria	Housekeeper	1808	1808(4):28A
Davise, Allen & wife Ann	Alexandria	Resident	1800	1800(4):09B
Davise, Allen, watchman	Alexandria	Head	1800	1800(4):09A
Davise, Mary	Alexandria	Boarder	1800	1800(4):10A
Davise, Mary	Alexandria	Resident	1800	1800(4):07B
Davise, Prissellere	Alexandria	Resident	1800	1800(4):10B
Davise, Prissey, [spinster]	Alexandria	Boarder	1800	1800(4):10A
Davison, Lancelot, master	Arlington	Respondent	1804	ACO:029
Davison, Lancelot, master	Arlington	Respondent	1805	ACO:035
Davison, Thomas & wife	Alexandria	Head	1795	1795(4):06
Davy, David	Alexandria	Deed	1795	CRI:049
Davy, David	Alexandria	Tax Charge	1796	Tax LP 1796:06
Davy, David	Alexandria	Tax Charge	1800	Tax PP 1800:06
Davy, David, King St.	Alexandria	Occupant	1790	Tax L 1790:12
Davy, M.	Alexandria	Reference	1808	1808(3):19B
Daw, John, b. Cornwall	Arlington	Alien Entry	1817	RA:22/12/17
Daw, Philip	Alexandria	Owner	1787	Tax L 1787:10
Daw, Philip	Alexandria	Tax Charge	1796	Tax LP 1796:06
Daw, Wm.	Alexandria	Boarder	1808	1808(1):02A

NAME OR SUBJECT	LOCATION	TYPE	YEAR	REFERENCE(S)
Dawe, Philip, Fairfax St.	Alexandria	Owner	1790	Tax L 1790:03
Dawe, Philip, Fairfax St.	Alexandria	Owner	1795	Tax L 1795:07
Dawe, Reuben	Arlington	Apprentice	1822	OCR1822:030
Dawes, Edward	Alexandria	Tax Charge	1799	Tax PP 1799:09
Dawes, Edward, shoemaker	Alexandria	Head	1810	1810(1):01A
Dawes, Edwd.	Alexandria	Tax Charge	1798	Tax PP 1798:04
Dawes, Isaac, currier	Alexandria	Housekeeper	1808	1808(3):21A
Dawkins, Thos.	Alexandria	Boarder	1808	1808(4):29A
Daws, Henry, shoemaker	Alexandria	Tax Charge	1800	Tax PP 1800:07
Dawson, Ben (C), laborer	Alexandria	Housekeeper	1808	1808(1):07A
Dawson, Benn, labourer	Alexandria	Head	1810	1810(1):09A
Dawson, John	Alexandria	Tax Charge	1799	Tax PP 1799:10
Dawson, John	Alexandria	Tax Charge	1800	Tax PP 1800:06
Dawson, Saml.	Alexandria	Tax Charge	1798	Tax PP 1798:04
Dawson, Samuel	Arlington	Ordinary	1802	OBL1(np)
Dawson, Thomas	Alexandria	Tax Charge	1800	Tax PP 1800:06
Dawson, William	Alexandria	Tax Charge	1799	Tax PP 1799:09
Dawson, Wm. & wife, goldsmith	Alexandria	Housekeeper	1799	1799(2):15A
Dawson, Wm. & wife Elisabeth	Alexandria	Resident	1800	1800(4):05B
Dawson, Wm., silversmith	Alexandria	Head	1800	1800(4):05A
Day, George	Alexandria	Tax Charge	1789	Tax PP 1789:04
Day, Lewis	Alexandria	Tax Charge	1796	Tax PP 1796:04
Day, Samuel	Alexandria	Will	1875	WB1:161; LP
Dayes, Henry	Alexandria	Tax Charge	1798	Tax PP 1798:04
Dayley, Edward & wife, carpenter	Alexandria	Housekeeper	1799	1799(2):10A
Daylor, G., Fairfax St.	Alexandria	Occupant	1795	Tax L 1795:02
Days, Henry	Alexandria	Tax Charge	1800	Tax PP 1800:06
Days, Henry & wife, shoemaker	Alexandria	Housekeeper	1799	1799(2):09A
Daywood, Peter	Alexandria	Tax Charge	1796	Tax LP 1796:06
Deagan, Charlotte [Jacobs]	Arlington	Defendant	(nd)	LSA:124
Deagan, Henry	Arlington	Account	1833	LVA-LP
Deagan, Henry	Arlington	Account	1834	AB7:333; LVA-LP
Deagan, Henry B.	Arlington	Inventory	1826	AB6:180
Deagan, Henry B.	Arlington	Sale	1826	AB6:206
Deagan, Henry B.	Arlington	Account	1826	AB6:244; LVA-LP
Deagan, Henry B.	Arlington	Bond	1826	WB3:231
Deagan, Henry B.	Arlington	Will	1826	WB3:229, File #240A
Deagan, Henry B.	Arlington	Account	1830	AB7:330; LVA-LP
Deagan, Henry B.	Arlington	Account	1835	AB7:335; LVA-LP
Deagan, Henry B.	Arlington	Account	1837	AB7:335; LVA-LP
Deagan, Henry B.	Arlington	Account	1839	AB7:330; LVA-LP
Deagans, Henry B.	Arlington	Account	1835	AB7:333; LVA-LP
Deagen, Henry B., grantee	Arlington	Indenture D.	1812	ID2:180
Deakins, Ambrose, sick man	Alexandria	Housekeeper	1808	1808(4):29A
Deakins, Joseph	Arlington	Guard. Acct.	1824	AB5:325; LVA-LP
Deakins, Joseph Milburn	Arlington	Guard.	1821	WB3:033
Deakins, Margaret	Arlington	Guard.	1821	WB3:033
Deakins, Margaret	Arlington	Guard. Acct.	1824	AB5:325; LVA-LP
Deakins, Margaret	Arlington	Will	1862	WB8:141; File #594A
Deakins, Margaret	Arlington	Account	1865	WB8:286
Deakins, Margaret	Arlington	Inventory	1865	WB8:235
Deakins, Margaret	Arlington	Appraisal	1865	WB8:234
Dean, Charity, weaver	Alexandria	Housekeeper	1808	1808(2):16A
Dean, Jos. & wife, merchant	Alexandria	Housekeeper	1799	1799(2):06A
Dean, Joseph	Alexandria	Mer. License	1798	Tax PP 1798:20-2
Dean, Joseph	Alexandria	Tax Charge	1798	Tax PP 1798:05
Dean, Joseph	Alexandria	Tax Charge	1799	Tax PP 1799:09
Dean, Joseph	Arlington	Plaintiff	1802	PA:287, 290
Dean, Joseph	Arlington	Inventory	1818	AB3:134; LVA-LP
Dean, Joseph	Arlington	Will	1818	WB2:232; File #150A
Dean, Joseph	Arlington	Sale	1819	AB3:339

NAME OR SUBJECT	LOCATION	TYPE	YEAR	REFERENCE(S)
Dean, Joseph	Arlington	Account	1819	AB3:341; LVA-LP
Dean, Joseph	Arlington	Account	1820	AB4:103; LVA-LP
Dean, Joseph	Arlington	Account	1829	AB6:491; LVA-LP
Dean, Joseph, def.	Alexandria	Suit	1810	CRH:197
Dean, Joseph, merchant	Alexandria	Housekeeper	1808	1808(1):05A
Dean, Joseph, merchant	Alexandria	Head	1810	1810(1):03A
Dean, Josh.	Alexandria	Tax Charge	1800	Tax PP 1800:06
Dean, Samuel	Arlington	Inventory	1827	AB6:276; LVA-LP
Dean, Samuel [Catharine]	Arlington	Admin.	1827	OCR1822:132a
Dean, Thomas	Alexandria	Tithable +16	1788	Tax PP 1788:07
Dean, William, miller	Alexandria	Head	1810	1810(3):02A
Deane & Gardner	Alexandria	Mer. License	1800	Tax PP 1800:54(12)r
Deane, Joseph	Alexandria	Mer. License	1799	Tax PP 1799:52-02w
Deane, Joseph	Arlington	Account	1823	LVA-LP
Deane, Joseph plt.	Alexandria	Suit	1812	CRK:002
Deane, Samuel	Arlington	Admin.	1827	WB3:276
Deane, William, c/o Samuel	Arlington	Guard.	1830	WB3:377
Deatley, Matthew	Arlington	Bond	1854	BB(np)
Deatley, Matthew	Arlington	Will	1854	WB6:340; File #508A
Deatly, Matthew	Arlington	Inventory	1856	WB7:058; LVA-LP
Deatly, Matthew	Arlington	Account	1856	WB7:049; LVA-LP
Deatly, Matthew	Arlington	Account	1856	WB7:151; LVA-LP
Deblois, James S.	Arlington	Will	1805	WBB:152; File #009A
Deblois, James S.	Arlington	Bond	1805	WBB:165
Deblois, James S.	Arlington	Debts	1806	WBB:269
Deblois, James S.	Arlington	Inventory	1806	WBB:268; LVA-LP
Deblois, James S.	Arlington	Sale	1807	WBB:525
Deblois, James S.	Arlington	Account	1807	WBB:523; LVA-LP
Deblois, Lewis	Arlington	Defendant	1808	ACO:083, 087, 088
Deblois, Lewis	Arlington	Defendant	1809	ACO:108
Deblois, Lewis, merchant	Alexandria	Housekeeper	1808	1808(1):01A
Deblois, Lewis, merchant	Alexandria	Head	1810	1810(1):02A
Deblois, Lewis, plt.	Alexandria	Suit	1809	CRH:423
Deboltin, Elin, (1), seamstress	Alexandria	Head	1796	1796(3):7
DeBruin, Ben	Arlington	Sale	1862	WB8:138
Debutts, Samuel	Alexandria	Letters	1805	CRG:227-232
Debutts, Samuel, plt.	Alexandria	Suit	1807	CRG:211
DeButts, John	Arlington	Account	1835	AB7:144
DeButts, John H.	Arlington	Guard. Acct.	1832	AB7:053
DeButts, John H.	Arlington	Account	1834	LVA-LP
DeButts, John H.	Arlington	Account	1836	LVA-LP (Accounts 2nd)
DeButts, John H.	Arlington	Inventory	1841	AB8:207
DeButts, John Henry	Arlington	Will	1832	WB3:371; File #291A
DeButts, Mary	Arlington	Will	1828	WB3:304; File #265A
DeButts, Mary	Arlington	Guard. Acct.	1832	AB7:049
DeButts, Mary	Arlington	Account	1833	AB7:052; LVA-LP
DeButts, Mary	Arlington	Distribution	1833	AB7:049; LVA-LP
DeButts, Mary	Arlington	Account	1834	AB7:245; LVA-LP
DeButts, Mary	Arlington	Distribution	1835	AB7:136
DeButts, Mary	Arlington	Account	1835	AB7:133; LVA-LP
DeButts, Mary	Arlington	Account	1837	AB7:245; LVA-LP
DeButts, Mary W.	Arlington	Guard. Acct.	1835	AB7:150
DeButts, Mary W., c/o John H.	Arlington	Guard. Acct.	1833	LVA-LP (Accounts 2nd)
DeButts, Mary Welby	Arlington	Guard. Acct.	1832	AB7:046
DeButts, Mary Welby	Arlington	Guard. Acct.	1837	AB7:248
DeButts, Melescent Welby, c/o Richard	Arlington	Guard.	1816	WB2:134
DeButts, Richard	Arlington	Admin.	1816	WB2:135
DeButts, Richard Earle	Arlington	Guard. Acct.	1832	AB7:051
DeButts, Richard Earle	Arlington	Guard. Acct.	1835	AB7:148
DeButts, Richard Earle	Arlington	Guard. Acct.	1837	AB7:240
DeButts, Richardetta	Arlington	Guard. Acct.	1832	AB7:062; LVA-LP

NAME OR SUBJECT	LOCATION	TYPE	YEAR	REFERENCE(S)
DeButts, Richardetta	Arlington	Guard. Acct.	1835	AB7:140; LVA-LP
DeButts, Richardetta, c/o Richard	Arlington	Guard.	1816	WB2:134
DeButts, Richardetta, c/o Richard	Arlington	Guard. Acct.	1833	AB7:063; LVA-LP
DeButts, Richardetta [Armistead]	Arlington	Guard. Acct.	1836	AB7:239, 242
DeButts, Richardetta [Armistead]	Arlington	Guard. Acct.	1839	AB8:132; LVA-LP
DeButts, Richardetta [Armistead]	Arlington	Guard. Acct.	1840	AB8:132
DeButts, Richardetta [Carter]	Arlington	Guard. Acct.	1835	AB7:149; LVA-LP
DeButts, Samuel Welby	Arlington	Guard. Acct.	1832	AB7:061; LVA-LP(2)
DeButts, Samuel Welby	Arlington	Guard. Acct.	1835	AB7:139
DeButts, Samuel Welby	Arlington	Guard. Acct.	1835	AB7:145; LVA-LP
DeButts, Samuel Welby	Arlington	Guard. Acct.	1836	AB7:241
DeButts, Samuel Welby, c/o Richard	Arlington	Guard. Acct.	1833	AB7:061; LVA-LP
Decker, John	Alexandria	Tax Charge	1800	Tax PP 1800:07
DeCourcy, Eliza (Rozer), w/o William H.	Arlington	Defendant	1837	LSA:017
DeCourcy, William H.	Arlington	Defendant	1837	LSA:017
Deeble, Edward, c/o Mary Duffey	Arlington	Apprentice	1805	OCR1801:324
Deeble, Sam.	Alexandria	Boarder	1808	1808(2):13A
Deeble, Samuel, c/o Mary Duffey	Arlington	Apprentice	1804	OCR1801:165
Deeble, Samuel, c/o Mary Duffey	Arlington	Apprentice	1804	OCR1801:218
Deeble, William	Arlington	Account	1806	WBB:320
Deeble, Wm.	Alexandria	Tax Charge	1795	Tax PP 1795:07
Deeton, Chris., taylor	Alexandria	Housekeeper	1808	1808(2):13A
Deeton, Christopher, taylor	Alexandria	Head	1810	1810(2):03A
Deeton, Isabell(a)	Arlington	Will	1852	WB6:100; File #476A
Deford, Benjamin	Arlington	Will	1881	WB10:019; File #706A
Degart, Samuel	Alexandria	Tax Charge	1788	Tax PP 1788:05
Degert, Samuel	Alexandria	Tax Charge	1789	Tax PP 1789:05
Degge, Robert F.	Arlington	Defendant	1823	ACO:222
Degge, Robert F.	Arlington	Defendant	1825	ACO:253, 258
Degge, Robert F.	Arlington	Defendant	1826	ACO:264
Degge, Robert F.	Arlington	Defendant	1827	ACO:267, 274
Degge, Robert F., assignees of	Arlington	Plaintiffs	1823	ACO:219
Degge, Robert F., assignees of	Arlington	Plaintiffs	1823	ACO:222
Degge, Robet F.	Arlington	Defendant	1824	ACO:242, 248
Dekeyser, Anne	Alexandria	Boarder	1799	1799(2):10A
Delacour, Josua	Alexandria	Tax Charge	1788	Tax PP 1788:04
Delahay, Jos.	Alexandria	Tax Charge	1795	Tax PP 1795:07
Delahay, Joseph	Alexandria	Tax Charge	1796	Tax PP 1796:04
Delahay, Joseph	Alexandria	Tax Charge	1798	Tax PP 1798:04
Delahay, Joseph	Alexandria	Tax Charge	1799	Tax PP 1799:09
Delahaye, Joseph	Alexandria	Tax Charge	1796	Tax LP 1796:06
Delahunt, John	Arlington	Apprentice	1813	OCR1811:193
Delahunt, Patrick	Arlington	Apprentice	1813	OCR1811:177
Delany, Wm., constable	Alexandria	Housekeeper	1808	1808(3):18A
Delaplane, Joseph, at his house	Arlington	Ordinary	1829	OBL4(np)
Delaplane, Joseph, in Alexandria Co.	Arlington	Ordinary	1828	OBL4(np)
Delarue, A., King St.	Alexandria	Occupant	1787	Tax L 1787:10
Delarue, Agustus	Alexandria	Owner	1787	Tax L 1787:10
Delarue, Augustus	Alexandria	Tax Charge	1787	Tax PP 1787:04
Delarue, Augustus	Alexandria	Tax Charge	1788	Tax PP 1788:04
Delarue, Augustus, King St.	Alexandria	Occupant	1787	Tax L 1787:19
Delarue, Augustus, King St.	Alexandria	Owner	1795	Tax L 1795:07
Delarue, Joseph	Alexandria	Tax Charge	1788	Tax PP 1788:04
Delehay, Josh.	Alexandria	Tax Charge	1800	Tax PP 1800:06
Delerock, Michael	Alexandria	Tax Charge	1787	Tax PP 1787:04
Dells, John	Arlington	Sale	1812	AB1:215
Dells, John	Arlington	Inventory	1812	AB1:213; LVA-LP
Dells, John	Arlington	Sale	1812	AB1:214
Dells, John	Arlington	Account	1812	LVA-LP
Dells, John	Arlington	Admin.	1812	WB1:146
Dells, John, retailer	Alexandria	Housekeeper	1808	1808(3):20A

NAME OR SUBJECT	LOCATION	TYPE	YEAR	REFERENCE(S)
Dells, John, shopkeeper	Alexandria	Head	1810	1810(3):04A
Delow, Alexander, c/o Anthony	Arlington	Apprentice	1802	OCR1801:026
Delphey, Orlando, grantor	Arlington	Indenture D.	1833	ID:420
Delphey, Orlando, in confinement	Arlington	Insolvent	1833	ID:418
Delphy, Bartholomew, c/o Richard	Arlington	Apprentice	1815	OCR1811:269
Delphy, Matilda	Arlington	Guard.	1817	WB2:211
Delphy, Richard	Arlington	Admin.	1835	WB4:088
Delvin, Peter (non-citizen; servant)	Alexandria	Tithable +21	1787	Tax PP 1787:09
Delze, Michael	Alexandria	Tithable +16	1788	Tax PP 1788:06
Delze, Michael	Alexandria	Tithable +16	1789	Tax PP 1789:06
Demain, Elizabeth (Mankin), w/o Wm.	Arlington	Defendant	1841	LSA:070
Demain, William	Arlington	Defendant	1841	LSA:070
Demaine Elizabeth, w/o William	Arlington	Defendant	1842	LSA:087
Demaine, Job, weaver	Alexandria	Head	1810	1810(4):06A
Demaine, John	Arlington	Inventory	1857	WB7:206; LVA-LP
Demaine, William	Arlington	Defendant	1842	LSA:087
Dempsey, Hugh	Alexandria	Tax Charge	1788	Tax PP 1788:04
Dempsey, Thomas	Alexandria	Mer. License	1799	Tax PP 1799:52-02r
Dempsey, Thomas	Arlington	Juryman	1804	ACO:026
Dempsey, Thomas & Co.	Alexandria	Mer. License	1800	Tax PP 1800:54(12)r
Dempsey, Thomas & wife Kitty Fleming	Alexandria	Suit	1801	CRC:194
Dempsey, Thomas, grantee	Arlington	Indenture D.	1804	ID3:044
Dempsey, Thos.	Alexandria	Tax Charge	1798	Tax PP 1798:05
Dempsey, Thos.	Alexandria	Mer. License	1798	Tax PP 1798:20-2
Dempsey, Thos.	Alexandria	Tax Charge	1800	Tax PP 1800:06
Dempsey, Thos. & Co.	Alexandria	Tax Charge	1799	Tax PP 1799:09
Dempsey, Thos., druggist	Alexandria	Head	1810	1810(3):02A
Dempsey, Thos., druggist & apothecary	Alexandria	Housekeeper	1799	1799(2):03A
Dempster, Henry	Alexandria	Tithable +16	1788	Tax PP 1788:12
Dempster, Hugh	Alexandria	Tax Charge	1789	Tax PP 1789:05
Dempster, Hugh	Alexandria	Tax Charge	1790	Tax PP 1790:04
Dempster, Hugh, Union St.	Alexandria	Occupant	1790	Tax L 1790:04
Demuth, Jacob	Alexandria	Tax Charge	1787	Tax PP 1787:04
DeNalengen, Thomas P., grantor	Arlington	Indenture D.	1812	ID2:114
DeNalengen, Thomas P., in jail bounds	Arlington	Insolvent	1812	ID2:112
Deneal, Geo., Duke St.	Alexandria	Occupant	1787	Tax L 1787:27
Deneal, George	Alexandria	Tax Charge	1796	Tax LP 1796:06
Deneal, George	Alexandria	Tax Charge	1800	Tax PP 1800:06
Deneal, George & Co., St. Asaph St.	Alexandria	Occupant	1787	Tax L 1787:03
Deneal, George, clarke of county	Alexandria	Head	1800	1800(4):15A
Deneal, George, clerk	Alexandria	Head	1795	1795(4):09
Deneal, Goerge, clerk	Alexandria	Boarder	1799	1799(2):10A
Deneale, Edward	Arlington	Admin.	1803	WBA:133
Deneale, Edward	Arlington	Account	1804	WBB:045; LVA-LP
Deneale, Edward	Arlington	Account	1812	AB1:217; LVA-LP
Deneale, G.	Alexandria	Reference	1808	1808(4):28A
Deneale, Geo.	Alexandria	Tax Charge	1795	Tax PP 1795:06
Deneale, Geo.	Alexandria	Tax Charge	1798	Tax PP 1798:04
Deneale, Geo. & wife, clerk of the Cnty.	Alexandria	Housekeeper	1799	1799(2):13A
Deneale, Geo., C.C.D., Alexa.	Alexandria	Housekeeper	1808	1808(3):20A
Deneale, Geo., clerk of the court	Alexandria	Head	1810	1810(3):04A
Deneale, Geo., Duke St.	Alexandria	Occupant	1790	Tax L 1790:03
Deneale, Geo., Duke St.	Alexandria	Owner	1790	Tax L 1790:03
Deneale, Geo., Duke St.	Alexandria	Owner	1795	Tax L 1795:06
Deneale, Geo., Duke St.	Alexandria	Occupant	1795	Tax L 1795:06
Deneale, George	Alexandria	Tax Charge	1787	Tax PP 1787:04
Deneale, George	Alexandria	Tax Charge	1788	Tax PP 1788:04
Deneale, George	Alexandria	Tax Charge	1789	Tax PP 1789:05
Deneale, George	Alexandria	Tax Charge	1790	Tax PP 1790:03
Deneale, George	Alexandria	Tax Charge	1799	Tax PP 1799:10
Deneale, George	Alexandria	Deed	1815	CRL:490

NAME OR SUBJECT	LOCATION	TYPE	YEAR	REFERENCE(S)
Deneale, George	Arlington	Will	1818	WB2:241; LVA-LP
Deneale, George	Arlington	Inventory	1819	AB3:289; LVA-LP
Deneale, George	Arlington	Account	1820	AB4:135; LVA-LP
Deneale, George	Arlington	Sale	1821	AB4:323
Deneale, George	Arlington	Settlement	1822	LVA-LP
Deneale, George	Arlington	Admin.	1823	OCR1822:038a
Deneale, George	Arlington	Bond	1823	WB3:090
Deneale, George & wife Mary	Alexandria	Serv./Appt.	1800	1800(4):15B
Deneale, George, as Clerk	Arlington	Bill	1807	ACO:075
Deneale, George, Clerk	Arlington	Appointment	1801	ACO:001, 006
Deneale, George, Clerk	Arlington	Payment	1808	ACO:095
Deneale, George, plt.	Alexandria	Suit	1812	CRK:002
Deneale, George, trustee, def.	Alexandria	Suit	1821	CRL:038
Deneale, Hugh	Alexandria	Boarder	1808	1808(3):20A
Deneale, Hugh W.	Arlington	Inventory	1815	AB2:230; LVA-LP
Deneale, Hugh W.	Arlington	Admin.	1815	WB2:097
Deneale, Hugh W.	Arlington	Account	1823	LVA-LP
Deneale, Hugh W., Capt.	Arlington	Sale	1816	AB2:253
Deneale, James	Arlington	Apprentice	1826	OCR1822:112a
Deneale, James, assignee, plt.	Alexandria	Suit	1802	CRD:051
Deneale, Margaret Lowe	Arlington	Admin.	1803	WBA:133
Deneale, Mary	Arlington	Bond	1841	WB4:292
Deneale, Mary	Arlington	Will	1841	WB4:291; File #385A
Deneale, William	Arlington	Apprentice	1824	OCR1822:059a
Deneale's Exrx. v. Stump's Exors.	Arlington	Suit	1837	LVA-LP (Judgments)
Dennett, John L.	Arlington	Sale	1811	AB1:092
Dennett, John L.	Arlington	Account	1811	AB1:093; LVA-LP
Dennett, John L.	Arlington	Inventory	1811	AB1:091; LVA-LP
Dennis, Clement	Alexandria	Tax Charge	1800	Tax PP 1800:07
Dennis, Jas.	Alexandria	Boarder	1808	1808(2):13A
Dennison, John	Alexandria	Tithable +16	1788	Tax PP 1788:03
Dennison, John	Alexandria	Tithable +16	1790	Tax PP 1790:03
Denois, Peter, 2, merchant	Alexandria	Head	1796	1796(3):6
Dent, Geo. W.	Alexandria	Tax Charge	1796	Tax PP 1796:04
Dent, George, as marshal	Arlington	Letter Patent	1801	ACO:001
Dent, Lewis	Alexandria	Tax Charge	1796	Tax PP 1796:04
Dent, Walter	Alexandria	Tithable +21	1787	Tax PP 1787:09
Denty, Matilda (C), sempstress	Alexandria	Housekeeper	1808	1808(4):24A
Dermott, James	Alexandria	Tax Charge	1790	Tax PP 1790:03
Derrick, Jno.	Alexandria	Tax Charge	1795	Tax PP 1795:07
Derrough, Amos	Alexandria	Tax Charge	1798	Tax PP 1798:04
Dertz, Adam, b. Hattenberg	Arlington	Alien Entry	1816	RA:06/06/16
Deshields, Jos.	Alexandria	License Due	1800	Tax PP 1800:54(24)
Deshiels, Thos., clerk	Alexandria	Boarder	1799	1799(2):08A
Desmond, Maurice	Alexandria	Will	1896	WB2:177; LP
Desmond, Tim.	Alexandria	Tax Charge	1795	Tax PP 1795:08
Desnoe, Peter	Alexandria	Tax Charge	1796	Tax PP 1796:04
Detcher, Leonard	Alexandria	Tax Charge	1799	Tax PP 1799:09
Detcher, Leond.	Alexandria	Tax Charge	1798	Tax PP 1798:04
Detcher, Leond.	Alexandria	Tax Charge	1800	Tax PP 1800:06
Devalingen, Thos. P., merchant	Alexandria	Head	1810	1810(1):11A
Devaughn, John, c/o Ann	Arlington	Apprentice	1815	OCR1811:227
Devaughn, Saml., shoemaker	Alexandria	Housekeeper	1808	1808(2):13A
Devaughn, Samuel	Arlington	Apprentice	1816	OCR1811:342
Devaughn, Samuel, c/o Anna	Arlington	Apprentice	1813	OCR1811:191
Devaughn, Thomas, c/o Polly Ogden	Arlington	Apprentice	1811	OCR1811:037
Devaughn, William	Arlington	Apprentice	1814	OCR1811:209
Devaughn, William, c/o Samuel	Arlington	Apprentice	1813	OCR1811:005
Devaughn, William, grantor	Arlington	Indenture D.	1826	ID:032
Devaughn, William, in jail	Arlington	Insolvent	1826	ID:029
DeVaughn, Addison, c/o William	Arlington	Guard. Acct.	1864	WB8:215, 511

NAME OR SUBJECT	LOCATION	TYPE	YEAR	REFERENCE(S)
DeVaughn, Alice, c/o William	Arlington	Guard. Acct.	1864	WB8:215, 511
DeVaughn, James H.	Alexandria	Will	1900	WB2:357; LP
DeVaughn, Susan	Arlington	Dower	1864	WB8:192
DeVaughn, William	Arlington	Inventory	1864	WB8:216
DeVaughn, William	Arlington	Account	1864	WB8:215, 322
DeVaughn, William	Arlington	Appraisal	1864	WB8:181
Devitt, Thomas	Alexandria	Will	1887	WB1:480; LP
Devoise, [blank], Washington St.	Alexandria	Occupant	1795	Tax L 1795:16
Dewees, Dav. P.	Alexandria	Boarder	1808	1808(2):10A
Dick, David	Alexandria	Tax Charge	1800	Tax PP 1800:06
Dick, David, Jr., grantee	Arlington	Indenture D.	1830	ID:258
Dick, David, shoemaker	Alexandria	Housekeeper	1808	1808(1):02A
Dick, David, shoemaker	Alexandria	Head	1810	1810(1):02A
Dick, E.C.	Alexandria	Tax Charge	1795	Tax PP 1795:08
Dick, E.C.	Alexandria	Tax Charge	1798	Tax PP 1798:04
Dick, E.C.	Alexandria	Tax Charge	1800	Tax PP 1800:06
Dick, E.C. & wife, physician	Alexandria	Housekeeper	1799	1799(2):02A
Dick, E.C., Royal St.	Alexandria	Occupant	1790	Tax L 1790:12
Dick, Elisha C.	Alexandria	Tax Charge	1796	Tax LP 1796:07
Dick, Elisha C.	Alexandria	Tax Charge	1796	Tax PP 1796:04
Dick, Elisha C.	Alexandria	Tax Charge	1799	Tax PP 1799:10
Dick, Elisha C.	Arlington	Defendant	1802	PA:040
Dick, Elisha C.	Alexandria	Deposition	1808	CRH:119
Dick, Elisha C. & wife, doctor	Alexandria	Head	1795	1795(4a):10
Dick, Elisha C., Dr.	Alexandria	Tax Charge	1790	Tax PP 1790:03
Dick, Elisha C., Dr.	Alexandria	Deposition	1802	CRI:085
Dick, Elisha C., Duke St.	Alexandria	Occupant	1795	Tax L 1795:07
Dick, Elisha C., physician	Alexandria	Housekeeper	1808	1808(1):02A
Dick, Elisha C., physician	Alexandria	Head	1810	1810(1):01A
Dick, Elisha C., plt.	Alexandria	Suit	1801	CRB:139
Dick, Elisha Cullen	Alexandria	Deed	1795	CRI:045
Dick, Elisha Cullen & wife Hannah	Alexandria	Deed	1796	CRI:314
Dick, Elisha, Dr.	Alexandria	Deed	1786	CRI:310
Dick, Hannah	Arlington	Will P.	1844	OCR1842:059
Dick, Hannah	Arlington	Will	1844	WB4:375; File #411A
Dick, Samuel & wife, mariner	Alexandria	Head	1795	1795(4):05
Dicksan, Thomas	Arlington	Apprentice	1827	OCR1822:140a
Dickson, Robert, of Norfolk	Alexandria	Deposition	1805	CRF:243
Diedel, Adolph	Alexandria	Will	1888	WB1:498; LP
Dier, Elizabeth, sempstress	Alexandria	Housekeeper	1808	1808(1):07A
Dier, Thomas, fisherman	Alexandria	Head	1800	1800(4):14A
Dietz, Adam	Arlington	Inventory	1831	LVA-LP
Diez, Adam	Arlington	Bond	1831	WB4:018
Diez, Adam	Arlington	Will	1831	WB4:018; File #305A
Diez, Dorothee, c/o Catharine	Arlington	Guard. Acct.	1833	LVA-LP
Diez, Dorothy	Arlington	Guard. Acct.	1839	AB8:033; LVA-LP
Diez, Dorothy	Arlington	Guard. Acct.	1840	AB8:133
Diez, Dorothy	Arlington	Guard. Acct.	1841	AB8:247
Diez, Dorothy, c/o Adam	Arlington	Guard. Acct.	1834	LVA-LP
Diez, Dorothy, c/o Catharine	Arlington	Guard. Acct.	1835	LVA-LP
Diez, Dorothy, c/o Adam	Arlington	Guard. Acct.	1842	AB8:310; LVA-LP
Diez, Dorothy, c/o Catharine	Arlington	Guard. Acct.	1843	AB8:358; LVA-LP
Diez, Dorothy, c/o Adam	Arlington	Guard. Acct.	1844	AB8:493; LVA-LP
Diez, Mary D., c/o Adam	Arlington	Guard.	1831	WB4:019
Diez, Rosena, c/o Catharine	Arlington	Guard. Acct.	1835	LVA-LP
Diez, Rosina	Arlington	Guard. Acct.	1839	AB8:033; LVA-LP
Diez, Rosina	Arlington	Guard. Acct.	1840	AB8:133
Diez, Rosina	Arlington	Guard. Acct.	1841	AB8:247
Diez, Rosina, c/o Adam	Arlington	Guard. Acct.	1834	LVA-LP
Diez, Rosina, c/o Adam	Arlington	Guard. Acct.	1842	AB8:310; LVA-LP
Diez, Rosina, c/o Adam	Arlington	Guard. Acct.	1844	AB8:494; LVA-LP

NAME OR SUBJECT	LOCATION	TYPE	YEAR	REFERENCE(S)
Diez, Rosina, c/o Adam	Arlington	Guard. Acct.	1846	AB9:190; LVA-LP
Diez, Rosine, c/o Catharine	Arlington	Guard. Acct.	1833	LVA-LP
Diez, Rosinna, c/o Catharine	Arlington	Guard. Acct.	1843	AB8:358; LVA-LP
Diez, Susannah R., c/o Adam	Arlington	Guard.	1831	WB4:019
Diez [Dietz], Rosina, c/o Adam	Arlington	Guard. Acct.	1845	AB9:076; LVA-LP
Digges, Richard (C)	Arlington	Apprentice	1846	OCR1842:176
Diggle, Charles	Arlington	Seaman	1803	ACO:007
Diggs, Thomas A., def.	Alexandria	Suit	1801	CRB:307
Diggs, Thomas A., plt.	Alexandria	Suit	1801	CRB:302
Dill, Nicho.	Alexandria	Tax Charge	1798	Tax PP 1798:04
Dill, Nicholas	Alexandria	Tax Charge	1790	Tax PP 1790:03
Dill, [blank], Princess St.	Alexandria	Occupant	1790	Tax L 1790:12
Diment, Elizabeth	Arlington	Guard.	1809	WBC:199
Diment, Thomas Kelley, c/o Elizabeth	Arlington	Apprentice	1815	OCR1811:252
Dinmore, Richard, for advertising sale	Arlington	Payment	1805	ACO:037
Dinnett, John L.	Arlington	Admin.	1811	WB1:030
Ditcher, Elmira	Alexandria	Will	1890	WB1:556; LP
Ditcher, Henry	Alexandria	Will	1890	WB1:555; LP
Dix, John	Alexandria	Boarder	1808	1808(2):11A
Dixon, Daniel (C), laborer	Alexandria	Housekeeper	1808	1808(1):05A
Dixon, Eleanor, seamstress	Alexandria	Head	1810	1810(1):01A
Dixon, George O.	Arlington	Will	1862	WB8:135; File #592A
Dixon, George O.	Arlington	Appraisal	1863	WB8:170
Dixon, George O.	Arlington	Account C.	1865	WB8:268
Dixon, James	Alexandria	Tax Charge	1796	Tax LP 1796:06
Dixon, James	Alexandria	Tax Charge	1799	Tax PP 1799:10
Dixon, James	Arlington	Will	1800	CRA:314
Dixon, James	Arlington	Account	1801	WBA:032; LVA-LP
Dixon, James, w2, innkeeper	Alexandria	Head	1796	1796(3):6
Dixon, John	Arlington	Libellant	1805	ACO:045
Dixon, John	Arlington	Admin.	1806	WBB:306
Dixon, John	Arlington	Will	1806	WBB:294; File #020A
Dixon, John	Arlington	Ordinary	1810	OBL2(np)
Dixon, John	Arlington	Ordinary	1810	OBL2(np)
Dixon, John	Arlington	Ordinary	1810	OBL2(np)
Dixon, John	Arlington	Account	1816	AB2:320; LVA-LP
Dixon, John	Arlington	Admin.	1841	WB4:292
Dixon, John A.	Alexandria	Will	1896	WB2:138; LP
Dixon, John B.	Arlington	Inventory	1818	AB3:195; LVA-LP
Dixon, John, baker	Alexandria	Head	1810	1810(1):12A
Dixon, John, Estate, plt.	Alexandria	Suit	1806	CRF:109
Dixon, John, of White Haven, Eng.	Arlington	Will	1802	DBD:157; DBAA:453
Dixon, John, of Whitehaven	Alexandria	Will	1798	CRF:116
Dixon, John, retailer	Alexandria	Housekeeper	1808	1808(1):03A
Dixon, John, retailer & tavern lic.	Alexandria	Housekeeper	1808	1808(1):03A
Dixon, John, seaman	Alexandria	Head	1810	1810(1):03A
Dixon, Mary Ann	Arlington	Admin.	1830	WB3:377
Dixon, Mary J.	Alexandria	Renounce	1871	LP
Dixon, Mary J.	Alexandria	Will	1871	WB1:012; LP
Dixon, Mary Jane, w/o Turner	Arlington	Complainant	1834	LSA:001
Dixon, Mildred	Arlington	Admin.	1819	WB2:335
Dixon, Patrick	Arlington	Will	1834	WB4:078; File #331A
Dixon, Patrick	Arlington	Account	1838	AB8:089; LVA-LP
Dixon, Patrick	Arlington	Account	1840	AB8:089
Dixon, Patrick [Henrietta]	Arlington	Citation	1841	LVA-LP (Box 214)
Dixon, Saml. & wife, shoemaker	Alexandria	Housekeeper	1799	1799(2):14A
Dixon, Samuel	Alexandria	Tax Charge	1788	Tax PP 1788:04
Dixon, Samuel	Alexandria	Tax Charge	1799	Tax PP 1799:09
Dixon, Samuel	Alexandria	Tax Charge	1800	Tax PP 1800:07
Dixon, Samuel, shoemaker	Alexandria	Housekeeper	1808	1808(1):04A
Dixon, Samul & wife Jane	Alexandria	Resident	1800	1800(4):10B

NAME OR SUBJECT	LOCATION	TYPE	YEAR	REFERENCE(S)
Dixon, Samul, shoemaker	Alexandria	Head	1800	1800(4):10A
Dixon, Solomon (C)	Alexandria	Boarder	1808	1808(3):22B
Dixon, Turner	Arlington	Complainant	1834	LSA:001
Dixon, Turner	Arlington	Fid. Bond	1865	FBB(np)
Dixon, Turner, at Lynchburg VA	Arlington	Will (NR)	1865	File #081A; CLOB2:593
Dixon v. Miller	Arlington	Citation Ans.	1841	LVA-LP (Box 214)
Dixon, William (C)	Arlington	Crime	1797	OT:09/06/1797
Dixson, James	Alexandria	Tax Charge	1795	Tax PP 1795:06
Dixson, James	Alexandria	Tax Charge	1796	Tax PP 1796:05
Dixson, Jas., btw. Union	Alexandria	Occupant	1795	Tax L 1795:03
Dixson, Jas., btw. Union	Alexandria	Owner	1795	Tax L 1795:06
Dobbin, Archd.	Alexandria	Tax Charge	1796	Tax LP 1796:06
Dobbin, Archd., Fairfax St.	Alexandria	Occupant	1795	Tax L 1795:28
Dobbin, Archd., Pitt St.	Alexandria	Occupant	1795	Tax L 1795:33
Dobbin, Archibald	Alexandria	Tithable +21	1787	Tax PP 1787:09
Dobbin, Archibald	Alexandria	Tithable +16	1788	Tax PP 1788:10
Dobbin, Archibald	Alexandria	Tax Charge	1795	Tax PP 1795:07
Dobbin, Archibald, w2, merchant	Alexandria	Head	1796	1796(3):1
Dobbin, Henry, b. Wexford	Arlington	Alien Entry	1819	RA:14/07/19
Dobbin, John, b. Wexford	Arlington	Alien Entry	1819	RA:14/07/19
Dobbin, Martha	Arlington	Admin.	1843	OCR1842:043
Dobbin, Martha	Arlington	Will	1843	WB4:335; File #402A
Dobbin, Martha	Arlington	Bond	1843	WB4:370
Dobbin, Martha	Arlington	Inventory	1844	AB8:465; LVA-LP
Dobbins, Archd.	Alexandria	Tithable +16	1790	Tax PP 1790:09
Dobbins, Archibald	Alexandria	Tithable +16	1789	Tax PP 1789:11
Dobey, Joseph Alfred	Arlington	Apprentice	1844	OCR1842:066
Dobey, William	Arlington	Apprentice	1843	OCR1842:037
Dobson, James	Alexandria	Tax Charge	1787	Tax PP 1787:04
Docket, Robert	Alexandria	Will	1899	WB2:323; LP
Dodd, James	Alexandria	Tax Charge	1796	Tax LP 1796:06
Dodd, James	Alexandria	Tax Charge	1799	Tax PP 1799:09
Dodd, James	Alexandria	Tax Charge	1800	Tax PP 1800:06
Dodd, James & wife, brickmaker	Alexandria	Head	1795	1795(4):08
Dodd, Jas.	Alexandria	Tax Charge	1795	Tax PP 1795:07
Dodd, Jas.	Alexandria	Tax Charge	1798	Tax PP 1798:04
Dodge, Robert P.	Arlington	Will	1893	WB10:257; File #759A
Dodson, Charles	Arlington	Apprentice	1828	OCR1822:156a
Dodson, Henry	Alexandria	Tax Charge	1799	Tax PP 1799:09
Dodson, Henry, clerk	Alexandria	Boarder	1799	1799(2):06A
Dodson, Hy.	Alexandria	Tax Charge	1798	Tax PP 1798:04
Dodson, James	Alexandria	Tax Charge	1796	Tax LP 1796:06
Dodson, Jas.	Alexandria	Tax Charge	1795	Tax PP 1795:06
Dodson, Wm.	Alexandria	Boarder	1799	1799(2):08A
Dodson, Wm.	Alexandria	Boarder	1808	1808(1):01A
Doe, Dearborn	Arlington	Admin.	1818	WB2:238
Doen, Geo.	Alexandria	Tax Charge	1795	Tax PP 1795:07
Dogan, Geo. G., l.b. baker	Alexandria	Housekeeper	1808	1808(3):19A
Dogan, Henry, l.b. baker	Alexandria	Housekeeper	1808	1808(3):19A
Dogan, Philip & wife (C), labourer	Alexandria	Housekeeper	1799	1799(2):15A
Doge, Wm.	Alexandria	Tithable +16	1789	Tax PP 1789:03
Doger, Samul, labourrer	Alexandria	Boarder	1800	1800(4):13A
Dogherty, James	Alexandria	Tax Charge	1796	Tax PP 1796:05
Dogherty, Jas.	Alexandria	Tax Charge	1795	Tax PP 1795:06
Dogherty, Jas.	Alexandria	Tax Charge	1795	Tax PP 1795:07
Dogherty, Jas., Cameron St.	Alexandria	Occupant	1795	Tax L 1795:09
Dogherty, Robert	Alexandria	Tax Charge	1796	Tax PP 1796:05
Dogherty, Robt.	Alexandria	Tax Charge	1795	Tax PP 1795:06
Dogherty, Robt., Princess St.	Alexandria	Occupant	1795	Tax L 1795:12
Doing, Joshua	Alexandria	Tax Charge	1798	Tax PP 1798:04
Doing, Joshua	Arlington	Juryman	1808	ACO:081

NAME OR SUBJECT	LOCATION	TYPE	YEAR	REFERENCE(S)
Doing, Joshua, St. Commr.	Alexandria	Housekeeper	1808	1808(4):25A
Doings, Joshua	Alexandria	Tax Charge	1799	Tax PP 1799:09
Dolton, Ann	Alexandria	Resident	1800	1800(4):11B
Dolton, Ann, spinster	Alexandria	Head	1800	1800(4):11A
Dolton, Daniel	Alexandria	Resident	1800	1800(4):11B
Domestic Manufacture Co., plt.	Alexandria	Suit	1812	CRK:002
Donaldson, Andrew	Arlington	Inventory	1815	AB2:204; LVA-LP
Donaldson, Andrew	Arlington	Will	1815	WB2:082
Donaldson, Elizabeth	Arlington	Will	1885	WB10:068; File #719A
Donaldson, John	Alexandria	Tithable +16	1788	Tax PP 1788:14
Donaldson, John	Alexandria	Tithable +16	1789	Tax PP 1789:15
Donaldson, John	Alexandria	Tithable +16	1790	Tax PP 1790:12
Donaldson, John	Arlington	Sale	1856	WB7:108; LVA-LP
Donaldson, John	Arlington	Appraisal	1856	WB7:107; LVA-LP
Donaldson, John T.	Arlington	Account	1858	WB7:293; LVA-LP
Donaldson, Matthew	Alexandria	Tithable +16	1788	Tax PP 1788:04
Donaldson, Mitchel	Alexandria	Tithable +16	1790	Tax PP 1790:04
Donaldson, R., Prince St.	Alexandria	Occupant	1787	Tax L 1787:20
Donaldson, Richd.	Alexandria	Tax Charge	1788	Tax PP 1788:04
Donaldson, Robert	Alexandria	Tax Charge	1787	Tax PP 1787:04
Donaldson, Robert	Alexandria	Tax Charge	1789	Tax PP 1789:05
Donaldson, Robert	Alexandria	Tax Charge	1790	Tax PP 1790:04
Donaldson, Robert, at his house	Arlington	Ordinary	1828	OBL4(np)
Donaldson, Robt., dec.	Alexandria	Tax Charge	1796	Tax LP 1796:07
Donaldson, Robt., Prince St.	Alexandria	Occupant	1790	Tax L 1790:06
Donaldson, Thomas	Arlington	Apprentice	1811	OCR1811:042
Donaldson, Thomas	Arlington	Apprentice	1812	OCR1811:132
Donaldson, Thomas	Arlington	Admin.	1835	WB4:105
Donaldson, Thomas	Arlington	Citation	1844	OCR1842:085
Donaldson, Thomas	Arlington	Account	1845	AB9:042; LVA-LP
Donaldson, Thos., house joiner	Alexandria	Head	1810	1810(3):07A
Donaldson, William	Arlington	Appraisal	1832	LVA-LP
Donaldson, William	Arlington	Admin.	1832	WB4:051
Donlon, Mary, w/o John	Alexandria	Will	1881	WB1:344; LP
Donnaldson, Robt., Duke St.	Alexandria	Owner	1795	Tax L 1795:07
Donnaldson, Robt., Fairfax St.	Alexandria	Owner	1795	Tax L 1795:07
Donnaldson, Robt., King St.	Alexandria	Owner	1795	Tax L 1795:07(4)
Donnaldson, Robt., Prince St.	Alexandria	Owner	1795	Tax L 1795:07
Donnaldson, Robt., Royal St.	Alexandria	Owner	1795	Tax L 1795:07
Donnaldson, Robt., wharf	Alexandria	Owner	1795	Tax L 1795:07
Donnell, Harry (C), drayman	Alexandria	Housekeeper	1808	1808(4):28A
Donnelson, Robert, in Alexandria Co.	Arlington	Ordinary	1827	OBL4(np)
Donnison, P., Duke St.	Alexandria	Occupant	1795	Tax L 1795:02
Donohoe, Patrick	Alexandria	Tax Charge	1787	Tax PP 1787:04
Dorcus, George	Alexandria	Tax Charge	1790	Tax PP 1790:03
Dorman, Thomas	Arlington	Apprentice	1822	OCR1822:026a
Dorman, thos., seaman & shopkeeper	Alexandria	Housekeeper	1808	1808(2):16A
Dorsey, Edward	Arlington	Bond	1852	BB(np)
Dorsey, Edward J.	Arlington	Insolvent	1826	ID:006
Dorsey, Edward J., grantor	Arlington	Indenture D.	1826	ID:009
Dorsey, Edwd.	Alexandria	Boarder	1808	1808(4):27A
Dorsey, Elizabeth	Alexandria	Will	1883	WB1:378; LP
Dorsey, H. Carter	Arlington	Account	1869	WB9:147
Dorsey, Henry Carter	Arlington	Guard.	1841	WB4:293
Dorsey, Henry Carter	Arlington	Will	1863	WB8:171; File #603A
Dorsey, Henry Carter	Arlington	Account	1866	WB8:393, 400
Dorsey, Jane P.	Arlington	Admin.	1843	OCR1842:040
Dorsey, Jane P.	Arlington	Bond	1843	WB4:357
Dorsey, Jane P.	Arlington	Will	1843	WB4:319; File #394A
Dorsey, Jane P.	Arlington	Petition	1844	LVA-LP (Box 214)
Dorsey, Jane P.	Arlington	Account	1850	WB5:296; LVA-LP

NAME OR SUBJECT	LOCATION	TYPE	YEAR	REFERENCE(S)
Dorsey, Jane Prince	Arlington	Inventory	1844	AB8:422; LVA-LP
Dorsey, Jane V.	Arlington	Will P.	1843	OCR1842:027, 028
Dorsey, Matthew	Arlington	Crime	1795	OT:15/12/1795
Dorsey, Mial	Alexandria	Tax Charge	1796	Tax PP 1796:04
Dorsey, Mial	Alexandria	Tax Charge	1798	Tax PP 1798:04
Dorsey, Mial	Alexandria	Tax Charge	1799	Tax PP 1799:09
Dorsey, Mial	Arlington	Admin.	1827	OCR1822:142
Dorsey, Mial, coachmaker	Alexandria	Head	1810	1810(3):03A
Dorsey, Mial, def.	Alexandria	Suit	1801	CRB:302
Dorsey, Mils	Alexandria	Tax Charge	1800	Tax PP 1800:05
Dorsey, Mi'al	Arlington	Admin.	1827	WB3:197
Dorsey, Richard, Capt.	Arlington	Deposition	1822	WB3:065
Doubledee, Sarah	Alexandria	Boarder	1799	1799(2):08A
Dougherty, Daniel	Arlington	Inventory	1823	AB5:151; LVA-LP
Dougherty, Daniel	Arlington	Sale	1823	AB5:164
Dougherty, Daniel	Arlington	Admin.	1823	OCR1822:030a
Dougherty, Daniel	Arlington	Admin.	1823	WB3:081
Dougherty, Daniel	Arlington	Account	1824	AB5:227; LVA-LP
Dougherty, Daniel	Arlington	Account	1825	AB5:381
Dougherty, Daniel	Arlington	Account	1826	AB6:199; LVA-LP
Dougherty, Daniel, c/o Margaret	Arlington	Apprentice	1801	OCR1801:017
Dougherty, Daniel, merchant	Alexandria	Head	1810	1810(3):03A
Dougherty, James	Alexandria	Tax Charge	1796	Tax LP 1796:06
Dougherty, Mary	Arlington	Inventory	1817	AB3:009; LVA-LP
Dougherty, Mary	Arlington	Admin.	1817	WB2:182
Dougherty, Mary, retailer	Alexandria	Housekeeper	1808	1808(2):16A
Dougherty, Richard, b. Wexford	Arlington	Alien Entry	1826	RA:21/11/26
Dougherty, Robert	Alexandria	Tax Charge	1796	Tax LP 1796:06
Dougherty, Robert, Queen St.	Alexandria	Occupant	1790	Tax L 1790:09
Doughety, Robt.	Alexandria	Tax Charge	1788	Tax PP 1788:04
Douglas, Archibald, c/o Daniel	Arlington	Guard.	1812	WB1:176
Douglas, Charles	Alexandria	Mer. License	1798	Tax PP 1798:20-2
Douglas, Charles	Alexandria	Tax Charge	1799	Tax PP 1799:09
Douglas, Charles	Alexandria	License Due	1800	Tax PP 1800:54(24)
Douglas, Charles	Arlington	Admin.	1824	WB3:119
Douglas, Charles, (1)1, doctor	Alexandria	Head	1796	1796(3):3
Douglas, Charles, at Bermuda	Arlington	Will	1823	LVA-LP (Sherron Acct.)
Douglas, Daniel	Alexandria	Tithable +16	1788	Tax PP 1788:15
Douglas, Daniel	Alexandria	Tax Charge	1800	Tax PP 1800:06
Douglas, Daniel	Arlington	Inventory	1803	WBA:235; LVA-LP
Douglas, Daniel	Arlington	Admin.	1803	WBA:218
Douglas, Daniel	Arlington	Account	1805	LVA-LP
Douglas, Daniel	Arlington	Sale	1805	WBB:159
Douglas, Daniel	Arlington	Account	1805	WBB:209, 212
Douglas, Daniel	Arlington	Account	1806	WBB:344; LVA-LP
Douglas, Daniel	Arlington	Account	1807	WBB:528; LVA-LP
Douglas, Daniel	Arlington	Account	1809	WBC:241; LVA-LP
Douglas, Daniel	Arlington	Account	1812	AB1:221
Douglas, Daniel P.P., c/o A.P.	Arlington	Guard.	1829	WB3:353
Douglas, James	Arlington	Admin.	1828	OCR1822:166a
Douglas, James	Arlington	Admin. Bond	1847	ABB(np)
Douglas, John, c/o Daniel	Arlington	Guard.	1812	WB1:176
Douglas, Rebecca, c/o A.P.	Arlington	Guard.	1829	WB3:353
Douglas, Thomas	Alexandria	Tax Charge	1798	Tax PP 1798:04
Douglas, William	Arlington	Will	1884	WB10:053
Douglas, William James	Arlington	Will	1889	WB10:153; File #741A
Douglass & Mandeville, def.	Alexandria	Suit	1805	CRF:010
Douglass, Charles	Arlington	Will P.	1824	OCR1822:063
Douglass, Charles	Arlington	Account	1827	LVA-LP
Douglass, Charles & wife, physician	Alexandria	Housekeeper	1799	1799(2):13A
Douglass, Charles B.R.	Arlington	Inventory	1826	AB6:224

NAME OR SUBJECT	LOCATION	TYPE	YEAR	REFERENCE(S)
Douglass, Charles B.R.	Arlington	Sale	1826	AB6:232
Douglass, Charles B.R.	Arlington	Admin.	1826	WB3:251
Douglass, Charlotte, c/o John	Arlington	Guard.	1829	WB3:353
Douglass, Chas.	Alexandria	Mer. License	1799	Tax PP 1799:52-03r
Douglass, Chas., Doctr.	Alexandria	Head	1810	1810(4):07A
Douglass, Chas., Jr.	Alexandria	Boarder	1808	1808(4):24A
Douglass, Chas., physician	Alexandria	Housekeeper	1808	1808(4):24A
Douglass, Chs.	Alexandria	Tax Charge	1800	Tax PP 1800:06
Douglass, Daniel	Alexandria	Tax Charge	1796	Tax PP 1796:04
Douglass, Daniel	Alexandria	Tax Charge	1799	Tax PP 1799:09
Douglass, Daniel & wife, flour inspector	Alexandria	Head	1795	1795(4):02
Douglass, Danl.	Alexandria	Tithable +16	1790	Tax PP 1790:14
Douglass, Danl.	Alexandria	Tax Charge	1795	Tax PP 1795:07
Douglass, Danl.	Alexandria	Tax Charge	1796	Tax LP 1796:07
Douglass, Danl.	Alexandria	Tax Charge	1798	Tax PP 1798:04
Douglass, Danl. & wife, four inspector	Alexandria	Housekeeper	1799	1799(2):15A
Douglass, Elizabeth, c/o John	Arlington	Guard.	1829	WB3:353
Douglass, Heath, c/o Dr. Charles	Arlington	Apprentice	1802	OCR1801:035
Douglass, Heatley A.	Arlington	Libellant	1813	ACO:137
Douglass, Jacob	Alexandria	Boarder	1808	1808(2):11A
Douglass, James	Alexandria	Tax Charge	1789	Tax PP 1789:04
Douglass, James	Alexandria	Tax Charge	1790	Tax PP 1790:03
Douglass, James	Arlington	Admin.	1828	WB3:333
Douglass, James, King St.	Alexandria	Occupant	1790	Tax L 1790:11
Douglass, James, merchant	Alexandria	Head	1810	1810(4):03A
Douglass, James, retailer	Alexandria	Housekeeper	1808	1808(4):25A
Douglass, James, retailer	Alexandria	Housekeeper	1808	1808(3):23A
Douglass, John, physician	Alexandria	Head	1810	1810(1):01A
Douglass, Margaret	Arlington	Guard. Acct.	1839	AB8:088; LVA-LP
Douglass, Margaret	Arlington	Guard. Acct.	1840	AB8:088
Douglass, Margaret, c/o John	Arlington	Guard.	1838	WB4:171
Douglass, Margaret H., c/o John	Arlington	Guard.	1829	WB3:353
Douglass, Mary, c/o John	Arlington	Guard.	1829	WB3:353
Douglass, Thompson	Alexandria	Boarder	1808	1808(4):25A
Douglass v. Buckingham	Arlington	Suit	1846	LVA-LP (Box 214)
Douglass, Wm.	Alexandria	Boarder	1808	1808(3):22A
Douglass, Wm., merchant	Alexandria	Housekeeper	1808	1808(3):20A
Dousher, George	Alexandria	Tax Charge	1789	Tax PP 1789:05
Douthat, Grundy et al., def.	Alexandria	Suit	1807	CRF:203, 340
Douthat, Robert, def.	Alexandria	Suit	1807	CRF:203, 340
Dove, Benjamin	Alexandria	Tax Charge	1789	Tax PP 1789:05
Dove, Nancy	Arlington	Witness	1794	OT:07/11/1794
Dove, Thos., labourer	Alexandria	Head	1810	1810(3):09A
Dover, Sam, drayman	Alexandria	Housekeeper	1808	1808(4):28A
Dover, Samuel	Alexandria	Head	1810	1810(4):09A
Dowdall, John	Alexandria	Tax Charge	1788	Tax PP 1788:04
Dowdle, Jas.	Alexandria	Tax Charge	1795	Tax PP 1795:07
Dowell, Albert, c/o Jeremiah	Arlington	Guard.	1833	WB4:068
Dowell, George, c/o Jeremiah	Arlington	Guard.	1833	WB4:068
Dowell, James, b/o Jeremiah	Arlington	Apprentice	1815	OCR1811:282
Dowell, James, c/o Jeremiah	Arlington	Guard.	1833	WB4:068
Dowell, Jeremiah	Arlington	Inventory	1823	AB5:204; LVA-LP
Dowell, Jeremiah	Arlington	Sale	1823	AB5:218
Dowell, Jeremiah	Arlington	Admin.	1823	OCR1822:055
Dowell, Jeremiah	Arlington	Admin.	1823	WB3:116
Dowell, Jeremiah	Arlington	Account	1825	AB5:384
Dowell, Jeremiah	Arlington	Guard. Acct.	1835	AB7:192; LVA-LP
Dowell, Jeremiah, children of	Arlington	Guard. Acct.	1836	AB7:192
Dowings, Joshua	Alexandria	Tax Charge	1800	Tax PP 1800:07
Dowings, Joshua, paver	Alexandria	Head	1810	1810(4):04A
Dowins, Joshua & wife, labourer	Alexandria	Housekeeper	1799	1799(2):10A

NAME OR SUBJECT	LOCATION	TYPE	YEAR	REFERENCE(S)
Dowles, Saml. & wife, plaisterer	Alexandria	Housekeeper	1799	1799(2):11A
Dowles, Saml., plasterer	Alexandria	Head	1810	1810(4):05A
Dowles, Saml., shopkeeper	Alexandria	Housekeeper	1808	1808(4):26A
Dowling, Anthony, grantee	Arlington	Indenture D.	1827	ID:106
Dowling, Daniel	Alexandria	Tax Charge	1800	Tax PP 1800:06
Dowling, Daniel	Arlington	Deposition	1802	PA:258
Dowling, Danl., clerk	Alexandria	Boarder	1799	1799(2):02A
Downe, Joseph Gundry	Arlington	P. of Atty.	1811	LVA-LP
Downey, Thomas	Alexandria	Will	1887	WB1:444; LP
Downing, Michl., Estate	Alexandria	Tax Charge	1796	Tax LP 1796:06
Downs, Lemuel	Alexandria	Tax Charge	1800	Tax PP 1800:06
Doxey, Thos., carpenter	Alexandria	Boarder	1799	1799(2):06A
Doxy, Thos., carpenter	Alexandria	Boarder	1799	1799(2):18A
Doyl, Garret	Alexandria	Tax Charge	1800	Tax PP 1800:06
Doyle, Ann, sempstress	Alexandria	Housekeeper	1808	1808(1):04A
Doyle, Conrod	Alexandria	Tax Charge	1787	Tax PP 1787:04
Doyle, Conrod, Royal St.	Alexandria	Occupant	1787	Tax L 1787:06
Doyle, Garret	Alexandria	Tax Charge	1795	Tax PP 1795:08
Doyle, Garret & wife	Alexandria	Head	1795	1795(4):05
Doyle, Garrett	Alexandria	Tax Charge	1796	Tax PP 1796:04
Doyle, Garrett	Alexandria	Tax Charge	1798	Tax PP 1798:04
Doyle, Garrett	Alexandria	Tax Charge	1799	Tax PP 1799:09
Doyle, Gerard	Alexandria	Tax Charge	1796	Tax LP 1796:06
Doyle, James	Alexandria	Tax Charge	1796	Tax LP 1796:06
Doyle, John	Alexandria	Tithable +21	1787	Tax PP 1787:08
Doyle, John	Alexandria	Tax Charge	1788	Tax PP 1788:04
Doyle, Mary, c/o Garret	Arlington	Apprentice	1804	OCR1801:204
Doyle, Nimrod	Alexandria	Tithable +16	1788	Tax PP 1788:14
Doyle, Nimrod	Alexandria	Tithable +16	1789	Tax PP 1789:16
Doyle, Richd.	Alexandria	Tax Charge	1796	Tax PP 1796:05
Doyle, William (non-citizen, servant)	Alexandria	Tithable +21	1787	Tax PP 1787:07
Doyle, William, c/o Garret	Arlington	Apprentice	1805	OCR1801:300
Doysey, [blank], Washington St.	Alexandria	Occupant	1795	Tax L 1795:16
Dozars, Geo., Gretter's alley	Alexandria	Owner	1795	Tax L 1795:06
Drake, Edward	Alexandria	Tax Charge	1799	Tax PP 1799:09
Drake, Edward	Alexandria	Tax Charge	1800	Tax PP 1800:07
Drake, Edwd., carpenter	Alexandria	Housekeeper	1808	1808(4):26A
Drake, Julia	Arlington	Inventory	1840	AB8:162; LVA-LP
Drake, Julia	Arlington	Bond	1840	WB4:278
Drake, Julia	Arlington	Will	1840	WB4:277; File #382A
Drake, Julia	Arlington	Account	1841	AB8:279; LVA-LP
Drake, Julia	Arlington	Account	1842	AB8:279
Drake, Julia	Arlington	Account	1842	AB8:323; LVA-LP
Drake, Julia	Arlington	Account	1842	OCR1842:015
Drake, Julia	Arlington	Account	1843	AB8:392; LVA-LP
Drake, Julia	Arlington	Account	1844	AB9:010
Drake, Julia	Arlington	Account	1845	AB9:126; LVA-LP
Drake, Julia	Arlington	Account	1846	AB9:249
Drake, Julian, seamstress	Alexandria	Head	1810	1810(4):02A
Drake, [blank] & wife, carpenter	Alexandria	Housekeeper	1799	1799(2):14A
Draper, Ida M., of Chicago IL	Arlington	Will	1898	WB10:359; File #784A
Drayman, Alexander	Arlington	Account	1806	WBB:320; LVA-LP
Drayman, John Jones	Arlington	Apprentice	1812	OCR1811:046
Dreadnaught, Ferdinando	Arlington	Suit	1841	LSA:142, 145
Drean, Thomas, cooper	Alexandria	Head	1810	1810(1):08A
Dressler, Lewis, w(3), wheelwright	Alexandria	Head	1796	1796(3):3
Drew, Alice, c/o Solomon (1)	Arlington	Alien Entry	1818	RA:30/11/18
Drew, Charles, grantor	Arlington	Indenture D.	1812	ID2:120
Drew, Charles, in jail bounds	Arlington	Insolvent	1812	ID2:118
Drew, Charles, mariner	Alexandria	Head	1810	1810(1):10A
Drew, Edward Martin, c/o Solomon (7)	Arlington	Alien Entry	1818	RA:30/11/18

NAME OR SUBJECT	LOCATION	TYPE	YEAR	REFERENCE(S)
Drew, Elizabeth, c/o Solomon (12)	Arlington	Alien Entry	1818	RA:30/11/18
Drew, Solomon, b. Helstone	Arlington	Alien Entry	1818	RA:30/11/18
Drew, Susana, c/o Solomon (5)	Arlington	Alien Entry	1818	RA:30/11/18
Driesorynf, Francis, Rev., b. Poland	Arlington	Alien Entry	1822	RA:14/06/22
Drinker, Geo.	Alexandria	Tax Charge	1795	Tax PP 1795:07
Drinker, Geo.	Alexandria	Tax Charge	1798	Tax PP 1798:04
Drinker, Geo.	Alexandria	Mer. License	1800	Tax PP 1800:54(12)r
Drinker, Geo. & wife, merchant	Alexandria	Housekeeper	1799	1799(2):07A
Drinker, Geo., miller & retail shop	Alexandria	Housekeeper	1808	1808(3):20A
Drinker, George	Alexandria	Tax Charge	1796	Tax LP 1796:07
Drinker, George	Alexandria	Tax Charge	1796	Tax PP 1796:05
Drinker, George	Alexandria	Mer. License	1798	Tax PP 1798:20-2
Drinker, George	Alexandria	Tax Charge	1799	Tax PP 1799:10
Drinker, George	Alexandria	Tax Charge	1800	Tax PP 1800:06
Drinker, George	Arlington	Will P.	1846	OCR1842:166
Drinker, George	Arlington	Will	1846	WB4:418; File #431A
Drinker, George	Arlington	Account	1849	WB5:014
Drinker, George, failed to appear as	Arlington	Juryman	1808	ACO:082
Drinker, George, w2, merchant	Alexandria	Head	1796	1796(3):5
Drinker, George [Ruth]	Arlington	Inventory	1846	AB9:169; LVA-LP
Droll, Andrew	Alexandria	Tax Charge	1790	Tax PP 1790:03
Drown, Thomas	Alexandria	Tax Charge	1798	Tax PP 1798:04
Drown, Thomas	Alexandria	Tax Charge	1799	Tax PP 1799:09
Drown, Thomas	Alexandria	Tax Charge	1800	Tax PP 1800:07
Drown, Thos., taylor	Alexandria	Housekeeper	1808	1808(3):22A
Drowns, John	Alexandria	Head	1810	1810(4):06A
Drue, Ezra, grantee	Arlington	Indenture D.	1812	ID2:120
Drum, C., Princess St.	Alexandria	Occupant	1787	Tax L 1787:19
Drumm, Charles	Alexandria	Tax Charge	1787	Tax PP 1787:04
Drummond, John	Alexandria	Tithable +16	1788	Tax PP 1788:10
Drury, John C.	Arlington	Inventory	1822	AB5:032; LVA-LP
Drury, John C.	Arlington	Admin.	1822	WB3:044
Drury, Thomas, c/o Anna	Arlington	Apprentice	1816	OCR1811:325
Drury, William	Arlington	Apprentice	1824	OCR1822:063a
Drydle, Fredk.	Alexandria	Tax Charge	1798	Tax PP 1798:04
Drydle, Fredk.	Alexandria	Tax Charge	1799	Tax PP 1799:10
Drynan, Alexr.	Alexandria	Tax Charge	1800	Tax PP 1800:06
Drynan, Thomas	Alexandria	Resident	1800	1800(4):16B
Drynan, Thomas, coopper	Alexandria	Boarder	1800	1800(4):16A
Dublois, Charlotte Rebecca, c/o Lewis	Arlington	Guard.	1810	WBC:431
Dublois, Eliza, c/o Lewis	Arlington	Guard.	1810	WBC:431
Dublois, John Dalton, c/o Lewis	Arlington	Guard.	1810	WBC:431
Dublois, Mary Ann, c/o Lewis	Arlington	Guard.	1810	WBC:431
Dublois, Matilda, c/o Lewis	Arlington	Guard.	1810	WBC:431
Dublois, Robert, def.	Alexandria	Suit	1801	CRB:329
Dubois, Robert, def.	Alexandria	Suit	1801	CRB:313
Dudley, James	Arlington	Apprentice	1825	OCR1822:097a
Dudley, Joseph	Alexandria	Tithable +16	1788	Tax PP 1788:02
Dudley, Joseph	Alexandria	Tax Charge	1796	Tax LP 1796:06
Dudley, Joseph	Alexandria	Tax Charge	1796	Tax PP 1796:05
Dudley, Joseph	Alexandria	Tax Charge	1798	Tax PP 1798:04
Dudley, Joseph	Alexandria	Tax Charge	1799	Tax PP 1799:09
Dudley, Joseph, painter	Alexandria	Head	1810	1810(3):08A
Dudley, Joseph, painter & shopkeeper	Alexandria	Housekeeper	1808	1808(3):22A
Dudly, Joseph	Alexandria	Tax Charge	1800	Tax PP 1800:06
Duff, James	Alexandria	Tax Charge	1788	Tax PP 1788:04
Duff, James	Alexandria	Tithable +16	1789	Tax PP 1789:05
Duff, James	Alexandria	Tax Charge	1789	Tax PP 1789:05
Duff, James	Alexandria	Tax Charge	1796	Tax LP 1796:06
Duff, James	Alexandria	Tax Charge	1799	Tax PP 1799:10
Duff, James	Alexandria	Tax Charge	1800	Tax PP 1800:07

NAME OR SUBJECT	LOCATION	TYPE	YEAR	REFERENCE(S)
Duff, James	Arlington	Inventory	1831	LVA-LP
Duff, James	Arlington	Bond	1831	WB4:025
Duff, James	Arlington	Will	1831	WB4:024; File #309A
Duff, James	Arlington	Account	1835	AB7:163; LVA-LP
Duff [Daff], John	Arlington	Apprentice	1805	OCR1801:293
Duff, Jno.	Alexandria	Tax Charge	1798	Tax PP 1798:05
Duff, Jno., market	Alexandria	Occupant	1795	Tax L 1795:04
Duff, John	Alexandria	Tax Charge	1787	Tax PP 1787:04
Duff, John	Alexandria	Tax Charge	1788	Tax PP 1788:04
Duff, John	Alexandria	Tax Charge	1795	Tax PP 1795:06
Duff, John	Alexandria	Tax Charge	1796	Tax LP 1796:06
Duff, John	Alexandria	Tax Charge	1799	Tax PP 1799:10
Duff, John	Alexandria	Tax Charge	1800	Tax PP 1800:06
Duff, John	Arlington	Will	1807	WBB:526; File #033A
Duff, John	Arlington	Bond	1807	WBB:527
Duff, John	Arlington	Inventory	1807	WBB:531; LVA-LP
Duff, John	Arlington	Account	1808	WBC:107; LVA-LP
Duff, John, a.k.a. Nelson	Arlington	Defendant	1805	ACO:040, 041
Duff, John, a.k.a. Nelson	Arlington	Defendant	1806	ACO:050
Duff, John, a.k.a. Nelson	Arlington	Respondent	1808	ACO:081
Duff, Sarah, shopkeeper & sempstress	Alexandria	Housekeeper	1808	1808(3):19A
Duffe, Jno.	Alexandria	Tax Charge	1795	Tax PP 1795:06
Duffe, John	Alexandria	Tax Charge	1796	Tax PP 1796:05
Duffe, John, w(5)1, comb maker	Alexandria	Head	1796	1796(3):4
Duffey, Bartho.	Alexandria	Tax Charge	1788	Tax PP 1788:04
Duffey, Bartholomew	Alexandria	Tax Charge	1789	Tax PP 1789:05
Duffey, Catharine	Arlington	Guard.	1827	WB3:299
Duffey, Catharine, c/o George H.	Arlington	Guard.	1827	OCR1822:151a
Duffey, Christopher Philip, c/o John	Arlington	Apprentice	1803	OCR1801:092
Duffey, George	Alexandria	Will	1896	WB2:155; LP
Duffey, Jno.	Alexandria	Tax Charge	1795	Tax PP 1795:06
Duffey, Jno. & wife, comb maker	Alexandria	Housekeeper	1799	1799(2):02A
Duffey, John	Alexandria	Tax Charge	1789	Tax PP 1789:05
Duffey, John, assee. Philip Russell est.	Arlington	Bond	1804	ID3:089
Duffey, John, grantee	Arlington	Indenture	1804	ID3:090
Duffy, B., King St.	Alexandria	Occupant	1787	Tax L 1787:19
Duffy, Bartel	Alexandria	Boarder	1808	1808(2):10A
Duffy, Barth., c/o Marg. Duffy McClish	Arlington	Apprentice	1802	OCR1801:051
Duffy, Bartholomew	Alexandria	Tax Charge	1787	Tax PP 1787:04
Duffy, Bartholw.	Alexandria	Tax Charge	1790	Tax PP 1790:03
Duffy, Barthw., King St.	Alexandria	Occupant	1790	Tax L 1790:05
Duffy, George	Arlington	Ordinary	1821	OBL3(np)
Duffy, George H., on Royal St.	Arlington	Ordinary	1824	OBL3(np)
Duffy, Jno.	Alexandria	Tax Charge	1798	Tax PP 1798:04
Duffy, John	Alexandria	Tax Charge	1790	Tax PP 1790:04
Duffy, John	Alexandria	Tax Charge	1796	Tax LP 1796:06
Duffy, John	Alexandria	Tax Charge	1799	Tax PP 1799:09
Duffy, John	Alexandria	Tax Charge	1800	Tax PP 1800:07
Duffy, John, alley btw. Union & W.	Alexandria	Occupant	1795	Tax L 1795:02
Duffy, John, comb maker	Alexandria	Head	1810	1810(2):03A
Duffy, John, retailer	Alexandria	Housekeeper	1808	1808(2):13A
Duffy, John, Royal St.	Alexandria	Occupant	1790	Tax L 1790:01
Duffy, Kesiah, washwoman	Alexandria	Housekeeper	1808	1808(1):03A
Duffy, [blank], King St.	Alexandria	Occupant	1795	Tax L 1795:16
Dugan, Anthony	Alexandria	Will	1879	WB1:265; LP
Dugan, Margaret	Alexandria	Will	1898	WB2:297; LP
Dugan, Philip (C), laborer	Alexandria	Housekeeper	1808	1808(1):09A
Dugan, Phillip & wife Florrer	Alexandria	Resident	1800	1800(4):03B
Dugan, Phillip, hosler	Alexandria	Head	1800	1800(4):03A
Duglass, Charles & wife Susanah	Alexandria	Serv./Appt.	1800	1800(4):15B
Duglass, Charles, doctor	Alexandria	Head	1800	1800(4):15A

NAME OR SUBJECT	LOCATION	TYPE	YEAR	REFERENCE(S)
Duglass, Nancey	Alexandria	Boarder	1800	1800(4):04A
Dugless, Daniel & wife Charlet	Alexandria	Resident	1800	1800(4):04B
Dugless, Daniel, flower inspector	Alexandria	Head	1800	1800(4):04A
Duke, James, seaman	Alexandria	Head	1810	1810(3):08A
Dulaney, Benja.	Alexandria	Tax Charge	1796	Tax LP 1796:07
Dulaney, Benjn., gentleman	Alexandria	Housekeeper	1808	1808(3):20A
Dulaney, John	Arlington	Will	1867	WB8:532; File #653A
Dulany, Benj.	Alexandria	Tax Charge	1798	Tax PP 1798:05
Dulany, Benj.	Alexandria	Tax Charge	1800	Tax PP 1800:06
Dulany, Benj., Duke St.	Alexandria	Owner	1795	Tax L 1795:08
Dulany, Benja.	Alexandria	Tax Charge	1788	Tax PP 1788:04
Dulany, Benja. & wife	Alexandria	Housekeeper	1799	1799(2):11A
Dulany, Benjamin	Alexandria	Tax Charge	1787	Tax PP 1787:04
Dulany, Benjamin	Alexandria	Tax Charge	1799	Tax PP 1799:09
Dulany, Benjamin	Arlington	Juryman	1808	ACO:081
Dulany, Benjamin	Arlington	Admin.	1818	WB2:264
Dulany, Benjamin	Arlington	Account	1820	AB4:094; LVA-LP
Dulany, Benjamin	Arlington	Report	1821	LVA-LP
Dulany, Benjamin, plt.	Alexandria	Suit	1802	CRC:180
Dulany, Benjamin, plt.	Alexandria	Suit	1808	CRG:077
Dulany, Constance Seaton	Alexandria	Will	1886	WB1:439; LP
Dulany, Eliza	Arlington	Sale	1822	AB5:083
Dulany, Eliza	Arlington	Inventory	1822	AB5:077; LVA-LP
Dulany, Eliza	Arlington	Admin.	1822	OCR1822:011a
Dulany, Eliza	Arlington	Will	1822	WB3:053; File #207A
Dulany, Eliza	Arlington	Bond	1822	WB3:054
Dulany, Eliza	Arlington	Account	1823	AB5:169; LVA-LP
Dulany, Eliza	Arlington	Account	1825	AB5:379
Dulany, Eliza	Arlington	Account	1827	AB6:434; LVA-LP
Dulany, Eliza	Arlington	Account F.	1828	AB6:447; LVA-LP
Dulany, Rebecca Ann, c/o Henry R.	Arlington	Guard.	1836	WB4:115
Dulany, William	Arlington	Inventory	1820	AB4:106; LVA-LP
Dulany, William	Arlington	Admin.	1820	WB2:343
Dulany, William A.	Arlington	Admin.	1839	WB4:238
Dulany, William, constable	Alexandria	Head	1810	1810(3):01A
Dull, John	Alexandria	Boarder	1808	1808(3):21A
Dumaix, Andw.	Alexandria	Tax Charge	1798	Tax PP 1798:04
Dumas, Andw., l.b. baker	Alexandria	Housekeeper	1808	1808(3):21A
Dumax, Andrew	Alexandria	Tax Charge	1799	Tax PP 1799:09
Dumax, Andrew, baker	Alexandria	Head	1810	1810(3):04A
Dumax, Andw.	Alexandria	Tax Charge	1795	Tax PP 1795:06
Dumax, Andw.	Alexandria	Tax Charge	1800	Tax PP 1800:06
Dunbar, Alexander	Arlington	Ordinary	1806	OBL2(np)
Dunbar, Alexander	Arlington	Ordinary	1807	OBL2(np)
Dunbar, Alexander	Arlington	Ordinary	1808	OBL2(np)
Dunbar, Alexander	Arlington	Ordinary	1811	OBL2(np)
Dunbar, Alexr., shopkeeper & tavern lic.	Alexandria	Housekeeper	1808	1808(1):03A
Dunbar, Elizabeth	Arlington	Guard. Acct.	1825	AB5:391
Dunbar, Elizabeth	Arlington	Guard. Acct.	1825	OCR1822:087a
Dunbar, Elizabeth	Arlington	Guard.	1825	WB3:168
Dunbar, Elizabeth	Arlington	Guard. Acct.	1826	AB6:209; LVA-LP
Dunbar, Elizabeth	Arlington	Guard. Acct.	1829	AB6:492; LVA-LP
Dunbar, Jesse	Alexandria	Tax Charge	1796	Tax LP 1796:06
Dunbar, Laura	Arlington	Guard. Acct.	1825	AB5:391
Dunbar, Laura	Arlington	Guard. Acct.	1825	OCR1822:087a
Dunbar, Laura	Arlington	Guard.	1825	WB3:167
Dunbar, Laura	Arlington	Guard. Acct.	1826	LVA-LP
Dunbar, Laura	Arlington	Guard. Acct.	1829	AB6:492; LVA-LP
Dunbar, Laura	Arlington	Guard. Rel.	1839	WB4:233
Dunbar, Laura & Elizabeth	Arlington	Guard. Acct.	1827	AB6:413; LVA-LP
Dunbar, Peter	Arlington	Inventory	1821	AB4:297; LVA-LP

NAME OR SUBJECT	LOCATION	TYPE	YEAR	REFERENCE(S)
Dunbar, Peter	Arlington	Admin.	1821	WB3:007
Dunbar, Peter	Arlington	Sale	1822	AB5:099
Dunbar, Peter	Arlington	Account	1822	AB5:101; LVA-LP
Dunbar, Peter	Arlington	Distribution	1825	AB5:390
Dunbar, Peter, children of	Arlington	Guard.	1827	OCR1822:133a
Duncan, Charles, waiter	Alexandria	Head	1810	1810(1):10A
Duncan, Geo., Estate, nr. Royal St.	Alexandria	Owner	1790	Tax L 1790:03
Duncan, Geo., Estate, Royal St.	Alexandria	Owner	1795	Tax L 1795:07
Duncan, George	Alexandria	Tithable +16	1790	Tax PP 1790:06
Duncan, George, Estate	Alexandria	Tax Charge	1796	Tax LP 1796:06
Duncan, Henry	Alexandria	Tithable +16	1789	Tax PP 1789:08
Duncan, Henry	Alexandria	Tithable +16	1790	Tax PP 1790:06
Duncan, John	Arlington	Will	1896	WB10:341; File #774A
Dundas, Agnes	Arlington	Inventory	1820	AB4:145; LVA-LP
Dundas, Agnes	Arlington	Will	1820	WB2:365; File #177A
Dundas, Agnes	Arlington	Admin.	1823	OCR1822:053a
Dundas, Agnes	Arlington	Bond	1823	WB3:109
Dundas, Eliza	Arlington	Suit	1853	BB(np)
Dundas, Jno.	Alexandria	Tax Charge	1798	Tax PP 1798:04
Dundas, Jno., King St.	Alexandria	Owner	1795	Tax L 1795:06
Dundas, Jno., Pitt St.	Alexandria	Owner	1795	Tax L 1795:06
Dundas, Jno., Princess St.	Alexandria	Owner	1795	Tax L 1795:06
Dundas, Jno., Princess St.	Alexandria	Occupant	1795	Tax L 1795:06
Dundas, John	Alexandria	Tithable +21	1787	Tax PP 1787:06
Dundas, John	Alexandria	Tithable +16	1788	Tax PP 1788:07
Dundas, John	Alexandria	Tithable +16	1789	Tax PP 1789:08
Dundas, John	Arlington	Witness	1795	OT:22/06/1795
Dundas, John	Alexandria	Agreement	1796	CRE:016
Dundas, John	Alexandria	Agreement	1796	CRC:303, 305
Dundas, John	Alexandria	Tax Charge	1796	Tax PP 1796:04
Dundas, John	Alexandria	Tax Charge	1799	Tax PP 1799:10
Dundas, John	Alexandria	Deed	1800	CRE:332
Dundas, John	Alexandria	Deed	1800	CRC:299
Dundas, John	Alexandria	Deed	1800	CRE:221
Dundas, John	Alexandria	Tax Charge	1800	Tax PP 1800:06
Dundas, John	Arlington	Inventory	1813	AB1:331; LVA-LP
Dundas, John	Arlington	Will	1813	WB1:239; File #111A
Dundas, John	Arlington	Bond	1813	WB1:250
Dundas, John	Arlington	Account F.	1815	AB2:121; LVA-LP
Dundas, John, def.	Alexandria	Suit	1805	CRE:001
Dundas, John, gentleman	Alexandria	Head	1810	1810(3):09A
Dundas, John, plt.	Alexandria	Suit	1802	CRC:155
Dundass, Jas.	Alexandria	Boarder	1808	1808(3):18A
Dundass, John	Alexandria	Tithable +16	1790	Tax PP 1790:06
Dundass, John	Alexandria	Tax Charge	1796	Tax LP 1796:06
Dundass, John, gentleman	Alexandria	Housekeeper	1808	1808(3):18A
Dunington, John	Alexandria	Tax Charge	1795	Tax PP 1795:07
Dunington, Wm. P.	Alexandria	Boarder	1808	1808(1):02A
Dunkin, Charles	Alexandria	Resident	1800	1800(4):02B
Dunkin, Charles, lofe bread baker	Alexandria	Head	1800	1800(4):02A
Dunkin, George, Estate	Alexandria	Owner	1787	Tax L 1787:10
Dunlap & Craige, Fairfax St.	Alexandria	Occupant	1790	Tax L 1790:06
Dunlap, Elizabeth, gentlewoman	Alexandria	Housekeeper	1808	1808(1):08A
Dunlap, Jno. & wife, merchant	Alexandria	Housekeeper	1799	1799(2):15A
Dunlap, Jno., Prince St.	Alexandria	Occupant	1795	Tax L 1795:15
Dunlap, John	Alexandria	Tax Charge	1787	Tax PP 1787:04
Dunlap, John	Alexandria	Tax Charge	1788	Tax PP 1788:04
Dunlap, John	Alexandria	Tax Charge	1790	Tax PP 1790:03
Dunlap, John	Alexandria	Tax Charge	1795	Tax PP 1795:07
Dunlap, John	Alexandria	Tax Charge	1796	Tax LP 1796:06
Dunlap, John	Alexandria	Tax Charge	1796	Tax PP 1796:04

NAME OR SUBJECT	LOCATION	TYPE	YEAR	REFERENCE(S)
Dunlap, John	Alexandria	Tax Charge	1798	Tax PP 1798:05
Dunlap, John	Alexandria	Tax Charge	1799	Tax PP 1799:10
Dunlap, John	Alexandria	Deed	1800	CRC:143
Dunlap, John	Alexandria	License Due	1800	Tax PP 1800:54(24)
Dunlap, John	Alexandria	Mer. License	1800	Tax PP 1800:54(12)r
Dunlap, John	Arlington	Juryman	1804	ACO:023
Dunlap, John	Arlington	Juryman	1804	ACO:026
Dunlap, John	Arlington	Bond	1806	WBB:361
Dunlap, John	Arlington	Will	1806	WBB:361; File #023A
Dunlap, John	Arlington	Inventory	1806	WBB:389; LVA-LP
Dunlap, John	Arlington	Sale	1807	WBB:438; LVA-LP
Dunlap, John	Arlington	Account	1807	WBB:541; LVA-LP
Dunlap, John	Arlington	Account	1808	WBC:069
Dunlap, John	Arlington	Debts	1808	WBC:082
Dunlap, John & Co., complt.	Alexandria	Suit	1816	CRK:236
Dunlap, John & wife Elisabeth	Alexandria	Resident	1800	1800(4):05B
Dunlap, John, def.	Alexandria	Suit	1800	CRF:096
Dunlap, John, merchant	Alexandria	Head	1800	1800(4):05A
Dunlap, John, plt.	Alexandria	Suit	1800	CRF:097
Dunlap, John, plt.	Alexandria	Suit	1801	CRC:138
Dunlap, John, Prince St.	Alexandria	Occupant	1787	Tax L 1787:15
Dunlap, Mary	Arlington	Guard. Acct.	1808	WBC:027; LVA-LP
Dunlap, Mary, c/o John	Arlington	Guard.	1806	WBB:363
Dunlap, Saml., clerk	Alexandria	Boarder	1799	1799(2):15A
Dunlap, Samuel, clerk	Alexandria	Boarder	1800	1800(4):05A
Dunlap, William	Arlington	Inventory	1827	LVA-LP
Dunlap, William	Arlington	Admin.	1827	OCR1822:142
Dunlap, William	Arlington	Admin.	1827	WB3:297
Dunlap, William	Arlington	Account	1828	AB6:451; LVA-LP
Dunlap, William, soap boiler	Alexandria	Head	1810	1810(2):01A
Dunlap, Wm., porter merchant	Alexandria	Housekeeper	1808	1808(2):11A
Dunlop, John	Alexandria	Tax Charge	1800	Tax PP 1800:07
Dunlop, John & Co., def.	Alexandria	Suit	1801	CRC:282
Dunlop, John & Co., plt.	Alexandria	Suit	1805	CRE:001
Dunn, J., King St.	Alexandria	Occupant	1787	Tax L 1787:26
Dunn, James W.	Arlington	Guard.	1818	WB2:231
Dunn, John, of Loudoun Co.	Alexandria	Deposition	1822	CRL:539
Dunn, Mrs., King St.	Alexandria	Occupant	1790	Tax L 1790:12
Dunn, William	Alexandria	Tax Charge	1787	Tax PP 1787:04
Dunnington, Elijah	Alexandria	Boarder	1799	1799(2):06A
Dunscomb, Andrew	Arlington	Plaintiff	1802	PA:342
Durant, William	Arlington	Apprentice	1816	OCR1811:337
Duron, Lewis	Alexandria	Tithable +21	1787	Tax PP 1787:11
Dushay, Mons.	Alexandria	Boarder	1808	1808(1):04A
Dusieul, Adelaide	Arlington	Admin.	1808	WBC:108; LVA-LP
Dusieul, Adelaide	Arlington	Appraisal	1809	WBC:110
Dusieul, Adelaide	Arlington	Sale	1809	WBC:269
Dusieul, Adelaide	Arlington	Account	1809	WBC:302
Dusky, Jesse	Alexandria	Tithable +16	1789	Tax PP 1789:07
Duval, Gabriella A.	Alexandria	Will	1879	WB1:274; LP
Duval, William, Fairfax St.	Alexandria	Occupant	1787	Tax L 1787:23
Duvall, Rezin, Princess St.	Alexandria	Owner	1795	Tax L 1795:06
Duvall, William	Alexandria	Owner	1787	Tax L 1787:10
Duvall, William	Alexandria	Tax Charge	1787	Tax PP 1787:04
Duvall, William	Alexandria	Tax Charge	1788	Tax PP 1788:04
Duvall, William	Alexandria	Tax Charge	1789	Tax PP 1789:05
Duvall, William	Alexandria	Tax Charge	1790	Tax PP 1790:03
Duvall, William, Fairfax St.	Alexandria	Owner	1790	Tax L 1790:03
Duvall, Wm., Fairfax St.	Alexandria	Occupant	1787	Tax L 1787:10
Duvall, Wm., Fairfax St.	Alexandria	Occupant	1790	Tax L 1790:03
Dwyer, Anthony	Alexandria	Will	1899	WB2:310; LP

NAME OR SUBJECT	LOCATION	TYPE	YEAR	REFERENCE(S)
Dwyer, Susan	Alexandria	Will	1884	WB1:403; LP
Dwyer, Thomas	Alexandria	Will	1879	WB1:263; LP
Dyckes, Mungo, w(1)2, carpenter	Alexandria	Head	1796	1796(3):1
Dye, Reuben	Arlington	Will	1815	WB2:092
Dye, Reuben	Arlington	Inventory	1816	AB2:245; LVA-LP
Dye, Reuben	Arlington	Account	1817	AB3:011; LVA-LP
Dye, Reuben, sea captain	Alexandria	Housekeeper	1808	1808(1):07A
Dyer, Anthony, merchant	Alexandria	Head	1810	1810(1):04A
Dyer, Anthony, sea captain	Alexandria	Housekeeper	1808	1808(1):04A
Dyer, Benjamin	Arlington	Libellant	1811	ACO:119
Dyer, John W.	Arlington	Apprentice	1845	OCR1842:136
Dyer, Margaret M.	Arlington	Will	1866	WB8:388; File #647A
Dyer, Robert	Arlington	Will	1895	WB10:294
Dyer, Thomas & wife Susaner	Alexandria	Resident	1800	1800(4):14B
Dyer, Thomas, plt.	Alexandria	Suit	1801	CRB:332
Dyer, Thomas, plt.	Alexandria	Suit	1801	CRC:095
Dyer, Thomas, plt.	Alexandria	Suit	1803	CRD:093
Dyer, Walter	Alexandria	Boarder	1808	1808(3):21A
Dyke, James	Alexandria	Tax Charge	1800	Tax PP 1800:07
Dykes, Fleming & Co., Fairfax St.	Alexandria	Occupant	1790	Tax L 1790:02
Dykes, James	Alexandria	Tax Charge	1796	Tax PP 1796:05
Dykes, James	Alexandria	Tax Charge	1798	Tax PP 1798:04
Dykes, James	Alexandria	Tax Charge	1799	Tax PP 1799:09
Dykes, James, plt.	Alexandria	Suit	1802	CRC:262
Dykes, John	Alexandria	Tax Charge	1796	Tax LP 1796:06
Dykes, Mungo	Alexandria	Tax Charge	1787	Tax PP 1787:04
Dykes, Mungo	Alexandria	Tax Charge	1788	Tax PP 1788:05
Dykes, Mungo	Alexandria	Tax Charge	1789	Tax PP 1789:04
Dykes, Mungo	Alexandria	Tax Charge	1790	Tax PP 1790:03
Dykes, Mungo	Alexandria	Tax Charge	1795	Tax PP 1795:08
Dykes, Mungo	Alexandria	Tax Charge	1796	Tax LP 1796:07
Dykes, Mungo	Alexandria	Tax Charge	1796	Tax PP 1796:04
Dykes, Mungo	Alexandria	Tax Charge	1798	Tax PP 1798:04
Dykes, Mungo, Fairfax St.	Alexandria	Owner	1790	Tax L 1790:03
Dykes, Mungo, Fairfax St.	Alexandria	Occupant	1790	Tax L 1790:03
Dykes, Mungo, St. Asaph St.	Alexandria	Owner	1795	Tax L 1795:07
Dykes, Mungo, St. Asaph St.	Alexandria	Occupant	1795	Tax L 1795:07
Dynes, Wade (C), laborer	Alexandria	Housekeeper	1808	1808(1):09A
Dyson, George T.	Arlington	Apprentice	1812	OCR1811:119
Dyson, George T.	Arlington	Guard. Acct.	1814	AB2:001; LVA-LP
Dyson, George T.	Arlington	Guard. Acct.	1815	AB2:084; LVA-LP
Dyson, George T.	Arlington	Guard. Acct.	1820	AB4:164; LVA-LP
Dyson, George T., c/o Joseph	Arlington	Guard.	1812	WB1:177
Dyson, George Thomas	Arlington	Guard. Acct.	1818	AB3:194; LVA-LP
Dyson, Hannah, shopkeeper	Alexandria	Head	1810	1810(1):01A
Dyson, James L.	Alexandria	Will	1890	WB1:554; LP
Dyson, Jos. & wife, retailer	Alexandria	Housekeeper	1799	1799(2):01A
Dyson, Joseph	Alexandria	Tax Charge	1796	Tax LP 1796:06
Dyson, Joseph	Alexandria	Tax Charge	1796	Tax PP 1796:05
Dyson, Joseph	Alexandria	Tax Charge	1798	Tax PP 1798:04
Dyson, Joseph	Alexandria	Mer. License	1798	Tax PP 1799:52-11r
Dyson, Joseph	Alexandria	Tax Charge	1799	Tax PP 1799:09
Dyson, Joseph	Alexandria	Mer. License	1799	Tax PP 1799:52-02r
Dyson, Joseph	Alexandria	Mer. License	1800	Tax PP 1800:54(12)r
Dyson, Joseph	Arlington	Defendant	1802	PA:144
Dyson, Joseph	Arlington	Defendant	1802	PA:043
Dyson, Joseph	Arlington	Admin.	1804	WBA:282
Dyson, Joseph	Arlington	Inventory	1804	WBB:042; LVA-LP
Dyson, Joseph	Arlington	Account	1805	WBB:225; LVA-LP
Dyson, Joseph	Arlington	Account	1807	WBC:025; LVA-LP
Dyson, Joseph	Arlington	Admin.	1813	WB1:205

NAME OR SUBJECT	LOCATION	TYPE	YEAR	REFERENCE(S)
Dyson, Joseph	Arlington	Account	1816	AB2:344; LVA-LP
Dyson, Joseph, for retailing liquors	Arlington	Defendant	1802	PA:005
Dyson, Joseph, w(2)2, shopkeeper	Alexandria	Head	1796	1796(3):6
Dyson, Joseph [wife Hannah]	Arlington	Defendant	1802	PA:057
Dyson, Josh.	Alexandria	Tax Charge	1800	Tax PP 1800:06

NAME OR SUBJECT	LOCATION	TYPE	YEAR	REFERENCE(S)
E				
Eaches, Eliza	Arlington	Guard.	1839	WB4:235
Eaches, Joseph	Arlington	Will	1858	WB7:277; File #551A
Eaches, Joseph	Arlington	Account	1859	WB7:432; LVA-LP
Eaches, Mary	Arlington	Guard.	1839	WB4:235
Eaches, Mary M.	Arlington	Will	1858	WB7:277; File #550A
Eaches, William	Arlington	Inventory	1856	WB7:140; LVA-LP
Eaches, William	Arlington	Appraisal	1856	WB7:107; LVA-LP
Eaches, William	Arlington	Account	1859	WB7:431; LVA-LP
Eagan, Honora	Alexandria	Will	1893	WB2:065; LP
Eaker, Matthew	Alexandria	Tax Charge	1799	Tax PP 1799:11
Eakin, Frederic, confectioner	Alexandria	Housekeeper	1808	1808(2):10A
Eakin, Matthew	Arlington	Inventory	1807	WBB:514; LVA-LP
Eakin, Matthew	Arlington	Admin.	1807	WBB:508
Eakin, Matthew	Arlington	Account	1808	WBC:101; LVA-LP
Earl, David, Estate, Duke St.	Alexandria	Owner	1795	Tax L 1795:08
Earl, David, Estate, Fairfax St.	Alexandria	Owner	1795	Tax L 1795:08
Earl, David, Estate, Royal St.	Alexandria	Owner	1795	Tax L 1795:08
Earl, David, Estate, Water St.	Alexandria	Owner	1795	Tax L 1795:08
Earl, Eliner, widow, 2	Alexandria	Head	1795	1796(3):7
Earl, Henry S.	Alexandria	Tax Charge	1795	Tax PP 1795:08
Earl, Henry S.	Alexandria	Tax Charge	1796	Tax LP 1796:08
Earl, Henry S.	Alexandria	Tax Charge	1796	Tax PP 1796:05
Earl, Henry S.	Alexandria	Tax Charge	1798	Tax PP 1798:05
Earl, Henry S.	Alexandria	Mer. License	1798	Tax PP 1798:20-2
Earl, Henry S.	Alexandria	Tax Charge	1799	Tax PP 1799:11
Earl, Henry S.	Alexandria	Mer. License	1799	Tax PP 1799:52-03r
Earl, Henry S.	Alexandria	Mer. License	1800	Tax PP 1800:54(12)r
Earl, Henry S.	Alexandria	Tax Charge	1800	Tax PP 1800:08
Earl, Henry S.	Arlington	Inventory	1816	AB2:396; LVA-LP
Earl, Henry S.	Arlington	Account	1818	AB3:115; LVA-LP
Earl, Henry S., Capt.	Arlington	Sale	1816	AB2:399
Earl, Henry S., King St.	Alexandria	Occupant	1795	Tax L 1795:19
Earl, Henry S., merchant	Alexandria	Housekeeper	1808	1808(3):20A
Earl, Henry S., merchant	Alexandria	Head	1810	1810(3):02A
Earl, Henry S., w(1), shopkeeper	Alexandria	Head	1796	1796(3):5
Earl, Saml., Duke St.	Alexandria	Owner	1795	Tax L 1795:08
Earl, Saml., Fairfax St.	Alexandria	Owner	1795	Tax L 1795:08(2)
Earle, Abbott	Arlington	Admin.	1804	WBA:239
Earle, Abbott	Arlington	Account	1804	WBA:268; LVA-LP
Earle, Abbott	Arlington	Sale	1804	WBA:267
Earle, Abbott	Arlington	Inventory	1804	WBA:266; LVA-LP
Earle, Esaias	Arlington	Will	1827	WB3:292; File #261A
Earle, Henry S. & wife, grocer	Alexandria	Housekeeper	1799	1799(2):08A
Earle, Henry Stanton	Arlington	Admin.	1816	WB2:131
Earle, Richard	Alexandria	Tax Charge	1795	Tax PP 1795:09
Earll, James & wife Ann	Alexandria	Resident	1800	1800(4):08B
Early, Francis	Alexandria	Tax Charge	1796	Tax PP 1796:05
Early, Francis	Alexandria	Tax Charge	1798	Tax PP 1798:05
Early, Nathl.	Alexandria	Boarder	1808	1808(2):13A
Earp, Caleb	Alexandria	Tithable +21	1787	Tax PP 1787:05
Earp, Caleb	Alexandria	Tax Charge	1789	Tax PP 1789:06
Earp, Caleb	Alexandria	Tax Charge	1790	Tax PP 1790:04
Earp, Caleb	Alexandria	Tax Charge	1795	Tax PP 1795:08
Earp, Caleb	Alexandria	Tax Charge	1796	Tax LP 1796:08
Earp, Caleb	Alexandria	Tax Charge	1796	Tax PP 1796:05
Earp, Caleb, King St.	Alexandria	Owner	1790	Tax L 1790:03
Earp, Caleb, King St.	Alexandria	Occupant	1795	Tax L 1795:08
Earp, Caleb, King St.	Alexandria	Owner	1795	Tax L 1795:08
Earp, Caleb, shopkeeper	Alexandria	Head	1796	1796(3):4
Earp [Erp], Caleb	Alexandria	Tax Charge	1787	Tax PP 1787:05

NAME OR SUBJECT	LOCATION	TYPE	YEAR	REFERENCE(S)
Easby, William, of Washington DC	Arlington	Will	1890	WB10:166; File #745A
Easlyhy [Herlihy], Morris	Alexandria	Tax Charge	1787	Tax PP 1787:05
Eastburn, Joseph	Alexandria	Tax Charge	1795	Tax PP 1795:09
Easton, David	Alexandria	Tax Charge	1796	Tax LP 1796:08
Easton, David	Alexandria	Housekeeper	1808	1808(1):10A
Easton, David, (1)1, merchant	Alexandria	Head	1796	1796(3):6
Easton, David (C)	Alexandria	Tax Charge	1799	Tax PP 1799:11
Easton, David (C)	Arlington	Apprentice	1826	OCR1822:115
Easton, David, def.	Alexandria	Suit	1802	CRD:163
Easton, David, Prince St.	Alexandria	Occupant	1795	Tax L 1795:15
Easton, Hanner	Alexandria	Serv./Appt.	1800	1800(4):15B
Easton, John	Arlington	Apprentice	1823	OCR1822:054a
Easton, Maria	Arlington	Apprentice	1822	OCR1822:023a
Easton, William (C), c/o Caroline Butler	Arlington	Apprentice	1813	OCR1811:156
Easton, William (C), c/o Kesiah Tate	Arlington	Apprentice	1827	OCR1822:138a
Easton [Aston], David	Alexandria	Tax Charge	1800	Tax PP 1800:01
Eawens, John, blacksmith	Alexandria	Head	1810	1810(4):04A
Ebert [Eibert], Adam	Alexandria	Tax Charge	1787	Tax PP 1787:04
Ebhart, Adam, King St., tanyard	Alexandria	Occupant	1790	Tax L 1790:12
Eccleston, Samuel	Arlington	Will	1859	WB7:406; File #564A
Eckford, Walter	Alexandria	Tax Charge	1798	Tax PP 1798:05
Eddick, Geo., b. porter	Alexandria	Housekeeper	1808	1808(2):14A
Eddicks, George	Alexandria	Tax Charge	1799	Tax PP 1799:11
Eddoch, George (C)	Alexandria	Tax Charge	1800	Tax PP 1800:08
Edelin, Robert J.	Alexandria	Will	1880	WB1:302; LP
Edgar, Thomas, of Greenbrier Co.	Alexandria	Deed	1799	CRF:322
Edie, Robert	Alexandria	Tax Charge	1799	Tax PP 1799:11
Edie, Robert & Co.	Alexandria	Mer. License	1799	Tax PP 1799:52-03r
Edmond, Edmond, w(1), schoolmaster	Alexandria	Head	1796	1796(3):3
Edmonds, Courtney Ann Hite	Arlington	Will	1839	WB4:210; File #370A
Edmonds, Edmd., schoolmaster	Alexandria	Housekeeper	1808	1808(1):07A
Edmonds, Edmond	Alexandria	Tax Charge	1787	Tax PP 1787:05
Edmonds, Edmond	Alexandria	Tax Charge	1789	Tax PP 1789:05
Edmonds, Edmond	Alexandria	Tax Charge	1800	Tax PP 1800:08
Edmonds, Edmond & wife, teacher	Alexandria	Housekeeper	1799	1799(2):17A
Edmonds, Edmond & wife Sarah	Alexandria	Resident	1800	1800(4):12B
Edmonds, Edmond, teacher	Alexandria	Head	1810	1810(1):04A
Edmonds, Edmund	Alexandria	Tax Charge	1788	Tax PP 1788:05
Edmonds, Edmund	Alexandria	Tax Charge	1790	Tax PP 1790:04
Edmonds, Edmund	Alexandria	Tax Charge	1799	Tax PP 1799:11
Edmonds, Edmund	Arlington	Admin	1824	OCR1822:065
Edmonds, Edmund	Arlington	Admin.	1824	WB3:122
Edmonds, Edmund, scoolmaster	Alexandria	Head	1800	1800(4):12A
Edmonds, Edward	Alexandria	Tax Charge	1796	Tax LP 1796:08
Edmonds, Elias, at his house	Arlington	Ordinary	1838	OBL5(np)
Edmonds, Elias, at his house	Arlington	Ordinary	1839	OBL5(np)
Edmonds, Geo. W., merchant	Alexandria	Head	1810	1810(3):05A
Edmonds, Meredith M., at his house	Arlington	Ordinary	1839	OBL5(np)
Edmondson, Mary	Arlington	Will	1815	WB2:088
Edmunds, Edm.	Alexandria	Tax Charge	1795	Tax PP 1795:08
Edmunds, Edmd.	Alexandria	Tax Charge	1798	Tax PP 1798:05
Edmunds, Edmd., Fairfax St.	Alexandria	Occupant	1795	Tax L 1795:13
Edmunds, Edmond, nr. Fairfax St.	Alexandria	Occupant	1790	Tax L 1790:06
Edmunds, Edmund	Alexandria	Tax Charge	1796	Tax PP 1796:05
Edmunds, Edmund	Arlington	Account	1824	AB5:262
Edmunds, J., Royal St.	Alexandria	Occupant	1787	Tax L 1787:12
Edward Stabler & Son	Arlington	Inventory	1831	LVA-LP
Edwards, Ann	Alexandria	Resident	1800	1800(4):08B
Edwards, Ann, labourrer	Alexandria	Boarder	1800	1800(4):08A
Edwards, David	Alexandria	Tax Charge	1789	Tax PP 1789:05
Edwards, Elizabeth	Arlington	Apprentice	1827	OCR1822:130a

NAME OR SUBJECT	LOCATION	TYPE	YEAR	REFERENCE(S)
Edwards, Jared	Alexandria	Boarder	1808	1808(4):24A
Edwards, Meredith M.	Arlington	Ordinary	1841	OBL6(np)
Edwards, Wm.	Alexandria	Boarder	1808	1808(4):24A
Egan, William	Alexandria	Will	1876	WB1:177; LP
Egolff, John Valentine	Alexandria	Tax Charge	1799	Tax PP 1799:11
Egolph, John V.	Alexandria	Tax Charge	1800	Tax PP 1800:08
Ehlers, Catharine	Arlington	Account	1827	AB6:439; LVA-LP
Ehlers, Catherine	Arlington	Inventory	1827	AB6:279; LVA-LP
Ehlers, Catherine	Arlington	Will	1827	WB3:272; File #255A
Ehlers, Catherine	Arlington	Bond	1827	WB3:274
Ehlers, John C.	Arlington	Inventory	1821	AB4:235; LVA-LP
Ehlers, John C.	Arlington	Will	1821	WB2:415; File #189A
Ehlers, John C.	Arlington	Admin.	1821	WB2:416
Ehlers, John C.	Arlington	Account	1823	AB5:145; LVA-LP
Ehrmann, Anna Catharina	Alexandria	Will	1886	WB1:441; LP
Eibert, Adam	Alexandria	Tax Charge	1790	Tax PP 1790:04
Eibert, Adam	Alexandria	Tithable +16	1790	Tax PP 1790:08
Eiles, Samuel	Alexandria	Tax Charge	1790	Tax PP 1790:04
Eisler, George, w, cooper	Alexandria	Head	1796	1796(3):4
Ekin, Mathews	Alexandria	Tax Charge	1800	Tax PP 1800:08
Eldridge, Levi, wheelwright	Alexandria	Head	1810	1810(1):05A
Eldrige, Levi, wheelwright	Alexandria	Housekeeper	1808	1808(1):03A
Eldrige, Robt.	Alexandria	Boarder	1808	1808(2):12A
Ellendorf, Henry & wife, carpenter	Alexandria	Housekeeper	1799	1799(2):16A
Ellice, Sarah	Alexandria	Serv./Appr.	1800	1800(4):10B
Ellicot, Mary	Arlington	Account	1842	OCR1842:011
Ellicott, Andrew	Arlington	Will	1879	WB10:013; File #704A
Ellicott, Evan T., Jr.	Arlington	Will	1881	WB10:016; File #705A
Ellicott, John M.	Arlington	Will	1841	WB4:327; File #399A
Ellicott, John M.	Arlington	Will P.	1843	OCR1842:034
Ellicott, Mary	Arlington	Will	1842	WB4:305; File #389A
Ellicott, Mary	Arlington	Bond	1842	WB4:307
Ellicott, Mary	Arlington	Inventory	1843	AB8:357, 371; LVA-LP
Ellicott, Mary	Arlington	Account	1843	AB8:390; LVA-LP
Ellicott, Mary	Arlington	Appraisers	1843	OCR1842:034
Ellicott, Mary	Arlington	Account	1844	AB9:008; LVA-LP
Ellicott, Mary	Arlington	Petition	1844	LVA-LP (Box 214)
Ellicott, Mary	Arlington	Account	1845	AB9:120
Ellicott, Mary	Arlington	Account	1846	AB9:180; LVA-LP
Ellicott, Mary	Arlington	Account	1852	WB6:063; LVA-LP
Elliot, Francis	Alexandria	Tithable +16	1789	Tax PP 1789:08
Elliot, Francis	Alexandria	Tithable +16	1790	Tax PP 1790:06
Ellis, Aminta	Arlington	Apprentice	1822	OCR1822:023a
Ellis, Ann Maria, w/o Joshua	Alexandria	Will	1892	WB2:006; LP
Ellis, John	Arlington	Ordinary	1803	OBL1(np)
Ellis, John	Arlington	Admin.	1822	WB3:062
Ellis, Philippe	Arlington	Guard.	1808	WBC:067
Ellis, Samuel	Arlington	Apprentice	1822	OCR1822:022
Ellis, William	Arlington	Apprentice	1822	OCR1822:022
Ellis, Wm., Estate	Alexandria	Owner	1787	Tax L 1787:10
Ellis, [blank], heirs, nr. Water St.	Alexandria	Owner	1790	Tax L 1790:03
Elliss, George, labourer	Alexandria	Head	1810	1810(1):12A
Ellwood, William	Alexandria	Deposition	1806	CRG:286
Ellzey, Lewis	Alexandria	Tax Charge	1796	Tax PP 1796:05
Ellzey, William, Jr., plt.	Alexandria	Suit	1802	CRC:047
Elwine, Francis	Arlington	Admin.	1806	WBB:290
Emack, William	Alexandria	Tax Charge	1799	Tax PP 1799:11
Emack, William	Alexandria	Mer. License	1799	Tax PP 1799:52-03r
Emack, William	Alexandria	Tax Charge	1800	Tax PP 1800:08
Emack, Willm.	Alexandria	Mer. License	1798	Tax PP 1798:20-2
Emack, Wm.	Alexandria	Tax Charge	1798	Tax PP 1798:05

NAME OR SUBJECT	LOCATION	TYPE	YEAR	REFERENCE(S)
Emack, Wm. & wife, grocer	Alexandria	Housekeeper	1799	1799(2):15A
Emack, Wm. & wife Ana	Alexandria	Resident	1800	1800(4):06B
Emack, Wm., shopkeeper	Alexandria	Head	1800	1800(4):06A
Emerson, Aquila	Arlington	Ordinary	1821	OBL3(np)
Emerson, Aquila	Arlington	Exor. Bond	1850	EBB(np)
Emerson, Aquila, at his house	Arlington	Ordinary	1830	OBL4(np)
Emerson, Aquila, at his house	Arlington	Ordinary	1831	OBL4(np)
Emerson, Aquila, at his house	Arlington	Ordinary	1832	OBL4(np)
Emerson, Aquilla	Arlington	Ordinary	1808	OBL2(np)
Emerson, Aquilla	Arlington	Inventory	1859	WB7:464; LVA-LP
Emerson, Aquilla	Arlington	Sale	1859	WB7:466; LVA-LP
Emerson, Aquilla, at his house	Arlington	Ordinary	1833	OBL5(np)
Emerson, Aquilla, at his house	Arlington	Ordinary	1834	OBL5(np)
Emerson, Ellen	Arlington	Account	1856	WB7:114; LVA-LP
Emerson, John P.	Alexandria	Will	1883	WB1:417; LP
Emerson, John S., grantee	Arlington	Indenture D.	1831	ID:340
Emerson, John Simpson, s/o Aquila	Arlington	Apprentice	1813	OCR1811:160
Emerson, John W., at his house	Arlington	Ordinary	1833	OBL5(np)
Emerson, Prudence	Alexandria	Will	1900	WB2:384; LP
Emerson, Richard D., grantor	Arlington	Indenture D.	1828	ID:208
Emerson, Richard D., in prison bounds	Arlington	Insolvent	1828	ID:205
Emery, William	Alexandria	Tax Charge	1789	Tax PP 1789:05
Emmerson, Aquilla	Arlington	Will	1850	WB5:215; File #456A
Emmerson, Eleanor	Arlington	Appraisal	1855	WB6:426; LVA-LP
Emmerson, John S.	Arlington	Will	1865	WB8:260; File #631A
Emmet, Josiah	Alexandria	Tithable +16	1789	Tax PP 1789:07
Emmet, Josiah & wife, turner	Alexandria	Head	1795	1795(4):06
Emmet, Josiah & wife, turner	Alexandria	Housekeeper	1799	1799(2):13A
Emmett, Josiah	Alexandria	Tax Charge	1790	Tax PP 1790:04
Emmett, Josiah	Alexandria	Tax Charge	1795	Tax PP 1795:08
Emmett, Josiah	Alexandria	Tax Charge	1796	Tax LP 1796:08
Emmett, Josiah	Alexandria	Tax Charge	1796	Tax PP 1796:05
Emmett, Josiah	Alexandria	Tax Charge	1798	Tax PP 1798:05
Emmett, Josiah, back building	Alexandria	Occupant	1795	Tax L 1795:02
Emmett, Josiah, Fairfax St.	Alexandria	Occupant	1795	Tax L 1795:11
Emmit, Josiah	Alexandria	Tax Charge	1788	Tax PP 1788:05
Emmit, Josiah	Alexandria	Tax Charge	1799	Tax PP 1799:11
Emmit, Josiah	Alexandria	Tax Charge	1800	Tax PP 1800:08
Emmit, Josies & wife Cartharine	Alexandria	Resident	1800	1800(4):11B
Emmit, Josies, turner	Alexandria	Head	1800	1800(4):11A
Emmonds, William	Alexandria	Tax Charge	1800	Tax PP 1800:08
Emmons, Willm. & wife, sea captain	Alexandria	Housekeeper	1799	1799(2):04A
Emmons, Wm. & wife Hannah	Alexandria	Resident	1800	1800(4):12B
Emmons, Wm., marriner	Alexandria	Head	1800	1800(4):12A
Engle, Henry & wife, ironmonger	Alexandria	Housekeeper	1799	1799(2):03A
Engle, Jos. & wife, cabinet maker	Alexandria	Housekeeper	1799	1799(2):03A
Englin, Joseph, w(1)1, cabinet maker	Alexandria	Head	1796	1796(3):3
English, James	Arlington	Appraisal	1863	WB8:147
English, James	Arlington	Sale	1863	WB8:162
English, James	Arlington	Will	1863	WB8:143; File #595A
English, James	Arlington	Account	1865	WB8:240
English, James, at his house	Arlington	Ordinary	1825	OBL4(np)
English, James, at his house	Arlington	Ordinary	1827	OBL4(np)
English, James, at his house	Arlington	Ordinary	1828	OBL4(np)
English, James, at his house	Arlington	Ordinary	1830	OBL4(np)
English, James, at his house	Arlington	Ordinary	1831	OBL4(np)
English, James, at his house	Arlington	Ordinary	1832	OBL4(np)
English, James, at his house	Arlington	Ordinary	1834	OBL5(np)
English, James, at his house	Arlington	Ordinary	1835	OBL5(np)
English, James, at his house	Arlington	Ordinary	1837	OBL5(np)
English, James, at his house	Arlington	Ordinary	1842	OBL6(np)

NAME OR SUBJECT	LOCATION	TYPE	YEAR	REFERENCE(S)
English, James, at his house	Arlington	Ordinary	1848	OBL6(np)
English, James, at his house	Arlington	Ordinary	1849	OBL6(np)
English, James, his house Cameron St.	Arlington	Ordinary	1833	OBL5(np)
English, James, his house Cameron St.	Arlington	Ordinary	1838	OBL5(np)
English, James, in Alexandria Co.	Arlington	Ordinary	1824	OBL3(np)
English, James, in Alexandria Co.	Arlington	Ordinary	1847	OBL6(np)
English, James, on Cameron St.	Arlington	Ordinary	1841	OBL6(np)
English, James, on Cameron St.	Arlington	Ordinary	1843	OBL6(np)
English, James, on Cameron St.	Arlington	Ordinary	1844	OBL6(np)
English, James, on Cameron St.	Arlington	Ordinary	1845	OBL6(np)
English, Josph.	Alexandria	Tax Charge	1795	Tax PP 1795:08
English, Zelph, of Baltimore Co. MD	Alexandria	Will	1877	WB1:221; LP
Entwisle, Isa., retailer & brewer, T.L.	Alexandria	Housekeeper	1808	1808(1):03A
Entwisle, Isaac	Arlington	Ordinary	1802	OBL1(np)
Entwisle, Isaac	Arlington	Ordinary	1803	OBL1(np)
Entwisle, Isaac	Arlington	Ordinary	1804	OBL1(np)
Entwisle, Isaac	Arlington	Ordinary	1805	OBL1(np)
Entwisle, Isaac	Arlington	Ordinary	1808	OBL2(np)
Entwisle, Isaac	Arlington	Ordinary	1809	OBL2(np)
Entwisle, Isaac	Arlington	Ordinary	1810	OBL2(np)
Entwisle, Isaac	Arlington	Inventory	1821	AB4:295; LVA-LP
Entwisle, Isaac	Arlington	Sale	1821	AB4:320
Entwisle, Isaac	Arlington	Admin.	1821	WB3:008, 106
Entwisle, Isaac	Arlington	Account	1822	AB5:107; LVA-LP
Entwisle, Isaac	Arlington	Account	1830	AB6:519; LVA-LP
Entwisle, Isaac, b. Bolton, Lincolnshire	Arlington	Alien Entry	1817	RA:22/12/17
Entwisle, Isaac, brewer	Alexandria	Head	1810	1810(1):07A
Entwisle, Isaac, brewer	Arlington	Witness	1820	ACO:175, 176
Entwisle, Isaac, Jr.	Arlington	Ordinary	1821	OBL3(np)
Entwisle, James	Arlington	Inventory	1821	AB5:008
Entwisle, James	Arlington	Admin.	1821	WB3:027
Entwisle, James	Arlington	Admin.	1828	OCR1822:162a
Entwisle, James	Arlington	Admin.	1829	OCR1822:172
Entwisle, James	Alexandria	Will	1876	WB1:197; LP
Episcopal Church, Fairfax Parish	Alexandria	Survey	1770	CRI:170
Episcopal Church, Fairfax Parish, def.	Alexandria	Suit	1813	CRI:158
Erel, James, ship carpenter	Alexandria	Head	1800	1800(4):08A
Erena, Herculus, b. Dublin	Arlington	Alien Entry	1802	RA:21/01/02
Erinshaw, Westly, c/o Eleanor	Arlington	Apprentice	1804	OCR1801:167
Erly, William	Alexandria	Deposition	(nd)	CRE:347
Erly [Oxley], William, Plt.	Alexandria	Suit	1804	CRE:139
Ermage, Anthony	Alexandria	Tax Charge	1789	Tax PP 1789:05
Ervin, Thos., Union St.	Alexandria	Owner	1795	Tax L 1795:08
Ervin, William, w(1)2, cabinet maker	Alexandria	Head	1796	1796(3):2
Ervin, Wm., St. Asaph St.	Alexandria	Occupant	1795	Tax L 1795:08
Ervin, Wm., St. Asaph St.	Alexandria	Owner	1795	Tax L 1795:08
Ervine, Thos., Union St.	Alexandria	Occupant	1795	Tax L 1795:08
Ervine, Wm.	Alexandria	Tax Charge	1795	Tax PP 1795:08
Erwin, Wm.	Alexandria	Tax Charge	1796	Tax PP 1796:05
Eskew, John	Arlington	Will	1812	WB1:179; File #102A
Essex, Wm., labourer	Alexandria	Head	1810	1810(1):04A
Estaave, Andw.	Alexandria	Tax Charge	1798	Tax PP 1798:05
Estave, Andrew	Alexandria	Tax Charge	1796	Tax PP 1796:05
Estave, Andrew, w(1)1, baker	Alexandria	Head	1796	1796(3):5
Estaves, Andw.	Alexandria	Tax Charge	1796	Tax LP 1796:08
Evans, E., Fairfax St.	Alexandria	Occupant	1787	Tax L 1787:12
Evans, Edward, of PA	Alexandria	Will	1890	WB1:563; LP
Evans, Eliza	Alexandria	Boarder	1799	1799(2):07A
Evans, Elizabeth	Arlington	Will	1836	WB4:123; File #343A
Evans, Ephm.	Alexandria	Tax Charge	1795	Tax PP 1795:08
Evans, Ephm., Royal St.	Alexandria	Occupant	1795	Tax L 1795:08

NAME OR SUBJECT	LOCATION	TYPE	YEAR	REFERENCE(S)
Evans, Ephraim	Alexandria	Tax Charge	1787	Tax PP 1787:05
Evans, Ephraim	Alexandria	Tax Charge	1788	Tax PP 1788:05
Evans, Ephraim	Alexandria	Tax Charge	1789	Tax PP 1789:06
Evans, Ephraim	Alexandria	Tax Charge	1790	Tax PP 1790:04
Evans, Ephraim	Alexandria	Tax Charge	1796	Tax LP 1796:08
Evans, Ephraim	Alexandria	Tax Charge	1796	Tax PP 1796:05
Evans, Ephraim	Alexandria	Tax Charge	1799	Tax PP 1799:11
Evans, Ephraim	Alexandria	Tax Charge	1800	Tax PP 1800:08
Evans, Ephraim & wife, chair maker	Alexandria	Housekeeper	1799	1799(2):08A
Evans, Ephraim, chairmaker	Alexandria	Housekeeper	1808	1808(1):04A
Evans, Ephraim, chairmaker	Alexandria	Head	1810	1810(1):04A
Evans, Ephraim, Fairfax St.	Alexandria	Occupant	1795	Tax L 1795:06
Evans, Ephraim, Royal St.	Alexandria	Owner	1795	Tax L 1795:08
Evans, Ephraim, w(3)1, chairmaker	Alexandria	Head	1796	1796(3):1
Evans, Epm.	Alexandria	Tax Charge	1798	Tax PP 1798:05
Evans, George	Alexandria	Mer. License	1799	Tax PP 1799:52-03r
Evans, James, brickmaker	Alexandria	Head	1810	1810(4):03A
Evans, Jno.	Alexandria	Tax Charge	1795	Tax PP 1795:08
Evans, Jno.	Alexandria	Tax Charge	1796	Tax PP 1796:05
Evans, Jno. & wife, waterman	Alexandria	Housekeeper	1799	1799(2):11A
Evans, Jno. & wife, merchant	Alexandria	Housekeeper	1799	1799(2):17A
Evans, Jno., taylor	Alexandria	Boarder	1799	1799(2):03A
Evans, John	Alexandria	Tax Charge	1800	Tax PP 1800:08
Evans, John	Alexandria	Tax Charge	1800	Tax PP 1800:08
Evans, John	Alexandria	Suit	1802	CRB:220
Evans, John & Co., Duke St.	Alexandria	Occupant	1787	Tax L 1787:15
Evans, John, boatman	Alexandria	Housekeeper	1808	1808(2):16A
Evans, John, cooper	Alexandria	Head	1810	1810(1):13A
Evans, John, def.	Alexandria	Suit	1809	CRH:182
Evans, John, labourer	Alexandria	Head	1810	1810(2):08A
Evans, John, of Washington DC	Alexandria	Will	1900	WB2:398; LP
Evans, John, ship carpenter	Alexandria	Head	1810	1810(2):08A
Evans, John, w, labourer	Alexandria	Head	1796	1796(3):6
Evans, Joseph, Jr., assignee, plt.	Alexandria	Suit	1801	CRB:243
Evans, Robert	Alexandria	Tax Charge	1787	Tax PP 1787:05
Evans, Robert	Alexandria	Tax Charge	1788	Tax PP 1788:05
Evans, Robert	Alexandria	Tax Charge	1789	Tax PP 1789:05
Evans, Robert	Alexandria	Tax Charge	1790	Tax PP 1790:04
Evans, Robert	Alexandria	Tax Charge	1795	Tax PP 1795:08
Evans, Robert	Alexandria	Tax Charge	1796	Tax LP 1796:08
Evans, Robert	Alexandria	Mer. License	1799	Tax PP 1799:52-03r
Evans, Robert	Alexandria	Tax Charge	1799	Tax PP 1799:11
Evans, Robert	Alexandria	Mer. License	1799	Tax PP 1799:52-03(2)r
Evans, Robert	Alexandria	Tax Charge	1800	Tax PP 1800:08
Evans, Robert	Arlington	Defendant	1802	PA:280
Evans, Robert	Arlington	Inventory	1810	AB1:014
Evans, Robert	Arlington	Ordinary	1810	OBL2(np)
Evans, Robert	Arlington	Ordinary	1810	OBL2(np)
Evans, Robert	Arlington	Admin.	1810	WB1:015
Evans, Robert	Arlington	Inventory	1811	AB1:090; LVA-LP
Evans, Robert	Arlington	Account	1812	AB1:167
Evans, Robert F., grantor	Arlington	Indenture D.	1832	ID:388
Evans, Robert F., in jail bounds	Arlington	Insolvent	1832	ID:387
Evans, Robert, nr. Adams' wharf	Alexandria	Occupant	1790	Tax L 1790:03
Evans, Robert, nr. Adams' wharf	Alexandria	Owner	1790	Tax L 1790:03
Evans, Robert, ret. liquor w/o license	Arlington	Defendant	1802	PA:323
Evans, Robert, shoemaker	Alexandria	Head	1810	1810(1):03A
Evans, Robert, shopkeeper	Alexandria	Head	1810	1810(1):12A
Evans, Robert, Union St.	Alexandria	Occupant	1787	Tax L 1787:01
Evans, Robert, w(3), express rider	Alexandria	Head	1796	1796(3):5
Evans, Robt.	Alexandria	Boarder	1808	1808(1):08A

NAME OR SUBJECT	LOCATION	TYPE	YEAR	REFERENCE(S)
Evans, Robt. & wife, huckster	Alexandria	Housekeeper	1799	1799(2):03A
Evans, Robt., Prince St.	Alexandria	Occupant	1795	Tax L 1795:08
Evans, Robt., Prince St.	Alexandria	Owner	1795	Tax L 1795:08
Evans, Robt., shopkeeper	Alexandria	Housekeeper	1808	1808(1):03A
Evans, Saml., wheelwright	Alexandria	Boarder	1799	1799(2):04A
Evans, Samuel	Alexandria	Tax Charge	1795	Tax PP 1795:08
Evans, Samuel	Alexandria	Tax Charge	1796	Tax PP 1796:05
Evans, Samuel	Alexandria	Tax Charge	1799	Tax PP 1799:11
Evans, Samuel	Alexandria	Tax Charge	1800	Tax PP 1800:08
Evans, Thomas	Alexandria	Tithable +16	1788	Tax PP 1788:05
Evans, Thomas	Alexandria	Tithable +16	1789	Tax PP 1789:06
Evans, Thomas	Alexandria	Tithable +16	1790	Tax PP 1790:04
Evans, Thomas	Alexandria	Tax Charge	1799	Tax PP 1799:11
Evans, Thomas & wife, chairmaker	Alexandria	Head	1795	1795(4):07
Evans, Thos.	Alexandria	Tax Charge	1795	Tax PP 1795:08
Evans, Thos.	Alexandria	Tax Charge	1796	Tax PP 1796:05
Evans, Thos.	Alexandria	Tax Charge	1798	Tax PP 1798:05
Evans, Thos.	Alexandria	Tax Charge	1800	Tax PP 1800:08
Evans, Thos. & wife, chair maker	Alexandria	Housekeeper	1799	1799(2):10A
Evans, William, shopkeeper	Alexandria	Head	1810	1810(3):02A
Eve, Francis, Capt., of Bermuda	Arlington	Account	1812	AB1:183; LVA-LP
Eve, George W.	Alexandria	Will	1875	WB1:137; LP
Eveleth, Ebenezer	Alexandria	Tax Charge	1799	Tax PP 1799:11
Eveleth, Ebenezer	Arlington	Defendant	1802	PA:297
Eveleth, Ebenezer	Arlington	Defendant	1802	PA:307
Eveleth, Ebenezer	Arlington	Inventory	1815	AB2:157; LVA-LP
Eveleth, Ebenezer	Arlington	Admin.	1815	WB2:059
Evens, Susaner, labourrer	Alexandria	Boarder	1800	1800(4):13A
Everard & Johnson	Alexandria	Mer. License	1798	Tax PP 1798:20-2
Everard, Wm.	Alexandria	Tax Charge	1798	Tax PP 1798:05
Everet, Henry W., Master	Arlington	Respondent	1827	ACO:269, 270
Everett, A., King St.	Alexandria	Occupant	1787	Tax L 1787:26
Everett, Eli	Arlington	Apprentice	1802	OCR1801:070
Evert, Adam	Alexandria	Tax Charge	1788	Tax PP 1788:05
Evert, Adam	Alexandria	Tax Charge	1789	Tax PP 1789:05
Eves, Benjamin, stage driver	Alexandria	Head	1810	1810(3):06A
Ewell, Thomas	Arlington	Plaintiff	1815	ACO:142, 144, 147
Ewers, E.	Alexandria	Boarder	1808	1808(1):04A
Ewing, Cornelia L.	Arlington	Guard.	1851	BB(np)
Ewing, James H.	Arlington	Guard.	1851	BB(np)
Ewing, Laura B.	Arlington	Guard.	1851	BB(np)
Ewing, Maskell	Arlington	Guard.	1851	BB(np)

NAME OR SUBJECT	LOCATION	TYPE	YEAR	REFERENCE(S)
F				
Fadley, Elizabeth, shopkeeper	Alexandria	Housekeeper	1808	1808(4):25A
Fagan, Polly, c/o Nicholas	Arlington	Apprentice	1805	OCR1801:236
Fagen, Saml. B.	Alexandria	Tithable +16	1789	Tax PP 1789:07
Fair, Mary (C)	Arlington	Apprentice	1845	OCR1842:105
Fair, Stephen, grave digger	Alexandria	Housekeeper	1808	1808(3):18A
Fairall, Sarah	Alexandria	Will	1881	WBC1:038; LP
Fairchild, Aaron	Alexandria	Tithable +16	1788	Tax PP 1788:18
Fairfax, Albert	Alexandria	Will	1887	WB1:481; LP
Fairfax, Ann, plt.	Alexandria	Suit	1805	CRF:135
Fairfax, Bryan, Estate (heirs), def.	Alexandria	Suit	1813	CRH:512
Fairfax, Bryan, Estate, def.	Alexandria	Suit	1805	CRF:135
Fairfax, Bryan, Estate, *Mount Eagle*	Alexandria	Division	1789	CRH:553
Fairfax, Ferdinando	Alexandria	Deposition	(nd)	CRK:119
Fairfax, Ferdinando	Alexandria	Deposition	(nd)	CRL:140
Fairfax, Ferdinando	Alexandria	Account B.	1800	CRK:105
Fairfax, Ferdinando	Alexandria	Account B.	1800	CRL:124
Fairfax, Ferdinando	Alexandria	Deed	1814	CRK:434
Fairfax, Ferdinando, complt.	Alexandria	Suit	1818	CRK:390
Fairfax, Ferdinando, Jefferson Co.	Alexandria	Deed	1811	CRK:415
Fairfax, Ferdinando, of Washington	Alexandria	Deposition	1818	CRK:356
Fairfax, Ferdinando, plt.	Alexandria	Suit	(nd)	CRK:430
Fairfax, Mary Randolph	Alexandria	Will	1887	WB1:478; LP
Fairfax, O.	Alexandria	Will	1893	WB2:047; LP
Fairfax, Sarah	Arlington	Will	1813	WB1:268; File #059A
Fairfax, Thomas	Alexandria	Deposition	1814	CRL:145
Fairfax, Thomas	Alexandria	Deposition	1816	CRK:124
Fairfax, Thomas, def.	Alexandria	Suit	1805	CRF:135
Fairfax, Thomas, def.	Alexandria	Suit	1813	CRH:512
Fairfax, Thomas, def.	Alexandria	Suit	1815	CRK:127
Falconer, William	Alexandria	Tax Charge	1798	Tax PP 1798:05
Falconer, William & Co.	Alexandria	Mer. License	1798	Tax PP 1798:20-2
Fall, Basil & wife (C), labourer	Alexandria	Housekeeper	1799	1799(2):14A
Faller, Jacob	Arlington	Apprentice	1803	OCR1801:085
Falls, Basil (C), ship carpenter	Alexandria	Housekeeper	1808	1808(1):07A
Faner, John	Alexandria	Tax Charge	1796	Tax PP 1796:06
Fanner, John	Alexandria	Tax Charge	1798	Tax PP 1798:06
Fanning, David, grantor	Arlington	Indenture D.	1804	ID3:031
Fanning, David, in jail	Arlington	Insolvent	1804	ID3:029
Fannon, Michael	Alexandria	Will	1896	WB2:154; LP
Fant, John	Arlington	Ordinary	1820	OBL3(np)
Fant, John	Arlington	Ordinary	1821	OBL3(np)
Fant, John	Arlington	Account	1825	AB6:093; LVA-LP
Fant, John	Arlington	Will (N)	1825	WB3:178; File #232A
Fant, John	Arlington	Bond	1825	WB3:179
Fant, John, near the market	Arlington	Ordinary	1822	OBL3(np)
Fant [Fouts], John	Arlington	Inventory	1825	AB6:092; LVA-LP
Fare, Priscilla	Arlington	Bond	1852	BB(np)
Farlee, William A.	Arlington	Will	1887	WB10:094
Farmer, Ann	Alexandria	Housekeeper	1799	1799(2):18A
Farmer, Ann, seamstress	Alexandria	Head	1810	1810(4):05A
Farmer, Ann, sempstress	Alexandria	Housekeeper	1808	1808(4):28A
Farnow, Philip, w(3), carpenter	Alexandria	Head	1796	1796(3):1
Farnsworth, James	Alexandria	Tax Charge	1800	Tax PP 1800:09
Farr, Abram	Alexandria	Tax Charge	1796	Tax PP 1796:06
Farr, Francis, sempstress	Alexandria	Housekeeper	1808	1808(3):22A
Farr, George, c/o Frances Ballenger	Arlington	Apprentice	1816	OCR1811:326
Farr, Joshua	Arlington	Apprentice	1813	OCR1811:173
Farr, Mary, seamstress	Alexandria	Head	1810	1810(4):02A
Farrel, Thos. & wife, sea captain	Alexandria	Housekeeper	1799	1799(2):13A
Farrel, Wm., Fairfax St.	Alexandria	Occupant	1790	Tax L 1790:01

NAME OR SUBJECT	LOCATION	TYPE	YEAR	REFERENCE(S)
Farrell, Ann Morgan, c/o Mary Humes	Arlington	Apprentice	1803	OCR1801:097
Farrell, Edward	Alexandria	Tithable +21	1787	Tax PP 1787:08
Farrell, John	Alexandria	Tithable +16	1789	Tax PP 1789:02
Farrell, John	Alexandria	Tax Charge	1789	Tax PP 1789:06
Farrell, John	Arlington	Guard. Acct.	1812	AB1:219; LVA-LP
Farrell, John	Arlington	Account	1813	AB1:291; LVA-LP
Farrell, John	Arlington	Apprentice	1814	OCR1811:232
Farrell, John	Arlington	Guard.	1815	WB2:067
Farrell, John	Arlington	Guard. Acct.	1816	AB2:384
Farrell, John	Arlington	Guard. Acct.	1817	AB3:071
Farrell, John	Arlington	Inventory	1822	AB5:087; LVA-LP
Farrell, John	Arlington	Admin.	1822	OCR1822:015a
Farrell, John	Arlington	Admin.	1822	WB3:057
Farrell, John	Arlington	Account	1824	AB5:307
Farrell, John	Arlington	Account	1825	AB5:307; LVA-LP
Farrell, John & wife Ann	Alexandria	Resident	1800	1800(4):12B
Farrell, John, c/o Thomas	Arlington	Guard.	1809	WBC:317
Farrell, John, c/o Thomas	Arlington	Guard. Acct.	1811	AB1:031; LVA-LP
Farrell, John Thos.	Alexandria	Tax Charge	1800	Tax PP 1800:09
Farrell, Nancy, gentlewoman	Alexandria	Housekeeper	1808	1808(1):06A
Farrell, Thomas	Alexandria	Tax Charge	1799	Tax PP 1799:12
Farrell, Thomas	Arlington	Admin.	1804	WBB:096
Farrell, Thomas	Arlington	Inventory	1804	WBB:104; LVA-LP
Farrell, Thomas	Arlington	Sale	1806	WBB:321
Farrell, Thomas	Arlington	Account	1806	WBB:277
Farrell, Thomas	Arlington	Account	1807	WBB:528; LVA-LP
Farrell, Thomas, Capt.	Arlington	Account	1810	WBC:337; LVA-LP
Farrell, Thomas, marrener	Alexandria	Head	1800	1800(4):12A
Farrell, Thos.	Alexandria	Tax Charge	1798	Tax PP 1798:06
Farrell, William	Alexandria	Tax Charge	1790	Tax PP 1790:04
Farrell, William, Royal St.	Alexandria	Occupant	1790	Tax L 1790:12
Farrelton, Bennet, gc/o Eliza. Mandley	Arlington	Apprentice	1815	OCR1811:314
Farris, Thomas	Alexandria	Tax Charge	1799	Tax PP 1799:12
Faucet, John & wife, blacksmith	Alexandria	Head	1795	1795(4):01
Faucet, [blank], Wilks St.	Alexandria	Occupants	1790	Tax L 1790:13
Faucett, John	Alexandria	Tax Charge	1790	Tax PP 1790:04
Faulkner, Jacob, Water St.	Alexandria	Owner	1795	Tax L 1795:09
Faulkner's Estate	Alexandria	Tax Charge	1796	Tax LP 1796:09
Fauntleroy, Ann L.	Arlington	Fid. Bond	1854	FBB(np)
Fauquier & Alexandria Turnpike Co.	Alexandria	Stockholders	1820	CRL:227
Faw, Abm.	Alexandria	Tax Charge	1798	Tax PP 1798:05
Faw, Abraham	Alexandria	Deed	1795	CRI:049
Faw, Abraham	Alexandria	Account B.	1795	CRI:091, 103
Faw, Abraham	Alexandria	Deed	1796	CRI:055
Faw, Abraham	Alexandria	Account B.	1797	CRI:058, 063
Faw, Abraham	Alexandria	Deed	1799	CRI:064
Faw, Abraham	Arlington	Juryman	1804	ACO:026
Faw, Abraham	Alexandria	Rents	1805	CRF:064
Faw, Abraham	Alexandria	Head	1810	1810(3):01A
Faw, Abraham	Arlington	Sale	1828	LVA-LP
Faw, Abraham	Arlington	Will P.	1828	OCR1822:164
Faw, Abraham	Arlington	Will	1828	WB3:306; File #266A
Faw, Abraham	Arlington	Bond	1828	WB3:318, 379
Faw, Abraham	Arlington	Account	1829	AB6:495; LVA-LP
Faw, Abraham	Arlington	Account	1829	AB6:499; LVA-LP
Faw, Abraham	Arlington	Account	1830	AB6:495, 499
Faw, Abraham & wife	Alexandria	Housekeeper	1799	1799(2):06A
Faw, Abraham, def.	Alexandria	Suit	1801	CRB:298
Faw, Abraham, def.	Alexandria	Suit	1804	CRF:057
Faw, Abraham, plt.	Alexandria	Suit	1809	CRI:001
Faw, Abraham, w(4)2, gentleman	Alexandria	Head	1796	1796(3):1

NAME OR SUBJECT	LOCATION	TYPE	YEAR	REFERENCE(S)
Faw, Abram	Alexandria	Tax Charge	1799	Tax PP 1799:12
Faw, Abram	Alexandria	Tax Charge	1800	Tax PP 1800:09
Faw, Abram, gentleman	Alexandria	Housekeeper	1808	1808(3):21A
Faw, Abram.	Alexandria	Tax Charge	1796	Tax LP 1796:09
Faw, Jonathan	Alexandria	Boarder	1799	1799(2):06A
Faw, Jonathan	Alexandria	Tax Charge	1799	Tax PP 1799:12
Faw, Jonathan	Alexandria	Tax Charge	1800	Tax PP 1800:09
Faw, Jonathan	Arlington	Defendant	1802	PA:054
Fawcett, Children	Arlington	Guard. Acct.	1860	LVA-LP
Fawcett, Edward S.	Arlington	Guard. Acct.	1854	WB6:343
Fawcett, Edward S.	Arlington	Guard. Acct.	1855	WB7:120, 234
Fawcett, Edward S.	Arlington	Guard. Acct.	1855	WB7:001; LVA-LP
Fawcett, Edward S.	Arlington	Guard. Acct.	1858	WB7:357, 476; LVA-LP
Fawcett, Edward S.	Arlington	Guard. Acct.	1860	WB8:006, 197, 256
Fawcett, Eugenia	Arlington	Guard. Acct.	1854	WB6:342; LVA-LP
Fawcett, Eugenia G.	Arlington	Guard. Acct.	1855	WB7:003; LVA-LP
Fawcett, Eugenia G.	Arlington	Guard. Acct.	1855	WB7:119, 235
Fawcett, Eugenia G.	Arlington	Guard. Acct.	1858	WB7:359, 477; LVA-LP
Fawcett, Eugenia G.	Arlington	Guard. Acct.	1860	WB8:005, 197, 256
Fawcett, Harriet S.	Arlington	Guard. Acct.	1854	WB6:344; LVA-LP
Fawcett, Harriet S.	Arlington	Guard. Acct.	1855	WB7:004; LVA-LP
Fawcett, Harriet S.	Arlington	Guard. Acct.	1855	WB7:121, 233
Fawcett, Harriet S.	Arlington	Guard. Acct.	1858	WB7:359, 474
Fawcett, Harriet S.	Arlington	Guard. Acct.	1860	WB8:007, 197, 256
Fawcett, Heirs	Arlington	Settlement	1867	WB8:539
Fawcett, Henrietta	Arlington	Guard. Acct.	1854	WB6:343
Fawcett, Henrietta	Arlington	Guard. Acct.	1855	WB7:005; LVA-LP
Fawcett, Henrietta	Arlington	Guard. Acct.	1855	WB7:119, 233
Fawcett, Henrietta	Arlington	Guard. Acct.	1856	LVA-LP
Fawcett, Henrietta	Arlington	Guard. Acct.	1860	WB8:006, 197, 256
Fawcett, Henrietta	Arlington	Guard. Acct.	1861	WB7:361, 477; LVA-LP
Fawcett, Henrietta	Arlington	Guard. Acct.	1870	WB9:259
Fawcett, Henrietta	Arlington	Guard. Acct.	1870	WB9:242
Fawcett, Henrietta	Arlington	Guard. Acct.	1871	WB9:319
Fawcett, Joseph	Arlington	Guard. Acct.	1854	WB6:343
Fawcett, Joseph	Arlington	Guard. Acct.	1855	WB7:005; LVA-LP
Fawcett, Joseph	Arlington	Guard. Acct.	1855	WB7:122, 232
Fawcett, Joseph	Arlington	Guard. Acct.	1858	WB7:360, 475; LVA-LP
Fawcett, Joseph	Arlington	Guard. Acct.	1860	WB8:004, 197, 256
Fawcett, Joseph	Arlington	Guard. Acct.	1870	WB9:258
Fawcett, Joseph	Arlington	Guard. Acct.	1870	WB9:243
Fawcett, Joseph, c/o Willis	Arlington	Guard.	1853	BB(np)
Fawcett, Lucy F.	Arlington	Guard. Acct.	1854	WB6:342
Fawcett, Lucy F.	Arlington	Guard. Acct.	1855	WB7:123, 235
Fawcett, Lucy F.	Arlington	Guard. Acct.	1855	WB7:002; LVA-LP
Fawcett, Lucy F.	Arlington	Guard. Acct.	1856	LVA-LP
Fawcett, Lucy F.	Arlington	Guard. Acct.	1858	WB7:358, 476; LVA-LP
Fawcett, Lucy F.	Arlington	Guard. Acct.	1860	WB8:008, 197
Fawcett, Virginia	Arlington	Guard. Acct.	1854	WB6:342
Fawcett, Virginia	Arlington	Guard. Acct.	1855	WB7:001; LVA-LP
Fawcett, Virginia	Arlington	Guard. Acct.	1855	WB7:123, 232
Fawcett, Virginia	Arlington	Guard. Acct.	1858	WB7:357, 478; LVA-LP
Fawcett, Virginia, c/o Willis	Arlington	Guard.	1853	BB(np) (2)
Fawcett, Virginia [Moore]	Arlington	Guard. Acct.	1860	WB8:008, 197
Faxon, Joaish, 1, merchant	Alexandria	Head	1796	1796(3):6
Faxon, Jonah	Alexandria	License Due	1800	Tax PP 1800:54(24)
Faxon, Jos.	Alexandria	Boarder	1808	1808(2):15A
Faxon, Josiah	Alexandria	Tax Charge	1795	Tax PP 1795:09
Faxon, Josiah	Alexandria	Tax Charge	1798	Tax PP 1798:06
Faxon, Josiah	Alexandria	Mer. License	1799	Tax PP 1799:52-03r
Faxon, Josiah	Alexandria	Tax Charge	1799	Tax PP 1799:12

NAME OR SUBJECT	LOCATION	TYPE	YEAR	REFERENCE(S)
Faxon, Josiah	Alexandria	Tax Charge	1800	Tax PP 1800:09
Faxon, Josiah & Co., plt.	Alexandria	Suit	1801	CRC:111
Faxon, Josiah & Co., plt.	Alexandria	Suit	1803	CRD:101
Faxon, Josiah, for playing Faro	Arlington	Defendant	1801	PA:132
Faxon, Josiah, merchant	Alexandria	Head	1810	1810(1):01A
Faxon, Josiah, Prince St.	Alexandria	Occupant	1795	Tax L 1795:15
Faxon, Metcalf & Co., def.	Alexandria	Suit	1817	CRK:256
Faxon, Metcalf & Co., def.	Alexandria	Suit	1817	CRL:015
Faxon, Michael, merchant	Alexandria	Housekeeper	1808	1808(1):02A
Faxon, R.	Alexandria	Reference	1808	1808(3):21B
Faxson, Josiah	Alexandria	Mer. License	1798	Tax PP 1798:20-2
Faxton, Josiah	Alexandria	Tax Charge	1796	Tax LP 1796:09
Febrey, John E.	Arlington	Will	1893	WB10:261; File #760A
Febrey, Nicholas	Arlington	Inventory	1868	WB9:103
Febrey, Nicholas	Arlington	Will	1868	WB9:015
Febrey, Nicholas	Arlington	Account	1869	WB9:167
Febrey, Nicholas	Arlington	Account	1870	WB9:276
Feddon, John T.	Alexandria	Will	1890	WB1:575; LP
Fegan, Hugh	Alexandria	Appraisal	1884	WBC1:043
Fegan, John, of DC	Alexandria	Will	1896	WB2:142; LP
Feiner, William, b. Munster	Arlington	Alien Entry	1822	RA:14/06/22
Feiser, Adam	Alexandria	Tax Charge	1788	Tax PP 1788:05
Feiser [Faisar], Adam	Alexandria	Tax Charge	1789	Tax PP 1789:06
Feizer [Fiezer], Adam	Alexandria	Tax Charge	1790	Tax PP 1790:04
Feizer [Fizer], Adam	Alexandria	Tax Charge	1787	Tax PP 1787:05
Felps, Joseph	Alexandria	Tithable +16	1788	Tax PP 1788:15
Feltcher, William, c/o William	Arlington	Apprentice	1812	OCR1811:091
Fendal, P., Washington St.	Alexandria	Occupant	1787	Tax L 1787:10
Fendal, Philip	Alexandria	Owner	1787	Tax L 1787:10
Fendal, Philip R.	Alexandria	Tax Charge	1787	Tax PP 1787:05
Fendall, Benjamin T.	Arlington	Exor. Bond	1849	EBB(np)
Fendall, Benjamin T.	Arlington	Will	1849	WB5:181; File #455A
Fendall, Benjamin T.	Arlington	Inventory	1849	WB5:195; LVA-LP
Fendall, Benjamin T.	Arlington	Account	1851	WB6:001; LVA-LP
Fendall, Benjamin T.	Arlington	Account	1851	WB6:173; LVA-LP
Fendall, Mary, gentlewoman	Alexandria	Housekeeper	1808	1808(3):22A
Fendall, Mary T.S., of Pr. Geo. Co. MD	Alexandria	Will	1897	WB2:244; LP
Fendall, Mrs.	Alexandria	Head	1810	1810(3):09A
Fendall, P.R.	Alexandria	Tax Charge	1796	Tax LP 1796:09
Fendall, P.R.	Alexandria	Tax Charge	1798	Tax PP 1798:06
Fendall, P.R., Oronoko St.	Alexandria	Occupant	1795	Tax L 1795:10
Fendall, P.R., Oronoko St.	Alexandria	Owner	1795	Tax L 1795:10
Fendall, P.R., Washington St.	Alexandria	Owner	1795	Tax L 1795:10(2)
Fendall, P.R., Washington St.	Alexandria	Occupant	1795	Tax L 1795:10
Fendall, Phil. R.	Alexandria	Tax Charge	1795	Tax PP 1795:10
Fendall, Phil. R.	Alexandria	Tax Charge	1799	Tax PP 1799:12
Fendall, Philip R.	Alexandria	Tax Charge	1789	Tax PP 1789:06
Fendall, Philip R.	Alexandria	Tax Charge	1790	Tax PP 1790:04
Fendall, Philip R.	Alexandria	Tax Charge	1796	Tax PP 1796:06
Fendall, Philip R., Hon.	Arlington	Resignation	1826	OCR1822:120a
Fendall, Philip R., Oronoka St.	Alexandria	Occupant	1790	Tax L 1790:04
Fendall, Philip R., Oronoka St.	Alexandria	Owner	1790	Tax L 1790:04
Fendall, Philip Richard	Alexandria	Deed	1803	CRH:220, 223
Fendall, Philip Richard	Arlington	Will	1805	WBB:137; File #011A
Fendall, Philip Richard	Arlington	Trustee Acct.	1807	LVA-LP
Fendall, Philip Richard, plt.	Alexandria	Suit	1803	CRH:219
Fendall, Philip Richd.	Alexandria	Tax Charge	1788	Tax PP 1788:06
Fendall, Richd. P.	Alexandria	Tax Charge	1800	Tax PP 1800:09
Fentham, Jno. G.	Alexandria	Tax Charge	1798	Tax PP 1798:05
Fentham, Jno. G.	Alexandria	Tax Charge	1800	Tax PP 1800:09
Fentham, John G.	Alexandria	Tax Charge	1799	Tax PP 1799:12

NAME OR SUBJECT	LOCATION	TYPE	YEAR	REFERENCE(S)
Fenwick, Francis	Alexandria	Tax Charge	1799	Tax PP 1799:12
Fenwick, Francis	Alexandria	Tax Charge	1800	Tax PP 1800:09
Fenwick, Jno.	Alexandria	Boarder	1808	1808(1):03A
Ferguson & Co.	Alexandria	Tax Charge	1798	Tax PP 1798:05
Ferguson, Cumb.	Alexandria	Tax Charge	1790	Tax PP 1790:04
Ferguson, Cumbd.	Alexandria	Tax Charge	1795	Tax PP 1795:10
Ferguson, Cumbd.	Alexandria	Tax Charge	1798	Tax PP 1798:05
Ferguson, Cumbd.	Alexandria	Tax Charge	1799	Tax PP 1799:12
Ferguson, Cumbd.	Alexandria	Tax Charge	1800	Tax PP 1800:09
Ferguson, Cumbd., Hooe's wharf	Alexandria	Occupant	1790	Tax L 1790:04
Ferguson, Cumbd., Hooe's wharf	Alexandria	Owner	1790	Tax L 1790:04
Ferguson, Cumberland	Alexandria	Tax Charge	1789	Tax PP 1789:06
Ferguson, Cumberland	Alexandria	Tax Charge	1796	Tax LP 1796:09
Ferguson, Cumberland	Alexandria	Tax Charge	1796	Tax PP 1796:06
Ferguson, Cumberland & wife, bdnghse.	Alexandria	Head	1795	1795(4):01
Ferguson, Cumberland & wife, carpenter	Alexandria	Housekeeper	1799	1799(2):16A
Ferguson, Cumberland & wife Mary	Alexandria	Resident	1800	1800(4):02B
Ferguson, Cumberland, ship joiner	Alexandria	Head	1800	1800(4):02A
Ferguson, Cumberld.	Alexandria	Tax Charge	1788	Tax PP 1788:06
Ferguson, Dennis (C)	Arlington	Apprentice	1826	OCR1822:124
Ferguson, Edward	Alexandria	Tax Charge	1796	Tax PP 1796:06
Ferguson, John	Alexandria	Tax Charge	1799	Tax PP 1799:12
Ferguson, Joshua	Arlington	Fid. Bond	1854	FBB(np)
Ferguson, Joshua	Arlington	Account	1857	WB7:210; LVA-LP
Ferguson, Margaret	Arlington	Crime	1796	OT:10/08/1796
Ferguson, Mrs., Princess St.	Alexandria	Occupant	1795	Tax L 1795:12
Ferguson, Robertson & Co.	Alexandria	Tax Charge	1799	Tax PP 1799:12
Ferguson, Robertson & Co.	Alexandria	Mer. License	1798	Tax PP 1798:20-2
Ferguson, William	Arlington	Apprentice	1829	OCR1822:172a
Ferguson, William, grantor	Arlington	Indenture D.	1829	ID:225
Ferguson, William, in jail	Arlington	Insolvent	1829	ID:223
Ferguson, William J., grantee	Arlington	Indenture D.	1829	ID:229
Ferguson, William James, in jail	Arlington	Insolvent	1829	ID:227
Ferguson, Wm.	Alexandria	Boarder	1808	1808(1):05A
Fergusson, Cumberland	Alexandria	Tax Charge	1787	Tax PP 1787:05
Fergusson, Dennis	Arlington	Apprentice	1829	OCR1822:168a
Fergusson, Mary	Arlington	Guard.	1827	OCR1822:143a
Ferneau, Elizabeth	Arlington	Sale	1817	AB3:060
Ferno, Philip	Alexandria	Tax Charge	1795	Tax PP 1795:09
Ferno, Philip	Alexandria	Tax Charge	1799	Tax PP 1799:12
Fernow, Philip	Alexandria	Tax Charge	1796	Tax LP 1796:09
Fernow, Philip & wife, carpenter	Alexandria	Housekeeper	1799	1799(2):11A
Ferral, Capt. & wife, mariner	Alexandria	Head	1795	1795(4):09
Ferral, Jeremiah	Alexandria	Tax Charge	1790	Tax PP 1790:04
Ferral, Wm.	Alexandria	Tithable +16	1788	Tax PP 1788:05
Ferrall, Jas.	Alexandria	Tax Charge	1795	Tax PP 1795:09
Ferrall, Jas., King St.	Alexandria	Occupant	1795	Tax L 1795:25
Ferrall, Thomas	Alexandria	Tax Charge	1796	Tax PP 1796:06
Ferrall, Thos., Capt.	Alexandria	Tax Charge	1796	Tax LP 1796:09
Ferrel, Jeremiah	Alexandria	Tax Charge	1788	Tax PP 1788:06
Ferrel, John	Alexandria	Tax Charge	1788	Tax PP 1788:05
Ferrell, Jeremiah	Alexandria	Tax Charge	1789	Tax PP 1789:06
Ferrell, Tho., Royal St.	Alexandria	Occupant	1795	Tax L 1795:09
Ferrell, Thos., Royal St.	Alexandria	Owner	1795	Tax L 1795:09
Ferrell, William	Alexandria	Tax Charge	1789	Tax PP 1789:06
Fetter, Daniel	Alexandria	Deposition	1802	CRD:139
Fichter, George, at his house	Arlington	Ordinary	1828	OBL4(np)
Fichter, George, at his house	Arlington	Ordinary	1831	OBL4(np)
Fichter, George, in Alexandria Co.	Arlington	Ordinary	1827	OBL4(np)
Field, Horace	Arlington	Ordinary	1824	OBL3(np)
Field, Horace, at his house	Arlington	Ordinary	1827	OBL4(np)

NAME OR SUBJECT	LOCATION	TYPE	YEAR	REFERENCE(S)
Field, Horace, at his house	Arlington	Ordinary	1828	OBL4(np)
Field, Horace, at his house	Arlington	Ordinary	1829	OBL4(np)
Field, Horace, in Alexandria Co.	Arlington	Ordinary	1826	OBL4(np)
Field, Horace, in Alexandria Co.	Arlington	Ordinary	1825	OBL4(np)
Field, Horace, retailer & nailor	Alexandria	Housekeeper	1808	1808(1):05A
Field, Horrace, nailor	Alexandria	Head	1810	1810(1):03A
Field, J. Albert	Alexandria	Will	1897	WB2:246; LP
Field, Jona.	Alexandria	Boarder	1808	1808(3):22A
Field, Jonathan, nailor	Alexandria	Head	1810	1810(1):12A
Field, Josa.	Alexandria	Boarder	1808	1808(1):05A
Field, Stephen, grantee	Arlington	Indenture D.	1827	ID:139
Fielding, Elizabeth, washwoman	Alexandria	Housekeeper	1808	1808(1):10A
Fielding, John, c/o Michael	Arlington	Apprentice	1805	OCR1801:244
Fielding, Nancy, c/o Michael	Arlington	Apprentice	1804	OCR1801:215
Fielding, Nancy, c/o Michael	Arlington	Apprentice	1805	OCR1801:283
Fielding, Winny, c/o Michael	Arlington	Apprentice	1805	OCR1801:282
Fields, William	Alexandria	Tax Charge	1788	Tax PP 1788:05
Fig, Elizabeth	Alexandria	Housekeeper	1799	1799(2):14A
Figg, Elizebeth, sumpster	Alexandria	Head	1800	1800(4):10A
Figg, Matilda	Arlington	Guard.	1816	WB2:125
Filbert, Chloe, washer woman	Alexandria	Housekeeper	1799	1799(2):02A
Filbert, Patsey	Alexandria	Head	1810	1810(2):07A
Finch, Joseph M., Rev.	Arlington	Ordination	1851	BB(np)
Findlay, David	Alexandria	Tithable +16	1788	Tax PP 1788:17
Findlay, David	Alexandria	Tithable +16	1789	Tax PP 1789:20
Findlay, Robert, Jr., plt.	Alexandria	Suit	1802	CRB:168
Findlay, William	Alexandria	Tax Charge	1789	Tax PP 1789:06
Findley, Oliver P., merchant	Alexandria	Housekeeper	1808	1808(1):01A
Findley, William	Alexandria	Tax Charge	1788	Tax PP 1788:05
Findley, William	Alexandria	Tax Charge	1790	Tax PP 1790:05
Findly, Henry	Alexandria	Tax Charge	1800	Tax PP 1800:09
Fineacy, James	Arlington	Will	1869	WB9:062; File #662A
Finley, David	Alexandria	Tithable +16	1790	Tax PP 1790:11
Finley, Henry	Alexandria	Tax Charge	1799	Tax PP 1799:12
Finley, Hugh	Alexandria	Tax Charge	1796	Tax LP 1796:09
Finley, Oliver P.	Alexandria	Deed	1804	CRG:324
Finley, Oliver P.	Alexandria	Agreement	1805	CRG:352
Finley, Oliver P.	Arlington	Account	1835	AB7:190; LVA-LP
Finley, Oliver P.	Arlington	Account	1836	AB7:190
Finley, Oliver P., complt.	Alexandria	Suit	1809	CRG:300
Finley, Oliver Phelps	Arlington	Admin.	1831	WB4:037
Finly, William	Alexandria	Tithable +21	1787	Tax PP 1787:05
Firoud, Mary, pauper	Alexandria	Housekeeper	1808	1808(3):22A
Fish, Ann Becraft	Alexandria	Will	1887	WB1:455; LP
Fisher, Amos	Alexandria	Tax Charge	1796	Tax LP 1796:09
Fisher, Amos	Alexandria	Tax Charge	1796	Tax PP 1796:06
Fisher, Amos	Alexandria	Mer. License	1798	Tax PP 1798:20-2
Fisher, Ann	Alexandria	Will	1872	WB1:046; LP
Fisher, George W.	Alexandria	Will	1897	WB2:234; LP
Fisher, Henrietta	Alexandria	Will	1896	WB2:163; LP
Fisher, James C., of Philadelphia	Alexandria	Deed	1811	CRK:048
Fisher, John	Alexandria	Tax Charge	1795	Tax PP 1795:09
Fisher, Jonas	Alexandria	Will	1890	WB1:552; LP
Fisher, Jos.	Alexandria	Boarder	1799	1799(2):04A
Fisher, Joseph	Alexandria	Tax Charge	1799	Tax PP 1799:12
Fisher, Thomas	Alexandria	Tax Charge	1796	Tax LP 1796:09
Fisher, Thomas	Alexandria	Tax Charge	1799	Tax PP 1799:12
Fisher, Thomas	Alexandria	Tax Charge	1800	Tax PP 1800:09
Fisher, Thos., Washington St.	Alexandria	Occupant	1795	Tax L 1795:20
Fisher, William	Alexandria	Tithable +16	1788	Tax PP 1788:05
Fisher, William	Alexandria	Tax Charge	1789	Tax PP 1789:06

NAME OR SUBJECT	LOCATION	TYPE	YEAR	REFERENCE(S)
Fisher, William	Alexandria	Tax Charge	1790	Tax PP 1790:05
Fisher, William	Alexandria	Tax Charge	1796	Tax PP 1796:06
Fitzgerald, Andrew	Alexandria	Tax Charge	1795	Tax PP 1795:09
Fitzgerald, Andrew	Alexandria	Tax Charge	1796	Tax PP 1796:06
Fitzgerald, Ann	Arlington	Guard.	1812	WB1:171
Fitzgerald, Charlotta (C), washwoman	Alexandria	Housekeeper	1808	1808(3):23A
Fitzgerald, Charlotte, washerwoman	Alexandria	Head	1810	1810(4):09A
Fitzgerald, Col. & wife	Alexandria	Head	1795	1795(4):03
Fitzgerald, Geo.	Alexandria	Boarder	1808	1808(3):22A
Fitzgerald, Jno., Duke St.	Alexandria	Occupant	1795	Tax L 1795:22
Fitzgerald, Jno., Fairfax St.	Alexandria	Occupant	1787	Tax L 1787:11
Fitzgerald, Jno., Fairfax St.	Alexandria	Owner	1795	Tax L 1795:09(3)
Fitzgerald, Jno., St. Asaph St.	Alexandria	Owner	1795	Tax L 1795:09
Fitzgerald, Jno., Union St.	Alexandria	Owner	1795	Tax L 1795:09
Fitzgerald, Jno., Water St.	Alexandria	Owner	1795	Tax L 1795:10
Fitzgerald, John	Alexandria	Owner	1787	Tax L 1787:11
Fitzgerald, John	Alexandria	Tax Charge	1787	Tax PP 1787:05
Fitzgerald, John	Alexandria	Tithable +16	1789	Tax PP 1789:05
Fitzgerald, John	Alexandria	Tax Charge	1789	Tax PP 1789:06
Fitzgerald, John	Alexandria	Tax Charge	1790	Tax PP 1790:04
Fitzgerald, John	Alexandria	Tax Charge	1795	Tax PP 1795:10
Fitzgerald, John	Alexandria	Tax Charge	1796	Tax LP 1796:09
Fitzgerald, John	Alexandria	Tax Charge	1796	Tax LP 1796:09
Fitzgerald, John	Alexandria	Tax Charge	1796	Tax PP 1796:06
Fitzgerald, John	Arlington	Account	1801	WBA:044
Fitzgerald, John & wife, naval officer	Alexandria	Head	1795	1795(4a):08
Fitzgerald, John, Estate, def.	Alexandria	Suit	1801	CRB:307
Fitzgerald, John, Fairfax St.	Alexandria	Owner	1790	Tax L 1790:04(3)
Fitzgerald, John, King St.	Alexandria	Owner	1790	Tax L 1790:04
Fitzgerald, John, ropemaker, factor	Alexandria	Head	1795	1795(4a):05
Fitzgerald, John, Wolf St.	Alexandria	Owner	1790	Tax L 1790:04
Fitzgerald, John, Wolf St.	Alexandria	Occupant	1790	Tax L 1790:04
Fitzgerald, John, Wolfe St.	Alexandria	Occupant	1790	Tax L 1790:07
Fitzgerald, Richard	Alexandria	Tax Charge	1790	Tax PP 1790:04
Fitzgerald, Richard Stanley	Arlington	Apprentice	1804	OCR1801:171
Fitzgerald, Thomas	Alexandria	Tax Charge	1788	Tax PP 1788:05
Fitzgerald, Thomas	Arlington	Crime	1796	OT:26/09/1796
Fitzgerald, Thos.	Alexandria	Tax Charge	1789	Tax PP 1789:06
Fitzhugh, A.M., of *Ravensworth*	Alexandria	Will	1873	WB1:104; LP
Fitzhugh, A.M., of *Ravensworth*	Alexandria	Plat	1873	WB1:104; LP
Fitzhugh, Ann G.	Alexandria	Renounce	1870	LP
Fitzhugh, Augustine	Alexandria	Boarder	1808	1808(2):16A
Fitzhugh, Augustine, grantee	Arlington	Indenture D.	1812	ID2:166
Fitzhugh, Augustine, grantee	Arlington	Indenture D.	1813	ID2:342
Fitzhugh, Daniel & wife, brewer	Alexandria	Head	1795	1795(4):03
Fitzhugh, Edmund	Alexandria	Deposition	1822	CRL:534
Fitzhugh, Harrison, gentleman	Alexandria	Head	1810	1810(3):02A
Fitzhugh, Harrison, gentleman	Alexandria	Head	1810	1810(3):05A
Fitzhugh, John	Alexandria	Will	1870	WB1:011
Fitzhugh, John, of Pr. Wm. Co.	Alexandria	Will	1870	WB1:011; LP
Fitzhugh, Lawrence	Arlington	Guard.	1821	WB2:402
Fitzhugh, Lucretia, c/o Norman R.	Arlington	Suit	1842	LVA-LP
Fitzhugh, Lucretia, c/o Norman R.	Arlington	Guard.	1850	GBB(np)
Fitzhugh, Lucretia, c/o Norman R.	Arlington	Guard.	1853	WB6:218; LVA-LP
Fitzhugh, Margaretta, c/o Norman R.	Arlington	Suit	1842	LVA-LP
Fitzhugh, Mary Ann	Arlington	Admin.	1841	WB4:280
Fitzhugh, Mary Ann	Arlington	Account	1842	AB8:320; LVA-LP
Fitzhugh, Mary Ann	Arlington	Inventory	1842	AB8:285; LVA-LP
Fitzhugh, Mary Ann	Arlington	Account	1842	OCR1842:009
Fitzhugh, Mary Ann	Arlington	Distribution	1845	AB9:026
Fitzhugh, Mary Ann	Arlington	Account	1845	AB9:026; LVA-LP

NAME OR SUBJECT	LOCATION	TYPE	YEAR	REFERENCE(S)
Fitzhugh, Mary Ann	Arlington	Citation	1845	OCR1842:098
Fitzhugh, McCarty	Alexandria	Account B.	1795	CRC:065
Fitzhugh, McCarty, def.	Alexandria	Suit	1801	CRC:062
Fitzhugh, Nicholas	Arlington	Bond	1814	WB1:332
Fitzhugh, Nicholas	Arlington	Will	1815	WB1:329
Fitzhugh, Nicholas	Arlington	Account	1818	AB3:274; LVA-LP
Fitzhugh, Nicholas, Guardian	Arlington	Plaintiff	1802	PA:284
Fitzhugh, Nicholas, Hon.	Arlington	Inventory	1815	AB2:087; LVA-LP
Fitzhugh, Nicholas, judge	Alexandria	Housekeeper	1808	1808(2):16A
Fitzhugh, Nichs., judge	Alexandria	Head	1810	1810(1):08A
Fitzhugh, Norman, c/o Norman R.	Arlington	Guard.	1850	GBB(np)
Fitzhugh, Norman R.	Arlington	Appraisal	1835	LVA-LP
Fitzhugh, Norman R.	Arlington	Will	1835	WB4:094; File #337A
Fitzhugh, Norman R.	Arlington	Bond	1835	WB4:097, 279
Fitzhugh, Norman R.	Arlington	Account	1839	AB8:125; LVA-LP
Fitzhugh, Norman R.	Arlington	Account	1840	AB8:125
Fitzhugh, Norman R., grantee	Arlington	Indenture D.	1826	ID:060
Fitzhugh, Norman R., orphans of	Arlington	Suit	1842	LVA-LP
Fitzhugh, Norman R., orphans of	Arlington	Guard.	1853	WB6:218; LVA-LP
Fitzhugh, Philip & wife Charlotte	Alexandria	Deed	1802	CRI:338
Fitzhugh, Philip, Pr. George's Co. Md.	Alexandria	Deed	1801	CRI:324
Fitzhugh, Philip, Pr. George's Co. Md.	Alexandria	Deed	1801	CRI:330
Fitzhugh, Thomas V., c/o Norman R.	Arlington	Suit	1842	LVA-LP
Fitzhugh, Thomas Vowell, c/o Norman	Arlington	Guard.	1850	GBB(np)
Fitzhugh, William	Alexandria	Tax Charge	1798	Tax PP 1798:06
Fitzhugh, William	Alexandria	Tax Charge	1799	Tax PP 1799:12
Fitzhugh, William	Alexandria	Tax Charge	1800	Tax PP 1800:09
Fitzhugh, William	Arlington	Will	1809	WBC:308; File #046A
Fitzhugh, William	Arlington	Bond	1809	WBC:314
Fitzhugh, William Henry, c/o William	Arlington	Guard.	1810	WBC:335
Fitzhugh, William, of *Chatham*	Arlington	Inventory	1809	WBC:318; LVA-LP
Fitzhugh, William, of *Chatham*	Arlington	Account	1811	AB1:074
Fitzhugh, William, of *Chatham*	Arlington	Account	1812	AB1:180; LVA-LP
Fitzhugh, Wm., gentleman	Alexandria	Housekeeper	1808	1808(3):22A
Fitzpatrick, Mary, boarding house	Alexandria	Housekeeper	1799	1799(2):09A
Fitzpatrick, Tho., Duke St.	Alexandria	Occupant	1795	Tax L 1795:09
Fitzpatrick, Thomas	Alexandria	Owner	1787	Tax L 1787:10
Fitzpatrick, Thomas	Alexandria	Tax Charge	1787	Tax PP 1787:05
Fitzpatrick, Thomas	Alexandria	Tax Charge	1788	Tax PP 1788:06
Fitzpatrick, Thomas	Alexandria	Tax Charge	1789	Tax PP 1789:06
Fitzpatrick, Thomas	Alexandria	Tax Charge	1790	Tax PP 1790:04
Fitzpatrick, Thomas	Alexandria	Tax Charge	1795	Tax PP 1795:10
Fitzpatrick, Thomas	Alexandria	Tax Charge	1796	Tax LP 1796:09
Fitzpatrick, Thomas	Alexandria	Tax Charge	1796	Tax PP 1796:06
Fitzpatrick, Thomas, w, shopkeeper	Alexandria	Head	1796	1796(3):2
Fitzpatrick, Thos., Duke St.	Alexandria	Occupant	1787	Tax L 1787:10
Fitzpatrick, Thos., Duke St.	Alexandria	Owner	1790	Tax L 1790:04
Fitzpatrick, Thos., Duke St.	Alexandria	Occupant	1790	Tax L 1790:04
Fitzpatrick, Thos., Duke St.	Alexandria	Owner	1795	Tax L 1795:09
Flannagan, Clarissa	Arlington	Guard.	1808	WBC:065
Flannan, John	Alexandria	Tax Charge	1790	Tax PP 1790:04
Flannery, Michael	Arlington	Inventory	1813	AB1:338; LVA-LP
Flannery, Michael	Arlington	Admin.	1813	WB1:263
Flannery, Michael	Arlington	Sale	1814	AB2:004
Flannery, Michael	Arlington	Account	1814	AB2:051; LVA-LP
Flannery, Michael	Arlington	Account	1816	AB2:378
Flannery, Michael	Arlington	Account	1817	AB3:039; LVA-LP
Flannery, Michael, clerk in bank	Alexandria	Head	1810	1810(4):04A
Flannery, Michael, [Alexa. Bank] teller	Alexandria	Housekeeper	1808	1808(4):25A
Flannery, Michl.	Alexandria	Tithable +16	1790	Tax PP 1790:06
Flannery, Michl.	Alexandria	Tax Charge	1798	Tax PP 1798:05

NAME OR SUBJECT	LOCATION	TYPE	YEAR	REFERENCE(S)
Flannery, Michl.	Alexandria	Tax Charge	1799	Tax PP 1799:12
Flanny, Michael	Alexandria	Tax Charge	1800	Tax PP 1800:09
Flavel, Caleb	Alexandria	Tithable +16	1788	Tax PP 1788:10
Flavel, Caleb	Alexandria	Tithable +16	1789	Tax PP 1789:11
Flavel, Richard	Alexandria	Tithable +16	1788	Tax PP 1788:10
Flecher, James, plasterrer	Alexandria	Head	1800	1800(4):12A
Fleming, Andrew	Alexandria	Tax Charge	1790	Tax PP 1790:04
Fleming, Andrew	Alexandria	Tax Charge	1796	Tax PP 1796:06
Fleming, Andrew	Alexandria	Tax Charge	1800	Tax PP 1800:09
Fleming, Andrew	Arlington	Inventory	1820	AB4:166; LVA-LP
Fleming, Andrew	Arlington	Admin.	1820	WB2:377
Fleming, Andrew, c/o Andrew	Arlington	Guard.	1829	WB3:352
Fleming, Andw.	Alexandria	Tax Charge	1795	Tax PP 1795:09
Fleming, Andw.	Alexandria	Tax Charge	1798	Tax PP 1798:06
Fleming, Andw.	Alexandria	Tax Charge	1799	Tax PP 1799:12
Fleming, Andw., carpenter	Alexandria	Housekeeper	1808	1808(2):14A
Fleming, Andw., Fairfax St.	Alexandria	Occupant	1795	Tax L 1795:30
Fleming, Archibald, at market house	Arlington	Ordinary	1842	OBL6(np)
Fleming, Bitty	Alexandria	Tax Charge	1787	Tax PP 1787:05
Fleming, Eliza, c/o Andrew	Arlington	Guard.	1829	WB3:352
Fleming, Eliza.	Alexandria	Tax Charge	1790	Tax PP 1790:05
Fleming, Eliza., Duke St.	Alexandria	Owner	1790	Tax L 1790:04
Fleming, Eliza., Duke St.	Alexandria	Occupant	1790	Tax L 1790:04
Fleming, Eliza., Union St.	Alexandria	Owner	1790	Tax L 1790:04
Fleming, Eliza., Water St.	Alexandria	Owner	1790	Tax L 1790:04
Fleming, Hugh	Alexandria	Tax Charge	1787	Tax PP 1787:05
Fleming, Isabella, c/o Andrew	Arlington	Guard.	1829	WB3:352
Fleming, John, c/o Andrew	Arlington	Guard.	1829	WB3:352
Fleming, Kathrine	Alexandria	Boarder	1795	1795(4a):03
Fleming, Mary, washwoman	Alexandria	Housekeeper	1808	1808(4):29A
Fleming, Miss, Duke St.	Alexandria	Occupant	1795	Tax L 1795:09
Fleming, Mrs., Duke St.	Alexandria	Occupant	1787	Tax L 1787:11
Fleming, Robert F.	Alexandria	Will	1871	WB1:035; LP
Fleming, Thomas, Estate	Alexandria	Owner	1787	Tax L 1787:11
Fleming, Thos., Estate, Duke St.	Alexandria	Owner	1795	Tax L 1795:09
Fleming, Thos., Estate, Union St.	Alexandria	Owner	1795	Tax L 1795:09
Fleming, Thos., ship carpenter, Estate	Alexandria	Suit	1801	CRC:194
Flemings, Miss	Alexandria	Tax Charge	1796	Tax PP 1796:06
Flemming, Andrew	Alexandria	Tax Charge	1796	Tax LP 1796:09
Flemming, Andrew, house joiner	Alexandria	Head	1810	1810(2):07A
Flemming, Andw.	Alexandria	Tithable +16	1789	Tax PP 1789:04
Flemming, Elizabeth	Alexandria	Tax Charge	1788	Tax PP 1788:06
Flemming, Elizabeth	Alexandria	Tax Charge	1789	Tax PP 1789:06
Flemming, Mary	Arlington	Will	1815	WB1:340
Flemming, Nancy	Alexandria	Boarder	1799	1799(2):03A
Flemming, Widow	Alexandria	Tax Charge	1796	Tax LP 1796:09
Fletcher & Finley	Alexandria	Owner	1787	Tax L 1787:10
Fletcher & Finley, Wilks St.	Alexandria	Occupant	1787	Tax L 1787:10
Fletcher & Finly	Alexandria	Tax Charge	1787	Tax PP 1787:05
Fletcher & Otway	Alexandria	Tax Charge	1796	Tax LP 1796:09
Fletcher, Aaron (C), stevedore	Alexandria	Housekeeper	1808	1808(1):06A
Fletcher, Aaron & wife (C), labourer	Alexandria	Housekeeper	1799	1799(2):18A
Fletcher, Aaron & wife Nancey	Alexandria	Resident	1800	1800(4):03B
Fletcher, Aaron, seeman [seaman]	Alexandria	Head	1800	1800(4):03A
Fletcher, Ann, seamstress	Alexandria	Head	1810	1810(1):05A
Fletcher, Edward C.	Alexandria	Will	1877	WB1:211; LP
Fletcher, George	Arlington	Bond	1855	BB(np)
Fletcher, George	Arlington	Inventory	1856	WB7:153; LVA-LP
Fletcher, George	Arlington	Account	1857	WB7:169; LVA-LP
Fletcher, James	Alexandria	Tithable +21	1787	Tax PP 1787:05
Fletcher, James	Alexandria	Tithable +16	1788	Tax PP 1788:05

NAME OR SUBJECT	LOCATION	TYPE	YEAR	REFERENCE(S)
Fletcher, James	Alexandria	Tax Charge	1789	Tax PP 1789:06
Fletcher, James	Alexandria	Tax Charge	1790	Tax PP 1790:04
Fletcher, James	Alexandria	Tax Charge	1795	Tax PP 1795:10
Fletcher, James	Alexandria	Tax Charge	1796	Tax LP 1796:09
Fletcher, James	Alexandria	Tax Charge	1796	Tax PP 1796:06
Fletcher, James	Alexandria	Tax Charge	1798	Tax PP 1798:05
Fletcher, James	Alexandria	Tax Charge	1799	Tax PP 1799:12
Fletcher, James	Alexandria	Tax Charge	1800	Tax PP 1800:09
Fletcher, James & wife, plaisterer	Alexandria	Head	1795	1795(4):07
Fletcher, James & wife, plaisterer	Alexandria	Housekeeper	1799	1799(2):19A
Fletcher, James & wife Mary	Alexandria	Resident	1800	1800(4):12B
Fletcher, James, Wilkes St.	Alexandria	Occupant	1790	Tax L 1790:04
Fletcher, James, Wilkes St.	Alexandria	Owner	1790	Tax L 1790:04
Fletcher, James, Wilks St.	Alexandria	Owner	1795	Tax L 1795:09
Fletcher, Jas., Wilks St.	Alexandria	Occupant	1795	Tax L 1795:09
Fletcher, Jno. W. & wife, merchant	Alexandria	Housekeeper	1799	1799(2):09A
Fletcher, Jno. W., Prince St.	Alexandria	Owner	1795	Tax L 1795:09
Fletcher, Jno. W., Prince St.	Alexandria	Occupant	1795	Tax L 1795:09
Fletcher, John W.	Alexandria	Tax Charge	1795	Tax PP 1795:09
Fletcher, John W.	Alexandria	Tax Charge	1796	Tax PP 1796:06
Fletcher, John W.	Alexandria	Tax Charge	1798	Tax PP 1798:06
Fletcher, John W.	Alexandria	Tax Charge	1799	Tax PP 1799:12
Fletcher, John W., Estate	Alexandria	Tax Charge	1800	Tax PP 1800:09
Fletcher, John W., w(7)4, merchant	Alexandria	Head	1796	1796(3):2
Fletcher, John Walter	Alexandria	Will	1894	WB2:086; LP
Fletcher, Mary	Alexandria	Head	1810	1810(4):03A
Fletcher, Mary, gentlewoman	Alexandria	Housekeeper	1808	1808(4):25A
Fletcher, Matilda	Alexandria	Will	1880	WB1:293; LP
Fletcher, Simeon, in jail	Arlington	Libel	1819	ACO:164
Fletcher, Thomas	Arlington	Will	1813	WB1:258; File #113A
Fletcher, Walter	Arlington	Will	1834	WB4:076; File #328A
Fletcher, Walter, c/o Mary	Arlington	Apprentice	1802	OCR1801:032
Fletcher, William	Arlington	Apprentice	1812	OCR1811:126
Fletcher, William	Alexandria	Tax Charge	1799	Tax PP 1799:12
Fletcher, William	Alexandria	Tax Charge	1800	Tax PP 1800:09
Fletcher, William	Alexandria	Head	1810	1810(4):04A
Fletcher, Wm.	Alexandria	Tax Charge	1798	Tax PP 1798:06
Fletcher, Wm. & wife, brass founder	Alexandria	Housekeeper	1799	1799(2):04A
Fletcher, Wm., brass founder	Alexandria	Housekeeper	1808	1808(2):15A
Fleury, Victor	Arlington	Apprentice	1823	OCR1822:057
Flinn, Michael	Alexandria	Tithable +21	1787	Tax PP 1787:16
Flinn, Michael	Alexandria	Tax Charge	1788	Tax PP 1788:05
Flood, Andrew	Alexandria	Tax Charge	1799	Tax PP 1799:12
Flood, Charles	Alexandria	Will	1892	WB2:033; LP
Flood, James, packer	Alexandria	Head	1810	1810(3):09A
Flood, Jas., laborer	Alexandria	Housekeeper	1808	1808(2):15A
Flood, Joseph	Arlington	Apprentice	1826	OCR1822:123
Flood, Thomas	Alexandria	Suit	1814	CRK:001
Flood, Thomas, plt.	Alexandria	Suit	1814	CRI:459
Flood, Thos., street cleaner	Alexandria	Head	1810	1810(3):08A
Flood, William	Alexandria	Tax Charge	1799	Tax PP 1799:12
Flood, Wm., physician	Alexandria	Boarder	1799	1799(2):03A
Flower, Saml.	Alexandria	Tax Charge	1795	Tax PP 1795:09
Flower, Samuel	Alexandria	Tax Charge	1796	Tax PP 1796:06
Flowers, David	Alexandria	Tax Charge	1796	Tax LP 1796:09
Floyd, Jacob	Alexandria	Tax Charge	1790	Tax PP 1790:05
Floyd, Mary T.C.	Arlington	Guard.	1801	CRA:335
Floyd, Saml. & wife, cooper	Alexandria	Housekeeper	1799	1799(2):08A
Floyd, Samuel	Alexandria	Tax Charge	1799	Tax PP 1799:12
Floyd, Thomas	Arlington	Admin.	1800	CRA:336
Floyd, Thomas, Dr.	Arlington	Account	1804	WBA:329; LVA-LP

NAME OR SUBJECT	LOCATION	TYPE	YEAR	REFERENCE(S)
Focke, [blank], merchant	Alexandria	Boarder	1799	1799(2):02A
Foley, Dennis	Alexandria	Tax Charge	1795	Tax PP 1795:09
Foley, Dennis	Alexandria	Tax Charge	1796	Tax LP 1796:09
Foley, Dennis	Alexandria	Tax Charge	1796	Tax PP 1796:06
Foley, Dennis	Alexandria	Tax Charge	1798	Tax PP 1798:05
Foley, Dennis	Alexandria	Mer. License	1798	Tax PP 1798:20-2
Foley, Dennis	Alexandria	Mer. License	1799	Tax PP 1799:52-03r
Foley, Dennis	Alexandria	Tax Charge	1799	Tax PP 1799:12
Foley, Dennis & wife, grocer	Alexandria	Housekeeper	1799	1799(2):09A
Foley, Dennis, def.	Alexandria	Suit	1801	CRB:066
Foley, Dennis, King St.	Alexandria	Occupant	1795	Tax L 1795:32
Foley, Elizabeth	Arlington	Will	1818	WB2:230; File #149A
Foley, Elizabeth, seamstress	Alexandria	Head	1810	1810(4):04A
Foley, Jeremiah	Alexandria	Will	1898	WB2:285; LP
Foley, John	Alexandria	Boarder	1808	1808(1):03A
Foley, Richard	Alexandria	Tax Charge	1799	Tax PP 1799:12
Foling, Wm., ship carpenter	Alexandria	Housekeeper	1808	1808(3):21A
Follin, Edward, b/o William	Arlington	Apprentice	1805	OCR1801:255
Follin, William	Alexandria	Tax Charge	1799	Tax PP 1799:12
Follin, William	Alexandria	Tax Charge	1800	Tax PP 1800:09
Follin, William	Arlington	Ordinary	1810	OBL2(np)
Follin, William, grantor	Arlington	Indenture D.	1804	ID3:066
Follin, William, house joiner	Alexandria	Head	1810	1810(3):05A
Follin, William, in jail	Arlington	Insolvent	1804	ID3:060
Follin, Wm.	Alexandria	Tax Charge	1798	Tax PP 1798:05
Folly, Dennis, 4, shopkeeper	Alexandria	Head	1796	1796(3):2
Folly, Elizabeth, (2), shopkeeper	Alexandria	Head	1796	1796(3):3
Folman, Christian	Arlington	Inventory	1857	WB7:270; LVA-LP
Folnie [Fowle], William	Alexandria	Tax Charge	1799	Tax PP 1799:12
Folson, Anthony (C), laborer	Alexandria	Housekeeper	1808	1808(1):08A
Folton, Mary	Alexandria	Resident	1800	1800(4):08B
Folton, Mary, sempster	Alexandria	Head	1800	1800(4):08A
Foly, Dennis	Alexandria	Tax Charge	1800	Tax PP 1800:09
Foote, Mary Marshall	Alexandria	Will	1880	WB1:323; LP
Forbes, Bennett	Alexandria	Tithable +16	1790	Tax PP 1790:10
Forbes, William	Arlington	Guard.	1816	WB2:114
Forbury, George	Alexandria	Tithable +21	1787	Tax PP 1787:07
Ford, Andrew	Alexandria	Tax Charge	1795	Tax PP 1795:10
Ford, Andrew	Alexandria	Tax Charge	1796	Tax PP 1796:06
Ford, Andrew	Alexandria	Tax Charge	1798	Tax PP 1798:05
Ford, Andrew	Alexandria	Tax Charge	1799	Tax PP 1799:12
Ford, Andw., schoolmaster	Alexandria	Boarder	1795	1795(4a):11
Ford, Andw., St. Asaph St.	Alexandria	Occupant	1795	Tax L 1795:24
Ford, Daniel	Arlington	Apprentice	1822	OCR1822:003
Ford, E., Fairfax St.	Alexandria	Occupant	1787	Tax L 1787:22
Ford, James	Alexandria	Resident	1800	1800(4):12B
Ford, James, sergent	Alexandria	Boarder	1800	1800(4):12A
Ford, John E.	Alexandria	Tithable +21	1787	Tax PP 1787:15
Ford, John Edwd.	Alexandria	Tithable +16	1788	Tax PP 1788:16
Ford, John, of Cecil Co. MD	Alexandria	Will	1892	WB2:036; LP
Ford, Josiah	Alexandria	Will	1878	WB1:235; LP
Ford, Patton & Co., King St.	Alexandria	Occupant	1795	Tax L 1795:07
Ford, Patton & Co.	Alexandria	Tax Charge	1795	Tax PP 1795:23
Ford, Patton & Co.	Alexandria	Tax Charge	1796	Tax LP 1796:09
Ford, Patton & Co.	Alexandria	Tax Charge	1796	Tax PP 1796:06
Ford, Thomas R.	Arlington	Will	1816	WB2:108; File #129A
Ford, Thomas R.	Arlington	Bond	1816	WB2:109
Ford, Thomas R.	Arlington	Sale	1817	AB3:001
Ford, Thomas R.	Arlington	Account	1825	AB5:404
Forester, Jane, washwoman	Alexandria	Housekeeper	1808	1808(4):25A
Forester, Wm. (C)	Alexandria	Boarder	1808	1808(4):25B

NAME OR SUBJECT	LOCATION	TYPE	YEAR	REFERENCE(S)
Formann, Ann (McKnight), w/o Joseph	Arlington	Defendant	1842	LSA:082
Formann, Joseph	Arlington	Defendant	1842	LSA:082
Forneau, Philip	Alexandria	Tax Charge	1790	Tax PP 1790:05
Forrest, Joseph	Alexandria	Tax Charge	1796	Tax LP 1796:09
Forrester, Jno. (C)	Alexandria	Boarder	1808	1808(2):13B
Forrister, Jane	Alexandria	Resident	1800	1800(4):13B
Forrister, Jane, sumpster	Alexandria	Boarder	1800	1800(4):13A
Forst, Abm.	Alexandria	Tax Charge	1795	Tax PP 1795:09
Fort Washington	Alexandria	Expenses	1814	CRL:353
Forteney, Jacob	Arlington	Will	1818	WB2:273
Forteney, Jacob	Arlington	Bond	1818	WB2:275
Forteney, Jacob	Arlington	Admin.	1820	WB2:370
Forteney, Jacob, Jr.	Arlington	Account	1819	AB3:347; LVA-LP
Forteney, Jacob, Jr.	Arlington	Sale	1819	AB3:340
Forteney, Jacob, Jr.	Arlington	Inventory	1819	AB3:286; LVA-LP
Forteney, Jacob, Jr.	Arlington	Sale	1819	AB3:296
Fortney, Edwin W.	Arlington	Guard. Acct.	1819	AB3:288; LVA-LP
Fortney, Edwin W.	Arlington	Guard. Acct.	1820	AB4:107; LVA-LP
Fortney, Edwin W.	Arlington	Guard. Acct.	1821	AB4:227
Fortney, Edwin W.	Arlington	Guard.	1821	WB2:421
Fortney, Edwin W.	Arlington	Guard. Acct.	1822	AB5:037; LVA-LP
Fortney, Edwin W.	Arlington	Guard. Acct.	1822	OCR1822:002a
Fortney, Edwin W.	Arlington	Guard. Acct.	1823	AB5:159; LVA-LP
Fortney, Edwin W.	Arlington	Guard. Acct.	1825	AB5:388
Fortney, Edwin W.	Arlington	Guard. Acct.	1825	OCR1822:083
Fortney, Edwin W.	Arlington	Guard. Acct.	1826	AB6:157; LVA-LP
Fortney, Edwin W.	Arlington	Guard. Acct.	1827	AB6:222; LVA-LP
Fortney, Edwin W.	Arlington	Guard. Acct.	1828	AB6:444; LVA-LP
Fortney, Edwin W.	Arlington	Guard. Acct.	1829	AB6:480; LVA-LP
Fortney, Edwin W.	Arlington	Guard. Acct.	1830	AB6:512; LVA-LP
Fortney, Edwin W.	Arlington	Guard. Acct.	1831	AB7:003
Fortney, Edwin W.	Arlington	Guard. Acct.	1832	AB7:035; LVA-LP
Fortney, Edwin W.	Arlington	Guard. Acct.	1834	AB7:337; LVA-LP
Fortney, Edwin W.	Arlington	Guard. Acct.	1835	AB7:337; LVA-LP
Fortney, Edwin W.	Arlington	Guard. Acct.	1836	AB8:337; LVA-LP
Fortney, Edwin W.	Arlington	Guard. Acct.	1837	AB7:339; LVA-LP
Fortney, Edwin W.	Arlington	Guard. Acct.	1838	AB7:339; LVA-LP
Fortney, Edwin W.	Arlington	Guard. Acct.	1839	AB7:337
Fortney, Edwin Washington, c/o Jacob	Arlington	Guard.	1817	WB2:214
Fortney, Geo., blacksmith	Alexandria	Head	1810	1810(2):05A
Fortney, George	Arlington	Bond	1817	WB2:207
Fortney, George	Arlington	Will	1817	WB2:207
Fortney, George	Arlington	Account	1818	AB3:211; LVA-LP
Fortney, George	Arlington	Account	1841	AB8:240; LVA-LP
Fortney, George	Arlington	Account	1846	AB9:252; LVA-LP
Fortney, George, grantor	Arlington	Indenture D.	1812	ID2:180
Fortney, George, in jail bounds	Arlington	Insolvent	1812	ID2:176
Fortney, J., Royal St.	Alexandria	Occupant	1787	Tax L 1787:27
Fortney, Jacob	Alexandria	Owner	1787	Tax L 1787:10
Fortney, Jacob	Alexandria	Tax Charge	1787	Tax PP 1787:05
Fortney, Jacob	Alexandria	Tax Charge	1788	Tax PP 1788:05
Fortney, Jacob	Alexandria	Tax Charge	1789	Tax PP 1789:06
Fortney, Jacob	Alexandria	Tax Charge	1790	Tax PP 1790:04
Fortney, Jacob	Alexandria	Tax Charge	1795	Tax PP 1795:09
Fortney, Jacob	Alexandria	Tax Charge	1796	Tax LP 1796:09
Fortney, Jacob	Alexandria	Tax Charge	1796	Tax PP 1796:06
Fortney, Jacob	Alexandria	Tax Charge	1798	Tax PP 1798:05
Fortney, Jacob	Alexandria	Tax Charge	1799	Tax PP 1799:12
Fortney, Jacob	Alexandria	Boarder	1808	1808(2):14A
Fortney, Jacob	Arlington	Inventory	1816	AB2:400; LVA-LP
Fortney, Jacob	Arlington	Admin.	1816	WB2:157

NAME OR SUBJECT	LOCATION	TYPE	YEAR	REFERENCE(S)
Fortney, Jacob	Arlington	Sale	1817	AB2:421, 424
Fortney, Jacob	Arlington	Account	1817	AB3:108; LVA-LP
Fortney, Jacob	Arlington	Account	1817	AB3:016; LVA-LP
Fortney, Jacob	Arlington	Account F.	1818	AB3:157; LVA-LP
Fortney, Jacob	Arlington	Will	1819	WB2:273; File #157A
Fortney, Jacob, blacksmith	Alexandria	Housekeeper	1808	1808(2):14A
Fortney, Jacob, blacksmith	Alexandria	Head	1810	1810(2):05A
Fortney, Jacob, Cameron St.	Alexandria	Owner	1795	Tax L 1795:09
Fortney, Jacob, King St.	Alexandria	Occupant	1787	Tax L 1787:10
Fortney, Jacob, King St.	Alexandria	Owner	1790	Tax L 1790:04
Fortney, Jacob, King St.	Alexandria	Occupant	1790	Tax L 1790:04
Fortney, Jacob, King St.	Alexandria	Owner	1795	Tax L 1795:09
Fortney, Jacob, Queen St.	Alexandria	Owner	1795	Tax L 1795:09
Fortney, Jacob, Royal St.	Alexandria	Owner	1795	Tax L 1795:09
Fortney, Jacob, Royal St.	Alexandria	Occupant	1795	Tax L 1795:09
Fortney, Nancy	Arlington	Guard.	1817	WB2:172
Fortney, Nancy	Arlington	Guard. Acct.	1818	AB3:113; LVA-LP
Fortny, George	Alexandria	Tax Charge	1800	Tax PP 1800:09
Fortny, Jacob	Alexandria	Tax Charge	1800	Tax PP 1800:09
Fosset, John	Alexandria	Tax Charge	1795	Tax PP 1795:10
Fossett, James	Alexandria	Will	1879	WB1:281; LP
Fossett, John	Alexandria	Tax Charge	1789	Tax PP 1789:06
Fossett, John B.	Alexandria	Will	1883	WB1:394; LP
Foster, Elizabeth, seamstress	Alexandria	Head	1810	1810(2):06A
Foster, Francis, clerk	Alexandria	Boarder	1799	1799(2):02A
Foster, Jno.	Alexandria	Tax Charge	1795	Tax PP 1795:09
Foster, Jno.	Alexandria	Tax Charge	1798	Tax PP 1798:06
Foster, Jno.	Alexandria	Tax Charge	1800	Tax PP 1800:09
Foster, Jno. & Co., King St.	Alexandria	Occupant	1795	Tax L 1795:14
Foster, Jno. & wife	Alexandria	Housekeeper	1799	1799(2):02A
Foster, John	Alexandria	Tax Charge	1790	Tax PP 1790:04
Foster, John	Alexandria	Tax Charge	1796	Tax LP 1796:09
Foster, John	Alexandria	Tax Charge	1796	Tax PP 1796:06
Foster, John	Alexandria	Mer. License	1799	Tax PP 1799:52-03w
Foster, John	Alexandria	Tax Charge	1799	Tax PP 1799:12
Foster, John	Alexandria	Mer. License	1800	Tax PP 1800:54(13)r
Foster, John	Arlington	Defendant	1802	PA:149
Foster, John	Arlington	Defendant	1802	PA:287, 290
Foster, John	Arlington	Will	1806	WBB:345; File #022A
Foster, John	Arlington	Bond	1806	WBB:351
Foster, John	Arlington	Inventory	1807	WBB:499; LVA-LP
Foster, John	Arlington	Sale	1807	WBB:498
Foster, John	Arlington	Account	1810	WBC:451; LVA-LP
Foster, John	Arlington	Account	1812	AB1:236; LVA-LP
Foster, John	Arlington	Settlement	1813	AB1:289; LVA-LP
Foster, John, def.	Alexandria	Suit	1802	CRC:051
Foster, John, def.	Alexandria	Suit	1803	CRD:172
Foster, John, for playing Faro	Arlington	Defendant	1801	PA:125
Foster, John, w1, merchant	Alexandria	Head	1796	1796(3):4
Foster, William, in jail	Arlington	Insolvent	1817	ID2:430
Foster, Wm., labourer	Alexandria	Head	1810	1810(1):05A
Foucard, John A.	Arlington	Bond	1833	WB4:058
Foucard, John A.	Arlington	Will	1833	WB4:057; File #321A
Foucard, John A.	Arlington	Account	1834	AB7:111; LVA-LP
Foucard, John A.	Arlington	Account	1835	AB7:195; LVA-LP
Foucard, John A.	Arlington	Account	1836	AB7:195
Foucard, John A.	Arlington	Account	1838	AB7:272; LVA-LP
Foucard, John, grantee	Arlington	Indenture D.	1831	ID:346
Fouch, Ira	Alexandria	Boarder	1808	1808(4):25A
Fouch, Isaac, c/o Betsy Fouch Smith	Arlington	Apprentice	1802	OCR1801:037
Fouch, Isaac, c/o Betsy Fouch Smith	Arlington	Apprentice	1803	OCR1801:073

NAME OR SUBJECT	LOCATION	TYPE	YEAR	REFERENCE(S)
Fouchee, Jno.	Alexandria	Tax Charge	1798	Tax PP 1798:05
Fouchee, John	Alexandria	Tax Charge	1796	Tax PP 1796:06
Fouchee, John	Alexandria	Tax Charge	1799	Tax PP 1799:12
Foushea, Elizabeth, seamstress	Alexandria	Head	1810	1810(4):07A
Foushee, George	Alexandria	Tax Charge	1787	Tax PP 1787:15
Foushee, Jno., Washington St.	Alexandria	Occupant	1795	Tax L 1795:10
Foushee, John	Alexandria	Tax Charge	1787	Tax PP 1787:05
Foushee, John	Alexandria	Tax Charge	1788	Tax PP 1788:05
Foushee, John	Alexandria	Tax Charge	1789	Tax PP 1789:06
Foushee, John	Alexandria	Tax Charge	1790	Tax PP 1790:04
Foushee, John	Alexandria	Tax Charge	1800	Tax PP 1800:09
Foushee, John, nr. Adams' wharf	Alexandria	Occupant	1790	Tax L 1790:04
Foushee, John, nr. Adams' wharf	Alexandria	Owner	1790	Tax L 1790:04
Foushee, Thomas A., Culpeper Co.	Arlington	P. of Atty.	1860	WB7:526
Fowle, Ann Eliza	Arlington	Guard. Acct.	1839	AB8:015
Fowle, Ann Eliza	Arlington	Guard. Acct.	1841	AB8:196
Fowle, Ann Eliza	Arlington	Guard. Acct.	1845	AB9:074; LVA-LP
Fowle, Eliza T.	Arlington	Account	1870	WB9:279
Fowle, Eliza T.	Arlington	Account	1870	WB9:261
Fowle, Eliza T., w/o William H.	Arlington	Will	1869	WB9:170; File #671A
Fowle, George D.	Arlington	Inventory	1877	WB9:467
Fowle, Holmes	Arlington	Deposition	1812	ACR:060
Fowle, Holmes, master	Arlington	Respondent	1812	ACR:050
Fowle, Holms, master	Arlington	Respondent	1812	ACO:127-128, 132-135
Fowle, Homes, master of *Wilhelmina*	Arlington	Cargo	1812	ACR:061
Fowle, John Charles	Arlington	Guard. Acct.	1839	AB8:015
Fowle, John Charles	Arlington	Guard. Acct.	1841	AB8:196
Fowle, John, Col.	Arlington	Account	1839	AB8:014; LVA-LP
Fowle, John, Col.	Arlington	Account	1841	AB8:194
Fowle, John, Col.	Arlington	Account	1845	AB9:066; LVA-LP
Fowle, John, Col.	Arlington	Account	1847	AB9:308
Fowle, John, Maj.	Arlington	Will	1838	WB4:165; File #355A
Fowle, Paulina Adeline	Arlington	Guard. Acct.	1839	AB8:015
Fowle, Paulina Adeline	Arlington	Guard. Acct.	1841	AB8:196
Fowle, Paulina Adeline	Arlington	Guard. Acct.	1845	AB9:072; LVA-LP
Fowle, Paulina Adeline	Arlington	Guard. Acct.	1847	AB9:312
Fowle, Susan	Arlington	Will	1865	WB8:223; File #619A
Fowle? [Folnie], William	Alexandria	Tax Charge	1799	Tax PP 1799:12
Fowle, William	Arlington	Account	1844	AB8:445
Fowle, William	Arlington	Will	1862	WB7:505; File #571A
Fowle, William H.	Arlington	Will	1870	WB9:212; File #677A
Fowle, William H.	Arlington	Account	1877	WB9:438
Fowle, Wm., merchant	Alexandria	Housekeeper	1808	1808(1):01A
Fowle, Wm., merchant	Alexandria	Head	1810	1810(1):08A
Fowler, Benjamin, Alexandria Co.	Arlington	Ordinary	1839	OBL5(np)
Fowler, Benjamin, at his house	Arlington	Ordinary	1838	OBL5(np)
Fowler, Benjamin, near Geo'tn. Ferry	Arlington	Ordinary	1841	OBL6(np)
Fowler, Geo., Estate	Alexandria	Owner	1787	Tax L 1787:10
Fowler, George, Estate, Fairfax St.	Alexandria	Owner	1790	Tax L 1790:07
Fowler, John	Arlington	Admin.	1806	WBB:267
Fowler, Matilda, washwoman	Alexandria	Housekeeper	1808	1808(3):23A
Fowler, Molly	Alexandria	Housekeeper	1799	1799(2):16A
Fowler, Wm.	Alexandria	Tax Charge	1796	Tax LP 1796:23
Fox, Daniel (C)	Arlington	Apprentice	1828	OCR1822:156
Fox, Fitzwilliam, c/o Lycurgus	Arlington	Guard.	1852	BB(np)
Fox, George, of Philadelphia	Alexandria	Deed	1811	CRK:048
Fox, L.F.	Arlington	Petition	1844	LVA-LP (Box 214)
Fox, Lycurgus F.	Arlington	Admin.	1844	OCR1842:064
Fox, Lycurgus Fitzwilliam [Elizabeth K.]	Arlington	Summons	1843	OCR1842:056
Fox, Monica, in Alexandria Co.	Arlington	Ordinary	1848	OBL6(np)
Fox, William	Arlington	Juryman	1808	ACO:081

NAME OR SUBJECT	LOCATION	TYPE	YEAR	REFERENCE(S)
Fox, William, marshall	Alexandria	Head	1810	1810(3):03A
Fox, Wm., retailer	Alexandria	Housekeeper	1808	1808(3):22A
Foxall, Henry, of Washington Co., def.	Alexandria	Suit	1822	CRL:544
Foxton, William	Alexandria	Tax Charge	1799	Tax PP 1799:12
Foxton, Wm.	Alexandria	Tax Charge	1798	Tax PP 1798:05
Foy, James	Alexandria	Mer. License	1799	Tax PP 1799:52-03r
Foy, Jas. & wife, grocer	Alexandria	Housekeeper	1799	1799(2):08A
Foy, Monica	Arlington	Ordinary	1846	OBL6(np)
Foy, Monica, her house Alexandria Co.	Arlington	Ordinary	1849	OBL6(np)
Foy, Monica, on Peyton St.	Arlington	Ordinary	1847	OBL6(np)
Foy, Patrick, at his house	Arlington	Ordinary	1832	OBL4(np)
Foy, Patrick, his house King St.	Arlington	Ordinary	1833	OBL5(np)
Foye, James	Alexandria	Mer. License	1798	Tax PP 1798:20-2
Foye, James	Alexandria	Tax Charge	1799	Tax PP 1799:12
Foye, Jas.	Alexandria	Tax Charge	1798	Tax PP 1798:05
Fraiser, William	Alexandria	Tax Charge	1800	Tax PP 1800:09
France, Hanner	Alexandria	Serv./Appr.	1800	1800(4):04B
France, Philip	Alexandria	Tax Charge	1788	Tax PP 1788:05
France, Philip	Alexandria	Tax Charge	1789	Tax PP 1789:06
France, Philip	Alexandria	Tax Charge	1796	Tax LP 1796:09
France, Philip	Alexandria	Tax Charge	1798	Tax PP 1798:05
France, Philip	Alexandria	Tax Charge	1799	Tax PP 1799:12
France, Philip	Alexandria	Tax Charge	1800	Tax PP 1800:09
France, Philip	Arlington	Will	1802	WBA:067
France, Philip	Arlington	Admin.	1802	WBA:068
France, Philip	Arlington	Inventory	1802	WBA:071; LVA-LP
Francis, Edward	Arlington	Will	1851	WB5:303; File #464A
Francis, Emanuel	Alexandria	Will	1897	WB2:183; LP
Francis, Hannah	Arlington	Will	1853	WB6:265; File #502A
Francis, John G.	Arlington	Ordinary	1809	OBL2(np)
Francis, John G., shoemaker	Alexandria	Housekeeper	1808	1808(3):21A
Francis, John G., shoemaker	Alexandria	Head	1810	1810(1):04A
Francis, Peter	Alexandria	Will	1889	WB1:525; LP
Franklin, Cora	Arlington	Apprentice	1843	OCR1842:027
Franklin, Elenor, shopkeeper	Alexandria	Head	1810	1810(2):04A
Franklin, J.	Alexandria	Tax Charge	1796	Tax PP 1796:06
Franklin, James, breeches maker	Alexandria	Head	1810	1810(1):04A
Franklin, Jas., breeches maker	Alexandria	Housekeeper	1808	1808(2):14A
Franklin, Thos.	Alexandria	Tax Charge	1798	Tax PP 1798:05
Franklin, Thos.	Alexandria	Tax Charge	1800	Tax PP 1800:09
Frantz, Philip, Princess	Alexandria	Occupant	1795	Tax L 1795:23
Fraser, Anthony R.	Arlington	Will	1881	WB10:008; File #702A
Fraser, Cornelia	Alexandria	Will	1895	WB2:118; LP
Fraser, Linney	Arlington	Apprentice	1828	OCR1822:154
Fraser, Mary	Arlington	Apprentice	1828	OCR1822:154
Fraser, Peter, confectioner	Alexandria	Housekeeper	1808	1808(3):20A
Fraser, William	Alexandria	Tax Charge	1799	Tax PP 1799:12
Fraser, William	Arlington	Inventory	1826	AB6:210
Fraser, William	Arlington	Account	1827	AB6:432; LVA-LP
Fraser, Wm., Jr.	Alexandria	Boarder	1808	1808(1):04A
Frasier, Daniel, blacksmith	Alexandria	Head	1810	1810(3):01A
Frazer, Anthony R.	Arlington	Complainant	1840	LSA:048
Frazer, Colin	Alexandria	Tax Charge	1789	Tax PP 1789:06
Frazer, Elizabeth, washerwoman	Alexandria	Head	1810	1810(1):12A
Frazer, George, b/o Henry	Arlington	Apprentice	1804	OCR1801:200
Frazer, Henry	Alexandria	Tax Charge	1796	Tax PP 1796:06
Frazer, Henry, nailor	Alexandria	Head	1810	1810(1):03A
Frazer, John	Arlington	Apprentice	1801	OCR1801:014
Frazer, Joseph	Alexandria	Tax Charge	1789	Tax PP 1789:06
Frazer, Joseph	Arlington	Will	1858	WB7:333; File #552A
Frazer, Rezin, on Union St.	Arlington	Ordinary	1841	OBL6(np)

NAME OR SUBJECT	LOCATION	TYPE	YEAR	REFERENCE(S)
Frazer, William	Arlington	Will	1826	WB3:233; File #247A
Frazer, William	Arlington	Bond	1826	WB3:236
Frazer, Wm. & wife, blacksmith	Alexandria	Housekeeper	1799	1799(2):05A
Frazier, Francis	Arlington	Crime	1796	OT:03/11/1796
Frazier, Jeremiah H.	Alexandria	Will	1897	WB2:206; LP
Frazier, Joseph	Alexandria	Tax Charge	1790	Tax PP 1790:04
Frazier, Lucy	Arlington	Admin. Bond	1850	ABB(np)
Frazier, William	Alexandria	Tax Charge	1790	Tax PP 1790:05
Frazier, William	Arlington	Ordinary	1804	OBL1(np)
Frazier, William	Arlington	Ordinary	1805	OBL1(np)
Frazier, William, def.	Alexandria	Suit	1801	CRC:118
Frederick, Henry	Alexandria	Tax Charge	1788	Tax PP 1788:05
Frederick, Henry	Alexandria	Tax Charge	1789	Tax PP 1789:06
Frederick, Henry, drayman	Alexandria	Boarder	1799	1799(2):04A
Freeborn, Joseph	Arlington	Apprentice	1804	OCR1801:189
Freeland, Benj., c/o Benj., Calvert Co.	Arlington	Apprentice	1811	OCR1811:081
Freeland, Richard, b/o Nancy	Arlington	Apprentice	1812	OCR1811:138
Freeman, Adam	Arlington	Apprentice	1803	OCR1801:123
Freeman, Bennett, cartman	Alexandria	Housekeeper	1808	1808(1):01A
Freeman, Eleanor, c/o William	Arlington	Apprentice	1805	OCR1801:314
Freeman, Jno.	Alexandria	Boarder	1808	1808(1):05A
Freeman, Nathaniel, Master	Arlington	Defendant	1819	ACO:164
Freeman, Wm., cartman	Alexandria	Housekeeper	1808	1808(1):03A
Freman, Philip, carpenter	Alexandria	Housekeeper	1808	1808(4):26A
French, Clarence E.	Alexandria	Will	1900	WB2:364; LP
French, Henry	Alexandria	Tithable +16	1788	Tax PP 1788:08
French, Henry	Alexandria	Tax Charge	1789	Tax PP 1789:06
French, John, c/o Susanna McCarty	Arlington	Apprentice	1803	OCR1801:088
French, Mary E.	Alexandria	Will	1892	WB2:011; LP
French, Samuel, seaman	Alexandria	Head	1810	1810(1):06A
French, Virginia C.	Alexandria	Will	1894	WB2:091; LP
Frenchman, Fairfax St.	Alexandria	Occupant	1795	Tax L 1795:30
Frenchman, King St.	Alexandria	Occupant	1795	Tax L 1795:32
Freud, James	Alexandria	Tax Charge	1788	Tax PP 1788:05
Freud, James	Alexandria	Tax Charge	1789	Tax PP 1789:06
Fridell, William, c/o Mary	Arlington	Apprentice	1815	OCR1811:271
Friend, Catharine, sempstress	Alexandria	Housekeeper	1808	1808(3):18A
Friend, William	Alexandria	Tax Charge	1799	Tax PP 1799:12
Frignet, John, shopkeeper	Alexandria	Head	1810	1810(1):02A
Fristo, John	Alexandria	Mer. License	1799	Tax PP 1799:52-03r
Fristoe, John, of Pr. William Co.	Alexandria	Bond	1801	CRB:098
Fristow, Jno. & wife	Alexandria	Boarder	1799	1799(2):01A
Frizzel, John, aged 41	Alexandria	Deposition	1767	CRI:267
Frizzell, John	Arlington	Apprentice	1843	OCR1842:033
Froud, Mary, nr. Royal St.	Alexandria	Occupant	1790	Tax L 1790:10
Froxous, Hampshire	Arlington	Will	1889	WB10:156; File #742A
Fruner, Phil.	Alexandria	Tax Charge	1795	Tax PP 1795:09
Frush, John (C)	Alexandria	Boarder	1808	1808(3):21B
Fry, Christopher	Alexandria	Deposition	1805	CRF:251
Fry, Christopher, plt.	Alexandria	Suit	1806	CRG:037
Fry, Daniel	Alexandria	Tax Charge	1790	Tax PP 1790:04
Frye, Margaret	Arlington	Inventory	1843	AB8:404; LVA-LP
Frye, Margaret	Arlington	Debts	1843	AB8:405
Frye, Margaret	Arlington	Petition	1843	LVA-LP (Box 214)
Frye, Margaret	Arlington	Will P.	1843	OCR1842:043
Frye, Margaret	Arlington	Sale	1843	OCR1842:056
Frye, Margaret	Arlington	Will	1843	WB4:364; File #407A
Frye, Margaret	Arlington	Account	1845	AB9:078
Frye, Margaret	Arlington	Account	1846	AB9:234; LVA-LP
Frye, Margaret	Arlington	Account	1846	AB9:258; LVA-LP
Fugett, Jarrett	Arlington	Inventory	1822	AB5:056; LVA-LP

NAME OR SUBJECT	LOCATION	TYPE	YEAR	REFERENCE(S)
Fugett, Jarrett	Arlington	Sale	1822	AB5:078
Fugett, Jarrett	Arlington	Account	1822	LVA-LP
Fugett, Jarrett	Arlington	Admin.	1822	OCR1822:007
Fugett, Jarrett	Arlington	Admin.	1822	WB3:050
Fugett, Jarrett	Arlington	Account F.	1836	AB7:213; LVA-LP
Fugitt, Gerrard	Arlington	Receipt	1822	AB5:079
Fugitt, James, grantor	Arlington	Indenture D.	1827	ID:109
Fugitt, James, in jail	Arlington	Insolvent	1827	ID:107
Fulford, Mary, Fairfax St.	Alexandria	Occupant	1795	Tax L 1795:09
Fulford, Polly	Alexandria	Boarder	1795	1795(4):04
Fulkason, Richd.	Alexandria	Tax Charge	1795	Tax PP 1795:10
Fuller, Lynne	Arlington	Will	1860	WB8:027; File #578A
Fullerson, John	Alexandria	Tithable +21	1787	Tax PP 1787:08
Fullerton, William	Alexandria	Tax Charge	1789	Tax PP 1789:06
Fullmer, Joseph, w(2), carpenter	Alexandria	Head	1796	1796(3):1
Fullum, Daniel	Arlington	Appraisal	1866	WB8:404
Fullum, Daniel	Arlington	Inventory	1866	WB8:389
Fulmer, Jos., St. Asaph St.	Alexandria	Occupant	1795	Tax L 1795:09
Fulmer, Joseph	Alexandria	Tax Charge	1787	Tax PP 1787:05
Fulmer, Joseph	Alexandria	Tax Charge	1789	Tax PP 1789:06
Fulmer, Joseph	Alexandria	Tax Charge	1796	Tax PP 1796:06
Fulmer, Joseph	Alexandria	Tax Charge	1798	Tax PP 1798:06
Fulmer, Joseph, St. Asaph St.	Alexandria	Occupant	1787	Tax L 1787:12
Fulmer, Joseph, St. Asaph St.	Alexandria	Owner	1795	Tax L 1795:09
Fulmore, Joseph	Alexandria	Tax Charge	1788	Tax PP 1788:06
Fulmore, Joseph	Alexandria	Tax Charge	1790	Tax PP 1790:05
Fulmore, Joseph	Alexandria	Tax Charge	1796	Tax LP 1796:09
Fulmore, Joseph, St. Asaph St.	Alexandria	Occupant	1790	Tax L 1790:04
Fulmore, Joseph, St. Asaph St.	Alexandria	Owner	1790	Tax L 1790:04
Fulton, Alexander W., c/o Ann	Arlington	Apprentice	1823	OCR1822:038a
Fulton, Jacob C., c/o Virginia	Arlington	Guard.	1823	OCR1822:046
Fulton, Jacob C., c/o Joseph	Arlington	Guard.	1823	WB3:100
Fulton, John	Alexandria	Tax Charge	1787	Tax PP 1787:05
Fulton, Joseph	Arlington	Admin.	1823	OCR1822:046
Fulton, Joseph	Arlington	Admin.	1823	WB3:094
Fulton, Joseph, c/o Mary Fulton Wico	Arlington	Apprentice	1802	OCR1801:025
Fulton, Mary	Alexandria	Housekeeper	1799	1799(2):19A
Fulton, Robert	Alexandria	Tax Charge	1788	Tax PP 1788:06
Fulton, Robert	Alexandria	Tax Charge	1789	Tax PP 1789:06
Fulton, Robert	Alexandria	Tax Charge	1790	Tax PP 1790:05
Fulton, Robert	Alexandria	Tax Charge	1796	Tax LP 1796:09
Fulton, Robert	Alexandria	Tax Charge	1796	Tax PP 1796:06
Fulton, Robert	Arlington	Defendant	1819	ACO:157, 160-163
Fulton, Robert, Fairfax St.	Alexandria	Owner	1790	Tax L 1790:04
Fulton, Robert, Fairfax St.	Alexandria	Occupant	1790	Tax L 1790:04
Fulton, Robert, Fairfax St.	Alexandria	Owner	1795	Tax L 1795:09
Fulton, Robert, St. Asaph St.	Alexandria	Owner	1795	Tax L 1795:09
Fulton, Robt.	Alexandria	Tax Charge	1795	Tax PP 1795:09
Fulton, Robt. & wife, carpenter	Alexandria	Head	1795	1795(4):04
Fulton, Robt., Fairfax St.	Alexandria	Occupant	1795	Tax L 1795:09
Furguson, Benjamin, Owner	Arlington	Respondent	1823	ACO:232
Furguson, Jno. & wife, labourer	Alexandria	Housekeeper	1799	1799(2):12A
Furguson, Robt., merchant	Alexandria	Boarder	1799	1799(2):02A
Furlong, John, b. Wexford	Arlington	Alien Entry	1818	RA:30/11/18
Furlong, John, b. Wexford, Ireland	Arlington	Citizenship	1823	ACO:231
Furneau, Philip	Alexandria	Tax Charge	1796	Tax PP 1796:06
Furnis, John	Arlington	Ordinary	1803	OBL1(np)
Furno, Philip	Alexandria	Tax Charge	1798	Tax PP 1798:05
Furno, Philip	Alexandria	Tax Charge	1800	Tax PP 1800:09
Furnough, Phillip, house joiner	Alexandria	Head	1810	1810(3):09A

NAME OR SUBJECT	LOCATION	TYPE	YEAR	REFERENCE(S)
G				
Gadsby, Jno.	Alexandria	Tax Charge	1798	Tax PP 1798:06
Gadsby, John	Alexandria	Tax Charge	1796	Tax LP 1796:10
Gadsby, John	Alexandria	Tax Charge	1796	Tax PP 1796:07
Gadsby, John	Alexandria	Tax Charge	1799	Tax PP 1799:15
Gadsby, John	Alexandria	Tax Charge	1800	Tax PP 1800:11
Gadsby, John	Arlington	Defendant	1801	PA:159
Gadsby, John	Arlington	Ordinary	1802	OBL1(np)
Gadsby, John	Arlington	Plaintiff	1802	PA:317, 320
Gadsby, John	Arlington	Defendant	1802	PA:144
Gadsby, John	Arlington	Ordinary	1803	OBL1(np)
Gadsby, John	Arlington	Ordinary	1804	OBL1(np)
Gadsby, John	Arlington	Ordinary	1806	OBL1(np)
Gadsby, John	Arlington	Ordinary	1807	OBL2(np)
Gadsby, John, def.	Alexandria	Suit	1802	CRC:277
Gadsby, John, tavern keeper	Alexandria	Housekeeper	1808	1808(2):15A
Gadsby, John, w(3)3, innkeeper	Alexandria	Head	1795	1796(3):7
Gadsby, Samuel & wife, ship carpenter	Alexandria	Head	1795	1795(4):04
Gahagan, Michael	Alexandria	Tax Charge	1787	Tax PP 1787:05
Gahagan, Michael	Alexandria	Tithable +16	1789	Tax PP 1789:15
Gal?, Thos.	Alexandria	Boarder	1808	1808(2):14A
Galbraith, Jas.	Alexandria	Tax Charge	1798	Tax PP 1798:06
Galbreath, James	Alexandria	Tax Charge	1800	Tax PP 1800:11
Galbreath, James, a cripple	Alexandria	Housekeeper	1808	1808(4):28A
Galbreath, John	Alexandria	Tax Charge	1800	Tax PP 1800:11
Gale, James	Alexandria	Tax Charge	1799	Tax PP 1799:15
Gale, James	Alexandria	Tax Charge	1800	Tax PP 1800:11
Gale, James, b. Scotland	Arlington	Alien Entry	1801	RA:06/07/01
Gale, Jas.	Alexandria	Tax Charge	1798	Tax PP 1798:06
Gale, Levin (C)	Alexandria	Tax Charge	1800	Tax PP 1800:11
Gale, Sally (C), n/o Nancy Watkins	Arlington	Apprentice	1823	OCR1822:039
Gale, Thadeus, schoolmaster	Alexandria	Housekeeper	1808	1808(2):14A
Gale, Theodore, teacher	Alexandria	Head	1810	1810(1):08A
Gales, Moses (C)	Arlington	Apprentice	1822	OCR1822:030
Galett, Helen, sometimes Gary	Arlington	Will	1857	WB7:260; File #548A
Gallagher, Ann Jane, of Geneva NY	Alexandria	Will	1887	WB1:484; LP
Gallagher, Margaret S.	Alexandria	Will	1890	WB1:567
Gallat, Charles & wife, tailor	Alexandria	Housekeeper	1799	1799(2):04A
Gallaudet, Peter W.	Arlington	Deposition	1831	ACR:084
Gallaway, Jerramia, marriner	Alexandria	Head	1800	1800(4):05A
Galloway, Jerrimier & Mary	Alexandria	Resident	1800	1800(4):05B
Galloway, John, blacksmith	Alexandria	Housekeeper	1808	1808(3):19A
Gallup, Asa O.	Arlington	Fid. Bond	1865	FBB(np)
Galt, Eve	Arlington	Account	1829	AB6:484; LVA-LP
Galt, Eve	Arlington	Account	1831	AB7:017; LVA-LP
Galt, Eve	Arlington	Guard. Acct.	1835	AB7:017; LVA-LP
Galt, Fanny	Arlington	Guard. Acct.	1829	AB6:485
Galt, Jacob	Arlington	Guard.	1827	OCR1822:148
Galt, Jacob	Arlington	Guard. Acct.	1829	AB6:485
Galt, Jacob	Arlington	Guard. Acct.	1831	AB7:019
Galt, James	Arlington	Juryman	1824	ACO:237
Galt, James, grantee	Arlington	Indenture D.	1804	ID3:023
Galt, James M.	Arlington	Guard.	1827	OCR1822:148
Galt, James M.	Arlington	Guard. Acct.	1831	AB7:019
Galt, James Madison	Arlington	Guard. Acct.	1829	AB6:485
Galt, James, silversmith	Alexandria	Housekeeper	1808	1808(1):02A
Galt, James, watchmaker	Alexandria	Head	1810	1810(1):02A
Galt, Tamany	Arlington	Guard.	1827	OCR1822:148
Galt, Tamany	Arlington	Guard. Acct.	1831	AB7:019
Galvan, Jno. & wife, carpenter	Alexandria	Housekeeper	1799	1799(2):17A
Galvan, John	Alexandria	Tax Charge	1799	Tax PP 1799:14

NAME OR SUBJECT	LOCATION	TYPE	YEAR	REFERENCE(S)
Gamalry, Jos.	Alexandria	Boarder	1808	1808(3):20A
Gamberg, Gure	Arlington	Admin.	1804	WBB:106
Gamberg, Gure	Arlington	Sale	1804	WBB:181
Gamberg, Gure	Arlington	Account	1805	WBB:182
Gamble, Samuel	Alexandria	Tax Charge	1789	Tax PP 1789:07
Ganett, Enoch, boatman	Alexandria	Housekeeper	1808	1808(1):01A
Gantt, Nancy (C), washwoman	Alexandria	Housekeeper	1808	1808(2):17A
Gardiner, Zachariah	Alexandria	Tax Charge	1799	Tax PP 1799:14
Gardner, Eliza F.	Arlington	Appraisal	1857	WB7:224; LVA-LP
Gardner, Eliza F.	Arlington	Account	1858	WB7:354; LVA-LP
Gardner, Eliza F.	Arlington	Report	1859	WB7:425; LVA-LP
Gardner, Eliza F.	Arlington	Report	1859	WB7:548; LVA-LP
Gardner, Eliza F.	Arlington	Account	1868	WB9:026
Gardner, Eliza Frances	Arlington	Will	1857	WB7:184; File #538A
Gardner, Henry	Alexandria	Tax Charge	1787	Tax PP 1787:05
Gardner, John	Alexandria	Tax Charge	1799	Tax PP 1799:14
Gardner, John Peter P.	Alexandria	Tithable +16	1789	Tax PP 1789:02
Gardner, Joseph	Alexandria	Tax Charge	1788	Tax PP 1788:06
Gardner, Joseph	Alexandria	Tax Charge	1789	Tax PP 1789:07
Gardner, Joseph, Union St.	Alexandria	Occupant	1787	Tax L 1787:01
Gardner, Rebeckah, labourrer	Alexandria	Boarder	1800	1800(4):09A
Gardner, Thomas	Alexandria	Tax Charge	1788	Tax PP 1788:06
Gardner, William	Arlington	Ordinary	1810	OBL2(np)
Gardner, William C.	Arlington	Defendant	1839	LSA:039
Gardner, William C.	Arlington	Will P.	1845	OCR1842:102, 103
Gardner, William C.	Arlington	Will	1845	WB4:390; File #419A
Gardner, William F., c/o Eliza F.	Arlington	Guard.	1858	WB7:351; LVA-LP
Gardner, William F., c/o Eliza F.	Arlington	Guard. Acct.	1859	WB7:427; LVA-LP
Gardner, William F., c/o Eliza F.	Arlington	Guard.	1859	WB7:550; LVA-LP
Gardner, Zacarier, murchant	Alexandria	Head	1800	1800(4):15A
Gardner, Zach.	Alexandria	Mer. License	1799	Tax PP 1799:52-04w
Gardner, Zachariah	Alexandria	Tax Charge	1800	Tax PP 1800:11
Gardner, Zachariah	Arlington	Inventory	1825	AB6:001; LVA-LP
Gardner, Zachariah	Arlington	Sale	1825	AB6:079
Gardner, Zachariah	Arlington	Admin.	1825	OCR1822:090a
Gardner, Zachariah	Arlington	Admin	1825	WB3:177
Gardner, Zachariah	Arlington	Account	1826	AB6:190; LVA-LP
Gardner, Zachariah	Arlington	Account	1827	AB6:438; LVA-LP
Gardner, Zachariah	Arlington	Account	1828	AB6:459; LVA-LP
Gardner, Zachariah	Arlington	Account	1831	AB7:007
Gardner, Zachariah	Arlington	Account	1833	AB7:072; LVA-LP
Gardner, Zachariah & wife, merchant	Alexandria	Housekeeper	1799	1799(2):13A
Gardner, Zacrier & wife Betsy	Alexandria	Serv./Appt.	1800	1800(4):15B
Garland, Jno. & wife, shoemaker	Alexandria	Housekeeper	1799	1799(2):09A
Garland, John	Alexandria	Tax Charge	1799	Tax PP 1799:14
Garlick, Elizabeth	Alexandria	Head	1810	1810(2):06A
Garner, Margaret	Arlington	Ordinary	1820	OBL3(np)
Garner, Margaret	Arlington	Ordinary	1822	OBL3(np)
Garner, Margaret	Arlington	Ordinary	1823	OBL3(np)
Garner, Margaret	Arlington	Admin. Bond	1848	ABB(np)
Garner, Margaret	Arlington	Account	1849	LVA-LP
Garner, Margaret, at her house	Arlington	Ordinary	1826	OBL4(np)
Garner, Margaret, at her house	Arlington	Ordinary	1837	OBL5(np)
Garner, Margaret, at her house	Arlington	Ordinary	1841	OBL6(np)
Garner, Margaret, in Alexandria Co.	Arlington	Ordinary	1824	OBL3(np)
Garner, Margaret, in Alexandria Co.	Arlington	Ordinary	1825	OBL4(np)
Garner, William	Arlington	Ordinary	1809	OBL2(np)
Garner, Wm.	Alexandria	Boarder	1808	1808(1):04A
Garner, Wm., retailer	Alexandria	Housekeeper	1808	1808(1):03A
Garner, Wm., shopkeeper	Alexandria	Head	1810	1810(1):12A
Garnett, Obadiah	Arlington	Admin.	1811	WB1:028

NAME OR SUBJECT	LOCATION	TYPE	YEAR	REFERENCE(S)
Garratt, Enoch, labourer	Alexandria	Head	1810	1810(1):03A
Garretson, Frances	Alexandria	Resident	1800	1800(4):06B
Garretson, Frances, semster	Alexandria	Boarder	1800	1800(4):06A
Garvey's Estate	Alexandria	Tax Charge	1796	Tax LP 1796:10
Garvey, [blank], Estate, Fairfax St.	Alexandria	Owner	1795	Tax L 1795:10
Garvy, Lewis, Estate	Alexandria	Owner	1787	Tax L 1787:12
Gary, John G.	Arlington	Ordinary	1823	OBL3(np)
Gater, Elizebeth, labourrer	Alexandria	Boarder	1800	1800(4):09A
Gates, Elizabeth	Alexandria	Resident	1800	1800(4):09B
Gates, Margaret	Arlington	Guard.	1819	WB2:270
Gates, William	Alexandria	Tax Charge	1800	Tax PP 1800:11
Gates, William	Arlington	Admin.	1836	WB4:107
Gates, William (aka John White)	Arlington	Will (N)	1836	WB4:107
Gathagan, Mathias P.	Arlington	Apprentice	1812	OCR1811:090
Gatton, Azariah	Arlington	Inventory	1815	AB2:176; LVA-LP
Gatton, Azariah	Arlington	Admin.	1815	WB2:068
Gatton, Azariah	Arlington	Account	1816	AB2:296; LVA-LP
Gatton, Azariah	Arlington	Sale	1816	AB2:239
Gatton, Azariah	Arlington	Account F.	1817	AB3:001; LVA-LP
Gavin, John	Arlington	Apprentice	1827	OCR1822:134
Gawler, Charles B.	Arlington	Guard.	1838	WB4:172
Gay, James & wife Elizebeth	Alexandria	Resident	1800	1800(4):10B
Gay, James, shoemaker	Alexandria	Head	1800	1800(4):10A
Gaytor & Griffith, watchmakers	Alexandria	Head	1810	1810(1):02A
Gaytor, Ann, seamstress	Alexandria	Head	1810	1810(1):12A
Geary, Mary	Alexandria	Will	1897	WB2:191; LP
Gebard, Peggy, Queen St.	Alexandria	Occupant	1787	Tax L 1787:06
Gebo, John	Alexandria	Owner	1787	Tax L 1787:12
Gebo, John, King St.	Alexandria	Occupant	1787	Tax L 1787:12
Geddis, Margaret, alias Marks	Arlington	Crime	1794	OT:03/07/1794
Gee, Mary Ann	Arlington	Guard.	1807	WBB:348m
Gee, Saml.	Alexandria	Boarder	1799	1799(2):10A
Gee, Saml.	Alexandria	Boarder	1808	1808(4):25A
Geeslin, Ezekiel	Arlington	Apprentice	1826	OCR1822:107
Geeslin, William L.	Arlington	Apprentice	1826	OCR1822:107
Geiger, Jacob	Alexandria	Tax Charge	1800	Tax PP 1800:11
Geiger, Jacob, plt.	Alexandria	Suit	1801	CRD:038
Geilchrist, Alexander	Alexandria	Tithable +16	1790	Tax PP 1790:04
Geisendaffer, William, on King St.	Arlington	Ordinary	1845	OBL6(np)
Geisendaffer, William, on King St.	Arlington	Ordinary	1846	OBL6(np)
Geislin, Ezekiel G.	Arlington	Apprentice	1829	OCR1822:168a
Geislin, William L.	Arlington	Apprentice	1829	OCR1822:168a
Gelston, Charles W.	Arlington	Suit	1823	ACO:232
Gelston, Charles W.	Arlington	Respondent	1823	ACO:208, 209
Geltson, Charles W.	Arlington	Respondent	1823	ACO:218
Gemeny, John	Arlington	Ordinary	1821	OBL3(np)
Gemeny, John	Arlington	Ordinary	1823	OBL3(np)
Gemeny, John, at his house	Arlington	Ordinary	1828	OBL4(np)
Gemeny, John, in Alexandria Co.	Arlington	Ordinary	1822	OBL3(np)
Gemeny, John, in Alexandria Co.	Arlington	Ordinary	1824	OBL3(np)
Gemeny, John, in Alexandria Co.	Arlington	Ordinary	1825	OBL4(np)
Gemeny, John, in Alexandria Co.	Arlington	Ordinary	1826	OBL4(np)
Gemeny, John, in Alexandria Co.	Arlington	Ordinary	1830	OBL4(np)
Generis, [blank], dancing master	Alexandria	Housekeeper	1808	1808(1):03A
Generis, [blank], dancing master	Alexandria	Head	1810	1810(1):07A
Genigal, Enos	Alexandria	Tax Charge	1798	Tax PP 1798:06
Genigle, Enos	Alexandria	Tax Charge	1796	Tax PP 1796:07
Genigle, Enos	Alexandria	Tax Charge	1799	Tax PP 1799:14
George, Anna S.	Alexandria	Will	1877	WB1:227; LP
George, Isaac	Arlington	Appraisal	1862	WB8:142; LVA-LP
George, Isaac	Arlington	Will	1862	WB8:137; File #593A

NAME OR SUBJECT	LOCATION	TYPE	YEAR	REFERENCE(S)
George, Isaac	Arlington	Will (Error)	1865	WD0.200
George, Isaac, b. Cornwall	Arlington	Alien Entry	1818	RA:03/12/18
George, Jno., gunsmith	Alexandria	Housekeeper	1808	1808(2):14A
Georgetown & Alexandria Turnpike Co.	Alexandria	Suit	1809	CRG:187
German, John George	Arlington	Apprentice	1843	OCR1842:055
Gerrard, John	Arlington	Admin.	1821	WB2:428
Ghequere, Bernd.	Alexandria	Tax Charge	1796	Tax LP 1796:10
Ghequiere, Bernard	Alexandria	Tax Charge	1796	Tax PP 1796:07
Ghequiere, Bernard	Alexandria	Mer. License	1798	Tax PP 1798:20-3
Ghequiere, Bernard	Alexandria	Tax Charge	1799	Tax PP 1799:14
Ghequiere, Bernard	Alexandria	Mer. License	1800	Tax PP 1800:54(13)r
Ghequiere, Bernard, merchant	Alexandria	Boarder	1799	1799(2):02A
Ghequiere, Bernd., Fairfax St.	Alexandria	Occupant	1795	Tax L 1795:25
Ghequiere, Mr., Union St.	Alexandria	Occupant	1795	Tax L 1795:08
Ghequire, Berd.	Alexandria	Tax Charge	1798	Tax PP 1798:06
Ghequire, Berd.	Alexandria	Tax Charge	1800	Tax PP 1800:11
Ghequire, Bernard	Alexandria	Mer. License	1799	Tax PP 1799:52-04w
Ghequire, Bernd.	Alexandria	Tax Charge	1795	Tax PP 1795:10
Gibbons, John	Arlington	Deposition	1806	ACR:025
Gibbons, Patrick	Alexandria	Tithable +16	1789	Tax PP 1789:05
Gibbs, James	Alexandria	Tax Charge	1799	Tax PP 1799:14
Gibbs, James (C)	Alexandria	Tax Charge	1800	Tax PP 1800:11
Gibbs, James & wife Bettey	Alexandria	Resident	1800	1800(4):13B
Gibbs, James, labourer	Alexandria	Head	1810	1810(4):09A
Gibbs, James, labourrer	Alexandria	Head	1800	1800(4):13A
Gibbs, Theodore, grantor	Arlington	Indenture D.	1828	ID:185
Gibbs, Theodore, in jail	Arlington	Insolvent	1828	ID:183
Gibby, John	Arlington	Apprentice	1804	OCR1801:208
Gibby, John, gc/o Sophia Crout	Arlington	Apprentice	1801	OCR1801:016
Gibney, Hugh, Estate	Alexandria	Owner	1787	Tax L 1787:12
Gibney, Jno. F. & wife, merchant	Alexandria	Housekeeper	1799	1799(2):03A
Gibney, John F.	Alexandria	Tax Charge	1799	Tax PP 1799:14
Gibo, John	Alexandria	Tax Charge	1787	Tax PP 1787:05
Giborey, John	Alexandria	Tax Charge	1796	Tax PP 1796:07
Gibory, Jno.	Alexandria	Tax Charge	1795	Tax PP 1795:15
Gibory, Jno.	Alexandria	Tax Charge	1798	Tax PP 1798:06
Gibory, Jno., Fairfax St.	Alexandria	Occupant	1795	Tax L 1795:11
Gibory, John & wife, schoolmaster	Alexandria	Head	1795	1795(4a):03
Gibson, A.	Alexandria	Tax Charge	1796	Tax PP 1796:07
Gibson, Agusta	Alexandria	Head	1810	1810(2):07A
Gibson, Alfred (C)	Arlington	Apprentice	1827	OCR1822:137
Gibson, Emily	Alexandria	Will	1899	WB2:355; LP
Gibson, Guss, flour brander	Alexandria	Housekeeper	1808	1808(2):17A
Gibson, Isa.	Alexandria	Reference	1808	1808(3):20B
Gibson, Isaac	Alexandria	Tax Charge	1798	Tax PP 1798:06
Gibson, Isaac	Alexandria	Mer. License	1799	Tax PP 1799:52-04r
Gibson, Isaac	Alexandria	Mer. License	1800	Tax PP 1800:54(13)r
Gibson, Isaac	Alexandria	Tax Charge	1800	Tax PP 1800:11
Gibson, Isaac	Arlington	Inventory	1826	AB6:175
Gibson, Isaac	Arlington	Admin.	1826	OCR1822:110a
Gibson, Isaac	Arlington	Admin.	1826	WB3:223
Gibson, Isaac	Arlington	Account	1827	AB6:417; LVA-LP
Gibson, Isaac	Arlington	Account	1828	AB6:450; LVA-LP
Gibson, Isaac	Arlington	Account	1828	AB6:451; LVA-LP
Gibson, Isaac & wife, merchant	Alexandria	Housekeeper	1799	1799(2):06A
Gibson, Isaac, merchant	Alexandria	Housekeeper	1808	1808(4):27A
Gibson, Isaac [Susannah]	Arlington	Admin.	1826	OCR1822:109
Gibson, Isaac [Susannah]	Arlington	Renounce	1826	OCR1822:110a
Gibson, John H., at his house	Arlington	Ordinary	1837	OBL5(np)
Gibson, John H., at his house	Arlington	Ordinary	1838	OBL5(np)
Gibson, John, of Pr. William Co.	Alexandria	Affidavit	1806	CRE:076

NAME OR SUBJECT	LOCATION	TYPE	YEAR	REFERENCE(S)
Gibson, John, plt.	Alexandria	Suit	1801	CRC:194
Gibson, Robert	Alexandria	Deposition	1805	CRF:240
Gibson, Sarah, washwoman	Alexandria	Housekeeper	1808	1808(4):25A
Gibson, William	Alexandria	Will	1892	WB2:005; LP
Gibson, Wm., ex. parson	Alexandria	Housekeeper	1808	1808(4):29A
Gibson, Wm. L., dr. of divinity	Alexandria	Head	1810	1810(1):08A
Gifford, Robert	Alexandria	Boarder	1808	1808(2):16A
Giilbery, James, w(5), drayman	Alexandria	Head	1796	1796(3):1
Gilbert, Jno.	Alexandria	Boarder	1808	1808(4):24A
Gilbert, Peter	Arlington	Libellant	1803	ACO:007
Gilbert, Peter, re: Ship *Governor Strong*	Arlington	Bond	1801	ACO:006
Gilda, John	Alexandria	Tax Charge	1800	Tax PP 1800:11
Gildee, John	Alexandria	Tax Charge	1799	Tax PP 1799:14
Giles, David M., of Nantucket, Mass.	Alexandria	Deposition	1818	CRK:469
Gilham, William, as witness	Arlington	Payment	1808	ACO:086
Gilham, Wm., merchant	Alexandria	Housekeeper	1808	1808(2):16A
Gill, Jno.	Alexandria	Tax Charge	1795	Tax PP 1795:11
Gill, Jno., Prince St.	Alexandria	Occupant	1795	Tax L 1795:15
Gill, John	Alexandria	Tithable +16	1790	Tax PP 1790:09
Gill, John	Alexandria	Tax Charge	1796	Tax LP 1796:10
Gill, John	Alexandria	Tax Charge	1796	Tax PP 1796:07
Gill, John	Alexandria	Tax Charge	1798	Tax PP 1798:06
Gill, John	Alexandria	Tax Charge	1799	Tax PP 1799:14
Gill, Nathaniel	Alexandria	Tax Charge	1799	Tax PP 1799:14
Gill, Nathaniel & wife, shoemaker	Alexandria	Housekeeper	1799	1799(2):08A
Gillbraith, Jas. & wife, drayman	Alexandria	Housekeeper	1799	1799(2):11A
Gillham, William, merchant	Alexandria	Head	1810	1810(2):02A
Gillies, James	Alexandria	Tax Charge	1796	Tax PP 1796:07
Gillies, James	Alexandria	Tax Charge	1798	Tax PP 1798:07
Gillies, James	Alexandria	Tax Charge	1799	Tax PP 1799:15
Gillies, James	Arlington	Admin.	1807	WBB:524
Gillies, James	Arlington	Inventory	1807	WBB:537; LVA-LP
Gillies, James, def.	Alexandria	Suit	1801	CRB:252
Gillies, James, Princess St.	Alexandria	Occupant	1795	Tax L 1795:12
Gillies, Lucinda, c/o James	Arlington	Guard.	1807	WBC:022
Gillingham, Samuel	Alexandria	Will	1890	WB1:576; LP
Gillis, James	Alexandria	Tax Charge	1800	Tax PP 1800:11
Gillis, James, M.D.	Alexandria	Tax Charge	1795	Tax PP 1795:10
Gilliss, Francis, gentlewoman	Alexandria	Housekeeper	1808	1808(2):14A
Gillman, Ephraim, merchant	Alexandria	Head	1810	1810(2):03A
Gilman, Ephraim, trunkmaker & retailer	Alexandria	Housekeeper	1808	1808(2):13A
Gilpin, Benjamin N.	Alexandria	Tax Charge	1788	Tax PP 1788:06
Gilpin, Geo. & wife, merchant	Alexandria	Housekeeper	1799	1799(2):07A
Gilpin, Geo., post master	Alexandria	Head	1810	1810(2):01A
Gilpin, Geo., retailer	Alexandria	Housekeeper	1808	1808(2):11A
Gilpin, Geo., Water St.	Alexandria	Occupant	1795	Tax L 1795:08
Gilpin, Geo., wharf	Alexandria	Occupant	1795	Tax L 1795:07
Gilpin, Geo., Wolf St.	Alexandria	Occupant	1787	Tax L 1787:14
Gilpin, George	Alexandria	Owner	1787	Tax L 1787:11
Gilpin, George	Alexandria	Tax Charge	1789	Tax PP 1789:07
Gilpin, George	Alexandria	Tax Charge	1790	Tax PP 1790:05
Gilpin, George	Alexandria	Tax Charge	1795	Tax PP 1795:11
Gilpin, George	Alexandria	Tax Charge	1796	Tax LP 1796:10
Gilpin, George	Alexandria	Tax Charge	1796	Tax PP 1796:07
Gilpin, George	Alexandria	Mer. License	1798	Tax PP 1798:20-3
Gilpin, George	Alexandria	Tax Charge	1798	Tax PP 1798:06
Gilpin, George	Alexandria	Mer. License	1799	Tax PP 1799:52-04w
Gilpin, George	Alexandria	Tax Charge	1799	Tax PP 1799:14
Gilpin, George	Alexandria	Tax Charge	1800	Tax PP 1800:11
Gilpin, George	Alexandria	Mer. License	1800	Tax PP 1800:54(13)r
Gilpin, George	Arlington	Commission	1801	WBA:332, 336

NAME OR SUBJECT	LOCATION	TYPE	YEAR	REFERENCE(S)
Gilpin, George	Alexandria	Deposition	1808	CRH:125, 127
Gilpin, George	Arlington	Will	1814	WB1:280; File #115A
Gilpin, George	Arlington	Bond	1814	WB1:281
Gilpin, George	Arlington	Account	1815	AB2:155; LVA-LP
Gilpin, George	Arlington	Sale	1815	AB2:153
Gilpin, George	Arlington	Admin.	1838	WB4:186
Gilpin, George, Fairfax St.	Alexandria	Occupant	1787	Tax L 1787:12
Gilpin, George, Prince St.	Alexandria	Occupant	1790	Tax L 1790:06
Gilpin, George, surveyor	Arlington	Inventory	1814	AB2:025; LVA-LP
Gilpin, George, Union St.	Alexandria	Occupant	1790	Tax L 1790:04
Gilpin, George, Union St.	Alexandria	Owner	1790	Tax L 1790:04
Gilpin, George, w(8)6, merchant	Alexandria	Head	1795	1796(3):7
Gilpin, George, Water & Union sts.	Alexandria	Occupant	1787	Tax L 1787:11
Gilpin, George, wharf	Alexandria	Owner	1795	Tax L 1795:07
Gilpin, Jane	Arlington	Renounce	1814	WB1:281
Gilpin, John	Alexandria	Boarder	1808	1808(2):11A
Gilpin, Jos. & Thos., Estate, Water St.	Alexandria	Owner	1795	Tax L 1795:08
Gilpin, Jos. & Thos., Estate, Union St.	Alexandria	Owner	1795	Tax L 1795:08
Gilpin, Joseph	Alexandria	Owner	1787	Tax L 1787:11
Gilpin, Joseph	Alexandria	Tithable +16	1789	Tax PP 1789:11
Gilpin, Joseph	Alexandria	Tithable +16	1790	Tax PP 1790:08
Gilpin, Joseph, heirs, Union St.	Alexandria	Owner	1790	Tax L 1790:04
Gilpin, Joseph, heirs, Water St.	Alexandria	Owner	1790	Tax L 1790:04
Gilpin, Josh. & Thos.	Alexandria	Tax Charge	1796	Tax LP 1796:10
Gilpin, Mary	Arlington	Will	1860	WB7:531; File #574A
Gilpin, Thomas, Estate	Alexandria	Owner	1787	Tax L 1787:11
Gilpin, Thos.	Alexandria	Boarder	1808	1808(2):11A
Gilpin, Thos., heirs, Union St.	Alexandria	Owner	1790	Tax L 1790:04
Gilpin, Thos., heirs, Water St.	Alexandria	Owner	1790	Tax L 1790:04
Gilpin, [blank]	Alexandria	Boarder	1808	1808(2):13A
Gilroy, Mark	Arlington	Bond	1853	BB(np)
Gird, Chris., barber	Alexandria	Housekeeper	1808	1808(2):11A
Gird, Christopher	Alexandria	Tax Charge	1799	Tax PP 1799:14
Gird, Christopher	Alexandria	Tax Charge	1800	Tax PP 1800:11
Gird, Christopher	Arlington	Inventory	1819	AB3:349; LVA-LP
Gird, Christopher	Arlington	Will	1819	WB2:305; File #164A
Gird, Christopher	Arlington	Bond	1819	WB2:305
Gird, Christopher	Arlington	Admin.	1828	WB3:339
Gird, Christopher, barber	Alexandria	Head	1810	1810(2):01A
Gird, Edward, c/o Henry of Berkeley Co.	Arlington	Apprentice	1805	OCR1801:298
Gird, Edwd.	Alexandria	Boarder	1808	1808(2):16A
Gird, Eliza M., c/o John	Arlington	Guard.	1835	WB4:090
Gird, Henry	Alexandria	Tax Charge	1796	Tax LP 1796:10
Gird, Henry	Arlington	Will	1807	WBB:472; File #032A
Gird, Henry	Arlington	Bond	1807	WBB:474
Gird, Henry	Arlington	Account	1808	WBC:063; LVA-LP
Gird, Henry, Jr.	Alexandria	Tax Charge	1799	Tax PP 1799:14
Gird, Henry, Sr.	Alexandria	Tax Charge	1796	Tax PP 1796:07
Gird, Hy., Jr.	Alexandria	Tax Charge	1796	Tax PP 1796:07
Gird, Hy., Jr.	Alexandria	Tax Charge	1798	Tax PP 1798:06
Gird, John	Arlington	Defendant	1822	ACO:205
Gird, John	Arlington	Defendant	1823	ACO:213, 225
Gird, John	Arlington	Defendant	1824	ACO:235
Gird, John, grantee	Arlington	Indenture D.	1811	ID2:047
Gird, John H., c/o John	Arlington	Guard.	1835	WB4:090
Gird, John H., c/o John W.	Arlington	Guard.	1839	WB4:231
Gird, Jos.	Alexandria	Boarder	1808	1808(2):11A
Gird, Joseph C.	Arlington	Inventory	1819	AB4:009; LVA-LP
Gird, Joseph C.	Arlington	Will	1819	WB2:336
Gird, Joseph C.	Arlington	Bond	1819	WB2:337
Gird, William	Alexandria	Tax Charge	1799	Tax PP 1799:14

NAME OR SUBJECT	LOCATION	TYPE	YEAR	REFERENCE(S)
Gird, William	Alexandria	Tax Charge	1800	Tax PP 1800:11
Gird, Wm. F., watchmaker & shopkpr.	Alexandria	Housekeeper	1808	1808(2):10A
Gird, Wm. F., watchmaker	Alexandria	Head	1810	1810(2):02A
Gladin, William, age near 77	Alexandria	Deposition	1767	CRI:245
Glander, Anthony	Alexandria	Tax Charge	1796	Tax PP 1796:07
Glander, Anthony	Alexandria	Tax Charge	1798	Tax PP 1798:07
Glander, Anthony, w(1), baker	Alexandria	Head	1796	1796(3):1
Glanders, Tabitha	Alexandria	Housekeeper	1799	1799(2):11A
Glanoler, Anthony	Alexandria	Tax Charge	1790	Tax PP 1790:05
Glanville, Joseph	Arlington	Inventory	1818	AB3:177; LVA-LP
Glanville, Joseph	Arlington	Admin.	1818	WB2:243
Glascock, Sarah, sempstress	Alexandria	Housekeeper	1808	1808(1):01A
Glascock, William & wife, painter	Alexandria	Head	1795	1795(4):09
Glascock, William R.	Arlington	Suit	1853	BB(np)
Glascock, Wm. & wife, jack of all trades	Alexandria	Head	1795	1795(4a):08
Glassa, Michael	Alexandria	Tax Charge	1787	Tax PP 1787:06
Glasscock, Jas.	Alexandria	Boarder	1808	1808(3):18A
Glasscock, Sarah, seamstress	Alexandria	Head	1810	1810(1):10A
Glasscock, William	Alexandria	Tax Charge	1795	Tax PP 1795:11
Glasscock, William	Alexandria	Tax Charge	1796	Tax PP 1796:07
Glasscock, William	Alexandria	Tax Charge	1798	Tax PP 1798:06
Glasscock, William	Alexandria	Tax Charge	1799	Tax PP 1799:14
Glasscock, William	Alexandria	Tax Charge	1800	Tax PP 1800:11
Glasscock, William, w(2), painter	Alexandria	Head	1796	1796(3):1
Glasscock, [blank]	Alexandria	Tax Charge	1796	Tax LP 1796:10
Glasser, John	Alexandria	Tithable +16	1789	Tax PP 1789:15
Glasser, Michael	Alexandria	Tax Charge	1788	Tax PP 1788:06
Glasser, Michael	Alexandria	Tax Charge	1790	Tax PP 1790:05
Glassing, John	Alexandria	Tithable +16	1788	Tax PP 1788:13
Glassing, John	Alexandria	Tithable +16	1790	Tax PP 1790:12
Gleece, John	Alexandria	Mer. License	1799	Tax PP 1799:52-04r
Gleese, Jno.	Alexandria	Boarder	1799	1799(2):04A
Gleese, John	Alexandria	Tax Charge	1799	Tax PP 1799:14
Gleese, John	Arlington	Account	1804	LVA-LP
Gleman, Jacob, w(1), merchant	Alexandria	Head	1796	1796(3):2
Glenn, Robert, b. Galway	Arlington	Alien Entry	1820	RA:20/12/20
Glocester, Baptist	Alexandria	Tithable +16	1790	Tax PP 1790:06
Glouster, James Nott, c/o James	Arlington	Apprentice	1813	OCR1811:186
Glover, J., Royal St.	Alexandria	Occupant	1787	Tax L 1787:23
Glover, Thomas	Alexandria	Tax Charge	1787	Tax PP 1787:06
Glover, Thomas	Alexandria	Tax Charge	1789	Tax PP 1789:07
Glover, Thomas	Alexandria	Tax Charge	1790	Tax PP 1790:05
Glover, Thomas	Alexandria	Tax Charge	1796	Tax PP 1796:07
Glover, Thomas	Alexandria	Tax Charge	1799	Tax PP 1799:14
Glover, Thomas & wife Mary	Alexandria	Resident	1800	1800(4):02B
Glover, Thomas, hatter	Alexandria	Head	1800	1800(4):02A
Glover, Thos.	Alexandria	Tax Charge	1796	Tax LP 1796:10
Glover, Thos.	Alexandria	Tax Charge	1798	Tax PP 1798:06
Glover, Thos.	Alexandria	Tax Charge	1800	Tax PP 1800:11
Glover, Thos. & wife, hatter	Alexandria	Housekeeper	1799	1799(2):20A
Glover, Wm.	Alexandria	Boarder	1808	1808(2):15A
Goches, Peter	Alexandria	Boarder	1808	1808(3):20A
Goddard, William	Alexandria	Tax Charge	1799	Tax PP 1799:14
Goddard, William	Alexandria	Tax Charge	1800	Tax PP 1800:11
Goddard, William	Arlington	Account	1816	AB3:006; LVA-LP
Goddard, William	Arlington	Inventory	1816	AB2:249
Goddard, William	Arlington	Bond	1816	WB2:107, 310
Goddard, William	Arlington	Will	1816	WB2:105; File #128A
Goddard, William	Arlington	Account	1817	AB3:006
Goddard, William	Arlington	Account	1821	AB4:315; LVA-LP
Goddard, William	Arlington	Account	1822	AB5:139

NAME OR SUBJECT	LOCATION	TYPE	YEAR	REFERENCE(S)
Goddard, William	Arlington	Account	1823	AB5:202; LVA-LP
Goddard, William	Arlington	Account	1825	AB5:411; LVA-LP
Goddard, William	Arlington	Account	1826	AB6:293; LVA-LP
Goddard, William	Arlington	Account	1827	AB6:293; LVA-LP
Goddard, William [Nelly]	Arlington	Terms	1825	OCR1822:086a
Goddard, Wm. & wife (C), carpenter	Alexandria	Housekeeper	1799	1799(2):12A
Godred, Wm. & wife Elender	Alexandria	Resident	1800	1800(4):14B
Godred, Wm., carpenter	Alexandria	Head	1800	1800(4):14A
Godridg, Birnet	Alexandria	Serv./Appr.	1800	1800(4):09B
Gody, John W.	Arlington	Guard.	1834	WB4:102
Gohegan, Jno., bricklayer	Alexandria	Boarder	1799	1799(2):20A
Goines, James, w(4)1, carpenter	Alexandria	Head	1796	1796(3):2
Going, William & wife, laborer	Alexandria	Head	1795	1795(4):05
Going, Wm.	Alexandria	Boarder	1808	1808(1):02A
Going, Wm. (C), laborer	Alexandria	Housekeeper	1808	1808(1):09A
Goings, Susan, w/o John	Arlington	Will	1884	WB10:058; File #716A
Golden, Alexr.	Alexandria	Tax Charge	1795	Tax PP 1795:10
Golden, James	Alexandria	Tithable +16	1789	Tax PP 1789:03
Golden, James	Alexandria	Tithable +16	1790	Tax PP 1790:08
Goldsberry, Nealey, labourer	Alexandria	Head	1810	1810(1):12A
Goldsmith, Catharine	Arlington	Guard.	1804	WBB:107
Goldsmith, James	Arlington	Apprentice	1802	OCR1801:024
Goldy, William	Arlington	Admin. Bond	1848	ABB(np)
Golt, Joseph	Alexandria	Tithable +21	1787	Tax PP 1787:03
Good, Benjamin	Alexandria	Tithable +16	1790	Tax PP 1790:01
Goodes, Benja.	Alexandria	Tithable +16	1789	Tax PP 1789:02
Goodes, Geo., Estate, Wilks St.	Alexandria	Owner	1795	Tax L 1795:10
Goodes, George	Alexandria	Tax Charge	1788	Tax PP 1788:06
Goodes, George	Alexandria	Tax Charge	1789	Tax PP 1789:07
Goodes, George	Alexandria	Tax Charge	1790	Tax PP 1790:05
Goodes, George, Wolf St.	Alexandria	Owner	1790	Tax L 1790:04
Goodes, George, Wolf St.	Alexandria	Occupant	1790	Tax L 1790:04
Goodes, Saml., Water St.	Alexandria	Occupant	1795	Tax L 1795:04
Goodes, Samuel	Alexandria	Tithable +16	1788	Tax PP 1788:06
Goodes, Samuel	Alexandria	Tax Charge	1789	Tax PP 1789:07
Goodes, Samuel	Alexandria	Tax Charge	1790	Tax PP 1790:05
Goodes, Samuel	Alexandria	Tax Charge	1795	Tax PP 1795:11
Goodes, Susan, Wilks St.	Alexandria	Occupant	1795	Tax L 1795:10
Gooding, Dorcus, seamstress	Alexandria	Head	1810	1810(1):12A
Goodrich, Russel	Alexandria	Tax Charge	1788	Tax PP 1788:06
Goodrich, Russel	Alexandria	Tax Charge	1790	Tax PP 1790:05
Goodrich, Russell	Alexandria	Tithable +21	1787	Tax PP 1787:12
Goodrick, John	Arlington	Admin.	1811	WB1:118
Goodrick, Russell	Alexandria	Tax Charge	1789	Tax PP 1789:07
Goodridge, Bernard Nash	Arlington	Apprentice	1804	OCR1801:217
Goods, Benjamin, c/o Ebby	Arlington	Apprentice	1801	OCR1801:010
Goods, Ebbey	Alexandria	Resident	1800	1800(4):10B
Goods, Ebbey, sumpster	Alexandria	Head	1800	1800(4):10A
Goods, Ebe	Alexandria	Housekeeper	1799	1799(2):19A
Goods, Elizey, labourer	Alexandria	Boarder	1800	1800(4):04A
Goods, Geo.	Alexandria	Boarder	1808	1808(2):16A
Goods, George	Alexandria	Tax Charge	1787	Tax PP 1787:06
Goods, George, c/o Susanna G. Rinker	Arlington	Apprentice	1803	OCR1801:076
Goods, Jer. & wife, ship builder	Alexandria	Head	1795	1795(4a):07
Goods, Saml., Water St.	Alexandria	Occupant	1790	Tax L 1790:02
Goods, Widow	Alexandria	Tax Charge	1796	Tax LP 1796:10
Goods, William	Arlington	Admin.	1821	WB3:007
Goods, William, c/o Susanna Rinker	Arlington	Apprentice	1805	OCR1801:306
Goodwin, Robert	Alexandria	Tax Charge	1800	Tax PP 1800:11
Goodwin, Robt.	Alexandria	Boarder	1799	1799(2):11A
Goodwin, Thomas	Arlington	Libellant	1803	ACO:007

NAME OR SUBJECT	LOCATION	TYPE	YEAR	REFERENCE(S)
Goody, Susannah	Alexandria	Head	1795	1795(4):07
Gordon, Alex.	Alexandria	Tax Charge	1796	Tax LP 1796:10
Gordon, Alexa., nr. King St.	Alexandria	Occupant	1790	Tax L 1790:04
Gordon, Alexander	Alexandria	Tax Charge	1788	Tax PP 1788:06
Gordon, Alexander	Alexandria	Tax Charge	1789	Tax PP 1789:07
Gordon, Alexander	Arlington	Ordinary	1808	OBL2(np)
Gordon, Alexander, nr. King St.	Alexandria	Owner	1790	Tax L 1790:04
Gordon, Alexander, w(6)3, shopkeeper	Alexandria	Head	1796	1796(3):4
Gordon, Alexr.	Alexandria	Tax Charge	1790	Tax PP 1790:05
Gordon, Alexr.	Alexandria	Tax Charge	1795	Tax PP 1795:10
Gordon, Alexr.	Alexandria	Tax Charge	1796	Tax PP 1796:07
Gordon, Alexr.	Alexandria	Housekeeper	1808	1808(2):17A
Gordon, Alexr.	Arlington	Ordinary	1808	OBL2(np)
Gordon, Alexr., tavern keeper	Alexandria	Housekeeper	1808	1808(3):23A
Gordon, Ann	Arlington	Admin.	1825	WB3:202
Gordon, Caroline Virginia	Arlington	Guard.	1844	OCR1842:071
Gordon, Geo., wheelright	Alexandria	Head	1810	1810(4):01A
Gordon, Geo., wheelwright	Alexandria	Housekeeper	1808	1808(4):28A
Gordon, Jno.	Alexandria	Tax Charge	1798	Tax PP 1798:06
Gordon, Jno. & Thos. Cole, butchers	Alexandria	Housekeeper	1799	1799(2):18A
Gordon, Jno. & wife, merchant	Alexandria	Housekeeper	1799	1799(2):06A
Gordon, John	Alexandria	Tithable +16	1789	Tax PP 1789:16
Gordon, John	Alexandria	Tax Charge	1796	Tax LP 1796:10
Gordon, John	Alexandria	Tax Charge	1796	Tax PP 1796:07
Gordon, John	Alexandria	Mer. License	1798	Tax PP 1798:20-3
Gordon, John	Alexandria	Tax Charge	1799	Tax PP 1799:14
Gordon, John	Alexandria	Tax Charge	1800	Tax PP 1800:11
Gordon, John	Arlington	Will	1836	WB4:120; File #340A
Gordon, John, Col.	Alexandria	Account B.	1796	CRB:071
Gordon, John, def.	Alexandria	Suit	1801	CRB:069
Gordon, John, def.	Alexandria	Suit	1802	CRB:132
Gordon, John, w(3)1, shopkeeper	Alexandria	Head	1796	1796(3):4
Gordon, Robert	Alexandria	Tax Charge	1799	Tax PP 1799:14
Gordon, Robert	Alexandria	Tax Charge	1800	Tax PP 1800:11
Gordon, Robert	Alexandria	Mer. License	1800	Tax PP 1800:54(13)r
Gordon, Robert, ret. liquor w/o license	Arlington	Defendant	1802	PA:226
Gordon, Will (C), gardener	Alexandria	Housekeeper	1808	1808(4):24A
Gordon, Will, Jr. (C)	Alexandria	Boarder	1808	1808(4):24B
Gordon, William, gardner	Alexandria	Head	1810	1810(4):08A
Gore, William	Alexandria	Tax Charge	1800	Tax PP 1800:11
Gore, William	Arlington	Defendant	1804	ACO:028
Gore, William	Arlington	Defendant	1805	ACO:031, 032
Gore, William	Arlington	Defendant	1805	ACO:045
Gore, Wm.	Alexandria	Resident	1800	1800(4):14B
Gore, Wm., murchant	Alexandria	Boarder	1800	1800(4):14A
Gorham, Catherine A.	Alexandria	Will	1900	WB2:365; LP
Gormley, Samuel	Alexandria	Tax Charge	1787	Tax PP 1787:06
Gormley, Samuel, Admor.	Arlington	Defendant	1802	PA:259
Goryell, George	Alexandria	Tax Charge	1799	Tax PP 1799:06
Gosser, Emeline, c/o John	Arlington	Guard.	1843	WB4:357
Gosser, Emeline, c/o John	Arlington	Petition	1844	LVA-LP (Box 214)
Gosser, John, c/o John	Arlington	Guard.	1843	OCR1842:039
Gosser, John, c/o John	Arlington	Guard.	1843	WB4:357
Gosser, John, c/o John	Arlington	Petition	1844	LVA-LP (Box 214)
Gosser, John, children of	Arlington	Petition	1844	LVA-LP (Box 214)
Gosser, John, children of	Arlington	Guard.	1844	OCR1842:094
Gosser, John, children of	Arlington	Guard.	1845	OCR1842:100, 110
Gosser, Virginia, c/o John	Arlington	Guard.	1843	OCR1842:039
Gosser, Virginia, c/o John	Arlington	Guard.	1843	WB4:357
Gosser, Virginia, c/o John	Arlington	Petition	1844	LVA-LP (Box 214)
Gosser, William, c/o John	Arlington	Guard.	1843	OCR1842:039

NAME OR SUBJECT	LOCATION	TYPE	YEAR	REFERENCE(S)
Gosser, William, c/o John	Alexandria	Guard.	1843	WB4:357
Gosser, William, c/o John	Arlington	Petition	1844	LVA-LP (Box 214)
Gosson, William, age 69	Alexandria	Deposition	1767	CRI:219
Gother, Matthew, Washington St.	Alexandria	Occupant	1795	Tax L 1795:07
Gotier, Matthew	Alexandria	Tax Charge	1796	Tax LP 1796:10
Gotier, Matthew	Alexandria	Tax Charge	1796	Tax PP 1796:07
Gotier, Matthew	Alexandria	Tax Charge	1799	Tax PP 1799:14
Gotier, Matthew & wife, plaisterer	Alexandria	Housekeeper	1799	1799(2):10A
Gotier, Mattw.	Alexandria	Tax Charge	1798	Tax PP 1798:06
Gould, Jno.	Alexandria	Tax Charge	1798	Tax PP 1798:06
Gould, John	Alexandria	Tax Charge	1799	Tax PP 1799:14
Gould, John	Alexandria	Mer. License	1799	Tax PP 1799:52-04r
Gould, John	Alexandria	Tax Charge	1800	Tax PP 1800:11
Gould, John	Arlington	Defendant	1802	PA:043
Gould, John	Arlington	Admin.	1824	OCR1822:064
Gould, John	Arlington	Will	1824	WB3:124; File #222A
Gould, John & wife, storekeeper	Alexandria	Housekeeper	1799	1799(2):01A
Gouldsmith, William Copeland	Alexandria	Deposition	1802	CRD:136
Gourdon, Robt., grocer	Alexandria	Housekeeper	1799	1799(2):05A
Gover, Anthony	Alexandria	Boarder	1808	1808(1):04A
Gover, Anthony P., defendant	Arlington	Suit	1841	LSA:145
Gover, Robt.	Alexandria	Boarder	1808	1808(1):02A
Gowns, Daniel, c/o Susanna Cooper	Arlington	Apprentice	1812	OCR1811:049
Gowns, Ezekiel, c/o Susanna	Arlington	Apprentice	1804	OCR1801:213
Gowns, John	Arlington	Apprentice	1812	OCR1811:046
Gowns, John, c/o Susan Cooper	Arlington	Apprentice	1811	OCR1811:063
Gowns, John, c/o Susan Cooper	Arlington	Apprentice	1811	OCR1811:027
Grace, John	Arlington	Will	1800	CRA:321
Grace, John	Arlington	Account	1804	WBA:251; LVA-LP
Grace, John	Arlington	Sale	1804	WBA:246; LVA-LP
Grace, John	Arlington	Account	1804	WBB:056
Grace, John, Estate, def.	Alexandria	Suit	1801	CRB:294
Grace, John, Estate, def.	Alexandria	Suit	1801	CRB:283, 287, 290
Grady, Gregory, def.	Alexandria	Suit	1802	CRC:180
Grady, Grigsberry and Ann Eliza	Alexandria	Inventory	1871	WB1:014
Graffort, Thos.	Alexandria	Tax Charge	1795	Tax PP 1795:11
Graffort, Thos.	Alexandria	Tax Charge	1796	Tax PP 1796:07
Graffort, Thos.	Alexandria	Tax Charge	1798	Tax PP 1798:06
Graham, Ann, washerwoman	Alexandria	Head	1810	1810(4):01A
Graham, Charles	Alexandria	Will	1873	WB1:052; LP
Graham, Charles, at his house	Arlington	Ordinary	1848	OBL6(np)
Graham, Charles, at his house	Arlington	Ordinary	1849	OBL6(np)
Graham, Curtis B.	Arlington	Will	1900	WB10:433
Graham, David	Alexandria	Tax Charge	1800	Tax PP 1800:11
Graham, David	Arlington	Admin.	1803	WBA:192
Graham, David	Arlington	Inventory	1803	WBB:073; LVA-LP
Graham, David	Arlington	Sale	1804	WBB:074
Graham, David	Arlington	Account	1805	WBB:172, 328; LVA-LP
Graham, David	Arlington	Account	1806	LVA-LP
Graham, David & wife, merchant	Alexandria	Housekeeper	1799	1799(2):16A
Graham, David & wife Mary	Alexandria	Resident	1800	1800(4):04B
Graham, David, merchant	Alexandria	Head	1800	1800(4):04A
Graham, Edward	Alexandria	Deposition	(nd)	CRE:343
Graham, Edward	Alexandria	Deposition	1801	CRE:286
Graham, Edward, at Kanawha	Alexandria	Letter	1799	CRE:323
Graham, Edward, plt.	Alexandria	Suit	1802	CRC:170
Graham, Fanny (C)	Arlington	Apprentice	1823	OCR1822:040
Graham, Geo.	Alexandria	Boarder	1808	1808(3):20A
Graham, Geo., merchant	Alexandria	Boarder	1799	1799(2):12A
Graham, George	Alexandria	Tax Charge	1795	Tax PP 1795:11
Graham, George	Alexandria	Tax Charge	1799	Tax PP 1799:14

NAME OR SUBJECT	LOCATION	TYPE	YEAR	REFERENCE(S)
Graham, James & wife, tallow chandler	Alexandria	Head	1795	1795(4a):03
Graham, Jehab, plt.	Alexandria	Ejectment	1802	CRE:242
Graham, Jno.	Alexandria	Tax Charge	1798	Tax PP 1798:06
Graham, John	Alexandria	Owner	1787	Tax L 1787:12
Graham, John	Alexandria	Tax Charge	1787	Tax PP 1787:06
Graham, John	Alexandria	Tax Charge	1788	Tax PP 1788:06
Graham, John	Alexandria	Tax Charge	1789	Tax PP 1789:07
Graham, John	Alexandria	Tax Charge	1790	Tax PP 1790:05
Graham, John & Co., Fairfax St.	Alexandria	Occupant	1787	Tax L 1787:12
Graham, John C.	Alexandria	Will	1883	WBC1:041; LP
Graham, John, Fairfax St.	Alexandria	Occupant	1790	Tax L 1790:04
Graham, John, Fairfax St.	Alexandria	Owner	1790	Tax L 1790:04
Graham, John, shopkeeper	Alexandria	Housekeeper	1808	1808(1):02A
Graham, John, Washington St.	Alexandria	Occupant	1787	Tax L 1787:04
Graham, Mary, plt.	Alexandria	Ejectment	1802	CRE:242
Graham, Peggy, plt.	Alexandria	Ejectment	1802	CRE:242
Graham, Penny, washerwoman	Alexandria	Head	1810	1810(1):07A
Graham, Polly, plt.	Alexandria	Ejectment	1802	CRE:242
Graham, Sarah M., c/o Sarah	Arlington	Guard.	1852	BB(np)
Graham, Susanna, plt.	Alexandria	Ejectment	1802	CRE:242
Graham, Weedon S.	Arlington	Apprentice	1826	OCR1822:107a
Graham, William	Alexandria	Agreement	1796	CRE:016
Graham, William, Estate, plt.	Alexandria	Suit	1802	CRC:170
Graham, William, heirs of, plt.	Alexandria	Ejectment	1802	CRE:242
Graham, William, of Rockbridge Co.	Alexandria	Agreement	1796	CRC:303, 305
Graham, William, plt.	Alexandria	Ejectment	1802	CRE:242
Graisberry, James	Alexandria	Tax Charge	1789	Tax PP 1789:07
Graisberry, James	Alexandria	Tax Charge	1790	Tax PP 1790:05
Grant, Catharine	Arlington	Will	1864	WB8:184; File #609A
Grant, Catharine	Arlington	Account	1866	WB8:366
Grant, John W., grantor	Arlington	Indenture D.	1827	ID:106
Grant, John W., in jail	Arlington	Insolvent	1827	ID:104
Grant, Tibbey (C), washwoman	Alexandria	Housekeeper	1808	1808(4):26A
Grant, Tibby	Alexandria	Head	1810	1810(4):05A
Grant, Wm. (C)	Alexandria	Boarder	1808	1808(1):02B
Graves, John	Arlington	Admin.	1830	OCR1822:174
Gray, Ann	Alexandria	Mer. License	1799	Tax PP 1799:52-04r
Gray, Anna (C), sempstress	Alexandria	Housekeeper	1808	1808(1):07A
Gray, Anna, Prince St.	Alexandria	Occupant	1790	Tax L 1790:06
Gray, Edward	Alexandria	Tax Charge	1796	Tax PP 1796:07
Gray, Edward	Alexandria	Tax Charge	1798	Tax PP 1798:06
Gray, Edward	Alexandria	Tax Charge	1799	Tax PP 1799:14
Gray, Edward & wife, mariner	Alexandria	Head	1795	1795(4):04
Gray, Edward & wife, mariner	Alexandria	Housekeeper	1799	1799(2):19A
Gray, Esther, c/o Margaret Cook	Arlington	Apprentice	1804	OCR1801:183
Gray, Hannah (C), labourer	Alexandria	Head	1795	1795(4):01
Gray, Hugh	Alexandria	Reference	1808	1808(3):18B
Gray, Jane	Alexandria	Boarder	1799	1799(2):17A
Gray, Jane	Alexandria	Resident	1800	1800(4):13B
Gray, Jane, visiter	Alexandria	Boarder	1800	1800(4):13A
Gray, John, bookbinder	Alexandria	Head	1810	1810(4):05A
Gray, John H.	Alexandria	Will	1890	WB1:583; LP
Gray, Kitty, labourrer	Alexandria	Boarder	1800	1800(4):06A
Gray, Robert, bookstore	Alexandria	Housekeeper	1808	1808(2):10A
Gray, Robert, plt.	Alexandria	Suit	1814	CRK:136
Gray, Robt., bookbinder	Alexandria	Head	1810	1810(2):01A
Gray, Robt., taylor	Alexandria	Head	1810	1810(2):04A
Gray, Sarah A.	Alexandria	Will	1893	WB2:040
Gray, Spencer	Arlington	Inventory	1822	AB5:130; LVA-LP
Gray, Spencer	Arlington	Will	1822	WB3:077; File #214A
Gray, Spencer	Arlington	Bond	1822	WB3:078

NAME OR SUBJECT	LOCATION	TYPE	YEAR	REFERENCE(S)
Gray, Spencer	Arlington	Sale	1823	AB5:163
Gray, Spencer	Arlington	Account	1824	AB5:341; LVA-LP
Gray, Spencer	Arlington	Account	1824	AB5:219; LVA-LP
Gray, Spencer	Arlington	Account F.	1825	AB5:374
Gray, Theophilus	Arlington	Will (NP)	1805	File #012A
Gray, Vincent	Alexandria	Tax Charge	1795	Tax PP 1795:10
Gray, Vincent	Alexandria	Tax Charge	1796	Tax LP 1796:10
Gray, Vincent	Alexandria	Tax Charge	1796	Tax PP 1796:07
Gray, Vincent	Alexandria	Tax Charge	1798	Tax PP 1798:06
Gray, Vincent	Alexandria	Tax Charge	1800	Tax PP 1800:11
Gray, Vincent, Fairfax St.	Alexandria	Occupant	1795	Tax L 1795:13
Gray, William	Arlington	Plaintiff	1802	PA:297
Gray, William	Arlington	Defendant	1821	ACO:191
Gray, William	Arlington	Guard.	1825	WB3:206
Gray, William	Arlington	Will	1891	WB10:188; File #750A
Gray, Wm.	Alexandria	Boarder	1808	1808(3):19A
Graysbury, Jas.	Alexandria	Tax Charge	1787	Tax PP 1787:06
Grayson, Geo., sawyer & shopkeeper	Alexandria	Housekeeper	1808	1808(1):01A
Green, Adelaide H., c/o William P.	Arlington	Guard.	1850	GBB(np)
Green, Charles, b. Sheffield, Eng.	Arlington	Alien Entry	1818	RA:30/3/18
Green, Clement	Alexandria	Tax Charge	1799	Tax PP 1799:14
Green, Clement	Alexandria	Tax Charge	1800	Tax PP 1800:11
Green, Clement, clerk	Alexandria	Boarder	1799	1799(2):09A
Green, Edward, b. Co. Kent, Eng.	Arlington	Alien Entry	1822	RA:18/05/22
Green, Francis, def.	Alexandria	Suit	1810	CRH:197
Green, Geo.	Alexandria	Boarder	1808	1808(1):04A
Green, George H.	Alexandria	Will	1892	WB2:020; LP
Green, George Wakefield, c/o S. Allison	Arlington	Apprentice	1804	OCR1801:202
Green, Henry	Alexandria	Will	1897	WB2:192
Green, James	Alexandria	Will	1880	WB1:313; LP
Green, James, b. Sheffield, Eng.	Arlington	Alien Entry	1818	RA:30/3/18
Green, James H., c/o William P.	Arlington	Guard.	1850	GBB(np)
Green, James W.	Arlington	Receipt	1851	FBB(np)
Green, Jane O'Brien, c/o John F.	Arlington	Guard.	1840	WB4:239
Green, Jesse	Alexandria	Tax Charge	1799	Tax PP 1799:14
Green, Jesse, plt.	Alexandria	Suit	1003	CRD:185
Green, Jno.	Alexandria	Reference	1808	1808(2):16B
Green, Job	Alexandria	Tax Charge	1795	Tax PP 1795:10
Green, Job	Alexandria	Tax Charge	1796	Tax PP 1796:07
Green, Job, St. Asaph St.	Alexandria	Occupant	1795	Tax L 1795:25
Green, Job, w1, mariner	Alexandria	Head	1796	1796(3):1
Green, John	Alexandria	Mer. License	1798	Tax PP 1798:20-3
Green, John	Alexandria	Mer. License	1799	Tax PP 1799:52-04r
Green, John	Alexandria	Tax Charge	1799	Tax PP 1799:14
Green, John	Alexandria	Tax Charge	1800	Tax PP 1800:11
Green, John	Alexandria	Mer. License	1800	Tax PP 1800:54(13)r
Green, John	Arlington	Apprentice	1804	OCR1801:147
Green, John	Arlington	Ordinary	1805	OBL1(np)
Green, John	Arlington	Ordinary	1810	OBL2(np)
Green, John	Arlington	Ordinary	1820	OBL3(np)
Green, John	Arlington	Apprentice	1822	OCR1822:030
Green, John	Arlington	Inventory	1843	AB8:401; LVA-LP
Green, John	Arlington	Admin.	1843	OCR1842:041
Green, John	Arlington	Will P.	1843	OCR1842:044
Green, John	Arlington	Bond	1843	WB4:362
Green, John	Arlington	Will	1843	WB4:360; File #405A
Green, John, b. Co. Kent, Eng.	Arlington	Alien Entry	1822	RA:27/05/22
Green, John, drayman	Alexandria	Head	1810	1810(3):08A
Green, John E., grantor	Arlington	Indenture D.	1827	ID:125
Green, John E., in jail	Arlington	Insolvent	1827	ID:124
Green, John, house joiner	Alexandria	Head	1810	1810(3):09A

NAME OR SUBJECT	LOCATION	TYPE	YEAR	REFERENCE(S)
Green, John, in Alexandria Co.	Arlington	Ordinary	1822	OBL3(np)
Green, John, laborer	Alexandria	Housekeeper	1808	1808(4):29A
Green, John, laborer, a stranger	Alexandria	Boarder	1795	1795(4a):11
Green, John, retailer	Alexandria	Housekeeper	1808	1808(2):14A
Green, John, shopkeeper	Alexandria	Head	1810	1810(2):04A
Green, John, shopkeeper, drayman	Alexandria	Housekeeper	1808	1808(3):18A
Green, John Westly	Arlington	Apprentice	1804	OCR1801:158
Green, Levi	Alexandria	Tax Charge	1787	Tax PP 1787:06
Green, Levi	Alexandria	Tax Charge	1798	Tax PP 1798:06
Green, Levi & Co., Water St.	Alexandria	Occupant	1787	Tax L 1787:19
Green, Levi, Royal St.	Alexandria	Occupant	1790	Tax L 1790:10
Green, Levy	Alexandria	Tax Charge	1790	Tax PP 1790:05
Green, Mary	Alexandria	Boarder	1795	1795(4a):04
Green, Mary	Arlington	Account	1869	WB9:207
Green, Mary	Arlington	Will	1869	WB9:169; File #670A
Green, Mary	Arlington	Inventory	1869	WB9:184
Green, Sarah, semstress	Alexandria	Head	1795	1795(4):05
Green, Shadrack (C)	Arlington	Apprentice	1844	OCR1842:091
Green, Suckey, labourrer	Alexandria	Boarder	1800	1800(4):08A
Green, Susan, seamstress	Alexandria	Head	1810	1810(2):08A
Green, Susanah, washwoman	Alexandria	Housekeeper	1808	1808(1):03A
Green, Thomas	Alexandria	Serv./Appr.	1800	1800(4):11B
Green, Thomas	Arlington	Ordinary	1805	OBL1(np)
Green, Thomas, turner	Alexandria	Head	1810	1810(1):05A
Green, Victoria H., c/o William P.	Arlington	Guard.	1850	GBB(np)
Green, William	Arlington	Sale	1824	AB5:326
Green, William	Arlington	Inventory	1824	AB5:276
Green, William	Arlington	Admin.	1824	OCR1822:067
Green, William	Arlington	Admin.	1824	WB3:126
Green, William	Arlington	Account	1825	LVA-LP
Green, William	Arlington	Account	1826	AB6:214
Green, William	Arlington	Account	1835	AB7:188; LVA-LP
Green, William	Arlington	Account	1835	AB7:237; LVA-LP
Green, William	Arlington	Account	1836	AB7:237
Green, William	Arlington	Account F.	1836	AB7:188
Green, William, b. Sheffield, Eng.	Arlington	Alien Entry	1818	RA:30/3/18
Greenleaf, Thomas	Arlington	Inventory	1826	AB6:202
Greenleaf, Thomas	Arlington	Will	1826	WB3:237; File #248A
Greenleaf, Thomas	Arlington	Bond	1826	WB3:238
Greenway, Joseph	Alexandria	Owner	1787	Tax L 1787:12
Greenway, Joseph	Alexandria	Tax Charge	1787	Tax PP 1787:05
Greenway, Joseph	Alexandria	Tax Charge	1788	Tax PP 1788:06
Greenway, Joseph	Alexandria	Tax Charge	1789	Tax PP 1789:07
Greenway, Joseph	Alexandria	Tax Charge	1790	Tax PP 1790:05
Greenway, Joseph	Arlington	Apprentice	1801	OCR1801:003
Greenway, Joseph, Fairfax St.	Alexandria	Occupant	1787	Tax L 1787:14
Greenway, Joseph, Prince St.	Alexandria	Occupant	1787	Tax L 1787:19
Greenway, Joseph, Wilkes St.	Alexandria	Occupant	1790	Tax L 1790:11
Greenway, Rebecca	Alexandria	Head	1795	1795(4):05
Greenway, Rebecca	Alexandria	Tax Charge	1796	Tax LP 1796:10
Greenway, Rebecca	Arlington	Admin.	1809	WBC:215
Greenway, Rebecca, Estate, plt.	Alexandria	Suit	1821	CRL:369
Greenway, Rebecca, Fairfax St.	Alexandria	Owner	1795	Tax L 1795:10
Greenway, Robt., Fairfax St.	Alexandria	Occupant	1795	Tax L 1795:10
Greenwood, Benjamin	Arlington	Defendant	1801	PA:195
Greenwood, Charles W.	Alexandria	Will	1900	WB2:362; LP
Greenwood, Jno.	Alexandria	Tax Charge	1798	Tax PP 1798:06
Greenwood, Jno. & wife, carpenter	Alexandria	Housekeeper	1799	1799(2):12A
Greenwood, John	Alexandria	Tax Charge	1796	Tax LP 1796:10
Greenwood, John	Alexandria	Tax Charge	1799	Tax PP 1799:14
Greenwood, John	Alexandria	Tax Charge	1800	Tax PP 1800:11

NAME OR SUBJECT	LOCATION	TYPE	YEAR	REFERENCE(S)
Greenwood, John & wife, turner	Alexandria	Head	1795	1795(4):03
Greenwood, John, carpenter	Alexandria	Housekeeper	1808	1808(3):23A
Greenwood, John, w(1), carpenter	Alexandria	Head	1795	1796(3):7
Greenwood, William, age 33	Alexandria	Deposition	1767	CRI:223
Greer, A.	Alexandria	Tax Charge	1796	Tax PP 1796:07
Gregg, Jacob, machine maker	Alexandria	Head	1810	1810(1):04A
Gregg, Jacob, silversmith	Alexandria	Housekeeper	1808	1808(1):04A
Greggory, Thomas	Alexandria	Tax Charge	1799	Tax PP 1799:14
Gregory, Alexander B.	Arlington	Admin.	1835	WB4:085
Gregory, Alexander B.	Arlington	Account	1836	AB7:253; LVA-LP
Gregory, Alexander B.	Arlington	Account	1837	AB7:253; LVA-LP
Gregory, Alexander B.	Arlington	Account	1838	AB7:308; LVA-LP
Gregory, Alexander B.	Arlington	Account F.	1839	AB7:308
Gregory, Charles N.	Arlington	Inventory	1868	WB9:084
Gregory, Charles N.	Arlington	Stock Sale	1868	WB9:064
Gregory, James	Arlington	Will	1818	WB2:221; File #147A
Gregory, James S., b. Kilmarnock	Arlington	Alien Entry	1819	RA:04/05/19
Gregory, Mary D.	Alexandria	Will	1896	WB2:158; LP
Gregory, Thomas & wife, blacksmith	Alexandria	Housekeeper	1799	1799(2):16A
Gregory, William	Alexandria	Will	1872	WB1:154, 165; LP
Gregory, William B.	Alexandria	Will	1887	WB1:465; LP
Gregory, Wm.	Alexandria	Boarder	1808	1808(2):10A
Gregory, Wm.	Alexandria	Boarder	1808	1808(2):10A
Greiling, Bernard	Alexandria	Tithable +16	1789	Tax PP 1789:12
Greiling, Burnard (servant)	Alexandria	Tithable +21	1787	Tax PP 1787:10
Greling, Bernard	Alexandria	Tithable +16	1788	Tax PP 1788:11
Grenalds, Ignatious, seaman	Alexandria	Head	1810	1810(2):01A
Gretter, Betty	Alexandria	Tax Charge	1796	Tax LP 1796:10
Gretter, Charles	Alexandria	Tax Charge	1799	Tax PP 1799:14
Gretter, Charles, taylor	Alexandria	Boarder	1799	1799(2):03A
Gretter, Eliza., King St.	Alexandria	Occupant	1790	Tax L 1790:04
Gretter, Eliza., King St.	Alexandria	Owner	1790	Tax L 1790:04
Gretter, Jno.	Alexandria	Tax Charge	1798	Tax PP 1798:06
Gretter, Jno., King St.	Alexandria	Owner	1795	Tax L 1795:10
Gretter, John	Alexandria	Owner	1787	Tax L 1787:11
Gretter, John	Alexandria	Tax Charge	1787	Tax PP 1787:05
Gretter, John	Alexandria	Tax Charge	1788	Tax PP 1788:06
Gretter, John	Alexandria	Tax Charge	1789	Tax PP 1789:07
Gretter, John	Alexandria	Tax Charge	1790	Tax PP 1790:05
Gretter, John	Alexandria	Tax Charge	1795	Tax PP 1795:10
Gretter, John	Alexandria	Tax Charge	1796	Tax LP 1796:10
Gretter, John	Alexandria	Tax Charge	1796	Tax PP 1796:07
Gretter, John	Alexandria	Tax Charge	1799	Tax PP 1799:14
Gretter, John	Arlington	Admin.	1802	WBA:063
Gretter, John	Arlington	Inventory	1802	WBB:018; LVA-LP
Gretter, John	Arlington	Account	1804	WBB:065
Gretter, John, King St.	Alexandria	Occupant	1787	Tax L 1787:11
Gretter, John, King St.	Alexandria	Occupant	1790	Tax L 1790:04
Gretter, John, King St.	Alexandria	Owner	1790	Tax L 1790:04
Gretter, Jonn	Arlington	Sale	1804	WBB:064
Gretter, Joseph, Estate	Alexandria	Tax Charge	1800	Tax PP 1800:11
Gretter, Margaret	Arlington	Crime	1798	OT:04/04/1798
Gretter, Margaret	Arlington	Admin.	1802	WBA:064
Gretter, Margaret	Arlington	Inventory	1802	WBB:019; LVA-LP
Gretter, Margaret	Arlington	Account	1804	WBB:066
Gretter, Michael	Alexandria	Owner	1787	Tax L 1787:12
Gretter, Michael	Alexandria	Tax Charge	1787	Tax PP 1787:05
Gretter, Michael	Alexandria	Tax Charge	1788	Tax PP 1788:06
Gretter, Michael	Alexandria	Tax Charge	1789	Tax PP 1789:07
Gretter, Michael	Alexandria	Tax Charge	1790	Tax PP 1790:05
Gretter, Michael	Alexandria	Tax Charge	1796	Tax PP 1796:07

NAME OR SUBJECT	LOCATION	TYPE	YEAR	REFERENCE(S)
Gretter, Michael, Love alley	Alexandria	Occupant	1787	Tax L 1787:12
Gretter, Michael, Love alley	Alexandria	Owner	1790	Tax L 1790:04
Gretter, Michael, Queen St.	Alexandria	Owner	1790	Tax L 1790:04
Gretter, Michl.	Alexandria	Tax Charge	1796	Tax LP 1796:10
Gretter, Michl., Gretter's alley	Alexandria	Occupant	1795	Tax L 1795:10
Gretter, Michl., Gretter's alley	Alexandria	Owner	1795	Tax L 1795:10(2)
Gretter, Michl., King St.	Alexandria	Owner	1795	Tax L 1795:10
Gretter, Michl., Love alley	Alexandria	Occupant	1787	Tax L 1787:02
Gretter, Michl., Queen St.	Alexandria	Occupant	1787	Tax L 1787:12
Gretter, Michl., Queen St.	Alexandria	Owner	1795	Tax L 1795:10(3)
Gretter, Mrs., King St.	Alexandria	Occupant	1787	Tax L 1787:12
Gretter, Mrs., King St.	Alexandria	Occupant	1795	Tax L 1795:10
Grew, Rebecca W.	Arlington	Guard. Acct.	1842	AB8:263
Grew, Rebecca W.	Arlington	Guard. Acct.	1843	AB8:349
Grew, Rebecca W.	Arlington	Guard. Acct.	1844	AB8:444
Grew, Rebecca W.	Arlington	Guard. Acct.	1844	OCR1842:068
Grew, Rebecca W.	Arlington	Guard. Acct.	1847	AB9:266
Grew, Rebecca W.	Arlington	Guard. Acct.	Mult.	LVA-LP (Box 214)
Grew, Rebecca Wainwright	Arlington	Guard. Acct.	1841	AB8:205
Grew, Rebecca Wainwright	Arlington	Guard. Acct.	1845	AB9:024
Grew, Rebecca Wainwright	Arlington	Guard. Acct.	1846	AB9:147
Grew, Rebecca Wainwright, c/o John	Arlington	Guard.	1836	WB4:112
Grey, Ann, millener	Alexandria	Housekeeper	1799	1799(2):03A
Griffin, Daniel P.	Alexandria	Will	1899	WB2:320; LP
Griffin, Frankey	Arlington	Guard.	1818	WB2:222
Griffin, John, labourer	Alexandria	Head	1810	1810(2):07A
Griffin, Richard B.	Arlington	Apprentice	1826	OCR1822:125
Griffin, Spencer	Alexandria	Tax Charge	1796	Tax PP 1796:07
Griffin, Thos.	Alexandria	Boarder	1808	1808(2):14A
Griffiss, Joseph	Arlington	Admin.	1818	WB2:260
Griffith, Alfred, M.G.	Alexandria	Will	1871	WB1:033; LP
Griffith, Camillus, heirs of	Arlington	Execution	1812	LVA-LP
Griffith, Cammillus	Alexandria	Boarder	1808	1808(4):27A
Griffith, Charles, age 70 or thereabouts	Alexandria	Deposition	1767	CRI:262
Griffith, David, Jr.	Alexandria	Tax Charge	1788	Tax PP 1788:06
Griffith, David, Jr.	Alexandria	Tax Charge	1789	Tax PP 1789:07
Griffith, Edward	Alexandria	Resident	1800	1800(4):06B
Griffith, Edward, clerk	Alexandria	Boarder	1800	1800(4):06A
Griffith, Frances	Alexandria	Resident	1800	1800(4):06B
Griffith, Frances, semster	Alexandria	Boarder	1800	1800(4):06A
Griffith, Frederick L.	Arlington	Admin.	1832	WB4:048; LVA-LP
Griffith, Frederick L.	Arlington	Account	1833	AB7:087; LVA-LP
Griffith, H., Mrs.	Alexandria	Tax Charge	1800	Tax PP 1800:11
Griffith, Hannah	Alexandria	Tax Charge	1796	Tax PP 1796:07
Griffith, Hannah	Alexandria	Tax Charge	1798	Tax PP 1798:07
Griffith, Hannah	Alexandria	Tax Charge	1799	Tax PP 1799:14
Griffith, Hannah	Alexandria	Head	1810	1810(3):06A
Griffith, Hannah, boarding house	Alexandria	Housekeeper	1799	1799(2):02A
Griffith, Hannah, gentlewoman	Alexandria	Housekeeper	1808	1808(3):19A
Griffith, Hannah, Royal St.	Alexandria	Occupant	1795	Tax L 1795:31
Griffith, Kinsey	Arlington	Inventory	1846	AB9:230; LVA-LP
Griffith, Kinsey	Arlington	Citation	1846	OCR1842:181
Griffith, Kinsey	Arlington	Will P.	1846	OCR1842:178
Griffith, Kinsey	Arlington	Will	1846	WB4:424; File #434A
Griffith, Kinsey	Arlington	Account	1847	WB5:026
Griffith, Mrs. H.	Alexandria	Tax Charge	1795	Tax PP 1795:11
Griffith, Nehemiah	Alexandria	Tax Charge	1796	Tax LP 1796:10
Griffith, Richard, Rev.	Arlington	Account	1820	LVA-LP
Griffith, Sally W.	Arlington	Will	1865	WB8:263; File #576A
Griffith, Sally W.	Arlington	Account	1868	WB9:112
Griffith, Saml. G.	Alexandria	Tax Charge	1800	Tax PP 1800:11

NAME OR SUBJECT	LOCATION	TYPE	YEAR	REFERENCE(S)
Griffith, Samuel	Alexandria	Resident	1800	1800(4):06B
Griffith, Samuel G., for playing Faro	Arlington	Defendant	1801	PA:112
Griffith, Samuel, murchant	Alexandria	Head	1800	1800(4):06A
Griffith, Sarah	Arlington	Apprentice	1843	OCR1842:027
Griffith, Sarah P.	Arlington	Guard.	1820	WB2:376
Griffith, Sarah P.	Arlington	Guard. Acct.	1821	AB4:273; LVA-LP
Griffith, Sarah P.	Arlington	Guard. Acct.	1822	AB5:111; LVA-LP
Griffith, Sarah Pleasants	Arlington	Guard. Acct.	1820	AB4:161; LVA-LP
Griffith, Widow	Alexandria	Tax Charge	1796	Tax LP 1796:10
Griffiths, Edward, clerk	Alexandria	Boarder	1799	1799(2):18A
Grigg, James	Alexandria	Will	1898	WB2:289; LP
Grigg, Joseph	Arlington	Will	1869	WB9:189; File #673A
Grigg, Joseph	Arlington	Appraisal	1870	WB9:263
Grigg, Joseph	Arlington	Account	1870	WB9:290
Grigg, Joseph	Arlington	Sale	1870	WB9:267
Grigg, Mary Ann Newton	Alexandria	Will	1898	WB2:272; LP
Grigsberry, Wilkinson, waggoner	Alexandria	Housekeeper	1808	1808(4):28A
Grigsby, James	Arlington	Admin.	1822	OCR1822:021a
Grigsby, James	Arlington	Admin.	1822	WB3:064
Grigsby, James	Arlington	Inventory	1823	AB5:162; LVA-LP
Grimbler, Michael	Alexandria	Tax Charge	1790	Tax PP 1790:05
Grimes, Elizabeth	Alexandria	Boarder	1799	1799(2):10A
Grimes, Enoch	Arlington	Apprentice	1828	OCR1822:167
Grimes, George	Alexandria	Tax Charge	1787	Tax PP 1787:05
Grimes, George	Alexandria	Tax Charge	1789	Tax PP 1789:07
Grimes, James	Alexandria	Owner	1787	Tax L 1787:12
Grimes, James	Alexandria	Tax Charge	1787	Tax PP 1787:06
Grimes, James	Alexandria	Tax Charge	1788	Tax PP 1788:06
Grimes, James	Alexandria	Tax Charge	1795	Tax PP 1795:11
Grimes, James	Alexandria	Tax Charge	1796	Tax LP 1796:10
Grimes, James	Alexandria	Tax Charge	1796	Tax PP 1796:07
Grimes, James	Alexandria	Tax Charge	1798	Tax PP 1798:06
Grimes, James	Alexandria	Tax Charge	1799	Tax PP 1799:14
Grimes, James	Arlington	Apprentice	1825	OCR1822:102
Grimes, James & wife, carpenter	Alexandria	Housekeeper	1799	1799(2):17A
Grimes, James, Fairfax St.	Alexandria	Occupant	1787	Tax L 1787:05
Grimes, James Grandison	Arlington	Apprentice	1824	OCR1822:075
Grimes, James M., c/o Mary N.	Arlington	Guard.	1842	OCR1842:005
Grimes, James, Pitt St.	Alexandria	Occupant	1795	Tax L 1795:22
Grimes, James, Water St.	Alexandria	Occupant	1787	Tax L 1787:12
Grimes, Jno. & wife, carpenter	Alexandria	Housekeeper	1799	1799(2):10A
Grimes, John	Alexandria	Tax Charge	1790	Tax PP 1790:05
Grimes, John	Alexandria	Tax Charge	1796	Tax LP 1796:10
Grimes, John	Alexandria	Tax Charge	1799	Tax PP 1799:14
Grimes, John	Alexandria	Tax Charge	1800	Tax PP 1800:11
Grimes, Joseph	Arlington	Apprentice	1825	OCR1822:086a
Grimes, Lettetia	Arlington	Guard. Acct.	1822	AB5:137; LVA-LP
Grimes, Lettetia, late Hepburn	Arlington	Guard. Acct.	1823	AB5:196; LVA-LP
Grimes, Philip H.	Arlington	Debts	1852	WB6:045; LVA-LP
Grimes, Philip H.	Arlington	Account	1853	WB6:262; LVA-LP
Grimes, Robert T.	Alexandria	Will	1899	WB2:354; LP
Grimes, Sarah	Alexandria	Boarder	1799	1799(2):17A
Grimes, Stephen	Alexandria	Tithable +16	1788	Tax PP 1788:04
Grimes, Thomas E.	Arlington	Guard. Acct.	1869	WB9:158
Grimes, Thomas E.	Arlington	Guard. Acct.	1870	WB9:288
Grimes, Thomas Edward	Arlington	Guard. Acct.	1866	WB8:437
Grimes, William	Alexandria	Tax Charge	1789	Tax PP 1789:07
Grimes, William	Alexandria	Tax Charge	1790	Tax PP 1790:05
Grimes, William	Alexandria	Tax Charge	1799	Tax PP 1799:14
Grimes, William	Alexandria	Tax Charge	1800	Tax PP 1800:11
Grimes, William	Alexandria	Will	1875	WB1:138; LP

NAME OR SUBJECT	LOCATION	TYPE	YEAR	REFERENCE(S)
Grimes, William, c/o Cath. G. Green	Arlington	Apprentice	1803	OCR1801:106
Grimes, William, taylor	Alexandria	Head	1810	1810(2):06A
Grimes, Wm.	Alexandria	Tax Charge	1795	Tax PP 1795:10
Grimes, Wm.	Alexandria	Tax Charge	1796	Tax LP 1796:10
Grimes, Wm.	Alexandria	Tax Charge	1796	Tax PP 1796:07
Grimes, Wm.	Alexandria	Tax Charge	1798	Tax PP 1798:06
Grimes, Wm., Fairfax St.	Alexandria	Occupant	1795	Tax L 1795:10
Grimmer, Michael	Alexandria	Tax Charge	1789	Tax PP 1789:07
Grimshaw, Thos., ropemaker	Alexandria	Head	1810	1810(3):10A
Grimshaw, Thos., shopkeeper	Alexandria	Housekeeper	1808	1808(3):20A
Grinnalds, Elijah, c/o John	Arlington	Apprentice	1814	OCR1811:231
Grinnolds, John	Alexandria	Deposition	1816	CRK:253
Grinnolds, John, seaman	Alexandria	Head	1810	1810(1):04A
Grinolds, John, sea captain	Alexandria	Housekeeper	1808	1808(1):10A
Grinshaw, Thomas, in prison bounds	Arlington	Insolvent	1812	ID2:181
Griswold, Nathaniel S., N.Y.	Alexandria	Deposition	1805	CRF:249
Gross, William	Arlington	Will (N)	1832	WB4:049; File #320A
Gross, William	Arlington	Admin.	1832	WB4:049
Gross, William, mariner	Arlington	Petition	1832	LVA-LP (Box 214)
Groverman, William	Arlington	Defendant	1802	PA:287, 290
Groverman, William	Arlington	Defendant	1802	PA:149
Groverman, William, def.	Alexandria	Suit	1801	CRB:322
Groverman, William, def.	Alexandria	Suit	1802	CRC:051
Groverman, William, grantee	Arlington	Indenture D.	1812	ID2:096
Groverman, William, plt.	Alexandria	Suit	1801	CRD:001
Groverman, Wm.	Alexandria	Tax Charge	1798	Tax PP 1798:06
Groverman, Wm.	Alexandria	Tax Charge	1799	Tax PP 1799:15
Groverman, Wm. & wife, merchant	Alexandria	Housekeeper	1799	1799(2):03A
Groverman, Wm., broker	Alexandria	Housekeeper	1808	1808(1):06A
Groverman, Wm., broker	Alexandria	Head	1810	1810(1):09A
Groves, Caleb, c/o Ann Violett	Arlington	Apprentice	1805	OCR1801:267
Grubb, George, grantor	Arlington	Indenture D.	1831	ID:359
Grubb, George, in jail bounds	Arlington	Insolvent	1831	ID:356
Grubb, James H.	Alexandria	Will	1875	WB1:168; LP
Grubb, John	Arlington	Admin. Bond	1849	ABB(np)
Grubb, John	Arlington	Account	1850	WB5:240; LVA-LP
Grubb, John H.	Arlington	Account	1850	WB5:275; LVA-LP
Gruber, David	Arlington	Sale	1817	AB3:024
Gruber, David	Arlington	Inventory	1817	AB3:045; LVA-LP
Gruber, David	Arlington	Admin.	1817	WB2:191
Gruber, David	Arlington	Account	1818	AB3:153; LVA-LP
Grundy, George, def.	Alexandria	Suit	1807	CRF:203, 340
Grundy, George, plt.	Alexandria	Suit	1821	CRK:321
Gruver, George, grantee	Arlington	Indenture D.	1831	ID:359
Gruver, John	Arlington	Admin.	1829	WB3:350; LVA-LP
Gruver, John	Arlington	Account	1830	AB6:502; LVA-LP
Grymes, James M., c/o Charles	Arlington	Guard.	1842	WB4:304
Grymes, James M., c/o Charles	Arlington	Guard. Acct.	1846	AB9:180; LVA-LP
Grymes, Wm., taylor	Alexandria	Housekeeper	1808	1808(4):29A
Guest, Robt., hatter	Alexandria	Housekeeper	1799	1799(2):04A
Guinn, David H.	Arlington	Inventory	1852	WB6:081; LVA-LP
Guinn, David H.	Arlington	Sale	1852	WB6:096; LVA-LP
Guinn, David H.	Arlington	Account	1853	WB6:270; LVA-LP
Guionnet, Susanna	Arlington	Will	1837	WB4:142; File #351A
Gullat, James, baker	Alexandria	Head	1810	1810(2):07A
Gullatt, Charles	Alexandria	Tax Charge	1799	Tax PP 1799:14
Gullatt, James	Alexandria	Tax Charge	1799	Tax PP 1799:15
Gullatt, James	Alexandria	Tax Charge	1800	Tax PP 1800:11
Gullatt, James	Alexandria	Deposition	1808	CRI:089
Gullatt, Jas., b. baker	Alexandria	Housekeeper	1808	1808(2):17A
Gullatt, John	Alexandria	Boarder	1808	1808(2):17A

NAME OR SUBJECT	LOCATION	TYPE	YEAR	REFERENCE(S)
Gullatt, William, grantor	Arlington	Indenture D.	1811	ID2:105
Gullatt, William, house joiner	Alexandria	Head	1810	1810(4):06A
Gullatt, William, in jail bounds	Arlington	Insolvent	1811	ID2:060 (partial)
Gullatt, William, in jail bounds	Arlington	Insolvent	1811	ID2:106
Gullits, Thomas, d(r)ayman	Alexandria	Head	1800	1800(4):11A
Gumberg, Gurie	Arlington	Account	1805	LVA-LP
Gun, Obedier & wife Ann	Alexandria	Resident	1800	1800(4):09B
Gun, Obedier, drayman	Alexandria	Head	1800	1800(4):09A
Gunnell, Henry, Maj., Fairfax Co.	Alexandria	Deposition	1815	CRK:123
Gunnell, Henry, Maj., of Fairfax Co.	Alexandria	Deposition	1815	CRL:144
Gunnell, Ira	Arlington	Guard. Acct.	1806	WBB:340
Gunnell, Ira	Arlington	Guard. Acct.	1811	AB1:077
Gunnell, Ira	Arlington	Guard. Acct.	1814	AB2:037; LVA-LP
Gunnell, Ira, c/o Presley	Arlington	Guard.	1810	WBC:383
Gunnell, Ira, c/o Presley	Arlington	Guard. Acct.	1812	AB1:188; LVA-LP
Gunnell, Ira, c/o Presley	Arlington	Guard. Acct.	1813	AB1:317; LVA-LP
Gunnell, Ira, c/o Presley	Arlington	Payment	1814	AB2:002
Gunnell, Jannett, c/o Presley	Arlington	Guard.	1810	WBC:340
Gunnell, Jennet	Arlington	Guard. Acct.	1811	AB1:077
Gunnell, Jennet	Arlington	Guard. Acct.	1814	AB2:037; LVA-LP
Gunnell, Jennet, c/o Presley	Arlington	Guard. Acct.	1812	AB1:188; LVA-LP
Gunnell, Jennet, c/o Presley	Arlington	Guard. Acct.	1813	AB1:317; LVA-LP
Gunnell, Jennett [Haycock], c/o Presley	Arlington	Payment	1814	AB2:002
Gunnell, Mr., *Towlston* from Fairfax	Alexandria	Lease	(nd)	CRH:553
Gunnell, Presley	Arlington	Bond	1806	WBB:340
Gunnell, Presley	Arlington	Will	1806	WBB:339; File #021A
Gunnell, Presley	Arlington	Sale	1807	WBB:492; LVA-LP
Gunnell, Presley	Arlington	Inventory	1807	WBB:488; LVA-LP
Gunnell, Presley	Arlington	Account	1807	WBB:534; LVA-LP
Gunnell, Presley	Arlington	Account	1810	WBC:495; LVA-LP
Gunnell, Presley	Arlington	Division	1814	AB2:002; LVA-LP
Gunnell, Sally, c/o Presley	Arlington	Guard.	1810	WBC:383
Gunnell, Sally [McEndree], c/o Presley	Arlington	Payment	1814	AB2:002
Gunnell, Sarah	Arlington	Guard. Acct.	1811	AB1:077
Gunnell, Sarah	Arlington	Guard. Acct.	1814	AB2:037; LVA-LP
Gunnell, Sarah, c/o Presley	Arlington	Guard. Acct.	1812	AB1:189; LVA-LP
Gunnell, Sarah, c/o Presley	Arlington	Guard. Acct.	1813	AB1:317; LVA-LP
Gunnell, William	Arlington	Guard. Acct.	1811	AB1:077
Gunnell, William	Arlington	Guard. Acct.	1814	AB2:037; LVA-LP
Gunnell, William	Arlington	Guard. Acct.	1815	AB2:162; LVA-LP
Gunnell, William, c/o Presley	Arlington	Guard.	1810	WBC:383
Gunnell, William H.	Arlington	Guard. Acct.	1816	AB2:298; LVA-LP
Gunnell, William H.	Arlington	Guard. Acct.	1817	AB3:041
Gunnell, William H.	Arlington	Guard. Acct.	1818	AB3:209; LVA-LP
Gunnell, William H.	Arlington	Guard. Acct.	1821	AB4:275; LVA-LP
Gunnell, William H., c/o Presley	Arlington	Guard. Acct.	1812	AB1:189; LVA-LP
Gunnell, William H., c/o Presley	Arlington	Guard. Acct.	1813	AB1:317; LVA-LP
Gunning, James	Alexandria	Tax Charge	1796	Tax PP 1796:07
Gunning, Jas., Water St.	Alexandria	Occupant	1795	Tax L 1795:22
Guss, Peter	Arlington	Admin.	1803	WBA:130
Guss, Peter	Arlington	Sale	1804	WBB:055
Guss, Peter	Arlington	Account	1804	WBB:055
Guss [Gust], Peter	Arlington	Inventory	1803	LVA-LP
Gust, P., back building	Alexandria	Occupant	1795	Tax L 1795:03
Guthery, Mrs., seamstress	Alexandria	Head	1810	1810(1):08A
Guthrie, Jno. & wife, sail maker	Alexandria	Housekeeper	1799	1799(2):20A
Guthrie, John & wife Elisabeth	Alexandria	Resident	1800	1800(4):04B
Guthrie, John, Cap.	Alexandria	Tax Charge	1800	Tax PP 1800:11
Guthrie, John, marriner	Alexandria	Head	1800	1800(4):04A
Guthrie, John, sea captain	Alexandria	Housekeeper	1808	1808(1):08A
Guthrie, Jos. (sail maker)	Alexandria	Tax Charge	1800	Tax PP 1800:11

NAME OR SUBJECT	LOCATION	TYPE	YEAR	REFERENCE(S)
Guthrie, Mary Ann	Arlington	Guard.	1816	WB2:160
Guthrie, Mathew & wife, plaisterer	Alexandria	Head	1795	1795(4):08
Guthry, John & wife, sail maker	Alexandria	Head	1795	1795(4):07
Gutrey, [blank]	Alexandria	Occupant	1795	Tax L 1795:08
Gutrie, John, sailmaker	Alexandria	Head	1800	1800(4):08A
Gutterick, Jno.	Alexandria	Tax Charge	1798	Tax PP 1798:06
Guttery, Jno.	Alexandria	Tax Charge	1795	Tax PP 1795:11
Guttery, John	Alexandria	Tax Charge	1796	Tax PP 1796:07
Guttery, John	Alexandria	Tax Charge	1799	Tax PP 1799:14
Guttree, John & wife Mary	Alexandria	Resident	1800	1800(4):08B
Guttrick, John	Alexandria	Tax Charge	1790	Tax PP 1790:05
Guy, Charles, c/o Susanna D.	Arlington	Apprentice	1815	OCR1811:298
Guy, Charles, grantee	Arlington	Indenture D.	1827	ID:113
Guy, Frances C.	Alexandria	Will	1900	WB2:367; LP
Guy, John M.	Arlington	Apprentice	1823	OCR1822:043a
Guy, William	Arlington	Apprentice	1815	OCR1811:309
Guyer, John	Arlington	Apprentice	1824	OCR1822:077
Gwathmey, Owen	Alexandria	Tax Charge	1798	Tax PP 1798:06
Gwathmey, Owen, clerk	Alexandria	Boarder	1799	1799(2):13A
Gwatkin, Edward	Arlington	Guard.	1811	WB1:027
Gwyn, John	Arlington	Admin.	1815	WB2:060

NAME OR SUBJECT	LOCATION	TYPE	YEAR	REFERENCE(S)
H				
Haas, J.F.	Arlington	Inventory	1875	WB9:374
Haden, Ellen, grantor	Arlington	Indenture D.	1813	ID2:228
Haden, Ellen, in jail	Arlington	Insolvent	1813	ID2:224
Haden, Garret	Arlington	Ordinary	1805	OBL1(np)
Hadley, Paul	Alexandria	Tax Charge	1796	Tax PP 1796:08
Hagan, Francis	Arlington	Will	1830	WB3:375; File #292A
Hagan, Francis	Arlington	Account	1832	AB7:200; LVA-LP
Hagan, Francis	Arlington	Account	1836	AB7:200
Hagan, Francis	Arlington	Account	1838	AB7:266; LVA-LP
Hageman, Henry	Arlington	Admin.	1811	WB1:148
Hagemann, Nicholas, b. Bremen	Arlington	Alien Entry	1822	RA:19/03/22
Hagen, Roger	Alexandria	Tithable +16	1788	Tax PP 1788:04
Hagen, Roger	Alexandria	Tax Charge	1789	Tax PP 1789:09
Hagerty, Patrick	Alexandria	Tax Charge	1788	Tax PP 1788:07
Hagerty, Patrick	Alexandria	Tax Charge	1789	Tax PP 1789:07
Hagerty, Patrick, plaisterer	Alexandria	Boarder	1799	1799(2):19A
Haggerty, Patrick	Alexandria	Tax Charge	1787	Tax PP 1787:06
Haggerty, Patrick	Alexandria	Tax Charge	1790	Tax PP 1790:06
Hagner & Starr, King St.	Alexandria	Occupant	1795	Tax L 1795:03
Hagner, Martin	Alexandria	Tax Charge	1795	Tax PP 1795:12
Hagner, Martin	Alexandria	Tax Charge	1796	Tax PP 1796:08
Hagner, Martin	Alexandria	Tax Charge	1799	Tax PP 1799:18
Hagner, Martin	Alexandria	Tax Charge	1800	Tax PP 1800:15
Hagner, Michl.	Alexandria	Tax Charge	1796	Tax LP 1796:11
Hague, John	Alexandria	Tax Charge	1788	Tax PP 1788:08
Haines, Daniel, grantor	Arlington	Indenture D.	1817	ID2:421
Haines, Daniel, in jail	Arlington	Insolvent	1817	ID2:417
Hainey, Lydia (C)	Arlington	Apprentice	1845	OCR1842:129, 130
Hale, Amos	Alexandria	Tithable +16	1788	Tax PP 1788:08
Hale, Amos	Alexandria	Tithable +16	1789	Tax PP 1789:09
Hale, George	Alexandria	Tax Charge	1787	Tax PP 1787:06
Hale, George	Alexandria	Tax Charge	1788	Tax PP 1788:08
Hale, George	Alexandria	Tax Charge	1789	Tax PP 1789:09
Hale, George	Alexandria	Tax Charge	1790	Tax PP 1790:07
Hale, George	Alexandria	Tax Charge	1796	Tax PP 1796:08
Hale, George & wife, bricklayer	Alexandria	Head	1795	1795(4):08
Hale, George, Duke St.	Alexandria	Occupant	1790	Tax L 1790:06
Hale, George, Duke St.	Alexandria	Owner	1790	Tax L 1790:06
Hale, Phineas	Alexandria	Tax Charge	1796	Tax PP 1796:08
Haley, William, n/o John Lanham	Arlington	Apprentice	1823	OCR1822:050a
Hall, Andrew J.	Alexandria	Will	1896	WB2:151; LP
Hall, Bazil	Arlington	Will	1888	WB10:137; File #736A
Hall, Charles	Alexandria	Tax Charge	1789	Tax PP 1789:07
Hall, Charles	Alexandria	Tax Charge	1790	Tax PP 1790:07
Hall, Ellener, sumpster	Alexandria	Boarder	1800	1800(4):11A
Hall, Frances	Arlington	Account	1859	WB7:441; LVA-LP
Hall, Francis	Alexandria	Boarder	1808	1808(2):10A
Hall, Francis I.	Arlington	Ordinary	1809	OBL2(np)
Hall, James	Alexandria	Tax Charge	1799	Tax PP 1799:17
Hall, James, c/o William James	Arlington	Guard.	1812	WB1:181
Hall, John J., in Alexandria Co.	Arlington	Ordinary	1849	OBL6(np)
Hall, Jona., heirs, Union St.	Alexandria	Owner	1790	Tax L 1790:06
Hall, Jona., heirs, Water St.	Alexandria	Owner	1790	Tax L 1790:06
Hall, Mary, c/o William James	Arlington	Guard.	1812	WB1:179
Hall, Milly (C), washwoman	Alexandria	Housekeeper	1808	1808(4):24A
Hall, Peter, grantor	Arlington	Indenture D.	1831	ID:312
Hall, Peter, in jail bounds	Arlington	Insolvent	1831	ID:310
Hall, Philip, labourer	Alexandria	Head	1810	1810(1):11A
Hall, Robert	Arlington	Ordinary	1820	OBL3(np)
Hall, Robert	Arlington	Juryman	1824	ACO:237

NAME OR SUBJECT	LOCATION	TYPE	YEAR	REFERENCE(S)
Hall, Robert	Arlington	Account	1857	WB7:258; LVA-LP
Hall, Robert	Arlington	Inventory	1857	WB7:262; LVA-LP
Hall, Robert	Arlington	Sale	1858	WB7:279; LVA-LP
Hall, Robt., taylor	Alexandria	Housekeeper	1808	1808(2):13A
Hall, Robt., taylor	Alexandria	Head	1810	1810(2):03A
Hall, Talbot, tavern keeper	Alexandria	Head	1810	1810(2):02A
Hall, W.J.	Alexandria	Tax Charge	1796	Tax LP 1796:12
Hall, William	Alexandria	Tax Charge	1789	Tax PP 1789:09
Hall, William	Alexandria	Tax Charge	1790	Tax PP 1790:07
Hall, William	Alexandria	Tax Charge	1796	Tax PP 1796:08
Hall, William	Alexandria	Tax Charge	1799	Tax PP 1799:16
Hall, William J.	Alexandria	Tax Charge	1796	Tax PP 1796:08
Hall, William J.	Alexandria	Tax Charge	1798	Tax PP 1798:07
Hall, William J.	Alexandria	Tax Charge	1799	Tax PP 1799:18
Hall, William J.	Alexandria	Tax Charge	1800	Tax PP 1800:13
Hall, William J.	Arlington	Defendant	1808	ACO:082
Hall, William J.	Arlington	Defendant	1808	ACO:085
Hall, William J.	Arlington	Defendant	1808	ACO:091
Hall, William J.	Arlington	Defendant	1809	ACO:106, 109
Hall, William J.	Arlington	Account	1813	AB1:287; LVA-LP
Hall, William J.	Arlington	Account	1813	AB1:291; LVA-LP
Hall, William J.	Arlington	Account	1821	AB4:251
Hall, William James	Arlington	Admin.	1810	WBC:427
Hall, Willliam	Alexandria	Tithable +16	1788	Tax PP 1788:05
Hall, Wm.	Alexandria	Boarder	1808	1808(2):12A
Hall, Wm.	Alexandria	Head	1810	1810(1):03A
Hall, Wm. (C), laborer	Alexandria	Housekeeper	1808	1808(4):28A
Hall, Wm. J., merchant	Alexandria	Housekeeper	1808	1808(1):06A
Hallam, Jno. & wife, carpenter	Alexandria	Housekeeper	1799	1799(2):11A
Halley, Esther	Arlington	Will	1831	WB4:027; File #311A
Halley, Esther	Arlington	Bond	1831	WB4:028
Halley, James	Alexandria	Tax Charge	1788	Tax PP 1788:08
Halley, William	Arlington	Will (NR)	(nd)	File #1832-4m
Halley, William	Alexandria	Tax Charge	1788	Tax PP 1788:07
Halley, William	Alexandria	Tax Charge	1790	Tax PP 1790:06
Halley, William	Alexandria	Tax Charge	1799	Tax PP 1799:17
Halley, William	Alexandria	Tax Charge	1800	Tax PP 1800:13
Halley, William	Arlington	Bond	1808	WBC:157
Halley, William	Arlington	Will	1808	WBC:152; File #035A
Halley, William	Arlington	Account	1810	WBC:449; LVA-LP
Halley, William	Arlington	Account	1832	LVA-LP
Halley, William, Fairfax St.	Alexandria	Occupant	1790	Tax L 1790:09
Halley, William, Pitt St.	Alexandria	Occupant	1787	Tax L 1787:17
Halley, Wm.	Alexandria	Tax Charge	1795	Tax PP 1795:14
Halley, Wm.	Alexandria	Tax Charge	1796	Tax LP 1796:11
Halley, Wm.	Alexandria	Tax Charge	1796	Tax PP 1796:09
Halley, Wm.	Alexandria	Tax Charge	1798	Tax PP 1798:08
Halley, Wm. & wife, millstone maker	Alexandria	Housekeeper	1799	1799(2):05A
Halley, Wm., King St.	Alexandria	Owner	1795	Tax L 1795:14(2)
Halley, Wm., King St.	Alexandria	Occupant	1795	Tax L 1795:14
Halley, Wm., King St.	Alexandria	Occupant	1795	Tax L 1795:19
Halliday, Charles	Alexandria	Tithable +16	1789	Tax PP 1789:15
Halls, Jonathan, Estate	Alexandria	Owner	1787	Tax L 1787:14
Halls, Nommy, nurse	Alexandria	Head	1810	1810(2):05A
Hally, William	Alexandria	Tax Charge	1787	Tax PP 1787:06
Hally, William, w(2)4, millstone maker	Alexandria	Head	1796	1796(3):3
Halmuth, Valentine	Alexandria	Will	1872	WB1:051; LP
Halteifer, Jos., Fairfax St.	Alexandria	Occupant	1787	Tax L 1787:12
Halterfer, John	Alexandria	Tax Charge	1787	Tax PP 1787:07
Hambleton, Susanna	Arlington	Inventory	1807	WBB:539; LVA-LP
Hambleton, Susanna	Arlington	Bond	1807	WBB:536

NAME OR SUBJECT	LOCATION	TYPE	YEAR	REFERENCE(S)
Hambleton, Susanna	Arlington	Will	1807	WBB:535; File #027A
Hambleton, Susanna	Arlington	Account	1809	WBC:283
Hambleton, Wesley	Arlington	Will P.	1843	OCR1842:046
Hambleton, Wesley	Arlington	Will	1843	WB4:371; File #408A
Hamersley, James F.	Alexandria	Will	1900	WB2:363; LP
Hamilton, Alfred	Alexandria	Will	1887	WB1:469; LP
Hamilton, James	Alexandria	Tax Charge	1796	Tax LP 1796:11
Hamilton, James	Alexandria	Tax Charge	1799	Tax PP 1799:17
Hamilton, James	Alexandria	Tax Charge	1800	Tax PP 1800:15
Hamilton, James, Merchant	Arlington	Victim	1802	PA:217
Hamilton, Jas. & wife, merchant	Alexandria	Housekeeper	1799	1799(2):06A
Hamilton, Jno.	Alexandria	Boarder	1808	1808(2):12A
Hamilton, John	Alexandria	Tithable +21	1787	Tax PP 1787:06
Hamilton, John	Alexandria	Tithable +16	1788	Tax PP 1788:07
Hamilton, John	Alexandria	Tax Charge	1789	Tax PP 1789:08
Hamilton, John Milroy	Alexandria	Will	1896	WB2:140; LP
Hamilton, Mary	Alexandria	Resident	1800	1800(4):02B
Hamilton, Mary, labourer	Alexandria	Boarder	1800	1800(4):02A
Hamilton, Maurice W.	Arlington	Guard. Acct.	1868	WB9:047
Hamilton, N.W., Miss	Arlington	Guard.	1859	WB7:419; LVA-LP
Hamilton, Nannie Whiting, c/o Henry	Arlington	Guard.	1853	BB(np)
Hamilton, Patty	Alexandria	Resident	1800	1800(4):10B
Hamilton, Patty	Alexandria	Head	1800	1800(4):10A
Hamilton, Patty (C)	Alexandria	Housekeeper	1799	1799(2):13A
Hamilton, Philip	Alexandria	Will	1875	WB1:122; LP
Hamilton, Phillip	Arlington	Will	1863	WB8:175; File #605A
Hamilton, Robert	Alexandria	Tithable +16	1790	Tax PP 1790:09
Hamilton, Robert	Alexandria	Tax Charge	1796	Tax PP 1796:09
Hamilton, Robert	Alexandria	Mer. License	1799	Tax PP 1799:52-05w
Hamilton, Robert	Alexandria	Tax Charge	1799	Tax PP 1799:17
Hamilton, Robert	Alexandria	Head	1800	1800(4):13A
Hamilton, Robert	Alexandria	Tax Charge	1800	Tax PP 1800:15
Hamilton, Robert, w4, merchant	Alexandria	Head	1796	1796(3):5
Hamilton, Robt.	Alexandria	Tithable +16	1789	Tax PP 1789:11
Hamilton, Robt.	Alexandria	Tax Charge	1795	Tax PP 1795:14
Hamilton, Robt.	Alexandria	Tax Charge	1796	Tax LP 1796:12
Hamilton, Robt.	Alexandria	Tax Charge	1798	Tax PP 1798:07
Hamilton, Robt. & wife, merchant	Alexandria	Housekeeper	1799	1799(2):17A
Hamilton, Robt., Prince St.	Alexandria	Owner	1795	Tax L 1795:11
Hamilton, Robt., Prince St.	Alexandria	Occupant	1795	Tax L 1795:11
Hamilton, Robt., wharf	Alexandria	Owner	1795	Tax L 1795:11
Hamilton, Robt., wharf	Alexandria	Occupant	1795	Tax L 1795:11
Hamilton, Sarah	Arlington	Guard.	1816	WB2:113
Hamilton, Silas M.	Alexandria	Will	1896	WB2:130; LP
Hamilton, Susannah	Alexandria	Owner	1787	Tax L 1787:13
Hamilton, Susannah	Arlington	Account	1808	LVA-LP
Hamilton, Thomas & wife Sarah	Alexandria	Resident	1800	1800(4):08B
Hamilton, Thomas, Dr., def.	Alexandria	Suit	1802	CRC:245, 249
Hamilton, Thos.	Alexandria	Tax Charge	1800	Tax PP 1800:15
Hamiltons, Robert & wife Esther	Alexandria	Resident	1800	1800(4):13B
Hamiltton, Thomas, doctor	Alexandria	Head	1800	1800(4):08A
Hammatt, John B., Jr., in jail bounds	Arlington	Insolvent	1830	ID:250
Hammatt, John B., Jr., grantor	Arlington	Indenture D.	1830	ID:252
Hammerdinger, John C.	Arlington	Appraisal	1863	WB8:149
Hammill, Francis P., c/o Patrick	Arlington	Guard. Acct.	1870	WB9:292
Hammill, George W., c/o Patrick	Arlington	Guard. Acct.	1870	WB9:291
Hammill, John H., c/o Patrick	Arlington	Guard. Acct.	1870	WB9:292
Hammill, Kate F., c/o Patrick	Arlington	Guard. Acct.	1870	WB9:293
Hammilton, James, merchant	Alexandria	Head	1810	1810(3):01A
Hammond, Abijah, New York	Alexandria	Deed	1811	CRK:048
Hammond, James	Arlington	Ordinary	1803	OBL1(np)

NAME OR SUBJECT	LOCATION	TYPE	YEAR	REFERENCE(S)
Hammond, James	Arlington	Ordinary	1805	OBL1(np)
Hammond, James	Arlington	Ordinary	1805	OBL1(np)
Hammond, James	Arlington	Ordinary	1806	OBL2(np)
Hammond, James	Alexandria	Head	1810	1810(3):03A
Hammond, Jas. (C), oysterman	Alexandria	Housekeeper	1808	1808(3):20A
Hamp, B. & Co., Prince St.	Alexandria	Occupant	1787	Tax L 1787:15
Hamp, B.A., King St.	Alexandria	Occupant	1787	Tax L 1787:27
Hamp, Benja. A., King St.	Alexandria	Occupant	1790	Tax L 1790:09
Hamp, Benjamin A.	Alexandria	Tax Charge	1787	Tax PP 1787:06
Hamp, Benjamin A.	Alexandria	Tax Charge	1788	Tax PP 1788:07
Hamp, Benjamin A.	Alexandria	Tax Charge	1789	Tax PP 1789:08
Hamp, Benjamin A.	Alexandria	Tax Charge	1790	Tax PP 1790:06
Hampson & Williams, Prince St.	Alexandria	Occupant	1790	Tax L 1790:10
Hampson, Benjamin	Alexandria	Tax Charge	1790	Tax PP 1790:07
Hampson, Bryan	Alexandria	Tax Charge	1795	Tax PP 1795:13
Hampson, Bryan	Alexandria	Tax Charge	1796	Tax LP 1796:12
Hampson, Bryan	Alexandria	Tax Charge	1796	Tax PP 1796:09
Hampson, Bryan	Alexandria	Tax Charge	1798	Tax PP 1798:08
Hampson, Bryan	Alexandria	Mer. License	1798	Tax PP 1798:20-3
Hampson, Bryan	Alexandria	Mer. License	1799	Tax PP 1799:52-05w
Hampson, Bryan	Alexandria	Tax Charge	1799	Tax PP 1799:17
Hampson, Bryan	Alexandria	Tax Charge	1800	Tax PP 1800:15
Hampson, Bryan	Alexandria	Mer. License	1800	Tax PP 1800:54(14)r
Hampson, Bryan & wife, merchant	Alexandria	Housekeeper	1799	1799(2):02A
Hampson, Bryan, Fairfax St.	Alexandria	Occupant	1795	Tax L 1795:21
Hampson, Bryan, grantor	Arlington	Indenture D.	1830	ID:307
Hampson, Bryan, in prison bounds	Arlington	Insolvent	1830	ID:304
Hampson, Bryan, merchant	Alexandria	Housekeeper	1808	1808(1):02A
Hampson, Bryan, merchant	Alexandria	Head	1810	1810(1):01A
Hampson, Bryan, w(1)7, merchant	Alexandria	Head	1796	1796(3):4
Hampson, Bryan, Water St.	Alexandria	Occupant	1795	Tax L 1795:29
Hampson, John L., grantee	Arlington	Indenture D.	1832	ID:391a
Hampson, John L., grantee	Arlington	Indenture D.	1833	ID:420
Hampson, Joseph H., grantor	Arlington	Indenture D.	1828	ID:156
Hampson, Joseph H., in jail	Arlington	Insolvent	1828	ID:153
Hampton, Ann F.	Alexandria	Boarder	1799	1799(2):04A
Hampton, Jeremiah, age 50 or upwards	Alexandria	Deposition	1768	CRI:273
Hancock, Andrew	Arlington	Apprentice	1822	OCR1822:026a
Hancock, John B., constable	Arlington	Appointment	1852	BB(np)
Hancock, Michael W.	Arlington	Defendant	1821	ACO:192
Hand, Caleb, merchant	Alexandria	Housekeeper	1808	1808(1):06A
Hand, John, Capt., plt.	Alexandria	Suit	1801	CRC:082
Hand, John, sea captain	Alexandria	Housekeeper	1808	1808(1):07A
Handless, Moses (C), c/o Robert	Arlington	Guard.	1850	GBB(np)
Handless, William	Arlington	Guard.	1822	WB3:061
Haney, Martin	Arlington	Apprentice	1824	OCR1822:075
Hanly, Eugene	Arlington	Admin.	1805	WBB:174
Hanly, Eugene	Arlington	Sale	1807	WBB:537; LVA-LP
Hanly, Eugene	Arlington	Account	1807	WBB:537
Hanly, Eugene	Arlington	Account	1808	WBC:097; LVA-LP
Hannah, Alex.	Alexandria	Tax Charge	1796	Tax LP 1796:12
Hannah, Alexander	Alexandria	Tax Charge	1799	Tax PP 1799:17
Hannah, Alexandr. & wife, labourer	Alexandria	Head	1795	1795(4):08
Hannah, Alexr.	Alexandria	Tax Charge	1796	Tax PP 1796:08
Hannah, Alexr.	Alexandria	Tax Charge	1798	Tax PP 1798:08
Hannah, Alexr.	Alexandria	Tax Charge	1800	Tax PP 1800:13
Hannah, Alexr. & wife, sexton	Alexandria	Housekeeper	1799	1799(2):18A
Hannah, Elizabeth, merchant	Alexandria	Head	1795	1795(4):03
Hannah, Elizth., Duke St.	Alexandria	Occupant	1795	Tax L 1795:11
Hannah, Elizth., Duke St.	Alexandria	Owner	1795	Tax L 1795:11
Hannah, Elizth., Fairfax St.	Alexandria	Owner	1795	Tax L 1795:11

NAME OR SUBJECT	LOCATION	TYPE	YEAR	REFERENCE(S)
Hannah, George, c/o Nicholas	Arlington	Guard.	1806	WBB:362
Hannah, George Emperor	Arlington	Will	1811	WB1:067; File #092A
Hannah, Jas., shoemaker	Alexandria	Boarder	1799	1799(2):19A
Hannah, Nich. & wife, capt. U.S. army	Alexandria	Head	1795	1795(4a):03
Hannah, Nicholas	Alexandria	Tax Charge	1787	Tax PP 1787:06
Hannah, Nicholas	Alexandria	Tax Charge	1788	Tax PP 1788:08
Hannah, Nicholas	Alexandria	Tax Charge	1789	Tax PP 1789:09
Hannah, Nicholas	Alexandria	Tax Charge	1790	Tax PP 1790:07
Hannah, Nicholas, Duke St.	Alexandria	Occupant	1787	Tax L 1787:05
Hannah, Nicholas, Duke St.	Alexandria	Owner	1790	Tax L 1790:06
Hannah, Nicholas, Duke St.	Alexandria	Occupant	1790	Tax L 1790:06
Hannah, Nicholas, Fairfax St.	Alexandria	Occupant	1787	Tax L 1787:19
Hannah, Thos., Queen St.	Alexandria	Occupant	1790	Tax L 1790:01
Hannahan, Michael	Arlington	Libellant	1811	ACO:119
Hannan, Robert	Arlington	Apprentice	1824	OCR1822:064a
Hanner, Alexander & wife Mary	Alexandria	Resident	1800	1800(4):13B
Hanner, Alexander, rings the church bell	Alexandria	Head	1800	1800(4):13A
Hannon, Francis Oscar, c/o William H.	Arlington	Guard.	1822	OCR1822:009
Hannon, Francis Oscar, c/o William H.	Arlington	Guard.	1822	WB3:052
Hannon, Julia	Arlington	Inventory	1845	AB9:109; LVA-LP
Hannon, Julia	Arlington	Petition	1845	LVA-LP (Box 214)
Hannon, Julia	Arlington	Sale	1845	OCR1842:133
Hannon, Julia	Arlington	Will P.	1845	OCR1842:112
Hannon, Julia	Arlington	Will	1845	WB4:395; File #423A
Hannon, Julia	Arlington	Renounce	1845	WB4:396
Hannon, Julia	Arlington	Account	1846	AB9:268; LVA-LP
Hannon, Julia	Arlington	Account	1847	AB9:268
Hannon, Martha Ann, c/o William	Arlington	Guard.	1822	OCR1822:009
Hannon, Martha Ann, c/o William H.	Arlington	Guard.	1822	WB3:052
Hannon, Thomas L., c/o Henry M.	Arlington	Guard.	1848	GBB(np)
Hannon, Thomas L., gc/o Julia	Arlington	Guard.	1846	OCR1842:196
Hannon, Thomas, s/o Henry M.	Arlington	Guard.	1846	CF# Hannon v.
Hannon, William H.	Arlington	Sale	1822	AB5:059
Hannon, William H.	Arlington	Inventory	1822	AB5:039; LVA-LP
Hannon, William H.	Arlington	Inventory	1822	OCR1822:003
Hannon, William H.	Arlington	Admin.	1822	OCR1822:002
Hannon, William H.	Arlington	Admin.	1822	WB3:047
Hannon, William H.	Arlington	Account	1823	LVA-LP
Hannon, William H.	Arlington	Account	1825	LVA-LP
Hanson & Bond, Prince St.	Alexandria	Occupant	1790	Tax L 1790:12
Hanson, Ignatius (C)	Alexandria	Boarder	1808	1808(4):27B
Hanson, Mark & wife (C), labourer	Alexandria	Housekeeper	1799	1799(2):14A
Hanson, Mark, stevedore	Alexandria	Housekeeper	1808	1808(4):27A
Hanson, Marke & wife Rachel	Alexandria	Resident	1800	1800(4):10B
Hanson, Marke, rigger	Alexandria	Head	1800	1800(4):10A
Hanson, S., St. Asaph St.	Alexandria	Occupant	1787	Tax L 1787:22
Hanson, Sam. laborer	Alexandria	Housekeeper	1808	1808(2):16A
Hanson, Saml., St. Asaph St.	Alexandria	Occupant	1790	Tax L 1790:06
Hanson, Samuel	Alexandria	Tax Charge	1787	Tax PP 1787:07
Hanson, Samuel	Alexandria	Tax Charge	1788	Tax PP 1788:08
Hanson, Samuel	Alexandria	Tax Charge	1789	Tax PP 1789:09
Hanson, Samuel, of Sam.	Alexandria	Tax Charge	1790	Tax PP 1790:07
Hanson, Samuel, St. Asaph St.	Alexandria	Owner	1790	Tax L 1790:06
Hanson, Thos., Fairfax St.	Alexandria	Occupant	1787	Tax L 1787:07
Haragan, Jeremiah	Alexandria	Tax Charge	1788	Tax PP 1788:07
Harbaugh, David	Alexandria	Boarder	1808	1808(2):15A
Harbaugh, Saml.	Alexandria	Boarder	1808	1808(2):15A
Harbaugh, [blank]	Alexandria	Boarder	1808	1808(2):12A
Harclay, James	Alexandria	Tax Charge	1796	Tax PP 1796:08
Harclay, James	Alexandria	Mer. License	1798	Tax PP 1798:20-3
Harden, Harriet Eliza	Arlington	Guard. Acct.	1820	AB4:188; LVA-LP

NAME OR SUBJECT	LOCATION	TYPE	YEAR	REFERENCE(S)
Harden, Harriet Eliza	Arlington	Guard. Acct.	1825	AB6:138; LVA-LP
Harden, Harriet Eliza, c/o Thomas G.	Arlington	Guard.	1815	WB2:007
Harden, Harriet Eliza, c/o Thos. Green	Arlington	Guard.	1821	WB2:432
Harden, Mary Ann	Arlington	Guard. Acct.	1820	AB4:188; LVA-LP
Harden, Mary Ann	Arlington	Guard. Acct.	1825	AB6:138; LVA-LP
Harden, Mary Ann, c/o Thomas G.	Arlington	Guard.	1815	WB2:007
Harden, Mary Ann, c/o Thomas Green	Arlington	Guard.	1821	WB2:432
Harden, Nancy, c/o Thomas Green	Arlington	Guard.	1815	WB2:007
Harden, Sinclair	Arlington	Guard. Acct.	1825	AB6:138
Harden, Thomas	Arlington	Account	1815	LVA-LP
Harden, Thomas G.	Arlington	Account	1817	AB3:017; LVA-LP
Harden, Thomas G.	Arlington	Bond	1815	WB2:003
Harden, Thomas G.	Arlington	Will	1815	WB2:002
Harden, Thomas G.	Arlington	Sale	1816	AB2:280
Harden, Thomas Green	Arlington	Receipt	1825	AB6:139
Harden, Thomas Sinclair, c/o Thos. G.	Arlington	Guard.	1815	WB2:007
Harden, Thos. Sinclair, c/o Thos. Green	Arlington	Guard.	1821	WB2:432
Harden, William	Alexandria	Tax Charge	1788	Tax PP 1788:07
Harden, William	Arlington	Appraisal	1828	LVA-LP
Harden, William	Arlington	Will P.	1828	OCR1822:165
Harden, William	Arlington	Will	1828	WB3:324; File #275A
Harden, William	Arlington	Account	1831	AB7:016; LVA-LP
Harden, William, c/o Thomas G.	Arlington	Guard.	1815	WB2:007
Harden, William [Ann C.]	Arlington	Admin.	1828	OCR1822:165
Hardin, Ann E.	Arlington	P. of Atty.	1838	LVA-LP (Accounts)
Hardin, Henry (C), alias Hyson	Arlington	Apprentice	1845	OCR1842:138
Hardin, Thomas G.	Arlington	Inventory	1815	AB2:098
Harding, Ann (Adams)	Arlington	Defendant	1841	LSA:075
Harding, Presley	Arlington	Apprentice	1826	OCR1822:124
Harding, Presley	Arlington	Apprentice	1826	OCR1822:120
Hardy, Charles, b. Co. Tyrone	Arlington	Alien Entry	1816	RA:02/09/16
Hardy, Frederick	Arlington	Libellant	1804	ACO:029
Hardy, Frederick	Arlington	Libellant	1805	ACO:036
Hardy, Letitia S.	Alexandria	Boarder	1799	1799(2):04A
Hardy, Thomas	Alexandria	Tithable +21	1787	Tax PP 1787:04
Hare, Betsey	Alexandria	Boarder	1799	1799(2):05A
Hare, Geo.	Alexandria	Boarder	1808	1808(1):01A
Hare, Mary, washwoman	Alexandria	Housekeeper	1808	1808(3):22A
Hare, Polly	Alexandria	Boarder	1799	1799(2):05A
Hargerty, Patrick, Oronoka St.	Alexandria	Occupant	1790	Tax L 1790:05
Harl, Robert (C)	Alexandria	Tax Charge	1787	Tax PP 1787:06
Harle, Robert	Alexandria	Tax Charge	1796	Tax PP 1796:09
Harle, Robert (C)	Alexandria	Tax Charge	1790	Tax PP 1790:06
Harle, Robert, Royal St.	Alexandria	Owner	1790	Tax L 1790:05(2)
Harle, Robert, Royal St.	Alexandria	Occupant	1790	Tax L 1790:05(2)
Harle, Robt. (C)	Alexandria	Tax Charge	1795	Tax PP 1795:12
Harle, Robt., Queen St.	Alexandria	Owner	1795	Tax L 1795:12(2)
Harle, Robt., Royal St.	Alexandria	Owner	1795	Tax L 1795:13
Harley, Ann, seamstress	Alexandria	Head	1810	1810(4):06A
Harley, John, laborer	Alexandria	Housekeeper	1808	1808(1):06A
Harlow, Michael	Alexandria	Will	1879	WBC1:031; LP
Harman, Jacob, merchant, of Pa.	Alexandria	Deed	1779	CRI:298
Harman, Jacob, of Philadelphia	Alexandria	Will	1780	CRI:302
Harmon, Aaron D.	Arlington	Juryman	1824	ACO:237
Harnerd, John & wife, ship builder	Alexandria	Head	1795	1795(4a):06
Harper & Davis	Alexandria	Tax Charge	1796	Tax LP 1796:12
Harper & Davis	Alexandria	Mer. License	1798	Tax PP 1798:20-3
Harper & Janney	Alexandria	Mer. License	1798	Tax PP 1798:20-3
Harper, Anthony F.	Alexandria	Will	1880	WB1:284; LP
Harper, Catharine Ann, c/o William A.	Arlington	Guard.	1836	WB4:111
Harper, Charles	Alexandria	Tax Charge	1798	Tax PP 1798:07

NAME OR SUBJECT	LOCATION	TYPE	YEAR	REFERENCE(S)
Harper, Charles & wife, merchant	Alexandria	Head	1795	1795(4):05
Harper, Charles A.	Alexandria	Deposition	1810	CRK:171
Harper, Chas. & Co., Union St.	Alexandria	Occupant	1795	Tax L 1795:18
Harper, Chas., Fairfax St.	Alexandria	Owner	1795	Tax L 1795:11
Harper, Edward	Alexandria	Tax Charge	1787	Tax PP 1787:08
Harper, Edward	Alexandria	Tax Charge	1788	Tax PP 1788:08
Harper, Edward	Alexandria	Tax Charge	1789	Tax PP 1789:07
Harper, Edward	Alexandria	Tax Charge	1795	Tax PP 1795:12
Harper, Edward	Alexandria	Tax Charge	1796	Tax LP 1796:13
Harper, Edward	Alexandria	Tax Charge	1796	Tax PP 1796:08
Harper, Edward	Alexandria	Tax Charge	1798	Tax PP 1798:08
Harper, Edward	Alexandria	Tax Charge	1799	Tax PP 1799:17
Harper, Edward	Alexandria	Tax Charge	1800	Tax PP 1800:15
Harper, Edward & wife, naval officer	Alexandria	Head	1795	1795(4):05
Harper, Edward & wife	Alexandria	Housekeeper	1799	1799(2):13A
Harper, Edward & wife Rose	Alexandria	Serv./Appt.	1800	1800(4):15B
Harper, Edward, waymaster	Alexandria	Head	1800	1800(4):15A
Harper, Edwd.	Alexandria	Occupant	1795	Tax L 1795:15
Harper, Edwd., Prince St.	Alexandria	Occupant	1787	Tax L 1787:16
Harper, Elizabeth	Alexandria	Will	1897	WB2:190; LP
Harper, George	Arlington	Apprentice	1829	OCR1822:172a
Harper, Hannah Ann, c/o John	Arlington	Guard.	1838	WB4:161
Harper, Hannah, Prince St.	Alexandria	Occupant	1790	Tax L 1790:12
Harper, J. & Saml.	Alexandria	Tax Charge	1795	Tax PP 1795:13
Harper, James & Joshua, in jail	Arlington	Insolvents	1828	ID:171
Harper, James, grantor	Arlington	Indenture D.	1828	ID:174
Harper, James, plt.	Alexandria	Suit	1822	CRL:232
Harper, Jas.	Alexandria	Boarder	1808	1808(4):27A
Harper, Jno.	Alexandria	Reference	1808	1808(2):10B
Harper, Jno. & wife, tailor	Alexandria	Housekeeper	1799	1799(2):04A
Harper, Jno. & wife	Alexandria	Housekeeper	1799	1799(2):13A
Harper, Jno., King St.	Alexandria	Owner	1795	Tax L 1795:13
Harper, Jno., taylor	Alexandria	Housekeeper	1808	1808(2):10A
Harper, John	Alexandria	Owner	1787	Tax L 1787:15
Harper, John	Alexandria	Owner	1787	Tax L 1787:16
Harper, John	Alexandria	Tax Charge	1787	Tax PP 1787:06
Harper, John	Alexandria	Tax Charge	1788	Tax PP 1788:07
Harper, John	Alexandria	Tax Charge	1789	Tax PP 1789:08
Harper, John	Alexandria	Tax Charge	1790	Tax PP 1790:06
Harper, John	Arlington	Witness	1795	OT:28/07/1795
Harper, John	Alexandria	Tax Charge	1795	Tax PP 1795:12
Harper, John	Alexandria	Tax Charge	1796	Tax LP 1796:11
Harper, John	Alexandria	Tax Charge	1796	Tax PP 1796:08
Harper, John	Alexandria	Tax Charge	1798	Tax PP 1798:07
Harper, John	Alexandria	Tax Charge	1798	Tax PP 1798:08
Harper, John	Alexandria	Tax Charge	1799	Tax PP 1799:16
Harper, John	Arlington	Defendant	1802	PA:051
Harper, John	Arlington	Will	1804	WBB:025, 32; LVA-LP
Harper, John	Arlington	Bond	1804	WBB:034
Harper, John	Arlington	Inventory	1804	WBB:060; LVA-LP
Harper, John	Arlington	Account	1805	WBB:160, 288; LVA-LP
Harper, John	Arlington	Account	1809	WBC:303; LVA-LP
Harper, John	Arlington	Account	1811	AB1:079
Harper, John	Arlington	Apprentice	1815	OCR1811:350
Harper, John	Arlington	Account	1833	AB7:070; LVA-LP
Harper, John	Arlington	Admin.	1834	WB4:160
Harper, John	Arlington	Debts Due	1839	AB8:041
Harper, John	Arlington	Inventory	1839	AB8:039
Harper, John	Arlington	Account	1839	AB8:037; LVA-LP
Harper, John (taylor)	Alexandria	Tax Charge	1800	Tax PP 1800:13
Harper, John & wife Mary	Alexandria	Resident	1800	1800(4):16B

NAME OR SUBJECT	LOCATION	TYPE	YEAR	REFERENCE(S)
Harper, John, at Caton's Tavern	Alexandria	Deposition	1808	CRH:120
Harper, John C., grantor	Arlington	Indenture D.	1827	ID:075
Harper, John C., in jail	Arlington	Insolvent	1827	ID:073
Harper, John, Capn.	Alexandria	Tax Charge	1800	Tax PP 1800:15
Harper, John, Capt.	Alexandria	Tax Charge	1796	Tax LP 1796:12
Harper, John, Capt.	Arlington	Account	1812	AB1:209; LVA-LP
Harper, John, Capt., Fairfax St.	Alexandria	Owner	1790	Tax L 1790:06
Harper, John, Capt., Prince St.	Alexandria	Owner	1790	Tax L 1790:06(8)
Harper, John, Fairfax St.	Alexandria	Occupant	1787	Tax L 1787:09
Harper, John, Fairfax St.	Alexandria	Owner	1795	Tax L 1795:15
Harper, John, Gibbon St.	Alexandria	Occupant	1787	Tax L 1787:04
Harper, John, Gibbon St.	Alexandria	Occupant	1787	Tax L 1787:04
Harper, John H.	Arlington	Account	1815	AB2:194
Harper, John, heirs of	Arlington	Suit	1839	AB8:042
Harper, John, King St.	Alexandria	Occupant	1790	Tax L 1790:05
Harper, John, King St.	Alexandria	Owner	1790	Tax L 1790:05
Harper, John, mariner	Alexandria	Head	1810	1810(1):09A
Harper, John, marriner	Alexandria	Head	1800	1800(4):16A
Harper, John, Pitt St.	Alexandria	Occupant	1790	Tax L 1790:05
Harper, John, plt.	Alexandria	Suit	1801	CRB:261
Harper, John, Prince St.	Alexandria	Owner	1795	Tax L 1795:15(10)
Harper, John, Royal St.	Alexandria	Occupant	1795	Tax L 1795:31
Harper, John, sea captain	Alexandria	Housekeeper	1808	1808(1):08A
Harper, John, Sr.	Alexandria	Tax Charge	1799	Tax PP 1799:17
Harper, John, Sr.	Arlington	Admin.	1832	WB4:056; LVA-LP
Harper, John, taylor	Alexandria	Housekeeper	1808	1808(1):02A
Harper, John, taylor	Alexandria	Head	1810	1810(2):02A
Harper, John W.	Arlington	Inventory	1814	AB2:039; LVA-LP
Harper, John W.	Arlington	Admin.	1814	WB1:285
Harper, John W.	Arlington	Account	1816	AB2:326; LVA-LP
Harper, John, w(6), taylor	Alexandria	Head	1795	1796(3):7
Harper, Jos.	Alexandria	Tax Charge	1795	Tax PP 1795:13
Harper, Joseph	Alexandria	Tax Charge	1796	Tax PP 1796:08
Harper, Joseph	Alexandria	Tax Charge	1798	Tax PP 1798:07
Harper, Joseph	Alexandria	Tax Charge	1799	Tax PP 1799:17
Harper, Joseph	Alexandria	Tax Charge	1800	Tax PP 1800:15
Harper, Joseph	Arlington	Inventory	1809	WBC:322; LVA-LP
Harper, Joseph	Arlington	Admin.	1809	WBC:304
Harper, Joseph	Arlington	Account	1811	AB1:081
Harper, Joseph & S., Prince St.	Alexandria	Occupant	1795	Tax L 1795:15
Harper, Joseph & Saml.	Alexandria	Mer. License	1798	Tax PP 1798:20-3
Harper, Joseph & Samuel	Alexandria	Tax Charge	1796	Tax PP 1796:08
Harper, Joseph & wife, merchant	Alexandria	Head	1795	1795(4):09
Harper, Joseph, ropemaker	Alexandria	Housekeeper	1808	1808(3):18A
Harper, Joseph, Royal St.	Alexandria	Occupant	1795	Tax L 1795:04
Harper, Josh. & Saml.	Alexandria	Tax Charge	1796	Tax LP 1796:12
Harper, Joshua, grantor	Arlington	Indenture D.	1828	ID:177
Harper, Mary	Alexandria	Head	1810	1810(4):07A
Harper, Mary Ann	Arlington	Exor. Bond	1849	EBB(np) (2)
Harper, Mary Ann	Arlington	Will	1849	WB5:141; File #450A
Harper, Mary, c/o Edward	Arlington	Guard.	1806	WBB:353
Harper, Mary, gentlewoman	Alexandria	Housekeeper	1808	1808(4):27A
Harper, Pierson	Arlington	Guard. Acct.	1812	AB1:232; LVA-LP
Harper, Pierson	Arlington	Apprentice	1815	OCR1811:287
Harper, Pierson, c/o Joseph	Arlington	Guard.	1811	WB1:064
Harper, Robert	Arlington	Guard. Acct.	1812	AB1:232; LVA-LP
Harper, Robert, mariner	Alexandria	Head	1810	1810(1):09A
Harper, Robert Parke, c/o Joseph	Arlington	Guard.	1811	WB1:064
Harper, Saml. & wife, merchant	Alexandria	Housekeeper	1799	1799(2):19A
Harper, Saml., nr. Wolfe St.	Alexandria	Occupant	1790	Tax L 1790:05
Harper, Saml., nr. Wolfe St.	Alexandria	Owner	1790	Tax L 1790:05

NAME OR SUBJECT	LOCATION	TYPE	YEAR	REFERENCE(S)
Harper, Saml., retailer	Alexandria	Housekeeper	1808	1808(1):02A
Harper, Samuel	Alexandria	Tax Charge	1790	Tax PP 1790:06
Harper, Samuel	Alexandria	Tax Charge	1795	Tax PP 1795:13
Harper, Samuel	Alexandria	Tax Charge	1798	Tax PP 1798:08
Harper, Samuel	Alexandria	Tax Charge	1799	Tax PP 1799:17
Harper, Samuel	Alexandria	Mer. License	1799	Tax PP 1799:52-04r
Harper, Samuel	Alexandria	Mer. License	1800	Tax PP 1800:54(14)r
Harper, Samuel	Alexandria	Tax Charge	1800	Tax PP 1800:13
Harper, Samuel	Arlington	Account	1840	AB8:071; LVA-LP
Harper, Samuel & wife, merchant	Alexandria	Head	1795	1795(4):02
Harper, Samuel B.	Arlington	Admin.	1838	WB4:181
Harper, Samuel, c/o John	Arlington	Guard.	1838	WB4:161
Harper, Samuel, ropemaker	Alexandria	Head	1810	1810(1):11A
Harper, Samul & wife Sarrah	Alexandria	Resident	1800	1800(4):09B
Harper, Samul, murchant	Alexandria	Head	1800	1800(4):09A
Harper, Sarah	Alexandria	Head	1810	1810(3):06A
Harper, Sarah, c/o Edward	Arlington	Guard.	1806	WBB:353
Harper, Sarah Wells	Arlington	Guard. Acct.	1812	AB1:232; LVA-LP
Harper, Sarah Wells, c/o Joseph	Arlington	Guard.	1811	WB1:064
Harper, Washington	Arlington	Plat	1839	LSA:047
Harper, Washington T.	Arlington	Appraisal	1860	WB7:498; LVA-LP
Harper, Washington T.	Arlington	Sale	1860	WB7:501
Harper, William	Alexandria	Tax Charge	1787	Tax PP 1787:07
Harper, William	Alexandria	Tax Charge	1788	Tax PP 1788:08
Harper, William	Alexandria	Tax Charge	1789	Tax PP 1789:09
Harper, William	Alexandria	Tax Charge	1790	Tax PP 1790:06
Harper, William	Alexandria	Tax Charge	1799	Tax PP 1799:17
Harper, William	Alexandria	Tax Charge	1800	Tax PP 1800:15
Harper, William	Alexandria	Mer. License	1800	Tax PP 1800:54(14)r
Harper, William	Arlington	Account	1831	AB7:001
Harper, William	Arlington	Appraisal	1831	LVA-LP
Harper, William	Arlington	Account	1845	AB9:052; LVA-LP
Harper, William	Arlington	Account	1846	AB9:216; LVA-LP
Harper, William	Arlington	Citation	1846	OCR1842:170, 172
Harper, William	Arlington	Will	1852	WB6:151; File #485A
Harper, William	Arlington	Account	1856	WB7:116; LVA-LP
Harper, William & wife, carpenter	Alexandria	Head	1795	1795(4):02
Harper, William A.	Arlington	Will	1821	WB3:024; File #200A
Harper, William A.	Arlington	Bond	1821	WB3:025
Harper, William A.	Arlington	Inventory	1822	AB5:054; LVA-LP
Harper, William A.	Arlington	Sale	1822	AB5:089
Harper, William A.	Arlington	Admin.	1822	OCR1822:004
Harper, William A., grantee	Arlington	Indenture D.	1812	ID2:169
Harper, William A., grantee	Arlington	Indenture D.	1812	ID2:114
Harper, William A., orphans of	Arlington	Guard.	1827	OCR1822:130a
Harper, William, Capt.	Arlington	Will	1830	WB3:340; File #279A
Harper, William, Wolf St.	Alexandria	Occupant	1790	Tax L 1790:05
Harper, William, Wolf St.	Alexandria	Owner	1790	Tax L 1790:05
Harper, Wm.	Alexandria	Tax Charge	1795	Tax PP 1795:13
Harper, Wm.	Alexandria	Tax Charge	1796	Tax LP 1796:12
Harper, Wm.	Alexandria	Tax Charge	1796	Tax PP 1796:08
Harper, Wm.	Alexandria	Tax Charge	1798	Tax PP 1798:07
Harper, Wm.	Alexandria	Mer. License	1799	Tax PP 1799:52-05r
Harper, Wm.	Alexandria	Boarder	1808	1808(2):10A
Harper, Wm. & wife, lumber merchant	Alexandria	Housekeeper	1799	1799(2):15A
Harper, Wm. & wife Mary	Alexandria	Resident	1800	1800(4):06B
Harper, Wm., murchant	Alexandria	Head	1800	1800(4):06A
Harper, Wm., ropemaker	Alexandria	Head	1810	1810(1):06A
Harper, Wm., tavern lic. & merchant	Alexandria	Housekeeper	1808	1808(1):08A
Harper, Wm., Wolf St.	Alexandria	Occupant	1787	Tax L 1787:16
Harper, Wm., Wolf St.	Alexandria	Owner	1795	Tax L 1795:14(3)

NAME OR SUBJECT	LOCATION	TYPE	YEAR	REFERENCE(S)
Harper, Wm., Wolf St.	Alexandria	Occupant	1795	Tax L 1795:14
Harrigan, Jeremiah	Alexandria	Tithable +21	1787	Tax PP 1787:08
Harrington, Danl.	Alexandria	Mer. License	1798	Tax PP 1798:20-3
Harrington, Richard H., at his house	Arlington	Ordinary	1832	OBL4(np)
Harrington, Richard H., on Union St.	Arlington	Ordinary	1833	OBL5(np)
Harris, Andw. & wife, mariner	Alexandria	Head	1795	1795(4):06
Harris, Arthur C.	Arlington	Apprentice	1828	OCR1822:165a
Harris, Creesy, shopkeeper	Alexandria	Housekeeper	1808	1808(1):01A
Harris, Hanner	Alexandria	Resident	1800	1800(4):10B
Harris, Hanner, laundress	Alexandria	Head	1800	1800(4):10A
Harris, Henry	Alexandria	Tax Charge	1799	Tax PP 1799:16
Harris, Henry	Alexandria	Tax Charge	1799	Tax PP 1799:17
Harris, Henry (C)	Arlington	Apprentice	1829	OCR1822:170
Harris, Henry & wife	Alexandria	Housekeeper	1799	1799(2):14A
Harris, Henry & wife, bricklayer	Alexandria	Housekeeper	1799	1799(2):17A
Harris, Hugh, laborer	Alexandria	Housekeeper	1808	1808(2):14A
Harris, James	Arlington	Ordinary	1804	OBL1(np)
Harris, James	Arlington	Ordinary	1805	OBL1(np)
Harris, James	Arlington	Account	1838	AB7:271; LVA-LP
Harris, James	Arlington	Will	1838	WB4:162; File #354A
Harris, James	Arlington	Bond	1838	WB4:163
Harris, James, bailiff, def.	Alexandria	Suit	1804	CRF:001
Harris, James, market master	Alexandria	Head	1810	1810(3):06A
Harris, jas., shopkeeper	Alexandria	Housekeeper	1808	1808(2):10A
Harris, Joe	Alexandria	Head	1810	1810(4):05A
Harris, Joe (C), laborer	Alexandria	Housekeeper	1808	1808(4):28A
Harris, John	Alexandria	Tax Charge	1787	Tax PP 1787:07
Harris, John	Alexandria	Tax Charge	1790	Tax PP 1790:06
Harris, John L.	Arlington	Bond	1850	BB(np)
Harris, Jos., clerk	Alexandria	Boarder	1799	1799(2):07A
Harris, Joseph	Alexandria	Tax Charge	1788	Tax PP 1788:08
Harris, Joseph	Alexandria	Tax Charge	1789	Tax PP 1789:08
Harris, Joseph	Alexandria	Tax Charge	1790	Tax PP 1790:06
Harris, Joseph	Alexandria	Tax Charge	1799	Tax PP 1799:17
Harris, Joseph	Alexandria	Deposition	1822	CRL:534
Harris, Joseph, U.S. officer	Alexandria	Housekeeper	1808	1808(1):07A
Harris, Louden, seaman	Alexandria	Head	1810	1810(4):04A
Harris, Loudon (C), cooper	Alexandria	Housekeeper	1808	1808(4):24A
Harris, Lucy (C), washwoman	Alexandria	Housekeeper	1808	1808(4):28A
Harris, Mary	Alexandria	Resident	1800	1800(4):02B
Harris, Mary, laundress	Alexandria	Head	1800	1800(4):02A
Harris, Mrs., Royal St.	Alexandria	Occupant	1795	Tax L 1795:02
Harris, Pompey P.	Arlington	Inventory	1823	AB5:211; LVA-LP
Harris, Pompey P.	Arlington	Admin.	1823	OCR1822:053a
Harris, Pompey P.	Arlington	Account	1824	AB5:366; LVA-LP
Harris, Pompey Pohra	Arlington	Will	1823	WB3:111; File #220A
Harris, Pompey Pohra	Arlington	Bond	1823	WB3:114
Harris, Samuel	Arlington	Apprentice	1842	OCR1842:019
Harris, [Sarchy] (C), washwoman	Alexandria	Housekeeper	1808	1808(4):28A
Harris, Searchy	Alexandria	Head	1810	1810(4):02A
Harris, Susan (C), washwoman	Alexandria	Housekeeper	1808	1808(3):21A
Harris, Theoph.	Alexandria	Tax Charge	1795	Tax PP 1795:12
Harris, Theoph.	Alexandria	Tax Charge	1798	Tax PP 1798:07
Harris, Theoph., Royal St.	Alexandria	Occupant	1795	Tax L 1795:20
Harris, Theophilus	Alexandria	Tax Charge	1796	Tax LP 1796:11
Harris, Theophilus	Alexandria	Tax Charge	1796	Tax PP 1796:08
Harris, Theophilus	Alexandria	Mer. License	1798	Tax PP 1798:20-3
Harris, Theophilus	Alexandria	Tax Charge	1799	Tax PP 1799:16
Harris, Theophilus	Alexandria	Mer. License	1799	Tax PP 1799:52-04r
Harris, Theophilus, def.	Alexandria	Suit	1800	CRF:097
Harris, Theophilus, def.	Alexandria	Suit	1801	CRF:074

NAME OR SUBJECT	LOCATION	TYPE	YEAR	REFERENCE(S)
Harris, Theophilus, plt.	Alexandria	Suit	1800	CRF:096
Harris, Theophis.	Alexandria	Tax Charge	1800	Tax PP 1800:13
Harris, Walter	Arlington	Will	1866	WB8:418; File #650A
Harris, Walter	Arlington	Appraisal	1867	WB8:449
Harris, William	Arlington	Apprentice	1823	OCR1822:057a
Harris, William (C), c/o Mary Keeler	Arlington	Apprentice	1823	OCR1822:038
Harris, William, house joiner	Alexandria	Head	1810	1810(4):03A
Harris, William P., plt.	Alexandria	Suit	1803	CRD:099
Harrison, Alexr., seaman & shopkeeper	Alexandria	Housekeeper	1808	1808(1):03A
Harrison, Amie, washerwoman	Alexandria	Head	1810	1810(3):09A
Harrison, Elias, Rev.	Arlington	Will	1863	WB8:144; File #596A
Harrison, Elias, Rev.	Arlington	Account	1865	WB8:242
Harrison, George, of Philadelphia	Alexandria	Deed	1811	CRK:048
Harrison, Jacob	Alexandria	Tax Charge	1789	Tax PP 1789:08
Harrison, John	Alexandria	Tax Charge	1799	Tax PP 1799:16
Harrison, John	Alexandria	Tax Charge	1800	Tax PP 1800:13
Harrison, John (C), c/o Fanny	Arlington	Apprentice	1801	OCR1801:015
Harrison, John D.	Arlington	Bond	1853	BB(np)
Harrison, John D.	Arlington	Will	1853	WB6:189; File #491A
Harrison, John D.	Arlington	Inventory	1861	WB8:075
Harrison, John D. [Martha Lunt]	Arlington	Renounce	1853	WB6:191; LVA-LP
Harrison, Joseph	Alexandria	Tax Charge	1788	Tax PP 1788:09
Harrison, Joseph W.	Alexandria	Owner	1787	Tax L 1787:12
Harrison, Kartherren, laburrer	Alexandria	Boarder	1800	1800(4):12A
Harrison, Mary	Alexandria	Resident	1800	1800(4):02B
Harrison, Mary M.	Alexandria	Will	1899	WB2:346; LP
Harrison, Mary, sempstress	Alexandria	Head	1800	1800(4):02A
Harrison, Mrs.	Alexandria	Tax Charge	1796	Tax LP 1796:12
Harrison, Richard	Alexandria	Tithable +16	1790	Tax PP 1790:07
Harrison, Robert	Alexandria	Tax Charge	1799	Tax PP 1799:16
Harrison, Robert	Arlington	Will	1874	WB9:364; File #691A
Harrison, Robert, b. Yorkshire, Eng.	Arlington	Alien Entry	1820	RA:11/01/20
Harrison, Robert H.	Alexandria	Owner	1787	Tax L 1787:13
Harrison, Robert H., Estate, Water St.	Alexandria	Owner	1790	Tax L 1790:05(2)
Harrison, Robert W.	Arlington	Bond	1819	WB2:341
Harrison, Robert W.	Arlington	Will	1819	WB2:340; File #169A
Harrison, Robert W.	Arlington	Inventory	1820	AB4:101; LVA-LP
Harrison, Robert W.	Arlington	Account	1821	AB4:284; LVA-LP
Harrison, Robt.	Alexandria	Boarder	1808	1808(1):02A
Harrison, Robt. H.	Alexandria	Tax Charge	1788	Tax PP 1788:08
Harrison, Sam. (C)	Alexandria	Boarder	1808	1808(1):01B
Harrison, Saml., Fairfax St.	Alexandria	Owner	1790	Tax L 1790:05
Harrison, Saml., King St.	Alexandria	Owner	1790	Tax L 1790:05
Harrison, Saml., King St.	Alexandria	Occupant	1790	Tax L 1790:05
Harrison, Samuel	Arlington	Will (NR)	(nd)	File #1801-2m
Harrison, Samuel	Alexandria	Tax Charge	1790	Tax PP 1790:06
Harrison, Samuel	Arlington	Guard.	1804	WBB:078
Harrison, Samuel & wife Barbara	Arlington	Settlement	1803	WBA:109
Harrison, Samuel, Capt.	Arlington	Account	1803	LVA-LP
Harrison, sempstress	Alexandria	Housekeeper	1808	1808(4):29A
Harrison, Thomas, grantee	Arlington	Indenture D.	1831	ID:312
Harrison, Widow, 2, widow	Alexandria	Head	1796	1796(3):4
Harrison, William, c/o Hugh Monroe	Arlington	Apprentice	1813	OCR1811:213
Harriss, Hugh, seaman	Alexandria	Head	1810	1810(1):05A
Harriss, Joseph, tide waiter	Alexandria	Head	1810	1810(1):11A
Harriss, William	Arlington	Apprentice	1823	OCR1822:040
Harrow, Gilbert	Alexandria	Tax Charge	1787	Tax PP 1787:06
Harrow, Gilbert	Alexandria	Tax Charge	1788	Tax PP 1788:07
Harrow, Gilbert	Alexandria	Tax Charge	1789	Tax PP 1789:09
Harrow, Gilbert	Alexandria	Tax Charge	1790	Tax PP 1790:07
Harrow, Gilbert, Cameron St.	Alexandria	Occupant	1787	Tax L 1787:01

NAME OR SUBJECT	LOCATION	TYPE	YEAR	REFERENCE(S)
Harrow, Gilbert, Duke St.	Alexandria	Occupant	1790	Tax L 1790:08
Harrowsan, J.	Alexandria	Boarder	1808	1808(2):16A
Harshman, Henry	Alexandria	Tax Charge	1798	Tax PP 1798:07
Harshman, Henry	Arlington	Crime	1799	OT:12/11/1799
Harshman, Henry	Alexandria	Tax Charge	1799	Tax PP 1799:16
Harshman, Henry & wife Susaner	Alexandria	Resident	1800	1800(4):05B
Harshman, Henry, painter	Alexandria	Head	1800	1800(4):05A
Hart, Anna (M)	Arlington	Apprentice	1804	OCR1801:192
Hart, Anna (M), c/o Anna	Arlington	Apprentice	1803	OCR1801:091
Hart, Frederick William	Arlington	Guard. Acct.	1869	WB9:150
Hart, James	Alexandria	Will	1891	WB1:591; LP
Hart, Robert, weaver	Alexandria	Head	1810	1810(4):06A
Hart, William	Arlington	Crime	1795	OT:28/07/1795
Hart, William	Arlington	Crime	1795	OT:28/07/1795
Hartley, Catharine	Alexandria	Will	1889	WB1:529; LP
Hartley, Elizabeth, c/o James	Arlington	Guard.	1810	WB1:004
Hartley, Geo., shoemaker	Alexandria	Housekeeper	1808	1808(4):26A
Hartley, Geo., shoemaker	Alexandria	Head	1810	1810(4):02A
Hartley, George	Alexandria	Tax Charge	1798	Tax PP 1798:07
Hartley, George	Alexandria	Tax Charge	1799	Tax PP 1799:18
Hartley, George, b. Cairn, Ireland	Arlington	Alien Entry	1801	RA:08/07/01
Hartley, James	Alexandria	Tax Charge	1796	Tax LP 1796:12
Hartley, James	Alexandria	Tax Charge	1799	Tax PP 1799:16
Hartley, James & wife, cooper	Alexandria	Head	1795	1795(4):02
Hartley, James & wife, cooper	Alexandria	Housekeeper	1799	1799(2):15A
Hartley, James, Fairfax St.	Alexandria	Owner	1795	Tax L 1795:11
Hartley, Jas.	Alexandria	Tax Charge	1795	Tax PP 1795:13
Hartley, Jas.	Alexandria	Tax Charge	1798	Tax PP 1798:08
Hartley, Jas., Fairfax St.	Alexandria	Occupant	1795	Tax L 1795:11
Hartley, Jas., Fairfax St.	Alexandria	Occupant	1795	Tax L 1795:22
Hartley, Leticisa	Alexandria	Resident	1800	1800(4):05B
Hartley, Leticita	Alexandria	Resident	1800	1800(4):05B
Hartley, Leticita, shopkeeper	Alexandria	Head	1800	1800(4):05A
Hartley, Letitia, Admx. of James, def.	Alexandria	Suit	1799	CRB:041
Hartley, Mrs.	Alexandria	License Due	1800	Tax PP 1800:54(24)
Hartley, Thomas	Alexandria	Will	1883	WB1:377; LP
Hartly, George	Alexandria	Tax Charge	1800	Tax PP 1800:13
Hartly, George, w(1), shoemaker	Alexandria	Head	1796	1796(3):6
Harton, William (C)	Arlington	Apprentice	1804	OCR1801:229
Hartshorne & Donaldson, Hooe's wharf	Alexandria	Occupant	1790	Tax L 1790:06
Hartshorne & Donaldson, Kirk's wharf	Alexandria	Occupant	1790	Tax L 1790:06
Hartshorne & Sons	Alexandria	Mer. License	1798	Tax PP 1798:20-3
Hartshorne & Watson	Alexandria	Tax Charge	1796	Tax LP 1796:13
Hartshorne, Susan	Arlington	Sale	1821	AB4:243
Hartshorne, Susan	Arlington	Inventory	1821	AB4:231; LVA-LP
Hartshorne, Susan	Arlington	Will	1821	WB2:424; File #193A
Hartshorne, Susan	Arlington	Bond	1821	WB2:425
Hartshorne, Susanna	Arlington	Account	1822	AB5:074; LVA-LP
Hartshorne, Susanna	Arlington	Account	1823	AB5:179; LVA-LP
Hartshorne, William	Alexandria	Deed	1778	CRI:285, 290
Hartshorne, William	Alexandria	Owner	1787	Tax L 1787:13
Hartshorne, William	Alexandria	Mer. License	1799	Tax PP 1799:52-05w
Hartshorne, William	Alexandria	Deposition	1808	CRH:116
Hartshorne, William	Arlington	Inventory	1818	AB3:137; LVA-LP
Hartshorne, William	Arlington	Will	1818	WB2:201; File #142A
Hartshorne, William	Arlington	Admin.	1818	WB2:235
Hartshorne, William	Arlington	Account	1820	AB4:186; LVA-LP
Hartshorne, William	Arlington	Sale	1820	AB4:183
Hartshorne, William & Co., plt.	Alexandria	Suit	1800	CRC:034
Hartshorne, William & wife Susanna	Alexandria	Deed	1779	CRI:298
Hartshorne, William, Fairfax St.	Alexandria	Owner	1790	Tax L 1790:06

NAME OR SUBJECT	LOCATION	TYPE	YEAR	REFERENCE(S)
Hartshorne, William, Hooe's wharf	Alexandria	Owner	1790	Tax L 1790:06
Hartshorne, William, Jr.	Alexandria	Deposition	1805	CRF:245
Hartshorne, William, King St.	Alexandria	Occupant	1787	Tax L 1787:02
Hartshorne, William, King St.	Alexandria	Owner	1790	Tax L 1790:06
Hartshorne, William, Kirk's wharf	Alexandria	Owner	1790	Tax L 1790:06
Hartshorne, William, plt.	Alexandria	Suit	1801	CRB:349
Hartshorne, William, Prince St.	Alexandria	Owner	1790	Tax L 1790:06(3)
Hartshorne, William, Washington St.	Alexandria	Occupant	1787	Tax L 1787:03
Hartshorne, Wm.	Alexandria	Tax Charge	1787	Tax PP 1787:07
Hartshorne, Wm.	Alexandria	Tax Charge	1788	Tax PP 1788:07
Hartshorne, Wm.	Alexandria	Tax Charge	1789	Tax PP 1789:09
Hartshorne, Wm.	Alexandria	Tax Charge	1796	Tax LP 1796:11
Hartshorne, Wm.	Alexandria	License Due	1800	Tax PP 1800:54(24)
Hartshorne, Wm. & Co., Union St.	Alexandria	Occupant	1795	Tax L 1795:04
Hartshorne, Wm. & Others, Union wharf	Alexandria	Occupant	1787	Tax L 1787:14
Hartshorne, Wm. & Sons	Alexandria	Tax Charge	1796	Tax LP 1796:13
Hartshorne, Wm., Jr.	Alexandria	Tax Charge	1799	Tax PP 1799:18
Hartshorne, Wm., Jr.	Alexandria	Tax Charge	1798	Tax PP 1798:08
Hartshorne, Wm., King St.	Alexandria	Owner	1795	Tax L 1795:14
Hartshorne, Wm., merchant	Alexandria	Housekeeper	1808	1808(1):05A
Hartshorne, Wm., Prince St.	Alexandria	Occupant	1787	Tax L 1787:13
Hartshorne, Wm., Sr.	Alexandria	Tax Charge	1796	Tax PP 1796:08
Hartshorne, Wm., Sr.	Alexandria	Tax Charge	1800	Tax PP 1800:15
Hartshorne, Wm., Union St.	Alexandria	Occupant	1787	Tax L 1787:14
Hartshorne, Wm., Union St.	Alexandria	Occupant	1795	Tax L 1795:17
Hartshorne, Wm., Water St.	Alexandria	Owner	1795	Tax L 1795:14
Hartshorne, Wm., wharf	Alexandria	Occupant	1795	Tax L 1795:07
Hartsock, Philip	Alexandria	Tax Charge	1790	Tax PP 1790:07
Hartsock [Hartsok], Philip	Alexandria	Tax Charge	1788	Tax PP 1788:07
Harvey, William	Alexandria	Tax Charge	1790	Tax PP 1790:06
Harwell, Richard	Alexandria	Mer. License	1800	Tax PP 1800:54(14)r
Harwood, Charles, c/o Samuel	Arlington	Apprentice	1811	OCR1811:082
Haskins, Jno.	Alexandria	Tax Charge	1795	Tax PP 1795:12
Haslip, Roger	Alexandria	Boarder	1808	1808(2):15A
Hastings, Jonathan, plt.	Alexandria	Suit	1801	CRB:208
Hatan, John & wife, ship builder	Alexandria	Head	1795	1795(4a):10
Hathaway, Jethro	Alexandria	Tax Charge	1800	Tax PP 1800:15
Hathaway, Jetro & wife, mariner	Alexandria	Housekeeper	1799	1799(2):16A
Hatherley, Nathan	Alexandria	Tax Charge	1795	Tax PP 1795:14
Hatherley, Nathan	Alexandria	Tax Charge	1796	Tax PP 1796:09
Hatherley, Nathan	Alexandria	Tax Charge	1799	Tax PP 1799:17
Hatherly, Nathan	Alexandria	Tax Charge	1796	Tax LP 1796:11
Hatherly, Nathan, Princess St.	Alexandria	Occupant	1795	Tax L 1795:12
Hatherly, Nathanl.	Alexandria	Tax Charge	1798	Tax PP 1798:08
Hathuyson & Cox, plt.	Alexandria	Suit	1809	CRG:238
Hathuyson & Cox, plt.	Alexandria	Suit	1809	CRG:345
Hathway, Joshua	Alexandria	Tax Charge	1799	Tax PP 1799:18
Hatsock, Philip	Alexandria	Tax Charge	1799	Tax PP 1799:17
Hatteking, Thos., cartman	Alexandria	Housekeeper	1808	1808(3):23A
Hatten, Saml., tailor	Alexandria	Boarder	1799	1799(2):04A
Hatterslay, Saml., glover	Alexandria	Housekeeper	1808	1808(3):19A
Hattersley, Geo.	Alexandria	Boarder	1808	1808(1):05A
Hattersley, Josiah	Alexandria	Tax Charge	1790	Tax PP 1790:07
Hattersly, Saml., glover	Alexandria	Head	1810	1810(3):05A
Hatton, Casey (C), washwoman	Alexandria	Housekeeper	1808	1808(1):07A
Hatton, Cassa, washerwoman	Alexandria	Head	1810	1810(1):09A
Hatton, John Mc., Capt.	Alexandria	Deposition	1808	CRI:401
Hatton, Wm.	Alexandria	Boarder	1808	1808(2):10A
Hatton, Wm., retailer	Alexandria	Housekeeper	1808	1808(2):11A
Hauck, Peter	Alexandria	Tax Charge	1796	Tax PP 1796:08
Hauck, Peter	Alexandria	Tax Charge	1798	Tax PP 1798:08

NAME OR SUBJECT	LOCATION	TYPE	YEAR	REFERENCE(S)
Hauck, Peter	Alexandria	Tax Charge	1799	Tax PP 1799:17
Hauk, Peter & wife, hatter	Alexandria	Head	1795	1795(4):02
Havard, John	Alexandria	Tithable +21	1787	Tax PP 1787:11
Havener, Thos.	Alexandria	Boarder	1808	1808(2):17A
Havens, Thomas	Arlington	Witness	1812	ACR:060
Hawk, George	Alexandria	Tax Charge	1788	Tax PP 1788:08
Hawke, Charles	Arlington	Admin.	1820	WB2:357
Hawke, George	Alexandria	Tax Charge	1789	Tax PP 1789:09
Hawke, George	Alexandria	Tax Charge	1790	Tax PP 1790:07
Hawkins, Jno., Fairfax St.	Alexandria	Occupant	1787	Tax L 1787:11
Hawkins, John	Alexandria	Owner	1787	Tax L 1787:15
Hawkins, John	Alexandria	Tax Charge	1790	Tax PP 1790:07
Hawkins, John, Fairfax St.	Alexandria	Occupant	1790	Tax L 1790:02
Hawkins, John, Fayette Co. Ky.	Alexandria	Plat	1790	CRH:387
Hawkins, Peter Francis (C)	Arlington	Apprentice	1844	OCR1842:084
Hawkins, Peter Francis (C)	Arlington	Apprentice	1847	OCR1842:199
Hawkins, Thos.	Alexandria	Tax Charge	1798	Tax PP 1798:07
Hawks, Jacob & wife, drayman	Alexandria	Head	1795	1795(4a):06
Hawley, James	Alexandria	Tax Charge	1789	Tax PP 1789:09
Hawley, William	Alexandria	Tax Charge	1789	Tax PP 1789:08
Hawley, William	Arlington	Admin.	1832	WB4:032
Haws, Abraham	Arlington	Inventory	1828	LVA-LP
Haws, Milly, washwoman	Alexandria	Housekeeper	1808	1808(4):24A
Hawthorn, Thomas, def.	Alexandria	Suit	1801	CRC:227
Hawuk, Fanny, seamstress	Alexandria	Head	1810	1810(1):11A
Hay, Jno. & Co., Royal St.	Alexandria	Occupant	1787	Tax L 1787:10
Haycock, William	Alexandria	Tax Charge	1787	Tax PP 1787:06
Haycock, William	Alexandria	Tax Charge	1788	Tax PP 1788:07
Haycock, William	Alexandria	Tax Charge	1789	Tax PP 1789:07
Haycock, William, Royal St.	Alexandria	Occupant	1787	Tax L 1787:23
Hayes, Andrew	Alexandria	Tax Charge	1788	Tax PP 1788:08
Hayes, Andrew	Alexandria	Tax Charge	1796	Tax PP 1796:08
Hayes, Andrew	Alexandria	Tax Charge	1799	Tax PP 1799:17
Hayes, Andrew, Prince St.	Alexandria	Owner	1790	Tax L 1790:05
Hayes, Andrew, Prince St.	Alexandria	Owner	1795	Tax L 1795:11(2)
Hayes, Andrew, w(5), sadler	Alexandria	Head	1796	1796(3):3
Hayes, Andw.	Alexandria	Tax Charge	1795	Tax PP 1795:13
Hayes, Andw., Prince St.	Alexandria	Occupant	1790	Tax L 1790:05
Hayes, Andw., Prince St.	Alexandria	Occupant	1795	Tax L 1795:11
Hayes, Jno.	Alexandria	Tax Charge	1795	Tax PP 1795:12
Hayes, John	Alexandria	Tax Charge	1796	Tax PP 1796:08
Hayes, John, sadler	Alexandria	Head	1810	1810(3):02A
Hayes, John, sadler & shopkeeper	Alexandria	Housekeeper	1808	1808(3):20A
Hayes, Mary	Arlington	Ordinary	1811	OBL2(np)
Hayley, Elizabeth, seampstress	Alexandria	Head	1810	1810(1):02A
Hayley, Geo. & wife, labourer	Alexandria	Housekeeper	1799	1799(2):07A
Hayley, George	Alexandria	Tax Charge	1799	Tax PP 1799:17
Hayman, Caspar	Arlington	Ordinary	1807	OBL2(np)(2)
Hayman, Casper, shopkeeper	Alexandria	Head	1810	1810(2):04A
Hayman, Gasper, seaman, shopkpr. T.L.	Alexandria	Housekeeper	1808	1808(2):14A
Haynes, Eliza Ann	Arlington	Guard. Acct.	1813	LVA-LP
Haynes, Eliza Ann	Arlington	Guard. Acct.	1814	AB2:059
Haynes, Eliza Ann	Arlington	Guard. Acct.	1816	AB2:270; LVA-LP
Haynes, Eliza Ann	Arlington	Guard. Acct.	1818	AB3:267
Haynes, Eliza Ann	Arlington	Guard. Acct.	1825	AB6:069; LVA-LP
Haynes, Elizabeth	Arlington	Guard.	1826	WB3:222
Haynes, Elizabeth Ann	Arlington	Guard.	1826	OCR1822:110
Haynes, Elizabeth Ann, c/o John	Arlington	Guard.	1812	WB1:186
Haynes, John	Arlington	Inventory	1812	AB1:233; LVA-LP
Haynes, John	Arlington	Admin.	1812	WB1:167
Haynes, John	Arlington	Distribution	1813	AB1:305; LVA-LP

NAME OR SUBJECT	LOCATION	TYPE	YEAR	REFERENCE(S)
Haynes, John	Arlington	Account	1813	AB1:302; LVA-LP
Haynes, John	Arlington	Admin.	1834	WB4:099
Haynes, John, b. Plymouth, Eng.	Arlington	Alien Entry	1802	RA:01/06/02
Haynes, John, mariner	Alexandria	Head	1810	1810(1):09A
Hays, Andrew	Alexandria	Tax Charge	1787	Tax PP 1787:07
Hays, Andrew	Alexandria	Tax Charge	1790	Tax PP 1790:06
Hays, Andrew	Alexandria	Tax Charge	1800	Tax PP 1800:13
Hays, Andrew, Prince St.	Alexandria	Occupant	1787	Tax L 1787:11
Hays, Andw., sadler	Alexandria	Housekeeper	1808	1808(1):03A
Hays, George	Alexandria	Tithable +16	1788	Tax PP 1788:06
Hays, Jane, labourrer	Alexandria	Boarder	1800	1800(4):12A
Hays, Jeremiah	Alexandria	Will	1883	WB1:379; LP
Hays, John, Queen St.	Alexandria	Occupant	1795	Tax L 1795:12
Hays, Robert	Alexandria	Tax Charge	1787	Tax PP 1787:07
Hays, William H., grantor	Arlington	Indenture D.	1812	ID2:166
Hays, William H., in jail	Arlington	Insolvent	1812	ID2:163
Hays, [blank], Royal St.	Alexandria	Occupant	1795	Tax L 1795:13
Hayse, Abraham	Alexandria	Tax Charge	1789	Tax PP 1789:09
Headen, Garret	Arlington	Ordinary	1804	OBL1(np)
Headen, Garrett, in jail	Arlington	Insolvent	1806	ID3:214
Headley, Julia A.	Arlington	Guard. Acct.	1842	AB8:303
Headley, Julia R.	Arlington	Account	1833	AB7:091, 100
Headley, Julia R.	Arlington	Guard. Acct.	1840	AB8:177; LVA-LP
Headley, Julia R.	Arlington	Guard. Acct.	1841	AB8:177
Headley, Julia R.	Arlington	Guard. Acct.	1843	AB8:344; LVA-LP
Headley, Julia Rebecca	Arlington	Guard.	1832	WB4:044
Headley, Julia Rebecca	Arlington	Guard. Acct.	1834	AB7:091; LVA-LP
Headley, Julia Rebecca	Arlington	Guard. Acct.	1834	AB7:100; LVA-LP
Headley, Julia Rebecca	Arlington	Guard. Acct.	1835	AB7:172; LVA-LP
Headley, Julia Rebecca	Arlington	Guard. Acct.	1836	AB7:208; LVA-LP
Headley, Julia Rebecca	Arlington	Guard. Acct.	1837	AB7:305; LVA-LP
Headley, Julia Rebecca	Arlington	Guard. Acct.	1837	LVA-LP
Headley, Julia Rebecca	Arlington	Guard. Acct.	1838	AB7:305
Headley, Julia Rebecca	Arlington	Guard. Acct.	1839	AB7:323; LVA-LP
Headley, Julia Rebecca	Arlington	Guard. Acct.	1839	AB8:050; LVA-LP
Headley, Priscilla	Arlington	Will	1831	WB4:042; File #315A
Headley, Priscilla	Arlington	Bond	1831	WB4:043
Headley, Priscilla	Arlington	Account	1832	AB7:065
Headley, Priscilla	Arlington	Appraisal	1832	LVA-LP
Headley, Priscilla	Arlington	Account	1833	AB7:065; LVA-LP
Headley, Robert P.	Arlington	Account	1827	AB6:433
Headley, Robert P.	Arlington	Admin.	1827	OCR1822:143a
Headley, Robert P.	Arlington	Admin.	1827	WB3:298
Headon, Ellen, sempstress	Alexandria	Housekeeper	1808	1808(2):16A
Heale, Geo.	Alexandria	Tax Charge	1796	Tax LP 1796:12
Heale, Geo.	Alexandria	Tax Charge	1798	Tax PP 1798:07
Heard, Bennet	Alexandria	Tax Charge	1787	Tax PP 1787:07
Heard, George	Alexandria	Tithable +16	1790	Tax PP 1790:07
Heard, John	Alexandria	Tithable +16	1790	Tax PP 1790:13
Heard, Joseph	Alexandria	Tithable +16	1789	Tax PP 1789:03
Heard, Joseph	Alexandria	Tithable +16	1790	Tax PP 1790:03
Hearlihy, Kitty	Arlington	Guard.	1813	WB2:091
Hearlihy, Maurice	Arlington	Guard.	1813	WB2:091
Hearlihy, Morris	Arlington	Sale	1804	WBB:083
Hearlihy, Morris	Arlington	Admin.	1804	WBB:068
Heartly, Thomas	Arlington	Apprentice	1813	OCR1811:180
Heartly, Thomas	Arlington	Guard.	1813	WB1:238
Heath, Andw.	Alexandria	Boarder	1808	1808(4):25A
Heath, Fortu., clerk	Alexandria	Boarder	1799	1799(2):02A
Heath, John K.	Arlington	Guard.	1837	WB4:114
Heath, Milly (C)	Alexandria	Reference	1808	1808(4):24A

NAME OR SUBJECT	LOCATION	TYPE	YEAR	REFERENCE(S)
Heath, [blank], sadler	Alexandria	Head	1810	1810(4):05A
Heatland, Phebe	Arlington	Guard. Acct.	1822	AB5:129; LVA-LP
Heavey, Isaac	Alexandria	Tax Charge	1795	Tax PP 1795:12
Hebb, John, grantor	Arlington	Indenture D.	1831	ID:364
Hebb, John, in jail	Arlington	Insolvent	1831	ID:361
Hebb, Susanna	Alexandria	Head	1810	1810(1):10A
Heddick, Geo., waiter at bank	Alexandria	Head	1810	1810(3):03A
Heddrick, Anthy.	Alexandria	Tax Charge	1790	Tax PP 1790:07
Heddrick, Robert	Alexandria	Tax Charge	1790	Tax PP 1790:07
Heddrick, Thomas	Alexandria	Tax Charge	1790	Tax PP 1790:07
Heden, Eleanor	Arlington	Ordinary	1810	OBL2(np)
Heden, Garret	Arlington	Ordinary	1806	OBL2(np)
Hedges, Fredk., clerk	Alexandria	Boarder	1799	1799(2):08A
Hedges, Hanson, grantor	Arlington	Indenture D.	1811	ID2:026
Hedges, Hanson, in jail	Arlington	Insolvent	1809	ID2:023
Hedley, Jacob	Alexandria	Tax Charge	1788	Tax PP 1788:09
Hedley, Paul	Alexandria	Tax Charge	1796	Tax LP 1796:11
Hedrick, Anthony	Alexandria	Tax Charge	1789	Tax PP 1789:09
Hedrick, John, c/o Catherine	Arlington	Apprentice	1803	OCR1801:133
Hedrick, Kitty	Alexandria	Housekeeper	1799	1799(2):06A
Hedrick, Robert	Alexandria	Tax Charge	1787	Tax PP 1787:07
Hedrick, Robert	Alexandria	Tax Charge	1788	Tax PP 1788:07
Hedrick, Thomas	Alexandria	Tax Charge	1787	Tax PP 1787:08
Hedrick, Thomas	Alexandria	Tax Charge	1788	Tax PP 1788:08
Hedrick, Thomas	Arlington	Apprentice	1802	OCR1801:048
Hedrick, Thomas, Fairfax St.	Alexandria	Occupant	1787	Tax L 1787:06
Hedrick, Thos.	Alexandria	Tax Charge	1789	Tax PP 1789:09
Hedricks, Thomas	Arlington	Apprentice	1801	OCR1801:017
Heerman, Frederick	Arlington	Admin.	1808	WBC:162
Heflebower, Samuel	Alexandria	Will	1876	WB1:179; LP
Heide, Philip	Alexandria	Tax Charge	1790	Tax PP 1790:06
Heidic, [blank], nr. Union St.	Alexandria	Occupant	1790	Tax L 1790:11
Heies, Andw.	Alexandria	Tax Charge	1796	Tax LP 1796:12
Heinaman, Jacob	Alexandria	Tax Charge	1790	Tax PP 1790:06
Heinegan, Edward, for playing Faro	Arlington	Defendant	1802	PA:066
Heineman, Ann, widow (1)	Alexandria	Head	1795	1796(3):7
Heineman, Conrod	Alexandria	Tax Charge	1790	Tax PP 1790:06
Heineman, Jacob, Washington St.	Alexandria	Occupant	1790	Tax L 1790:05
Heineman, Jacob, Washington St.	Alexandria	Owner	1790	Tax L 1790:05
Heinemann, Jacob	Alexandria	Tax Charge	1788	Tax PP 1788:07
Heinemann, Jacob	Alexandria	Tax Charge	1789	Tax PP 1789:08
Heints, Mary, labourrer	Alexandria	Boarder	1800	1800(4):05A
Heirs, William	Alexandria	Tithable +16	1789	Tax PP 1789:20
Heiskill, Peter	Alexandria	Tax Charge	1800	Tax PP 1800:13
Heister, John, cooper	Alexandria	Housekeeper	1808	1808(3):21A
Heitzer, Henry	Alexandria	Tax Charge	1787	Tax PP 1787:07
Heitzer, Henry	Alexandria	Tax Charge	1788	Tax PP 1788:09
Helliman, Conrad	Alexandria	Tax Charge	1788	Tax PP 1788:08
Helliman, Conrod	Alexandria	Tax Charge	1789	Tax PP 1789:08
Hellmuth, Louis	Arlington	Appraisal	1864	WB8:207
Hellrigel, Christian L.	Arlington	Account	1811	AB1:062
Hellrigel, Christian Ludwick	Arlington	Will	1810	WBC:326; File #051A
Hellrigel, Christian Ludwick	Arlington	Inventory	1810	WBC:328
Hellrigel, Christian Ludwick	Arlington	Bond	1810	WBC:327
Hellrigel, Philip, c/o Barbary	Arlington	Apprentice	1811	OCR1811:064
Hellrigell, Philip, c/o Barbary	Arlington	Apprentice	1811	OCR1811:029
Hellriggle, Barbara	Alexandria	Head	1810	1810(1):10A
Hellriggle, Christian, ship carpenter	Alexandria	Housekeeper	1808	1808(1):06A
Hellrigle, Christian L.	Arlington	Admin.	1829	WB3:347
Helm, Thomas	Arlington	Plaintiff	1802	PA:338
Helm, William, plt.	Alexandria	Suit	1801	CRC:118

NAME OR SUBJECT	LOCATION	TYPE	YEAR	REFERENCE(S)
Helmes, Elizabeth, washwoman	Alexandria	Housekeeper	1808	1808(4):24A
Helms, John	Alexandria	Tax Charge	1790	Tax PP 1790:07
Helms, John	Alexandria	Tax Charge	1796	Tax PP 1796:09
Helms, John	Alexandria	Tax Charge	1799	Tax PP 1799:17
Helms, John	Alexandria	Tax Charge	1800	Tax PP 1800:13
Helms, John, w(2), carpenter	Alexandria	Head	1796	1796(3):1
Helms, Mrs., seamstress	Alexandria	Head	1810	1810(4):08A
Helmsley, Geo.	Alexandria	Boarder	1808	1808(4):26A
Heming, Thos., Estate	Alexandria	Tax Charge	1795	Tax PP 1795:10
Hemmersly, William, at his house	Arlington	Ordinary	1849	OBL6(np)
Hemp, five tons of	Arlington	Suit	1821	ACO:201, 204
Hendall, John	Alexandria	Tax Charge	1800	Tax PP 1800:15
Henderson, Alexander, def.	Alexandria	Suit	1819	CRK:438
Henderson, Alexander, in prison rules	Arlington	Insolvent	1806	ID3:139
Henderson, Alexander, Jr.	Arlington	Respondent	1808	ACO:100
Henderson, Alexander, Jr., grantee	Arlington	Indenture D.	1806	ID3:154
Henderson, Alexander, Jr., plt.	Alexandria	Suit	1801	CRB:085
Henderson, Alexander, Jr.	Arlington	Witness	1801	ACO:006
Henderson, Alexander, plt.	Alexandria	Suit	1801	CRC:194
Henderson, Alexander, plt.	Alexandria	Suit	1803	CRE:071
Henderson, Alexander, s/o Archd.	Arlington	Schedule	1806	ID3:147
Henderson, Anne	Arlington	Will	1857	WB7:204; File #542A
Henderson, Anne	Arlington	Account	1857	WB7:226; LVA-LP
Henderson, Anne	Arlington	Account	1858	WB7:348; LVA-LP
Henderson, Anne	Arlington	Account	1859	WB7:416; LVA-LP
Henderson, Anny, washerwoman	Alexandria	Head	1810	1810(2):05A
Henderson, David	Alexandria	Tax Charge	1796	Tax PP 1796:09
Henderson, David	Alexandria	Tax Charge	1798	Tax PP 1798:07
Henderson, David	Alexandria	Tax Charge	1799	Tax PP 1799:16
Henderson, David	Alexandria	Tax Charge	1800	Tax PP 1800:13
Henderson, David	Arlington	Plaintiff	1802	PA:180
Henderson, David	Arlington	Guard.	1802	WBA:081
Henderson, David & wife, baker	Alexandria	Housekeeper	1799	1799(2):05A
Henderson, Dorcas	Arlington	Ordinary	1810	OBL2(np)
Henderson, George	Arlington	Inventory	1820	AB4:111; LVA-LP
Henderson, George	Arlington	Admin.	1820	WB2:349
Henderson, Hannah	Arlington	Guard.	1802	WBA:081
Henderson, Harry, seaman	Alexandria	Housekeeper	1808	1808(3):18A
Henderson, Jesse	Arlington	Will P.	1823	OCR1822:040a
Henderson, Jesse	Arlington	Will	1824	WB3:391a; File #295A
Henderson, John E.	Arlington	Appraisal	1863	WB8:153
Henderson, John E.	Arlington	Account	1867	WB8:543
Henderson, John W.	Alexandria	Will	1894	WB2:074; LP
Henderson, Margaret	Alexandria	Will	1882	WB1:331; LP
Henderson Octavius Cazenove	Alexandria	Will	1897	WB2:248; LP
Henderson, Robert	Alexandria	Tax Charge	1796	Tax LP 1796:13
Henderson, Robert, shopkeeper	Alexandria	Head	1795	1796(3):7
Henderson, Robt.	Alexandria	Tax Charge	1795	Tax PP 1795:13
Henderson, Robt.	Alexandria	Boarder	1808	1808(3):18A
Henderson, Sarah	Arlington	Guard.	1820	WB2:375
Hendricks, James	Alexandria	Owner	1787	Tax L 1787:14
Hendricks, James	Alexandria	Tax Charge	1787	Tax PP 1787:07
Hendricks, James	Alexandria	Tax Charge	1788	Tax PP 1788:07
Hendricks, James, King St.	Alexandria	Occupant	1787	Tax L 1787:14
Hendricks, John	Alexandria	Tax Charge	1787	Tax PP 1787:07
Hendricks, John	Alexandria	Tax Charge	1788	Tax PP 1788:07
Hendricks, John	Alexandria	Tax Charge	1789	Tax PP 1789:09
Hendricks, John, Fairfax St.	Alexandria	Occupant	1787	Tax L 1787:01
Hendricks, John, King St.	Alexandria	Occupant	1787	Tax L 1787:01
Hendrickson, Joseph, shopkeeper	Alexandria	Housekeeper	1808	1808(1):09A
Hendron, John	Alexandria	Tax Charge	1789	Tax PP 1789:07

NAME OR SUBJECT	LOCATION	TYPE	YEAR	REFERENCE(S)
Henigan, Timothy, b. Corke	Arlington	Alien Entry	1821	RA:12/06/21
Henley, David	Alexandria	Owner	1787	Tax L 1787:13
Henley, David, Wilks St.	Alexandria	Occupant	1787	Tax L 1787:03
Henley, Zenus, tanner	Alexandria	Head	1810	1810(4):09A
Henly, D., Fairfax St.	Alexandria	Occupant	1787	Tax L 1787:13
Henly, David, Duke St.	Alexandria	Owner	1790	Tax L 1790:06
Henly, David, Wolfe St.	Alexandria	Owner	1790	Tax L 1790:06
Hennekin, Thomas, c/o Anne Brammel	Arlington	Apprentice	1805	OCR1801:307
Henona, William (non-citizen, servant)	Alexandria	Tithable +21	1787	Tax PP 1787:05
Henretty, Bridget	Alexandria	Will	1878	WB1:237; LP
Henry, Aron	Alexandria	Tax Charge	1799	Tax PP 1799:16
Henry, Bitsey	Arlington	Guard.	1820	WB2:393
Henry, Daniel	Alexandria	Tax Charge	1796	Tax PP 1796:08
Henry, Danl.	Alexandria	Tax Charge	1798	Tax PP 1798:08
Henry, James	Arlington	P. of Atty.	1816	WB2:174
Henry, John	Arlington	Inventory	1800	CRA:328
Henry, John	Arlington	Admin.	1808	WBC:078
Henry, John	Arlington	Respondent	1821	ACO:198
Henry, John	Arlington	Respondent	1822	ACO:205
Henry, John	Arlington	Respondent	1823	ACO:211
Henry, John, of Richmond	Arlington	Will (NP)	1808	File #030A
Henry, Thomas	Arlington	Guard.	1820	WB2:393
Henry, William, Genl.	Alexandria	Deposition	1808	CRI:425, 432
Henson & Welden, house joiners	Alexandria	Head	1810	1810(2):06A
Henson, Mark, labourer	Alexandria	Head	1810	1810(3):07A
Henson, Saml., labourer	Alexandria	Head	1810	1810(2):08A
Hepburn & Dundas	Alexandria	Owner	1787	Tax L 1787:17
Hepburn & Dundas	Alexandria	Owner	1787	Tax L 1787:16
Hepburn & Dundas	Alexandria	Tax Charge	1787	Tax PP 1787:06
Hepburn & Dundas	Alexandria	Tax Charge	1796	Tax PP 1796:08
Hepburn & Dundas	Alexandria	Mer. License	1798	Tax PP 1798:20-3
Hepburn & Dundas	Alexandria	Mer. License	1799	Tax PP 1799:52-04r
Hepburn & Dundas	Alexandria	Tax Charge	1799	Tax PP 1799:18
Hepburn & Dundas	Alexandria	License Due	1800	Tax PP 1800:54(24)
Hepburn & Dundas	Arlington	Plaintiffs	1802	PA:304
Hepburn & Dundas, complt.	Alexandria	Suit	1805	CRE:171
Hepburn & Dundas, King St.	Alexandria	Occupant	1787	Tax L 1787:17
Hepburn & Dundas, King St.	Alexandria	Occupant	1787	Tax L 1787:16
Hepburn & Dundas, Oronoko St.	Alexandria	Owner	1795	Tax L 1795:06
Hepburn & Dundas, plt.	Alexandria	Suit	1801	CRC:282
Hepburn & Dundas, plt.	Alexandria	Suit	1803	CRD:071
Hepburn & Dundas, Union St.	Alexandria	Occupant	1787	Tax L 1787:17
Hepburn & Dundas, wharf	Alexandria	Owner	1795	Tax L 1795:06
Hepburn & Dundass	Alexandria	Tax Charge	1796	Tax LP 1796:11
Hepburn & Dundass, King St.	Alexandria	Occupant	1790	Tax L 1790:05
Hepburn & Dundass, King St.	Alexandria	Owner	1790	Tax L 1790:05(3)
Hepburn & Dundass, Oronoka St.	Alexandria	Owner	1790	Tax L 1790:05
Hepburn & Dundass, Pitt St.	Alexandria	Owner	1790	Tax L 1790:05
Hepburn & Dundass, Princess St.	Alexandria	Owner	1790	Tax L 1790:05
Hepburn & Dundass, Union St.	Alexandria	Owner	1790	Tax L 1790:05(2)
Hepburn & Dundass, Union St.	Alexandria	Occupant	1790	Tax L 1790:05
Hepburn, John E.	Arlington	Guard. Acct.	1822	AB5:135
Hepburn, Julia	Arlington	Guard. Acct.	1821	AB4:315
Hepburn, Julia Ann E.	Arlington	Guard. Acct.	1829	AB6:509; LVA-LP
Hepburn, Julia Ann E.	Arlington	Guard. Acct.	1830	AB6:509
Hepburn, Julia Ann E.	Arlington	Guard. Acct.	1831	AB7:015; LVA-LP
Hepburn, Julia Ann Eliza, c/o William	Arlington	Guard.	1818	WB2:250
Hepburn, Julia Ann Eliza	Arlington	Guard. Acct.	1823	AB5:201; LVA-LP
Hepburn, Julia Ann Eliza	Arlington	Guard. Acct.	1826	AB6:257; LVA-LP
Hepburn, Julia Ann Eliza	Arlington	Guard.	1830	WB3:379
Hepburn, Julia Ann Eliza [Waring]	Arlington	Guard. Acct.	1832	AB7:142; LVA-LP

NAME OR SUBJECT	LOCATION	TYPE	YEAR	REFERENCE(S)
Hepburn, Julian Eliza	Arlington	Guard. Acct.	1822	AB5:135; LVA-LP
Hepburn, Julian Eliza	Arlington	Guard.	1827	OCR1822:135, 136a
Hepburn, Juliana Eliza	Arlington	Guard. Acct.	1818	AB3:243; LVA-LP
Hepburn, Juliana Eliza	Arlington	Guard. Acct.	1819	AB3:381; LVA-LP
Hepburn, Julianna E.	Arlington	Payment	1828	OCR1822:165
Hepburn, Julianna E.	Arlington	Petition	1829	OCR1822:175
Hepburn, Julianna E.	Arlington	Petition	1829	OCR1822:167a
Hepburn, Julianna Eliza	Arlington	Guard. Acct.	1819	AB3:311; LVA-LP
Hepburn, Julianna [Waring]	Arlington	Guard. Acct.	1835	AB7:142
Hepburn, Letitia	Arlington	Guard. Acct.	1819	AB3:311; LVA-LP
Hepburn, Letitia	Arlington	Guard. Acct.	1819	AB3:381; LVA-LP
Hepburn, Lettetia	Arlington	Guard. Acct.	1818	AB3:241; LVA-LP
Hepburn, Lettetia, c/o William	Arlington	Guard.	1818	WB2:250
Hepburn, Lettetia [Grimes]	Arlington	Guard. Acct.	1823	AB5:196; LVA-LP
Hepburn, Moses	Arlington	Guard. Acct.	1818	AB3:239; LVA-LP
Hepburn, Moses	Arlington	Petition	1818	WB3:282
Hepburn, Moses	Arlington	Guard. Acct.	1819	AB3:383; LVA-LP
Hepburn, Moses	Arlington	Guard. Acct.	1819	AB3:309; LVA-LP
Hepburn, Moses	Arlington	Guard. Acct.	1821	AB4:311; LVA-LP
Hepburn, Moses	Arlington	Guard. Acct.	1822	AB5:135; LVA-LP
Hepburn, Moses	Arlington	Guard. Acct.	1823	AB5:200; LVA-LP
Hepburn, Moses	Arlington	Guard. Acct.	1826	AB6:256; LVA-LP
Hepburn, Moses	Arlington	Guard. Acct.	1826	OCR1822:127a
Hepburn, Moses	Arlington	Guard. Acct.	1827	AB6:409; LVA-LP
Hepburn, Moses	Arlington	Guard.	1827	OCR1822:135, 136a
Hepburn, Moses	Arlington	Guard. Acct.	1829	AB6:508; LVA-LP
Hepburn, Moses	Arlington	Petition	1829	OCR1822:167a
Hepburn, Moses	Arlington	Petition	1829	OCR1822:175
Hepburn, Moses	Arlington	Guard. Acct.	1830	AB6:508
Hepburn, Moses	Arlington	Guard. Acct.	1832	AB7:143; LVA-LP
Hepburn, Moses	Arlington	Guard. Acct.	1832	AB7:037; LVA-LP
Hepburn, Moses, c/o William	Arlington	Guard.	1818	WB2:250
Hepburn, Moses, of Chester Co. PA	Arlington	Will	1861	WB8:050; File #580A
Hepburn v. McClean	Arlington	Petition	1829	WBB:281; LVA-LP
Hepburn, William	Alexandria	Tax Charge	1789	Tax PP 1789:08
Hepburn, William	Alexandria	Tax Charge	1790	Tax PP 1790:06
Hepburn, William	Arlington	Witness	1794	OT:25/07/1794
Hepburn, William	Alexandria	Agreement	1796	CRC:303, 305
Hepburn, William	Alexandria	Agreement	1796	CRE:016
Hepburn, William	Alexandria	Tax Charge	1796	Tax PP 1796:08
Hepburn, William	Alexandria	Tax Charge	1799	Tax PP 1799:18
Hepburn, William	Alexandria	Deed	1800	CRE:332
Hepburn, William	Alexandria	Deed	1800	CRE:221
Hepburn, William	Alexandria	Deed	1800	CRC:299
Hepburn, William	Arlington	Sale	1817	AB3:058
Hepburn, William	Arlington	Inventory	1817	AB3:057; LVA-LP
Hepburn, William	Arlington	Admin.	1817	WB2:196
Hepburn, William	Arlington	Will	1817	WB2:186; File #140A
Hepburn, William	Arlington	Account	1818	AB3:199; LVA-LP
Hepburn, William	Arlington	Account	1819	AB3:313; LVA-LP
Hepburn, William	Arlington	Account	1819	AB3:385; LVA-LP
Hepburn, William	Arlington	Account	1822	AB5:137
Hepburn, William, def.	Alexandria	Suit	1805	CRE:001
Hepburn, William, def.	Alexandria	Suit	1816	CRK:236
Hepburn, William, plt.	Alexandria	Suit	1802	CRC:155
Hepburn, Wm.	Alexandria	Tithable +21	1787	Tax PP 1787:06
Hepburn, Wm.	Alexandria	Tax Charge	1788	Tax PP 1788:07
Hepburn, Wm.	Alexandria	Tax Charge	1796	Tax LP 1796:11
Hepburn, Wm.	Alexandria	Tax Charge	1798	Tax PP 1798:07
Hepburn, Wm., gentleman	Alexandria	Housekeeper	1808	1808(2):16A
Hepburn, Wm., King St.	Alexandria	Owner	1795	Tax L 1795:12

NAME OR SUBJECT	LOCATION	TYPE	YEAR	REFERENCE(S)
Hepburn, Wm., King St.	Alexandria	Occupant	1795	Tax L 1795:12
Hepburn, Wm., Princess St.	Alexandria	Owner	1795	Tax L 1795:12(13)
Hepburn, Wm., Queen St.	Alexandria	Owner	1795	Tax L 1795:12
Hepburn [H.] & Dundas	Alexandria	Tax Charge	1798	Tax PP 1798:07
Hepurn, Lettetia	Arlington	Guard. Acct.	1821	AB4:313; LVA-LP
Herbert & Potts	Alexandria	Owner	1787	Tax L 1787:12
Herbert & Potts, Fairfax St.	Alexandria	Occupant	1787	Tax L 1787:12
Herbert & Potts, nr. Royal St.	Alexandria	Owner	1790	Tax L 1790:06
Herbert, Betsey	Arlington	Account C.	1867	WB8:484
Herbert, Betsey	Arlington	Account C.	1869	WB9:195
Herbert, Betsey & Kitty	Arlington	Account C.	1868	WB9:142
Herbert, George	Alexandria	Owner	1787	Tax L 1787:13
Herbert, George, Wilks St.	Alexandria	Occupant	1787	Tax L 1787:13
Herbert, Jno. C.	Alexandria	Tax Charge	1800	Tax PP 1800:15
Herbert, John C.	Alexandria	Tax Charge	1799	Tax PP 1799:16
Herbert, John D., def.	Alexandria	Suit	1822	CRL:232
Herbert, Kitty	Arlington	Account C.	1867	WB8:484
Herbert, Noblet, attorney	Arlington	Proof	1805	ACO:044
Herbert, Noblet	Arlington	Inventory	1825	AB6:110, 139; LVA-LP
Herbert, Noblet	Arlington	Sale	1825	AB6:143
Herbert, Noblet	Arlington	Will	1825	WB3:189; File #237A
Herbert, Noblet	Arlington	Bond	1825	WB3:190
Herbert, Noblet	Arlington	Account	1826	AB6:220; LVA-LP
Herbert, Noblet	Arlington	Account	1829	AB6:473; LVA-LP
Herbert, Noblet	Arlington	Account	1836	AB7:214; LVA-LP
Herbert, Noblet, def.	Alexandria	Suit	1820	CRL:036
Herbert, Noblet, def.	Alexandria	Suit	1821	CRL:365
Herbert, Noblet, def.	Alexandria	Suit	1822	CRL:389
Herbert, Noblet, grantee	Arlington	Indenture D.	1812	ID2:102
Herbert, Noblett, lawyer	Alexandria	Housekeeper	1808	1808(2):15A
Herbert, Tho., Fairfax St.	Alexandria	Owner	1795	Tax L 1795:13
Herbert, Thomas	Alexandria	Owner	1787	Tax L 1787:13
Herbert, Thomas	Alexandria	Tax Charge	1796	Tax LP 1796:11
Herbert, Thomas	Alexandria	Tax Charge	1799	Tax PP 1799:17
Herbert, Thomas	Alexandria	Deposition	1808	CRE:324
Herbert, Thomas	Alexandria	Deposition	1808	CRI:093
Herbert, Thomas	Arlington	Will P.	1825	OCR1822:105a
Herbert, Thomas	Arlington	Inventory	1826	AB6:219
Herbert, Thomas	Arlington	Admin.	1826	OCR1822:119
Herbert, Thomas	Arlington	Will P.	1826	OCR1822:108a
Herbert, Thomas	Arlington	Will P.	1826	OCR1822:119
Herbert, Thomas	Arlington	Will	1826	WB3:247; File #251A
Herbert, Thomas	Arlington	Bond	1826	WB3:249
Herbert, Thomas, def.	Alexandria	Suit	1820	CRL:036
Herbert, Thomas, Fairfax St.	Alexandria	Owner	1790	Tax L 1790:05
Herbert, Thos.	Alexandria	Tax Charge	1798	Tax PP 1798:07
Herbert, Thos.	Alexandria	Tax Charge	1800	Tax PP 1800:15
Herbert, Thos.	Alexandria	Boarder	1808	1808(2):15A
Herbert, Thos., Cameron St.	Alexandria	Occupant	1787	Tax L 1787:13
Herbert, Thos., gentleman	Alexandria	Housekeeper	1808	1808(2):15A
Herbert, Thos., gentleman	Alexandria	Head	1810	1810(2):04A
Herbert, W., Fairfax St.	Alexandria	Occupant	1787	Tax L 1787:15
Herbert, W., Oronoka St.	Alexandria	Occupant	1787	Tax L 1787:15
Herbert, William	Alexandria	Owner	1787	Tax L 1787:15
Herbert, William	Alexandria	Tax Charge	1787	Tax PP 1787:07
Herbert, William	Alexandria	Tax Charge	1788	Tax PP 1788:07
Herbert, William	Alexandria	Tax Charge	1789	Tax PP 1789:07
Herbert, William	Alexandria	Tax Charge	1790	Tax PP 1790:07
Herbert, William	Alexandria	Tax Charge	1795	Tax PP 1795:12
Herbert, William	Alexandria	Tax Charge	1796	Tax PP 1796:09
Herbert, William	Alexandria	Deed	1798	CRF:197

NAME OR SUBJECT	LOCATION	TYPE	YEAR	REFERENCE(S)
Herbert, William	Alexandria	Tax Charge	1798	Tax PP 1798:08
Herbert, William	Alexandria	Tax Charge	1799	Tax PP 1799:16
Herbert, William	Alexandria	Tax Charge	1800	Tax PP 1800:15
Herbert, William	Alexandria	Deed	1806	CRH:227
Herbert, William	Arlington	Admin.	1819	WB2:289
Herbert, William	Alexandria	Deposition	1822	CRL:536
Herbert, William, def.	Alexandria	Suit	1822	CRL:600
Herbert, William, Fairfax St.	Alexandria	Occupant	1787	Tax L 1787:15
Herbert, William, Jr., def.	Alexandria	Suit	1821	CRL:172
Herbert, William, Jr., grantee	Arlington	Indenture D.	1809	ID2:015
Herbert, William, Jr., grantee	Arlington	Indenture D.	1810	ID2:006
Herbert, William, Jr., grantee	Arlington	Indenture D.	1812	ID2:128
Herbert, William, Jr., grantee	Arlington	Indenture D.	1816	ID2:386
Herbert, William, Jr., trustee, plt.	Alexandria	Suit	1812	CRH:492
Herbert, William, nr. Fairfax St.	Alexandria	Occupant	1790	Tax L 1790:06
Herbert, William, nr. Fairfax St.	Alexandria	Owner	1790	Tax L 1790:06(3)
Herbert, William, Oronoka St.	Alexandria	Owner	1790	Tax L 1790:06
Herbert, William, plt.	Alexandria	Suit	1813	CRI:158
Herbert, William, pres. of bank	Alexandria	Head	1810	1810(2):02A
Herbert, William, trustee, def.	Alexandria	Suit	1810	CRH:197
Herbert, William, Water St.	Alexandria	Owner	1790	Tax L 1790:06
Herbert, Wm.	Alexandria	Tax Charge	1796	Tax LP 1796:11
Herbert, Wm.	Alexandria	Boarder	1808	1808(2):12A
Herbert, Wm. & Co., Wilks St.	Alexandria	Occupant	1787	Tax L 1787:03
Herbert, Wm., Fairfax St.	Alexandria	Occupant	1795	Tax L 1795:13
Herbert, Wm., Fairfax St.	Alexandria	Owner	1795	Tax L 1795:13(4)
Herbert, Wm., gentleman	Alexandria	Housekeeper	1808	1808(2):12A
Herbert, Wm., Oronoko St.	Alexandria	Owner	1795	Tax L 1795:13
Herbert, Wm., Water St.	Alexandria	Owner	1795	Tax L 1795:13
Herd, John	Alexandria	Tithable +16	1789	Tax PP 1789:17
Herenshaw, Jno.	Alexandria	Boarder	1808	1808(1):01A
Herenshaw, Thos.	Alexandria	Boarder	1808	1808(1):01A
Herenshaw, Westly	Alexandria	Boarder	1808	1808(1):01A
Herley, Morris	Alexandria	Tax Charge	1796	Tax PP 1796:09
Herlihy, M., Princess St.	Alexandria	Occupant	1795	Tax L 1795:12
Herlihy, Maurice	Alexandria	Tax Charge	1799	Tax PP 1799:16
Herlihy, Morris	Alexandria	Tax Charge	1789	Tax PP 1789:08
Herlihy, Morris	Alexandria	Tax Charge	1798	Tax PP 1798:08
Herlihy, Morris	Arlington	Account	1811	AB1:123; LVA-LP
Herlihy, Morris, Princess St.	Alexandria	Owner	1795	Tax L 1795:12
Herlihy [Easlyhy], Morris	Alexandria	Tax Charge	1787	Tax PP 1787:05
Herlihy [Hearlihy], Morris	Arlington	Inventory	1804	WBB:081; LVA-LP
Herlughy, Morris	Alexandria	Tax Charge	1795	Tax PP 1795:12
Hern, William, b. Lismore	Arlington	Alien Entry	1819	RA:07/09/19
Herrick, William T.	Alexandria	Will	1893	WBC1:064; LP
Herringshaw, John, c/o Eleanor	Arlington	Apprentice	1803	OCR1801:110
Herrington, Mich.	Alexandria	Tax Charge	1795	Tax PP 1795:14
Hersh, Robert	Arlington	Inventory	1872	WB9:340
Hertson, Charles	Arlington	Defendant	1811	ACO:115
Heshuyson, Lewis D.	Alexandria	Tax Charge	1790	Tax PP 1790:06
Heshuyson, [L.D.], Fairfax St.	Alexandria	Occupant	1790	Tax L 1790:12
Heslop, Robert, b. Maryport	Arlington	Alien Entry	1818	RA:24/11/18
Hess, Barbary	Alexandria	Tax Charge	1788	Tax PP 1788:07
Hess, Barbary	Alexandria	Tax Charge	1789	Tax PP 1789:08
Hess, Jacob	Alexandria	Owner	1787	Tax L 1787:13
Hess, Jacob	Alexandria	Tax Charge	1787	Tax PP 1787:06
Hess, Jacob, King St.	Alexandria	Occupant	1787	Tax L 1787:13
Hessey, Caleb, cutler	Alexandria	Housekeeper	1808	1808(2):13A
Hetherly, Nathan	Alexandria	Tax Charge	1800	Tax PP 1800:13
Hewes & Miller	Alexandria	Mer. License	1800	Tax PP 1800:54(14)w
Hewes & Miller, plt.	Alexandria	Suit	1803	CRD:166

NAME OR SUBJECT	LOCATION	TYPE	YEAR	REFERENCE(S)
Hewes, A., Fairfax St.	Alexandria	Occupant	1795	Tax L 1795:14
Hewes, A., Prince St.	Alexandria	Occupant	1795	Tax L 1795:14
Hewes, Aaron	Alexandria	Tax Charge	1788	Tax PP 1788:08
Hewes, Aaron	Alexandria	Tax Charge	1790	Tax PP 1790:06
Hewes, Aaron	Alexandria	Tax Charge	1796	Tax LP 1796:12
Hewes, Aaron	Alexandria	Tax Charge	1799	Tax PP 1799:17
Hewes, Aaron	Arlington	Admin.	1819	WB2:304
Hewes, Aaron & wife, hatter	Alexandria	Housekeeper	1799	1799(2):02A
Hewes, Aaron, hatter	Alexandria	Head	1810	1810(1):01A
Hewes, Aaron, Prince St.	Alexandria	Owner	1790	Tax L 1790:05
Hewes, Aaron, Prince St.	Alexandria	Occupant	1790	Tax L 1790:05
Hewes, Abm.	Alexandria	Tax Charge	1795	Tax PP 1795:13
Hewes, Abm.	Alexandria	Tax Charge	1798	Tax PP 1798:07
Hewes, Abraham	Arlington	Account	1824	AB5:356; LVA-LP
Hewes, Abraham	Arlington	Account	1828	AB6:442; LVA-LP
Hewes, Abram	Alexandria	Tax Charge	1796	Tax LP 1796:12
Hewes, Abram	Alexandria	Tax Charge	1796	Tax PP 1796:08
Hewes, Abram	Alexandria	Tax Charge	1799	Tax PP 1799:17
Hewes, Abram	Alexandria	Tax Charge	1800	Tax PP 1800:13
Hewes, Abram	Arlington	Inventory	1805	WBB:206, 224
Hewes, Abram	Arlington	Admin.	1805	WBB:201
Hewes, Abram	Arlington	Sale	1806	WBB:244
Hewes, Abram	Arlington	Account	1807	WBB:470
Hewes, Abram	Arlington	Account	1813	AB1:320; LVA-LP
Hewes, Abram & wife, merchant	Alexandria	Housekeeper	1799	1799(2):17A
Hewes, Abrm.	Alexandria	Tax Charge	1798	Tax PP 1798:07
Hewes, Abrm., Prince St.	Alexandria	Occupant	1795	Tax L 1795:18
Hewes, Aron	Alexandria	Tax Charge	1795	Tax PP 1795:13
Hewes, Aron	Alexandria	Tax Charge	1796	Tax PP 1796:08
Hewes, Aron, Fairfax St.	Alexandria	Owner	1795	Tax L 1795:14
Hewes, Aron, Prince St.	Alexandria	Owner	1795	Tax L 1795:14
Hewes, Aron, w(4)1, hatter	Alexandria	Head	1796	1796(3):4
Hewes, Deborah, c/o Abram	Arlington	Guard.	1813	WB1:262
Hewes, Eliza	Arlington	Account	1844	AB8:490; LVA-LP
Hewes, Eliza	Arlington	Exor.	1844	AB8:441
Hewes, Eliza	Arlington	Inventory	1844	AB8:449; LVA-LP
Hewes, Eliza	Arlington	Will P.	1844	OCR1842:063
Hewes, Eliza	Arlington	Will P.	1844	OCR1842:067
Hewes, Eliza	Arlington	Will	1844	WB4:377; File #412A
Hewes, Elizabeth	Arlington	Admin.	1812	WB1:173
Hewes, Jno., Water St.	Alexandria	Occupant	1795	Tax L 1795:33
Hewes, John, ship carpenter	Alexandria	Head	1810	1810(1):10A
Hewes, Lydia	Arlington	Bond	1853	BB(np)
Hewes, Lydia	Arlington	Will	1853	WB6:260; File #501A
Hewes, Maria	Arlington	Apprentice	1813	OCR1811:201
Hewes, Robert & wife, laborer	Alexandria	Head	1800	1800(4):12A
Hewes, Sarah Ann	Alexandria	Will	1879	WB1:262; LP
Hewes, Sarah Ann, c/o Abram	Arlington	Guard.	1813	WB1:262
Hewes [Hughs], William H.	Arlington	Account	1828	AB6:446; LVA-LP
Hewett, Rachel	Alexandria	Tax Charge	1800	Tax PP 1800:13
Hewett, Richard	Arlington	Debts	1821	AB4:283; LVA-LP
Hewett, Richard L.	Arlington	Account	1816	AB2:338
Hewett, Richd., gentleman	Alexandria	Head	1810	1810(3):06A
Hewitt, Capt.	Alexandria	Tax Charge	1796	Tax LP 1796:11
Hewitt, James, orphans of	Arlington	Guard.	1816	WB2:144
Hewitt, Margaret B.	Arlington	Will	1854	WB6:354; File #509A
Hewitt, Margaret B.	Arlington	Appraisal	1854	WB6:365; LVA-LP
Hewitt, Margaret B.	Arlington	Account	1857	WB7:211; LVA-LP
Hewitt, Margaret B., heirs of	Arlington	Account	1857	WB7:213; LVA-LP
Hewitt, Peter, grantor	Arlington	Indenture D.	1828	ID:181
Hewitt, Peter, in jail	Arlington	Insolvent	1828	ID:179

NAME OR SUBJECT	LOCATION	TYPE	YEAR	REFERENCE(S)
Hewitt, Rd.	Alexandria	Reference	1808	1808(4):24A
Hewitt, Richard	Alexandria	Tax Charge	1796	Tax PP 1796:08
Hewitt, Richard	Alexandria	Tax Charge	1799	Tax PP 1799:17
Hewitt, Richard	Alexandria	Tax Charge	1800	Tax PP 1800:13
Hewitt, Richard L.	Arlington	Account	1814	LVA-LP
Hewitt, Richard L.	Arlington	Bond	1814	WB1:292
Hewitt, Richard L.	Arlington	Will	1814	WB1:293; File #120A
Hewitt, Richd.	Alexandria	Tax Charge	1795	Tax PP 1795:12
Hewitt, Richd.	Alexandria	Tax Charge	1798	Tax PP 1798:08
Hewitt, Richd., Royal St.	Alexandria	Owner	1795	Tax L 1795:13
Hewitt, Thomas M., c/o Margaret B.	Arlington	Guard.	1854	BB(np)
Hewitt, Thomas W., c/o Margaret B.	Arlington	Guard.	1854	WB6:354
Hewitt, Thos. W.	Alexandria	Boarder	1808	1808(2):11A
Hewitt, William	Alexandria	Tax Charge	1800	Tax PP 1800:15
Hews, A.	Alexandria	Reference	1808	1808(4):27B
Hews, Aaron, hatter	Alexandria	Housekeeper	1808	1808(1):02A
Hews, Johh, ship carpenter	Alexandria	Housekeeper	1808	1808(1):06A
Hews, John	Alexandria	Tax Charge	1800	Tax PP 1800:13
Hews, Wm.	Alexandria	Boarder	1808	1808(1):06A
Heyes, Aw.	Alexandria	Tax Charge	1798	Tax PP 1798:07
Hibb, Thomas	Arlington	Account	1812	AB1:216
Hickling, Phebe	Arlington	Guard. Acct.	1822	AB5:129
Hickman, Jno.	Alexandria	Tithable +21	1787	Tax PP 1787:07
Hickman, Jno. & Co., King St.	Alexandria	Occupant	1795	Tax L 1795:07
Hickman, Jno. & Co., Union St.	Alexandria	Occupant	1795	Tax L 1795:18
Hickman, John	Alexandria	Tithable +16	1788	Tax PP 1788:07
Hickman, Thomas	Alexandria	Tithable +21	1787	Tax PP 1787:07
Hickman, Thomas	Alexandria	Tithable +16	1788	Tax PP 1788:07
Hickman, Thomas	Alexandria	Tithable +16	1789	Tax PP 1789:08
Hickman, William	Alexandria	Tax Charge	1787	Tax PP 1787:07
Hickman, William	Alexandria	Tax Charge	1789	Tax PP 1789:08
Hickman, William	Alexandria	Tax Charge	1790	Tax PP 1790:06
Hickman, William & wife, merchant	Alexandria	Head	1795	1795(4):09
Hickman, William, King St.	Alexandria	Occupant	1790	Tax L 1790:08
Hickman, William, St. Asaph St.	Alexandria	Owner	1790	Tax L 1790:05
Hickman, William, St. Asaph St.	Alexandria	Occupant	1790	Tax L 1790:05
Hickman, Wm.	Alexandria	Tax Charge	1788	Tax PP 1788:07
Hickman, Wm.	Alexandria	Tax Charge	1795	Tax PP 1795:14
Hickman, Wm.	Alexandria	Tax Charge	1796	Tax LP 1796:12
Hickman, Wm.	Alexandria	Tax Charge	1796	Tax PP 1796:08
Hickman, Wm.	Alexandria	Tax Charge	1798	Tax PP 1798:08
Hickman, Wm., St. Asaph St.	Alexandria	Owner	1795	Tax L 1795:11
Hickman, Wm., St. Asaph St.	Alexandria	Occupant	1795	Tax L 1795:11
Hicks, Isaac	Alexandria	Boarder	1808	1808(1):04A
Hicks, James, labourer	Alexandria	Head	1810	1810(1):10A
Hicks, Jas., lawyer	Alexandria	Housekeeper	1808	1808(1):10A
Hicks, John	Alexandria	Boarder	1808	1808(1):10A
Hicks, Nehemiah, at his house	Arlington	Ordinary	1827	OBL4(np)
Hicks, Nehemiah, at his house	Arlington	Ordinary	1828	OBL4(np)
Hicks, Nehemiah, at his house	Arlington	Ordinary	1831	OBL4(np)
Hicks, Nehemiah, his house Union/Duke	Arlington	Ordinary	1833	OBL5(np)
Hide, Jno.	Alexandria	Tax Charge	1795	Tax PP 1795:12
Higdon, Jno.	Alexandria	Tax Charge	1798	Tax PP 1798:07
Higdon, Jno. & wife, bricklayer	Alexandria	Housekeeper	1799	1799(2):12A
Higdon, John	Alexandria	Tax Charge	1799	Tax PP 1799:17
Higdon, John	Alexandria	Tax Charge	1800	Tax PP 1800:13
Higginson, Henry, owner	Arlington	Respondent	1811	ACO:119
Hiker, Henry, King St.	Alexandria	Occupant	1790	Tax L 1790:01
Hilaman, Conrad	Alexandria	Tax Charge	1799	Tax PP 1799:16
Hilaman, Conrod	Alexandria	Tax Charge	1795	Tax PP 1795:12
Hileman, Conrod	Alexandria	Tax Charge	1787	Tax PP 1787:07

NAME OR SUBJECT	LOCATION	TYPE	YEAR	REFERENCE(S)
Hileman, Peter	Alexandria	Tax Charge	1787	Tax PP 1787:07
Hill, Asa	Alexandria	Tax Charge	1795	Tax PP 1795:12
Hill, Asa	Alexandria	Tax Charge	1796	Tax LP 1796:11
Hill, Asa	Alexandria	Tax Charge	1796	Tax PP 1796:07
Hill, Asa	Alexandria	Tax Charge	1798	Tax PP 1798:08
Hill, Asa	Alexandria	Tax Charge	1799	Tax PP 1799:16
Hill, Asa	Alexandria	Tax Charge	1800	Tax PP 1800:13
Hill, Asa, def.	Alexandria	Suit	1801	CRC:022, 026
Hill, Asa, Fairfax St.	Alexandria	Occupant	1795	Tax L 1795:03
Hill, Bennett, bricklayer	Alexandria	Head	1810	1810(4):01A
Hill, Caddus, cooper	Alexandria	Head	1810	1810(4):08A
Hill, David, c/o Elizabeth	Arlington	Apprentice	1812	OCR1811:145
Hill, E., Union St.	Alexandria	Occupant	1787	Tax L 1787:20
Hill, Eliza., Duke St.	Alexandria	Occupant	1790	Tax L 1790:03
Hill, Geo.	Alexandria	Tax Charge	1796	Tax LP 1796:12
Hill, Geo. & wife, cooper	Alexandria	Housekeeper	1799	1799(2):16A
Hill, Geo., shopkeeper	Alexandria	Housekeeper	1808	1808(1):03A
Hill, Geo., Union St.	Alexandria	Occupant	1795	Tax L 1795:01
Hill, Geo., Water St.	Alexandria	Occupant	1795	Tax L 1795:21
Hill, George	Alexandria	Tax Charge	1787	Tax PP 1787:07
Hill, George	Alexandria	Tax Charge	1788	Tax PP 1788:08
Hill, George	Alexandria	Tax Charge	1789	Tax PP 1789:09
Hill, George	Alexandria	Tax Charge	1790	Tax PP 1790:07
Hill, George	Alexandria	Tax Charge	1795	Tax PP 1795:14
Hill, George	Alexandria	Tax Charge	1796	Tax PP 1796:08
Hill, George	Alexandria	Tax Charge	1798	Tax PP 1798:07
Hill, George	Alexandria	Tax Charge	1799	Tax PP 1799:17
Hill, George	Alexandria	Tax Charge	1800	Tax PP 1800:13
Hill, George & wife, cooper	Alexandria	Head	1795	1795(4):03
Hill, George & wife Elisebeth	Alexandria	Resident	1800	1800(4):03B
Hill, George, cooper	Alexandria	Head	1800	1800(4):03A
Hill, George, cooper	Alexandria	Head	1810	1810(1):12A
Hill, George, nr. Water St.	Alexandria	Occupant	1790	Tax L 1790:03
Hill, James, grantee	Arlington	Indenture D.	1815	ID2:390
Hill, James, grantor	Arlington	Indenture D.	1817	ID2:410
Hill, James, in jail	Arlington	Insolvent	1817	ID2:406, 407
Hill, Jno. & wife, blacksmith	Alexandria	Housekeeper	1799	1799(2):16A
Hill, Jno., Water St.	Alexandria	Occupant	1795	Tax L 1795:14
Hill, Jno., Water St.	Alexandria	Owner	1795	Tax L 1795:14
Hill, Jno., Water St.	Alexandria	Occupant	1795	Tax L 1795:17
Hill, John	Alexandria	Tithable +16	1788	Tax PP 1788:18
Hill, John	Alexandria	Tax Charge	1789	Tax PP 1789:09
Hill, John	Alexandria	Tax Charge	1790	Tax PP 1790:07
Hill, John	Alexandria	Tax Charge	1795	Tax PP 1795:13
Hill, John	Alexandria	Tax Charge	1796	Tax LP 1796:13
Hill, John	Alexandria	Tax Charge	1796	Tax PP 1796:09
Hill, John	Alexandria	Tax Charge	1798	Tax PP 1798:07
Hill, John	Alexandria	Tax Charge	1799	Tax PP 1799:17
Hill, John	Alexandria	Tax Charge	1800	Tax PP 1800:15
Hill, John	Arlington	Admin.	1804	WBB:080
Hill, John	Arlington	Inventory	1804	WBB:083; LVA-LP
Hill, John	Arlington	Account	1805	WBB:221, 236; LVA-LP
Hill, John & wife, smith	Alexandria	Head	1795	1795(4):01
Hill, John & wife Mary	Alexandria	Resident	1800	1800(4):04B
Hill, John, at his house	Arlington	Ordinary	1829	OBL4(np)
Hill, John, grantor	Arlington	Indenture D.	1831	ID:295
Hill, John, in jail bounds	Arlington	Insolvent	1831	ID:293
Hill, John, labourer	Alexandria	Head	1810	1810(3):07A
Hill, John, smith	Alexandria	Head	1800	1800(4):04A
Hill, John T.	Alexandria	Will	1890	WB1:552; LP
Hill, John Thomas	Arlington	Apprentice	1842	OCR1842:005

NAME OR SUBJECT	LOCATION	TYPE	YEAR	REFERENCE(S)
Hill, Jos.	Alexandria	Boarder	1808	1808(4):27A
Hill, Joseph, retailer	Alexandria	Housekeeper	1808	1808(2):11A
Hill, Josiah	Alexandria	Tax Charge	1800	Tax PP 1800:13
Hill, Josiah, paver	Alexandria	Head	1810	1810(1):10A
Hill, Josias	Alexandria	Tax Charge	1799	Tax PP 1799:18
Hill, Josias & wife, drayman	Alexandria	Housekeeper	1799	1799(2):12A
Hill, Josias, laborer	Alexandria	Housekeeper	1808	1808(4):29A
Hill, Lawrence, cooper	Alexandria	Head	1810	1810(1):03A
Hill, Lucey, laundress	Alexandria	Head	1800	1800(4):13A
Hill, Lucy	Alexandria	Resident	1800	1800(4):13B
Hill, Mary Ellen	Alexandria	Will	1889	LP
Hill, Samuel	Alexandria	Mer. License	1800	Tax PP 1800:54(14)r
Hill, Samuel, in Alexandria Co.	Arlington	Ordinary	1825	OBL4(np)
Hill, Willam B., of Baltimore MD	Alexandria	Will	1879	WB1:253; LP
Hillis, Michael J.	Arlington	Appraisal	1874	WB9:370
Hillman, Thomas	Alexandria	Tithable +16	1789	Tax PP 1789:10
Hills, Eliza, c/o Samuel	Arlington	Guard.	1831	WB4:041
Hills, Josiah B., grantee	Arlington	Indenture D.	1833	ID:412
Hills, Luther, c/o Samuel	Arlington	Guard.	1831	WB4:041
Hills, Reuben, at his house	Arlington	Ordinary	1834	OBL5(np)
Hills, Samuel Edwin, c/o Samuel	Arlington	Guard.	1831	WB4:041
Hills, Samuel, grantor	Arlington	Indenture D.	1833	ID:412
Hills, Samuel, in jail	Arlington	Insolvent	1833	ID:410
Hilman, Thomas	Alexandria	Tithable +21	1787	Tax PP 1787:08
Hilman, Thomas	Alexandria	Tithable +16	1788	Tax PP 1788:01
Hilton, Hannah	Arlington	Will P. (N)	1843	OCR1842:034, 035
Hilton, Hannah	Arlington	Will (N)	1843	WB4:324; File #349A
Hilton, Henry	Arlington	Will	1806	WBB:256
Hilton, James	Arlington	Appraisal	1875	WB9:383
Hilton, Saml.	Alexandria	Tax Charge	1798	Tax PP 1798:07
Hilton, Saml.	Alexandria	Head	1800	1800(4):03A
Hilton, Saml. & wife, innkeeper	Alexandria	Housekeeper	1799	1799(2):07A
Hilton, Samuel	Alexandria	Tax Charge	1799	Tax PP 1799:18
Hilton, Samuel	Alexandria	Tax Charge	1800	Tax PP 1800:15
Hilton, Wm., seaman	Alexandria	Head	1810	1810(1):05A
Hinds, Jno.	Alexandria	Boarder	1799	1799(2):18A
Hineman, Jacob	Alexandria	Tax Charge	1787	Tax PP 1787:07
Hineman, Mrs.	Alexandria	Head	1795	1795(4):07
Hingson, N.	Alexandria	License Due	1800	Tax PP 1800:54(24)
Hingston, Nicholas	Alexandria	Mer. License	1798	Tax PP 1798:20-3
Hingston, Nicholas	Alexandria	Mer. License	1799	Tax PP 1799:52-05r
Hingston, Nicholas	Alexandria	Tax Charge	1799	Tax PP 1799:16
Hingston, Nicholas	Alexandria	Tax Charge	1800	Tax PP 1800:15
Hingston, Nicholas	Arlington	Inventory	1830	LVA-LP
Hingston, Nicholas	Arlington	Bond	1830	WB3:358
Hingston, Nicholas	Arlington	Will	1830	WB3:357; File #283A
Hingston, Nicholas & wife, grocer	Alexandria	Housekeeper	1799	1799(2):08A
Hingston, Nicholas, retailer	Alexandria	Housekeeper	1808	1808(1):04A
Hingston, Nichs., bottanist	Alexandria	Head	1810	1810(1):04A
Hinkle, Nathaniel A., in Alexandria Co.	Arlington	Ordinary	1827	OBL4(np)
Hinkley, Ebenezer, N., Seaman	Arlington	Libellant	1818	ACO:152
Hipkins, Lewis	Alexandria	Boarder	1808	1808(3):18A
Hipkins, Lewis, Estate (children), def.	Alexandria	Suit	1803	CRH:219
Hipkins, Lewis, of Fairfax Co.	Alexandria	Will	1794	CRH:337
Hipkins, Lewis, of Washington DC	Alexandria	Will	1888	WB1:499; LP
Hipkins, Susanna, relict of Lewis	Alexandria	Deed	1797	CRH:341
Hiseler, Charles	Alexandria	Tax Charge	1796	Tax LP 1796:11
Hitson, Henry	Alexandria	Tax Charge	1789	Tax PP 1789:09
Hixson, Jno.	Alexandria	Boarder	1808	1808(4):25A
Hoaff, John	Alexandria	Serv./Appt.	1800	1800(4):15B
Hoaks, Richd., labourer	Alexandria	Head	1810	1810(4):04A

NAME OR SUBJECT	LOCATION	TYPE	YEAR	REFERENCE(S)
Hoar [Hore], James	Arlington	Sale	1858	WB7:338; LVA-LP
Hoar [Hore], James	Arlington	Appraisal	1858	WB7:337; LVA-LP
Hobbs, Sally	Arlington	Apprentice	1816	OCR1811:324
Hobrook, Abiel	Arlington	Defendant	1823	ACO:222
Hobs, Jeremh.	Alexandria	Tax Charge	1795	Tax PP 1795:13
Hobson, William	Alexandria	Tithable +21	1787	Tax PP 1787:12
Hodge, John, apprentice cooper	Alexandria	Boarder	1795	1795(4a):01
Hodge, Morgan	Alexandria	Tax Charge	1789	Tax PP 1789:08
Hodges, Hanson (C)	Alexandria	Boarder	1808	1808(4):27B
Hodges, J.	Alexandria	Tax Charge	1799	Tax PP 1799:16
Hodgkin, John	Alexandria	Tax Charge	1799	Tax PP 1799:17
Hodgkin, John	Arlington	Ordinary	1802	OBL1(np)
Hodgkin, John	Arlington	Ordinary	1803	OBL1(np)
Hodgkin, John	Arlington	Ordinary	1807	OBL2(np)
Hodgkin, John	Arlington	Apprentice	1815	OCR1811:261
Hodgkin, John	Arlington	Apprentice	1816	OCR1811:262
Hodgkin, John, def.	Alexandria	Suit	1808	CRG:077
Hodgkin, Robert	Alexandria	Will	1876	WB1:181; LP
Hodgkin, Walter	Alexandria	Tax Charge	1798	Tax PP 1798:08
Hodgkin, Walter	Alexandria	Tax Charge	1799	Tax PP 1799:16
Hodgkins, James	Arlington	Apprentice	1827	OCR1822:140a
Hodgkins, John	Arlington	Ordinary	1804	OBL1(np)
Hodgkins, John	Arlington	Ordinary	1806	OBL1(np)
Hodgkins, John	Arlington	Ordinary	1809	OBL2(np)
Hodgkins, John	Arlington	Inventory	1811	AB1:124; LVA-LP
Hodgkins, John	Arlington	Will	1811	WB1:089; File #094A
Hodgkins, John	Arlington	Bond	1811	WB1:090
Hodgkins, John	Arlington	Account	1812	AB1:263
Hodgkins, John	Arlington	Sale	1812	AB1:262; LVA-LP
Hodgkins, John	Arlington	Account	1815	AB2:195; LVA-LP
Hodgkins, John	Arlington	Account	1832	LVA-LP
Hodgkins, John, plt.	Alexandria	Suit	1801	CRB:099
Hodgkins, Rachael	Arlington	Renounce	1812	WB1:191
Hodgkins, Thomas	Arlington	Inventory	1805	WBB:148
Hodgkins, Thomas	Arlington	Sale	1805	WBB:157
Hodgkins, Thomas	Arlington	Admin.	1805	WBB:144
Hodgkins, Thomas	Arlington	Account	1808	WBC:147; LVA-LP
Hodgkinson, Anthony	Arlington	Admin.	1827	OCR1822:140
Hodgkinson, Anthony	Arlington	Will (N)	1827	WB3:290; File #259A
Hodgkinson, Anthony	Arlington	Bond	1827	WB3:290
Hodgkinson, Elizabeth	Alexandria	Boarder	1799	1799(2):02A
Hodgskin, Susanah, shopkeeper	Alexandria	Head	1810	1810(2):07A
Hodgskins, John	Arlington	Ordinary	1808	OBL2(np)
Hodgskins, John, tavern keeper	Alexandria	Head	1810	1810(3):03A
Hodgson, Cornelia L.	Arlington	Appraisal	1860	WB7:544; LVA-LP
Hodgson, John	Alexandria	Tax Charge	1788	Tax PP 1788:08
Hodgson, John	Arlington	Plaintiff	1802	PA:310
Hodgson, John Edmund	Arlington	Apprentice	1805	OCR1801:303
Hodgson v. Hodgson	Arlington	Suit	1840	LVA-LP (Box 214)
Hodgson, William	Alexandria	Tithable +16	1788	Tax PP 1788:14
Hodgson, William	Alexandria	Tax Charge	1789	Tax PP 1789:08
Hodgson, William	Alexandria	Tax Charge	1790	Tax PP 1790:06
Hodgson, William	Alexandria	Tax Charge	1795	Tax PP 1795:14
Hodgson, William	Alexandria	Tax Charge	1796	Tax PP 1796:09
Hodgson, William	Alexandria	Tax Charge	1798	Tax PP 1798:08
Hodgson, William	Alexandria	Mer. License	1799	Tax PP 1799:52-05w
Hodgson, William	Alexandria	Tax Charge	1799	Tax PP 1799:16
Hodgson, William	Alexandria	Tax Charge	1799	Tax PP 1799:17
Hodgson, William	Alexandria	Freight	1800	CRD:202
Hodgson, William	Alexandria	Mer. License	1800	Tax PP 1800:54(14)w
Hodgson, William	Alexandria	Tax Charge	1800	Tax PP 1800:13

NAME OR SUBJECT	LOCATION	TYPE	YEAR	REFERENCE(S)
Hodgson, William	Alexandria	Account B.	1807	CRL:034
Hodgson, William	Arlington	Defendant	1808	ACO:085
Hodgson, William	Arlington	Defendant	1808	ACO:081, 082
Hodgson, William	Arlington	Defendant	1808	ACO:091
Hodgson, William	Arlington	Defendant	1809	ACO:106, 109
Hodgson, William	Arlington	Inventory	1821	AB4:225; LVA-LP
Hodgson, William	Arlington	Admin.	1821	WB2:414
Hodgson, William	Arlington	Account	1826	AB6:204; LVA-LP
Hodgson, William	Arlington	Admin.	1832	WB4:053
Hodgson, William	Arlington	Admin.	1841	WB4:302
Hodgson, William & Co.	Arlington	Inventory	1819	AB4:084
Hodgson, William & wife Portia	Alexandria	Deed	1800	CRL:030
Hodgson, William, 2, merchant	Alexandria	Head	1796	1796(3):6
Hodgson, William, assignee, plt.	Alexandria	Suit	1801	CRB:122
Hodgson, William, def.	Alexandria	Suit	1803	CRD:095
Hodgson, William, def.	Alexandria	Suit	1810	CRG:369
Hodgson, William, def.	Alexandria	Suit	1813	CRK:186
Hodgson, William, Fairfax St.	Alexandria	Owner	1790	Tax L 1790:05
Hodgson, William L.	Arlington	Library	1842	AB8:282
Hodgson, William L.	Arlington	Inventory	1842	AB8:281; LVA-LP
Hodgson, William L.	Arlington	Account	1842	OCR1842:008
Hodgson, William L.	Arlington	Account	1843	AB8:386; LVA-LP
Hodgson, William L.	Arlington	Account	1847	WB5:061; LVA-LP
Hodgson, William L., grantee	Arlington	Indenture D.	1827	ID:122
Hodgson, William L., grantee	Arlington	Indenture D.	1832	ID:381
Hodgson, William Ludwell	Arlington	Will	1841	WB4:297; File #387A
Hodgson, William Ludwell	Arlington	Bond	1841	WB4:298
Hodgson, William Ludwell, grantee	Arlington	Indenture D.	1829	ID:234
Hodgson, William, on Colchester Road	Frederick	Plat	1820	E
Hodgson, William, on the wharf	Alexandria	Occupant	1790	Tax L 1790:01
Hodgson, William, plt.	Alexandria	Suit	1801	CRB:069
Hodgson, William, plt.	Alexandria	Suit	1801	CRB:135
Hodgson, William, plt.	Alexandria	Suit	1801	CRB:113
Hodgson, William, plt.	Alexandria	Suit	1802	CRD:193
Hodgson, William, plt.	Alexandria	Suit	1803	CRD:090
Hodgson, William, plt.	Alexandria	Suit	1805	CRG:242
Hodgson, William, plt.	Alexandria	Suit	1807	CRF:159
Hodgson, William, Prince St.	Alexandria	Owner	1790	Tax L 1790:05
Hodgson, William, Prince St.	Alexandria	Occupant	1790	Tax L 1790:06
Hodgson, William, Prince St.	Alexandria	Occupant	1790	Tax L 1790:12
Hodgson, William, Water St.	Alexandria	Owner	1790	Tax L 1790:05
Hodgson, William, Water St.	Alexandria	Occupant	1790	Tax L 1790:05
Hodgson, Wm.	Alexandria	Tax Charge	1796	Tax LP 1796:12
Hodgson, Wm., merchant	Alexandria	Housekeeper	1808	1808(1):02A
Hodgson, Wm., Prince St.	Alexandria	Owner	1795	Tax L 1795:11
Hodgson, Wm., wharf & warehouse	Alexandria	Occupant	1795	Tax L 1795:01
Hodgson, Wm., wholesale merchant	Alexandria	Housekeeper	1799	1799(2):02A
Hoenstein, Frederick	Arlington	Will (NR)	1877	COB2:054; File #084A
Hoff, John, clerk	Alexandria	Head	1810	1810(2):05A
Hoffman, Daniel (servant)	Alexandria	Tithable +21	1787	Tax PP 1787:11
Hoffman, Jacob	Alexandria	Tax Charge	1798	Tax PP 1798:07
Hoffman, Jacob	Alexandria	Mer. License	1798	Tax PP 1798:20-3
Hoffman, Jacob	Alexandria	Tax Charge	1799	Tax PP 1799:16
Hoffman, Jacob	Alexandria	Mer. License	1799	Tax PP 1799:52-04w
Hoffman, Jacob	Alexandria	Agreement	1800	CRC:165
Hoffman, Jacob	Alexandria	Mer. License	1800	Tax PP 1800:54(14)w
Hoffman, Jacob	Alexandria	Tax Charge	1800	Tax PP 1800:15
Hoffman, Jacob & wife, merchant	Alexandria	Housekeeper	1799	1799(2):03A
Hoffman, Jacob, merchant	Alexandria	Housekeeper	1808	1808(3):18A
Hoffman, Jacob, plt	Alexandria	Suit	1801	CRB:183
Hoffman, Jacob, plt.	Alexandria	Suit	1801	CRB:356

NAME OR SUBJECT	LOCATION	TYPE	YEAR	REFERENCE(S)
Hoffman, Jacob, plt.	Alexandria	Suit	1802	CRC:161
Hoffman, Peter, of Baltimore MD	Arlington	Will	1853	WB6:233; File #498A
Hog, James	Alexandria	Deposition	1805	CRE:266
Hogan, Edmd.	Alexandria	Tax Charge	1798	Tax PP 1798:07
Hogan, Edmund	Alexandria	Tax Charge	1799	Tax PP 1799:17
Hogland, John	Alexandria	Boarder	1808	1808(2):10A
Hoke, George	Arlington	Admin.	1805	WBB:178
Hoke, George	Arlington	Sale	1805	WBB:184
Hoke, George	Arlington	Inventory	1805	WBB:180
Hoke, George	Arlington	Account	1806	WBB:331; LVA-LP
Hokes, Geo.	Alexandria	Tax Charge	1795	Tax PP 1795:12
Hokes, Geo.	Alexandria	Tax Charge	1796	Tax LP 1796:11
Hokes, Geo.	Alexandria	Tax Charge	1798	Tax PP 1798:08
Hokes, Geo. & wife, musician	Alexandria	Housekeeper	1799	1799(2):11A
Hokes, Geo., Royal St.	Alexandria	Occupant	1795	Tax L 1795:27
Hokes, George	Alexandria	Tax Charge	1799	Tax PP 1799:18
Hokes, George	Alexandria	Tax Charge	1800	Tax PP 1800:13
Hokes, Jacob	Arlington	Witness	1794	OT:07/11/1794
Hokes, Jacob	Alexandria	Tax Charge	1795	Tax PP 1795:12
Hokes, Jacob	Alexandria	Tax Charge	1796	Tax LP 1796:11
Hokes, Jacob	Alexandria	Tax Charge	1796	Tax PP 1796:08
Hokes, Jacob	Alexandria	Tax Charge	1798	Tax PP 1798:07
Hokes, Jacob	Alexandria	Tax Charge	1799	Tax PP 1799:17
Hokes, Jacob	Alexandria	Tax Charge	1800	Tax PP 1800:15
Hokes, Jacob & wife, drayman	Alexandria	Housekeeper	1799	1799(2):19A
Hokes, Jacob & wife Mary	Alexandria	Resident	1800	1800(4):09B
Hokes, Jacob, drayman	Alexandria	Head	1800	1800(4):09A
Hokes, Jacob, drayman	Alexandria	Head	1810	1810(1):10A
Hokes, Jacob, Fairfax St.	Alexandria	Occupant	1795	Tax L 1795:11
Hokes, Jacob, Fairfax St.	Alexandria	Owner	1795	Tax L 1795:11
Holbroke, John, master	Arlington	Respondent	1803	ACO:022, 023
Holbrook Abiel	Arlington	Defendant	1824	ACO:248
Holbrook Abiel	Arlington	Defendant	1825	ACO:253, 258
Holbrook, Abiel	Arlington	Defendant	1826	ACO:264
Holbrook, Abiel	Arlington	Defendant	1827	ACO:268, 274
Holbrook, Abiel, def.	Alexandria	Suit	1819	CRK:501
Holbrook, Abiel, grantor	Arlington	Indenture D.	1827	ID:122
Holbrook, Abiel, in jail	Arlington	Insolvent	1827	ID:120
Holbrook, Abiel, plt., plt.	Alexandria	Suit	1820	CRL:213
Holbrook, Alice	Alexandria	Boarder	1808	1808(3):22A
Holland, Levi, plt.	Alexandria	Suit	1802	CRD:188, 190
Holliday, Betty	Alexandria	Resident	1800	1800(4):14B
Holliday, Betty, labourer	Alexandria	Boarder	1800	1800(4):14A
Holliday, James, Wolfe St.	Alexandria	Occupant	1787	Tax L 1787:12
Holliday, Jas.	Alexandria	Tax Charge	1787	Tax PP 1787:07
Hollingsworth, Jesse	Alexandria	Owner	1787	Tax L 1787:12
Hollingsworth, Jesse, Fairfax St.	Alexandria	Owner	1795	Tax L 1795:11
Hollingsworth, Paschall, of Philadelphia	Alexandria	Deed	1811	CRK:048
Hollingsworth, [blank]	Alexandria	Tax Charge	1796	Tax LP 1796:12
Hollinsberry, John, brickmaker	Alexandria	Housekeeper	1808	1808(3):22A
Hollinsberry, John, brickmaker	Alexandria	Head	1810	1810(3):08A
Hollinsbury, Jno.	Alexandria	Tax Charge	1800	Tax PP 1800:13
Hollinsbury, John	Alexandria	Tax Charge	1799	Tax PP 1799:17
Hollis, Chas. (C)	Alexandria	Boarder	1808	1808(2):13B
Hollis, Dennis	Arlington	Guard.	1816	WB2:112
Hollis, Sarah	Arlington	Guard.	1816	WB2:112
Hollory, Francis	Arlington	Crime	1795	OT:18/04/1795
Holly, Harry, labourer	Alexandria	Head	1810	1810(3):07A
Holly, Hester	Alexandria	Head	1810	1810(3):01A
Holly, Wm.	Alexandria	Reference	1808	1808(3):21B
Holmes, Benjamin, def.	Alexandria	Suit	1801	CRB:139

NAME OR SUBJECT	LOCATION	TYPE	YEAR	REFERENCE(S)
Holmes, Bridgett	Alexandria	Will	1874	WBC1:003; LP
Holmes, Isaac	Alexandria	Tax Charge	1795	Tax PP 1795:13
Holmes, Isaac	Alexandria	Tax Charge	1799	Tax PP 1799:18
Holmes, Jeremh.	Alexandria	Tax Charge	1795	Tax PP 1795:13
Holmes, Samuel Morris	Arlington	Crime	1794	OT:01/11/1794
Holms, Stephen	Alexandria	Tax Charge	1787	Tax PP 1787:07
Holwell, Chas.	Alexandria	Boarder	1808	1808(1):04A
Homes, Bridgett	Alexandria	Will	1874	WB1:111
Homes, Elizabeth, labourer	Alexandria	Boarder	1800	1800(4):03A
Honesty, John (C), c/o Hannah	Arlington	Apprentice	1804	OCR1801:164
Honisty, John (C)	Alexandria	Boarder	1808	1808(2):11B
Hood, Thomas	Arlington	Ordinary	1806	OBL1(np)
Hooe & Harrison, Prince St.	Alexandria	Occupant	1790	Tax L 1790:05
Hooe & Harrison, wharf	Alexandria	Occupant	1790	Tax L 1790:05
Hooe, Bernard, grantee	Arlington	Indenture D.	1829	ID:225
Hooe, Bernard, grantee	Arlington	Indenture D.	1829	ID:229
Hooe, Bernard, Jr.	Alexandria	Inventory	1871	WB1:013
Hooe, Bernard, plt.	Alexandria	Suit	1801	CRB:125
Hooe, Bernard, register of wills	Arlington	Appointment	1843	OCR1842:029
Hooe, Daniel F.	Arlington	Will	1865	WB8:247; File #625A
Hooe, Daniel F.	Arlington	Appraisal	1873	WB9:346
Hooe, Daniel F.	Arlington	Account	1877	WB9:460
Hooe, Howson L., grantor	Arlington	Indenture D.	1826	ID:014
Hooe, Howson L., grantor	Arlington	Indenture D.	1832	ID:399
Hooe, Howson L., in jail	Arlington	Insolvent	1826	ID:011
Hooe, Howson L., in jail	Arlington	Insolvent	1832	ID:397
Hooe, James	Alexandria	Tithable +16	1789	Tax PP 1789:09
Hooe, James	Alexandria	Tithable +16	1790	Tax PP 1790:07
Hooe, James	Alexandria	Tax Charge	1800	Tax PP 1800:13
Hooe, James H.	Alexandria	Tax Charge	1795	Tax PP 1795:13
Hooe, James H., def.	Alexandria	Suit	1801	CRC:039
Hooe, James H., def.	Alexandria	Suit	1822	CRL:389
Hooe, James H., merchant	Alexandria	Head	1810	1810(1):04A
Hooe, Jas. H., merchant	Alexandria	Housekeeper	1808	1808(1):04A
Hooe, Jas., merchant	Alexandria	Boarder	1799	1799(2):08A
Hooe, Junia S.	Arlington	Guard. Acct.	1836	AB7:227; LVA-LP
Hooe, Junia Servilia, c/o James H.	Arlington	Guard.	1831	WB4:034
Hooe, Lucy E.	Arlington	Guard. Acct.	1836	AB7:229; LVA-LP
Hooe, Lucy Engenia, c/o James H.	Arlington	Guard.	1831	WB4:034
Hooe, Margaret	Arlington	Appraisal	1837	LVA-LP
Hooe, Margaret	Arlington	Bond	1837	WB4:138
Hooe, Margaret	Arlington	Will	1837	WB4:137; File #348A
Hooe, Margaret	Arlington	Account	1843	AB8:384; LVA-LP
Hooe, Margaret	Arlington	Account	1843	AB8:391; LVA-LP
Hooe, Margaret	Arlington	Receipt	1844	AB8:420
Hooe, Mary Dade	Alexandria	Will	1872	WB1:058; LP
Hooe, Nancy, washwoman	Alexandria	Housekeeper	1808	1808(1):09A
Hooe, R.	Alexandria	Tax Charge	1795	Tax PP 1795:13
Hooe, R., Prince St.	Alexandria	Owner	1795	Tax L 1795:11
Hooe, R., Water St.	Alexandria	Owner	1795	Tax L 1795:11
Hooe, R.T.	Alexandria	Tax Charge	1796	Tax LP 1796:12
Hooe, R.T.	Alexandria	Tax Charge	1798	Tax PP 1798:07
Hooe, R.T.	Alexandria	Tax Charge	1799	Tax PP 1799:18
Hooe, R.T. & Co., Water St.	Alexandria	Occupant	1787	Tax L 1787:13
Hooe, Robert T.	Alexandria	Owner	1787	Tax L 1787:14
Hooe, Robert T.	Alexandria	Tax Charge	1787	Tax PP 1787:07
Hooe, Robert T.	Alexandria	Tax Charge	1790	Tax PP 1790:07
Hooe, Robert T.	Alexandria	Mer. License	1799	Tax PP 1799:52-05w
Hooe, Robert T.	Arlington	Account	1812	AB1:239; LVA-LP
Hooe, Robert T.	Arlington	Account	1821	AB4:240
Hooe, Robert T. & Co., def.	Alexandria	Suit	1801	CRD:001

NAME OR SUBJECT	LOCATION	TYPE	YEAR	REFERENCE(S)
Hooe, Robert T., 8, merchant	Alexandria	Head	1796	1796(3):5
Hooe, Robert T., def.	Alexandria	Suit	1801	CRC:039
Hooe, Robert T., Prince St.	Alexandria	Occupant	1787	Tax L 1787:14
Hooe, Robert T., Prince St.	Alexandria	Owner	1790	Tax L 1790:05
Hooe, Robert T., Water St.	Alexandria	Occupant	1787	Tax L 1787:14
Hooe, Robert T., wharf	Alexandria	Owner	1790	Tax L 1790:05(2)
Hooe, Robert Townshend	Arlington	Will	1809	WBC:185; File #039A
Hooe, Robert Townshend	Arlington	Bond	1809	WBC:196
Hooe, Robert Townshend	Arlington	Inventory	1809	WBC:201; LVA-LP
Hooe, Robert Townshend	Arlington	Sale	1810	WBC:436
Hooe, Robert Townshend, Col.	Arlington	Account	1810	WBC:442; LVA-LP
Hooe, Robt. T.	Alexandria	Tax Charge	1788	Tax PP 1788:08
Hooe, Robt. T.	Alexandria	Tax Charge	1789	Tax PP 1789:09
Hooe, Robt. T.	Alexandria	Tax Charge	1796	Tax PP 1796:09
Hooe, Robt. T. & Co.	Alexandria	Mer. License	1800	Tax PP 1800:54(14)w
Hooe, Robt. T., merchant	Alexandria	Housekeeper	1799	1799(2):08A
Hooe, Robt. T., merchant	Alexandria	Housekeeper	1808	1808(1):04A
Hooe, Rt. T., Prince St.	Alexandria	Occupant	1795	Tax L 1795:11
Hooe, Thomas P.	Arlington	Stock	1844	OCR1842:066
Hooe, Thomas P., Sr.	Arlington	Admin.	1844	OCR1842:060
Hooe, Thomas P., the Elder	Arlington	Petition	1844	LVA-LP (Box 214)
Hooe, Thomas Pratt, Sr.	Arlington	Account	1844	AB8:421; LVA-LP
Hooe, Thomas Pratt, Sr.	Arlington	Inventory	1844	AB8:420; LVA-LP
Hooe v. Hamilton's Heirs	Arlington	Suit	1833	LVA-LP (Accounts)
Hooe, Virginia L.	Arlington	Will	1832	WB4:048; File #319A
Hooe [Hoe], Robert T.	Alexandria	Tax Charge	1800	Tax PP 1800:13
Hoof, L., King St.	Alexandria	Occupant	1787	Tax L 1787:12
Hoof, Lawrence	Alexandria	Owner	1787	Tax L 1787:12
Hoof, Lawrence	Alexandria	Tax Charge	1796	Tax LP 1796:11
Hoof, Lawrence, Sr., farmer	Alexandria	Head	1810	1810(2):04A
Hooff, Ann	Arlington	Will	1836	WB4:116; File #338A
Hooff, John	Alexandria	Serv./Appt.	1800	1800(4):15B
Hooff, John	Arlington	Will	1860	WB7:543
Hooff, John, [Alexa. Bank] Clerk	Alexandria	Housekeeper	1808	1808(4):25A
Hooff, Lau.	Alexandria	Boarder	1808	1808(2):13A
Hooff, Laurence	Alexandria	Tax Charge	1789	Tax PP 1789:08
Hooff, Laurence	Alexandria	Tax Charge	1790	Tax PP 1790:07
Hooff, Laurence	Alexandria	Tax Charge	1796	Tax PP 1796:08
Hooff, Laurence	Alexandria	Tax Charge	1798	Tax PP 1798:07
Hooff, Laurence, at Brooke's Tavern	Alexandria	Deposition	1810	CRH:130
Hooff, Laurence, def.	Alexandria	Suit	1801	CRB:195
Hooff, Lawr., King St.	Alexandria	Occupant	1795	Tax L 1795:13
Hooff, Lawrence	Alexandria	Tax Charge	1787	Tax PP 1787:06
Hooff, Lawrence	Alexandria	Tax Charge	1788	Tax PP 1788:07
Hooff, Lawrence	Alexandria	Tax Charge	1795	Tax PP 1795:12
Hooff, Lawrence	Alexandria	Tax Charge	1799	Tax PP 1799:16
Hooff, Lawrence	Alexandria	Tax Charge	1800	Tax PP 1800:13
Hooff, Lawrence	Alexandria	Deposition	1822	CRL:531
Hooff, Lawrence	Arlington	Inventory	1837	LVA-LP
Hooff, Lawrence	Arlington	Bond	1837	WB4:153
Hooff, Lawrence	Arlington	Account	1842	OCR1842:012
Hooff, Lawrence	Arlington	Account	1843	AB8:361; LVA-LP
Hooff, Lawrence, def.	Alexandria	Suit	1801	CRB:356
Hooff, Lawrence, Duke St.	Alexandria	Owner	1790	Tax L 1790:05
Hooff, Lawrence, Duke St.	Alexandria	Owner	1795	Tax L 1795:13
Hooff, Lawrence, Jr.	Arlington	Juryman	1804	ACO:026
Hooff, Lawrence, King St.	Alexandria	Owner	1790	Tax L 1790:05(2)
Hooff, Lawrence, King St.	Alexandria	Occupant	1790	Tax L 1790:05
Hooff, Lawrence, King St.	Alexandria	Owner	1795	Tax L 1795:13(3)
Hooff, Lawrence, plt.	Alexandria	Suit	1803	CRD:095
Hooff, Lawrence, Sr.	Alexandria	Deposition	1819	CRK:453

NAME OR SUBJECT	LOCATION	TYPE	YEAR	REFERENCE(S)
Hooff, Lawrence, Sr.	Arlington	Will	1834	WB4:070
Hooff, Lewis	Alexandria	Boarder	1808	1808(2):13A
Hooff, Margaret	Alexandria	Owner	1787	Tax L 1787:14
Hooff, Margaret	Arlington	Will	1811	WB1:130; File #133A
Hooff, Margaret	Arlington	Bond	1812	WB1:147
Hooff, Margaret	Arlington	Account	1813	AB1:293; LVA-LP
Hooff, Margaret	Arlington	Account	1814	AB2:036; LVA-LP
Hooff, Margaret	Arlington	Settlement	1816	AB2:252
Hooff, Margaret, Fairfax St.	Alexandria	Owner	1790	Tax L 1790:06
Hooff, Margaret, Fairfax St.	Alexandria	Owner	1795	Tax L 1795:14
Hoofman, Jacob, merchant	Alexandria	Head	1810	1810(3):07A
Hoogs, George, w1, shopkeeper	Alexandria	Head	1796	1796(3):4
Hook, Andrew	Alexandria	Tithable +16	1789	Tax PP 1789:17
Hooke, Michael	Alexandria	Tithable +21	1787	Tax PP 1787:04
Hookes, Jacob, cartman	Alexandria	Housekeeper	1808	1808(1):07A
Hookes, Mary Ann	Arlington	Guard.	1822	WB3:056
Hooks, George	Alexandria	Tax Charge	1788	Tax PP 1788:07
Hooks, George	Alexandria	Tax Charge	1789	Tax PP 1789:08
Hooks, George	Alexandria	Tax Charge	1790	Tax PP 1790:06
Hooks, Jacob & wife, drayman	Alexandria	Head	1795	1795(4):07
Hooper, Charles, c/o Rebecca	Arlington	Apprentice	1814	OCR1811:226
Hooper, Edward	Arlington	Apprentice	1829	OCR1822:173
Hooper, Mary, seamstress	Alexandria	Head	1810	1810(3):07A
Hooper, Rebecca	Alexandria	Boarder	1795	1795(4a):05
Hooper, Rebecca, washwoman	Alexandria	Housekeeper	1808	1808(4):25A
Hooper, Sarah	Alexandria	Housekeeper	1799	1799(2):14A
Hooper, Sarah, semstress	Alexandria	Head	1795	1795(4):04
Hoopper, Sarah	Alexandria	Resident	1800	1800(4):10B
Hoopper, Sarah, sumpster	Alexandria	Head	1800	1800(4):10A
Hoover, Andrew	Arlington	Inventory	1857	LVA-LP
Hopcroft, Edward	Arlington	Will	1886	WB10:076; File #724A
Hope, Patty (C), washwoman	Alexandria	Housekeeper	1808	1808(4):24A
Hope, Thomas	Arlington	Admin.	1828	OCR1822:162a
Hopewell, Hugh, grantor	Arlington	Indenture D.	1812	ID2:139
Hopewell, Hugh, in prison bounds	Arlington	Insolvent	1812	ID2:136
Hopewell, Julia	Arlington	Guard.	1806	WBB:291
Hopkins, Cornelia	Arlington	Will	1817	WB2:198; File #141A
Hopkins, John	Alexandria	Tax Charge	1800	Tax PP 1800:15
Hopkins, John	Alexandria	Deed	1807	CRK:101
Hopkins, John	Alexandria	Deed	1807	CRL:120
Hopkins, John	Alexandria	Agreement	1811	CRK:112
Hopkins, John, complt.	Alexandria	Suit	1815	CRK:076
Hopkins, John, complt.	Alexandria	Suit	1817	CRK:260
Hopkins, John, def.	Alexandria	Suit	1818	CRL:092
Hopkins, John, def.	Alexandria	Suit	1818	CRK:330
Hopkins, John, def.	Alexandria	Suit	1818	CRK:390
Hopkins, John, gentleman	Alexandria	Housekeeper	1808	1808(1):02A
Hopkins, Louisa F.	Arlington	Will	1881	WB10:011; File #703A
Hopkins, Wm.	Alexandria	Boarder	1808	1808(4):24A
Hopwood, John, taylor	Alexandria	Housekeeper	1808	1808(2):13A
Hopwood, Thomas	Arlington	Apprentice	1823	OCR1822:050a
Horde, Reuben, carpenter	Alexandria	Boarder	1799	1799(2):09A
Hore, Nathaniel, Mariner	Arlington	Defendant	1802	PA:307
Hore, William, c/o Elias	Arlington	Apprentice	1801	OCR1801:010
Horner, Jno.	Alexandria	Tax Charge	1795	Tax PP 1795:13
Horner, Jno.	Alexandria	Tax Charge	1800	Tax PP 1800:13
Horner, Jno. & wife, wheelwright	Alexandria	Housekeeper	1799	1799(2):04A
Horner, Jno. & wife, ship builder	Alexandria	Housekeeper	1799	1799(2):17A
Horner, Jno., Prince St.	Alexandria	Occupant	1795	Tax L 1795:13
Horner, Jno., ship carpenter, Wilks St.	Alexandria	Occupant	1795	Tax L 1795:11
Horner, Jno., Wilks St.	Alexandria	Owner	1795	Tax L 1795:11

NAME OR SUBJECT	LOCATION	TYPE	YEAR	REFERENCE(S)
Horner, John	Alexandria	Tithable +16	1788	Tax PP 1788:03
Horner, John	Alexandria	Tax Charge	1789	Tax PP 1789:09
Horner, John	Alexandria	Tax Charge	1790	Tax PP 1790:07
Horner, John	Alexandria	Tax Charge	1796	Tax LP 1796:11
Horner, John	Alexandria	Tax Charge	1796	Tax LP 1796:13
Horner, John	Alexandria	Tax Charge	1796	Tax PP 1796:08
Horner, John	Alexandria	Tax Charge	1799	Tax PP 1799:18
Horner, John	Alexandria	Tax Charge	1799	Tax PP 1799:17
Horner, John	Arlington	Inventory	1825	AB6:067; LVA-LP
Horner, John	Arlington	Admin.	1825	OCR1822:092
Horner, John	Arlington	Will	1825	WB3:180; File #233A
Horner, John	Arlington	Bond	1825	WB3:182
Horner, John	Arlington	Account	1826	AB6:221; LVA-LP
Horner, John (S.C.)	Alexandria	Tax Charge	1800	Tax PP 1800:15
Horner, John, Jr., grantor	Arlington	Indenture D.	1810	ID2:032
Horner, John, Jr., in jail bounds	Arlington	Insolvent	1810	ID2:028
Horner, John, Jr., wheelwright	Alexandria	Housekeeper	1808	1808(4):25A
Horner, John, Prince St.	Alexandria	Owner	1795	Tax L 1795:13
Horner, John, ship carpenter	Alexandria	Head	1800	1800(4):07A
Horner, John, w2, wheelwright	Alexandria	Head	1796	1796(3):4
Horner, John, wheelwright	Alexandria	Housekeeper	1808	1808(1):01A
Horner, John, wheelwright	Alexandria	Head	1810	1810(1):02A
Horner, Louisa	Arlington	Will	1887	WB10:085; File #726A
Horner, Sarah	Alexandria	Boarder	1799	1799(2):13A
Horrer, John & wife Elizabeth	Alexandria	Resident	1800	1800(4):07B
Horsburg, Jno., merchant	Alexandria	Housekeeper	1799	1799(2):05A
Horsburg, John	Alexandria	Mer. License	1798	Tax PP 1798:20-3
Horsburg, John	Alexandria	Tax Charge	1798	Tax PP 1798:07
Horsburgh, John	Alexandria	Tax Charge	1799	Tax PP 1799:16
Horsburgh, John	Alexandria	Mer. License	1799	Tax PP 1799:52-04r
Horsburgh, John	Alexandria	Mer. License	1800	Tax PP 1800:54(14)r
Horsburgh, John	Alexandria	Deposition	1804	CRE:340
Horsburgh, John	Alexandria	Deposition	1808	CRE:326
Horsbury, Jno.	Alexandria	Boarder	1808	1808(2):10A
Horseman, Elijah, in Alexandria Co.	Arlington	Ordinary	1849	OBL6(np)
Horseman, James E.	Arlington	Appraisal	1867	WB8:550
Horwell, Ann	Alexandria	Boarder	1799	1799(2):01A
Horwell, Charles	Alexandria	Tax Charge	1800	Tax PP 1800:13
Horwell, John	Alexandria	Tax Charge	1800	Tax PP 1800:13
Horwell, Richard	Alexandria	Mer. License	1799	Tax PP 1799:52-04r
Horwell, Richard	Alexandria	Tax Charge	1799	Tax PP 1799:17
Horwell, Richard	Alexandria	Tax Charge	1800	Tax PP 1800:13
Horwell, Richard, taylor	Alexandria	Head	1810	1810(1):03A
Horwell, Richd. & wife, taylor	Alexandria	Housekeeper	1799	1799(2):07A
Horwell, Richd., habitmaker	Alexandria	Housekeeper	1808	1808(1):05A
Hosburg, John	Alexandria	Tax Charge	1796	Tax LP 1796:12
Hosburg, John	Alexandria	Tax Charge	1800	Tax PP 1800:13
Hoskins, Jas.	Alexandria	Boarder	1808	1808(2):11A
Hoskins, John	Alexandria	Tax Charge	1798	Tax PP 1798:07
Hoskins, John, tavernkeeper	Alexandria	Housekeeper	1808	1808(3):22A
Hoskins, Susanah, shopkeeper	Alexandria	Housekeeper	1808	1808(2):16A
Houck, Peter & wife, hatter	Alexandria	Housekeeper	1799	1799(2):04A
Hough, Mahlon	Alexandria	Tax Charge	1796	Tax LP 1796:11
Hough, Susan Alice	Alexandria	Will	1886	WB1:429; LP
Hough, William	Arlington	Account	1833	LVA-LP
Hough, William S.	Alexandria	Will	1887	WB1:443; LP
Hough, Wm.	Alexandria	Tax Charge	1796	Tax LP 1796:11
House, David	Alexandria	Tax Charge	1796	Tax LP 1796:11
House, David	Alexandria	Tax Charge	1796	Tax PP 1796:08
House, David	Alexandria	Tax Charge	1799	Tax PP 1799:16
House, David	Alexandria	Tax Charge	1800	Tax PP 1800:13

NAME OR SUBJECT	LOCATION	TYPE	YEAR	REFERENCE(S)
House, David	Arlington	Ordinary	1810	OBL2(np)
House, David	Arlington	Ordinary	1810	OBL2(np)
House, David & wife, blacksmith	Alexandria	Housekeeper	1799	1799(2):11A
House, David, blacksmith	Alexandria	Housekeeper	1808	1808(4):26A
House, David, blacksmith	Alexandria	Head	1810	1810(3):02A
House, David, blacksmith	Alexandria	Head	1810	1810(4):02A
Houston, Mary, children of	Arlington	Guard.	1843	OCR1842:048
How, William, grantor	Arlington	Indenture D.	1827	ID:148
How, William, in jail	Arlington	Insolvent	1827	ID:146
Howard & Snyder v. Urie's Admx.	Arlington	Suit	1845	LVA-LP (Box 214)
Howard & Snyder v. Hart	Arlington	Suit	1846	OCR1842:170
Howard, Ann	Arlington	Inventory	1824	AB5:355; LVA-LP
Howard, Ann	Arlington	Will P.	1824	OCR1822:077a
Howard, Ann	Arlington	Bond	1824	WB3:144
Howard, Ann	Arlington	Will	1824	WB3:144; File #225A
Howard, Ann	Arlington	Account	1825	AB6:129; LVA-LP
Howard, Ann R.	Arlington	Guard.	1822	WB3:062
Howard, Annie E.	Alexandria	Will	1898	WB2:299
Howard, B.	Alexandria	Reference	1808	1808(4):29A
Howard, B., Washington St.	Alexandria	Occupant	1795	Tax L 1795:12
Howard, Beal	Alexandria	Tax Charge	1787	Tax PP 1787:07
Howard, Beal	Alexandria	Tax Charge	1788	Tax PP 1788:07
Howard, Beal	Alexandria	Tax Charge	1789	Tax PP 1789:08
Howard, Beal	Alexandria	Tax Charge	1790	Tax PP 1790:07
Howard, Beal	Alexandria	Tax Charge	1796	Tax LP 1796:11
Howard, Beal	Alexandria	Tax Charge	1800	Tax PP 1800:15
Howard, Beale	Alexandria	Tax Charge	1795	Tax PP 1795:12
Howard, Beale	Alexandria	Tax Charge	1796	Tax PP 1796:09
Howard, Beale	Alexandria	Tax Charge	1798	Tax PP 1798:08
Howard, Beale	Alexandria	Tax Charge	1799	Tax PP 1799:18
Howard, Beale	Arlington	Inventory	1821	AB4:222; LVA-LP
Howard, Beale	Arlington	Sale	1821	AB4:239
Howard, Beale	Arlington	Will	1821	WB2:403
Howard, Beale	Arlington	Bond	1821	WB2:404
Howard, Beale	Arlington	Account	1822	AB5:075; LVA-LP
Howard, Beale	Arlington	Inventory	1824	AB5:363; LVA-LP
Howard, Beale	Arlington	Sale	1824	AB5:364
Howard, Beale	Arlington	Admin.	1824	OCR1822:077a
Howard, Beale	Arlington	Admin. DBN	1824	WB3:143
Howard, Beale	Arlington	Account	1825	AB6:130; LVA-LP
Howard, Beale	Arlington	Guard. Acct.	1825	AB6:132
Howard, Beale	Arlington	Guard. Acct.	1829	AB6:477; LVA-LP
Howard, Beale, Washington St.	Alexandria	Owner	1795	Tax L 1795:12
Howard, Catharine	Arlington	Guard. Acct.	1829	AB6:475; LVA-LP
Howard, Catherine	Arlington	Guard. Acct.	1825	AB6:132
Howard, Elizabeth Ann, c/o John	Arlington	Guard.	1830	WB3:386
Howard, Elizabeth, c/o John	Arlington	Guard. Acct.	1830	AB6:525; LVA-LP
Howard, Henry, c/o James	Arlington	Guard.	1813	WB1:209
Howard, Jane	Arlington	Guard.	1818	WB2:262
Howard, Jno.	Alexandria	Boarder	1808	1808(2):12A
Howard, John	Alexandria	Tax Charge	1787	Tax PP 1787:07
Howard, John	Alexandria	Tax Charge	1788	Tax PP 1788:08
Howard, John	Alexandria	Tax Charge	1789	Tax PP 1789:09
Howard, John	Alexandria	Tax Charge	1790	Tax PP 1790:07
Howard, John	Arlington	Inventory	1822	AB5:035; LVA-LP
Howard, John	Arlington	Account	1822	LVA-LP
Howard, John	Arlington	Will	1822	WB3:042
Howard, John	Arlington	Bond	1822	WB3:043
Howard, John, c/o John	Arlington	Guard. Acct.	1830	AB6:525; LVA-LP
Howard, John, Fairfax St.	Alexandria	Occupant	1787	Tax L 1787:13
Howard, Julia	Alexandria	Boarder	1799	1799(2):19A

NAME OR SUBJECT	LOCATION	TYPE	YEAR	REFERENCE(S)
Howard, Julia	Alexandria	Resident	1800	1800(4):07B
Howard, Julia, sempster	Alexandria	Boarder	1800	1800(4):07A
Howard, Margaret	Arlington	Guard. Acct.	1825	AB6:132; LVA-LP
Howard, Margaret	Arlington	Guard. Acct.	1829	AB6:476; LVA-LP
Howard, Margaret Beale	Arlington	Guard.	1824	WB3:183
Howard, Martha Ann	Arlington	Guard.	1824	WB3:183
Howard, Martha S.	Alexandria	Will	1894	WB2:094; LP
Howard, Mrs.	Alexandria	Boarder	1795	1795(4):04
Howard, William R., c/o John	Arlington	Guard.	1830	WB3:386
Howard, [blank], Fairfax St.	Alexandria	Occupant	1790	Tax L 1790:07
Howell, Charles	Alexandria	Tax Charge	1799	Tax PP 1799:16
Howell, Jno.	Alexandria	Tax Charge	1798	Tax PP 1798:07
Howell, John	Alexandria	Tax Charge	1799	Tax PP 1799:16
Howell, Joseph M.	Alexandria	Will	1882	WB1:350; LP
Howell, Richd.	Alexandria	Tax Charge	1798	Tax PP 1798:07
Howell, Samuel	Alexandria	Tax Charge	1799	Tax PP 1799:16
Howell, Sarah	Alexandria	Resident	1800	1800(4):10B
Howell, Sarah, shopkeeper	Alexandria	Head	1800	1800(4):10A
Howland, Thomas H., owner	Arlington	Libellant	1818	ACO:152
Howsen, William	Arlington	Admin.	1812	WB1:170
Hoxley, Elizabeth	Arlington	Will	1818	WB2:230
Hoxton, Llewellyn, c/o William W.	Arlington	Guard.	1855	WB7:013
Hoxton, Mary S., c/o William W.	Arlington	Guard.	1855	WB7:013
Hoxton, Sally G., c/o William W.	Arlington	Guard.	1855	WB7:013
Hoxton, William, c/o William W.	Arlington	Guard.	1855	WB7:013
Hoxton, William W., Dr.	Arlington	Will	1855	WB7:013; File #523A
Hoxton, Winslow, c/o William W.	Arlington	Guard.	1855	WB7:013
Hoy, France, labourrer	Alexandria	Head	1800	1800(4):13A
Hoy, Francis & wife Milley	Alexandria	Resident	1800	1800(4):13B
Hoy, William	Alexandria	Mer. License	1799	Tax PP 1799:52-04r
Hoy, William, w(2), merchant	Alexandria	Head	1796	1796(3):6
Hoye, Francis	Alexandria	Tax Charge	1799	Tax PP 1799:16
Hoye, Francis & wife (C), labourer	Alexandria	Housekeeper	1799	1799(2):14A
Hoye, Francis, laborer	Alexandria	Housekeeper	1808	1808(4):24A
Hoye, William	Alexandria	Tax Charge	1799	Tax PP 1799:17
Hoye, William	Arlington	Will	1800	CRA:305
Hoye, Wm.	Alexandria	Tax Charge	1795	Tax PP 1795:13
Hoye, Wm.	Alexandria	Tax Charge	1796	Tax LP 1796:12
Hoye, Wm.	Alexandria	Tax Charge	1796	Tax PP 1796:08
Hoye, Wm.	Alexandria	Mer. License	1798	Tax PP 1798:20-3
Hoye, Wm.	Alexandria	Tax Charge	1798	Tax PP 1798:07
Hoye, Wm. & wife, grocer	Alexandria	Housekeeper	1799	1799(2):07A
Hoye, Wm., Wolf St.	Alexandria	Owner	1795	Tax L 1795:14
Hoye, Wm., Wolf St.	Alexandria	Occupant	1795	Tax L 1795:14
Hubball, Elicia	Arlington	Guard.	1815	WB2:068
Hubball, Jno.	Alexandria	Tax Charge	1795	Tax PP 1795:13
Hubball, Jno.	Alexandria	Tax Charge	1798	Tax PP 1798:07
Hubball, Jno. & wife, cabinet maker	Alexandria	Housekeeper	1799	1799(2):15A
Hubball, John	Alexandria	Tax Charge	1796	Tax LP 1796:12
Hubball, John	Alexandria	Tax Charge	1799	Tax PP 1799:16
Hubball, John	Alexandria	Tax Charge	1800	Tax PP 1800:15
Hubball, John	Arlington	Ordinary	1803	OBL1(np)
Hubball, John	Arlington	Inventory	1804	WBA:310; LVA-LP
Hubball, John	Arlington	Will	1804	WBA:293; LVA-LP
Hubball, John	Arlington	Bond	1804	WBA:294
Hubball, John	Arlington	Account	1806	WBB:288; LVA-LP
Hubball, John & wife, cabinet maker	Alexandria	Head	1795	1795(4):02
Hubball, John, cabinet maker	Alexandria	Head	1800	1800(4):05A
Hubball, John, Fairfax St.	Alexandria	Occupant	1795	Tax L 1795:08
Hubball, Mary	Arlington	Ordinary	1804	OBL1(np)
Hubball, William	Arlington	Guard.	1815	WB2:068

NAME OR SUBJECT	LOCATION	TYPE	YEAR	REFERENCE(S)
Hubball, William, c/o Mary Drew	Arlington	Apprentice	1814	OCR1811:242
Hubbard, Dyer, cabinet maker	Alexandria	Housekeeper	1808	1808(2):14A
Hubbard, Jeremiah, at his house	Arlington	Ordinary	1834	OBL5(np)
Hubbard, Jeremiah, at his house	Arlington	Ordinary	1836	OBL5(np)
Hubbard, Jeremiah, grantor	Arlington	Indenture D.	1831	ID:331
Hubbard, Jeremiah, in jail bounds	Arlington	Insolvent	1831	ID:329
Hubbell, John & wife Mary	Alexandria	Resident	1800	1800(4):05B
Huber, William	Arlington	Inventory	1807	WBC:018, 062; LVA-LP
Huber, William	Arlington	Admin.	1807	WBB:530
Huber, William	Arlington	Account	1808	WBC:100; LVA-LP
Hucorn, Francis	Alexandria	Tax Charge	1800	Tax PP 1800:13
Hucorn, Francis	Arlington	Ordinary	1803	OBL1(np)
Hucorn, Francis	Arlington	Ordinary	1805	OBL1(np)
Hucorn, Francis	Arlington	Ordinary	1806	OBL1(np)
Hucorn, Francis	Arlington	Ordinary	1807	OBL2(np)
Hucorn, Francis	Arlington	Ordinary	1809	OBL2(np)
Hucorn, Francis	Arlington	Ordinary	1810	OBL2(np)
Hucorn, Francis	Arlington	Sale	1814	AB2:062
Hucorn, Francis, tavern keeper	Alexandria	Housekeeper	1808	1808(2):15A
Hucorne, Francis	Arlington	Account	1813	AB2:063; LVA-LP
Hucorne, Francis	Arlington	Inventory	1813	AB1:337; LVA-LP
Hucorne, Francis	Arlington	Receipt	1813	LVA-LP
Hucorne, Francis	Arlington	Admin.	1813	WB1:264
Hucorne, Francis, tavern keeper	Alexandria	Head	1810	1810(2):06A
Hudgins, James	Arlington	Admin. Bond	1848	ABB(np)
Hudgins, James, at his house	Arlington	Ordinary	1832	OBL4(np)
Hudson, James	Alexandria	Tax Charge	1799	Tax PP 1799:17
Hudson, James, lamp lighter	Alexandria	Head	1810	1810(3):09A
Hudson, Jas., watchman	Alexandria	Housekeeper	1808	1808(3):22A
Hudson, Mariah	Alexandria	Will	1894	WB2:104; LP
Hudson, Mary Ann	Arlington	Guard.	1824	WB3:129
Huey, James, grantor	Arlington	Indenture D.	1805	ID3:101
Huey, James, in gaol bounds	Arlington	Insolvent	1805	ID3:092
Hughes & Towers	Alexandria	Tax Charge	1800	Tax PP 1800:13
Hughes, Aaron	Alexandria	Tax Charge	1800	Tax PP 1800:13
Hughes, James, def.	Alexandria	Suit	1806	CRI1:344
Hughes, Jno. & wife, ship builder	Alexandria	Housekeeper	1799	1799(2):07A
Hughes, Jno., Water St.	Alexandria	Occupant	1795	Tax L 1795:14
Hughes, John	Alexandria	Tax Charge	1789	Tax PP 1789:09
Hughes, John	Alexandria	Tax Charge	1795	Tax PP 1795:12
Hughes, John	Alexandria	Tax Charge	1796	Tax PP 1796:08
Hughes, John	Alexandria	Tax Charge	1798	Tax PP 1798:08
Hughes, John	Alexandria	Tax Charge	1799	Tax PP 1799:16
Hughes, John	Arlington	Will	1831	WB4:029; File #312A
Hughes, John	Arlington	Bond	1831	WB4:030
Hughes, John & wife, ship builder	Alexandria	Head	1795	1795(4a):04
Hughes, Richardson H., grantor	Arlington	Indenture D.	1813	ID2:157
Hughes, Richardson H., in jail bounds	Arlington	Involvent	1813	ID2:152
Hughes, Thomas	Alexandria	Tax Charge	1798	Tax PP 1798:07
Hughes, Thomas	Alexandria	Mer. License	1798	Tax PP 1798:20-3
Hughes, Thomas	Alexandria	Tax Charge	1799	Tax PP 1799:17
Hughes, Thomas	Alexandria	Tax Charge	1800	Tax PP 1800:13
Hughes, Thomas, in Alexandria Co.	Arlington	Ordinary	1847	OBL6(np)
Hughes, Thomas, in Alexandria Co.	Arlington	Ordinary	1848	OBL6(np)
Hughes, Thomas, in Alexandria Co.	Arlington	Ordinary	1849	OBL6(np)
Hughes, Thomas, ret. liquor w/o license	Arlington	Defendant	1802	PA:239
Hughes, William	Arlington	Admin.	1827	OCR1822:132
Hughes, William	Arlington	Admin.	1827	WB3:274
Hughes, [blank], nr. Union St.	Alexandria	Occupant	1790	Tax L 1790:11
Hughes [Hewes], William H.	Arlington	Account	1828	AB6:446; LVA-LP
Hughs, A., Fairfax St.	Alexandria	Occupant	1787	Tax L 1787:24

NAME OR SUBJECT	LOCATION	TYPE	YEAR	REFERENCE(S)
Hughs, Aaron	Alexandria	Owner	1787	Tax L 1787:14
Hughs, Aaron, Prince St.	Alexandria	Occupant	1787	Tax L 1787:16
Hughs, Aaron, Prince St.	Alexandria	Occupant	1787	Tax L 1787:14
Hughs, Aaron, Washington St.	Alexandria	Occupant	1787	Tax L 1787:04
Hughs, Thos. (bottler?)	Alexandria	Tax Charge	1800	Tax PP 1800:13
Hughs [Hewes], Aaron	Alexandria	Tax Charge	1787	Tax PP 1787:06
Huguely, Elishabah	Arlington	Guard. Acct.	1814	AB2:152, 311
Huguely, Elishabah	Arlington	Guard. Acct.	1814	AB2:003; LVA-LP
Huguely, Elizabeth F.	Arlington	Guard. Acct.	1816	LVA-LP
Huguely, Elizabeth Harris, c/o George	Arlington	Guard.	1811	WB1:117
Huguely, George	Arlington	Account	1811	AB1:131; LVA-LP
Huguely, George	Arlington	Inventory	1811	AB1:111; LVA-LP
Huguely, George	Arlington	Admin.	1811	WB1:085
Huguely, George	Arlington	Guard. Acct.	1815	AB2:152; LVA-LP
Huguely, George	Arlington	Account	1816	LVA-LP
Huguely, George	Arlington	Division S.	1823	AB5:224
Huguely, George	Arlington	Division S.	1823	OCR1822:050
Huguely, George	Arlington	Guard.	1823	OCR1822:058a
Huguely, George, children of	Arlington	Guard. Acct.	1812	AB1:259; LVA-LP
Huguely, George F.	Arlington	Guard. Acct.	1814	AB2:152, 311
Huguely, George F.	Arlington	Guard. Acct.	1814	AB2:003; LVA-LP
Huguely, George F.	Arlington	Guard. Acct.	1816	LVA-LP
Huguely, George F.	Arlington	Guard. Acct.	1818	AB3:269
Huguely, George F.	Arlington	Guard. Acct.	1819	AB3:397; LVA-LP
Huguely, George F.	Arlington	Guard. Acct.	1821	AB4:291; LVA-LP
Huguely, George F.	Arlington	Guard. Acct.	1822	AB5:113
Huguely, George F.	Arlington	Account	1827	AB6:430
Huguely, George F.	Arlington	Guard. Acct.	1827	OCR1822:140; LVA-LP
Huguely, George Fendall	Arlington	Guard.	1823	WB3:132
Huguely, George Fendall, c/o George	Arlington	Guard.	1811	WB1:117
Huguely, Matilda L.	Arlington	Guard. Acct.	1816	LVA-LP
Huguely, Matilda L.	Arlington	Guard. Acct.	1818	AB3:269; LVA-LP
Huguely, Matilda L.	Arlington	Guard. Acct.	1819	AB3:397; LVA-LP
Huguely, Matilda L.	Arlington	Guard. Acct.	1821	AB4:293; LVA-LP
Huguely, Matilda L.	Arlington	Guard. Acct.	1822	AB5:115; LVA-LP
Huguely, Matilda Lee	Arlington	Guard. Acct.	1814	AB2:003, 152, 311
Huguely, Matilda Lee, c/o George	Arlington	Guard.	1811	WB1:117
Huguely, Sarah	Arlington	Account	1819	AB3:395; LVA-LP
Huguely, Sarah	Arlington	Bond	1819	WB2:300
Huguely, Sarah	Arlington	Will	1819	WB2:291; File #161A
Huguely, Sarah	Arlington	Account	1820	AB4:128; LVA-LP
Huguely, Sarah	Arlington	Admin.	1823	OCR1822:058a
Huguely [Hughly], Matilda L.	Arlington	Guard. Acct.	1823	AB5:223; LVA-LP
Huguly, Geo., shopkeeper	Alexandria	Head	1810	1810(3):04A
Hulbert, Thomas J.	Arlington	Will	1883	WB10:043; File #714A
Hull, George	Alexandria	Tithable +16	1788	Tax PP 1788:07
Hull, John	Alexandria	Tax Charge	1796	Tax LP 1796:13
Hull, John	Alexandria	Tax Charge	1796	Tax PP 1796:07
Hull, John	Alexandria	Tax Charge	1798	Tax PP 1798:08
Hull, John	Alexandria	Tax Charge	1799	Tax PP 1799:17
Hull, John	Alexandria	Tax Charge	1800	Tax PP 1800:15
Hull, John	Arlington	Sale	1803	WBA:205
Hull, John	Arlington	Appraisal	1803	WBA:188
Hull, John	Arlington	Bond	1803	WBA:187
Hull, John	Arlington	Account	1804	WBB:069
Hull, John	Arlington	Order	1805	WBB:210
Hull, John	Arlington	Account	1808	WBC:030; LVA-LP
Hull, John	Arlington	Account	1810	WBC:533
Hull, John & wife, labourer	Alexandria	Housekeeper	1799	1799(2):18A
Hull, Robt., Estate	Alexandria	Tax Charge	1798	Tax PP 1798:07
Hulls, Esther	Arlington	Guard.	1815	WB2:072

NAME OR SUBJECT	LOCATION	TYPE	YEAR	REFERENCE(S)
Hulls, John	Arlington	Will	1803	WBA:185; LVA-LP
Hulls, John	Arlington	Account	1806	WBB:384; LVA-LP
Hulls, John	Arlington	Account	1808	WBC:300; LVA-LP
Hulls, John	Arlington	Account	1808	WBC:159; LVA-LP
Hulls, John	Arlington	Account	1811	AB1:130; LVA-LP
Hulls, John	Arlington	Account	1812	AB1:257; LVA-LP
Hulls, John	Arlington	Account	1813	AB1:339; LVA-LP
Hulls, John	Arlington	Account	1814	AB2:062; LVA-LP
Hulls, John	Arlington	Guard. Acct.	1818	AB3:118; LVA-LP
Hulls, John & wife Ann	Alexandria	Resident	1800	1800(4):12B
Hulls, John, children of	Arlington	Guard. Acct.	1816	AB2:236
Hulls, John, children of	Arlington	Guard. Acct.	1817	AB2:416
Hulls, John, labourrer	Alexandria	Head	1800	1800(4):12A
Hulls, Mary	Arlington	Guard.	1815	WB2:072
Hulls, Nancy	Arlington	Apprentice	1812	OCR1811:068
Hulls, Nanny (C), shopkeeper	Alexandria	Housekeeper	1808	1808(2):14A
Hulls, Robert	Alexandria	Tax Charge	1796	Tax LP 1796:11
Hume, David	Arlington	Account	1858	WB7:366, 479; LVA-LP
Hume, David	Arlington	Account	1860	WB8:039; LVA-LP
Humphrey, Mary Ann	Arlington	Guard.	1819	WB2:326
Humphreys, Elizabeth	Arlington	Admin.	1823	OCR1822:043a
Humphreys, Elizabeth	Arlington	Admin.	1823	WB3:094
Humphreys, John S.	Arlington	Citation	1844	OCR1842:096
Humphreys, John S.	Arlington	Citation	1845	OCR1842:101
Humphries, John S.	Arlington	Inventory	1839	AB8:011; LVA-LP
Humphries, John S.	Arlington	Will	1839	WB4:208; File #365A
Humphries, John S.	Arlington	Bond	1839	WB4:210
Humphries, John S.	Arlington	Account	1840	AB8:130
Humphries, John S.	Arlington	Account	1843	OCR1842:038
Humphries, Mary (C), washwoman	Alexandria	Housekeeper	1808	1808(2):15A
Humphries, Richd., carpenter	Alexandria	Housekeeper	1808	1808(1):06A
Hunt, Maria, bonnetmaker	Alexandria	Housekeeper	1808	1808(1):01A
Hunt, Offy (C), washwoman	Alexandria	Housekeeper	1808	1808(4):28A
Hunt, Robert, seaman	Alexandria	Head	1810	1810(1):09A
Hunter & Allison	Alexandria	Owner	1787	Tax L 1787:15
Hunter & Allison	Alexandria	Tax Charge	1787	Tax PP 1787:06
Hunter & Allison, Union St.	Alexandria	Occupant	1787	Tax L 1787:15
Hunter, Alexander	Alexandria	Deposition	1822	CRL:533
Hunter, Alexander	Arlington	Exor. Bond	1849	EBB(np)
Hunter, Alexander	Arlington	Will	1849	WB5:128; File #448A
Hunter, Alexander	Arlington	Inventory	1850	WB5:226; LVA-LP
Hunter, Alexander	Arlington	Debts	1850	WB5:267
Hunter, Alexander, Gen.	Arlington	Account	1877	WB9:480
Hunter, Alexander, Lt.	Arlington	Account	1851	LVA-LP
Hunter, Allison & Co.	Alexandria	Tax Charge	1789	Tax PP 1789:08
Hunter, Ann S.	Arlington	Will P.	1843	OCR1842:038
Hunter, Ann S.	Arlington	Will	1843	WB4:333
Hunter, Christiana, gentlewoman	Alexandria	Housekeeper	1808	1808(1):07A
Hunter, Collin, block maker	Alexandria	Head	1810	1810(1):08A
Hunter, Collin, brickmaker	Alexandria	Housekeeper	1808	1808(1):08A
Hunter, G.	Alexandria	Tax Charge	1796	Tax LP 1796:11
Hunter, Geo., Fairfax St.	Alexandria	Occupant	1795	Tax L 1795:14
Hunter, Geo., Fairfax St.	Alexandria	Owner	1795	Tax L 1795:14
Hunter, George	Alexandria	Owner	1787	Tax L 1787:14
Hunter, George	Alexandria	Tax Charge	1788	Tax PP 1788:08
Hunter, George	Alexandria	Tax Charge	1789	Tax PP 1789:08
Hunter, George	Alexandria	Tax Charge	1790	Tax PP 1790:07
Hunter, George	Alexandria	Tax Charge	1796	Tax PP 1796:07
Hunter, George, Fairfax St.	Alexandria	Occupant	1787	Tax L 1787:14
Hunter, George, Fairfax St.	Alexandria	Owner	1790	Tax L 1790:06
Hunter, George, Fairfax St.	Alexandria	Occupant	1790	Tax L 1790:06

NAME OR SUBJECT	LOCATION	TYPE	YEAR	REFERENCE(S)
Hunter, Icabod	Alexandria	Tithable +16	1788	Tax PP 1788:14
Hunter, Ichabod	Alexandria	Tithable +21	1787	Tax PP 1787:10
Hunter, Ichabod	Alexandria	Tithable +16	1789	Tax PP 1789:08
Hunter, Ichabod	Alexandria	Tithable +16	1790	Tax PP 1790:06
Hunter, Jackson	Alexandria	Tax Charge	1789	Tax PP 1789:09
Hunter, Jackson	Alexandria	Tax Charge	1790	Tax PP 1790:07
Hunter, Jackson, widow of	Alexandria	Head	1795	1795(4a):05
Hunter, James	Alexandria	Tithable +16	1788	Tax PP 1788:06
Hunter, Jane	Alexandria	Housekeeper	1808	1808(1):08A
Hunter, Jane, seamstress	Alexandria	Head	1810	1810(1):06A
Hunter, Jno. & wife, ship builder	Alexandria	Housekeeper	1799	1799(2):17A
Hunter, Jno., Duke St.	Alexandria	Occupant	1787	Tax L 1787:14
Hunter, Jno., Prince St.	Alexandria	Occupant	1795	Tax L 1795:11
Hunter, Jno., Water St.	Alexandria	Occupant	1795	Tax L 1795:13
Hunter, John	Alexandria	Owner	1787	Tax L 1787:14
Hunter, John	Alexandria	Tax Charge	1788	Tax PP 1788:08
Hunter, John	Alexandria	Tax Charge	1789	Tax PP 1789:09
Hunter, John	Alexandria	Tax Charge	1790	Tax PP 1790:07
Hunter, John	Alexandria	Tax Charge	1795	Tax PP 1795:14
Hunter, John	Alexandria	Tax Charge	1796	Tax PP 1796:08
Hunter, John	Alexandria	Tax Charge	1798	Tax PP 1798:08
Hunter, John	Alexandria	Tax Charge	1799	Tax PP 1799:18
Hunter, John	Alexandria	Tax Charge	1800	Tax PP 1800:15
Hunter, John	Arlington	Inventory	1826	AB6:247
Hunter, John	Arlington	Admin.	1826	OCR1822:124
Hunter, John	Arlington	Admin.	1826	WB3:262
Hunter, John	Arlington	Account	1827	AB6:435; LVA-LP
Hunter, John (h. carpenter)	Alexandria	Tax Charge	1796	Tax LP 1796:13
Hunter, John (Scotch)	Alexandria	Tax Charge	1796	Tax LP 1796:11
Hunter, John & wife, ship carpenter	Alexandria	Head	1795	1795(4):04
Hunter, John & wife Dayley	Alexandria	Resident	1800	1800(4):07B
Hunter, John C.	Alexandria	Tax Charge	1796	Tax LP 1796:12
Hunter, John Chapman, Duke St.	Alexandria	Owner	1790	Tax L 1790:06
Hunter, John, Fairfax St.	Alexandria	Occupant	1790	Tax L 1790:06
Hunter, John, Fairfax St.	Alexandria	Owner	1790	Tax L 1790:06
Hunter, John, Fairfax St.	Alexandria	Owner	1795	Tax L 1795:13
Hunter, John, ship carpenter	Alexandria	Housekeeper	1808	1808(1):08A
Hunter, John, ship carpenter	Alexandria	Head	1800	1800(4):07A
Hunter, John, ship carpenter	Alexandria	Head	1810	1810(1):08A
Hunter, Kitty, d/o Richard Arell, plt.	Alexandria	Suit	1809	CRG:131
Hunter, Louisa, of Washington DC	Arlington	Will	1866	WB8:300; File #641A
Hunter, Malcolm	Alexandria	Boarder	1808	1808(1):08A
Hunter, Nathaniel	Alexandria	Owner	1787	Tax L 1787:13
Hunter, Nathaniel C., P. Bank clerk	Alexandria	Housekeeper	1808	1808(4):26A
Hunter, Nathaniel Chapman, c/o Na. C.	Arlington	Apprentice	1811	OCR1811:003
Hunter, Nathaniel, clerk in bank	Alexandria	Head	1810	1810(4):09A
Hunter, Nathaniel, Fairfax St.	Alexandria	Owner	1790	Tax L 1790:07
Hunter, Nathaniel, Fairfax St.	Alexandria	Owner	1795	Tax L 1795:14
Hunter, Nathl.	Alexandria	Tax Charge	1796	Tax LP 1796:12
Hunter, Richard, carpenter	Alexandria	Head	1810	1810(1):06A
Hunter, Richd.	Alexandria	Boarder	1808	1808(1):07A
Hunter, Rob.	Alexandria	Boarder	1808	1808(1):08A
Hunter, Robert	Alexandria	Tithable +16	1788	Tax PP 1788:08
Hunter, Robert	Arlington	Will	1857	WB7:167; File #535A
Hunter, Robert W.	Arlington	Appraisal	1859	WB7:410
Hunter, Robert W.	Arlington	Inventory	1859	WB7:410; LVA-LP
Hunter, Robert W., Pr. Geo. Co. MD	Arlington	Will	1858	WB7:375; File #563A
Hunter, Sally	Alexandria	Will	1898	WB2:282; LP
Hunter, Samuel Arell, c/o William	Arlington	Guard.	1810	WB1:003
Hunter, Will., Jr., Fairfax St.	Alexandria	Owner	1790	Tax L 1790:05
Hunter, Will., Jr., Prince St.	Alexandria	Owner	1790	Tax L 1790:05

NAME OR SUBJECT	LOCATION	TYPE	YEAR	REFERENCE(S)
Hunter, Will., Jr., Queen St.	Alexandria	Owner	1790	Tax L 1790:05
Hunter, Will., Jr., Union St.	Alexandria	Owner	1790	Tax L 1790:05
Hunter, Will., Jr., Wilkes St.	Alexandria	Owner	1790	Tax L 1790:05
Hunter, William	Alexandria	Owner	1787	Tax L 1787:14
Hunter, William	Alexandria	Tax Charge	1788	Tax PP 1788:08
Hunter, William	Arlington	Crime	1796	OT:26/11/1796
Hunter, William	Alexandria	Tax Charge	1799	Tax PP 1799:17
Hunter, William	Alexandria	Tax Charge	1800	Tax PP 1800:15
Hunter, William	Arlington	Apprentice	1801	OCR1801:009
Hunter, William	Arlington	Inventory	1804	WBA:316; LVA-LP
Hunter, William	Arlington	Admin.	1804	WBA:284
Hunter, William	Arlington	Account	1809	WBC:251; LVA-LP
Hunter, William & wife Catherine, def.	Alexandria	Suit	1801	CRC:115
Hunter, William, def.	Alexandria	Suit	1802	CRD:054
Hunter, William, def.	Alexandria	Suit	1803	CRD:068
Hunter, William, Fairfax St.	Alexandria	Occupant	1790	Tax L 1790:05
Hunter, William, Jr.	Alexandria	Owner	1787	Tax L 1787:13
Hunter, William, Jr.	Alexandria	Tax Charge	1787	Tax PP 1787:08
Hunter, William, Jr.	Alexandria	Tax Charge	1788	Tax PP 1788:08
Hunter, William, Jr.	Alexandria	Tax Charge	1789	Tax PP 1789:09
Hunter, William, Jr.	Alexandria	Tax Charge	1790	Tax PP 1790:06
Hunter, William, Sr., Fairfax St.	Alexandria	Owner	1790	Tax L 1790:07
Hunter, William, Sr., Union St.	Alexandria	Owner	1790	Tax L 1790:07
Hunter, William, Sr., Wilkes St.	Alexandria	Owner	1790	Tax L 1790:07
Hunter, William, Union St.	Alexandria	Occupant	1790	Tax L 1790:05
Hunter, William W., grantor	Arlington	Indenture D.	1831	ID:317
Hunter, William W., in jail	Arlington	Insolvent	1831	ID:315
Hunter, William, Water St.	Alexandria	Occupant	1790	Tax L 1790:10
Hunter, William, Wilks St.	Alexandria	Occupant	1787	Tax L 1787:03
Hunter, Wm.	Alexandria	Tax Charge	1787	Tax PP 1787:07
Hunter, Wm.	Alexandria	Tax Charge	1796	Tax LP 1796:12
Hunter, Wm.	Alexandria	Tax Charge	1796	Tax LP 1796:12
Hunter, Wm.	Alexandria	Tax Charge	1798	Tax PP 1798:08
Hunter, Wm.	Alexandria	Boarder	1808	1808(1):07A
Hunter, Wm. & wife	Alexandria	Housekeeper	1799	1799(2):19A
Hunter, Wm. & wife Christianney	Alexandria	Resident	1800	1800(4):08B
Hunter, Wm., Estate, Water St.	Alexandria	Owner	1795	Tax L 1795:12
Hunter, Wm., Fairfax St.	Alexandria	Occupant	1787	Tax L 1787:17
Hunter, Wm., Fairfax St.	Alexandria	Owner	1795	Tax L 1795:11
Hunter, Wm., gentelmen	Alexandria	Head	1800	1800(4):08A
Hunter, Wm., Jr., Fairfax St.	Alexandria	Occupant	1787	Tax L 1787:13
Hunter, Wm., Jr., Queen St.	Alexandria	Occupant	1787	Tax L 1787:13
Hunter, Wm., Jr., Union St.	Alexandria	Occupant	1787	Tax L 1787:18
Hunter, Wm., Jr., Water St.	Alexandria	Occupant	1787	Tax L 1787:22
Hunter, Wm., Jr., Wilks St.	Alexandria	Occupant	1787	Tax L 1787:13
Hunter, Wm., Prince St.	Alexandria	Occupant	1787	Tax L 1787:24
Hunter, Wm., Wilks St.	Alexandria	Occupant	1787	Tax L 1787:14
Hunter, Wm., Wolf St.	Alexandria	Owner	1795	Tax L 1795:11
Huntin, Chas., merchant	Alexandria	Head	1810	1810(3):08A
Huntington, Mary Ellen	Arlington	Apprentice	1844	OCR1842:092
Hurdle, Clement W., shopkeeper	Alexandria	Head	1810	1810(4):04A
Hurdle, Jesse, c/o Delia	Arlington	Apprentice	1805	OCR1801:256
Hurdle, Thomas T.	Alexandria	Will	1891	WB1:586; LP
Hurle, Robert (C)	Alexandria	Tax Charge	1788	Tax PP 1788:08
Hurle, Robert (C)	Alexandria	Tax Charge	1789	Tax PP 1789:07
Hurley, Colly, c/o Cornelius	Arlington	Apprentice	1804	OCR1801:194
Hurley, Enoch, pump maker	Alexandria	Head	1810	1810(1):11A
Hurley, Enock	Arlington	Ordinary	1805	OBL1(np)
Hurley, Jane, seamstress	Alexandria	Head	1810	1810(2):07A
Hurley, John	Arlington	Crime	1796	OT:19/04/1796
Hurley, John	Arlington	Crime	1796	OT:14/11/1796

NAME OR SUBJECT	LOCATION	TYPE	YEAR	REFERENCE(S)
Hurley, Mathew, laborer	Alexandria	Housekeeper	1808	1808(1):06A
Hurley, Morris	Arlington	Account	1811	AB1:123; LVA-LP
Hurley, Morris & wife, bricklayer	Alexandria	Housekeeper	1799	1799(2):01A
Hurley, Thomas, c/o Cornelius	Arlington	Apprentice	1803	OCR1801:140
Hurley, Thos.	Alexandria	Boarder	1808	1808(1):02A
Hurlley, Jany, sempstress	Alexandria	Housekeeper	1808	1808(2):17A
Hurlughy, Morris	Alexandria	Tax Charge	1800	Tax PP 1800:13
Hurly, Morrice & wife, bricklayer	Alexandria	Head	1795	1795(4a):03
Hurly, Morris	Alexandria	Tax Charge	1796	Tax LP 1796:11
Hurst, John, Capt.	Alexandria	Deposition	1808	CRI:425
Hurst, Richard	Arlington	Apprentice	1826	OCR1822:126a
Hussey, Barzilla, of Nantucket MA	Alexandria	Deposition	1818	CRK:471
Hussey, Henry	Arlington	Will	1807	WBB:506
Hussey, Samuel B., of Durham ME	Arlington	Will	1861	WB8:077; File #586A
Hustin, Wm., printer	Alexandria	Housekeeper	1808	1808(3):22A
Huston, William	Alexandria	Tax Charge	1800	Tax PP 1800:13
Hutchens, Ann, c/o Thomas	Arlington	Guard.	1812	WB1:146
Hutchens, Ann, c/o James	Arlington	Guard.	1818	WB2:243
Hutchens, John, c/o Mercy	Arlington	Apprentice	1813	OCR1811:176
Hutchens, Margaret	Arlington	Will	1814	WB1:289; File #118A
Hutchens, Margaret	Arlington	Bond	1814	WB1:292
Hutchens, Thomas	Arlington	Inventory	1811	AB1:073; LVA-LP
Hutchens, Thomas	Arlington	Will	1811	WB1:023; File #090A
Hutchens, Thomas	Arlington	Bond	1811	WB1:022
Hutchens, Thomas	Arlington	Account	1812	AB1:166; LVA-LP
Hutchins, Ann, c/o Thomas	Arlington	Inventory	1818	AB3:193; LVA-LP
Hutchins, Benjamin F., c/o William	Arlington	Guard.	1850	GBB(np)
Hutchins, Margaret	Arlington	Sale	1814	AB2:057
Hutchins, Margaret	Arlington	Inventory	1814	AB2:054; LVA-LP
Hutchins, Martha, seamstress	Alexandria	Head	1810	1810(1):05A
Hutchins, Massey, waterman	Alexandria	Housekeeper	1808	1808(2):17A
Hutchins, Thos., shopkeeper	Alexandria	Head	1810	1810(4):04A
Hutchison, Eleanor, c/o Mary	Arlington	Apprentice	1803	OCR1801:098
Hutchison, James C., b. Killala	Arlington	Alien Entry	1819	RA:02/07/19
Hutchison, Robert	Arlington	Apprentice	1802	OCR1801:065
Hutton, George	Alexandria	Will	1876	WB1:178; LP
Hutton, Samuel & Elisebeth	Alexandria	Resident	1800	1800(4):03B
Hyday, [blank]	Alexandria	Tax Charge	1796	Tax LP 1796:11
Hyde, Charles K.	Arlington	Exor. Bond	1850	EBB(np)
Hyde, Charles K.	Arlington	Will	1850	WB5:223; File #457A
Hyde, Eugenia C.	Alexandria	Will	1880	WB1:285; LP
Hyde, Philip	Alexandria	Tithable +16	1788	Tax PP 1788:15
Hyde, Philip	Alexandria	Tax Charge	1789	Tax PP 1789:09
Hyees, Andw. & wife, sadler	Alexandria	Housekeeper	1799	1799(2):09A
Hyleman, Ann	Alexandria	Boarder	1799	1799(2):06A
Hylton, Wm., waterman	Alexandria	Housekeeper	1808	1808(1):08A
Hymandinen, John C., grantor	Arlington	Indenture D.	1827	ID:129
Hymandinen, John C., in jail	Arlington	Insolvent	1827	ID:127
Hyne, William	Alexandria	Tax Charge	1787	Tax PP 1787:06
Hyneman, Ann	Alexandria	Tax Charge	1796	Tax LP 1796:11
Hynes, Penney (C)	Alexandria	Housekeeper	1808	1808(1):09A
Hyseler, John	Alexandria	Tax Charge	1796	Tax PP 1796:08
Hyseller, Jno.	Alexandria	Tax Charge	1795	Tax PP 1795:12
Hyseller, Jno., King St.	Alexandria	Occupant	1795	Tax L 1795:13
Hyseller, John, King St.	Alexandria	Owner	1795	Tax L 1795:13
Hyson, Henry (C), alias Hardin	Arlington	Apprentice	1845	OCR1842:138
Hyson, John, plaisterer	Alexandria	Housekeeper	1808	1808(3):21A
Hyson, Samuel	Arlington	Will	1855	WB6:445; File #520A

NAME OR SUBJECT	LOCATION	TYPE	YEAR	REFERENCE(S)
I				
Ike, Albert	Arlington	Fid. Bond	1860	FBB(np)
Immohr, Frederick	Arlington	Admin.	1830	WB3:385
Improving navigation, lottery for	Alexandria	Schedule	1812	CRK:138, 140
Ingersoll, Adeline M., of Brooklyn NY	Arlington	Will	1892	WB10:232; File #755A
Ingle, Henry	Alexandria	Mer. License	1799	Tax PP 1799:52-05r
Ingle, Henry	Alexandria	Tax Charge	1799	Tax PP 1799:20
Ingle, Henry	Alexandria	Tax Charge	1800	Tax PP 1800:19
Ingle, Henry	Arlington	Plaintiff	1802	PA:197
Ingle, Jos., Royal St.	Alexandria	Occupant	1795	Tax L 1795:15
Ingle, Joseph	Alexandria	Tax Charge	1795	Tax PP 1795:14
Ingle, Joseph	Alexandria	Tax Charge	1796	Tax PP 1796:09
Ingle, Joseph	Alexandria	Tax Charge	1798	Tax PP 1798:09
Ingle, Joseph	Alexandria	Tax Charge	1799	Tax PP 1799:20
Ingle, Joseph	Alexandria	Tax Charge	1800	Tax PP 1800:19
Ingle, Joseph	Arlington	Inventory	1818	AB3:257; LVA-LP
Ingle, Joseph	Arlington	Admin.	1818	WB2:254
Ingle, Joseph	Arlington	Account	1820	AB4:188; LVA-LP
Ingle, Joseph	Arlington	Account	1821	AB4:301; LVA-LP
Ingle, Joseph, cabinetmaker	Alexandria	Head	1810	1810(2):01A
Ingle, Joseph, cabinetmaker	Alexandria	Housekeeper	1808	1808(2):10A
Ingle, Joseph, def.	Alexandria	Suit	1801	CRB:349
Ingle, Joseph, Royal St.	Alexandria	Owner	1795	Tax L 1795:15
Ingles, Joseph	Alexandria	Tax Charge	1796	Tax LP 1796:15
Ingraham, Nathl.	Alexandria	Tax Charge	1790	Tax PP 1790:08
Insurance coverage of cargo	Alexandria	List	1805	CRF:276
Irish, Geo.	Alexandria	Owner	1795	Tax L 1795:15
Irish, Geo.	Alexandria	Tax Charge	1795	Tax PP 1795:14
Irish, Geo.	Alexandria	Tax Charge	1798	Tax PP 1798:09
Irish, Geo. & wife, merchant	Alexandria	Housekeeper	1799	1799(2):08A
Irish, George	Alexandria	Tax Charge	1796	Tax PP 1796:09
Irish, George	Alexandria	Tax Charge	1799	Tax PP 1799:20
Irish, George	Alexandria	Tax Charge	1800	Tax PP 1800:19
Irspis?, Jas.	Alexandria	Boarder	1808	1808(1):01A
Irvin, David, seaman	Alexandria	Head	1810	1810(1):04A
Irvin, James	Alexandria	Tax Charge	1796	Tax LP 1796:15
Irvin, James	Alexandria	Tax Charge	1796	Tax PP 1796:10
Irvin, James, rope walk	Alexandria	Owner	1795	Tax L 1795:16
Irvin, James, Washington St.	Alexandria	Owner	1795	Tax L 1795:16(3)
Irvin, Jas.	Alexandria	Tax Charge	1795	Tax PP 1795:15
Irvin, Jas.	Alexandria	Reference	1808	1808(2):16B
Irvin, Jas., rope walk	Alexandria	Occupant	1795	Tax L 1795:16
Irvin, Jas., Washington St.	Alexandria	Occupant	1795	Tax L 1795:16
Irvin, Tho., Union St.	Alexandria	Occupant	1795	Tax L 1795:16
Irvin, Thos.	Alexandria	Tax Charge	1795	Tax PP 1795:15
Irvin, Thos.	Alexandria	Tax Charge	1800	Tax PP 1800:19
Irvin, Thos., merchant	Alexandria	Head	1810	1810(3):06A
Irvin, Thos., St. Asaph St.	Alexandria	Occupant	1795	Tax L 1795:16
Irvin, Thos., Union St.	Alexandria	Owner	1795	Tax L 1795:16
Irvine, Elizabeth [Bailey]	Arlington	P. of Atty.	1828	LVA-LP (Accounts)
Irvine, Thomas	Alexandria	Tax Charge	1789	Tax PP 1789:10
Irvine, Thomas, Fairfax St.	Alexandria	Occupant	1790	Tax L 1790:10
Irving, John, assignee, plt.	Alexandria	Suit	1809	CRH:484
Irwin, Ann B.	Arlington	Trustee Acct.	1860	LVA-LP
Irwin, Elizabeth	Arlington	Exor. Bond	1847	EBB(np)
Irwin, Elizabeth	Arlington	Will	1847	WB5:007; File #440A
Irwin, Elizabeth	Arlington	Inventory	1847	WB5:010; LVA-LP
Irwin, Elizabeth	Arlington	Account	1849	WB5:202; LVA-LP
Irwin, Fred., Sr.	Arlington	Appraisal	1829	LVA-LP
Irwin, James	Alexandria	Tax Charge	1790	Tax PP 1790:08
Irwin, James	Arlington	Will	1857	WB7:176; File #536A

NAME OR SUBJECT	LOCATION	TYPE	YEAR	REFERENCE(S)
Irwin, Mary	Alexandria	Will	1875	WBC1:022; LP
Irwin, Thomas	Alexandria	Tax Charge	1790	Tax PP 1790:07
Irwin, Thomas	Alexandria	Tax Charge	1796	Tax LP 1796:15
Irwin, Thomas	Alexandria	Tax Charge	1796	Tax PP 1796:09
Irwin, Thomas	Alexandria	Tax Charge	1799	Tax PP 1799:20
Irwin, Thomas	Arlington	Plaintiff	1802	PA:277
Irwin, Thomas	Arlington	Juryman	1804	ACO:026
Irwin, Thomas	Arlington	Sale	1814	AB2:061
Irwin, Thomas	Arlington	Inventory	1815	AB2:091; LVA-LP
Irwin, Thomas	Arlington	Admin.	1815	WB1:324
Irwin, Thomas	Arlington	Account	1817	AB3:047; LVA-LP
Irwin, Thomas	Arlington	Inventory	1827	AB6:397, 412; LVA-LP
Irwin, Thomas	Arlington	Will P.	1827	OCR1822:130
Irwin, Thomas	Arlington	Bond	1827	WB3:270
Irwin, Thomas	Arlington	Will	1827	WB3:269; File #253A
Irwin, Thomas	Arlington	Partition	1835	LVA-LP
Irwin, Thomas	Arlington	Distribution	1839	AB7:339
Irwin, Thomas & wife, merchant	Alexandria	Head	1795	1795(4):09
Irwin, Thomas, Plaisterer	Arlington	Account	1828	AB6:455; LVA-LP
Irwin, Thos.	Alexandria	Mer. License	1798	Tax PP 1798:20-3
Irwin, Thos.	Alexandria	Tax Charge	1798	Tax PP 1798:09
Irwin, Thos., retailer	Alexandria	Housekeeper	1808	1808(3):18A
Irwin, William	Alexandria	Tax Charge	1800	Tax PP 1800:01
Irwin, William, plt.	Alexandria	Suit	1802	CRC:207
Irwin, Wm.	Alexandria	Tax Charge	1796	Tax LP 1796:15
Irwin, Wm. & wife, joiner	Alexandria	Head	1795	1795(4a):09
Isaac, Elizabeth	Arlington	Inventory	1808	WBC:076
Isaac, Elizabeth	Arlington	Sale	1808	WBC:077
Isaac, Elizabeth	Arlington	Admin.	1808	WBC:075
Isaac, Elizabeth	Arlington	Account	1810	WBC:449
Isaac, Mary	Arlington	Guard. Acct.	1822	AB5:129; LVA-LP
Isaac, Phoebe Heathland, c/o Elizabeth	Arlington	Guard.	1810	WBC:469
Isaac, Polly Jane, c/o Elizabeth	Arlington	Guard.	1810	WBC:469
Isaac, Samuel, taylor	Alexandria	Head	1810	1810(3):01A
Isaacs, Samuel	Arlington	Exor. Bond	1848	EBB(np)
Isaacs, Samuel	Arlington	Will	1848	WB5:072
Isaacs, Sarah	Arlington	Will	1866	WB8:298; File #639A
Isabel, Jonah	Alexandria	Tax Charge	1795	Tax PP 1795:14
Isabel, Jonah	Alexandria	Tax Charge	1799	Tax PP 1799:20
Isabel, Jonah, merchant	Alexandria	Head	1810	1810(2):01A
Isabel, William	Alexandria	Mer. License	1799	Tax PP 1799:52-05r
Isabel, William	Alexandria	Tax Charge	1799	Tax PP 1799:20
Isabel, William	Alexandria	Tax Charge	1800	Tax PP 1800:19
Isabel, William	Arlington	Account	1828	AB6:456; LVA-LP
Isabel, William	Arlington	Account	1828	AB6:513; LVA-LP
Isabel, Wm.	Alexandria	Tax Charge	1798	Tax PP 1798:09
Isabel, Wm.	Alexandria	Mer. License	1800	Tax PP 1800:54(15)r
Isabel, Wm., retailer	Alexandria	Boarder	1799	1799(2):01A
Isabel, Wm., retailer	Alexandria	Housekeeper	1808	1808(1):02A
Isabell, Jonah	Alexandria	Tax Charge	1796	Tax PP 1796:10
Isabell, Jonah, retailer	Alexandria	Housekeeper	1808	1808(2):11A
Isabell, William	Arlington	Sale	1827	AB6:399
Isabell, William	Arlington	Inventory	1827	AB6:280; LVA-LP
Isabell, William	Arlington	Bond	1827	WB3:281
Isabell, William	Arlington	Will	1827	WB3:280; File #257A
Isabell, William	Arlington	Account	1830	AB6:513
Isabell, William, shopkeeper	Alexandria	Head	1810	1810(1):01A
Isabell, Wm.	Alexandria	Tax Charge	1796	Tax PP 1796:09
Isabell, Wm.	Alexandria	Mer. License	1798	Tax PP 1798:20-3
Isaloan, Jasper, Cameron St.	Alexandria	Occupant	1790	Tax L 1790:03
Isborne, Washington, hatter	Alexandria	Boarder	1799	1799(2):01A

NAME OR SUBJECT	LOCATION	TYPE	YEAR	REFERENCE(S)
Iseler, Geo.	Alexandria	Tax Charge	1795	Tax PP 1795:14
Iseler, Geo., King St.	Alexandria	Occupant	1795	Tax L 1795:05
Iseler, George	Alexandria	Tax Charge	1796	Tax LP 1796:15
Iseler, George	Alexandria	Tax Charge	1796	Tax PP 1796:09
Iserloan, Jasper	Alexandria	Tax Charge	1789	Tax PP 1789:10
Iserloan, Jasper	Alexandria	Tax Charge	1790	Tax PP 1790:07
Iservey, Anth.	Alexandria	Tax Charge	1795	Tax PP 1795:15
Island, estate called	Arlington	Suit	1835	LSA:010
Iver, John, barber	Alexandria	Head	1810	1810(1):02A
Ivery, Chas.	Alexandria	Boarder	1808	1808(1):09A
Ivins, Robert	Alexandria	Tax Charge	1796	Tax PP 1796:09
Ivins, Robert	Alexandria	Tax Charge	1798	Tax PP 1798:09

NAME OR SUBJECT	LOCATION	TYPE	YEAR	REFERENCE(S)
J				
Jackson, Amashack & wife Easter	Alexandria	Resident	1800	1800(4):09B
Jackson, Amashack, labourrer	Alexandria	Head	1800	1800(4):09A
Jackson, Ann	Alexandria	Resident	1800	1800(4):12B
Jackson, Ann Eliz. (C), c/o Julia Morris	Arlington	Apprentice	1845	OCR1842:140
Jackson, Ann, laundress	Alexandria	Head	1800	1800(4):12A
Jackson, annas, seaman	Alexandria	Housekeeper	1808	1808(1):05A
Jackson, Annas, Capt.	Arlington	Inventory	1808	WBC:080; LP
Jackson, Annas, Capt.	Arlington	Admin.	1808	WBC:079
Jackson, Annas, Capt.	Arlington	Inventory	1809	WBC:238
Jackson, Annas, Capt.	Arlington	Account	1809	WBC:237; LVA-LP
Jackson, Archibald, c/o Meshack	Arlington	Apprentice	1803	OCR1801:130
Jackson, Archy (C), s/o Esther	Alexandria	Boarder	1808	1808(1):09A
Jackson, Bridgett	Arlington	Account	1836	AB7:211; LVA-LP
Jackson, Charles	Alexandria	Will	1898	WB2:284
Jackson, David, Estate	Alexandria	Owner	1787	Tax L 1787:17
Jackson, David, heirs, Fairfax St.	Alexandria	Owner	1790	Tax L 1790:07
Jackson, Esther (C), washwoman	Alexandria	Housekeeper	1808	1808(1):09A
Jackson, Esther, washerwoman	Alexandria	Head	1810	1810(1):06A
Jackson, George, w(3)1, doctor	Alexandria	Head	1796	1796(3):3
Jackson, Hannah	Arlington	Will	1827	WB3:291; File #260A
Jackson, Hannah (C), washwoman	Alexandria	Housekeeper	1808	1808(1):07A
Jackson, Hannah, washerwoman	Alexandria	Head	1810	1810(1):10A
Jackson, Harriet H.	Arlington	Appraisal	1834	LVA-LP
Jackson, Harriet Hannah	Arlington	Bond	1834	WB4:071
Jackson, Harriet Hannah	Arlington	Will	1834	WB4:071; File #325A
Jackson, Harriet M.	Arlington	Account	1835	AB7:161; LVA-LP
Jackson, Harriet, seamstress	Alexandria	Head	1810	1810(1):11A
Jackson, John	Alexandria	Tax Charge	1796	Tax LP 1796:15
Jackson, John	Arlington	Will	1890	WB10:179; File #747A
Jackson, John, Fairfax St.	Alexandria	Owner	1795	Tax L 1795:16
Jackson, John, Jr.	Alexandria	Deposition	1815	CRL:147
Jackson, John, Sr.	Alexandria	Deposition	1815	CRK:126
Jackson, Joseph	Alexandria	Tax Charge	1789	Tax PP 1789:10
Jackson, Joseph	Alexandria	Tax Charge	1790	Tax PP 1790:08
Jackson, Landon	Alexandria	Will	1899	WB2:329; LP
Jackson, Lucy (C), washwoman	Alexandria	Housekeeper	1808	1808(1):07A
Jackson, M.	Alexandria	Tax Charge	1796	Tax PP 1796:09
Jackson, Mescheck	Alexandria	Tax Charge	1798	Tax PP 1798:09
Jackson, Mescheck	Alexandria	Tax Charge	1799	Tax PP 1799:20
Jackson, Meshack & wife, laborer	Alexandria	Head	1795	1795(4):05
Jackson, Mesheck	Alexandria	Tax Charge	1800	Tax PP 1800:19
Jackson, Mesheck (C)	Alexandria	Tax Charge	1795	Tax PP 1795:15
Jackson, Mesheck & wife (C), labourer	Alexandria	Housekeeper	1799	1799(2):20A
Jackson, Nancy K.	Arlington	Apprentice	1827	OCR1822:144
Jackson, Rebecca, King St.	Alexandria	Occupant	1795	Tax L 1795:16
Jackson, Robert A.	Arlington	Guard.	1813	WB1:251
Jackson, Robert A.	Alexandria	Will	1878	WB1:229; LP
Jackson, Tabitha	Arlington	Will	1815	WB2:071
Jackson, Thomas	Arlington	Apprentice	1803	OCR1801:132
Jackson, Thomas	Arlington	Admin.	1820	WB2:350
Jackson, Wall, drayman	Alexandria	Housekeeper	1808	1808(3):18A
Jackson, Wall, labourer	Alexandria	Head	1810	1810(3):09A
Jackson, William	Alexandria	Tax Charge	1788	Tax PP 1788:09
Jackson, William	Arlington	Apprentice	1827	OCR1822:141a
Jackson, William & wife Sally Fleming	Alexandria	Suit	1801	CRC:194
Jackson, William B., of DC	Alexandria	Will	1896	WB2:164; LP
Jackson, Wm.	Alexandria	Tax Charge	1796	Tax PP 1796:09
Jackson, Wm.	Alexandria	Tax Charge	1798	Tax PP 1798:09
Jackson, Wm., Estate	Alexandria	Tax Charge	1796	Tax LP 1796:15
Jackson, Wm., King St.	Alexandria	Owner	1795	Tax L 1795:16(2)

NAME OR SUBJECT	LOCATION	TYPE	YEAR	REFERENCE(S)
Jacob, Presley	Arlington	Bond	1852	BB(np)
Jacob, Thomas	Arlington	Inventory	1810	WBC:522
Jacob, Thomas	Arlington	Bond	1810	WBC:498
Jacob, Thomas	Arlington	Will	1810	WBC:491; File #048A
Jacob, Thos.	Alexandria	Tax Charge	1800	Tax PP 1800:19
Jacobes, Sarah, labourer	Alexandria	Boarder	1800	1800(4):03A
Jacobs, Almira	Arlington	Account C.	1853	WB6:282; LVA-LP
Jacobs, Almira	Arlington	Report	1855	WB6:455; LVA-LP
Jacobs, Charlotte	Alexandria	Will	1875	WB1:124; LP
Jacobs, Charlotte (Deagan), w/o Thos.	Arlington	Defendant	(nd)	LSA:124
Jacobs, Edward	Arlington	Ordinary	1808	OBL2(np)
Jacobs, Edward H., in Alexandria Co.	Arlington	Ordinary	1824	OBL3(np)
Jacobs, George	Arlington	Guard.	1818	WB2:269
Jacobs, Harrison	Alexandria	Will	1888	WB1:511; LP
Jacobs, John	Alexandria	Tithable +21	1787	Tax PP 1787:14
Jacobs, John	Alexandria	Tithable +16	1788	Tax PP 1788:07
Jacobs, Joshua	Alexandria	Tax Charge	1796	Tax PP 1796:09
Jacobs, Joshua	Alexandria	Tax Charge	1798	Tax PP 1798:09
Jacobs, Joshua	Alexandria	Tax Charge	1799	Tax PP 1799:20
Jacobs, Joshua	Alexandria	Tax Charge	1800	Tax PP 1800:19
Jacobs, Joshua, taylor	Alexandria	Housekeeper	1799	1799(2):07A
Jacobs, Liddey, labourer	Alexandria	Boarder	1800	1800(4):03A
Jacobs, Liddy	Alexandria	Resident	1800	1800(4):03B
Jacobs, Presley	Alexandria	Tax Charge	1800	Tax PP 1800:19
Jacobs, Presley	Arlington	Will	1852	WB6:115; File #481A
Jacobs, Presley	Arlington	Inventory	1852	WB6:152; LVA-LP
Jacobs, Presley	Arlington	Account	1855	WB6:442; LVA-LP
Jacobs, Presley	Arlington	Account	1856	WB6:273
Jacobs, Presley, taylor	Alexandria	Housekeeper	1808	1808(1):01A
Jacobs, Presley, taylor	Alexandria	Housekeeper	1808	1808(2):15A
Jacobs, Presly, taylor	Alexandria	Head	1810	1810(2):02A
Jacobs, Sarah	Alexandria	Resident	1800	1800(4):03B
Jacobs, Thomas	Arlington	Defendant	(nd)	LSA:124
Jacobs, Thomas	Alexandria	Tithable +16	1788	Tax PP 1788:07
Jacobs, Thomas	Alexandria	Tithable +16	1789	Tax PP 1789:08
Jacobs, Thomas	Alexandria	Tithable +16	1790	Tax PP 1790:06
Jacobs, Thomas	Alexandria	Tax Charge	1796	Tax LP 1796:15
Jacobs, Thomas	Alexandria	Tax Charge	1798	Tax PP 1798:09
Jacobs, Thomas	Alexandria	Tax Charge	1799	Tax PP 1799:20
Jacobs, Thomas	Arlington	Account	1812	AB1:265; LVA-LP
Jacobs, Thomas, taylor	Alexandria	Head	1810	1810(1):09A
Jacobs, Thos.	Alexandria	Boarder	1808	1808(4):26A
Jacobs, Thos. & wife, taylor	Alexandria	Housekeeper	1799	1799(2):06A
Jacobs, Thos., merchant	Alexandria	Head	1810	1810(2):01A
Jacobs, Thos., taylor	Alexandria	Housekeeper	1808	1808(4):26A
Jacobs, Thos., taylor	Alexandria	Head	1810	1810(4):01A
Jacobs, William, c/o Edward H.	Arlington	Apprentice	1811	OCR1811:021
Jameison, Andrew	Alexandria	Tax Charge	1790	Tax PP 1790:07
James, Harry, baker	Alexandria	Head	1810	1810(4):05A
James, Henry, b. baker	Alexandria	Housekeeper	1808	1808(2):14A
James Russell & Co.	Alexandria	Mer. License	1799	Tax PP 1799:52-09r
James Russell & Co.	Alexandria	Mer. License	1800	Tax PP 1800:54(19)r
James, Samuel	Alexandria	Tax Charge	1787	Tax PP 1787:08
James, William	Alexandria	Tax Charge	1790	Tax PP 1790:08
Jamesson, R.B.	Alexandria	Tax Charge	1798	Tax PP 1798:09
Jamesson, R.B.	Alexandria	Mer. License	1800	Tax PP 1800:54(15)r
Jamesson, R.B., Fairfax St.	Alexandria	Occupant	1795	Tax L 1795:13
Jamesson, Robert B.	Alexandria	Tax Charge	1799	Tax PP 1799:20
Jamesson, Robert B., def.	Alexandria	Suit	1801	CRB:108, 111
Jamesson, Robert B., def.	Alexandria	Suit	1801	CRB:342
Jamesson, Robert B., def.	Alexandria	Suit	1802	CRC:255

NAME OR SUBJECT	LOCATION	TYPE	YEAR	REFERENCE(S)
Jamesson, Robert B., def.	Alexandria	Suit	1806	CRH:176
Jamesson, Robert B., def.	Alexandria	Suit	1809	CRH:156
Jamesson, Robert B., grantor	Arlington	Indenture D.	1806	ID3:245
Jamesson, Robert Brown, prison bounds	Arlington	Insolvent	1806	ID3:234
Jamesson, Robt. B.	Alexandria	Tax Charge	1795	Tax PP 1795:14
Jamesson, Robt. B.	Alexandria	Tax Charge	1796	Tax PP 1796:09
Jamesson, Robt. B.	Alexandria	Tax Charge	1800	Tax PP 1800:19
Jamesson, Robt. B., def.	Alexandria	Suit	1807	CRF:151
Jamesson, William	Alexandria	Will	1873	WB1:103; LP
Jamieson & Anderson	Alexandria	Tax Charge	1799	Tax PP 1799:20
Jamieson & Anderson, Water St.	Alexandria	Occupant	1795	Tax L 1795:01
Jamieson & Bartleman	Alexandria	Mer. License	1798	Tax PP 1798:20-3
Jamieson & Bartleman	Alexandria	Tax Charge	1798	Tax PP 1798:09
Jamieson, Andrew	Alexandria	Tithable +16	1788	Tax PP 1788:01
Jamieson, Andrew	Alexandria	Tax Charge	1789	Tax PP 1789:10
Jamieson, Andrew	Alexandria	Tax Charge	1796	Tax PP 1796:09
Jamieson, Andrew	Alexandria	Tax Charge	1799	Tax PP 1799:20
Jamieson, Andrew	Alexandria	Deposition	1805	CRE:264
Jamieson, Andrew	Arlington	Inventory	1823	AB5:181; LVA-LP
Jamieson, Andrew	Arlington	Will P.	1823	OCR1822:044
Jamieson, Andrew	Arlington	Will	1823	WB3:098; File #445A
Jamieson, Andrew	Arlington	Bond	1823	WB3:095
Jamieson, Andrew	Arlington	Account	1824	AB5:343; LVA-LP
Jamieson, Andrew	Arlington	Debts Due	1824	AB5:345; LVA-LP
Jamieson, Andrew	Arlington	Account	1825	AB6:076; LVA-LP
Jamieson, Andrew	Arlington	Account	1834	AB7:121; LVA-LP
Jamieson, Andrew	Arlington	Account	1839	AB7:347
Jamieson, Andrew & wife, baker	Alexandria	Head	1795	1795(4):01
Jamieson, Andw.	Alexandria	Tax Charge	1796	Tax LP 1796:15
Jamieson, Andw.	Alexandria	Tax Charge	1798	Tax PP 1798:09
Jamieson, Andw., merchant & b. baker	Alexandria	Housekeeper	1808	1808(2):16A
Jamieson, Andw., Union St.	Alexandria	Occupant	1795	Tax L 1795:17
Jamieson, Charles	Alexandria	Tax Charge	1796	Tax PP 1796:09
Jamieson, Charles	Alexandria	Tax Charge	1799	Tax PP 1799:20
Jamieson, Charles	Alexandria	Resident	1800	1800(4):16B
Jamieson, Charles	Arlington	Admin.	1804	WBB:037
Jamieson, Charles	Arlington	Inventory	1804	WBB:085; LVA-LP
Jamieson, Charles	Arlington	Sale	1804	WBB:089
Jamieson, Charles	Arlington	Account	1806	WBB:255; LVA-LP
Jamieson, Charles & sister, grocer	Alexandria	Housekeeper	1799	1799(2):07A
Jamieson, Charles, coopper	Alexandria	Head	1800	1800(4):16A
Jamieson, Charles, mariner	Alexandria	Boarder	1795	1795(4a):01
Jamieson, Charles, ret. liquors w/o lic.	Arlington	Defendant	1802	PA:009
Jamieson, Chas., Union St.	Alexandria	Occupant	1795	Tax L 1795:05
Jamieson, Chs.	Alexandria	Tax Charge	1796	Tax LP 1796:15
Jamieson, Elizabeth J.	Alexandria	Will	1890	WB1:572; LP
Jamieson, John, b. baker	Alexandria	Housekeeper	1808	1808(2):16A
Jamieson, John, grantor	Arlington	Indenture D.	1811	ID2:058
Jamieson, John, in jail bounds	Arlington	Insolvent	1811	ID2:054
Jamieson, John J.	Alexandria	Will	1899	WB2:311; LP
Jamieson, John, owner	Arlington	Respondent	1805	ACO:045
Jamieson, John, trustee, grantee	Arlington	Indenture D.	1811	ID2:039
Jamieson, Maria C.	Arlington	Will	1869	WB9:190; File #674A
Jamieson, Maria C.	Arlington	Appraisal	1869	WB9:205
Jamieson, Mary	Arlington	Renounce	1823	OCR1822:044
Jamieson, Mary	Arlington	Will P.	1824	OCR1822:072
Jamieson, Mary	Arlington	Will	1824	WB3:128; File #224A
Jamieson, Mary, of Lawrenceville NJ	Alexandria	Will	1898	WB2:264
Jamieson, R.B., nr. Fairfax St.	Alexandria	Occupant	1790	Tax L 1790:06
Jamieson, Robert	Alexandria	Tax Charge	1796	Tax LP 1796:15
Jamieson, Robert	Arlington	Will	1863	WB8:176; File #606A

NAME OR SUBJECT	LOCATION	TYPE	YEAR	REFERENCE(S)
Jamieson, Robert	Arlington	Appraisal	1865	WB8:265
Jamieson, Robert B., plt.	Alexandria	Suit	1802	CRC:231
Jamieson, Robert Brown	Alexandria	Tax Charge	1790	Tax PP 1790:07
Jamieson, Robt. B.	Alexandria	Tithable +16	1788	Tax PP 1788:02
Jamieson, Robt. B.	Alexandria	Tax Charge	1789	Tax PP 1789:10
Jamieson, T.S.	Arlington	Account	1858	LVA-LP
Jamiesson, Andrew	Alexandria	Tax Charge	1795	Tax PP 1795:15
Jamiesson, Robert B.	Arlington	Plaintiff	1802	PA:259
Jamiesson, Robert B., merchant	Arlington	Defendant	1802	PA:217
Jamison & Anderson	Alexandria	Tax Charge	1800	Tax PP 1800:19
Jamison, Andrew	Alexandria	Tithable +21	1787	Tax PP 1787:08
Jamison, Andrew	Alexandria	Tax Charge	1800	Tax PP 1800:19
Jamison, Andrew & Co.	Alexandria	Tax Charge	1787	Tax PP 1787:08
Jamison, Charles	Alexandria	Mer. License	1799	Tax PP 1799:52-05r
Jamison, Charles	Alexandria	Tax Charge	1800	Tax PP 1800:19
Jamison, Charles, shopkeeper	Alexandria	Head	1795	1796(3):7
Jamison, Robert B.	Alexandria	Mer. License	1799	Tax PP 1799:52-05r
Jammesson, Andrew, baker	Alexandria	Head	1810	1810(2):08A
Jane, Peter	Arlington	Guard.	1804	WBB:059
Janney & Graham	Alexandria	Mer. License	1800	Tax PP 1800:54(15)r
Janney & Grayham	Alexandria	Mer. License	1799	Tax PP 1799:52-05r
Janney & Irish	Alexandria	Tax Charge	1796	Tax LP 1796:15
Janney & Irish	Alexandria	Mer. License	1798	Tax PP 1798:20-3
Janney & Irish	Alexandria	Tax Charge	1798	Tax PP 1798:09
Janney & Irish	Alexandria	Mer. License	1799	Tax PP 1799:52-05r
Janney & Irish	Alexandria	Mer. License	1800	Tax PP 1800:54(15)r
Janney [Janny], Abel	Alexandria	Tax Charge	1800	Tax PP 1800:19
Janney [Janny], Abel, collector	Alexandria	Head	1810	1810(4):07A
Janney, Abel	Alexandria	Tax Charge	1799	Tax PP 1799:20
Janney, Abel & wife, merchant	Alexandria	Housekeeper	1799	1799(2):12A
Janney, Abel, collector	Alexandria	Housekeeper	1808	1808(4):30A
Janney, Abijah, Mrs.	Arlington	Receipt	1845	LVA-LP
Janney, Aquila	Arlington	Account	1824	AB5:226; LVA-LP
Janney, Aquilla	Arlington	Inventory	1805	WBB:156
Janney, Aquilla	Arlington	Will	1805	WBB:125; File #001A
Janney, Aquilla	Arlington	Bond	1805	WBB:126
Janney, Aquilla	Arlington	Sale	1807	WBB:482
Janney, Aquilla	Arlington	Account	1808	WBC:056; LVA-LP
Janney, Cosmelia	Arlington	Will	1834	WB4:079; File #332A
Janney, Cosmelia	Arlington	Bond	1834	WB4:081
Janney, Cosmelia	Arlington	Account	1836	AB7:260; LVA-LP
Janney, Cosmelia	Arlington	Account	1836	AB7:261; LVA-LP
Janney, Cosmelia	Arlington	Account	1837	AB7:260
Janney, Elisha	Alexandria	Tax Charge	1795	Tax PP 1795:15
Janney, Elisha	Alexandria	Tax Charge	1798	Tax PP 1798:09
Janney, Elisha	Alexandria	Tax Charge	1799	Tax PP 1799:20
Janney, Elisha	Alexandria	Tax Charge	1800	Tax PP 1800:19
Janney, Elisha & wife, merchant	Alexandria	Housekeeper	1799	1799(2):07A
Janney, Elisha & wife Mary	Alexandria	Deed	1809	CRK:062
Janney, Elisha, merchant	Alexandria	Housekeeper	1808	1808(1):04A
Janney, Elisha, w1, merchant	Alexandria	Head	1796	1796(3):1
Janney, Elizabeth	Alexandria	Will	1899	WB2:353; LP
Janney, Elizabeth, w/o Samuel H.	Alexandria	Will	1884	WB1:408; LP
Janney, Francis H.	Arlington	Guard. Acct.	1845	AB9:123
Janney, Francis H.	Arlington	Guard. Acct.	1846	AB9:256; LVA-LP
Janney, Francis H., c/o Abijah & Mary E.	Arlington	Guard.	1843	WB4:326
Janney, Jane	Arlington	Guard. Acct.	1845	AB9:122
Janney, Jane, c/o Abijah & Mary E.	Arlington	Guard.	1843	WB4:326
Janney, Jno.	Alexandria	Tax Charge	1795	Tax PP 1795:15
Janney, Jno.	Alexandria	Tax Charge	1798	Tax PP 1798:09
Janney, Jno. & wife, merchant	Alexandria	Head	1795	1795(4):09

NAME OR SUBJECT	LOCATION	TYPE	YEAR	REFERENCE(S)
Janney, Jno. & wife, merchant	Alexandria	Housekeeper	1799	1799(2):09A
Janney, John	Alexandria	Tax Charge	1796	Tax LP 1796:15
Janney, John	Alexandria	Tax Charge	1796	Tax LP 1796:15
Janney, John	Alexandria	Tax Charge	1796	Tax PP 1796:10
Janney, John	Alexandria	Mer. License	1798	Tax PP 1798:20-3
Janney, John	Alexandria	Mer. License	1799	Tax PP 1799:52-05w
Janney, John	Alexandria	Tax Charge	1799	Tax PP 1799:20
Janney, John	Alexandria	Mer. License	1800	Tax PP 1800:54(15)w
Janney, John	Alexandria	Tax Charge	1800	Tax PP 1800:19
Janney, John	Alexandria	Suit	1801	CRB:158
Janney [Janny], John, merchant	Alexandria	Head	1810	1810(4):04A
Janney, John	Arlington	Inventory	1823	AB5:176; LVA-LP
Janney, John	Arlington	Admin.	1823	OCR1822:039a
Janney, John	Arlington	Will P.	1823	OCR1822:039a
Janney, John	Arlington	Bond	1823	WB3:092
Janney, John	Arlington	Will	1823	WB3:093; File #217A
Janney, John	Arlington	Account	1824	AB5:281; LVA-LP
Janney, John	Arlington	Debts Due	1824	AB5:293
Janney, John	Arlington	Inventory	1824	LVA-LP
Janney, John	Arlington	Account	1825	AB5:421; LVA-LP
Janney, John	Arlington	Account	1826	LVA-LP
Janney, John	Arlington	Account	1827	AB6:284, 292; LVA-LP
Janney, John	Arlington	Account	1829	LVA-LP
Janney, John	Arlington	Account	1831	LVA-LP
Janney, John	Arlington	Account	1841	AB8:242; LVA-LP
Janney, John, Fairfax St.	Alexandria	Owner	1795	Tax L 1795:16
Janney, John, Fairfax St.	Alexandria	Occupant	1795	Tax L 1795:22
Janney, John H.	Arlington	Guard.	1825	WB3:209
Janney, John H.	Arlington	Guard. Acct.	1828	AB6:453; LVA-LP
Janney, John, Jr., of Loudoun Co.	Alexandria	Will	1899	WB2:351; LP
Janney, John, King St.	Alexandria	Occupant	1795	Tax L 1795:27
Janney, John, merchant	Alexandria	Housekeeper	1808	1808(4):25A
Janney, John, plt.	Alexandria	Suit	1801	CRB:161
Janney, John, St. Asaph St.	Alexandria	Owner	1795	Tax L 1795:16
Janney, Jonathan	Arlington	Inventory	1839	AB8:046; LVA-LP
Janney, Jonathan	Arlington	Will	1839	WB4:187; File #361A
Janney, Jonathan	Arlington	Bond	1839	WB4:188
Janney, Jonathan	Arlington	Account	1840	AB8:127; LVA-LP
Janney, Jonathan	Arlington	Account	1843	AB8:388; LVA-LP
Janney, Jos., clerk	Alexandria	Boarder	1799	1799(2):09A
Janney, Joseph	Alexandria	Boarder	1808	1808(2):10A
Janney, Joseph	Arlington	Claim	1812	ACO:124
Janney, Joseph	Arlington	Juryman	1824	ACO:237
Janney, Joseph	Arlington	Renounce	1853	WB6:244
Janney, Joseph & Co., St. Asaph St.	Alexandria	Occupant	1787	Tax L 1787:03
Janney, Joseph & Co.	Alexandria	Owner	1787	Tax L 1787:17
Janney, Joseph, Fairfax St.	Alexandria	Owner	1790	Tax L 1790:07
Janney, Joseph, of Baltimore MD	Arlington	Will	1853	WB6:238; File #499A
Janney, Joseph, retailer	Alexandria	Housekeeper	1808	1808(2):11A
Janney, M. & J., shoemakers	Alexandria	Housekeeper	1808	1808(1):02A
Janney, Mahlon H.	Alexandria	Will	1882	WB1:373; LP
Janney, Mary E.	Arlington	Inventory	1843	AB8:369; LVA-LP
Janney, Mary E.	Arlington	Will P.	1843	OCR1842:034
Janney, Mary E.	Arlington	Will	1843	WB4:325; File #398A
Janney, Mary E.	Arlington	Account	1844	AB9:006; LVA-LP
Janney, Mary E.	Arlington	Account	1845	AB9:128; LVA-LP
Janney, Mary E.	Arlington	Petition	1845	LVA-LP (Box 214)
Janney, Mary E.	Arlington	Account	1846	AB9:254; LVA-LP
Janney, Mary E.	Arlington	Account	1852	WB6:039; LVA-LP
Janney, Mary E., children of	Arlington	Guard.	1843	OCR1842:034
Janney, Phineas	Alexandria	Mer. License	1800	Tax PP 1800:54(15)r

NAME OR SUBJECT	LOCATION	TYPE	YEAR	REFERENCE(3)
Janney, Phineas	Alexandria	Tax Charge	1800	Tax PP 1800:19
Janney, Phineas	Arlington	Bond	1852	BB(np)
Janney, Phineas	Arlington	Will	1852	WB6:128; File #484A
Janney, Phineas	Arlington	Account	1853	WB6:360; LVA-LP
Janney, Phineas	Arlington	Account	1853	WB6:252; LVA-LP
Janney, Phineas	Arlington	Debts	1853	WB6:224; LVA-LP
Janney, Phineas	Arlington	Account	1856	WB7:112, 162; LVA-LP
Janney, Phineas	Arlington	Account	1857	WB7:350
Janney, Phineas	Arlington	Account	1858	WB7:350; LVA-LP
Janney, Phineas	Arlington	Account	1859	WB7:383; LVA-LP
Janney, Phineas	Arlington	Account	1860	WB7:504; LVA-LP
Janney, Phineas	Arlington	Account	1867	WB9:009
Janney, Phineas	Arlington	Account	1868	WB9:121
Janney, Phinias, merchant	Alexandria	Housekeeper	1808	1808(3):20A
Janney, Rachel E.	Arlington	Guard. Acct.	1845	AB9:122
Janney, Rachel E.	Arlington	Guard. Acct.	1846	AB9:256; LVA-LP
Janney, Rachel E., c/o Abijah & Mary E.	Arlington	Guard.	1843	WB4:326
Janney, Rebecca	Arlington	Guard. Acct.	1845	AB9:123
Janney, Rebecca	Arlington	Guard. Acct.	1846	AB9:254
Janney, Rebecca, c/o Abijah & Mary E.	Arlington	Guard.	1843	WB4:326
Janney, Samuel H.	Alexandria	Will	1887	WB1:452
Janney, Sarah S.	Arlington	Account	1855	LVA-LP
Janney, Sarah S.	Arlington	Account	1856	LVA-LP
Janney, Sarah S., of Alexandria	Frederick	Will	1853	CF1884-019CC
Janney, Susannah	Alexandria	Resident	1800	1800(4):09B
Janney, Thomas	Alexandria	Mer. License	1800	Tax PP 1800:54(15)r
Janney, Thomas	Arlington	Respondent	1812	ACO:123, 125
Janney, Thomas, plt.	Alexandria	Suit	1822	CRL:578
Janney, Thos.	Alexandria	Tax Charge	1800	Tax PP 1800:19
Janney [Janny], Thos., merchant	Alexandria	Head	1810	1810(4):02A
Janney, Thos., merchant	Alexandria	Housekeeper	1808	1808(4):27A
Janney [Janny], Abel	Alexandria	Tax Charge	1800	Tax PP 1800:19
Janny, Abel, collector	Alexandria	Head	1810	1810(4):07A
Janny, John, merchant	Alexandria	Head	1810	1810(4):04A
Janny, Thos., merchant	Alexandria	Head	1810	1810(4):02A
Jarbar, Martha	Alexandria	Boarder	1795	1795(4a):04
Jarbo, Bennitt, retailer & shopkeeper	Alexandria	Housekeeper	1808	1808(2):12A
Jarbo, Ignatius, waterman	Alexandria	Housekeeper	1808	1808(1):09A
Jarbo, Joseph, waterman	Alexandria	Housekeeper	1808	1808(1):07A
Jarbo, Vernon	Arlington	Ordinary	1807	OBL2(np)
Jarbo, Vernon, seaman, shopkpr. & T.L.	Alexandria	Housekeeper	1808	1808(1):05A
Jarbo, Wm., seaman	Alexandria	Housekeeper	1808	1808(1):03A
Jarboe, Ignatius	Arlington	Ordinary	1809	OBL2(np)(2)
Jarbos, Joseph, grantor	Arlington	Indenture D.	1805	ID3:106
Jarbos, Joseph, in gaol	Arlington	Insolvent	1805	ID3:104
Jarvis, John, at his house	Arlington	Ordinary	1824	OBL3(np)
Jarvis, Wm., labourer	Alexandria	Head	1810	1810(1):03A
Jasper, Jahrell	Arlington	Libellant	1813	ACO:137
Javens, Thompson, grantor	Arlington	Indenture D.	1826	ID:064
Javens, Thompson, in jail	Arlington	Insolvent	1826	ID:062
Javins, John D.	Arlington	Apprentice	1826	OCR1822:110a
Javins, John, in Alexandria Co.	Arlington	Ordinary	1825	OBL4(np)
Jebo, John	Alexandria	Tax Charge	1788	Tax PP 1788:09
Jefferies, Hannah	Alexandria	Resident	1800	1800(4):16B
Jefferson, Elizabeth	Arlington	Apprentice	1843	OCR1842:033
Jefferson, Frederick (C)	Arlington	Apprentice	1815	OCR1811:323
Jefferson, Frederick (C)	Arlington	Apprentice	1823	OCR1822:041a
Jefferson, Hamilton, n/o Benjamin	Arlington	Apprentice	1812	OCR1811:071
Jefferson, Jas., shoemaker	Alexandria	Housekeeper	1808	1808(4):25A
Jefferson, Jeremiah, c/o Sarah	Arlington	Apprentice	1822	OCR1822:025
Jefferson, Jeremiah, labourer	Alexandria	Head	1810	1810(4):05A

NAME OR SUBJECT	LOCATION	TYPE	YEAR	REFERENCE(S)
Jefferson, Jerre, waggoner	Alexandria	Housekeeper	1808	1808(3):20A
Jefferson, Jno.	Alexandria	Tax Charge	1795	Tax PP 1795:14
Jefferson, Jno., Royal St.	Alexandria	Occupant	1795	Tax L 1795:32
Jefferson, John	Alexandria	Tithable +16	1788	Tax PP 1788:12
Jefferson, John	Alexandria	Tithable +16	1789	Tax PP 1789:14
Jefferson, John	Alexandria	Tithable +16	1790	Tax PP 1790:11
Jefferson, John	Alexandria	Tax Charge	1796	Tax LP 1796:15
Jefferson, John	Alexandria	Tax Charge	1796	Tax PP 1796:09
Jefferson, Lucy & child, washwoman	Alexandria	Housekeeper	1808	1808(2):16A
Jefferson, Nancy	Alexandria	Will	1891	WB1:601; LP
Jefferson, Thomas	Alexandria	Tax Charge	1799	Tax PP 1799:20
Jefferson, Thos.	Alexandria	Tax Charge	1800	Tax PP 1800:19
Jefferson, Thos., tailor	Alexandria	Boarder	1799	1799(2):04A
Jefferson, Thos., taylor	Alexandria	Boarder	1799	1799(2):18A
Jefferson, Wilhelmina	Arlington	Apprentice	1844	OCR1842:083
Jeffrey, Ann	Arlington	Will	1840	WB4:283; File #383A
Jeffreys, Geo.	Alexandria	Boarder	1799	1799(2):17A
Jeffries, Hugh	Alexandria	Tax Charge	1796	Tax LP 1796:15
Jeffris, Hanah, labourrer	Alexandria	Boarder	1800	1800(4):16A
Jenckes, Crawford	Alexandria	Tax Charge	1788	Tax PP 1788:09
Jenckes, Crawford	Alexandria	Tithable +16	1789	Tax PP 1789:20
Jenckes, Winsor & Co., King St.	Alexandria	Owner	1790	Tax L 1790:07
Jenckes, Winsor & Co.	Alexandria	Tax Charge	1790	Tax PP 1790:07
Jencks & Winsor, King St.	Alexandria	Occupant	1787	Tax L 1787:11
Jencks, Joseph	Alexandria	Tax Charge	1787	Tax PP 1787:08
Jencks, William	Alexandria	Tithable +16	1790	Tax PP 1790:07
Jenegel, Ignatius	Alexandria	Mer. License	1799	Tax PP 1799:52-05r
Jenifer, Daniel	Arlington	Admin.	1812	WB1:165
Jenigal, Enos	Alexandria	Mer. License	1798	Tax PP 1798:20-3
Jenings, Henry	Alexandria	Boarder	1808	1808(2):12A
Jenizel, Enos	Alexandria	Tax Charge	1800	Tax PP 1800:19
Jenkes & Winsor	Alexandria	Tax Charge	1796	Tax LP 1796:15
Jenkin & Burn, Water St.	Alexandria	Occupant	1787	Tax L 1787:11
Jenkin, Wm.	Alexandria	Tax Charge	1798	Tax PP 1798:18
Jenkins & Potts	Alexandria	Tax Charge	1798	Tax PP 1798:09
Jenkins, Alonzo	Arlington	Apprentice	1822	OCR1822:012
Jenkins, Charles	Alexandria	Tax Charge	1799	Tax PP 1799:20
Jenkins, Daniel	Arlington	Will	1818	WB2:265; File #155A
Jenkins, Daniel	Arlington	Appraisal	1832	LVA-LP
Jenkins, David	Alexandria	Tax Charge	1800	Tax PP 1800:19
Jenkins, David, def.	Alexandria	Suit	1802	CRC:044
Jenkins, David, for playing Faro	Arlington	Defendant	1801	PA:082
Jenkins, David, taylor	Alexandria	Housekeeper	1808	1808(2):11A
Jenkins, David, taylor	Alexandria	Head	1810	1810(2):02A
Jenkins, Eleanor, d/o Mary	Alexandria	Suit	1809	CRG:131
Jenkins, George	Arlington	Will	1831	WB3:387; File #293A
Jenkins, George	Arlington	Account	1839	AB8:051; LVA-LP
Jenkins, George, plt.	Alexandria	Suit	1801	CRB:102
Jenkins, Jas., merchant	Alexandria	Housekeeper	1808	1808(1):08A
Jenkins, Jemima	Arlington	Bond	1832	WB4:047
Jenkins, Jemima	Arlington	Will	1832	WB4:047; File #318A
Jenkins, John T.	Arlington	Complainant	1838	LSA:034
Jenkins, Johnson	Alexandria	Tithable +16	1788	Tax PP 1788:09
Jenkins, Johnson	Alexandria	Tithable +16	1789	Tax PP 1789:10
Jenkins, Johnson	Alexandria	Tax Charge	1790	Tax PP 1790:08
Jenkins, Johnson	Alexandria	Tax Charge	1799	Tax PP 1799:20
Jenkins, Johnson & wife, sail maker	Alexandria	Housekeeper	1799	1799(2):14A
Jenkins, Johnston	Alexandria	Tax Charge	1800	Tax PP 1800:19
Jenkins, Joseph	Arlington	Admin.	1828	OCR1822:163a
Jenkins, Joseph	Arlington	Will P.	1828	OCR1822:163a
Jenkins, Joseph	Arlington	Admin.	1828	WB3:337; LVA-LP

NAME OR SUBJECT	LOCATION	TYPE	YEAR	REFERENCE(S)
Jenkins, Joseph	Arlington	Account	1829	AB6:487; LVA-LP
Jenkins, Joseph, at his house	Arlington	Ordinary	1824	OBL3(np)
Jenkins, Joseph, in Alexandria Co.	Arlington	Ordinary	1825	OBL4(np)
Jenkins, Joseph, near Wash. Bridge	Arlington	Ordinary	1823	OBL3(np)
Jenkins, Richard	Alexandria	Tax Charge	1787	Tax PP 1787:08
Jenkins, Richard	Alexandria	Tax Charge	1788	Tax PP 1788:09
Jenkins, Richard	Alexandria	Tax Charge	1789	Tax PP 1789:10
Jenkins, Richard	Alexandria	Tax Charge	1790	Tax PP 1790:08
Jenkins, Richard	Alexandria	Tax Charge	1795	Tax PP 1795:15
Jenkins, Richard	Alexandria	Tax Charge	1796	Tax PP 1796:09
Jenkins, Richard	Alexandria	Tax Charge	1798	Tax PP 1798:09
Jenkins, Richard	Alexandria	Tax Charge	1799	Tax PP 1799:20
Jenkins, Richard	Alexandria	Tax Charge	1800	Tax PP 1800:19
Jenkins, Richard, Water St.	Alexandria	Occupant	1790	Tax L 1790:04
Jenkins, Richd.	Alexandria	Tax Charge	1796	Tax LP 1796:15
Jenkins, Richd., laborer	Alexandria	Housekeeper	1808	1808(1):09A
Jenkins, Richd., labourer	Alexandria	Head	1810	1810(3):01A
Jenkins, Sarah	Arlington	Apprentice	1805	OCR1801:258
Jenkins, William	Arlington	Apprentice	1828	OCR1822:166
Jenkins, William	Arlington	Guard. Acct.	1829	AB6:489; LVA-LP
Jenkins, William, c/o Joseph	Arlington	Guard.	1828	OCR1822:164a
Jenkins, William H.	Arlington	Guard. Acct.	1833	AB7:083; LVA-LP
Jenkins, William Henry	Arlington	Guard.	1828	WB3:336
Jenks & Winsor, Estate, King St.	Alexandria	Owner	1795	Tax L 1795:34
Jenks, William	Arlington	Admin.	1859	WB7:446
Jenks, William	Arlington	Inventory	1859	WB7:446; LVA-LP
Jenney, Elieser, w1, merchant	Alexandria	Head	1796	1796(3):1
Jennings, Daniel & wife Ann	Alexandria	Deed	1770	CRI:171
Jennings, Isaac, tanner	Alexandria	Boarder	1799	1799(2):12A
Jennings, Jesse, seaman	Alexandria	Head	1810	1810(1):11A
Jennings, Jno.	Alexandria	Tax Charge	1795	Tax PP 1795:14
Jennings, [blank]	Alexandria	Tax Charge	1796	Tax LP 1796:04
Jenzel, Enos	Alexandria	Mer. License	1800	Tax PP 1800:54(15)r
Jepson, Saml., hatter	Alexandria	Head	1810	1810(1):04A
Jervey, Thomas Hall, Charleston S.C.	Alexandria	Deposition	1810	CRK:181
Jewell, Elisha	Arlington	Ordinary	1805	OBL1(np)
Jewell, Elisha	Arlington	Will	1834	WB4:083; File #334A
Jewell, Elisha, farmer	Alexandria	Housekeeper	1808	1808(3):21A
Jewell, Emma, of Kansas City MO	Arlington	Will	1899	WB10:391; File #086A
Jewell, William, of Georgetown DC	Arlington	Will	1856	WB10:139; File #737A
Jewett, Joseph G., in confinement	Arlington	Insolvent	1813	ID2:189
Jewett, Joseph, grantor	Arlington	Indenture D.	1813	ID2:194
Jinkings, Jonson & wife Sarah	Alexandria	Resident	1800	1800(4):10B
Jinkings, Jonston, sailmaker	Alexandria	Head	1800	1800(4):10A
Jinkins, George, w(5)4, gentleman	Alexandria	Head	1795	1796(3):7
Jinkins, Thomas	Arlington	Apprentice	1813	OCR1811:200
Job, Joel	Alexandria	Tax Charge	1795	Tax PP 1795:14
Job, Joel, wheelright	Alexandria	Head	1810	1810(4):05A
Jobson, David	Alexandria	Boarder	1808	1808(2):16A
Jobson, James	Alexandria	Tax Charge	1796	Tax PP 1796:10
Jobson, Jas.	Alexandria	Tax Charge	1795	Tax PP 1795:15
John Anderson & Co.	Alexandria	Tax Charge	1796	Tax PP 1796:01
John Dunlap & Co., complt.	Alexandria	Suit	1816	CRK:236
John Dunlop & Co., def.	Alexandria	Suit	1801	CRC:282
John Dunlop & Co., plt.	Alexandria	Suit	1805	CRE:001
John, George	Alexandria	Tax Charge	1799	Tax PP 1799:20
John W. Massie & Co.	Arlington	Inventory	1819	AB4:062
John, Walter	Alexandria	Tax Charge	1799	Tax PP 1799:20
Johns, Elias, c/o Dezina Workinson	Arlington	Apprentice	1815	OCR1811:306
Johns, George	Alexandria	Tax Charge	1800	Tax PP 1800:19
Johns, George	Arlington	Admin.	1822	OCR1822:005

NAME OR SUBJECT	LOCATION	TYPE	YEAR	REFERENCE(S)
Johns, George	Arlington	Admin.	1822	WB3:050
Johns, George	Arlington	Account	1823	AB5:171; LVA-LP
Johns, John	Arlington	Apprentice	1804	OCR1801:151
Johns, John, fishmonger	Alexandria	Housekeeper	1808	1808(2):17A
Johns, Peter	Alexandria	Tax Charge	1800	Tax PP 1800:19
Johns, Peter, seaman	Alexandria	Head	1810	1810(2):06A
Johns, Richard H.	Alexandria	Deposition	1818	CRK:465
Johns, Widow, seamstress	Alexandria	Head	1810	1810(4):06A
Johns, William	Alexandria	Tax Charge	1800	Tax PP 1800:19
Johns, Wm.	Alexandria	Tax Charge	1796	Tax LP 1796:15
Johns, Wm.	Alexandria	Tax Charge	1798	Tax PP 1798:09
Johnson & Marks, Fairfax St.	Alexandria	Occupant	1795	Tax L 1795:27
Johnson, Alexander McK.	Arlington	Will	1828	WB3:355
Johnson, Alexious	Arlington	Inventory	1843	AB8:368; LVA-LP
Johnson, Alexious	Arlington	Will P.	1843	OCR1842:031
Johnson, Alexious	Arlington	Will	1843	WB4:323; File #396A
Johnson, Alexis	Arlington	Account	1844	AB9:004; LVA-LP
Johnson, Alexis	Arlington	Account	1847	AB9:267
Johnson, Andrew Gill	Arlington	Will	1900	WB10:445; File #801A
Johnson, Charles F.M.	Arlington	Inventory	1872	WB9:341
Johnson, Charles F.M.	Arlington	Sale	1872	WB9:342
Johnson, D.M.	Alexandria	Tax Charge	1798	Tax PP 1798:09
Johnson, D.M.	Alexandria	Tax Charge	1799	Tax PP 1799:20
Johnson, D.M.	Alexandria	Tax Charge	1800	Tax PP 1800:19
Johnson, David	Alexandria	Tithable +16	1788	Tax PP 1788:11
Johnson, Dennis & wife, sea captain	Alexandria	Housekeeper	1799	1799(2):19A
Johnson, Dennis M., sea captain	Alexandria	Housekeeper	1808	1808(1):07A
Johnson, George	Arlington	Ordinary	1820	OBL3(np)
Johnson, Harry	Alexandria	Tax Charge	1799	Tax PP 1799:20
Johnson, Harry	Alexandria	Tax Charge	1800	Tax PP 1800:19
Johnson, Henry & wife (C)	Alexandria	Housekeeper	1799	1799(2):12A
Johnson, Isaac	Alexandria	Tax Charge	1796	Tax PP 1796:09
Johnson, Isaac	Alexandria	Tax Charge	1798	Tax PP 1798:09
Johnson, J.B., of Washington DC	Alexandria	Will	1893	WB2:068; LP
Johnson, John	Alexandria	Tithable +16	1788	Tax PP 1788:01
Johnson, John	Alexandria	Tax Charge	1795	Tax PP 1795:15
Johnson, John	Alexandria	Tax Charge	1796	Tax LP 1796:15
Johnson, John	Alexandria	Tax Charge	1798	Tax PP 1798:09
Johnson, John	Alexandria	Tax Charge	1799	Tax PP 1799:20
Johnson, John T., c/o John T.	Arlington	Guard. Acct.	1868	WB9:050
Johnson, Mary	Alexandria	Head	1810	1810(4):08A
Johnson, Rebecca J., of Pr. Wm. Co.	Alexandria	Will	1874	WB1:113; LP
Johnson, Robert (C)	Arlington	Apprentice	1827	OCR1822:148a
Johnson, Thomas	Arlington	Will (NR)	1867	File #082A
Johnson, Virginia Page, c/o John T.	Arlington	Guard. Acct.	1868	WB9:050
Johnson, Walter	Alexandria	Tithable +16	1788	Tax PP 1788:03
Johnson, Walter	Arlington	Witness	1794	OT:07/11/1794
Johnson, Walter	Alexandria	Tax Charge	1798	Tax PP 1798:09
Johnson, Walther, w(1), carpenter	Alexandria	Head	1796	1796(3):1
Johnson, William	Alexandria	Tax Charge	1799	Tax PP 1799:20
Johnson, William	Alexandria	Tax Charge	1800	Tax PP 1800:19
Johnson, William	Arlington	Apprentice	1812	OCR1811:047
Johnson, William	Arlington	Guard. Acct.	1816	AB2:397
Johnson, William A.	Alexandria	Will	1879	WB1:282; LP
Johnston, Alexander M.	Arlington	Guard. Acct.	1814	AB1:354; LVA-LP
Johnston, Alexander M.	Arlington	Guard. Acct.	1818	AB3:187; LVA-LP
Johnston, Alexander M.	Arlington	Guard. Acct.	1824	AB5:322; LVA-LP
Johnston, Alexander M., c/o Dennis M.	Arlington	Guard. Acct.	1823	AB5:186; LVA-LP
Johnston, Alexander McKenzie	Arlington	Will	1830	WB3:355; File #281A
Johnston, Andrew R.	Arlington	Admin.	1815	WB2:072
Johnston, Antoinette F.	Arlington	Will	1891	WB10:180; File #748A

NAME OR SUBJECT	LOCATION	TYPE	YEAR	REFERENCE(S)
Johnston, Capt.	Alexandria	Tax Charge	1796	Tax LP 1796:15
Johnston, Charles A., grantee	Arlington	Indenture D.	1828	ID:189
Johnston, Charles P.	Arlington	Guard. Acct.	1814	AB1:354; LVA-LP
Johnston, Charles P.	Arlington	Guard. Acct.	1818	AB3:185; LVA-LP
Johnston, Charles P.	Arlington	Guard. Acct.	1824	AB5:322; LVA-LP
Johnston, Charles P., c/o Dennis M.	Arlington	Guard. Acct.	1823	AB5:186
Johnston, Dennis M.	Arlington	Account	1818	AB3:181; LVA-LP
Johnston, Dennis M.	Arlington	Account	1823	AB5:185; LVA-LP
Johnston, Dennis M.	Arlington	Account	1824	AB5:321; LVA-LP
Johnston, Dennis M., Capt., orphans of	Arlington	Guard.	1823	OCR1822:048a
Johnston, Dennis M., children of	Arlington	Guard. Acct.	1829	AB6:490; LVA-LP
Johnston, Dennis M., plt.	Alexandria	Suit	1801	CRF:074
Johnston, Dennis, mariner	Alexandria	Head	1810	1810(1):10A
Johnston, Dennis Mc.	Arlington	Admin.	1811	WB1:125
Johnston, Dennis McCarty	Arlington	Account	1812	AB1:165; LVA-LP
Johnston, Dennis McCarty, Capt.	Arlington	Sale	1812	AB1:163
Johnston, Dennis McCarty, Capt.	Arlington	Inventory	1812	AB1:159; LVA-LP
Johnston, Dennis McCarty, children	Arlington	Guard. Acct.	1813	AB1:288; LVA-LP
Johnston, Dennis McCarty, orphans of	Arlington	Guard.	1811	WB1:126
Johnston, Eleanor, c/o William	Arlington	Guard.	1815	WB2:061
Johnston, Geo.	Alexandria	Tax Charge	1795	Tax PP 1795:14
Johnston, Geo. C.S.	Arlington	Apprentice	1822	OCR1822:029a
Johnston, George	Arlington	Will	1897	WB10:344; File #777A
Johnston, George	Alexandria	Will	1897	WB2:229; LP
Johnston, Hezekiah, cooper	Alexandria	Head	1810	1810(4):02A
Johnston, Horace S.	Arlington	Will	1893	WB10:248
Johnston, James	Alexandria	Tax Charge	1787	Tax PP 1787:08
Johnston, James T.	Alexandria	Will	1876	WB1:208; LP
Johnston, Jane	Alexandria	Will	1884	WB1:406; LP
Johnston, Jno. & wife, hatter	Alexandria	Housekeeper	1799	1799(2):03A
Johnston, Jno., Fairfax St.	Alexandria	Occupant	1795	Tax L 1795:26
Johnston, John	Alexandria	Mer. License	1799	Tax PP 1799:52-05r
Johnston, John D.	Arlington	Guard. Acct.	1814	AB1:352; LVA-LP
Johnston, John D.	Arlington	Guard. Acct.	1818	AB3:183; LVA-LP
Johnston, John D.	Arlington	Guard. Acct.	1820	LVA-LP
Johnston, John D.	Arlington	Guard. Acct.	1824	AB5:322; LVA-LP
Johnston, John D., c/o Dennis M.	Arlington	Guard. Acct.	1823	AB5:186; LVA-LP
Johnston, John, hatter	Alexandria	Housekeeper	1808	1808(4):26A
Johnston, John, hatter	Alexandria	Head	1810	1810(4):05A
Johnston, John, labourer	Alexandria	Head	1810	1810(2):06A
Johnston, John M., seaman	Alexandria	Head	1810	1810(2):07A
Johnston, John R.	Arlington	Will	1882	WB10:029
Johnston, John, seaman & shopkeeper	Alexandria	Housekeeper	1808	1808(1):03A
Johnston, John, w(2)3, hatter	Alexandria	Head	1796	1796(3):5
Johnston, Joshua (C)	Arlington	Crime	1799	OT:06/11/1799
Johnston, Josiah, c/o William	Arlington	Guard.	1815	WB2:297
Johnston, Levi, c/o Jane	Arlington	Apprentice	1803	OCR1801:138
Johnston, Margaret Louisa (C)	Arlington	Will	1859	WB7:412; File #566A
Johnston, Margery	Arlington	Will	1839	WB4:223; File #367A
Johnston, Martha D.	Arlington	Guard.	1840	WB4:271
Johnston, Mary (C), washwoman	Alexandria	Housekeeper	1808	1808(4):24A
Johnston, Mary, seamstress	Alexandria	Head	1810	1810(4):01A
Johnston, Matthew	Alexandria	Deposition	1822	CRL:472
Johnston, Mr.	Alexandria	Boarder	1808	1808(4):26A
Johnston, Philip, c/o Wm. of King Geo.	Arlington	Apprentice	1816	OCR1811:346
Johnston, Reuben	Arlington	Deposition	1806	ACR:029
Johnston, Reuben	Arlington	Will	1840	WB4:263; File #379A
Johnston, Reuben	Arlington	Bond	1840	WB4:272
Johnston, Reuben	Arlington	Inventory	1841	AB8:176a; LVA-LP
Johnston, Reuben	Arlington	Debts Due	1841	AB8:178
Johnston, Reuben	Arlington	Account	1842	AB8:277; LVA-LP

NAME OR SUBJECT	LOCATION	TYPE	YEAR	REFERENCE(S)
Johnston, Reuben	Arlington	Account	1842	OCR1842:007
Johnston, Reuben	Arlington	Account	1843	AB8:418; LVA-LP
Johnston, Reuben	Arlington	Petition	1843	LVA-LP (Box 214)
Johnston, Reuben	Arlington	Deed/Trust	1855	WB7:018
Johnston, Reuben, grantee	Arlington	Indenture D.	1832	ID:388
Johnston, Reuben, merchant	Alexandria	Head	1810	1810(1):06A
Johnston, Reuben, sea captain	Alexandria	Housekeeper	1808	1808(1):09A
Johnston, Reuben, the Elder	Arlington	Account	1842	OCR1842:008
Johnston, Richard	Alexandria	Tax Charge	1796	Tax LP 1796:15
Johnston, Samuel	Arlington	Apprentice	1815	OCR1811:353
Johnston, Samuel, c/o Susanna	Arlington	Apprentice	1803	OCR1801:094
Johnston, Samuel, c/o William	Arlington	Guard.	1815	WB2:297
Johnston, Sarah M.	Arlington	Guard. Acct.	1814	AB1:352; LVA-LP
Johnston, Sarah M.	Arlington	Guard. Acct.	1818	AB3:183; LVA-LP
Johnston, Sarah M., c/o Dennis M.	Arlington	Guard. Acct.	1823	AB5:185
Johnston, Suky (C), washwoman	Alexandria	Housekeeper	1808	1808(3):20A
Johnston, Susanah, washwoman	Alexandria	Housekeeper	1808	1808(4):26A
Johnston, Thomas	Arlington	Will	1867	File #082A
Johnston v. Lawrason	Arlington	Suit	1805	LVA-LP (Accounts)
Johnston, Walter	Alexandria	Tax Charge	1795	Tax PP 1795:15
Johnston, William	Arlington	Libellant	1811	ACO:119
Johnston, William	Arlington	Libellant	1821	ACO:198
Johnston, William	Arlington	Libellant	1822	ACO:205
Johnston, William	Arlington	Libellant	1823	ACO:211
Johnston, William, children of	Arlington	Guard. Acct.	1819	AB3:328; LVA-LP
Johnston, William, grantor	Arlington	Indenture D.	1828	ID:189
Johnston, William, in jail	Arlington	Insolvent	1828	ID:187
Johnston, Wm.	Alexandria	Serv./Appr.	1800	1800(4):04B
Johnston, Wm. & wife, shoemaker	Alexandria	Housekeeper	1799	1799(2):14A
Johnston, Wm., shoemaker	Alexandria	Housekeeper	1808	1808(3):21A
Joice, Pierce	Alexandria	Tax Charge	1799	Tax PP 1799:20
Joliff, Wm. & Brown, merchants	Alexandria	Housekeeper	1808	1808(3):19A
Jolliffe, William, merchant	Alexandria	Head	1810	1810(4):07A
Jolly, Christianna A.	Alexandria	Will	1880	WBC1:033; LP
Jolly, J., Prince St.	Alexandria	Occupant	1787	Tax L 1787:24
Jolly, Jno.	Alexandria	Tax Charge	1795	Tax PP 1795:15
Jolly, Jno.	Alexandria	Tax Charge	1798	Tax PP 1798:09
Jolly, John	Alexandria	Owner	1787	Tax L 1787:17
Jolly, John	Alexandria	Tax Charge	1787	Tax PP 1787:08
Jolly, John	Alexandria	Tax Charge	1788	Tax PP 1788:09
Jolly, John	Alexandria	Tax Charge	1789	Tax PP 1789:10
Jolly, John	Alexandria	Tax Charge	1790	Tax PP 1790:07
Jolly, John, Fairfax St.	Alexandria	Occupant	1787	Tax L 1787:22
Jonekin, Wm., w(2), joiner	Alexandria	Head	1796	1796(3):4
Jones, Butler	Alexandria	Tax Charge	1795	Tax PP 1795:15
Jones, Catesby	Arlington	Guard.	1808	WBC:066
Jones, Charles	Alexandria	Tax Charge	1796	Tax LP 1796:15
Jones, Charles	Alexandria	Tax Charge	1796	Tax PP 1796:09
Jones, Charles	Alexandria	Tax Charge	1800	Tax PP 1800:19
Jones, Charles	Arlington	Defendant	1802	PA:197
Jones, Charles, carriage maker	Alexandria	Agreement	1798	CRB:340
Jones, Charles, def.	Alexandria	Suit	1801	CRB:335
Jones, Colin	Alexandria	Boarder	1808	1808(3):21A
Jones, Daniel (C)	Alexandria	Boarder	1808	1808(3):20B
Jones, Daniel (C), laborer	Alexandria	Housekeeper	1808	1808(2):14A
Jones, Daniel, labourer	Alexandria	Head	1810	1810(2):04A
Jones, David	Alexandria	Owner	1787	Tax L 1787:17
Jones, David	Alexandria	Tax Charge	1787	Tax PP 1787:08
Jones, David	Alexandria	Tax Charge	1788	Tax PP 1788:09
Jones, David, c/o Anne	Arlington	Apprentice	1804	OCR1801:152
Jones, David, Princess St.	Alexandria	Occupant	1787	Tax L 1787:17

NAME OR SUBJECT	LOCATION	TYPE	YEAR	REFERENCE(S)
Jones, David, Union St.	Alexandria	Occupant	1787	Tax L 1787:19
Jones, Dudley	Arlington	Apprentice	1823	OCR1822:040
Jones, Dudley	Arlington	Apprentice	1823	OCR1822:038
Jones, Edward, weaver	Alexandria	Head	1810	1810(1):12A
Jones, Edwd., shopkeeper	Alexandria	Housekeeper	1808	1808(1):05A
Jones, Elizabeth, washwoman	Alexandria	Housekeeper	1808	1808(1):05A
Jones, Emanuel	Alexandria	Will	1891	WB1:600; LP
Jones, Ezekiel	Alexandria	Will	1870	WBC1:047; LP
Jones, Ezra	Alexandria	Boarder	1808	1808(3):21A
Jones, Geo. & wife, labourer	Alexandria	Housekeeper	1799	1799(2):13A
Jones, Grace	Arlington	Admin.	1836	WB4:104
Jones, Henry (C)	Arlington	Apprentice	1844	OCR1842:084
Jones, Henry (C)	Arlington	Apprentice	1845	OCR1842:130
Jones, Jas., tanner	Alexandria	Boarder	1799	1799(2):12A
Jones, Jno. & wife, shoemaker	Alexandria	Housekeeper	1799	1799(2):17A
Jones, Job	Alexandria	Boarder	1808	1808(4):24A
Jones, John	Alexandria	Tax Charge	1798	Tax PP 1798:09
Jones, John	Alexandria	Tax Charge	1799	Tax PP 1799:20
Jones, John	Alexandria	Tax Charge	1800	Tax PP 1800:19
Jones, John & wife Sary Ann	Alexandria	Resident	1800	1800(4):07B
Jones, John A.	Alexandria	Will	1900	WB2:409; LP
Jones, John, c/o Anne	Arlington	Apprentice	1804	OCR1801:155
Jones, John, shoemaker	Alexandria	Head	1800	1800(4):07A
Jones, John W.	Arlington	Inventory	1800	CRA:332
Jones, John W.	Arlington	Account	1802	WBA:078; LVA-LP
Jones, Joseph	Alexandria	Serv./Appr.	1800	1800(4):05B
Jones, Levi	Arlington	Will	1886	WB10:073; File #722A
Jones, Lewin	Alexandria	Tax Charge	1799	Tax PP 1799:20
Jones, Lewin, c/o Margaret	Arlington	Apprentice	1803	OCR1801:111
Jones, Lucy (C), c/o Polly Cole	Arlington	Apprentice	1812	OCR1811:048
Jones, Martha	Arlington	Appraisal	1836	LVA-LP
Jones, Martha	Arlington	Admin.	1836	WB4:106
Jones, Martha	Arlington	Account	1837	AB7:262a; LVA-LP
Jones, Nelly, sempstress	Alexandria	Housekeeper	1808	1808(2):13A
Jones, Peggy	Alexandria	Head	1810	1810(4):07A
Jones, Rich.	Alexandria	Boarder	1808	1808(3):20A
Jones, Sarah (C)	Arlington	Apprentice	1827	OCR1822:129
Jones, Selina, c/o Nancy	Arlington	Apprentice	1842	OCR1842:002
Jones, Thomas H., b. Ireland	Arlington	Alien Entry	1801	RA:24/01/01
Jones, Thomas, seaman	Alexandria	Head	1810	1810(1):10A
Jones, Thos., merchant	Alexandria	Housekeeper	1808	1808(3):19A
Jones, Walter	Alexandria	Tax Charge	1799	Tax PP 1799:20
Jones, Walter	Alexandria	Tax Charge	1800	Tax PP 1800:19
Jones, Walter & wive Ann Lucinda	Alexandria	Deed	1820	CRL:499
Jones, Walter, attorney at law	Alexandria	Boarder	1799	1799(2):02A
Jones, Walter, attorney at law	Alexandria	Housekeeper	1799	1799(2):08A
Jones, Walter, def.	Alexandria	Suit	1819	CRK:497
Jones, Walter, Jr., def.	Alexandria	Suit	1803	CRD:099
Jones, Walter, Jr., U.S. Attorney	Arlington	Payment	1808	ACO:096
Jones, Walter, lawyer	Alexandria	Housekeeper	1808	1808(2):13A
Jones, William	Alexandria	Tax Charge	1787	Tax PP 1787:08
Jones, William	Alexandria	Tithable +16	1788	Tax PP 1788:08
Jones, William	Alexandria	Tax Charge	1788	Tax PP 1788:09
Jones, William H.	Arlington	Inventory	1825	AB6:134; LVA-LP
Jones, William H.	Arlington	Admin.	1825	OCR1822:102
Jones, William H.	Arlington	Account	1826	AB6:171; LVA-LP
Jones, William, house joiner	Alexandria	Head	1810	1810(3):08A
Jones, William Loftus, c/o Elizabeth	Arlington	Apprentice	1813	OCR1811:204
Jones, Wm.	Alexandria	Boarder	1808	1808(3):20A
Jones, Wm., waterman	Alexandria	Housekeeper	1808	1808(2):17A
Jones, [blank]	Alexandria	Tax Charge	1796	Tax LP 1796:15

NAME OR SUBJECT	LOCATION	TYPE	YEAR	REFERENCE(S)
Jonston, Denniel & wife Jane	Alexandria	Resident	1800	1800(4):08B
Jonston, Denniel, marrener	Alexandria	Head	1800	1800(4):08A
Jonston, Sarah, laundress	Alexandria	Head	1800	1800(4):10A
Jonston, Wm. & wife Mary	Alexandria	Resident	1800	1800(4):11B
Jonston, Wm., shoemaker	Alexandria	Head	1800	1800(4):11A
Jordan, Thompson, c/o William	Arlington	Apprentice	1813	OCR1811:182
Jordon, Alexr., King St.	Alexandria	Occupant	1795	Tax L 1795:18
Jordon, John, grantor	Arlington	Indenture D.	1831	ID:353
Jordon, John, in jail	Arlington	Insolvent	1831	ID:349
Jordon, Thompson, grantee	Arlington	Indenture D.	1831	ID:353
Joseph, Jno. & wife (C), labourer	Alexandria	Housekeeper	1799	1799(2):15A
Joseph Riddle & Co.	Alexandria	Tax Charge	1799	Tax PP 1799:35
Joseph Riddle & Co.	Alexandria	Mer. License	1799	Tax PP 1799:52-09w
Joseph Riddle & Co.	Alexandria	Mer. License	1800	Tax PP 1800:54(19)r
Joseph Riddle & Co., plt.	Alexandria	Suit	1801	CRC:062
Joseph Riddle & Co., plt.	Alexandria	Suit	1802	CRC:255
Joseph Riddle & Co., plt.	Alexandria	Suit	1805	CRG:009
Joseph Riddle & Co., plt.	Alexandria	Suit	1807	CRG:104
Josiah Faxon & Co., plt.	Alexandria	Suit	1801	CRC:111
Josiah Faxon & Co., plt.	Alexandria	Suit	1803	CRD:101
Joy, Wm.	Alexandria	Boarder	1808	1808(2):16A
Joyce, Pearce	Alexandria	Tax Charge	1798	Tax PP 1798:09
Joye, Anne	Alexandria	Resident	1800	1800(4):04B
Joye, Anne, labourer	Alexandria	Boarder	1800	1800(4):04A
Judge's Estate, Queen St.	Alexandria	Occupant	1787	Tax L 1787:17
Julias, Thomas	Arlington	Inventory	1823	AB5:191; LVA-LP
Julis, Thomas	Alexandria	Tax Charge	1799	Tax PP 1799:20
Julis, Thos. (C)	Alexandria	Tax Charge	1800	Tax PP 1800:19
Julius, Thom. (C), drayman	Alexandria	Housekeeper	1808	1808(4):25A
Julius, Thomas	Arlington	Will P.	1823	OCR1822:048
Julius, Thomas	Arlington	Bond	1823	WB3:104
Julius, Thomas	Arlington	Will	1823	WB3:103; File #218A
Julius, Thomas	Arlington	Account	1824	AB5:332; LVA-LP
Julius, Thomas	Arlington	Sale	1824	AB5:350
Julius, Thomas	Arlington	Account	1828	AB6:448; LVA-LP
Julius, Thos. & wife (C), labourer	Alexandria	Housekeeper	1799	1799(2):14A
Julius, Thos., drayman	Alexandria	Head	1810	1810(4):08A
Jullits, Thomas & wife Cloey	Alexandria	Resident	1800	1800(4):11B
Junicle, Enas, shopkeeper	Alexandria	Head	1796	1796(3):6
Junigal, Enos	Alexandria	Tax Charge	1796	Tax LP 1796:15
Junigel, Ignatius	Arlington	Sale	1810	WBC:535
Junigel, Ignatius	Arlington	Bond	1810	WBC:496
Junigel, Ignatius	Arlington	Inventory	1810	WBC:530
Junigel, Ignatius	Arlington	Will	1810	WBC:495; File #047A
Junigel, Ignatius	Arlington	Account	1812	AB1:175; LVA-LP
Junigel, Ignatius, retailer	Alexandria	Housekeeper	1799	1799(2):01A
Junigle, Ignatius, shopkeeper	Alexandria	Head	1810	1810(1):01A
Junigle, Ignel	Alexandria	Tax Charge	1795	Tax PP 1795:15
Junizell, Ignatius, retailer	Alexandria	Housekeeper	1808	1808(1):02A
Justa, Mathew	Arlington	Apprentice	1805	OCR1801:320

NAME OR SUBJECT	LOCATION	TYPE	YEAR	REFERENCE(S)
K				
Kallahan, James	Alexandria	Tax Charge	1789	Tax PP 1789:10
Kane, James	Alexandria	Tax Charge	1796	Tax PP 1796:10
Kase, John	Alexandria	Tax Charge	1796	Tax PP 1796:10
Kaufman, Rosa	Alexandria	Will	1893	WB2:054; LP
Kays, Elizabeth, seamstress	Alexandria	Head	1810	1810(3):04A
Keach, Saml.	Alexandria	Tax Charge	1796	Tax LP 1796:16
Keach, Samuel	Alexandria	Tax Charge	1796	Tax PP 1796:10
Keach, Samul & wife Mary	Alexandria	Resident	1800	1800(4):08B
Keach, Samul, house carpenter	Alexandria	Head	1800	1800(4):08A
Kean, J., Fairfax St.	Alexandria	Occupant	1787	Tax L 1787:25
Kean, John	Alexandria	Tax Charge	1787	Tax PP 1787:08
Kean, John	Alexandria	Tax Charge	1790	Tax PP 1790:08
Kean, John, Fairfax St.	Alexandria	Occupant	1790	Tax L 1790:02
Kean, Patric	Alexandria	Tax Charge	1800	Tax PP 1800:21
Kean, Thos.	Alexandria	Tax Charge	1796	Tax PP 1796:10
Keane, Newton, merchant	Alexandria	Head	1810	1810(3):10A
Keane, Thos.	Alexandria	Tax Charge	1795	Tax PP 1795:16
Keath, James	Alexandria	Tax Charge	1796	Tax LP 1796:16
Keating, Edmd., shopkeeper	Alexandria	Housekeeper	1808	1808(3):18A
Keating, Edward	Alexandria	Tax Charge	1800	Tax PP 1800:21
Keating, Edwd., house joiner	Alexandria	Head	1810	1810(3):06A
Keating, George W., c/o Mary	Arlington	Apprentice	1815	OCR1811:273
Keating, James	Alexandria	Tax Charge	1795	Tax PP 1795:16
Keating, James	Alexandria	Tax Charge	1796	Tax PP 1796:10
Keating, James	Alexandria	Tax Charge	1798	Tax PP 1798:10
Keating, James	Alexandria	Tax Charge	1799	Tax PP 1799:21
Keating, James, w(2), bricklayer	Alexandria	Head	1796	1796(3):2
Keating, Jas. & wife, bricklayer	Alexandria	Housekeeper	1799	1799(2):06A
Keating, Jas., St. Asaph St.	Alexandria	Occupant	1795	Tax L 1795:18
Keating, Jas., St. Asaph St.	Alexandria	Owner	1795	Tax L 1795:18
Keating, Lofty	Alexandria	Tax Charge	1798	Tax PP 1798:10
Keaton, Lucy	Arlington	Guard.	1807	WBB:540
Keech, Saml. & wife, carpenter	Alexandria	Housekeeper	1799	1799(2):19A
Keech, Samuel	Alexandria	Tax Charge	1795	Tax PP 1795:16
Keech, Samuel	Alexandria	Tax Charge	1798	Tax PP 1798:10
Keech, Samuel	Alexandria	Tax Charge	1799	Tax PP 1799:21
Keech, Samuel	Alexandria	Tax Charge	1800	Tax PP 1800:21
Keech, William	Alexandria	Tax Charge	1790	Tax PP 1790:08
Keech, William, King St.	Alexandria	Occupant	1790	Tax L 1790:05
Keechall, Mrs., Princess St.	Alexandria	Occupant	1795	Tax L 1795:12
Keene, Ann M.	Arlington	Guard.	1855	BB(np)
Keene, Ann M., c/o Moses	Arlington	Guard.	1854	BB(np)
Keene, Clarintine V.	Arlington	Guard.	1855	BB(np)
Keene, Clarintine V., c/o Moses	Arlington	Guard.	1854	BB(np)
Keene, Eleanor	Arlington	Apprentice	1823	OCR1822:037a
Keene, George (C)	Arlington	Apprentice	1823	OCR1822:038
Keene, James N.	Arlington	Account	1859	WB7:481; LVA-LP
Keene, James W.	Arlington	Account	1860	WB8:018; LVA-LP
Keene, Matthew	Arlington	Bond Made	1808	ACR:048
Keene, Matthew	Arlington	Defendant	1821	ACO:198
Keene, Matthew, apellt.	Alexandria	Suit	1808	CRF:281
Keene, Newton, def.	Alexandria	Suit	1822	CRL:232
Keene, Newton, plaintiff	Arlington	Suit	1841	LSA:142
Keiger, Daniel, plt.	Alexandria	Suit	1807	CRI:372
Keiger, George, plt.	Alexandria	Suit	1807	CRI:372
Keiger [Kygan], George	Alexandria	Owner	1787	Tax L 1787:17
Keiger [Kyger], George	Alexandria	Plats	1792	CRI:414-415
Keiger [Kyger], George	Alexandria	Plats	1792	CRI:409-410
Kein, Benjn.	Alexandria	Resident	1800	1800(4):02B
Kein, Benjn., ship carpenter	Alexandria	Boarder	1800	1800(4):02A

NAME OR SUBJECT	LOCATION	TYPE	YEAR	REFERENCE(S)
Keitch, Samuel	Alexandria	Tithable +16	1788	Tax PP 1788:06
Keitch, Samuel	Alexandria	Tax Charge	1789	Tax PP 1789:10
Keitch, William	Alexandria	Tax Charge	1787	Tax PP 1787:08
Keitch, William	Alexandria	Tax Charge	1788	Tax PP 1788:09
Keitch, William	Alexandria	Tax Charge	1789	Tax PP 1789:10
Keith, Alexander	Alexandria	Tax Charge	1787	Tax PP 1787:08
Keith, Alexander	Alexandria	Tax Charge	1788	Tax PP 1788:09
Keith, Elizabeth	Alexandria	Resident	1800	1800(4):06B
Keith, Elizabeth	Arlington	Inventory	1828	LVA-LP
Keith, Elizabeth	Arlington	Admin.	1828	OCR1822:154
Keith, Elizabeth	Arlington	Account	1829	AB6:474; LVA-LP
Keith, Elizabeth C.	Arlington	Admin.	1828	WB3:329
Keith, Elizabeth C.	Arlington	Account	1838	AB7:268; LVA-LP
Keith, Isaac L.	Alexandria	Tax Charge	1788	Tax PP 1788:09
Keith, Ja.	Alexandria	Tax Charge	1796	Tax PP 1796:10
Keith, James	Alexandria	Owner	1787	Tax L 1787:17
Keith, James	Alexandria	Tax Charge	1787	Tax PP 1787:08
Keith, James	Alexandria	Tax Charge	1788	Tax PP 1788:09
Keith, James	Alexandria	Tax Charge	1789	Tax PP 1789:10
Keith, James	Alexandria	Tax Charge	1790	Tax PP 1790:08
Keith, James	Alexandria	Tax Charge	1795	Tax PP 1795:16
Keith, James	Alexandria	Deed	1796	CRL:383
Keith, James	Alexandria	Deposition	1797	CRE:239
Keith, James	Alexandria	Tax Charge	1798	Tax PP 1798:10
Keith, James	Alexandria	Tax Charge	1799	Tax PP 1799:21
Keith, James	Alexandria	Tax Charge	1800	Tax PP 1800:21
Keith, James	Alexandria	Deposition	1802	CRI:070
Keith, James	Alexandria	Deposition	1803	CRE:268
Keith, James	Alexandria	Deposition	1805	CRE:296
Keith, James & wife	Alexandria	Head	1795	1795(4):03
Keith, James & wife, councellor	Alexandria	Housekeeper	1799	1799(2):17A
Keith, James & wife Elizabeth	Alexandria	Resident	1800	1800(4):06B
Keith, James, at Mott's Tavern	Alexandria	Deposition	1805	CRE:313
Keith, James Contee	Alexandria	Tithable +16	1788	Tax PP 1788:09
Keith, James, def.	Alexandria	Suit	1801	CRB:307
Keith, James, Georgetown DC	Alexandria	Will	1874	WB1:115; LP
Keith, James, Gibbon St.	Alexandria	Occupant	1787	Tax L 1787:04
Keith, James, Jr.	Alexandria	Tithable +16	1788	Tax PP 1788:09
Keith, James, Jr.	Alexandria	Tithable +16	1789	Tax PP 1789:10
Keith, James, Jr.	Alexandria	Tithable +16	1790	Tax PP 1790:08
Keith, James, Jr.	Alexandria	Mer. License	1799	Tax PP 1799:52-06w
Keith, James, Jr.	Alexandria	Resident	1800	1800(4):06B
Keith, James, Jr.	Alexandria	License Due	1800	Tax PP 1800:54(24)
Keith, James, Jr., def.	Alexandria	Suit	1822	CRL:389
Keith, James, Jr., merchant	Alexandria	Boarder	1800	1800(4):06A
Keith, James, Sr., conveyancer	Alexandria	Head	1810	1810(1):08A
Keith, James, Sr., lawyer	Alexandria	Head	1800	1800(4):06A
Keith, James, Water St.	Alexandria	Occupant	1787	Tax L 1787:09
Keith, James, Water St.	Alexandria	Occupant	1787	Tax L 1787:17
Keith, James, Water St.	Alexandria	Occupant	1790	Tax L 1790:07
Keith, James, Water St.	Alexandria	Owner	1790	Tax L 1790:07
Keith, Jane	Alexandria	Resident	1800	1800(4):06B
Keith, Jane A.	Arlington	Bond	1854	BB(np)
Keith, Jane A.C.	Arlington	Account	1855	WB6:417; LVA-LP
Keith, Jas., mas. chan'y.	Alexandria	Housekeeper	1808	1808(1):08A
Keith, Jas., Water St.	Alexandria	Occupant	1795	Tax L 1795:17
Keith, Jas., Water St.	Alexandria	Owner	1795	Tax L 1795:17
Keith, John	Alexandria	Tithable +16	1789	Tax PP 1789:10
Keith, John	Alexandria	Tithable +16	1790	Tax PP 1790:08
Keith, John	Alexandria	Resident	1800	1800(4):06B
Keith, John	Alexandria	Boarder	1800	1800(4):06A

NAME OR SUBJECT	LOCATION	TYPE	YEAR	REFERENCE(S)
Keith, Kitty	Alexandria	Resident	1800	1800(4):06B
Keith, Margaret S.	Arlington	Account	1860	WB7:502; LVA-LP
Keith, Mary	Alexandria	Resident	1800	1800(4):06B
Keith, Mary E.	Arlington	Guard. Acct.	1848	WB5:102; LVA-LP
Keith, Mary Eliza	Arlington	Guard. Acct.	1848	WB5:179; LVA-LP
Keith, Mary Eliza	Arlington	Guard. Acct.	1851	WB5:276; LVA-LP
Keith, Mary Eliza	Arlington	Guard. Acct.	1852	WB6:013; LVA-LP
Keith, Mary Eliza	Arlington	Guard. Acct.	1852	WB6:245; LVA-LP
Keith, Mary Eliza, c/o John C.	Arlington	Guard.	1846	OCR1842:188
Keith, Mary Elizabeth	Arlington	Guard.	1863	WB6:246
Keith, Peggy	Alexandria	Resident	1800	1800(4):06B
Keith, Saml. S.	Alexandria	Tithable +16	1790	Tax PP 1790:05
Keith, Samuel & wife, shopkeeper	Alexandria	Head	1795	1795(4):05
Keith, Smith	Alexandria	Tithable +16	1788	Tax PP 1788:09
Keith, Smith	Alexandria	Tithable +16	1789	Tax PP 1789:11
Keith, Smith	Alexandria	Tax Charge	1796	Tax PP 1796:10
Keith, Smith	Alexandria	Tax Charge	1798	Tax PP 1798:10
Keith, Smith	Alexandria	Tax Charge	1799	Tax PP 1799:21
Keith, Smith	Alexandria	Tax Charge	1800	Tax PP 1800:21
Keith, Smith & wife, taylor	Alexandria	Housekeeper	1799	1799(2):06A
Keith, William, seaman	Alexandria	Head	1810	1810(2):06A
Keith, William, seaman	Alexandria	Head	1810	1810(3):04A
Kell, Isaac	Alexandria	Tax Charge	1800	Tax PP 1800:21
Kell, Isaac, for playing Faro	Arlington	Defendant	1801	PA:102
Kell, Isaac, grantor	Arlington	Indenture D.	1806	ID3:163
Kell, Isaac, grantor	Arlington	Indenture D.	1831	ID:326
Kell, Isaac, in jail bounds	Arlington	Insolvent	1831	ID:324
Kell, Isaac, in prison bounds	Arlington	Insolvent	1806	ID3:157
Kell, Isaac, plt.	Alexandria	Suit	1801	CRC:054
Kell, Isaac, Sr.	Arlington	Inventory	1845	AB9:111; LVA-LP
Kell, Isaac, Sr.	Arlington	Admin.	1845	OCR1842:104
Kell, Isaac, tinman	Alexandria	Housekeeper	1808	1808(2):11A
Kell, Isaac, tinman	Alexandria	Head	1810	1810(1):04A
Kell, John, grantee	Arlington	Indenture D.	1831	ID:326
Kelloy, James	Alexandria	Tax Charge	1796	Tax LP 1796:16
Kelley, James	Alexandria	Tax Charge	1796	Tax PP 1796:10
Kelley, Jno.	Alexandria	Tax Charge	1795	Tax PP 1795:16
Kelley, John	Alexandria	Tax Charge	1796	Tax LP 1796:16
Kelley, Nancy	Alexandria	Occupant	1795	Tax L 1795:08
Kelly, Anne E.	Arlington	Will	1865	WB8:278; File #635A
Kelly, Edmund	Alexandria	Tithable +16	1789	Tax PP 1789:21
Kelly, Elizabeth	Alexandria	Head	1795	1795(4a):05
Kelly, Elizabeth	Alexandria	Housekeeper	1799	1799(2):18A
Kelly, Ellen, c/o Mary Ann	Arlington	Guard.	1817	WB2:214
Kelly, Henry, c/o Nancy	Arlington	Apprentice	1802	OCR1801:072
Kelly, Jas.	Alexandria	Tax Charge	1798	Tax PP 1798:10
Kelly, Jas.	Alexandria	Boarder	1808	1808(1):04A
Kelly, John	Alexandria	Tithable +16	1788	Tax PP 1788:08
Kelly, John	Alexandria	Tax Charge	1796	Tax PP 1796:10
Kelly, John	Alexandria	Will	1889	WB1:515; LP
Kelly, John B.	Alexandria	Tithable +21	1787	Tax PP 1787:05
Kelly, John L.	Alexandria	Will	1895	WB2:123; LP
Kelly, Jos., bricklayer	Alexandria	Boarder	1799	1799(2):05A
Kelly, Joseph	Alexandria	Tax Charge	1799	Tax PP 1799:21
Kelly, Joseph	Alexandria	Tax Charge	1800	Tax PP 1800:21
Kelly, Joseph, plt.	Alexandria	Suit	1801	CRB:318
Kelly, Mary Ann, c/o James	Arlington	Apprentice	1805	OCR1801:323
Kelly, Vincent	Alexandria	Tax Charge	1789	Tax PP 1789:10
Kelly, Vincent	Alexandria	Tax Charge	1790	Tax PP 1790:08
Kelly, William	Alexandria	Tax Charge	1799	Tax PP 1799:21
Kelly, Wm., tailor	Alexandria	Boarder	1799	1799(2):04A

NAME OR SUBJECT	LOCATION	TYPE	YEAR	REFERENCE(S)
Kelton, Elizabeth, shopkeeper	Alexandria	Head	1810	1810(3):05A
Kelton, Geo.	Alexandria	Tax Charge	1798	Tax PP 1798:10
Kelton, George	Alexandria	Tax Charge	1799	Tax PP 1799:21
Kelton, George	Alexandria	Tax Charge	1800	Tax PP 1800:21
Kemp, Henry, school boy	Alexandria	Boarder	1800	1800(4):05A
Kemp, Jno. C. & wife, schrivener	Alexandria	Housekeeper	1799	1799(2):09A
Kempff, Jno. C.	Alexandria	Tax Charge	1798	Tax PP 1798:10
Kempff, John C.	Alexandria	Tax Charge	1796	Tax PP 1796:10
Kempff, John C.	Alexandria	Tax Charge	1799	Tax PP 1799:21
Kempff, John C., w, scrivener	Alexandria	Head	1796	1796(3):2
Kempff, John Christr.	Alexandria	Tax Charge	1789	Tax PP 1789:10
Kempff, Kesiah, gentlewoman	Alexandria	Housekeeper	1808	1808(4):27A
Kempff, Peter	Arlington	Defendant	1802	PA:180
Kemph, Christopher & wife, scrivener	Alexandria	Head	1795	1795(4a):09
Kemph, Jno. C.	Alexandria	Tax Charge	1800	Tax PP 1800:21
Kemph, John Christopher	Alexandria	Tax Charge	1790	Tax PP 1790:08
Kenna, Jacob	Alexandria	Tax Charge	1795	Tax PP 1795:16
Kenna, James	Alexandria	Tax Charge	1790	Tax PP 1790:08
Kenna, James	Alexandria	Tax Charge	1796	Tax PP 1796:10
Kennady, James	Alexandria	Tithable +21	1787	Tax PP 1787:03
Kennady, James	Alexandria	Mer. License	1799	Tax PP 1799:52-06r
Kennady, James, Dr.	Alexandria	Mer. License	1799	Tax PP 1799:52-06r
Kennady, James, Sr.	Alexandria	Tax Charge	1800	Tax PP 1800:21
Kennady, James, Sr.	Alexandria	Tax Charge	1800	Tax PP 1800:21
Kennedy, Andrew T.	Arlington	Appraisal	1829	LVA-LP
Kennedy, Andrew T.	Arlington	Account	1831	AB7:004; LVA-LP
Kennedy, Andrew Thomas	Arlington	Bond	1829	WB3:317
Kennedy, Andrew Thomas	Arlington	Will	1829	WB3:315; File #272A
Kennedy, Andw. T.	Alexandria	Boarder	1808	1808(2):10A
Kennedy, Catherine	Arlington	Guard.	1822	WB3:038
Kennedy, David	Alexandria	Owner	1787	Tax L 1787:17
Kennedy, David, King St.	Alexandria	Occupant	1787	Tax L 1787:02
Kennedy, Doctr.	Alexandria	Head	1810	1810(2):06A
Kennedy, J., Dr.	Alexandria	Tax Charge	1796	Tax LP 1796:16
Kennedy, James	Alexandria	Tax Charge	1788	Tax PP 1788:09
Kennedy, James	Alexandria	Tax Charge	1790	Tax PP 1790:08
Kennedy, James	Alexandria	Tax Charge	1796	Tax LP 1796:16
Kennedy, James	Alexandria	Tax Charge	1796	Tax PP 1796:10
Kennedy, James	Arlington	Plaintiff	1802	PA:149
Kennedy, James	Arlington	Account	1817	AB2:425; LVA-LP
Kennedy, James	Arlington	Will	1820	WB2:401; File #183A
Kennedy, James	Arlington	Settlement	1821	AB5:011; LVA-LP
Kennedy, James	Arlington	Inventory	1821	AB4:233; LVA-LP
Kennedy, James	Arlington	Bond	1821	WB2:427
Kennedy, James	Arlington	Defendant	1823	ACO:215
Kennedy, James, Dr.	Alexandria	Tax Charge	1789	Tax PP 1789:10
Kennedy, James, Dr.	Arlington	Sale	1816	AB2:360
Kennedy, James, druggist	Alexandria	Housekeeper	1808	1808(2):16A
Kennedy, James, Jr.	Arlington	Inventory	1816	AB2:354; LVA-LP
Kennedy, James, Jr.	Arlington	Admin.	1816	WB2:103
Kennedy, James, Jr.	Arlington	Debts Due	1817	AB3:015
Kennedy, James, Jr.	Arlington	Account	1820	AB4:108; LVA-LP
Kennedy, James, Jr., Dr.	Alexandria	Mer. License	1800	Tax PP 1800:54(15)r
Kennedy, James, Jr., Dr.	Arlington	Inventory	1816	AB2:247; LVA-LP
Kennedy, James, Jr., plt.	Alexandria	Suit	1798	CRC:030
Kennedy, James, Jr., plt.	Alexandria	Suit	1808	CRG:155
Kennedy, James, Sr.	Alexandria	Tax Charge	1799	Tax PP 1799:21
Kennedy, James, Sr.	Alexandria	Mer. License	1800	Tax PP 1800:54(15)r
Kennedy, James, Sr., stationer	Alexandria	Head	1810	1810(2):02A
Kennedy, James, w(1)3, druggist	Alexandria	Head	1795	1796(3):7
Kennedy, Jas.	Alexandria	Tax Charge	1795	Tax PP 1795:16(2)

NAME OR SUBJECT	LOCATION	TYPE	YEAR	REFERENCE(S)
Kennedy, Jas.	Alexandria	Tax Charge	1795	Tax PP 1795:16
Kennedy, Jas.	Alexandria	Tax Charge	1796	Tax PP 1796:10
Kennedy, Jas.	Alexandria	Tax Charge	1798	Tax PP 1798:10
Kennedy, Jas.	Alexandria	Tax Charge	1798	Tax PP 1798:10
Kennedy, Jas. & wife, apoth. & druggist	Alexandria	Housekeeper	1799	1799(2):04A
Kennedy, Jas., bookstore	Alexandria	Housekeeper	1808	1808(2):10A
Kennedy, Jas., Fairfax St.	Alexandria	Owner	1795	Tax L 1795:17
Kennedy, Jas., Fairfax St.	Alexandria	Occupant	1795	Tax L 1795:17
Kennedy, Jas. Jr.	Alexandria	Mer. License	1798	Tax PP 1798:20-4
Kennedy, Jas., King St.	Alexandria	Occupant	1795	Tax L 1795:26
Kennedy, Jas., Sr.	Alexandria	Mer. License	1798	Tax PP 1798:20-4
Kennedy, Joseph	Arlington	Ordinary	1803	OBL1(np)
Kennedy, Nicholas	Arlington	Libellant	1811	ACO:119
Kennedy, Susanna	Arlington	Inventory	1845	AB9:113; LVA-LP
Kennedy, Susanna	Arlington	Will P.	1845	OCR1842:131
Kennedy, Susanna	Arlington	Account	1846	AB9:236; LVA-LP
Kennedy, Susannah	Arlington	Will	1845	WB4:405; File #427A
Kennedy, Thomas Wilson, c/o Wm. D.	Arlington	Apprentice	1815	OCR1811:250
Kenner, George	Arlington	Ordinary	1810	OBL2(np)(2)
Kenner, George	Arlington	Will P.	1823	OCR1822:056a, 58
Kenner, George	Arlington	Will	1823	WB3:390; File #294A
Kenner, George	Arlington	Inventory	1824	AB5:225; LVA-LP
Kenner, George	Arlington	Admin.	1824	OCR1822:059a
Kenner, George	Arlington	Bond	1824	WB3:118
Kenner, George, shopkeeper	Alexandria	Head	1810	1810(1):01A
Kenner, James	Alexandria	Tax Charge	1799	Tax PP 1799:21
Kenner, James	Alexandria	Tax Charge	1800	Tax PP 1800:21
Kenner, James	Arlington	Ordinary	1808	OBL2(np)
Kenner, James	Arlington	Ordinary	1809	OBL2(np)
Kenner, James, def.	Alexandria	Suit	1801	CRB:147
Kenner, James, shopkeeper	Alexandria	Head	1810	1810(1):13A
Kenner, Jas.	Alexandria	Tax Charge	1798	Tax PP 1798:10
Kenner, Rebecca	Alexandria	Deed	1798	CRF:197
Kenner, William	Arlington	Apprentice	1827	OCR1822:149a
Kenner, Wm.	Alexandria	Boarder	1808	1808(2):11A
Kensal, Michl.	Alexandria	Tithable +16	1788	Tax PP 1788:15
Kensel, Michael	Alexandria	Tax Charge	1790	Tax PP 1790:10
Kent, Ann	Arlington	Guard.	1818	WB2:249
Kent, L.	Alexandria	Boarder	1808	1808(4):25A
Kent, Wm.	Alexandria	Serv./Appr.	1800	1800(4):11B
Kenworth, Wm. & wife Rebecah	Alexandria	Resident	1800	1800(4):14B
Kenworthy, Willm.	Alexandria	Tax Charge	1800	Tax PP 1800:21
Kenworthy, Wm., scoolmaster	Alexandria	Head	1800	1800(4):14A
Kenzie, Ezra, tanner	Alexandria	Housekeeper	1799	1799(2):12A
Keogh, Patrick	Arlington	Guard.	1813	WB1:238
Keogh, Patrick, c/o Jane	Arlington	Apprentice	1813	OCR1811:187
Keough, John	Arlington	Apprentice	1816	OCR1811:338
Kephart, Jacob	Alexandria	Serv./Appr.	1800	1800(4):09B
Kerchner, Frederick	Alexandria	Tax Charge	1799	Tax PP 1799:21
Kerchner, Jonah, c/o Fredrick	Arlington	Apprentice	1813	OCR1811:179
Kerr, Alexander	Alexandria	Mer. License	1799	Tax PP 1799:52-06w
Kerr, Alexander	Alexandria	Tax Charge	1799	Tax PP 1799:21
Kerr, Alexander	Alexandria	Mer. License	1800	Tax PP 1800:54(15)r
Kerr, Alexander, def.	Alexandria	Suit	1801	CRC:227
Kerr, Alexander, plt.	Alexandria	Suit	1801	CRD:034
Kerr, Alexr. & wife, merchant	Alexandria	Housekeeper	1799	1799(2):03A
Kerr, James	Alexandria	Tax Charge	1795	Tax PP 1795:16
Kerr, Jas., Princess St.	Alexandria	Occupant	1795	Tax L 1795:12
Kerwan, Peter	Arlington	Crime	1797	OT:18/12/1797
Kesler, John	Alexandria	Resident	1800	1800(4):12B
Kesler, John, plasterrer	Alexandria	Boarder	1800	1800(4):12A

NAME OR SUBJECT	LOCATION	TYPE	YEAR	REFERENCE(S)
Kester, Charles	Alexandria	Resident	1800	1800(4):14B
Kester, Charles, tanner	Alexandria	Boarder	1800	1800(4):14A
Ketcham & Co., Union St.	Alexandria	Occupant	1795	Tax L 1795:09
Ketcham, Danl. & Co., Union St.	Alexandria	Owner	1795	Tax L 1795:17(2)
Ketcham, Danl. & Co., Union St.	Alexandria	Occupant	1795	Tax L 1795:17(2)
Ketcham, Danl. & Co., Water St.	Alexandria	Owner	1795	Tax L 1795:17
Ketcham, Danl. & Co., Water St.	Alexandria	Occupant	1795	Tax L 1795:17
Kethard, Sally	Alexandria	Boarder	1799	1799(2):12A
Keveland [Kevelin], Thomas	Arlington	Account	1812	AB1:170; LVA-LP
Kevelin, Mary, c/o Thomas	Arlington	Guard.	1812	WB1:148
Kevelin, Thomas	Arlington	Admin.	1803	WBA:135
Kevelin, Thomas	Arlington	Account	1804	WBB:047; LVA-LP
Kevelin, Thomas	Arlington	Sale	1804	WBB:047
Kevelin, Thomas	Arlington	Inventory	1804	WBB:046; LVA-LP
Key, Francis S.	Alexandria	Deposition	1822	CRL:571
Keys, William	Arlington	Ordinary	1809	OBL2(np)
Kibbey, William B., b. Devon., Eng.	Arlington	Alien Entry	1827	RA:11/04/27
Kibbs, Jas. & wife (C), labourer	Alexandria	Housekeeper	1799	1799(2):14A
Kibby, Chas.	Alexandria	Boarder	1808	1808(2):16A
Kidd, David	Arlington	Admin.	1800	CRA:300
Kidd, David, Estate	Alexandria	Tax Charge	1796	Tax LP 1796:16
Kidd, David, Estate, King St.	Alexandria	Owner	1795	Tax L 1795:17(2)
Kidd, David, Estate, Queen St.	Alexandria	Owner	1795	Tax L 1795:16(2)
Kidd, Wm.	Alexandria	Tax Charge	1799	Tax PP 1799:21
Kidwell, Elijah	Alexandria	Tax Charge	1798	Tax PP 1798:10
Kidwell, Elijah	Alexandria	Tax Charge	1799	Tax PP 1799:21
Kidwell, Elijah, drayman	Alexandria	Housekeeper	1799	1799(2):11A
Kidwell, Elijah, drayman	Alexandria	Head	1810	1810(4):02A
Kidwell, Elisha, cartman	Alexandria	Housekeeper	1808	1808(4):27A
Kidwell, Elizabeth	Alexandria	Boarder	1799	1799(2):11A
Kidwell, Hezekiah, c/o Pricey	Arlington	Apprentice	1812	OCR1811:129
Kidwell, Mary	Alexandria	Boarder	1799	1799(2):11A
Kidwell, Rebecca	Alexandria	Boarder	1799	1799(2):11A
Kilbraith, James	Alexandria	Tax Charge	1799	Tax PP 1799:21
Kilbride, Michael	Arlington	Inventory	1827	AB6:423; LVA-LP
Kilbride, Michael	Arlington	Admin.	1827	OCR1822:137a
Kilbride, Michael	Arlington	Admin.	1827	WB3:287
Killbreath, John, blacksmith	Alexandria	Head	1810	1810(4):06A
Killigan, Jas.	Alexandria	Tax Charge	1795	Tax PP 1795:16
Kilton, Eliza	Arlington	Guard.	1805	WBB:132
Kilton, Eliza	Arlington	Guard. Acct.	1806	WBB:232; LVA-LP
Kilton, Eliza Mary	Arlington	Guard.	1805	WB2:209
Kilton, Eliza Mary	Arlington	Release	1816	WB2:209
Kilton, Elizabeth	Arlington	Renounce	1803	WBA:181
Kilton, Elizabeth, shopkeeper	Alexandria	Housekeeper	1808	1808(3):20A
Kilton, George	Arlington	Admin.	1803	WBA:180
Kilton, George	Arlington	Inventory	1803	WBA:229; LVA-LP
Kilton, George	Arlington	Account	1805	WBB:143; LVA-LP
Kilton, Georgiana	Arlington	Guard.	1805	WB2:209
Kilton, Georgianna	Arlington	Guard.	1805	WBB:132
Kilton, Georgianna	Arlington	Guard. Acct.	1806	WBB:232; LVA-LP
Kilton, Mary	Arlington	Guard.	1805	WBB:132
Kilton, Mary	Arlington	Guard. Acct.	1806	WBB:232
Kilty, William, chief judge	Arlington	Oath	1801	ACO:005
Kilty, William, Hon., ill with fever	Arlington	Letter	1803	ACO:017
Kim, Julia, gentlewoman	Alexandria	Housekeeper	1808	1808(4):25A
Kimber, Joseph	Alexandria	Tax Charge	1788	Tax PP 1788:09
Kimber, Joseph	Alexandria	Tax Charge	1789	Tax PP 1789:10
Kimble, Joseph	Alexandria	Tithable +16	1789	Tax PP 1789:09
Kimbo, John	Alexandria	Tax Charge	1790	Tax PP 1790:08
Kimbo, John, nr. Royal St.	Alexandria	Occupant	1790	Tax L 1790:10

NAME OR SUBJECT	LOCATION	TYPE	YEAR	REFERENCE(S)
Kincade, John	Alexandria	Mer. License	1799	Tax PP 1799:52-00r
Kincaid, Archd.	Alexandria	Boarder	1808	1808(2):11A
Kincaid, Archibald, c/o John	Arlington	Debt	1800	OT:05/07/1800
Kincaid, George	Alexandria	Deposition	1814	CRI:500
Kincaid, James, clerk	Alexandria	Head	1810	1810(3):06A
Kincaid, Jas.	Alexandria	Boarder	1808	1808(4):26A
Kincaid, Jno.	Alexandria	Tax Charge	1798	Tax PP 1798:10
Kincaid, Jno.	Alexandria	Boarder	1808	1808(4):26A
Kincaid, John	Alexandria	Mer. License	1798	Tax PP 1798:20-4
Kincaid, John	Alexandria	Tax Charge	1799	Tax PP 1799:21
Kincaid, John	Alexandria	Tax Charge	1800	Tax PP 1800:21
Kincaid, John	Alexandria	Mer. License	1800	Tax PP 1800:54(15)r
Kincaid, John	Arlington	Juryman	1804	ACO:026
Kincaid, John	Arlington	Admin.	1810	WB1:024
Kincaid, John	Arlington	Inventory	1811	AB1:047; LVA-LP
Kincaid, John	Arlington	Debts	1811	AB1:052
Kincaid, John	Arlington	Account	1812	AB1:171; LVA-LP
Kincaid, John, grocer	Alexandria	Housekeeper	1808	1808(3):22A
Kincaid, John, merchant	Alexandria	Head	1810	1810(3):04A
Kincaid, John, s/o John	Alexandria	Boarder	1808	1808(3):22A
Kincaid, John [Lucy]	Arlington	Receipt	1812	LVA-LP
King, Benjamin	Arlington	Defendant	1820	ACO:182
King, Benjamin	Arlington	Defendant	1820	ACO:173, 178, 180
King, Benjn., house carpenter	Alexandria	Housekeeper	1808	1808(1):06A
King, Charles, at his house	Arlington	Ordinary	1836	OBL5(np)
King, Charles, at his house	Arlington	Ordinary	1837	OBL5(np)
King, Charles, at his house	Arlington	Ordinary	1838	OBL5(np)
King, Charles, shopkeeper	Alexandria	Housekeeper	1808	1808(2):16A
King, Chas., labourer	Alexandria	Head	1810	1810(2):07A
King, Edward	Arlington	Will	1868	CLOB3:042
King, Edwin H., c/o Richard	Arlington	Guard.	1841	WB4:288
King, Eugenia, c/o Richard	Arlington	Guard.	1841	WB4:288
King, Ignatius, in Alexandria Co.	Arlington	Ordinary	1822	OBL3(np)
King, James Andrew, c/o Richard	Arlington	Guard.	1841	WB4:288
King, James, blacksmith	Alexandria	Head	1810	1810(4):05A
King, Jno. & wife, mariner	Alexandria	Housekeeper	1799	1799(2):11A
King, Joanna M., c/o Richard	Arlington	Guard.	1841	WB4:288
King, John	Alexandria	Tax Charge	1789	Tax PP 1789:10
King, John	Alexandria	Tax Charge	1790	Tax PP 1790:08
King, John	Alexandria	Tax Charge	1798	Tax PP 1798:10
King, John	Arlington	Inventory	1804	WBB:078; LVA-LP
King, John	Arlington	Sale	1804	WBB:080
King, John	Arlington	Account	1805	WBB:192; LVA-LP
King, John	Arlington	Inventory	1827	LVA-LP
King, John	Arlington	Account	1829	AB6:488; LVA-LP
King, John, Capt.	Arlington	Admin.	1804	WBA:320
King, John, seaman	Alexandria	Head	1810	1810(2):06A
King, John Y.	Arlington	Admin.	1827	OCR1822:150a
King, Leonard, laborer	Alexandria	Housekeeper	1808	1808(2):16A
King, Leonard, labourer	Alexandria	Head	1810	1810(2):08A
King, Margaret S. (McKnight), w/o Robt.	Arlington	Defendant	1842	LSA:082
King, Mary	Arlington	Guard.	1824	WB3:128
King, Norvell, c/o Richard	Arlington	Guard.	1841	WB4:288
King, Patrick, grantee	Arlington	Indenture D.	1827	ID:071
King, Polly & Sally	Alexandria	Housekeeper	1808	1808(2):17A
King, Richard Henry, c/o Joanna	Arlington	Apprentice	1815	OCR1811:283
King, Robert	Arlington	Defendant	1842	LSA:082
King, Suky, Fairfax St.	Alexandria	Occupant	1790	Tax L 1790:01
King, Thomas, b. Coston, Leisc., Eng.	Arlington	Alien Entry	1826	RA:05/05/26
King, Thos.?, washwoman	Alexandria	Housekeeper	1808	1808(3):20A
King, William	Alexandria	Head	1810	1810(1):01A

NAME OR SUBJECT	LOCATION	TYPE	YEAR	REFERENCE(S)
King, William, def.	Alexandria	Suit	1810	CRH:009
King, Wm.	Alexandria	Tax Charge	1795	Tax PP 1795:16
King, Wm., gentleman	Alexandria	Housekeeper	1808	1808(1):02A
Kingsbury, Henry W.	Alexandria	Will	1870	WB1:001
Kingsbury, Henry W., U.S.A.	Alexandria	Will	1870	WB1:001; LP
Kingston, Thomas, grantor	Arlington	Indenture D.	1829	ID:238
Kingston, Thomas, in jail	Arlington	Insolvent	1829	ID:235
Kingston [Hingston], Nicholas	Arlington	Will	1830	WB3:357
Kinner, Geo., seaman & shopkeeper	Alexandria	Housekeeper	1808	1808(2):15A
Kinsey, Ezra	Alexandria	Tax Charge	1798	Tax PP 1798:10
Kinsey, Ezra	Alexandria	Tax Charge	1799	Tax PP 1799:21
Kinsey, Ezra	Alexandria	Resident	1800	1800(4):14B
Kinsey, Ezra	Arlington	Inventory	1819	AB4:054
Kinsey, Ezra	Arlington	Inventory	1826	AB6:226
Kinsey, Ezra	Arlington	Will	1826	WB3:245; File #250A
Kinsey, Ezra	Arlington	Bond	1826	WB3:246
Kinsey, Ezra	Arlington	Account	1828	AB6:465; LVA-LP
Kinsey, Ezra, tanner	Alexandria	Head	1795	1795(4):08
Kinsey, Ezra, tanner	Alexandria	Head	1800	1800(4):14A
Kinsey, Ezra, tanner	Alexandria	Housekeeper	1808	1808(4):24A
Kinsey, Ezra, tanner	Alexandria	Head	1810	1810(4):09A
Kinsey, Zenas, tanner	Alexandria	Head	1810	1810(3):02A
Kinsey, Zinas, currier	Alexandria	Housekeeper	1808	1808(3):21A
Kinzer, J. Lewis	Arlington	Sale	1872	WB9:353
Kinzer, J. Louis	Arlington	Will	1863	WB8:160; File #600A
Kinzer, J. Louis	Arlington	Trustee Acct.	1866	WB8:310, 495, 568
Kinzer, Lewis, notary public	Arlington	Appointment	1851	BB(np)
Kinzey, Ezra	Alexandria	Tax Charge	1800	Tax PP 1800:21
Kirby, Cloe, seamstress	Alexandria	Head	1810	1810(4):08A
Kirby, John, laborer	Alexandria	Housekeeper	1808	1808(4):29A
Kirby, John, labourer	Alexandria	Head	1810	1810(4):03A
Kirby, Richard	Arlington	Admin.	1810	WBC:422
Kirby, Richard	Arlington	Will	1831	WB4:026; File #310A
Kirby, Richard	Arlington	Account	1835	AB7:186; LVA-LP
Kirby, Richard	Arlington	Account	1836	AB7:186
Kirchener, Fredk., shopkpr. & l.b. baker	Alexandria	Housekeeper	1808	1808(4):30A
Kirchner, Frederic	Alexandria	Tax Charge	1800	Tax PP 1800:21
Kirk & Fleming, Duke St.	Alexandria	Occupant	1795	Tax L 1795:09
Kirk, Betty, def.	Alexandria	Suit	1801	CRC:194
Kirk, Bridget	Alexandria	Tax Charge	1787	Tax PP 1787:08
Kirk, Bridget	Alexandria	Tax Charge	1788	Tax PP 1788:09
Kirk, Bridget	Alexandria	Tax Charge	1790	Tax PP 1790:08
Kirk, Bridget	Alexandria	Head	1795	1795(4):02
Kirk, Bridget	Alexandria	Tax Charge	1795	Tax PP 1795:16
Kirk, Bridget	Alexandria	Tax Charge	1796	Tax PP 1796:10
Kirk, Bridget	Arlington	Account	1802	WBA:061; LVA-LP
Kirk, Bridget, King St.	Alexandria	Owner	1795	Tax L 1795:18
Kirk, Bridget, Union St.	Alexandria	Owner	1795	Tax L 1795:17(2)
Kirk, Bridget, Water St.	Alexandria	Owner	1795	Tax L 1795:18
Kirk, Bridget, Water St.	Alexandria	Owner	1795	Tax L 1795:17
Kirk, Bridget, Wolf St.	Alexandria	Owner	1795	Tax L 1795:17
Kirk, Bridget, Wolfe St.	Alexandria	Owner	1790	Tax L 1790:07
Kirk, Bridgett	Alexandria	Tax Charge	1789	Tax PP 1789:10
Kirk, Grafton, constable	Alexandria	Tax Charge	1789	Tax PP 1789:10
Kirk, Hannah Harriet, def.	Alexandria	Suit	1801	CRC:194
Kirk, Harvey	Arlington	Apprentice	1826	OCR1822:119a
Kirk, James, Estate	Alexandria	Owner	1787	Tax L 1787:18
Kirk, Jas.	Alexandria	Tax Charge	1798	Tax PP 1798:10
Kirk, Mrs., Duke St.	Alexandria	Occupant	1795	Tax L 1795:09
Kirk, Mrs., Union St.	Alexandria	Occupant	1787	Tax L 1787:18
Kirk, R.W.	Arlington	Guard. Acct.	1804	WBA:296; LVA-LP

NAME OR SUBJECT	LOCATION	TYPE	YEAR	REFERENCE(S)
Kirk, R.W.	Arlington	Wharf Acct.	1804	WBA:302; LVA-LP
Kirk, Robert, def.	Alexandria	Suit	1801	CRD:206
Kirk, Robert W.	Arlington	Guard. Acct.	1804	WBB:063; LVA-LP
Kirk, Robert W.	Arlington	Bond	1811	WB1:136
Kirk, Robert W.	Arlington	Will	1811	WB1:132
Kirk, Robert W.	Arlington	Account	1812	AB1:249; LVA-LP
Kirk, Saml.	Alexandria	Tax Charge	1798	Tax PP 1798:10
Kirk, Saml.	Alexandria	Boarder	1808	1808(3):21A
Kirk, Saml. & wife, taylor	Alexandria	Housekeeper	1799	1799(2):06A
Kirk, Saml., cryer & bellman	Alexandria	Housekeeper	1808	1808(4):27A
Kirk, Samuel	Alexandria	Tax Charge	1799	Tax PP 1799:21
Kirk, Samuel	Alexandria	Tax Charge	1800	Tax PP 1800:21
Kirk, Samuel, bellman	Arlington	Payment	1805	ACO:037
Kirk, Samuel, sadler	Alexandria	Head	1810	1810(3):04A
Kirk, Samuel, umbrella maker	Alexandria	Head	1810	1810(3):01A
Kirk, Widow, Estate	Alexandria	Tax Charge	1796	Tax LP 1796:16
Kirk, Wm., seaman	Alexandria	Housekeeper	1808	1808(3):22A
Kirkmore, Frederick, carpenter	Alexandria	Boarder	1799	1799(2):01A
Kirkpatrick, Thomas, Estate	Alexandria	Owner	1787	Tax L 1787:18
Kirkpatrick, Thomas, Estate, plt.	Alexandria	Suit	1801	CRC:194
Kirkpatrick, Thomas, Exrs., plt.	Alexandria	Suit	1801	CRB:072
Kirkpatrick, Thos., Estate, Queen St.	Alexandria	Owner	1795	Tax L 1795:17
Kirkpatrick, Thos., Estate, Water St.	Alexandria	Owner	1790	Tax L 1790:07(2)
Kirkpatrick, Thos., Estate, Water St.	Alexandria	Owner	1795	Tax L 1795:17(3)
Kirkpatrick, William	Alexandria	Tax Charge	1799	Tax PP 1799:21
Kirkpatrick, Willm.	Alexandria	Tax Charge	1800	Tax PP 1800:21
Kirkpatrick, Wm.	Alexandria	Tax Charge	1788	Tax PP 1788:09
Kirkpatrick, Wm.	Alexandria	Tax Charge	1788	Tax PP 1788:09
Kirkpatrick, Wm.	Alexandria	Tax Charge	1789	Tax PP 1789:10
Kirtz, Nicholas	Alexandria	Tax Charge	1790	Tax PP 1790:08
Kisendaffer, John, grantor	Arlington	Indenture D.	1830	ID:258
Kisendaffer, John, in jail	Arlington	Insolvent	1830	ID:255
Kitchen, James, laborer	Alexandria	Housekeeper	1808	1808(4):29A
Kitcher, Danl.	Alexandria	Tax Charge	1795	Tax PP 1795:16
Kitely, James	Alexandria	Tax Charge	1799	Tax PP 1799:21
Kitson, Elizabeth	Alexandria	Deposition	1814	CRI:498
Kitten, John	Alexandria	Tax Charge	1795	Tax PP 1795:16
Kitten, John	Alexandria	Tax Charge	1796	Tax LP 1796:16
Kitten, John	Alexandria	Tax Charge	1796	Tax PP 1796:10
Kivasirick, Simon	Arlington	Libellant	1811	ACO:119
Klinehoof, Sarah	Alexandria	Resident	1800	1800(4):05B
Klinehoof, Sarah, housekeeper	Alexandria	Boarder	1800	1800(4):05A
Klipstein, William B.	Alexandria	Will	1881	WB1:347; LP
Kloptore, Philip	Alexandria	Tax Charge	1799	Tax PP 1799:21
Knight, Ferdinand	Arlington	Apprentice	1844	OCR1842:089
Knight, Ferdinand	Alexandria	Will	1894	WB2:096; LP
Knight, John	Arlington	Insolvent	1811	ID2:018
Knight, John, grantor	Arlington	Indenture D.	1811	ID2:021
Knight, John, sadler	Alexandria	Housekeeper	1808	1808(1):01A
Knight, John, sadler	Alexandria	Head	1810	1810(3):02A
Knokes, Frances, c/o Fanny	Arlington	Apprentice	1815	OCR1811:280
Knower, Andrew, Prince St.	Alexandria	Occupant	1790	Tax L 1790:02
Knox & Crawford, plt.	Alexandria	Suit	1804	CRF:067
Knox, William, plt.	Alexandria	Suit	1804	CRF:067
Koon, Eleanor M.	Arlington	Will	1896	WB10:338; File #773A
Koones, Charles	Arlington	Fid. Bond	1857	FBB(np)
Koones, Charles	Arlington	Account	1859	WB7:395; LVA-LP
Koones, Charles	Arlington	Account	1859	WB7:393; LVA-LP
Koones, Frederick	Alexandria	Account B.	1793	CRC:022
Koones, Frederick	Arlington	Ordinary	1802	OBL1(np)
Koones, Frederick	Arlington	Ordinary	1804	OBL1(np)

NAME OR SUBJECT	LOCATION	TYPE	YEAR	REFERENCE(S)
Koones, Frederick, baker	Alexandria	Head	1810	1810(3):01A
Koones, Frederick, def.	Alexandria	Suit	1802	CRC:019
Koones, Fredk., bread baker & confect.	Alexandria	Housekeeper	1808	1808(2):10A
Koontz & Ober	Alexandria	Account B.	1793	CRH:030
Koontz, John, def.	Alexandria	Suit	1807	CRH:017
Kooper, William	Arlington	Apprentice	1823	OCR1822:040a
K. & Wisemiller	Alexandria	Tax Charge	1798	Tax PP 1798:10
Korn & Weismiller, St. Asaph St.	Alexandria	Occupants	1790	Tax L 1790:13
Korn & Wisemiller	Alexandria	Tax Charge	1795	Tax PP 1795:33
Korn & Wisemiller	Alexandria	Tax Charge	1796	Tax LP 1796:16
Korn & Wisemiller	Alexandria	Tax Charge	1796	Tax PP 1796:10
Korn & Wisemiller	Alexandria	Mer. License	1798	Tax PP 1798:20-4
Korn & Wisemiller	Alexandria	Tax Charge	1799	Tax PP 1799:21
Korn & Wisemiller	Alexandria	Mer. License	1799	Tax PP 1799:52-06w
Korn & Wisemiller	Alexandria	Tax Charge	1800	Tax PP 1800:21
Korn & Wisemiller	Alexandria	Mer. License	1800	Tax PP 1800:54(15)r
Korn & Wisemiller, def.	Alexandria	Suit	1801	CRD:152
Korn & Wisemiller, def.	Alexandria	Suit	1808	CRG:332
Korn & Wisemiller, def.	Alexandria	Suit	1809	CRG:238
Korn & Wisemiller, def.	Alexandria	Suit	1810	CRH:154
Korn & Wisemiller, merchants	Alexandria	Head	1810	1810(4):05A
Korn & Wisemiller, St. Asaph St.	Alexandria	Occupant	1795	Tax L 1795:33
Korn & Wisemiller, St. Asaph St.	Alexandria	Owner	1795	Tax L 1795:33
Korn, Chas.	Alexandria	Boarder	1808	1808(4):25A
Korn, Jno.	Alexandria	Tax Charge	1795	Tax PP 1795:16
Korn, Jno. & wife, baker	Alexandria	Housekeeper	1799	1799(2):10A
Korn, John	Alexandria	Tax Charge	1787	Tax PP 1787:08
Korn, John	Alexandria	Tax Charge	1788	Tax PP 1788:09
Korn, John	Alexandria	Tax Charge	1789	Tax PP 1789:10
Korn, John	Alexandria	Tax Charge	1790	Tax PP 1790:08
Korn, John, def.	Alexandria	Suit	1801	CRD:152
Korn, John, def.	Alexandria	Suit	1809	CRG:238
Korn, John, def.	Alexandria	Suit	1809	CRG:345
Korn, John, Prince St.	Alexandria	Owner	1790	Tax L 1790:07
Korn, John, Prince St.	Alexandria	Occupant	1790	Tax L 1790:07
Korn, John, w(4), baker	Alexandria	Head	1796	1796(3):2
Korn, John, [biscuit baker]	Alexandria	Housekeeper	1808	1808(4):25A
Korn, William F., c/o John	Arlington	Apprentice	1815	OCR1811:264
Krouse, Catharine, seamstress	Alexandria	Head	1810	1810(4):08A
Krower, Andrew	Alexandria	Tax Charge	1789	Tax PP 1789:10
Kurtz, John	Arlington	Defendant	1810	ACO:114
Kurtz, John, plt.	Alexandria	Suit	1818	CRK:458
Kygan [Keiger], George	Alexandria	Owner	1787	Tax L 1787:17
Kyger [Keiger], George	Alexandria	Plats	1792	CRI:414-415
Kyger [Keiger], George	Alexandria	Plats	1792	CRI:409-410

NAME OR SUBJECT	LOCATION	TYPE	YEAR	REFERENCE(S)
L				
Labille, Lewis	Alexandria	Tax Charge	1798	Tax PP 1798:11
Labille, Lewis	Alexandria	Tax Charge	1799	Tax PP 1799:23
Lacey, Isaac	Alexandria	Tax Charge	1796	Tax PP 1796:11
Lacey, William	Alexandria	Tax Charge	1799	Tax PP 1799:23
Lacey, Wm., brewer	Alexandria	Housekeeper	1799	1799(2):12A
Lackey, Joanna L.	Arlington	Fid. Bond	1855	FBB(np)
Lackey, Leila L.	Arlington	Guard. Acct.	1868	WB9:052
Lackey, Leila L.	Arlington	Guard. Acct.	1869	WB9:177
Lackey, Leila L.	Arlington	Guard. Acct.	1870	WB9:268
Lackey, Lelia L.	Arlington	Guard. Acct.	1867	WB8:532
Lacton, William	Alexandria	Tax Charge	1795	Tax PP 1795:17
Lacy, Martha, gc/o William Bladen	Arlington	Apprentice	1802	OCR1801:033
Lacy, Patsey	Alexandria	Head	1810	1810(2):07A
Lacy, William	Alexandria	Tax Charge	1800	Tax PP 1800:23
Ladd, Harriot V.	Alexandria	Will	1875	WB1:125; LP
Ladd, Jno. G.	Alexandria	Tax Charge	1798	Tax PP 1798:11
Ladd, Jno. G.	Alexandria	Mer. License	1798	Tax PP 1798:20-4
Ladd, Jno. G. & wife, merchant	Alexandria	Housekeeper	1799	1799(2):13A
Ladd, John G.	Alexandria	Tax Charge	1796	Tax LP 1796:17
Ladd, John G.	Alexandria	Tax Charge	1796	Tax PP 1796:11
Ladd, John G.	Alexandria	Tax Charge	1799	Tax PP 1799:23
Ladd, John G.	Alexandria	Mer. License	1799	Tax PP 1799:52-06w
Ladd, John G.	Alexandria	Tax Charge	1800	Tax PP 1800:23
Ladd, John G.	Alexandria	Mer. License	1800	Tax PP 1800:54(16)r
Ladd, John G.	Arlington	Defendant	1817	ACO:149
Ladd, John G.	Arlington	Inventory	1819	AB3:333, 335; LVA-LP
Ladd, John G.	Arlington	Sale	1820	AB4:112
Ladd, John G.	Arlington	Account	1821	AB4:335; LVA-LP
Ladd, John G.	Arlington	Account	1823	AB5:209; LVA-LP
Ladd, John G.	Arlington	Account	1825	LVA-LP
Ladd, John G. & wife Sarrah	Alexandria	Serv./Appt.	1800	1800(4):15B
Ladd, John G., merchant	Alexandria	Housekeeper	1808	1808(1):08A
Ladd, John G., merchant	Alexandria	Head	1810	1810(4):06A
Ladd, John G., murchant	Alexandria	Head	1800	1800(4):15A
Ladd, John G., plt.	Alexandria	Suit	1802	CRB:231, 235
Ladd, John Gardner	Arlington	Bond	1819	WB2:383, 293
Ladd, John Gardner	Arlington	Will	1819	WB2:278; File #159A
Ladd, John Gardner	Arlington	Account	1820	AB4:153; LVA-LP
Ladd, John H. & Co.	Arlington	Libellant	1823	ACO:206, 208, 209
Ladd, John H. & Co.	Arlington	Libellant	1823	ACO:218
Ladd, John H. & Co.	Arlington	Libellant	1823	ACO:232
Ladd, Sally Easton	Arlington	Guard. Acct.	1830	AB6:518; LVA-LP
Ladd, Sally Easton	Arlington	Guard. Acct.	1831	AB7:020; LVA-LP
Ladd, Sally Easton	Arlington	Guard. Acct.	1833	AB7:086; LVA-LP
Ladd, Sally Easton	Arlington	Guard. Acct.	1835	AB7:169; LVA-LP
Ladd, Sarah	Arlington	Renounce	1819	WB2:303
Ladd, Sarah	Arlington	Will P.	1846	OCR1842:180
Ladd, Sarah Easton	Arlington	Guard.	1819	WB2:293
Ladd, Sarah Easton	Arlington	Guard. Acct.	1826	AB6:249; LVA-LP
Ladd, Sarah Easton	Arlington	Guard. Acct.	1826	OCR1822:124
Ladd, Sarah Easton	Arlington	Guard.	1826	OCR1822:123a
Ladd, Sarah Easton	Arlington	Guard.	1826	WB3:162
Ladd, Sarah Easton	Arlington	Guard. Acct.	1827	AB6:441
Ladd, Sarah Easton	Arlington	Guard. Acct.	1828	AB6:464; LVA-LP(2)
Ladd, Sarah Easton	Arlington	Guard. Acct.	1829	AB6:493; LVA-LP
Ladd, Sarah, w/o John G.	Arlington	Renounce	1819	WB4:423
Ladd, Thomas, at Richmond	Alexandria	Deposition	1817	CRK:372
Laferty, Daniel, labourer	Alexandria	Head	1796	1796(3):6
Lafferty, Mrs.	Arlington	Sale	1818	AB3:140
Laird, John, of Georgetown DC	Arlington	Deposition	1830	ACR:076

NAME OR SUBJECT	LOCATION	TYPE	YEAR	REFERENCE(S)
Lake, Ann, King St.	Alexandria	Owner	1795	Tax L 1795:19
Lake, Ann, washwoman	Alexandria	Housekeeper	1808	1808(3):23A
Lake, Anna, King St.	Alexandria	Occupant	1790	Tax L 1790:07
Lake, Anna, King St.	Alexandria	Owner	1790	Tax L 1790:07
Lake, George	Arlington	Libellant	1819	ACO:156
Lamar, William, def.	Alexandria	Suit	1801	CRD:104
Lamason, Benjamin Poulton	Arlington	Will	1892	WB10:240; File #757A
Lambdin, Elizabeth Hines, of DC	Alexandria	Will	1898	WB2:250; LP
Lambert, Benjamin H.	Alexandria	Will	1873	WB1:087; LP
Lambert, Geo.	Alexandria	Boarder	1808	1808(1):04A
Lambert, Jacob	Alexandria	Resident	1800	1800(4):14B
Lambert, Jacob, tanner	Alexandria	Boarder	1800	1800(4):14A
Lambert, Mary, seamstress	Alexandria	Head	1810	1810(1):05A
Lambert, Thomas, laborer	Alexandria	Housekeeper	1808	1808(4):29A
Lambert, [blank]	Alexandria	Boarder	1808	1808(2):13A
Lambeth, Dorah, c/o Wm. M./Georg.	Arlington	Guard.	1855	BB(np)
Lambeth, Fanny, c/o Wm. M./Georg.	Arlington	Guard.	1855	BB(np)
Lambrie, John	Alexandria	Tax Charge	1800	Tax PP 1800:23
Lammond, Alexander	Arlington	Will	1806	WBB:388; File #024A
Lammond, Alexander	Arlington	Admin.	1807	WBC:016
Lammond, Alexander	Arlington	Account	1808	WBC:037; LVA-LP
Lammond, Charlotte, seamstress	Alexandria	Head	1810	1810(1):11A
Lamoin, John	Alexandria	Mer. License	1799	Tax PP 1799:52-06r
Lamphier, Going	Alexandria	Tax Charge	1790	Tax PP 1790:08
Lamphier [Langfare], Going	Alexandria	Tax Charge	1795	Tax PP 1795:17
Lamphier [Langfare], Robt.	Alexandria	Tax Charge	1795	Tax PP 1795:17
Lamphiere, Gowen, house joiner	Alexandria	Head	1810	1810(3):08A
Lamphiere, William, custom house ofcr.	Alexandria	Head	1810	1810(3):08A
Lancaster, Thomas	Alexandria	Tax Charge	1796	Tax PP 1796:11
Lancaster, Thos.	Alexandria	Tax Charge	1798	Tax PP 1798:11
Landres, Henry W., grantor	Arlington	Indenture D.	1813	ID2:198
Landres, Henry W., in jail	Arlington	Insolvent	1813	ID2:196
Landris, Henry W.	Alexandria	Boarder	1808	1808(1):03A
Lane, James	Alexandria	Tithable +16	1789	Tax PP 1789:08
Lane, Mary (C), washwoman	Alexandria	Housekeeper	1808	1808(3):23A
Langdon, Elias	Arlington	Guard.	1817	WB2:183
Langdon, James	Arlington	Apprentice	1827	OCR1822:130a
Langfair, George, w(1)1, carpenter	Alexandria	Head	1796	1796(3):1
Langfare, Going, Queen St.	Alexandria	Occupant	1795	Tax L 1795:24
Langfew, Gowin	Alexandria	Tax Charge	1787	Tax PP 1787:09
Langfier, Gowen	Alexandria	Tax Charge	1796	Tax LP 1796:17
Langfier, Robert	Alexandria	Tax Charge	1796	Tax LP 1796:17
Langfore, G., Wolf St.	Alexandria	Occupant	1787	Tax L 1787:26
Langherty, Margaret	Arlington	Will	1813	WB1:279
Langley, Edward, in jail bounds	Arlington	Insolvent	1812	ID2:184
Langley, Elizabeth	Alexandria	Housekeeper	1799	1799(2):16A
Langley, Elizabeth, seamstress	Alexandria	Head	1810	1810(1):11A
Langly, Edwd., hatter	Alexandria	Head	1810	1810(4):03A
Langolon, [blank], nr. Duke St.	Alexandria	Occupant	1790	Tax L 1790:02
Langston, Benja.	Alexandria	Tax Charge	1796	Tax LP 1796:17
Langston, Benja. & wife, painter	Alexandria	Housekeeper	1799	1799(2):01A
Langston, Benjamin	Alexandria	Tax Charge	1790	Tax PP 1790:09
Langston, Benjamin	Arlington	Admin.	1803	WBA:230
Langston, Benjamin	Arlington	Inventory	1803	WBA:233; LVA-LP
Langston, Benjamin	Arlington	Account	1805	WBB:116; LVA-LP
Langston, Joseph, c/o Hannah	Arlington	Apprentice	1804	OCR1801:198
Langston, Reuben Y.	Arlington	Account	1819	AB3:307; LVA-LP
Langston, Reuben Y.	Arlington	Admin.	1819	WB2:272
Lanham, Eli, waterman	Alexandria	Head	1810	1810(1):05A
Lanham, Geo. H.	Alexandria	Boarder	1799	1799(2):07A
Lanham, Horatio	Alexandria	Tax Charge	1799	Tax PP 1799:23

NAME OR SUBJECT	LOCATION	TYPE	YEAR	REFERENCE(S)
Lanham, Jacob	Alexandria	Tax Charge	1799	Tax PP 1799:23
Lanham, Jacob & wife, shoemaker	Alexandria	Housekeeper	1799	1799(2):11A
Lanham, Jno. B.	Alexandria	Tax Charge	1798	Tax PP 1798:11
Lanham, Jno. B. & wife, shoemaker	Alexandria	Housekeeper	1799	1799(2):17A
Lanham, John	Alexandria	Tax Charge	1796	Tax PP 1796:11
Lanham, John	Arlington	Ordinary	1806	OBL1(np)
Lanham, John	Arlington	Ordinary	1806	OBL1(np)
Lanham, John B.	Alexandria	Tax Charge	1796	Tax PP 1796:11
Lanham, John B.	Alexandria	Tax Charge	1799	Tax PP 1799:23
Lanham, John B.	Alexandria	Tax Charge	1800	Tax PP 1800:23
Lanham, John, baker	Alexandria	Head	1810	1810(1):02A
Lanham, John, labourer	Alexandria	Head	1810	1810(1):04A
Lanham, John, shopkeeper	Alexandria	Housekeeper	1808	1808(4):27A
Lannam, Esa	Alexandria	Serv./Appr.	1800	1800(4):12B
Lannan, Joanna V., w/o John	Alexandria	Will	1883	WB1:382; LP
Lannan, John	Alexandria	Will	1887	WB1:433; LP
Lannon, John	Alexandria	Will	1880	LP
Lanphier, Going	Alexandria	Tax Charge	1796	Tax PP 1796:11
Lanphier, Going	Alexandria	Tax Charge	1798	Tax PP 1798:11
Lanphier, Going	Alexandria	Tax Charge	1799	Tax PP 1799:23
Lanphier, Going	Alexandria	Tax Charge	1800	Tax PP 1800:23
Lanphier, Going, carpenter	Alexandria	Housekeeper	1808	1808(3):19A
Lanphier, Going, def.	Alexandria	Suit	1801	CRB:072
Lanphier, Robert	Alexandria	Tax Charge	1796	Tax PP 1796:10
Lanphier, Robert G.	Alexandria	Tax Charge	1799	Tax PP 1799:23
Lanphier, Robt. G.	Alexandria	Tax Charge	1800	Tax PP 1800:23
Lanphier, Robt., house joiner	Alexandria	Head	1810	1810(3):03A
Lanphier, Robt., shopkeeper	Alexandria	Housekeeper	1808	1808(3):22A
Lanphier, Robt., St. Asaph St.	Alexandria	Occupant	1795	Tax L 1795:19
Lanphier, Robt., St. Asaph St.	Alexandria	Owner	1795	Tax L 1795:19
Lanphier, Rt. G.	Alexandria	Tax Charge	1798	Tax PP 1798:11
Lanphier, William	Alexandria	Tax Charge	1799	Tax PP 1799:23
Lanphier, William	Alexandria	Tax Charge	1800	Tax PP 1800:23
Lanphier, Wm.	Alexandria	Tax Charge	1796	Tax PP 1796:10
Lanphier, Wm.	Alexandria	Tax Charge	1798	Tax PP 1798:11
Lanphier, Wm.	Alexandria	Letter	1801	Tax PP 1800:54(26)
Lanphier, Wm., U.S. office	Alexandria	Housekeeper	1808	1808(3):19A
Lanston, Benj.	Alexandria	Tax Charge	1795	Tax PP 1795:17
Lanston, Benj.	Alexandria	Tax Charge	1798	Tax PP 1798:11
Lanston, Benjamin	Alexandria	Tax Charge	1789	Tax PP 1789:11
Lanston, Benjamin	Alexandria	Tax Charge	1796	Tax PP 1796:10
Lanston, Benjamin	Alexandria	Tax Charge	1799	Tax PP 1799:23
Lanston, Benjn.	Alexandria	Tax Charge	1788	Tax PP 1788:10
Lanston, Benjn., King St.	Alexandria	Owner	1795	Tax L 1795:20
Lanston, Benjn., King St.	Alexandria	Occupant	1795	Tax L 1795:20
Lapham, Oliver, at his house	Arlington	Ordinary	1821	OBL3(np)
Lapham, Oliver, at his house	Arlington	Ordinary	1825	OBL4(np)
Lapham, Oliver, at his house	Arlington	Ordinary	1826	OBL4(np)
Laphen, Mary Louisa	Alexandria	Will	1897	WB2:233; LP
Lapp, John	Alexandria	Boarder	1808	1808(3):18A
Larkin, Joseph	Alexandria	Tax Charge	1789	Tax PP 1789:11
Larkin, Joseph	Alexandria	Tax Charge	1790	Tax PP 1790:08
Larkin, Joseph, Fairfax St.	Alexandria	Occupant	1790	Tax L 1790:10
Larmor, Saml. B.	Alexandria	Boarder	1808	1808(2):12A
Larmour, Jane H., c/o Samuel B.	Arlington	Guard.	1851	BB(np)
Larmour, Jane H., c/o Samuel B.	Arlington	Guard. Acct.	1868	WB9:095
Larmour, John W., c/o Samuel B.	Arlington	Guard.	1851	BB(np)
Larmour, John W., c/o Samuel B.	Arlington	Guard. Acct.	1868	WB9:091
Larmour, Samuel B.	Arlington	Complainant	1839	LSA:039
Larmour, Samuel B.	Arlington	Plat	1839	LSA:047
Larmour, Samuel B.	Arlington	Account	1847	LVA-LP

NAME OR SUBJECT	LOCATION	TYPE	YEAR	REFERENCE(S)
Larmour, Samuel B.	Arlington	Inventory	1847	WB5:037; LVA-LP
Larmour, Samuel B.	Arlington	Sale	1847	WB5:073; LVA-LP
Larnum, John B.	Alexandria	Tax Charge	1796	Tax LP 1796:17
Larrance, Vintal	Alexandria	Tithable +21	1787	Tax PP 1787:10
Larson, John	Arlington	Bond	1851	BB(np)
Lary, Andrew, white smith	Alexandria	Head	1810	1810(2):08A
Laskin, Joseph	Alexandria	Tithable +16	1788	Tax PP 1788:11
Latham, Edward	Arlington	Inventory	1840	AB8:123; LVA-LP
Latham, Edward	Arlington	Will	1840	WB4:247; File #377A
Latham, Edward, c/o William	Arlington	Apprentice	1805	OCR1801:278
Latham, Elizabeth, shopkeeper	Alexandria	Housekeeper	1808	1808(1):03A
Latham, Richard, clerk	Alexandria	Boarder	1799	1799(2):17A
Latham, Wm., ditcher	Alexandria	Housekeeper	1808	1808(3):18A
Lathan, Jno. & wife, brickmaker	Alexandria	Housekeeper	1799	1799(2):09A
Lathan, Richard	Alexandria	Tax Charge	1800	Tax PP 1800:23
Lathan, Richard & Co.	Alexandria	Mer. License	1799	Tax PP 1799:52-06r
Latimer, Alexander	Alexandria	Tax Charge	1796	Tax PP 1796:11
Latimer, Alexander	Alexandria	Mer. License	1798	Tax PP 1798:20-4
Latimer, Alexander	Alexandria	Tax Charge	1798	Tax PP 1798:11
Latimer, Alexander	Alexandria	Tax Charge	1799	Tax PP 1799:24
Latimer, Alexander	Alexandria	Tax Charge	1800	Tax PP 1800:23
Latimer, Alexander	Arlington	Ordinary	1802	OBL1(np)
Latimer, Alexander	Arlington	Ordinary	1803	OBL1(np)
Latimer, Alexander	Arlington	Ordinary	1804	OBL1(np)
Latimer, Alexander	Arlington	Ordinary	1805	OBL1(np)
Latimer, Alexander	Arlington	Ordinary	1806	OBL2(np)
Latimer, Alexander	Arlington	Will	1810	WBC:474; File #055A
Latimer, Alexander	Arlington	Account	1810	WBC:433
Latimer, Henry	Alexandria	Tax Charge	1796	Tax LP 1796:17
Latimer, Henry	Alexandria	Tax Charge	1799	Tax PP 1799:23
Latimer, Henry, Fairfax St.	Alexandria	Occupant	1795	Tax L 1795:30
Latimer, Henry, mariner	Alexandria	Tax Charge	1795	Tax PP 1795:17
Latimer, Mary	Arlington	Ordinary	1807	OBL2(np)
Latimore, Alexander	Arlington	Sale	1807	WBB:407
Latimore, Alexander	Arlington	Admin.	1807	WBB:394
Latimore, Marcy, tavern license	Alexandria	Housekeeper	1808	1808(2):15A
Latimore [Latimer], Alexander	Arlington	Inventory	1807	WBB:405; LVA-LP
Lattimer, Henry (C)	Alexandria	Tax Charge	1789	Tax PP 1789:11
Lattimer, Henry (M)	Alexandria	Tax Charge	1790	Tax PP 1790:09
Lattimore, Harry, nr. Princess St.	Alexandria	Occupant	1790	Tax L 1790:01
Lattimore, Henry	Alexandria	Tax Charge	1800	Tax PP 1800:23
Laugherty, Margaret	Alexandria	Head	1810	1810(2):06A
Laugherty, Margaret	Arlington	Will	1814	WB1:279; File #114A
Laugherty, Margaret	Arlington	Account	1818	AB3:141; LVA-LP
Laugherty, Margaret, washwoman	Alexandria	Housekeeper	1808	1808(2):15A
Laurason, James	Alexandria	Tax Charge	1799	Tax PP 1799:23
Laurason, James	Alexandria	Tax Charge	1800	Tax PP 1800:23
Laurason, Jas.	Alexandria	Tax Charge	1798	Tax PP 1798:11
Laurason, Thomas	Arlington	Inventory	1819	AB3:361; LVA-LP
Laurason, Thomas	Arlington	Account	1820	AB4:170; LVA-LP
Laurence, Rebecca, merchant	Alexandria	Head	1810	1810(2):02A
Lavely, Thomas	Alexandria	Tithable +16	1788	Tax PP 1788:11
Lavender, Robert	Arlington	Apprentice	1826	OCR1822:121a
Lawerd, Edward, murchant	Alexandria	Boarder	1800	1800(4):07A
Lawler, Edward F.	Alexandria	Will	1883	WB1:395; LP
Lawrason & Fowle	Alexandria	Housekeeper	1808	1808(4):25A
Lawrason & Smoot, def.	Alexandria	Suit	1804	CRF:039
Lawrason, Ann Carson, c/o Thomas	Arlington	Guard.	1820	WB2:376
Lawrason, Ann Carson, c/o Thomas	Arlington	Guard.	1841	AB8:230
Lawrason, Elizabeth	Alexandria	Boarder	1795	1795(4a):11
Lawrason, Elizabeth	Alexandria	Boarder	1799	1799(2):08A

NAME OR SUBJECT	LOCATION	TYPE	YEAR	REFERENCE(S)
Lawrason, George C., c/o Thomas	Arlington	Guard.	1841	AB8:230
Lawrason, George Carson, c/o Thomas	Arlington	Guard.	1820	WB2:376
Lawrason, James	Alexandria	Tax Charge	1787	Tax PP 1787:09
Lawrason, James	Alexandria	Tax Charge	1788	Tax PP 1788:10
Lawrason, James	Alexandria	Tax Charge	1789	Tax PP 1789:11
Lawrason, James	Alexandria	Tax Charge	1790	Tax PP 1790:08
Lawrason, James	Alexandria	Tax Charge	1796	Tax LP 1796:17
Lawrason, James	Alexandria	Tax Charge	1796	Tax PP 1796:11
Lawrason, James	Alexandria	Mer. License	1800	Tax PP 1800:54(16)r
Lawrason, James	Arlington	Plat	1808	WB3:138-141
Lawrason, James	Arlington	Inventory	1824	AB5:349; LVA-LP
Lawrason, James	Arlington	Will P.	1824	OCR1822:065
Lawrason, James	Arlington	Admin.	1824	OCR1822:066
Lawrason, James	Arlington	Bond	1824	WB3:123
Lawrason, James	Arlington	Will	1824	WB3:133
Lawrason, James	Arlington	Sale	1825	AB5:411
Lawrason, James	Arlington	Account	1825	AB6:078; LVA-LP
Lawrason, James & wife, merchant	Alexandria	Head	1795	1795(4):08
Lawrason, James, Admor.	Arlington	Suit	1825	LVA-LP
Lawrason, James, Capt.	Arlington	Account	1825	AB5:403; LVA-LP
Lawrason, James, Fairfax St.	Alexandria	Owner	1790	Tax L 1790:07
Lawrason, James, Fairfax St.	Alexandria	Owner	1795	Tax L 1795:18
Lawrason, James, plt.	Alexandria	Suit	1809	CRH:423
Lawrason, James, St. Asaph St.	Alexandria	Occupant	1790	Tax L 1790:07
Lawrason, James, St. Asaph St.	Alexandria	Owner	1790	Tax L 1790:07
Lawrason, James, St. Asaph St.	Alexandria	Occupant	1790	Tax L 1790:10
Lawrason, James, St. Asaph St.	Alexandria	Owner	1795	Tax L 1795:18
Lawrason, James Thomas, c/o Thomas	Arlington	Guard.	1820	WB2:376
Lawrason, James Thomas, c/o Thomas	Arlington	Guard.	1841	AB8:230
Lawrason, Jas.	Alexandria	Tax Charge	1795	Tax PP 1795:18
Lawrason, Jas. & wife, merchant	Alexandria	Housekeeper	1799	1799(2):13A
Lawrason, Jas., merchant	Alexandria	Housekeeper	1808	1808(4):25A
Lawrason, Jas., St. Asaph St.	Alexandria	Occupant	1795	Tax L 1795:18
Lawrason, Jas., St. Asaph St.	Alexandria	Occupant	1795	Tax L 1795:27
Lawrason, Samuel C., c/o Thomas	Arlington	Guard.	1841	AB8:230
Lawrason, Samuel Carson, c/o Thomas	Arlington	Guard.	1820	WB2:376
Lawrason, Thomas	Arlington	Defendant	1817	ACO:149
Lawrason, Thomas	Arlington	Suit	1819	LVA-LP
Lawrason, Thomas	Arlington	Admin.	1819	WB2:307
Lawrason, Thomas	Arlington	Account	1823	AB5:183; LVA-LP
Lawrason, William Wilson, c/o Thomas	Arlington	Guard.	1820	WB2:376
Lawrason, William Wilson, c/o Thomas	Arlington	Guard.	1841	AB8:230
Lawrence, John	Arlington	Deposition	1806	ACR:014
Lawrence, John, seaman	Alexandria	Housekeeper	1808	1808(1):06A
Lawrence, Rebecca, retailer	Alexandria	Housekeeper	1808	1808(2):10A
Lawrence, Richard	Arlington	Apprentice	1844	OCR1842:095
Lawreson, James	Alexandria	Owner	1787	Tax L 1787:18
Lawreson, James, St. Asaph St.	Alexandria	Occupant	1787	Tax L 1787:18
Lawreson, Jas., merchant	Alexandria	Head	1810	1810(4):07A
Lawreson, Thos., merchant	Alexandria	Head	1810	1810(4):01A
Lawrison, James & wife Alcia	Alexandria	Serv./Appt.	1800	1800(4):15B
Lawrison, James, murchant	Alexandria	Head	1800	1800(4):15A
Laws, Belitha, bricklayer	Alexandria	Head	1810	1810(3):05A
Laws, Bolitha, bricklayer	Alexandria	Housekeeper	1808	1808(3):19A
Laws, Elizabeth, at the theatre tavern	Arlington	Ordinary	1823	OBL3(np)
Laws, Joshua	Alexandria	Reference	1808	1808(2):17B
Laws, Joshua, coach maker	Alexandria	Housekeeper	1808	1808(2):14A
Laws, Joshua, coach maker	Alexandria	Head	1810	1810(2):07A
Laws v. Russell's Exor.	Arlington	Suit	1816	LVA-LP
Lawson, Anthony, b. Northumberland	Arlington	Alien Entry	1817	RA:22/12/17
Lawson, John	Arlington	Ordinary	1821	OBL3(np)

NAME OR SUBJECT	LOCATION	TYPE	YEAR	REFERENCE(S)
Lawson, John	Arlington	Proceedings	1833	WB4:054
Lawson, John	Arlington	Inventory	1851	WB6:015, 051; LVA-LP
Lawson, John	Arlington	Sale	1851	WB5:331; LVA-LP
Lawson, John	Arlington	Will	1851	WB5:317; File #468A
Lawson, John	Arlington	Debts	1851	WB5:318; LVA-LP
Lawson, John	Arlington	Inventory	1851	WB6:127; LVA-LP
Lawson, John	Arlington	Debts	1852	WB6:051
Lawson, John	Arlington	Sale S.	1852	WB6:126; LVA-LP
Lawson, John	Arlington	Account	1852	WB6:133; LVA-LP
Lawson, John	Arlington	Account	1852	WB6:162; LVA-LP
Lawson, John	Arlington	Account	1857	WB7:201; LVA-LP
Lawson, John, at his house	Arlington	Ordinary	1822	OBL3(np)
Lawson, John, at his house	Arlington	Ordinary	1825	OBL4(np)
Lawson, John, at his house	Arlington	Ordinary	1827	OBL4(np)
Lawson, John, at his house	Arlington	Ordinary	1828	OBL4(np)
Lawson, John, at his house	Arlington	Ordinary	1829	OBL4(np)
Lawson, John, at his house	Arlington	Ordinary	1830	OBL4(np)
Lawson, John, at his house	Arlington	Ordinary	1831	OBL4(np)
Lawson, John, at his house	Arlington	Ordinary	1832	OBL4(np)
Lawson, John, at his house	Arlington	Ordinary	1834	OBL5(np)
Lawson, John, at his house	Arlington	Ordinary	1835	OBL5(np)
Lawson, John, at his house	Arlington	Ordinary	1836	OBL5(np)
Lawson, John, at his house	Arlington	Ordinary	1837	OBL5(np)
Lawson, John, b. Northumberland, Eng.	Arlington	Alien Entry	1827	RA:09/04/27
Lawson, John, grantee	Arlington	Indenture D.	1828	ID:185
Lawson, John, grantee	Arlington	Indenture D.	1830	ID:263
Lawson, John, grantee	Arlington	Indenture D.	1831	ID:336
Lawson, John, his house Cameron St.	Arlington	Ordinary	1833	OBL5(np)
Lawson, John, his house Cameron St.	Arlington	Ordinary	1838	OBL5(np)
Lawson, John, in Alexandria Co.	Arlington	Ordinary	1824	OBL3(np)
Lawson, John, in Alexandria Co.	Arlington	Ordinary	1826	OBL4(np)
Lawson, John, on Cameron St.	Arlington	Ordinary	1823	OBL3(np)
Lawson, Mary Seymour	Arlington	Guard.	1822	WB3:058
Lawson, Robert, Admor.	Arlington	Plaintiff	1802	PA:155
Lawson, Robert, Estate, plt.	Alexandria	Suit	1801	CRB:102
Lawwell, Samuel [sic]	Arlington	Ordinary	1808	OBL2(np)
Lawyed, John & wife Rebeccah	Alexandria	Resident	1800	1800(4):09B
Lawyed, John, hatter	Alexandria	Head	1800	1800(4):09A
Lawyrd, Edward	Alexandria	Resident	1800	1800(4):07B
Lazy, [blank]	Alexandria	Tax Charge	1796	Tax PP 1796:11
Leadbeater, Edward Stabler	Alexandria	Will	1899	WB2:350; LP
Leadbeater, John	Arlington	Will	1860	WB7:513; File #572A
Leadbeater, John	Arlington	Appraisal	1865	WB8:293
Leadbeater, John	Arlington	Account	1865	WB8:290
Leadbeater, Mary P.	Arlington	Will	1865	WB8:248; File #626A
Leadbeater, Mary P.	Arlington	Account	1865	WB8:288, 424; LVA-LP
Leadbeater, Mary P.	Arlington	Appraisal	1865	WB8:293
Leadbeater, Mary P.	Arlington	Account	1869	WB9:191
Leadbeater, Thomas	Arlington	Guard. Acct.	1866	WB8:427
Leadbeater, Thomas	Arlington	Guard. Acct.	1869	WB9:193
Leadbeater, Thomas	Alexandria	Will	1895	WB2:117; LP
Leake, Ann	Alexandria	Owner	1787	Tax L 1787:18
Leake, Ann, King St.	Alexandria	Occupant	1787	Tax L 1787:18
Leaky, Dennis	Alexandria	Tithable +21	1787	Tax PP 1787:12
Leap, Jacob	Alexandria	Tax Charge	1787	Tax PP 1787:09
Leap, Jacob	Alexandria	Tax Charge	1788	Tax PP 1788:10
Leap, Jacob	Alexandria	Tax Charge	1789	Tax PP 1789:11
Leap, Jacob	Alexandria	Tax Charge	1795	Tax PP 1795:18
Leap, Jacob	Alexandria	Tax Charge	1796	Tax LP 1796:17
Leap, Jacob	Alexandria	Tax Charge	1796	Tax PP 1796:11
Leap, Jacob	Alexandria	Tax Charge	1798	Tax PP 1798:11

NAME OR SUBJECT	LOCATION	TYPE	YEAR	REFERENCE(S)
Leap, Jacob	Alexandria	Mer. License	1798	Tax PP 1798:20-4
Leap, Jacob	Alexandria	Tax Charge	1799	Tax PP 1799:23
Leap, Jacob	Arlington	Ordinary	1803	OBL1(np)
Leap, Jacob	Arlington	Ordinary	1804	OBL1(np)
Leap, Jacob	Arlington	Ordinary	1807	OBL2(np)
Leap, Jacob	Arlington	Ordinary	1808	OBL2(np)
Leap, Jacob	Arlington	Ordinary	1809	OBL2(np)
Leap, Jacob	Arlington	Ordinary	1810	OBL2(np)
Leap, Jacob	Arlington	Inventory	1821	AB4:195; LVA-LP
Leap, Jacob	Arlington	Bond	1821	WB2:407
Leap, Jacob	Arlington	Will	1821	WB2:405; File #186A
Leap, Jacob	Arlington	Account	1823	AB5:145; LVA-LP
Leap, Jacob & wife, grocer	Alexandria	Housekeeper	1799	1799(2):07A
Leap, Jacob Jr. c/o Jacob Sr.	Arlington	Apprentice	1802	OCR1801:045
Leap, Jacob, shopkeeper	Alexandria	Head	1810	1810(1):13A
Leap, Jacob, shopkeeper & tavern lic.	Alexandria	Housekeeper	1808	1808(1):03A
Leap, Jacob, Union St.	Alexandria	Occupant	1795	Tax L 1795:18
Leap, Jacob, w(2), shopkeeper	Alexandria	Head	1795	1796(3):7
Leap [Leep], Jacob	Alexandria	Tax Charge	1800	Tax PP 1800:23
Lear, Tobias	Alexandria	Tax Charge	1796	Tax LP 1796:17
Lear, Tobias, def.	Alexandria	Suit	1801	CRB:076
Lear, Tobias, def.	Alexandria	Suit	1801	CRC:183
Leary, William B., b. Youghal	Arlington	Alien Entry	1818	RA:08/06/18
Leasy, Isaac, w, ship carpenter	Alexandria	Head	1796	1796(3):3
Lebillé, Lewis	Alexandria	Tax Charge	1800	Tax PP 1800:23
Leddy, Hugh, b. Co. Cavan, Ulster	Arlington	Alien Entry	1824	RA:26/02/24
Lee, Annie, w/o Samuel	Alexandria	Will	1882	WB1:363; LP
Lee, Arthur	Alexandria	Owner	1787	Tax L 1787:18
Lee, Arthur & Co., St. Asaph St.	Alexandria	Occupant	1787	Tax L 1787:03
Lee, Arthur, Princess St.	Alexandria	Occupant	1790	Tax L 1790:05
Lee, Arthur, St. Asaph St.	Alexandria	Occupant	1787	Tax L 1787:18
Lee, Cassius F.	Alexandria	Will	1890	WB1:548; LP
Lee, Cassius F., Jr.	Alexandria	Will	1892	WB2:028; LP
Lee, Charles	Alexandria	Deposition	(nd)	CRK:119
Lee, Charles	Alexandria	Owner	1787	Tax L 1787:18
Lee, Charles	Alexandria	Tax Charge	1787	Tax PP 1787:09
Lee, Charles	Alexandria	Tax Charge	1788	Tax PP 1788:10
Lee, Charles	Alexandria	Tax Charge	1789	Tax PP 1789:11
Lee, Charles	Alexandria	Tax Charge	1790	Tax PP 1790:09
Lee, Charles	Alexandria	Tax Charge	1795	Tax PP 1795:17
Lee, Charles	Alexandria	Tax Charge	1796	Tax LP 1796:17
Lee, Charles	Alexandria	Tax Charge	1796	Tax PP 1796:11
Lee, Charles	Alexandria	Tax Charge	1798	Tax PP 1798:11
Lee, Charles	Alexandria	Tax Charge	1800	Tax PP 1800:23
Lee, Charles	Alexandria	Deposition	1808	CRH:106
Lee, Charles	Arlington	Admin.	1815	WB2:074
Lee, Charles	Arlington	Sale	1816	AB2:334, 337
Lee, Charles, Cameron St.	Alexandria	Occupant	1790	Tax L 1790:03
Lee, Charles J., Exor., plt.	Alexandria	Suit	1801	CRB:205
Lee, Charles, prosecutor	Arlington	Appointment	1794	OT:03/07/1794
Lee, Charles, Queen St.	Alexandria	Owner	1790	Tax L 1790:08
Lee, Charles, Queen St.	Alexandria	Occupant	1790	Tax L 1790:08
Lee, Charles, Washington St.	Alexandria	Occupant	1787	Tax L 1787:18
Lee, Chas., atty. at law	Alexandria	Head	1810	1810(3):09A
Lee, Chas., lawyer	Alexandria	Housekeeper	1808	1808(3):22A
Lee, Chas., Oronoko St.	Alexandria	Owner	1795	Tax L 1795:19
Lee, Chas., Oronoko St.	Alexandria	Occupant	1795	Tax L 1795:19
Lee, Chas., Princess St.	Alexandria	Occupant	1795	Tax L 1795:19(2)
Lee, Chas., Princess St.	Alexandria	Owner	1795	Tax L 1795:19(2)
Lee, Edmd. J., lawyer	Alexandria	Housekeeper	1808	1808(3):18A
Lee, Edmund J.	Alexandria	Tax Charge	1798	Tax PP 1798:11

NAME OR SUBJECT	LOCATION	TYPE	YEAR	REFERENCE(S)
Lee, Edmund J.	Alexandria	Tax Charge	1799	Tax PP 1799:23
Lee, Edmund J.	Alexandria	Tax Charge	1800	Tax PP 1800:23
Lee, Edmund J.	Alexandria	Deed	1814	CRK:434
Lee, Edmund J.	Alexandria	Deposition	1817	CRK:430
Lee, Edmund J.	Alexandria	Deposition	1818	CRK:386
Lee, Edmund J.	Alexandria	Deed	1820	CRL:499
Lee, Edmund J.	Arlington	Will P.	1843	OCR1842:030, 033
Lee, Edmund J.	Arlington	Will	1843	WB4:320; File #395A
Lee, Edmund J.	Arlington	Library	1844	AB8:473
Lee, Edmund J.	Arlington	Sale	1844	AB8:479
Lee, Edmund J.	Arlington	Inventory	1844	AB8:472; LVA-LP
Lee, Edmund J.	Arlington	Account	1846	AB9:226; LVA-LP
Lee, Edmund J.	Arlington	Citation	1846	OCR1842:164
Lee, Edmund J., atty. at law	Alexandria	Head	1810	1810(3):09A
Lee, Edmund J., def.	Alexandria	Suit	1818	CRL:035
Lee, Edmund J., def.	Alexandria	Suit	1819	CRL:024
Lee, Edmund J., def.	Alexandria	Suit	1819	CRK:497
Lee, Edmund J., def.	Alexandria	Suit	1821	CRL:089
Lee, Edmund J., def.	Alexandria	Suit	1821	CRL:162
Lee, Edmund J., def.	Alexandria	Suit	1821	CRL:159
Lee, Edmund J., def.	Alexandria	Suit	1822	CRL:576
Lee, Edmund J., Jr.	Arlington	Renounce	1843	WB4:322
Lee, Edmund J., plt.	Alexandria	Suit	1813	CRI:158
Lee, Edmund J., plt.	Alexandria	Suit	1822	CRL:232
Lee, Edmund J., the Younger	Arlington	Renounce	1843	OCR1842:030
Lee, Edmund J., trustee, plt.	Alexandria	Suit	1807	CRF:140
Lee, Edmund Jennings	Alexandria	Deed	1803	CRH:220, 223
Lee, Edmund Jennings, clerk	Arlington	Appointment	1818	ACO:150
Lee, Edmund Jennings, def.	Alexandria	Suit	1810	CRH:197
Lee, Edmune J., Attorney	Arlington	Proof	1801	ACO:001
Lee, Essex (C)	Arlington	Apprentice	1815	OCR1811:300
Lee, Fanny	Arlington	Will	1851	WB6:020; File #472A
Lee, Francis L., lawyer	Alexandria	Housekeeper	1808	1808(3):22A
Lee, H., Princess St.	Alexandria	Occupant	1787	Tax L 1787:08
Lee, Henry & wife Ann, Westmoreland	Alexandria	Deed	1797	CRI:320
Lee, Henry, Jr.	Alexandria	Owner	1787	Tax L 1787:19
Lee, Henry, of Westmoreland Co.	Alexandria	Deed	1796	CRI:314
Lee, Ikanah (C), washwoman	Alexandria	Housekeeper	1808	1808(1):08A
Lee, Jack (C)	Alexandria	Boarder	1808	1808(4):24B
Lee, James, seaman	Alexandria	Head	1810	1810(2):06A
Lee, Jas., seaman	Alexandria	Housekeeper	1808	1808(2):11A
Lee, John F.	Arlington	Guard.	1830	WB3:387
Lee, Julia A.	Alexandria	Will	1886	WB1:427; LP
Lee, Lewis (C)	Arlington	Apprentice	1827	OCR1822:129
Lee, Lucy	Alexandria	Head	1810	1810(4):09A
Lee, Lucy (C), washwoman	Alexandria	Housekeeper	1808	1808(4):24A
Lee, Lucy, Miss	Alexandria	Tax Charge	1800	Tax PP 1800:23
Lee, Ludwell	Alexandria	Tax Charge	1789	Tax PP 1789:11
Lee, Ludwell	Alexandria	Tax Charge	1790	Tax PP 1790:09
Lee, Ludwell	Alexandria	Deposition	1822	CRL:541
Lee, Ludwell, def.	Alexandria	Suit	1801	CRB:102
Lee, Ludwell, def.	Alexandria	Suit	1812	CRH:492
Lee, Ludwell, Wilkes St.	Alexandria	Occupant	1790	Tax L 1790:07
Lee, Mary	Arlington	Guard.	1831	WB4:038
Lee, Mary	Arlington	Guard. Acct.	1832	LVA-LP
Lee, Mary	Arlington	Account	1833	AB7:355; LVA-LP
Lee, Mary	Arlington	Account	1834	AB7:357; LVA-LP
Lee, Mary	Arlington	Guard. Acct.	1839	AB7:353
Lee, N.A.	Arlington	Appraisal	1867	WB8:567
Lee, Philip, drayman	Alexandria	Housekeeper	1808	1808(4):30A
Lee, Philip, drayman	Alexandria	Head	1810	1810(1):02A

NAME OR SUBJECT	LOCATION	TYPE	YEAR	REFERENCE(S)
Lee, Richard B.	Alexandria	Inventory	1807	CRK:110
Lee, Richard Bland	Alexandria	Account B.	1807	CRK:086, 096, 098
Lee, Richard Bland	Alexandria	Mil. Lands	1807	CRK:100
Lee, Richard Bland	Alexandria	Account B.	1807	CRK:114
Lee, Richard Bland	Alexandria	Account B.	1807	CRL:106, 118
Lee, Richard Bland	Alexandria	Account B.	1807	CRK:341, 349
Lee, Richard Bland	Alexandria	Inventory	1807	CRL:130
Lee, Richard Bland	Alexandria	Account B.	1811	CRK:267
Lee, Richard Bland	Alexandria	Will	1875	WB1:162; LP
Lee, Richard Bland & wife Elizabeth	Alexandria	Deed	1807	CRK:101
Lee, Richard Bland & wife Elizabeth	Alexandria	Deed	1807	CRL:120
Lee, Richard Bland, def.	Alexandria	Suit	1810	CRH:197
Lee, Richard Bland, def.	Alexandria	Suit	1815	CRK:076
Lee, Richard Bland, def.	Alexandria	Suit	1817	CRK:260
Lee, Richard Bland, of Fairfax Co.	Alexandria	Deed	1806	CRH:227
Lee, Richard Bland, plt.	Alexandria	Suit	1818	CRL:092
Lee, Richard Bland, plt.	Alexandria	Suit	1818	CRK:330
Lee, Richard Bland, re: *Hillsdale*	Alexandria	Land Sale	1807	CRL:119
Lee, Richd. Bland, gentleman	Alexandria	Head	1810	1810(1):01A
Lee, Sarah	Alexandria	Tax Charge	1796	Tax LP 1796:17
Lee, Theodorick	Alexandria	Tithable +16	1788	Tax PP 1788:17
Lee, Theodorick	Alexandria	Tax Charge	1789	Tax PP 1789:11
Lee, William Ludwell	Arlington	Will	1807	WBB:543; File #026A
Lee, William Ludwell	Arlington	Inventory	1807	WBC:003; LVA-LP
Lee, William Ludwell	Arlington	Bond	1807	WBB:547
Lee, Wm.	Alexandria	Boarder	1808	1808(1):03A
Lee, Zenobia	Arlington	Guard.	1822	OCR1822:001a
Lee, Zenobia	Arlington	Guard.	1822	WB3:046
Leech, Nancy, c/o Samuel	Arlington	Guard.	1817	WB2:181
Leeds, Jedediah	Alexandria	Agreement	1800	CRK:233
Leeds, Jedediah	Alexandria	Account B.	1802	CRK:232
Leeds, Jedediah, complt.	Alexandria	Suit	1817	CRK:359
Leeds, Jedediah, def.	Alexandria	Suit	1814	CRH:565
Leeds, Jedediah, def.	Alexandria	Suit	1815	CRK:389
Leep, Jacob	Alexandria	Mer. License	1799	Tax PP 1799:52-06r
Leep, Jacob	Arlington	Ordinary	1805	OBL1(np)
Leesburg, [blank], seaman	Alexandria	Head	1810	1810(1):03A
Lefevre, Ceaser, dancing master	Alexandria	Boarder	1799	1799(2):05A
LeFevre, Casar	Alexandria	Tax Charge	1799	Tax PP 1799:24
Legg, Eli	Arlington	Ordinary	1823	OBL3(np)
Legg, Eli, at his house	Arlington	Ordinary	1822	OBL3(np)
Leigh, George H.	Alexandria	Tax Charge	1788	Tax PP 1788:10
Leigh, J.H., Fairfax St.	Alexandria	Occupant	1787	Tax L 1787:13
Leip, Jacob	Alexandria	Mer. License	1800	Tax PP 1800:54(16)r
Lemmon, Alexr. & wife	Alexandria	Boarder	1799	1799(2):15A
Lemmon, Charlotte, gentlewoman	Alexandria	Housekeeper	1808	1808(1):07A
Lemoin, Jno.	Alexandria	Tax Charge	1795	Tax PP 1795:17
Lemoin, John	Alexandria	Tax Charge	1800	Tax PP 1800:23
Lemoine, Jno.	Alexandria	Tax Charge	1798	Tax PP 1798:11
Lemoine, Jno. & wife, broker	Alexandria	Housekeeper	1799	1799(2):08A
Lemoine, John	Alexandria	Tax Charge	1796	Tax LP 1796:17
Lemoine, John	Alexandria	Tax Charge	1796	Tax PP 1796:11
Lemoine, John	Alexandria	Tax Charge	1799	Tax PP 1799:23
Lemoine, John	Alexandria	Mer. License	1800	Tax PP 1800:54(16)r
Lemoine, John	Arlington	Inventory	1802	WBA:095; LVA-LP
Lemoine, John	Arlington	Sale	1802	WBA:093
Lemoine, John	Arlington	Admin.	1802	WBA:077
Lemoine, John	Arlington	Account	1805	WBB:146; LVA-LP
Lemoine, John	Alexandria	Boarder	1808	1808(3):21A
Lemoine, John, plt.	Alexandria	Suit	1801	CRB:250
Lemoine, John, plt.	Alexandria	Suit	1801	CRB:247

NAME OR SUBJECT	LOCATION	TYPE	YEAR	REFERENCE(S)
Lemoine, John, w(2)2, sadler	Alexandria	Head	1796	1796(3):4
Lennox, Walter	Arlington	Trustee	1862	WB8:121
Lenon & Maitland, def.	Alexandria	Suit	1804	CRG:191
Lenon, James, def.	Alexandria	Suit	1807	CRG:206
Lenox & Maitland, plt.	Alexandria	Suit	1801	CRB:001, 004
Lenox, David, complt.	Alexandria	Suit	1815	CRK:030
Lenox, David, of Philadelphia	Alexandria	Deed	1811	CRK:048
Lenox, James	Arlington	Plaintiff	1802	PA:345
Lenox, James, plt.	Alexandria	Suit	1801	CRB:001, 004, 008
Lenox, James, plt.	Alexandria	Suit	1801	CRB:013, 016
Lenox, Margaret, Queen St.	Alexandria	Occupant	1795	Tax L 1795:16
Lenter, Julia Wise	Arlington	Guard.	1813	WB1:271
Lenter, Julia Wise, c/o William	Arlington	Guard.	1817	WB2:182
Lenter, William	Arlington	Inventory	1810	AB1:019; LVA-LP
Lenter, William	Arlington	Admin.	1810	WB1:009
Lenter, William	Arlington	Account	1811	AB1:105; LVA-LP
Lenter, William, Capt.	Arlington	Sale	1811	AB1:021
Leonard, John	Alexandria	Will	1888	WB1:490; LP
Lesby, Joseph	Alexandria	Tax Charge	1799	Tax PP 1799:23
Lesley, Benjn.	Alexandria	Boarder	1808	1808(4):24A
Levaux, T.	Arlington	Admin.	1842	AB8:313
Leveaux, J.	Arlington	Account	1840	AB8:313; LVA-LP
Levering, Elizabeth	Arlington	Will	1854	WB6:326; File #507A
Levering, Elizebeth	Arlington	Account	1856	WB7:092; LVA-LP
Levering, John	Arlington	Apprentice	1805	OCR1801:256
Levering, Septimus, grantor	Arlington	Indenture D.	1804	ID3:016
Levering, Septimus, in jail	Arlington	Insolvent	1804	ID3:012
Levering, Septimus, sea captain	Alexandria	Housekeeper	1808	1808(1):07A
Levering, Septs., mariner	Alexandria	Head	1810	1810(1):10A
Levering, Wm., architect	Alexandria	Housekeeper	1808	1808(1):04A
Levi, John	Alexandria	Boarder	1808	1808(2):16A
Levring, Septemus	Alexandria	Serv./Appt.	1800	1800(4):15B
Lewin, Peggy	Alexandria	Resident	1800	1800(4):10B
Lewin, Peggy, laundress	Alexandria	Head	1800	1800(4):10A
Lewis, Ambrose	Arlington	Admin.	1833	WB4:067
Lewis, Benjamin, n/o William	Arlington	Apprentice	1812	OCR1811:049
Lewis, Benjamin, n/o William	Arlington	Apprentice	1812	OCR1811:065
Lewis, Cuthbert	Alexandria	Tax Charge	1789	Tax PP 1789:11
Lewis, Dav.	Alexandria	Boarder	1808	1808(2):15A
Lewis, Edward	Alexandria	Tax Charge	1795	Tax PP 1795:18
Lewis, Edward	Alexandria	Tax Charge	1796	Tax LP 1796:17
Lewis, Edward	Alexandria	Tax Charge	1796	Tax PP 1796:11
Lewis, Edward	Alexandria	Tax Charge	1798	Tax PP 1798:11
Lewis, Edward	Alexandria	Tax Charge	1799	Tax PP 1799:23
Lewis, Edward	Arlington	Will	1800	CRA:299
Lewis, Edward & wife, blacksmith	Alexandria	Housekeeper	1799	1799(2):07A
Lewis, Edward, Union St.	Alexandria	Occupant	1795	Tax L 1795:02
Lewis, Henry	Alexandria	Tax Charge	1799	Tax PP 1799:24
Lewis, Hugh, shoemaker	Alexandria	Housekeeper	1808	1808(1):05A
Lewis, James	Arlington	Guard.	1823	WB3:085
Lewis, James, c/o Kitty	Arlington	Guard.	1823	OCR1822:034a
Lewis, John A.	Arlington	Will	1873	WB9:356; File #689A
Lewis, Joseph	Alexandria	Tithable +16	1788	Tax PP 1788:08
Lewis, Joseph	Alexandria	Tithable +16	1789	Tax PP 1789:09
Lewis, Joseph	Alexandria	Tithable +16	1790	Tax PP 1790:07
Lewis, Lucy, washwoman	Alexandria	Housekeeper	1808	1808(1):06A
Lewis, Magnus M.	Alexandria	Will	1884	WB1:399; LP
Lewis, Mordecai, of Philadelphia	Alexandria	Deed	1786	CRI:310
Lewis, Richard	Alexandria	Tax Charge	1799	Tax PP 1799:24
Lewis, Richard	Alexandria	Tax Charge	1800	Tax PP 1800:23
Lewis, Richard	Arlington	Defendant	1802	PA:051

NAME OR SUBJECT	LOCATION	TYPE	YEAR	REFERENCE(S)
Lewis, Richard	Arlington	Defendant	1802	PA:294
Lewis, Richard	Arlington	Defendant	1802	PA:280
Lewis, Richard	Arlington	Defendant	1802	PA:274
Lewis, Richard	Arlington	Defendant	1802	PA:300
Lewis, Richard, assessor	Alexandria	Head	1810	1810(3):04A
Lewis, Richard, def.	Alexandria	Suit	1802	CRC:213
Lewis, Richard, def.	Alexandria	Suit	1803	CRD:086
Lewis, Richd.	Alexandria	Tax Charge	1798	Tax PP 1798:11
Lewis, Richd.	Alexandria	Mer. License	1798	Tax PP 1798:20-4
Lewis, Richd. & wife	Alexandria	Housekeeper	1799	1799(2):06A
Lewis, Richd., St. Commr.	Alexandria	Housekeeper	1808	1808(3):19A
Lewis, Samuel	Arlington	Sale	1804	WBA:290
Lewis, Samuel	Arlington	Inventory	1804	WBA:289; LVA-LP
Lewis, Samuel	Arlington	Admin.	1804	WBA:274
Lewis, Samuel	Arlington	Account	1804	WBB:070
Lewis, T., Fairfax St.	Alexandria	Occupant	1787	Tax L 1787:07
Lewis, Thomas	Alexandria	Tax Charge	1787	Tax PP 1787:09
Lewis, William late mate S. *Enterprize*	Arlington	Respondent	1805	ACO:035
Lewis, William, plasterer	Alexandria	Head	1810	1810(4):06A
Lewis, Wm., plaisterer	Alexandria	Housekeeper	1808	1808(1):02A
Leyne, Patrick, b. Killarney	Arlington	Alien Entry	1819	RA:30/11/19
Libbey, Richard L.	Arlington	Inventory	1822	OCR1822:005
Libbey, Richd.	Alexandria	Boarder	1799	1799(2):08A
Libby & Carne	Alexandria	Tax Charge	1800	Tax PP 1800:23
Libby & Carne	Alexandria	Tax Charge	1799	Tax PP 1799:23
Libby, Richard	Alexandria	Letter	1801	CRE:343
Libby, Richard	Arlington	Sale	1821	AB5:022
Libby, Richard	Arlington	Bond	1821	WB3:029
Libby, Richard	Arlington	Will	1821	WB3:028; File #201A
Libby, Richard	Arlington	Inventory	1822	AB5:042; LVA-LP
Libby, Richard	Arlington	Account	1823	AB5:161
Libby, Richard	Arlington	Account	1824	AB5:264; LVA-LP
Libby, Ro., merchant	Alexandria	Housekeeper	1808	1808(1):04A
Licklace, [blank]	Alexandria	Tax Charge	1796	Tax PP 1796:11
Lickless, D.	Alexandria	Boarder	1808	1808(2):12A
Lieberman, Louisa Catherine	Arlington	Will	1861	WB8:050; File #582A
Lightfoot, Harriet	Arlington	Apprentice	1815	OCR1811:320
Lightfoot, John	Arlington	Admin.	1807	WBB:402
Lightfoot, John	Arlington	Inventory	1807	WBB:415; LVA-LP
Lightfoot, John	Arlington	Account	1809	WBC:181; LVA-LP
Lightfoot, Saml.	Alexandria	Reference	1808	1808(4):29B
Lightfoot, William & carpenter	Alexandria	Head	1795	1795(4):07
Lightfoot, William & wife, labourer	Alexandria	Head	1795	1795(4):08
Lightfoot, William, Jr.	Alexandria	Tax Charge	1799	Tax PP 1799:23
Lightfoot, William, Jr.	Alexandria	Tax Charge	1800	Tax PP 1800:23
Lightfoot, Wm.	Alexandria	Tax Charge	1796	Tax LP 1796:17
Lightfoot, Wm.	Alexandria	Housekeeper	1799	1799(2):11A
Lightfoot, Wm.	Alexandria	Boarder	1808	1808(4):29A
Lightfoot, Wm. & daughter, drayman	Alexandria	Head	1795	1795(4a):07
Lightfoot, Wm. & wife, labourer	Alexandria	Housekeeper	1799	1799(2):18A
Lightfoot, Wm., Jr.	Alexandria	Tax Charge	1795	Tax PP 1795:18
Lightfoot, Wm., Jr.	Alexandria	Tax Charge	1796	Tax LP 1796:17
Lightfoot, Wm., Jr.	Alexandria	Tax Charge	1796	Tax PP 1796:11
Lightfoot, Wm., Jr.	Alexandria	Tax Charge	1798	Tax PP 1798:11
Lightfoot, Wm., Sr.	Alexandria	Tax Charge	1795	Tax PP 1795:18
Lightfoot, Wm., Sr.	Alexandria	Tax Charge	1796	Tax PP 1796:11
Lightfoot, Wm., Sr.	Alexandria	Tax Charge	1799	Tax PP 1799:24
Lightfoot, Wm., Sr., Royal St.	Alexandria	Occupant	1795	Tax L 1795:08
Liles, Susanna	Alexandria	Will	1887	WB1:458; LP
Liles, Zacriah, overseer of the streets	Alexandria	Head	1800	1800(4):09A
Liles, Zacrier & wife Mary	Alexandria	Resident	1800	1800(4):09B

NAME OR SUBJECT	LOCATION	TYPE	YEAR	REFERENCE(S)
Lillefrow, Andrew, w1, taylor	Alexandria	Head	1796	1796(3):4
Limbrick, John	Alexandria	Mer. License	1800	Tax PP 1800:54(16)r
Lime Kiln, in Berkeley Co., tract called	Arlington	Suit	1840	LSA:054
Limmrick, John	Alexandria	Tax Charge	1796	Tax LP 1796:17
Limrick, John	Alexandria	Tax Charge	1795	Tax PP 1795:17
Limrick, John	Alexandria	Tax Charge	1796	Tax PP 1796:11
Limrick, John	Alexandria	Mer. License	1798	Tax PP 1798:20-4
Limrick, John	Alexandria	Tax Charge	1798	Tax PP 1798:11
Limrick, John	Arlington	Ordinary	1803	OBL1(np)
Limrick, John	Arlington	Sale	1806	WBB:312
Limrick, John	Arlington	Admin.	1806	WBB:271
Limrick, John	Arlington	Inventory	1806	WBB:286; LVA-LP
Limrick, John	Arlington	Account	1806	WBB:384; LVA-LP
Limrick, John, Fairfax St.	Alexandria	Occupant	1795	Tax L 1795:01
Linaway, Sharlet, labourrer	Alexandria	Boarder	1800	1800(4):07A
Linch, Daniel	Alexandria	Tax Charge	1787	Tax PP 1787:09
Linde, Abraham, def.	Alexandria	Suit	1807	CRG:163
Lindell, John, b. Stockholm, Swe.	Arlington	Alien Entry	1817	RA:03/12/17
Lindo, Abram	Arlington	Ordinary	1809	OBL2(np)
Lindon, Abram, merchant	Alexandria	Housekeeper	1808	1808(3):19A
Lindsay, Benjamin & wife, taylor	Alexandria	Head	1795	1795(4):06
Lindsay, John, merchant, plt.	Alexandria	Suit	1805	CRE:001
Lindsay, Opie, cartman	Alexandria	Housekeeper	1808	1808(3):23A
Lindsay, Opie, drayman	Alexandria	Head	1810	1810(3):07A
Lindsay, Saml.	Alexandria	Boarder	1808	1808(1):05A
Lindsay, Samuel	Arlington	Will	1857	WB7:223; File #544A
Lindsay, Samuel D.	Arlington	Inventory	1817	AB3:031, 091; LVA-LP
Lindsay, Samuel D.	Arlington	Admin.	1817	WB2:195
Lindsay, Samuel, grantee	Arlington	Indenture D.	1829	ID:242
Lindsey, Benj.	Alexandria	Tax Charge	1795	Tax PP 1795:17
Linn [Lynn], Catharine	Alexandria	Tax Charge	1787	Tax PP 1787:09
Linsey, Robert	Alexandria	Serv./Appr.	1800	1800(4):14B
Linter, Wm., retailer	Alexandria	Housekeeper	1808	1808(1):09A
Linter, Wm., shopkeeper	Alexandria	Head	1810	1810(1):06A
Linton, George, seaman	Alexandria	Head	1810	1810(1):03A
Lippitt, Edward R.	Arlington	Complainant	1835	LSA:005
Lippitt, Mary F.	Arlington	Will	1882	WB10:037; File #711A
Lippitt, Mary Frances, w/o Edward R.	Arlington	Complainant	1835	LSA:005
Litefoot, Wm. & wife Mary	Alexandria	Resident	1800	1800(4):13B
Litefoot, Wm., carter	Alexandria	Head	1800	1800(4):13A
Litle, Hannah	Arlington	Will	1817	WB2:225; File #148A
Litle, Hannah	Arlington	Bond	1817	WB2:227
Litle, Hannah	Arlington	Account	1823	AB5:237, 239; LVA-LP
Litle, Hannah	Arlington	Account	1824	AB5:237
Litle, Hannah	Arlington	Admin.	1825	OCR1822:085a
Litle, John	Arlington	Admin.	1823	WB3:161
Litle, Richard H.	Arlington	Sale	1825	AB6:066
Litle, Richard H.	Arlington	Inventory	1825	AB6:045; LVA-LP
Litle, Richard H.	Arlington	Admin.	1825	OCR1822:085
Litle, Richard H.	Arlington	Admin.	1825	WB3:166
Litle, Richard H.	Arlington	Account	1826	AB6:200; LVA-LP
Litle, Richard H.	Arlington	Account	1827	AB6:422; LVA-LP
Little, Charles	Alexandria	Tax Charge	1796	Tax PP 1796:11
Little, Rd.	Alexandria	Boarder	1808	1808(4):25A
Little River Turnpike Co.	Alexandria	Stockholders	1820	CRL:225
Littlefield, Theodore	Arlington	Bond	1851	BB(np)
Littlefield, Theodore	Arlington	Appraisal	1852	WB6:056; LVA-LP
Liverpool ware	Arlington	Suit	1827	ACO:275
Livers, Anthony	Alexandria	Tax Charge	1799	Tax PP 1799:23
Livers, Antoney	Alexandria	Resident	1800	1800(4):14B
Livers, Antoney, tanner	Alexandria	Boarder	1800	1800(4):14A

NAME OR SUBJECT	LOCATION	TYPE	YEAR	REFERENCE(S)
Livingston, John	Alexandria	Tax Charge	1796	Tax LP 1796:17
Livingston, John	Alexandria	Tax Charge	1799	Tax PP 1799:23
Livingston, John	Alexandria	Tax Charge	1800	Tax PP 1800:23
Livres, Anthony, tanner	Alexandria	Boarder	1799	1799(2):12A
Lloyd, Anne H.	Arlington	Will	1865	WB8:274; File #634A
Lloyd, Edmund J.	Alexandria	Will	1889	WB1:546; LP
Lloyd, Edward	Alexandria	Tax Charge	1800	Tax PP 1800:23
Lloyd, Edward	Arlington	Account	1821	AB4:337, 343, 347
Lloyd, Edward	Arlington	Will P.	1828	OCR1822:156
Lloyd, Edward	Arlington	Admin.	1828	OCR1822:158
Lloyd, Edward	Arlington	Bond	1828	WB3:303, 345
Lloyd, Edward	Arlington	Will	1828	WB3:302; File #264A
Lloyd, Edward	Arlington	Account	1838	LVA-LP (Accounts 2nd)
Lloyd, Edward	Arlington	Account	1839	AB8:109; LVA-LP
Lloyd, Edward	Arlington	Guard. Acct.	1839	AB8:103; LVA-LP
Lloyd, Edward	Arlington	Account	1840	AB8:110; LVA-LP
Lloyd, Edward	Arlington	Guard. Acct.	1840	AB8:107; LVA-LP
Lloyd, Edward	Arlington	Account	1841	AB8:202; LVA-LP
Lloyd, Edward	Arlington	Account	1842	OCR1842:009
Lloyd, Edward	Arlington	Account	1842	OCR1842:015
Lloyd, Edward, children of	Arlington	Guard.	1828	OCR1822:162a
Lloyd, Edward, children of	Arlington	Guard. Acct.	1840	AB8:103
Lloyd, Edward, def.	Alexandria	Suit	1803	CRD:182
Lloyd, Edward, def.	Alexandria	Suit	1803	CRD:175
Lloyd, Edward, def.	Alexandria	Suit	1822	CRL:232
Lloyd, Edwd.	Alexandria	Boarder	1808	1808(2):10A
Lloyd, Francis B.	Arlington	Guard. Acct.	1821	AB4:341, 345, 351
Lloyd, Francis B.	Arlington	Guard. Acct.	1838	LVA-LP (Accounts 2nd)
Lloyd, Francis B.	Arlington	Guard. Acct.	1839	AB8:110; LVA-LP
Lloyd, Francis B.L., plaintiff	Arlington	Suit	1843	LSA:155
Lloyd, Francis, c/o Edward	Arlington	Guard.	1828	WB3:330; WB4:055
Lloyd, Francis L.B.	Arlington	Account	1854	LVA-LP
Lloyd, Frederick	Arlington	Account	1870	WB9:250
Lloyd, Frederick	Arlington	Account	1871	WB9:295
Lloyd, Frederick	Arlington	Inventory	1872	WB9:338
Lloyd, Harriet M.	Arlington	Proceedings	1833	WB4:054, 55
Lloyd, Harriet M., defendant	Arlington	Defendant	1843	LSA:155
Lloyd, Harriet Mason	Arlington	Will	1854	WB6:325; File #506A
Lloyd, Henry	Arlington	Guard. Acct.	1821	AB4:341, 345, 351
Lloyd, Henry	Arlington	Guard. Acct.	1838	LVA-LP (Accounts 2nd)
Lloyd, Henry	Arlington	Will (NR)	1867	File #083A; OB2:468
Lloyd, Henry, c/o Edward	Arlington	Guard.	1828	WB3:330; WB4:055
Lloyd, Henry, defendant	Arlington	Defendant	1843	LSA:155
Lloyd, Joanna L.	Arlington	Guard. Acct.	1839	AB8:111; LVA-LP
Lloyd, Joanna L.	Arlington	Guard. Acct.	1840	AB8:204; LVA-LP
Lloyd, Joanna L.	Arlington	Guard. Acct.	1841	AB8:204
Lloyd, Joanna L., c/o Edward	Arlington	Guard.	1828	WB3:330; WB4:055
Lloyd, Joanna L., c/o Edward	Arlington	Guard. Acct.	1840	AB8:111; LVA-LP
Lloyd, Johanna L.	Arlington	Guard. Acct.	1821	AB4:341, 345, 351
Lloyd, Johanna L.	Arlington	Guard. Acct.	1838	LVA-LP (Accounts 2nd)
Lloyd, Johanna L., defendant	Arlington	Defendant	1843	LSA:155
Lloyd, John	Alexandria	Tax Charge	1798	Tax PP 1798:11
Lloyd, John	Alexandria	Tax Charge	1799	Tax PP 1799:23
Lloyd, John	Alexandria	Tax Charge	1800	Tax PP 1800:23
Lloyd, John	Arlington	Claim	1812	ACO:124
Lloyd, John	Arlington	Respondent	1812	ACO:123, 125
Lloyd, John	Arlington	Will	1854	WB6:369; File #511A
Lloyd, John	Arlington	Fid. Bond	1865	FBB(np)
Lloyd, John J.	Arlington	Will	1871	WB9:316
Lloyd, John, merchant	Alexandria	Housekeeper	1808	1808(1):01A
Lloyd, John, merchant	Alexandria	Head	1810	1810(1):01A

NAME OR SUBJECT	LOCATION	TYPE	YEAR	REFERENCE(S)
Lloyd, Lucy L.	Alexandria	Will	1875	WB1:147; LP
Lloyd, Richard B.	Arlington	Guard. Acct.	1821	AB4:341, 345, 351
Lloyd, Richard B.	Arlington	Guard. Acct.	1838	LVA-LP (Accounts 2nd)
Lloyd, Richard B.	Arlington	Will	1872	WB9:335; File #684A
Lloyd, Richard B., at Head Quarters	Arlington	Ordinary	1846	OBL6(np)
Lloyd, Richard B., c/o Edward	Arlington	Guard.	1828	WB3:330; WB4:055
Lloyd, Richard B., defendant	Arlington	Defendant	1843	LSA:155
Lloyd, Richard B., on Cameron St.	Arlington	Ordinary	1845	OBL6(np)
Lloyd, Richard H.	Arlington	Will	1883	WB10:040; File #713A
Lloyd [Lawyed], John, hatter	Alexandria	Head	1800	1800(4):09A
Locher, John	Alexandria	Boarder	1808	1808(3):21A
Locke, Jonathan	Arlington	Libellant	1827	ACO:275
Locke, Joseph	Arlington	Apprentice	1813	OCR1811:144
Locke, Joseph	Arlington	Apprentice	1815	OCR1811:267
Locke, Joseph	Arlington	Apprentice	1815	OCR1811:171
Locke, Joseph	Arlington	Apprentice	1815	OCR1811:288
Locke, Joseph, c/o Catherine	Arlington	Apprentice	1812	OCR1811:111
Locke, Thomas	Alexandria	Tax Charge	1799	Tax PP 1799:23
Locke, Thomas	Alexandria	Tax Charge	1800	Tax PP 1800:23
Locke, Thomas E., rector	Arlington	Will	1897	WB10:342; File #775A
Locke, Thomas, ret. liquor w/o license	Arlington	Defendant	1802	PA:243
Locke, Thos.	Alexandria	Tax Charge	1798	Tax PP 1798:11
Locke, Thos. & wife, measurer of lumber	Alexandria	Housekeeper	1799	1799(2):01A
Locke, Thos., wood measurer	Alexandria	Housekeeper	1808	1808(1):05A
Locker, Francis, c/o Sarah	Arlington	Apprentice	1815	OCR1811:291
Lockey, Andrew, grantor	Arlington	Indenture D.	1832	ID:403
Lockey, Andrew R., in jail bounds	Arlington	Insolvent	1832	ID:401
Logan, Billy & wife, black labourer	Alexandria	Housekeeper	1799	1799(2):03A
Logan, Elizabeth, seamstress	Alexandria	Head	1810	1810(4):07A
Logan, Hugh, c/o Samuel	Arlington	Apprentice	1813	OCR1811:151
Logan, Loyd, shopkeeper	Alexandria	Housekeeper	1808	1808(3):18A
Logan, Peter	Alexandria	Tax Charge	1796	Tax PP 1796:11
Logan, Peter	Alexandria	Tax Charge	1798	Tax PP 1798:11
Logan, Peter	Alexandria	Tax Charge	1800	Tax PP 1800:23
Logan, Peter (C)	Alexandria	Tax Charge	1795	Tax PP 1795:18
Logan, Peter (C), ship carpenter	Alexandria	Housekeeper	1808	1808(4):24A
Logan, Peter & wife, ship carpenter	Alexandria	Head	1795	1795(4):08
Logan, Peter & wife, ship carpenter	Alexandria	Housekeeper	1799	1799(2):12A
Logan, Peter & wife Sarah	Alexandria	Resident	1800	1800(4):14B
Logan, Peter, Cook	Arlington	Libellant	1818	ACO:152
Logan, Peter, ship carpenter	Alexandria	Head	1800	1800(4):14A
Logan, Peter, ship carpenter	Alexandria	Head	1810	1810(4):08A
Logan, Randall, carpenter	Alexandria	Boarder	1799	1799(2):05A
Logan, Randolph	Arlington	Defendant	1802	PA:271
Logan, Randolph	Arlington	Admin.	1805	WBB:210
Logan, Randolph	Arlington	Inventory	1805	WBB:219
Logan, Randolph	Arlington	Account	1808	WBC:030; LVA-LP
Logan, Rudolph	Alexandria	Will	1899	WB2:349; LP
Logan, Saml.	Alexandria	Tax Charge	1796	Tax PP 1796:11
Logan, Saml., tavern license	Alexandria	Housekeeper	1808	1808(2):15A
Logan, Samuel	Alexandria	Tithable +16	1788	Tax PP 1788:03
Logan, Samuel	Alexandria	Tax Charge	1789	Tax PP 1789:11
Logan, Samuel	Arlington	Ordinary	1803	OBL1(np)
Logan, Samuel	Arlington	Ordinary	1804	OBL1(np)
Logan, Samuel	Arlington	Ordinary	1805	OBL1(np)
Logan, Samuel	Arlington	Ordinary	1806	OBL2(np)
Logan, Samuel	Arlington	Ordinary	1807	OBL2(np)
Logan, Samuel	Arlington	Ordinary	1808	OBL2(np)
Logan, Samuel	Arlington	Ordinary	1809	OBL2(np)
Logan, Samuel	Arlington	Ordinary	1810	OBL2(np)
Logan, Samuel, tavern keeper	Alexandria	Head	1810	1810(2):05A

NAME OR SUBJECT	LOCATION	TYPE	YEAR	REFERENCE(S)
Lokey, Thomas, wood corder	Alexandria	Head	1810	1810(1):03A
Loll, John	Alexandria	Tithable +21	1787	Tax PP 1787:11
Lomax, Caleb, c/o Mary	Arlington	Apprentice	1803	OCR1801:120
Lomax, Caroline	Alexandria	Head	1810	1810(4):06A
Lomax, John	Arlington	Ordinary	1803	OBL1(np)
Lomax, John	Arlington	Ordinary	1806	OBL2(np)
Lomax, John	Arlington	Ordinary	1807	OBL2(np)
Lomax, John	Arlington	Ordinary	1808	OBL2(np)
Lomax, John, b. Bolton	Arlington	Alien Entry	1801	RA:27/07/01
Lomax, John, Estate, Princess St.	Alexandria	Owner	1790	Tax L 1790:07
Lomax, John, Jr.	Arlington	Apprentice	1814	OCR1811:238
Lomax, John Jr., c/o John Sr.	Arlington	Apprentice	1814	OCR1811:050
Lomax, John, shopkeeper	Alexandria	Head	1810	1810(1):01A
Lomax, John, tavern keeper	Alexandria	Housekeeper	1808	1808(1):04A
Lomax, Rachael	Alexandria	Tax Charge	1788	Tax PP 1788:10
Lomax, Rachel	Alexandria	Owner	1787	Tax L 1787:18
Lomax, Rachel	Alexandria	Tax Charge	1787	Tax PP 1787:09
Lomax, Rachel, Princess St.	Alexandria	Occupant	1787	Tax L 1787:18
Lomax's Estate, Princess St.	Alexandria	Occupant	1787	Tax L 1787:17
Lon & Carr	Alexandria	Tax Charge	1787	Tax PP 1787:09
Lon, Thomas	Alexandria	Tithable +21	1787	Tax PP 1787:09
Lonagan, Edward	Alexandria	Tax Charge	1800	Tax PP 1800:23
Lonergan, Edmd., tallow chandler	Alexandria	Boarder	1800	1800(4):02A
Lonergan, Edmd.	Alexandria	Resident	1800	1800(4):02B
Long, George	Arlington	Apprentice	1828	OCR1822:159a
Long, James	Arlington	Witness	1794	OT:25/07/1794
Long, Jesse, laborer	Alexandria	Housekeeper	1808	1808(1):03A
Long, John	Alexandria	Tax Charge	1789	Tax PP 1789:11
Long, John	Alexandria	Tithable +16	1790	Tax PP 1790:08
Long, Robert	Alexandria	Tax Charge	1796	Tax PP 1796:11
Long, Samuel	Arlington	Inventory	1806	LVA-LP
Long, Samuel	Arlington	Sale	1806	WBB:313
Long, Samuel	Arlington	Account	1808	WBC:106; LVA-LP
Longden, Abel	Alexandria	Tax Charge	1798	Tax PP 1798:11
Longden, Abel	Alexandria	Tax Charge	1799	Tax PP 1799:23
Longden, Adam	Arlington	Bond	1803	WBA:174
Longden, Adam	Arlington	Will	1803	WBA:173; LVA-LP
Longden, Jno., Princess St.	Alexandria	Owner	1795	Tax L 1795:20
Longden, Jno., Royal St.	Alexandria	Occupant	1795	Tax L 1795:20
Longden, Jno., Royal St.	Alexandria	Owner	1795	Tax L 1795:20(2)
Longden, John	Alexandria	Tax Charge	1789	Tax PP 1789:11
Longden, John	Alexandria	Tax Charge	1795	Tax PP 1795:17
Longden, John	Alexandria	Tax Charge	1796	Tax PP 1796:11
Longden, John	Alexandria	Tax Charge	1799	Tax PP 1799:23
Longden, John	Arlington	Account	1830	AB6:522; LVA-LP
Longden, John	Arlington	Appraisal	1830	LVA-LP
Longden, John	Arlington	Will	1830	WB3:366; File #290A
Longden, John	Arlington	Order	1832	LVA-LP (Accounts)
Longden, John, plt.	Alexandria	Suit	1812	CRK:002
Longden, John, taylor	Alexandria	Head	1810	1810(2):02A
Longden, John, w(3)1, taylor	Alexandria	Head	1796	1796(3):4
Longden, Julia Ann	Arlington	Guard.	1830	WB3:370
Longden, Julia Ann	Arlington	Guard. Acct.	1832	AB7:039; LVA-LP
Longden, Julia Ann	Arlington	Guard. Acct.	1836	AB7:232; LVA-LP
Longden, Maria	Arlington	Guard.	1816	WB2:115
Longden, Ralph	Alexandria	Tax Charge	1789	Tax PP 1789:11
Longden, Ralph	Alexandria	Tax Charge	1795	Tax PP 1795:17
Longden, Ralph	Alexandria	Tax Charge	1796	Tax PP 1796:11
Longden, Ralph	Alexandria	Tax Charge	1798	Tax PP 1798:11
Longden, Ralph	Alexandria	Tax Charge	1799	Tax PP 1799:23
Longden, Ralph	Arlington	Sale	1815	AB2:083

NAME OR SUBJECT	LOCATION	TYPE	YEAR	REFERENCE(S)
Longden, Ralph	Arlington	Inventory	1815	AB2:081; LVA-LP
Longden, Ralph	Arlington	Admin.	1815	WB1:328
Longden, Ralph	Arlington	Account	1816	AB2:274; LVA-LP
Longden, Ralph	Arlington	Receipts	1817	AB3:014
Longden, Ralph, bricklayer	Alexandria	Housekeeper	1808	1808(3):22A
Longden, Ralph, bricklayer	Alexandria	Head	1810	1810(3):09A
Longden, Ralph, Princess St.	Alexandria	Occupant	1795	Tax L 1795:06
Longden, Robert	Arlington	Inventory	1800	WBA:131; LVA-LP
Longden, Robert	Arlington	Account	1803	WBA:132
Longden, Thomas	Arlington	Inventory	1820	AB4:096; LVA-LP
Longden, Thomas	Arlington	Admin.	1820	WB2:342
Longden, Walter, labourer	Alexandria	Head	1810	1810(3):08A
Longdon, Abe; & wife, cooper	Alexandria	Housekeeper	1799	1799(2):17A
Longdon, Abel	Alexandria	Tax Charge	1800	Tax PP 1800:23
Longdon, Abel	Alexandria	Tax Charge	1796	Tax LP 1796:17
Longdon, Able & wife Susaner	Alexandria	Resident	1800	1800(4):07B
Longdon, Able, ship carpenter	Alexandria	Head	1800	1800(4):07A
Longdon, Elizabeth, sempstress	Alexandria	Housekeeper	1808	1808(1):06A
Longdon, Jno.	Alexandria	Tax Charge	1798	Tax PP 1798:11
Longdon, Jno. & wife, ship builder	Alexandria	Housekeeper	1799	1799(2):16A
Longdon, John	Alexandria	Owner	1787	Tax L 1787:18
Longdon, John	Alexandria	Tax Charge	1787	Tax PP 1787:08
Longdon, John	Alexandria	Tax Charge	1788	Tax PP 1788:09
Longdon, John	Alexandria	Tax Charge	1790	Tax PP 1790:08
Longdon, John	Alexandria	Tax Charge	1796	Tax LP 1796:17
Longdon, John	Alexandria	Tax Charge	1799	Tax PP 1799:23
Longdon, John	Arlington	Juryman	1804	ACO:026
Longdon, John	Arlington	Juryman	1804	ACO:023
Longdon, John (cooper)	Alexandria	Tax Charge	1800	Tax PP 1800:23
Longdon, John, Royal St.	Alexandria	Occupant	1787	Tax L 1787:18
Longdon, John, Royal St.	Alexandria	Owner	1790	Tax L 1790:07
Longdon, John, Royal St.	Alexandria	Occupant	1790	Tax L 1790:07
Longdon, John, taylor	Alexandria	Housekeeper	1808	1808(2):14A
Longdon, Ralph	Alexandria	Tax Charge	1787	Tax PP 1787:08
Longdon, Ralph	Alexandria	Tax Charge	1788	Tax PP 1788:10
Longdon, Ralph	Alexandria	Tax Charge	1790	Tax PP 1790:09
Longdon, Ralph	Alexandria	Tax Charge	1796	Tax LP 1796:17
Longdon, Ralph	Alexandria	Tax Charge	1800	Tax PP 1800:23
Longdon, Ralph, Fairfax St.	Alexandria	Occupant	1790	Tax L 1790:07
Longdon, Thomas, grantor	Arlington	Indenture D.	1812	ID2:169
Longdon, Thomas, in jail bounds	Arlington	Insolvent	1812	ID2:168
Longdon, [blank]	Alexandria	Boarder	1808	1808(2):13A
Longmair, John, Merchant, plt.	Alexandria	Suit	1805	CRE:001
Longston, Benjamin, w(4)1, painter	Alexandria	Head	1796	1796(3):6
Longston, Geo.	Alexandria	Boarder	1808	1808(4):24A
Lothrup, Seth, Jr.	Arlington	Will	1800	CRA:318
Lott, William	Alexandria	Tax Charge	1788	Tax PP 1788:10
Lott, William	Alexandria	Tax Charge	1789	Tax PP 1789:11
Lottery for improving nagivation	Alexandria	Schedule	1812	CRK:138, 140
Louder, Mons. & wife	Alexandria	Head	1795	1795(4a):11
Lougherty, Margaret	Arlington	Inventory	1814	AB2:003a; LVA-LP
Loundes, James	Alexandria	Tax Charge	1790	Tax PP 1790:09
Loundes, John	Alexandria	Tithable +16	1790	Tax PP 1790:09
Loury, William	Alexandria	Tax Charge	1799	Tax PP 1799:24
Love, Charles	Alexandria	Tax Charge	1796	Tax PP 1796:11
Love, Charles	Alexandria	Tax Charge	1799	Tax PP 1799:23
Love, Charles	Alexandria	Tax Charge	1800	Tax PP 1800:23
Love, Charles & wife, merchant	Alexandria	Housekeeper	1799	1799(2):10A
Love, Charles, def.	Alexandria	Suit	1802	CRB:273
Love, Charles Jones, plt.	Alexandria	Suit	1801	CRB:335
Love, Charles, w2, bank officer	Alexandria	Head	1796	1796(3):1

NAME OR SUBJECT	LOCATION	TYPE	YEAR	REFERENCE(S)
Love, Chas.	Alexandria	Tax Charge	1798	Tax PP 1798:11
Love, Chas., St. Asaph St.	Alexandria	Occupant	1795	Tax L 1795:25
Love, J., Princess St.	Alexandria	Occupant	1787	Tax L 1787:18
Love, John	Alexandria	Tax Charge	1787	Tax PP 1787:09
Love, John	Alexandria	Tax Charge	1788	Tax PP 1788:10
Love, John	Alexandria	Tax Charge	1789	Tax PP 1789:11
Love, Saml.	Alexandria	Tax Charge	1796	Tax LP 1796:17
Love, Samuel, Estate, plt.	Alexandria	Suit	1801	CRB:205
Love, Samuel, Estate, plt.	Alexandria	Suit	1801	CRB:335
Love, Samuel, *Salisbury*, Loudoun Co.	Alexandria	Agreement	1798	CRB:340
Lovell, Wm.	Alexandria	Boarder	1808	1808(1):05A
Lovely, Juliana, c/o Elizabeth	Arlington	Apprentice	1814	OCR1811:228
Lovely, Thomas	Alexandria	Tithable +16	1789	Tax PP 1789:13
Lovely, Thomas	Alexandria	Tithable +16	1790	Tax PP 1790:10
Low, James	Alexandria	Tithable +16	1788	Tax PP 1788:07
Low, Thomas, children of	Arlington	Guard. Acct.	1811	AB1:145; LVA-LP
Low, Thomas, children of	Arlington	Guard. Acct.	1813	AB1:284; LVA-LP
Low, Thomas, children of	Arlington	Trustee Acct.	1816	AB2:237
Lowe, Ann Magruder	Arlington	Guard.	1821	WB3:022
Lowe, Children	Arlington	Account	1810	WBC:341
Lowe, Children	Arlington	Trustee Acct.	1814	AB2:001; LVA-LP
Lowe, Children	Arlington	Trustee Acct.	1815	AB2:080
Lowe, Christiana	Alexandria	Will	1872	WB1:056; LP
Lowe, E.M.	Alexandria	Will	1879	WB1:264; LP
Lowe, Henry	Alexandria	Tax Charge	1790	Tax PP 1790:09
Lowe, Henry	Alexandria	Tax Charge	1796	Tax LP 1796:17
Lowe, Henry F., Queen St.	Alexandria	Occupant	1795	Tax L 1795:10
Lowe, Henry T.	Alexandria	Tax Charge	1795	Tax PP 1795:17
Lowe, James, b. Perthshire, Scot.	Arlington	Alien Entry	1819	RA:03/12/19
Lowe, James R.M.	Arlington	Ordinary	1803	OBL1(np)
Lowe, James R.M. & wife Kitty, plt.	Alexandria	Suit	1809	CRG:131
Lowe, Jane	Arlington	Inventory	1814	WB1:320; LVA-LP
Lowe, Jane	Arlington	Admin.	1814	WB1:320
Lowe, Margaret	Arlington	Admin.	1802	WBA:217
Lowe, Margaret	Arlington	Inventory	1804	WBA:270; LVA-LP
Lowe, Margaret	Arlington	Sale	1804	WBA:272
Lowe, Margaret	Arlington	Account	1805	WBB:188; LVA-LP
Lowe, Orphans, c/o Margaret	Arlington	Account	1805	WBB:188; LVA-LP
Lowe, Rector M., clerk	Alexandria	Housekeeper	1808	1808(1):06A
Lowe, Richd. M., clerk	Alexandria	Head	1810	1810(1):09A
Lowe, Samuel	Alexandria	Tax Charge	1799	Tax PP 1799:23
Lowe, Samuel	Alexandria	Tax Charge	1800	Tax PP 1800:23
Lowe, Sophia E.	Alexandria	Will	1871	WBC1:001; LP
Lowe, Sophia E.	Alexandria	Sale	1872	WBC1:011
Lowe, Sophia E.	Alexandria	Inventory	1872	WBC1:004
Lowe, Thomas	Alexandria	Tax Charge	1799	Tax PP 1799:23
Lowe, Thomas	Alexandria	Deposition	1801	CRE:328
Lowe, Thomas, children	Arlington	Account	1810	WBC:341; LVA-LP
Lowe, Thomas, children of	Arlington	Trustee Acct.	1817	AB2:407; LVA-LP
Lowe, Thomas, orphans of	Arlington	Guard.	1823	OCR1822:048a
Lowe, Thos.	Alexandria	Tax Charge	1800	Tax PP 1800:23
Lowe, Thos. & wife, tavern keeper	Alexandria	Housekeeper	1799	1799(2):01A
Lower, Joseph	Alexandria	Tax Charge	1795	Tax PP 1795:17
Lowman, Henry	Alexandria	Tax Charge	1799	Tax PP 1799:23
Lowndes, Hyat	Alexandria	Tithable +16	1790	Tax PP 1790:13
Lowndes, John	Alexandria	Account B.	1800	CRD:157
Lowndes, John, plt.	Alexandria	Suit	1801	CRD:152
Lownds, John	Arlington	Admin.	1800	CRA:362
Lownes, Hiett	Alexandria	Tithable +16	1789	Tax PP 1789:17
Lownes, Hyett	Alexandria	Tithable +16	1788	Tax PP 1788:15
Lownes, J., Prince St.	Alexandria	Occupant	1787	Tax L 1787:16

NAME OR SUBJECT	LOCATION	TYPE	YEAR	REFERENCE(S)
Lownes, James	Alexandria	Tax Charge	1787	Tax PP 1787:09
Lownes, James	Alexandria	Tax Charge	1788	Tax PP 1788:10
Lownes, James	Alexandria	Tax Charge	1789	Tax PP 1789:11
Lownes, James	Alexandria	Tax Charge	1796	Tax LP 1796:17
Lownes, James, Prince St.	Alexandria	Occupant	1790	Tax L 1790:08
Lownes, James, Washington St.	Alexandria	Owner	1795	Tax L 1795:20
Lowns, James, Washington St.	Alexandria	Occupant	1787	Tax L 1787:04
Lowrey, Agnes	Arlington	Will	1844	WB4:379; File #414A
Lowrey, Agnes	Arlington	Account	1845	AB9:136; LVA-LP
Lowrey, Agnes	Arlington	Account	1847	AB9:316
Lowrey, William, Fairfax St.	Alexandria	Occupant	1790	Tax L 1790:07
Lowry, John	Arlington	Suit Bond	1827	ACO:273
Lowry, William	Alexandria	Tax Charge	1787	Tax PP 1787:09
Lowry, William	Alexandria	Tax Charge	1788	Tax PP 1788:10
Lowry, William	Alexandria	Tax Charge	1789	Tax PP 1789:11
Lowry, William	Alexandria	Tax Charge	1790	Tax PP 1790:09
Lowry, William	Alexandria	Tax Charge	1798	Tax PP 1798:11
Lowry, William	Alexandria	Tax Charge	1800	Tax PP 1800:23
Lowry, William, store in *Arlington*	Arlington	Suit	1803	ACO:016
Lowry, Wm. & Co., wharf	Alexandria	Occupant	1790	Tax L 1790:02
Lowry, Wm. & Co., Prince St.	Alexandria	Occupant	1790	Tax L 1790:05
Lowry, Wm. & wife, merchant	Alexandria	Housekeeper	1799	1799(2):08A
Lowry, Wm., Prince St.	Alexandria	Occupant	1787	Tax L 1787:15
Loyd, Jno. & wife, hatter	Alexandria	Housekeeper	1799	1799(2):20A
Loyd, John	Alexandria	Tax Charge	1796	Tax PP 1796:11
Loyd, Thomas	Alexandria	Tax Charge	1796	Tax PP 1796:11
Lucas, Alexander	Arlington	Apprentice	1803	OCR1801:086
Lucas, Kitty	Arlington	Apprentice	1803	OCR1801:101
Lucas, Molly (C)	Alexandria	Housekeeper	1799	1799(2):17A
Lucas, Monica	Arlington	Will	1864	WB8:205; File #614A
Lucas, Wilhiaminer	Arlington	Guard.	1846	LVA-LP (Box 214)
Lucket, Capt., seaman	Alexandria	Head	1810	1810(4):08A
Luckett, Fielder	Alexandria	Boarder	1808	1808(1):06A
Luckett, Fielder	Arlington	Appraisal	1828	LVA-LP
Luckett, Fielder	Arlington	Will	1828	WB3:300
Luckett, Fielder	Arlington	Bond	1828	WB3:330
Ludwig, Frederick	Alexandria	Will	1876	WB1:202; LP
Lugenbeel, James W.	Arlington	Will	1857	WB7:257; File #547A
Luke, John	Arlington	Admin.	1810	WB1:001
Luke, John	Arlington	Sale	1811	AB1:037
Luke, John, def.	Alexandria	Suit	1801	CRB:261
Luke [Lucke], John	Arlington	Inventory	1811	AB1:035; LVA-LP
Lukes, John	Alexandria	Tithable +16	1788	Tax PP 1788:10
Lukes, John	Alexandria	Tithable +16	1789	Tax PP 1789:11
Lukes, Michael	Alexandria	Tax Charge	1788	Tax PP 1788:10
Lukes, Michael	Alexandria	Tax Charge	1789	Tax PP 1789:11
Lumsdon, Catharine, c/o John	Arlington	Guard.	1821	WB3:006
Lumsdon, John	Arlington	Admin.	1806	WBB:343
Lumsdon, John	Arlington	Inventory	1806	WBB:346; LVA-LP
Lumsdon, John	Arlington	Sale	1806	WBB:354
Lumsdon, John	Arlington	Account	1808	WBC:058, 494; LVA-LP
Lumsdon, John	Arlington	Account	1821	AB4:252
Lumsdon, Margery, retailer	Alexandria	Housekeeper	1808	1808(2):10A
Lumsdon, Mary Ann, c/o John	Arlington	Guard.	1821	WB3:006
Lumsdon, Mrs., merchant	Alexandria	Head	1810	1810(2):02A
Lumsdon, William, c/o John	Arlington	Guard.	1821	WB3:006
Lunbeck, William, c/o Margaret	Arlington	Apprentice	1804	OCR1801:222
Lunbeck, Wm.	Alexandria	Boarder	1808	1808(1):01A
Lunt & Cook, partnership	Arlington	Account	1839	LVA-LP
Lunt, Agothian	Arlington	Appraisal	1857	WB7:231; LVA-LP
Lunt, Ann, boarding house keeper	Alexandria	Housekeeper	1808	1808(4):27A

NAME OR SUBJECT	LOCATION	TYPE	YEAR	REFERENCE(S)
Lunt, Elizabeth H., c/o Samuel	Arlington	Guard.	1852	BB(np)
Lunt, Ezra	Alexandria	Tax Charge	1799	Tax PP 1799:23
Lunt, Ezra	Alexandria	Tax Charge	1800	Tax PP 1800:23
Lunt, Ezra	Arlington	Will	1805	WBB:136; File #007A
Lunt, Ezra	Alexandria	Boarder	1808	1808(4):24A
Lunt, Ezra	Arlington	Inventory	1812	AB1:177; LVA-LP
Lunt, Ezra	Arlington	Account	1812	AB1:191
Lunt, Ezra	Arlington	Admin.	1812	WB1:155
Lunt, Ezra	Arlington	Bond	1852	BB(np)
Lunt, Ezra & wife, tobacconist	Alexandria	Housekeeper	1799	1799(2):04A
Lunt, Ezra, c/o Ann	Arlington	Apprentice	1805	OCR1801:260
Lupton, David, Jr.	Arlington	Bond	1814	WB1:312
Lupton, David, Jr.	Arlington	Will	1814	WB1:311; File #123A
Lupton, David, Jr.	Arlington	Inventory	1815	AB2:103; LVA-LP
Lupton, David, Jr.	Arlington	Inventory	1816	AB2:351
Lupton, David, Jr.	Arlington	Account	1816	AB2:370
Lupton, David, Jr.	Arlington	Account	1818	AB3:129; LVA-LP
Lupton, David, Jr.	Arlington	Debts Due	1820	AB4:193
Lupton, David, Jr.	Arlington	Account	1820	AB4:192; LVA-LP
Lupton, David, Jr.	Arlington	Settlement	1821	AB4:277
Lupton, David, Jr. [Ann]	Arlington	Sale	1815	AB4:193
Lupton, Nathan, grantee	Arlington	Indenture D.	1817	ID2:421
Lutes's Estate	Alexandria	Tax Charge	1796	Tax LP 1796:17
Lutz, Cath., washwoman	Alexandria	Housekeeper	1808	1808(4):24A
Lutz, Catharine	Alexandria	Housekeeper	1799	1799(2):18A
Lutz, Catherine	Alexandria	Head	1810	1810(4):09A
Lutz, Cathren	Alexandria	Resident	1800	1800(4):13B
Lutz, Cathrin, tanner	Alexandria	Head	1800	1800(4):13A
Lutz, Michael	Alexandria	Tax Charge	1787	Tax PP 1787:09
Lutz, Michael	Alexandria	Tax Charge	1790	Tax PP 1790:09
Lutz, Michael	Alexandria	Tax Charge	1795	Tax PP 1795:18
Lutz, Michael & wife, tanner	Alexandria	Head	1795	1795(4a):09
Lutz, Michael, Estate	Alexandria	Tax Charge	1796	Tax PP 1796:11
Lutz, Michael, Estate	Alexandria	Tax Charge	1798	Tax PP 1798:11
Lutz, Michael, Wilkes St.	Alexandria	Occupant	1790	Tax L 1790:07
Lutz, Michael, Wilkes St.	Alexandria	Owner	1790	Tax L 1790:07
Lutz, Michael	Alexandria	Owner	1787	Tax L 1787:18
Lutz, Michl.	Alexandria	Boarder	1808	1808(3):21A
Lutz, Michl., St. Asaph St.	Alexandria	Occupant	1787	Tax L 1787:18
Lutz, Michl., St. Asaph St.	Alexandria	Owner	1795	Tax L 1795:19
Lutz, Michl., St. Asaph St.	Alexandria	Occupant	1795	Tax L 1795:19
Lutz, Sophia	Arlington	Guard.	1810	WBC:466
Lyle, Enoch	Alexandria	Boarder	1799	1799(2):02A
Lyle, Martha, btw. Fairfax	Alexandria	Owner	1795	Tax L 1795:19
Lyle, Martha, Fairfax St.	Alexandria	Owner	1795	Tax L 1795:19
Lyle, R., Jr., Queen St.	Alexandria	Occupant	1787	Tax L 1787:18
Lyle, Robert	Alexandria	Owner	1787	Tax L 1787:19
Lyle, Robert	Alexandria	Tax Charge	1788	Tax PP 1788:10
Lyle, Robert	Alexandria	Tax Charge	1789	Tax PP 1789:11
Lyle, Robert	Alexandria	Tax Charge	1790	Tax PP 1790:09
Lyle, Robert	Alexandria	Tax Charge	1795	Tax PP 1795:17
Lyle, Robert	Arlington	Defendant	1802	PA:155
Lyle, Robert, def.	Alexandria	Suit	1801	CRB:094
Lyle, Robert, Estate, alley	Alexandria	Owner	1790	Tax L 1790:07
Lyle, Robert, Estate, Fairfax St.	Alexandria	Owner	1790	Tax L 1790:07(2)
Lyle, Robert, Estate, Royal St.	Alexandria	Owner	1790	Tax L 1790:07
Lyle, Robert, Fairfax & Lyle's alley	Alexandria	Occupant	1787	Tax L 1787:19
Lyle, Robert, Fairfax St.	Alexandria	Occupant	1787	Tax L 1787:02
Lyle, Robert, Jr.	Alexandria	Owner	1787	Tax L 1787:18
Lyle, Robert, Jr.	Alexandria	Tax Charge	1788	Tax PP 1788:10
Lyle, Robert, Jr., plt.	Alexandria	Suit	1820	CRL:022

NAME OR SUBJECT	LOCATION	TYPE	YEAR	REFERENCE(S)
Lyle, Robert, of Pr. William Co.	Alexandria	Bond	1801	CRB:098
Lyle, Robert, Queen St.	Alexandria	Occupant	1790	Tax L 1790:07
Lyle, Robert, Queen St.	Alexandria	Owner	1790	Tax L 1790:07
Lyle, Robt., btw. Fairfax	Alexandria	Owner	1795	Tax L 1795:19
Lyle, Robt., btw. Fairfax	Alexandria	Occupant	1795	Tax L 1795:19
Lyle, Robt., Fairfax St.	Alexandria	Owner	1795	Tax L 1795:19
Lyle, Robt., Queen St.	Alexandria	Owner	1795	Tax L 1795:19
Lyle, Robt., Royal St.	Alexandria	Owner	1795	Tax L 1795:19
Lyle, William	Alexandria	Tithable +16	1788	Tax PP 1788:01
Lyle, William	Arlington	Guard.	1820	WB2:390
Lyle, William	Arlington	Will	1836	WB4:119; File #339A
Lyle, William, c/o Robert	Arlington	Guard.	1805	WBB:122
Lyle, Wm.	Alexandria	Tax Charge	1795	Tax PP 1795:17
Lyle, Zacchariah	Alexandria	Tax Charge	1796	Tax PP 1796:11
Lyle, Zach.	Alexandria	Tax Charge	1798	Tax PP 1798:11
Lyles & Harper, plt.	Alexandria	Suit	1801	CRB:197
Lyles, Emily	Arlington	Apprentice	1846	OCR1842:171
Lyles, Enoch H.	Alexandria	Will	1877	WB1:228; LP
Lyles, Enoch M.	Alexandria	Tax Charge	1800	Tax PP 1800:23
Lyles, Enoch M.	Arlington	Dispute	1811	AB1:068
Lyles, Enoch Magruder	Arlington	Bond	1805	WBB:186
Lyles, Enoch Magruder	Arlington	Will	1805	WBB:185; File #008A
Lyles, Enoch Magruder	Arlington	Debts	1806	WBB:253
Lyles, Enoch Magruder	Arlington	Inventory	1806	WBB:314; LVA-LP
Lyles, Enoch Magruder	Arlington	Sale	1806	WBB:318
Lyles, George N., grantor	Arlington	Indenture D.	1806	ID3:123
Lyles, George N., in jail	Arlington	Insolvent	1806	ID3:119
Lyles, Henry, Estate	Alexandria	Tax Charge	1796	Tax LP 1796:17
Lyles, Henry, sailor	Alexandria	Housekeeper	1808	1808(3):18A
Lyles, Hezekiah, c/o Zacharia	Arlington	Apprentice	1805	OCR1801:242
Lyles, John	Alexandria	Tithable +16	1788	Tax PP 1788:17
Lyles, Kitty	Alexandria	Tax Charge	1787	Tax PP 1787:09
Lyles, Kitty	Alexandria	Tax Charge	1788	Tax PP 1788:10
Lyles, Kitty	Alexandria	Tax Charge	1789	Tax PP 1789:11
Lyles, Kitty	Alexandria	Tax Charge	1790	Tax PP 1790:09
Lyles, Robert	Alexandria	Tax Charge	1787	Tax PP 1787:09
Lyles, Robert	Alexandria	Tax Charge	1796	Tax LP 1796:17
Lyles, Robert, Jr.	Alexandria	Tax Charge	1787	Tax PP 1787:09
Lyles, W. & Co., Union & Wolf sts.	Alexandria	Occupant	1787	Tax L 1787:23
Lyles, W. & H., Fairfax St.	Alexandria	Occupant	1787	Tax L 1787:02
Lyles, William	Alexandria	Owner	1787	Tax L 1787:18
Lyles, William	Alexandria	Tax Charge	1787	Tax PP 1787:09
Lyles, William	Alexandria	Deposition	1808	CRH:099
Lyles, William	Arlington	Ordinary	1810	OBL2(np)
Lyles, William	Alexandria	Will	1874	WB1:100; LP
Lyles, William, Fairfax Parish	Alexandria	Deed	1793	CRH:080
Lyles, William, Jr. Pr. George's Co. Md.	Alexandria	Deed	1790	CRH:090
Lyles, William, Prince St.	Alexandria	Occupant	1787	Tax L 1787:16
Lyles, William, Wolf St.	Alexandria	Occupant	1787	Tax L 1787:18
Lyles, Wm., cooper	Alexandria	Head	1810	1810(1):12A
Lyles, Wm., Fairfax St.	Alexandria	Occupant	1787	Tax L 1787:17
Lyles, Zac.	Alexandria	Boarder	1808	1808(1):09A
Lyles, Zachariah	Arlington	Witness	1794	OT:07/11/1794
Lyles, Zachariah	Alexandria	Tax Charge	1799	Tax PP 1799:23
Lyles, Zachariah	Alexandria	Tax Charge	1800	Tax PP 1800:23
Lyles, Zachariah	Arlington	Apprentice	1801	OCR1801:018
Lyles, Zachariah & wife, drayman	Alexandria	Head	1795	1795(4a):06
Lyles, Zachariah & wife	Alexandria	Housekeeper	1799	1799(2):18A
Lyles, Zachh.	Alexandria	Tax Charge	1796	Tax LP 1796:17
Lymbrick, John	Alexandria	Mer. License	1799	Tax PP 1799:52-06r
Lynch, Barton	Alexandria	Tax Charge	1796	Tax PP 1796:11

NAME OR SUBJECT	LOCATION	TYPE	YEAR	REFERENCE(S)
Lynch, Barton	Alexandria	Tax Charge	1799	Tax PP 1799:24
Lynch, James H., at Richmond	Alexandria	Deposition	1817	CRK:363
Lynch, John	Alexandria	Will	1898	WB2:281; LP
Lyne, Cathrine, (1)1, widow	Alexandria	Head	1796	1796(3):3
Lynn & Walden, King St.	Alexandria	Occupant	1790	Tax L 1790:07
Lynn, Adam	Alexandria	Tax Charge	1796	Tax LP 1796:17
Lynn, Adam	Alexandria	Tax Charge	1796	Tax PP 1796:11
Lynn, Adam	Alexandria	Tax Charge	1798	Tax PP 1798:11
Lynn, Adam	Alexandria	Mer. License	1798	Tax PP 1798:20-4
Lynn, Adam	Alexandria	Tax Charge	1799	Tax PP 1799:23
Lynn, Adam	Alexandria	Mer. License	1799	Tax PP 1799:52-06r
Lynn, Adam	Alexandria	Mer. License	1800	Tax PP 1800:54(16)r
Lynn, Adam	Alexandria	Tax Charge	1800	Tax PP 1800:23
Lynn, Adam	Alexandria	Account B.	1802	CRG:329
Lynn, Adam	Alexandria	Account B.	1804	CRG:354
Lynn, Adam	Alexandria	Deed	1804	CRG:324
Lynn, Adam	Alexandria	Agreement	1805	CRG:352
Lynn, Adam, def.	Alexandria	Suit	1809	CRG:300
Lynn, Adam, Estate	Alexandria	Owner	1787	Tax L 1787:19
Lynn, Adam, Estate	Alexandria	Tax Charge	1796	Tax LP 1796:17
Lynn, Adam, Estate, King St.	Alexandria	Owner	1790	Tax L 1790:07
Lynn, Adam, Estate, King St.	Alexandria	Owner	1795	Tax L 1795:19(3)
Lynn, Adam, merchant	Alexandria	Head	1810	1810(3):01A
Lynn, Adam, silversmith & retailer	Alexandria	Housekeeper	1808	1808(3):21A
Lynn, Adam & mother	Alexandria	Housekeeper	1799	1799(2):05A
Lynn [Linn], Catharine	Alexandria	Tax Charge	1787	Tax PP 1787:09
Lynn, Catharine, King St.	Alexandria	Occupant	1795	Tax L 1795:19
Lynn, Catherine	Alexandria	Tax Charge	1799	Tax PP 1799:23
Lynn, Joseph	Alexandria	Tax Charge	1795	Tax PP 1795:17
Lynn, Mrs., King St.	Alexandria	Occupant	1787	Tax L 1787:19
Lynsey & Ferguson	Alexandria	Tax Charge	1796	Tax LP 1796:17
Lyon, Andrew	Alexandria	Tax Charge	1796	Tax PP 1796:11
Lyon, Andrew	Alexandria	Tax Charge	1799	Tax PP 1799:24
Lyon, Andrew, blacksmith	Alexandria	Head	1810	1810(1):04A
Lyon, Andw.	Alexandria	Tax Charge	1798	Tax PP 1798:11
Lyon, Andw., carpenter	Alexandria	Housekeeper	1808	1808(4):26A
Lyon, George, b. Liverpool	Arlington	Alien Entry	1817	RA:22/12/17
Lyon, Walter	Alexandria	Tax Charge	1795	Tax PP 1795:17
Lyons, John	Alexandria	Tithable +16	1789	Tax PP 1789:16
Lyons, John, c/o John	Arlington	Apprentice	1844	OCR1842:076
Lyons, Michael, c/o Ann	Arlington	Apprentice	1822	OCR1822:020
Lyons, Vincent, c/o Andrew	Arlington	Apprentice	1811	OCR1811:055

NAME OR SUBJECT	LOCATION	TYPE	YEAR	REFERENCE(S)
M				
Machen, Thomas	Alexandria	Tax Charge	1787	Tax PP 1787:10
MacIntosh, Jno.	Alexandria	Boarder	1799	1799(2):03A
Mackafee, John & wife, weaver	Alexandria	Head	1795	1795(4):01
Mackall, Geo.	Alexandria	Boarder	1808	1808(4):24A
Mackall, Geo., tanner	Alexandria	Housekeeper	1808	1808(4):29A
Mackay, Michael	Alexandria	Boarder	1799	1799(2):06A
Mackenzie, Alexr. & wife, merchant	Alexandria	Housekeeper	1799	1799(2):07A
Mackenzie, Jas. & wife, sea captain	Alexandria	Housekeeper	1799	1799(2):07A
Mackie, Griffin	Arlington	Defendant	1821	ACO:197
MacLeod, John	Arlington	Ordinary	1807	OBL2(np)
MacNamarra, Patrick & wife, mariner	Alexandria	Head	1795	1795(4):01
MacPherson, Robert Hector	Arlington	Bond	1821	WB3:008
Madden, Hannah, heirs of	Arlington	Sale	1822	LVA-LP
Madden, Mary F.	Arlington	Guard.	1807	WBB:523
Madden, Michael	Alexandria	Owner	1787	Tax L 1787:20
Madden, Michael	Alexandria	Tax Charge	1787	Tax PP 1787:10
Madden, Michael	Alexandria	Tax Charge	1788	Tax PP 1788:11
Madden, Michael	Alexandria	Tax Charge	1789	Tax PP 1789:13
Madden, Michael, Prince St.	Alexandria	Owner	1790	Tax L 1790:08(2)
Madden, Michael, Wolf St.	Alexandria	Occupant	1787	Tax L 1787:14
Madden, Michl.	Alexandria	Tax Charge	1790	Tax PP 1790:10
Madden, Michl.	Alexandria	Tax Charge	1796	Tax LP 1796:18
Madden, Michl., nr. Royal St.	Alexandria	Occupant	1790	Tax L 1790:03
Madden, Michl., Prince St.	Alexandria	Owner	1795	Tax L 1795:21
Madden, S.W.	Alexandria	Will	1896	WB2:150; LP
Maddock, Ann B., c/o James	Arlington	Guard.	1813	WB1:233
Maddocks, Erasmus	Alexandria	Tax Charge	1796	Tax PP 1796:13
Maddox, Joseph H.	Alexandria	Will	1887	WB1:463; LP
Maffet, Wm.	Alexandria	Boarder	1799	1799(2):13A
Maffitt, William	Alexandria	Tax Charge	1799	Tax PP 1799:28
Maffitt, Wm., Rev.	Alexandria	Tax Charge	1798	Tax PP 1798:13
Maffitt, [blank]	Alexandria	Tax Charge	1796	Tax PP 1796:12
Magee, Charles E., master	Arlington	Respondent	1811	ACO:119
Magee, Henry & wife, drayman	Alexandria	Head	1795	1795(4):02
Magee, Mansfield	Alexandria	Tax Charge	1798	Tax PP 1798:13
Magee, William	Arlington	Account	1826	LVA-LP
Magill, Charles, at Winchester	Alexandria	Deposition	1810	CRH:030
Magin, E.M., back building	Alexandria	Occupant	1795	Tax L 1795:03
Magrath, Owen F.	Arlington	Inventory	1810	WBC:347
Magrath, Owen F.	Arlington	Bond	1810	WBC:350
Magrath, Owen F.	Arlington	Will	1810	WBC:346; File #085A
Magrath, Owen F.	Arlington	Sale	1810	WBC:385
Magrath, Owen F., Rev.	Arlington	Account	1811	AB1:033; LVA-LP
Magrath, Owen F., Rev.	Arlington	Account	1812	AB1:195; LVA-LP
Magruder, Basil	Arlington	Will	1803	WBA:105; LVA-LP
Magruder, Capt. & wife, mariner	Alexandria	Boarder	1795	1795(4):05
Magruder, Dennis	Alexandria	Boarder	1800	1800(4):05A
Magruder, Dennis, def.	Alexandria	Suit	1802	CRC:161
Magruder, Dennis, of MD	Alexandria	Agreement	1800	CRC:165
Magruder, John	Alexandria	Boarder	1800	1800(4):05A
Magruder, Margaret	Arlington	Admin.	1801	WBA:037
Magruder, Margaret	Arlington	Renounce	1801	WBA:036
Magruder, Margaret A.	Arlington	Will	1896	WB10:328; File #771A
Magruder, Margarett	Alexandria	Head	1810	1810(3):03A
Magruder, Philip	Alexandria	Tax Charge	1796	Tax PP 1796:12
Magruder, Philip	Alexandria	Tax Charge	1798	Tax PP 1798:13
Magruder, Philip	Alexandria	Tax Charge	1799	Tax PP 1799:27
Magruder, Philip	Alexandria	Tax Charge	1800	Tax PP 1800:26
Magruder, Philip	Arlington	Property	1801	WBA:035
Magruder, Philip	Arlington	Will	1801	WBA:034; LVA-LP

NAME OR SUBJECT	LOCATION	TYPE	YEAR	REFERENCE(S)
Magruder, Philip	Arlington	Account	1804	WBA:278; LVA-LP
Magruder, Philip	Arlington	Inventory	1804	WBA:275; LVA-LP
Magruder, Philip & wife, sea captain	Alexandria	Housekeeper	1799	1799(2):09A
Magruder, Philip [Margaret]	Arlington	Admin.	1801	LVA-LP
Magruder, Thomas	Alexandria	Tax Charge	1798	Tax PP 1798:12
Magruder, Thomas	Alexandria	Mer. License	1798	Tax PP 1798:20-4
Magruder, Thomas	Alexandria	Tax Charge	1799	Tax PP 1799:26
Magruder, Thos. & wife, merchant	Alexandria	Housekeeper	1799	1799(2):03A
Maguire, James	Alexandria	Tax Charge	1798	Tax PP 1798:12
Maguire, James	Alexandria	Tax Charge	1799	Tax PP 1799:26
Maguire, James	Alexandria	Tax Charge	1800	Tax PP 1800:26
Mahaffey, Thomas J.	Alexandria	Will	1887	WB1:445; LP
Mahall, James	Alexandria	Tax Charge	1795	Tax PP 1795:18
Mahall, James	Alexandria	Tax Charge	1796	Tax PP 1796:13
Mahall, James	Alexandria	Tax Charge	1798	Tax PP 1798:12
Mahall, Jas., Princess St.	Alexandria	Occupant	1795	Tax L 1795:12
Mahall, Saml., Princess St.	Alexandria	Occupant	1795	Tax L 1795:12
Mahall, Samuel	Alexandria	Tax Charge	1795	Tax PP 1795:19
Mahaney, Thomas & wife Sarah	Alexandria	Resident	1800	1800(4):03B
Mahaney, Thomas, taylor	Alexandria	Head	1800	1800(4):03A
Maher, John & wife, laborer	Alexandria	Head	1795	1795(4):02
Mahon, Nicholas, plt.	Alexandria	Suit	1801	CRB:283, 287, 290
Mahon, Nicholas, plt.	Alexandria	Suit	1801	CRB:294
Mahone, Thomas	Alexandria	Tax Charge	1788	Tax PP 1788:11
Mahoney, John	Alexandria	Tax Charge	1798	Tax PP 1798:12
Mahoney, John	Alexandria	Tax Charge	1799	Tax PP 1799:27
Mahony, John	Alexandria	Tax Charge	1800	Tax PP 1800:27
Mahony, Thos.	Alexandria	Tax Charge	1800	Tax PP 1800:27
Maile, James	Alexandria	Tax Charge	1796	Tax PP 1796:12
Mains, Archibald, plt.	Alexandria	Suit	1821	CRL:365
Mains, William, Estate, plt.	Alexandria	Suit	1821	CRL:365
Maitland, William	Arlington	Plaintiff	1802	PA:345
Maitland, William, def.	Alexandria	Suit	1807	CRG:206
Maitland, William, plt.	Alexandria	Suit	1801	CRB:013, 016
Maitland, William, plt.	Alexandria	Suit	1801	CRB:001, 004, 008
Major, Elizabeth B. (Crook), w/o James	Arlington	Defendant	1841	LSA:062
Major, Henry, c/o John	Arlington	Guard.	1836	WB4:111
Major, James	Arlington	Defendant	1841	LSA:062
Major, John	Arlington	Admin.	1834	WB4:100
Major, John	Arlington	Appraisal	1834	LVA-LP
Major, John	Arlington	Account	1835	AB7:202, 204; LVA-LP
Major, John	Arlington	Account	1836	AB7:202
Major, Margaret, c/o John	Arlington	Guard.	1836	WB4:111
Major, Prudence T., c/o John	Arlington	Guard.	1836	WB4:111
Majorfield, William	Arlington	Admin.	1813	WB1:235
Makey, Richd., seaman	Alexandria	Head	1810	1810(4):01A
Malban, Joseph	Alexandria	Tithable +16	1789	Tax PP 1789:03
Malrooney, James, from Ireland	Arlington	Apprentice	1828	OCR1822:154
Man, Bernard	Alexandria	Tax Charge	1788	Tax PP 1788:12
Man, Bernard	Alexandria	Tax Charge	1790	Tax PP 1790:10
Manchester goods	Arlington	Suit	1806	ACO:051
Manchester goods	Arlington	Suit	1808	ACO:081
Manchester goods, bundles of	Arlington	Suit	1805	ACO:041
Mandaville, John	Alexandria	Tax Charge	1800	Tax PP 1800:27
Mandaville, Jona.	Alexandria	Tax Charge	1800	Tax PP 1800:26
Mandaville, Jonathan	Alexandria	Mer. License	1799	Tax PP 1799:52-07r
Mandaville, Joseph	Alexandria	Tax Charge	1800	Tax PP 1800:26
Mandell, John C., cryer	Arlington	Appointment	1821	ACO:184
Mandell, John C., grantee	Arlington	Indenture D.	1811	ID2:105
Mandell, John, shopkeeper	Alexandria	Head	1810	1810(3):05A
Mandevill, John (non-citizen)	Alexandria	Tithable +21	1787	Tax PP 1787:03

NAME OR SUBJECT	LOCATION	TYPE	YEAR	REFERENCE(S)
M. & Jamesson	Alexandria	Tax Charge	1798	Tax PP 1798:12
Mandeville & Jamesson	Alexandria	Mer. License	1798	Tax PP 1798:20-5
Mandeville & Jamesson	Alexandria	Suit	1807	CRF:298
Mandeville & Jamesson	Alexandria	Suit	1807	CRG:210
Mandeville & Jamesson, def.	Alexandria	Suit	1801	CRB:108, 111
Mandeville & Jamesson, def.	Alexandria	Suit	1809	CRG:290
Mandeville & Jamesson, def.	Alexandria	Suit	1809	CRH:156
Mandeville & Jamesson, def.	Alexandria	Suit	1814	CRK:013
Mandeville & Jamieson, plt.	Alexandria	Suit	1802	CRC:231
Mandeville & Sampson, def.	Alexandria	Suit	1805	CRG:009
Mandeville, Ann, c/o Jonathan	Arlington	Guard.	1811	WB1:053
Mandeville, Elizabeth, seamstress	Alexandria	Head	1810	1810(3):07A
Mandeville, J., Queen St.	Alexandria	Occupant	1787	Tax L 1787:24
Mandeville, Jno.	Alexandria	Tax Charge	1795	Tax PP 1795:22
Mandeville, Jno.	Alexandria	Tax Charge	1798	Tax PP 1798:12
Mandeville, John	Alexandria	Tax Charge	1787	Tax PP 1787:09
Mandeville, John	Alexandria	Tax Charge	1788	Tax PP 1788:11
Mandeville, John	Alexandria	Tax Charge	1789	Tax PP 1789:12
Mandeville, John	Alexandria	Tax Charge	1790	Tax PP 1790:09
Mandeville, John	Alexandria	Tax Charge	1796	Tax LP 1796:18
Mandeville, John	Alexandria	Tax Charge	1796	Tax PP 1796:13
Mandeville, John	Alexandria	Tax Charge	1799	Tax PP 1799:26
Mandeville, John	Alexandria	Deposition	1810	CRH:136
Mandeville, John, def.	Alexandria	Suit	1803	CRD:095
Mandeville, John, farmer	Alexandria	Head	1810	1810(2):05A
Mandeville, John, King St.	Alexandria	Occupant	1790	Tax L 1790:08
Mandeville, John, Queen St.	Alexandria	Occupant	1790	Tax L 1790:08
Mandeville, John, Queen St.	Alexandria	Owner	1790	Tax L 1790:08
Mandeville, John, Queen St.	Alexandria	Owner	1795	Tax L 1795:20(2)
Mandeville, John, Queen St.	Alexandria	Occupant	1795	Tax L 1795:20
Mandeville, John, Royal St.	Alexandria	Owner	1795	Tax L 1795:20
Mandeville, John, supt. police	Alexandria	Enumerator	1808	1808(4):31
Mandeville, John, supt. police	Alexandria	Housekeeper	1808	1808(2):15A
Mandeville, Johnn.	Alexandria	Tax Charge	1796	Tax LP 1796:19
Mandeville, Jonathan	Alexandria	Tax Charge	1788	Tax PP 1788:11
Mandeville, Jonathan	Alexandria	Tax Charge	1789	Tax PP 1789:12
Mandeville, Jonathan	Alexandria	Tax Charge	1790	Tax PP 1790:09
Mandeville, Jonathan	Alexandria	Tax Charge	1795	Tax PP 1795:22
Mandeville, Jonathan	Alexandria	Tax Charge	1795	Tax PP 1795:20
Mandeville, Jonathan	Alexandria	Tax Charge	1796	Tax PP 1796:13
Mandeville, Jonathan	Alexandria	Tax Charge	1798	Tax PP 1798:13
Mandeville, Jonathan	Alexandria	Mer. License	1798	Tax PP 1798:20-4
Mandeville, Jonathan	Alexandria	Tax Charge	1799	Tax PP 1799:26
Mandeville, Jonathan	Alexandria	License Due	1800	Tax PP 1800:54(24)
Mandeville, Jonathan	Arlington	Inventory	1809	WBC:290; LVA-LP
Mandeville, Jonathan	Arlington	Admin.	1809	WBC:287
Mandeville, Jonathan	Arlington	Account	1810	AB1:009
Mandeville, Jonathan	Arlington	Sale	1810	WBC:338
Mandeville, Jonathan	Arlington	Account	1812	AB1:251; LVA-LP
Mandeville, Jonathan, King St.	Alexandria	Occupant	1795	Tax L 1795:23
Mandeville, Jonathan, King St.	Alexandria	Occupant	1795	Tax L 1795:20
Mandeville, Jonathan, retailer	Alexandria	Housekeeper	1808	1808(2):13A
Mandeville, Jos. & wife, merchant	Alexandria	Housekeeper	1799	1799(2):04A
Mandeville, Jos. H.	Alexandria	Boarder	1808	1808(2):15A
Mandeville, Joseph	Alexandria	Tax Charge	1796	Tax LP 1796:18
Mandeville, Joseph	Alexandria	Tax Charge	1796	Tax PP 1796:13
Mandeville, Joseph	Alexandria	Tax Charge	1798	Tax PP 1798:12
Mandeville, Joseph	Alexandria	Tax Charge	1799	Tax PP 1799:26
Mandeville, Joseph	Alexandria	Agreement	1818	CRL:169
Mandeville, Joseph	Arlington	Will	1837	WB4:143; File #352A
Mandeville, Joseph	Arlington	Bond	1837	WB4:146

NAME OR SUBJECT	LOCATION	TYPE	YEAR	REFERENCE(S)
Mandeville, Joseph	Arlington	Inventory	1837	LVA-LP
Mandeville, Joseph	Arlington	Account	1839	AB8:059; LVA-LP
Mandeville, Joseph	Arlington	Account	1839	AB8:119; LVA-LP
Mandeville, Joseph	Arlington	Account	1840	AB8:119
Mandeville, Joseph	Arlington	Account	1840	AB8:058
Mandeville, Joseph	Arlington	Account	1841	AB8:212
Mandeville, Joseph	Arlington	Account	1842	AB8:305; LVA-LP
Mandeville, Joseph	Arlington	Account	1842	AB8:304; LVA-LP
Mandeville, Joseph	Arlington	Account	1843	AB8:381; LVA-LP
Mandeville, Joseph	Arlington	Admin.	1845	OCR1842:103
Mandeville, Joseph, def.	Alexandria	Suit	1801	CRD:056
Mandeville, Joseph, def.	Alexandria	Suit	1801	CRB:108, 111
Mandeville, Joseph, def.	Alexandria	Suit	1802	CRC:255
Mandeville, Joseph, def.	Alexandria	Suit	1807	CRF:151
Mandeville, Joseph, def.	Alexandria	Suit	1809	CRH:156
Mandeville, Joseph, def.	Alexandria	Suit	1816	CRK:276
Mandeville, Joseph, def.	Alexandria	Suit	1821	CRL:165
Mandeville, Joseph, def.	Alexandria	Suit	1822	CRL:232
Mandeville, Joseph, Exor. of	Arlington	Defendant	1839	LSA:039
Mandeville, Joseph, Fairfax St.	Alexandria	Occupant	1795	Tax L 1795:31
Mandeville, Joseph H.	Arlington	Admin.	1813	WB1:265
Mandeville, Joseph H.	Arlington	Inventory	1814	AB2:005; LVA-LP
Mandeville, Joseph H.	Arlington	Debts Due	1814	AB2:009
Mandeville, Joseph H.	Arlington	Account	1815	AB2:139
Mandeville, Joseph H.	Arlington	Account	1818	AB3:225; LVA-LP
Mandeville, Joseph H., def.	Alexandria	Suit	1811	CRI:124
Mandeville, Joseph, Jr., grantee	Arlington	Indenture D.	1804	ID3:086
Mandeville, Joseph, Jr., plt.	Alexandria	Suit	1801	CRB:188
Mandeville, Joseph, merchant	Alexandria	Housekeeper	1808	1808(2):12A
Mandeville, Joseph, plt.	Alexandria	Suit	1802	CRC:231
Mandeville, Joseph, Sr.	Alexandria	Tax Charge	1799	Tax PP 1799:27
Mandeville, Joseph, Sr., merchant	Alexandria	Head	1810	1810(2):02A
Mandeville, Julia	Arlington	Will	1858	WB7:303; File #554A
Mandeville, Mary	Arlington	Account	1861	LVA-LP
Mandeville, Mary	Arlington	Will	1861	WB8:080; File #587A
Mandeville, Mary	Arlington	Report	1864	WB8:189
Mandeville, Mary	Arlington	Account	1866	WB8:348, 474
Mandeville, Mary	Arlington	Account	1868	WB9:042
Mandeville, Mary	Arlington	Account	1869	WB9:161
Mandeville, Mary	Arlington	Account	1870	WB9:220
Mandeville, Mary	Arlington	Account	1871	WB9:304
Mandeville, Mary	Arlington	Account	1875	WB9:377
Mandeville, Robt.	Alexandria	Boarder	1808	1808(2):15A
Mandeville, Susannah, c/o Jonathan	Arlington	Guard.	1809	WBC:289
Mandeville v. Sanderson's Admr.	Arlington	Suit	1835	LVA-LP (Judgments)
Manery, Elizabeth	Arlington	Will P.	1846	OCR1842:174
Manery, John	Arlington	Ordinary	1821	OBL3(np)
Manery, John	Arlington	Ordinary	1823	OBL3(np)
Manery, John	Arlington	Ordinary	1826	OBL4(np)
Manery, John	Arlington	Will	1850	WB5:295; File #462A
Manery, John, at his house	Arlington	Ordinary	1825	OBL4(np)
Manery, John, at his house	Arlington	Ordinary	1827	OBL4(np)
Manery, John, at his house	Arlington	Ordinary	1831	OBL4(np)
Manery, John, in Alexandria Co.	Arlington	Ordinary	1822	OBL3(np)
Manery, John, in Alexandria Co.	Arlington	Ordinary	1824	OBL3(np)
Manery, John, in Alexandria Co.	Arlington	Ordinary	1830	OBL4(np)
Maneyham, Norry, sempstress	Alexandria	Head	1800	1800(4):03A
Mankin, Charles	Arlington	Inventory	1841	AB8:171; LVA-LP
Mankin, Charles	Arlington	Petition	1842	OCR1842:018
Mankin, Charles	Arlington	Account	1842	AB8:316; LVA-LP
Mankin, Charles	Arlington	Account	1842	OCR1842:007, 011

NAME OR SUBJECT	LOCATION	TYPE	YEAR	REFERENCE(S)
Mankin, Charles	Arlington	Account	1843	OCR1842:032
Mankin, Charles	Arlington	Bond	1845	OCR1842:142, 144
Mankin, Charles	Arlington	Account	1845	AB9:132; LVA-LP
Mankin, Charles	Alexandria	Will	1879	WB1:280; LP
Mankin, Charles [Elizabeth]	Arlington	Defendant	1841	LSA:070
Mankin, Chas., cooper	Alexandria	Head	1810	1810(4):02A
Mankin, David	Alexandria	Tax Charge	1796	Tax LP 1796:18
Mankin, David	Arlington	Bond	1824	WB3:148
Mankin, David	Arlington	Will	1824	WB3:146; File #226A
Mankin, David, grantee	Arlington	Indenture D.	1806	ID3:179
Mankin, David, shopkeeper	Alexandria	Head	1810	1810(3):03A
Mankin, James E.	Arlington	Defendant	1841	LSA:070
Mankin, John J.	Arlington	Defendant	1841	LSA:070
Mankin, Mark M.	Arlington	Will	1866	WB8:384; File #643A
Mankin v. Mankin's Admor.	Arlington	Suit	1845	OCR1842:114
Mankin, William	Arlington	Defendant	1841	LSA:070
Mankings, Kitty	Alexandria	Serv./Appt.	1800	1800(4):15B
Mankins, Charles	Alexandria	Tax Charge	1800	Tax PP 1800:27
Mankins, Charles	Arlington	Admin.	1840	WB4:279
Mankins, Chas., cooper	Alexandria	Housekeeper	1808	1808(4):26A
Mankins, David	Alexandria	Tax Charge	1796	Tax PP 1796:13
Mankins, David	Alexandria	Tax Charge	1798	Tax PP 1798:13
Mankins, David	Alexandria	Tax Charge	1799	Tax PP 1799:27
Mankins, David	Alexandria	Tax Charge	1800	Tax PP 1800:27
Mankins, David	Arlington	Ordinary	1803	OBL1(np)
Mankins, David	Arlington	Ordinary	1806	OBL2(np)
Mankins, David	Arlington	Ordinary	1807	OBL2(np)
Mankins, David	Arlington	Ordinary	1810	OBL2(np)
Mankins, David	Arlington	Ordinary	1810	OBL2(np)
Mankins, David	Arlington	Ordinary	1820	OBL3(np)
Mankins, David	Arlington	Inventory	1824	AB5:367; LVA-LP
Mankins, David	Arlington	Account	1826	AB6:158; LVA-LP
Mankins, David	Arlington	Distribution	1830	AB6:516
Mankins, David, retailer & tavern lic.	Alexandria	Housekeeper	1808	1808(1):03A
Mankins, Elizabeth, wid/o Charles	Arlington	Defendant	1842	LSA:087
Mankins, John, ac/o David & Ann	Arlington	Apprentice	1801	OCR1801:010
Mankins, John J.	Arlington	Defendant	1842	LSA:087
Mankins, William	Arlington	Complainant	1842	LSA:087
Mankins, [blank]	Alexandria	Reference	1808	1808(4):26B
Manley, Barbara	Arlington	Guard.	1807	WBB:539
Manley, Elizabeth, weaver	Alexandria	Housekeeper	1808	1808(2):11A
Manley, Jane, labourer	Alexandria	Boarder	1800	1800(4):02A
Manley, John H., grantor	Arlington	Indenture D.	1814	ID2:380
Manley, John H., in jail	Arlington	Insolvent	1815	ID2:376
Manley, John, schoolmaster	Alexandria	Head	1810	1810(3):02A
Manley, John, shop & school	Alexandria	Housekeeper	1808	1808(3):20A
Manley, Washington, c/o John	Arlington	Apprentice	1811	OCR1811:025
Manly, Barbara, c/o Elizabeth	Arlington	Apprentice	1804	OCR1801:150
Manly, Elizabeth	Alexandria	Housekeeper	1799	1799(2):17A
Manly, John H., grantee	Arlington	Indenture D.	1811	ID2:026
Manly, Jos. Wray, c/o Priscilla Hessian	Arlington	Apprentice	1802	OCR1801:022
Mann, Bernard	Alexandria	Tax Charge	1789	Tax PP 1789:13
Mann, Bernhard, Water St.	Alexandria	Occupant	1790	Tax L 1790:08
Mann, Bernhard, Water St.	Alexandria	Owner	1790	Tax L 1790:08
Mann, James	Alexandria	Tax Charge	1796	Tax LP 1796:18
Mann, Katharine, Wales' alley	Alexandria	Occupant	1795	Tax L 1795:21
Mann, Mrs., alley nr. Union St.	Alexandria	Occupant	1790	Tax L 1790:08
Mannecks, Jane	Alexandria	Housekeeper	1799	1799(2):10A
Mannery, Elizabeth	Arlington	Inventory	1846	AB9:260; LVA-LP
Mannery, Elizabeth	Arlington	Will	1846	WB4:420; File #433A
Mannery, Elizabeth	Arlington	Account	1847	AB9:272

NAME OR SUBJECT	LOCATION	TYPE	YEAR	REFERENCE(S)
Manning, Ignatius	Alexandria	Tax Charge	1800	Tax PP 1800:27
Manning, Ignatius	Arlington	Deposition	1802	PA:194
Manning, William, Capt.	Alexandria	Account B.	1799	CRB:182
Manning, William, def.	Alexandria	Suit	1802	CRB:177
Manning, Wm., mariner	Alexandria	Head	1810	1810(1):11A
Manning, Wm., sea captain	Alexandria	Housekeeper	1808	1808(3):18A
Mannyham, Norry	Alexandria	Resident	1800	1800(4):03B
Manor, Zacariah, sea captain	Alexandria	Housekeeper	1808	1808(1):04A
Mansfield, Henry	Arlington	Account	1864	WB8:206, 284
Mansfield, Wm.	Alexandria	Tax Charge	1795	Tax PP 1795:18
Mapins, Mr., Fairfax St.	Alexandria	Occupant	1795	Tax L 1795:30
Mara, John	Arlington	Apprentice	1804	OCR1801:211
Mara, John	Arlington	Apprentice	1811	OCR1811:012
Marble, Charles	Arlington	Guard.	1822	WB3:072
Marbury, Elizabeth	Arlington	Guard.	1839	WB4:236
Marbury, Francis F., grantee	Arlington	Indenture D.	1828	ID:156
Marbury, Jack (non-citizen, servant)	Alexandria	Tithable +21	1787	Tax PP 1787:07
Marbury, Joseph	Arlington	Admin.	1825	WB3:202
Marbury, Joseph C.	Arlington	Admin.	1825	OCR1822:102
Marbury, Robert (C)	Alexandria	Tax Charge	1789	Tax PP 1789:13
Marbury, William H.	Arlington	Inventory	1817	AB3:026; LVA-LP
Marbury, William H.	Arlington	Admin.	1817	WB2:193; LVA-LP
Marbury, William H.	Arlington	Sale	1819	AB4:007
Marbury, William H.	Arlington	Inventory	1819	AB3:369; LVA-LP
Marbury, William H.	Arlington	Account	1822	AB5:085; LVA-LP
Marbury, William H.	Alexandria	Will	1900	WB2:392; LP
Marcey, James, c/o Samuel	Arlington	Guard.	1823	WB3:085
Marcey, James, c/o Jane	Arlington	Guard.	1823	OCR1822:032a
Marcey, Lewis, c/o Jane	Arlington	Guard.	1823	OCR1822:032a
Marcey, Lewis, c/o Samuel	Arlington	Guard.	1823	WB3:085
Marcey, Robert Henry	Arlington	Will	1883	WB10:031; File #708A
Marcey, Samuel	Arlington	Admin.	1823	OCR1822:032a
Marcey, Samuel	Arlington	Inventory	1823	AB5:159; LVA-LP
Marcey, Samuel	Arlington	Admin.	1823	WB3:084
Marcey, Samuel	Arlington	Account	1824	AB5:318; LVA-LP
Marcey, William	Arlington	Appraisal	1854	WB6:306; LVA-LP
Marcey, William, c/o Samuel	Arlington	Guard.	1823	WB3:085
Marcey, William, c/o Jane	Arlington	Guard.	1823	OCR1822:032a
Marchant, William	Alexandria	Tax Charge	1787	Tax PP 1787:11
Marcher, James	Arlington	Will (NP)	1871	WB10:063
Marckley, Elizabeth, c/o William	Arlington	Guard.	1823	WB3:105
Marckley, Joanna	Arlington	Will	1868	WB9:090; File #664A
Marckley, Mary, c/o William	Arlington	Guard.	1823	WB3:105
Marckley, Sarah Ann, c/o William	Arlington	Guard.	1823	WB3:105
Marckley, Susana, c/o William	Arlington	Guard.	1823	WB3:105
Marckley, William	Arlington	Inventory	1822	AB5:030; LVA-LP
Marckley, William	Arlington	Will	1822	WB3:040; File #204A
Marckley, William	Arlington	Bond	1822	WB3:041
Marckley, William	Arlington	Account	1823	AB5:182; LVA-LP
Marckley, William, c/o William	Arlington	Guard.	1823	WB3:105
Marckley, Wm., seaman	Alexandria	Housekeeper	1808	1808(1):07A
Marcy, William	Arlington	Bond	1853	BB(np)
Marcy, William	Arlington	Bond	1854	BB(np)
Marine Insurance Co.	Alexandria	Suit	1810	CRG:369
Marine Insurance Co., complt.	Alexandria	Suit	1813	CRK:186
Marine Insurance Co., def.	Alexandria	Suit	1800	CRK:209
Marine Insurance Co., def.	Alexandria	Suit	1805	CRG:242
Marine Insurance Co., def.	Alexandria	Suit	1805	CRF:218
Marine Insurance Co., def.	Alexandria	Suit	1807	CRF:159
Marine Insurance Co., def.	Alexandria	Suit	1817	CRK:359
Maris, Samuel W.	Alexandria	Will	1890	WB1:549; LP

NAME OR SUBJECT	LOCATION	TYPE	YEAR	REFERENCE(S)
Maris, Samuel W.	Alexandria	Inventory	1890	WB1:519; LP
Mark, Ellen M.	Alexandria	Will	1892	WBC1:063; LP
Mark, Lydia	Alexandria	Will	1891	WB1:599
Mark, Lydia	Alexandria	Will	1891	WBC1:057; LP
Markell, George H.	Alexandria	Will	1888	WB1:509; LP
Markham, Joseph	Arlington	Will	1885	WB10:062
Markham, Mary Ann	Alexandria	Will	1897	WB2:224; LP
Markland, John, waterman	Alexandria	Housekeeper	1808	1808(3):22A
Marks, Margaret, alias Geddis	Arlington	Crime	1794	OT:03/07/1794
Marks, Will. G.	Alexandria	Tax Charge	1800	Tax PP 1800:26
Marks, William	Alexandria	Tax Charge	1790	Tax PP 1790:09
Marks, William G.	Arlington	Witness	1794	OT:03/07/1794
Marks, William G.	Alexandria	Tax Charge	1799	Tax PP 1799:27
Marks, Wm.	Alexandria	Tax Charge	1796	Tax LP 1796:19
Marks, Wm. & wife, sadler	Alexandria	Housekeeper	1799	1799(2):09A
Marks, Wm., Fairfax St.	Alexandria	Occupant	1790	Tax L 1790:01
Marks, Wm. G.	Alexandria	Tax Charge	1795	Tax PP 1795:21
Marks, Wm. G.	Alexandria	Tax Charge	1796	Tax PP 1796:14
Marks, Wm. G.	Alexandria	Tax Charge	1798	Tax PP 1798:13
Marks, Wm. Gough	Alexandria	Tithable +16	1789	Tax PP 1789:14
Markward, Charles B., c/o William	Arlington	Apprentice	1815	OCR1811:310
Marl, Elizabeth, sempstress	Alexandria	Housekeeper	1808	1808(3):22A
Marl, Hannah, labourer	Alexandria	Boarder	1800	1800(4):04A
Marl, Joseph & wife Elisebeth	Alexandria	Resident	1800	1800(4):04B
Marl, Joseph, marrener	Alexandria	Head	1800	1800(4):04A
Marle, Hannah	Arlington	Guard.	1808	WBC:164
Marle, Jos. & wife, waterman	Alexandria	Housekeeper	1799	1799(2):15A
Marle, Joseph	Alexandria	Tax Charge	1796	Tax PP 1796:12
Marle, Joseph	Alexandria	Tax Charge	1798	Tax PP 1798:12
Marle, Joseph	Arlington	Admin.	1807	WBC:015
Marle, Joseph	Arlington	Inventory	1807	WBC:017; LVA-LP
Marle, Joseph	Arlington	Account	1808	WBC:068; LVA-LP
Marle, Rebecca	Alexandria	Boarder	1799	1799(2):09A
Marll, David	Arlington	Admin.	1827	WB3:284
Marll, David [Elizabeth]	Arlington	Admin.	1827	OCR1822:134a
Marmeduke, John	Alexandria	Resident	1800	1800(4):16B
Marmeduke, John, clarke	Alexandria	Boarder	1800	1800(4):16A
Marr, John	Alexandria	Tax Charge	1795	Tax PP 1795:21
Marr, Mrs., Fairfax St.	Alexandria	Occupant	1787	Tax L 1787:09
Marr, Mrs., Fairfax St.	Alexandria	Occupant	1790	Tax L 1790:12
Marra, Capt.	Alexandria	Boarder	1795	1795(4):03
Marsailes, Wm. & wife, ship builder	Alexandria	Housekeeper	1799	1799(2):08A
Marshal, Henry, carpenter & shopkeeper	Alexandria	Housekeeper	1808	1808(2):13A
Marshall, Benjamin	Alexandria	Tax Charge	1795	Tax PP 1795:21
Marshall, E.C.	Alexandria	Will	1890	WB1:519; LP
Marshall, George, c/o Ann	Arlington	Apprentice	1801	OCR1801:001a
Marshall, Henry, shopkeeper	Alexandria	Head	1810	1810(2):03A
Marshall, Jas., clerk	Alexandria	Boarder	1799	1799(2):03A
Marshall, John	Alexandria	Plat	1784	CRH:396
Marshall, John, Jr., Fayette Co. KY	Alexandria	Plats	1784	CRH:380-385
Marshall, Maria R., plaintiff	Arlington	Suit	(nd)	LSA:134
Marshall, Richard	Alexandria	Tithable +16	1790	Tax PP 1790:16
Marshall, Teresia, sempstress	Alexandria	Head	1800	1800(4):02A
Marshall, Terrence	Alexandria	Housekeeper	1799	1799(2):16A
Marshall, Terresia	Alexandria	Resident	1800	1800(4):02B
Marshall, Thomas, plt.	Alexandria	Suit	1801	CRB:239
Marshall, Wm.	Alexandria	Boarder	1808	1808(1):03A
Marshall, [blank], Fairfax St.	Alexandria	Occupant	1795	Tax L 1795:32
Marsteller & Young, def.	Alexandria	Suit	1811	CRI:116
Marsteller, Ferdinand	Arlington	Juryman	1808	ACO:081
Marsteller, Ferdinand	Arlington	Admin.	1817	WB2:180

NAME OR SUBJECT	LOCATION	TYPE	YEAR	REFERENCE(S)
Marsteller, Ferdinand	Arlington	Account	1818	AB3:122; LVA-LP
Marsteller, Ferdinand, b. baker	Alexandria	Housekeeper	1808	1808(4):25A
Marsteller, Ferdinand, def.	Alexandria	Suit	1811	CRI:116
Marsteller, Ferdinand, merchant	Alexandria	Head	1810	1810(4):04A
Marsteller, Ferdinand, plt.	Alexandria	Suit	1804	CRF:057
Marsteller, Mary Magdalene	Arlington	Admin.	1815	WB2:066
Marsteller, Mary Magdalene	Arlington	Inventory	1815	AB2:167a; LVA-LP
Marsteller, P., Water St.	Alexandria	Occupant	1787	Tax L 1787:20
Marsteller, P.G.	Alexandria	Tax Charge	1796	Tax LP 1796:18
Marsteller, P.G.	Alexandria	Mer. License	1799	Tax PP 1799:52-07w
Marsteller, P.G.	Alexandria	License Due	1800	Tax PP 1800:54(24)
Marsteller, P.G.	Alexandria	Tax Charge	1800	Tax PP 1800:28
Marsteller, P.G. & wife, vendue master	Alexandria	Housekeeper	1799	1799(2):07A
Marsteller, P.G., King St.	Alexandria	Occupant	1795	Tax L 1795:21
Marsteller, P.G., vendue master	Alexandria	Head	1810	1810(1):03A
Marsteller, Phil. G., King St.	Alexandria	Owner	1795	Tax L 1795:21
Marsteller, Phil. G., vendue master	Alexandria	Housekeeper	1808	1808(1):05A
Marsteller, Phil., Water St.	Alexandria	Occupant	1795	Tax L 1795:04
Marsteller, Philip	Alexandria	Tax Charge	1787	Tax PP 1787:11
Marsteller, Philip	Alexandria	Owner	1787	Tax L 1787:20
Marsteller, Philip	Alexandria	Tax Charge	1788	Tax PP 1788:12
Marsteller, Philip	Alexandria	Tax Charge	1789	Tax PP 1789:12
Marsteller, Philip	Alexandria	Tax Charge	1790	Tax PP 1790:10
Marsteller, Philip	Alexandria	Tax Charge	1795	Tax PP 1795:20
Marsteller, Philip	Alexandria	Tax Charge	1796	Tax PP 1796:12
Marsteller, Philip	Alexandria	Tax Charge	1796	Tax LP 1796:19
Marsteller, Philip	Alexandria	Tax Charge	1798	Tax PP 1798:12
Marsteller, Philip	Alexandria	Tax Charge	1799	Tax PP 1799:27
Marsteller, Philip	Alexandria	Tax Charge	1800	Tax PP 1800:28
Marsteller, Philip	Arlington	Inventory	1804	WBB:038; LVA-LP
Marsteller, Philip	Arlington	Admin.	1804	WBA:265
Marsteller, Philip & Co., Prince St.	Alexandria	Occupant	1787	Tax L 1787:11
Marsteller, Philip, Col.	Arlington	Account	1805	WBB:108; LVA-LP
Marsteller, Philip, Estate, plt.	Alexandria	Suit	1804	CRF:057
Marsteller, Philip G.	Alexandria	Tax Charge	1796	Tax PP 1796:13
Marsteller, Philip G.	Alexandria	Tax Charge	1799	Tax PP 1799:27
Marsteller, Philip G.	Arlington	Defendant	1802	PA:057
Marsteller, Philip G., at Caton's Tavern	Alexandria	Deposition	1808	CRH:122
Marsteller, Philip G., plt.	Alexandria	Suit	1809	CRG:131
Marsteller, Philip G., w(2)4, merchant	Alexandria	Head	1796	1796(3):5
Marsteller, Philip, Jr.	Alexandria	Tithable +16	1788	Tax PP 1788:12
Marsteller, Philip, Jr.	Alexandria	Tithable +16	1789	Tax PP 1789:12
Marsteller, Philip, Jr.	Alexandria	Tithable +16	1790	Tax PP 1790:10
Marsteller, Philip, w(3)2, merchant	Alexandria	Head	1796	1796(3):1
Marsteller, Philip, Water St.	Alexandria	Owner	1790	Tax L 1790:08
Marsteller, Philip, Water St.	Alexandria	Occupant	1790	Tax L 1790:08
Marsteller, Philip, Water St.	Alexandria	Owner	1795	Tax L 1795:22
Marsteller, Philip, Water St.	Alexandria	Occupant	1795	Tax L 1795:22
Marsteller, Php. G.	Alexandria	Tax Charge	1795	Tax PP 1795:21
Marston, Joshua, grantor	Arlington	Indenture D.	1812	ID2:160
Marston, Joshua, in jail	Arlington	Insolvent	1813	ID2:159
Martin, Ann	Arlington	Account	1830	LVA-LP
Martin, Ann	Arlington	Inventory	1830	LVA-LP
Martin, Ann	Arlington	Will	1830	WB3:358; File #284A
Martin, David	Alexandria	Tithable +21	1787	Tax PP 1787:08
Martin, David	Arlington	Library	1832	LVA-LP
Martin, David	Arlington	Inventory	1832	LVA-LP
Martin, David	Arlington	Admin.	1832	WB4:050; LVA-LP
Martin, David	Arlington	Account	1833	AB7:217; LVA-LP
Martin, David	Arlington	Account	1836	AB7:217
Martin, David	Arlington	Account	1841	AB8:222; LVA-LP

NAME OR SUBJECT	LOCATION	TYPE	YEAR	REFERENCE(S)
Martin, Edward	Alexandria	Tax Charge	1800	Tax PP 1800:27
Martin, Edward & wife, blacksmith	Alexandria	Housekeeper	1799	1799(2):06A
Martin, Edward, blacksmith	Alexandria	Head	1810	1810(4):01A
Martin, Elizabeth	Arlington	Guard.	1813	WB1:229
Martin, Ellen F.	Alexandria	Will	1893	WB2:063; LP
Martin, Henry	Alexandria	Boarder	1808	1808(3):20A
Martin, Henry, b/o John	Arlington	Apprentice	1811	OCR1811:016
Martin, Hezekiah, b/o John	Arlington	Apprentice	1815	OCR1811:286
Martin, James	Alexandria	Tithable +21	1787	Tax PP 1787:10
Martin, James	Alexandria	Tax Charge	1788	Tax PP 1788:11
Martin, James	Alexandria	Tax Charge	1789	Tax PP 1789:12
Martin, James	Alexandria	Tax Charge	1790	Tax PP 1790:09
Martin, James, c/o Ann	Arlington	Apprentice	1822	OCR1822:004a
Martin, James Warden, c/o Elijah	Arlington	Apprentice	1805	OCR1801:292
Martin, Jas., Princess St.	Alexandria	Occupant	1795	Tax L 1795:20
Martin, John (C), ship carpenter	Alexandria	Housekeeper	1808	1808(1):06A
Martin, Jos. & wife, grocer	Alexandria	Housekeeper	1799	1799(2):09A
Martin, Joseph	Alexandria	Tax Charge	1795	Tax PP 1795:19
Martin, Joseph	Alexandria	Mer. License	1798	Tax PP 1798:20-4
Martin, Joseph	Alexandria	Tax Charge	1798	Tax PP 1798:12
Martin, Joseph	Alexandria	Mer. License	1799	Tax PP 1799:52-07r
Martin, Joseph	Alexandria	Tax Charge	1799	Tax PP 1799:26
Martin, Joseph	Alexandria	Tax Charge	1800	Tax PP 1800:27
Martin, Joseph	Alexandria	Mer. License	1800	Tax PP 1800:54(16)r
Martin, Mary Ann	Arlington	Admin.	1814	WB1:300
Martin, Mary Ann	Arlington	Inventory	1814	AB2:064; LVA-LP
Martin, Mary Ann	Arlington	Account	1815	AB2:219; LVA-LP
Martin, Mary Ann, boarding house	Alexandria	Head	1810	1810(2):04A
Martin, Mrs.	Arlington	Sale	1815	AB2:095
Martin, Nancy	Alexandria	Housekeeper	1808	1808(2):15A
Martin, Priscilla (C), washwoman	Alexandria	Housekeeper	1808	1808(1):07A
Martin, Prissey	Alexandria	Head	1810	1810(1):11A
Martin, Stephen, at his house	Arlington	Ordinary	1832	OBL4(np)
Martin, Tho.	Alexandria	Tax Charge	1795	Tax PP 1795:21
Martin, Thomas	Alexandria	Tax Charge	1796	Tax PP 1796:14
Martin, Thomas, c/o James	Arlington	Apprentice	1812	OCR1811:162
Martin, Thomas J., at his house	Arlington	Ordinary	1837	OBL5(np)
Martin, Thos.	Alexandria	Tax Charge	1798	Tax PP 1798:13
Martin, William	Arlington	Inventory	1809	WBC:294; LVA-LP
Martin, William	Arlington	Admin.	1809	WBC:259
Martin, William	Arlington	Account	1811	AB1:107; LVA-LP
Martin, William, blacksmith	Alexandria	Head	1810	1810(3):02A
Martin, Wm., blacksmith	Alexandria	Housekeeper	1808	1808(3):20A
Martin, Wm., sea captain	Alexandria	Housekeeper	1808	1808(4):25A
Martinell, Elianor	Arlington	Guard.	1822	WB3:056
Marting, John	Alexandria	Serv./Appr.	1800	1800(4):11B
Martinure, Antonio	Arlington	Libellant	1811	ACO:119
Marvel, Israel	Alexandria	Will	1887	WB1:470; LP
Marvell, Charity, washerwoman	Alexandria	Head	1810	1810(1):06A
Marvell, Henry	Arlington	Apprentice	1812	OCR1811:102
Marvell, Henry	Arlington	Guard.	1812	WB1:202
Marvell, Jacob	Arlington	Apprentice	1805	OCR1801:313
Marvell, Robert	Arlington	Apprentice	1805	OCR1801:312
Marybren, John	Alexandria	Tax Charge	1796	Tax LP 1796:19
Maryman, Horatio R.	Arlington	Receipt	1831	LVA-LP
Maryman, Horatio R., c/o Richard	Arlington	Guard.	1830	WB3:379
Masclay, [blank], mariner	Alexandria	Head	1810	1810(1):09A
Maservey, Thos., Fairfax St.	Alexandria	Occupant	1790	Tax L 1790:03
Mason & Moore	Alexandria	Mer. License	1798	Tax PP 1798:20-5
Mason, Betsey C., w/o Thomson F.	Alexandria	Will	1873	WB1:074; LP
Mason, Betty	Alexandria	Housekeeper	1799	1799(2):16A

NAME OR SUBJECT	LOCATION	TYPE	YEAR	REFERENCE(S)
Mason, Billy	Alexandria	Boarder	1795	1795(4a):04
Mason, Elizabeth	Alexandria	Resident	1800	1800(4):02B
Mason, Elizabeth	Alexandria	Resident	1800	1800(4):02B
Mason, Elizabeth, Jr., boarding house	Alexandria	Head	1800	1800(4):02A
Mason, Elizabeth, Sr., labourer	Alexandria	Head	1800	1800(4):02A
Mason, Elizabeth, washer woman	Alexandria	Housekeeper	1799	1799(2):16A
Mason, Elizabeth, widow, 2	Alexandria	Head	1795	1796(3):7
Mason, Geo.	Alexandria	Tax Charge	1795	Tax PP 1795:21
Mason, Geo.	Alexandria	Tax Charge	1796	Tax LP 1796:21
Mason, Geo., Duke St.	Alexandria	Occupant	1795	Tax L 1795:08
Mason, George	Alexandria	Tax Charge	1787	Tax PP 1787:10
Mason, George	Alexandria	Tax Charge	1788	Tax PP 1788:12
Mason, George	Alexandria	Tax Charge	1789	Tax PP 1789:13
Mason, George	Alexandria	Tax Charge	1790	Tax PP 1790:10
Mason, George	Alexandria	Tax Charge	1796	Tax PP 1796:13
Mason, George	Alexandria	Will	1888	WB1:500; LP
Mason, George T.	Arlington	Petition	1846	LVA-LP (Box 214)
Mason, George T., Lieut. 2nd Reg.	Arlington	Admin.	1846	OCR1842:190, 191
Mason, Jno.	Alexandria	Tax Charge	1795	Tax PP 1795:20
Mason, Jno.	Alexandria	Tax Charge	1798	Tax PP 1798:12
Mason, Jno., King St.	Alexandria	Occupant	1795	Tax L 1795:23
Mason, John	Alexandria	Tax Charge	1796	Tax LP 1796:18
Mason, John	Alexandria	Tax Charge	1796	Tax LP 1796:19
Mason, John	Alexandria	Tax Charge	1796	Tax PP 1796:12
Mason, John	Alexandria	Tax Charge	1799	Tax PP 1799:26
Mason, John, complt.	Alexandria	Suit	1822	CRL:389
Mason, John T., plt.	Alexandria	Suit	1802	CRD:149
Mason, John, watchmaker	Alexandria	Housekeeper	1808	1808(3):22A
Mason, John, watchmaker	Alexandria	Head	1810	1810(3):04A
Mason, Mary, sempstress	Alexandria	Housekeeper	1808	1808(2):16A
Mason, Matilda (Somers)	Arlington	Suit	1841	LSA:076
Mason, Richard B.	Arlington	Admin.	1843	OCR1842:022, 077
Mason, Richard B.	Arlington	Admin.	1843	WB4:316
Mason, Richard B.	Arlington	Inventory	1843	AB8:429
Mason, Richard B.	Arlington	Account	1844	AB8:429; LVA-LP
Mason, Richard B. and wife	Arlington	Defendant	1837	LSA:024
Mason, Richard Patton	Arlington	Will	1848	WB5:078; File #443A
Mason, Sarah	Arlington	Bond	1806	WBB:238
Mason, Sarah	Arlington	Will	1806	WBB:237; File #016A
Mason, Thomas, plt.	Alexandria	Suit	1804	CRF:039
Mason, Thomson F.	Arlington	Will	1839	WB4:188; File #362A
Mason, Thomson F.	Arlington	Bond	1839	WB4:190
Mason, Thomson F., Hon.	Arlington	Inventory	1841	AB8:232; LVA-LP
Massett, [blank], Union St.	Alexandria	Occupant	1790	Tax L 1790:05
Massey & Wheeler	Arlington	Sale	1842	OCR1842:011
Massey, Hartless (C)	Alexandria	Tax Charge	1788	Tax PP 1788:11
Massey, Henry W., grantor	Arlington	Indenture D.	1814	ID2:348
Massey, Henry W., in jail	Arlington	Insolvent	1814	ID2:345
Massey, John H.	Arlington	Apprentice	1829	OCR1822:173a
Massey, John W.	Arlington	Account	1842	OCR1842:003
Massey, John W.	Arlington	Account	1842	AB8:332; LVA-LP
Massey, Mary, w/o Robert	Arlington	Will	1870	WB9:225; File #678A
Massey, Robert, grantor	Arlington	Indenture D.	1814	ID2:354
Massey, Robert, in jail bounds	Arlington	Insolvent	1814	ID2:351
Massey, William	Arlington	Apprentice	1829	OCR1822:173a
Massie, John W.	Alexandria	Boarder	1808	1808(3):20A
Massie, John W.	Arlington	Bond	1840	WB4:260
Massie, John W.	Arlington	Will	1840	WB4:257; File #378A
Massie, John W.	Arlington	Inventory	1840	AB8:156; LVA-LP
Massie, John W.	Arlington	Account	1841	AB8:249; LVA-LP
Massie, John W.	Arlington	Petition	1842	LVA-LP (Box 214)

NAME OR SUBJECT	LOCATION	TYPE	YEAR	REFERENCE(S)
Massie, John W.	Arlington	Account	1843	AB9:016; LVA-LP
Massie, John W.	Arlington	Account	1843	AB8:426; LVA-LP
Massie, John W.	Arlington	Account	1843	AB8:332
Massie, John W.	Arlington	Account	1844	AB9:018; LVA-LP
Massie, John W.	Arlington	Account	1844	AB9:016; LVA-LP
Massie, John W.	Arlington	Petition	1844	LVA-LP (Box 214)
Massie, John W.	Arlington	Will P.	1844	OCR1842:090, 093
Massie, John W.	Arlington	Will P.	1845	OCR1842:140
Massie, John W.	Arlington	Account	1845	AB9:124; LVA-LP
Massie, John W.	Arlington	Account	1846	AB9:250
Massie, John W.	Arlington	Account C.	1847	WB5:216; LVA-LP
Massie, John W.	Arlington	Account C.	1847	WB5:016, 112; LVA-LP
Massie, John W.	Arlington	Account	1850	WB5:281; LVA-LP
Massie, John W.	Arlington	Account	1852	WB6:164; LVA-LP
Massie, John W.	Arlington	Account	1852	WB6:350; LVA-LP
Massie, John W.	Arlington	Account	1852	WB6:031; LVA-LP
Massie, John W.	Arlington	Account	1854	WB6:459; LVA-LP
Massie, John W.	Arlington	Account	1854	WB6:404; LVA-LP
Massie, John W. & Co.	Arlington	Inventory	1819	AB4:062
Massie, Mary S.	Alexandria	Will	1878	WB1:233; LP
Massoletti, Vincent, in Alexandria Co.	Arlington	Ordinary	1822	OBL3(np)
Masters, John Reece, s/o John I.	Alexandria	Will	1878	WB1:245; LP
Masters, Richd.	Alexandria	Tax Charge	1798	Tax PP 1798:12
Masters, Richd.	Alexandria	Mer. License	1798	Tax PP 1798:20-4
Masters, S.S. & Son	Arlington	Trustee Acct.	1859	WB7:405; LVA-LP
Masters, Samuel	Arlington	Sale	1859	LVA-LP
Masters, Wm.	Alexandria	Tax Charge	1796	Tax LP 1796:18
Masterson, Francis	Arlington	Guard. Acct.	1834	AB7:128; LVA-LP
Masterson, Francis H., c/o Laughlin	Arlington	Guard.	1834	WB4:101
Masterson, Laughlin	Arlington	Admin.	1827	OCR1822:143
Masterson, Laughlin	Arlington	Admin.	1827	WB3:298
Masterson, Laughlin	Arlington	Account	1834	AB7:154; LVA-LP
Masterson, Laughlin, b. Co. Cavan	Arlington	Alien Entry	1817	RA:26/11/17
Masterson, Laughlin, children of	Arlington	Guard. Acct.	1834	AB7:120; LVA-LP
Masterson, Laughton	Arlington	Inventory	1827	LVA-LP
Masterson, Laughton	Arlington	Account	1835	AB7:154
Masterson, Mark E.	Arlington	Guard. Acct.	1835	AB7:158
Masterson, Mark E., c/o Laughlin	Arlington	Guard.	1834	WB4:101; LVA-LP
Masterson, Mary A., Washington DC	Alexandria	Will	1882	WB1:355; LP
Masterson, Sarah	Arlington	Will	1803	WBA:160; LVA-LP
Mastin, John	Arlington	Receipt	1861	LVA-LP
Mastin, John	Arlington	Will	1861	WB8:074; File #585A
Mastin, John, in Alexandria Co.	Arlington	Ordinary	1847	OBL6(np)
Mastin, John, in Alexandria Co.	Arlington	Ordinary	1848	OBL6(np)
Mathers, James G.	Arlington	Apprentice	1828	OCR1822:161a
Mathers, Sarah	Arlington	Will (NR)	1821	File #061A
Matheson, Kenneth	Arlington	Admin.	1804	WBA:285
Matheson, Kenneth	Arlington	Inventory	1804	WBB:022; LVA-LP
Matheson, Kenneth	Arlington	Account	1805	WBB:214; LVA-LP
Mathews, Lastley	Arlington	Inventory	1813	AB1:323; LVA-LP
Mathews, Lastley, Rev.	Arlington	Sale	1813	AB1:323
Mathews, Patrick	Alexandria	Tax Charge	1789	Tax PP 1789:12
Mathews, Patty	Alexandria	Boarder	1799	1799(2):06A
Mathews, Thomas	Alexandria	Mer. License	1799	Tax PP 1799:52-07r
Mathews, Thos. & wife, merchant	Alexandria	Housekeeper	1799	1799(2):06A
Mathiesen, Albert, at his house	Arlington	Ordinary	1836	OBL5(np)
Matkins, Phil., Mariner	Alexandria	Tax Charge	1795	Tax PP 1795:19
Matteson, Lorenzo D., of DC	Alexandria	Will	1899	WB2:303; LP
Mattheson, Kenneth, b. North Britain	Arlington	Alien Entry	1801	RA:24/06/01
Matthews, Lastly	Arlington	Will	1813	WB1:227; File #109A
Matthews, Lastly, Rev.	Arlington	Sale	1814	AB2:027

NAME OR SUBJECT	LOCATION	TYPE	YEAR	REFERENCE(S)
Matthews, Lastly, Rev.	Arlington	Account	1814	AB2:027; LVA-LP
Matthews, Thomas	Alexandria	Mer. License	1798	Tax PP 1798:20-4
Matthews, Thomas	Alexandria	Tax Charge	1798	Tax PP 1798:12
Matthews, Thomas	Alexandria	Tax Charge	1799	Tax PP 1799:26
Matthews, Thomas	Alexandria	Tax Charge	1800	Tax PP 1800:27
Matthews, Thomas	Alexandria	Mer. License	1800	Tax PP 1800:54(16)r
Matthews, Thomas, of Philadelphia PA	Arlington	Will (NP)	1832	WB4:324; File #397A
Matthieson, Mary ann, b. London	Arlington	Alien Entry	1801	RA:24/06/01
Mattimor, Elizabeth	Alexandria	Resident	1800	1800(4):02B
Mattimor, Elizabeth, labourer	Alexandria	Boarder	1800	1800(4):02A
Mattingly, John E.	Arlington	Apprentice	1828	OCR1822:163a
Mattocks, Mary	Arlington	Guard.	1804	WBB:011
Maul, John	Arlington	Defendant	1824	ACO:249
Maund, Henry L.	Arlington	Admin.	1822	OCR1822:001, 002a
Maund, Henry L.	Arlington	Admin.	1822	WB3:045
Maund, Henry L.	Arlington	Inventory	1823	AB5:154; LVA-LP
Maund, Henry L.	Arlington	Account	1825	AB5:387
Maxfield, Matthew, mate	Arlington	Libellant	1818	ACO:152
Maxwell, Alvira V.	Alexandria	Will	1895	WB2:116; LP
Maxwell, Close	Alexandria	Mer. License	1798	Tax PP 1798:20-4
Maxwell, Close	Alexandria	Tax Charge	1799	Tax PP 1799:27
Maxwell, Close	Alexandria	Tax Charge	1800	Tax PP 1800:27
Maxwell, Close & wife, retailer	Alexandria	Housekeeper	1799	1799(2):01A
Maxwell, George W.	Arlington	Will	1861	WB8:091; File #589A
Maxwell, Hugh	Alexandria	Tax Charge	1799	Tax PP 1799:27
Maxwell, James	Alexandria	Deposition	1806	CRG:284
Maxwell, Thomas	Alexandria	Tithable +16	1788	Tax PP 1788:05
May & Tasize, Pitt St.	Alexandria	Occupant	1795	Tax L 1795:21
May & Tasize, Pitt St.	Alexandria	Owner	1795	Tax L 1795:21
May, Edward	Alexandria	Mer. License	1798	Tax PP 1798:20-4
May, Edward	Alexandria	Tax Charge	1799	Tax PP 1799:27
May, Edward	Alexandria	Tax Charge	1800	Tax PP 1800:26
May, Edward	Arlington	Will	1810	WBC:467; File #052A
May, Edward	Arlington	Appraisal	1810	WBC:469
May, Edward	Arlington	Bond	1810	WBC:468
May, Edward	Arlington	Account	1811	AB1:145; LVA-LP
May, Edward & wife, taylor	Alexandria	Housekeeper	1799	1799(2):11A
May, Edward, w(6), merchant	Alexandria	Head	1796	1796(3):4
May, Edwd.	Alexandria	Boarder	1808	1808(1):05A
May, Edwd.	Alexandria	Reference	1808	1808(4):28B
May, Francis, carpenter	Alexandria	Housekeeper	1808	1808(4):29A
May, Francis R.	Arlington	Apprentice	1813	OCR1811:190
May, Francis Russell, c/o Mary	Arlington	Apprentice	1812	OCR1811:105
May, Frederick	Arlington	Bond	1853	BB(np)
May, Frederick, of Washington DC	Arlington	Will (NR)	1847	File #076A
May, Henry K.	Arlington	Defendant	1808	ACO:082, 089
May, Henry K.	Arlington	Passenter	1812	ACR:054
May, Henry K., merchant	Alexandria	Housekeeper	1808	1808(4):30A
May, John	Alexandria	Boarder	1808	1808(1):02A
May, John	Arlington	Inventory	1817	AB2:417; LVA-LP
May, John	Arlington	Sale	1817	AB2:428
May, John	Arlington	Will	1817	WB2:178; File #138A
May, John	Arlington	Bond	1817	WB2:179
May, John	Arlington	Account	1818	AB3:119; LVA-LP
May, John	Arlington	Account	1819	AB3:283; LVA-LP
May, John R.	Arlington	Apprentice	1812	OCR1811:050
May, Jona.	Alexandria	Boarder	1808	1808(1):05A
May, Richard, w, labourer	Alexandria	Head	1796	1796(3):3
May, Richd.	Alexandria	Tax Charge	1795	Tax PP 1795:20
May, Richd. & wife	Alexandria	Housekeeper	1799	1799(2):04A
May, Thompson	Arlington	Guard.	1819	WB2:333

NAME OR SUBJECT	LOCATION	TYPE	YEAR	REFERENCE(S)
May, Thompson	Arlington	Account	1819	AB3:403; LVA-LP
May, Thompson	Arlington	Guard. Acct.	1826	AB6:218; LVA-LP
May, Thompson	Arlington	Guard. Acct.	1826	OCR1822:118a
Mayer, Anna Rogers	Arlington	Will	1900	WB10:430; File #796A
Mayhall, Hy.	Alexandria	Boarder	1808	1808(3):20A
Mayhall, James	Alexandria	Tithable +16	1788	Tax PP 1788:01
Mayhall, James	Alexandria	Tithable +16	1789	Tax PP 1789:10
Mayhall, James	Alexandria	Tithable +16	1790	Tax PP 1790:01
Mayhall, James, w, baker	Alexandria	Head	1796	1796(3):1
Mayhall, Jas., baker	Alexandria	Housekeeper	1808	1808(1):03A
Mayhall, Rezin	Alexandria	Tax Charge	1799	Tax PP 1799:27
Mayhall, Rezin	Alexandria	Tax Charge	1800	Tax PP 1800:27
Mayhall, Rezin & wife, drayman	Alexandria	Housekeeper	1799	1799(2):11A
Mayhall, Samuel	Arlington	Will	1814	WB1:020; File #089A
Mayhall, Walter	Alexandria	Tithable +16	1788	Tax PP 1788:01
Mayhall, Walter	Alexandria	Tithable +16	1789	Tax PP 1789:10

Mc

NAME OR SUBJECT	LOCATION	TYPE	YEAR	REFERENCE(S)
Mc___, Jas. M.	Alexandria	Tax Charge	1788	Tax PP 1788:10
McAchran, Angus, shopkeeper	Alexandria	Housekeeper	1808	1808(1):09A
McAfee, Mary	Arlington	Guard.	1816	WB2:114
McAffry, Pat.	Alexandria	Tax Charge	1795	Tax PP 1795:20
McAlister, Daniel	Alexandria	Tax Charge	1799	Tax PP 1799:27
McAlister, Jas., carpenter	Alexandria	Boarder	1799	1799(2):11A
McAlister, Nathaniel	Arlington	Bond	1816	WB2:163
McAlister, Nathaniel	Arlington	Will	1816	WB2:161; File #136A
McAlister, Nathaniel	Arlington	Inventory	1817	AB2:402; LVA-LP
McAlister, Nathl.	Alexandria	Tax Charge	1795	Tax PP 1795:19
McAlister, Nathnl.	Alexandria	Tax Charge	1799	Tax PP 1799:26
McAllister, Daniel	Arlington	Account	1801	WBA:032
McAllister, John, plt.	Alexandria	Suit	1805	CRF:010
McAllister, Nathaniel	Arlington	Ordinary	1811	OBL2(np)
McAllister, Nathaniel & wife, carpenter	Alexandria	Housekeeper	1799	1799(2):11A
McAllister, Nathaniel, shopkeeper	Alexandria	Head	1810	1810(3):01A
McAllister, Nathaniel, shopkpr. & carp.	Alexandria	Housekeeper	1808	1808(3):20A
McAllister, Natl.	Alexandria	Tax Charge	1800	Tax PP 1800:26
McAllister, Tracy, washwoman	Alexandria	Housekeeper	1808	1808(2):16A
McArthur, John	Alexandria	Tax Charge	1795	Tax PP 1795:21
McBride, John	Alexandria	Tax Charge	1787	Tax PP 1787:11
McBride, John	Alexandria	Tax Charge	1788	Tax PP 1788:10
McBride, Phenix	Alexandria	Tax Charge	1796	Tax PP 1796:13
McBride, William	Alexandria	Tax Charge	1790	Tax PP 1790:09
McBride, Wm.	Alexandria	Tax Charge	1789	Tax PP 1789:12
McBurney, Agnes	Alexandria	Will	1893	WB2:067; LP
McBurney, Alexander	Alexandria	Will	1890	WBC1:055; LP
McBurney, George	Alexandria	Will	1885	WB1:412; LP
McCabe, Edward	Alexandria	Tax Charge	1796	Tax PP 1796:12
McCabe, Edward, taylor	Alexandria	Head	1796	1796(3):5
McCaffry, Patrick	Arlington	Witness	1795	OT:22/06/1795
McCaine, Robert R.R.	Alexandria	Will	1874	WB1:089; LP
McCall, Archd.	Alexandria	Tax Charge	1800	Tax PP 1800:27
McCall, Archd., nail maker	Alexandria	Housekeeper	1799	1799(2):08A
McCall, Archibald	Alexandria	Tax Charge	1799	Tax PP 1799:26
McCall, Archibald, of Philadelphia	Alexandria	Deed	1811	CRK:048
McCall, Wm.	Alexandria	Tax Charge	1795	Tax PP 1795:20
McCan, Neil	Alexandria	Tax Charge	1790	Tax PP 1790:10
McCann, Neal	Alexandria	Tithable +21	1787	Tax PP 1787:09
McCarter, John	Alexandria	Tax Charge	1796	Tax PP 1796:12
McCarthy, Mary	Alexandria	Will	1897	WB2:189; LP
McCartney, Margarett, seamstress	Alexandria	Head	1810	1810(1):05A
McCarty, Arthur	Alexandria	Tax Charge	1789	Tax PP 1789:12

NAME OR SUBJECT	LOCATION	TYPE	YEAR	REFERENCE(S)
McCarty, Benjamin	Arlington	Apprentice	1815	OCR1811:245
McCarty, Daniel	Alexandria	Account B.	1800	CRC:106
McCarty, Daniel, def.	Alexandria	Suit	1802	CRC:103
McCarty, Dennis	Alexandria	Tax Charge	1788	Tax PP 1788:12
McCarty, Dennis	Alexandria	Tax Charge	1789	Tax PP 1789:13
McCarty, Dennis	Arlington	Admin.	1811	WB1:125
McCarty, Francis X., of Staunton	Alexandria	Will	1900	WB2:390; LP
McCarty, John, c/o [Susan?]	Arlington	Apprentice	1803	OCR1801:136
McCarty, Mary, sempstress	Alexandria	Housekeeper	1808	1808(2):13A
McCarty, Michael, b. Cork, Ire.	Arlington	Alien Entry	1829	RA:31/10/29
McCarty, Timothy	Alexandria	Tax Charge	1799	Tax PP 1799:26
McCarty, Timothy, b. Co. Cork	Arlington	Alien Entry	1825	RA:10/11/25
McCarty, William H.	Arlington	Apprentice	1842	OCR1842:014
McCaughen, Hugh	Alexandria	Tax Charge	1789	Tax PP 1789:12
McCay, Benjamin	Arlington	Sale	1820	AB4:144
McCay, Benjamin	Arlington	Account	1820	AB4:138
McCay, Elizabeth	Arlington	Will	1819	WB2:317; File #166A
McCay, Elizabeth	Arlington	Inventory	1819	AB3:373; LVA-LP
McCay, Elizabeth	Arlington	Bond	1819	WB2:318, 342
McCay, Mary, seamstress	Alexandria	Head	1810	1810(2):05A
McClae, James	Arlington	Guard.	1813	WB1:256
McClae, John	Arlington	Apprentice	1802	OCR1801:062
McClanahan, Jas.	Alexandria	Tax Charge	1788	Tax PP 1788:11
McClanahan, John, Prince St.	Alexandria	Occupant	1790	Tax L 1790:08
McClanahan, John, Prince St.	Alexandria	Owner	1790	Tax L 1790:08
McClanahan, John, Union St.	Alexandria	Occupant	1790	Tax L 1790:08
McClanahan, John, Union St.	Alexandria	Owner	1790	Tax L 1790:08
McClasky, Thomas	Alexandria	Tax Charge	1787	Tax PP 1787:10
McClaud, Hugh	Alexandria	Boarder	1808	1808(2):13A
McClaud, Saml. & Hugh	Alexandria	Tax Charge	1798	Tax PP 1798:13
McClaud, Saml. & Hugh	Alexandria	Tax Charge	1799	Tax PP 1799:26
McClaud, Saml., retailer	Alexandria	Housekeeper	1808	1808(2):13A
McClay, James	Arlington	Apprentice	1813	OCR1811:198
McClay, [blank]	Alexandria	Boarder	1808	1808(2):16A
McClean, Abigail	Arlington	Account	1824	LVA-LP
McClean, Arch. & wife Mary	Alexandria	Resident	1800	1800(4):02B
McClean, Arch., schoolmaster	Alexandria	Head	1800	1800(4):02A
McClean, Archd.	Alexandria	Tax Charge	1796	Tax LP 1796:21
McClean, Archd., schoolmaster	Alexandria	Boarder	1795	1795(4a):01
McClean, Archibald & wife, teacher	Alexandria	Housekeeper	1799	1799(2):17A
McClean, Archibald & wife Christiana	Alexandria	Suit	1809	CRG:131
McClean, Archibald, def.	Alexandria	Suit	1803	CRD:086
McClean, B., Queen St.	Alexandria	Occupant	1787	Tax L 1787:22
McClean, Daniel	Alexandria	Mer. License	1799	Tax PP 1799:52-07r
McClean, Daniel	Alexandria	Tax Charge	1800	Tax PP 1800:26
McClean, Daniel	Arlington	Will P.	1823	OCR1822:033a
McClean, Daniel	Arlington	Admin.	1823	OCR1822:035
McClean, Daniel	Arlington	Inventory	1823	AB5:165; LVA-LP
McClean, Daniel	Arlington	Sale	1824	AB5:295
McClean, Daniel	Arlington	Debts Due	1824	AB5:301
McClean, Daniel	Arlington	Account	1834	LVA-LP
McClean, Daniel, def.	Alexandria	Suit	1808	CRG:086
McClean, Daniel, merchant	Alexandria	Head	1810	1810(1):11A
McClean, Danl.	Alexandria	Tax Charge	1795	Tax PP 1795:20
McClean, Danl.	Alexandria	Tax Charge	1796	Tax LP 1796:19
McClean, Danl. & wife, baker	Alexandria	Housekeeper	1799	1799(2):02A
McClean, Evan, Prince St.	Alexandria	Occupant	1787	Tax L 1787:06
McClean, Mary	Alexandria	Resident	1800	1800(4):02B
McClean, Mary, visitor	Alexandria	Boarder	1800	1800(4):02A
McClean, Samuel	Alexandria	Owner	1787	Tax L 1787:20
McClean, Sauel, Queen St.	Alexandria	Occupant	1787	Tax L 1787:20

NAME OR SUBJECT	LOCATION	TYPE	YEAR	REFERENCE(S)
McClean, Thomas	Alexandria	Tax Charge	1799	Tax PP 1799:26
McClean, William, labourer	Alexandria	Head	1810	1810(2):01A
McClean, Wm. & wife, ship builder	Alexandria	Housekeeper	1799	1799(2):20A
McClean, Wm. & wife Agness	Alexandria	Resident	1800	1800(4):08B
McClean, Wm., ship carpenter	Alexandria	Head	1800	1800(4):08A
McClean's Estate	Alexandria	Tax Charge	1796	Tax LP 1796:18
McCleane, Daniel	Alexandria	Tax Charge	1799	Tax PP 1799:26
McCleesh, Archd., cooper	Alexandria	Head	1810	1810(1):12A
McCleish, Ann Elizabeth	Arlington	Guard.	1826	WB3:256
McCleish, Archibald	Arlington	Admin.	1819	WB2:300
McCleish, Archibald	Arlington	Account	1820	AB4:142; LVA-LP
McCleish, Archibald	Arlington	Admin.	1825	WB3:205
McCleish, James	Arlington	Account	1826	AB6:238; LVA-LP
McCleish, Virginia Sarah	Arlington	Guard.	1826	WB3:256
McClenachan, John	Alexandria	Tax Charge	1789	Tax PP 1789:12
McClenachan, John	Alexandria	Tax Charge	1790	Tax PP 1790:10
McClenahan, J., Prince St.	Alexandria	Occupant	1787	Tax L 1787:20
McClenahan, J., Union St.	Alexandria	Occupant	1787	Tax L 1787:20
McClenahan, J., Union St.	Alexandria	Occupant	1787	Tax L 1787:16
McClenahan, Jno., Prince St.	Alexandria	Occupant	1787	Tax L 1787:10
McClenahan, Jno., Union St.	Alexandria	Owner	1795	Tax L 1795:21
McClenahan, Jno., Water St.	Alexandria	Owner	1795	Tax L 1795:21
McClenahan, Jno., Wilks St.	Alexandria	Occupant	1787	Tax L 1787:24
McClenahan, Jno., Wolfe St.	Alexandria	Occupant	1787	Tax L 1787:10
McClenahan, John	Alexandria	Owner	1787	Tax L 1787:20
McClenahan, John	Alexandria	Tax Charge	1787	Tax PP 1787:10
McClenechan, James	Alexandria	Deposition	1805	CRG:025
McCleod & Lumsdon	Alexandria	Tax Charge	1800	Tax PP 1800:26
McCleod, Daniel, painter	Alexandria	Head	1810	1810(2):01A
McCleod, Jno. & wife, beer house	Alexandria	Housekeeper	1799	1799(2):04A
McCleod, John, def.	Alexandria	Suit	1802	CRD:048
McCleod, John, ret. liquors w/o license	Arlington	Defendant	1802	PA:001
McCliesh, Archibald	Alexandria	Tithable +16	1789	Tax PP 1789:12
McCliesh, Archibald	Arlington	Inventory	1819	AB3:331; LVA-LP
McCliesh, George	Alexandria	Will	1880	WB1:301; LP
McCliesh, James	Alexandria	Tax Charge	1789	Tax PP 1789:12
McCliesh, James	Arlington	Admin.	1825	OCR1822:103
McClish, Arbhibald	Arlington	Account	1823	AB5:215; LVA-LP
McClish, Arch. & wife Elisibeth	Alexandria	Resident	1800	1800(4):02B
McClish, Arch., cooper	Alexandria	Head	1800	1800(4):02A
McClish, Archd.	Alexandria	Tax Charge	1795	Tax PP 1795:22
McClish, Archd.	Alexandria	Tax Charge	1796	Tax LP 1796:21
McClish, Archd.	Alexandria	Tax Charge	1796	Tax LP 1796:19
McClish, Archd.	Alexandria	Tax Charge	1798	Tax PP 1798:12
McClish, Archd.	Alexandria	Tax Charge	1800	Tax PP 1800:26
McClish, Archd. & wife, cooper	Alexandria	Housekeeper	1799	1799(2):16A
McClish, Archd., cooper	Alexandria	Housekeeper	1808	1808(1):05A
McClish, Archibald	Alexandria	Tithable +21	1787	Tax PP 1787:11
McClish, Archibald	Alexandria	Tithable +16	1788	Tax PP 1788:11
McClish, Archibald	Alexandria	Tax Charge	1796	Tax PP 1796:14
McClish, Archibald	Alexandria	Tax Charge	1799	Tax PP 1799:26
McClish, Archibald	Arlington	Libellant	1813	ACO:137
McClish, Archibald, c/o James	Arlington	Apprentice	1805	OCR1801:289
McClish, Archibald plt.	Alexandria	Suit	1812	CRK:002
McClish, Archibal[d]	Alexandria	Tithable +16	1790	Tax PP 1790:09
McClish, James	Alexandria	Tax Charge	1787	Tax PP 1787:11
McClish, James	Alexandria	Tax Charge	1788	Tax PP 1788:11
McClish, James	Alexandria	Tax Charge	1790	Tax PP 1790:09
McClish, James	Alexandria	Tax Charge	1796	Tax LP 1796:18
McClish, James	Alexandria	Tax Charge	1799	Tax PP 1799:28
McClish, James	Alexandria	Tax Charge	1800	Tax PP 1800:27

NAME OR SUBJECT	LOCATION	TYPE	YEAR	REFERENCE(S)
McClish, James	Arlington	Debts	1825	AB6:137
McClish, James	Arlington	Inventory	1825	AB6:135; LVA-LP
McClish, James, cooper	Alexandria	Housekeeper	1808	1808(2):15A
McClish, James, cooper	Alexandria	Head	1810	1810(2):06A
McClish, James, def.	Alexandria	Suit	1798	CRC:030
McClish, James, def.	Alexandria	Suit	1801	CRC:066
McClish, James, Union St.	Alexandria	Occupant	1787	Tax L 1787:08
McClish, Jas.	Alexandria	Tax Charge	1795	Tax PP 1795:19
McClish, Jas.	Alexandria	Tax Charge	1796	Tax PP 1796:12
McClish, Jas.	Alexandria	Tax Charge	1798	Tax PP 1798:12
McCloud, Daniel, w(4)1, painter	Alexandria	Head	1796	1796(3):3
McCloud, Donald	Alexandria	Boarder	1808	1808(2):12A
McCloud, John, agt. for d. warehouse	Alexandria	Head	1810	1810(3):03A
McCloud, John, tavern license	Alexandria	Housekeeper	1808	1808(2):12A
McCloud, Saml.	Alexandria	Tax Charge	1796	Tax LP 1796:18
McCloud, Saml.	Alexandria	Mer. License	1800	Tax PP 1800:54(16)r
McCloud, Saml. & Hugh	Alexandria	Tax Charge	1800	Tax PP 1800:26
McCloud, Samuel	Alexandria	Mer. License	1798	Tax PP 1798:20-4
McCloud, Samuel	Alexandria	Mer. License	1799	Tax PP 1799:52-07r
McCobb, John	Arlington	Account	1823	LVA-LP
McCobb, John, captain	Alexandria	Head	1810	1810(1):04A
McCobb, John, sea captain	Alexandria	Housekeeper	1808	1808(1):04A
McComb, Henry S.	Arlington	Will	1887	WB10:104; File #729A
McCommick, James	Alexandria	Tax Charge	1787	Tax PP 1787:11
McConnel, Corry, b. Armagh	Arlington	Alien Entry	1819	RA:16/01/19
McConnell, Alex.	Alexandria	Tax Charge	1796	Tax LP 1796:21
McConnell, Alexander	Arlington	Witness	1794	OT:25/07/1794
McConnell, Alexander	Alexandria	Tax Charge	1795	Tax PP 1795:22
McConnell, Alexander	Arlington	Witness	1795	OT:28/07/1795
McConnell, Alexander	Alexandria	Tax Charge	1796	Tax PP 1796:13
McConnell, Alexander, w(4)1, shopkpr.	Alexandria	Head	1796	1796(3):5
McConnell, Alexr., Prince St.	Alexandria	Occupant	1795	Tax L 1795:30
McConnell, Alexr., Water St.	Alexandria	Owner	1795	Tax L 1795:22
McConnell, Francis, Fayette Co. Ky.	Alexandria	Plat	1779	CRH:391
McCormick, John	Alexandria	Boarder	1795	1795(4):03
McCormick, John	Arlington	Admin. Bond	1850	ABB(np)
McCormick, John	Arlington	Trustee Acct.	1859	LVA-LP
McCormick, Luther	Arlington	Trustee Acct.	1860	WB8:032; LVA-LP
McCormick, Thomas & wife	Arlington	Trustee Acct.	1860	WB8:029, 36; LVA-LP
McCosland, Marcus, Fairfax St.	Alexandria	Owner	1795	Tax L 1795:21
McCowen, Hugh	Alexandria	Tax Charge	1795	Tax PP 1795:19
McCoy, Benjamin	Arlington	Admin.	1820	WB2:362
McCoy, William Henry (C)	Arlington	Apprentice	1847	OCR1842:204
McCracken, Jane	Alexandria	Will	1880	WB1:298; LP
McCrasay, Anthony	Alexandria	Tax Charge	1796	Tax PP 1796:12
McCrea & Mease	Alexandria	Owner	1787	Tax L 1787:19
McCrea & Mease, Royal St.	Alexandria	Occupant	1787	Tax L 1787:19
McCrea, James	Alexandria	Tax Charge	1787	Tax PP 1787:11
McCrea, James	Alexandria	Tax Charge	1789	Tax PP 1789:12
McCrea, James	Alexandria	Tax Charge	1796	Tax LP 1796:19
McCrea, Jas. M. & wife, postmaster	Alexandria	Housekeeper	1799	1799(2):07A
McCrea, John	Alexandria	Tithable +16	1789	Tax PP 1789:12
McCrea, John	Alexandria	Tithable +16	1790	Tax PP 1790:09
McCrea, Robert	Alexandria	Tax Charge	1787	Tax PP 1787:11
McCrea, Robert	Alexandria	Tax Charge	1790	Tax PP 1790:09
McCrea, Robert, alley nr. Union St.	Alexandria	Owner	1790	Tax L 1790:08
McCrea, Robert, merchant	Alexandria	Boarder	1799	1799(2):05A
McCrea, Robert, Royal St.	Alexandria	Occupant	1790	Tax L 1790:08
McCrea, Robert, Royal St.	Alexandria	Owner	1790	Tax L 1790:08
McCrea, Robert, Union St.	Alexandria	Owner	1790	Tax L 1790:08
McCrea, Robt.	Alexandria	Tax Charge	1788	Tax PP 1788:10

NAME OR SUBJECT	LOCATION	TYPE	YEAR	REFERENCE(S)
McCrea, Robt.	Alexandria	Tax Charge	1789	Tax PP 1789:12
McCrea, Robt. & Co., retailers	Alexandria	Housekeeper	1808	1808(2):10A
McCrea, William	Alexandria	Tax Charge	1790	Tax PP 1790:10
McCrea, Wm.	Alexandria	Tithable +16	1788	Tax PP 1788:10
McCrea, Wm.	Alexandria	Tax Charge	1789	Tax PP 1789:12
McCrea, Wm.	Alexandria	Boarder	1799	1799(2):07A
McCready, James, w(5), shoemaker	Alexandria	Head	1796	1796(3):7
McCredy, James	Alexandria	Tax Charge	1790	Tax PP 1790:10
McCrocklin, J., Queen St.	Alexandria	Occupant	1787	Tax L 1787:22
McCue, Henry	Alexandria	Tax Charge	1788	Tax PP 1788:11
McCue, Henry	Alexandria	Tax Charge	1789	Tax PP 1789:12
McCue, Henry	Alexandria	Tax Charge	1790	Tax PP 1790:09
McCue, Henry	Alexandria	Tax Charge	1795	Tax PP 1795:19
McCue, Henry	Alexandria	Tax Charge	1796	Tax PP 1796:13
McCue, Henry	Alexandria	Tax Charge	1796	Tax LP 1796:18
McCue, Henry	Alexandria	Tax Charge	1799	Tax PP 1799:27
McCue, Henry	Alexandria	Tax Charge	1800	Tax PP 1800:26
McCue, Henry	Arlington	Defendant	1802	PA:342
McCue, Henry	Arlington	Ordinary	1804	OBL1(np)
McCue, Henry	Arlington	Ordinary	1804	OBL1(np)
McCue, Henry	Arlington	Ordinary	1805	OBL1(np)
McCue, Henry	Alexandria	Housekeeper	1808	1808(2):17A
McCue, Henry	Alexandria	Head	1810	1810(2):07A
McCue, Henry	Arlington	Inventory	1811	AB1:119; LVA-LP
McCue, Henry	Arlington	Sale	1811	AB1:129
McCue, Henry	Arlington	Will	1811	WB1:086; File #093A
McCue, Henry	Arlington	Account	1812	AB1:234; LVA-LP
McCue, Henry, Princess St.	Alexandria	Owner	1795	Tax L 1795:20(2)
McCue, Henry, ret. liquor w/o license	Arlington	Defendant	1802	PA:230
McCue, Henry, Royal St.	Alexandria	Occupant	1790	Tax L 1790:01
McCue, Hy.	Alexandria	Tax Charge	1798	Tax PP 1798:12
McCue, Hy., Princess St.	Alexandria	Occupant	1795	Tax L 1795:20
McCue, Mary, sempstress	Alexandria	Housekeeper	1808	1808(4):26A
McCuen, Mary	Alexandria	Head	1810	1810(2):07A
McCuen, Robert	Alexandria	Will	1873	WB1:061; LP
McCulloch, John	Alexandria	Mer. License	1798	Tax PP 1798:20-4
McCulloch, John	Alexandria	Tax Charge	1799	Tax PP 1799:27
McCulloch, John	Alexandria	Tax Charge	1800	Tax PP 1800:26
McCullock, Jno.	Alexandria	Tax Charge	1798	Tax PP 1798:12
McCullock, John	Alexandria	Mer. License	1799	Tax PP 1799:52-07r
McCullock, John	Alexandria	Mer. License	1800	Tax PP 1800:54(17)r
McCullock, John, assault and battery	Arlington	Defendant	1802	PA:327
McCullock, [blank]	Alexandria	Tax Charge	1796	Tax PP 1796:13
McCurdy, Richard, of Lyme, Conn.	Alexandria	Deposition	1805	CRF:253
McCustis, George	Arlington	Crime	1798	OT:25/06/1798
McCutchen, Eleaner, c/o Jacobina	Arlington	Apprentice	1802	OCR1801:043
McCutchen, Eleanor, c/o Jacobine	Arlington	Apprentice	1805	OCR1801:281
McCutcheon, Eleanor	Arlington	Guard.	1808	WBC:061
McCutchison, Patrick, [biscuit] baker	Alexandria	Housekeeper	1808	1808(4):29A
McDade, Jno.	Alexandria	Tax Charge	1795	Tax PP 1795:19
McDade, John	Alexandria	Tax Charge	1796	Tax LP 1796:19
McDaniel, Alexander	Arlington	Apprentice	1805	OCR1801:252
McDaniel, Ann	Arlington	Bond	1803	WBA:175
McDaniel, Ann	Arlington	Sale	1805	WBB:115
McDaniel, Ann	Arlington	Account	1805	WBB:116; LVA-LP
McDaniel, Ann	Arlington	Inventory	1805	WBB:113
McDaniel, Anthony	Alexandria	Tax Charge	1790	Tax PP 1790:10
McDaniel, Charles	Alexandria	Tax Charge	1790	Tax PP 1790:10
McDaniel, George	Alexandria	Tithable +16	1788	Tax PP 1788:10
McDaniel, James, in Alexandria Co.	Arlington	Ordinary	1830	OBL4(np)
McDannick, James, wheelwright	Alexandria	Head	1810	1810(1):02A

NAME OR SUBJECT	LOCATION	TYPE	YEAR	REFERENCE(S)
McDennick, James	Arlington	Ordinary	1809	OBL2(np)
McDennick, James, coach maker	Alexandria	Housekeeper	1808	1808(2):17A
McDermit, Martin	Alexandria	Tax Charge	1788	Tax PP 1788:11
McDermot, Martin	Alexandria	Tax Charge	1787	Tax PP 1787:11
McDermott, Edwd., shoemaker	Alexandria	Housekeeper	1808	1808(3):22A
McDonald, Andrew, plt.	Alexandria	Suit	1801	CRC:203
McDonald, Charles	Alexandria	Tithable +16	1788	Tax PP 1788:08
McDonald, Charles	Alexandria	Tax Charge	1789	Tax PP 1789:13
McDonald, Frances	Arlington	Apprentice	1846	OCR1842:171
McDonald, James	Alexandria	Tax Charge	1788	Tax PP 1788:12
McDonald, Jas.	Alexandria	Boarder	1808	1808(1):08A
McDonald, John	Alexandria	Tax Charge	1789	Tax PP 1789:12
McDonald, John, def.	Alexandria	Suit	1802	CRC:006
McDonald, John, grantee	Arlington	Indenture D.	1827	ID:109
McDonald, John, grantor	Arlington	Indenture D.	1812	ID2:102
McDonald, John, in jail bounds	Arlington	Insolvent	1812	ID2:099
McDonald, John, plt.	Alexandria	Suit	1801	CRB:217
McDonald, John, retailer	Alexandria	Housekeeper	1808	1808(1):08A
McDonald, Margaret	Arlington	Guard.	1816	WB2:156
McDonald, Molly	Alexandria	Boarder	1795	1795(4):01
McDonald, William King	Arlington	Guard.	1816	WB2:128
McDonald, Wm.	Alexandria	Tithable +16	1788	Tax PP 1788:05
McDonald, [blank]	Alexandria	Tax Charge	1796	Tax PP 1796:12
McDonnald, John, storekeeper	Alexandria	Head	1810	1810(1):09A
McDougal, Danl.	Alexandria	Tax Charge	1796	Tax LP 1796:06
McDougal, Danl.	Alexandria	Tax Charge	1796	Tax LP 1796:20
McDougal, Danl., sailmaker	Alexandria	Housekeeper	1808	1808(2):10A
McDougall, Daniel	Alexandria	Tax Charge	1799	Tax PP 1799:26
McDougall, Daniel	Arlington	Inventory	1816	AB2:322; LVA-LP
McDougall, Daniel M.	Arlington	Admin.	1816	WB2:129
McDougall, Danl.	Alexandria	Tax Charge	1798	Tax PP 1798:12
McDougall, Danl., sail maker	Alexandria	Housekeeper	1799	1799(2):07A
McDougall, Dougall	Alexandria	Tax Charge	1788	Tax PP 1788:10
McDouglass, Daniel	Arlington	Ordinary	1810	OBL2(np)
McDowell, James, taylor	Alexandria	Head	1810	1810(1):03A
McDugal, Daniel, sail maker	Alexandria	Head	1810	1810(2):02A
McElhinney, John Joyce	Arlington	Will	1895	WB10:299; File #765A
McEwen, Thomas	Arlington	Will	1869	WB9:144; File #667A
McEwen, Thomas	Arlington	Account	1870	WB9:253
McFadden, James	Alexandria	Tax Charge	1799	Tax PP 1799:26
McFaddin, Bella	Arlington	Apprentice	1801	OCR1801:012
McFadon, James & wife, baker	Alexandria	Housekeeper	1799	1799(2):10A
McFarlane, John, b. Sterling, Scot.	Arlington	Alien Entry	1823	RA:04/03/23
McFarlin, George	Alexandria	Resident	1800	1800(4):04B
McFarlin, George	Alexandria	Serv./Appr.	1800	1800(4):04B
McFee, John, shopkeeper	Alexandria	Housekeeper	1808	1808(1):01A
McFee, John, weaver	Alexandria	Head	1810	1810(1):02A
McFey, John	Alexandria	Tax Charge	1796	Tax LP 1796:19
McGahan, Hugh	Alexandria	Tax Charge	1787	Tax PP 1787:10
McGahan, Hugh	Alexandria	Tax Charge	1788	Tax PP 1788:11
McGahan, Hugh	Alexandria	Tax Charge	1796	Tax PP 1796:13
McGahan, Hugh	Alexandria	Tax Charge	1798	Tax PP 1798:12
McGahan, Hugh	Alexandria	Tax Charge	1799	Tax PP 1799:27
McGahan, Hugh	Alexandria	Tax Charge	1800	Tax PP 1800:26
McGahan, Hugh, Cameron St.	Alexandria	Occupant	1795	Tax L 1795:03
McGahan, James	Alexandria	Tax Charge	1796	Tax LP 1796:18
McGahan, Thos.	Alexandria	Boarder	1808	1808(2):16A
McGahen, Hugh	Alexandria	Tax Charge	1790	Tax PP 1790:10
McGahen, Hugh, Fairfax St.	Alexandria	Occupant	1790	Tax L 1790:08
McGahen, Hugh, Fairfax St.	Alexandria	Owner	1790	Tax L 1790:08
McGahon, Angus, segar maker	Alexandria	Head	1810	1810(1):06A

NAME OR SUBJECT	LOCATION	TYPE	YEAR	REFERENCE(S)
McGaw & Clingham	Alexandria	Tax Charge	1796	Tax LP 1796:04
McGaw, James, w(1), merchant	Alexandria	Head	1796	1796(3):6
McGaw, Jas.	Alexandria	Tax Charge	1796	Tax PP 1796:12
McGaw, Juliana M., of Baltimore MD	Alexandria	Will	1880	WB1:309; LP
McGBride, Wm., Fairfax St.	Alexandria	Occupant	1790	Tax L 1790:01
McGee, Henry	Alexandria	Tax Charge	1795	Tax PP 1795:21
McGee, John	Alexandria	Tax Charge	1787	Tax PP 1787:10
McGee, Randall	Alexandria	Tax Charge	1796	Tax PP 1796:13
McGee, Randolph	Alexandria	Tax Charge	1796	Tax LP 1796:18
McGee, Samuel	Arlington	Apprentice	1816	OCR1811:333
McGender, Margret, gentlewoman	Alexandria	Housekeeper	1808	1808(3):22A
McGettigan, Rosina	Arlington	Will	1826	WB3:254
McGettigan, William	Arlington	Inventory	1826	AB6:236
McGettigan, William	Arlington	Admin.	1826	WB3:255
McGettigan, William	Arlington	Sale	1826	AB6:240
McGettigan, William	Arlington	Account	1827	AB6:436; LVA-LP
McGettigan, William	Arlington	Account	1830	AB6:524; LVA-LP
McGhee, John	Alexandria	Tax Charge	1788	Tax PP 1788:11
McGhow, Henry	Alexandria	Tithable +16	1788	Tax PP 1788:07
McGigor [McGreegor], John	Arlington	Ordinary	1804	OBL1(np)
McGill, Jno.	Alexandria	Boarder	1808	1808(2):10A
McGill, John	Alexandria	Tax Charge	1800	Tax PP 1800:27
McGill, John, tallow chandler	Arlington	Plaintiff	1802	PA:204
McGin, Abe, seamstress	Alexandria	Head	1810	1810(4):04A
McGin, Ebbey	Alexandria	Resident	1800	1800(4):10B
McGin, Ebbey, sumpster	Alexandria	Boarder	1800	1800(4):10A
McGindley, Andrew	Arlington	Admin.	1818	WB2:251
McGinnis, James	Arlington	Account	1867	WB8:449
McGinnis, John	Arlington	Crime	1798	OT:09/06/1798
McGiven, Edwd.	Alexandria	Tax Charge	1788	Tax PP 1788:11
McGoah, Henry, Duke St.	Alexandria	Occupant	1795	Tax L 1795:23
McGouden, Jeremiah	Alexandria	Tax Charge	1787	Tax PP 1787:10
McGough, Henry	Alexandria	Tax Charge	1789	Tax PP 1789:12
McGough, Henry	Alexandria	Tax Charge	1798	Tax PP 1798:13
McGough, Henry & wife, drayman	Alexandria	Housekeeper	1799	1799(2):15A
McGrath, Owen F., schoolmaster	Alexandria	Housekeeper	1808	1808(2):14A
McGregor, Robert	Arlington	Account	1860	WB7:540; LVA-LP
McGruder, Capt.	Alexandria	Tax Charge	1796	Tax LP 1796:19
McGruder, Philip & wife, shipmaster	Alexandria	Head	1795	1795(4a):05
McGruder, Philip, Fairfax St.	Alexandria	Owner	1795	Tax L 1795:22
McGruder, Philip, w(1)1, mariner	Alexandria	Head	1796	1796(3):2
McGue, Henry	Alexandria	Tax Charge	1796	Tax LP 1796:21
McGuire, James	Alexandria	Tithable +16	1790	Tax PP 1790:02
McGuire, James	Alexandria	Tax Charge	1795	Tax PP 1795:21
McGuire, James	Alexandria	Tax Charge	1796	Tax LP 1796:18
McGuire, James	Arlington	Plaintiff	1802	PA:203
McGuire, James	Arlington	Inventory	1850	WB5:301; LVA-LP
McGuire, James	Arlington	Bond	1850	BB(np) (2)
McGuire, James	Arlington	Sale	1851	WB5:313; LVA-LP
McGuire, James	Arlington	Fid. Bond	1851	FBB(np)
McGuire, James, for playing Faro	Arlington	Defendant	1801	PA:092
McGuire, James, lumber merchant	Alexandria	Head	1810	1810(2):05A
McGuire, James, plt.	Alexandria	Suit	1802	CRD:062
McGuire, Jas.	Alexandria	Reference	1808	1808(4):29B
McGuire, Jas., lumber merchant	Alexandria	Housekeeper	1808	1808(2):14A
McGunn, Edw. & wife, grain measurer	Alexandria	Head	1795	1795(4a):08
McHenry, J.	Alexandria	Tax Charge	1796	Tax LP 1796:18
McHenry, James	Alexandria	Tax Charge	1789	Tax PP 1789:12
McHenry, James	Alexandria	Tax Charge	1790	Tax PP 1790:09
McHenry, James	Alexandria	Tax Charge	1795	Tax PP 1795:19
McHenry, James	Alexandria	Tax Charge	1796	Tax PP 1796:12

NAME OR SUBJECT	LOCATION	TYPE	YEAR	REFERENCE(S)
McHenry, James, Princess St.	Alexandria	Owner	1790	Tax L 1790:08
McHenry, James, Princess St.	Alexandria	Occupant	1790	Tax L 1790:08
McHenry, Jas., Water St.	Alexandria	Owner	1795	Tax L 1795:22
McHenry, Manasses, in jail	Arlington	Insolvent	1805	ID3:109
Mcliver, Sarah	Alexandria	Serv./Appr.	1800	1800(4):05B
McIlroy, James	Alexandria	Tithable +21	1787	Tax PP 1787:13
McIlroy, William	Alexandria	Tithable +21	1787	Tax PP 1787:13
McIntosh, Alexander	Alexandria	Tax Charge	1795	Tax PP 1795:18
McIntosh, Francis M., c/o John	Arlington	Guard.	1858	WB7:374; LVA-LP
McIntosh, James	Alexandria	Tax Charge	1795	Tax PP 1795:18
McIntosh, James E.	Arlington	Will	1900	WB10:414; File #793A
McIntosh, John	Alexandria	Tax Charge	1799	Tax PP 1799:27
McIntosh, Joseph, c/o John	Arlington	Guard.	1858	WB7:374
McInty, John	Alexandria	Tithable +16	1788	Tax PP 1788:13
McIver, C. & Co., King St.	Alexandria	Occupant	1787	Tax L 1787:27
McIver, Charles	Alexandria	Tax Charge	1787	Tax PP 1787:11
McIver, Colin	Alexandria	Tax Charge	1787	Tax PP 1787:10
McIver, Colin, Union St.	Alexandria	Occupant	1787	Tax L 1787:19
McIver, Evander, def.	Alexandria	Suit	1821	CRL:347
McIver, Jno.	Alexandria	Tax Charge	1795	Tax PP 1795:22
McIver, Jno., Prince St.	Alexandria	Occupant	1795	Tax L 1795:22
McIver, Jno., Prince St.	Alexandria	Owner	1795	Tax L 1795:22
McIver, Jno., Union St.	Alexandria	Occupant	1795	Tax L 1795:01
McIver, John	Alexandria	Tithable +21	1787	Tax PP 1787:10
McIver, John	Alexandria	Tax Charge	1788	Tax PP 1788:11
McIver, John	Alexandria	Tax Charge	1789	Tax PP 1789:12
McIver, John	Alexandria	Tax Charge	1790	Tax PP 1790:10
McIver, John	Alexandria	Tax Charge	1796	Tax PP 1796:12
McIver, John	Alexandria	Tax Charge	1796	Tax LP 1796:19
McIver, John	Alexandria	Tax Charge	1800	Tax PP 1800:27
McIver, John, accomptant	Alexandria	Head	1810	1810(4):01A
McIver, John, assignee, complt.	Alexandria	Suit	1804	CRG:191
McIver, John, assignee, def.	Alexandria	Suit	1807	CRI:372
McIver, John, assignee, plt.	Alexandria	Suit	1801	CRC:166
McIver, John, clerk	Alexandria	Housekeeper	1808	1808(4):26A
McIver, John, def.	Alexandria	Suit	1821	CRL:347
McIver, John, Fairfax St.	Alexandria	Owner	1790	Tax L 1790:08
McIver, John, grantee	Arlington	Indenture D.	1806	ID3:154
McIver, John, King St.	Alexandria	Occupant	1790	Tax L 1790:01
McIver, John, trustee, def.	Alexandria	Suit	1821	CRL:038
McIver, John, Union St.	Alexandria	Occupant	1790	Tax L 1790:08
McIver, Jon	Alexandria	Tax Charge	1799	Tax PP 1799:27
McKan, John	Alexandria	Tithable +16	1790	Tax PP 1790:03
McKay, Benjamin	Arlington	Inventory	1820	LVA-LP
McKay [McCay], Catherine	Arlington	Will (NR)	1838	File #073A
McKeel, John	Arlington	Inventory	1822	AB5:084; LVA-LP
McKeel, John	Arlington	Admin.	1822	WB3:057
McKeel, John	Arlington	Sale	1822	AB5:095
McKeel, John	Arlington	Account	1823	AB5:162; LVA-LP
McKenna, Alicia	Arlington	Bond	1825	WB3:157
McKenna, Alicia	Arlington	Will	1825	WB3:156; File #229A
McKenna, Charles	Alexandria	Boarder	1799	1799(2):04A
McKenna, James	Alexandria	Tax Charge	1787	Tax PP 1787:09
McKenna, James	Alexandria	Tax Charge	1789	Tax PP 1789:12
McKenna, James	Alexandria	Tax Charge	1790	Tax PP 1790:09
McKenna, James	Alexandria	Tax Charge	1796	Tax PP 1796:12
McKenna, James	Alexandria	Tax Charge	1799	Tax PP 1799:27
McKenna, James	Alexandria	Tax Charge	1800	Tax PP 1800:27
McKenna, James & wife	Alexandria	Head	1795	1795(4a):10
McKenna, James, clerk	Alexandria	Head	1810	1810(3):06A
McKenna, James, King St.	Alexandria	Occupant	1787	Tax L 1787:16

NAME OR SUBJECT	LOCATION	TYPE	YEAR	REFERENCE(S)
McKenna, James, King St.	Alexandria	Occupant	1790	Tax L 1790:05
McKenna, Jas.	Alexandria	Tax Charge	1795	Tax PP 1795:21
McKenna, Jas.	Alexandria	Tax Charge	1798	Tax PP 1798:12
McKenna, Miss	Alexandria	Boarder	1799	1799(2):04A
McKenna, Peter	Alexandria	Tax Charge	1787	Tax PP 1787:11
McKenna, Peter	Alexandria	Tax Charge	1788	Tax PP 1788:12
McKenney, Alvin, gentleman	Alexandria	Housekeeper	1808	1808(3):18A
McKenney, James, w(3)1, bank officer	Alexandria	Head	1796	1796(3):3
McKenney, Jas.	Alexandria	Boarder	1808	1808(3):18A
McKenney, William	Arlington	Defendant	1823	ACO:213, 215, 216
McKenny, Edward, c/o Henrietta Linton	Arlington	Apprentice	1816	OCR1811:331
McKenzey, [blank], Union St.	Alexandria	Occupant	1795	Tax L 1795:09
McKenzie, Alexander	Alexandria	Tax Charge	1796	Tax PP 1796:13
McKenzie, Alexander	Alexandria	Mer. License	1798	Tax PP 1798:20-4
McKenzie, Alexander	Alexandria	Tax Charge	1799	Tax PP 1799:27
McKenzie, Alexander	Arlington	Inventory	1834	LVA-LP
McKenzie, Alexander	Arlington	Bond	1834	WB4:135
McKenzie, Alexander	Arlington	Account	1834	AB7:107; LVA-LP
McKenzie, Alexander	Arlington	Will	1834	WB4:077; File #330A
McKenzie, Alexander	Alexandria	Will	1878	WB1:242; LP
McKenzie, Alexr.	Alexandria	Tax Charge	1798	Tax PP 1798:13
McKenzie, Alexr., merchant	Alexandria	Head	1810	1810(1):03A
McKenzie, Elizabeth	Arlington	Inventory	1844	AB8:446; LVA-LP
McKenzie, Elizabeth	Arlington	Account	1844	AB9:010; LVA-LP
McKenzie, Elizabeth	Arlington	Renounce	1844	LVA-LP (Box 214)
McKenzie, Elizabeth	Arlington	Admin.	1844	OCR1842:064
McKenzie, Elizabeth	Arlington	Distributees	1845	OCR1842:113
McKenzie, Elizabeth	Arlington	Account	1845	AB9:092
McKenzie, Ezra	Alexandria	Tax Charge	1796	Tax PP 1796:14
McKenzie, Lewis	Alexandria	Will	1895	WB2:120; LP
McKenzie, William	Alexandria	Will	1872	WB1:057; LP
McKenzy, Alexr.	Alexandria	Tax Charge	1796	Tax LP 1796:19
McKey, Elijah, labourer	Alexandria	Head	1810	1810(3):05A
McKim, N.B.	Alexandria	Boarder	1808	1808(2):15A
McKin, Aby, washwoman	Alexandria	Housekeeper	1808	1808(4):25A
McKinna, George	Alexandria	Tithable +16	1788	Tax PP 1788:10
McKinney, James	Alexandria	Tax Charge	1788	Tax PP 1788:10
McKinney, John	Alexandria	Head	1810	1810(3):03A
McKinney, John plt.	Alexandria	Suit	1812	CRK:002
McKinney, John, U.S. office	Alexandria	Housekeeper	1808	1808(3):20A
McKinney, Mary	Arlington	Guard.	1818	WB2:236
McKinsey, Alexander, 1, merchant	Alexandria	Head	1796	1796(3):6
McKinsey, James, seaman	Alexandria	Head	1810	1810(3):02A
McKinsie, Alexr.	Alexandria	Tithable +16	1789	Tax PP 1789:12
McKinzey, Alexr.	Alexandria	Tax Charge	1800	Tax PP 1800:26
McKinzey, James	Alexandria	Tax Charge	1800	Tax PP 1800:26
McKinzie, Alexander, def.	Alexandria	Suit	1802	CRC:231
McKinzie, Alexr.	Alexandria	License Due	1800	Tax PP 1800:54(24)
McKinzie, Alexr., retailer merchant	Alexandria	Housekeeper	1808	1808(1):05A
McKinzie, James, sea captain	Alexandria	Housekeeper	1808	1808(3):20A
McKinzie, William, plt.	Alexandria	Suit	1809	CRH:466
McKinzy, Alexanr.	Alexandria	Mer. License	1799	Tax PP 1799:52-07r
McKnab, Thomas	Alexandria	Tax Charge	1787	Tax PP 1787:11
McKnab, Thomas	Alexandria	Tax Charge	1790	Tax PP 1790:10
McKnab, Thomas, Fairfax St.	Alexandria	Occupant	1790	Tax L 1790:02
McKnight, Catharine	Arlington	Defendant	1842	LSA:082
McKnight, Catharine, w/o John	Arlington	Defendant	1842	LSA:082
McKnight, Ch.	Alexandria	Tax Charge	1800	Tax PP 1800:26
McKnight, Charles	Arlington	Witness	1794	OT:25/07/1794
McKnight, Charles	Alexandria	Tax Charge	1799	Tax PP 1799:26
McKnight, Charles	Arlington	Ordinary	1822	OBL3(np)

NAME OR SUBJECT	LOCATION	TYPE	YEAR	REFERENCE(S)
McKnight, Charles	Arlington	Complainant	1842	LSA:082
McKnight, Charles	Arlington	Appraisal	1853	WB6:232; LVA-LP
McKnight, Charles	Arlington	Will	1853	WB6:220; File #496A
McKnight, Charles	Arlington	Bond	1853	BB(np)
McKnight, Charles	Arlington	Account	1854	WB6:377; LVA-LP
McKnight, Charles	Arlington	Account	1866	WB8:396
McKnight, Charles, for playing Faro	Arlington	Defendant	1801	PA:087
McKnight, Charles, plt.	Alexandria	Suit	1809	CRG:121, 128
McKnight, Chas.	Alexandria	Tax Charge	1795	Tax PP 1795:20
McKnight, Chas.	Alexandria	Tax Charge	1796	Tax PP 1796:14
McKnight, Chas.	Alexandria	Boarder	1808	1808(2):13A
McKnight, Chas. & Wm.	Alexandria	Tax Charge	1798	Tax PP 1798:12
McKnight, Chas., King St.	Alexandria	Owner	1795	Tax L 1795:21
McKnight, Chs.	Alexandria	Tax Charge	1796	Tax LP 1796:19
McKnight, George	Arlington	Defendant	1842	LSA:082
McKnight, John	Alexandria	Tithable +16	1788	Tax PP 1788:10
McKnight, John	Alexandria	Tax Charge	1800	Tax PP 1800:27
McKnight, John	Arlington	Juryman	1808	ACO:081
McKnight, John	Arlington	Defendant	1811	ACO:115
McKnight, John	Arlington	Will	1834	WB4:081; File #333A
McKnight, John	Arlington	Bond	1834	WB4:109
McKnight, John	Arlington	Appraisal	1836	LVA-LP
McKnight, John	Arlington	Account	1838	AB7:312; LVA-LP
McKnight, John	Arlington	Account	1839	AB7:312a
McKnight, John C.	Arlington	Defendant	1842	LSA:082
McKnight, John, Capt., seaman	Alexandria	Head	1810	1810(4):03A
McKnight, John H., heirs of	Arlington	Defendants	1842	LSA:082
McKnight, John, sea captain	Alexandria	Housekeeper	1808	1808(4):25A
McKnight, Mary	Arlington	Defendant	1842	LSA:082
McKnight, William	Alexandria	Tax Charge	1787	Tax PP 1787:09
McKnight, William	Alexandria	Tax Charge	1790	Tax PP 1790:10
McKnight, William	Alexandria	Tithable +16	1790	Tax PP 1790:08
McKnight, William	Alexandria	Tax Charge	1799	Tax PP 1799:26
McKnight, William	Alexandria	Tax Charge	1800	Tax PP 1800:27
McKnight, William	Arlington	Account	1812	AB1:255
McKnight, William	Arlington	Inventory	1812	LVA-LP
McKnight, William	Arlington	Admin.	1812	WB1:187
McKnight, William	Arlington	Account F.	1814	AB2:041; LVA-LP
McKnight, William H.	Arlington	Defendant	1842	LSA:082
McKnight, William, King St.	Alexandria	Occupant	1790	Tax L 1790:08
McKnight, William, King St.	Alexandria	Owner	1790	Tax L 1790:08(2)
McKnight, William, shopkeeper	Alexandria	Head	1810	1810(2):03A
McKnight, Wm.	Alexandria	Tax Charge	1788	Tax PP 1788:10
McKnight, Wm.	Alexandria	Tax Charge	1789	Tax PP 1789:12
McKnight, Wm.	Alexandria	Tax Charge	1795	Tax PP 1795:20
McKnight, Wm.	Alexandria	Tax Charge	1796	Tax PP 1796:13
McKnight, Wm.	Alexandria	Tax Charge	1796	Tax LP 1796:18
McKnight, Wm., gentleman	Alexandria	Housekeeper	1808	1808(2):13A
McKnight, Wm., King St.	Alexandria	Owner	1795	Tax L 1795:20(2)
McKnight, [blank], Royal St.	Alexandria	Occupant	1795	Tax L 1795:07
McKNight, Wm., King St.	Alexandria	Occupant	1795	Tax L 1795:20
McKutchin, Jacobina, seamstress	Alexandria	Head	1810	1810(4):03A
McLanahan, Sarah, formerly Murray	Arlington	Account	1844	AB9:004
McLauchlin, Tho.	Alexandria	Tax Charge	1795	Tax PP 1795:19
McLauchlin, Thomas	Alexandria	Tax Charge	1799	Tax PP 1799:26
McLaughlin, Edward	Arlington	Admin.	1834	WB4:232
McLaughlin, Edward	Arlington	Debts Due	1834	LVA-LP
McLaughlin, John	Alexandria	Boarder	1808	1808(2):15A
McLaughlin, Polly	Alexandria	Boarder	1799	1799(2):12A
McLaughlin, Thos.	Alexandria	Tax Charge	1800	Tax PP 1800:27
McLay, Dav.	Alexandria	Boarder	1808	1808(1):04A

NAME OR SUBJECT	LOCATION	TYPE	YEAR	REFERENCE(S)
McLean, Archd.	Alexandria	Tax Charge	1798	Tax PP 1798:13
McLean, Archd.	Alexandria	Tax Charge	1800	Tax PP 1800:27
McLean, Archibald	Alexandria	Tax Charge	1799	Tax PP 1799:27
McLean, Archibd.	Alexandria	Tax Charge	1796	Tax PP 1796:12
McLean, Barnett	Alexandria	Tax Charge	1787	Tax PP 1787:09
McLean, Catharine, c/o D.	Arlington	Guard. Acct.	1837	LVA-LP
McLean, Daniel	Alexandria	Mer. License	1798	Tax PP 1799:52-11r
McLean, Daniel	Alexandria	Deposition	1822	CRL:529
McLean, Daniel	Arlington	Bond	1823	WB3:088
McLean, Daniel	Arlington	Account	1824	AB5:309; LVA-LP
McLean, Daniel	Arlington	Inventory	1824	LVA-LP
McLean, Daniel	Arlington	Account	1826	AB6:178; LVA-LP
McLean, Daniel	Arlington	Account	1835	LVA-LP
McLean, Daniel	Arlington	Guard. Acct.	1837	LVA-LP
McLean, Daniel, sugar refiner	Arlington	Will	1823	WB3:087; File #216A
McLean, Danl.	Alexandria	Tax Charge	1798	Tax PP 1798:12
McLean, Danl., merchant	Alexandria	Housekeeper	1808	1808(1):07A
McLean, Douglas	Arlington	Guard. Acct.	1837	LVA-LP
McLean Estate	Arlington	Vouchers	1838	LVA-LP
McLean, Evan	Alexandria	Tax Charge	1787	Tax PP 1787:10
McLean, Evan	Alexandria	Tax Charge	1788	Tax PP 1788:12
McLean, Evan	Alexandria	Tax Charge	1789	Tax PP 1789:12
McLean, Hannah	Arlington	Guard. Acct.	1831	LVA-LP
McLean, Hannah, c/o D.	Arlington	Guard. Acct.	1837	LVA-LP
McLean, Isaac	Alexandria	Tax Charge	1800	Tax PP 1800:26
McLean, Isaac, carpenter	Alexandria	Housekeeper	1808	1808(3):20A
McLean, Lucy Minor Tebbs	Alexandria	Will	1898	WB2:255; LP
McLean, Miss, wife of Howson Hooe	Arlington	Guard.	1838	LVA-LP (Accounts)
McLean, Richard	Arlington	Apprentice	1815	OCR1811:260
McLean, Saml., Estate, Queen St.	Alexandria	Owner	1795	Tax L 1795:21(2)
McLean, Samuel	Alexandria	Tax Charge	1787	Tax PP 1787:10
McLean, Samuel, Queen St.	Alexandria	Owner	1790	Tax L 1790:08
McLean, Sarah	Alexandria	Will	1884	WB1:409; LP
McLeod & Lumsdon	Alexandria	Tax Charge	1796	Tax PP 1796:12
McLeod & Lumsdon	Alexandria	Mer. License	1798	Tax PP 1798:20-4
McLeod & Lumsdon	Alexandria	Tax Charge	1798	Tax PP 1798:12
McLeod & Yeatman	Alexandria	Tax Charge	1796	Tax LP 1796:19
McLeod, Daniel	Alexandria	Tax Charge	1799	Tax PP 1799:26
McLeod, Daniel, painter	Alexandria	Housekeeper	1808	1808(2):11A
McLeod, George, c/o Daniel	Arlington	Apprentice	1812	OCR1811:096
McLeod, Hugh	Alexandria	Tax Charge	1796	Tax PP 1796:12
McLeod, John	Alexandria	Tax Charge	1796	Tax PP 1796:12
McLeod, John	Alexandria	Tax Charge	1799	Tax PP 1799:28
McLeod, John	Alexandria	Tax Charge	1800	Tax PP 1800:26
McLeod, John	Arlington	Ordinary	1805	OBL1(np)
McLeod, Samuel	Alexandria	Tax Charge	1796	Tax PP 1796:12
McLiesh, James, Union St.	Alexandria	Owner	1790	Tax L 1790:08
McLiesh, James, Union St.	Alexandria	Occupant	1790	Tax L 1790:08
McLish, Jas., Queen St.	Alexandria	Occupant	1795	Tax L 1795:17
McLish, Jas., Water St.	Alexandria	Occupant	1795	Tax L 1795:17
McMahan, James, w(1), farmer	Alexandria	Head	1795	1796(3):7
McMahan, Jeremiah	Arlington	Account	1824	AB5:317; LVA-LP
McMahan, Nancy, Princess St.	Alexandria	Occupant	1787	Tax L 1787:01
McMahan, Thomas	Alexandria	Tax Charge	1799	Tax PP 1799:27
McMahon, Jeremiah	Arlington	Admin.	1823	OCR1822:047a
McMahon, Jeremiah	Arlington	Admin.	1823	WB3:102
McMahon, Jeremiah	Arlington	Will (NR)	1823	File #062A
McMahon, Nancy	Alexandria	Tax Charge	1787	Tax PP 1787:10
McMahon, Sarah	Alexandria	Housekeeper	1799	1799(2):18A
McMahon, Wm., shopkeeper	Alexandria	Head	1810	1810(1):06A
McMan, Roger	Alexandria	Tax Charge	1795	Tax PP 1795:21

NAME OR SUBJECT	LOCATION	TYPE	YEAR	REFERENCE(S)
McMan, Thos.	Alexandria	Tax Charge	1795	Tax PP 1795:19
McMann, Neal	Alexandria	Tax Charge	1787	Tax PP 1787:09
McMann, Thomas	Alexandria	Tax Charge	1796	Tax LP 1796:18
McMann, Thomas	Alexandria	Tax Charge	1796	Tax PP 1796:14
McManning, John, cooper	Alexandria	Housekeeper	1808	1808(1):04A
McMasters, Andrew	Alexandria	Tax Charge	1787	Tax PP 1787:10
McMasters, Andrew	Alexandria	Tax Charge	1788	Tax PP 1788:11
McMasters, Mary	Arlington	Inventory	1795	WBA:004; LVA-LP
McMasters, Mary	Arlington	Sale	1795	WBA:005
McMasters, Mary	Arlington	Account	1801	WBA:006; LVA-LP
McMath, James	Alexandria	Tax Charge	1790	Tax PP 1790:10
McMeant, Geo.	Alexandria	Reference	1808	1808(4):25A
McMechen, Jas.	Alexandria	Boarder	1799	1799(2):02A
McMechen, William	Alexandria	Mer. License	1799	Tax PP 1799:52-07r
McMechen, William	Alexandria	Tax Charge	1799	Tax PP 1799:26
McMechen, Wm.	Alexandria	Mer. License	1798	Tax PP 1798:20-4
McMechen, Wm.	Alexandria	Tax Charge	1798	Tax PP 1798:12
McMechen, Wm. & wife, merchant	Alexandria	Housekeeper	1799	1799(2):03A
McMechen, Wm., retailer	Alexandria	Housekeeper	1808	1808(2):13A
McMechin, William, grantee	Arlington	Indenture D.	1832	ID:403
McMillan, Samuel	Alexandria	Deposition	1808	CRI:405
McMinn, Thomas	Alexandria	Tax Charge	1799	Tax PP 1799:26
McMunn, Elizabeth, tinner	Alexandria	Head	1810	1810(2):01A
McMunn, G.	Alexandria	Tax Charge	1796	Tax LP 1796:18
McMunn, Geo.	Alexandria	Tax Charge	1798	Tax PP 1798:12
McMunn, Geo. & wife, coppersmith	Alexandria	Housekeeper	1799	1799(2):02A
McMunn, Geo., Gretter's alley	Alexandria	Owner	1795	Tax L 1795:21
McMunn, Geo., King St.	Alexandria	Occupant	1795	Tax L 1795:21
McMunn, Geo., King St.	Alexandria	Owner	1795	Tax L 1795:21
McMunn, Geo., King St.	Alexandria	Occupant	1795	Tax L 1795:21
McMunn, Geo., Prince St.	Alexandria	Owner	1795	Tax L 1795:21
McMunn, Geo., Prince St.	Alexandria	Occupant	1795	Tax L 1795:21
McMunn, Geo., tinman	Alexandria	Housekeeper	1808	1808(2):11A
McMunn, George	Alexandria	Tax Charge	1796	Tax PP 1796:13
McMunn, George	Alexandria	Tax Charge	1799	Tax PP 1799:26
McMunn, George	Alexandria	Tax Charge	1800	Tax PP 1800:27
McMunn, George	Alexandria	Suit	1802	CRD:149
McMunn, George	Arlington	Bond	1810	WBC:355
McMunn, George	Arlington	Will	1810	WBC:354; File #049A
McMunn, George	Arlington	Inventory	1810	WBC:356
McMunn, George	Arlington	Sale	1811	AB1:023
McMunn, George	Arlington	Account	1811	AB1:025; LVA-LP
McMunn, George	Arlington	Account	1812	AB1:261; LVA-LP
McMunn, George	Arlington	Account	1813	LVA-LP(3)
McMunn, George	Arlington	Account	1815	AB2:123
McMunn, George	Arlington	Sale	1815	AB2:122
McMunn, George	Arlington	Account	1817	AB3:081
McMunn, George, def.	Alexandria	Suit	1801	CRB:259
McMunn, George, for debt	Arlington	Defendant	1802	PA:070
McMunn, Robert, def.	Alexandria	Suit	1802	CRC:107
McNab, J., Fairfax St.	Alexandria	Occupant	1787	Tax L 1787:07
McNab, Thomas	Alexandria	Tax Charge	1789	Tax PP 1789:13
McNab, Thos.	Alexandria	Tax Charge	1788	Tax PP 1788:12
McNair, William, at the Little Falls	Arlington	Ordinary	1805	OBL1(np)
McNamara, John, mariner	Alexandria	Head	1810	1810(1):10A
McNamara, Patrick, Water St.	Alexandria	Occupant	1795	Tax L 1795:23
McNamara, Wm., sea captain	Alexandria	Housekeeper	1808	1808(1):07A
McNeal, Eliza	Alexandria	Resident	1800	1800(4):04B
McNeal, Elizey, labourer	Alexandria	Boarder	1800	1800(4):04A
McNeal, Hugh	Alexandria	Tax Charge	1789	Tax PP 1789:12
McNight, W., King St.	Alexandria	Occupant	1787	Tax L 1787:20

NAME OR SUBJECT	LOCATION	TYPE	YEAR	REFERENCE(S)
McNight, William	Alexandria	Owner	1787	Tax L 1787:20
McNight, William, King St.	Alexandria	Occupant	1787	Tax L 1787:18
McNulty, Henry	Arlington	Will	1852	WB6:107; File #477A
McNunn, Geo.	Alexandria	Tax Charge	1795	Tax PP 1795:20
McPharson, Isaac, (2)2, merchant	Alexandria	Head	1796	1796(3):1
McPherson, D. & I., Prince St.	Alexandria	Occupant	1787	Tax L 1787:16
McPherson, Daniel	Alexandria	Tax Charge	1789	Tax PP 1789:13
McPherson, Daniel & Isaac	Alexandria	Tax Charge	1790	Tax PP 1790:10
McPherson, Daniel, merchant	Alexandria	Head	1810	1810(4):04A
McPherson, Danl.	Alexandria	Tax Charge	1788	Tax PP 1788:12
McPherson, Danl.	Alexandria	Tithable +16	1790	Tax PP 1790:10
McPherson, Danl. & I.	Alexandria	Tax Charge	1787	Tax PP 1787:10
McPherson, Danl. & Isaac, Prince St.	Alexandria	Occupant	1790	Tax L 1790:11
McPherson, Danl. & Isaac, Prince St.	Alexandria	Owner	1790	Tax L 1790:08
McPherson, E. & I., Prince St.	Alexandria	Occupant	1790	Tax L 1790:08
McPherson, Isaac	Alexandria	Tithable +21	1787	Tax PP 1787:10
McPherson, Isaac	Alexandria	Tithable +16	1788	Tax PP 1788:12
McPherson, Isaac	Alexandria	Tithable +16	1789	Tax PP 1789:13
McPherson, Isaac	Alexandria	Tithable +16	1790	Tax PP 1790:10
McPherson, Isaac	Alexandria	Tax Charge	1795	Tax PP 1795:21
McPherson, Isaac	Alexandria	Tax Charge	1796	Tax PP 1796:13
McPherson, Isaac	Alexandria	Tax Charge	1796	Tax LP 1796:19
McPherson, Isaac	Alexandria	Mer. License	1798	Tax PP 1798:20-5
McPherson, Isaac	Alexandria	Tax Charge	1798	Tax PP 1798:13
McPherson, Isaac	Alexandria	Account B.	1799	CRB:192
McPherson, Isaac	Alexandria	Tax Charge	1799	Tax PP 1799:27
McPherson, Isaac, def.	Alexandria	Suit	1801	CRB:188
McPherson, Isaac, def.	Alexandria	Suit	1801	CRB:135
McPherson, Isaac, def.	Alexandria	Suit	1801	CRC:147
McPherson, Isaac, def.	Alexandria	Suit	1801	CRB:105
McPherson, Isaac, King St.	Alexandria	Occupants	1790	Tax L 1790:13
McPherson, Isaac, Prince St.	Alexandria	Owner	1795	Tax L 1795:22
McPherson, Isaac, St. Asaph St.	Alexandria	Owner	1795	Tax L 1795:22
McPherson, Isaac, St. Asaph St.	Alexandria	Occupant	1795	Tax L 1795:22
McPherson, Isaac, Union St.	Alexandria	Occupant	1795	Tax L 1795:18
McPherson, John & Co.	Arlington	Suit	1806	ID3:139
McPherson, Jonas	Alexandria	Tithable +16	1790	Tax PP 1790:10
McPherson, Robert Hector	Arlington	Will	1818	WB2:352; File #173A
McPHerson, Isaac & wife, merchant	Alexandria	Housekeeper	1799	1799(2):10A
McQuam, Edwd.	Alexandria	Tax Charge	1795	Tax PP 1795:20
McQuan, Hanah	Alexandria	Head	1810	1810(4):06A
McQueen, Christina Jane	Arlington	Will	1900	WB10:457; File #804A
McQueen, Hannah (C), sempstress	Alexandria	Housekeeper	1808	1808(4):28A
McRady, James	Alexandria	Tax Charge	1789	Tax PP 1789:12
McRea, Ann, c/o James M.	Arlington	Guard.	1815	WB2:017
McRea, Catharine	Arlington	Renounce	1809	WBC:212
McRea, Henry, c/o James M.	Arlington	Guard.	1815	WB2:017
McRea, James, c/o James M.	Arlington	Guard.	1815	WB2:017
McRea, James M.	Alexandria	Tax Charge	1796	Tax PP 1796:12
McRea, James M.	Alexandria	Tax Charge	1799	Tax PP 1799:27
McRea, James M.	Alexandria	Tax Charge	1800	Tax PP 1800:26
McRea, James M.	Arlington	Admin.	1809	WBC:212
McRea, James M.	Arlington	Account	1810	WBC:432; LVA-LP
McRea, James M., clerk P. Bank	Alexandria	Housekeeper	1808	1808(2):13A
McRea, James Mease	Arlington	Inventory	1809	WBC:238; LVA-LP
McRea, James, w(4)6, merchant	Alexandria	Head	1796	1796(3):5
McRea, Jas.	Alexandria	Tax Charge	1795	Tax PP 1795:21
McRea, Jas.	Alexandria	Occupant	1795	Tax L 1795:31
McRea, Jas. M.	Alexandria	Tax Charge	1798	Tax PP 1798:13
McRea, Jno.	Alexandria	Tax Charge	1798	Tax PP 1798:13
McRea, John W.	Arlington	Guard.	1809	WBC:217

NAME OR SUBJECT	LOCATION	TYPE	YEAR	REFERENCE(S)
McRea, Kitty, c/o James M.	Arlington	Guard.	1815	WB2:017
McRea, Robt.	Alexandria	Boarder	1808	1808(2):13A
McRea, William, c/o James M.	Arlington	Guard.	1815	WB2:017
McRea [McCrea], Robert	Alexandria	Tax Charge	1787	Tax PP 1787:11
McReady, J., Queen St.	Alexandria	Occupant	1787	Tax L 1787:22
McReady, James	Alexandria	Tax Charge	1787	Tax PP 1787:12
McReady, James	Alexandria	Tax Charge	1788	Tax PP 1788:11
McReady, James	Alexandria	Tax Charge	1796	Tax PP 1796:13
McReady, James	Alexandria	Tax Charge	1796	Tax LP 1796:19
McReady, James, Prince St.	Alexandria	Occupant	1790	Tax L 1790:06
McReady, Jas.	Alexandria	Tax Charge	1795	Tax PP 1795:19
McReady, Jas., btw. Union	Alexandria	Occupant	1795	Tax L 1795:06
McSweeney, Felix	Alexandria	Tax Charge	1799	Tax PP 1799:27
McSweeney, Philip	Alexandria	Tax Charge	1796	Tax PP 1796:12
McSweeny, Felix, w(2), blacksmith	Alexandria	Head	1796	1796(3):2
McSweeny, Phenix	Alexandria	Tax Charge	1796	Tax LP 1796:21
McSweeny, Philip	Alexandria	Tax Charge	1796	Tax LP 1796:26
McVeigh, William N.	Alexandria	Will	1889	WB1:536; LP
McWhir, William	Alexandria	Tax Charge	1789	Tax PP 1789:13
McWhir, William	Alexandria	Tax Charge	1790	Tax PP 1790:10
McWhir, William, Wolfe St.	Alexandria	Occupant	1790	Tax L 1790:06
McWhir, Wm.	Alexandria	Tax Charge	1788	Tax PP 1788:12
McWilliams, Henry	Alexandria	Will	1892	WB2:031; LP
Mead, Saml.	Alexandria	Boarder	1808	1808(3):19A
Mead, Wm.	Alexandria	Boarder	1808	1808(3):19A
Meade & Eaches	Arlington	Stock	1856	WB7:099; LVA-LP
Meade, Theodore, grantee	Arlington	Indenture D.	1828	ID:164
Meade, Theodore, grantee	Arlington	Indenture D.	1833	ID:407
Meades, Samuel, drayman	Alexandria	Head	1810	1810(3):03A
Meagher, Mathew	Arlington	Will	1861	WB8:072; File #584A
Meara, Francis	Alexandria	Tithable +16	1790	Tax PP 1790:04
Meara [O'Meara], Nancy	Arlington	Account	1818	AB3:203; LVA-LP
Meary, Jno.	Alexandria	Boarder	1808	1808(4):25A
Mease & McRea, Wales' alley	Alexandria	Owner	1795	Tax L 1795:21(2)
Mease, Allison & Hooe	Alexandria	Property	1810	CRH:150
Mease, Robert	Alexandria	Tax Charge	1787	Tax PP 1787:11
Mease, Robert	Alexandria	Tax Charge	1790	Tax PP 1790:09
Mease, Robert	Alexandria	Tax Charge	1796	Tax PP 1796:13
Mease, Robert	Alexandria	Tax Charge	1799	Tax PP 1799:26
Mease, Robert	Alexandria	Tax Charge	1800	Tax PP 1800:26
Mease, Robt.	Alexandria	Tax Charge	1788	Tax PP 1788:10
Mease, Robt.	Alexandria	Tithable +16	1789	Tax PP 1789:12
Mease, Robt.	Alexandria	Tax Charge	1795	Tax PP 1795:20
Mease, Robt.	Alexandria	Tax Charge	1796	Tax LP 1796:19
Mease, Robt.	Alexandria	Tax Charge	1798	Tax PP 1798:13
Mease, Robt., King St.	Alexandria	Occupant	1795	Tax L 1795:26
Mease, Robt., Union St.	Alexandria	Owner	1795	Tax L 1795:21
Mecain, Harriet	Arlington	Guard.	1823	WB3:080
Mechanics Bank of Alexandria, def.	Alexandria	Suit	1817	CRK:301
Mechanics Bank of Alexandria, plt.	Alexandria	Suit	1818	CRK:317
Mechever, Jacob, c/o Mary Yash	Arlington	Apprentice	1805	OCR1801:235
Meclin, Jno.	Alexandria	Tax Charge	1795	Tax PP 1795:19
Meekes, Edward	Alexandria	Resident	1800	1800(4):16B
Meekes, Mary	Alexandria	Serv./Appr.	1800	1800(4):02B
Meekes, Mary	Alexandria	Resident	1800	1800(4):02B
Meeks, Edward	Alexandria	Tax Charge	1800	Tax PP 1800:27
Meeks, Edward, murchant	Alexandria	Boarder	1800	1800(4):16A
Meeks, Elizabeth	Alexandria	Head	1795	1795(4):04
Meins, Andrew, cooper	Alexandria	Boarder	1799	1799(2):04A

NAME OR SUBJECT	LOCATION	TYPE	YEAR	REFERENCE(S)
Mellan, Jacob, c/o Elizabeth	Arlington	Apprentice	1816	OCR1811:341
Mellon, James, lumber merchant	Alexandria	Head	1810	1810(3):07A
Mellson, Jas., carpenter	Alexandria	Housekeeper	1808	1808(3):23A
Melow, John, c/o Anthony	Arlington	Apprentice	1802	OCR1801:028
Mencher, J., Thorn alley	Alexandria	Occupant	1787	Tax L 1787:25
Mendenhall, Martha	Alexandria	Housekeeper	1799	1799(2):06A
Mendenhall, William	Arlington	Inventory	1800	CRA:351
Mendenhall, William	Arlington	Guard. Acct.	1812	AB1:237; LVA-LP
Mendenhall, William	Arlington	Guard. Acct.	1818	AB3:123; LVA-LP
Mendenhall, Wm.	Alexandria	Tax Charge	1795	Tax PP 1795:20
Mendenhall, Wm.	Alexandria	Tax Charge	1796	Tax LP 1796:19
Mendenhall, Wm.	Alexandria	Tax Charge	1796	Tax PP 1796:12
Mendinhall, William, w, shopkeeper	Alexandria	Head	1796	1796(3):4
Menix, Mary Ann, c/o Kitty Hutton	Arlington	Apprentice	1803	OCR1801:083
Menix, Philip, c/o Kitty Hutton	Arlington	Apprentice	1803	OCR1801:082
Mercer, Bessie B., of Savannah GA	Alexandria	Will	1893	WB2:050; LP
Merchant, Alban H., c/o John B.	Arlington	Guard.	1854	BB(np)
Merchant, Eugene, port warden	Alexandria	Deposition	1822	CRL:598
Merchant, Thomas, grantor	Arlington	Indenture D.	1826	ID:022
Merchant, Thomas, in jail bounds	Arlington	Insolvent	1826	ID:020
Merchant, William, Royal St.	Alexandria	Occupant	1787	Tax L 1787:02
Merifield, Mary	Arlington	Account	1853	WB6:258; LVA-LP
Merony, Joseph	Alexandria	Tithable +16	1790	Tax PP 1790:15
Merrick, Alfred (C)	Alexandria	Will	1890	WB1:571; LP
Merrick, Nancy, washer	Alexandria	Head	1795	1795(4):07
Merrick, Wm.	Alexandria	Tax Charge	1795	Tax PP 1795:22
Merriken, Joseph	Arlington	Will	1848	WB5:036; File #442A
Merriken, Joseph	Arlington	Exor. Bond	1848	EBB(np)
Merriken, Joseph	Arlington	Account	1849	WB5:188; LVA-LP
Merryman & Greene, Fairfax St.	Alexandria	Occupant	1790	Tax L 1790:07
Merryman, Joshua	Alexandria	Tax Charge	1787	Tax PP 1787:10
Merryman, Joshua	Alexandria	Tax Charge	1789	Tax PP 1789:12
Merryman, Joshua	Alexandria	Tax Charge	1790	Tax PP 1790:09
Merryman, Jos[h]ua	Alexandria	Tax Charge	1788	Tax PP 1788:11
Merryman, [blank]	Alexandria	Tax Charge	1796	Tax PP 1796:12
Mertland, Jno.	Alexandria	Tax Charge	1798	Tax PP 1798:13
Mertland, John	Alexandria	Tax Charge	1796	Tax PP 1796:13
Mertland, John	Alexandria	Tax Charge	1799	Tax PP 1799:26
Mertland, John	Arlington	Bond	1800	CRA:358
Mertland, John, Duke St.	Alexandria	Occupant	1790	Tax L 1790:06
Mertlin, Susanah, seamstress	Alexandria	Head	1810	1810(3):08A
Mescrop, Henry, teacher	Alexandria	Housekeeper	1808	1808(4):27A
Meservey, Jonatha.	Alexandria	Tax Charge	1790	Tax PP 1790:10
Meservy, Thomas	Alexandria	Tax Charge	1790	Tax PP 1790:10
Messenger, Wm.	Alexandria	Boarder	1808	1808(1):05A
Messersmith, Samual	Arlington	Petition	1842	LVA-LP (Box 214)
Messersmith, Samuel	Arlington	Will	1840	WB4:274; File #381A
Messersmith, Samuel	Arlington	Bond	1840	WB4:275
Messersmith, Samuel	Arlington	Inventory	1841	AB8:179; LVA-LP
Messersmith, Samuel	Arlington	Account	1841	AB8:273; LVA-LP
Messersmith, Samuel	Arlington	Account	1842	OCR1842:007
Messersmith, Samuel	Arlington	Account	1842	OCR1842:004, 005
Messersmith, Samuel	Arlington	Account	1842	AB8:273
Messersmith, Samuel	Arlington	Account	1843	AB8:366; LVA-LP
Messersmith, Samuel	Arlington	Account	1843	AB8:384; LVA-LP
Messersmith, Samuel	Arlington	Account	1843	AB8:364; LVA-LP
Messersmith, Samuel	Arlington	Account	1843	AB8:382; LVA-LP
Messersmith, Samuel	Arlington	Petition	1843	OCR1842:038; LVA-LP
Messersmith, Samuel	Arlington	Debts Due	1844	AB8:450
Messersmith, Samuel	Arlington	Account	1844	AB8:466; LVA-LP
Messersmith, Samuel	Arlington	Sale	1844	AB8:453

NAME OR SUBJECT	LOCATION	TYPE	YEAR	REFERENCE(S)
Messersmith, Samuel	Arlington	Account	1845	AB9:044; LVA-LP
Metcalf, Dwight	Arlington	Will	1857	WB7:256; File #546A
Metcalf, Dwight	Arlington	Inventory	1857	WB7:269; LVA-LP
Meyenberg, Simon	Arlington	Will	1856	WB7:070; File #528A
Meyers, Wm.	Alexandria	Boarder	1799	1799(2):06A
Mezarvey, Ephraim, c/o Thomas	Arlington	Apprentice	1802	OCR1801:044
Mezarvey, Thomas	Alexandria	Tax Charge	1796	Tax PP 1796:13
Mezarvey, Thomas	Alexandria	Tax Charge	1799	Tax PP 1799:27
Mezarvey, Thos.	Alexandria	Tax Charge	1795	Tax PP 1795:20
Mezarvey, Thos.	Alexandria	Mer. License	1798	Tax PP 1798:20-4
Mezarvey, Thos.	Alexandria	Tax Charge	1798	Tax PP 1798:12
Mezarvey, Thos., Union St.	Alexandria	Occupant	1795	Tax L 1795:21
Mezarvey, Thos., Union St.	Alexandria	Owner	1795	Tax L 1795:21
Mezarvy, Thos. & wife, retailer	Alexandria	Housekeeper	1799	1799(2):01A
Mezarvy, Thos., retailer	Alexandria	Housekeeper	1808	1808(2):11A
Mezervey, Thomas, shopkeeper	Alexandria	Head	1810	1810(1):12A
Mezervey, Thomas, w(1)2, shopkeeper	Alexandria	Head	1796	1796(3):6
Mezervey, Thos.	Alexandria	Tax Charge	1796	Tax LP 1796:19
Mezervy, Thos.	Alexandria	Tax Charge	1800	Tax PP 1800:27
Middleton, John	Alexandria	Tithable +16	1788	Tax PP 1788:02
Middleton, John	Alexandria	Tithable +16	1790	Tax PP 1790:02
Miens, Andw., cooper	Alexandria	Boarder	1799	1799(2):15A
Milbourn, Jos.	Alexandria	Mer. License	1800	Tax PP 1800:54(16)r
Milbourn, Joseph	Alexandria	Tax Charge	1798	Tax PP 1798:12
Milbourn, Joseph	Alexandria	Tax Charge	1799	Tax PP 1799:27
Milbourn, Joseph, tavern license	Alexandria	Housekeeper	1808	1808(2):12A
Milbun, Joseph, w(2), joiner	Alexandria	Head	1796	1796(3):6
Milburn, Ann, labourer	Alexandria	Boarder	1800	1800(4):03A
Milburn, Benedict	Arlington	Account	1870	WB9:239
Milburn, Benedict C.	Arlington	Will	1867	WB8:528; File #652A
Milburn, Benedict C.	Arlington	Account	1868	WB9:114
Milburn, Joseph	Alexandria	Mer. License	1798	Tax PP 1798:20-4
Milburn, Joseph	Alexandria	Mer. License	1799	Tax PP 1799:52-07r
Milburn, Joseph	Alexandria	Tax Charge	1800	Tax PP 1800:27
Milburn, Joseph	Arlington	Ordinary	1803	OBL1(np)
Milburn, Joseph	Arlington	Ordinary	1804	OBL1(np)
Milburn, Joseph	Arlington	Ordinary	1805	OBL1(np)
Milburn, Joseph	Arlington	Ordinary	1807	OBL2(np)
Milburn, Joseph	Arlington	Ordinary	1807	OBL2(np)
Milburn, Joseph	Arlington	Ordinary	1808	OBL2(np)
Milburn, Joseph	Arlington	Ordinary	1809	OBL2(np)
Milburn, Joseph	Arlington	Ordinary	1810	OBL2(np)
Milburn, Joseph	Arlington	Bond	1821	WB3:032
Milburn, Joseph	Arlington	Inventory	1821	AB5:006; LVA-LP
Milburn, Joseph	Arlington	Will	1821	WB3:030; File #202A
Milburn, Joseph	Arlington	Account	1823	AB5:188l; LVA-LP
Milburn, Joseph	Arlington	Account	1824	AB5:323; LVA-LP
Milburn, Sarah Florence	Arlington	Guard. Acct.	1868	WB9:110
Milburn, Thomas	Arlington	Will P.	1822	OCR1822:029a
Milburn, Thomas	Arlington	Inventory	1822	AB5:142; LVA-LP
Milburn, Thomas	Arlington	Admin.	1822	OCR1822:030
Milburn, Thomas	Arlington	Bond	1822	WB3:076
Milburn, Thomas	Arlington	Will	1822	WB3:075; File #213A
Mile, James	Alexandria	Tithable +16	1790	Tax PP 1790:13
Miles & Cole, plt.	Alexandria	Suit	1802	CRB:177
Miles, Mary Susan	Alexandria	Will	1887	WB1:474; LP
Miles, Peter, plt.	Alexandria	Suit	1802	CRB:177
Miles, Thomas F., c/o James	Arlington	Apprentice	1812	OCR1811:059
Millan, George	Alexandria	Boarder	1808	1808(3):21A
Millan, James	Arlington	Defendant	1805	ACO:032
Millan, William	Arlington	Guard.	1819	WB2:290

NAME OR SUBJECT	LOCATION	TYPE	YEAR	REFERENCE(S)
Millar, Jacob	Alexandria	Tithable +16	1789	Tax PP 1789:11
Millbourne, Joseph, tavern keeper	Alexandria	Head	1810	1810(2):01A
Miller & Hewes	Alexandria	Mer. License	1799	Tax PP 1799:52-07w
Miller, Absolom	Arlington	Admin.	1809	WBC:242
Miller, Anna	Alexandria	Will	1880	WB1:411; LP
Miller, Benjamin C., grantor	Arlington	Indenture D.	1827	ID:091
Miller, Benjamin C., in jail	Arlington	Insolvent	1827	ID:089
Miller, Benjamin E., grantee	Arlington	Indenture D.	1826	ID:009
Miller, Capt.	Alexandria	Tax Charge	1796	Tax LP 1796:21
Miller, Elisha J.	Alexandria	Will	1895	WB2:125; LP
Miller, Elizabeth, c/o Joseph H.	Arlington	Guard.	1853	BB(np)
Miller, Elizabeth H.	Arlington	Guard. Acct.	1858	WB7:326; LVA-LP
Miller, Enoch	Alexandria	Tax Charge	1795	Tax PP 1795:22
Miller, Eoch, journeyman cooper	Alexandria	Reference	1795	1795(4a):11
Miller, Frederick	Alexandria	Will	1875	WB1:129; LP
Miller, Frederick, blacksmith	Alexandria	Reference	1795	1795(4a):11
Miller, J. Hartshorne	Arlington	Guard. Acct.	1860	WB8:044; LVA-LP
Miller, Jacob	Alexandria	Tithable +16	1788	Tax PP 1788:10
Miller, Jacob	Alexandria	Tax Charge	1790	Tax PP 1790:10
Miller, Jacob	Alexandria	Serv./Appt.	1800	1800(4):16B
Miller, Jacob	Alexandria	Resident	1800	1800(4):16B
Miller, Jacob (non-citizen, servant)	Alexandria	Tithable +21	1787	Tax PP 1787:09
Miller, Jacob, n/o Valentine	Arlington	Apprentice	1814	OCR1811:225
Miller, James	Alexandria	Tax Charge	1800	Tax PP 1800:26
Miller, James, grantor	Arlington	Indenture D.	1827	ID:068
Miller, James, in jail	Arlington	Insolvent	1826	ID:066
Miller, John	Alexandria	Mer. License	1799	Tax PP 1799:52-07r
Miller, John	Alexandria	Tax Charge	1799	Tax PP 1799:26
Miller, John S., of Philadelphia PA	Alexandria	Will	1879	WB1:267; LP
Miller, Mor., merchant	Alexandria	Housekeeper	1808	1808(3):21A
Miller, Mordacai	Alexandria	Tax Charge	1800	Tax PP 1800:27
Miller, Mordecai	Alexandria	Tax Charge	1788	Tax PP 1788:11
Miller, Mordecai	Alexandria	Tax Charge	1789	Tax PP 1789:13
Miller, Mordecai	Alexandria	Tax Charge	1790	Tax PP 1790:10
Miller, Mordecai	Alexandria	Tax Charge	1795	Tax PP 1795:21
Miller, Mordecai	Alexandria	Tax Charge	1796	Tax LP 1796:19
Miller, Mordecai	Alexandria	Tax Charge	1796	Tax PP 1796:13
Miller, Mordecai	Alexandria	Tax Charge	1798	Tax PP 1798:13
Miller, Mordecai	Alexandria	Mer. License	1798	Tax PP 1798:20-4
Miller, Mordecai	Alexandria	Mer. License	1799	Tax PP 1799:52-07r
Miller, Mordecai	Alexandria	Head	1810	1810(3):01A
Miller, Mordecai	Arlington	Claim	1812	ACO:124
Miller, Mordecai	Arlington	Bond	1832	WB4:046
Miller, Mordecai	Arlington	Will	1832	WB4:044; File #300A
Miller, Mordecai	Arlington	Account	1833	AB7:089; LVA-LP
Miller, Mordecai	Arlington	Account	1835	AB7:187; LVA-LP
Miller, Mordecai	Arlington	Account	1836	AB7:187
Miller, Mordecai	Arlington	Account	1841	AB8:248; LVA-LP
Miller, Mordecai, Fairfax St.	Alexandria	Occupant	1790	Tax L 1790:10
Miller, Mordecai, Fairfax St.	Alexandria	Occupant	1795	Tax L 1795:15
Miller, Mordecai, grantee	Arlington	Indenture D.	1828	ID:174
Miller, Mordecai, grantee	Arlington	Indenture D.	1828	ID:177
Miller, Mordecai, Owner	Arlington	Libellant	1818	ACO:152
Miller, Mordecai, Prince St.	Alexandria	Occupant	1795	Tax L 1795:21
Miller, Mordecai, Prince St.	Alexandria	Owner	1795	Tax L 1795:21
Miller, Mordecai, w(1)4, watch maker	Alexandria	Head	1796	1796(3):5
Miller, Peter	Alexandria	Tax Charge	1800	Tax PP 1800:27
Miller, Peter	Alexandria	Boarder	1808	1808(3):20A
Miller, Philip	Alexandria	Tax Charge	1796	Tax PP 1796:13
Miller, Phineas J.	Arlington	Guard. Acct.	1854	WB6:371; LVA-LP
Miller, Phineas J., c/o Robert H.	Arlington	Guard.	1853	BB(np)

NAME OR SUBJECT	LOCATION	TYPE	YEAR	REFERENCE(S)
Miller, Rebecca	Alexandria	Will	1891	WB1:584; LP
Miller, Richard, c/o Elizabeth & Peter	Arlington	Apprentice	1802	OCR1801:041
Miller, Robert	Alexandria	Tax Charge	1796	Tax PP 1796:12
Miller, Robert H.	Arlington	Juryman	1824	ACO:237
Miller, Robert H.	Alexandria	Will	1874	WB1:092; LP
Miller, Robert H., grantee	Arlington	Indenture D.	1830	ID:307
Miller, Robert H., lessee, plaintiff	Arlington	Suit	1841	LSA:152
Miller, Robt., house joiner	Alexandria	Head	1810	1810(3):09A
Miller, Robt., shopkeeper	Alexandria	Housekeeper	1808	1808(3):18A
Miller, Samuel	Alexandria	Will	1876	WB1:197; LP
Miller, William	Alexandria	Tax Charge	1790	Tax PP 1790:09
Miller, William	Alexandria	Tax Charge	1800	Tax PP 1800:27
Miller, William H., grantee	Arlington	Indenture D.	1827	ID:132
Miller, William H., grantee	Arlington	Indenture D.	1827	ID:129
Miller, [blank]	Alexandria	Boarder	1808	1808(2):13A
Milligan, Robert	Arlington	Admin.	1807	WBC:014
Milligan, Robert	Arlington	Admin.	1807	WBB:477
Milligan, Robert	Arlington	Will	1807	WBC:005; File #031A
Milligan, Robert	Arlington	Sale	1810	AB1:005
Milligan, Robert	Arlington	Account	1810	AB1:002
Milligan, Samuel	Arlington	Will	1820	WB2:391; File #181A
Milligan, Samuel	Arlington	Bond	1820	WB2:392
Milligan, Samuel	Arlington	Inventory	1820	AB4:185; LVA-LP
Millner, Wm.	Alexandria	Tax Charge	1798	Tax PP 1798:13
Mills, Catherine Ann	Arlington	Guard.	1839	WB4:228
Mills, Dyson	Arlington	Admin.	1815	WB2:100
Mills, Dyson, labourer	Alexandria	Head	1810	1810(1):06A
Mills, Edward, grantor	Arlington	Indenture D.	1805	ID3:115
Mills, Edward, in gaol	Arlington	Insolvent	1805	ID3:114
Mills, Elizabeth	Arlington	Inventory	1840	AB8:165; LVA-LP
Mills, Elizabeth	Arlington	Admin.	1840	WB4:278
Mills, Elizabeth	Arlington	Account	1841	AB8:226; LVA-LP
Mills, Ephm.	Alexandria	Tax Charge	1798	Tax PP 1798:12
Mills, Ephm.	Alexandria	Tax Charge	1799	Tax PP 1799:27
Mills, Ephraim	Alexandria	Boarder	1799	1799(2):16A
Mills, Ephraim	Alexandria	Tax Charge	1800	Tax PP 1800:27
Mills, Ephraim	Arlington	Inventory	1812	AB1:157, 160; LVA-LP
Mills, Ephraim	Arlington	Admin.	1812	WB1:138
Mills, Ephraim	Arlington	Account	1812	AB1:220; LVA-LP
Mills, Ephraim & wife Rebeca	Alexandria	Resident	1800	1800(4):03B
Mills, Ephraim, laborer	Alexandria	Housekeeper	1808	1808(1):05A
Mills, Ephraim, wh. rite [wheelwright]	Alexandria	Head	1800	1800(4):03A
Mills, Ephraim, wheelwright	Alexandria	Head	1810	1810(1):03A
Mills, Francis	Alexandria	Tax Charge	1789	Tax PP 1789:12
Mills, Francis	Alexandria	Tax Charge	1796	Tax LP 1796:19
Mills, Harvey O.	Arlington	Guard.	1839	WB4:229
Mills, John	Alexandria	Boarder	1808	1808(3):19A
Mills, John	Arlington	Bond	1822	WB3:334
Mills, John	Arlington	Apprentice	1826	OCR1822:119a
Mills, John	Arlington	Account	1846	WB5:099; LVA-LP
Mills, John	Arlington	Admin.	1846	OCR1842:192
Mills, John	Arlington	Inventory	1847	AB9:264; LVA-LP
Mills, John	Arlington	Account	1851	WB5:278; LVA-LP
Mills, John	Arlington	Account	1853	WB6:245; LVA-LP
Mills, John	Arlington	Account	1853	WB6:398; LVA-LP
Mills, John, Jr., def.	Alexandria	Suit	1809	CRH:466
Mills, John P.	Arlington	Guard.	1839	WB4:228
Mills, John S., grantee	Arlington	Indenture D.	1828	ID:181
Mills, John, Sr., of Co. Kent	Arlington	Will	1822	WB3:355
Mills, John, w, waterman	Alexandria	Head	1795	1796(3):7
Mills, Margarett, boarding house	Alexandria	Head	1810	1810(4):02A

NAME OR SUBJECT	LOCATION	TYPE	YEAR	REFERENCE(S)
Mills, Margery, sempstress	Alexandria	Housekeeper	1808	1808(4):26A
Mills, Mary Rebecca	Arlington	Guard.	1839	WB4:228
Mills, Nellie	Arlington	Will	1841	WB3:394
Mills, Rebecca	Arlington	Inventory	1834	LVA-LP
Mills, Rebecca	Arlington	Admin.	1834	WB4:098
Mills, Robert	Arlington	Inventory	1854	WB6:403; LVA-LP
Mills, Robert A.	Arlington	Defendant	1823	ACO:220, 223
Mills, Robert A.	Arlington	Defendant	1824	ACO:241, 243, 247
Mills, Robert A.	Arlington	Defendant	1825	ACO:252, 257
Mills, Robert A.	Arlington	Defendant	1826	ACO:260, 263
Mills, Robert A.	Arlington	Defendant	1827	ACO:266, 273
Mills, Robert A., assignee of	Arlington	Plaintiff	1823	ACO:220, 221
Mills, Robert, c/o William	Arlington	Apprentice	1804	OCR1801:230
Mills, Thomas	Alexandria	Tax Charge	1796	Tax PP 1796:13
Mills, William	Alexandria	Tax Charge	1799	Tax PP 1799:27
Mills, William	Alexandria	Tax Charge	1800	Tax PP 1800:27
Mills, William	Arlington	Admin.	1804	WBA:295
Mills, William	Arlington	Inventory	1804	WBB:011; LVA-LP
Mills, William	Arlington	Will	1870	WB9:238; File #681A
Mills, William, c/o William	Arlington	Apprentice	1804	OCR1801:231
Mills, William, c/o Margery	Arlington	Apprentice	1812	OCR1811:125
Mills, William N.	Arlington	Ordinary	1808	OBL2(np)(2)
Mills, William N.	Arlington	Ordinary	1809	OBL2(np)
Mills, William N.	Arlington	Defendant	1823	ACO:221, 222, 224
Mills, William N.	Arlington	Defendant	1824	ACO:242
Mills, William N.	Arlington	Defendant	1824	ACO:240
Mills, William N.	Arlington	Defendant	1825	ACO:253, 258
Mills, William N.	Arlington	Defendant	1826	ACO:261, 263
Mills, William N.	Arlington	Defendant	1827	ACO:267, 273
Mills, William N.	Arlington	Fid. Bond	1852	FBB(np)
Mills, William N., merchant	Alexandria	Head	1810	1810(3):06A
Mills, Wm.	Alexandria	Tax Charge	1795	Tax PP 1795:20
Mills, Wm.	Alexandria	Tax Charge	1796	Tax LP 1796:19
Mills, Wm.	Alexandria	Tax Charge	1796	Tax PP 1796:12
Mills, Wm.	Alexandria	Tax Charge	1798	Tax PP 1798:12
Mills, Wm., biscuit baker	Alexandria	Housekeeper	1808	1808(1):04A
Mills, Wm. N., merchant	Alexandria	Housekeeper	1808	1808(3):19A
Mills, Wm., w(2)1, mariner	Alexandria	Head	1795	1796(3):7
Mills, [blank], clerk	Alexandria	Boarder	1799	1799(2):06A
Milner, Nathan, Wolf St.	Alexandria	Occupant	1795	Tax L 1795:14
Milner, Wm.	Alexandria	Tax Charge	1796	Tax PP 1796:13
Milner, Wm. & wife, sail maker	Alexandria	Head	1795	1795(4):03
Milnor, William, Jr.	Alexandria	Tax Charge	1799	Tax PP 1799:27
Milnor, Wm. & Co.	Alexandria	Tax Charge	1796	Tax LP 1796:19
Milnor, Wm. & wife, sail maker	Alexandria	Housekeeper	1799	1799(2):18A
Milton, Henry	Arlington	Will	1806	WBB:256; File #015A
Milton, Henry	Arlington	Bond	1806	WBB:262
Minchen, John	Alexandria	Tax Charge	1787	Tax PP 1787:10
Minchin, John	Alexandria	Tax Charge	1788	Tax PP 1788:11
Minchin, John	Alexandria	Tax Charge	1789	Tax PP 1789:12
Miner, John	Alexandria	Resident	1800	1800(4):05B
Miner, John, doctor	Alexandria	Boarder	1800	1800(4):05A
Minicks, John	Alexandria	Head	1800	1800(4):09A
Minicks, John & wife Jinney	Alexandria	Resident	1800	1800(4):09B
Minitree, John	Alexandria	Boarder	1800	1800(4):02A
Minitree, John	Alexandria	Resident	1800	1800(4):02B
Minnigerode, Charles	Alexandria	Will	1895	WB2:106; LP
Minnigerode, Mary	Alexandria	Will	1898	WBC1:078; LP
Minor, Ann	Arlington	Admin.	1846	OCR1842:187
Minor, Ann	Arlington	Account	1846	WB5:119; LVA-LP
Minor, Ann	Arlington	Inventory	1846	AB9:245; LVA-LP

NAME OR SUBJECT	LOCATION	TYPE	YEAR	REFERENCE(S)
Minor, Ann	Arlington	Account	1847	AB9:318
Minor, Daniel	Alexandria	Deposition	1822	CRL:527
Minor, Daniel	Arlington	Trans. Slave	1853	BB(np)
Minor, Daniel	Arlington	Will	1865	WB8:281; File #637A
Minor, Daniel	Arlington	Account	1867	WB8:480, 530
Minor, Daniel, marshall	Alexandria	Head	1810	1810(3):07A
Minor, Elizabeth A.	Arlington	Will	1886	WB10:072; File #721A
Minor, Ellen M.	Arlington	Will	1836	WB4:121; File #342A
Minor, Gilbert S.	Alexandria	Appraisal	1870	WB1:025
Minor, Gilbert S.	Alexandria	Appraisal	1870	WB1:025
Minor, Gilbert S.	Alexandria	Inventory	1871	WB1:026
Minor, Hugh	Arlington	Witness	1804	ACO:023
Minor, John	Alexandria	Tax Charge	1799	Tax PP 1799:27
Minor, John	Alexandria	Tax Charge	1800	Tax PP 1800:26
Minor, Ph. H.	Alexandria	Boarder	1808	1808(2):13A
Minor, Smith	Arlington	Defendant	1841	LSA:075
Minor, Smith and wife	Arlington	Complainant	1837	LSA:024
Minor, William	Arlington	Appraisal	1860	WB7:526; LVA-LP
Minor, William, of *Springfield*	Arlington	Will	1859	WB7:442; LVA-LP
Minor, [blank]	Alexandria	Boarder	1808	1808(4):25A
Minot, Mary (Somers), w/o Smith	Arlington	Defendant	1841	LSA:075
Minter, William, ship carpenter	Alexandria	Head	1810	1810(1):13A
Mire, Thos. Wm.	Alexandria	Tax Charge	1789	Tax PP 1789:13
Mirtland, John	Alexandria	Tax Charge	1789	Tax PP 1789:12
Mirtlin, John	Alexandria	Tax Charge	1788	Tax PP 1788:12
Mitcham, Thos., Pitt St.	Alexandria	Owner	1795	Tax L 1795:22
Mitchel, Benjamin	Alexandria	Tax Charge	1800	Tax PP 1800:27
Mitchel, James & wife, mariner	Alexandria	Head	1795	1795(4):04
Mitchel, John, w(1), merchant	Alexandria	Head	1796	1796(3):5
Mitchel, Wm. (seaman)	Alexandria	Tax Charge	1800	Tax PP 1800:27
Mitchell, Benj.	Alexandria	Tax Charge	1798	Tax PP 1798:12
Mitchell, Benjamin	Alexandria	Tax Charge	1799	Tax PP 1799:26
Mitchell, Elizabeth, sempstress	Alexandria	Housekeeper	1808	1808(3):22A
Mitchell, Horace (C), c/o Peggy	Arlington	Apprentice	1812	OCR1811:108
Mitchell, James	Arlington	Admin.	1805	WBB:163
Mitchell, James & wife, waterman	Alexandria	Housekeeper	1799	1700(2):19A
Mitchell, John	Alexandria	Tax Charge	1796	Tax LP 1796:21
Mitchell, John	Alexandria	Tax Charge	1796	Tax PP 1796:13
Mitchell, John	Alexandria	Tax Charge	1796	Tax PP 1796:12
Mitchell, John Francis	Arlington	Apprentice	1844	OCR1842:085
Mitchell, Judson	Arlington	Appraisal	1852	WB6:174; LVA-LP
Mitchell, Judson	Arlington	Bond	1852	BB(np)
Mitchell, Judson	Arlington	Store Inv.	1853	WB6:212; LVA-LP
Mitchell, Judson	Arlington	Account	1854	WB6:302; LVA-LP
Mitchell, Mary, c/o Mary	Arlington	Apprentice	1805	OCR1801:291
Mitchell, Peggy (C), washwoman	Alexandria	Housekeeper	1808	1808(4):28A
Mitchell, Peggy, washwoman	Alexandria	Housekeeper	1808	1808(2):17A
Mitchell, Samuel	Arlington	Apprentice	1815	OCR1811:352
Mitchell, Sarah	Alexandria	Head	1810	1810(3):03A
Mitchell, Sarah, sempstress	Alexandria	Housekeeper	1808	1808(3):18A
Mitchell, Walter	Alexandria	Tax Charge	1796	Tax PP 1796:12
Mitchell, William	Alexandria	Tax Charge	1799	Tax PP 1799:26
Mitchell, William	Alexandria	Tax Charge	1799	Tax PP 1799:27
Mitchell, William	Arlington	Will	1803	WBA:147; LVA-LP
Mitchell, William	Arlington	Bond	1803	WBA:150
Mitchell, William	Arlington	Inventory	1804	WBB:040; LVA-LP
Mitchell, William	Arlington	Sale	1804	WBB:049
Mitchell, William	Arlington	Account	1808	WBC:059; LVA-LP
Mitchell, William, drayman	Arlington	Admin.	1807	WBB:416
Mitchell, William, drayman	Arlington	Inventory	1807	WBB:476; LVA-LP
Mitchell, William, drayman	Arlington	Sale	1807	WBB:476

NAME OR SUBJECT	LOCATION	TYPE	YEAR	REFERENCE(S)
Mitchell, William Thomas	Alexandria	Will	1878	WB1:248; LP
Mitchell, Wm.	Alexandria	Tax Charge	1788	Tax PP 1788:11
Mitchell, Wm.	Alexandria	Tax Charge	1798	Tax PP 1798:13
Mitchell, Wm. (draym.)	Alexandria	Tax Charge	1800	Tax PP 1800:27
Mitchell, Wm., Capt.	Alexandria	Tax Charge	1796	Tax LP 1796:21
Mitchem, Thomas	Alexandria	Owner	1787	Tax L 1787:20
Mitchem, Thomas, Pitt St.	Alexandria	Occupant	1787	Tax L 1787:20
Mitchum, Thomas	Alexandria	Tax Charge	1796	Tax LP 1796:19
Mix, Thomas & wife Ann	Alexandria	Resident	1800	1800(4):10B
Mix, Thomas, blacksmith	Alexandria	Head	1800	1800(4):10A
Mockaby, Sarah, shopkeeper	Alexandria	Housekeeper	1808	1808(4):29A
Moffett, John	Arlington	Admin.	1842	WB4:311
Moffett, Robert	Arlington	Ordinary	1821	OBL3(np)
Moffett, Robert, at his house	Arlington	Ordinary	1822	OBL3(np)
Moffit, John	Arlington	Inventory	1842	AB8:315
Moffitt, John	Arlington	Account	1843	AB8:408; LVA-LP
Moffitt, John, c/o Hannah	Arlington	Admin.	1842	OCR1842:014
Moffitt, John, grantee	Arlington	Indenture D.	1831	ID:331
Molds, Ann, Fairfax St.	Alexandria	Occupant	1790	Tax L 1790:02
Mollahon, Thomas	Alexandria	Tax Charge	1790	Tax PP 1790:10
Moloa, James	Alexandria	Tax Charge	1788	Tax PP 1788:11
Moloch, Michael	Arlington	Admin. Bond	1848	ABB(np)
Moncaster, Zaccheus, clerk	Alexandria	Boarder	1799	1799(2):08A
Money, Melinda	Alexandria	Head	1810	1810(2):05A
Monk, William	Alexandria	Tithable +21	1787	Tax PP 1787:17
Monroe, Adam (C)	Alexandria	Tax Charge	1795	Tax PP 1795:21
Monroe, Adam (C)	Alexandria	Tax Charge	1800	Tax PP 1800:26
Monroe, Adam (C), ship carpenter	Alexandria	Housekeeper	1808	1808(1):09A
Monroe, Adam & wife, ship carpenter	Alexandria	Head	1795	1795(4):06
Monroe, Adam & wife (C), ship carp.	Alexandria	Housekeeper	1799	1799(2):13A
Monroe, Adam & wife Caran	Alexandria	Resident	1800	1800(4):16B
Monroe, Daniel	Arlington	Admin.	1839	WB4:237
Monroe, Daniel	Arlington	Inventory	1839	AB8:012; LVA-LP
Monroe, Daniel	Arlington	Debts	1840	AB8:112
Monroe, Daniel	Arlington	Account	1840	AB8:168; LVA-LP
Monroe, Daniel	Arlington	Account	1841	AB8:236; LVA-LP
Monroe, Daniel	Arlington	Account	1841	AB8:276; LVA-LP
Monroe, Daniel	Arlington	Account	1841	AB8:184
Monroe, Daniel	Arlington	Account	1842	OCR1842:009
Monroe, Daniel	Arlington	Account	1842	AB8:276
Monroe, Daniel	Arlington	Account	1843	AB8:412; LVA-LP
Monroe, Daniel	Arlington	Distribution	1843	AB8:413
Monroe, Daniel	Arlington	Account	1845	AB9:048; LVA-LP
Monroe, Daniel	Arlington	Account S.	1846	AB9:286; LVA-LP
Monroe, Daniel	Arlington	Account	1846	AB9:289; LVA-LP
Monroe, Daniel	Arlington	Account F.	1847	AB9:292
Monroe, Daniel	Arlington	Account	1847	AB9:286, 289
Monroe, Daniel	Arlington	Receipt	1847	AB9:324
Monroe, Daniel, children of	Arlington	Guard. Acct.	1842	AB8:321
Monroe, Daniel, infants of	Arlington	Petition	1845	LVA-LP (Box 214)
Monroe, Edwin	Arlington	Guard. Acct.	1841	AB8:238
Monroe, Edwin	Arlington	Guard. Acct.	1842	AB8:322; LVA-LP
Monroe, Edwin	Arlington	Guard. Acct.	1847	AB9:287
Monroe, Edwin	Arlington	Guard. Acct.	1847	AB9:290
Monroe, Edwin, b. 3 MAR 1826	Arlington	Guard. Acct.	1843	AB8:416
Monroe, Edwin, c/o Daniel	Arlington	Guard.	1840	WB4:253
Monroe, Edwin, c/o Daniel	Arlington	Guard.	1845	OCR1842:137
Monroe, Edwin, c/o Daniel	Arlington	Guard. Acct.	1852	WB6:104
Monroe, Elizabeth	Arlington	Renounce	1839	WB4:237
Monroe, Harrison L., constable	Arlington	Appointment	1852	BB(np)
Monroe, James T.	Arlington	Guard. Acct.	1841	AB8:239

NAME OR SUBJECT	LOCATION	TYPE	YEAR	REFERENCE(S)
Monroe, James T.	Arlington	Guard. Acct.	1842	AB8:322; LVA-LP
Monroe, James T., b. 21 APR 1824	Arlington	Guard. Acct.	1843	AB8:415
Monroe, James Thomas, c/o Daniel	Arlington	Guard.	1840	WB4:254
Monroe, John M., grantor	Arlington	Indenture D.	1827	ID:095
Monroe, John M., in prison bounds	Arlington	Insolvent	1827	ID:093
Monroe, Marietta E.	Arlington	Guard. Acct.	1841	AB8:237
Monroe, Marietta E.	Arlington	Guard. Acct.	1842	AB8:322; LVA-LP
Monroe, Marietta E.	Arlington	Guard. Acct.	1846	AB9:291; LVA-LP
Monroe, Marietta E., b. 5 NOV 1827	Arlington	Guard. Acct.	1843	AB8:416
Monroe, Marietta E., b. 5 NOV 1827	Arlington	Guard. Acct.	1847	AB9:288, 291
Monroe, Marietta E., c/o Daniel	Arlington	Guard. Acct.	1852	WB6:103; LVA-LP
Monroe, Marietta Elizabeth, c/o Daniel	Arlington	Guard.	1840	WB4:256
Monroe, Marietta Elizabeth, c/o Daniel	Arlington	Guard.	1845	OCR1842:137
Monroe, Robert	Arlington	Will	1852	WB6:054; File #474A
Monroe, Robert M.	Arlington	Will	1858	WB7:374; File #562A
Monroe, Robert Ross	Arlington	Apprentice	1816	OCR1811:343
Monroe, Sarah	Arlington	Inventory	1840	AB8:129; LVA-LP
Monroe, Sarah	Arlington	Will	1840	WB4:245; File #376A
Monroe, Sarah	Arlington	Account	1841	AB8:275; LVA-LP
Monroe, Sarah	Arlington	Account	1842	AB8:275
Monroe, Sarah	Arlington	Account	1843	AB8:409; LVA-LP
Monroe, Shearman	Alexandria	Tax Charge	1795	Tax PP 1795:18
Monroe, Slighter S.	Arlington	Guard. Acct.	1841	AB8:238
Monroe, Slighter S.	Arlington	Guard. Acct.	1842	AB8:322; LVA-LP
Monroe, Slighter S.	Arlington	Guard. Acct.	1843	AB8:414, 415; LVA-LP
Monroe, Slighter S., c/o Daniel	Arlington	Guard.	1840	WB4:255
Monroe, Slighter S., c/o Daniel	Arlington	Release	1845	OCR1842:101
Monroe, Thomas	Arlington	Inventory	1839	AB8:025; LVA-LP
Monroe, Thomas	Arlington	Will	1839	WB4:216; File #366A
Monroe, Thomas	Arlington	Bond	1839	WB4:217
Monroe, Thomas	Arlington	Account	1840	AB8:137; LVA-LP
Monroe, Thomas L.	Alexandria	Will	1891	WB2:002; LP
Monroe, Thomas, plt.	Alexandria	Suit	1801	CRB:264, 269
Monrow, Adam, ship carpenter	Alexandria	Head	1800	1800(4):16A
Monrow, Thos. & wife, hatter	Alexandria	Housekeeper	1799	1799(2):20A
Montacue, Henry, ship carpenter	Alexandria	Head	1810	1810(1):08A
Montague, Lucinda	Alexandria	Will	1900	WB2:383; LP
Montgomerie, Peter	Alexandria	Tax Charge	1790	Tax PP 1790:10
Montgomery, Alexr.	Alexandria	Tax Charge	1795	Tax PP 1795:20
Montgomery, James	Arlington	Apprentice	1812	OCR1811:070
Montgomery, Matthew	Arlington	Letter	1807	WBB:410
Moody, Benjamin	Alexandria	Tax Charge	1800	Tax PP 1800:26
Moody, John	Alexandria	Boarder	1808	1808(3):21A
Moody, Margaret, washer woman	Alexandria	Housekeeper	1799	1799(2):05A
Moon, Henry, weaver	Alexandria	Head	1810	1810(4):06A
Mooney, Mary	Arlington	Inventory	1844	AB8:461; LVA-LP
Mooney, Mary	Arlington	Will P.	1844	OCR1842:067
Mooney, Mary	Arlington	Will	1844	WB4:378; File #413A
Mooney, Neal	Alexandria	Tax Charge	1796	Tax LP 1796:18
Mooney, Neale, bricklayer	Alexandria	Head	1810	1810(2):08A
Mooney, Neil	Alexandria	Tax Charge	1788	Tax PP 1788:11
Mooney, Neil	Alexandria	Tax Charge	1789	Tax PP 1789:11
Mooney, Neil	Alexandria	Tax Charge	1790	Tax PP 1790:09
Mooney, Neil	Alexandria	Deposition	1808	CRH:112
Mooney, Neil & Co., St. Asaph St.	Alexandria	Occupant	1787	Tax L 1787:03
Mooney, Neil, at Brooke's Tavern	Alexandria	Deposition	1810	CRH:133
Mooney, Neil, bricklayer	Alexandria	Housekeeper	1808	1808(2):16A
Mooney, Neil, Oronoka St.	Alexandria	Occupant	1790	Tax L 1790:06
Mooney, Niel	Alexandria	Tax Charge	1795	Tax PP 1795:22
Mooney, Niel	Alexandria	Tax Charge	1796	Tax PP 1796:14
Mooney, Niel, Oronoko St.	Alexandria	Occupant	1795	Tax L 1795:13

NAME OR SUBJECT	LOCATION	TYPE	YEAR	REFERENCE(S)
Mooney, Niell	Alexandria	Tax Charge	1798	Tax PP 1798:12
Mooney, Niell	Alexandria	Tax Charge	1799	Tax PP 1799:28
Moony, Neal	Alexandria	Tax Charge	1800	Tax PP 1800:27
Moony, Neil	Alexandria	Tax Charge	1787	Tax PP 1787:11
Moore, Aaron	Alexandria	Tax Charge	1800	Tax PP 1800:26
Moore, Aaron B., silversmith	Alexandria	Head	1810	1810(4):02A
Moore, Aaron B., watch mender	Alexandria	Housekeeper	1808	1808(4):26A
Moore, Aaron, silversmith	Alexandria	Boarder	1799	1799(2):12A
Moore, Alexander	Alexandria	Deposition	1814	CRI:525
Moore, Alexander	Arlington	Death	1843	OCR1842:029
Moore, Alexr., notary public	Alexandria	Housekeeper	1808	1808(1):02A
Moore, Annie L., w/o W.S.	Alexandria	Will	1900	WB2:394; LP
Moore, Aron	Alexandria	Tax Charge	1799	Tax PP 1799:26
Moore, Bettey	Alexandria	Serv./Appr.	1800	1800(4):08B
Moore, Capt.	Alexandria	Tax Charge	1796	Tax LP 1796:21
Moore, Christr. S.	Alexandria	Boarder	1808	1808(3):22A
Moore, Cleon	Alexandria	Land War.	1783	CRH:400
Moore, Cleon	Alexandria	Tax Charge	1787	Tax PP 1787:10
Moore, Cleon	Alexandria	Tax Charge	1788	Tax PP 1788:11
Moore, Cleon	Alexandria	Tax Charge	1789	Tax PP 1789:13
Moore, Cleon	Alexandria	Tax Charge	1790	Tax PP 1790:10
Moore, Cleon	Alexandria	Tax Charge	1796	Tax PP 1796:12
Moore, Cleon	Alexandria	Tax Charge	1796	Tax LP 1796:21
Moore, Cleon	Alexandria	Tax Charge	1798	Tax PP 1798:13
Moore, Cleon	Alexandria	Tax Charge	1799	Tax PP 1799:27
Moore, Cleon	Alexandria	Tax Charge	1800	Tax PP 1800:26
Moore, Cleon	Arlington	Commission	1801	WBA:334
Moore, Cleon & wife, notary public	Alexandria	Head	1795	1795(4):08
Moore, Cleon & wife, notary public	Alexandria	Housekeeper	1799	1799(2):13A
Moore, Cleon & wife Margret	Alexandria	Serv./Appt.	1800	1800(4):15B
Moore, Cleon, Cameron St.	Alexandria	Occupant	1787	Tax L 1787:08
Moore, Cleon, def.	Alexandria	Suit	1803	CRE:071
Moore, Cleon, lawyer	Alexandria	Head	1800	1800(4):15A
Moore, Cleon, Mason Co. KY	Alexandria	Plat	1796	CRH:392
Moore, Cleon, Mason Co. KY	Alexandria	Plat	1796	CRH:401
Moore, Cleon, N.P. [notary public]	Alexandria	Housekeeper	1808	1808(4):25A
Moore, Cleon, notary public	Alexandria	Head	1810	1810(4):07A
Moore, Cleon, plt.	Alexandria	Suit	1806	CRH:344
Moore, Cleon, St. Asaph St.	Alexandria	Occupant	1790	Tax L 1790:08
Moore, Cleon, St. Asaph St.	Alexandria	Owner	1790	Tax L 1790:08
Moore, Cleon, St. Asaph St.	Alexandria	Occupant	1795	Tax L 1795:09
Moore, Elizabeth, spinster	Alexandria	Head	1795	1795(4):07
Moore, Harrison, gc/o John	Arlington	Apprentice	1804	OCR1801:190
Moore, Harry	Alexandria	Boarder	1808	1808(4):25A
Moore, Henry	Alexandria	Tax Charge	1798	Tax PP 1798:13
Moore, Henry	Alexandria	Tax Charge	1800	Tax PP 1800:26
Moore, Henry	Alexandria	Serv./Appt.	1800	1800(4):15B
Moore, Henry	Arlington	Plaintiff	1802	PA:061
Moore, Henry	Arlington	Admin.	1826	OCR1822:112
Moore, Henry & Thos.	Alexandria	License Due	1800	Tax PP 1800:54(24)
Moore, Jacob	Alexandria	Tax Charge	1787	Tax PP 1787:09
Moore, James	Alexandria	Tithable +16	1788	Tax PP 1788:07
Moore, Jesse, def.	Alexandria	Suit	1801	CRC:166
Moore, Jno. & wife, butcher	Alexandria	Housekeeper	1799	1799(2):16A
Moore, Jno., clerk	Alexandria	Boarder	1799	1799(2):06A
Moore, John	Alexandria	Tax Charge	1799	Tax PP 1799:27
Moore, John	Alexandria	Tax Charge	1800	Tax PP 1800:26
Moore, John	Arlington	Apprentice	1803	OCR1801:141
Moore, John, hatter	Alexandria	Head	1810	1810(1):05A
Moore, Joseph H.	Alexandria	Will	1878	WB1:243; LP
Moore, Julius	Arlington	Inventory	1877	WB9:466

NAME OR SUBJECT	LOCATION	TYPE	YEAR	REFERENCE(S)
Moore, Lewis (C)	Arlington	Apprentice	1811	OCR1811:043
Moore, Ludwell	Alexandria	Boarder	1808	1808(4):25A
Moore, Ludwell Lee, c/o Cleon	Arlington	Apprentice	1802	OCR1801:058
Moore, Mary C.	Alexandria	Will	1883	WB1:353; LP
Moore, Peter	Arlington	Bond	1854	BB(np)
Moore, Peter	Arlington	Account	1858	WB7:295; LVA-LP
Moore, Robt.	Alexandria	Boarder	1808	1808(1):01A
Moore, Sandy	Alexandria	Boarder	1808	1808(4):25A
Moore, Step.	Alexandria	Reference	1808	1808(4):24B
Moore, Steph.	Alexandria	Tax Charge	1798	Tax PP 1798:13
Moore, Stephen	Alexandria	Tax Charge	1796	Tax PP 1796:13
Moore, Stephen	Alexandria	Tax Charge	1799	Tax PP 1799:27
Moore, Stephen	Alexandria	Tax Charge	1800	Tax PP 1800:26
Moore, Stephen	Arlington	Ordinary	1803	OBL1(np)
Moore, Stephen	Arlington	Admin.	1815	WB2:016
Moore, Stephen	Arlington	Inventory	1815	AB2:120; LVA-LP
Moore, Stephen & wife, sea captain	Alexandria	Housekeeper	1799	1799(2):12A
Moore, Stephen, marrener	Alexandria	Head	1800	1800(4):14A
Moore, Stephen, Prince St.	Alexandria	Occupant	1795	Tax L 1795:28
Moore, Stephen, retailer	Alexandria	Housekeeper	1808	1808(4):27A
Moore, Stephen, seaman	Alexandria	Head	1810	1810(4):07A
Moore, Steven & Pheb	Alexandria	Resident	1800	1800(4):14B
Moore, Thomas	Alexandria	Serv./Appt.	1800	1800(4):15B
Moore, Thomas	Arlington	Plaintiff	1802	PA:061
Moore, Thomas, def.	Alexandria	Suit	1801	CRB:099
Moore, Thomas, def.	Alexandria	Suit	1803	CRD:071
Moore, Thos.	Alexandria	Tax Charge	1800	Tax PP 1800:26
Moore, Thos., clerk in bank	Alexandria	Head	1810	1810(4):04A
Moore, Thos., [P. Bank] clerk	Alexandria	Housekeeper	1808	1808(4):27A
Moore, William	Arlington	Guard.	1817	WB2:218
Moore, William	Arlington	Sale	1820	AB4:122
Moore, William	Arlington	Inventory	1820	AB4:097; LVA-LP
Moore, William	Arlington	Account	1822	AB5:103; LVA-LP
Moore, William	Arlington	Apprentice	1827	OCR1822:138
Moore, William S.	Alexandria	Will	1894	WB2:081; LP
Moore, William S., merchant	Alexandria	Head	1810	1810(3):05A
Moore, William S., plt.	Alexandria	Suit	1813	CRI:158
Moore, Wilson Lee	Arlington	Admin.	1825	WB3:201
Moore, Wm. S., soap boiler & merchant	Alexandria	Housekeeper	1808	1808(3):19A
Moorefield, tract called	Arlington	Reference	1840	LSA:055
Moreland, George, on Wolfe St.	Arlington	Ordinary	1822	OBL3(np)
Moreland, Hanson	Alexandria	Boarder	1808	1808(1):05A
Moreland, Leven, carpenter	Alexandria	Housekeeper	1808	1808(4):30A
Moreland, Levin, house joiner	Alexandria	Head	1810	1810(4):02A
Morfet, Wm., preacher	Alexandria	Boarder	1800	1800(4):11A
Morfit, Wm.	Alexandria	Resident	1800	1800(4):11B
Morgan, Ann, c/o Elizabeth	Arlington	Guard.	1804	WBA:291
Morgan, Billy (C)	Alexandria	Boarder	1808	1808(4):27B
Morgan, Billy (C)	Alexandria	Boarder	1808	1808(3):23B
Morgan, Elizabeth, washwoman	Alexandria	Housekeeper	1808	1808(4):27A
Morgan, James, c/o Elizabeth	Arlington	Guard.	1804	WBA:291
Morgan, John	Arlington	Defendant	1823	ACO:225, 226
Morgan, Joshua, c/o Hieram	Arlington	Apprentice	1846	OCR1842:175
Morgan, Susanna, c/o Elizabeth	Arlington	Guard.	1804	WBA:291
Morgan, Thomas, c/o Elizabeth	Arlington	Apprentice	1803	OCR1801:137
Morgan, Thomas, c/o Elizabeth	Arlington	Guard.	1804	WBA:291
Morgan v. Halley's Admr.	Arlington	Suit	1836	LVA-LP (Judgments)
Morgan v. Thompson	Arlington	Suit	1845	LVA-LP (Box 214) (2)
Morgan, William	Alexandria	Tax Charge	1790	Tax PP 1790:09
Morgan, William	Arlington	Inventory	1821	AB4:307; LVA-LP
Morgan, William	Arlington	Admin.	1821	WB3:015

NAME OR SUBJECT	LOCATION	TYPE	YEAR	REFERENCE(S)
Morgan, William (M)	Alexandria	Tax Charge	1790	Tax PP 1790:09
Morgan, William, cooper	Alexandria	Head	1810	1810(4):03A
Morgan, William, Fairfax St.	Alexandria	Occupant	1790	Tax L 1790:07
Morgan, William, shoemaker	Alexandria	Head	1810	1810(3):08A
Morgan, Wm.	Alexandria	Tax Charge	1796	Tax PP 1796:12
Morgan, Wm.	Alexandria	Tax Charge	1798	Tax PP 1798:13
Morgan, Wm.	Alexandria	Serv./Appr.	1800	1800(4):02B
Morgan, Wm.	Alexandria	Boarder	1808	1808(3):21A
Morgan, Wm. & wife Elender	Alexandria	Resident	1800	1800(4):14B
Morgan, Wm., drayman	Alexandria	Head	1800	1800(4):14A
Morgan, Wm., drayman	Alexandria	Head	1810	1810(1):09A
Morgan, [blank], Queen St.	Alexandria	Occupant	1790	Tax L 1790:10
Morhouse, Abm., King St.	Alexandria	Owner	1795	Tax L 1795:21
Morhouse, Abm., King St.	Alexandria	Occupant	1795	Tax L 1795:21
Morison, Hugh, w(3), silver smith	Alexandria	Head	1796	1796(3):6
Morrill, William	Arlington	Inventory	1843	AB8:401; LVA-LP
Morrill, William	Arlington	Guard. Acct.	1843	AB8:417
Morrill, William	Arlington	Will P.	1843	OCR1842:046
Morrill, William	Arlington	Bond	1843	WB4:370
Morrill, William	Arlington	Will	1843	WB4:368
Morrill, William	Arlington	Account	1845	AB9:044; LVA-LP
Morrill, William	Arlington	Receipt	1847	AB9:324
Morris, Daniel	Alexandria	Tax Charge	1800	Tax PP 1800:27
Morris, Daniel, labourer	Alexandria	Head	1810	1810(4):03A
Morris, Elias	Alexandria	Tax Charge	1795	Tax PP 1795:19
Morris, Elias	Alexandria	Tax Charge	1796	Tax PP 1796:12
Morris, Elias	Alexandria	Tax Charge	1798	Tax PP 1798:12
Morris, Elias, w(3), hatter	Alexandria	Head	1796	1796(3):6
Morris, Frederick West	Arlington	Apprentice	1814	OCR1811:219
Morris, James	Alexandria	Tax Charge	1800	Tax PP 1800:27
Morris, James	Alexandria	Head	1810	1810(4):05A
Morris, James (C), laborer	Alexandria	Housekeeper	1808	1808(4):28A
Morris, James, at his house	Arlington	Ordinary	1830	OBL4(np)
Morris, James, at his house	Arlington	Ordinary	1831	OBL4(np)
Morris, Jno.	Alexandria	Tax Charge	1795	Tax PP 1795:20
Morris, Jno.	Alexandria	Tax Charge	1798	Tax PP 1798:12
Morris, John	Alexandria	Tax Charge	1796	Tax LP 1796:19
Morris, John	Alexandria	Tax Charge	1796	Tax PP 1796:13
Morris, John	Alexandria	Tax Charge	1799	Tax PP 1799:26
Morris, John	Alexandria	Tax Charge	1800	Tax PP 1800:27
Morris, John, Fairfax St.	Alexandria	Occupant	1795	Tax L 1795:09
Morris, John Hart, c/o Lucinda	Arlington	Apprentice	1814	OCR1811:220
Morris, John, laborer	Alexandria	Housekeeper	1808	1808(2):16A
Morris, Mark, seaman	Alexandria	Head	1810	1810(3):09A
Morris, Owen, age about 65	Alexandria	Deposition	1767	CRI:246
Morris, Susannah, washer woman	Alexandria	Housekeeper	1799	1799(2):10A
Morrison, Elias	Alexandria	Tax Charge	1796	Tax LP 1796:18
Morrison, Hugh	Alexandria	Tax Charge	1789	Tax PP 1789:13
Morrison, Hugh	Alexandria	Tax Charge	1790	Tax PP 1790:10
Morrison, Hugh	Alexandria	Tax Charge	1799	Tax PP 1799:28
Morrison, Hugh	Alexandria	Tax Charge	1800	Tax PP 1800:26
Morrison, Hugh & wife, silversmith	Alexandria	Head	1795	1795(4):02
Morrison, Hugh & wife, silversmith	Alexandria	Housekeeper	1799	1799(2):19A
Morrison, Hugh & wife Mary	Alexandria	Resident	1800	1800(4):13B
Morrison, Hugh, silversmith	Alexandria	Head	1800	1800(4):13A
Morrison, Hugh, silversmith	Alexandria	Housekeeper	1808	1808(1):04A
Morrison, James	Alexandria	Tax Charge	1787	Tax PP 1787:11
Morrison, James	Alexandria	Tithable +21	1787	Tax PP 1787:11
Morrison, James	Alexandria	Tax Charge	1788	Tax PP 1788:12
Morrison, James	Alexandria	Tax Charge	1789	Tax PP 1789:13
Morrison, James	Alexandria	Tax Charge	1790	Tax PP 1790:09

NAME OR SUBJECT	LOCATION	TYPE	YEAR	REFERENCE(S)
Morrison, James	Alexandria	Tax Charge	1799	Tax PP 1799:27
Morrison, James, Fairfax St.	Alexandria	Occupant	1787	Tax L 1787:07
Morrison, Jas. & wife (C), Laborer	Alexandria	Housekeeper	1799	1799(2):10A
Morrison, John J., of Allegany Co. MD	Alexandria	Will	1889	WB1:531; LP
Morrison, Mary, teacher	Alexandria	Head	1810	1810(1):04A
Morrison, William	Alexandria	Tax Charge	1799	Tax PP 1799:26
Morriss, Charles	Alexandria	Will	1882	WB1:348; LP
Morriss, John	Arlington	Will	1826	WB3:257
Morrow, James, b. Co. Down, Ire.	Arlington	Alien Entry	1823	RA:04/03/23
Morrow, Robert	Alexandria	Tax Charge	1799	Tax PP 1799:26
Morrow, Robert	Arlington	Complainant	1838	LSA:034
Morse, Hannah M., c/o Orland S.	Arlington	Guard.	1835	WB4:088
Morse, Julius	Arlington	Appraisal	1866	WB8:446
Morse, Julius	Arlington	Account	1867	WB8:452
Morse, Sarah, c/o Orland S.	Arlington	Guard.	1835	WB4:088
Morsey, Mial, coach maker	Alexandria	Housekeeper	1808	1808(3):18A
Mortar, Archibald	Alexandria	Tithable +16	1789	Tax PP 1789:02
Mortimer, George W.	Arlington	Guard.	1818	WB2:252
Mortimer, Sarah, sempstress	Alexandria	Housekeeper	1808	1808(4):24A
Mortmer, Sarah, seamstress	Alexandria	Head	1810	1810(4):08A
Morton, Archd.	Alexandria	Tax Charge	1790	Tax PP 1790:10
Morton, Peter, c/o Elizabeth Dunlap	Arlington	Apprentice	1813	OCR1811:157
Morven, tract called	Arlington	Suit	1840	LSA:055, 056, 059
Moseley, Wm.	Alexandria	Tax Charge	1795	Tax PP 1795:19
Moseley, Wm.	Alexandria	Tax Charge	1796	Tax LP 1796:18
Moss, John	Alexandria	Tithable +16	1788	Tax PP 1788:11
Moss, John	Alexandria	Tithable +16	1789	Tax PP 1789:11
Moss, Martha	Arlington	Admin.	1837	WB4:155
Moss, Martha	Arlington	Inventory	1838	LVA-LP (Accounts)
Moss, Martha	Arlington	Account	1838	LVA-LP
Moss, Martha	Arlington	Account	1838	AB7:364; LVA-LP
Moss, Martha	Arlington	Account	1839	AB7:365
Moss, Martha	Arlington	Inventory	1839	AB7:363
Moss, Obediah, c/o Nancy	Arlington	Apprentice	1815	OCR1811:251
Moss, Robert, def.	Alexandria	Suit	1807	CRG:104
Moss, Robert, def.	Alexandria	Suit	1808	CRH:001
Moss, Robt., d. marshall	Alexandria	Housekeeper	1808	1808(4):25A
Moss, Thos. & wife, soldier	Alexandria	Head	1795	1795(4a):07
Moss, Wm.	Alexandria	Serv./Appt.	1800	1800(4):15B
Moss, Wm.	Alexandria	Serv./Appt.	1800	1800(4):15B
Moss, Wm., clerk	Alexandria	Boarder	1799	1799(2):13A
Moten, Fanney, labourrer	Alexandria	Boarder	1800	1800(4):05A
Mott, Randolph	Arlington	Ordinary	1802	OBL1(np)
Mott, Randolph	Arlington	Ordinary	1803	OBL1(np)
Mott, Randolph	Arlington	Ordinary	1804	OBL1(np)
Mott, Randolph	Arlington	Ordinary	1805	OBL1(np)
Mott, Randolph	Arlington	Ordinary	1807	OBL2(np)
Mott, Randolph	Arlington	Ordinary	1810	OBL2(np)
Mott, Randolph	Arlington	Ordinary	1810	OBL2(np)
Mott, Randolph	Arlington	Admin.	1818	WB2:234
Mott, Randolph	Arlington	Inventory	1818	AB3:145; LVA-LP
Mott, Randolph	Arlington	Account	1819	AB3:359; LVA-LP
Mott, Randolph	Arlington	Account	1821	AB5:003; LVA-LP
Mott, Randolph, in[n]keeper	Alexandria	Head	1810	1810(1):04A
Mott, Randolph, tavern keeper	Alexandria	Housekeeper	1808	1808(2):10A
Mott, Randolph [Ann]	Arlington	Dower	1819	AB4:008; LVA-LP
Mott, Thos. R.	Alexandria	Boarder	1808	1808(2):10A
Mouet, Joseph	Alexandria	Tax Charge	1796	Tax PP 1796:13
Mouncey, William, plt.	Alexandria	Suit	1801	CRC:227
Mounsher, William, Royal St.	Alexandria	Occupant	1787	Tax L 1787:18
Mounsher, Wm.	Alexandria	Tax Charge	1787	Tax PP 1787:10

NAME OR SUBJECT	LOCATION	TYPE	YEAR	REFERENCE(S)
Mounsher, Wm.	Alexandria	Tax Charge	1788	Tax PP 1788:12
Mount, Thomas	Arlington	Juryman	1824	ACO:237
Mount, Thomas, grantee	Arlington	Indenture D.	1831	ID:285
Mount, Thos.	Alexandria	Boarder	1808	1808(2):10A
Mount, Thos., merchant	Alexandria	Head	1810	1810(2):03A
Mount, Wm.	Alexandria	Boarder	1808	1808(1):05A
Moxley, Ann Maria	Arlington	Guard.	1810	WBC:329
Moxley, Benjamin, c/o Martha	Arlington	Apprentice	1801	OCR1801:005
Moxley, Benjamin, cooper	Alexandria	Head	1810	1810(3):04A
Moxley, D.	Alexandria	Reference	1808	1808(2):17B
Moxley, Daniel	Alexandria	Tithable +16	1788	Tax PP 1788:06
Moxley, Daniel	Alexandria	Tithable +16	1789	Tax PP 1789:06
Moxley, Daniel	Alexandria	Tax Charge	1796	Tax PP 1796:12
Moxley, Daniel & wife, carpenter	Alexandria	Head	1795	1795(4a):10
Moxley, Danl.	Alexandria	Tax Charge	1795	Tax PP 1795:18
Moxley, Danl.	Alexandria	Tax Charge	1796	Tax LP 1796:18
Moxley, Danl.	Alexandria	Tax Charge	1798	Tax PP 1798:13
Moxley, Danl., Fairfax St.	Alexandria	Owner	1795	Tax L 1795:20
Moxley, Esther	Alexandria	Tax Charge	1788	Tax PP 1788:10
Moxley, George, carpenter	Alexandria	Head	1810	1810(1):07A
Moxley, Harry (C), laborer	Alexandria	Housekeeper	1808	1808(1):09A
Moxley, Harry & wife, carpenter	Alexandria	Head	1795	1795(4):02
Moxley, Henry, ship carpenter	Alexandria	Head	1810	1810(1):06A
Moxley, Mr., *Towlston* from Fairfax	Alexandria	Lease	(nd)	CRH:553
Moxley, Mrs., Oronoka St.	Alexandria	Occupant	1787	Tax L 1787:20
Moxley, Thomas, Estate	Alexandria	Owner	1787	Tax L 1787:20
Moxley, Thomas, Estate	Alexandria	Tax Charge	1787	Tax PP 1787:11
Moxley, William	Alexandria	Tax Charge	1788	Tax PP 1788:11
Moxley, William	Alexandria	Tax Charge	1799	Tax PP 1799:26
Moxley, Wm.	Alexandria	Tax Charge	1795	Tax PP 1795:19
Moxley, Wm.	Alexandria	Tax Charge	1796	Tax LP 1796:18
Moxley, Wm.	Alexandria	Tax Charge	1796	Tax PP 1796:12
Moxley, Wm.	Alexandria	Tax Charge	1798	Tax PP 1798:12
Moxley, Wm., Queen St.	Alexandria	Occupant	1795	Tax L 1795:19
Moyers, Marion T.	Alexandria	Will	1893	WB2:071; LP
Mozengo, Elizabeth, c/o James F.	Arlington	Guard.	1816	WB2:130
Mozengo, Elizabeth, c/o James F.	Arlington	Guard.	1819	WB2:310
Mozengo, William Henry, c/o James F.	Arlington	Guard.	1816	WB2:130
Mozengo, William Henry, c/o James F.	Arlington	Guard.	1819	WB2:310
Mozey, William	Arlington	Apprentice	1823	OCR1822:040
Muckleroy, Jane	Arlington	Apprentice	1805	OCR1801:234
Mudd, Aloysius	Arlington	Apprentice	1812	OCR1811:072
Mudd, George W., c/o Elizabeth	Arlington	Apprentice	1825	OCR1822:095
Muir, Elizabeth L.	Alexandria	Will	1876	WB1:203; LP
Muir [Mure], James, minister	Alexandria	Head	1800	1800(4):11A
Muir, James	Arlington	Inventory	1820	AB4:172; LVA-LP
Muir, James	Arlington	Admin.	1820	WB2:381
Muir, James & wife, minister	Alexandria	Head	1795	1795(4a):07
Muir, James, D.D.	Alexandria	Tax Charge	1796	Tax PP 1796:14
Muir, James, D.D.	Alexandria	Tax Charge	1799	Tax PP 1799:26
Muir, James, doctor of divinity	Alexandria	Head	1810	1810(1):07A
Muir, James, Rev.	Alexandria	Tax Charge	1789	Tax PP 1789:13
Muir, James, Rev.	Alexandria	Tax Charge	1790	Tax PP 1790:11
Muir, James, Rev.	Arlington	Witness	1794	OT:03/07/1794
Muir, Jas. & wife, minister of the gospel	Alexandria	Housekeeper	1799	1799(2):13A
Muie [Muyr], James & wife Elizebeth	Alexandria	Resident	1800	1800(4):11B
Muir, Jas., D.D.	Alexandria	Tax Charge	1798	Tax PP 1798:13
Muir, Jas., M.D.	Alexandria	Tax Charge	1795	Tax PP 1795:22
Muir, Jas., Rev., gentleman	Alexandria	Housekeeper	1808	1808(1):06A
Muir, Jno.	Alexandria	Tax Charge	1795	Tax PP 1795:21
Muir, Jno.	Alexandria	Tax Charge	1798	Tax PP 1798:12

NAME OR SUBJECT	LOCATION	TYPE	YEAR	REFERENCE(S)
Muir, John	Alexandria	Owner	1787	Tax L 1787:20
Muir, John	Alexandria	Tax Charge	1787	Tax PP 1787:10
Muir, John	Alexandria	Tax Charge	1788	Tax PP 1788:11
Muir, John	Alexandria	Tax Charge	1789	Tax PP 1789:12
Muir, John	Alexandria	Tax Charge	1790	Tax PP 1790:09
Muir, John	Alexandria	Tax Charge	1799	Tax PP 1799:26
Muir, John	Alexandria	Tax Charge	1800	Tax PP 1800:27
Muir, John	Arlington	Admin.	1815	WB2:005
Muir, John	Arlington	Inventory	1815	AB2:097; LVA-LP
Muir, John	Arlington	Sale	1816	AB2:339
Muir, John	Arlington	Account	1817	AB3:072; LVA-LP
Muir, John	Arlington	Account	1817	AB3:003
Muir, John	Arlington	Inventory	1817	LVA-LP
Muir, John, cabiner maker	Alexandria	Head	1810	1810(2):01A
Muir, John, cabinet maker	Alexandria	Housekeeper	1808	1808(3):18A
Muir, John, Duke St.	Alexandria	Owner	1790	Tax L 1790:08
Muir, John, King St.	Alexandria	Occupant	1787	Tax L 1787:20
Muir, John, King St.	Alexandria	Occupant	1790	Tax L 1790:08
Muir, John, King St.	Alexandria	Owner	1790	Tax L 1790:08(3)
Muir, John, orphans of	Arlington	Guard.	1817	WB2:202
Muir, John, Royal St.	Alexandria	Owner	1790	Tax L 1790:08
Muir, Josh. (C)	Alexandria	Tax Charge	1796	Tax LP 1796:19
Muir, Moses, Rev. & wife, minister	Alexandria	Head	1795	1795(4):09
Muir, Robert, Estate	Alexandria	Owner	1787	Tax L 1787:19
Muir, Robert, heirs, King St.	Alexandria	Owner	1790	Tax L 1790:08
Muir, William H.	Alexandria	Will	1891	WB1:597; LP
Mulledy, Thomas F., Frederick Co. MD	Alexandria	Will	1871	WB1:030; LP
Mullen, Bryan	Alexandria	Boarder	1808	1808(1):02A
Mullican, Betty, alias Bell, def.	Alexandria	Suit	1802	CRC:220
Mullikin, John	Alexandria	Tax Charge	1789	Tax PP 1789:12
Mullikin, John	Alexandria	Tax Charge	1790	Tax PP 1790:10
Mullikin, John, Oronoka St.	Alexandria	Owner	1790	Tax L 1790:08(2)
Mullikin, John, Oronoka St.	Alexandria	Occupant	1790	Tax L 1790:08
Mullin, Daniel	Alexandria	Tax Charge	1799	Tax PP 1799:26
Mullowney, John	Alexandria	Tax Charge	1799	Tax PP 1799:28
Mumford, John	Arlington	Account	1804	WBA:318, LVA-LP
Mumford, John	Arlington	Settlement	1816	AB2:398
Mumford, Timothy	Alexandria	Boarder	1808	1808(2):11A
Munaster, John	Arlington	Defendant	1805	ACO:038, 039
Muncaster, Jno.	Alexandria	Tax Charge	1795	Tax PP 1795:21
Muncaster, Jno.	Alexandria	Tax Charge	1798	Tax PP 1798:12
Muncaster, Jno. & wife, merchant	Alexandria	Housekeeper	1799	1799(2):15A
Muncaster, John	Alexandria	Tax Charge	1796	Tax PP 1796:14
Muncaster, John	Alexandria	Tax Charge	1799	Tax PP 1799:27
Muncaster, John	Arlington	Defendant	1805	ACO:033, 034
Muncaster, John	Alexandria	Deed	1815	CRL:490
Muncaster, John	Alexandria	Deed	1820	CRL:499
Muncaster, John	Arlington	Admin.	1829	WB3:346
Muncaster, John	Arlington	Admin.	1829	OCR1822:175a
Muncaster, John	Arlington	Inventory	1830	LVA-LP
Muncaster, John	Arlington	Admin.	1843	OCR1842:036
Muncaster, John	Arlington	Account F.	1845	AB9:056; LVA-LP
Muncaster, John	Arlington	Admin.	1854	WB4:352
Muncaster, John & Elisebeth Arll	Alexandria	Resident	1800	1800(4):04B
Muncaster, John & wife Elizabeth	Alexandria	Suit	1809	CRG:131
Muncaster, John, def.	Alexandria	Suit	1801	CRC:039
Muncaster, John, def.	Alexandria	Suit	1822	CRL:389
Muncaster, John, merchant	Alexandria	Housekeeper	1808	1808(1):09A
Muncaster, John, merchant	Alexandria	Head	1810	1810(1):06A
Muncaster, Zach.	Alexandria	Tax Charge	1800	Tax PP 1800:26
Muncaster [Moncaster], Jno.	Alexandria	Tax Charge	1800	Tax PP 1800:26

NAME OR SUBJECT	LOCATION	TYPE	YEAR	REFERENCE(S)
Munford, John	Arlington	Account	1808	WBC:050; LVA-LP
Munford, Peggy (C)	Alexandria	Housekeeper	1799	1799(2):14A
Mung, Jas.	Alexandria	Tax Charge	1795	Tax PP 1795:19
Munkaster, John, merchant	Alexandria	Head	1800	1800(4):04A
Munn, James, churchwarden	Alexandria	Deed	1770	CRI:172
Munn, John	Alexandria	Tax Charge	1796	Tax PP 1796:13
Munroe, Adam	Alexandria	Tax Charge	1796	Tax PP 1796:14
Munroe, Adam & wife, ship builder	Alexandria	Head	1795	1795(4a):07
Munroe, Adam, Royal St.	Alexandria	Occupant	1795	Tax L 1795:22
Munroe, Adam, Royal St.	Alexandria	Owner	1795	Tax L 1795:22
Munroe, Thomas	Alexandria	Tithable +16	1789	Tax PP 1789:16
Munroe, Thomas, postmaster in D.C.	Alexandria	Deposition	1811	CRK:072
Munroe, Thos.	Alexandria	Tithable +16	1788	Tax PP 1788:14
Munroe, Thos.	Alexandria	Tax Charge	1798	Tax PP 1798:12
Munroe, Thos., Royal St.	Alexandria	Occupant	1795	Tax L 1795:26
Munrowe, Carey, labourer	Alexandria	Head	1810	1810(1):12A
Murdaugh, Roberta Shield	Alexandria	Will	1900	WB2:408; LP
Murdock, John	Alexandria	Tax Charge	1796	Tax LP 1796:18
Murgatroyd, Samuel	Arlington	Admin.	1808	WBC:035
Murphey, Francis	Alexandria	Tax Charge	1800	Tax PP 1800:26
Murphy, Francis	Alexandria	Mer. License	1800	Tax PP 1800:54(16)r
Murphy, Francis James	Alexandria	Will	1877	WBC1:025; LP
Murphy, Francis, merchant	Alexandria	Head	1810	1810(2):01A
Murphy, Francis, retailer	Alexandria	Housekeeper	1808	1808(2):11A
Murphy, Jas.	Alexandria	Boarder	1808	1808(2):12A
Murphy, John	Alexandria	Tithable +16	1788	Tax PP 1788:12
Murphy, John Parker	Arlington	Will	1899	WB10:365; File #786A
Murphy, John, plt.	Alexandria	Suit	1821	CRL:162
Murphy, Michael	Alexandria	Tithable +16	1788	Tax PP 1788:05
Murphy, Owen	Alexandria	Tithable +21	1787	Tax PP 1787:08
Murphy, Owen	Alexandria	Tithable +16	1788	Tax PP 1788:01
Murphy, Owen	Alexandria	Tithable +16	1789	Tax PP 1789:10
Murphy, Owen	Alexandria	Tithable +16	1790	Tax PP 1790:01
Murphy, Owen	Alexandria	Tax Charge	1795	Tax PP 1795:18
Murphy, Owen	Alexandria	Tax Charge	1796	Tax PP 1796:13
Murphy, Patrick	Alexandria	Tithable +16	1788	Tax PP 1788:12
Murphy, Robert	Alexandria	Tax Charge	1796	Tax PP 1796:12
Murphy, Thos.	Alexandria	Tax Charge	1788	Tax PP 1788:12
Murphy, Wm.	Alexandria	Tax Charge	1796	Tax LP 1796:18
Murran, Roger & wife, ship carpenter	Alexandria	Head	1795	1795(4):04
Murray & Porter	Alexandria	Tax Charge	1796	Tax LP 1796:21
Murray & Wheaton	Alexandria	Tax Charge	1790	Tax PP 1790:09
Murray, Ann O., c/o Ignatius	Arlington	Guard.	1841	WB4:286
Murray, Charles, b. Londonderry	Arlington	Alien Entry	1821	RA:01/03/21
Murray, Edward	Alexandria	Tax Charge	1799	Tax PP 1799:26
Murray, George	Alexandria	Tithable +16	1788	Tax PP 1788:17
Murray, George W.	Alexandria	Tithable +16	1790	Tax PP 1790:09
Murray, Ignatius, taylor	Alexandria	Housekeeper	1808	1808(1):08A
Murray, James	Alexandria	Tax Charge	1789	Tax PP 1789:12
Murray, James	Alexandria	Tax Charge	1790	Tax PP 1790:10
Murray, James	Alexandria	Tax Charge	1796	Tax PP 1796:13
Murray, James	Alexandria	Tax Charge	1796	Tax LP 1796:18
Murray, James	Alexandria	Tax Charge	1799	Tax PP 1799:26
Murray, James, taylor	Alexandria	Head	1810	1810(2):05A
Murray, Jas.	Alexandria	Tax Charge	1798	Tax PP 1798:12
Murray, Jas., Fairfax St.	Alexandria	Occupant	1795	Tax L 1795:05
Murray, Jas., taylor & shopkeeper	Alexandria	Housekeeper	1808	1808(2):14A
Murray, John	Alexandria	Tax Charge	1787	Tax PP 1787:11
Murray, John	Alexandria	Tax Charge	1788	Tax PP 1788:11
Murray, John	Alexandria	Tithable +16	1788	Tax PP 1788:08
Murray, John	Alexandria	Tax Charge	1789	Tax PP 1789:12

NAME OR SUBJECT	LOCATION	TYPE	YEAR	REFERENCE(S)
Murray, John	Alexandria	Tax Charge	1790	Tax PP 1790:10
Murray, John	Alexandria	Tax Charge	1796	Tax LP 1796:19
Murray, John & Co., Prince St.	Alexandria	Owner	1795	Tax L 1795:22
Murray, John, Duke St.	Alexandria	Owner	1795	Tax L 1795:22
Murray, John, Pitt St.	Alexandria	Occupant	1787	Tax L 1787:15
Murray, John, Prince St.	Alexandria	Occupant	1787	Tax L 1787:18
Murray, John, Prince St.	Alexandria	Occupant	1790	Tax L 1790:08
Murray, John, Prince St.	Alexandria	Owner	1790	Tax L 1790:08
Murray, John, Sr., at New York City	Alexandria	Deposition	1805	CRF:248
Murray, John, Water St.	Alexandria	Occupant	1790	Tax L 1790:12
Murray, Nace, taylor	Alexandria	Head	1810	1810(4):06A
Murray, P., Prince St.	Alexandria	Occupant	1787	Tax L 1787:20
Murray, Patrick	Alexandria	Owner	1787	Tax L 1787:20
Murray, Patrick	Alexandria	Tax Charge	1787	Tax PP 1787:10
Murray, Patrick	Alexandria	Tax Charge	1788	Tax PP 1788:11
Murray, Patrick	Alexandria	Tax Charge	1789	Tax PP 1789:13
Murray, Patrick	Alexandria	Tax Charge	1790	Tax PP 1790:10
Murray, Patrick	Arlington	Will	1802	WBA:069; LVA-LP
Murray, Patrick, Prince St.	Alexandria	Occupant	1790	Tax L 1790:08
Murray, Patrick, Prince St.	Alexandria	Owner	1790	Tax L 1790:08
Murray, Patrick, St. Asaph St.	Alexandria	Occupant	1787	Tax L 1787:03
Murray, Peter	Alexandria	Tithable +16	1788	Tax PP 1788:11
Murray, Peter	Alexandria	Tithable +16	1789	Tax PP 1789:13
Murray, Peter	Alexandria	Tithable +16	1790	Tax PP 1790:10
Murray, Sarah	Arlington	Account	1832	AB7:041; LVA-LP
Murray, Sarah	Arlington	Guard. Acct.	1838	AB8:146; LVA-LP
Murray, Sarah	Arlington	Guard. Acct.	1840	AB8:146; LVA-LP
Murray, Sarah Ann	Arlington	Guard.	1832	WB4:067
Murray, Sarah [McLanahan]	Arlington	Account	1844	AB9:004; LVA-LP
Murray, Thomas	Alexandria	Tax Charge	1799	Tax PP 1799:26
Murray, Thomas	Arlington	Guard.	1802	WBA:089
Murray, Thomas	Arlington	Will	1821	WB2:422; File #192A
Murray, Thomas	Arlington	Inventory	1821	AB4:230; LVA-LP
Murray, Thomas	Arlington	Bond	1821	WB2:423
Murray, Thomas	Arlington	Sale	1822	AB5:073
Murray, Thomas	Arlington	Account	1822	AB5:071; LVA-LP
Murray, Thomas	Arlington	Account	1839	LVA-LP
Murray, Thomas	Arlington	Distribution	1840	AB8:117
Murray, Thomas, w(1)1, carpenter	Alexandria	Head	1796	1796(3):3
Murray, Thos.	Alexandria	Tax Charge	1796	Tax PP 1796:12
Murray, Thos.	Alexandria	Tax Charge	1796	Tax LP 1796:19
Murray, Thos.	Alexandria	Reference	1808	1808(4):29B
Murray, Thos. & wife, carpenter	Alexandria	Housekeeper	1799	1799(2):11A
Murray, William	Alexandria	Will	1899	WB2:346; LP
Murray, [blank], shoemaker	Alexandria	Boarder	1799	1799(2):04A
Murry, James	Alexandria	Tax Charge	1800	Tax PP 1800:27
Murry, Sarah Edmonds, c/o Thomas	Arlington	Guard.	1821	WB3:026
Murry, Thos.	Alexandria	Tax Charge	1800	Tax PP 1800:26
Murtland, John	Alexandria	Tax Charge	1796	Tax LP 1796:18
Murtland, Robert, c/o Susannah Massey	Arlington	Apprentice	1804	OCR1801:173
Murtlin, Jno., Washington St.	Alexandria	Occupant	1795	Tax L 1795:20
Murtlin, John, Washington St.	Alexandria	Owner	1795	Tax L 1795:20
Muse, Jno.	Alexandria	Tax Charge	1795	Tax PP 1795:21
Muse, Waker, plt.	Alexandria	Suit	1803	CRH:219
Musgrave, Israel	Alexandria	Tax Charge	1798	Tax PP 1798:12
Musgrave, Israel & wife, carpenter	Alexandria	Housekeeper	1799	1799(2):20A
Musklan, James	Alexandria	Tax Charge	1787	Tax PP 1787:11
Mussleman, Jacob, plt.	Alexandria	Ejectment	1802	CRE:242
Mutton, John & wife, mariner	Alexandria	Head	1795	1795(4):01
Mutual Assurance Society & Co., plt.	Alexandria	Suit	1814	CRI:363
Mutual Assurance Society, plt.	Alexandria	Suit	1808	CRG:332

NAME OR SUBJECT	LOCATION	TYPE	YEAR	REFERENCE(S)
Mutual Assurance Society, plt.	Alexandria	Suit	1808	CRG:337, 343
Mutual Assurance Society, plt.	Alexandria	Suit	1810	CRH:154
Mutual Assurance Society, plt.	Alexandria	Suit	1817	CRL:015
Mutual Assurance Society, plt.	Alexandria	Suit	1817	CRK:256
Myers, Alexander, at his house	Arlington	Ordinary	1836	OBL5(np)
Myers, Catherine	Arlington	Guard.	1817	WB2:216
Myers, Elizabeth	Arlington	Guard.	1827	OCR1822:143a
Myers, George	Arlington	Guard. Acct.	1811	AB1:109; LVA-LP
Myers, George	Arlington	Guard. Acct.	1812	AB1:253; LVA-LP
Myers, George	Arlington	Guard. Acct.	1813	AB1:329; LVA-LP
Myers, George, c/o John	Arlington	Guard. Acct.	1806	WBB:311; LVA-LP
Myers, George, c/o John	Arlington	Guard.	1806	WBB:230
Myers, Jno., bottler	Alexandria	Boarder	1799	1799(2):15A
Myers, John	Alexandria	Tax Charge	1799	Tax PP 1799:27
Myers, John	Alexandria	Tax Charge	1800	Tax PP 1800:27
Myers, John	Arlington	Inventory	1802	WBA:066; LVA-LP
Myers, John	Arlington	Admin.	1802	WBA:065
Myers, John	Arlington	Account	1805	WBB:119, 310; LVA-LP
Myers, John	Arlington	Account	1806	LVA-LP
Myers, Joseph	Alexandria	Tax Charge	1799	Tax PP 1799:27
Myers, Joseph	Alexandria	Tax Charge	1800	Tax PP 1800:26
Myers, Joseph	Arlington	Inventory	1816	AB2:299; LVA-LP
Myers, Joseph	Arlington	Admin.	1816	WB2:121
Myers, Joseph	Arlington	Account	1818	AB3:191; LVA-LP
Myers, Joseph, carpenter & shopkeeper	Alexandria	Housekeeper	1808	1808(1):08A
Myers, Joseph, house joiner	Alexandria	Head	1810	1810(3):06A
Myers, Margaret	Arlington	Ordinary	1805	OBL1(np)
Myers, Marian Twiggs	Alexandria	Will	1892	WB2:071
Myers, Moses	Alexandria	Deposition	1805	CRF:273
Myers, Rebecca	Arlington	Guard.	1822	WB3:043
Myers, William	Alexandria	Tax Charge	1799	Tax PP 1799:27
Myers, William	Alexandria	Tax Charge	1800	Tax PP 1800:26
Myers, Wm.	Alexandria	Tax Charge	1798	Tax PP 1798:12
Myers, Wm.	Alexandria	Mer. License	1799	Tax PP 1799:52-07r
Myers, Wm.	Alexandria	Reference	1808	1808(3):20B
Myler, James	Alexandria	Tax Charge	1787	Tax PP 1787:11
Myler, James, Union St.	Alexandria	Occupant	1787	Tax L 1787:01
Mylisher, Wm.	Alexandria	Boarder	1808	1808(3):22A
Myres, Alexander K.	Arlington	Complainant	(nd)	LSA:124
Myres, Rebecca (Suter), w/o Alexander	Arlington	Complainant	(nd)	LSA:124
Myrtland, John	Alexandria	Tax Charge	1800	Tax PP 1800:27

NAME OR SUBJECT	LOCATION	TYPE	YEAR	REFERENCE(S)
N				
Nagel, Jacob	Alexandria	Will	1878	WB1:230; LP
Nailer, Allison	Arlington	Apprentice	1826	OCR1822:117
Nailor, Allison	Arlington	Apprentice	1825	OCR1822:098
Nailor, Thomas	Arlington	Apprentice	1825	OCR1822:100a
Nailor, Thompson	Arlington	Ordinary	1821	OBL3(np)
Nailor, Thompson	Arlington	Inventory	1823	LVA-LP
Nailor, Thompson	Arlington	Admin.	1823	OCR1822:053
Nailor, Thompson	Arlington	Admin.	1823	WB3:108
Nailor, Thompson, in Alexandria Co.	Arlington	Ordinary	1822	OBL3(np)
Nairn, James, retailer	Alexandria	Housekeeper	1808	1808(3):20A
Nalls, James W.	Alexandria	Will	1888	WB1:495; LP
Nals, Geo. W.	Alexandria	Boarder	1808	1808(4):25A
Nanter, Henny, sempster	Alexandria	Boarder	1800	1800(4):08A
Naris, Charles	Arlington	Inventory	1823	AB5:203
Nash, Hanner	Alexandria	Resident	1800	1800(4):07B
Nash, Hanner, laundress	Alexandria	Boarder	1800	1800(4):07A
Nash, Michael Henry	Alexandria	Will	1898	WB2:302
Nash, Robert	Arlington	Inventory	1814	AB2:043; LVA-LP
Nash, Robert	Arlington	Admin.	1814	WB1:288
Nash, Robert, c/o Robert	Arlington	Guard.	1821	WB3:037
Nash, Robt., gunsmith	Alexandria	Housekeeper	1808	1808(2):11A
Nash, Robt., gunsmith	Alexandria	Head	1810	1810(2):01A
Natcellus, Leoly (C)	Arlington	Apprentice	1813	OCR1811:196
Neal, Daniel & wife Susanner	Alexandria	Resident	1800	1800(4):08B
Neal, Danil, carpenter	Alexandria	Head	1800	1800(4):08A
Neal, Edward	Alexandria	Mer. License	1799	Tax PP 1799:52-08r
Neal, John	Alexandria	Tax Charge	1796	Tax LP 1796:22
Neal, Nancey	Alexandria	Serv./Appt.	1800	1800(4):15B
Neal, Rebecca, Mrs.	Arlington	Inventory	1832	LVA-LP
Neale, Ann Olivia, c/o Jeremiah A.	Arlington	Guard.	1817	WB2:119
Neale, Christopher	Arlington	Family III	1845	OCR1842:135
Neale, Christopher	Arlington	Will	1863	WB8:172; File #604A
Neale, Christopher, Attorney	Arlington	Oath	1826	ACO:262
Neale, Christopher, grantee	Arlington	Indenture D.	1826	ID:044
Neale, Christopher, grantee	Arlington	Indenture D.	1827	ID:136
Neale, Christopher, grantee	Arlington	Indenture D.	1828	ID:200
Neale, Christopher, grantee	Arlington	Indenture D.	1828	ID:217
Neale, Christopher, grantee	Arlington	Indenture D.	1830	ID:273
Neale, Christopher, grantee	Arlington	Indenture D.	1830	ID:278
Neale, Christopher, grantee	Arlington	Indenture D.	1831	ID:295
Neale, Christopher, Hon.	Arlington	Appointment	1826	OCR1822:121
Neale, Christopher, merchant	Alexandria	Head	1810	1810(2):03A
Neale, Francis, schooner owner	Arlington	Respondent	1804	ACO:029
Neale, Francis, schooner owner	Arlington	Respondent	1805	ACO:035
Neale, Harriet	Arlington	Will P.	1846	OCR1842:189
Neale, Harriet	Arlington	Will	1846	WB4:430; File #437A
Neale, J.A.	Arlington	Sale	1816	AB2:276
Neale, J.A., tavern keeper	Alexandria	Head	1810	1810(2):01A
Neale, Jeremiah A.	Arlington	Ordinary	1808	OBL2(np)
Neale, Jeremiah A.	Arlington	Ordinary	1809	OBL2(np)
Neale, Jeremiah A.	Arlington	Ordinary	1810	OBL2(np)
Neale, Jeremiah A.	Arlington	Inventory	1815	AB2:231; LVA-LP
Neale, Jeremiah A.	Arlington	Will	1815	WB2:075
Neale, Jeremiah A.	Arlington	Bond	1815	WB2:098
Neale, Jeremiah A.	Arlington	Account	1816	AB2:368
Neale, Jeremiah, boarding house	Alexandria	Head	1810	1810(1):01A
Neale, Jno. B.	Alexandria	Tax Charge	1798	Tax PP 1798:14
Neale, John B.	Alexandria	Mer. License	1798	Tax PP 1798:20-5
Neale, Joseph & J.R.	Alexandria	Tax Charge	1799	Tax PP 1799:30
Neale, Lizzie E.	Alexandria	Will	1878	WB1:247; LP

NAME OR SUBJECT	LOCATION	TYPE	YEAR	REFERENCE(S)
Neale, Mary Carlin, c/o Jeremiah A.	Arlington	Guard.	1817	WB2:119
Neale, Sarah M.	Arlington	Defendant	1838	LSA:034
Neale, Thomas	Alexandria	Tax Charge	1799	Tax PP 1799:30
Neale, William	Arlington	Defendant	1819	ACO:157, 160-163
Neale, William, schooner owner	Arlington	Respondent	1804	ACO:029
Neale, William, schooner owner	Arlington	Respondent	1805	ACO:035
Neblon, Jno. Jas.	Alexandria	Mer. License	1798	Tax PP 1798:20-5
Neblon, Jno. Jas.	Alexandria	Tax Charge	1798	Tax PP 1798:14
Neblon, John	Alexandria	Tax Charge	1796	Tax LP 1796:22
Negro London (C)	Alexandria	Tax Charge	1788	Tax PP 1788:10
Negro London (C)	Alexandria	Tax Charge	1789	Tax PP 1789:11
Negro London (C)	Alexandria	Tax Charge	1790	Tax PP 1790:09
Negro London, a pauper, plt.	Alexandria	Suit	1805	CRF:102
Neil, Jeremiah	Alexandria	Tithable +16	1788	Tax PP 1788:03
Neil, John, w, merchant	Alexandria	Head	1796	1796(3):5
Neil, William	Arlington	Admin. Bond	1848	ABB(np)
Neill, Jno.	Alexandria	Tax Charge	1795	Tax PP 1795:22
Neill, Jno.	Alexandria	Boarder	1808	1808(2):12A
Neill, John	Alexandria	Tax Charge	1796	Tax PP 1796:14
Neill, John	Arlington	Plaintiff	1801	PA:172
Neill, Lemuel Charity, c/o John	Arlington	Apprentice	1815	OCR1811:292
Neill, Mary A., c/o Rebecca	Arlington	Guard.	1832	WB4:023
Neill, Rebecca	Arlington	Bond	1831	WB4:023
Neill, Rebecca	Arlington	Will	1831	WB4:022; File #306A
Neill, Rebecca	Arlington	Account	1832	LVA-LP
Neill, Rebecca	Arlington	Account	1835	AB7:142
Neill, Samuel, c/o John	Arlington	Apprentice	1815	OCR1811:302
Neille, Macalina	Arlington	Apprentice	1823	OCR1822:051a
Nelson, Elizabeth C.	Arlington	Will	1895	WB10:306; File #767A
Nelson, Fame	Arlington	Inventory	1812	AB1:151; LVA-LP
Nelson, Fame	Arlington	Admin.	1812	WB1:135
Nelson, Fame	Arlington	Account	1813	AB1:283; LVA-LP
Nelson, Fanny, sempstress	Alexandria	Housekeeper	1808	1808(4):24A
Nelson, Hendley	Arlington	Ordinary	1810	OBL2(np)
Nelson, Hendley	Arlington	Ordinary	1810	OBL2(np)
Nelson, Henley	Arlington	Ordinary	1810	OBL2(np)
Nelson, John, alias Duff	Arlington	Defendant	1805	ACO:040
Nelson, John, alias Duff	Arlington	Defendant	1806	ACO:050
Nelson, John, alias Duff	Arlington	Respondent	1808	ACO:081
Nelson, John, sailor & retailer	Alexandria	Housekeeper	1808	1808(3):21A
Nelson, John, seaman	Alexandria	Housekeeper	1808	1808(2):10A
Nelson, John, seaman	Alexandria	Head	1810	1810(3):01A
Nelson, Phanie, seamstress	Alexandria	Head	1810	1810(4):08A
Nelson, Philip	Alexandria	Tithable +16	1788	Tax PP 1788:08
Nesbett, Robert	Arlington	Debts Due	1821	AB5:018
Nesbett, Robert	Arlington	Sale	1821	AB5:010
Nesbett, Robert	Arlington	Admin.	1821	WB3:022
Nesbitt, Robert	Arlington	Inventory	1821	AB4:332; LVA-LP
Nevan, Duncan	Alexandria	Tax Charge	1796	Tax LP 1796:22
Nevett, Chas. L., merchant	Alexandria	Head	1810	1810(4):08A
Nevett, Joseph, at his house	Arlington	Ordinary	1837	OBL5(np)
Nevett, Joseph, at his house	Arlington	Ordinary	1838	OBL5(np)
Nevett, Joseph, at his house	Arlington	Ordinary	1841	OBL6(np)
Nevin, Duncan	Alexandria	Tax Charge	1790	Tax PP 1790:11
Nevin, Duncan	Alexandria	Tax Charge	1795	Tax PP 1795:22
Nevin, Duncan	Alexandria	Tax Charge	1796	Tax PP 1796:14
Nevin, Duncan	Alexandria	Tax Charge	1798	Tax PP 1798:14
Nevin, Duncan	Alexandria	Tax Charge	1799	Tax PP 1799:30
Nevin, Duncan	Alexandria	Tax Charge	1800	Tax PP 1800:31
Nevin, Duncan	Arlington	Defendant	1802	PA:155
Nevin, Duncan	Arlington	Defendant	1802	PA:141

NAME OR SUBJECT	LOCATION	TYPE	YEAR	REFERENCE(S)
Nevin, Duncan	Arlington	Sale	1806	WBB:282
Nevin, Duncan	Arlington	Inventory	1806	WBB:264; LVA-LP
Nevin, Duncan	Arlington	Admin.	1806	WBB:263
Nevin, Duncan	Arlington	Account	1807	WBB:501
Nevitt & Baden, merchants	Alexandria	Housekeeper	1808	1808(3):19A
Nevitt, Benj. Alexander, c/o Charles L.	Arlington	Guard.	1814	WB1:284
Nevitt, Charles L., merchant	Alexandria	Housekeeper	1808	1808(4):29A
Nevitt, George G., c/o Charles L.	Arlington	Guard.	1811	WB1:066
Nevitt, Harriet B., c/o Charles L.	Arlington	Guard.	1811	WB1:066
Nevitt, Henry J.	Alexandria	Will	1899	WB2:316
Nevitt, John	Alexandria	Tax Charge	1800	Tax PP 1800:31
Nevitt, John	Alexandria	Boarder	1808	1808(2):17A
Newby, Exum	Arlington	Admin.	1818	WB2:228
Newby, Richard	Alexandria	Tithable +16	1790	Tax PP 1790:16
Newhouse, John H.	Alexandria	Boarder	1808	1808(3):22A
Newman, Ann	Alexandria	Head	1795	1795(4a):08
Newman, Ann, Fairfax St.	Alexandria	Occupant	1790	Tax L 1790:02
Newman, Elias	Alexandria	Tax Charge	1795	Tax PP 1795:22
Newman, Geo.	Alexandria	Head	1810	1810(4):08A
Newman, Geo. (C), gardener	Alexandria	Housekeeper	1808	1808(4):24A
Newman, James	Arlington	Apprentice	1815	OCR1811:258
Newman, John	Arlington	Apprentice	1815	OCR1811:253
Newman, Land & Hunt, plt.	Alexandria	Suit	1801	CRB:344
Newman, Mary A.	Alexandria	Will	1890	WB1:581; LP
Newmann, Elias	Alexandria	Tax Charge	1796	Tax PP 1796:14
Newton & Roby	Alexandria	Tax Charge	1799	Tax PP 1799:30
Newton, A.G., at Marshal House	Arlington	Ordinary	1847	OBL6(np)
Newton, Agusta, merchant	Alexandria	Head	1810	1810(2):01A
Newton, Albert G., at his house	Arlington	Ordinary	1849	OBL6(np)
Newton, Albert G., in Alexandria Co.	Arlington	Ordinary	1848	OBL6(np)
Newton, Albert G., on King St.	Arlington	Ordinary	1845	OBL6(np)
Newton, Albert O., c/o William	Arlington	Guard.	1817	WB2:169
Newton, Albert, on King St.	Arlington	Ordinary	1846	OBL6(np)
Newton, Augustine	Arlington	Defendant	1824	ACO:242, 248
Newton, Augustine	Arlington	Defendant	1826	ACO:261, 264
Newton, Augustine	Arlington	Defendant	1827	ACO:267, 274
Newton, Augustine	Arlington	Debts	1844	AB8:504
Newton, Augustine	Arlington	Inventory	1844	AB8:498; LVA-LP
Newton, Augustine	Arlington	Petition	1844	LVA-LP (Box 214)
Newton, Augustine	Arlington	Citation	1845	OCR1842:117, 119
Newton, Augustine	Arlington	Sale	1846	AB9:220
Newton, Augustine	Arlington	Sale of Wine	1846	AB9:224
Newton, Augustine	Arlington	Creditors	1846	AB9:218
Newton, Augustine	Arlington	Account	1846	AB9:216
Newton, Augustine, assignees of	Arlington	Plaintiffs	1823	ACO:228
Newton, Augustine, at Alexandria	Arlington	Ordinary	1833	OBL5(np)
Newton, Augustine, at his house	Arlington	Ordinary	1827	OBL4(np)
Newton, Augustine, at his house	Arlington	Ordinary	1828	OBL4(np)
Newton, Augustine, at his house	Arlington	Ordinary	1829	OBL4(np)
Newton, Augustine, at his house	Arlington	Ordinary	1831	OBL4(np)
Newton, Augustine, at his house	Arlington	Ordinary	1832	OBL4(np)
Newton, Augustine, at his house	Arlington	Ordinary	1835	OBL5(np)
Newton, Augustine, at Marshal House	Arlington	Ordinary	1843	OBL6(np)
Newton, Augustine, def.	Alexandria	Suit	1820	CRL:022
Newton, Augustine F., c/o William	Arlington	Guard.	1817	WB2:166
Newton, Augustine, grantee	Arlington	Indenture D.	1811	ID2:058
Newton, Augustine, grantee	Arlington	Indenture D.	1827	ID:148
Newton, Augustine, in Alexandria Co.	Arlington	Ordinary	1830	OBL4(np)
Newton, Augustine, retailer	Alexandria	Housekeeper	1808	1808(2):13A
Newton, Augustine [Ann Sophia]	Arlington	Bond	1844	OCR1842:078
Newton, Augustine [Ann Sophia]	Arlington	Sale	1844	OCR1842:082; LVA-LP

NAME OR SUBJECT	LOCATION	TYPE	YEAR	REFERENCE(S)
Newton, Edwin B., c/o William	Arlington	Guard.	1817	WB2:167
Newton, Henry C., c/o William	Arlington	Guard.	1817	WB2:165
Newton, Horace	Alexandria	Boarder	1808	1808(2):10A
Newton, Jane E., c/o William	Arlington	Guard.	1817	WB2:165
Newton, Jno.	Alexandria	Tax Charge	1795	Tax PP 1795:22
Newton, John	Alexandria	Tax Charge	1796	Tax PP 1796:14
Newton, John & wife, ship carpenter	Alexandria	Head	1795	1795(4):08
Newton, John & wife Filey	Alexandria	Resident	1800	1800(4):13B
Newton, John, ship carpenter	Alexandria	Head	1800	1800(4):13A
Newton, Joseph M., c/o William	Arlington	Guard.	1817	WB2:170
Newton, Patty	Alexandria	Boarder	1799	1799(2):06A
Newton, Sinay Ann, c/o William	Arlington	Guard.	1817	WB2:168
Newton, Thomas W., c/o William	Arlington	Guard.	1817	WB2:169
Newton, Virginia Sophia, c/o Augustine	Arlington	Apprentice	1845	OCR1842:125
Newton, W., King St.	Alexandria	Occupant	1787	Tax L 1787:26
Newton, W.C., shopkeeper	Alexandria	Head	1810	1810(4):02A
Newton, Will. C.	Alexandria	Tax Charge	1800	Tax PP 1800:31
Newton, William	Alexandria	Tax Charge	1787	Tax PP 1787:11
Newton, William	Alexandria	Tax Charge	1788	Tax PP 1788:12
Newton, William	Alexandria	Tax Charge	1789	Tax PP 1789:14
Newton, William	Alexandria	Tax Charge	1790	Tax PP 1790:11
Newton, William	Alexandria	Tax Charge	1800	Tax PP 1800:31
Newton, William	Arlington	Admin.	1814	WB1:321
Newton, William	Arlington	Inventory	1815	AB2:111; LVA-LP
Newton, William	Arlington	Sale	1815	AB2:168a, 171
Newton, William	Arlington	Account	1816	AB2:254; LVA-LP
Newton, William	Arlington	Account	1817	AB3:063; LVA-LP
Newton, William	Arlington	Account	1821	AB4:299
Newton, William	Arlington	Guard. Acct.	1821	AB4:302; LVA-LP
Newton, William C.	Alexandria	Mer. License	1799	Tax PP 1799:52-08r
Newton, William C.	Alexandria	Tax Charge	1799	Tax PP 1799:30
Newton, William C.	Arlington	Ordinary	1810	OBL2(np)
Newton, William C.	Arlington	Will P.	1827	OCR1822:137a
Newton, William C.	Arlington	Will	1827	WB3:285
Newton, William, def.	Alexandria	Suit	1809	CRH:466
Newton, William, King St.	Alexandria	Occupant	1790	Tax L 1790:11
Newton, William, merchant	Alexandria	Head	1810	1810(3):05A
Newton, William S., c/o William	Arlington	Guard.	1817	WB2:171
Newton, William, w(2)4, merchant	Alexandria	Head	1796	1796(3):2
Newton, Wm.	Alexandria	Tax Charge	1795	Tax PP 1795:22
Newton, Wm.	Alexandria	Tax Charge	1796	Tax PP 1796:14
Newton, Wm.	Alexandria	Tax Charge	1799	Tax PP 1799:30
Newton, Wm. & wife, merchant	Alexandria	Housekeeper	1799	1799(2):06A
Newton, Wm. C.	Alexandria	Tax Charge	1798	Tax PP 1798:14
Newton, Wm. C.	Alexandria	Mer. License	1798	Tax PP 1798:20-5
Newton, Wm. C., no business	Alexandria	Housekeeper	1808	1808(4):30A
Newton, Wm., merchant	Alexandria	Housekeeper	1808	1808(3):19A
Niblon, Jno., Fairfax St.	Alexandria	Owner	1795	Tax L 1795:22
Niblon, Jno., King St.	Alexandria	Owner	1795	Tax L 1795:22
Niblon, John	Alexandria	Tax Charge	1796	Tax PP 1796:14
Niblon, John, Fairfax St.	Alexandria	Occupant	1795	Tax L 1795:08
Niblon, John Jas. & wife, merchant	Alexandria	Head	1795	1795(4):03
Nice, Henry, plt.	Alexandria	Ejectment	1802	CRE:242
Nichol, John, Jr.	Arlington	Admin.	1815	WB2:098
Nichol, John, Jr.	Arlington	Inventory	1816	AB2:321; LVA-LP
Nicholas, Lewis, Brig. Gen.	Arlington	Inventory	1809	WBC:241; LVA-LP
Nicholas, Lewis, Brig. Gen.	Arlington	Bond	1809	WBC:220
Nicholas, Lewis, Brig. Gen.	Arlington	Will	1809	WBC:218; File #041A
Nicholas, Marsalena (C)	Arlington	Apprentice	1828	OCR1822:165
Nicholls, Ely	Alexandria	Tax Charge	1796	Tax LP 1796:22
Nicholls, Isaac	Arlington	Will (NR)	1834	File #063A

NAME OR SUBJECT	LOCATION	TYPE	YEAR	REFERENCE(S)
Nicholls, J.B.	Alexandria	Tax Charge	1796	Tax LP 1796:22
Nicholls, James B.	Alexandria	Tax Charge	1796	Tax PP 1796:14
Nicholls, James B.	Arlington	Account	1832	AB7:047; LVA-LP
Nicholls, James Bruce	Arlington	Account	1831	AB7:029; LVA-LP
Nicholls, James Bruce	Arlington	Account	1831	AB7:047
Nicholls, James Bruce	Arlington	Bond	1831	WB4:007
Nicholls, James Bruce	Arlington	Will	1831	WB4:001; File #297A
Nicholls, James Bruce	Arlington	Account	1833	AB7:069; LVA-LP
Nicholls, James Bruce, assignee	Arlington	Plaintiff	1802	PA:186
Nicholls, Jas. B.	Alexandria	Tax Charge	1795	Tax PP 1795:22
Nicholls, Mary Lee	Arlington	Guard. Acct.	1839	AB7:355
Nicholls, Mary Lee	Arlington	Guard. Acct.	1839	AB8:029; LVA-LP
Nicholls, Saml., Jr.	Alexandria	Tax Charge	1796	Tax LP 1796:22
Nichols, Celina, teacher	Alexandria	Head	1810	1810(1):04A
Nichols, E. & J., Fairfax St.	Alexandria	Occupant	1787	Tax L 1787:25
Nichols, Eli	Alexandria	Owner	1787	Tax L 1787:21
Nichols, Eli, nr. Wilkes St.	Alexandria	Owner	1790	Tax L 1790:09
Nichols, Eli, Wilks St.	Alexandria	Occupant	1787	Tax L 1787:21
Nichols, Isaac	Alexandria	Owner	1787	Tax L 1787:21
Nichols, Isaac, nr. Fairfax St.	Alexandria	Owner	1790	Tax L 1790:09
Nichols, Isaac, Wilks St.	Alexandria	Occupant	1787	Tax L 1787:21
Nichols, James B., w2, merchant	Alexandria	Head	1796	1796(3):1
Nichols, Mary Lee	Arlington	Guard. Acct.	1835	LVA-LP
Nichols, Samuel	Arlington	Will	1825	WB3:266
Nichols, Selina, schoolmistress	Alexandria	Housekeeper	1808	1808(1):02A
Nicholson & Co., Fairfax St.	Alexandria	Occupant	1790	Tax L 1790:04
Nicholson, Henry	Alexandria	Tax Charge	1795	Tax PP 1795:22
Nicholson, Henry	Alexandria	Tax Charge	1796	Tax LP 1796:22
Nicholson, Henry	Alexandria	Mer. License	1798	Tax PP 1798:20-5
Nicholson, Henry	Alexandria	Tax Charge	1799	Tax PP 1799:30
Nicholson, Henry	Alexandria	Mer. License	1799	Tax PP 1799:52-08r
Nicholson, Henry	Alexandria	Tax Charge	1800	Tax PP 1800:31
Nicholson, Henry	Alexandria	Mer. License	1800	Tax PP 1800:54(18)r
Nicholson, Henry	Arlington	Bond	1821	WB3:037
Nicholson, Henry	Arlington	Will	1821	WB3:035; File #203A
Nicholson, Henry	Arlington	Inventory	1822	AB5:055; LVA-LP
Nicholson, Henry	Arlington	Sale	1822	AB5:079
Nicholson, Henry	Arlington	Account	1822	OCR1822:001a
Nicholson, Henry	Arlington	Account	1823	AB5:143; LVA-LP
Nicholson, Henry	Arlington	Account	1824	AB5:257; LVA-LP
Nicholson, Henry	Arlington	Account	1833	LVA-LP
Nicholson, Henry	Arlington	Account	1839	AB7:373
Nicholson, Henry, b. baker & merchant	Alexandria	Housekeeper	1808	1808(2):15A
Nicholson, Henry, def.	Alexandria	Suit	1815	CRK:245
Nicholson, Henry, merchant	Alexandria	Head	1810	1810(2):04A
Nicholson, Henry, plt.	Alexandria	Suit	1817	CRL:001
Nicholson, Hy.	Alexandria	Tax Charge	1798	Tax PP 1798:14
Nicholson, John	Arlington	Guard. Acct.	1825	AB5:399
Nicholson, John Y., c/o Henry	Arlington	Guard.	1823	OCR1822:058
Nicholson, John Y., c/o Henry	Arlington	Guard.	1823	WB3:130
Nicholson, Lionel	Arlington	Guard. Acct.	1825	AB5:399
Nicholson, Lionel	Arlington	Apprentice	1827	OCR1822:139
Nicholson, Lionel	Arlington	Receipt	1833	LVA-LP
Nicholson, Lionel, c/o Henry	Arlington	Guard.	1823	OCR1822:058
Nicholson, Lionel, c/o Henry	Arlington	Guard.	1823	WB3:132
Nicholson, Margaret, c/o Henry	Arlington	Guard.	1822	WB3:078, 130, 133
Nicholson, Mary Ann, c/o Henry	Arlington	Guard.	1822	WB3:078
Nicholson, Resdin (C)	Arlington	Apprentice	1827	OCR1822:148a
Nicholson, Saml.	Alexandria	Tithable +21	1787	Tax PP 1787:04
Nickens, John, labourer	Alexandria	Head	1810	1810(3):03A
Nickens, Matilda, seamstress	Alexandria	Head	1810	1810(4):05A

NAME OR SUBJECT	LOCATION	TYPE	YEAR	REFERENCE(S)
Nickens, William	Arlington	Guard.	1819	WB2:286
Nickens, Wm.	Alexandria	Will	1874	WB1:112; LP
Nickins, Polly (C), washwoman	Alexandria	Housekeeper	1808	1808(3):19A
Nickoll, Henry	Alexandria	Tax Charge	1798	Tax PP 1798:14
Nickolls, James B., def.	Alexandria	Suit	1806	CRE:065
Nickolls, James Bruce	Arlington	Inventory	1831	LVA-LP
Nickolls, Jas. B., King St.	Alexandria	Occupant	1795	Tax L 1795:06
Nickolls, Saml., Fairfax St.	Alexandria	Owner	1795	Tax L 1795:22
Nickolls' Exors. v. McIver's Admr.	Arlington	Suit	1835	LVA-LP (Judgments)
Nickolson & Co.	Alexandria	Occupant	1795	Tax L 1795:31
Nickolson, Henry	Alexandria	Tax Charge	1796	Tax PP 1796:14
Nickolson, Henry, Fairfax St.	Alexandria	Occupant	1795	Tax L 1795:31
Nicoll, John, Jr.	Arlington	Account	1817	AB2:412
Nicoll, John, Jr.	Arlington	Account F.	1817	AB3:010; LVA-LP
Nicoll, Walter A.	Arlington	Will	1840	WB4:373; File #409A
Nicoll, Walter A.	Arlington	Renounce	1845	OCR1842:132
Nicoll, Walter A.	Arlington	Will P.	1845	OCR1842:133
Niel, John, constable	Alexandria	Housekeeper	1808	1808(3):21A
Niell, Rosannah	Alexandria	Boarder	1795	1795(4a):01
Night, Robert	Alexandria	Tax Charge	1799	Tax PP 1799:30
Nightingill, James	Arlington	Will	1865	WB8:279; File #636A
Nightingill, James	Arlington	Appraisal	1867	WB8:521
Nikolls, Jas. B.	Alexandria	Tax Charge	1798	Tax PP 1798:14
Ninde, Alexander B.	Arlington	Admin.	1838	WB4:176
Ninde, Alexander B.	Arlington	Account	1839	AB8:034; LVA-LP
Nitingale, James	Alexandria	Tax Charge	1800	Tax PP 1800:31
Nivan, Duncan	Alexandria	Tax Charge	1788	Tax PP 1788:05
Niven, Duncan	Alexandria	Tax Charge	1787	Tax PP 1787:11
Niven, Duncan	Alexandria	Tithable +16	1789	Tax PP 1789:04
Niven, Duncan	Arlington	Account	1807	LVA-LP
Nix, Chas. (C), stevedore	Alexandria	Housekeeper	1808	1808(3):18A
Nix, Chas., labourer	Alexandria	Head	1810	1810(3):10A
Noble, Jos.	Alexandria	Boarder	1799	1799(2):15A
Noble, Wm. S.	Alexandria	Housekeeper	1799	1799(2):05A
Noble, Wm. S.	Alexandria	Tax Charge	1799	Tax PP 1799:30
Noland, Dennis, corn measurer	Alexandria	Head	1810	1810(1):06A
Noland, Edward (M), c/o Sarah Watts	Arlington	Apprentice	1802	OCR1801:047
Noland, Eliza, mantuamaker	Alexandria	Head	1810	1810(1):02A
Noland, Eliza, sempstress	Alexandria	Housekeeper	1808	1808(1):02A
Noland, John, carpenter	Alexandria	Head	1810	1810(1):06A
Noland, Peter	Alexandria	Tax Charge	1800	Tax PP 1800:31
Nooff, Laurence, butcher	Alexandria	Housekeeper	1808	1808(2):13A
Nore, Ephraim	Arlington	Libellant	1811	ACO:119
Norman, David	Arlington	Bond	1815	WB2:005
Norman, David	Arlington	Will	1815	WB2:004
Norman, Virginia A., w/o John S.	Alexandria	Will	1882	WB1:368; LP
Normyle, Michael	Alexandria	Will	1882	WB1:349; LP
Norris, Catherine	Arlington	Will	1847	WB5:001; File #438A
Norris, Charles	Arlington	Inventory	1823	LVA-LP
Norris, Charles	Arlington	Admin.	1823	OCR1822:054
Norris, Charles	Arlington	Admin.	1823	WB3:114
Norris, Charles	Arlington	Account	1824	AB5:362; LVA-LP
Norris, Charles	Arlington	Account	1827	LVA-LP
Norris, Clara, washwoman	Alexandria	Housekeeper	1808	1808(4):27A
Norris, Clary	Alexandria	Head	1810	1810(4):06A
Norris, Dawes, c/o Sarah	Arlington	Apprentice	1801	OCR1801:007
Norris, Edward	Arlington	Guard.	1827	WB3:284
Norris, Eliza	Arlington	Guard.	1827	WB3:284
Norris, Eliza M.	Arlington	Guard. Rel.	1838	WB4:232
Norris, James	Alexandria	Deposition	1822	CRL:572
Norris, James	Arlington	Appraisal	1835	LVA-LP

NAME OR SUBJECT	LOCATION	TYPE	YEAR	REFERENCE(S)
Norris, James	Arlington	Admin.	1835	WB4:086
Norris, Mark	Alexandria	Tax Charge	1800	Tax PP 1800:31
Norris, Mark	Arlington	Inventory	1815	AB2:137; LVA-LP
Norris, Mark	Arlington	Division S.	1818	AB3:161
Norris, Mark	Arlington	Inventory	1818	LVA-LP
Norris, Mark	Arlington	Sale	1819	AB3:299
Norris, Mark	Arlington	Inventory	1819	AB3:297; LVA-LP
Norris, Mark	Arlington	Account	1819	AB3:401; LVA-LP
Norris, Mark, grantee	Arlington	Indenture D.	1814	ID2:354
Norris, Mark, waterman	Alexandria	Housekeeper	1808	1808(3):18A
Norris, Mary	Alexandria	Resident	1800	1800(4):12B
Norris, Mary (C)	Arlington	Apprentice	1843	OCR1842:034
Norris, Mary, sumpster	Alexandria	Boarder	1800	1800(4):12A
Norris, Oliver	Arlington	Admin.	1825	OCR1822:098a
Norris, Oliver	Arlington	Admin.	1825	WB3:199
Norris, Oliver	Arlington	Account	1826	AB6:254; LVA-LP
Norris, Oliver	Arlington	Account	1833	AB7:073; LVA-LP
Norris, Oliver, Rev.	Alexandria	Statement	1815	CRL:495
Norris, Oliver, Rev.	Arlington	Sale	1825	AB6:120, 124
Norris, Oliver, Rev.	Arlington	Inventory	1825	AB6:113; LVA-LP
Norris, Polly	Alexandria	Boarder	1799	1799(2):17A
Norris, Richard	Arlington	Will	1900	WB10:438; File #799A
Norris, William	Alexandria	Tax Charge	1788	Tax PP 1788:12
Norris, William	Alexandria	Tax Charge	1789	Tax PP 1789:14
Norris, William	Alexandria	Tax Charge	1790	Tax PP 1790:11
Norris, William H.	Arlington	Guard.	1827	WB3:284
Norris, William Herbert	Arlington	Guard.	1838	WB4:232
Norris, William, nr. Royal St.	Alexandria	Occupant	1790	Tax L 1790:12
Norriss, Catharine, c/o Mark	Arlington	Guard.	1819	WB2:311
Norriss, Edward G.	Arlington	Apprentice	1827	OCR1822:144a
Norriss, John, c/o Mark	Arlington	Guard.	1819	WB2:311
Norriss, Mark	Arlington	Admin.	1815	WB2:017, 283
Norriss, Mark, c/o Mark	Arlington	Guard.	1819	WB2:311
Norriss, Tabitha	Arlington	Guard.	1819	WB2:285
Norton, Ann Burwell	Alexandria	Will	1896	WBC1:069; LP
Norton, Courtney, c/o Charles M.	Arlington	Guard.	1835	WB4:085
Norton, George Hatley, Rev.	Alexandria	Will	1893	WBC1:065; LP
Norton, Henny, washerwoman	Alexandria	Head	1810	1810(2):07A
Norton, Henny, washwoman	Alexandria	Housekeeper	1808	1808(2):17A
Norton, John	Arlington	Guard.	1818	WB2:252
Norton, Louisa, c/o Charles M.	Arlington	Guard.	1835	WB4:085
Norton, Mary, millioner	Alexandria	Head	1810	1810(1):02A
Norton, Sarah, c/o Charles M.	Arlington	Guard.	1835	WB4:085
Norwood, Jno.	Alexandria	Tax Charge	1795	Tax PP 1795:22
Norwood, Jno.	Alexandria	Tax Charge	1798	Tax PP 1798:14
Norwood, Jno.	Alexandria	Boarder	1799	1799(2):07A
Norwood, Jno.	Alexandria	Boarder	1808	1808(2):13A
Norwood, Jno., King St.	Alexandria	Occupant	1795	Tax L 1795:28
Norwood, Jno., Royal St.	Alexandria	Occupant	1795	Tax L 1795:28
Norwood, John	Alexandria	Tax Charge	1796	Tax LP 1796:22
Norwood, John	Alexandria	Tax Charge	1796	Tax PP 1796:14
Norwood, John	Alexandria	Tax Charge	1799	Tax PP 1799:30
Norwood, John	Alexandria	Tax Charge	1800	Tax PP 1800:31
Norwood, John, plt.	Alexandria	Suit	1808	CRG:001
Nottingham, Olivia	Arlington	Will	1898	WB10:355; File #781A
Nourse, Charles J.	Arlington	Depoisition	1830	ACR:075, 084
Nourse, Joseph	Arlington	Plaintiff	1830	ACR:063
Nourse, Michael	Arlington	Deposition	1830	ACR:073, 085
Nowland, Catharine	Alexandria	Will	1900	WB2:389; LP
Nowland, Peter	Alexandria	Tax Charge	1799	Tax PP 1799:30
Nowland, Peter & wife, hairdresser	Alexandria	Housekeeper	1799	1799(2):03A

NAME OR SUBJECT	LOCATION	TYPE	YEAR	REFERENCE(S)
Nowling, Eleanor	Arlington	Will (NR)	1813	File #058A
Nugent, Owen	Alexandria	Will	1887	WB1:456; LP
Nulty, Stephen	Alexandria	Boarder	1808	1808(3):19A
Nutt, James	Alexandria	Serv./Appt.	1800	1800(4):15B
Nutt, James	Arlington	Inventory	1814	AB2:055; LVA-LP
Nutt, James	Arlington	Admin.	1814	WB1:291
Nutt, James	Arlington	Account	1816	AB2:348; LVA-LP
Nutt, James	Arlington	Inventory	1822	AB5:088; LVA-LP
Nutt, James	Arlington	Bond	1822	WB3:059
Nutt, James	Arlington	Will	1822	WB3:059; File #208A
Nutt, James	Arlington	Account	1824	LVA-LP
Nutt, James (C)	Arlington	Will P.	1822	OCR1822:016a
Nutt, James (C)	Arlington	Account	1832	AB7:040; LVA-LP
Nutt, James, merchant	Alexandria	Housekeeper	1808	1808(4):30A
Nutt, James, merchant	Alexandria	Head	1810	1810(4):02A
Nutt, James, shopkeeper	Alexandria	Housekeeper	1808	1808(1):01A
Nutt, James, soapmaker	Alexandria	Head	1810	1810(1):02A
Nutt, Jas. (C), labourer	Alexandria	Housekeeper	1799	1799(2):17A
Nutt, Violet, washerwoman	Alexandria	Head	1810	1810(1):11A
Nutt, Voilet	Alexandria	Resident	1800	1800(4):07B
Nutt, Voilet, laundress	Alexandria	Head	1800	1800(4):07A
Nutt, William D.	Alexandria	Will	1888	WB1:512; LP

NAME OR SUBJECT	LOCATION	TYPE	YEAR	REFERENCE(S)
O				
O__, Christopher	Alexandria	Tax Charge	1787	Tax PP 1787:11
O'Brien, Lewis	Arlington	Libellant	1805	ACO:046
O'Brien, Thomas	Arlington	Libellant	1806	ACO:051
O'Connell, Patrick	Arlington	Apprentice	1828	OCR1822:159a
O'Connelly, Patrick	Arlington	Admin.	1828	OCR1822:166a
O'Conner, John	Arlington	Crime	1797	OT:18/12/1797
O'Conner, John	Alexandria	Tax Charge	1799	Tax PP 1799:31
O'Conner, William, barber	Alexandria	Head	1810	1810(2):03A
O'Conner, Wm., barber	Alexandria	Housekeeper	1808	1808(1):02A
O'Connor, Daniel	Arlington	Account	1867	WB8:576
O'Connor, John	Alexandria	Tax Charge	1788	Tax PP 1788:12
O'Connor, John	Alexandria	Tax Charge	1800	Tax PP 1800:32
O'Daniel, Hugh	Alexandria	Tax Charge	1799	Tax PP 1799:31
O'Dowd, Richard	Arlington	Will	1899	WB10:390
O'Mara, Michl.	Alexandria	Tax Charge	1796	Tax LP 1796:19
O'Meara, Michael	Arlington	Account	1820	AB4:092; LVA-LP
O'Meara, Michael	Arlington	Account	1825	AB6:154; LVA-LP
O'Meara, Michael, at Brooke's Tavern	Alexandria	Deposition	1810	CRH:134
O'Meara, Michael, of West End	Arlington	Inventory	1815	WB1:328
O'Meara, Michael, of West End	Arlington	Will	1815	WB1:326; File #125A
O'Meara, Michl., Prince St.	Alexandria	Owner	1795	Tax L 1795:23
O'Meara, Michl., Wales' alley	Alexandria	Owner	1795	Tax L 1795:23(2)
O'Meara, Nancy	Arlington	Inventory	1815	AB2:156; LVA-LP
O'Meara, Nancy	Arlington	Sale	1815	AB2:156
O'Meara, Nancy	Arlington	Admin.	1815	WB1:325
O'Meara, Nancy	Arlington	Account	1818	AB3:203; LVA-LP
O'Neal, Ann	Arlington	Apprentice	1811	OCR1811:060
O'Neal, Ferdinando, aged 50	Alexandria	Deposition	1767	CRI:269
O'Neal, Francis	Arlington	Apprentice	1812	OCR1811:073
O'Neal, Francis	Arlington	Apprentice	1814	OCR1811:221
O'Neal, Israel C.	Alexandria	Will	1894	WB2:311
O'Neale, Ann	Arlington	Apprentice	1811	OCR1811:040
O'Neale, Charles	Alexandria	Tax Charge	1796	Tax PP 1796:14
O'Neale, Ferdinand, at his house	Arlington	Ordinary	1832	OBL4(np)
O'Neale, Ferdinand, at his house	Arlington	Ordinary	1849	OBL6(np)
O'Neale, Ferdinand, in Alexandria Co.	Arlington	Ordinary	1848	OBL6(np)
O'Neale, Ferdinand, in Alexandria Co.	Arlington	Ordinary	1850	OBL6(np)
O'Neale, Hugh	Alexandria	Tax Charge	1798	Tax PP 1798:14
O'Neale, Hugh	Alexandria	Tax Charge	1799	Tax PP 1799:31
O'Neale, William	Arlington	Libellant	1805	ACO:045
O'Neale [Neale], Ferdinando	Arlington	Ordinary	1831	OBL4(np)
O'Neall, Ferdinand, at Alexandria	Arlington	Ordinary	1833	OBL5(np)
O'Neall, Ferdinand, at his house	Arlington	Ordinary	1834	OBL5(np)
O'Neill, Hugh	Alexandria	Mer. License	1798	Tax PP 1798:20-5
O'Neill, Hugh & wife, grocer	Alexandria	Housekeeper	1799	1799(2):05A
O'Reiley, Henry	Arlington	Account	1816	AB2:266; LVA-LP
O'Reily, Elizabeth, c/o Henry	Arlington	Guard.	1814	WB1:284
O'Reily, Henry	Arlington	Admin.	1813	WB1:225
O'Reily, Henry	Arlington	Sale	1813	AB1:333
O'Reily, Henry	Arlington	Account	1814	AB2:059; LVA-LP
O'Reily, Henry	Arlington	Inventory	1814	AB1:330; LVA-LP
O'Reily, Henry	Arlington	Account	1819	AB3:371; LVA-LP
O'Reily, Louisa, c/o Henry	Arlington	Guard.	1814	WB1:284
O'Reily, Maria, c/o Henry	Arlington	Guard.	1814	WB1:284
O'Sullivan, Jane	Arlington	Ordinary	1848	OBL6(np)
O'Sullivan, Jno., merchant	Alexandria	Boarder	1799	1799(2):02A
O'Sullivan, Matthew	Arlington	Will	1844	WB4:382; File #415A
O'Sullivan, Matthew	Arlington	Inventory	1844	AB8:481; LVA-LP
O'Sullivan, Matthew	Arlington	Sale	1844	AB8:487
O'Sullivan, Matthew	Arlington	Will P.	1844	OCR1842:075

NAME OR SUBJECT	LOCATION	TYPE	YEAR	REFERENCE(S)
O'Sullivan, Matthew	Arlington	Account	1845	AB9:088
O'Sullivan, Matthew [Jane]	Arlington	Renounce	1844	OCR1842:075
Oakely, John	Alexandria	Tax Charge	1799	Tax PP 1799:31
Oakley, Jno.	Alexandria	Tax Charge	1795	Tax PP 1795:23
Oakley, Jno. & wife, brickmaker	Alexandria	Housekeeper	1799	1799(2):12A
Oakley, John	Alexandria	Tax Charge	1789	Tax PP 1789:14
Oakley, John	Alexandria	Tax Charge	1790	Tax PP 1790:11
Oakley, John	Alexandria	Tax Charge	1796	Tax PP 1796:14
Oakly, John	Alexandria	Tax Charge	1800	Tax PP 1800:32
Oates, William, b. Cornwall	Arlington	Alien Entry	1817	RA:22/12/17
Ober, Robert	Arlington	Defendant	1823	ACO:214
Obrie, Nichl.	Alexandria	Tax Charge	1796	Tax LP 1796:22
Obrié, Nicholas	Alexandria	Tax Charge	1795	Tax PP 1795:23
Obrié, Nicholas	Alexandria	Tax Charge	1796	Tax PP 1796:14
Obrié, Nicholas	Alexandria	Tax Charge	1798	Tax PP 1798:14
Obrié, Nicholas	Alexandria	Mer. License	1798	Tax PP 1798:20-5
Obrien, Lewis	Arlington	Libellant	1805	ACO:042
Oden, William	Arlington	Witness	1795	OT:22/06/1795
Odlen, John	Arlington	Defendant	1809	ACO:108
Offutt, Francis, grantor	Arlington	Indenture D.	1829	ID:247
Offutt, Francis, in jail	Arlington	Insolvent	1829	ID:245
Offutt, Sarah B., of Montgomery Co. MD	Arlington	Will	1859	WB7:471; File #570A
Ogden, Elisha L.	Arlington	Apprentice	1826	OCR1822:120
Ogden, Rezin L., grantor	Arlington	Indenture D.	1827	ID:099
Ogden, Rezin L., in jail	Arlington	Insolvent	1827	ID:097
Ogden, Thomas C.	Arlington	Apprentice	1826	OCR1822:120
Ogden, Thomas C.	Arlington	Apprentice	1829	OCR1822:173
Ogle, J., Queen St.	Alexandria	Occupant	1787	Tax L 1787:22
Oiley, Wm. & Co.	Alexandria	License Due	1800	Tax PP 1800:54(24)
Oldham, Edward	Arlington	Will	1860	WB8:038; File #579A
Olive, Colkett & Britton, of London, plt.	Alexandria	Suit	1801	CRD:042
Olton, John, w(1), shopkeeper	Alexandria	Head	1796	1796(3):1
Oneal, Chas.	Alexandria	Tax Charge	1795	Tax PP 1795:23
Oneil, Chas., Princess St.	Alexandria	Occupant	1795	Tax L 1795:12
Oneshear, Martin, plasterer	Alexandria	Head	1810	1810(3):08A
Ord, James	Arlington	Defendant	1825	ACO:255
Ord, Thomas	Arlington	Sale S.	1834	LVA-LP
Orde, Catherine	Arlington	Guard.	1832	WB4:052
Orde, Thomas	Arlington	Admin.	1829	WB3:249
Orde, Thomas	Arlington	Account	1829	AB6:485a; LVA-LP
Orme, Archibald, c/o John	Arlington	Apprentice	1811	OCR1811:001
Oronoko and West Streets	Alexandria	Plat	1810	CRH:153
Orr, Alexander	Arlington	Crime	1794	OT:25/07/1794
Orr, Alexander D.	Alexandria	Deposition	1807	CRH:375
Orr, Cragos, washer	Alexandria	Head	1795	1795(4):04
Orr, J.D., Doctr.	Alexandria	Tax Charge	1796	Tax LP 1796:22
Orr, James L.	Alexandria	Tax Charge	1799	Tax PP 1799:31
Orr, John D., M.D., Fairfax St.	Alexandria	Occupant	1795	Tax L 1795:04
Orr, John D., M.D.	Alexandria	Tax Charge	1796	Tax PP 1796:14
Orr, John D., w(1)6, doctor	Alexandria	Head	1796	1796(3):5
Osborne, Archibald	Arlington	Ordinary	1820	OBL3(np)
Osborne, Archibald	Arlington	Bond	1823	WB3:084
Osborne, Archibald	Arlington	Will	1823	WB3:083; File #215A
Osburn, Archibald	Alexandria	Tithable +16	1789	Tax PP 1789:04
Osburn, Archibald	Arlington	Will P.	1823	OCR1822:031
Osburn, Thomas	Alexandria	Tax Charge	1796	Tax PP 1796:14
Osburn, Thomas	Alexandria	Tax Charge	1799	Tax PP 1799:31
Osburn, Thos.	Alexandria	Tax Charge	1800	Tax PP 1800:32
Osburne, Archibald	Arlington	Inventory	1823	AB5:153; LVA-LP

NAME OR SUBJECT	LOCATION	TYPE	YEAR	REFERENCE(S)
Osburne, Archibald, at Potomac Bridge	Arlington	Ordinary	1822	OBL3(np)
Oten, Jno. & wife, ship builder	Alexandria	Housekeeper	1799	1799(2):19A
Otley, James, painter	Alexandria	Head	1810	1810(1):02A
Oton, John	Alexandria	Tax Charge	1796	Tax LP 1796:22
Otterson, James, of Philadelphia PA	Arlington	Will	1891	WB10:181; File #749A
Otway, Thomas	Arlington	Crime	1800	OT:05/07/1800
Outon, John	Alexandria	Tax Charge	1800	Tax PP 1800:32
Overall, Jno.	Alexandria	Tax Charge	1798	Tax PP 1798:14
Overall, Jno. & wife, merchant	Alexandria	Housekeeper	1799	1799(2):06A
Overall, John	Alexandria	Mer. License	1798	Tax PP 1798:20-5
Overall, John	Alexandria	Tax Charge	1799	Tax PP 1799:31
Overall, John	Alexandria	Mer. License	1799	Tax PP 1799:52-08r
Overall, John	Arlington	Account	1800	LVA-LP
Overall, John	Arlington	Inventory	1800	LVA-LP
Overall, John	Arlington	Ordinary	1802	OBL1(np)
Overseers of the Poor, Princess St.	Alexandria	Occupant	1795	Tax L 1795:26
Owen, Edmund B.	Alexandria	Deposition	1801	CRG:331
Owen, William, c/o Elenor	Arlington	Apprentice	1804	OCR1801:170
Owen, Wm.	Alexandria	Tax Charge	1798	Tax PP 1798:14
Owenbread, William	Alexandria	Tax Charge	1790	Tax PP 1790:11
Owenbread, William, Prince St.	Alexandria	Owner	1790	Tax L 1790:09
Owenbread, Wm.	Alexandria	Tax Charge	1788	Tax PP 1788:12
Owenbread, Wm.	Alexandria	Tax Charge	1789	Tax PP 1789:14
Owens, Elias	Arlington	Apprentice	1845	OCR1842:151
Owens, James, c/o Martha	Arlington	Apprentice	1813	OCR1811:170
Owens, James H.	Arlington	Sale	1816	AB2:350
Owens, James H.	Arlington	Inventory	1816	AB2:316; LVA-LP
Owens, James H.	Arlington	Admin.	1816	WB2:124
Owens, Jas.	Alexandria	Boarder	1808	1808(1):03A
Owens, Thomas	Alexandria	Tax Charge	1799	Tax PP 1799:31
Owens, Thomas, b. Holywell	Arlington	Alien Entry	1819	RA:22/01/19
Owens, William	Alexandria	Tax Charge	1788	Tax PP 1788:12
Owens, William	Arlington	Admin.	1800	CRA:308
Owens, William	Arlington	Account	1806	WBB:293; LVA-LP
Owing, James	Arlington	Account	1817	AB3:050
Owing, James	Arlington	Account	1817	AB3:039
Ownbread, William, Prince St.	Alexandria	Occupant	1790	Tax L 1790:09
Oxley, Jefferson, at his house	Arlington	Ordinary	1830	OBL4(np)
Oxley, William & Co., plt.	Alexandria	Suit	1801	CRB:195
Oxley, William, def.	Alexandria	Suit	1803	CRD:068
Oxley, William, grantor	Arlington	Indenture D.	1806	ID3:259
Oxley, William, in confinement	Arlington	Insolvent	1806	ID3:249
Oxley, Wm., merchant	Alexandria	Boarder	1799	1799(2):02A

NAME OR SUBJECT	LOCATION	TYPE	YEAR	REFERENCE(S)

P

NAME OR SUBJECT	LOCATION	TYPE	YEAR	REFERENCE(S)
Packett, John	Alexandria	Tithable +16	1789	Tax PP 1789:20
Padgett, John G., c/o James Cooper	Arlington	Apprentice	1828	OCR1822:164
Padgett, Lucretia	Alexandria	Will	1889	WB1:530; LP
Padgett, William L.	Alexandria	Will	1890	WB1:582; LP
Page, Charles	Alexandria	Tithable +16	1789	Tax PP 1789:14
Page, Charles	Alexandria	Tax Charge	1800	Tax PP 1800:33
Page, Charles	Arlington	Will	1839	WB4:226; File #368A
Page, Charles	Arlington	Bond	1839	WB4:228
Page, Charles	Arlington	Inventory	1840	AB8:073; LVA-LP
Page, Charles	Arlington	Account	1841	AB8:198
Page, Charles	Arlington	Account	1842	AB8:271; LVA-LP
Page, Charles	Arlington	Account	1842	OCR1842:006
Page, Charles	Arlington	Account	1843	AB8:348; LVA-LP
Page, Charles	Arlington	Account	1844	AB8:438; LVA-LP
Page, Charles	Arlington	Account	1845	AB9:048; LVA-LP
Page, Charles	Arlington	Account	1846	AB9:178; LVA-LP
Page, Charles	Arlington	Account	1847	AB9:293
Page, Charles	Arlington	Account	1848	WB5:053; LVA-LP
Page, Charles	Arlington	Account	1848	WB5:180
Page, Charles	Arlington	Account	1849	LVA-LP
Page, Charles	Arlington	Account	1851	WB5:249; LVA-LP
Page, Charles	Arlington	Account	1852	WB6:052; LVA-LP
Page, Charles	Arlington	Account C.	1852	WB6:257; LVA-LP
Page, Charles	Arlington	Account C.	1852	WB6:339; LVA-LP
Page, Charles	Arlington	Account	1855	LVA-LP
Page, Charles	Arlington	Account	1855	WB7:014, 139
Page, Charles	Arlington	Account	1857	WB7:254; LVA-LP
Page, Charles	Arlington	Account	1858	WB7:364; LVA-LP
Page, Charles	Arlington	Account	1859	WB7:457; LVA-LP
Page, Charles	Arlington	Account	1860	WB8:469
Page, Charles	Arlington	Account	1860	WB8:028; LVA-LP
Page, Charles, cashier	Alexandria	Head	1810	1810(1):02A
Page, Charles Craig, c/o William	Arlington	Guard.	1852	BB(np)
Page, Charles, servants of	Arlington	Births	1840	AB8:074
Page, Chas.	Alexandria	Tax Charge	1798	Tax PP 1798:14
Page, Chas., cashr. Po. Bank	Alexandria	Housekeeper	1808	1808(1):01A
Page, Chas., Union St.	Alexandria	Occupant	1795	Tax L 1795:31
Page, Elias H.	Arlington	Guard.	1865	FBB(np)
Page, Mann	Arlington	Bond	1820	WB2:368
Page, Mann	Arlington	Will	1820	WB2:369
Page, Peyton Randolph	Alexandria	Deposition	1802	CRC:042
Page, Washington C.	Arlington	Bond	1854	BB(np)
Page, Will. B.	Alexandria	Tax Charge	1800	Tax PP 1800:33
Page, William	Alexandria	Tax Charge	1789	Tax PP 1789:14
Page, William	Alexandria	Tax Charge	1790	Tax PP 1790:11
Page, William	Alexandria	Tithable +16	1790	Tax PP 1790:10
Page, William	Arlington	Bond	1851	BB(np)
Page, William Byrd	Alexandria	Deed	1800	CRL:030
Page, William Byrd, def.	Alexandria	Suit	1810	CRH:197
Page, William Byrd, Estate, def.	Alexandria	Suit	1819	CRL:024
Page, William H.	Arlington	Suit	1858	LVA-LP
Page, William, Union St.	Alexandria	Occupant	1790	Tax L 1790:12
Page, Wm.	Alexandria	Tax Charge	1796	Tax LP 1796:23
Page, Wm. B.	Alexandria	Tax Charge	1798	Tax PP 1798:14
Page, Wm. B.	Alexandria	Tax Charge	1799	Tax PP 1799:33
Pain, London (C)	Alexandria	Tax Charge	1800	Tax PP 1800:33
Paine, John	Alexandria	Tax Charge	1796	Tax PP 1796:15
Paine, Landon (C), carpenter	Alexandria	Boarder	1799	1799(2):19A
Paine, Lund	Alexandria	Tax Charge	1796	Tax PP 1796:15
Paine, Samuel, at Richmond	Alexandria	Deposition	1817	CRK:367

NAME OR SUBJECT	LOCATION	TYPE	YEAR	REFERENCE(S)
Paine, Samuel, at Richmond	Alexandria	Deposition	1818	CRK:383
Painter, George	Alexandria	Tax Charge	1796	Tax PP 1796:15
Paisley, John	Alexandria	Tax Charge	1790	Tax PP 1790:11
Paisley, John, King St.	Alexandria	Occupant	1790	Tax L 1790:08
Paler, Thornton, c/o Mary Williams	Arlington	Apprentice	1805	OCR1801:302
Palmer, Colin	Alexandria	Boarder	1808	1808(3):21A
Palmer, John R., sadler	Alexandria	Head	1810	1810(3):02A
Palmer, Mary, sempstress	Alexandria	Housekeeper	1808	1808(4):29A
Palmer, Roger, c/o Mary	Arlington	Apprentice	1801	OCR1801:005
Palmer, Roger, c/o Mary	Arlington	Apprentice	1803	OCR1801:084
Pancoast, David, Estate, St. Asaph St.	Alexandria	Owner	1790	Tax L 1790:09
Pancoast, Jonathan	Alexandria	Account B.	1799	CRC:114
Pancoast, Jonathan	Alexandria	Tax Charge	1799	Tax PP 1799:32
Pancoast, Jonathan	Alexandria	Tax Charge	1800	Tax PP 1800:33
Pancoast, Jonathan & wife, bricklayer	Alexandria	Housekeeper	1799	1799(2):08A
Pancoast, Jonathan, def.	Alexandria	Suit	1801	CRB:202
Pancoast, Jonathan, def.	Alexandria	Suit	1801	CRC:111
Pancoast, Jonathan, def.	Alexandria	Suit	1803	CRD:101
Pancoast, Jonathan, grantor	Arlington	Indenture D.	1806	ID3:184
Pancoast, Jonathan, in jail bounds	Arlington	Insolvent	1806	ID3:181
Pancoast, Sarah	Alexandria	Boarder	1799	1799(2):09A
Pancoast, Sarah	Arlington	Will	1819	WB2:298; File #163A
Pancoast, Sarah, St. Asaph St.	Alexandria	Owner	1795	Tax L 1795:24
Pancost, D., Estate, Washington St.	Alexandria	Occupant	1787	Tax L 1787:04
Pancost, Sarah	Alexandria	Tax Charge	1796	Tax LP 1796:24
Pane, London	Alexandria	Tax Charge	1796	Tax LP 1796:23
Panwright, Ennis	Alexandria	Tax Charge	1788	Tax PP 1788:13
Pape, Sarah	Arlington	Exor. Bond	1847	EBB(np)
Pape, Sarah	Arlington	Will	1847	WB5:003; File #439A
Pape, Sarah	Arlington	Inventory	1847	WB5:009; LVA-LP
Pape, Sarah	Arlington	Account	1848	WB5:083; LVA-LP
Paradise, John	Arlington	Inventory	1818	AB3:117; LVA-LP
Paradise, John	Arlington	Admin.	1818	WB2:218
Paradise, John A.	Arlington	Apprentice	1827	OCR1822:147a
Paradise, John, schoolmaster	Alexandria	Housekeeper	1808	1808(3):19A
Paradise, William	Arlington	Apprentice	1804	OCR1801:223
Paris, Peter	Arlington	Will	1837	WB4:134; File #069A
Paris, Peter	Arlington	Account	1838	AB7:307; LVA-LP
Paris, Peter	Arlington	Account F.	1839	AB7:306
Paris, Peter, labourer	Alexandria	Head	1810	1810(3):04A
Paris, Peter, shopkpr. & oysters r.	Alexandria	Housekeeper	1808	1808(3):20A
Paris, Polly (C), washer woman	Alexandria	Housekeeper	1799	1799(2):12A
Park, James	Arlington	Admin.	1804	WBB:048
Park, Jane, b. Peterhead, Aberdeen	Arlington	Alien Entry	1824	RA:17/11/24
Park, John, b. Peterhead, Aberdeen	Arlington	Alien Entry	1824	RA:17/11/24
Park, John, b. Peterhead, Aberdeen	Arlington	Alien Entry	1824	RA:17/11/24
Parke, Alexander, b. Peterhead, Scot.	Arlington	Alien Entry	1824	RA:17/11/24
Parke, Jannett, b. Peterhead, Scot.	Arlington	Alien Entry	1824	RA:17/11/24
Parke, Matthew, master	Arlington	Respondent	1805	ACO:045
Parker, Fielder	Arlington	Defendant	1815	ACO:142, 144, 147
Parker, Geo. (C), shopkeeper	Alexandria	Housekeeper	1808	1808(3):20A
Parker, Geo., shopkeeper	Alexandria	Head	1810	1810(3):04A
Parker, George	Arlington	Ordinary	1805	OBL1(np)
Parker, George	Arlington	Ordinary	1806	OBL1(np)
Parker, George	Arlington	Ordinary	1809	OBL2(np)
Parker, George S., of Washington DC	Arlington	Will	1896	WB10:329; File #772A
Parker, Johh, ship carpenter	Alexandria	Housekeeper	1808	1808(1):06A
Parker, John	Alexandria	Serv./Appt.	1800	1800(4):16B
Parker, John	Alexandria	Resident	1800	1800(4):16B
Parker, John, joiner	Alexandria	Head	1810	1810(1):10A
Parker, Philip	Arlington	Apprentice	1823	OCR1822:040a

NAME OR SUBJECT	LOCATION	TYPE	YEAR	REFERENCE(S)
Parker, Robert & wife Sarah	Alexandria	Resident	1800	1800(4):14B
Parker, Robert, labourrer	Alexandria	Head	1800	1800(4):14A
Parker, Sarah	Alexandria	Resident	1800	1800(4):16B
Parker, Sarah, labourrer	Alexandria	Boarder	1800	1800(4):16A
Parker, Thomas, Frederick Co.	Alexandria	Deed	1811	CRK:415
Parnel, Jessee & wife, carpenter	Alexandria	Head	1795	1795(4):08
Parnell, George, c/o Sally	Arlington	Apprentice	1822	OCR1822:014a
Parris, Mary	Alexandria	Serv./Appt.	1800	1800(4):15B
Parris, Mary, laundress	Alexandria	Head	1800	1800(4):15A
Parry, William H.	Arlington	Defendant	1808	ACO:103
Parry, William H.	Arlington	Ordinary	1810	OBL2(np)
Parry, Wm. H., clerk	Alexandria	Housekeeper	1808	1808(4):26A
Parry, Wm. H., clerk	Alexandria	Head	1810	1810(1):01A
Parry, Wm. H., grantor	Arlington	Indenture D.	1812	ID2:096
Parry, Wm. H., in jail bounds	Arlington	Insolvent	1812	ID2:089
Parson, James, Estate	Alexandria	Tax Charge	1787	Tax PP 1787:11
Parsons, Eliza.	Alexandria	Tax Charge	1790	Tax PP 1790:11
Parsons, Eliza., Cameron St.	Alexandria	Occupant	1790	Tax L 1790:09
Parsons, Elizabeth	Alexandria	Tax Charge	1788	Tax PP 1788:13
Parsons, Elizabeth	Alexandria	Tax Charge	1789	Tax PP 1789:14
Parsons, Elizabeth	Alexandria	Tax Charge	1799	Tax PP 1799:32
Parsons, Elizabeth, Cameron St.	Alexandria	Owner	1790	Tax L 1790:09
Parsons, Elizabeth, Fairfax St.	Alexandria	Owner	1790	Tax L 1790:09
Parsons, Elizh.	Alexandria	Tax Charge	1796	Tax LP 1796:23
Parsons, Elizh.	Alexandria	Tax Charge	1796	Tax LP 1796:23
Parsons, Elizth.	Alexandria	Tax Charge	1800	Tax PP 1800:33
Parsons, Elizth., Cameron St.	Alexandria	Occupant	1795	Tax L 1795:23
Parsons, Elizth., Cameron St.	Alexandria	Owner	1795	Tax L 1795:23
Parsons, Elizth., King St.	Alexandria	Owner	1795	Tax L 1795:23(3)
Parsons, George M.	Arlington	Ordinary	1822	OBL3(np)
Parsons, George M.	Arlington	Ordinary	1825	OBL4(np)
Parsons, George M., at Washington Inn	Arlington	Ordinary	1823	OBL3(np)
Parsons, George M., grantor	Arlington	Indenture D.	1827	ID:087
Parsons, George M., in jail	Arlington	Insolvent	1827	ID:084
Parsons, James	Arlington	Will	1823	WB3:277
Parsons, James	Arlington	Account	1826	AB6:246; LVA-LP
Parsons, James	Arlington	Inventory	1826	AB6:156
Parsons, James	Arlington	Will P.	1826	OCR1822:125
Parsons, James	Arlington	Will P.	1826	OCR1822:107
Parsons, James	Arlington	Bond	1826	WB3:212
Parsons, James	Arlington	Account	1827	AB6:278; LVA-LP
Parsons, James, Estate	Alexandria	Owner	1787	Tax L 1787:21
Parsons, James, Estate	Alexandria	Tax Charge	1796	Tax PP 1796:15
Parsons, John	Alexandria	Tithable +16	1788	Tax PP 1788:13
Parsons, John	Arlington	Defendant	1802	PA:310
Parsons, John	Arlington	Ordinary	1807	OBL2(np)
Parsons, John	Arlington	Ordinary	1808	OBL2(np)
Parsons, John, grantor	Arlington	Indenture D.	1831	ID:301
Parsons, John, in jail	Arlington	Insolvent	1831	ID:298
Parsons, John, shopkeeper & tavern lic.	Alexandria	Housekeeper	1808	1808(4):28A
Parsons, Marshfield	Alexandria	Deposition	1805	CRF:250
Parsons, Mrs.	Alexandria	Head	1810	1810(3):04A
Parsons, Mrs., Cameron St.	Alexandria	Occupant	1787	Tax L 1787:21
Parsons, Solomon	Alexandria	Tax Charge	1799	Tax PP 1799:32
Parsons, Solomon	Alexandria	Tax Charge	1800	Tax PP 1800:33
Parsons, Solomon, clerk	Alexandria	Boarder	1799	1799(2):08A
Parsons, Solomon, clerk	Alexandria	Head	1810	1810(1):08A
Parsons, Thomas, c/o Jonathan C.	Arlington	Apprentice	1814	OCR1811:233
Parsons, Thomas, grantee	Arlington	Indenture D.	1831	ID:301
Parsons, Thomas, Jr.	Arlington	Apprentice	1825	OCR1822:096
Pasco, Charles	Alexandria	Tax Charge	1800	Tax PP 1800:33

NAME OR SUBJECT	LOCATION	TYPE	YEAR	REFERENCE(S)
Pascoe, Charles	Alexandria	Tax Charge	1799	Tax PP 1799:32
Pascoe, Charles	Arlington	Juryman	1824	ACO:237
Pascoe, Charles, as witness	Arlington	Payment	1808	ACO:090
Pascoe, Chas.	Alexandria	Tax Charge	1798	Tax PP 1798:14
Pascoe, Chas., choemaker	Alexandria	Head	1810	1810(2):03A
Pascoe, Chas., shoemaker	Alexandria	Housekeeper	1808	1808(2):13A
Pascoe v. Daugherty	Arlington	Suit	1818	LVA-LP
Pascoe, William	Arlington	Inventory	1833	LVA-LP
Pascoe, William	Arlington	Admin.	1833	WB4:066
Pascoe, William	Arlington	Account	1834	AB7:105; LVA-LP
Pascue, John	Alexandria	Tax Charge	1787	Tax PP 1787:12
Pasquale, Peter	Arlington	Admin.	1812	WB1:156
Pasquall, Frederick	Arlington	Apprentice	1822	OCR1822:025a
Pasquall, Peter	Arlington	Inventory	1812	AB1:178; LVA-LP
Pasquall, Peter	Arlington	Account	1813	AB1:293; LVA-LP
Pasquall, Peter, seaman	Alexandria	Housekeeper	1808	1808(4):30A
Pasquall, Peter, seaman	Alexandria	Head	1810	1810(4):02A
Pasque, John	Alexandria	Tax Charge	1788	Tax PP 1788:13
Paterson, Wm. P. & wife, callico printer	Alexandria	Housekeeper	1799	1799(2):09A
Paton & Butcher	Alexandria	Tax Charge	1788	Tax PP 1788:13
Paton & Butcher	Alexandria	Tax Charge	1789	Tax PP 1789:14
Paton & Butcher	Alexandria	Tax Charge	1796	Tax LP 1796:23
Paton & Butcher	Alexandria	Tax Charge	1796	Tax LP 1796:02
Paton & Butcher	Alexandria	Tax Charge	1796	Tax PP 1796:15
Paton & Butcher	Alexandria	Mer. License	1798	Tax PP 1798:20-5
Paton & Butcher	Alexandria	Tax Charge	1799	Tax PP 1799:32
Paton & Butcher	Alexandria	Mer. License	1799	Tax PP 1799:52-08r
Paton & Butcher	Alexandria	Mer. License	1800	Tax PP 1800:54(18)r
Paton & Butcher	Arlington	Claim	1812	ACO:124
Paton & Butcher	Arlington	Inventory	1819	AB4:011
Paton & Butcher	Arlington	Account	1826	AB6:203; LVA-LP
Paton & Butcher, Fairfax St.	Alexandria	Occupant	1790	Tax L 1790:01
Paton & Butcher, Fairfax St.	Alexandria	Occupant	1790	Tax L 1790:10
Paton & Butcher, Fairfax St.	Alexandria	Owner	1795	Tax L 1795:04
Paton & Butcher, Fairfax St.	Alexandria	Occupant	1795	Tax L 1795:04
Paton & Butcher, Fairfax St.	Alexandria	Occupant	1795	Tax L 1795:27
Paton & Butcher, King St.	Alexandria	Occupant	1790	Tax L 1790:01
Paton & Butcher, Royal St.	Alexandria	Owner	1795	Tax L 1795:04
Paton, Ann B.	Arlington	Guard. Acct.	1822	AB5:045; LVA-LP
Paton, Ann B.	Arlington	Guard. Acct.	1823	AB5:222; LVA-LP
Paton, Ann B.	Arlington	Guard. Acct.	1823	AB5:172; LVA-LP
Paton, Ann B.	Arlington	Guard. Acct.	1825	AB5:377; LVA-LP
Paton, Ann B.	Arlington	Guard. Acct.	1826	AB6:159; LVA-LP
Paton, Ann B.	Arlington	Guard. Acct.	1827	AB6:291; LVA-LP
Paton, Ann B.	Arlington	Guard. Acct.	1828	LVA-LP
Paton, Ann B.	Arlington	Guard. Acct.	1830	LVA-LP
Paton, Ann B.	Arlington	Complainant	1834	LSA:001
Paton, Ann Butcher, c/o John B.	Arlington	Guard.	1820	WB2:364
Paton, Ann Maria	Arlington	Inventory	1828	LVA-LP
Paton, Ann Maria	Arlington	Account	1834	AB7:106; LVA-LP
Paton, Ann Rebecca	Arlington	Guard. Acct.	1834	LVA-LP
Paton, James	Alexandria	Tithable +16	1788	Tax PP 1788:08
Paton, John B.	Arlington	Inventory	1819	AB3:355
Paton, John B.	Arlington	Admin.	1819	WB2:277
Paton, John B.	Arlington	Account	1820	AB4:130
Paton, John B.	Arlington	Guard. Acct.	1825	AB5:377
Paton, John B.	Arlington	Account	1826	AB6:206
Paton, John B.	Arlington	Account	1830	AB6:521
Paton, John B.	Arlington	Account F.	1834	AB7:110
Paton, John B., orphans of	Arlington	Guard.	1822	OCR1822:005
Paton, John B., orphans of	Arlington	Guard. Acct.	1827	OCR1822:135a

NAME OR SUBJECT	LOCATION	TYPE	YEAR	REFERENCE(S)
Paton, John B., orphans of	Arlington	Guard. Acct.	1829	OCR1822:169
Paton, Mary Jane	Arlington	Guard. Acct.	1822	AB5:047; LVA-LP
Paton, Mary Jane	Arlington	Guard. Acct.	1823	AB5:172; LVA-LP
Paton, Mary Jane	Arlington	Guard. Acct.	1823	AB5:221
Paton, Mary Jane	Arlington	Guard. Acct.	1824	AB5:221; LVA-LP
Paton, Mary Jane	Arlington	Guard. Acct.	1825	AB5:375
Paton, Mary Jane	Arlington	Guard. Acct.	1826	AB6:161
Paton, Mary Jane	Arlington	Guard. Acct.	1827	AB6:290; LVA-LP
Paton, Mary Jane	Arlington	Guard. Acct.	1832	LVA-LP
Paton, Mary Jane, c/o John B.	Arlington	Guard.	1820	WB2:364
Paton, Rebecca	Arlington	Guard. Acct.	1822	AB5:045; LVA-LP
Paton, Rebecca	Arlington	Guard. Acct.	1823	AB5:220
Paton, Rebecca	Arlington	Guard. Acct.	1823	AB5:171
Paton, Rebecca	Arlington	Guard. Acct.	1824	LVA-LP
Paton, Rebecca	Arlington	Guard. Acct.	1825	AB5:376
Paton, Rebecca	Arlington	Guard. Acct.	1826	AB6:160
Paton, Rebecca	Arlington	Guard. Acct.	1827	AB6:290
Paton, Rebecca	Arlington	Guard. Acct.	1834	AB7:207; LVA-LP
Paton, Rebecca	Arlington	Defendant	1834	LSA:001
Paton, Rebecca	Arlington	Guard. Acct.	1836	AB7:207
Paton, Rebecca, c/o John B.	Arlington	Guard.	1820	WB2:364
Paton, Richard	Alexandria	Tithable +16	1788	Tax PP 1788:07
Paton, Will.	Alexandria	Tax Charge	1800	Tax PP 1800:33
Paton, William	Alexandria	Tax Charge	1787	Tax PP 1787:12
Paton, William	Alexandria	Tax Charge	1788	Tax PP 1788:13
Paton, William	Alexandria	Tax Charge	1799	Tax PP 1799:32
Paton, William	Arlington	Will P.	1825	OCR1822:086a
Paton, William	Arlington	Bond	1825	WB3:173
Paton, William	Arlington	Will	1825	WB3:170; File #231A
Paton, William	Arlington	Inventory	1826	AB6:230; LVA-LP
Paton, William	Arlington	Account	1831	AB7:009
Paton, William	Arlington	Receipt	1834	LVA-LP
Paton, William	Arlington	Account	1839	AB7:321
Paton, William, Jr.	Arlington	Admin.	1815	WB2:202
Paton, William, Jr.	Arlington	Inventory	1817	AB3:085; LVA-LP
Paton, William, Jr.	Arlington	Sale	1817	AB3:088
Paton, William, Jr.	Arlington	Admin.	1825	OCR1822:098a
Paton, William, Jr.	Arlington	Bond	1825	WB3:200
Paton, William, Pitt St.	Alexandria	Occupant	1790	Tax L 1790:09
Paton, William, Pitt St.	Alexandria	Owner	1790	Tax L 1790:09
Paton, Wm.	Alexandria	Tax Charge	1795	Tax PP 1795:24
Paton, Wm. & wife, merchant	Alexandria	Housekeeper	1799	1799(2):13A
Paton, Wm., Jr.	Alexandria	Tax Charge	1799	Tax PP 1799:33
Paton, Wm., Jr., clerk	Alexandria	Boarder	1799	1799(2):02A
Paton, Wm., merchant	Alexandria	Head	1810	1810(1):08A
Paton, Wm., Pitt St.	Alexandria	Occupant	1795	Tax L 1795:23
Paton, Wm., Pitt St.	Alexandria	Owner	1795	Tax L 1795:23
Patrick, William (C)	Arlington	Apprentice	1827	OCR1822:146a
Patten & Dykes	Alexandria	Mer. License	1798	Tax PP 1798:20-5
Patten, Alexr.	Alexandria	Boarder	1808	1808(2):16A
Patten, James	Alexandria	Tax Charge	1800	Tax PP 1800:33
Patten, James	Arlington	Invoice	1808	ACR:043
Patten, James & wife, merchant	Alexandria	Housekeeper	1799	1799(2):10A
Patten, James, merchant	Alexandria	Head	1810	1810(4):01A
Patten, John	Alexandria	Tithable +16	1790	Tax PP 1790:08
Patten, John	Arlington	Account	1839	AB7:313
Patten, Robert	Alexandria	Tax Charge	1800	Tax PP 1800:33
Patten, T. & Co., Prince St.	Alexandria	Occupant	1795	Tax L 1795:15
Patten, Tho.	Alexandria	Tax Charge	1798	Tax PP 1798:15
Patten, Tho.	Alexandria	Tax Charge	1799	Tax PP 1799:33
Patten, Thomas	Alexandria	Tax Charge	1796	Tax PP 1796:15

NAME OR SUBJECT	LOCATION	TYPE	YEAR	REFERENCE(S)
Patten, Thomas, def.	Alexandria	Suit	1801	CRB:083
Patten, Thomas, def.	Alexandria	Suit	1801	CRB:122
Patten, Thomas, late of Alexa.	Arlington	Insolvent	1812	ID2:085
Patten, Thos.	Alexandria	Tax Charge	1795	Tax PP 1795:24
Patten, Thos.	Alexandria	Tax Charge	1800	Tax PP 1800:34
Patten, Thos. & wife, merchant	Alexandria	Housekeeper	1799	1799(2):18A
Patten, Thos., King St.	Alexandria	Owner	1795	Tax L 1795:23
Patten, Thos., merchant	Alexandria	Head	1810	1810(3):01A
Patten, Thos., Princess St.	Alexandria	Owner	1795	Tax L 1795:23
Patten, Thos., sea captain	Alexandria	Housekeeper	1808	1808(2):11A
Patten, Thos., Union St.	Alexandria	Occupant	1795	Tax L 1795:23
Patten, Thos., Union St.	Alexandria	Owner	1795	Tax L 1795:23
Patten, Thos., Water St.	Alexandria	Occupant	1795	Tax L 1795:11
Patten, Thos., Water St.	Alexandria	Owner	1795	Tax L 1795:23(2)
Patten, William	Alexandria	Tax Charge	1790	Tax PP 1790:11
Patterson, Alexander, clerk	Alexandria	Boarder	1800	1800(4):07A
Patterson, Alexr., clerk	Alexandria	Boarder	1799	1799(2):17A
Patterson, Benjamin D.	Arlington	Inventory	1816	AB2:302; LVA-LP
Patterson, Benjamin D.	Arlington	Admin.	1816	WB2:134
Patterson, Benjamin D.	Arlington	Account	1817	AB3:035; LVA-LP
Patterson, Benjamin D.	Arlington	Sale	1817	AB3:019
Patterson, Benjamin D.	Arlington	Account	1818	AB3:145; LVA-LP
Patterson, Benjamin, house joiner	Alexandria	Head	1810	1810(4):03A
Patterson, Edgar	Arlington	Defendant	1824	ACO:237
Patterson, Hugh	Alexandria	Tithable +21	1787	Tax PP 1787:05
Patterson, James, tanner	Alexandria	Head	1810	1810(4):09A
Patterson, John	Alexandria	Tax Charge	1789	Tax PP 1789:14
Patterson, Thomas, Master	Arlington	Respondent	1827	ACO:275
Patterson, William	Alexandria	Tax Charge	1790	Tax PP 1790:12
Patterson, William	Alexandria	Tax Charge	1799	Tax PP 1799:32
Patterson, William	Arlington	Ordinary	1804	OBL1(np)
Patterson, William	Arlington	Ordinary	1805	OBL1(np)
Patterson, William	Arlington	Ordinary	1806	OBL2(np)
Patterson, William	Arlington	Inventory	1816	AB2:300; LVA-LP
Patterson, William	Arlington	Ordinary	1823	OBL3(np)
Patterson, William, plt.	Alexandria	Suit	1801	CRB:083
Patterson, William, Queen St.	Alexandria	Occupants	1790	Tax L 1790:13
Patterson, William, Sr.	Arlington	Bond	1816	WB2:117
Patterson, William, Sr.	Arlington	Will	1816	WB2:116; File #096A
Patterson, William to Sarah Patterson	Arlington	Sale	1817	LVA-LP (Accounts)
Patterson, Wm.	Alexandria	Tax Charge	1795	Tax PP 1795:23
Patterson, Wm.	Alexandria	Tax Charge	1795	Tax PP 1795:23
Patterson, Wm.	Alexandria	Tax Charge	1796	Tax PP 1796:15
Patterson, Wm.	Alexandria	Tax Charge	1798	Tax PP 1798:15
Patterson, Wm.	Alexandria	Tax Charge	1800	Tax PP 1800:33
Patterson, Wm., gunner	Alexandria	Head	1810	1810(1):11A
Patterson, Wm., Water St.	Alexandria	Occupant	1795	Tax L 1795:26
Pattinson, Jas., tanner	Alexandria	Housekeeper	1808	1808(4):24A
Pattinson, Wm.	Alexandria	Boarder	1808	1808(2):12A
Pattinson, Wm., blacksmith	Alexandria	Housekeeper	1808	1808(3):19A
Pattison, Benjamin, carpenter	Alexandria	Housekeeper	1808	1808(4):29A
Pattison, Wm.	Alexandria	Tax Charge	1799	Tax PP 1799:33
Patton & Butcher	Alexandria	Owner	1787	Tax L 1787:21
Patton & Butcher, Fairfax St.	Alexandria	Occupant	1787	Tax L 1787:02
Patton & Butcher, Fairfax St.	Alexandria	Occupant	1787	Tax L 1787:24
Patton & Butcher, Fairfax St.	Alexandria	Occupant	1787	Tax L 1787:21
Patton, Alexander	Alexandria	Resident	1800	1800(4):07B
Patton, Ann	Alexandria	Resident	1800	1800(4):13B
Patton, Ann B.	Arlington	Guard. Acct.	1821	AB4:245
Patton, Ann Maria	Arlington	Bond	1828	WB3:322
Patton, Ann Maria	Arlington	Will	1828	WB3:309; File #267A

NAME OR SUBJECT	LOCATION	TYPE	YEAR	REFERENCE(S)
Patton, James	Alexandria	Tax Charge	1789	Tax PP 1789:14
Patton, James	Alexandria	Tax Charge	1790	Tax PP 1790:11
Patton, James	Alexandria	Tax Charge	1796	Tax LP 1796:23
Patton, James	Alexandria	Tax Charge	1796	Tax PP 1796:15
Patton, James	Alexandria	Tax Charge	1799	Tax PP 1799:33
Patton, James	Arlington	Defendant	1808	ACO:085
Patton, James	Arlington	Defendant	1808	ACO:091
Patton, James	Arlington	Defendant	1808	ACO:081
Patton, James	Arlington	Defendant	1809	ACO:106, 109
Patton, James	Arlington	Defendant	1812	ACO:122
Patton, James	Arlington	Defendant	1812	ACO:121
Patton, James & Co.	Alexandria	Tax Charge	1796	Tax LP 1796:23
Patton, James & Robert, Jr., def.	Alexandria	Suit	1817	CRL:001
Patton, James, def.	Alexandria	Suit	1802	CRC:047
Patton, James, King St.	Alexandria	Owner	1795	Tax L 1795:23
Patton, James, merchant	Alexandria	Housekeeper	1808	1808(4):26A
Patton, James, plt.	Alexandria	Suit	1802	CRC:262
Patton, James, plt.	Alexandria	Suit	1802	CRC:004
Patton, James, plt.	Alexandria	Suit	1808	CRF:188
Patton, Jane	Arlington	Guard. Acct.	1821	AB4:245
Patton, Jas.	Alexandria	Tax Charge	1795	Tax PP 1795:24
Patton, Jas.	Alexandria	Tax Charge	1798	Tax PP 1798:15
Patton, Jas., Fairfax St.	Alexandria	Occupant	1795	Tax L 1795:29
Patton, Jas., King St.	Alexandria	Occupant	1795	Tax L 1795:23
Patton, John	Alexandria	Tax Charge	1796	Tax LP 1796:23
Patton, John	Alexandria	Tax Charge	1796	Tax PP 1796:15
Patton, John	Alexandria	Tax Charge	1799	Tax PP 1799:32
Patton, John	Alexandria	Boarder	1808	1808(1):06A
Patton, John B., merchant	Alexandria	Head	1810	1810(2):02A
Patton, John, bricklayer	Alexandria	Housekeeper	1808	1808(3):23A
Patton, John Butcher	Alexandria	Resident	1800	1800(4):13B
Patton, Rebecca	Arlington	Guard. Acct.	1821	AB4:245
Patton, Robert	Alexandria	Tax Charge	1796	Tax LP 1796:23
Patton, Robert, Jr.	Arlington	Defendant	1808	ACO:081
Patton, Robert, Jr.	Arlington	Defendant	1812	ACO:122
Patton, Robert, Jr., def.	Alexandria	Suit	1801	CRD:023
Patton, Robert, Jr., plt.	Alexandria	Suit	1815	CRK:245
Patton, Robt.	Alexandria	Mer. License	1800	Tax PP 1800:54(18)r
Patton, Thomas	Alexandria	Tax Charge	1796	Tax LP 1796:23
Patton, Thomas & wife, merchant	Alexandria	Head	1795	1795(4):01
Patton, Thomas, def.	Alexandria	Suit	1806	CRE:065
Patton, William	Alexandria	Owner	1787	Tax L 1787:21
Patton, William	Alexandria	Tax Charge	1789	Tax PP 1789:14
Patton, William & wife, merchant	Alexandria	Head	1795	1795(4):09
Patton, William, Pitt St.	Alexandria	Occupant	1787	Tax L 1787:21
Patton, Wm.	Alexandria	Tax Charge	1796	Tax LP 1796:24
Patton, Wm.	Alexandria	Tax Charge	1798	Tax PP 1798:15
Patton, Wm.	Alexandria	Resident	1800	1800(4):13B
Patton, Wm.	Alexandria	Boarder	1808	1808(1):06A
Patton, Wm. & wife Mary	Alexandria	Resident	1800	1800(4):13B
Patton, Wm., merchant	Alexandria	Head	1800	1800(4):13A
Patton, Wm., merchant	Alexandria	Housekeeper	1808	1808(1):06A
Paxton, Joseph, grantor	Arlington	Indenture D.	1804	ID3:023
Paxton, Joseph, in jail bounds	Arlington	Insolvent	1804	ID3:019
Payne, Duval	Alexandria	Deposition	1807	CRH:395
Payne, Henry, retailer	Alexandria	Housekeeper	1808	1808(4):27A
Payne, James	Alexandria	Deposition	1822	CRL:535
Payne, James	Alexandria	Deposition	1822	CRL:474
Payne, John	Alexandria	Will	1887	WB1:451; LP
Payne, John, Genl., at George Town	Alexandria	Deposition	1808	CRI:422
Payne, Landon	Alexandria	Tax Charge	1799	Tax PP 1799:32

NAME OR SUBJECT	LOCATION	TYPE	YEAR	REFERENCE(S)
Payne, London	Arlington	Bond	1820	WB2:344
Payne, London	Arlington	Will	1820	WB2:344; File #170A
Payne, London, drummer	Alexandria	Housekeeper	1808	1808(4):29A
Payne, Loud., Queen St.	Alexandria	Occupant	1795	Tax L 1795:12
Payne, Louden, house joiner	Alexandria	Head	1810	1810(4):03A
Payne, Lundon (C)	Alexandria	Tax Charge	1795	Tax PP 1795:23
Payne, Thos.	Alexandria	Boarder	1808	1808(1):07A
Payne, Vilender	Alexandria	Tax Charge	1788	Tax PP 1788:13
Peacock, Robert Ware	Arlington	Defendant	1802	PA:338
Peacock, Robert Ware, counsellor	Arlington	Proof	1801	ACO:004
Pead, William	Arlington	Apprentice	1804	OCR1801:212
Peake, Charles Henry, c/o Nancy Black	Arlington	Apprentice	1824	OCR1822:074a
Peake, Humphrey	Alexandria	Tax Charge	1796	Tax PP 1796:15
Peake, Thomas	Alexandria	Tax Charge	1796	Tax PP 1796:15
Pearce, Allan	Arlington	Will	1873	WB9:361; File #690A
Pearce, Allen	Arlington	Appraisal	1873	WB9:363
Pearce, Morris, c/o Susanna	Arlington	Apprentice	1805	OCR1801:280
Pearson, George W.	Arlington	Account	1831	LVA-LP
Pearson, George W.	Arlington	Appraisal	1831	LVA-LP
Pearson, George W.	Arlington	Admin.	1831	WB4:041
Pearson, George W., c/o George W.	Arlington	Guard.	1832	WB4:050
Pearson, Jas., Estate	Alexandria	Tax Charge	1798	Tax PP 1798:15
Pearson, Polley, washwoman	Alexandria	Housekeeper	1808	1808(2):17A
Pearson, Sarah, sempstress	Alexandria	Housekeeper	1808	1808(3):23A
Pearson, Simon	Alexandria	Tax Charge	1798	Tax PP 1798:14
Pearson's, tract called	Arlington	Suit	1840	LSA:055
Peck, Adam	Alexandria	Tax Charge	1800	Tax PP 1800:33
Peck, James (C), Rev.	Arlington	Ordination	1865	FBB(np)
Peck, Joseph	Alexandria	Tax Charge	1796	Tax PP 1796:15
Peck, Joseph	Alexandria	Mer. License	1798	Tax PP 1798:20-5
Peck, Joseph	Alexandria	Tax Charge	1798	Tax PP 1798:15
Peck, Peter, plt.	Alexandria	Ejectment	1802	CRE:242
Peck, William T.	Arlington	Ordinary	1806	OBL2(np)
Peck, William I.	Arlington	Ordinary	1807	OBL2(np)
Peck, Wm. T., coachman & shop., T.L.	Alexandria	Housekeeper	1808	1808(2):16A
Pecks, Joseph	Alexandria	Tax Charge	1796	Tax LP 1796:23
Pecks, Joseph, w, shopkeeper	Alexandria	Head	1796	1796(3):6
Peed, James, carpenter	Alexandria	Head	1810	1810(1):12A
Peers, Valentine	Alexandria	Tax Charge	1796	Tax LP 1796:23
Peirce, Joshua	Alexandria	Tax Charge	1790	Tax PP 1790:11
Pelter, James	Alexandria	Deposition	1814	CRI:524
Pelter, James	Arlington	Sale	1815	AB2:135
Pelter, James	Arlington	Inventory	1815	AB2:135; LVA-LP
Pelter, James	Arlington	Admin.	1815	WB2:015
Pelter, James	Arlington	Account	1816	AB2:283; LVA-LP
Pelter, James, waggoner	Alexandria	Head	1810	1810(3):07A
Pelton, Enoch	Arlington	Ordinary	1809	OBL2(np)
Pelton, Enoch, at the Upper Ferry	Arlington	Ordinary	1823	OBL3(np)
Pelton, Enoch, orphans of	Arlington	Guard.	1819	WB2:308
Pelton, Enoch, shopkeeper & tavern lic.	Alexandria	Housekeeper	1808	1808(1):05A
Pelton, Enoch, tavern keeper	Alexandria	Head	1810	1810(2):05A
Pelton, Enock	Arlington	Ordinary	1810	OBL2(np)
Pendleton, Nathaniel	Alexandria	Deed	1805	CRI:360
Pendleton, Nathaniel, City of New York	Alexandria	Deed	1802	CRI:338
Pendleton, Nathaniel, City of New York	Alexandria	Deed	1803	CRI:347
Pendleton, Nathaniel, complt.	Alexandria	Suit	1811	CRI:176
Penn, Walter L., constable	Arlington	Appointment	1851	BB(np)
Penney, John & wife Elizebeth	Alexandria	Resident	1800	1800(4):16B
Penney, John, marriener	Alexandria	Head	1800	1800(4):16A
Pennoyer, John	Arlington	Account	1801	WBA:048; LVA-LP
Pennoyer, John, Capt.	Arlington	Statement	(nd)	LVA-LP

NAME OR SUBJECT	LOCATION	TYPE	YEAR	REFERENCE(S)
Penny, John	Alexandria	Tax Charge	1800	Tax PP 1800:34
Penoyer, John	Arlington	Admin.	1801	WBA:045
Penoyer, John	Arlington	Inventory	1801	WBA:047
Penoyer, John	Arlington	Account	1803	LVA-LP
Penoyer, John	Arlington	Account	1803	WBA:182
Pepper, Michael	Alexandria	Tax Charge	1796	Tax PP 1796:15
Pepper, Michael	Alexandria	Tax Charge	1799	Tax PP 1799:32
Pepper, Michael	Alexandria	Tax Charge	1800	Tax PP 1800:33
Pepper, Michael, Water St.	Alexandria	Occupant	1790	Tax L 1790:05
Pepper, Michl.	Alexandria	Tax Charge	1790	Tax PP 1790:11
Pepper, Michl.	Alexandria	Tax Charge	1795	Tax PP 1795:23
Pepper, Michl.	Alexandria	Tax Charge	1796	Tax LP 1796:23
Pepper, Michl.	Alexandria	Tax Charge	1798	Tax PP 1798:14
Percy, Henry, [sick] man	Alexandria	Housekeeper	1808	1808(4):27A
Perin & Brothers	Alexandria	Mer. License	1799	Tax PP 1799:52-08r
Perkins, Charles	Arlington	Admin.	1821	WB3:005
Perkins, John	Arlington	Defendant	1821	ACO:197
Perkins, Samuel	Arlington	Ordinary	1823	OBL3(np)
Perkins, Samuel, at his house	Arlington	Ordinary	1822	OBL3(np)
Perkins, Samuel, in Alexandria Co.	Arlington	Ordinary	1824	OBL3(np)
Perot, John, of Philadelphia	Alexandria	Deed	1811	CRK:045, 048
Perrin & Brother	Alexandria	Tax Charge	1799	Tax PP 1799:32
Perrin & Brother	Alexandria	Tax Charge	1800	Tax PP 1800:33
Perrin & Brothers	Alexandria	Tax Charge	1796	Tax PP 1796:15
Perrin & Brothers	Alexandria	Mer. License	1798	Tax PP 1798:20-5
Perrin & Brothers	Alexandria	Tax Charge	1798	Tax PP 1798:14
Perrin Brothers	Alexandria	Tax Charge	1796	Tax LP 1796:23
Perrin Brothers, retailers	Alexandria	Housekeeper	1808	1808(2):13A
Perrin, Joseph	Alexandria	Owner	1787	Tax L 1787:21
Perrin, Joseph	Alexandria	Tax Charge	1788	Tax PP 1788:13
Perrin, Joseph M.	Alexandria	Tax Charge	1787	Tax PP 1787:12
Perrin, Joseph M.	Alexandria	Tax Charge	1789	Tax PP 1789:14
Perrin, Joseph M.	Alexandria	Tax Charge	1790	Tax PP 1790:11
Perrin, Joseph M.	Alexandria	Tax Charge	1795	Tax PP 1795:23
Perrin, Joseph M., Royal St.	Alexandria	Occupant	1790	Tax L 1790:09
Perrin, Joseph M., Royal St.	Alexandria	Owner	1790	Tax L 1790:09
Perrin, Joseph M., Royal St.	Alexandria	Occupant	1795	Tax L 1795:24
Perrin, Joseph M., Royal St.	Alexandria	Owner	1795	Tax L 1795:24
Perrin, Joseph Marie	Arlington	Inventory	1808	WBC:088
Perrin, Joseph Marie	Arlington	Will	1808	WBC:047; File #034A
Perrin, Joseph Marie	Arlington	Bond	1808	WBC:048
Perrin, Joseph Marie	Arlington	Account	1809	WBC:213; LVA-LP
Perrin, Joseph, Royal St.	Alexandria	Occupant	1787	Tax L 1787:21
Perrin, Matalan	Alexandria	Tithable +16	1790	Tax PP 1790:11
Perrin, Mathurin	Alexandria	Tithable +21	1787	Tax PP 1787:12
Perrin, Mathurin	Alexandria	Tithable +16	1789	Tax PP 1789:14
Perrin, Mathurin	Arlington	Will	1814	WB1:315; File #124A
Perrin, Mathurin	Arlington	Account	1816	AB2:250; LVA-LP
Perrin, Mathurin	Arlington	Account	1819	AB3:279; LVA-LP
Perrin, Mathurin, merchant	Alexandria	Head	1810	1810(2):03A
Perrin, Matthurin	Alexandria	Tithable +16	1788	Tax PP 1788:13
Perrin, Matthurin	Arlington	Inventory	1815	AB2:093; LVA-LP
Perrin, Matthurin	Arlington	Account	1821	AB4:247
Perrin, Matthurin	Arlington	Account	1822	AB5:081; LVA-LP
Perrin, Matthurin	Arlington	Account	1823	AB5:149; LVA-LP
Perrin, Methurion	Alexandria	Tax Charge	1795	Tax PP 1795:23
Perry, Alex., Fairfax St.	Alexandria	Occupant	1790	Tax L 1790:09
Perry, Alexander	Alexandria	Tax Charge	1787	Tax PP 1787:12
Perry, Alexander	Alexandria	Tax Charge	1788	Tax PP 1788:13
Perry, Alexander	Alexandria	Tax Charge	1789	Tax PP 1789:15
Perry, Alexander	Alexandria	Tax Charge	1796	Tax PP 1796:15

NAME OR SUBJECT	LOCATION	TYPE	YEAR	REFERENCE(S)
Perry, Alexander	Alexandria	Tax Charge	1799	Tax PP 1799:32
Perry, Alexander	Alexandria	Tax Charge	1800	Tax PP 1800:33
Perry, Alexander	Arlington	Ordinary	1802	OBL1(np)
Perry, Alexander	Arlington	Ordinary	1803	OBL1(np)
Perry, Alexander	Arlington	Ordinary	1804	OBL1(np)
Perry, Alexander	Arlington	Defendant	1824	ACO:241, 247
Perry, Alexander	Arlington	Defendant	1825	ACO:252, 257
Perry, Alexander	Arlington	Defendant	1826	ACO:260, 263
Perry, Alexander	Arlington	Defendant	1827	ACO:266, 273
Perry, Alexander	Arlington	Inventory	1831	LVA-LP
Perry, Alexander	Arlington	Will	1831	WB4:015; File #304A
Perry, Alexander	Arlington	Bond	1831	WB4:015
Perry, Alexander	Arlington	Account	1832	AB7:143; LVA-LP
Perry, Alexander	Arlington	Account F.	1835	AB7:143
Perry, Alexander, def.	Alexandria	Suit	1801	CRB:247
Perry, Alexander, def.	Alexandria	Suit	1801	CRB:147
Perry, Alexander, def.	Alexandria	Suit	1801	CRB:217
Perry, Alexander, def.	Alexandria	Suit	1801	CRC:199
Perry, Alexander, Fairfax St.	Alexandria	Owner	1790	Tax L 1790:09
Perry, Alexander, Jr., grantee	Arlington	Indenture D.	1817	ID2:427
Perry, Alexander, retailer	Alexandria	Housekeeper	1808	1808(3):21A
Perry, Alexander, soap boiler	Alexandria	Head	1810	1810(3):02A
Perry, Alexander, trustee, grantee	Arlington	Indenture D.	1812	ID2:074
Perry, Alexander, trustee, grantee	Arlington	Indenture D.	1813	ID2:204
Perry, Alexr.	Alexandria	Owner	1787	Tax L 1787:21
Perry, Alexr.	Alexandria	Tax Charge	1790	Tax PP 1790:11
Perry, Alexr.	Alexandria	Tax Charge	1795	Tax PP 1795:23
Perry, Alexr.	Alexandria	Tax Charge	1796	Tax LP 1796:23
Perry, Alexr.	Alexandria	Tax Charge	1798	Tax PP 1798:14
Perry, Alexr.	Alexandria	Reference	1808	1808(2):10B
Perry, Alexr., Duke St.	Alexandria	Occupant	1787	Tax L 1787:05
Perry, Alexr., Fairfax St.	Alexandria	Occupant	1787	Tax L 1787:21
Perry, Alexr., Gretter's alley	Alexandria	Occupant	1795	Tax L 1795:06
Perry, Alexr., s/o Alexander	Alexandria	Boarder	1808	1808(3):21A
Perry, Alexr., Wilks St.	Alexandria	Occupant	1787	Tax L 1787:06
Perry, Edwd.	Alexandria	Boarder	1808	1808(1):03A
Perry, Elisha	Alexandria	Tax Charge	1800	Tax PP 1800:33
Perry, Fewell A., in Alexandria Co.	Arlington	Ordinary	1825	OBL4(np)
Perry, Henrietta	Arlington	Will	1841	WB4:284; File #369A
Perry, James	Arlington	Admin.	1819	WB2:272
Perry, James, brickmaker	Alexandria	Housekeeper	1808	1808(3):19A
Perry, John	Alexandria	Will	1893	WB2:061; LP
Perry, John T.B.	Arlington	Inventory	1859	WB7:412; LVA-LP
Perry, Mary Anna	Alexandria	Will	1895	WB2:111; LP
Peter, Bohrer, Estate, plt.	Alexandria	Suit	1803	CRD:068
Peter, John, w, mariner	Alexandria	Head	1796	1796(3):4
Peter, Sarah	Arlington	Guard. Acct.	1804	LVA-LP
Peterkin, Thomas, def.	Alexandria	Suit	1801	CRB:079
Peterkin, Thos.	Alexandria	Tithable +16	1789	Tax PP 1789:12
Peters, John	Alexandria	Tax Charge	1796	Tax LP 1796:23
Peters, John, mariner	Alexandria	Tax Charge	1795	Tax PP 1795:23
Peters, Mary, Queen St.	Alexandria	Occupant	1795	Tax L 1795:16
Peterson & Taylor, Prince St.	Alexandria	Occupant	1787	Tax L 1787:13
Peterson, Henry	Alexandria	Tax Charge	1788	Tax PP 1788:13
Peterson, Henry	Arlington	Claim	1812	ACO:124
Peterson, Henry, Jr.	Alexandria	Tax Charge	1789	Tax PP 1789:15
Peterson, J., Water St.	Alexandria	Occupant	1787	Tax L 1787:15
Peterson, Peter	Alexandria	Tax Charge	1787	Tax PP 1787:12
Peterson, Peter	Alexandria	Tax Charge	1788	Tax PP 1788:13
Petit, Jesse, c/o Elizabeth	Arlington	Apprentice	1803	OCR1801:090
Petit, John	Alexandria	Tax Charge	1788	Tax PP 1788:13

NAME OR SUBJECT	LOCATION	TYPE	YEAR	REFERENCE(S)
Petit, John	Alexandria	Tax Charge	1789	Tax PP 1789:14
Petit, John	Arlington	Will (NR)	1836	File #068A
Pettit, John	Alexandria	Tax Charge	1787	Tax PP 1787:11
Pettit, John, Fairfax St.	Alexandria	Occupant	1790	Tax L 1790:07
Pettit, John, King St.	Alexandria	Owner	1790	Tax L 1790:09
Pettit, John, King St.	Alexandria	Occupant	1790	Tax L 1790:09
Pettitt & Blondelet, Fairfax St.	Alexandria	Occupant	1787	Tax L 1787:19
Pettitt & Blondelet, King St.	Alexandria	Occupant	1787	Tax L 1787:21
Pettitt, John	Alexandria	Owner	1787	Tax L 1787:21
Pettitt, John	Alexandria	Tax Charge	1790	Tax PP 1790:11
Pettitt, John, King St.	Alexandria	Occupant	1787	Tax L 1787:21
Petty, James	Arlington	Apprentice	1824	OCR1822:079a
Peverill, George	Arlington	Will	1872	WB9:352; File #688A
Peyton & Gibson	Alexandria	Mer. License	1798	Tax PP 1798:20-5
Peyton, Alfred	Arlington	Will	1841	WB4:296; File #386A
Peyton, Ann	Alexandria	Tax Charge	1790	Tax PP 1790:12
Peyton, Ann	Alexandria	Housekeeper	1799	1799(2):06A
Peyton, Ann	Alexandria	Tax Charge	1799	Tax PP 1799:32
Peyton, Ann	Alexandria	Head	1810	1810(3):04A
Peyton, Ann	Arlington	Inventory	1826	AB6:172
Peyton, Ann	Arlington	Will P.	1826	OCR1822:108a
Peyton, Ann	Arlington	Admin.	1826	OCR1822:109
Peyton, Ann	Arlington	Bond	1826	WB3:219
Peyton, Ann	Arlington	Will	1826	WB3:218; File #244A
Peyton, Ann	Arlington	Account	1827	AB6:436; LVA-LP
Peyton, Ann, Mrs.	Alexandria	Tax Charge	1800	Tax PP 1800:33
Peyton, F. & Co., King St.	Alexandria	Occupant	1787	Tax L 1787:21
Peyton, Francis	Alexandria	Deposition	(nd)	CRI:085
Peyton, Francis	Alexandria	Tax Charge	1787	Tax PP 1787:12
Peyton, Francis	Alexandria	Tax Charge	1788	Tax PP 1788:13
Peyton, Francis	Alexandria	Tax Charge	1789	Tax PP 1789:14
Peyton, Francis	Alexandria	Tax Charge	1790	Tax PP 1790:11
Peyton, Francis	Alexandria	Tax Charge	1790	Tax PP 1790:11
Peyton, Francis	Arlington	Witness	1795	OT:28/07/1795
Peyton, Francis	Alexandria	Tax Charge	1795	Tax PP 1795:24
Peyton, Francis	Alexandria	Tax Charge	1796	Tax LP 1796:23
Peyton, Francis	Alexandria	Tax Charge	1796	Tax PP 1796:15
Peyton, Francis	Alexandria	Tax Charge	1798	Tax PP 1798:14
Peyton, Francis	Alexandria	Tax Charge	1799	Tax PP 1799:32
Peyton, Francis	Alexandria	Tax Charge	1800	Tax PP 1800:33
Peyton, Francis	Alexandria	Deposition	1808	CRI:092
Peyton, Francis	Arlington	Inventory	1836	LVA-LP
Peyton, Francis	Arlington	Will	1836	WB4:124; File #344A
Peyton, Francis	Arlington	Bond	1836	WB4:113
Peyton, Francis	Arlington	Account	1838	LVA-LP
Peyton, Francis	Arlington	Defendant	1842	LSA:094
Peyton, Francis, at Heiskell's Tavern	Alexandria	Deposition	1802	CRI:080
Peyton, Francis, gentlewoman	Alexandria	Housekeeper	1808	1808(2):13A
Peyton, Francis, King St.	Alexandria	Owner	1790	Tax L 1790:09
Peyton, Francis, King St.	Alexandria	Occupant	1790	Tax L 1790:09
Peyton, Francis, King St.	Alexandria	Owner	1795	Tax L 1795:24(2)
Peyton, Francis, King St.	Alexandria	Occupant	1795	Tax L 1795:24
Peyton, Francis, M.D.	Alexandria	Tax Charge	1798	Tax PP 1798:15
Peyton, Francis, plt.	Alexandria	Suit	1803	CRD:084
Peyton, Francis, Prince St.	Alexandria	Owner	1795	Tax L 1795:24
Peyton, Francis, Prince St.	Alexandria	Occupant	1795	Tax L 1795:24
Peyton, Francis, St. Asaph St.	Alexandria	Occupant	1790	Tax L 1790:09
Peyton, Francis, Union St.	Alexandria	Owner	1795	Tax L 1795:24
Peyton, Francis, Union St.	Alexandria	Occupant	1795	Tax L 1795:24
Peyton, George Dallas	Arlington	Guard. Acct.	1852	WB6:076; LVA-LP
Peyton, George Dallas, c/o Wm. Henry	Arlington	Guard.	1852	BB(np)

NAME OR SUBJECT	LOCATION	TYPE	YEAR	REFERENCE(S)
Peyton, Henry	Arlington	Defendant	1842	LSA:094
Peyton, John	Arlington	Defendant	1842	LSA:094
Peyton, John B.	Arlington	Account	1834	LVA-LP (Accounts 2nd)
Peyton, John B.	Arlington	Complainant	1842	LSA:094
Peyton, John S.	Arlington	Bond	1853	BB(np)
Peyton, John S.	Arlington	Appraisal	1853	WB6:261; LVA-LP
Peyton, John S., at his house	Arlington	Ordinary	1841	OBL6(np)
Peyton, Lavinia	Arlington	Guard.	1836	WB4:114
Peyton, Lucian	Arlington	Defendant	1842	LSA:094
Peyton, Lucien, comr. of revenue	Arlington	Appointment	1850	BB(np)
Peyton, Lucien, notary public	Arlington	Appointment	1851	BB(np)
Peyton, Mrs., Wilkes St.	Alexandria	Occupant	1790	Tax L 1790:05
Peyton, Sarah	Arlington	Exor. Bond	1849	EBB(np)
Peyton, Sarah	Arlington	Will	1849	WB5:143; File #451A
Peyton, Sarah Payne, c/o Valentine	Arlington	Guard.	1812	WB1:198
Peyton, Sarah, washerwoman	Alexandria	Head	1810	1810(1):09A
Peyton, Sarah, wid/o Francis	Arlington	Defendant	1842	LSA:094
Peyton, Susan P., w/o Valentine W.	Arlington	Guard. Acct.	1814	AB2:029; LVA-LP
Peyton, Thomas J.	Arlington	Defendant	1842	LSA:094
Peyton, Thomas J.	Arlington	Admin.	1844	OCR1842:062
Peyton, Thomas J.	Arlington	Account	1845	AB9:050
Peyton, Thomas Jefferson	Arlington	Inventory	1844	AB8:447; LVA-LP
Peyton, Thomas W.	Arlington	Insolvent	1817	ID2:393
Peyton, Thomas W., def.	Alexandria	Suit	1810	CRK:162
Peyton, Thomas W., def.	Alexandria	Suit	1816	CRK:156
Peyton, Thomas W., grantor	Arlington	Indenture D.	1817	ID2:397
Peyton, Thomas West, plt.	Alexandria	Suit	1810	CRK:164
Peyton, Thos. W.	Alexandria	Boarder	1799	1799(2):06A
Peyton, West	Alexandria	Tax Charge	1800	Tax PP 1800:33
Peyton, William	Arlington	Account	1834	LVA-LP (Accounts 2nd)
Peyton, William H.	Arlington	Account	1852	WB6:060; LVA-LP
Peyton, William H.	Arlington	Account	1852	WB6:095
Phearlow, Philip	Alexandria	Tax Charge	1788	Tax PP 1788:13
Phelps, John Wolcott, of Marlboro VT	Alexandria	Will	1886	WB1:436; LP
Pherno, Philip, St. Asaph St.	Alexandria	Occupant	1790	Tax L 1790:09
Pherno, Philip, St. Asaph St.	Alexandria	Owner	1790	Tax L 1790:09
Philbert, Martha, sempstress	Alexandria	Housekeeper	1808	1808(2):16A
Philbert, Patsey, c/o Chloe	Arlington	Apprentice	1801	OCR1801:004
Philips, Charles	Arlington	Apprentice	1804	OCR1801:197
Philips, John	Arlington	Ordinary	1827	OBL4(np)
Philips, John, cartman	Alexandria	Housekeeper	1808	1808(3):20A
Philips, John, grantee	Arlington	Indenture D.	1830	ID:268
Philips, John H.	Alexandria	Deposition	1819	CRK:454
Philips, John, in Alexandria Co.	Arlington	Ordinary	1825	OBL4(np)
Philips, John, taylor	Alexandria	Housekeeper	1808	1808(2):12A
Philips, M__gea	Alexandria	Serv./Appr.	1800	1800(4):12B
Philips, William, at his house	Arlington	Ordinary	1824	OBL3(np)
Philips, William, at the Cross Roads	Arlington	Ordinary	1823	OBL3(np)
Philips, William, c/o John H.	Arlington	Apprentice	1805	OCR1801:294
Philips, Zachariah	Alexandria	Tax Charge	1799	Tax PP 1799:32
Phillips, James	Arlington	Bond	1852	BB(np)
Phillips, James	Arlington	Inventory	1852	WB6:124; LVA-LP
Phillips, James	Arlington	Will	1852	WB6:112; File #480A
Phillips, James	Arlington	Account	1854	WB6:364; LVA-LP
Phillips, James B.	Arlington	Will	1876	WB9:385; File #694A
Phillips, James, on Columbus St.	Arlington	Ordinary	1849	OBL6(np)
Phillips, John, drayman	Alexandria	Head	1810	1810(3):08A
Phillips, John H.	Arlington	Will	1828	WB3:311; File #269A
Phillips, John, shopkeeper	Alexandria	Head	1810	1810(2):03A
Phillips, Joseph	Alexandria	Tithable +21	1787	Tax PP 1787:13
Phillips, L. Annette	Arlington	Will	1896	WB10:326; File #770A

NAME OR SUBJECT	LOCATION	TYPE	YEAR	REFERENCE(S)
Phillips, William	Arlington	Insolvent	1826	ID:037
Phillips, William, drayman	Alexandria	Head	1810	1810(3):06A
Phillips, William, grantor	Arlington	Indenture D.	1814	ID2:366
Phillips, William, grantor	Arlington	Indenture D.	1826	ID:039
Phillips, William Henry	Arlington	Apprentice	1845	OCR1842:098
Phillips, William, in jail	Arlington	Insolvent	1814	ID2:363
Phillips, Wm., drayman	Alexandria	Housekeeper	1808	1808(3):22A
Phippard, Sarah, of Washington DC	Arlington	Will	1899	WB10:402; File #790A
Phirno, Philip	Alexandria	Tax Charge	1789	Tax PP 1789:15
Piano fortes, barrel organs and music	Arlington	Suit	1808	ACO:096
Piano fortes, barrel organs and music	Arlington	Suit	1808	ACR:039
Piano fortes, barrel organs	Alexandria	Suit	1808	CRF:289
Pickerel, Richd.	Alexandria	Tax Charge	1796	Tax LP 1796:23
Pickerell, J.	Alexandria	Tax Charge	1796	Tax PP 1796:15
Pickerell, John	Arlington	Apprentice	1815	OCR1811:316
Pickerell, Richard	Alexandria	Tax Charge	1796	Tax PP 1796:15
Pickeril, Charles & sister	Alexandria	Boarder	1799	1799(2):17A
Pickering, Levi	Arlington	Ordinary	1821	OBL3(np)
Pickering, Levi	Arlington	Inventory	1835	LVA-LP
Pickering, Levi	Arlington	Admin.	1835	WB4:089
Pickering, Richd.	Alexandria	Tax Charge	1798	Tax PP 1798:14
Pickett, Charles	Alexandria	Tax Charge	1796	Tax PP 1796:15
Pickett, Thomas B.	Arlington	Inventory	1852	WB6:042; LVA-LP
Pickett, Thomas B.	Arlington	Sale	1852	WB6:038; LVA-LP
Pickett, William S., Exors., plt.	Alexandria	Suit	1801	CRB:094
Pickrell, Richd.	Alexandria	Tax Charge	1795	Tax PP 1795:23
Piell [Pile], Peter	Alexandria	Tax Charge	1788	Tax PP 1788:13
Pier, Jessey, labourrer	Alexandria	Boarder	1800	1800(4):11A
Pier, Jessey	Alexandria	Resident	1800	1800(4):11B
Pierce, Humphrey	Arlington	Suit	1805	ID3:099
Pierce, Humphrey, assignee of plt.	Alexandria	Suit	1801	CRB:054
Pierce, Humphrey, plt.	Alexandria	Suit	1807	CRF:193
Pierce, John, sadler	Alexandria	Housekeeper	1808	1808(3):21A
Pierce, Nathaniel	Arlington	Inventory	1809	WBC:325; LVA-LP
Pierce, Nathaniel	Arlington	Admin.	1809	WBC:315
Pierce, Nathaniel, Jr.	Arlington	Account	1812	LVA-LP
Pierce, Susannah, washwoman	Alexandria	Housekeeper	1808	1808(1):05A
Piercy, Catharine	Alexandria	Boarder	1799	1799(2):10A
Piercy, Henry	Alexandria	Tax Charge	1795	Tax PP 1795:24
Piercy, Henry	Alexandria	Tax Charge	1796	Tax LP 1796:23
Piercy, Henry	Alexandria	Tax Charge	1796	Tax PP 1796:15
Piercy, Henry	Alexandria	Tax Charge	1799	Tax PP 1799:32
Piercy, Henry	Arlington	Bond	1809	WBC:254
Piercy, Henry	Arlington	Will	1809	WBC:252; File #43A
Piercy, Henry	Arlington	Account	1815	AB2:133; LVA-LP
Piercy, Henry & wife, potter	Alexandria	Housekeeper	1799	1799(2):10A
Piercy, Henry, Capt.	Arlington	Inventory	1815	AB2:133; LVA-LP
Piercy, Henry, Duke St.	Alexandria	Occupant	1795	Tax L 1795:23
Piercy, Henry, Duke St.	Alexandria	Owner	1795	Tax L 1795:23
Piercy, Henry, King St.	Alexandria	Occupant	1795	Tax L 1795:32
Piercy, Henry, w(1)3, merchant	Alexandria	Head	1796	1796(3):5
Piercy, Hy.	Alexandria	Tax Charge	1798	Tax PP 1798:15
Pieres, Nat.	Alexandria	Boarder	1808	1808(1):04A
Pierson, Sarah, seamstress	Alexandria	Head	1810	1810(3):06A
Pigot, John	Arlington	Crime	1800	OT:04/10/1800
Pile, Jacob	Alexandria	Tithable +16	1790	Tax PP 1790:07
Pile, Jacob	Alexandria	Tax Charge	1796	Tax PP 1796:15
Pile, Jacob	Alexandria	Tax Charge	1799	Tax PP 1799:32
Pile, Jacob	Alexandria	Tax Charge	1800	Tax PP 1800:33
Pile, Lewis	Alexandria	Tax Charge	1799	Tax PP 1799:32
Pile, Peter	Alexandria	Tax Charge	1787	Tax PP 1787:01

NAME OR SUBJECT	LOCATION	TYPE	YEAR	REFERENCE(S)
Pile, Peter	Alexandria	Tax Charge	1788	Tax PP 1788:13
Pile, Peter	Alexandria	Tax Charge	1789	Tax PP 1789:14
Pile, Peter	Alexandria	Tax Charge	1790	Tax PP 1790:11
Pile, Peter	Alexandria	Tax Charge	1796	Tax PP 1796:15
Pile, Peter	Alexandria	Tax Charge	1798	Tax PP 1798:14
Pile, Peter	Alexandria	Tax Charge	1799	Tax PP 1799:32
Pile, Peter & wife, sausage maker	Alexandria	Housekeeper	1799	1799(2):06A
Pile, Peter, p. and [sausage] maker	Alexandria	Housekeeper	1808	1808(3):21A
Pile, Peter, Royal St.	Alexandria	Occupant	1790	Tax L 1790:01
Pile, Peter, w(4), tobacconist	Alexandria	Head	1796	1796(3):3
Pile, Phil., s/o Peter	Alexandria	Boarder	1808	1808(3):21A
Pile, Pter, Royal St.	Alexandria	Occupant	1787	Tax L 1787:19
Piles, Christian	Arlington	Inventory	1818	AB3:196; LVA-LP
Piles, Christian	Arlington	Will	1818	WB2:244; File #153A
Piles, Jacob, laborer	Alexandria	Housekeeper	1808	1808(4):27A
Piles, Jacob, labourer	Alexandria	Head	1810	1810(4):02A
Piles, Lewis	Alexandria	Tax Charge	1800	Tax PP 1800:33
Piles, Lewis	Arlington	Inventory	1842	AB8:314
Piles, Lewis	Arlington	Admin.	1842	OCR1842:006
Piles, Lewis	Arlington	Admin.	1842	WB4:304
Piles, Lewis	Arlington	Account	1843	OCR1842:038
Piles, Lewis	Arlington	Citation	1845	OCR1842:102
Piles, Lewis, assault and battery	Arlington	Defendant	1801	PA:168
Piles, Lewis, blacksmith	Alexandria	Boarder	1799	1799(2):04A
Piles, Lewis, blacksmith	Alexandria	Housekeeper	1808	1808(1):01A
Piles, Lewis, blacksmith	Alexandria	Head	1810	1810(4):04A
Piles, Mary Ann	Arlington	Apprentice	1846	OCR1842:171
Piles, Peter	Alexandria	Tax Charge	1796	Tax LP 1796:23
Piles, Peter	Alexandria	Tax Charge	1796	Tax LP 1796:23
Piles, Peter	Alexandria	Tax Charge	1800	Tax PP 1800:33
Piles, Peter	Arlington	Ordinary	1810	OBL2(np)
Piles, Peter	Arlington	Ordinary	1810	OBL2(np)
Piles, Peter	Arlington	Bond	1816	WB2:160, 195
Piles, Peter	Arlington	Will	1816	WB2:158; File #135A
Piles, Peter	Arlington	Inventory	1817	AB3:032; LVA-LP
Piles, Peter	Arlington	Sale	1817	AB3:064, 066
Piles, Peter	Arlington	Account	1818	AB3:189; LVA-LP
Piles, Peter	Arlington	Account F.	1819	AB3:321; LVA-LP
Piles, Peter, blacksmith	Alexandria	Housekeeper	1808	1808(4):26A
Piles, Peter, Jr.	Alexandria	Head	1810	1810(4):02A
Piles, Peter, Royal St.	Alexandria	Occupant	1795	Tax L 1795:01
Piles, Peter, tavern keeper	Alexandria	Head	1810	1810(3):01A
Piles, Susanna	Arlington	Apprentice	1846	OCR1842:171
Pilmere, Thos.	Alexandria	Tax Charge	1796	Tax LP 1796:24
Pilmore, Thomas	Alexandria	Tax Charge	1790	Tax PP 1790:12
Pinkton, Mary	Alexandria	Head	1800	1800(4):05A
Pinnock, William, at Norfolk	Alexandria	Deposition	1805	CRF:271
Piper, Harry	Arlington	Will	1802	DBD:151
Piper, Hugh, wheelwright	Alexandria	Head	1810	1810(1):05A
Piper, James	Arlington	Inventory	1813	AB1:329; LVA-LP
Piper, James	Arlington	Admin.	1813	WB1:234
Piper, James	Arlington	Apprentice	1829	OCR1822:172a
Piper, James, shopkeeper	Alexandria	Housekeeper	1808	1808(3):20A
Piper, Michael	Alexandria	Tax Charge	1788	Tax PP 1788:13
Piper, Michael	Alexandria	Tax Charge	1789	Tax PP 1789:15
Piper, Sarah, washerwoman	Alexandria	Head	1810	1810(1):07A
Piper, Thomas (C), c/o Hugh	Arlington	Apprentice	1846	OCR1842:178
Piper, William	Alexandria	Tithable +16	1788	Tax PP 1788:02
Piper, William	Alexandria	Tithable +16	1789	Tax PP 1789:03
Piper, William	Alexandria	Tax Charge	1799	Tax PP 1799:32
Piper, William	Alexandria	Tax Charge	1800	Tax PP 1800:33

NAME OR SUBJECT	LOCATION	TYPE	YEAR	REFERENCE(S)
Piper, William & wife	Alexandria	Head	1795	1795(4):06
Piper, Wm.	Alexandria	Tax Charge	1796	Tax LP 1796:24
Piper, Wm. (C)	Alexandria	Tax Charge	1795	Tax PP 1795:24
Piper, Wm. & wife Sarah	Alexandria	Resident	1800	1800(4):11B
Piper, Wm. & wife (C)	Alexandria	Housekeeper	1799	1799(2):13A
Piper, Wm., laborer	Alexandria	Housekeeper	1808	1808(4):24A
Pipper, Wm., laberrer	Alexandria	Head	1800	1800(4):11A
Pipsico, John	Arlington	Inventory	1843	AB8:352; LVA-LP
Pipsico, John	Arlington	Admin.	1843	OCR1842:021
Pipsico, John	Arlington	Bond	1854	WB4:314
Pipsico, John, Jr.	Arlington	Account	1844	AB8:458; LVA-LP
Pipsico, John, Sr.	Arlington	Will	1843	WB4:315; File #393A
Pitman, John	Alexandria	Tax Charge	1800	Tax PP 1800:33
Pitman, Mrs.	Alexandria	Head	1810	1810(4):01A
Pittman, Cath., sempstress	Alexandria	Housekeeper	1808	1808(4):27A
Pittman, Henry, c/o Catharine Ann	Arlington	Apprentice	1812	OCR1811:047
Pittman, Jno.	Alexandria	Tax Charge	1798	Tax PP 1798:15
Pittman, Jno. & wife, silversmith	Alexandria	Housekeeper	1799	1799(2):03A
Pittman, John	Alexandria	Tax Charge	1799	Tax PP 1799:32
Pitts, Thoimas	Alexandria	Tax Charge	1799	Tax PP 1799:32
Pitts, Thomas & wife Marthew	Alexandria	Resident	1800	1800(4):11B
Pitts, Thomas, coopper	Alexandria	Head	1800	1800(4):11A
Pitts, Thos.	Alexandria	Tax Charge	1800	Tax PP 1800:33
Pitts, [blank] & wife, mariner	Alexandria	Housekeeper	1799	1799(2):14A
Plain, Benjamin K., of Washington DC	Alexandria	Will	1893	WBC1:066; LP
Plain, George	Arlington	Appraisal	1858	WB7:311; LVA-LP
Plant, James, b. Sheffield, Eng.	Arlington	Alien Entry	1818	RA:30/3/18
Plater, Sarah, spinster	Alexandria	Head	1800	1800(4):14A
Platter, Sally	Alexandria	Resident	1800	1800(4):14B
Playford, Harriot, c/o Robert (18)	Arlington	Alien Entry	1818	RA:13/3/18
Playford, Robert, b. Westwinch, Eng.	Arlington	Alien Entry	1818	RA:13/3/18
Playford, Robert Wm., c/o Robert (20)	Arlington	Alien Entry	1818	RA:13/3/18
Playford, Sophia, c/o Robert (17)	Arlington	Alien Entry	1818	RA:13/3/18
Pleasant, Ned (C), laborer	Alexandria	Housekeeper	1808	1808(1):07A
Pleasants, Edwards, labourer	Alexandria	Head	1810	1810(1):07A
Pleasants, John	Alexandria	Tithable +16	1789	Tax PP 1789:20
Pleasants, John S.	Alexandria	Tithable +16	1788	Tax PP 1788:17
Pleffey, Rachel, laudress	Alexandria	Head	1800	1800(4):11A
Pleffy, Rachel	Alexandria	Resident	1800	1800(4):11B
Plowman, James	Alexandria	Tax Charge	1790	Tax PP 1790:11
Plum & Hughs	Alexandria	Tax Charge	1800	Tax PP 1800:33
Plum, Annis, c/o Lewis	Arlington	Guard.	1822	WB3:048
Plum, Benjamin, c/o Lewis W.	Arlington	Guard.	1822	OCR1822:002a
Plum, Benjamin, c/o Lewis	Arlington	Guard.	1822	WB3:048
Plum, Jacob Bend, c/o Lewis	Arlington	Guard.	1822	WB3:048
Plum, Jane, c/o Lewis	Arlington	Guard.	1822	WB3:048
Plum, Joseph, c/o Lewis W.	Arlington	Guard.	1822	OCR1822:002a
Plum, Joseph, c/o Lewis	Arlington	Guard.	1822	WB3:048
Plum, Lewis	Alexandria	Tax Charge	1799	Tax PP 1799:32
Plum, Lewis	Alexandria	Tax Charge	1800	Tax PP 1800:33
Plum, Lewis, potter	Alexandria	Housekeeper	1808	1808(4):24A
Plum, Lewis W.	Arlington	Inventory	1821	AB4:324; LVA-LP
Plum, Lewis W.	Arlington	Distribution	1822	AB5:049; LVA-LP
Plum, Lewis W.	Arlington	Account	1822	OCR1822:005a
Plum, Lewis Wilson	Arlington	Admin.	1821	WB3:020
Plum, Lewis Wilson, c/o Lewis	Arlington	Guard.	1822	WB3:048
Plum, Rebecca, c/o Lewis	Arlington	Guard.	1822	WB3:048
Plum, Sarah Fidelia, c/o Lewis	Arlington	Guard.	1822	WB3:048
Plum, Thomas Sanford, c/o Lewis	Arlington	Guard.	1822	WB3:048
Plumb, Lewis, potter	Alexandria	Head	1810	1810(4):09A
Plumber, Israel	Alexandria	Tax Charge	1796	Tax PP 1796:15

NAME OR SUBJECT	LOCATION	TYPE	YEAR	REFERENCE(S)
Plumber, Jerome, merchant	Alexandria	Head	1810	1810(4):01A
Plummer, Daniel, Seaman	Arlington	Libellant	1818	ACO:152
Plummer, Ezra	Alexandria	Tax Charge	1795	Tax PP 1795:24
Plummer, Jerome	Arlington	Sale	1817	AB2:403
Plummer, Jerome	Arlington	Inventory	1817	AB2:405; LVA-LP
Plummer, Jerome	Arlington	Account	1817	AB3:121; LVA-LP
Plummer, Jerome	Arlington	Admin.	1817	WB2:173
Plummer, Jerome	Arlington	Account	1818	AB3:121
Plummer, Jerome	Arlington	Account	1818	AB3:273; LVA-LP
Plummer, Jerome, merchant	Alexandria	Housekeeper	1808	1808(3):19A
Plummer, Samuel, grantor	Arlington	Indenture D.	1831	ID:321
Plummer, Samuel, in jail bounds	Arlington	Insolvent	1831	ID:319
Poe, David	Arlington	Crime	1797	OT:18/07/1797
Polkenhorn, Henry	Alexandria	Tax Charge	1795	Tax PP 1795:24
Polkinhorn & Andrews	Alexandria	Mer. License	1799	Tax PP 1799:52-08r
Polkinhorn, Henry	Alexandria	Tax Charge	1796	Tax LP 1796:23
Polkinhorne & Andrews	Alexandria	Tax Charge	1796	Tax PP 1796:15
Polkinhorne, Henry, Prince St.	Alexandria	Occupant	1795	Tax L 1795:07
Polkinhorne, [blank], (2), sadler	Alexandria	Head	1796	1796(3):5
Pollock, Elizabeth, c/o George W.	Arlington	Guard.	1817	WB2:210
Pollock, Geo., hatter	Alexandria	Housekeeper	1808	1808(4):25A
Pollock, Geo., hatter	Alexandria	Head	1810	1810(3):01A
Pollock, George W., c/o George W.	Arlington	Guard.	1817	WB2:210
Pollock, George W., grantor	Arlington	Indenture D.	1805	ID3:172
Pollock, George W., in jail	Arlington	Insolvent	1805	ID3:167
Polock, David & Co.	Alexandria	Mer. License	1798	Tax PP 1798:20-6
Polock, Steuart	Alexandria	Tax Charge	1798	Tax PP 1798:14
Pomeroy & Isabel	Alexandria	Tax Charge	1800	Tax PP 1800:33
Pomeroy, George	Alexandria	Tax Charge	1800	Tax PP 1800:33
Pomeroy, Richard	Alexandria	Tithable +21	1787	Tax PP 1787:04
Pomeroy, Walter, Prince St.	Alexandria	Occupant	1795	Tax L 1795:27
Pomery & Isabell	Alexandria	Tax Charge	1796	Tax LP 1796:23
Pomery & Isabell	Alexandria	Tax Charge	1796	Tax PP 1796:16
Pomery & Walcom	Alexandria	Mer. License	1799	Tax PP 1799:52-08r
Pomery & Walcom	Alexandria	Tax Charge	1800	Tax PP 1800:33
Pomery & Walkom	Alexandria	Tax Charge	1796	Tax LP 1796:23
Pomery & Walkom	Alexandria	Tax Charge	1798	Tax PP 1798:14
Pomery & Walkom	Alexandria	Mer. License	1798	Tax PP 1798:20-5
Pomery & Walkom	Alexandria	Tax Charge	1799	Tax PP 1799:32
Pomery & Walkom	Alexandria	Mer. License	1800	Tax PP 1800:54(18)r
Pomery & Walkom, ret. liquors w/o lic.	Arlington	Defendants	1802	PA:022
Pomery & Walkoms	Alexandria	Tax Charge	1796	Tax PP 1796:15
Pomery & Walter	Alexandria	Mer. License	1798	Tax PP 1798:20-5
Pomery, Geo.	Alexandria	Tax Charge	1798	Tax PP 1798:14
Pomery, Geo.	Alexandria	Mer. License	1800	Tax PP 1800:54(18)r
Pomery, Geo., retailer	Alexandria	Boarder	1799	1799(2):01A
Pomery, George	Alexandria	Mer. License	1798	Tax PP 1798:20-5
Pomery, George	Alexandria	Tax Charge	1799	Tax PP 1799:32
Pomery, George	Alexandria	Mer. License	1799	Tax PP 1799:52-08r
Pomery, George, ret. liquor w/o license	Arlington	Defendant	1802	PA:248
Pomery, John	Alexandria	Housekeeper	1808	1808(2):15A
Pomery, Walter	Alexandria	Tax Charge	1798	Tax PP 1798:14
Pomery, Walter	Alexandria	Mer. License	1799	Tax PP 1799:52-08r
Pomery, Walter	Alexandria	Tax Charge	1799	Tax PP 1799:32
Pomery, Walter	Alexandria	Mer. License	1800	Tax PP 1800:54(18)r
Pomery, Walter, w, merchant	Alexandria	Head	1796	1796(3):2
Pomery, William, plt.	Alexandria	Suit	1809	CRG:141
Pomery, Wm.	Alexandria	Reference	1808	1808(4):26B
Pomery, Wm., retailer	Alexandria	Boarder	1799	1799(2):01A
Pomery, Wm., retailer	Alexandria	Housekeeper	1808	1808(1):02A
Pommery, William, shopkeeper	Alexandria	Head	1810	1810(1):01A

NAME OR SUBJECT	LOCATION	TYPE	YEAR	REFERENCE(S)
Poor, Pompey	Alexandria	Tax Charge	1800	Tax PP 1800:33
Poorah, Pompey	Alexandria	Tax Charge	1799	Tax PP 1799:32
Pope, Thomas	Arlington	Apprentice	1812	OCR1811:100
Pope, Thomas S.	Alexandria	Tax Charge	1799	Tax PP 1799:32
Pope, Thos., taylor	Alexandria	Boarder	1799	1799(2):03A
Pope, William	Alexandria	Tax Charge	1789	Tax PP 1789:15
Popejoy, Wm.	Alexandria	Tax Charge	1795	Tax PP 1795:24
Popejoy, Wm.	Alexandria	Resident	1800	1800(4):11B
Popejoy, Wm., painter	Alexandria	Boarder	1800	1800(4):11A
Poplar, James	Arlington	Admin.	1814	WB1:323
Poplar, James, Capt.	Arlington	Sale	1815	AB2:118
Pora, Pompey (C), laborer	Alexandria	Housekeeper	1808	1808(4):24A
Pora, Pompy	Alexandria	Head	1810	1810(4):08A
Porer, Pompey & wife (C), drayman	Alexandria	Housekeeper	1799	1799(2):12A
Porrer, Pompy & Rose (C)	Alexandria	Head	1800	1800(4):14A
Port, Christopher	Alexandria	Tax Charge	1787	Tax PP 1787:12
Porter & Ingraham, Fairfax St.	Alexandria	Occupant	1787	Tax L 1787:10
Porter & Ingraham, Fairfax St.	Alexandria	Occupant	1790	Tax L 1790:03
Porter, James	Alexandria	Tax Charge	1796	Tax PP 1796:15
Porter, James	Alexandria	Mer. License	1798	Tax PP 1798:20-6
Porter, James	Alexandria	Tax Charge	1800	Tax PP 1800:33
Porter, James	Alexandria	Mer. License	1800	Tax PP 1800:54(18)w
Porter, James, Union St.	Alexandria	Occupant	1795	Tax L 1795:33
Porter, Jas.	Alexandria	Tax Charge	1795	Tax PP 1795:24
Porter, Jas.	Alexandria	Tax Charge	1798	Tax PP 1798:14
Porter, Parker	Alexandria	Boarder	1808	1808(1):03A
Porter, Sarah	Alexandria	Deed	1803	CRH:502
Porter, Sarah	Alexandria	Account B.	1803	CRH:500
Porter, Sarah, boarding house	Alexandria	Head	1810	1810(1):05A
Porter, Sarah, gentlewoman	Alexandria	Housekeeper	1808	1808(1):03A
Porter, Sarah, plt.	Alexandria	Suit	1811	CRH:496
Porter, Sinah Ball	Arlington	Will	1853	WB6:194; File #492A
Porter, Tho.	Alexandria	Tax Charge	1798	Tax PP 1798:15
Porter, Thomas	Alexandria	Tax Charge	1787	Tax PP 1787:12
Porter, Thomas	Alexandria	Tax Charge	1788	Tax PP 1788:13
Porter, Thomas	Alexandria	Tax Charge	1789	Tax PP 1789:14
Porter, Thomas	Alexandria	Tax Charge	1790	Tax PP 1790:11
Porter, Thomas	Alexandria	Tax Charge	1796	Tax LP 1796:23
Porter, Thomas	Alexandria	Tax Charge	1796	Tax PP 1796:16
Porter, Thomas	Arlington	Admin.	1800	CRA:325
Porter, Thomas	Arlington	Inventory	1803	WBA:152; LVA-LP
Porter, Thomas	Arlington	Account	1803	WBA:155; LVA-LP
Porter, Thomas, Royal St.	Alexandria	Owner	1790	Tax L 1790:09
Porter, Thos.	Alexandria	Tax Charge	1795	Tax PP 1795:24
Porter, Thos.	Alexandria	Tax Charge	1799	Tax PP 1799:33
Porter, Thos.	Alexandria	Tax Charge	1800	Tax PP 1800:33
Porter, Thos., Fairfax St.	Alexandria	Occupant	1795	Tax L 1795:07
Porter, Thos., Royal St.	Alexandria	Owner	1795	Tax L 1795:24
Posey, Benjamin	Arlington	Ordinary	1804	OBL1(np)
Posey, Benjamin	Arlington	Sale	1825	AB5:409
Posey, Benjamin	Arlington	Inventory	1825	AB5:402; LVA-LP
Posey, Benjamin	Arlington	Admin.	1825	WB3:158
Posey, Benjamin	Arlington	Will (NR)	1838	File #072A
Posey, Benjamin	Arlington	Inventory	1840	AB8:164; LVA-LP
Posey, Benjamin	Arlington	Admin.	1840	WB4:276, 287
Posey, Benjamin	Arlington	Inventory	1842	AB8:300; LVA-LP
Posey, Benjamin	Arlington	Account F.	1845	AB9:043; LVA-LP////
Posey, Benjamin	Arlington	Bond	1851	BB(np)
Posey, Henry	Arlington	Inventory	1823	AB5:168; LVA-LP
Posey, Henry	Arlington	Sale	1823	AB5:168
Posey, Henry	Arlington	Admin.	1823	OCR1822:035a

NAME OR SUBJECT	LOCATION	TYPE	YEAR	REFERENCE(S)
Posey, Henry	Arlington	Admin.	1823	WB3:086
Posey, Hezekiah, at his house	Arlington	Ordinary	1837	OBL5(np)
Posey, James	Arlington	Inventory	1837	LVA-LP
Posey, James	Arlington	Will	1837	WB4:140; File #070A
Posey, James	Arlington	Guard.	1838	WB4:143
Posey, James, at his house	Arlington	Ordinary	1833	OBL5(np)
Posey, James, at his house	Arlington	Ordinary	1834	OBL5(np)
Posey, James, at his house	Arlington	Ordinary	1835	OBL5(np)
Posey, James, at his house	Arlington	Ordinary	1836	OBL5(np)
Posey, James, at his house	Arlington	Ordinary	1837	OBL5(np)
Posey, John, at his house	Arlington	Ordinary	1830	OBL4(np)
Posey, Mary	Arlington	Account	1839	LVA-LP
Posey, Mary, at his house	Arlington	Ordinary	1838	OBL5(np)
Posey, Sarah	Arlington	Guard.	1825	WB3:157
Posset, John	Alexandria	Tithable +16	1788	Tax PP 1788:03
Poston, Frances & [Hoffman], carpenter	Alexandria	Housekeeper	1808	1808(3):20A
Poston, Francis	Alexandria	Tax Charge	1800	Tax PP 1800:33
Poston, Francis E.	Arlington	Will (NR)	1835	File #067A
Poston, Francis E., def.	Alexandria	Suit	1803	CRD:074
Poston, Francis, house joiner	Alexandria	Head	1810	1810(3):05A
Potten, John	Alexandria	Tax Charge	1800	Tax PP 1800:33
Potten, John	Arlington	Will	1835	WB4:091; File #335A
Potten, John	Arlington	Account	1836	AB7:222; LVA-LP
Potten, John	Arlington	Account	1838	AB7:313; LVA-LP
Potter, Chas.	Alexandria	Boarder	1800	1800(4):04A
Potter, Chas.	Alexandria	Resident	1800	1800(4):04B
Potter, Chas., painter	Alexandria	Housekeeper	1808	1808(3):19A
Potter, Chas., painter	Alexandria	Head	1810	1810(3):04A
Potter, Henry	Alexandria	Tax Charge	1788	Tax PP 1788:13
Potter, John	Arlington	Apprentice	1822	OCR1822:001a
Potter, John, bricklayer	Alexandria	Head	1810	1810(3):07A
Potter, Margaret A.	Arlington	Guard.	1825	WB3:251
Potter, Margaret Ann	Arlington	Apprentice	1825	OCR1822:085a
Potter, Margaret Ann, c/o John	Arlington	Guard.	1826	OCR1822:119a
Potter, Reuben	Arlington	Inventory	1845	AB9:114; LVA-LP
Potter, Reuben	Arlington	Will P.	1845	OCR1842:123
Potter, Reuben	Arlington	Will	1845	WB4:397; File #424A
Potter, Reuben	Arlington	Account	1846	AB9:235; LVA-LP
Potter, Virginia, c/o John	Arlington	Guard.	1825	WB3:250
Potter, Virginia, c/o John	Arlington	Guard.	1826	OCR1822:119a
Pottler, Charles, w, shopkeeper	Alexandria	Head	1796	1796(3):3
Potton, Jno.	Alexandria	Tax Charge	1798	Tax PP 1798:15
Potts, Jno & wife, merchant	Alexandria	Housekeeper	1799	1799(2):09A
Potts, Jno.	Alexandria	Tax Charge	1795	Tax PP 1795:24
Potts, Jno.	Alexandria	Tax Charge	1798	Tax PP 1798:15
Potts, Jno., King St.	Alexandria	Occupant	1795	Tax L 1795:06
Potts, Jno., St. Asaph St.	Alexandria	Occupant	1787	Tax L 1787:22
Potts, John	Alexandria	Tax Charge	1789	Tax PP 1789:15
Potts, John	Alexandria	Tax Charge	1796	Tax LP 1796:23
Potts, John	Alexandria	Tax Charge	1799	Tax PP 1799:33
Potts, John	Alexandria	Tax Charge	1800	Tax PP 1800:33
Potts, John	Alexandria	Reference	1808	1808(2):11B
Potts, John, def.	Alexandria	Suit	1801	CRD:178
Potts, John, def.	Alexandria	Suit	1802	CRB:174
Potts, John, grantor	Arlington	Indenture D.	1809	ID2:015
Potts, John, in prison rules	Arlington	Insolvent	1809	ID2:010
Potts, John, Jr.	Alexandria	Tax Charge	1787	Tax PP 1787:11
Potts, John, Jr.	Alexandria	Tax Charge	1790	Tax PP 1790:11
Potts, John, King St.	Alexandria	Occupant	1790	Tax L 1790:03
Potts, John, plt.	Alexandria	Suit	1801	CRB:051
Potts, Thomas	Alexandria	Tax Charge	1799	Tax PP 1799:32

NAME OR SUBJECT	LOCATION	TYPE	YEAR	REFERENCE(S)
Potts, Thomas, grantee	Arlington	Indenture D.	1806	ID3:129
Potts, Thos.	Alexandria	Tax Charge	1800	Tax PP 1800:33
Potts, Thos., tailor	Alexandria	Boarder	1799	1799(2):04A
Potts, Thos., taylor	Alexandria	Housekeeper	1808	1808(3):21A
Potts, Thos., taylor	Alexandria	Head	1810	1810(3):06A
Pouch, Elizabeth	Alexandria	Housekeeper	1799	1799(2):11A
Poultney, Thomas	Alexandria	Tax Charge	1789	Tax PP 1789:15
Poultney, Thomas	Alexandria	Tax Charge	1790	Tax PP 1790:11
Poultney, Thomas, Royal St.	Alexandria	Occupant	1790	Tax L 1790:12
Poura, Pompy & Rose	Alexandria	Resident	1800	1800(4):14B
Powell, Alfred	Arlington	Apprentice	1811	OCR1811:205
Powell, Alfred, c/o William L.	Arlington	Guard.	1853	BB(np)
Powell, Alfred H., c/o Ann M.	Arlington	Guard. Acct.	1855	WB7:007
Powell, Ann	Arlington	Guard. Acct.	1855	WB7:006; LVA-LP
Powell, Ann W., c/o William L.	Arlington	Guard.	1853	BB(np)
Powell, Burr	Arlington	Apprentice	1812	OCR1811:115
Powell, Burr, c/o Edea Isaacs	Arlington	Apprentice	1815	OCR1811:244
Powell, Charles L.	Alexandria	Will	1895	WB2:137; LP
Powell, Col., Duke St.	Alexandria	Owner	1795	Tax L 1795:23
Powell, Cuthbert	Alexandria	Tax Charge	1799	Tax PP 1799:32
Powell, Cuthbert	Alexandria	Tax Charge	1800	Tax PP 1800:34
Powell, Cuthbert, merchant	Alexandria	Housekeeper	1808	1808(2):11A
Powell, Cuthbert, merchant	Alexandria	Head	1810	1810(4):04A
Powell, Fanny, c/o William L.	Arlington	Guard.	1853	BB(np)
Powell, Fanny L., c/o Ann M.	Arlington	Guard. Acct.	1855	WB7:007
Powell, Harriet E.	Arlington	Guard.	1845	LVA-LP (Box 214)
Powell, Harriet E., c/o Alfred	Arlington	Guard.	1845	OCR1842:155
Powell, James	Alexandria	Tax Charge	1799	Tax PP 1799:32
Powell, John	Alexandria	Tax Charge	1800	Tax PP 1800:33
Powell, L. & C.	Alexandria	Tax Charge	1798	Tax PP 1798:15
Powell, L. & C.	Alexandria	Mer. License	1798	Tax PP 1798:20-6
Powell, Leven	Alexandria	Tax Charge	1795	Tax PP 1795:24
Powell, Leven, Jr.	Alexandria	Tax Charge	1796	Tax PP 1796:15
Powell, Leven, Prince St.	Alexandria	Occupant	1795	Tax L 1795:22
Powell, Levin	Alexandria	Tax Charge	1796	Tax LP 1796:24
Powell, Lucy P.	Alexandria	Will	1890	WB1:559; LP
Powell, Margaret	Arlington	Guard.	1822	WB3:074
Powell, Marietta F.	Alexandria	Will	1894	WB2:083; LP
Powell, Posey	Alexandria	Boarder	1808	1808(1):04A
Powell, Richd.	Alexandria	Tax Charge	1795	Tax PP 1795:23
Powell, Richd., Oronoko St.	Alexandria	Occupant	1795	Tax L 1795:24
Powell, Robert C.	Alexandria	Will	1890	WB1:557; LP
Powell, Robert C., c/o Ann M.	Arlington	Guard. Acct.	1855	WB7:007
Powell, Selina, w/o Charles L.	Alexandria	Will	1882	WB1:362; LP
Powell, Thos.	Alexandria	Tax Charge	1795	Tax PP 1795:23
Powell, Thos.	Alexandria	Boarder	1808	1808(2):11A
Powell, W.H., Fairfax St.	Alexandria	Occupant	1787	Tax L 1787:26
Powell, William	Alexandria	Tax Charge	1788	Tax PP 1788:13
Powell, William L.	Arlington	Account	1849	WB5:144; LVA-LP
Powell, William L.	Arlington	Bond	1853	BB(np)
Powell, William L.	Arlington	Inventory	1854	WB6:326; LVA-LP
Powell, William L.	Arlington	Sale	1854	WB6:331; LVA-LP
Powell, Wm. H.	Alexandria	Tax Charge	1787	Tax PP 1787:11
Powers, John B.	Arlington	Will	1900	WB10:428; File #795A
Powers, Thomas	Arlington	Inventory	1820	AB4:146
Powley, John	Alexandria	Tax Charge	1788	Tax PP 1788:13
Poyer, John, w(6)3, cooper	Alexandria	Head	1795	1796(3):7
Poyer, Philip, b. Barbadoes	Arlington	Alien Entry	1801	RA:07/07/01
Prater, Thomas	Alexandria	Tithable +16	1789	Tax PP 1789:01
Prater, Thomas	Alexandria	Tithable +16	1790	Tax PP 1790:11
Prather, Elisabeth	Alexandria	Serv./Appr.	1800	1800(4):04B

NAME OR SUBJECT	LOCATION	TYPE	YEAR	REFERENCE(S)
Prather, Thomas	Alexandria	Tithable +16	1788	Tax PP 1788:01
Pratt, Henry, of Philadelphia	Alexandria	Deed	1811	CRK:048
Pratt, Humphrey, of Saybrook, Conn.	Alexandria	Deposition	1805	CRF:246
Pratt, Leven	Alexandria	Tax Charge	1799	Tax PP 1799:32
Pratt, Thomas	Alexandria	Tax Charge	1789	Tax PP 1789:14
Pratt, William	Arlington	Exor. Bond	1847	EBB(np)
Pratt, William	Arlington	Will	1847	WB5:013; File #441A
Pratt's Estate, Fairfax St.	Alexandria	Occupant	1787	Tax L 1787:05
Presbury, Joseph	Alexandria	Tax Charge	1795	Tax PP 1795:24
Prescott, Hannah Eliz., c/o Oscar B.	Arlington	Guard.	1851	BB(np)
Prescott, Levi Plummer, c/o Oscar B.	Arlington	Guard.	1851	BB(np)
Prescott, Mary Amanda, c/o Oscar B.	Arlington	Guard.	1851	BB(np)
Prescott, Roger	Alexandria	Tax Charge	1790	Tax PP 1790:11
Preson, Thomas, crier	Arlington	Appointment	1824	ACO:234
Presstman, Stephen W., Abbeville NC	Arlington	Will	1868	WB9:134; File #666A
Prestman, Frank F.	Arlington	Guard. Acct.	1877	WB9:416
Prestman, Frank F.	Arlington	Inventory	1878	WB9:414
Prestman, Stephen W.	Arlington	Inventory	1877	WB9:445
Preston, Tho.	Alexandria	Tax Charge	1798	Tax PP 1798:15
Preston, Thomas	Alexandria	Tithable +16	1789	Tax PP 1789:17
Preston, Thomas	Alexandria	Tax Charge	1796	Tax PP 1796:15
Preston, Thomas	Alexandria	Mer. License	1798	Tax PP 1798:20-5
Preston, Thomas	Alexandria	Account B.	1799	CRC:251
Preston, Thomas	Alexandria	Mer. License	1799	Tax PP 1799:52-08r
Preston, Thomas	Alexandria	Tax Charge	1799	Tax PP 1799:32
Preston, Thomas	Alexandria	Deposition	1808	CRH:112
Preston, Thomas	Arlington	Account	1809	LVA-LP
Preston, Thomas, def.	Alexandria	Suit	1811	CRI:104
Preston, Thomas, grantee	Arlington	Indenture D.	1806	ID3:184
Preston, Thomas, joiner	Alexandria	Head	1810	1810(1):03A
Preston, Thomas, plt.	Alexandria	Suit	1802	CRC:249
Preston, Thomas, plt.	Alexandria	Suit	1806	CRE:082
Preston, Thos.	Alexandria	Tithable +16	1788	Tax PP 1788:14
Preston, Thos.	Alexandria	Tax Charge	1795	Tax PP 1795:24
Preston, Thos.	Alexandria	Tax Charge	1796	Tax LP 1796:24
Preston, Thos.	Alexandria	Tax Charge	1800	Tax PP 1800:33
Preston, Thos.	Alexandria	License Due	1800	Tax PP 1800:54(24)
Preston, Thos.	Alexandria	Reference	1808	1808(2):11B
Preston, Thos.	Alexandria	Reference	1808	1808(3):22B
Preston, Thos. & wife, house/ship joiner	Alexandria	Housekeeper	1799	1799(2):07A
Preston, Thos., lumber merchant & ret.	Alexandria	Housekeeper	1808	1808(1):05A
Preston, William	Alexandria	Tithable +16	1790	Tax PP 1790:13
Prettyman, David G.	Arlington	Inventory	1844	AB8:497; LVA-LP
Prettyman, David G.	Arlington	Admin.	1844	LVA-LP (Box 214)
Prettyman, David G.	Arlington	Bond	1844	OCR1842:079
Prettyman, David G.	Arlington	Account	1845	AB9:120
Price, Alfred, b/o David	Arlington	Apprentice	1824	OCR1822:075a
Price, Ann	Alexandria	Boarder	1799	1799(2):05A
Price, Ann, spinster	Alexandria	Boarder	1799	1799(2):02A
Price, Benjamin	Arlington	Apprentice	1824	OCR1822:074a
Price, Benjamin F.	Alexandria	Will	1894	WB2:082; LP
Price, Bennett King	Alexandria	Will	1900	WB2:403; LP
Price, David	Alexandria	Boarder	1808	1808(4):29A
Price, David	Arlington	Defendant	1841	LSA:062
Price, Ellice & wife Sarah	Alexandria	Resident	1800	1800(4):13B
Price, Ellis	Alexandria	Tithable +16	1788	Tax PP 1788:14
Price, Ellis	Alexandria	Tithable +16	1790	Tax PP 1790:11
Price, Ellis	Alexandria	Tax Charge	1795	Tax PP 1795:23
Price, Ellis	Alexandria	Tax Charge	1796	Tax LP 1796:23
Price, Ellis	Alexandria	Tax Charge	1796	Tax PP 1796:15
Price, Ellis	Alexandria	Tax Charge	1798	Tax PP 1798:14

NAME OR SUBJECT	LOCATION	TYPE	YEAR	REFERENCE(S)
Price, Ellis	Alexandria	Mer. License	1798	Tax PP 1798:20-5
Price, Ellis	Alexandria	Tax Charge	1799	Tax PP 1799:32
Price, Ellis	Alexandria	Tax Charge	1800	Tax PP 1800:33
Price, Ellis	Alexandria	Housekeeper	1808	1808(4):24A
Price, Ellis & wife, bookseller/stationer	Alexandria	Housekeeper	1799	1799(2):03A
Price, Ellis & wife Nancy Fleming, def.	Alexandria	Suit	1801	CRC:194
Price, Ellis, clerk in bank	Alexandria	Head	1810	1810(4):09A
Price, Ellis, grantor	Arlington	Indenture D.	1804	ID3:044
Price, Ellis, in jail bounds	Arlington	Insolvent	1804	ID3:035
Price, Ellis, printer	Alexandria	Head	1800	1800(4):13A
Price, George	Arlington	Apprentice	1824	OCR1822:074a
Price, Hezekiah	Alexandria	Tithable +16	1788	Tax PP 1788:06
Price, James	Alexandria	Tax Charge	1787	Tax PP 1787:12
Price, Jane	Alexandria	Mer. License	1798	Tax PP 1798:20-5
Price, Jane	Alexandria	Tax Charge	1799	Tax PP 1799:32
Price, Jeremiah	Arlington	Ordinary	1808	OBL2(np)
Price, Jeremiah	Arlington	Ordinary	1821	OBL3(np)
Price, Jeremiah, carpenter	Alexandria	Housekeeper	1808	1808(4):28A
Price, Jeremiah, grantor	Arlington	Indenture D.	1814	ID2:360
Price, Jeremiah, prison rules, carpenter	Arlington	Insolvent	1814	ID2:357
Price, John P., c/o Nancy	Arlington	Apprentice	1823	OCR1822:053a
Price, John T., in Alexandria Co.	Arlington	Ordinary	1850	OBL6(np)
Price, Kate F. (formerly Hammill)	Arlington	Guard. Acct.	1870	WB9:293
Price, Margaret (Crook), w/o David	Arlington	Defendant	1841	LSA:062
Price, Oliver	Alexandria	Owner	1787	Tax L 1787:21
Price, Oliver	Alexandria	Tax Charge	1787	Tax PP 1787:12
Price, Oliver	Alexandria	Tax Charge	1788	Tax PP 1788:13
Price, Oliver	Alexandria	Tax Charge	1789	Tax PP 1789:14
Price, Oliver	Alexandria	Tax Charge	1790	Tax PP 1790:11
Price, Oliver	Alexandria	Tax Charge	1795	Tax PP 1795:23
Price, Oliver	Alexandria	Tax Charge	1796	Tax LP 1796:23
Price, Oliver	Alexandria	Tax Charge	1796	Tax PP 1796:15
Price, Oliver, Fairfax St.	Alexandria	Occupant	1787	Tax L 1787:02
Price, Oliver, Fairfax St.	Alexandria	Occupant	1787	Tax L 1787:21
Price, Oliver, Fairfax St.	Alexandria	Occupant	1790	Tax L 1790:09
Price, Oliver, Fairfax St.	Alexandria	Owner	1790	Tax L 1790:09
Price, Oliver, Fairfax St.	Alexandria	Owner	1795	Tax L 1795:24
Price, Oliver, Fairfax St.	Alexandria	Occupant	1795	Tax L 1795:24
Price, Oliver, St. Asaph St.	Alexandria	Owner	1790	Tax L 1790:09
Price, Oliver, St. Asaph St.	Alexandria	Owner	1795	Tax L 1795:24
Price, Peter	Alexandria	Tax Charge	1796	Tax LP 1796:23
Price, Peter, St. Asaph St.	Alexandria	Occupant	1795	Tax L 1795:24
Primus, Anderson, labourer	Alexandria	Head	1810	1810(1):10A
Primus, J., Duke St.	Alexandria	Occupant	1787	Tax L 1787:07
Primus, Pompey (C), laborer	Alexandria	Housekeeper	1808	1808(1):07A
Prince, Sarah, sempstress	Alexandria	Housekeeper	1808	1808(4):26A
Prior, Allen, of Kanawha Co.	Alexandria	Deed	1799	CRF:322
Prise, Jane	Alexandria	Boarder	1800	1800(4):07A
Prise, Jane	Alexandria	Resident	1800	1800(4):07B
Proctor, John, grantor	Arlington	Indenture D.	1831	ID:340
Proctor, John, in jail bounds	Arlington	Insolvent	1831	ID:338
Proffits, Robt.	Alexandria	Boarder	1808	1808(4):27A
Proudfit, John, of Norfolk	Alexandria	Deposition	1805	CRF:242
Proudfoot, Mary	Arlington	Admin.	1806	WBB:352
Proudfoot, William	Arlington	Admin.	1812	WB1:152
Prout, Richd. & wife	Alexandria	Head	1795	1795(4a):08
Prue, Jeremiah	Arlington	Ordinary	1809	OBL2(np)
Prunell, Thamer	Arlington	Guard.	1818	WB2:262
Pugh, Isaac	Arlington	Guard.	1804	WBB:009
Pugh, Jesse	Alexandria	Tax Charge	1796	Tax LP 1796:24
Pugh, Jesse	Alexandria	Tax Charge	1799	Tax PP 1799:32

NAME OR SUBJECT	LOCATION	TYPE	YEAR	REFERENCE(S)
Pugh, Jesse	Alexandria	Tax Charge	1800	Tax PP 1800:33
Pugh, Jesse	Arlington	Admin.	1803	WBA:215
Pugh, Jesse	Arlington	Sale	1803	WBA:231
Pugh, Jesse	Arlington	Account	1804	WBB:010; LVA-LP
Pugh, Jesse & wife, grocer	Alexandria	Housekeeper	1799	1799(2):08A
Pugh, Sarah	Arlington	Guard.	1804	WBB:009
Pulman, Mary A.	Alexandria	Will	1897	WB2:241; LP
Pulman, Samuel	Alexandria	Will	1898	WB2:279; LP
Pulman, Thomas	Alexandria	Will	1883	WB1:396; LP
Pumroy, George	Arlington	Crime	1795	OT:09/01/1795
Pupo, Daniel	Alexandria	Resident	1800	1800(4):16B
Pupo, Daniel, inspecter	Alexandria	Boarder	1800	1800(4):16A
Puppo, D.C.	Alexandria	Tax Charge	1799	Tax PP 1799:33
Puppo, Daniel C.	Alexandria	Tax Charge	1796	Tax PP 1796:15
Puppo, Daniel C., orphans of	Arlington	Guard. Acct.	1820	LVA-LP
Puppo, Danl. C.	Alexandria	Tax Charge	1798	Tax PP 1798:15
Puppo, Danl. C.	Alexandria	Tax Charge	1800	Tax PP 1800:33
Purdie, Chas., labourer	Alexandria	Head	1810	1810(2):06A
Purdy, Charles, blacksmith	Alexandria	Housekeeper	1808	1808(2):16A
Purdy, George, c/o Patience	Arlington	Apprentice	1811	OCR1811:037
Purdy, John	Arlington	Apprentice	1814	OCR1811:241
Purdy, John, c/o Patience	Arlington	Apprentice	1812	OCR1811:079
Purkis, Thomas	Arlington	Ordinary	1802	OBL1(np)
Purkis, Thomas	Arlington	Ordinary	1803	OBL1(np)
Purkis, Thomas	Arlington	Ordinary	1804	OBL1(np)
Purkis, Thomas	Arlington	Ordinary	1805	OBL1(np)
Purkis, Thomas	Arlington	Insolvent	1813	ID2:211
Purkis, Thomas, grantor	Arlington	Indenture D.	1813	ID2:214
Purkis, Thos., laborer	Alexandria	Housekeeper	1808	1808(3):22A
Purley, Benjamin D.	Arlington	Apprentice	1826	OCR1822:120
Purley, Ebenezer	Arlington	Apprentice	1822	OCR1822:023
Purley, James	Arlington	Apprentice	1822	OCR1822:024
Purley, James	Arlington	Apprentice	1823	OCR1822:037
Purnell, Jesse	Alexandria	Tax Charge	1795	Tax PP 1795:24
Purnell, Jesse	Alexandria	Tax Charge	1798	Tax PP 1798:15
Purnell, Jesse & wife	Alexandria	Boarder	1795	1795(4a):09
Purnell, Thomas	Alexandria	Tax Charge	1788	Tax PP 1788:13
Purnell, Wm.	Alexandria	Tax Charge	1795	Tax PP 1795:24
Purnell, Wm.	Alexandria	Tax Charge	1796	Tax PP 1796:15
Purnell, Wm.	Alexandria	Tax Charge	1798	Tax PP 1798:15
Purnell, Wm. & wife, labourer	Alexandria	Head	1795	1795(4a):09
Pursley, Robert, waiter	Alexandria	Head	1810	1810(1):05A
Pye, Edward A.	Arlington	Defendant	1838	LSA:034
Pyle, Christian	Alexandria	Tax Charge	1796	Tax PP 1796:16
Pyle, Geo.	Alexandria	Tithable +16	1788	Tax PP 1788:13
Pyles, Christian	Alexandria	Tax Charge	1795	Tax PP 1795:24
Pyles, Jacob	Alexandria	Tax Charge	1795	Tax PP 1795:24
Pyles, Peter	Alexandria	Tax Charge	1795	Tax PP 1795:24
Pyne, Edward	Alexandria	Will	1876	WB1:183; LP

NAME OR SUBJECT	LOCATION	TYPE	YEAR	REFERENCE(S)

Q

NAME OR SUBJECT	LOCATION	TYPE	YEAR	REFERENCE(S)
Quabb, Wm. (C)	Alexandria	Tax Charge	1800	Tax PP 1800:36
Quick silver, wine, almonds, etc.	Arlington	Suit	1818	ACO:152
Quigley, James, c/o Michael	Arlington	Guard.	1821	WB3:019
Quigley, Mary Elizabeth, c/o Michael	Arlington	Guard.	1821	WB3:019
Quigley, Michael	Arlington	Sale	1818	AB3:152
Quigley, Michael	Arlington	Inventory	1818	AB3:133; LVA-LP
Quigley, Michael	Arlington	Admin.	1818	WB2:229
Quigley, Michael, c/o Michael	Arlington	Guard.	1821	WB3:019
Quigley, Michael, millstone maker	Alexandria	Housekeeper	1808	1808(3):23A
Quigley, Michael, millstone maker	Alexandria	Head	1810	1810(3):05A
Quigley, Thomas, c/o Michael	Arlington	Guard.	1821	WB3:019
Quinlen, Edward	Alexandria	Tithable +21	1787	Tax PP 1787:01
Quirk, Richard	Alexandria	Tax Charge	1799	Tax PP 1799:34
Quirk, Richard, marriner	Alexandria	Head	1800	1800(4):12A
Quirke, Richard & wife Mary	Alexandria	Resident	1800	1800(4):12B
Quisenberry, Edith	Arlington	Guard. Acct.	1869	WB9:162
Quisenberry, Edith	Arlington	Guard. Acct.	1871	WB9:299, 301
Quisenberry, Rebecca	Arlington	Bond	1851	BB(np)
Quisenberry, William P.	Arlington	Account	1866	WB8:350, 456
Quisenberry, William P.	Arlington	Account	1869	WB9:165
Quisenberry, William P.	Arlington	Account	1871	WB9:303
Quisenbury, Edith	Arlington	Guard. Acct.	1868	WB9:038
Quisenbury, Edith	Arlington	Guard. Acct.	1870	WB9:218
Quisenbury, Edith, c/o William P.	Arlington	Guard. Acct.	1864	WB8:204, 354, 471
Quisenbury, William P.	Arlington	Will	1864	WB8:204; File #614A
Quisenbury, William P.	Arlington	Renounce	1865	LVA-LP
Quisenbury, William P.	Arlington	Account	1868	WB9:040
Quisenbury, William P.	Arlington	Account	1870	WB9:217

R

NAME OR SUBJECT	LOCATION	TYPE	YEAR	REFERENCE(S)
Raborg, Christopher & Son, plt.	Alexandria	Suit	1816	CRK:156
Rabson, A.	Alexandria	Tax Charge	1796	Tax PP 1796:16
Radcliff, Ignatius, carpenter	Alexandria	Housekeeper	1808	1808(1):07A
Ragan, Basil, physician	Alexandria	Boarder	1799	1799(2):01A
Ragen, Jno.	Alexandria	Tax Charge	1795	Tax PP 1795:25
Raisins, Boxes of	Arlington	Suit	1818	ACO:152
Rambler, Charles	Arlington	Libellant	1803	ACO:007
Rammell, Ignatz	Alexandria	Will	1889	WB1:515; LP
Ramsay, A. & W.	Alexandria	Mer. License	1800	Tax PP 1800:54(19)w
Ramsay, A. & Wm.	Alexandria	Tax Charge	1799	Tax PP 1799:34
Ramsay, Amelia	Alexandria	Tax Charge	1788	Tax PP 1788:14
Ramsay, Amelia	Alexandria	Tax Charge	1789	Tax PP 1789:16
Ramsay, Amelia	Alexandria	Tax Charge	1790	Tax PP 1790:12
Ramsay, Amelia, Estate	Alexandria	Tax Charge	1795	Tax PP 1795:25
Ramsay, Amelia, Estate	Alexandria	Tax Charge	1796	Tax LP 1796:24
Ramsay, Amelia, Royal St.	Alexandria	Owner	1790	Tax L 1790:09
Ramsay, Amelia [Emelia]	Alexandria	Tax Charge	1787	Tax PP 1787:13
Ramsay, Andrew	Alexandria	Tithable +16	1790	Tax PP 1790:16
Ramsay, Andrew	Arlington	Plaintiff	1802	PA:054
Ramsay, Andrew & William, def.	Alexandria	Suit	1801	CRB:158
Ramsay, Andrew & William, def.	Alexandria	Suit	1801	CRB:161
Ramsay, Andrew & William, def.	Alexandria	Suit	1801	CRB:344
Ramsay, Andrew & William, def.	Alexandria	Suit	1801	CRD:042
Ramsay, Andrew & William, Estate	Alexandria	Account B.	1804	CRG:203, 208
Ramsay, Andrew & Wm.	Alexandria	Mer. License	1799	Tax PP 1799:52-09w
Ramsay, Andrew, def.	Alexandria	Suit	1801	CRB:008, 013, 016
Ramsay, Andrew, def.	Alexandria	Suit	1801	CRB:163, 166
Ramsay, Andrew, def.	Alexandria	Suit	1802	CRB:231, 235
Ramsay, Andrew William	Arlington	Defendant	1802	PA:141
Ramsay, Andw. & Wm., King St.	Alexandria	Occupant	1795	Tax L 1795:23
Ramsay, Andw. & Wm.	Alexandria	Tax Charge	1798	Tax PP 1798:15
Ramsay, Ann, c/o John	Arlington	Guard.	1821	WB3:018
Ramsay, Ann, c/o John	Arlington	Guard. Acct.	1824	AB5:236
Ramsay, Ann, Estate	Alexandria	Tax Charge	1787	Tax PP 1787:13
Ramsay, Anw. & Will.	Alexandria	Tax Charge	1800	Tax PP 1800:37
Ramsay, Catharine, c/o John	Arlington	Guard.	1821	WB3:018
Ramsay, Catharine R., c/o John	Arlington	Guard. Acct.	1824	AB5:236
Ramsay, D., Fairfax St.	Alexandria	Occupant	1787	Tax L 1787:22
Ramsay, D., Fairfax St.	Alexandria	Occupant	1787	Tax L 1787:21
Ramsay, D., Royal St.	Alexandria	Occupant	1787	Tax L 1787:22
Ramsay, D., Royal St.	Alexandria	Occupant	1787	Tax L 1787:21
Ramsay, Dannie	Alexandria	Owner	1787	Tax L 1787:23
Ramsay, Dennis	Alexandria	Owner	1787	Tax L 1787:22
Ramsay, Dennis	Alexandria	Tax Charge	1787	Tax PP 1787:13
Ramsay, Dennis	Alexandria	Tax Charge	1788	Tax PP 1788:14
Ramsay, Dennis	Alexandria	Tax Charge	1789	Tax PP 1789:16
Ramsay, Dennis	Alexandria	Tax Charge	1790	Tax PP 1790:12
Ramsay, Dennis	Alexandria	Tax Charge	1795	Tax PP 1795:25
Ramsay, Dennis	Alexandria	Tax Charge	1796	Tax LP 1796:24
Ramsay, Dennis	Alexandria	Tax Charge	1796	Tax PP 1796:16
Ramsay, Dennis	Alexandria	Tax Charge	1798	Tax PP 1798:16
Ramsay, Dennis	Alexandria	Tax Charge	1799	Tax PP 1799:34
Ramsay, Dennis	Alexandria	Tax Charge	1800	Tax PP 1800:37
Ramsay, Dennis	Alexandria	Head	1810	1810(2):02A
Ramsay, Dennis	Arlington	Inventory	1810	AB1:011
Ramsay, Dennis	Arlington	Admin.	1810	WBC:489
Ramsay, Dennis & wife Jane Allen, def.	Alexandria	Suit	1801	CRC:118
Ramsay, Dennis, Col.	Alexandria	Deposition	1802	CRI:078
Ramsay, Dennis, Col.	Arlington	Account	1812	AB1:187; LVA-LP
Ramsay, Dennis, Col.	Arlington	Sale	1812	AB1:185

NAME OR SUBJECT	LOCATION	TYPE	YEAR	REFERENCE(S)
Ramsay, Dennis, Fairfax St.	Alexandria	Occupant	1790	Tax L 1790:10
Ramsay, Dennis, Fairfax St.	Alexandria	Owner	1790	Tax L 1790:10(3)
Ramsay, Dennis, Fairfax St.	Alexandria	Owner	1795	Tax L 1795:25(3)
Ramsay, Dennis, Fairfax St.	Alexandria	Occupant	1795	Tax L 1795:25
Ramsay, Dennis, gentleman	Alexandria	Housekeeper	1808	1808(2):12A
Ramsay, Dennis, King St.	Alexandria	Occupant	1787	Tax L 1787:23
Ramsay, Dennis, plt.	Alexandria	Suit	1801	CRB:322
Ramsay, Dennis, Queen St.	Alexandria	Owner	1790	Tax L 1790:10
Ramsay, Dennis, Royal St.	Alexandria	Occupant	1787	Tax L 1787:23
Ramsay, Dennis, Royal St.	Alexandria	Owner	1790	Tax L 1790:10
Ramsay, Dennis, Royal St.	Alexandria	Owner	1795	Tax L 1795:25
Ramsay, Dennis, Water St.	Alexandria	Owner	1790	Tax L 1790:10
Ramsay, Edward	Alexandria	Owner	1787	Tax L 1787:23
Ramsay, Edward	Alexandria	Tax Charge	1787	Tax PP 1787:12
Ramsay, Edward	Alexandria	Tax Charge	1789	Tax PP 1789:15
Ramsay, Edward	Alexandria	Tax Charge	1790	Tax PP 1790:12
Ramsay, Edward, King St.	Alexandria	Occupant	1787	Tax L 1787:02
Ramsay, Edward, King St.	Alexandria	Owner	1790	Tax L 1790:09
Ramsay, Edward Mitchell	Alexandria	Tax Charge	1796	Tax PP 1796:16
Ramsay, Edwd.	Alexandria	Tax Charge	1788	Tax PP 1788:14
Ramsay, Edwd.	Alexandria	Tax Charge	1795	Tax PP 1795:25
Ramsay, Edwd.	Alexandria	Tax Charge	1796	Tax LP 1796:24
Ramsay, Edwd., King St.	Alexandria	Occupant	1795	Tax L 1795:10
Ramsay, Edwd. M.	Alexandria	Tax Charge	1798	Tax PP 1798:16
Ramsay, Edwd., Royal St.	Alexandria	Occupant	1787	Tax L 1787:20
Ramsay, Edwd., Royal St.	Alexandria	Occupant	1795	Tax L 1795:07
Ramsay, Eliza, w/o Robert T.	Arlington	Will	1868	WB9:036; File #660A
Ramsay, Elizabeth	Arlington	Admin.	1822	OCR1822:004
Ramsay, Elizabeth	Arlington	Admin.	1822	WB3:049
Ramsay, Elizabeth	Arlington	Account	1824	AB5:250; LVA-LP
Ramsay, James	Alexandria	Tax Charge	1787	Tax PP 1787:12
Ramsay, James	Alexandria	Tax Charge	1788	Tax PP 1788:14
Ramsay, James	Alexandria	Tax Charge	1789	Tax PP 1789:15
Ramsay, Jane A.	Arlington	Will	1850	WB5:260; File #460A
Ramsay, Jesse	Alexandria	Boarder	1808	1808(2):12A
Ramsay, Jesse T., grantee	Arlington	Indenture D.	1812	ID2:160
Ramsay, Jesse T., grantee	Arlington	Indenture D.	1814	ID2:366
Ramsay, Jesse T., grantee	Arlington	Indenture D.	1827	ID:118
Ramsay, Jesse T., grantee	Arlington	Indenture D.	1827	ID:095
Ramsay, Jesse T., grantee	Arlington	Indenture D.	1828	ID:151
Ramsay, Jesse T., grantee	Arlington	Indenture D.	1828	ID:168
Ramsay, Jesse T., grantee	Arlington	Indenture D.	1832	ID:377
Ramsay, Jno. & wife, merchant	Alexandria	Housekeeper	1799	1799(2):10A
Ramsay, Jno., clerk	Alexandria	Boarder	1799	1799(2):10A
Ramsay, John	Alexandria	Tithable +21	1787	Tax PP 1787:13
Ramsay, John	Alexandria	Mer. License	1798	Tax PP 1798:20-6
Ramsay, John	Alexandria	Tax Charge	1799	Tax PP 1799:34
Ramsay, John	Alexandria	Tax Charge	1800	Tax PP 1800:37
Ramsay, John	Arlington	Inventory	1821	AB5:027; LVA-LP
Ramsay, John	Arlington	Will	1821	WB3:017; File #199A
Ramsay, John	Arlington	Bond	1821	WB3:018
Ramsay, John	Arlington	Credits	1822	AB5:058
Ramsay, John	Arlington	Account	1822	LVA-LP
Ramsay, John	Arlington	Debts Due	1822	OCR1822:007a
Ramsay, John	Arlington	Account	1822	OCR1822:003
Ramsay, John	Arlington	Account	1824	AB5:233; LVA-LP
Ramsay, John	Arlington	Account	1829	AB6:481; LVA-LP
Ramsay, John	Arlington	Admin.	1842	OCR1842:019
Ramsay, John	Arlington	Admin.	1842	WB4:314
Ramsay, John	Arlington	Inventory	1843	AB8:353; LVA-LP
Ramsay, John, c/o John	Arlington	Guard.	1821	WB3:018

NAME OR SUBJECT	LOCATION	TYPE	YEAR	REFERENCE(S)
Ramsay, John, c/o John	Arlington	Guard. Acct.	1824	AB5:235
Ramsay, John, merchant	Alexandria	Housekeeper	1808	1808(3):21A
Ramsay, John, retailer	Alexandria	Housekeeper	1808	1808(2):11A
Ramsay, Margaret D.	Alexandria	Will	1884	WB1:401; LP
Ramsay, Mary	Arlington	Guard. Acct.	1824	AB5:236
Ramsay, Mary Ann, seamstress	Alexandria	Head	1810	1810(4):07A
Ramsay, Mary Ann, washwoman/semp.	Alexandria	Housekeeper	1808	1808(4):26A
Ramsay, Mary, c/o John	Arlington	Guard.	1821	WB3:018
Ramsay, Patrick	Alexandria	Boarder	1808	1808(2):10A
Ramsay, Patrick, def.	Alexandria	Suit	1807	CRF:140
Ramsay, Sally	Alexandria	Owner	1787	Tax L 1787:21
Ramsay, Sally	Alexandria	Tax Charge	1787	Tax PP 1787:13
Ramsay, Sally & Emelia	Alexandria	Owner	1787	Tax L 1787:21
Ramsay, Sarah, c/o John	Arlington	Guard.	1821	WB3:018
Ramsay, Sarah, c/o John	Arlington	Guard. Acct.	1824	AB5:235
Ramsay, Thomas	Alexandria	Tax Charge	1787	Tax PP 1787:13
Ramsay, Thos.	Alexandria	Tax Charge	1788	Tax PP 1788:14
Ramsay, Thos., Oronoko St.	Alexandria	Owner	1795	Tax L 1795:24
Ramsay, Wilhelmina	Arlington	Will	1866	WB8:387; File #646A
Ramsay, William	Alexandria	Owner	1787	Tax L 1787:21
Ramsay, William	Alexandria	Tax Charge	1787	Tax PP 1787:13
Ramsay, William	Alexandria	Tax Charge	1788	Tax PP 1788:14
Ramsay, William	Alexandria	Tax Charge	1789	Tax PP 1789:16
Ramsay, William	Alexandria	Tax Charge	1790	Tax PP 1790:12
Ramsay, William	Arlington	Plaintiff	1802	PA:054
Ramsay, William	Arlington	Deposition	1806	ACR:029
Ramsay, William, Admr.	Arlington	Respondent	1805	ACO:046
Ramsay, William, Admr.	Arlington	Respondent	1805	ACO:042
Ramsay, William, Admr.	Arlington	Respondent	1806	ACO:051
Ramsay, William, def.	Alexandria	Suit	1801	CRB:008, 013, 016
Ramsay, William, Estate	Alexandria	Owner	1787	Tax L 1787:22
Ramsay, William, Estate	Alexandria	Tax Charge	1787	Tax PP 1787:13
Ramsay, William, Estate	Alexandria	Tax Charge	1788	Tax PP 1788:14
Ramsay, William, Estate, def.	Alexandria	Suit	1806	CRF:109
Ramsay, William, Estate, nr. Royal St.	Alexandria	Owner	1790	Tax L 1790:10(2)
Ramsay, William, Fairfax St.	Alexandria	Occupant	1790	Tax L 1790:10
Ramsay, William H. Piper	Arlington	Will	1864	WB8:194; File #610A
Ramsay, Wm.	Alexandria	Boarder	1808	1808(2):12A
Ramsay, Wm., Dr., Estate	Alexandria	Tax Charge	1796	Tax LP 1796:25
Ramsay, Wm., Estate	Alexandria	Tax Charge	1789	Tax PP 1789:16
Ramsay, Wm., Estate	Alexandria	Tax Charge	1790	Tax PP 1790:13
Ramsay, Wm., Estate	Alexandria	Tax Charge	1795	Tax PP 1795:25
Ramsay, Wm., Fairfax St.	Alexandria	Owner	1790	Tax L 1790:10
Ramsay, Wm., M.D.	Alexandria	Tax Charge	1795	Tax PP 1795:25
Ramsay, Wm., M.D., Fairfax St.	Alexandria	Owner	1795	Tax L 1795:25
Ramsey, John	Alexandria	Mer. License	1799	Tax PP 1799:52-09r
Randal, Theophilus, ship carpenter	Alexandria	Housekeeper	1808	1808(1):08A
Randall, J.	Alexandria	Tax Charge	1796	Tax PP 1796:16
Randall, Orpha	Alexandria	Tithable +16	1788	Tax PP 1788:03
Randall, Theoph.	Alexandria	Tax Charge	1798	Tax PP 1798:16
Randall, Theophilus	Alexandria	Tax Charge	1796	Tax LP 1796:25
Randall, Theophilus	Alexandria	Tax Charge	1799	Tax PP 1799:34
Randall, Theophilus	Alexandria	Tax Charge	1800	Tax PP 1800:37
Randall, Theophilus & wife, ship builder	Alexandria	Head	1795	1795(4a):04
Randall, Theophilus & wife, ship builder	Alexandria	Housekeeper	1799	1799(2):16A
Randall, Theopholus, ship carpenter	Alexandria	Head	1810	1810(1):08A
Randell, Theophilus	Alexandria	Tax Charge	1789	Tax PP 1789:16
Randle, Theophilus & wife Rachel	Alexandria	Resident	1800	1800(4):02B
Randle, Theophilus, ship carpenter	Alexandria	Head	1800	1800(4):02A
Randolph, Cornelia Jefferson	Alexandria	Will	1872	WB1:047; LP
Randolph, Dav.	Alexandria	Boarder	1808	1808(2):15A

NAME OR SUBJECT	LOCATION	TYPE	YEAR	REFERENCE(S)
Randolph, David	Alexandria	Boarder	1808	1808(1):01A
Randolph, Martha E.	Arlington	Guard.	1834	WB4:103
Randolph, Mary J.	Alexandria	Will	1876	WB1:185; LP
Randolph, Peyton	Alexandria	Will	1891	WB1:594; LP
Randolph, [blank]	Alexandria	Boarder	1808	1808(2):16A
Ranger, Nichlas, labourer	Alexandria	Head	1810	1810(3):10A
Rankin, Robert	Arlington	Crime	1797	OT:10/04/1797
Rankins, Benj.	Alexandria	Tax Charge	1795	Tax PP 1795:26
Ranter, Henney	Alexandria	Resident	1800	1800(4):08B
Ranter, Henry	Alexandria	Boarder	1799	1799(2):19A
Rantons, R., Fairfax St.	Alexandria	Occupant	1795	Tax L 1795:02
Rantzel, Jacob	Alexandria	Tax Charge	1795	Tax PP 1795:26
Rantzell, Andrew	Alexandria	Tax Charge	1796	Tax PP 1796:16
Rantzell, Jacob, Water St.	Alexandria	Occupant	1795	Tax L 1795:10
Rantzill, Andw.	Alexandria	Tax Charge	1795	Tax PP 1795:25
Rantzill, Andw., Royal St.	Alexandria	Occupant	1795	Tax L 1795:01
Rape, Adam	Alexandria	Tax Charge	1790	Tax PP 1790:12
Rapley, Abraham, grantor	Arlington	Indenture D.	1829	ID:242
Rapley, Abraham, in jail	Arlington	Insolvent	1829	ID:240
Ratcliff, Ignatius	Alexandria	Tax Charge	1798	Tax PP 1798:16
Ratcliff, Ignatius, carpenter	Alexandria	Head	1810	1810(1):09A
Ratcliff, Richard	Alexandria	Owner	1787	Tax L 1787:22
Ratcliff, Richard, St. Asaph St.	Alexandria	Owner	1790	Tax L 1790:09(2)
Ratcliffe, Francis	Alexandria	Tax Charge	1795	Tax PP 1795:25
Ratcliffe, Ignatius	Alexandria	Tax Charge	1796	Tax PP 1796:16
Ratcliffe, Richard	Arlington	Plaintiff	1802	PA:051
Ratcliffe, Richd.	Alexandria	Tax Charge	1796	Tax LP 1796:25
Ratcliffe, Richd., St. Asaph St.	Alexandria	Owner	1795	Tax L 1795:25(2)
Ratlief, Ignatious & wife Viletter	Alexandria	Resident	1800	1800(4):09B
Ratlief, Ignatious, h. carpenter	Alexandria	Head	1800	1800(4):09A
Ratliff, Richd., Washington St.	Alexandria	Occupant	1787	Tax L 1787:01
Rattle, James	Alexandria	Tax Charge	1787	Tax PP 1787:12
Rattle, Jos., King St.	Alexandria	Occupant	1787	Tax L 1787:21
Rawlings, Jesse	Alexandria	Boarder	1808	1808(4):25A
Rawlings, Jno.	Alexandria	Tax Charge	1795	Tax PP 1795:25
Rawlings, John, Jr., grantor	Arlington	Indenture D.	1831	ID:336
Rawlings [Rolling], John, in jail	Arlington	Insolvent	1831	ID:333
Rawlingson, Polly, washwoman	Alexandria	Housekeeper	1808	1808(3):22A
Rawlins, John	Alexandria	Tax Charge	1796	Tax PP 1796:16
Rawlins, John, Washington St.	Alexandria	Occupant	1795	Tax L 1795:25
Rawlins, John, Washington St.	Alexandria	Owner	1795	Tax L 1795:25
Ray, Jno.	Alexandria	Tax Charge	1798	Tax PP 1798:15
Ray, John, coachmaker	Alexandria	Head	1810	1810(1):08A
Rayner, Joseph, b. Yorkshire	Arlington	Alien Entry	1819	RA:18/11/19
Rea, John, coachmaker	Alexandria	Housekeeper	1808	1808(1):04A
Read, James	Alexandria	Tax Charge	1796	Tax LP 1796:24
Read, Thomas	Arlington	Ordinary	1806	OBL2(np)
Read, Thomas	Arlington	Bond	1818	WB2:239
Reader, Cloe	Arlington	Will	1803	WBA:193; LVA-LP
Reader, Cloe	Arlington	Bond	1803	WBA:194
Reader, Cloe	Arlington	Account	1806	LVA-LP
Reader, Susaner	Alexandria	Resident	1800	1800(4):11B
Reader, Thomas	Arlington	Guard.	1804	WBA:283
Reader, Thomas	Arlington	Guard. Acct.	1808	WBC:025; LVA-LP
Readman, Thomas	Alexandria	Tax Charge	1787	Tax PP 1787:13
Ready, [blank]	Alexandria	Boarder	1808	1808(2):12A
Reagen, Michael, age near 67	Alexandria	Deposition	1767	CRI:221
Reardon, Cornelius	Arlington	Apprentice	1803	OCR1801:115
Reardon, Cornelius	Arlington	Guard.	1809	WBC:301
Reardon, Cornelius	Arlington	Guard. Acct.	1819	AB3:329
Reardon, Cornelius	Arlington	Guard. Acct.	1826	AB6:262

NAME OR SUBJECT	LOCATION	TYPE	YEAR	REFERENCE(S)
Reardon, Elizabeth	Arlington	Guard.	1809	WBC:301
Reardon, Elizabeth	Arlington	Guard. Acct.	1819	AB3:329
Reardon, Elizabeth, c/o Rachael	Arlington	Apprentice	1804	OCR1801:175
Reardon, Jno.	Alexandria	Tax Charge	1795	Tax PP 1795:26
Reardon, Jno.	Alexandria	Tax Charge	1798	Tax PP 1798:15
Reardon, Jno. & wife, cooper	Alexandria	Housekeeper	1799	1799(2):16A
Reardon, Jno., Union St.	Alexandria	Occupant	1795	Tax L 1795:01
Reardon, John	Alexandria	Tax Charge	1789	Tax PP 1789:16
Reardon, John	Alexandria	Tax Charge	1790	Tax PP 1790:12
Reardon, John	Alexandria	Tax Charge	1796	Tax LP 1796:25
Reardon, John	Alexandria	Tax Charge	1796	Tax PP 1796:16
Reardon, John	Alexandria	Tax Charge	1800	Tax PP 1800:37
Reardon, John	Arlington	Inventory	1803	WBA:196; LVA-LP
Reardon, John	Arlington	Admin.	1803	WBA:180
Reardon, John	Arlington	Sale	1805	WBB:166
Reardon, John	Arlington	Account	1805	WBB:167; LVA-LP
Reardon, John	Arlington	Account	1819	AB3:329
Reardon, John	Arlington	Guard. Acct.	1819	AB3:329
Reardon, John	Arlington	Guard. Acct.	1821	AB4:317; LVA-LP
Reardon, John & wife Rachel	Alexandria	Resident	1800	1800(4):02B
Reardon, John, c/o Ann	Arlington	Apprentice	1803	OCR1801:100
Reardon, John, children of	Arlington	Guard. Acct.	1810	AB1:001
Reardon, John, children of	Arlington	Guard. Acct.	1811	AB1:126
Reardon, John, children of	Arlington	Guard. Acct.	1815	AB2:163; LVA-LP
Reardon, John, children of	Arlington	Guard. Acct.	1819	AB3:385; LVA-LP
Reardon, John, cooper	Alexandria	Head	1800	1800(4):02A
Reardon, John, for retailing liquors	Arlington	Defendant	1802	PA:036
Reardon, John, heirs of	Arlington	Guard. Acct.	1812	AB1:267; LVA-LP
Reardon, John, heirs of	Arlington	Guard. Acct.	1814	AB2:036; LVA-LP
Reardon, John, heirs of	Arlington	Guard. Acct.	1817	AB3:038; LVA-LP
Reardon, John, orphans of	Arlington	Guard. Acct.	1818	AB3:249; LVA-LP
Reardon, John, w(3), cooper	Alexandria	Head	1795	1796(3):7
Reardon, Joseph	Arlington	Apprentice	1811	OCR1811:018
Reardon, Matthew D	Alexandria	Head	1810	1810(4):05A
Reardon, Michael	Alexandria	Tax Charge	1790	Tax PP 1790:12
Reardon, Michael	Arlington	Guard.	1809	WBC:301
Reardon, Michael	Arlington	Guard. Acct.	1819	AB3:329; LVA-LP
Reardon, Michael	Arlington	Guard. Acct.	1821	AB4:317; LVA-LP
Reardon, Michael	Arlington	Guard. Acct.	1826	AB6:262; LVA-LP
Reardon, Michl.	Alexandria	Tax Charge	1796	Tax LP 1796:25
Reardon, Michl., Wales' alley	Alexandria	Occupant	1795	Tax L 1795:23
Reardon, Pat.	Alexandria	Tax Charge	1795	Tax PP 1795:27
Reardon, Patrick	Alexandria	Tithable +16	1788	Tax PP 1788:08
Reardon, Wm.	Alexandria	Boarder	1808	1808(2):16A
Reason, Sarah	Arlington	Guard.	1806	WBB:377
Recklace, Isaac	Alexandria	Tax Charge	1799	Tax PP 1799:34
Recklace, Joseph	Alexandria	Tax Charge	1800	Tax PP 1800:37
Rector, Charles	Alexandria	Tax Charge	1796	Tax LP 1796:24
Reder, Susaner, sumpster	Alexandria	Boarder	1800	1800(4):11A
Redman, Edmd.	Alexandria	License Due	1800	Tax PP 1800:54(24)
Redman, Edwd., merchant	Alexandria	Head	1810	1810(2):05A
Redman, Sarah, seamstress	Alexandria	Head	1810	1810(1):05A
Redman, Thomas	Alexandria	Tax Charge	1788	Tax PP 1788:14
Redman, Thomas	Alexandria	Tax Charge	1789	Tax PP 1789:16
Redman, Thomas	Alexandria	Tax Charge	1790	Tax PP 1790:12
Redman, Thomas	Alexandria	Tax Charge	1796	Tax LP 1796:25
Redman, Thomas	Alexandria	Tax Charge	1796	Tax PP 1796:16
Redman, Thomas	Arlington	Will	1800	CRA:319
Redman, Thomas	Arlington	Inventory	1800	WBA:001; LVA-LP
Redman, Thomas	Arlington	Account	1800	WBA:002; LVA-LP
Redman, Thomas, Admr. of, def.	Alexandria	Suit	1801	CRB:045

NAME OR SUBJECT	LOCATION	TYPE	YEAR	REFERENCE(S)
Redman, Thomas, Prince St.	Alexandria	Occupant	1790	Tax L 1790:09
Redman, Thomas, Prince St.	Alexandria	Owner	1790	Tax L 1790:09
Redman, Thos.	Alexandria	Tax Charge	1795	Tax PP 1795:26
Redman, Thos. & wife, boarding house	Alexandria	Housekeeper	1799	1799(2):09A
Redman, Thos., Laborer	Alexandria	Tax Charge	1790	Tax PP 1790:12
Redman, Thos., Prince St.	Alexandria	Occupant	1787	Tax L 1787:11
Redman, Thos., Prince St.	Alexandria	Occupant	1795	Tax L 1795:25
Redman, Thos., Prince St.	Alexandria	Owner	1795	Tax L 1795:25
Redman, Wm. (C), laborer	Alexandria	Housekeeper	1808	1808(4):28A
Redmon, Edward	Alexandria	Tax Charge	1800	Tax PP 1800:37
Redmon, Sarah	Alexandria	Tax Charge	1800	Tax PP 1800:37
Redmon, Thos.	Alexandria	Tax Charge	1798	Tax PP 1798:15
Redmon, Thos.	Alexandria	Tax Charge	1799	Tax PP 1799:35
Redmond, Edward	Alexandria	Tax Charge	1799	Tax PP 1799:34
Redmond, Edwd., retailer	Alexandria	Housekeeper	1808	1808(2):14A
Redmond, Sarah, sempstress	Alexandria	Housekeeper	1808	1808(1):03A
Redmond, Thomas, w, innkeeper	Alexandria	Head	1796	1796(3):3
Redwood, James	Alexandria	Tax Charge	1789	Tax PP 1789:16
Reed & Gretter, Queen St.	Alexandria	Occupant	1787	Tax L 1787:17
Reed, Alexr.	Alexandria	Tax Charge	1798	Tax PP 1798:16
Reed, Ann (Spurling)	Arlington	Dispute	1816	AB2:390
Reed, Elizth., Queen St.	Alexandria	Occupant	1795	Tax L 1795:24
Reed, Francis Avery	Alexandria	Will	1895	WB2:127; LP
Reed, Hugh & wife, cooper	Alexandria	Head	1795	1795(4):03
Reed, James	Alexandria	Tax Charge	1796	Tax LP 1796:24
Reed, James	Alexandria	Tax Charge	1799	Tax PP 1799:34
Reed, James	Alexandria	Tax Charge	1800	Tax PP 1800:37
Reed, Jas.	Alexandria	Tax Charge	1795	Tax PP 1795:25
Reed, Jas.	Alexandria	Tax Charge	1795	Tax PP 1795:25
Reed, Marinda	Alexandria	Will	1898	WB2:286; LP
Reed, Nelson	Arlington	Will	1807	WBB:519; File #029A
Reed, Nelson	Arlington	Bond	1807	WBB:519
Reed, Nelson	Arlington	Account	1808	WBC:071; LVA-LP
Reed, Sandy	Alexandria	Tax Charge	1795	Tax PP 1795:26
Reed, Sawney	Alexandria	Tax Charge	1796	Tax PP 1796:17
Reed, Silas	Arlington	Account	1856	WB6:275; LVA-LP
Reed, Silas, of Scott Co. IL	Arlington	Will	1852	WB6:108; File #478A
Reed, Thomas	Alexandria	Owner	1787	Tax L 1787:22
Reed, Thomas	Arlington	Ordinary	1807	OBL2(np)
Reed, Thomas	Arlington	Will	1817	WB2:216; File #145A
Reed, Thomas, Queen St.	Alexandria	Occupant	1790	Tax L 1790:09
Reed, Thomas, Queen St.	Alexandria	Owner	1790	Tax L 1790:09(3)
Reed, Thos.	Alexandria	Boarder	1808	1808(3):22A
Reed [Read], Thomas	Arlington	Inventory	1818	AB3:163; LVA-LP
Reed, Thos., Estate	Alexandria	Tax Charge	1796	Tax LP 1796:24
Reed, Thos., Estate, Queen St.	Alexandria	Owner	1795	Tax L 1795:24(3)
Reed, Thos., painter	Alexandria	Head	1810	1810(4):07A
Reed, Thos., Queen St.	Alexandria	Occupant	1787	Tax L 1787:22
Reed, William	Arlington	Ordinary	1808	OBL2(np)
Reed, William	Arlington	Ordinary	1809	OBL2(np)
Reed, William	Arlington	Ordinary	1810	OBL2(np)
Reed, William	Arlington	Will	1814	WB1:335
Reed, William	Arlington	Inventory	1815	AB2:086; LVA-LP
Reed, William, grantor	Arlington	Indenture D.	1806	ID3:129
Reed, William, in jail bounds	Arlington	Insolvent	1806	ID3:126
Reed, Wm., baker	Alexandria	Head	1810	1810(1):12A
Reed, Wm., shopkeeper & tavern lic.	Alexandria	Housekeeper	1808	1808(2):13A
Reeder, Chloe	Arlington	Account	1806	WBB:370
Reeder, Hezekiah	Arlington	Apprentice	1804	OCR1801:210
Reeder, Jeremiah	Alexandria	Tithable +21	1787	Tax PP 1787:04
Reeder, Nancy	Alexandria	Boarder	1799	1799(2):09A

NAME OR SUBJECT	LOCATION	TYPE	YEAR	REFERENCE(S)
Reeder, Susannah	Alexandria	Boarder	1799	1799(2):13A
Reeder, Thomas	Arlington	Guard. Acct.	1808	WBC:025
Reen, Benjamin	Alexandria	Tax Charge	1799	Tax PP 1799:34
Reens, George, c/o Eliz. Mandeville	Arlington	Apprentice	1804	OCR1801:182
Rees, John W.	Arlington	Libellant	1820	ACO:181, 183
Rees, Polly	Alexandria	Serv./Appr.	1800	1800(4):04B
Reese, Mary	Arlington	Guard.	1805	WBB:225
Reese, Samuel	Arlington	Bond	1853	BB(np)
Reese, Samuel	Arlington	Will	1853	WB6:200; File #494A
Reese, Samuel	Arlington	Account	1854	WB6:400; LVA-LPS
Reese, Samuel	Arlington	Appraisal	1858	WB7:335; LVA-LP
Reeves, Charles F.	Arlington	Apprentice	1823	OCR1822:040
Reeves, Eliza	Arlington	Apprentice	1814	OCR1811:224
Reeves, Josiah W.	Arlington	Apprentice	1823	OCR1822:032
Reeves, Leoanrd, bricklayer	Alexandria	Housekeeper	1808	1808(2):16A
Reeves, Leonard	Alexandria	Tax Charge	1787	Tax PP 1787:13
Reeves, Leonard	Alexandria	Tax Charge	1788	Tax PP 1788:14
Reeves, Leonard	Alexandria	Tax Charge	1789	Tax PP 1789:16
Reeves, Leonard	Alexandria	Tax Charge	1790	Tax PP 1790:12
Reeves, Leonard	Alexandria	Tax Charge	1796	Tax LP 1796:25
Reeves, Leonard	Alexandria	Tax Charge	1796	Tax PP 1796:17
Reeves, Leonard	Alexandria	Tax Charge	1799	Tax PP 1799:35
Reeves, Leonard	Alexandria	Tax Charge	1800	Tax PP 1800:37
Reeves, Leonard & wife, bricklayer	Alexandria	Head	1795	1795(4a):10
Reeves, Leonard, Washington St.	Alexandria	Occupant	1795	Tax L 1795:07
Reeves, Leond.	Alexandria	Tax Charge	1795	Tax PP 1795:26
Reeves, [blank], nr. Union St.	Alexandria	Occupant	1790	Tax L 1790:11
Regan, Basil & wife	Alexandria	Housekeeper	1799	1799(2):12A
Regnigh, Willia, w(1), mariner	Alexandria	Head	1796	1796(3):1
Reid, Andrew	Alexandria	Tax Charge	1790	Tax PP 1790:12
Reid, James	Alexandria	Tax Charge	1796	Tax PP 1796:17
Reid, James H.	Arlington	Inventory	1869	WB9:181
Reid, James H.	Arlington	Account	1870	WB9:285
Reid, Jas.	Alexandria	Tax Charge	1798	Tax PP 1798:15
Reid, Thomas	Alexandria	Tax Charge	1787	Tax PP 1787:13
Reid, Thomas	Alexandria	Tax Charge	1788	Tax PP 1788:14
Reid, Thomas	Alexandria	Tax Charge	1789	Tax PP 1789:16
Reid, Thomas	Alexandria	Tax Charge	1790	Tax PP 1790:12
Reiley, Wm., merchant	Alexandria	Housekeeper	1808	1808(3):21A
Reily, Benneet	Alexandria	Tax Charge	1800	Tax PP 1800:37
Reily, Henry	Arlington	Account	1819	AB3:371; LVA-LP
Reily, William, merchant & wife Barbara	Alexandria	Deed	1793	CRD:142
Reily, William, plt.	Alexandria	Suit	1801	CRD:104
Reins, George	Arlington	Apprentice	1804	OCR1801:224
Reintzel, Andrew	Alexandria	Tax Charge	1800	Tax PP 1800:37
Reintzel, Andrew, w(2), blacksmith	Alexandria	Head	1796	1796(3):3
Reintzel, Andw., Fairfax St.	Alexandria	Occupant	1790	Tax L 1790:02
Reintzell, Andrew	Alexandria	Tax Charge	1789	Tax PP 1789:15
Reintzell, Andrew	Alexandria	Tax Charge	1790	Tax PP 1790:12
Reintzell, Andrew	Arlington	Witness	1794	OT:03/07/1794
Reintzell, Andrew	Alexandria	Tax Charge	1799	Tax PP 1799:34
Reintzell, Andrew	Arlington	Ordinary	1805	OBL1(np)
Reintzell, Andrew & wife, blacksmith	Alexandria	Housekeeper	1799	1799(2):11A
Reintzell, Andrew, blacksmith	Alexandria	Housekeeper	1808	1808(4):29A
Reintzell, Andrew, blacksmith	Alexandria	Head	1810	1810(4):06A
Reintzell, Andw.	Alexandria	Tax Charge	1798	Tax PP 1798:16
Reintzell, B. & N.	Alexandria	Tax Charge	1798	Tax PP 1798:16
Reintzell, Benja.	Alexandria	Tax Charge	1800	Tax PP 1800:37
Reintzell, Benjn.	Alexandria	Tax Charge	1799	Tax PP 1799:34
Reintzell, Benjn. & wife, sadler	Alexandria	Housekeeper	1799	1799(2):07A
Reintzell, Eliza Louisa, c/o Benjamin	Arlington	Apprentice	1805	OCR1801:288

NAME OR SUBJECT	LOCATION	TYPE	YEAR	REFERENCE(S)
Reintzell, Frederick, c/o Benjamin	Arlington	Apprentice	1805	OCR1801:286
Reintzell, Jacob	Alexandria	Tithable +16	1789	Tax PP 1789:15
Reintzell, Jacob	Alexandria	Tithable +16	1790	Tax PP 1790:12
Reintzell, Jacob	Alexandria	Tax Charge	1799	Tax PP 1799:35
Reintzell, Jacob & wife, carpenter	Alexandria	Housekeeper	1799	1799(2):01A
Reintzell, Jacob, blacksmith	Alexandria	Head	1810	1810(3):09A
Reintzell [Rantzel], Jacob	Alexandria	Tax Charge	1795	Tax PP 1795:26
Reintzell [Rantzill], Andw.	Alexandria	Tax Charge	1795	Tax PP 1795:25
Reintzle, Jacob, w(1), blacksmith	Alexandria	Head	1796	1796(3):6
Reinzel, Andrew	Alexandria	Tax Charge	1796	Tax LP 1796:25
Reiszler, Jacob	Alexandria	Tax Charge	1796	Tax LP 1796:25
Reler, Jesse, labourer	Alexandria	Head	1810	1810(1):05A
Reno, Hanson	Alexandria	Tax Charge	1798	Tax PP 1798:15
Reno, Hanson	Alexandria	Tax Charge	1799	Tax PP 1799:34
Reno, Hanson	Alexandria	Tax Charge	1800	Tax PP 1800:37
Reno, Hanson, def.	Alexandria	Suit	1802	CRD:062
Reno, Hanson, def.	Alexandria	Suit	1803	CRD:074
Renshaw, William	Arlington	Libellant	1819	ACO:166
Resler, Eve	Arlington	Guard.	1804	WBA:321
Resler, Jacob	Alexandria	Tax Charge	1790	Tax PP 1790:12
Resler, Jacob	Alexandria	Tax Charge	1795	Tax PP 1795:26
Resler, Jacob	Alexandria	Tax Charge	1796	Tax PP 1796:16
Resler, Jacob	Alexandria	Tax Charge	1798	Tax PP 1798:15
Resler, Jacob	Alexandria	Tax Charge	1799	Tax PP 1799:34
Resler, Jacob	Arlington	Will	1804	WBB:035; LVA-LP
Resler, Jacob	Arlington	Bond	1804	WBB:036
Resler, Jacob	Arlington	Inventory	1804	WBB:091; LVA-LP
Resler, Jacob	Arlington	Sale	1805	WBB:140
Resler, Jacob	Arlington	Account	1805	WBB:176; LVA-LP
Resler, Jacob, Prince St.	Alexandria	Occupant	1795	Tax L 1795:25
Resler, Jacob, Prince St.	Alexandria	Owner	1795	Tax L 1795:25
Resler, Mary	Arlington	Account	1827	AB6:435; LVA-LP
Resler, Mary	Arlington	Inventory	1827	AB6:424; LVA-LP
Resler, Mary	Arlington	Sale	1827	AB6:414
Resler, Mary	Arlington	Admin.	1827	OCR1822:137a
Resler, Mary	Arlington	Admin.	1827	WB3:287
Resler, Mary, tallow chandler	Alexandria	Housekeeper	1808	1808(1):04A
Resler, [blank], Royal St.	Alexandria	Occupant	1790	Tax L 1790:10
Ressler, Jacob & wife, tallow chandler	Alexandria	Housekeeper	1799	1799(2):03A
Ressler, Mary, tallow chandler	Alexandria	Head	1810	1810(1):05A
Reynolds & Barclay, King St.	Alexandria	Occupant	1787	Tax L 1787:17
Reynolds, Ann Eliza, c/o David	Arlington	Guard.	1823	WB3:101
Reynolds, David	Arlington	Inventory	1821	AB4:319; LVA-LP
Reynolds, David	Arlington	Bond	1821	WB3:014
Reynolds, David	Arlington	Will (N)	1821	WB3:016; File #198A
Reynolds, David, orphans of	Arlington	Guard.	1823	OCR1822:044a, 075
Reynolds, David, pilot	Alexandria	Housekeeper	1808	1808(2):11A
Reynolds, David, pilot	Alexandria	Head	1810	1810(1):03A
Reynolds, Elender Elvina, c/o David	Arlington	Guard.	1823	WB3:101
Reynolds, Ellen Malvena	Arlington	Guard. Acct.	1824	AB5:354
Reynolds [Raynolds], James	Arlington	Account	1824	AB5:353; LVA-LP
Reynolds, James David, c/o David	Arlington	Guard.	1823	WB3:101
Reynolds, John	Alexandria	Tax Charge	1787	Tax PP 1787:12
Reynolds, John	Alexandria	Tax Charge	1788	Tax PP 1788:14
Reynolds, John	Alexandria	Tax Charge	1789	Tax PP 1789:16
Reynolds, John	Alexandria	Tax Charge	1790	Tax PP 1790:12
Reynolds, John	Alexandria	Tax Charge	1795	Tax PP 1795:26
Reynolds, John	Alexandria	Tax Charge	1796	Tax LP 1796:24
Reynolds, John	Alexandria	Tax Charge	1796	Tax PP 1796:16
Reynolds, John & wife, waiter	Alexandria	Head	1795	1795(4a):08
Reynolds, John & wife, naval officer	Alexandria	Head	1795	1795(4):07

NAME OR SUBJECT	LOCATION	TYPE	YEAR	REFERENCE(S)
Reynolds, John, Gibbon St.	Alexandria	Occupant	1787	Tax L 1787:04
Reynolds, John, grantor	Arlington	Indenture D.	1806	ID3:179
Reynolds, John, in jail bounds	Arlington	Insolvent	1806	ID3:176
Reynolds, John, potter	Alexandria	Housekeeper	1808	1808(3):20A
Reynolds, John, Prince St.	Alexandria	Occupant	1790	Tax L 1790:06
Reynolds, John, Princess St.	Alexandria	Occupant	1790	Tax L 1790:09
Reynolds, John, Princess St.	Alexandria	Owner	1790	Tax L 1790:09
Reynolds, John, Royal St.	Alexandria	Occupant	1795	Tax L 1795:25
Reynolds, Levi	Alexandria	Tax Charge	1799	Tax PP 1799:34
Reynolds, Levi, nail maker	Alexandria	Housekeeper	1799	1799(2):09A
Reynolds, Margaret	Arlington	Will	1858	WB7:299; File #553A
Reynolds, Margaret, formerly Cohen	Arlington	Will	1857	WB7:299; File #552A
Reynolds, Michael	Alexandria	Tax Charge	1787	Tax PP 1787:13
Reynolds, Michael	Alexandria	Tax Charge	1789	Tax PP 1789:16
Reynolds, Michael, Fairfax St.	Alexandria	Occupant	1790	Tax L 1790:12
Reynolds, Michl.	Alexandria	Tax Charge	1788	Tax PP 1788:14
Reynolds, Michl.	Alexandria	Tax Charge	1790	Tax PP 1790:12
Reynolds, Michl., Fairfax St.	Alexandria	Occupant	1787	Tax L 1787:14
Reynolds, Rhinaldo, c/o David	Arlington	Guard.	1823	WB3:101
Reynolds, Sarah	Alexandria	Tax Charge	1798	Tax PP 1798:15
Reynolds, Tho.	Alexandria	Tax Charge	1795	Tax PP 1795:26
Reynolds, William	Alexandria	Tax Charge	1789	Tax PP 1789:15
Reynolds, William	Alexandria	Tax Charge	1799	Tax PP 1799:34
Reynolds, William	Alexandria	Tax Charge	1799	Tax PP 1799:35
Reynolds, William	Alexandria	Tax Charge	1800	Tax PP 1800:37
Reynolds, William	Arlington	Distribution	1830	AB6:517; LVA-LP
Reynolds, William	Arlington	Will	1830	WB3:363; File #289A
Reynolds, William (B.S.?)	Alexandria	Tax Charge	1800	Tax PP 1800:37
Reynolds, William, blacksmith	Alexandria	Head	1810	1810(4):06A
Reynolds, Wm.	Alexandria	Tax Charge	1795	Tax PP 1795:26
Reynolds, Wm.	Alexandria	Tax Charge	1795	Tax PP 1795:25
Reynolds, Wm.	Alexandria	Tax Charge	1796	Tax PP 1796:16
Reynolds, Wm.	Alexandria	Tax Charge	1796	Tax PP 1796:16
Reynolds, Wm.	Alexandria	Tax Charge	1796	Tax PP 1796:16
Reynolds, Wm.	Alexandria	Tax Charge	1798	Tax PP 1798:16
Reynolds, Wm.	Alexandria	Tax Charge	1798	Tax PP 1798:15
Reynolds, Wm.	Alexandria	Tax Charge	1799	Tax PP 1799:35
Reynolds, Wm.	Alexandria	Serv./Appr.	1800	1800(4):09B
Reynolds, Wm. & wife, shoemaker	Alexandria	Housekeeper	1799	1799(2):15A
Reynolds, Wm. & wife Sarrah	Alexandria	Resident	1800	1800(4):10B
Reynolds, Wm., blacksmith	Alexandria	Housekeeper	1808	1808(4):26A
Reynolds, Wm., Fairfax St.	Alexandria	Owner	1795	Tax L 1795:25
Reynolds, Wm., Fairfax St.	Alexandria	Occupant	1795	Tax L 1795:25
Reynolds, Wm., shoemaker	Alexandria	Head	1800	1800(4):10A
Reynolds, Wm., shoemaker	Alexandria	Housekeeper	1808	1808(1):09A
Reynolds, Wm., shoemaker	Alexandria	Head	1810	1810(1):07A
Rhay, John	Alexandria	Tax Charge	1795	Tax PP 1795:26
Rhea, Matsey	Alexandria	Boarder	1799	1799(2):11A
Rheem, John, grantor	Arlington	Indenture D.	1830	ID:273
Rheem, John, in prison walls	Arlington	Insolvent	1830	ID:271
Rhodes, Anthony	Arlington	Ordinary	1820	OBL3(np)
Rhodes, Anthony	Arlington	Ordinary	1822	OBL3(np)
Rhodes, Anthony, at his house	Arlington	Ordinary	1827	OBL4(np)
Rhodes, Anthony, at his house	Arlington	Ordinary	1829	OBL4(np)
Rhodes, Anthony, def.	Alexandria	Suit	1818	CRK:315
Rhodes, Anthony, in Alexandria Co.	Arlington	Ordinary	1824	OBL3(np)
Rhodes, Anthony, in Alexandria Co.	Arlington	Ordinary	1826	OBL4(np)
Rhodes, Anthony, in Alexandria Co.	Arlington	Ordinary	1828	OBL4(np)
Rhodes, Anthony, retailer	Alexandria	Housekeeper	1808	1808(1):02A
Rhodes, Anthony, shopkeeper	Alexandria	Head	1810	1810(1):01A
Rhodes, Jno.	Alexandria	Tax Charge	1798	Tax PP 1798:16

NAME OR SUBJECT	LOCATION	TYPE	YEAR	REFERENCE(S)
Rhodes, Jno. & wife, carpenter	Alexandria	Housekeeper	1799	1799(2):06A
Rhodes, John	Alexandria	Tax Charge	1796	Tax PP 1796:16
Rhodes, John	Alexandria	Tax Charge	1799	Tax PP 1799:34
Rhodes, John	Alexandria	Tax Charge	1800	Tax PP 1800:37
Rhodes, John & wife, carpenter	Alexandria	Head	1795	1795(4):07
Rhodes, Mary	Arlington	Apprentice	1825	OCR1822:102a
Rhodes, Thomas	Arlington	Ordinary	1809	OBL2(np)
Rhodes, Thompson	Alexandria	Boarder	1808	1808(3):19A
Rhodes, William	Alexandria	Tax Charge	1788	Tax PP 1788:13
Rhodes, William	Alexandria	Tax Charge	1789	Tax PP 1789:15
Rhodes, William	Alexandria	Tax Charge	1790	Tax PP 1790:12
Rhodes, William	Alexandria	Tax Charge	1799	Tax PP 1799:34
Rhodes, William	Alexandria	Tax Charge	1800	Tax PP 1800:37
Rhodes, William, Fairfax St.	Alexandria	Occupant	1790	Tax L 1790:09
Rhodes, William, Fairfax St.	Alexandria	Owner	1790	Tax L 1790:09
Rhodes, William H., c/o Drusilla	Arlington	Apprentice	1842	OCR1842:013
Rhodes, William, merchant	Alexandria	Head	1810	1810(3):03A
Rhodes, William, nr. Fairfax St.	Alexandria	Occupant	1790	Tax L 1790:09
Rhodes, William, plt.	Alexandria	Suit	1801	CRC:186
Rhodes, Wm.	Alexandria	Tax Charge	1795	Tax PP 1795:25
Rhodes, Wm.	Alexandria	Tax Charge	1796	Tax LP 1796:24
Rhodes, Wm.	Alexandria	Tax Charge	1796	Tax PP 1796:16
Rhodes, Wm.	Alexandria	Tax Charge	1798	Tax PP 1798:16
Rhodes, Wm., merchant A.G.	Alexandria	Housekeeper	1808	1808(3):19A
Rice, James	Alexandria	Will	1888	WB1:514; LP
Rice, William	Arlington	Admin.	1824	OCR1822:067a
Rice, William H.	Arlington	Inventory	1824	AB5:241; LVA-LP
Rice, William H.	Arlington	Account	1825	AB5:393
Rice, William H.	Arlington	Sale	1825	AB5:392
Rice, William H.	Arlington	Inventory	1825	LVA-LP
Rice, William H., b. London	Arlington	Alien Entry	1817	RA:03/12/17
Rice, William, on Union St.	Arlington	Ordinary	1844	OBL6(np)
Rice, William, at steam boat ferry wharf	Arlington	Ordinary	1843	OBL6(np)
Rice, Wm.	Alexandria	Boarder	1808	1808(2):11A
Richard, Francis	Arlington	Inventory	1805	WBB:170
Richard, Francis	Arlington	Admin.	1805	WBB:168
Richard, Francis	Arlington	Sale	1805	WBB:171
Richard, Francis	Arlington	Account	1807	WBB:467; LVA-LP
Richard Lathan & Co.	Alexandria	Mer. License	1799	Tax PP 1799:52-06r
Richard Veitch & Co., plt.	Alexandria	Suit	1810	CRK:162
Richards, Barber, Royal St.	Alexandria	Occupant	1787	Tax L 1787:20
Richards, Caleb	Arlington	Admin.	1822	WB3:079
Richards, Caleb	Arlington	Inventory	1823	AB5:155; LVA-LP
Richards, Caleb	Arlington	Sale	1823	AB5:157
Richards, Caleb	Arlington	Division S.	1823	OCR1822:041a
Richards, Caleb	Arlington	Account	1824	AB5:265; LVA-LP
Richards, Caleb	Arlington	Account	1826	AB6:164; LVA-LP
Richards, Doctr.	Alexandria	Head	1810	1810(3):06A
Richards, Francis P., c/o John	Arlington	Guard.	1851	BB(np)
Richards, George	Alexandria	Tax Charge	1787	Tax PP 1787:13
Richards, George	Alexandria	Tax Charge	1788	Tax PP 1788:14
Richards, George	Alexandria	Tax Charge	1789	Tax PP 1789:15
Richards, George, Fairfax St.	Alexandria	Occupant	1787	Tax L 1787:09
Richards, George S., c/o John	Arlington	Guard.	1851	BB(np)
Richards, John	Alexandria	Tax Charge	1800	Tax PP 1800:37
Richards, John	Arlington	Admin.	1841	WB4:293
Richards, John	Arlington	Inventory	1842	AB8:288; LVA-LP
Richards, John	Arlington	Will	1843	WB4:352; File #403A
Richards, John	Arlington	Bond	1843	WB4:356
Richards, John	Arlington	Account	1849	WB5:183, 184; LVA-LP
Richards, John	Arlington	Account	1852	WB6:036; LVA-LP

NAME OR SUBJECT	LOCATION	TYPE	YEAR	REFERENCE(S)
Richards, John	Arlington	Account	1856	WB7:152; LVA-LP
Richards, John, c/o John	Arlington	Guard.	1851	BB(np)
Richards, John, Dr.	Arlington	Account	1843	AB8:430; LVA-LP
Richards, John, Dr.	Arlington	Sale	1844	AB9:002
Richards, John, Dr.	Arlington	Account	1844	AB9:002; LVA-LP
Richards, John, Jr.	Arlington	Defendant	1842	LSA:094
Richards, John, M.D.	Arlington	Will P.	1843	OCR1842:039
Richards, John, physician	Alexandria	Housekeeper	1808	1808(3):19A
Richards, John, Sr., Dr.	Arlington	Inventory	1843	AB8:398; LVA-LP
Richards, Kitty	Alexandria	Boarder	1799	1799(2):10A
Richards, Laura, w/o John, Jr.	Arlington	Defendant	1842	LSA:094
Richards, Priscilla (Crook), w/o Wm. B.	Arlington	Complainant	1841	LSA:062
Richards, Thomas	Alexandria	Tax Charge	1787	Tax PP 1787:12
Richards, Thomas	Alexandria	Tax Charge	1787	Tax PP 1787:12
Richards, Thomas	Alexandria	Tax Charge	1789	Tax PP 1789:15
Richards, Thomas	Alexandria	Deed	1790	CRC:134
Richards, Thomas	Alexandria	Tax Charge	1790	Tax PP 1790:12
Richards, Thomas	Alexandria	Deed	1796	CRI:071
Richards, Thomas	Alexandria	Tax Charge	1796	Tax PP 1796:17
Richards, Thomas	Alexandria	Deed	1800	CRC:143
Richards, Thomas	Alexandria	Deposition	1808	CRI:090
Richards, Thomas	Arlington	Ordinary	1808	OBL2(np)
Richards, Thomas	Arlington	Ordinary	1809	OBL2(np)
Richards, Thomas	Arlington	Ordinary	1810	OBL2(np)
Richards, Thomas & wife Nancy, def.	Alexandria	Suit	1801	CRC:095
Richards, Thomas, def.	Alexandria	Suit	1801	CRB:056
Richards, Thomas, def.	Alexandria	Suit	1801	CRB:332
Richards, Thomas, def.	Alexandria	Suit	1801	CRC:127
Richards, Thomas, def.	Alexandria	Suit	1801	CRC:138
Richards, Thomas, def.	Alexandria	Suit	1802	CRC:175
Richards, Thomas, def.	Alexandria	Suit	1803	CRD:093
Richards, Thomas, Prince St.	Alexandria	Owner	1790	Tax L 1790:09
Richards, Thos.	Alexandria	Tax Charge	1788	Tax PP 1788:13
Richards, Thos.	Alexandria	Tax Charge	1796	Tax LP 1796:24
Richards, Thos.	Alexandria	Tax Charge	1798	Tax PP 1798:16
Richards, Thos.	Alexandria	License Due	1800	Tax PP 1800:54(24)
Richards, Thos.	Alexandria	Tax Charge	1800	Tax PP 1800:37
Richards, Thos., bot. of, Prince St.	Alexandria	Occupant	1795	Tax L 1795:30
Richards, Thos., King St.	Alexandria	Owner	1795	Tax L 1795:25(2)
Richards, Thos., King St.	Alexandria	Occupant	1795	Tax L 1795:25
Richards, Thos., retailer	Alexandria	Housekeeper	1808	1808(3):19A
Richards, Thos., Royal St.	Alexandria	Owner	1795	Tax L 1795:25
Richards, Thos., tavern keeper	Alexandria	Head	1810	1810(3):05A
Richards v. Mankin	Arlington	Suit	1844	LVA-LP (Box 214)
Richards, William B.	Arlington	Complainant	1841	LSA:062
Richards, William B.	Arlington	Inventory	1875	WB9:380
Richards, William B.	Alexandria	Will	1879	WB1:258; LP
Richardson, Callis	Alexandria	Reference	1808	1808(4):24B
Richardson, Daniel	Arlington	Apprentice	1822	OCR1822:003
Richardson, Elizabeth	Arlington	Guard.	1830	WB3:383
Richardson, Elizabeth, gentlewoman	Alexandria	Housekeeper	1808	1808(1):07A
Richardson, Elizabeth, mantuamaker	Alexandria	Head	1810	1810(1):10A
Richardson, F., Water St.	Alexandria	Occupant	1795	Tax L 1795:28
Richardson, Forrest	Alexandria	Tax Charge	1796	Tax PP 1796:16
Richardson, Forrest	Alexandria	Tax Charge	1798	Tax PP 1798:16
Richardson, Forrest	Alexandria	Tax Charge	1799	Tax PP 1799:34
Richardson, Forrest	Alexandria	Tax Charge	1800	Tax PP 1800:37
Richardson, Forrest	Arlington	Admin.	1807	WBB:517
Richardson, Forrest	Arlington	Inventory	1807	WBB:518; LVA-LP
Richardson, Forrest	Arlington	Sale	1807	WBB:530
Richardson, Forrest	Arlington	Account	1809	WBC:307; LVA-LP

NAME OR SUBJECT	LOCATION	TYPE	YEAR	REFERENCE(S)
Richardson, Forrest & wife	Alexandria	Head	1795	1795(4):02
Richardson, Forrest & wife, sea captain	Alexandria	Housekeeper	1799	1799(2):19A
Richardson, Hustley (C), washwoman	Alexandria	Housekeeper	1808	1808(3):23A
Richardson, Kitty	Arlington	Will P.	1846	OCR1842:157
Richardson, Kitty (C)	Arlington	Will	1846	WB4:417; File #430A
Richardson, William	Arlington	Libellant	1803	ACO:007
Richerson, Forrend & wife Elizebeth	Alexandria	Resident	1800	1800(4):08B
Richerson, Forrerd, marriner	Alexandria	Head	1800	1800(4):08A
Richie, John H., at his house	Arlington	Ordinary	1831	OBL4(np)
Richie, John H., in Alexandria Co.	Arlington	Ordinary	1830	OBL4(np)
Richter, Charles	Alexandria	Tax Charge	1799	Tax PP 1799:34
Richter, Chas.	Alexandria	Tax Charge	1795	Tax PP 1795:25
Richter, Jno.	Alexandria	Tax Charge	1798	Tax PP 1798:16
Richter, Jno., merchant	Alexandria	Housekeeper	1799	1799(2):11A
Richter, John	Alexandria	Mer. License	1798	Tax PP 1798:20-6
Richter, John	Alexandria	Mer. License	1799	Tax PP 1799:52-09r
Richter, John	Alexandria	Tax Charge	1799	Tax PP 1799:34
Richter, John	Alexandria	Tax Charge	1800	Tax PP 1800:37
Richter, John	Alexandria	Mer. License	1800	Tax PP 1800:54(19)r
Richter, John	Arlington	Inventory	1813	AB1:306; LVA-LP
Richter, John	Arlington	Sale	1813	AB1:310
Richter, John	Arlington	Account	1813	AB1:339a, 343; LVA-LP
Richter, John	Arlington	Will	1813	WB1:210; File #107A
Richter, John	Arlington	Sale	1814	AB2:044
Richter, John	Arlington	Account	1814	AB2:045; LVA-LP
Richter, John	Arlington	Account	1845	AB9:118
Richter, John, merchant	Alexandria	Housekeeper	1808	1808(3):20A
Richter, John, merchant	Alexandria	Head	1810	1810(3):02A
Rick, John, c/o Christian Hagner	Arlington	Apprentice	1805	OCR1801:321
Rick, William	Alexandria	Tithable +16	1789	Tax PP 1789:05
Rick, William	Arlington	Apprentice	1827	OCR1822:138
Rickard, William, w(1), taylor	Alexandria	Head	1796	1796(3):4
Rickard, Wm.	Alexandria	Tax Charge	1795	Tax PP 1795:26
Rickard, Wm.	Alexandria	Tax Charge	1796	Tax LP 1796:25
Rickard, Wm.	Alexandria	Tax Charge	1796	Tax PP 1796:16
Rickard, Wm.	Alexandria	Tax Charge	1798	Tax PP 1798:15
Rickard, Wm. & wife, taylor	Alexandria	Housekeeper	1799	1799(2):07A
Rickert, Adam, plt.	Alexandria	Ejectment	1802	CRE:242
Rickets, Caleb	Alexandria	Tax Charge	1800	Tax PP 1800:37
Ricketts & Newton	Alexandria	Tax Charge	1796	Tax LP 1796:24
Ricketts & Newton	Alexandria	Tax Charge	1798	Tax PP 1798:16
Ricketts & Newton	Alexandria	Mer. License	1798	Tax PP 1798:20-6
Ricketts & Newton	Alexandria	Mer. License	1799	Tax PP 1799:52-09r
Ricketts & Newton	Alexandria	Tax Charge	1799	Tax PP 1799:34
Ricketts & Newton	Alexandria	Mer. License	1800	Tax PP 1800:54(19)w
Ricketts & Newton, King St.	Alexandria	Occupant	1795	Tax L 1795:02
Ricketts & Newton, on wharf	Alexandria	Occupant	1795	Tax L 1795:33
Ricketts, Benja.	Alexandria	Boarder	1799	1799(2):05A
Ricketts, Benjamin	Arlington	Defendant	1808	ACO:103
Ricketts, Benjamin, grantor	Arlington	Indenture D.	1811	ID2:039
Ricketts, Benjamin, of Bonsal & Ricketts	Arlington	Insolvent	1811	ID2:034
Ricketts, Benjn., b. baker	Alexandria	Housekeeper	1808	1808(4):27A
Ricketts, Benjn., baker	Alexandria	Head	1810	1810(1):03A
Ricketts, C.	Alexandria	Boarder	1808	1808(4):27A
Ricketts, David	Arlington	Defendant	1823	ACO:228
Ricketts, David	Arlington	Defendant	1824	ACO:235
Ricketts, David, def.	Alexandria	Suit	1820	CRL:022
Ricketts, Jno. T. & wife, merchant	Alexandria	Housekeeper	1799	1799(2):05A
Ricketts, John T.	Alexandria	Tax Charge	1799	Tax PP 1799:35
Ricketts, John T.	Alexandria	Tax Charge	1800	Tax PP 1800:37
Ricketts, John Thomas	Arlington	Sale	1821	AB4:239

NAME OR SUBJECT	LOCATION	TYPE	YEAR	REFERENCE(S)
Ricketts, John Thomas	Arlington	Inventory	1821	AB4:237; LVA-LP
Ricketts, John Thomas	Arlington	Admin.	1821	WB2:431
Ricketts, John Thomas	Arlington	Account	1822	AB5:105; LVA-LP
Ricketts, John Thomas, def.	Alexandria	Suit	1806	CRE:065
Ricketts, John Thomas, def.	Alexandria	Suit	1820	CRL:022
Ricketts, Newton & Co., def.	Alexandria	Suit	1809	CRH:466
Ricketts, Thomas, def.	Alexandria	Suit	1809	CRH:466
Ricketts, William Stewart	Arlington	Apprentice	1823	OCR1822:038a
Rickett's Admr. v. Wherry & Metcalf	Arlington	Suit	1837	LVA-LP (Judgments)
Ricks, John	Alexandria	Tax Charge	1800	Tax PP 1800:37
Ricks, William, Fairfax St.	Alexandria	Occupant	1790	Tax L 1790:12
Riddle, James R.	Arlington	Inventory	1857	WB7:246; LVA-LP
Riddle, James R.	Arlington	Will	1857	WB7:229; File #545A
Riddle, James R.	Arlington	Account	1860	WB7:522; LVA-LP
Riddle, James R., merchant	Alexandria	Head	1810	1810(2):01A
Riddle, Jas. R., retailer	Alexandria	Housekeeper	1808	1808(2):11A
Riddle, Jos. & Co.	Alexandria	Mer. License	1800	Tax PP 1800:54(19)r
Riddle, Jos. & wife, merchant	Alexandria	Housekeeper	1799	1799(2):02A
Riddle, Joseph	Alexandria	Tax Charge	1795	Tax PP 1795:26
Riddle, Joseph	Alexandria	Tax Charge	1796	Tax PP 1796:17
Riddle, Joseph	Alexandria	Tax Charge	1798	Tax PP 1798:15
Riddle, Joseph	Alexandria	Tax Charge	1800	Tax PP 1800:37
Riddle, Joseph	Arlington	Respondent	1808	ACO:097
Riddle, Joseph	Alexandria	Merchant	1808	CRF:290
Riddle, Joseph & Co., Fairfax St.	Alexandria	Owner	1795	Tax L 1795:25
Riddle, Joseph & Co., Fairfax St.	Alexandria	Occupant	1795	Tax L 1795:19
Riddle, Joseph & Co., Fairfax St.	Alexandria	Occupant	1795	Tax L 1795:25
Riddle, Joseph & Co.	Alexandria	Mer. License	1798	Tax PP 1798:20-6
Riddle, Joseph & Co.	Alexandria	Tax Charge	1799	Tax PP 1799:35
Riddle, Joseph & Co.	Alexandria	Mer. License	1799	Tax PP 1799:52-09w
Riddle, Joseph & Co., plt.	Alexandria	Suit	1801	CRC:062
Riddle, Joseph & Co., plt.	Alexandria	Suit	1802	CRC:255
Riddle, Joseph & Co., plt.	Alexandria	Suit	1805	CRG:009
Riddle, Joseph & Co., plt.	Alexandria	Suit	1807	CRG:104
Riddle, Joseph, def.	Alexandria	Suit	1806	CRE:065
Riddle, Joseph, def.	Alexandria	Suit	1808	CRG:343
Riddle, Joseph, merchant	Alexandria	Housekeeper	1808	1808(2):11A
Riddle, Joseph, merchant	Alexandria	Head	1810	1810(2):01A
Riddle, Joseph, Merchant	Arlington	Suit	1808	ACR:042
Riddle, Joseph, plt.	Alexandria	Suit	1808	CRH:001
Riddle, Joseph, plt.	Alexandria	Suit	1810	CRH:009
Riddle, Joseph, w(2)2, merchant	Alexandria	Head	1796	1796(3):5
Riddle, Josh.	Alexandria	Tax Charge	1796	Tax LP 1796:24
Riddle, Joshua	Alexandria	Mer. License	1798	Tax PP 1798:20-6
Riddle, Joshua	Alexandria	Mer. License	1799	Tax PP 1799:52-09r
Riddle, Joshua	Alexandria	Tax Charge	1799	Tax PP 1799:35
Riddle, Joshua	Alexandria	Mer. License	1800	Tax PP 1800:54(19)r
Riddle, Joshua	Alexandria	Tax Charge	1800	Tax PP 1800:37
Riddle, Joshua & wife, merchant	Alexandria	Housekeeper	1799	1799(2):02A
Riddle, Joshua, assignee	Arlington	Plaintiff	1802	PA:253
Riddle, Joshua, clerk in bank	Alexandria	Head	1810	1810(4):03A
Riddle, Joshua, for playing Faro	Arlington	Defendant	1801	PA:129
Riddle, Joshua, gentleman	Alexandria	Housekeeper	1808	1808(1):08A
Riddle, Joshua, grantor	Arlington	Indenture D.	1811	ID2:047
Riddle, Joshua, heirs of	Arlington	Account	1845	AB9:141
Riddle, Joshua, in jail bounds	Arlington	Insolvent	1811	ID2:041
Ridgeway, Coats	Alexandria	Mer. License	1799	Tax PP 1799:52-09r
Ridgway, Coates	Alexandria	Mer. License	1798	Tax PP 1798:20-6
Ridgway, Coates	Alexandria	Tax Charge	1798	Tax PP 1798:16
Ridgway, Coats	Alexandria	Tax Charge	1799	Tax PP 1799:34
Ridgway, Coats	Alexandria	Tax Charge	1800	Tax PP 1800:37

NAME OR SUBJECT	LOCATION	TYPE	YEAR	REFERENCE(S)
Ridgway, Coats, merchant	Alexandria	Boarder	1799	1799(2):13A
Ridgway, Coats, plt.	Alexandria	Suit	1801	CRB:202
Ridley, Jno., merchant	Alexandria	Boarder	1799	1799(2):02A
Ridley, John	Alexandria	Mer. License	1799	Tax PP 1799:52-09w
Ridley, John	Alexandria	Tax Charge	1799	Tax PP 1799:34
Ridley, John	Alexandria	Resident	1800	1800(4):08B
Ridley, John, assignee, plt.	Alexandria	Suit	1801	CRB:091
Ridley, John, murchant	Alexandria	Head	1800	1800(4):08A
Ridley, John, plt.	Alexandria	Suit	1801	CRC:241
Ridly, John	Alexandria	Tax Charge	1800	Tax PP 1800:37
Rigg, John	Alexandria	Tax Charge	1787	Tax PP 1787:12
Rigg, John	Alexandria	Tax Charge	1789	Tax PP 1789:16
Rigg, John	Alexandria	Tax Charge	1790	Tax PP 1790:12
Rigg, John	Alexandria	Tax Charge	1796	Tax LP 1796:25
Rigg, John (C), plaisterer	Alexandria	Housekeeper	1808	1808(1):02A
Rigg, John, bricklayer, def.	Alexandria	Suit	1801	CRC:186
Rigg, John, Royal St.	Alexandria	Occupant	1787	Tax L 1787:02
Rigg, John, Royal St.	Alexandria	Owner	1790	Tax L 1790:09
Rigg, John, Royal St.	Alexandria	Occupant	1790	Tax L 1790:09
Rigg, Sukey	Alexandria	Head	1810	1810(2):08A
Rigg, Townley	Arlington	Will	1866	WB9:206; File #676A
Rigge, Jno.	Alexandria	Tax Charge	1798	Tax PP 1798:15
Rigge, John	Alexandria	Tax Charge	1796	Tax PP 1796:16
Rigge, John	Alexandria	Tax Charge	1799	Tax PP 1799:34
Riggs, Daniel	Arlington	Appraisal	1837	LVA-LP
Riggs, Daniel	Arlington	Will	1837	WB4:131; File #346A
Riggs, Daniel	Arlington	Bond	1837	WB4:134
Riggs, Daniel	Arlington	Account	1839	AB8:020; LVA-LP
Riggs, Isaac	Alexandria	Boarder	1799	1799(2):03A
Riggs, Jno. & wife, bricklayer	Alexandria	Housekeeper	1799	1799(2):03A
Riggs, John, w, bricklayer	Alexandria	Head	1796	1796(3):3
Riggs v. Swann	Arlington	Suit	1828	LVA-LP (Accounts)
Rigway, Coats	Alexandria	Resident	1800	1800(4):13B
Rigway, Coats, murchant	Alexandria	Boarder	1800	1800(4):13A
Riley, Bennet & wife, shoemaker	Alexandria	Housekeeper	1799	1799(2):08A
Riley, Patrick	Alexandria	Tithable +16	1788	Tax PP 1788:17
Riley, William R., of Washington DC	Alexandria	Will	1893	WB2:057; LP
Riley, William R., of Washington DC	Alexandria	Will	1900	WB2:368; LP
Rincker, Joseph	Alexandria	Tax Charge	1796	Tax PP 1796:16
Ringgold, Tench	Arlington	Inventory	1845	AB9:094; LVA-LP
Ringgold, Tench	Arlington	Admin.	1845	OCR1842:099
Ringgold, Tench, assignee, plt.	Alexandria	Suit	1801	CRB:108, 111
Rinker, James, port warden	Alexandria	Deposition	1822	CRL:598
Rinker, Jeremiah	Alexandria	Tax Charge	1796	Tax PP 1796:16
Rinker, Jeremiah	Alexandria	Tax Charge	1798	Tax PP 1798:15
Rinker, Jeremiah	Alexandria	Mer. License	1798	Tax PP 1798:20-6
Rinker, Jos. & wife, carpenter	Alexandria	Housekeeper	1799	1799(2):18A
Rinker, Joseph	Alexandria	Tax Charge	1798	Tax PP 1798:15
Rinker, Joseph	Alexandria	Tax Charge	1799	Tax PP 1799:34
Rinker, Joseph	Alexandria	Tax Charge	1800	Tax PP 1800:37
Rinker, Joseph & wife Susanah	Alexandria	Resident	1800	1800(4):09B
Rinker, Joseph, carpenter	Alexandria	Head	1800	1800(4):09A
Rinker, Joseph, carpenter	Alexandria	Housekeeper	1808	1808(4):24A
Rinker, Joseph, house joiner	Alexandria	Head	1810	1810(4):09A
Risan, John	Arlington	Guard.	1810	WBC:389
Rising, John	Arlington	Apprentice	1805	OCR1801:266
Rising, John	Arlington	Guard.	1805	WBB:148
Risings, John	Alexandria	Boarder	1808	1808(2):10A
Risler, Jacob	Alexandria	Tax Charge	1800	Tax PP 1800:37
Rison, Hanson	Arlington	Apprentice	1811	OCR1811:030
Riston, Bartil	Alexandria	Boarder	1808	1808(4):24A

NAME OR SUBJECT	LOCATION	TYPE	YEAR	REFERENCE(S)
Riston, John	Arlington	Appraisal	1860	WB7:530; LVA-LP
Ritchie, John H.	Arlington	Ordinary	1832	OBL4(np)
Ritson, John	Alexandria	Mer. License	1799	Tax PP 1799:52-09r
Rivers, John	Alexandria	Tax Charge	1799	Tax PP 1799:34
Rix, Henry, b/o Joseph Rix	Arlington	Apprentice	1804	OCR1801:163
Rix, James	Arlington	Apprentice	1803	OCR1801:118
Rix, Mrs., court square	Alexandria	Occupant	1787	Tax L 1787:02
Rixter, Eliza	Arlington	Guard.	1820	WB2:390
Rixter, John	Alexandria	Tax Charge	1796	Tax LP 1796:25
Rixton, John, shopkeeper	Alexandria	Housekeeper	1808	1808(1):03A
Rizinger, Geo.	Alexandria	Tax Charge	1795	Tax PP 1795:26
Roach, Ann, c/o John	Arlington	Guard. Acct.	1836	AB7:236a; LVA-LP
Roach, Anthony, c/o John	Arlington	Guard.	1831	WB4:017
Roach, Catharine, c/o John	Arlington	Guard. Acct.	1836	AB7:236a; LVA-LP
Roach, Catherine, c/o John	Arlington	Guard.	1831	WB4:017
Roach, Catherine, c/o John	Arlington	Guard.	1831	WB4:017
Roach, Geo., carpenter	Alexandria	Housekeeper	1808	1808(3):23A
Roach, Geo., house joiner	Alexandria	Head	1810	1810(3):07A
Roach, Georgianna, c/o John	Arlington	Guard.	1831	WB4:017
Roach, James	Arlington	Will	1865	WB8:227; File #621A
Roach, John	Arlington	Appraisal	1831	LVA-LP
Roach, John	Arlington	Bond	1831	WB4:017
Roach, John	Arlington	Will	1831	WB4:016
Roach, John	Arlington	Account	1832	LVA-LP
Roach, John	Arlington	Account	1836	AB7:236
Roach, John A.	Arlington	Will	1855	WB7:026
Roach, John A.	Arlington	Account	1857	WB7:198; LVA-LP
Roach, John A., c/o John	Arlington	Guard. Acct.	1836	AB7:236a; LVA-LP
Roach, John, c/o John	Arlington	Guard.	1831	WB4:017
Roach, John, heirs	Arlington	Release	1846	AB9:280; LVA-LP
Roach, John, heirs of	Arlington	Release	1847	AB9:280
Roach, John, heirs of	Arlington	Release	1847	OCR1842:200
Roach, John, orphans of	Arlington	Guard. Acct.	1839	AB8:027; LVA-LP
Roach, John, orphans of	Arlington	Account	1841	AB8:264; LVA-LP
Roach, John, orphans of	Arlington	Guard. Acct.	1842	AB8:348; LVA-LP
Roach, Melinda	Arlington	Guard.	1820	WB2:363
Roach, Philip	Arlington	Will	1838	WB4:168; File #356A
Roach, Philip	Arlington	Bond	1838	WB4:169
Roach, Philip	Arlington	Account	1840	AB8:131; LVA-LP
Roach, Philip	Arlington	Account	1843	AB8:393; LVA-LP
Roach, Richard	Arlington	Account	1847	AB9:300; LVA-LP
Roach, Thomas	Arlington	Account	1842	AB8:263
Roach, Thomas C., in jail bounds	Arlington	Insolvent	1833	ID:422
Roach, Thomas, orphans of	Arlington	Guard. Acct.	1842	AB8:264
Roach, William	Alexandria	Tax Charge	1787	Tax PP 1787:12
Robarts, Jno.	Alexandria	Boarder	1808	1808(1):05A
Robarts, John, merchant	Alexandria	Housekeeper	1808	1808(4):27A
Robarts, Wm. (C), laborer	Alexandria	Housekeeper	1808	1808(4):24A
Robbins, Isaac	Alexandria	Head	1810	1810(3):05A
Robbins, Isaac	Arlington	Inventory	1846	AB9:258; LVA-LP
Robbins, Isaac	Arlington	Will P.	1846	OCR1842:185, 186
Robbins, Isaac	Arlington	Will	1846	WB4:429; File #436A
Robbins, Isaac, def.	Alexandria	Suit	1821	CRL:369
Robbins, Isaac, grantee	Arlington	Indenture D.	1826	ID:027
Robbins, Isaac, merchant	Alexandria	Housekeeper	1808	1808(3):21A
Robbins, Luke, plt.	Alexandria	Suit	1802	CRB:224
Robbins, Mary Douglas	Arlington	Will	1855	WB7:012; File #522A
Roberdeau, D., Union St.	Alexandria	Occupant	1787	Tax L 1787:23
Roberdeau, Daniel	Alexandria	Owner	1787	Tax L 1787:23
Roberdeau, Daniel	Alexandria	Tax Charge	1788	Tax PP 1788:14
Roberdeau, Daniel	Alexandria	Tax Charge	1789	Tax PP 1789:16

NAME OR SUBJECT	LOCATION	TYPE	YEAR	REFERENCE(S)
Roberdeau, Daniel	Arlington	Admin.	1827	OCR1822:135
Roberdeau, Daniel	Arlington	Admin.	1827	WB3:283
Roberdeau, Daniel & wife	Alexandria	Head	1795	1795(4a):01
Roberdeau, Daniel, Estate, def.	Alexandria	Suit	1801	CRB:051
Roberdeau, Daniel, Water St.	Alexandria	Owner	1790	Tax L 1790:09
Roberdeau, Danl.	Alexandria	Tax Charge	1787	Tax PP 1787:12
Roberdeau, Danl.	Alexandria	Tax Charge	1790	Tax PP 1790:12
Roberdeau, Danl., Cameron St.	Alexandria	Occupant	1787	Tax L 1787:10
Roberdeau, Danl., Water St.	Alexandria	Occupant	1790	Tax L 1790:09
Roberdeau, Isaac	Alexandria	Tithable +21	1787	Tax PP 1787:12
Roberdeau, Isaac	Alexandria	Tithable +16	1789	Tax PP 1789:16
Roberdeau, Isaac	Alexandria	Tithable +16	1790	Tax PP 1790:12
Roberdeau, Isaac, Lt. Col. U.S.A.	Arlington	Will	1858	WB7:371; File #561A
Robert T. Hooe & Co.	Alexandria	Mer. License	1800	Tax PP 1800:54(14)w
Robert T. Hooe & Co., def.	Alexandria	Suit	1801	CRC:039
Robert T. Hooe & Co., def.	Alexandria	Suit	1801	CRD:001
Roberts & Griffith	Alexandria	Tax Charge	1799	Tax PP 1799:34
Roberts & Griffith	Alexandria	Mer. License	1799	Tax PP 1799:52-09r
Roberts & Griffith	Alexandria	Mer. License	1800	Tax PP 1800:54(19)r
Roberts & Griffith	Alexandria	Tax Charge	1800	Tax PP 1800:37
Roberts, Edward	Arlington	Appraisal	1870	WB9:211
Roberts, Jeffrey	Alexandria	Will	1892	WB2:018; LP
Roberts, Jno. & wife, merchant	Alexandria	Housekeeper	1799	1799(2):18A
Roberts, John	Alexandria	Tax Charge	1800	Tax PP 1800:37
Roberts, John	Arlington	Bond	1853	BB(np)
Roberts, John	Arlington	Will	1853	WB6:185; File #493A
Roberts, John	Arlington	Appraisal	1853	WB6:192; LVA-LP
Roberts, John	Arlington	Account	1854	WB6:345; LVA-LP
Roberts, John	Arlington	Account	1855	WB7:016; LVA-LP
Roberts, John & wife Ann	Alexandria	Resident	1800	1800(4):06B
Roberts, John, def.	Alexandria	Suit	1815	CRK:030
Roberts, John, merchant	Alexandria	Head	1810	1810(4):01A
Roberts, John, murchant	Alexandria	Head	1800	1800(4):06A
Roberts, John Wilmith	Arlington	Crime	1795	OT:22/06/1795
Roberts, Jonathan & wife Elizabeth	Alexandria	Suit	1821	CRL:369
Roberts, Jonathan, of Pa.	Alexandria	Deed	1817	CRL:382
Roberts, Nathan	Alexandria	Tax Charge	1800	Tax PP 1800:37
Roberts, Oscar C., s/o John	Arlington	Will	1857	WB7:160; File #533A
Roberts, Rachel & 2 children	Alexandria	Boarder	1799	1799(2):18A
Roberts, Reuben	Arlington	Will	1855	WB7:025; File #524A
Roberts, Reuben	Arlington	Account	1859	WB7:420; LVA-LP
Roberts, Robert	Arlington	Account	1816	LVA-LP
Roberts, Robert & wife Brigget	Alexandria	Resident	1800	1800(4):03B
Roberts, Robert, b. Hollyhead, N. Wales	Arlington	Alien Entry	1802	RA:28/10/02
Roberts, Robert B.	Arlington	Inventory	1814	AB2:079; LVA-LP
Roberts, Robert B.	Arlington	Admin.	1814	WB1:322
Roberts, Robert, marriener [mariner]	Alexandria	Head	1800	1800(4):03A
Roberts, Robt. B., seaman	Alexandria	Housekeeper	1808	1808(1):06A
Roberts, William	Alexandria	Head	1810	1810(3):07A
Roberts, [blank], mariner	Alexandria	Head	1810	1810(1):11A
Robertson, George	Arlington	Deposition	1806	ACR:034
Robertson, George	Alexandria	Deposition	1806	CRE:131
Robertson, James, of Allegany Co. MD	Arlington	Will	1866	WB8:415
Robertson, Jarret, merchant	Alexandria	Boarder	1799	1799(2):02A
Robertson, Jas., merchant	Alexandria	Boarder	1799	1799(2):02A
Robertson, John	Arlington	Will	1898	WB10:353; File #780A
Robertson, Mary E.	Arlington	Will	1892	WB10:230; File #754A
Robertson, Mathew	Alexandria	Tax Charge	1800	Tax PP 1800:37
Robertson, Matthew	Alexandria	Mer. License	1799	Tax PP 1799:52-09r
Robertson, Thomas, Scotland Co. MO	Arlington	Release	1845	AB9:091
Robertson, Thomas, Scotland Co. MO	Arlington	Release	1845	OCR1842:117

NAME OR SUBJECT	LOCATION	TYPE	YEAR	REFERENCE(S)
Robertson, Virginia, formerly Howard	Arlington	Release	1845	AB9:091
Robertson, William	Alexandria	Tax Charge	1789	Tax PP 1789:16
Robey, Hezekiah, at his house	Arlington	Ordinary	1836	OBL5(np)
Robey, Hezekiah, at Virginia Hotel	Arlington	Ordinary	1842	OBL6(np)
Robey, Hezekiah, at Virginia Tavern	Arlington	Ordinary	1843	OBL6(np)
Robey, Hezekiah, his house upper King	Arlington	Ordinary	1838	OBL5(np)
Robey, Hezekiah, upper end King St.	Arlington	Ordinary	1841	OBL6(np)
Robey, Joseph, c/o Machander	Arlington	Apprentice	1813	OCR1811:141
Robey, Josiah	Arlington	Ordinary	1810	OBL2(np)
Robey, Josiah, grocer	Alexandria	Housekeeper	1799	1799(2):04A
Robey, Macanda, seamstress	Alexandria	Head	1810	1810(4):06A
Robinson, Charles	Arlington	Defendant	1809	ACO:108, 109
Robinson, Christopher, clerk	Alexandria	Boarder	1799	1799(2):02A
Robinson, Elizabeth	Arlington	Admin.	1829	OCR1822:168
Robinson, Elizabeth	Arlington	Renounce	1829	OCR1822:168
Robinson, Elizabeth	Arlington	Will	1829	WB3:362a; File #288A
Robinson, Elizabeth	Arlington	Account	1839	AB7:314
Robinson, Helen	Alexandria	Will	1888	WB1:510; LP
Robinson, J.F., of Point of Rocks MD	Alexandria	Will	1895	WB2:112; LP
Robinson, Jeremiah	Alexandria	Will	1886	LP
Robinson, John	Arlington	Libellant	1813	ACO:137
Robinson, John, master	Arlington	Respondent	1813	ACO:137
Robinson, Margaret A.	Alexandria	Will	1888	WB1:503; LP
Robinson, Mathew	Alexandria	Tithable +16	1790	Tax PP 1790:09
Robinson, Mathew	Alexandria	Tax Charge	1790	Tax PP 1790:12
Robinson, Mathew	Arlington	Account	1830	AB6:501, 503
Robinson, Mathew	Arlington	Account	1834	AB7:119
Robinson, Mathew	Arlington	Account	1836	AB7:210
Robinson, Mathew & wife, merchant	Alexandria	Housekeeper	1799	1799(2):03A
Robinson, Mathew, merchant	Alexandria	Head	1810	1810(4):04A
Robinson, Matt.	Alexandria	Tax Charge	1795	Tax PP 1795:26
Robinson, Matthew	Alexandria	Tax Charge	1796	Tax PP 1796:16
Robinson, Matthew	Alexandria	Mer. License	1798	Tax PP 1799:52-11r
Robinson, Matthew	Alexandria	Tax Charge	1799	Tax PP 1799:34
Robinson, Matthew	Alexandria	Mer. License	1800	Tax PP 1800:54(19)r
Robinson, Matthew	Arlington	Admin.	1828	WB3:333
Robinson, Matthew	Arlington	Account	1844	AB8:458
Robinson, Matthew	Arlington	Account	1845	LVA-LP
Robinson, Matthew, def.	Alexandria	Suit	1801	CRB:294
Robinson, Matthew, def.	Alexandria	Suit	1801	CRB:283, 287, 290
Robinson, Mattw.	Alexandria	Tax Charge	1796	Tax LP 1796:25
Robinson, Mattw.	Alexandria	Tax Charge	1798	Tax PP 1798:16
Robinson, Patty	Alexandria	Boarder	1799	1799(2):11A
Robinson, Sanderson & Rumney	Alexandria	Tax Charge	1787	Tax PP 1787:12
Robinson, Sanderson & Rumney, plt.	Alexandria	Suit	1809	CRH:484
Robinson, Sarah E.	Arlington	Apprentice	1842	OCR1842:015
Robinson, William J.	Arlington	Inventory	1833	LVA-LP
Robinson, William Jerome	Arlington	Bond	1833	WB4:063
Robinson, William Jerome	Arlington	Will	1833	WB4:062; File #323A
Roby, Joshua T., at his house	Arlington	Ordinary	1839	OBL5(np)
Roby, Robt.	Alexandria	Boarder	1808	1808(1):08A
Rock, George W.	Arlington	Guard. Acct.	1839	AB7:367, 370
Rock, George W.	Arlington	Guard. Acct.	1847	AB9:300; LVA-LP
Rock, George W.	Alexandria	Will	1886	WB1:432; LP
Rock, George W., c/o Richard	Arlington	Guard.	1835	WB4:087
Rock, Margaret	Arlington	Will	1855	WB6:438; File #519A
Rock, Margaret	Arlington	Appraisal	1858	WB7:314; LVA-LP
Rock, Margaret E.	Arlington	Guard. Acct.	1847	AB9:304; LVA-LP
Rock, Margaret Ellen	Arlington	Guard. Acct.	1839	AB7:367, 371
Rock, Margaret Ellen, c/o Richard	Arlington	Guard.	1835	WB4:087
Rock, Mary Ann	Arlington	Guard. Acct.	1839	AB7:367, 370

NAME OR SUBJECT	LOCATION	TYPE	YEAR	REFERENCE(S)
Rock, Mary Ann, c/o Richard	Arlington	Guard.	1835	WB4:087
Rock, Rd.	Alexandria	Boarder	1808	1808(1):09A
Rock, Richard	Arlington	Admin.	1835	WB4:086
Rock, Richard	Arlington	Account	1836	AB7:212; LVA-LP
Rock, Richard	Arlington	Appraisal	1836	LVA-LP
Rock, Richard	Arlington	Guard. Acct.	1839	AB7:369, 371
Rock, Richard	Arlington	Guard. Acct.	1847	AB9:306; LVA-LP
Rock, Richard	Arlington	Account	1847	AB9:300; LVA-LP
Rock, Richard, orphans of	Arlington	Guard. Acct.	1840	LVA-LP
Rock, William	Alexandria	Tax Charge	1799	Tax PP 1799:34
Rock, William W.	Arlington	Guard. Acct.	1839	AB7:368, 371
Rock, William W., c/o Richard	Arlington	Guard.	1835	WB4:087
Rock, William Wells	Alexandria	Will	1887	WB1:473; LP
Roddey, Mary	Arlington	Account	1840	AB8:019; LVA-LP
Roddy, Fred. Y., children of	Arlington	Distribution	1841	AB8:174
Roddy, John Mc.	Arlington	Suit	1841	AB8:174
Roddy, Mary	Arlington	Admin.	1838	WB4:170
Roddy, Mary	Arlington	Account	1839	AB8:019
Roddy, Mary	Arlington	Bond	1839	WB4:231
Roddy, Mary	Arlington	Account	1841	AB8:168
Rodes, Charles & wife Cloey	Alexandria	Resident	1800	1800(4):12B
Rodes, Charles, sawyer	Alexandria	Head	1800	1800(4):12A
Rodgers, Samuel, Rev.	Arlington	Ordination	1851	BB(np)
Roe & Kershaw, of Manchester, plt.	Alexandria	Suit	1801	CRC:058
Roe, Abner, Fairfax St.	Alexandria	Occupant	1787	Tax L 1787:05
Roe, Absalom	Alexandria	Tax Charge	1789	Tax PP 1789:16
Roe, Absalon, w(4)6, wharf builder	Alexandria	Head	1795	1796(3):7
Roger, Herman	Alexandria	Tax Charge	1796	Tax LP 1796:24
Rogers, Hugh, of Loudoun Co.	Arlington	Will	1854	WB6:412; File #512A
Rogers, Joshua	Alexandria	Tax Charge	1790	Tax PP 1790:12
Rogers, Lambert	Alexandria	Tax Charge	1790	Tax PP 1790:12
Rogers, William H.	Arlington	Trustee Acct.	1858	WB7:339; LVA-LP
Rogerson & Dabney, Fairfax St.	Alexandria	Occupant	1790	Tax L 1790:06
Rogerson & Dabney, Washington St.	Alexandria	Owner	1795	Tax L 1795:07(2)
Rogerson, Tho.	Alexandria	Tax Charge	1798	Tax PP 1798:16
Rogerson, Thomas	Alexandria	Tithable +21	1787	Tax PP 1787:11
Rogerson, Thomas	Alexandria	Tax Charge	1789	Tax PP 1789:16
Rogerson, Thomas	Alexandria	Tax Charge	1790	Tax PP 1790:12
Rogerson, Thomas	Alexandria	Tax Charge	1796	Tax LP 1796:25
Rogerson, Thomas	Alexandria	Tax Charge	1796	Tax PP 1796:16
Rogerson, Thomas, w(3)2, merchant	Alexandria	Head	1796	1796(3):2
Rogerson, Thos.	Alexandria	Tax Charge	1788	Tax PP 1788:14
Rogerson, Thos.	Alexandria	Tax Charge	1795	Tax PP 1795:26
Rogerson, Thos. & Co.	Alexandria	Mer. License	1798	Tax PP 1798:20-6
Rogerson, Thos. & wife, shoe store	Alexandria	Housekeeper	1799	1799(2):08A
Rogerson, Thos., Prince St.	Alexandria	Occupant	1795	Tax L 1795:26
Roke, Andrew	Alexandria	Tax Charge	1796	Tax LP 1796:24
Roland, Dennis (C)	Alexandria	Boarder	1808	1808(1):09B
Rollings, Jesse, c/o John	Arlington	Apprentice	1804	OCR1801:219
Rollins, John	Alexandria	Tax Charge	1796	Tax LP 1796:24
Rollins, John, house joiner	Alexandria	Head	1810	1810(3):09A
Rollins, T., Pitt St.	Alexandria	Occupant	1787	Tax L 1787:13
Rollins, William, master	Arlington	Respondent	1823	ACO:232
Rollinson, Polly	Alexandria	Head	1810	1810(2):07A
Rombey, Samson & wife Lettey	Alexandria	Resident	1800	1800(4):11B
Roods, S., back building	Alexandria	Occupant	1795	Tax L 1795:03
Roper, Wm., clerk	Alexandria	Boarder	1799	1799(2):07A
Rose, Geo. N.	Alexandria	Boarder	1808	1808(2):13A
Rose, Alexander M.	Arlington	Appraisal	1834	LVA-LP
Rose, Alexander M.	Arlington	Admin.	1834	WB4:100
Rose, Alexander M.	Arlington	Account	1836	AB7:223; LVA-LP

NAME OR SUBJECT	LOCATION	TYPE	YEAR	REFERENCE(S)
Rose, Henry	Alexandria	Tax Charge	1795	Tax PP 1795:25
Rose, Henry	Alexandria	Tax Charge	1796	Tax PP 1796:17
Rose, Henry, def.	Alexandria	Suit	1803	CRD:090
Rose, Henry, Doctr.	Alexandria	Tax Charge	1796	Tax LP 1796:24
Rose, Henry, Fairfax St.	Alexandria	Occupant	1795	Tax L 1795:31
Rose, John	Alexandria	Boarder	1808	1808(2):16A
Rose, John	Arlington	Witness	1820	ACO:174
Rose, Thomas M., at his house	Arlington	Ordinary	1835	OBL5(np)
Rose, Thomas M., at his house	Arlington	Ordinary	1837	OBL5(np)
Rose, Thomas M., at his house	Arlington	Ordinary	1838	OBL5(np)
Rose, Thomas M., defendant	Arlington	Sui	1841	LSA:142
Rose, Thos. M., at Alexandria	Arlington	Ordinary	1836	OBL5(np)
Rose, Thos. M., on King St.	Arlington	Ordinary	1841	OBL6(np)
Rose, Virginia	Arlington	Guard.	1839	WB4:223
Rosebury, Kline, of Warren Co. NJ	Alexandria	Will	1875	WB1:130; LP
Ross, David & Jonathan, plt.	Alexandria	Suit	1819	CRK:501
Ross, David, merchant	Alexandria	Head	1810	1810(4):02A
Ross, Elizabeth, seamstress	Alexandria	Head	1810	1810(2):05A
Ross, Horatio	Alexandria	Tax Charge	1795	Tax PP 1795:26
Ross, Horatio, King St.	Alexandria	Occupant	1795	Tax L 1795:34
Ross, Horatio, Union St.	Alexandria	Occupant	1795	Tax L 1795:18
Ross, Isabella	Arlington	Renounce	1806	WBB:387
Ross, Isabella	Arlington	Account	1808	LVA-LP
Ross, Isabella	Arlington	Will	1813	WB1:223; File #108A
Ross, James	Arlington	Apprentice	1812	OCR1811:109
Ross, John, carpenter	Alexandria	Housekeeper	1808	1808(3):23A
Ross, John, grantee	Arlington	Indenture D.	1813	ID2:194
Ross, John, house joiner	Alexandria	Head	1810	1810(3):05A
Ross, William	Arlington	Sale	1807	WBB:401
Ross, William	Arlington	Inventory	1807	WBB:392; LVA-LP
Ross, William D.	Arlington	Admin.	1806	WBB:386
Ross, William D.	Arlington	Account	1807	WBC:019; LVA-LP
Ross, William D.	Arlington	Account	1812	AB1:173
Ross, William Henry, a pauper, plt.	Alexandria	Suit	1815	CRK:134
Rotchford, Bartholomew	Arlington	Appraisal	1857	WB7:207
Rotchford, Bartholomew	Arlington	Will	1857	WB7:196; File #539A
Rotchford, Bartholomew, b. Dublin	Arlington	Alien Entry	1812	RA:09/07/12
Rotchford, Patrick, b. Wexford	Arlington	Alien Entry	1825	RA:10/11/25
Rotchford, Philip	Arlington	Will	1878	WB9:518; File #697A
Rotchford, Philip, b. Wexford	Arlington	Alien Entry	1827	RA:07/11/27
Rotchford, Richard	Arlington	Guard.	1838	WB4:174
Rotchford, Richard L.	Alexandria	Will	1896	WB2:141; LP
Roundis, Benjn.	Alexandria	Boarder	1808	1808(3):21A
Rounsavell, Andrew	Arlington	Ordinary	1808	OBL2(np)
Rounsavell, Nathaniel	Alexandria	Deposition	1822	CRL:532
Rounsavelle, Andrew	Arlington	Account	1824	LVA-LP
Rounsavelle, Andrew	Arlington	Release	1845	OCR1842:117
Rounsaville, Andrew	Arlington	Ordinary	1808	OBL2(np)
Rounsaville, Andrew	Arlington	Ordinary	1809	OBL2(np)
Rounsaville, Andrew	Arlington	Ordinary	1810	OBL2(np)
Rounsaville, Andrew	Arlington	Inventory	1826	AB6:242
Rounsaville, Andrew	Arlington	Account	1826	LVA-LP
Rounsaville, Andrew	Arlington	Will	1826	WB3:258; File #252A
Rounsaville, Andrew	Arlington	Bond	1826	WB3:261
Rounsaville, Andrew	Arlington	Distribution	1827	AB6:437
Rounsaville, Andw.	Alexandria	Tax Charge	1795	Tax PP 1795:27
Rounsaville, Nathaniel, def.	Alexandria	Suit	1822	CRL:232
Rounsevel, Andrew	Alexandria	Tax Charge	1796	Tax LP 1796:24
Rounsevell, Andw., shopkeeper	Alexandria	Housekeeper	1808	1808(2):13A
Rourk, Andrew	Arlington	Witness	1794	OT:25/07/1794
Rourk, Catharine	Arlington	Witness	1794	OT:25/07/1794

NAME OR SUBJECT	LOCATION	TYPE	YEAR	REFERENCE(S)
Rourke, Amon	Alexandria	Tax Charge	1795	Tax PP 1795:25
Rourke, Andrew	Alexandria	Tax Charge	1796	Tax PP 1796:17
Rourke, Andrew	Alexandria	Tax Charge	1799	Tax PP 1799:35
Rourke, Andw.	Alexandria	Tax Charge	1798	Tax PP 1798:16
Rourke, Andw., Fairfax St.	Alexandria	Occupant	1795	Tax L 1795:31
Rourke, John	Alexandria	Tax Charge	1795	Tax PP 1795:25
Rouse, Daniel,, plt.	Alexandria	Ejectment	1802	CRE:242
Rouse, George, plt.	Alexandria	Ejectment	1802	CRE:242
Rouse, Henry, plt.	Alexandria	Ejectment	1802	CRE:242
Rouse, Jacob, plt.	Alexandria	Ejectment	1802	CRE:242
Rouse, John, plt.	Alexandria	Ejectment	1802	CRE:242
Rouse, Jonas, plt.	Alexandria	Ejectment	1802	CRE:242
Router, Robert	Alexandria	Tax Charge	1799	Tax PP 1799:35
Router, Robert	Alexandria	Tax Charge	1800	Tax PP 1800:37
Router, Robt.	Alexandria	Tax Charge	1795	Tax PP 1795:26
Router, Robt.	Alexandria	Tax Charge	1798	Tax PP 1798:16
Routter, Robert & wife	Alexandria	Head	1795	1795(4):05
Roux, Charles, grantor	Arlington	Indenture D.	1831	ID:346
Roux, Charles, in jail	Arlington	Insolvent	1831	ID:343
Rowan, Joseph, merchant	Alexandria	Head	1810	1810(3):05A
Rowe, Absalom	Alexandria	Tax Charge	1796	Tax LP 1796:25
Rowe, Absalom	Alexandria	Tax Charge	1796	Tax PP 1796:16
Rowe, Absalom & wife, ship builder	Alexandria	Head	1795	1795(4a):04
Rowe, Absalom, nr. Wilkes St.	Alexandria	Occupant	1790	Tax L 1790:09
Rowe, Francis Washington	Arlington	Apprentice	1824	OCR1822:064
Rowe, Geo.	Alexandria	Boarder	1808	1808(2):10A
Rowe, Giles	Alexandria	Tax Charge	1798	Tax PP 1798:15
Rowe, Giles, c/o Giles	Arlington	Apprentice	1812	OCR1811:088
Rowe, Gillis, laborer	Alexandria	Housekeeper	1808	1808(3):23A
Rowe, Jiles, labourer	Alexandria	Head	1810	1810(1):09A
Rowe, John Pomery	Arlington	Guard.	1820	WB2:374
Rowe, Richard H.	Alexandria	Will	1875	WB1:140; LP
Rowe, Thomas	Alexandria	Tax Charge	1796	Tax PP 1796:16
Rowe, Thos.	Alexandria	Tax Charge	1798	Tax PP 1798:16
Rowen, Joseph	Arlington	Bond	1838	WB4:184
Rowen, Joseph	Arlington	Will	1838	WB4:183; File #359A
Rowen, Joseph	Arlington	Sale	1840	AB8:055
Rowen [Rowan], Joseph	Arlington	Inventory	1839	AB8:053; LVA-LP
Rowlinson, David	Arlington	Apprentice	1812	OCR1811:107
Roxbury, Reuben	Arlington	Admin.	1833	WB4:069
Roxbury, Reuben, grantee	Arlington	Indenture D.	1827	ID:075
Royle, James, labourer	Alexandria	Boarder	1799	1799(2):19A
Roys, Betty, washwoman	Alexandria	Housekeeper	1808	1808(4):24A
Royson, William	Arlington	Apprentice	1811	OCR1811:036
Rozer, Charles B.	Arlington	Trustee Acct.	1856	WB7:044; LVA-LP
Rozer, Eliza [DeCourcy]	Arlington	Defendant	1837	LSA:017
Rozer, Francis E.	Arlington	Defendant	1837	LSA:017
Rozer, Francis W.	Arlington	Trustee Acct.	1856	WB7:044; LVA-LP
Rozer, Henry & Co., Wilks St.	Alexandria	Occupant	1787	Tax L 1787:03
Rudd, Ann T., c/o William	Arlington	Guard.	1822	WB3:051
Rudd, Elizabeth T., c/o William	Arlington	Guard.	1822	WB3:051
Rudd, James	Arlington	Apprentice	1829	OCR1822:169a
Rudd, James, c/o William	Arlington	Guard.	1822	WB3:051
Rudd, James T., at his house	Arlington	Ordinary	1848	OBL6(np)
Rudd, James T., in Alexandria Co.	Arlington	Ordinary	1848	OBL6(np)
Rudd, Joseph, c/o William	Arlington	Guard.	1822	WB3:051
Rudd, Kerenhappuck Totting'n, c/o Wm	Arlington	Guard.	1822	WB3:051
Rudd, Richard, c/o William	Arlington	Guard.	1822	WB3:051
Rudd, William	Arlington	Admin.	1822	OCR1822:007a
Rudd, William	Arlington	Admin.	1822	WB3:051
Rudd, William T., c/o William	Arlington	Guard.	1822	WB3:051

NAME OR SUBJECT	LOCATION	TYPE	YEAR	REFERENCE(S)
Rudd, Wm., painter	Alexandria	Head	1810	1810(1):04A
Rudd, Wm., shopkeeper	Alexandria	Housekeeper	1808	1808(4):26A
Ruddle, John (servant)	Alexandria	Tithable +21	1787	Tax PP 1787:12
Rudesel, James	Alexandria	Tithable +16	1788	Tax PP 1788:05
Rudesell, Jonas	Alexandria	Tithable +16	1789	Tax PP 1789:05
Ruffland, Peggy	Arlington	Crime	1794	OT:07/11/1794
Rum, puncheons of	Arlington	Suit	1811	ACO:116
Rum, puncheons of	Arlington	Suit	1813	ACO:136
Rumney, Adele, c/o Edward	Arlington	Guard.	1829	WB3:350
Rumney, Ann Eliza, c/o Edward	Arlington	Guard.	1829	WB3:350
Rumney, Edward	Arlington	Inventory	1823	AB5:175; LVA-LP
Rumney, Edward	Arlington	Admin.	1823	OCR1822:039a
Rumney, Edward	Arlington	Admin.	1823	WB3:092
Rumney, John	Alexandria	Tithable +21	1787	Tax PP 1787:12
Rumney, John	Alexandria	Tax Charge	1788	Tax PP 1788:14
Rumney, John	Arlington	Admin.	1837	WB4:156
Rumney, John, grantee	Arlington	Indenture D.	1830	ID:252
Rumney, Martha K. (McKnight)	Arlington	Defendant	1842	LSA:082
Rumney, Rumney, c/o Edward	Arlington	Guard.	1829	WB3:350
Runnells, John H., grantor	Arlington	Indenture D.	1828	ID:217
Runnells, John H., in jail bounds	Arlington	Insolvent	1828	ID:214
Rupner, Peter, plt.	Alexandria	Ejectment	1802	CRE:242
Rush, Richard	Arlington	Certificate	1830	ACR:089
Russel, James	Alexandria	Tax Charge	1800	Tax PP 1800:37
Russel, Jas. & wife, merchant	Alexandria	Housekeeper	1799	1799(2):03A
Russell, Cosmelia, w/o John	Arlington	Defendant	1842	LSA:094
Russell, George	Arlington	Will	1820	File #060A
Russell, George	Arlington	Inventory	1821	AB5:009; LVA-LP
Russell, George	Arlington	Admin.	1821	WB3:033, 165
Russell, George	Arlington	Sale	1822	AB5:036
Russell, George	Arlington	Account	1823	AB5:180; LVA-LP
Russell, George	Arlington	Account	1825	AB6:097; LVA-LP
Russell, George	Arlington	Inventory	1825	AB6:095; LVA-LP
Russell, George	Arlington	Division	1825	OCR1822:093
Russell, George	Arlington	Admin.	1825	OCR1822:085a
Russell, James	Alexandria	Tax Charge	1799	Tax PP 1799:34
Russell, James	Arlington	Inventory	1808	WBC:135; LP
Russell, James	Arlington	Will	1808	WBC:113; File #006A
Russell, James	Arlington	Bond	1808	WBC:115
Russell, James	Arlington	Debts	1809	WBC:247
Russell, James	Arlington	Sale	1809	WBC:222, 255
Russell, James	Arlington	Account	1810	WBC:417; LVA-LP
Russell, James	Arlington	Account	1811	AB1:143; LVA-LP
Russell, James	Arlington	Account	1816	AB2:290; LVA-LP
Russell, James	Arlington	Account	1818	AB3:201; LVA-LP
Russell, James	Arlington	Account	1831	AB7:002; LVA-LP
Russell, James & Co.	Alexandria	Mer. License	1798	Tax PP 1798:20-6
Russell, James & Co.	Alexandria	Mer. License	1799	Tax PP 1799:52-09r
Russell, James & Co.	Alexandria	Mer. License	1800	Tax PP 1800:54(19)r
Russell, James, d. 29 OCT 1808	Arlington	Admin.	1827	OCR1822:144a
Russell, James, merchant	Alexandria	Housekeeper	1808	1808(4):27A
Russell, Jas.	Alexandria	Tax Charge	1798	Tax PP 1798:16
Russell, John R.F.	Arlington	Defendant	1842	LSA:094
Russell, Joseph, of Boston MA	Alexandria	Deposition	1806	CRG:289
Russell, Margaret A.B.	Arlington	Bond	1853	BB(np)
Russell, Margaret A.B.	Arlington	Will	1853	WB6:267; File #503A
Russell, Margraet A.B.	Arlington	Appraisal	1854	WB6:310; LVA-LP
Russell, Moses	Arlington	Will	1868	WB9:103; File #665A
Russell, Moses	Arlington	Appraisal	1869	WB9:188
Russell, Moses	Arlington	Inventory	1877	WB9:413
Russell, Moses	Arlington	Account	1877	WB9:398

NAME OR SUBJECT	LOCATION	TYPE	YEAR	REFERENCE(S)
Russell, Philip	Arlington	Ordinary	1803	OBL1(np)
Russell, Philip, grantor	Arlington	Indenture	1804	ID3:090
Russell, Thomas	Alexandria	Tithable +16	1788	Tax PP 1788:03
Russell, Wm.	Alexandria	Boarder	1808	1808(1):02A
Russler, Jacob, w(1)1, chandler	Alexandria	Head	1796	1796(3):5
Rustin, John	Alexandria	Mer. License	1798	Tax PP 1798:20-6
Rustle, George, waterman	Alexandria	Housekeeper	1808	1808(4):26A
Rustman, William A.	Arlington	Guard. Acct.	1835	AB7:174; LVA-LP
Rustman, William Anthony	Arlington	Guard.	1830	WB3:384
Rutherford, J.C.	Arlington	Account	1818	AB3:248
Rutherford, J.C.	Arlington	Sale	1818	AB3:247
Rutherford, Joseph C.	Arlington	Inventory	1818	AB3:213; LVA-LP
Rutherford, Joseph C.	Arlington	Admin.	1818	WB2:228
Rutter, Charles	Arlington	Libellant	1804	ACO:029
Rutter, Charles	Arlington	Libellant	1805	ACO:035
Rutter, Edward, blacksmith	Alexandria	Boarder	1799	1799(2):06A
Rutter, Edwd.	Alexandria	Tax Charge	1798	Tax PP 1798:15
Rutter, Geo.	Alexandria	Tax Charge	1795	Tax PP 1795:26
Rutter, Geo.	Alexandria	Tax Charge	1798	Tax PP 1798:16
Rutter, Geo. & wife, boarding house	Alexandria	Housekeeper	1799	1799(2):01A
Rutter, Geo., Union St.	Alexandria	Owner	1795	Tax L 1795:25
Rutter, George	Alexandria	Tax Charge	1788	Tax PP 1788:14
Rutter, George	Alexandria	Tax Charge	1789	Tax PP 1789:16
Rutter, George	Alexandria	Tax Charge	1790	Tax PP 1790:12
Rutter, George	Alexandria	Tax Charge	1796	Tax LP 1796:24
Rutter, George	Alexandria	Tax Charge	1796	Tax PP 1796:16
Rutter, George	Alexandria	Tax Charge	1799	Tax PP 1799:35
Rutter, George	Alexandria	Tax Charge	1800	Tax PP 1800:37
Rutter, George, Prince St.	Alexandria	Occupant	1790	Tax L 1790:09
Rutter, George, Union St.	Alexandria	Occupant	1795	Tax L 1795:25
Rutter, George, w2, innkeeper	Alexandria	Head	1796	1796(3):6
Rutter, Robert & wife Ann	Alexandria	Resident	1800	1800(4):12B
Rutter, Robert, painter	Alexandria	Head	1800	1800(4):12A
Rutter, Robt., painter	Alexandria	Housekeeper	1808	1808(4):26A
Rutter, Robt., painter	Alexandria	Head	1810	1810(4):02A
Ryan, Ann	Arlington	Ordinary	1805	OBL1(np)
Ryan, Edward	Arlington	Admin.	1833	WB4:069
Ryan, James	Alexandria	Tax Charge	1799	Tax PP 1799:34
Ryan, James	Alexandria	Will	1895	WB2:116; LP
Ryan, John	Alexandria	Tax Charge	1787	Tax PP 1787:12
Ryan, Nathaniel	Arlington	Admin.	1836	WB4:106
Ryan, Philip	Arlington	Ordinary	1804	OBL1(np)
Rye, Jesse	Arlington	Guard.	1825	OCR1822:096
Ryeburn, John, plt.	Alexandria	Suit	1802	CRC:270
Ryley, John	Alexandria	Tax Charge	1799	Tax PP 1799:34
Ryley, Patrick	Alexandria	Tax Charge	1790	Tax PP 1790:13
Ryley, Patrick (non-citizen, servant)	Alexandria	Tax Charge	1787	Tax PP 1787:12
Ryon, Solomon	Alexandria	Deposition	1802	CRC:086

NAME OR SUBJECT	LOCATION	TYPE	YEAR	REFERENCE(S)
S				
Sachi, Philip, Rev., b. Moscow	Arlington	Alien Entry	1822	RA:14/06/22
Sage, Thomas	Alexandria	Tax Charge	1790	Tax PP 1790:14
Sails, Peter	Alexandria	Tax Charge	1800	Tax PP 1800:39
Sails, William	Alexandria	Tax Charge	1800	Tax PP 1800:39
Sales, George H.	Arlington	Guard.	1819	WB2:312
Sales, Quinlus	Alexandria	Head	1810	1810(4):05A
Sales, Thos. (C), seaman	Alexandria	Housekeeper	1808	1808(1):05A
Sales, Wm. (C), ship carpenter	Alexandria	Housekeeper	1808	1808(1):09A
Sales, Wm., ship carpenter	Alexandria	Head	1810	1810(1):07A
Salman, Isaac	Alexandria	Tax Charge	1799	Tax PP 1799:37
Salman, Isaac & wife Sarrah	Alexandria	Resident	1800	1800(4):07B
Salman, Isaac, d(r)ayman	Alexandria	Head	1800	1800(4):07A
Salmon, George	Arlington	Will	1818	WB2:220; File #146A
Salmon, Isaac	Alexandria	Tax Charge	1800	Tax PP 1800:40
Salmon, Isaac & wife, drayman	Alexandria	Housekeeper	1799	1799(2):14A
Salmon [Sammon], William, def.	Alexandria	Suit	1802	CRC:004
Salter, Fanny (C), washwoman	Alexandria	Housekeeper	1808	1808(1):09A
Salter, Fanny, washerwoman	Alexandria	Head	1810	1810(1):06A
Sambrey, Sampson (C), carpenter	Alexandria	Housekeeper	1808	1808(4):24A
Sample, Elizabeth, shopkeeper	Alexandria	Head	1810	1810(2):07A
Sample, Wm.	Alexandria	Tithable +16	1789	Tax PP 1789:10
Sampson, Alexr.	Alexandria	Tax Charge	1798	Tax PP 1798:17
Sampson, Alexr.	Alexandria	Mer. License	1798	Tax PP 1798:20-7
Sampson, Elias	Alexandria	Tax Charge	1796	Tax PP 1796:18
Sampson, Indiana (C)	Arlington	Apprentice	1805	OCR1801:309
Samson, Alexander	Alexandria	Tax Charge	1799	Tax PP 1799:37
Sanders, Dd.	Alexandria	Boarder	1808	1808(4):25A
Sanders, Gustavus J.	Arlington	Account	1835	AB7:171; LVA-LP
Sanders, Gustavus J., of LA	Arlington	Admin.	1833	WB4:066
Sanders, Hebert, labourer	Alexandria	Head	1810	1810(1):09A
Sanders, Hobbart, waterman	Alexandria	Housekeeper	1808	1808(2):14A
Sanders, John, Estate	Alexandria	Tax Charge	1790	Tax PP 1790:13
Sanders, Nelly, washerwoman	Alexandria	Head	1810	1810(2):04A
Sanders, Peter	Alexandria	Boarder	1808	1808(1):01A
Sanders, Peter, tanner	Alexandria	Head	1810	1810(4):03A
Sanderson, Capt., Lyle's alley	Alexandria	Occupant	1787	Tax L 1787:19
Sanderson, James	Arlington	Apprentice	1811	OCR1811:009
Sanderson, James	Arlington	Will	1831	WB4:019; File #307A
Sanderson, James	Arlington	Will	1834	WB4:082; File #307A
Sanderson, James	Arlington	Admin.	1834	WB4:020
Sanderson, James	Arlington	Account	1835	AB7:167; LVA-LP
Sanderson, James	Arlington	Inventory	1835	LVA-LP (Accounts)
Sanderson, James, def.	Alexandria	Suit	1822	CRL:232
Sanderson, James, merchant	Alexandria	Housekeeper	1808	1808(2):12A
Sanderson, Jas., clerk	Alexandria	Boarder	1799	1799(2):02A
Sanderson, John	Arlington	Guard.	1811	WB1:041
Sanderson, John	Arlington	Guard. Acct.	1841	AB8:233
Sanderson, John	Arlington	Guard. Acct.	1842	OCR1842:011
Sanderson, John F.	Arlington	Guard.	1839	WB4:234
Sanderson, John F.	Arlington	Guard. Acct.	1844	AB8:489; LVA-LP
Sanderson, John F.	Arlington	Guard. Acct.	1845	AB9:087
Sandford, Catha.	Alexandria	Tax Charge	1796	Tax LP 1796:26
Sandford, Edward & wife, silversmith	Alexandria	Head	1795	1795(4a):11
Sandford, Edwd.	Alexandria	Tax Charge	1788	Tax PP 1788:15
Sandford, Eliza	Alexandria	Will	1878	WB1:240; LP
Sandford, Jno. P.	Alexandria	Boarder	1808	1808(3):20A
Sandford, Thos., sailmaker	Alexandria	Housekeeper	1808	1808(1):05A
Sands, Robert	Arlington	Ordinary	1821	OBL3(np)
Sands, Robert, at his house	Arlington	Ordinary	1827	OBL4(np)
Sands, Robert, at his house	Arlington	Ordinary	1828	OBL4(np)

NAME OR SUBJECT	LOCATION	TYPE	YEAR	REFERENCE(S)
Sands, Robert, b. Dublin	Arlington	Alien Entry	1823	RA:31/01/23
Sands, Robert, in Alexandria Co.	Arlington	Ordinary	1822	OBL3(np)
Sands, Robert, in Alexandria Co.	Arlington	Ordinary	1823	OBL3(np)
Sands, Robert, in Alexandria Co.	Arlington	Ordinary	1824	OBL3(np)
Sands, Robert, in Alexandria Co.	Arlington	Ordinary	1825	OBL4(np)
Sands, Robert, in Alexandria Co.	Arlington	Ordinary	1826	OBL4(np)
Sanford, Andrew	Alexandria	Boarder	1799	1799(2):13A
Sanford, Ann, c/o John	Arlington	Guard.	1811	WB1:021
Sanford, Catharine	Alexandria	Owner	1787	Tax L 1787:23
Sanford, Catharine	Alexandria	Tax Charge	1787	Tax PP 1787:14
Sanford, Catharine, Fairfax St.	Alexandria	Occupant	1787	Tax L 1787:23
Sanford, Catharine, Fairfax St.	Alexandria	Owner	1790	Tax L 1790:10
Sanford, Catharine, Fairfax St.	Alexandria	Occupant	1790	Tax L 1790:10
Sanford, E., St. Asaph St.	Alexandria	Occupant	1787	Tax L 1787:24
Sanford, Edward	Alexandria	Tax Charge	1787	Tax PP 1787:14
Sanford, Edward	Alexandria	Tax Charge	1789	Tax PP 1789:17
Sanford, Edward	Alexandria	Tax Charge	1790	Tax PP 1790:13
Sanford, Edward, St. Asaph St.	Alexandria	Owner	1790	Tax L 1790:10
Sanford, Edward, St. Asaph St.	Alexandria	Occupant	1790	Tax L 1790:10
Sanford, Edwd., Fairfax St.	Alexandria	Occupant	1787	Tax L 1787:10
Sanford, Esther	Arlington	Will	1852	WB6:123; File #483A
Sanford, Esther	Arlington	Appraisal	1853	WB6:195; LVA-LP
Sanford, Esther	Arlington	Account	1854	WB6:317; LVA-LP
Sanford, Katharine, Fairfax St.	Alexandria	Occupant	1795	Tax L 1795:26
Sanford, Katharine, Fairfax St.	Alexandria	Owner	1795	Tax L 1795:26
Sanford, Margaret	Arlington	Will (N)	1817	WB2:205; File #144A
Sanford, Presley & wife, carpenter	Alexandria	Head	1795	1795(4a):06
Sanford, Thomas	Arlington	Will	1852	WB6:122; File #482A
Sanford, Thomas	Arlington	Appraisal	1853	WB6:193; LVA-LP
Sanford, Thomas	Arlington	Account	1853	WB6:261; LVA-LP
Sanford, Thomas, sailmaker	Alexandria	Head	1810	1810(1):06A
Sanford, Will.	Alexandria	Tax Charge	1800	Tax PP 1800:40
Sanford, William, def.	Alexandria	Suit	1802	CRC:210
Sanford, Wm.	Arlington	Defendant	1802	PA:297
Sanger, Stephen	Arlington	Ordinary	1810	OBL2(np)
Sanger, Stephen, retailer & tavern lic.	Alexandria	Housekeeper	1808	1808(2):12A
Sanger, Stephen S.	Arlington	Apprentice	1827	OCR1822:148a
Sanger, Stephen, seaman	Alexandria	Head	1810	1810(2):02A
Sangster, Alexr.	Alexandria	Boarder	1808	1808(2):10A
Sangster, Edward, sheriff	Arlington	Appointment	1854	BB(np)
Sangster, Thomas, grantor	Arlington	Indenture D.	1830	ID:278
Sangster, Thomas, in prison walls	Arlington	Insolvent	1830	ID:276
Sangster, Thos.	Alexandria	Boarder	1808	1808(2):15A
Sarrey, Mark? [damage]	Alexandria	Tax Charge	1796	Tax LP 1796:26
Sartin, James William	Arlington	Apprentice	1847	OCR1842:199
Satterwhite, Jeremiah	Alexandria	Tax Charge	1800	Tax PP 1800:39
Satterwhite, Jeremiah	Arlington	Apprentice	1822	OCR1822:029a
Satterwhite, Jeremiah, coach maker	Alexandria	Housekeeper	1808	1808(3):21A
Satterwhite, Jeremiah, coachmaker	Alexandria	Head	1810	1810(3):01A
Satterwhite, Jeremiah, grantor	Arlington	Indenture D.	1811	ID2:067
Satterwhite, Jeremiah, in jail	Arlington	Insolvent	1811	ID2:065
Satterwight, Jeremh.	Alexandria	Mer. License	1799	Tax PP 1799:52-10r
Saul, Jos. & wife, tea store	Alexandria	Housekeeper	1799	1799(2):05A
Saul, Joseph	Alexandria	Tax Charge	1795	Tax PP 1795:27
Saul, Joseph	Alexandria	Tax Charge	1798	Tax PP 1798:16
Saul, Joseph	Alexandria	Tax Charge	1799	Tax PP 1799:39
Saull, Wm.	Alexandria	Boarder	1799	1799(2):15A
Saunders, A.H.	Arlington	Admin.	1859	WB8:017
Saunders, A.H.	Arlington	Account	1860	WB8:542
Saunders, A.H.	Arlington	Account	1860	WB8:017; LVA-LP
Saunders, A.H.	Arlington	Commr.	1865	WB8:276

NAME OR SUBJECT	LOCATION	TYPE	YEAR	REFERENCE(S)
Saunders, Addison H.	Arlington	Account	1859	WB7:454; LVA-LP
Saunders, Charles, c/o Catharine Allen	Arlington	Apprentice	1805	OCR1801:318
Saunders, Chas.	Alexandria	Boarder	1808	1808(2):10A
Saunders, David	Arlington	Guard. Acct.	1804	LVA-LP
Saunders, David	Arlington	Guard. Acct.	1804	WBA:237
Saunders, David, gc/o Joseph	Arlington	Guard.	1804	WB4:237
Saunders, Jno., Prince St.	Alexandria	Occupant	1787	Tax L 1787:25
Saunders, John	Alexandria	Owner	1787	Tax L 1787:25
Saunders, John	Alexandria	Tax Charge	1787	Tax PP 1787:14
Saunders, John	Alexandria	Tax Charge	1788	Tax PP 1788:14
Saunders, John	Alexandria	Tax Charge	1789	Tax PP 1789:17
Saunders, John	Alexandria	Tax Charge	1796	Tax LP 1796:27
Saunders, John	Arlington	Account	1804	WBA:240
Saunders, John & Co., Wilks St.	Alexandria	Occupant	1787	Tax L 1787:03
Saunders, John, Estate, Prince St.	Alexandria	Owner	1790	Tax L 1790:11(2)
Saunders, John, Estate, Prince St.	Alexandria	Owner	1795	Tax L 1795:27(2)
Saunders, John W.	Arlington	Defendant	1821	ACO:198
Saunders, Joseph	Alexandria	Owner	1787	Tax L 1787:24
Saunders, Joseph	Arlington	Appraisal	1866	WB8:358
Saunders, Joseph	Arlington	Account	1867	WB8:522
Saunders, Mrs., Prince St.	Alexandria	Occupant	1790	Tax L 1790:11
Saunders, Peter	Arlington	Guard. Acct.	1804	WBA:237
Saunders, Peter, gc/o Joseph	Arlington	Guard.	1804	WB4:237
Saunders, Robert	Arlington	Will (N)	1815	WB2:006
Saunders, Sarah	Arlington	Guard. Acct.	1804	WBA:237
Saunders, Sarah, gc/o Joseph	Arlington	Guard.	1804	WB4:237
Saunders, Silas, at his house	Arlington	Ordinary	1849	OBL6(np)
Saunders, William, c/o Catharine Allen	Arlington	Apprentice	1805	OCR1801:319
Savori, Peter	Alexandria	Account B.	1794	CRC:038
Savori, Peter, of Maryland, def.	Alexandria	Suit	1800	CRC:034
Sawl, Joseph & wife Mary	Alexandria	Resident	1800	1800(4):07B
Sawl, Joseph, clerk to the bank	Alexandria	Head	1800	1800(4):07A
Sawyer, Lavinia, w/o Samuel	Arlington	Defendant	1842	LSA:094
Sawyer, Samuel	Arlington	Defendant	1842	LSA:094
Sayre, William R., of Newark NJ	Alexandria	Will	1880	WB1:316; LP
Sayres, Matilda A.	Arlington	Will	1845	WB4:392, File #420A
Sayres, Matilda R.	Arlington	Renounce	1845	WB4:392; File #420A
Sayrs, Charles E., c/o John J.	Arlington	Guard.	1848	GBB(np)
Sayrs, Henry S., c/o John J.	Arlington	Guard.	1848	GBB(np)
Sayrs, Jane J., c/o John J.	Arlington	Guard.	1848	GBB(np)
Sayrs, John J.	Arlington	Inventory	1845	AB9:096; LVA-LP
Sayrs, John J.	Arlington	Citation	1845	OCR1842:117
Sayrs, John J.	Arlington	Account	1846	AB9:148; LVA-LP
Sayrs, John J.	Arlington	Account	1847	AB9:272
Sayrs, John J., Dr.	Arlington	Creditors	1846	AB9:148
Sayrs, John J. [Matilda R.]	Arlington	Renounce	1845	OCR1842:099, 101
Sayrs, Matilda E., c/o John J.	Arlington	Guard.	1848	GBB(np)
Scallan, James, b. Waterford, Ire.	Arlington	Alien Entry	1812	RA:10/07/12
Scandlen, Danl.	Alexandria	Tithable +21	1787	Tax PP 1787:06
Scarce, William B., at his house	Arlington	Ordinary	1848	OBL6(np)
Scarce, William B., in Alexandria Co.	Arlington	Ordinary	1850	OBL6(np)
Scarce, William B., on King St.	Arlington	Ordinary	1844	OBL6(np)
Scarce, Wm. B., at Virginia House	Arlington	Ordinary	1847	OBL6(np)
Scarce, Wm. B., at his house	Arlington	Ordinary	1849	OBL6(np)
Scarce, Wm. B., on King St.	Arlington	Ordinary	1845	OBL6(np)
Scarce, Wm. B., on King St.	Arlington	Ordinary	1846	OBL6(np)
Scarce [Scearce], William B.	Arlington	Inventory	1861	WB8:067; LVA-LP
Scarce [Scearce], William B.	Arlington	Sale	1861	WB8:068; LVA-LP
Scarce [Scearce], William B.	Arlington	Will	1861	WB8:066; File #583A
Scarce [Scearce], William B.	Arlington	Account	1867	WB8:488, 492
Scarlet, Laurence	Arlington	Crime	1798	OT:05/03/1799

NAME OR SUBJECT	LOCATION	TYPE	YEAR	REFERENCE(S)
Scarlet, Lawrence	Alexandria	Housekeeper	1808	1808(1):09A
Scarlet, Lawrence & wife (C), labourer	Alexandria	Housekeeper	1799	1799(2):12A
Schafer, Christian, in Alexandria Co.	Arlington	Ordinary	1847	OBL6(np)
Schafizel, George	Arlington	Account	1832	AB7:038; LVA-LP
Schafizel, John	Arlington	Admin.	1831	WB4:039
Scheiss, Sebastian, King St.	Alexandria	Occupant	1787	Tax L 1787:18
Schekel, Dederick	Alexandria	Tax Charge	1789	Tax PP 1789:16
Schekel, Dedk.	Alexandria	Tax Charge	1788	Tax PP 1788:15
Schewe, Christo. F.	Alexandria	Tax Charge	1799	Tax PP 1799:37
Schewe, Christopher F., huckster	Alexandria	Housekeeper	1799	1799(2):04A
Schneider, Ernest A.	Arlington	Will	1898	WB10:376
Schnyder, Henry & Adam Brock, lab.	Alexandria	Housekeeper	1799	1799(2):18A
Schofield, Andrew	Arlington	Bond	1839	WB4:220
Schofield, Andrew	Arlington	Will	1839	WB4:218; File #373A
Schofield, Andrew	Arlington	Admin.	1845	OCR1842:146, 167
Schofield, Catharine	Arlington	Renounce	1839	WB4:252
Scholfield, Andrew	Alexandria	Tax Charge	1800	Tax PP 1800:39
Scholfield, Andrew	Arlington	Sale	1840	AB8:066
Scholfield, Andrew	Arlington	Inventory	1840	AB8:061; LVA-LP
Scholfield, Andrew	Arlington	Account	1840	AB8:186; LVA-LP
Scholfield, Andrew	Arlington	Account	1841	AB8:255; LVA-LP
Scholfield, Andrew	Arlington	Account	1841	AB8:186
Scholfield, Andrew	Arlington	Petition	1841	LVA-LP (Box 214)
Scholfield, Andrew	Arlington	Account	1843	AB8:336; LVA-LP
Scholfield, Andrew	Arlington	Account	1843	AB8:408; LVA-LP
Scholfield, Andrew	Arlington	Account	1843	AB9:022; LVA-LP
Scholfield, Andrew	Arlington	Account	1844	AB9:022
Scholfield, Andrew	Arlington	Petition	1844	LVA-LP (Box 214)
Scholfield, Andrew	Arlington	Loan	1844	OCR1842:091
Scholfield, Andrew	Arlington	Account	1845	AB9:130; LVA-LP(2)
Scholfield, Andrew	Arlington	Petition	1845	LVA-LP (Box 214)
Scholfield, Andrew	Arlington	Citation	1845	OCR1842:119, 120
Scholfield, Andrew	Arlington	Suit	1846	AB9:242
Scholfield, Andrew	Arlington	Account	1846	AB9:244
Scholfield, Andrew	Arlington	Account F.	1846	AB9:246; LVA-LP
Scholfield, Andrew, lumber merchant	Alexandria	Head	1810	1810(3):05A
Scholfield, Andw., lumber merchant	Alexandria	Housekeeper	1808	1808(3):19A
Scholfield, Jona., merchant	Alexandria	Housekeeper	1808	1808(3):19A
Scholfield, Jonathan, grantee	Arlington	Indenture D.	1810	ID2:032
Scholfield, Jonathan, merchant	Alexandria	Head	1810	1810(3):08A
Scholfield, Joshua	Alexandria	Agreement	1818	CRL:169
Scholfield, Joshua, plt.	Alexandria	Suit	1821	CRL:165
Scholfield, Lewis N., of Jefferson Co. IA	Arlington	P. of Atty.	1846	LVA-LP (Box 214)
Scholfield, Mahlon & Jona., merchants	Alexandria	Housekeeper	1808	1808(3):21A
Scholfield, Mahlon, merchant	Alexandria	Head	1810	1810(3):03A
Scholfield, Samuel, Montgomery Co. PA	Arlington	Will (NR)	1835	File #066A
Scholfield v. Waters	Arlington	Suit	1846	OCR1842:160-2
Schooner *Adventure*	Arlington	Suit	1805	ACO:045
Schooner *Ann*, and her tackle	Arlington	Suit	1803	ACO:022
Schooner *Betsey & Charlotte*	Arlington	Suit	1806	ACO:065
Schooner *Betsey & Charlotte*	Arlington	Suit	1806	ACO:053, 056, 063
Schooner *Betsey & Charlotte*	Arlington	Depositions	1806	ACO:056, 063
Schooner *Betsey & Charlotte*	Arlington	Seamen of	1806	ACR:022
Schooner *Betsey & Charlotte*	Arlington	Interrogatory	1806	ACR:007, 032, 035
Schooner *Betsey & Charlotte*	Arlington	Suit	1806	ACR:001
Schooner *Betsey & Fanny*	Arlington	Suit	1803	ACO:022, 023
Schooner *Betsy*	Arlington	Suit	1804	ACO:029
Schooner *Betsy*	Arlington	Suit	1805	ACO:035
Schooner *Brothers Return*	Arlington	Suit	1821	ACO:197
Schooner *Catharine*	Arlington	Suit	1821	ACO:198
Schooner Citizen, Elias Ceely, master	Alexandria	Survey	1815	CRK:489

NAME OR SUBJECT	LOCATION	TYPE	YEAR	REFERENCE(S)
Schooner *Eliza*	Arlington	Suit	1811	ACO:116, 117
Schooner *Eliza*	Arlington	Suit	1813	ACO:137
Schooner *Enterprize*	Arlington	Suit	1805	ACO:035
Schooner *General Pinckney*	Arlington	Reference	1806	ACR:023
Schooner *Highland*	Arlington	Suit	1806	ACO:070
Schooner *Hiland*	Arlington	Suit	1808	ACO:094
Schooner *Hiland*, by Young & Yeaton	Arlington	Reference	1806	ACR:024
Schooner *Hyland*	Arlington	Suit	1807	ACO:073, 074, 075
Schooner *Hyland*	Arlington	Suit	1807	ACO:076
Schooner *Industry*	Arlington	Suit	1819	ACO:177
Schooner *Industry*	Arlington	Suit	1819	ACO:165, 167-172
Schooner *Retaliation*	Arlington	Suit	1819	ACO:156
Schooner *Rose in Bloom*	Arlington	Suit	1827	ACO:269, 270
Schooner *Sea Flower*	Arlington	Suit	1808	ACR:045
Schooner *William & Mary*	Arlington	Suit	1808	ACO:098, 100
Schroeder, John	Arlington	Apprentice	1823	OCR1822:049a
Schroeder, John	Arlington	Apprentice	1823	OCR1822:036
Schroeder, John	Arlington	Apprentice	1824	OCR1822:066
Schwarz, Isaac	Alexandria	Will	1898	WB2:294; LP
Scisson, Geo. G., shopkeeper	Alexandria	Head	1810	1810(4):06A
Scollard, Anthy.	Alexandria	Tax Charge	1790	Tax PP 1790:13
Scott, Ann	Arlington	Petition	1846	LVA-LP (Box 214)
Scott, Bennet	Alexandria	Tax Charge	1799	Tax PP 1799:37
Scott, Bennet, taylor	Alexandria	Boarder	1799	1799(2):03A
Scott, Bennett	Alexandria	Tax Charge	1800	Tax PP 1800:39
Scott, Charles	Alexandria	Tithable +16	1789	Tax PP 1789:09
Scott, Charles	Alexandria	Tithable +16	1790	Tax PP 1790:06
Scott, Charles, def.	Alexandria	Suit	1805	CRF:102
Scott, Charles, grantee	Arlington	Indenture D.	1811	ID2:021
Scott, Charles, grantee	Arlington	Indenture D.	1813	ID2:221
Scott, Charles R.	Arlington	Witness	1795	OT:28/07/1795
Scott, Charles R.	Alexandria	Tax Charge	1796	Tax LP 1796:26
Scott, Charles R. & wife, merchant	Alexandria	Housekeeper	1799	1799(2):18A
Scott, Chas., merchant	Alexandria	Head	1810	1810(3):03A
Scott, Chas., merchant	Alexandria	Head	1810	1810(3):08A
Scott, Chas. R.	Alexandria	Tax Charge	1795	Tax PP 1795:27
Scott, Chas., shopkeeper	Alexandria	Housekeeper	1808	1808(3):22A
Scott, David W.	Alexandria	Tax Charge	1798	Tax PP 1798:16
Scott, David W.	Alexandria	Tax Charge	1800	Tax PP 1800:39
Scott, David Wilson	Alexandria	Tax Charge	1799	Tax PP 1799:38
Scott, David Wilson	Alexandria	Deposition	1805	CRG:023
Scott, David Wilson, plt.	Alexandria	Suit	1801	CRC:078
Scott, Dennis	Arlington	Inventory	1802	WBA:082; LVA-LP
Scott, Dennis	Arlington	Will	1802	WBA:072
Scott, Dennis	Arlington	Bond	1802	WBA:074
Scott, Esther E.	Alexandria	Will	1898	WB2:256; LP
Scott, Geo., labourer	Alexandria	Head	1810	1810(2):07A
Scott, George	Arlington	Account	1843	AB8:409
Scott, George	Arlington	Death	1845	OCR1842:146
Scott, George, at Geo: Town Ferry	Arlington	Ordinary	1824	OBL3(np)
Scott, George, in Alexandria Co.	Arlington	Ordinary	1825	OBL4(np)
Scott, Heirs	Arlington	Division	1815	AB2:134
Scott, Horatio	Alexandria	Boarder	1808	1808(3):19A
Scott, James	Alexandria	Tithable +16	1788	Tax PP 1788:07
Scott, James	Alexandria	Tithable +16	1789	Tax PP 1789:08
Scott, James	Alexandria	Tithable +16	1790	Tax PP 1790:06
Scott, James, labourer	Alexandria	Head	1810	1810(2):07A
Scott, James R., c/o James	Arlington	Guard.	1853	BB(np)
Scott, James S.	Alexandria	Tax Charge	1799	Tax PP 1799:37
Scott, James S., for playing Faro	Arlington	Defendant	1801	PA:117
Scott, James S., taylor	Alexandria	Head	1810	1810(1):05A

NAME OR SUBJECT	LOCATION	TYPE	YEAR	REFERENCE(S)
Scott, Jas. S., taylor	Alexandria	Housekeeper	1808	1808(2):10A
Scott, Jno.	Alexandria	Tax Charge	1795	Tax PP 1795:29
Scott, Jno. & Jas.	Alexandria	Tax Charge	1798	Tax PP 1798:17
Scott, Jno. & Jas. & wife, taylors/habitm.	Alexandria	Housekeeper	1799	1799(2):03A
Scott, John & James	Alexandria	Account B.	1798	CRC:244
Scott, John & James	Alexandria	Tax Charge	1800	Tax PP 1800:39
Scott, John & James S., def.	Alexandria	Suit	1801	CRB:275
Scott, John & James, def.	Alexandria	Suit	1801	CRC:241
Scott, John, for playing Faro	Arlington	Defendant	1801	PA:122
Scott, John R., c/o James	Arlington	Guard.	1853	BB(np)
Scott, R.M.	Alexandria	Tax Charge	1798	Tax PP 1798:18
Scott, Rebecca, c/o James	Arlington	Guard.	1853	BB(np)
Scott, Richard M.	Alexandria	Tithable +21	1787	Tax PP 1787:09
Scott, Richard M.	Alexandria	Tax Charge	1788	Tax PP 1788:14
Scott, Richard M.	Alexandria	Tax Charge	1789	Tax PP 1789:17
Scott, Richard M.	Alexandria	Tax Charge	1796	Tax PP 1796:18
Scott, Richard M.	Alexandria	Deposition	1812	CRK:073
Scott, Richard M., def.	Alexandria	Suit	1822	CRL:389
Scott, Richard Marshall	Arlington	Will	1833	WB4:199; File #364A
Scott, Richard Marshall	Arlington	Bond	1833	WB4:208
Scott, Richard Marshall	Arlington	Will (NR)	1856	CLOB1:512; File #078A
Scott, Richard Marshall, Fairfax Co.	Alexandria	Deed	1809	CRK:062
Scott, Richard, w7, gentleman	Alexandria	Head	1796	1796(3):1
Scott, Richd. M.	Alexandria	Tax Charge	1796	Tax LP 1796:26
Scott, Richd. M. & wife, merchant	Alexandria	Housekeeper	1799	1799(2):06A
Scott, Robert	Alexandria	Tithable +16	1789	Tax PP 1789:17
Scott, Robert	Alexandria	Tithable +16	1790	Tax PP 1790:13
Scott, Sabret	Arlington	Plaintiff	1821	ACO:198
Scott, Thos.	Alexandria	Tithable +16	1788	Tax PP 1788:08
Scott, Thos.	Alexandria	Boarder	1808	1808(2):10A
Scott, Watkin	Alexandria	Tax Charge	1790	Tax PP 1790:13
Scott, William	Alexandria	Tithable +16	1789	Tax PP 1789:08
Scott, William	Alexandria	Tithable +16	1790	Tax PP 1790:06
Scott, William H.	Arlington	Bond	1854	BB(np)
Scott's Exrx. v. Fairfax	Arlington	Suit	1835	LVA-LP (Judgments)
Scrags, Henry	Alexandria	Serv./Appr.	1800	1800(4):03B
Sea, Jacob	Alexandria	Tax Charge	1787	Tax PP 1787:14
Seabrooke, Thomas, b. London	Arlington	Alien Entry	1817	RA:23/12/17
Seahorn, Christopher	Alexandria	Tax Charge	1787	Tax PP 1787:13
Seahorn, John	Alexandria	Tax Charge	1787	Tax PP 1787:13
Seahorn, John	Alexandria	Tax Charge	1796	Tax PP 1796:17
Seahorne, Jno.	Alexandria	Tax Charge	1795	Tax PP 1795:27
Seahorne, Jno.	Alexandria	Tax Charge	1798	Tax PP 1798:18
Seahorne, Jno., Queen St.	Alexandria	Occupant	1795	Tax L 1795:03
Seahorne, John	Alexandria	Tax Charge	1799	Tax PP 1799:38
Seal, Moses	Arlington	Will	1828	WB3:325; File #276A
Seal, Wm.	Alexandria	Boarder	1808	1808(3):18A
Seale, Moses	Arlington	Admin.	1828	OCR1822:165a
Seale, Moses	Arlington	Will P.	1828	OCR1822:165a
Seam, John	Alexandria	Tax Charge	1800	Tax PP 1800:40
Sears, Charles L.	Arlington	Ordinary	1821	OBL3(np)
Sears, James W.	Arlington	Bond	1853	BB(np)
Sears, James W.	Arlington	Will	1853	WB6:247; File #500A
Sears, Winthrop	Arlington	Defendant	1817	ACO:149
Seaton, Anna Maria	Arlington	Guard.	1816	WB2:111
Seaton, Anna Maria	Arlington	Guard.	1819	WB2:313
Seaton, Eliza M.	Arlington	Guard.	1816	WB2:212
Seaton, Eliza W.	Arlington	Guard.	1817	WB2:111, 212
Seaton, George	Arlington	Will	1844	WB4:387; File #418A
Seaton, George	Arlington	Inventory	1845	AB9:098; LVA-LP
Seaton, George	Arlington	Will P.	1845	OCR1842:099

NAME OR SUBJECT	LOCATION	TYPE	YEAR	REFERENCE(S)
Seaton, George	Arlington	Account	1846	AB9:154; LVA-LP
Seaton, John A.	Alexandria	Will	1898	WB2:266; LP
Seaton, Louisa	Arlington	Guard.	1816	WB2:151
Seaton, Louisa	Arlington	Guard.	1818	WB2:250
Seaton, Louisa	Arlington	Guard.	1819	WB2:313
Seaton, Lucinda	Arlington	Will	1865	WB8:281; File #638A
Secrest, Michael, plt.	Alexandria	Ejectment	1802	CRE:242
Seddon, Joseph & Co.	Arlington	P. of Atty.	1812	LVA-LP
Sedwick, Benjamin	Arlington	Bond	1823	WB3:122
Sedwick, Benjamin	Arlington	Will	1823	WB3:120; File #221A
Sedwick, Benjamin	Arlington	Inventory	1824	AB5:242; LVA-LP
Sedwick, Benjamin	Arlington	Will P.	1824	OCR1822:063a
Sedwick, Benjamin	Arlington	Account	1825	AB5:400
Sedwick, Benjamin	Arlington	Account	1826	AB6:213; LVA-LP
Sedwick, Benjamin, Dr.	Arlington	Sale	1824	AB5:258
Sedwick, George W.	Arlington	Guard.	1825	OCR1822:086a
Sedwick, George W.	Arlington	Guard.	1825	WB3:176
Sedwick, John Alexander	Arlington	Guard.	1825	WB3:175
Sedwick, Sarah Ann	Arlington	Guard.	1825	OCR1822:086a
Sedwick, Sarah Ann	Arlington	Guard.	1825	WB3:175
Seekright, Aminadab	Arlington	Suit	1841	LSA:142, 145
Seekright, Aminadab, plt.	Alexandria	Ejectment	1802	CRE:242
Seekright, Aminidab, plt.	Alexandria	Ejectment	(nd)	CRI:282
Seidle, Hester, c/o Philip Henry	Arlington	Apprentice	1811	OCR1811:033
Seidle, John, c/o Philip Henry	Arlington	Apprentice	1811	OCR1811:014
Seimer, Paul, of Philadelphia	Alexandria	Deed	1811	CRK:048
Seivat, Nicholas	Alexandria	Tithable +16	1790	Tax PP 1790:10
Seiz, Chs. Frederick, b. Lindlefingen	Arlington	Alien Entry	1823	RA:15/11/23
Selden, L. Cary	Arlington	Will	1850	WB5:290; File #461A
Selden, L. Cary	Arlington	Inventory	1850	WB5:291; LVA-LP
Selden, Mary B.	Arlington	Defendant	1835	LSA:005
Selden, Mary B., w/o Wilson C.	Arlington	Complainant	1835	LSA:005
Selden, Wilson C.	Arlington	Complainant	1835	LSA:005
Selden, Wilson C., Jr.	Arlington	Complainant	1835	LSA:005
Seldon, Carey, merchant	Alexandria	Boarder	1799	1799(2):02A
Selfe, Jas.	Alexandria	Tax Charge	1795	Tax PP 1795:28
Selick, Thomas, seaman	Alexandria	Head	1810	1810(1):12A
Sellers, Ann Elizabeth	Arlington	Guard.	1822	WB3:055
Sellers, John	Arlington	Inventory	1809	WBC:244; LVA-LP
Sellers, John	Arlington	Admin.	1809	WBC:243
Sellers, John	Arlington	Sale	1809	WBC:271
Sellers, John	Arlington	Account	1811	AB1:109; LVA-LP
Sellers, John, musical instrument maker	Alexandria	Housekeeper	1808	1808(1):04A
Sellers, Richd.	Alexandria	Boarder	1808	1808(4):24A
Sellman, Deborah, widow, w(2)	Alexandria	Head	1796	1796(3):6
Selmen, James	Alexandria	Serv./Appr.	1800	1800(4):03B
Sely, Thomas	Alexandria	Tax Charge	1788	Tax PP 1788:15
Semmes, Charles	Arlington	Account	1839	AB8:021; LVA-LP
Semmes, Douglas Ramsay, c/o Thomas	Arlington	Guard.	1840	WB4:249
Semmes, Dr., physician	Alexandria	Housekeeper	1808	1808(1):02A
Semmes, Eliza F., guardian	Arlington	Suit	1851	FBB(np)
Semmes, Mary Elizabeth, c/o Thomas	Arlington	Guard.	1840	WB4:248
Semmes, Sarah Wilhemina, c/o Thomas	Arlington	Guard.	1840	WB4:248
Semmes, Sophia W.	Arlington	Bond	1839	WB4:215
Semmes, Sophia W.	Arlington	Will	1839	WB4:213; File #372A
Semmes, Sophia W.	Arlington	Inventory	1840	AB8:150; LVA-LP
Semmes, Sophia W.	Arlington	Library	1840	AB8:153
Semmes, Sophia W.	Arlington	Account	1841	AB8:219
Semmes, Sophia W.	Arlington	Account	1842	AB8:326; LVA-LP
Semmes, Sophia W.	Arlington	Will P.	1843	OCR1842:055, 060
Semmes, Sophia W.	Arlington	Account	1844	AB8:492; LVA-LP

NAME OR SUBJECT	LOCATION	TYPE	YEAR	REFERENCE(S)
Semmes, Sophia W.	Arlington	Account	1845	AB9:058; LVA-LP
Semmes, Sophia W.	Arlington	Account	1846	AB9:184; LVA-LP
Semmes, Sophia W.	Arlington	Account	1848	WB5:156; LVA-LP
Semmes, Thomas	Alexandria	Deposition	1814	CRI:523
Semmes, Thomas	Arlington	Will	1833	WB4:059; File #322A
Semmes, Thomas	Arlington	Bond	1833	WB4:060
Semmes, Thomas	Arlington	Will	1841	WB4:358
Semmes, Thomas	Arlington	Bond	1841	WB4:362
Semmes, Thomas	Arlington	Sale	1843	AB8:377
Semmes, Thomas	Arlington	Debts	1843	AB8:375
Semmes, Thomas	Arlington	Inventory	1843	AB8:373; LVA-LP
Semmes, Thomas	Arlington	Will P.	1843	OCR1842:041
Semmes, Thomas	Arlington	Will	1843	WB4:358; File #404A
Semmes, Thomas, def.	Alexandria	Suit	1822	CRL:389
Semmes, Thomas M.	Arlington	Suit	1851	FBB(np)
Semmes, Thomas M., c/o E.F.	Arlington	Guard.	1846	LVA-LP (Box 214)
Semmes, Thomas, M.D.	Alexandria	Deposition	1819	CRK:451
Semmes, Thomas Middleton, c/o Eliza	Arlington	Guard.	1845	OCR1842:151, 171
Semmes, Thomas, physician	Alexandria	Boarder	1799	1799(2):02A
Semmes, Thomas [Eliza F.]	Arlington	Renounce	1844	OCR1842:074
Semmes, William Hawley, c/o Thomas	Arlington	Guard.	1840	WB4:249
Semmes' Exors. v. Robey et al.	Arlington	Suit	1840	LVA-LP (Accounts)
Semms, Doctr.	Alexandria	Head	1810	1810(2):05A
Semple, Eliza	Alexandria	Mer. License	1798	Tax PP 1799:52-11r
Semple, Eliza	Alexandria	License Due	1800	Tax PP 1800:54(24)
Semple, Wm.	Alexandria	Tax Charge	1795	Tax PP 1795:27
Semple, Wm.	Alexandria	Tax Charge	1796	Tax PP 1796:18
Semple, Wm., Fairfax St.	Alexandria	Occupant	1795	Tax L 1795:01
Senior, John, b. Rowley, Yorkshire	Arlington	Alien Entry	1819	RA:17/11/19
Sepensons, Sippen & wife Mary	Alexandria	Resident	1800	1800(4):07B
Sequin, Andrew	Alexandria	Deposition	1822	CRL:599
Seratt, George	Arlington	Guard.	1832	WB4:050
Seratt, George D.	Arlington	Guard. Acct.	1838	AB7:329; LVA-LP
Seratt, George D.	Arlington	Guard. Acct.	1839	AB7:329
Seratt, John H.	Arlington	Guard.	1832	WB4:050
Seratt, John H.	Arlington	Guard. Acct.	1835	AB7:328; LVA-LP
Seratt, John H.	Arlington	Guard. Acct.	1839	AB7:328
Sergeant, Thos., meth. preacher	Alexandria	Housekeeper	1808	1808(4):27A
Serjinar, Jas.	Alexandria	Boarder	1808	1808(2):10A
Serratt, Saml.	Alexandria	Boarder	1808	1808(1):09A
Service, Mary	Arlington	Witness	1794	OT:25/07/1794
Set of tea china	Arlington	Suit	1827	ACO:275
Settler, Abm.	Alexandria	Tax Charge	1795	Tax PP 1795:27
Sevenson, Robert & wife Elizabeth	Alexandria	Resident	1800	1800(4):12B
Sevenson, Robert, carpenter	Alexandria	Head	1800	1800(4):12A
Sewall, Eleanor	Arlington	Will	1812	WB1:191; File #104A
Sewall, Joseph, grantor	Arlington	Indenture D.	1829	ID:221
Sewall, Joseph, in jail	Arlington	Insolvent	1829	ID:219
Sewell, Clement	Arlington	Ordinary	1802	OBL1(np)
Sewell, Clement	Arlington	Ordinary	1803	OBL1(np)
Sewell, Clement	Arlington	Ordinary	1807	OBL2(np)
Sewell, Clement, at George Town Ferry	Arlington	Ordinary	1805	OBL1(np)
Sewell, Clement, at George Town Ferry	Arlington	Ordinary	1806	OBL2(np)
Sexsmith & Bryan, Fairfax St.	Alexandria	Occupant	1795	Tax L 1795:25
Sexsmith, Geo.	Alexandria	Boarder	1808	1808(3):19A
Sexsmith, Mathew, shoemaker	Alexandria	Housekeeper	1808	1808(2):12A
Sexsmith, Mathew, shoemaker	Alexandria	Head	1810	1810(2):02A
Sexsmith, Matt.	Alexandria	Tax Charge	1795	Tax PP 1795:29
Sexsmith, Matthew	Alexandria	Tax Charge	1796	Tax LP 1796:26
Sexsmith, Matthew	Alexandria	Tax Charge	1796	Tax PP 1796:18
Sexsmith, Matthew	Alexandria	Tax Charge	1799	Tax PP 1799:38

NAME OR SUBJECT	LOCATION	TYPE	YEAR	REFERENCE(S)
Sexsmith, Matthew, grantor	Arlington	Indenture D.	1827	ID:079
Sexsmith, Matthew, in jail	Arlington	Insolvent	1827	ID:077
Sexsmith, Mattw.	Alexandria	Tax Charge	1798	Tax PP 1798:17
Sexsmith, Nathl.	Alexandria	Tax Charge	1800	Tax PP 1800:39
Shackelford, Richard	Arlington	Apprentice	1811	OCR1811:041
Shackleford, John	Arlington	Apprentice	1811	OCR1811:013
Shackleford, Richard	Arlington	Appraisal	1831	LVA-LP
Shackleford, Richard	Arlington	Admin.	1831	WB4:039
Shackleford, Richard	Arlington	Account	1832	AB7:033; LVA-LP
Shakes, Amanda U.R.V.	Arlington	Will	1861	WB8:053; File #581A
Shakes, John, brush maker	Alexandria	Housekeeper	1808	1808(3):21A
Shakes, John, brushmaker	Alexandria	Head	1810	1810(3):01A
Shakes, [blank], retailer	Alexandria	Housekeeper	1808	1808(2):10A
Shakespear, William	Alexandria	Tax Charge	1790	Tax PP 1790:13
Shakespear, Wm.	Alexandria	Tax Charge	1789	Tax PP 1789:17
Shakespear, Wm.	Alexandria	Tax Charge	1796	Tax LP 1796:26
Shakespear, Wm., Wilks St.	Alexandria	Occupant	1787	Tax L 1787:06
Shakespeare, William	Alexandria	Tax Charge	1788	Tax PP 1788:15
Shakespeare, William, Queen St.	Alexandria	Occupant	1790	Tax L 1790:08
Shanks, James	Arlington	Will	1806	WBB:334; File #014A
Shanks, James	Arlington	Bond	1806	WBB:335
Shanks, James	Arlington	Inventory	1806	WBB:338; LVA-LP
Shanks, James	Arlington	Account	1807	WBB:510; LVA-LP
Shanks, James	Arlington	Account	1809	WBC:178; LVA-LP
Shanks, James	Arlington	Account	1811	AB1:118; LVA-LP
Sharen, Martha, visiter	Alexandria	Boarder	1800	1800(4):09A
Sharon, Peter	Alexandria	Mer. License	1798	Tax PP 1798:20-7
Sharon, Peter	Alexandria	Tax Charge	1799	Tax PP 1799:37
Sharon, Peter	Alexandria	Tax Charge	1800	Tax PP 1800:39
Sharon, Peter, alias P. Nelly	Alexandria	Tax Charge	1798	Tax PP 1798:18
Sharron, Peter	Alexandria	Mer. License	1800	Tax PP 1800:54(20)r
Shartle, John	Alexandria	Tax Charge	1788	Tax PP 1788:14
Shattle, John	Alexandria	Tithable +21	1787	Tax PP 1787:01
Shaw, Alexander	Alexandria	Tax Charge	1799	Tax PP 1799:37
Shaw, Alexr.	Alexandria	Tax Charge	1798	Tax PP 1798:17
Shaw, Alexr. & wife, carpenter	Alexandria	Boarder	1799	1799(2):01A
Shaw, Catherine	Arlington	Guard.	1819	WB2:312
Shaw, Eleanor	Alexandria	Tax Charge	1788	Tax PP 1788:15
Shaw, Eleazor, Queen St.	Alexandria	Occupant	1790	Tax L 1790:11
Shaw, Eleazor, Queen St.	Alexandria	Owner	1790	Tax L 1790:11
Shaw, John	Alexandria	Tax Charge	1798	Tax PP 1798:17
Shaw, John	Arlington	Inventory	1812	AB1:190; LVA-LP
Shaw, John	Arlington	Admin.	1812	WB1:163
Shaw, John	Arlington	Account	1813	AB1:291; LVA-LP
Shaw, John, ship carpenter	Alexandria	Housekeeper	1808	1808(4):24A
Shaw, Mrs., Queen St.	Alexandria	Occupant	1787	Tax L 1787:23
Shaw, William	Alexandria	Tithable +16	1789	Tax PP 1789:02
Shaw, William	Alexandria	Tithable +16	1790	Tax PP 1790:01
Shaw, William, Estate	Alexandria	Owner	1787	Tax L 1787:23
Shay, Elijah, retailer	Alexandria	Housekeeper	1808	1808(1):02A
Sheahorne, John	Alexandria	Tax Charge	1796	Tax LP 1796:26
Shearman, Elizabeth	Arlington	Guard.	1805	WBB:200
Shearman, Mary	Arlington	Guard.	1805	WBB:169
Sheckel, Dedrick	Alexandria	Tax Charge	1800	Tax PP 1800:39
Sheckel, Dedrick	Arlington	Account	1829	AB6:506; LVA-LP
Sheckel, Dedrick	Arlington	Admin.	1829	OCR1822:171
Sheckel, Diederick, gentleman	Alexandria	Head	1796	1796(3):4
Sheckle, Dedrick	Alexandria	Tax Charge	1798	Tax PP 1798:16
Sheckle, Dedrick	Arlington	Bond	1829	WB3:325, 326, 351
Sheckle, Dedrick	Arlington	Will	1829	WB3:310; File #268A
Sheehy, Edward, b. Tiperara	Arlington	Alien Entry	1821	RA:26/05/21

NAME OR SUBJECT	LOCATION	TYPE	YEAR	REFERENCE(S)
Sheehy, James	Alexandria	Resident	1800	1800(4):02B
Sheehy, James	Alexandria	Tax Charge	1800	Tax PP 1800:40
Sheehy, James	Arlington	Inventory	1814	AB2:069; LVA-LP
Sheehy, James	Arlington	Will	1814	WB1:301; File #122A
Sheehy, James	Arlington	Sale	1815	AB2:084
Sheehy, James	Arlington	Account	1815	AB2:201; LVA-LP
Sheehy, James	Arlington	Account	1816	AB2:346; LVA-LP
Sheehy, James, chandler/soap boiler	Alexandria	Head	1800	1800(4):02A
Sheehy, James, plt.	Alexandria	Suit	1806	CRH:176
Sheehy, James, plt.	Alexandria	Suit	1809	CRH:156
Sheehy, James, plt.	Alexandria	Suit	1809	CRG:290
Sheehy, James, soap boiler	Alexandria	Head	1810	1810(2):03A
Sheeler, J.B.	Alexandria	Tax Charge	1796	Tax LP 1796:27
Sheeler, J.B.	Alexandria	Tax Charge	1796	Tax PP 1796:18
Sheeler, Jno.	Alexandria	Boarder	1808	1808(1):05A
Sheerman, Abraham, cooper	Alexandria	Head	1810	1810(2):08A
Sheese' Estate, King St.	Alexandria	Occupant	1795	Tax L 1795:32
Sheetz, Clement	Alexandria	Tax Charge	1800	Tax PP 1800:39
Sheffey, D.	Alexandria	Deposition	1803	CRE:283, 345
Shehee, James	Arlington	Defendant	1802	PA:204
Shehey, Jas., shopkeeper & soap boiler	Alexandria	Housekeeper	1808	1808(2):12A
Sheilds, Martin	Alexandria	Tax Charge	1787	Tax PP 1787:14
Shekel, Dedrick	Alexandria	Tax Charge	1790	Tax PP 1790:13
Shekel, Dedrick	Alexandria	Tax Charge	1796	Tax PP 1796:18
Shekel, Deedrick	Alexandria	Tax Charge	1795	Tax PP 1795:29
Shekle [Shakle], Dedrick	Arlington	Account	1830	AB6:506
Shekle, Dederick	Alexandria	Tax Charge	1796	Tax LP 1796:26
Shekle, Dederick	Alexandria	Tax Charge	1796	Tax LP 1796:27
Shekle, Dedrick	Alexandria	Tax Charge	1799	Tax PP 1799:37
Shekle, Dedrick, King St.	Alexandria	Occupant	1795	Tax L 1795:27
Shekle, Dedrick, King St.	Alexandria	Owner	1795	Tax L 1795:27
Shekle, Dedrick, Royal St.	Alexandria	Owner	1795	Tax L 1795:27
Sheler, Jno. B.	Alexandria	Tax Charge	1795	Tax PP 1795:29
Shelley, John	Alexandria	Tithable +21	1787	Tax PP 1787:14
Shelley, John	Alexandria	Tax Charge	1790	Tax PP 1790:14
Shelton, Henry	Alexandria	Will	1899	WB2:322; LP
Shepard, Thompson	Alexandria	Boarder	1808	1808(1):06A
Shepherd, John	Alexandria	Tithable +16	1789	Tax PP 1789:15
Shepherd, John	Alexandria	Tithable +16	1790	Tax PP 1790:10
Sheridan, Vincent	Alexandria	Tax Charge	1800	Tax PP 1800:39
Sherman, Elisha	Arlington	Will	1867	WB8:565; File #655A
Shermentine, Jas., shoemaker	Alexandria	Housekeeper	1808	1808(2):12A
Sherrard, Francis & wife, retailer	Alexandria	Housekeeper	1799	1799(2):01A
Sherron, Eleanor	Arlington	Will	1847	WB5:004; File #075A
Sherron, John, Co. Down, Ire.	Arlington	Claim	1824	OCR1822:069, 071a
Sherron, Peter	Arlington	Inventory	1821	AB4:214; LVA-LP
Sherron, Peter	Arlington	Will	1821	WB2:408; File #187A
Sherron, Peter	Arlington	Bond	1821	WB2:409
Sherron, Peter	Arlington	Account	1822	AB5:033; LVA-LP
Sherron, Peter	Arlington	Account	1823	AB5:173; LVA-LP
Sherron, Peter	Arlington	Will P.	1824	OCR1822:069a
Sherron, Peter	Arlington	Account	1825	AB5:385
Sherron, Peter & wife, merchant	Alexandria	Housekeeper	1799	1799(2):03A
Sherron, Peter, in prison bounds	Arlington	Insolvent	1833	ID1:001
Sherron, Peter, merchant	Alexandria	Head	1810	1810(2):03A
Sherron, Peter, plt.	Alexandria	Suit	1801	CRB:020
Sherron, Peter, plt.	Alexandria	Suit	1803	CRD:078
Sherron, Peter, retailer	Alexandria	Housekeeper	1808	1808(2):12A
Sherron v. Sherron	Arlington	Suit	1823	LVA-LP
Shertle, Luck, w(3)1, carpenter	Alexandria	Head	1796	1796(3):3
Shible, Mary	Alexandria	Will	1883	WB1:375; LP

NAME OR SUBJECT	LOCATION	TYPE	YEAR	REFERENCE(S)
Shields, Chas., ropemaker	Alexandria	Head	1810	1810(3):07A
Shields, Chas., ropemaker	Alexandria	Housekeeper	1808	1808(1):06A
Shields, John	Alexandria	Boarder	1808	1808(1):03A
Shields, John	Arlington	Libellant	1813	ACO:137
Shields, Mary Ann	Arlington	Guard.	1850	WB5:272; LVA-LP
Shields, Mary Ann, c/o Alfred Peyton	Arlington	Guard.	1846	OCR1842:190
Shields, Thomas	Arlington	Guard.	1807	WBB:447
Shields, Thomas	Arlington	Ordinary	1821	OBL3(np)
Shields, Thomas, c/o Ann Shields Tyler	Arlington	Apprentice	1802	OCR1801:038
Shields, Thos., barber	Alexandria	Head	1810	1810(2):03A
Shields, Thos., hairdresser	Alexandria	Housekeeper	1808	1808(1):02A
Shinlin, Daniel	Alexandria	Tithable +16	1789	Tax PP 1789:08
Ship *Argo*, from Liverpool	Arlington	Claims	1812	ACO:124, 125
Ship *Governor Strong*	Arlington	Bond	1801	ACO:006
Ship *Governor Strong*	Arlington	Suit	1801	ACO:007
Ship *Liberty*	Arlington	Suit	1818	ACO:152, 154
Ship *Monsoon*, from Liverpool	Arlington	Suit	1812	ACO:129, 130
Ship *Potomac*	Arlington	Suit	1820	ACO:181, 183
Ship *President*	Arlington	Suit	1806	ACO:052
Ship *Talbot*	Arlington	Suit	1819	ACO:164
Ship *United States*, merchandize on	Arlington	Suit	1805	ACO:041
Ship *United States*, merchandize on	Arlington	Suit	1806	ACO:050, 052
Ship *Wilhelmina*	Arlington	Suit	1812	ACO:127-128, 132-135
Ship *Wilhelmina*	Arlington	Suit	1812	ACR:050
Ship *William*	Arlington	Suit	1813	ACO:137
Ship *William & John*	Arlington	Suit	1805	ACO:033
Ship *William & John*	Arlington	Suit	1805	ACO:042
Ship *William & John*	Arlington	Suit	1806	ACO:049
Ship *William & John*, from Liverpool	Arlington	Suit	1808	ACR:039
Ship *William & John*	Arlington	Suit	1811	ACO:116
Ship's anchor, one	Arlington	Suit	1821	ACO:184, 189, 193
Shipman, John	Alexandria	Deposition	1805	CRF:246
Shirley, D.	Alexandria	Tax Charge	1798	Tax PP 1798:17
Shirley, Sarah C.	Alexandria	Will	1899	WB2:317; LP
Shirley, Theodore, brickmaker	Alexandria	Housekeeper	1808	1808(2):17A
Shirley, Theodosius	Alexandria	Tax Charge	1799	Tax PP 1799:37
Shively, John	Arlington	Apprentice	1802	OCR1801:052
Shoals, Manasa, fisherman	Alexandria	Head	1810	1810(3):09A
Shoemaker, Abram	Alexandria	Tax Charge	1796	Tax PP 1796:17
Shoemaker, Adam	Alexandria	Tax Charge	1799	Tax PP 1799:39
Shoemaker, Adam	Alexandria	Tax Charge	1800	Tax PP 1800:40
Shoemaker, Adam & wife, labourer	Alexandria	Housekeeper	1799	1799(2):12A
Shoemaker, Ann	Alexandria	Serv./Appr.	1800	1800(4):13B
Shoemaker, Elizabeth, c/o Elizabeth	Arlington	Apprentice	1803	OCR1801:119
Shoemaker, Frederick	Alexandria	Tax Charge	1790	Tax PP 1790:13
Shoemaker, Fredk.	Alexandria	Tax Charge	1788	Tax PP 1788:15
Shoemaker, Fredk.	Alexandria	Tax Charge	1789	Tax PP 1789:16
Shoemaker, Fredk., Princess St.	Alexandria	Occupant	1790	Tax L 1790:03
Shonnard, John	Alexandria	Tax Charge	1796	Tax PP 1796:17
Shook, Jacob	Alexandria	Tax Charge	1787	Tax PP 1787:14
Shook, Jacob	Alexandria	Tax Charge	1795	Tax PP 1795:28
Shook, Jacob & wife, carpenter	Alexandria	Head	1795	1795(4):02
Shook, Jacob, Duke St.	Alexandria	Owner	1795	Tax L 1795:28
Shook, Jacob, Duke St.	Alexandria	Occupant	1795	Tax L 1795:28
Shook, Jacob, Water St.	Alexandria	Owner	1795	Tax L 1795:26
Shooks, Jacob	Alexandria	Tax Charge	1796	Tax LP 1796:26
Shore, M., Fairfax St.	Alexandria	Occupant	1787	Tax L 1787:07
Shore, Michael	Alexandria	Tax Charge	1787	Tax PP 1787:14
Short, Edward	Alexandria	Tax Charge	1799	Tax PP 1799:38
Short, John	Alexandria	Owner	1787	Tax L 1787:24
Short, John	Alexandria	Tax Charge	1787	Tax PP 1787:14

NAME OR SUBJECT	LOCATION	TYPE	YEAR	REFERENCE(S)
Short, John	Alexandria	Tax Charge	1788	Tax PP 1788:15
Short, John, Duke St.	Alexandria	Occupant	1787	Tax L 1787:05
Short, John, Duke St.	Alexandria	Occupant	1787	Tax L 1787:24
Short, John, Prince St.	Alexandria	Occupant	1787	Tax L 1787:15
Shortell, Luke	Alexandria	Tax Charge	1788	Tax PP 1788:14
Shortell, Margarett, seamstress	Alexandria	Head	1810	1810(4):01A
Shorthill, Elizabeth	Arlington	Guard.	1806	WBB:366
Shorthill, Luke	Alexandria	Tax Charge	1790	Tax PP 1790:13
Shorthill, Luke	Alexandria	Tax Charge	1796	Tax PP 1796:18
Shorthill, Luke	Arlington	Bond	1802	WBA:075
Shorthill, Luke & wife, carpenter	Alexandria	Housekeeper	1799	1799(2):06A
Shorthill, Margret, washwoman	Alexandria	Housekeeper	1808	1808(4):26A
Shorthill, Robt.	Alexandria	Boarder	1808	1808(2):13A
Shortill, John	Alexandria	Tax Charge	1789	Tax PP 1789:18
Shortill, Luke	Alexandria	Tax Charge	1798	Tax PP 1798:17
Shortill, Luke	Alexandria	Tax Charge	1799	Tax PP 1799:37
Shortle, Luke	Alexandria	Tax Charge	1795	Tax PP 1795:29
Shortle, Luke, Pitt St.	Alexandria	Occupant	1795	Tax L 1795:33
Shortley, Luke	Alexandria	Tax Charge	1796	Tax LP 1796:26
Shortley, Luke, Water	Alexandria	Occupant	1790	Tax L 1790:12
Shortly, Luke	Alexandria	Tax Charge	1789	Tax PP 1789:17
Showlles, Manassa	Arlington	Will	1817	WB2:203; File #143A
Showman, Henry	Alexandria	Tax Charge	1787	Tax PP 1787:13
Showman, Henry	Alexandria	Tax Charge	1790	Tax PP 1790:13
Shownard, John	Alexandria	Tax Charge	1796	Tax LP 1796:26
Shreeder, John (servant)	Alexandria	Tithable +21	1787	Tax PP 1787:04
Shreeve & Lawreson, King St.	Alexandria	Occupant	1787	Tax L 1787:24
Shreeve, Benja.	Alexandria	Owner	1787	Tax L 1787:24
Shreeve, Benja., King St.	Alexandria	Occupant	1787	Tax L 1787:02
Shreeve, Benjamin, cooper	Alexandria	Head	1810	1810(2):01A
Shreeve, Benjamin, w(3)1, merchant	Alexandria	Head	1796	1796(3):2
Shreeve, Isaac	Arlington	Insolvent	1810	ID2:001
Shreeve, Isaac, grantor	Arlington	Indenture D.	1810	ID2:006
Shreeve, Reuben, w, merchant	Alexandria	Head	1796	1796(3):4
Shreeve, Thos., merchant	Alexandria	Head	1810	1810(4):04A
S. & Lawrason	Alexandria	Tax Charge	1798	Tax PP 1798:17
Shreve & Laurason	Alexandria	Tax Charge	1799	Tax PP 1799:38
Shreve & Lawrason	Alexandria	Tax Charge	1789	Tax PP 1789:17
Shreve & Lawrason	Alexandria	Tax Charge	1795	Tax PP 1795:18
Shreve & Lawrason	Alexandria	Tax Charge	1796	Tax LP 1796:27
Shreve & Lawrason	Alexandria	Tax Charge	1796	Tax PP 1796:17
Shreve & Lawrason	Alexandria	Mer. License	1798	Tax PP 1798:20-7
Shreve & Lawrason	Alexandria	Tax Charge	1800	Tax PP 1800:39
Shreve & Lawrason	Arlington	Plaintiffs	1802	PA:274
Shreve & Lawrason, Prince St.	Alexandria	Owner	1795	Tax L 1795:18
Shreve & Lawrason, St. Asaph St.	Alexandria	Owner	1790	Tax L 1790:10
Shreve & Lawrason, Union St.	Alexandria	Occupant	1790	Tax L 1790:04
Shreve & Lawrason, Union St.	Alexandria	Occupant	1790	Tax L 1790:06
Shreve & Lawrason, Union St.	Alexandria	Owner	1790	Tax L 1790:10(2)
Shreve & Lawrason, Union St.	Alexandria	Occupant	1790	Tax L 1790:10(2)
Shreve & Lawrason, Union St.	Alexandria	Owner	1795	Tax L 1795:18(7)
Shreve & Lawrason, Union St.	Alexandria	Occupant	1795	Tax L 1795:18
Shreve & Slimmer, retailers	Alexandria	Housekeeper	1808	1808(2):10A
Shreve, Bengemen	Alexandria	Serv./Appt.	1800	1800(4):15B
Shreve, Bengemen & wife Susanah	Alexandria	Serv./Appt.	1800	1800(4):15B
Shreve, Bengemen, murchant	Alexandria	Head	1800	1800(4):15A
Shreve, Benj.	Alexandria	Tax Charge	1795	Tax PP 1795:29
Shreve, Benj.	Alexandria	Tax Charge	1798	Tax PP 1798:17
Shreve, Benj., Duke St.	Alexandria	Occupant	1795	Tax L 1795:13
Shreve, Benj., Fairfax St.	Alexandria	Owner	1795	Tax L 1795:27(3)
Shreve, Benj., Jr.	Alexandria	Mer. License	1799	Tax PP 1799:52-10r

NAME OR SUBJECT	LOCATION	TYPE	YEAR	REFERENCE(S)
Shreve, Benj., King St.	Alexandria	Owner	1795	Tax L 1795:27(2)
Shreve, Benj., St. Asaph St.	Alexandria	Owner	1795	Tax L 1795:27
Shreve, Benja.	Alexandria	Tax Charge	1788	Tax PP 1788:15
Shreve, Benja.	Alexandria	Tax Charge	1790	Tax PP 1790:13
Shreve, Benja. & wife, merchant	Alexandria	Housekeeper	1799	1799(2):13A
Shreve, Benja., King St.	Alexandria	Occupant	1790	Tax L 1790:10
Shreve, Benja., Sr.	Alexandria	Tax Charge	1800	Tax PP 1800:39
Shreve, Benjamin	Alexandria	Tax Charge	1787	Tax PP 1787:13
Shreve, Benjamin	Alexandria	Tax Charge	1789	Tax PP 1789:17
Shreve, Benjamin	Alexandria	Tax Charge	1796	Tax PP 1796:17
Shreve, Benjamin	Alexandria	Tax Charge	1799	Tax PP 1799:38
Shreve, Benjamin	Arlington	Will	1801	WBA:048
Shreve, Benjamin	Arlington	Inventory	1801	WBA:056; LVA-LP
Shreve, Benjamin	Arlington	Bond	1801	WBA:053
Shreve, Benjamin	Arlington	Account	1804	WBA:253; LVA-LP
Shreve, Benjamin	Arlington	Account	1805	LVA-LP
Shreve, Benjamin	Arlington	Settlement	1805	WBB:154
Shreve, Benjamin	Arlington	Account	1806	WBB:285, 341; LVA-LP
Shreve, Benjamin	Arlington	Account	1807	WBB:521; LVA-LP
Shreve, Benjamin	Arlington	Account	1808	WBC:098; LVA-LP
Shreve, Benjamin	Arlington	Account	1808	WBC:281; LVA-LP
Shreve, Benjamin	Arlington	Account	1812	AB1:231; LVA-LP
Shreve, Benjamin	Arlington	Inventory	1815	AB2:165
Shreve, Benjamin	Arlington	Account	1816	AB2:272
Shreve, Benjamin	Arlington	Report	1822	AB5:051; LVA-LP
Shreve, Benjamin	Arlington	Inventory	1827	AB6:274; LVA-LP
Shreve, Benjamin	Arlington	Bond	1827	WB3:272
Shreve, Benjamin	Arlington	Will	1827	WB3:271; File #254A
Shreve, Benjamin	Arlington	Account	1828	AB6:463; LVA-LP
Shreve, Benjamin, Fairfax St.	Alexandria	Owner	1790	Tax L 1790:10(3)
Shreve, Benjamin, King St.	Alexandria	Owner	1790	Tax L 1790:10
Shreve, Benjamin, slaves of	Arlington	Births	1815	AB2:165
Shreve, Benjn.	Alexandria	Resident	1800	1800(4):02B
Shreve, Benjn., cooper	Alexandria	Boarder	1800	1800(4):02A
Shreve, Benjn., cooper	Alexandria	Housekeeper	1808	1808(1):07A
Shreve, Benjn., merchant	Alexandria	Housekeeper	1808	1808(1):05A
Shreve, Caleb	Alexandria	Tax Charge	1798	Tax PP 1798:17
Shreve, Caleb & Co.	Alexandria	Mer. License	1798	Tax PP 1798:20-7
Shreve, Caleb & Co.	Alexandria	Tax Charge	1799	Tax PP 1799:37
Shreve, Caleb & Co., plt.	Alexandria	Suit	1801	CRB:255
Shreve, Isaac, grantee	Arlington	Indenture D.	1806	ID3:191
Shreve, Isaac, retailer	Alexandria	Housekeeper	1808	1808(3):21A
Shreve, Margaret	Arlington	Will	1811	WB1:110; File #095A
Shreve, Margaret	Arlington	Sale	1815	AB2:165
Shreve, Margaret	Arlington	Inventory	1815	LVA-LP
Shreve, Saml.	Alexandria	Boarder	1808	1808(3):21A
Shreve, Samuel	Arlington	Inventory	1815	AB2:159; LVA-LP
Shreve, Samuel	Arlington	Will	1815	WB2:057
Shreve, Samuel	Arlington	Bond	1815	WB2:058
Shreve, Samuel	Arlington	Sale	1816	AB2:328
Shreve, Samuel	Arlington	Account	1816	AB2:324
Shreve, Samuel, Jr.	Arlington	Distribution	1828	LVA-LP
Shreve, Samuel, Jr.	Arlington	Inventory	1828	LVA-LP
Shreve, Samuel, Jr.	Arlington	Will (N)	1828	WB3:301; File #263A
Shreve, Samuel, Jr.	Arlington	Bond	1828	WB3:301
Shreve, Samul	Alexandria	Serv./Appt.	1800	1800(4):15B
Shreve, Thos.	Alexandria	Tax Charge	1796	Tax LP 1796:27
Shreve, Thos., retailer	Alexandria	Housekeeper	1808	1808(4):25A
Shreve, William	Arlington	Admin. DBN	1811	WB1:026
Shreve, William	Arlington	Account	1812	LVA-LP
Shreve, William James	Arlington	Admin.	1810	WBC:445

NAME OR SUBJECT	LOCATION	TYPE	YEAR	REFERENCE(S)
Shreve, William James	Arlington	Debts	1810	WBC:470
Shreve, William James	Arlington	Inventory	1810	WBC:455
Shreve, Wm.	Alexandria	Boarder	1808	1808(2):11A
Shreves, Benja.	Alexandria	Tax Charge	1796	Tax LP 1796:26
Shroeder, Elizabeth, seamstress	Alexandria	Head	1810	1810(4):06A
Shropsher, Wm., goldsmith	Alexandria	Head	1800	1800(4):10A
Shropshire, Will.	Alexandria	Tax Charge	1800	Tax PP 1800:40
Shropshire, William	Alexandria	Tax Charge	1799	Tax PP 1799:37
Shropshire, William	Arlington	Will	1801	CRA:338
Shropshire, William	Arlington	Inventory	1801	WBB:175
Shropshire, William	Arlington	Account	1805	WBB:178; LVA-LP
Shropshire, Wm.	Alexandria	Tax Charge	1798	Tax PP 1798:17
Shropshire, Wm. & wife, watchmaker	Alexandria	Housekeeper	1799	1799(2):10A
Shropshur, William & wife Elizabeth	Alexandria	Resident	1800	1800(4):10B
Shubarts, Zachh.	Alexandria	Tax Charge	1790	Tax PP 1790:14
Shuck, Frederick	Alexandria	Resident	1800	1800(4):04B
Shuck, Frederick	Arlington	Ordinary	1805	OBL1(np)
Shuck, Frederick	Arlington	Ordinary	1805	OBL1(np)
Shuck, Fredk., carpenter & shopkeeper	Alexandria	Housekeeper	1808	1808(1):08A
Shuck, Jacob	Alexandria	Tax Charge	1790	Tax PP 1790:14
Shuck, Jacob	Alexandria	Tax Charge	1800	Tax PP 1800:39
Shuck, Jacob	Arlington	Ordinary	1802	OBL1(np)
Shuck, Jacob	Arlington	Ordinary	1803	OBL1(np)
Shuck, Jacob & Barberry	Alexandria	Resident	1800	1800(4):04B
Shuck, Jacob & wife, carpenter	Alexandria	Housekeeper	1799	1799(2):15A
Shuck, Jacob, carpenter	Alexandria	Head	1810	1810(1):06A
Shuck, Jacob, carpenter & shopkeeper	Alexandria	Housekeeper	1808	1808(1):08A
Shuck, Jacob, def.	Alexandria	Suit	1803	CRD:185
Shuck, Jacob, Duke St.	Alexandria	Occupant	1790	Tax L 1790:11
Shuck, Jacob, Duke St.	Alexandria	Owner	1790	Tax L 1790:11
Shuck, Jacob, house carpenter	Alexandria	Head	1800	1800(4):04A
Shugars, Michl.	Alexandria	Tax Charge	1796	Tax LP 1796:27
Shugars, Zachary	Alexandria	Owner	1787	Tax L 1787:24
Shugars, Zachary, Water St.	Alexandria	Occupant	1787	Tax L 1787:24
Shugart, Michl.	Alexandria	Tithable +16	1790	Tax PP 1790:06
Shugarts, Zachariah, Water St.	Alexandria	Owner	1790	Tax L 1790:11
Shugarts, Zachariah, Water St.	Alexandria	Occupant	1790	Tax L 1790:11
Shuke, Jacob	Alexandria	Tax Charge	1788	Tax PP 1788:15
Shuke, Jacob	Alexandria	Tax Charge	1789	Tax PP 1789:17
Shuke, Jacob	Alexandria	Tax Charge	1796	Tax PP 1796:17
Shuke, Jacob	Alexandria	Tax Charge	1798	Tax PP 1798:18
Shuke, Jacob	Alexandria	Tax Charge	1799	Tax PP 1799:39
Shull, Will.	Alexandria	Tax Charge	1800	Tax PP 1800:39
Shull, Wm.	Alexandria	Boarder	1808	1808(1):08A
Shum, Adam	Alexandria	Tax Charge	1795	Tax PP 1795:27
Shurman, Abram, cooper	Alexandria	Housekeeper	1808	1808(2):16A
Shurman, Martin	Alexandria	Tax Charge	1787	Tax PP 1787:14
Shurn, Adam, Fairfax St.	Alexandria	Occupant	1795	Tax L 1795:01
Shuter's Hill estate	Alexandria	Suit	1809	CRH:065
Shuttle, [blank], Fairfax St.	Alexandria	Occupant	1790	Tax L 1790:08
Shutz, A. Conard	Arlington	Admin.	1817	WB2:197
Shutz, Ann	Alexandria	Boarder	1799	1799(2):08A
Shutz, Clement	Alexandria	Tax Charge	1799	Tax PP 1799:37
Shutz, Conrad	Alexandria	Boarder	1799	1799(2):08A
Shutz, Conrad A.	Arlington	Sale	1817	AB3:044
Shutz, Conrad A.	Arlington	Inventory	1817	AB3:037; LVA-LP
Shutz, Conrad A.	Arlington	Account	1818	AB3:179; LVA-LP
Shutz, Conrad A., retailer	Alexandria	Housekeeper	1808	1808(1):01A
Shutz, Kitty	Alexandria	Boarder	1799	1799(2):08A
Sidebothom, Henry	Arlington	Apprentice	1827	OCR1822:130
Sidebottom, Ann	Arlington	Will	1865	WB8:213; File #618A

NAME OR SUBJECT	LOCATION	TYPE	YEAR	REFERENCE(S)
Sidebottom, Ann	Arlington	Appraisal	1865	WB8:226
Sidles, Philip, labourer	Alexandria	Head	1810	1810(1):05A
Silkman, Henry & wife Mary	Alexandria	Resident	1800	1800(4):08B
Silkman, Henry, ship carpenter	Alexandria	Head	1800	1800(4):08A
Sillick, Thomas	Arlington	Ordinary	1808	OBL2(np)
Sillickman, Henry	Alexandria	Tax Charge	1799	Tax PP 1799:38
Sillikman, Henry & wife, ship builder	Alexandria	Housekeeper	1799	1799(2):19A
Silman, Deborah, Wales' alley	Alexandria	Occupant	1795	Tax L 1795:21
Silvers, Wm.	Alexandria	Tax Charge	1795	Tax PP 1795:29
Silversmith, John, Fairfax St.	Alexandria	Occupant	1787	Tax L 1787:14
Silverthorn, James	Arlington	Apprentice	1812	OCR1811:046
Sim, Jesse	Alexandria	Tax Charge	1795	Tax PP 1795:29
Simm, Robert, Princess St.	Alexandria	Occupants	1790	Tax L 1790:13
Simmes, Thomas	Arlington	Ordinary	1807	OBL2(np)
Simmon, Samuel	Alexandria	Owner	1787	Tax L 1787:25
Simmon, Samuel & Co., Fairfax St.	Alexandria	Occupant	1787	Tax L 1787:25
Simmonds, Saml.	Alexandria	Tax Charge	1798	Tax PP 1798:17
Simmonds, Saml.	Alexandria	Tax Charge	1800	Tax PP 1800:40
Simmonds, Saml., Fairfax St.	Alexandria	Occupant	1790	Tax L 1790:10
Simmonds, Saml., Fairfax St.	Alexandria	Owner	1795	Tax L 1795:26
Simmonds, Saml., Royal St.	Alexandria	Occupant	1795	Tax L 1795:26
Simmonds, Saml., Royal St.	Alexandria	Owner	1795	Tax L 1795:26(2)
Simmonds, Samuel	Alexandria	Tax Charge	1796	Tax PP 1796:18
Simmonds, Samuel	Alexandria	Tax Charge	1799	Tax PP 1799:38
Simmonds, Samuel, Fairfax St.	Alexandria	Owner	1790	Tax L 1790:10(2)
Simmonds, Samuel, Royal St.	Alexandria	Owner	1790	Tax L 1790:10
Simmons, John (C), seaman & shopkpr.	Alexandria	Housekeeper	1808	1808(1):02A
Simmons, John, labourer	Alexandria	Head	1810	1810(1):02A
Simmons, Saml.	Alexandria	Tax Charge	1788	Tax PP 1788:15
Simmons, Saml.	Alexandria	Tax Charge	1790	Tax PP 1790:13
Simmons, Saml.	Alexandria	Tax Charge	1795	Tax PP 1795:28
Simmons, Saml.	Alexandria	Tax Charge	1796	Tax LP 1796:27
Simmons, Saml. & wife, shoemaker	Alexandria	Housekeeper	1799	1799(2):18A
Simmons, Saml., shoemaker	Alexandria	Housekeeper	1808	1808(1):06A
Simmons, Samuel	Alexandria	Tax Charge	1787	Tax PP 1787:13
Simmons, Samuel	Alexandria	Tax Charge	1789	Tax PP 1789:17
Simmons, Samuel, w(3), shoemaker	Alexandria	Head	1796	1796(3):4
Simmons, Samul & wife Jane	Alexandria	Resident	1800	1800(4):12B
Simmons, Susanah	Alexandria	Tax Charge	1800	Tax PP 1800:39
Simmons, William Thomas	Arlington	Apprentice	1845	OCR1842:098
Simmons, Wm.	Alexandria	Tax Charge	1796	Tax LP 1796:26
Simmos, Samul, shoemaker	Alexandria	Head	1800	1800(4):12A
Simms, Agnes Virginia (C)	Arlington	Apprentice	1843	OCR1842:021
Simms, Alexander, vendue crier	Alexandria	Head	1810	1810(3):07A
Simms, Alexr., bellman	Alexandria	Housekeeper	1808	1808(3):22A
Simms, Alonzo Smith, c/o Bersheba	Arlington	Apprentice	1825	OCR1822:097
Simms, Charles	Alexandria	Owner	1787	Tax L 1787:25
Simms, Charles	Alexandria	Tax Charge	1787	Tax PP 1787:14
Simms, Charles	Alexandria	Tax Charge	1789	Tax PP 1789:17
Simms, Charles	Alexandria	Tax Charge	1790	Tax PP 1790:13
Simms, Charles	Alexandria	Tax Charge	1796	Tax PP 1796:17
Simms, Charles	Alexandria	Deed	1798	CRF:197
Simms, Charles	Alexandria	Tax Charge	1800	Tax PP 1800:40
Simms, Charles	Arlington	Claim	1812	ACO:124
Simms, Charles	Arlington	Sale	1820	AB4:158
Simms, Charles	Arlington	Inventory	1820	AB4:139; LVA-LP
Simms, Charles	Arlington	Bond	1820	WB2:368
Simms, Charles	Arlington	Will	1820	WB2:358; File #174A
Simms, Charles	Arlington	Admin.	1836	WB4:104
Simms, Charles	Arlington	Account	1838	AB8:021; LVA-LP
Simms, Charles	Arlington	Account	1840	AB8:144

NAME OR SUBJECT	LOCATION	TYPE	YEAR	REFERENCE(S)
Simms, Charles & wife, attorney at law	Alexandria	Housekeeper	1799	1799(2):09A
Simms, Charles, at Brooke's Tavern	Alexandria	Deposition	1810	CRH:135
Simms, Charles, Col.	Arlington	Account	1842	WB5:042
Simms, Charles, Pitt St.	Alexandria	Occupant	1787	Tax L 1787:25
Simms, Charles, Pitt St.	Alexandria	Occupant	1790	Tax L 1790:10
Simms, Charles, Pitt St.	Alexandria	Owner	1790	Tax L 1790:10
Simms, Charles, plt.	Alexandria	Suit	1813	CRI:158
Simms, Charles, Wilks St.	Alexandria	Occupant	1787	Tax L 1787:03
Simms, Chas.	Alexandria	Tax Charge	1788	Tax PP 1788:15
Simms, Chas.	Alexandria	Tax Charge	1795	Tax PP 1795:28
Simms, Chas.	Alexandria	Tax Charge	1798	Tax PP 1798:18
Simms, Chas.	Alexandria	Tax Charge	1799	Tax PP 1799:39
Simms, Chas., Duke St.	Alexandria	Owner	1795	Tax L 1795:28
Simms, Chas., lawyer	Alexandria	Housekeeper	1808	1808(4):25A
Simms, Chas., Pitt St.	Alexandria	Owner	1795	Tax L 1795:28(2)
Simms, Chas., Pitt St.	Alexandria	Occupant	1795	Tax L 1795:28(2)
Simms, Chs.	Alexandria	Tax Charge	1796	Tax LP 1796:27
Simms, Colnl., atty. at law	Alexandria	Head	1810	1810(4):04A
Simms, Eleanor	Arlington	Will	1805	WBB:203; File #004A
Simms, Eleanor	Arlington	Bond	1805	WBB:205
Simms, Eleanor	Arlington	Inventory	1806	WBB:274; LVA-LP
Simms, Eleanor	Arlington	Account	1808	WBC:021; LVA-LP
Simms, Emily	Arlington	Guard.	1822	WB3:070
Simms, G.W.	Alexandria	Will	1882	WB1:363; LP
Simms, Geo.	Alexandria	Boarder	1808	1808(3):20A
Simms, Geo., house joiner	Alexandria	Head	1810	1810(3):05A
Simms, George	Arlington	Admin.	1834	WB4:101
Simms, George	Arlington	Account	1835	AB7:168; LVA-LP
Simms, George	Arlington	Account F.	1835	AB7:177; LVA-LP
Simms, James, drayman	Alexandria	Head	1810	1810(3):09A
Simms, Jesse	Alexandria	Tithable +21	1787	Tax PP 1787:16
Simms, Jesse	Alexandria	Tithable +16	1788	Tax PP 1788:17
Simms, Jesse	Alexandria	Tithable +16	1789	Tax PP 1789:19
Simms, Jesse	Alexandria	Tithable +16	1790	Tax PP 1790:15
Simms, Jesse	Alexandria	Tax Charge	1796	Tax LP 1796:26
Simms, Jesse	Alexandria	Tax Charge	1796	Tax PP 1796:18
Simms, Jesse	Alexandria	Tax Charge	1798	Tax PP 1798:17
Simms, Jesse	Alexandria	Tax Charge	1799	Tax PP 1799:39
Simms, Jesse	Alexandria	Tax Charge	1800	Tax PP 1800:40
Simms, Jesse	Arlington	Defendant	1801	PA:163
Simms, Jesse	Alexandria	Deposition	1805	CRG:029
Simms, Jesse, def.	Alexandria	Suit	1801	CRB:091
Simms, Jesse, def.	Alexandria	Suit	1801	CRB:205
Simms, Jesse, def.	Alexandria	Suit	1801	CRB:264, 269
Simms, Jesse, def.	Alexandria	Suit	1804	CRF:030
Simms, Jesse, def.	Alexandria	Suit	1808	CRF:334
Simms, John	Arlington	Ordinary	1820	OBL3(np)
Simms, John	Arlington	Ordinary	1822	OBL3(np)
Simms, John	Arlington	Ordinary	1822	OBL3(np)
Simms, John, at his house	Arlington	Ordinary	1824	OBL3(np)
Simms, John, at his house	Arlington	Ordinary	1825	OBL4(np)
Simms, John, at his house	Arlington	Ordinary	1828	OBL4(np)
Simms, John, at his house	Arlington	Ordinary	1829	OBL4(np)
Simms, John, at his house	Arlington	Ordinary	1830	OBL4(np)
Simms, John, at his house	Arlington	Ordinary	1831	OBL4(np)
Simms, John D., attr. at law	Alexandria	Head	1810	1810(1):11A
Simms, John, in Alexandria Co.	Arlington	Ordinary	1826	OBL4(np)
Simms, John, in Alexandria Co.	Arlington	Ordinary	1827	OBL4(np)
Simms, Joseph, of Philadelphia	Alexandria	Deed	1811	CRK:048
Simms, Maria	Arlington	Admin.	1812	WB1:201
Simms, Matilda	Arlington	Guard.	1821	WB2:400

NAME OR SUBJECT	LOCATION	TYPE	YEAR	REFERENCE(S)
Simms, Nancy	Arlington	Renounce	1820	File #175A
Simms, Nancy	Arlington	Renounce	1820	WB2:360; File #175A
Simms, Richard Alex., c/o Bersheba	Arlington	Apprentice	1811	OCR1811:279
Simms, Robert	Alexandria	Tax Charge	1787	Tax PP 1787:15
Simms, Robert	Alexandria	Tax Charge	1789	Tax PP 1789:16
Simms, Robert	Alexandria	Tax Charge	1790	Tax PP 1790:13
Simms, Robert, Fairfax St.	Alexandria	Occupant	1787	Tax L 1787:15
Simms, Robt.	Alexandria	Tax Charge	1788	Tax PP 1788:15
Simms, Sampson, c/o Elizabeth	Arlington	Apprentice	1811	OCR1811:042
Simms, Thomas	Alexandria	Tax Charge	1796	Tax LP 1796:27
Simms, Thomas	Alexandria	Tax Charge	1796	Tax PP 1796:18
Simms, Thomas	Alexandria	Tax Charge	1799	Tax PP 1799:38
Simms, Thomas	Alexandria	Mer. License	1799	Tax PP 1799:52-10r
Simms, Thomas	Alexandria	Mer. License	1800	Tax PP 1800:54(20)r
Simms, Thomas	Arlington	Plaintiff	1802	PA:200
Simms, Thomas	Arlington	Ordinary	1803	OBL1(np)
Simms, Thomas	Arlington	Inventory	1808	LP
Simms, Thomas	Arlington	Admin.	1808	WBC:055
Simms, Thomas	Arlington	Inventory	1808	WBC:060
Simms, Thomas	Arlington	Account	1809	WBC:240; LVA-LP
Simms, Thomas	Arlington	Sale	1809	WBC:198
Simms, Thomas, ret. liquor w/o license	Arlington	Defendant	1802	PA:235
Simms, Thos.	Alexandria	Tax Charge	1798	Tax PP 1798:17
Simms, Thos.	Alexandria	Mer. License	1798	Tax PP 1798:20-7
Simms, Thos.	Alexandria	Tax Charge	1800	Tax PP 1800:39
Simms, Thos.	Alexandria	Reference	1808	1808(3):19B
Simms, Thos., retailer & tavern lic.	Alexandria	Housekeeper	1808	1808(1):02A
Simms, William	Arlington	Ordinary	1820	OBL3(np)
Simms, William	Arlington	Ordinary	1822	OBL3(np)
Simms, William, at his house	Arlington	Ordinary	1825	OBL4(np)
Simms, William, at his house	Arlington	Ordinary	1826	OBL4(np)
Simms, William, at his house	Arlington	Ordinary	1827	OBL4(np)
Simms, William, at his house	Arlington	Ordinary	1828	OBL4(np)
Simms, William, at his house	Arlington	Ordinary	1829	OBL4(np)
Simms, William Douglass, c/o Bersheba	Arlington	Apprentice	1822	OCR1822:017a
Simms, William, in Alexandria Co.	Arlington	Ordinary	1824	OBL3(np)
Simms, William, near the Market	Arlington	Ordinary	1823	OBL3(np)
Simms, William, on Sharp Shin Alley	Arlington	Ordinary	1823	OBL3(np)
Simms, Zarah Winkfield, c/o Bersheba	Arlington	Apprentice	1815	OCR1811:278
Simond, Lewis	Alexandria	Account B.	1803	CRD:175
Simond, Lewis, plt.	Alexandria	Suit	1803	CRD:172
Simpkins, Maria A.	Arlington	Guard.	1846	OCR1842:196
Simpson, Ann	Arlington	Guard.	1806	WBB:334
Simpson, Ann, c/o Mary	Arlington	Apprentice	1813	OCR1811:159
Simpson, Francis	Arlington	Inventory	1815	AB2:102; LVA-LP
Simpson, Francis	Arlington	Admin.	1815	WB1:342
Simpson, Francis	Arlington	Account	1816	AB2:376; LVA-LP
Simpson, Francis, on Royal St.	Arlington	Ordinary	1845	OBL6(np)
Simpson, Francis, sailmaker	Alexandria	Head	1810	1810(1):09A
Simpson, Geo.	Alexandria	Boarder	1808	1808(4):27A
Simpson, George	Arlington	Account	1812	AB1:179; LVA-LP
Simpson, George	Arlington	Admin.	1812	WB1:162
Simpson, Gilbert	Arlington	Apprentice	1822	OCR1822:023a
Simpson, Gilbert	Alexandria	Will	1880	WB1:305; LP
Simpson, Hanson	Arlington	Inventory	1845	AB9:108; LVA-LP
Simpson, Hanson	Arlington	Account	1846	AB9:225; LVA-LP
Simpson, Hanson	Arlington	Bond	1846	OCR1842:191
Simpson, Hanson	Arlington	Admin. Bond	1848	ABB(np)
Simpson, Hanson [Sarah]	Arlington	Admin.	1845	OCR1842:106
Simpson, Harriet Ann (C)	Arlington	Apprentice	1826	OCR1822:121
Simpson, Jane, seamstress	Alexandria	Head	1810	1810(1):09A

NAME OR SUBJECT	LOCATION	TYPE	YEAR	REFERENCE(S)
Simpson, John	Alexandria	Tithable +16	1788	Tax PP 1788:16
Simpson, John	Alexandria	Tithable +16	1789	Tax PP 1789:18
Simpson, John	Alexandria	Tithable +16	1790	Tax PP 1790:15
Simpson, John	Alexandria	Deed	1796	CRI:071
Simpson, Jos.	Alexandria	Boarder	1799	1799(2):05A
Simpson, Lewis	Alexandria	Tax Charge	1799	Tax PP 1799:39
Simpson, Lewis	Alexandria	Tax Charge	1800	Tax PP 1800:40
Simpson, Lewis	Arlington	Ordinary	1802	OBL1(np)
Simpson, Lewis	Arlington	Ordinary	1803	OBL1(np)
Simpson, Lewis	Arlington	Ordinary	1805	OBL1(np)
Simpson, Lewis	Arlington	Ordinary	1806	OBL2(np)
Simpson, Lewis	Arlington	Ordinary	1808	OBL2(np)
Simpson, Lewis, shoemaker	Alexandria	Head	1810	1810(4):07A
Simpson, Lewis, shopkpr. & tavern lic.	Alexandria	Housekeeper	1808	1808(2):13A
Simpson, Lucy	Arlington	Admin.	1838	WB4:170
Simpson, Lucy	Arlington	Account	1840	AB8:170; LVA-LP
Simpson, Lucy	Arlington	Account	1841	AB8:170
Simpson, Lucy	Arlington	Account	1842	AB8:324; LVA-LP
Simpson, Margaret, washerwoman	Alexandria	Head	1810	1810(1):03A
Simpson, Mary, washer	Alexandria	Head	1795	1795(4):04
Simpson, Mrs., Water St.	Alexandria	Occupant	1795	Tax L 1795:30
Simpson, Peggy, sempstress	Alexandria	Housekeeper	1808	1808(1):01A
Simpson, Peter	Arlington	Inventory	1813	LVA-LP
Simpson, Peter	Arlington	Account	1813	LVA-LP
Simpson, Peter	Arlington	Will (N)	1813	WB1:236; File #110A
Simpson, Thomas	Alexandria	Tax Charge	1796	Tax PP 1796:18
Simpson, Thos.	Alexandria	Tax Charge	1795	Tax PP 1795:29
Simpson, Thos.	Alexandria	Tax Charge	1795	Tax PP 1795:28
Simpson, Thos.	Alexandria	Tax Charge	1796	Tax LP 1796:26
Simpson, William	Arlington	Inventory	1817	AB3:023; LVA-LP
Simpson, William	Arlington	Admin.	1817	WB2:193
Simpson, William	Arlington	Apprentice	1829	OCR1822:174a
Simpson, [blank], King St.	Alexandria	Occupant	1795	Tax L 1795:05
Sims, Ann	Arlington	Ordinary	1841	OBL6(np)
Sims, Ann, at her house	Arlington	Ordinary	1837	OBL5(np)
Sims, Ann, at her house	Arlington	Ordinary	1838	OBL5(np)
Sims, Charles, w(7)7, lawyer	Alexandria	Head	1796	1796(3):2
Sims, Thomas, w(1)1, innkeeper	Alexandria	Head	1796	1796(3):6
Sims, Thos.	Alexandria	Tax Charge	1795	Tax PP 1795:29
Sims, Thos. & wife, retailer	Alexandria	Housekeeper	1799	1799(2):01A
Sims, Thos., Prince St.	Alexandria	Occupant	1795	Tax L 1795:23
Sinclair, Horatio	Alexandria	Serv./Appt.	1800	1800(4):15B
Sinclair, Horatio	Alexandria	Serv./Appt.	1800	1800(4):15B
Sinclair, Horatio, clerk	Alexandria	Boarder	1799	1799(2):13A
Sinclair, John	Arlington	Apprentice	1811	OCR1811:039
Sinclair, John, on Cameron St.	Arlington	Ordinary	1844	OBL6(np)
Sincox, Mary, w/o Aaron	Alexandria	Will	1873	WB1:080; LP
Singler, [blank], carpenter	Alexandria	Boarder	1799	1799(2):06A
Singleton, Geo. & wife, carpenter	Alexandria	Housekeeper	1799	1799(2):17A
Singleton, George	Alexandria	Tax Charge	1799	Tax PP 1799:38
Singleton, George	Alexandria	Tax Charge	1800	Tax PP 1800:40
Singleton, George	Arlington	Inventory	1807	WBB:507; LVA-LP
Singleton, George	Arlington	Admin.	1807	WBB:504
Singleton, Mary, washwoman	Alexandria	Housekeeper	1808	1808(1):08A
Singlton, George & wife Mary	Alexandria	Resident	1800	1800(4):02B
Singlton, George, house carpenter	Alexandria	Head	1800	1800(4):02A
Sinon, Michael	Arlington	Apprentice	1824	OCR1822:060a
Sippet, Jno.	Alexandria	Tax Charge	1795	Tax PP 1795:27
Sisson, Carrie R.	Arlington	Will	1899	WB10:373; File #787A
Sisson, George, paitner & shopkeeper	Alexandria	Housekeeper	1808	1808(4):28A
Sisson, Rachel Ann	Arlington	Guard.	1853	BB(np)

NAME OR SUBJECT	LOCATION	TYPE	YEAR	REFERENCE(S)
Sisson, Sarah, c/o Lucy	Arlington	Apprentice	1846	OCR1842:181
Sisson, William A.	Alexandria	Will	1892	WB2:013; LP
Sitler, Philip	Arlington	Ordinary	1838	OBL5(np)
Skam, John	Alexandria	Tax Charge	1799	Tax PP 1799:38
Skelly, Levin	Arlington	Guard.	1808	WBC:096
Skidmore, Edward	Arlington	Inventory	1828	LVA-LP
Skidmore, Edward	Arlington	Will P.	1828	OCR1822:155a
Skidmore, Edward	Arlington	Admin.	1828	OCR1822:155a
Skidmore, Edward	Arlington	Bond	1828	WB3:332
Skidmore, Edward	Arlington	Will	1828	WB3:392; File #296A
Skidmore, Edward	Arlington	Account	1829	AB6:505; LVA-LP
Skidmore, Edward	Arlington	Account	1830	AB6:505
Skidmore, Elizabeth	Arlington	Inventory	1874	WB9:372
Skidmore, Gerard	Arlington	Admin. Bond	1849	ABB(np)
Skidmore, Gerrard	Arlington	Inventory	1849	WB5:207; LVA-LP
Skidmore, Gerrard	Arlington	Account	1850	WB5:292; LVA-LP
Skidmore, Isaac P.	Arlington	Will	1883	WB10:039; File #712A
Skidmore, Lewis	Alexandria	Boarder	1808	1808(1):01A
Skidmore, Lewis, c/o Edward	Arlington	Apprentice	1805	OCR1801:276
Skidmore, Louis E.	Alexandria	Will	1900	WB2:396; LP
Skidmore, Sarah	Arlington	Will	1866	WB8:363; File #642A
Skinner, George	Arlington	Will	1816	WB2:118; File #130A
Skinner, Theodore	Arlington	Inventory	1815	AB2:108; LVA-LP
Skinner, Theodore	Arlington	Bond	1815	WB2:010
Skinner, Theodore	Arlington	Will	1815	WB2:009
Skinner, Theodore	Arlington	Account	1816	AB2:268; LVA-LP
Skinner, Theodore	Arlington	Account	1817	LVA-LP
Skinner, Theodore	Arlington	Account	1818	AB3:261; LVA-LP
Skinner, Theodore, seaman	Alexandria	Housekeeper	1808	1808(1):03A
Skinner, Theodore, seaman	Alexandria	Head	1810	1810(1):07A
Skipton, William	Alexandria	Tax Charge	1799	Tax PP 1799:38
Skipton, Wm.	Alexandria	Boarder	1799	1799(2):06A
Skull, William	Alexandria	Tax Charge	1799	Tax PP 1799:38
Skull, Wm.	Alexandria	Resident	1800	1800(4):06B
Skull, Wm., coach maker	Alexandria	Boarder	1800	1800(4):06A
Slacem, Gabriel	Alexandria	Owner	1787	Tax L 1787:24
Slacem, Gabriel	Alexandria	Tax Charge	1796	Tax LP 1796:27
Slacem, George	Alexandria	Tax Charge	1796	Tax LP 1796:27
Slack, Thomas A.	Arlington	Will	1897	WB10:345; File #778A
Slacum, Emeline, c/o George	Arlington	Guard.	1810	WBC:524
Slacum, Gabriel, Wilkes St.	Alexandria	Owner	1790	Tax L 1790:11
Slacum, Geo. & wife, ship master	Alexandria	Head	1795	1795(4a):05
Slacum, Geo. & wife	Alexandria	Housekeeper	1799	1799(2):19A
Slacum, Geo., merchant	Alexandria	Housekeeper	1808	1808(1):07A
Slacum, George	Alexandria	Tax Charge	1796	Tax PP 1796:18
Slacum, George	Alexandria	Tax Charge	1798	Tax PP 1798:17
Slacum, George	Alexandria	Mer. License	1798	Tax PP 1798:20-7
Slacum, George	Alexandria	Tax Charge	1799	Tax PP 1799:39
Slacum, George	Alexandria	Tax Charge	1800	Tax PP 1800:40
Slacum, George	Arlington	Juryman	1808	ACO:081
Slacum, George	Arlington	Bond Made	1808	ACR:048
Slacum, George	Arlington	Admin.	1810	WBC:497
Slacum, George	Arlington	Inventory	1811	AB1:056; LVA-LP
Slacum, George	Arlington	Account	1811	AB1:134; LVA-LP
Slacum, George	Arlington	Account	1813	LVA-LP
Slacum, George	Arlington	Defendant	1821	ACO:198
Slacum, George & wife, mariner	Alexandria	Head	1795	1795(4):04
Slacum, George & wife Jane Harriot	Alexandria	Resident	1800	1800(4):07B
Slacum, George, assignee, plt.	Alexandria	Suit	1804	CRF:030
Slacum, George, children listed	Arlington	Account	1811	AB1:141
Slacum, George, counselman	Alexandria	Head	1800	1800(4):07A

NAME OR SUBJECT	LOCATION	TYPE	YEAR	REFERENCE(S)
Slacum, George, def.	Alexandria	Suit	1809	CRG:141
Slacum, George, merchant	Alexandria	Head	1810	1810(1):10A
Slacum, George, plt.	Alexandria	Suit	1808	CRF:334
Slacum, George Wash., c/o George	Arlington	Guard.	1810	WBC:524
Slacum, George, Wilkes St.	Alexandria	Owner	1790	Tax L 1790:11
Slacum, Helen Adela, c/o George	Arlington	Guard.	1810	WBC:524
Slacum, Jane H.	Arlington	Appraisal	1842	AB8:350; LVA-LP
Slacum, Jane H.	Arlington	Admin.	1842	OCR1842:010
Slacum, Jane H.	Arlington	Account	1842	OCR1842:012
Slacum, Jane H.	Arlington	Admin.	1842	WB4:310
Slacum, Jane H.	Arlington	Account	1843	AB8:410; LVA-LP
Slacum, Jane H.	Arlington	Inventory	1843	AB8:350
Slacum, Jane H.	Arlington	Account	1845	AB9:028; LVA-LP
Slacum, Jane H.	Arlington	Account	1846	AB9:215; LVA-LP
Slacum, Jane Harriet, c/o George	Arlington	Guard.	1810	WBC:524
Slacum, Julia Matilda, c/o George	Arlington	Guard.	1810	WBC:524
Slacum, Mary Louisa, c/o George	Arlington	Guard.	1810	WBC:524
Slacum, William A.	Arlington	Admin.	1842	OCR1842:004
Slacum, William A.	Arlington	Account	1844	AB9:012; LVA-LP
Slacum, William A., s/o Jane H.	Arlington	Debts	1844	AB9:014
Slacum, William Augustus	Arlington	Bond	1839	WB4:225, 303
Slacum, William Augustus	Arlington	Will	1839	WB4:224; File #374A
Slacum, William Augustus, c/o George	Arlington	Guard.	1810	WBC:524
Slade & Carne	Alexandria	Tax Charge	1796	Tax LP 1796:04
Slade, Charles	Alexandria	Tax Charge	1795	Tax PP 1795:29
Slade, Charles	Alexandria	Tax Charge	1796	Tax PP 1796:17
Slade, Charles	Alexandria	Tax Charge	1798	Tax PP 1798:17
Slade, Charles	Alexandria	Tax Charge	1799	Tax PP 1799:38
Slade, Charles	Arlington	Respondent	1812	ACO:129, 130
Slade, Charles	Alexandria	Agreement	1818	CRL:169
Slade, Charles	Arlington	Will	1820	WB2:394; File #126A
Slade, Charles	Arlington	Bond	1820	WB2:395
Slade, Charles	Arlington	Inventory	1821	AB4:226; LVA-LP
Slade, Charles	Arlington	Debts Due	1821	AB4:257
Slade, Charles	Arlington	Settlement	1821	AB5:001
Slade, Charles	Arlington	Sale	1821	AB4:234
Slade, Charles	Arlington	Account	1823	AB5:173; LVA-LP
Slade, Charles	Arlington	Account	1825	LVA-LP
Slade, Charles & wife Mary	Alexandria	Resident	1800	1800(4):08B
Slade, Charles, merchant	Alexandria	Head	1810	1810(1):04A
Slade, Charles, murchant	Alexandria	Head	1800	1800(4):08A
Slade, Chas., merchant	Alexandria	Housekeeper	1808	1808(1):04A
Slade, Chas., Pitt St.	Alexandria	Occupant	1795	Tax L 1795:06
Slade, Richard	Alexandria	Agreement	1818	CRL:169
Slaid, Charles	Alexandria	Tax Charge	1800	Tax PP 1800:40
Slakum, Gabriel, Fairfax St.	Alexandria	Owner	1795	Tax L 1795:28
Slakum, George	Alexandria	Tax Charge	1795	Tax PP 1795:28
Slakum, George, Fairfax St.	Alexandria	Owner	1795	Tax L 1795:28
Slakum, George, Water St.	Alexandria	Owner	1795	Tax L 1795:28
Slakum, George, Wilks St.	Alexandria	Occupant	1795	Tax L 1795:28
Slakum, George, Wilks St.	Alexandria	Owner	1795	Tax L 1795:28
Slater, Andrew	Arlington	Apprentice	1802	OCR1801:067
Slater, David, plt.	Alexandria	Suit	1801	CRC:190
Slater, John	Arlington	Will	1883	WB10:034; File #710A
Slater, Josiah	Arlington	Apprentice	1816	OCR1811:332
Slater, Matilda	Arlington	Will	1879	WB10:001; File #698A
Slater, Thos. & wife (C), ship builder	Alexandria	Housekeeper	1799	1799(2):19A
Slatford, G. William	Arlington	Admin.	1815	WB2:091
Slatford, Geo.	Alexandria	Tax Charge	1796	Tax LP 1796:26
Slatford, Geo. W., drayman	Alexandria	Housekeeper	1808	1808(2):17A
Slatford, Geo. W., drayman	Alexandria	Head	1810	1810(2):06A

NAME OR SUBJECT	LOCATION	TYPE	YEAR	REFERENCE(S)
Slatford, Geo., Water St.	Alexandria	Occupant	1795	Tax L 1795:17
Slatford, Geo., Water St.	Alexandria	Occupant	1795	Tax L 1795:12
Slatford, George	Alexandria	Tax Charge	1789	Tax PP 1789:16
Slatford, George	Alexandria	Tax Charge	1790	Tax PP 1790:14
Slatford, George	Alexandria	Tax Charge	1795	Tax PP 1795:27
Slatford, George	Alexandria	Tax Charge	1796	Tax PP 1796:17
Slatford, George W.	Alexandria	Tax Charge	1800	Tax PP 1800:39
Slatford, George W.	Arlington	Sale	1816	AB2:238
Slatford, George W.	Arlington	Account	1817	AB3:007; LVA-LP
Slatford, George W.	Arlington	Admin.	1834	WB4:102
Slatford, George W.	Arlington	Account	1835	AB7:184; LVA-LP
Slatford, George W.	Arlington	Account F.	1836	AB7:184
Slatford, George William	Arlington	Inventory	1815	AB2:218; LVA-LP
Slatford, George Wm.	Alexandria	Tax Charge	1798	Tax PP 1798:17
Slatford, George Wm.	Alexandria	Tax Charge	1799	Tax PP 1799:38
Slatford, James	Arlington	Ordinary	1822	OBL3(np)
Slatford, James, at his house	Arlington	Ordinary	1822	OBL3(np)
Slatford, Robert	Arlington	Account	1833	AB7:067; LVA-LP
Slatford, Robert	Arlington	Account	1835	AB7:176; LVA-LP
Slatford, Sarah	Alexandria	Boarder	1800	1800(4):13A
Slatford, Sarah	Alexandria	Resident	1800	1800(4):13B
Slatford, Thomas, at his house	Arlington	Ordinary	1830	OBL4(np)
Slatter, Thomas & wife Florrer	Alexandria	Resident	1800	1800(4):03B
Slatter, Thomas, ship carpenter	Alexandria	Head	1800	1800(4):03A
Slaymaker, A.H.	Alexandria	Will	1889	WB1:547; LP
Slaymaker, Amos B.	Alexandria	Will	1894	WB2:103; LP
Slimmer, C., Prince St.	Alexandria	Occupant	1787	Tax L 1787:16
Slimmer, Chr.	Alexandria	Tax Charge	1798	Tax PP 1798:17
Slimmer, Christian	Alexandria	Owner	1787	Tax L 1787:24
Slimmer, Christian	Alexandria	Tax Charge	1787	Tax PP 1787:14
Slimmer, Christian	Alexandria	Tax Charge	1788	Tax PP 1788:15
Slimmer, Christian	Alexandria	Tax Charge	1789	Tax PP 1789:17
Slimmer, Christian	Alexandria	Tax Charge	1790	Tax PP 1790:13
Slimmer, Christian	Alexandria	Tax Charge	1796	Tax LP 1796:27
Slimmer, Christian, Prince St.	Alexandria	Owner	1795	Tax L 1795:28
Slimmer, Christian, Union St.	Alexandria	Owner	1790	Tax L 1790:11
Slimmer, Christian, Union St.	Alexandria	Owner	1795	Tax L 1795:26
Slimmer, Christian, Water St.	Alexandria	Occupant	1787	Tax L 1787:05
Slimmer, Christian, Water St.	Alexandria	Occupant	1787	Tax L 1787:24
Slimmer, Christian, Water St.	Alexandria	Owner	1790	Tax L 1790:11
Slimmer, Christian, Water St.	Alexandria	Occupant	1790	Tax L 1790:11
Slimmer, Christian, Water St.	Alexandria	Occupant	1795	Tax L 1795:28
Slimmer, Christian, Water St.	Alexandria	Owner	1795	Tax L 1795:28
Slimmer, Christn.	Alexandria	Tax Charge	1795	Tax PP 1795:28
Slimmer, Daniel, b/o Jacob	Arlington	Apprentice	1805	OCR1801:271
Slimmer, Danl.	Alexandria	Boarder	1808	1808(4):25A
Slimmer, Jacob	Alexandria	Boarder	1808	1808(2):11A
Slimmer, Jacob	Arlington	Inventory	1811	AB1:094; LVA-LP
Slimmer, Jacob	Arlington	Account	1811	AB1:127; LVA-LP
Slimmer, Jacob	Arlington	Sale	1811	AB1:097
Slimmer, Jacob	Arlington	Admin.	1811	WB1:027
Sloan, Jno.	Alexandria	Tax Charge	1798	Tax PP 1798:18
Sloan, Jno. & wife, painter	Alexandria	Housekeeper	1799	1799(2):09A
Sloan, Jno., Duke St.	Alexandria	Occupant	1795	Tax L 1795:28
Sloan, John	Alexandria	Tithable +16	1789	Tax PP 1789:11
Sloan, John	Alexandria	Tax Charge	1790	Tax PP 1790:14
Sloan, John	Alexandria	Tax Charge	1795	Tax PP 1795:29
Sloan, John	Alexandria	Tax Charge	1796	Tax PP 1796:17
Sloan, John	Alexandria	Tax Charge	1799	Tax PP 1799:38
Sloan, John	Alexandria	Tax Charge	1800	Tax PP 1800:39
Sloan, John	Arlington	Inventory	1815	AB2:188; LVA-LP

NAME OR SUBJECT	LOCATION	TYPE	YEAR	REFERENCE(S)
Sloan, John	Arlington	Sale	1815	AB2:190
Sloan, John	Arlington	Will	1815	WB2:010
Sloan, John	Arlington	Bond	1815	WB2:071
Sloan, John	Arlington	Account	1816	AB2:340; LVA-LP
Sloan, John, glazier	Alexandria	Head	1810	1810(3):01A
Sloan, John, painter	Alexandria	Housekeeper	1808	1808(3):21A
Sloan, John, w(2), painter	Alexandria	Head	1796	1796(3):2
Sloane, Adam	Alexandria	Tax Charge	1790	Tax PP 1790:14
Sloane, James	Alexandria	Tax Charge	1787	Tax PP 1787:13
Sloane, John	Alexandria	Tithable +16	1789	Tax PP 1789:02
Slone, John	Alexandria	Tax Charge	1796	Tax LP 1796:26
Sloop *Intercourse*	Arlington	Suit	1821	ACO:198
Sloop *Intercourse*	Arlington	Suit	1822	ACO:205
Sloop *Intercourse*	Arlington	Suit	1823	ACO:211
Sloop *Little Rebecca*	Arlington	Suit	1804	ACO:025, 028
Sloop *Theoderick Armistead*	Arlington	Suit	1823	ACO:232
Sloop *Theoderick Armistead*	Arlington	Suit	1824	ACO:235
Sloop *Theoderick Armistead*	Arlington	Suit	1824	ACO:245
Sloop *Theoderick Armistead*	Arlington	Suit	1825	ACO:256
Sly, Thomas	Alexandria	Tax Charge	1789	Tax PP 1789:17
Smallwood, Benja.	Alexandria	Boarder	1799	1799(2):03A
Smallwood, Eleanor	Alexandria	Boarder	1799	1799(2):03A
Smallwood, Eliza	Alexandria	Boarder	1799	1799(2):03A
Smallwood, Horatio	Arlington	Apprentice	1802	OCR1801:066
Smallwood, Saml.	Alexandria	Tax Charge	1800	Tax PP 1800:39
Smallwood, Saml., shoemaker	Alexandria	Housekeeper	1799	1799(2):03A
Smedley, David	Arlington	Inventory	1826	AB6:212
Smedley, David	Arlington	Sale	1826	AB6:216
Smedley, David	Arlington	Bond	1826	WB3:241
Smedley, David	Arlington	Will	1826	WB3:239; File #249A
Smedley, David	Arlington	Account	1827	AB6:420; LVA-LP
Smedley, David, merchant	Alexandria	Housekeeper	1808	1808(4):27A
Smedley, David, merchant	Alexandria	Head	1810	1810(4):01A
Smith & Gahagan, Royal St.	Alexandria	Occupant	1787	Tax L 1787:02
Smith & McLean	Alexandria	Mer. License	1800	Tax PP 1800:54(20)r
Smith, A., King St.	Alexandria	Occupant	1787	Tax L 1787:20
Smith, A., King St.	Alexandria	Occupant	1787	Tax L 1787:24
Smith, A.J., Doctr.	Alexandria	Head	1810	1810(4):10A
Smith, Alex., gentleman	Alexandria	Housekeeper	1808	1808(1):03A
Smith, Alexander	Alexandria	Tax Charge	1787	Tax PP 1787:13
Smith, Alexander	Alexandria	Tax Charge	1789	Tax PP 1789:17
Smith, Alexander	Alexandria	Tax Charge	1796	Tax PP 1796:18
Smith, Alexander	Alexandria	Tax Charge	1799	Tax PP 1799:37
Smith, Alexander	Alexandria	Tax Charge	1800	Tax PP 1800:39
Smith, Alexander	Arlington	Plaintiff	1802	PA:280
Smith, Alexander	Arlington	Renounce	1804	WBB:036
Smith, Alexander	Arlington	Ordinary	1809	OBL2(np)
Smith, Alexander & Son	Alexandria	Mer. License	1799	Tax PP 1799:52-10w
Smith, Alexander, def.	Alexandria	Suit	1801	CRB:051
Smith, Alexander, def.	Alexandria	Suit	1806	CRE:065
Smith, Alexander, King St.	Alexandria	Owner	1790	Tax L 1790:11(2)
Smith, Alexr.	Alexandria	Owner	1787	Tax L 1787:24
Smith, Alexr.	Alexandria	Tax Charge	1788	Tax PP 1788:15
Smith, Alexr.	Alexandria	Tax Charge	1790	Tax PP 1790:14
Smith, Alexr.	Alexandria	Tax Charge	1795	Tax PP 1795:28
Smith, Alexr.	Alexandria	Tax Charge	1796	Tax LP 1796:26
Smith, Alexr.	Alexandria	Mer. License	1798	Tax PP 1798:20-7
Smith, Alexr.	Alexandria	Tax Charge	1798	Tax PP 1798:18
Smith, Alexr. & wife, inspector	Alexandria	Head	1795	1795(4a):02
Smith, Alexr. & wife, merchant	Alexandria	Housekeeper	1799	1799(2):04A
Smith, Alexr. & wife Rachel	Alexandria	Resident	1800	1800(4):04B

NAME OR SUBJECT	LOCATION	TYPE	YEAR	REFERENCE(S)
Smith, Alexr., gentleman	Alexandria	Housekeeper	1808	1808(1):08A
Smith, Alexr., King St.	Alexandria	Owner	1795	Tax L 1795:28
Smith, Alexr., merchant	Alexandria	Head	1800	1800(4):04A
Smith, Alexr., Princess St.	Alexandria	Occupant	1795	Tax L 1795:12
Smith, Alexr., Royal St.	Alexandria	Owner	1795	Tax L 1795:28
Smith, Alexr., Water St.	Alexandria	Occupant	1790	Tax L 1790:12
Smith, Alexr., Water St.	Alexandria	Owner	1795	Tax L 1795:28
Smith, Alfred A.	Arlington	Guard. Acct.	1856	WB7:080, 142; LVA-LP
Smith, Alfred A.	Arlington	Guard. Acct.	1858	WB7:305; LVA-LP
Smith, Alfred A.	Arlington	Guard. Acct.	1858	WB7:387; LVA-LP
Smith, Alfred A.	Arlington	Guard. Acct.	1861	WB8:054; LVA-LP
Smith, Alfred A.	Arlington	Guard. Acct.	1861	WB8:343, 435
Smith, Alfred A.	Arlington	Guard. Acct.	1867	WB8:554
Smith, Alfred A.	Arlington	Trustee Acct.	1868	WB9:127
Smith, Alfred A.	Arlington	Trustee Acct.	1869	WB9:156
Smith, Ann (C), washwoman	Alexandria	Housekeeper	1808	1808(4):26A
Smith, Ann, Royal St.	Alexandria	Occupant	1795	Tax L 1795:02
Smith, Ann, washer	Alexandria	Head	1795	1795(4):06
Smith, Astun, w3, gentleman	Alexandria	Head	1796	1796(3):3
Smith, Augustine	Arlington	Statement	1830	LVA-LP
Smith, Augustine J. & wife Susannah	Alexandria	Suit	1801	CRC:118
Smith, Augustine J., def.	Alexandria	Suit	1801	CRB:255
Smith, Calvin	Arlington	Guard. Acct.	1839	AB8:028; LVA-LP
Smith, Calvin	Arlington	Guard. Acct.	1840	AB8:114; LVA-LP
Smith, Calvin	Arlington	Guard. Acct.	1842	AB8:264
Smith, Calvin Andrew, c/o John Y.	Arlington	Guard.	1837	WB4:156
Smith, Catharine	Arlington	Apprentice	1842	OCR1842:013
Smith, Charles	Arlington	Ordinary	1820	OBL3(np)
Smith, Charlotte E.	Alexandria	Will	1880	WBC1:035; LP
Smith, Courtland H.	Alexandria	Will	1892	WB2:022; LP
Smith, D. Boyd	Arlington	Will	1865	WB8:255; File #630A
Smith, Daniel	Alexandria	Tax Charge	1788	Tax PP 1788:14
Smith, Daniel	Alexandria	Tax Charge	1789	Tax PP 1789:17
Smith, Daniel	Alexandria	Tax Charge	1790	Tax PP 1790:13
Smith, Daniel	Alexandria	Deposition	1803	CRH:025
Smith, Daniel	Arlington	Bond	1803	WBA:178
Smith, Daniel	Arlington	Will	1803	WBA:177; LVA-LP
Smith, Daniel	Arlington	Inventory	1803	WBA:203; LVA-LP
Smith, Daniel	Arlington	Account	1805	WBB:150; LVA-LP
Smith, Daniel, King St., tanyard	Alexandria	Occupant	1790	Tax L 1790:12
Smith, Danl., tanner	Alexandria	Boarder	1799	1799(2):12A
Smith, David	Arlington	Admin.	1809	WBC:216
Smith, David, b. Sterling, Scot.	Arlington	Alien Entry	1823	RA:18/08/23
Smith, David Boy	Arlington	Suit	1855	BB(np)
Smith, Edward	Arlington	Admin. Bond	1849	ABB(np)
Smith, Edward, c/o Edward	Arlington	Guard.	1855	BB(np)
Smith, Elihu Platt	Alexandria	Tax Charge	1790	Tax PP 1790:13
Smith, Elizabeth	Arlington	Guard.	1807	WBB:450
Smith, Elizabeth J.	Arlington	Account	1856	WB7:067; LVA-LP
Smith, Elizabeth J.	Arlington	Inventory	1857	WB7:242; LVA-LP
Smith, Elizabeth J.	Arlington	Appraisal	1857	WB7:239; LVA-LP
Smith, Francis L.	Alexandria	Will	1877	WBC1:023; LP
Smith, George (C)	Arlington	Apprentice	1845	OCR1842:113
Smith, George A.	Alexandria	Will	1889	WB1:526; LP
Smith, Hannah	Arlington	Admin.	1820	WB2:399
Smith, Hannah	Arlington	Account	1822	AB5:141; LVA-LP
Smith, Hannah	Arlington	Admin.	1834	WB4:103
Smith, Hannah	Arlington	Account	1836	AB7:225; LVA-LP
Smith, Harrerd, labourrer	Alexandria	Boarder	1800	1800(4):16A
Smith, Harriet	Alexandria	Will	1874	WB1:097; LP
Smith, Henry Erric	Arlington	Guard. Acct.	1854	WB6:305, 447

NAME OR SUBJECT	LOCATION	TYPE	YEAR	REFERENCE(S)
Smith, Henry Errick	Arlington	Guard. Acct.	1855	WB7:029, 174, 291
Smith, Henry Errick	Arlington	Guard. Acct.	1858	WB7:380, 515
Smith, Henry Errick	Arlington	Guard. Acct.	1861	WB8:065, 202; LVA-LP
Smith, Henry Errick, c/o Sidney W.	Arlington	Guard. Acct.	1850	WB5:258, 310; LVA-LP
Smith, Hesselius	Arlington	Guard. Acct.	1854	WB6:305, 447
Smith, Hesselius	Arlington	Guard. Acct.	1855	WB7:030, 173, 290
Smith, Hesselius	Arlington	Guard. Acct.	1858	WB7:380, 514; LVA-LP
Smith, Hesselius, c/o Sidney W.	Arlington	Guard. Acct.	1850	WB5:259, 310; LVA-LP
Smith, Hesselius, c/o Sidney W.	Arlington	Guard.	1852	BB(np)
Smith, Hugh	Alexandria	Deed	1790	CRC:134
Smith, Hugh	Alexandria	Tax Charge	1798	Tax PP 1798:17
Smith, Hugh	Alexandria	Mer. License	1798	Tax PP 1798:20-7
Smith, Hugh	Alexandria	Mer. License	1799	Tax PP 1799:52-10r
Smith, Hugh	Alexandria	Tax Charge	1799	Tax PP 1799:38
Smith, Hugh	Alexandria	Mer. License	1800	Tax PP 1800:54(20)r
Smith, Hugh	Arlington	Respondent	1812	ACO:123, 125
Smith, Hugh	Arlington	Libellant	1824	ACO:235
Smith, Hugh	Arlington	Libellant	1824	ACO:245
Smith, Hugh	Arlington	Libellant	1825	ACO:256
Smith, Hugh	Arlington	Will	1856	WB7:134; File #531A
Smith, Hugh	Arlington	Account	1856	WB7:144; LVA-LP
Smith, Hugh	Arlington	Account	1856	WB7:306, 329; LVA-LP
Smith, Hugh	Arlington	Appraisal	1857	WB7:181; LVA-LP
Smith, Hugh	Arlington	Account	1859	LVA-LP
Smith, Hugh	Arlington	Account	1860	WB8:010, 551; LVA-LP
Smith, Hugh	Arlington	Account	1868	WB9:130
Smith, Hugh C.	Arlington	Account	1856	WB7:074; LVA-LP
Smith, Hugh C.	Arlington	Account	1856	WB7:148, 307
Smith, Hugh C.	Arlington	Account	1858	WB7:388; LVA-LP
Smith, Hugh C.	Arlington	Accoungt	1859	WB7:538, 541; LVA-LP
Smith, Hugh C.	Arlington	Trustee Acct.	1861	WB8:058, 340, 429
Smith, Hugh C.	Arlington	Guard. Acct.	1861	WB8:055; LVA-LP
Smith, Hugh C.	Arlington	Account	1867	WB8:559
Smith, Hugh C.	Arlington	Trustee Acct.	1867	WB8:558
Smith, Hugh C.	Arlington	Trustee Acct.	1868	WB9:128
Smith, Hugh C.	Arlington	Account	1869	WB9:152, 154
Smith, Hugh C.	Arlington	Trustee Acct.	1869	WB9:157
Smith, Hugh C.	Arlington	Account	1877	WB9:454
Smith, Hugh C., Jr.	Arlington	Trustee Acct.	1856	WB7:147; LVA-LP
Smith, Hugh C., Jr.	Arlington	Trustee Acct.	1856	WB7:309; LVA-LP
Smith, Hugh C., Jr.	Arlington	Trustee Acct.	1857	WB7:385
Smith, Hugh Charles	Arlington	Bond	1854	BB(np)
Smith, Hugh Charles	Arlington	Will	1854	WB6:357; File #510A
Smith, Hugh Charles	Arlington	Appraisal	1854	WB6:383; LVA-LP
Smith, Hugh Charles	Arlington	Trustee Acct.	1856	WB7:079; LVA-LP
Smith, Hugh Charles	Arlington	Account	1866	WB8:326, 331, 430
Smith, Hugh, merchant	Alexandria	Boarder	1799	1799(2):13A
Smith, Hugh, merchant	Alexandria	Housekeeper	1808	1808(3):18A
Smith, Hugh, merchant	Alexandria	Head	1810	1810(3):05A
Smith, Hugh, plt.	Alexandria	Suit	1801	CRC:127
Smith, Isaac, plaisterer	Alexandria	Housekeeper	1808	1808(1):03A
Smith, J. & Co., Pitt St.	Alexandria	Occupant	1787	Tax L 1787:17
Smith, Jacob	Alexandria	Resident	1800	1800(4):02B
Smith, Jacob	Arlington	Admin.	1803	WBA:216
Smith, Jacob	Arlington	Inventory	1804	WBA:286; LVA-LP
Smith, Jacob	Arlington	Account	1804	WBA:289
Smith, Jacob	Arlington	Account	1804	WBB:071
Smith, Jacob, painter	Alexandria	Boarder	1800	1800(4):02A
Smith, Jacquelin	Arlington	Guard. Acct.	1859	WB7:438; LVA-LP
Smith, James	Alexandria	Tax Charge	1787	Tax PP 1787:13
Smith, James	Alexandria	Tax Charge	1788	Tax PP 1788:14

NAME OR SUBJECT	LOCATION	TYPE	YEAR	REFERENCE(S)
Smith, James	Alexandria	Tax Charge	1788	Tax PP 1788:15
Smith, James	Alexandria	Tax Charge	1789	Tax PP 1789:16
Smith, James	Alexandria	Tax Charge	1790	Tax PP 1790:13
Smith, James	Alexandria	Tax Charge	1795	Tax PP 1795:28
Smith, James	Arlington	Will	1851	WB5:314; File #467A
Smith, James	Alexandria	Will	1899	WB2:342; LP
Smith, James & wife, carpenter	Alexandria	Head	1795	1795(4):01
Smith, James, teacher	Alexandria	Head	1810	1810(1):03A
Smith, Jane	Alexandria	Boarder	1799	1799(2):15A
Smith, Jane	Arlington	Will	1899	WB10:363; File #785A
Smith, Jas.	Alexandria	Boarder	1808	1808(3):21A
Smith, Jas., retailer	Alexandria	Housekeeper	1808	1808(1):05A
Smith, Jas., taylor	Alexandria	Boarder	1799	1799(2):07A
Smith, Jesse	Arlington	Ordinary	1821	OBL3(np)
Smith, Jesse	Arlington	Ordinary	1823	OBL3(np)
Smith, Jesse	Arlington	Inventory	1827	LVA-LP
Smith, Jesse	Arlington	Admin.	1827	OCR1822:150a
Smith, Jesse	Arlington	Admin.	1827	WB3:299
Smith, Jesse	Arlington	Account	1829	AB6:478; LVA-LP
Smith, Jesse, at his house	Arlington	Ordinary	1824	OBL3(np)
Smith, Jesse, at his house	Arlington	Ordinary	1826	OBL4(np)
Smith, Jesse, at his house	Arlington	Ordinary	1827	OBL4(np)
Smith, Jesse, in Alexandria Co.	Arlington	Ordinary	1822	OBL3(np)
Smith, Jesse, in Alexandria Co.	Arlington	Ordinary	1825	OBL4(np)
Smith, Jno.	Alexandria	Boarder	1808	1808(1):03A
Smith, John	Alexandria	Tax Charge	1787	Tax PP 1787:14
Smith, John	Alexandria	Tax Charge	1788	Tax PP 1788:14
Smith, John	Alexandria	Tax Charge	1789	Tax PP 1789:17
Smith, John	Alexandria	Tax Charge	1790	Tax PP 1790:14
Smith, John	Alexandria	Tax Charge	1796	Tax LP 1796:26
Smith, John	Alexandria	Tax Charge	1796	Tax LP 1796:26
Smith, John	Alexandria	Tax Charge	1796	Tax PP 1796:18
Smith, John	Alexandria	Tax Charge	1798	Tax PP 1798:16
Smith, John	Alexandria	Tax Charge	1799	Tax PP 1799:38
Smith, John	Alexandria	Tax Charge	1799	Tax PP 1799:38(2)
Smith, John	Alexandria	Tax Charge	1799	Tax PP 1799:37
Smith, John	Alexandria	Serv./Appr.	1800	1800(4):04B
Smith, John	Alexandria	Resident	1800	1800(4):04B
Smith, John	Alexandria	Resident	1800	1800(4):02B
Smith, John	Alexandria	Tax Charge	1800	Tax PP 1800:40
Smith, John	Arlington	Ordinary	1803	OBL1(np)
Smith, John	Arlington	Ordinary	1808	OBL2(np)
Smith, John	Arlington	Ordinary	1808	OBL2(np)
Smith, John	Arlington	Ordinary	1809	OBL2(np)
Smith, John	Arlington	Ordinary	1810	OBL2(np)
Smith, John	Arlington	Apprentice	1811	OCR1811:043
Smith, John	Arlington	Apprentice	1826	OCR1822:113a
Smith, John	Arlington	Guard.	1826	OCR1822:113a
Smith, John, assignee, plt.	Alexandria	Suit	1802	CRD:048
Smith, John B., c/o Edward	Arlington	Guard.	1855	BB(np)
Smith, John, c/o Jane	Arlington	Apprentice	1803	OCR1801:135
Smith, John F.	Arlington	Bond	1823	WB3:165
Smith, John F.	Arlington	Inventory	1825	AB5:418; LVA-LP
Smith, John F.	Arlington	Will P.	1825	OCR1822:084
Smith, John F.	Arlington	Will	1825	WB3:162; File #230A
Smith, John F.	Arlington	Admin.	1836	WB4:110, 156
Smith, John F.	Arlington	Sale	1837	LVA-LP
Smith, John F.	Arlington	Account	1837	LVA-LP(2)
Smith, John F.	Arlington	Account	1839	AB7:312
Smith, John, Fairfax St.	Alexandria	Occupant	1787	Tax L 1787:08
Smith, John, grantor	Arlington	Indenture D.	1811	ID2:052

NAME OR SUBJECT	LOCATION	TYPE	YEAR	REFERENCE(S)
Smith, John, in jail	Arlington	Insolvent	1811	ID2:049
Smith, John Jacqueline, c/o Francis L.	Arlington	Guard.	1853	BB(np)
Smith, John P., tavern keeper	Alexandria	Head	1810	1810(2):08A
Smith, John, pasterer	Alexandria	Head	1810	1810(4):02A
Smith, John, plaisterer	Alexandria	Boarder	1800	1800(4):02A
Smith, John, plt.	Alexandria	Suit	1821	CRL:369
Smith, John, retailer & shopkeeper	Alexandria	Housekeeper	1808	1808(2):12A
Smith, John W.	Arlington	Ordinary	1821	OBL3(np)
Smith, John W.	Arlington	Will (NR)	1839	File #074A
Smith, John W., at his house	Arlington	Ordinary	1824	OBL3(np)
Smith, John W., at his house	Arlington	Ordinary	1825	OBL4(np)
Smith, John W., at his house	Arlington	Ordinary	1827	OBL4(np)
Smith, John W., at his house	Arlington	Ordinary	1828	OBL4(np)
Smith, John W., at his house	Arlington	Ordinary	1830	OBL4(np)
Smith, John W., at his house	Arlington	Ordinary	1831	OBL4(np)
Smith, John W., at his house	Arlington	Ordinary	1832	OBL4(np)
Smith, John W., at his house	Arlington	Ordinary	1834	OBL5(np)
Smith, John W., at his house	Arlington	Ordinary	1835	OBL5(np)
Smith, John W., at Alexandria	Arlington	Ordinary	1836	OBL5(np)
Smith, John W., at his house	Arlington	Ordinary	1837	OBL5(np)
Smith, John W., at his house	Arlington	Ordinary	1838	OBL5(np)
Smith, John W., at his house	Arlington	Ordinary	1841	OBL6(np)
Smith, John W., at his house	Arlington	Ordinary	1849	OBL6(np)
Smith, John W., grantee	Arlington	Indenture D.	1833	ID:416
Smith, John W., in Alexandria Co.	Arlington	Ordinary	1822	OBL3(np)
Smith, John W., in Alexandria Co.	Arlington	Ordinary	1829	OBL4(np)
Smith, John W., on Cameron St.	Arlington	Ordinary	1823	OBL3(np)
Smith, John W., on Union St.	Arlington	Ordinary	1841	OBL6(np)
Smith, John W., on Cameron St.	Arlington	Ordinary	1842	OBL6(np)
Smith, John W., on Cameron St.	Arlington	Ordinary	1843	OBL6(np)
Smith, John W., on Cameron St.	Arlington	Ordinary	1846	OBL6(np)
Smith, John, Washington St.	Alexandria	Occupant	1790	Tax L 1790:11
Smith, John, Washington St.	Alexandria	Owner	1790	Tax L 1790:11
Smith, John Y.	Arlington	Admin.	1825	OCR1822:104
Smith, John Y.	Arlington	Admin.	1825	WB3:206
Smith, Joseph	Alexandria	Reference	1808	1808(3):19B
Smith, Joseph	Alexandria	Head	1810	1810(3):05A
Smith, Joseph	Arlington	Apprentice	1828	OCR1822:157
Smith, Joseph	Arlington	Inventory	1846	AB9:262; LVA-LP
Smith, Joseph	Arlington	Debts Due	1846	AB9:263
Smith, Joseph	Arlington	Will P.	1846	OCR1842:184, 185
Smith, Joseph	Arlington	Will	1846	WB4:426; File #435A
Smith, Joseph	Arlington	Account	1847	AB9:307
Smith, Joseph	Arlington	Exor. Bond	1848	EBB(np)
Smith, Joseph	Arlington	Account	1867	WB8:526
Smith, Joseph, failed to appear as	Arlington	Juryman	1808	ACO:104
Smith, Joseph, merchant	Alexandria	Housekeeper	1808	1808(3):19A
Smith, Joseph, plt.	Alexandria	Suit	1822	CRL:574
Smith, Julia	Arlington	Guard. Acct.	1819	AB3:317; LVA-LP
Smith, Julia, c/o Robert	Arlington	Guard.	1816	WB2:144
Smith, Louisa A.	Alexandria	Will	1871	WB1:013; LP
Smith, Louisa S.	Arlington	Guard. Acct.	1839	AB8:028; LVA-LP
Smith, Louisa S.	Arlington	Guard. Acct.	1840	AB8:138; LVA-LP
Smith, Louisa Staten, c/o John Y.	Arlington	Guard.	1837	WB4:156
Smith, Margaret (Sommers)	Arlington	Guard. Acct.	1839	AB8:031; LVA-LP
Smith, Margaret V.	Arlington	Guard. Acct.	1859	WB7:438; LVA-LP
Smith, Marsalena	Arlington	Guard. Acct.	1829	AB6:471; LVA-LP
Smith, Marsalena, c/o Robert	Arlington	Guard.	1816	WB2:144
Smith, Martha Ann	Arlington	Apprentice	1826	OCR1822:116a
Smith, Mary	Arlington	Guard. Acct.	1854	WB6:304, 446
Smith, Mary, c/o Sidney W.	Arlington	Guard. Acct.	1850	WB5:258, 310; LVA-LP

NAME OR SUBJECT	LOCATION	TYPE	YEAR	REFERENCE(S)
Smith, Mary Jane	Arlington	Guard. Acct.	1856	WB7:081, 143; LVA-LP
Smith, Mary Jane	Arlington	Guard. Acct.	1856	WB8:082
Smith, Mary Jane	Arlington	Guard. Acct.	1858	WB7:304; LVA-LP
Smith, Mary Jane	Arlington	Guard. Acct.	1858	WB7:386; LVA-LP
Smith, Mary Jane, c/o John	Arlington	Guard.	1854	BB(np)
Smith, Mary R.	Arlington	Guard. Acct.	1849	LVA-LP
Smith, Michael	Alexandria	Will	1888	WB1:489; LP
Smith, Nancy	Alexandria	Head	1810	1810(4):04A
Smith, Peggy, washwoman	Alexandria	Housekeeper	1808	1808(1):06A
Smith, Peter	Alexandria	Tax Charge	1799	Tax PP 1799:37
Smith, Peter & wife (C), labourer	Alexandria	Housekeeper	1799	1799(2):05A
Smith, Philip (C), c/o Celia	Arlington	Apprentice	1846	OCR1842:159
Smith, Philip D., c/o Edward	Arlington	Guard.	1855	BB(np)
Smith, Polly (M), washer woman	Alexandria	Housekeeper	1799	1799(2):01A
Smith, R., Oronoka St.	Alexandria	Occupant	1787	Tax L 1787:20
Smith, Rachel	Arlington	Guard. Acct.	1854	WB6:304, 448
Smith, Rachel	Arlington	Guard. Acct.	1855	WB7:028, 172, 290
Smith, Rachel	Arlington	Guard. Acct.	1857	WB7:289
Smith, Rachel, c/o Sidney W.	Arlington	Guard. Acct.	1850	WB5:258, 310; LVA-LP
Smith, Rachel, c/o Sidney W.	Arlington	Guard.	1852	BB(np)
Smith, Rd.	Alexandria	Boarder	1808	1808(1):04A
Smith, Rebecca	Arlington	Bond	1803	WBA:172
Smith, Rebecca	Arlington	Will	1803	WBA:171; LVA-LP
Smith, Rebecca	Arlington	Inventory	1804	LVA-LP
Smith, Rebecca	Arlington	Account	1806	WBB:248; LVA-LP
Smith, Rebecca	Arlington	Account	1809	WBC:260; LVA-LP
Smith, Rebecca	Arlington	Account	1812	AB1:158; LVA-LP
Smith, Richard, master	Arlington	Respondent	1805	ACO:046
Smith, Richard, master	Arlington	Respondent	1805	ACO:042
Smith, Richard, master	Arlington	Respondent	1806	ACO:051
Smith, Robert	Alexandria	Tax Charge	1787	Tax PP 1787:14
Smith, Robert	Alexandria	Mer. License	1798	Tax PP 1798:20-7
Smith, Robert	Alexandria	Tax Charge	1799	Tax PP 1799:37
Smith, Robert	Alexandria	Tax Charge	1799	Tax PP 1799:37
Smith, Robert	Alexandria	Tax Charge	1799	Tax PP 1799:38
Smith, Robert	Alexandria	Mer. License	1799	Tax PP 1799:62 10r
Smith, Robert	Alexandria	Tax Charge	1800	Tax PP 1800:39
Smith, Robert	Arlington	Defendant	1802	PA:200
Smith, Robert	Arlington	Plaintiff	1802	PA:294
Smith, Robert	Arlington	Defendant	1805	ACO:045
Smith, Robert	Arlington	Sale	1815	AB2:119
Smith, Robert	Arlington	Inventory	1815	AB2:107; LVA-LP
Smith, Robert	Arlington	Admin.	1815	WB2:014
Smith, Robert	Arlington	Account	1816	AB2:386; LVA-LP
Smith, Robert, Baltimore, Md.	Alexandria	Deed	1793	CRD:142, 145
Smith, Robert, def.	Alexandria	Suit	1801	CRD:111, 128
Smith, Robert J.	Arlington	Inventory	1868	WB9:088
Smith, Robert J., notary public	Arlington	Appointment	1854	BB(np)
Smith, Robert, of Philadelphia	Alexandria	Deed	1811	CRK:048
Smith, Robert, stone cutter	Alexandria	Head	1810	1810(1):10A
Smith, Robert, waiter	Alexandria	Head	1810	1810(1):02A
Smith, Robt. & Co.	Alexandria	Mer. License	1798	Tax PP 1798:20-7
Smith, Robt. & wife, merchant	Alexandria	Housekeeper	1799	1799(2):06A
Smith, Robt. & wife, merchant	Alexandria	Housekeeper	1799	1799(2):07A
Smith, Robt., stone cutter	Alexandria	Boarder	1799	1799(2):10A
Smith, Robt., stonecutter	Alexandria	Housekeeper	1808	1808(1):04A
Smith, Saml.	Alexandria	Tax Charge	1790	Tax PP 1790:13
Smith, Saml. & wife, grocer	Alexandria	Housekeeper	1799	1799(2):16A
Smith, Samuel	Alexandria	Owner	1787	Tax L 1787:24
Smith, Samuel	Alexandria	Tax Charge	1787	Tax PP 1787:14
Smith, Samuel	Alexandria	Tax Charge	1799	Tax PP 1799:38

NAME OR SUBJECT	LOCATION	TYPE	YEAR	REFERENCE(S)
Smith, Samuel	Alexandria	Mer. License	1800	Tax PP 1800:54(20)r
Smith, Samuel	Alexandria	Tax Charge	1800	Tax PP 1800:39
Smith, Samuel, def.	Alexandria	Suit	1808	CRG:177
Smith, Samuel, grantee	Arlington	Indenture D.	1827	ID:091
Smith, Samuel, grantor	Arlington	Indenture D.	1831	ID:285
Smith, Samuel, in jail bounds	Arlington	Insolvent	1830	ID:281
Smith, Samuel, merchant	Alexandria	Head	1810	1810(2):03A
Smith, Samuel, St. Asaph St.	Alexandria	Occupant	1787	Tax L 1787:24
Smith, Sarah J.	Arlington	Guard. Acct.	1841	AB8:241
Smith, Sarah Keightley	Arlington	Will	1864	WB8:191; File #612A
Smith, Sidney W.	Arlington	Admin. Bond	1848	ABB(np)
Smith, Sidney W.	Arlington	Account	1849	WB5:256
Smith, Sidney W.	Arlington	Account	1852	WB6:024; LVA-LP
Smith, Sidney W.	Arlington	Account C.	1854	WB6:445; LVA-LP
Smith, Sidney W.	Arlington	Rents	1854	WB6:303; LVA-LP
Smith, Sidney W., orphans of	Arlington	Guard. Acct.	1852	WB6:074; LVA-LP
Smith, Simon	Alexandria	Tax Charge	1790	Tax PP 1790:14
Smith, Sydney W.	Arlington	Rents	1855	WB7:027; LVA-LP
Smith, Sydney W.	Arlington	Rents	1858	WB7:381; LVA-LP
Smith, Sydney W., children of	Arlington	Guard. Acct.	1856	WB7:288; LVA-LP
Smith, Sydney W., children of	Arlington	Guard. Acct.	1857	WB7:171; LVA-LP
Smith, Sydney W., children of	Arlington	Guard. Acct.	1860	LVA-LP
Smith, Terry (C), washwoman	Alexandria	Housekeeper	1808	1808(3):20A
Smith, Theodore E.	Arlington	Apprentice	1826	OCR1822:119
Smith, Thomas	Arlington	Admin.	1803	WBA:169
Smith, Thomas	Arlington	Inventory	1804	WBB:012; LVA-LP
Smith, Thomas	Arlington	Account	1805	LVA-LP
Smith, Thomas	Arlington	Account	1805	WBB:120, 248, 398
Smith, Thomas	Arlington	Account	1807	LVA-LP
Smith, Thomas	Arlington	Apprentice	1815	OCR1811:289
Smith, Thomas	Arlington	Account F.	1818	AB3:125
Smith, Thomas L.	Arlington	Deposition	1831	ACR:082
Smith, Thomas, labourer	Alexandria	Head	1810	1810(1):02A
Smith, Thos.	Alexandria	Tax Charge	1800	Tax PP 1800:39
Smith, Thos.	Alexandria	License Due	1800	Tax PP 1800:54(24)
Smith, Thos.	Alexandria	Boarder	1808	1808(3):18A
Smith, Thos.	Alexandria	Boarder	1808	1808(3):20A
Smith, Thos., seaman	Alexandria	Housekeeper	1808	1808(1):06A
Smith, Thos., shoemaker	Alexandria	Housekeeper	1808	1808(4):25A
Smith to Cather	Arlington	Letter	1805	WBB:396
Smith, Townsend D., c/o Edward	Arlington	Guard.	1855	BB(np)
Smith, William	Alexandria	Tax Charge	1787	Tax PP 1787:15
Smith, William	Alexandria	Tax Charge	1799	Tax PP 1799:37
Smith, William	Alexandria	Tax Charge	1799	Tax PP 1799:38
Smith, William	Arlington	Inventory	1816	AB2:317; LVA-LP
Smith, William	Arlington	Sale	1816	AB2:320
Smith, William	Arlington	Bond	1816	WB2:127
Smith, William	Arlington	Will	1816	WB2:125; File #132A
Smith, William	Arlington	Account	1817	AB3:051; LVA-LP
Smith, William (C)	Arlington	Crime	1799	OT:06/11/1799
Smith, William A.	Alexandria	Will	1898	WB2:259; LP
Smith, William, c/o Nancy	Arlington	Apprentice	1815	OCR1811:236
Smith, William, c/o Nancy	Arlington	Apprentice	1817	OCR1811:356
Smith, William, Capn.	Alexandria	Tax Charge	1800	Tax PP 1800:40
Smith, William, labourer	Alexandria	Head	1810	1810(4):09A
Smith, William, merchant, plt.	Alexandria	Suit	1805	CRE:001
Smith, William Taylor	Arlington	Suit	1855	BB(np)
Smith, William, w(2), carpenter	Alexandria	Head	1796	1796(3):1
Smith, Wm.	Alexandria	Tax Charge	1795	Tax PP 1795:28
Smith, Wm.	Alexandria	Tax Charge	1795	Tax PP 1795:27
Smith, Wm.	Alexandria	Tax Charge	1796	Tax LP 1796:26

NAME OR SUBJECT	LOCATION	TYPE	YEAR	REFERENCE(S)
Smith, Wm.	Alexandria	Tax Charge	1796	Tax PP 1796:17
Smith, Wm.	Alexandria	Boarder	1808	1808(3):19A
Smith, Wm., Washington St.	Alexandria	Occupant	1795	Tax L 1795:26
Smith, Wm., Washington St.	Alexandria	Owner	1795	Tax L 1795:26
Smith, Wm., Wilks St.	Alexandria	Occupant	1787	Tax L 1787:06
Smith, [blank]	Alexandria	Boarder	1808	1808(4):24A
Smith [Smyth], William	Arlington	Guard. Acct.	1841	AB8:241
Smock, Rob.	Alexandria	Tax Charge	1798	Tax PP 1798:18
Smock, Robert	Alexandria	Tax Charge	1796	Tax LP 1796:27
Smock, Robert	Alexandria	Tax Charge	1799	Tax PP 1799:39
Smoot, Anna C.	Arlington	Guard. Acct.	1854	WB6:373; LVA-LP
Smoot, Bartin & wife, mariner	Alexandria	Head	1795	1795(4):07
Smoot, Charles C.	Arlington	Will	1867	WB9:001; File #656A
Smoot, Charles C.	Alexandria	Will	1882	WBC1:044; LP
Smoot, Christiana A.	Arlington	Guard. Acct.	1854	WB6:373; LVA-LP
Smoot, Christiana A., c/o James E.	Arlington	Guard.	1849	GBB(np)
Smoot, French	Alexandria	Will	1897	WB2:247; LP
Smoot, George H.	Arlington	Will	1870	WB9:234; File #679A
Smoot, George H.	Arlington	Account	1871	WB9:330
Smoot, George Hendly	Arlington	Apprentice	1816	OCR1811:345
Smoot, Hezekiah	Alexandria	Tax Charge	1795	Tax PP 1795:28
Smoot, Hezekiah	Alexandria	Tax Charge	1798	Tax PP 1798:17
Smoot, Hezekiah	Alexandria	Tax Charge	1799	Tax PP 1799:38
Smoot, Hezekiah	Alexandria	Mer. License	1799	Tax PP 1799:52-10w
Smoot, Hezekiah	Alexandria	Mer. License	1800	Tax PP 1800:54(20)r
Smoot, Hezekiah	Alexandria	Tax Charge	1800	Tax PP 1800:40
Smoot, Hezekiah	Arlington	Admin.	1804	WBB:095
Smoot, Hezekiah	Arlington	Inventory	1805	WBB:127
Smoot, Hezekiah	Arlington	Account	1805	WBB:214; LVA-LP
Smoot, Hezekiah	Arlington	Stock Sale	1805	WBB:215
Smoot, Hezekiah	Arlington	Sale	1805	WBB:130
Smoot, Hezekiah & wife, merchant	Alexandria	Housekeeper	1799	1799(2):13A
Smoot, Hezekiah B.	Arlington	Will	1857	WB7:160; File #534A
Smoot, Ida Virginia	Arlington	Guard. Acct.	1854	WB6:374; LVA-LP
Smoot, James E.	Arlington	Admin. Bond	1849	ABB(np)
Smoot, James H.	Arlington	Guard. Acct.	1816	AB2:382
Smoot, James Henley, c/o Hezekiah	Arlington	Guard.	1811	WB1:115
Smoot, James R.	Arlington	Guard. Acct.	1854	WB6:373; LVA-LP
Smoot, James R., c/o James E.	Arlington	Guard.	1849	GBB(np)
Smoot, Josiah H.D.	Alexandria	Will	1888	WBC1:052; LP
Smoot, Laura E.	Arlington	Guard. Acct.	1854	WB6:374; LVA-LP
Smoot, Susanna	Arlington	Guard. Acct.	1816	AB2:382
Smoot, Susanna, c/o Hezekiah	Arlington	Guard.	1811	WB1:115
Smoot, Susanna W.	Arlington	Guard.	1820	WB2:368
Smoot, William A.	Arlington	Guard. Acct.	1854	WB6:373; LVA-LP
Smoot, Wilson, clerk	Alexandria	Boarder	1799	1799(2):13A
Smoot, Wm., seaman	Alexandria	Head	1810	1810(1):12A
Smooth, Martin, Wales' alley	Alexandria	Occupant	1795	Tax L 1795:23
Smut, Wilson, clerk	Alexandria	Boarder	1800	1800(4):14A
Smute, Hezekel, murchant	Alexandria	Head	1800	1800(4):14A
Smute, Hezekiah & wife Elizebeth	Alexandria	Resident	1800	1800(4):14B
Smute, Wilson	Alexandria	Resident	1800	1800(4):14B
Smyth, Abram H.	Arlington	Guard. Acct.	1845	AB9:033; LVA-LP
Smyth, Abram H.	Arlington	Guard. Acct.	1846	AB9:158; LVA-LP
Smyth, Abram H.	Arlington	Guard. Acct.	1848	WB5:096; LVA-LP
Smyth, Abram H.	Arlington	Guard. Acct.	1848	WB5:165
Smyth, Abram H.	Arlington	Guard. Acct.	1849	LVA-LP
Smyth, Abram H.	Arlington	Guard. Acct.	1852	WB6:062; LVA-LP
Smyth, Abram Hewes	Arlington	Guard. Acct.	1842	AB8:290
Smyth, Abram Hewes	Arlington	Guard. Acct.	1844	AB8:455; LVA-LP
Smyth, Abram Hewes, c/o William	Arlington	Guard.	1840	WB4:269

NAME OR SUBJECT	LOCATION	TYPE	YEAR	REFERENCE(S)
Smyth, Abram Hewes, c/o William	Arlington	Guard. Acct.	1847	AB9:284
Smyth, Edward	Arlington	Inventory	1848	WB5:206; LVA-LP
Smyth, Edward	Arlington	Exor. Bond	1849	EBB(np)
Smyth, Edward	Arlington	Will	1849	WB5:167; File #452A
Smyth, Edward, b. Cavan	Arlington	Alien Entry	1819	RA:08/03/19
Smyth, Elizabeth	Alexandria	Will	1896	WB2:156; LP
Smyth, Mary M.	Alexandria	Will	1892	WB2:034; LP
Smyth, Mary R.	Arlington	Guard. Acct.	1848	WB5:097; LVA-LP
Smyth, Mary R., c/o William	Arlington	Guard.	1840	WB4:269
Smyth, Mary Russell	Arlington	Guard. Acct.	1842	AB8:290
Smyth, Mary Russell	Arlington	Guard. Acct.	1844	AB8:455; LVA-LP
Smyth, Mary Russell	Arlington	Guard. Acct.	1845	AB9:033; LVA-LP
Smyth, Mary Russell	Arlington	Guard. Acct.	1846	AB9:158; LVA-LP
Smyth, Mary Russell	Arlington	Guard. Acct.	1852	WB6:069; LVA-LP
Smyth, Mary Russell, c/o William	Arlington	Guard. Acct.	1847	AB9:284
Smyth, S.J.	Arlington	Guard. Acct.	1848	WB5:104
Smyth, Samuel, c/o William	Arlington	Guard.	1840	WB4:270
Smyth, Samuel M.	Arlington	Guard. Acct.	1841	AB8:289; LVA-LP
Smyth, Samuel M.	Arlington	Guard. Acct.	1842	AB8:289
Smyth, Samuel M.	Arlington	Guard. Acct.	1845	AB9:033; LVA-LP
Smyth, Samuel M.	Arlington	Guard. Acct.	1846	AB9:158; LVA-LP
Smyth, Samuel M.	Arlington	Guard. Acct.	1848	WB5:107; LVA-LP
Smyth, Samuel M.	Arlington	Guard. Acct.	1849	WB5:173; LVA-LP
Smyth, Samuel M.	Arlington	Guard. Acct.	1852	WB6:067; LVA-LP
Smyth, Samuel Miller	Arlington	Guard. Acct.	1844	AB8:455; LVA-LP
Smyth, Samuel Miller, c/o William	Arlington	Guard. Acct.	1847	AB9:284
Smyth, Sarah J.	Arlington	Guard. Acct.	1842	AB8:302
Smyth, Sarah J.	Arlington	Guard. Acct.	1844	AB8:425
Smyth, Sarah J.	Arlington	Guard. Acct.	1845	AB9:032; LVA-LP
Smyth, Sarah J.	Arlington	Guard. Acct.	1846	AB9:159; LVA-LP
Smyth, Sarah J.	Arlington	Guard. Acct.	1847	AB9:283
Smyth, Sarah J.	Arlington	Guard. Acct.	1848	WB5:094; LVA-LP
Smyth, Sarah J.	Arlington	Guard. Acct.	1849	WB5:164; LVA-LP
Smyth, Sarah J.	Arlington	Guard. Acct.	1852	WB6:058; LVA-LP
Smyth, Sarah J.	Arlington	Guard. Acct.	1852	WB6:070; LVA-LP
Smyth, Sarah Jane, c/o William	Arlington	Guard.	1840	WB4:251
Smyth, William	Arlington	Guard. Acct.	1842	AB8:302
Smyth, William	Arlington	Guard. Acct.	1844	AB8:425; LVA-LP
Smyth, William	Arlington	Guard. Acct.	1845	AB9:032; LVA-LP
Smyth, William	Arlington	Guard. Acct.	1846	AB9:159; LVA-LP
Smyth, William	Arlington	Guard. Acct.	1847	AB9:282
Smyth, William	Arlington	Guard. Acct.	1848	WB5:095; LVA-LP
Smyth, William	Arlington	Guard. Acct.	1848	WB5:166; LVA-LP
Smyth, William	Arlington	Guard. Acct.	1852	WB6:079; LVA-LP
Smyth, William	Arlington	Guard. Acct.	1852	WB6:057; LVA-LP
Smyth, William, c/o William	Arlington	Guard.	1840	WB4:251
Smyth, William, children of	Arlington	Guard. Acct.	1842	OCR1842:002
Smyth, William, orphans of	Arlington	Guard. Acct.	1841	AB8:289; LVA-LP
Snell, Catherine	Arlington	Guard.	1810	WBC:343
Snell, Leonard	Alexandria	Tax Charge	1799	Tax PP 1799:38
Snider, John	Alexandria	Tax Charge	1787	Tax PP 1787:14
Snider, John	Alexandria	Tax Charge	1788	Tax PP 1788:15
Snider, John	Alexandria	Tax Charge	1790	Tax PP 1790:14
Snow, Gideon	Alexandria	Tithable +16	1788	Tax PP 1788:13
Snow, Gideon	Alexandria	Tithable +16	1789	Tax PP 1789:14
Snow, Gideon	Alexandria	Tithable +16	1790	Tax PP 1790:11
Snowden, Edgar	Arlington	Guard.	1830	WB3:378
Snowden, Edgar	Alexandria	Will	1875	WB1:169; LP
Snowden, Louisa J.	Alexandria	Will	1897	WBC1:070; LP
Snowden, Saml., printer	Alexandria	Housekeeper	1808	1808(2):15A
Snowden, Samuel	Alexandria	Deposition	(nd)	CRE:346

NAME OR SUBJECT	LOCATION	TYPE	YEAR	REFERENCE(S)
Snowden, Samuel, printer	Alexandria	Housekeeper	1808	1808(1):01A
Snowden, Samuel, printer	Alexandria	Head	1810	1810(2):02A
Snowden, Sarah, washer woman	Alexandria	Housekeeper	1799	1799(2):05A
Snyder, Elizabeth Ann	Arlington	Appraisal	1865	WB8:258
Snyder, Elizabeth Ann	Arlington	Will	1865	WB8:249; File #627A
Snyder, Elizabeth Ann	Arlington	Inventory	1865	WB8:260
Snyder, John	Alexandria	Tax Charge	1789	Tax PP 1789:17
Snyder, John	Arlington	Objection	1862	LVA-LP
Snyder, Mat.	Alexandria	Boarder	1808	1808(3):21A
Snyder, Mathew, tinman	Alexandria	Housekeeper	1808	1808(3):21A
Snyder, Mathias	Arlington	Libellant	1804	ACO:025, 028
Snyder, Mathias, tinman	Alexandria	Head	1810	1810(4):01A
Snyder, Robert R.	Arlington	Will	1864	WB8:211; File #616A
Soap Factory	Arlington	Reference	1839	LSA:041, 044
Sobey, Linney	Alexandria	Resident	1800	1800(4):05B
Soloman, Jacob & wife, labourer	Alexandria	Head	1795	1795(4):05
Soloman, Sarah (C), washwoman	Alexandria	Housekeeper	1808	1808(3):20A
Solomon, Ann	Arlington	Will	1863	WB8:146; File #598A
Solomon, Ann	Arlington	Appraisal	1863	WB8:150
Solomon, Ann	Arlington	Account	1865	WB8:229
Solomon, Samuel	Arlington	Bond	1851	BB(np)
Solomon, Samuel	Arlington	Will	1851	WB5:308; File #466A
Solomon, William	Arlington	Proof	1858	LVA-LP
Solomon, William (C)	Arlington	Will	1858	WB7:364; File #559A
Sombey, Samson, ship carpenter	Alexandria	Head	1800	1800(4):11A
Somers, Abraham K.	Arlington	Defendant	1841	LSA:075
Somers, Adelina Virginia	Arlington	Defendant	1841	LSA:075
Somers, Ann Elizabeth	Arlington	Defendant	1841	LSA:075
Somers, Charles A.	Arlington	Defendant	1841	LSA:075
Somers, Eliza	Arlington	Defendant	1841	LSA:075
Somers, Henry, brickmaker	Alexandria	Boarder	1799	1799(2):12A
Somers, J.	Arlington	Plat	1841	LSA:080
Somers, John	Arlington	Inventory	1816	AB2:310; LVA-LP
Somers, John A., children of	Arlington	Defendant	1841	LSA:075
Somers, John, Capt.	Arlington	Account	1817	AB3:061; LVA-LP
Somers, John, in Fairfax Co.	Arlington	Inventory	1817	AB3:055, LVA-LP
Somers, John W.	Arlington	Defendant	1841	LSA:075
Somers, Simon, Col., d. 1836	Arlington	Suit	1837	LSA:025, 075
Somers, Simon, house of	Arlington	Plats	1837	LSA:029-032
Somers, Simon L.	Arlington	Defendant	1841	LSA:075
Somers, [blank], mariner	Alexandria	Head	1810	1810(1):08A
Somerville, estate called	Arlington	Suit	1837	LSA:075
Something, Fredk.	Alexandria	Boarder	1808	1808(4):25A
Something, John	Alexandria	Boarder	1808	1808(2):16A
Something, Thos. (non-citizen, servant)	Alexandria	Tithable +21	1787	Tax PP 1787:10
Sommers, A. Henry, c/o John A.	Arlington	Guard. Acct.	1844	AB8:496; LVA-LP
Sommers, Abram H., c/o John	Arlington	Guard.	1837	WB4:151
Sommers, Adelia V.	Arlington	Guard. Acct.	1839	AB8:043; LVA-LP
Sommers, Adelina Virginia	Arlington	Will	1890	WB10:175; File #746A
Sommers, Adelinah, c/o John	Arlington	Guard.	1837	WB4:157
Sommers, Ann E.	Arlington	Guard. Acct.	1839	AB8:043; LVA-LP
Sommers, Ann E.	Arlington	Guard. Acct.	1840	AB8:068; LVA-LP
Sommers, Ann E.	Arlington	Guard. Acct.	1841	AB8:201
Sommers, Ann Elizabeth	Arlington	Guard. Acct.	1846	AB9:154; LVA-LP
Sommers, Ann Elizabeth, c/o John A.	Arlington	Guard. Acct.	1844	AB8:496; LVA-LP
Sommers, Ann Elizabeth, c/o John A.	Arlington	Guard. Acct.	1844	AB8:495; LVA-LP
Sommers, Charles	Arlington	Guard. Acct.	1840	AB8:070; LVA-LP
Sommers, Charles A., c/o John	Arlington	Guard.	1837	WB4:149
Sommers, Charles Y.	Arlington	Guard. Acct.	1841	AB8:201
Sommers, Eliza	Arlington	Exor. Bond	1848	EBB(np)
Sommers, Eliza	Arlington	Inventory	1848	WB5:109

NAME OR SUBJECT	LOCATION	TYPE	YEAR	REFERENCE(S)
Sommers, Eliza	Arlington	Will	1848	WB5:107; File #447A
Sommers, Eliza	Arlington	Account	1851	WB5:209; LVA-LP
Sommers, Eliza	Arlington	Account	1851	WB5:315; LVA-LP
Sommers, Eliza	Arlington	Account	1852	WB6:160; LVA-LP
Sommers, Eliza	Arlington	Distribution	1860	WB8:013; LVA-LP
Sommers, Elizabeth A., c/o John	Arlington	Guard.	1837	WB4:149
Sommers, Henry	Arlington	Guard. Acct.	1839	AB8:045; LVA-LP
Sommers, Henry	Arlington	Guard. Acct.	1840	AB8:068; LVA-LP
Sommers, Henry	Arlington	Guard. Acct.	1841	AB8:200
Sommers, Henry, c/o John A.	Arlington	Guard. Acct.	1844	AB8:495; LVA-LP
Sommers, John	Arlington	Admin.	1816	WB2:123
Sommers, John A.	Arlington	Will	1828	WB3:326; File #277A
Sommers, John A.	Arlington	Bond	1828	WB3:327
Sommers, John A.	Arlington	Account	1839	AB8:078; LVA-LP
Sommers, John A.	Arlington	Account	1840	AB8:078
Sommers, John A., c/o John	Arlington	Guard.	1837	WB4:154
Sommers, John, children of	Arlington	Guard. Acct.	1839	AB8:036; LVA-LP
Sommers, John W.	Arlington	Guard. Acct.	1839	AB8:044; LVA-LP
Sommers, John W.	Arlington	Guard. Acct.	1840	AB8:067
Sommers, John W.	Arlington	Guard. Acct.	1840	AB8:200; LVA-LP
Sommers, John W.	Arlington	Guard. Acct.	1841	AB8:200
Sommers, Margaret [Smith]	Arlington	Guard. Acct.	1839	AB8:031; LVA-LP
Sommers, Simon	Arlington	Admin.	1836	WB4:110
Sommers, Simon	Arlington	Inventory	1837	LVA-LP
Sommers, Simon	Arlington	Account	1838	AB8:134; LVA-LP
Sommers, Simon	Arlington	Account	1839	AB8:017; LVA-LP
Sommers, Simon	Arlington	Account	1840	AB8:134
Sommers, Simon Fayette, c/o John	Arlington	Guard.	1837	WB4:150
Sommers, Simon, heirs of	Arlington	Account	1841	AB8:197
Sommers, Simon L.	Arlington	Guard. Acct.	1841	AB8:201
Sommers, Simon L., c/o John A.	Arlington	Guard. Acct.	1844	AB8:495; LVA-LP
Sommers, Simon L., surveyor	Arlington	Appointment	1852	BB(np)
Sommers, Simon LaFayette	Arlington	Guard. Acct.	1839	AB8:044; LVA-LP
Sommers, Simon LaFayette	Arlington	Guard. Acct.	1840	AB8:068; LVA-LP
Sommers, Susannah	Arlington	Will	1855	WB6:427; File #518A
Sommers, Susannah	Arlington	Appraisal	1855	WB6:458; LVA-LP
Sommers, Susannah	Arlington	Account	1857	WB7:214; LVA-LP
Sommers, Susannah	Arlington	Account	1860	WB8:041; LVA-LP
Sommers, Y. Charles	Arlington	Guard. Acct.	1839	AB8:043; LVA-LP
Soper, Leven, c/o Leonard	Arlington	Apprentice	1802	OCR1801:029
Southern, Richard	Arlington	Appraisal	1877	WB9:391
Southern, Richard	Arlington	Account	1877	WB9:393
Southern, Richard	Arlington	Will	1877	WB9:389; File #696A
Spadden, Ann	Alexandria	Tax Charge	1799	Tax PP 1799:38
Spadden, Ann, Cameron St.	Alexandria	Occupant	1795	Tax L 1795:26
Spadden, Ann, Cameron St.	Alexandria	Owner	1795	Tax L 1795:26
Spadding, Ann	Alexandria	Tax Charge	1796	Tax LP 1796:26
Spading, Ann, def.	Alexandria	Suit	1801	CRC:012
Spangingburg, Frederick	Alexandria	Tax Charge	1787	Tax PP 1787:14
Spangle, Geo.	Alexandria	Tax Charge	1795	Tax PP 1795:28
Spangle, George	Alexandria	Tax Charge	1796	Tax PP 1796:18
Spangleburgh, Fredk.	Alexandria	Tax Charge	1790	Tax PP 1790:14
Spangler, Balcher	Alexandria	Tax Charge	1796	Tax PP 1796:18
Spangler, Baltzer	Alexandria	Tax Charge	1796	Tax LP 1796:27
Spangler, Baltzer, Prince St.	Alexandria	Owner	1790	Tax L 1790:10
Spangler, Batzer, Prince St.	Alexandria	Owner	1795	Tax L 1795:27
Spangler, George	Alexandria	Tax Charge	1796	Tax PP 1796:18
Spangler, Goerge	Alexandria	Tax Charge	1796	Tax LP 1796:27
Speake, Edward, c/o Edward	Arlington	Apprentice	1814	OCR1811:211
Speake, Josias M.	Arlington	Respondent	1805	ACO:041
Speake, Josias M.	Arlington	Defendant	1808	ACO:086, 090, 092

NAME OR SUBJECT	LOCATION	TYPE	YEAR	REFERENCE(S)
Speake, Josias M.	Arlington	Defendant	1808	ACO:104, 105
Speake, Josias M.	Arlington	Defendant	1808	ACO:093
Speake, Josias M.	Arlington	Defendant	1809	ACO:108
Speake, Josias M., master	Arlington	Respondent	1806	ACO:050, 052
Speakes, Lucy	Alexandria	Boarder	1799	1799(2):14A
Speaks, Capt.	Alexandria	Tax Charge	1796	Tax LP 1796:27
Spear, Joseph	Arlington	Inventory	1819	AB3:323
Spear, Joseph	Arlington	Admin.	1819	WB2:288
Spears, Thomas G., c/o Hannah	Arlington	Apprentice	1822	OCR1822:020
Speck, Andw.	Alexandria	Boarder	1808	1808(4):29A
Spence, Jasper	Alexandria	Tax Charge	1799	Tax PP 1799:37
Spence, Richard	Alexandria	Tax Charge	1796	Tax PP 1796:17
Spence, William	Alexandria	Tax Charge	1789	Tax PP 1789:16
Spencer, Benjamin F., grantor	Arlington	Indenture D.	1833	ID:416
Spencer, Benjamin F., in jail bounds	Arlington	Insolvent	1833	ID:414
Spencer, Chas.	Alexandria	Tax Charge	1790	Tax PP 1790:14
Spencer, Jeremiah, b. Yorkshire	Arlington	Alien Entry	1819	RA:18/11/19
Spencer, Richard	Alexandria	Tax Charge	1796	Tax LP 1796:26
Spencer, Richard	Alexandria	Tax Charge	1798	Tax PP 1798:17
Spencer, Richard	Arlington	Admin.	1804	WBB:058
Spencer, Richard	Arlington	Inventory	1804	WBB:059; LVA-LP
Spengler, George, blacksmith	Alexandria	Head	1796	1796(3):4
Spicket, Charles	Alexandria	Resident	1800	1800(4):02B
Spicket, Charles, no trade	Alexandria	Boarder	1800	1800(4):02A
Spicott, Catharine, wharf	Alexandria	Occupant	1790	Tax L 1790:05
Spillman, Catherine	Alexandria	Will	1894	WB2:078; LP
Spilman, Armistead	Alexandria	Suit	1807	CRF:131
Spilman, James, grantor	Arlington	Indenture D.	1826	ID:027
Spilman, James, in jail	Arlington	Insolvent	1826	ID:025
Spinks, Geo.	Alexandria	Boarder	1808	1808(1):02A
Spinks, William Montgomery	Arlington	Apprentice	1844	OCR1842:089
Spires, Joshua	Alexandria	Tax Charge	1787	Tax PP 1787:13
Splain, Morris	Arlington	Account	1866	WB8:422
Sponagell, George	Alexandria	Tax Charge	1796	Tax LP 1796:26
Sponogle, Geo.	Alexandria	Tax Charge	1795	Tax PP 1795:27
Spooner, N., Wolf St.	Alexandria	Occupant	1787	Tax L 1787:17
Spooner, Nathaniel	Alexandria	Tax Charge	1787	Tax PP 1787:14
Spooner, Nathaniel	Alexandria	Tax Charge	1796	Tax PP 1796:18
Spooner, Nathaniel & wife, mariner	Alexandria	Head	1795	1795(4a):05
Spooner, Nathl.	Alexandria	Tax Charge	1790	Tax PP 1790:14
Spooner, Nathl.	Alexandria	Tax Charge	1796	Tax LP 1796:26
Spooner, Nathl., Wolfe St.	Alexandria	Occupant	1790	Tax L 1790:07
Spreeher, Andw.	Alexandria	Tax Charge	1789	Tax PP 1789:17
Sprig, Aaron & wife (C), labourer	Alexandria	Housekeeper	1799	1799(2):18A
Spriggs, Aron	Alexandria	Tax Charge	1799	Tax PP 1799:37
Sprigs, Kitty (C), washwoman	Alexandria	Housekeeper	1808	1808(1):06A
Springer, John, Duke St.	Alexandria	Occupant	1787	Tax L 1787:17
Spunaugle, George	Arlington	Apprentice	1811	OCR1811:052
Spunaugle, Samuel, c/o George	Arlington	Apprentice	1811	OCR1811:032
Spurling, Jeremiah	Arlington	Admin.	1811	WB1:111
Spurling, Jeremiah	Arlington	Account	1812	AB1:252; LVA-LP
Spurling, Jeremiah	Arlington	Inventory	1812	AB1:153; LVA-LP
Spurling, Jeremiah	Arlington	Account	1816	AB2:391; LVA-LP
Spurling, Jeremiah	Arlington	Sale	1816	AB2:372
Spurling, Jeremiah	Arlington	Division S.	1816	AB2:375
Spurling, Jeremiah	Arlington	Inventory	1816	AB2:390; LVA-LP
Spurr, John	Alexandria	Tax Charge	1789	Tax PP 1789:17
Squah, Wm., shopkeeper	Alexandria	Housekeeper	1808	1808(2):12A
Stabler, Anna, c/o Edward	Arlington	Guard.	1814	WB1:300
Stabler, Deborah H.	Alexandria	Will	1876	WB1:191; LP
Stabler, Doctor, apothory	Alexandria	Head	1800	1800(4):09A

NAME OR SUBJECT	LOCATION	TYPE	YEAR	REFERENCE(S)
Stabler, Edward	Alexandria	Tax Charge	1796	Tax LP 1796:27
Stabler, Edward	Alexandria	Tax Charge	1796	Tax PP 1796:17
Stabler, Edward	Alexandria	Mer. License	1798	Tax PP 1798:20-7
Stabler, Edward	Alexandria	Tax Charge	1799	Tax PP 1799:37
Stabler, Edward	Alexandria	Mer. License	1799	Tax PP 1799:52-10r
Stabler, Edward	Alexandria	Tax Charge	1800	Tax PP 1800:39
Stabler, Edward	Alexandria	Mer. License	1800	Tax PP 1800:54(20)r
Stabler, Edward	Arlington	Receipt Book	1825	LVA-LP
Stabler, Edward	Arlington	Inventory	1831	LVA-LP
Stabler, Edward	Arlington	Admin.	1831	WB4:032
Stabler, Edward	Arlington	Account	1832	AB7:353; LVA-LP
Stabler, Edward	Arlington	Account	1835	AB7:297; LVA-LP
Stabler, Edward	Arlington	Account	1836	AB7:286; LVA-LP
Stabler, Edward	Arlington	Account	1837	AB7:300; LVA-LP
Stabler, Edward	Arlington	Account	1837	LVA-LP
Stabler, Edward	Arlington	Distribution	1838	AB7:280
Stabler, Edward	Arlington	Account	1838	AB7:274, 284, 294
Stabler, Edward	Arlington	Account	1838	AB7:300; LVA-LP
Stabler, Edward	Arlington	Account	1839	AB8:085; LVA-LP
Stabler, Edward	Arlington	Account	1839	AB7:351
Stabler, Edward	Arlington	Account	1839	AB8:139; LVA-LP
Stabler, Edward	Arlington	Account	1840	AB8:139
Stabler, Edward	Arlington	Account	1840	AB8:085
Stabler, Edward	Arlington	Account	1841	AB8:208; LVA-LP
Stabler, Edward	Arlington	Account	1841	AB8:295; LVA-LP
Stabler, Edward	Arlington	Account	1842	AB8:295
Stabler, Edward	Arlington	Account	1843	AB8:338; LVA-LP
Stabler, Edward	Arlington	Account	1844	AB8:441, 442; LVA-LP
Stabler, Edward	Arlington	Account	1845	AB9:030; LVA-LP
Stabler, Edward	Arlington	Account	1846	AB9:152; LVA-LP
Stabler, Edward	Arlington	Account	1847	AB9:296
Stabler, Edward	Arlington	Account	1847	AB9:296; LVA-LP
Stabler, Edward	Arlington	Account	1848	WB5:055; LVA-LP
Stabler, Edward	Arlington	Account	1851	WB6:004; LVA-LP
Stabler, Edward	Arlington	Account	1851	WB5:237; LVA-LP
Stabler, Edward	Arlington	Account	1851	WB6:355; LVA-LP
Stabler, Edward	Arlington	Account	1851	WB6:118; LVA-LP
Stabler, Edward	Arlington	Account	1856	WB7:109; LVA-LP
Stabler, Edward & wife, druggist	Alexandria	Head	1795	1795(4):03
Stabler, Edward & wife, apothecary	Alexandria	Housekeeper	1799	1799(2):17A
Stabler, Edward & wife Mary	Alexandria	Resident	1800	1800(4):09B
Stabler, Edward, children of	Arlington	Guard. Acct.	1842	OCR1842:002
Stabler, Edward, druggist	Alexandria	Head	1810	1810(4):03A
Stabler, Edward H., c/o Edward	Arlington	Guard.	1831	WB4:033
Stabler, Edward, heirs of	Arlington	Account	1852	WB6:131; LVA-LP
Stabler, Edward S.	Arlington	Guard. Acct.	1856	WB7:124
Stabler, Edwd.	Alexandria	Tax Charge	1795	Tax PP 1795:29
Stabler, Edwd.	Alexandria	Tax Charge	1798	Tax PP 1798:18
Stabler, Edwd., druggist	Alexandria	Housekeeper	1808	1808(4):25A
Stabler, Edwd., Wolf St.	Alexandria	Occupant	1795	Tax L 1795:14
Stabler, Elizabeth, c/o Edward	Arlington	Guard.	1814	WB1:300
Stabler, Eugenia G.	Arlington	Guard. Acct.	1856	WB7:124
Stabler, Francis	Arlington	Guard. Acct.	1836	AB7:292; LVA-LP
Stabler, Francis	Arlington	Guard. Acct.	1837	AB7:297; LVA-LP
Stabler, Francis	Arlington	Guard. Acct.	1838	AB7:283, 292
Stabler, Francis	Arlington	Guard. Acct.	1838	AB7:303
Stabler, Francis	Arlington	Guard. Acct.	1839	AB8:136; LVA-LP
Stabler, Francis	Arlington	Guard. Acct.	1839	AB8:291; LVA-LP
Stabler, Francis	Arlington	Guard. Acct.	1840	AB8:136
Stabler, Francis	Arlington	Guard. Acct.	1841	AB8:210
Stabler, Francis	Arlington	Guard. Acct.	1842	AB8:291, 298

NAME OR SUBJECT	LOCATION	TYPE	YEAR	REFERENCE(S)
Stabler, Francis	Arlington	Guard. Acct.	1843	AB8:343
Stabler, Francis	Arlington	Guard. Acct.	1844	AB9:015; LVA-LP
Stabler, Francis	Arlington	Guard. Acct.	1844	AB8:438; LVA-LP
Stabler, Francis	Arlington	Guard. Acct.	1846	AB9:146; LVA-LP
Stabler, Francis	Arlington	Guard. Acct.	1847	AB9:298
Stabler, Harriet	Arlington	Guard. Acct.	1836	AB7:289; LVA-LP
Stabler, Harriet	Arlington	Guard. Acct.	1837	AB7:296; LVA-LP
Stabler, Harriet	Arlington	Guard. Acct.	1839	AB8:137; LVA-LP
Stabler, Harriet	Arlington	Guard. Acct.	1839	AB8:292; LVA-LP
Stabler, Harriet	Arlington	Guard. Acct.	1840	AB8:137
Stabler, Harriet	Arlington	Guard. Acct.	1842	AB8:292, 298
Stabler, Harriet	Arlington	Guard. Acct.	1843	AB8:342
Stabler, Harriet	Arlington	Guard. Acct.	1844	AB9:015
Stabler, Harriet	Arlington	Guard. Acct.	1844	AB8:440; LVA-LP
Stabler, Harriet	Arlington	Guard. Acct.	1846	AB9:145; LVA-LP
Stabler, Harriet	Arlington	Guard. Acct.	1847	AB9:299
Stabler, Harriet	Arlington	Guard. Acct.	1848	WB5:058
Stabler, Harriet	Arlington	Bond	1853	BB(np)
Stabler, Harriet	Arlington	Inventory	1853	WB6:269; LVA-LP
Stabler, Harriet	Arlington	Guard. Acct.	1854	WB6:398; LVA-LP
Stabler, Harriet, c/o Edward	Arlington	Guard.	1831	WB4:033
Stabler, Harriet, c/o Edward	Arlington	Guard. Acct.	1837	AB7:302; LVA-LP
Stabler, Harriet, c/o Edward	Arlington	Guard. Acct.	1848	WB5:060; LVA-LP
Stabler, Harriet S.	Arlington	Guard. Acct.	1856	WB7:124
Stabler, Harriett	Arlington	Guard. Acct.	1838	AB7:281, 289
Stabler, Henrietta	Arlington	Guard. Acct.	1856	WB7:124
Stabler, Henry	Arlington	Guard. Acct.	1836	AB7:293; LVA-LP
Stabler, Henry	Arlington	Guard. Acct.	1837	AB7:298; LVA-LP
Stabler, Henry	Arlington	Guard. Acct.	1838	AB7:283, 293, 298
Stabler, Henry	Arlington	Guard. Acct.	1838	AB7:304
Stabler, Henry	Arlington	Guard. Acct.	1839	AB8:292; LVA-LP
Stabler, Henry	Arlington	Guard. Acct.	1839	AB8:135; LVA-LP
Stabler, Henry	Arlington	Guard. Acct.	1840	AB8:135a
Stabler, Henry	Arlington	Guard. Acct.	1842	AB8:292
Stabler, Henry, c/o Edward	Arlington	Guard	1831	WB4:033
Stabler, Joseph	Arlington	Guard. Acct.	1856	WB7:124
Stabler, Lucy F.	Arlington	Guard. Acct.	1856	WB7:124
Stabler, Mary	Arlington	Will	1853	WB6:215; File #495A
Stabler, Mary	Arlington	Receipt	1854	LVA-LP
Stabler, Mary	Arlington	Account	1854	WB6:393; LVA-LP
Stabler, Mary	Arlington	Account	1856	WB7:111; LVA-LP
Stabler, Rebecca	Arlington	Guard. Acct.	1836	AB7:288; LVA-LP
Stabler, Rebecca	Arlington	Guard. Acct.	1837	AB7:298; LVA-LP
Stabler, Rebecca	Arlington	Guard. Acct.	1838	AB7:282, 288, 297
Stabler, Rebecca	Arlington	Guard. Acct.	1838	AB7:303
Stabler, Rebecca	Arlington	Will	1860	WB8:438; File #798A
Stabler, Rebecca	Arlington	Account	1867	WB8:536
Stabler, Rebecca, c/o Edward	Arlington	Guard.	1831	WB4:033
Stabler, Richard H.	Arlington	Guard. Acct.	1836	AB7:291; LVA-LP
Stabler, Richard H.	Arlington	Guard. Acct.	1837	AB7:296; LVA-LP
Stabler, Richard H.	Arlington	Guard. Acct.	1837	AB7:302; LVA-LP
Stabler, Richard H.	Arlington	Guard. Acct.	1838	AB7:302
Stabler, Richard H.	Arlington	Guard. Acct.	1838	AB7:281, 291, 296
Stabler, Richard H.	Arlington	Guard. Acct.	1839	AB8:136; LVA-LP
Stabler, Richard H.	Arlington	Guard. Acct.	1839	AB8:293; LVA-LP
Stabler, Richard H.	Arlington	Guard. Acct.	1840	AB8:136
Stabler, Richard H.	Arlington	Guard. Acct.	1841	AB8:211
Stabler, Richard H.	Arlington	Guard. Acct.	1842	AB8:293, 297
Stabler, Richard H.	Arlington	Guard. Acct.	1843	AB8:341
Stabler, Richard H.	Arlington	Release	1844	AB8:438; LVA-LP
Stabler, Richard H.	Arlington	Release	1844	OCR1842:069, 071

NAME OR SUBJECT	LOCATION	TYPE	YEAR	REFERENCE(S)
Stabler, Richard H.	Alexandria	Will	1878	WB1:249; LP
Stabler, Richard H., c/o Edward	Arlington	Guard.	1831	WB4:033; WB5:060
Stabler, Robinson, c/o Edward	Arlington	Guard.	1814	WB1:300
Stabler, Sarah	Arlington	Guard. Acct.	1836	AB7:290; LVA-LP
Stabler, Sarah	Arlington	Guard. Acct.	1837	AB7:297; LVA-LP
Stabler, Sarah	Arlington	Guard. Acct.	1838	AB7:282, 290
Stabler, Sarah	Arlington	Guard. Acct.	1838	AB7:304
Stabler, Sarah	Arlington	Guard. Acct.	1839	AB8:135; LVA-LP
Stabler, Sarah	Arlington	Guard. Acct.	1839	AB8:291; LVA-LP
Stabler, Sarah	Arlington	Guard. Acct.	1840	AB8:135a
Stabler, Sarah	Arlington	Guard. Acct.	1841	AB8:211
Stabler, Sarah	Arlington	Guard. Acct.	1842	AB8:291
Stabler, Sarah	Arlington	Guard. Acct.	1843	AB8:340
Stabler, Sarah	Arlington	Guard. Acct.	1844	AB8:440; LVA-LP
Stabler, Sarah	Arlington	Guard. Acct.	1844	AB9:016; LVA-LP
Stabler, Sarah	Arlington	Release	1844	OCR1842:095
Stabler, Sarah Frances, c/o Edward	Arlington	Guard.	1831	WB4:033; WB5:060
Stabler, Susan, c/o Edward	Arlington	Guard.	1831	WB4:033
Stabler, Thomas S., c/o Edward	Arlington	Guard.	1814	WB1:300
Stabler, Virginia	Arlington	Guard. Acct.	1856	WB7:124
Stabler, William	Arlington	Petition	1843	LVA-LP (Box 214)
Stabler, William	Arlington	Bond	1852	BB(np)
Stabler, William	Arlington	Will	1852	WB6:112; File #479A
Stabler, William	Arlington	Appraisal	1853	WB6:182; LVA-LP
Stabler, William	Arlington	Account	1854	WB6:453; LVA-LP
Stabler, William	Arlington	Account	1854	WB6:336; LVA-LP
Stabler, William	Arlington	Account	1854	WB6:337; LVA-LP
Stabler, William	Arlington	Account	1857	WB7:219; LVA-LP
Stabler, William	Arlington	Account	1860	WB8:042; LVA-LP
Stabler, William, c/o Edward	Arlington	Guard.	1814	WB1:300
Stafford, Wm.	Alexandria	Boarder	1808	1808(1):01A
Stafford, Wm.	Alexandria	Boarder	1808	1808(2):15A
Stagg, Cornelius	Alexandria	Tax Charge	1790	Tax PP 1790:13
Stair, Adam	Alexandria	Tax Charge	1787	Tax PP 1787:14
Stair, J., Fairfax St.	Alexandria	Occupant	1787	Tax L 1787:07
Stakey, Christopher	Alexandria	Tithable +16	1788	Tax PP 1788:03
Stangle, Christina, John A.	Arlington	Guard.	1848	GBB(np)
Stansbury, Joseph S.	Arlington	Trustee Acct.	1866	WB8:402
Stansbury, Saml.	Alexandria	Tax Charge	1796	Tax LP 1796:27
Stanton, Capt., seaman	Alexandria	Head	1810	1810(1):13A
Stanton, John, seaman	Alexandria	Housekeeper	1808	1808(1):06A
Stare, Adam	Alexandria	Tax Charge	1788	Tax PP 1788:15
Starr, Elisha	Alexandria	Tax Charge	1795	Tax PP 1795:27
Starr, Elisha	Alexandria	Tax Charge	1796	Tax LP 1796:26
Starr, Elisha	Alexandria	Tax Charge	1796	Tax PP 1796:18
Starr, Elisha	Alexandria	Tax Charge	1798	Tax PP 1798:18
Starr, Moses	Alexandria	Tax Charge	1796	Tax PP 1796:17
Statia, William	Alexandria	Tax Charge	1800	Tax PP 1800:40
Stavely, Jno.	Alexandria	Tax Charge	1798	Tax PP 1798:16
Steadicorn, Simon	Arlington	Ordinary	1802	OBL1(np)
Steavens, Russell	Arlington	Respondent	1812	ACO:122
Steber, Michael	Alexandria	Tax Charge	1800	Tax PP 1800:40
Stedecome, Mary	Alexandria	Tax Charge	1799	Tax PP 1799:38
Stedicorn, Mary, milliner	Alexandria	Housekeeper	1799	1799(2):08A
Steeber, Michl.	Alexandria	Tax Charge	1795	Tax PP 1795:28
Steeber, Michl.	Alexandria	Tax Charge	1796	Tax LP 1796:27
Steel, Horatio N., grantee	Arlington	Indenture D.	1828	ID:208
Steel, J., Queen St.	Alexandria	Occupant	1787	Tax L 1787:23
Steel, John	Alexandria	Tax Charge	1789	Tax PP 1789:17
Steel, Peter	Alexandria	Tax Charge	1788	Tax PP 1788:15
Steel, Peter	Alexandria	Tax Charge	1789	Tax PP 1789:17

NAME OR SUBJECT	LOCATION	TYPE	YEAR	REFERENCE(S)
Steel, Thomas, w(3), shoemaker	Alexandria	Head	1796	1796(3):6
Steel, Thos.	Alexandria	Tax Charge	1795	Tax PP 1795:29
Steel, Thos.	Alexandria	Tax Charge	1796	Tax LP 1796:27
Steel, Thos.	Alexandria	Tax Charge	1800	Tax PP 1800:39
Steel, Thos. & wife, shoemaker	Alexandria	Housekeeper	1799	1799(2):19A
Steel, Thos., shoemaker	Alexandria	Housekeeper	1808	1808(2):13A
Steel [Stell], John	Alexandria	Tax Charge	1787	Tax PP 1787:15
Steele, Jonathan H., grantee	Arlington	Indenture D.	1828	ID:196
Steele, Tho.	Alexandria	Tax Charge	1798	Tax PP 1798:17
Steele, Thomas	Alexandria	Tax Charge	1799	Tax PP 1799:37
Steele, Thomas	Arlington	Account	1830	AB6:526; LVA-LP
Steele, Thomas	Arlington	Admin.	1830	WB3:385
Steell, Thos., shoemaker	Alexandria	Head	1810	1810(3):01A
Steer, Adam	Alexandria	Tax Charge	1790	Tax PP 1790:14
Steer, Adam, Fairfax St.	Alexandria	Occupant	1790	Tax L 1790:02
Steiber, Michael	Alexandria	Owner	1787	Tax L 1787:23
Steiber, Michael	Alexandria	Tax Charge	1787	Tax PP 1787:13
Steiber, Michael, Royal St.	Alexandria	Occupant	1787	Tax L 1787:23
Steiber, Michl.	Alexandria	Tax Charge	1788	Tax PP 1788:15
Steiber, Michl.	Alexandria	Tax Charge	1789	Tax PP 1789:17
Steiber, Michl.	Alexandria	Tax Charge	1790	Tax PP 1790:13
Steir, Charles J.	Alexandria	Tax Charge	1800	Tax PP 1800:40
Steiver, Michael & wife, baker	Alexandria	Housekeeper	1799	1799(2):04A
Steiver, Michael, baker	Alexandria	Head	1810	1810(1):02A
Stephen, Adam	Alexandria	Death	1787	CRE:201
Stephens, Codger	Arlington	Libellant	1805	ACO:045
Stephens, George, c/o Levina	Arlington	Apprentice	1805	OCR1801:274
Stephens, Henry	Arlington	Libellant	1813	ACO:137
Stephens, James, c/o Levina	Arlington	Apprentice	1805	OCR1801:254
Stephens, James, def.	Alexandria	Suit	1802	CRC:217
Stephens, Russell	Arlington	Defendant	1809	ACO:108
Stephens, Russell	Arlington	Defendant	1812	ACO:126
Stephens, Russell, sea captain	Alexandria	Housekeeper	1808	1808(4):25A
Stephens, Russell, seaman	Alexandria	Head	1810	1810(1):04A
Stephens, Sarah, c/o Levina	Arlington	Apprentice	1805	OCR1801:263
Stephens, Steph.	Alexandria	Tax Charge	1800	Tax PP 1800:40
Stephens, Stephen	Alexandria	License Due	1800	Tax PP 1800:54(24)
Stephens, Stephen	Arlington	Suit	1802	PA:048
Stephens, Stephen, plt.	Alexandria	Suit	1803	CRD:175
Stephens, Stephen [Sephens, Sepen]	Alexandria	Head	1800	1800(4):07A
Stephenson, Clotworthy	Alexandria	Account B.	1799	CRB:321
Stephenson, Clotworthy, def.	Alexandria	Suit	1801	CRB:318
Stephenson, Jas.	Alexandria	Boarder	1808	1808(2):11A
Stephenson, Robt. & wife, carpenter	Alexandria	Housekeeper	1799	1799(2):19A
Stepper, Albert	Arlington	Apprentice	1843	OCR1842:046
Sterrett, James	Alexandria	Tax Charge	1796	Tax PP 1796:17
Steuart, Betty, King St.	Alexandria	Occupant	1790	Tax L 1790:10
Steuart, Betty, King St.	Alexandria	Owner	1790	Tax L 1790:10(2)
Steuart, Betty, Royal St.	Alexandria	Owner	1790	Tax L 1790:10
Steuart, Jno.	Alexandria	Tax Charge	1798	Tax PP 1798:18
Steuart, John	Alexandria	Mer. License	1798	Tax PP 1798:20-7
Steuart, John, Prince St.	Alexandria	Occupant	1790	Tax L 1790:11
Steuart, John, Prince St.	Alexandria	Owner	1790	Tax L 1790:11
Steuart, Mary	Alexandria	Will	1891	WB1:592; LP
Steuart, Mary (C), washwoman	Alexandria	Housekeeper	1808	1808(1):05A
Steuart, Robert	Alexandria	Tax Charge	1798	Tax PP 1798:17
Steuart, Robert	Alexandria	Tax Charge	1799	Tax PP 1799:39
Steuart, Sarah A.	Alexandria	Will	1900	WB2:379; LP
Steuart, Thomas	Alexandria	Tax Charge	1790	Tax PP 1790:13
Steuart, Thomas	Alexandria	Tax Charge	1795	Tax PP 1795:27
Steuart, Thomas	Alexandria	Tax Charge	1798	Tax PP 1798:17

NAME OR SUBJECT	LOCATION	TYPE	YEAR	REFERENCE(S)
Steuart, Thomas	Alexandria	Tax Charge	1799	Tax PP 1799:37
Steuart, Thos., Royal St.	Alexandria	Occupant	1795	Tax L 1795:26
Steuart, Thos., Royal St.	Alexandria	Owner	1795	Tax L 1795:26
Steuart, William, nail factor	Alexandria	Head	1810	1810(2):01A
Steuart, William, of Wm.	Alexandria	Tax Charge	1798	Tax PP 1798:17
Steuernagel, George	Alexandria	Will	1889	WB1:522; LP
Stevens, Chas., ship carpenter	Alexandria	Housekeeper	1808	1808(3):22A
Stevens, Elizabeth	Arlington	Guard.	1810	WBC:384
Stevens, Elizabeth, c/o Levena	Arlington	Apprentice	1804	OCR1801:184
Stevens, Henry	Arlington	Bond	1853	BB(np)
Stevens, Henry	Arlington	Inventory	1853	WB6:217; LVA-LP
Stevens, Henry	Arlington	Will	1853	WB6:181; File #490A
Stevens, Henry	Arlington	Account	1854	WB6:372; LVA-LP
Stevens, John, c/o Ann R.	Arlington	Apprentice	1822	OCR1822:024
Stevens, John R., c/o Russel	Arlington	Apprentice	1814	OCR1811:235
Stevens, Peter	Alexandria	Tax Charge	1798	Tax PP 1798:17
Stevens, Peter	Alexandria	Tax Charge	1799	Tax PP 1799:37
Stevens, Russell	Arlington	Defendant	1817	ACO:149
Stevens, Russell, master	Arlington	Respondent	1815	ACO:143
Stevens, Sarah	Arlington	Account	1820	AB4:160
Stevens, Sarah	Arlington	Inventory	1820	LVA-LP
Stevens, Sarah	Arlington	Admin.	1820	WB2:380
Stevens, Sarah	Arlington	Account	1823	AB5:199; LVA-LP
Stevenson, James	Alexandria	Tax Charge	1796	Tax PP 1796:18
Stevenson, Robert	Alexandria	Tax Charge	1799	Tax PP 1799:37
Stevenson, Robert	Alexandria	Tax Charge	1800	Tax PP 1800:40
Stevenson, Thomas	Arlington	Apprentice	1811	OCR1811:044
Stewart, Betty	Alexandria	Tax Charge	1788	Tax PP 1788:15
Stewart, Betty	Alexandria	Tax Charge	1789	Tax PP 1789:17
Stewart, Betty	Alexandria	Tax Charge	1790	Tax PP 1790:13
Stewart, David, clerk	Alexandria	Boarder	1799	1799(2):02A
Stewart, Henry	Arlington	Guard.	1810	WBC:499
Stewart, Ignatius, at his house	Arlington	Ordinary	1839	OBL5(np)
Stewart, Ignatius, at his house	Arlington	Ordinary	1842	OBL6(np)
Stewart, Ignatius, on Union St.	Arlington	Ordinary	1843	OBL6(np)
Stewart, Ignatius, on Union St.	Arlington	Ordinary	1844	OBL6(np)
Stewart, Ignatius, on Union St.	Arlington	Ordinary	1845	OBL6(np)
Stewart, James, Estate	Alexandria	Tax Charge	1796	Tax LP 1796:27
Stewart, James M.	Arlington	Exor. Bond	1849	EBB(np)
Stewart, James M.	Arlington	Will	1849	WB5:175; File #454A
Stewart, James Muir, c/o Robert	Arlington	Guard.	1817	WB2:209
Stewart, Jas., Estate, King St.	Alexandria	Owner	1795	Tax L 1795:26
Stewart, Jas., Estate, Royal St.	Alexandria	Owner	1795	Tax L 1795:26
Stewart, Jas. M.	Alexandria	Boarder	1808	1808(1):01A
Stewart, Jno.	Alexandria	Tax Charge	1795	Tax PP 1795:28
Stewart, Jno.	Alexandria	Tax Charge	1799	Tax PP 1799:39
Stewart, Jno. A.	Alexandria	Tax Charge	1800	Tax PP 1800:39
Stewart, Jno., clerk	Alexandria	Boarder	1799	1799(2):19A
Stewart, John	Alexandria	Tax Charge	1788	Tax PP 1788:15
Stewart, John	Alexandria	Tax Charge	1789	Tax PP 1789:17
Stewart, John	Alexandria	Tax Charge	1790	Tax PP 1790:14
Stewart, John	Alexandria	Tax Charge	1796	Tax LP 1796:26
Stewart, John	Alexandria	Tax Charge	1796	Tax PP 1796:17
Stewart, John	Alexandria	Tax Charge	1799	Tax PP 1799:37
Stewart, John	Alexandria	Tax Charge	1800	Tax PP 1800:39
Stewart, John	Arlington	Apprentice	1802	OCR1801:054
Stewart, John A.	Arlington	Juryman	1808	ACO:081
Stewart, John A.	Arlington	Admin.	1839	WB4:231
Stewart, John A., for playing Faro	Arlington	Defendant	1801	PA:136
Stewart, John A., grantee	Arlington	Indenture D.	1804	ID3:016
Stewart, John A., retailer	Alexandria	Housekeeper	1808	1808(2):13A

NAME OR SUBJECT	LOCATION	TYPE	YEAR	REFERENCE(S)
Stewart, John A., stationer	Alexandria	Head	1810	1810(2):03A
Stewart, John, c/o Robert	Arlington	Guard.	1817	WB2:209
Stewart, John, Jr.	Alexandria	Tax Charge	1799	Tax PP 1799:38
Stewart, John, merchant	Alexandria	Head	1810	1810(4):01A
Stewart, John P.	Arlington	Apprentice	1827	OCR1822:149
Stewart, John, Prince St.	Alexandria	Occupant	1795	Tax L 1795:28
Stewart, John, Prince St.	Alexandria	Owner	1795	Tax L 1795:28
Stewart, John, retailer	Alexandria	Housekeeper	1808	1808(4):27A
Stewart, John W.	Alexandria	Will	1885	WB1:423; LP
Stewart, John, w(3), cabinet maker	Alexandria	Head	1796	1796(3):1
Stewart, Margaret Milner	Alexandria	Will	1887	WB1:476; LP
Stewart, Mary	Alexandria	Resident	1800	1800(4):11B
Stewart, Mary Jane, c/o John A.	Arlington	Guard.	1837	WB4:154
Stewart, Robert	Alexandria	Tax Charge	1789	Tax PP 1789:16
Stewart, Robert	Alexandria	Tax Charge	1800	Tax PP 1800:39
Stewart, Robt.	Alexandria	Boarder	1808	1808(4):27A
Stewart, Sarah	Arlington	Apprentice	1805	OCR1801:262
Stewart, Thomas	Alexandria	Tax Charge	1788	Tax PP 1788:14
Stewart, Thomas	Alexandria	Tax Charge	1788	Tax PP 1788:15
Stewart, Thomas	Alexandria	Tax Charge	1789	Tax PP 1789:17
Stewart, Thomas	Alexandria	Tax Charge	1796	Tax PP 1796:18
Stewart, Thomas	Alexandria	Tax Charge	1800	Tax PP 1800:39
Stewart, Thos.	Alexandria	Tax Charge	1796	Tax LP 1796:26
Stewart, William	Arlington	Admin.	1816	WB2:223
Stewart, William	Arlington	Sale	1818	AB3:155
Stewart, William	Arlington	Inventory	1818	AB3:149; LVA-LP
Stewart, William	Arlington	Account	1820	AB4:132; LVA-LP
Stewart, William	Arlington	Inventory	1825	AB6:100; LVA-LP
Stewart, William	Arlington	Will P.	1825	OCR1822:096a
Stewart, William	Arlington	Admin.	1825	OCR1822:096a
Stewart, William	Arlington	Will	1825	WB3:184; File #234A
Stewart, William	Arlington	Bond	1825	WB3:185
Stewart, William	Arlington	Account	1826	AB6:222; LVA-LP
Stewart, William	Arlington	Sale	1826	AB6:155
Stewart, William B.	Arlington	Ordinary	1822	OBL3(np)
Stewart, William B.	Arlington	Ordinary	1827	OBL4(np)
Stewart, William B., at the ferry wharf	Arlington	Ordinary	1823	OBL3(np)
Stewart, William B., at steam boat hotel	Arlington	Ordinary	1824	OBL3(np)
Stewart, William B., at steamboat ferry	Arlington	Ordinary	1825	OBL4(np)
Stewart, William B., at his house	Arlington	Ordinary	1826	OBL4(np)
Stewart, William B., at his house	Arlington	Ordinary	1829	OBL4(np)
Stewart, William B., at his house	Arlington	Ordinary	1834	OBL5(np)
Stewart, William B., at his house	Arlington	Ordinary	1836	OBL5(np)
Stewart, William B., in Alexandria Co.	Arlington	Ordinary	1830	OBL4(np)
Stewart, William, c/o Robert	Arlington	Guard.	1817	WB2:209
Stewart, William D., c/o John A.	Arlington	Guard.	1837	WB4:154
Stewart, William, Jr., assignee, plt.	Alexandria	Suit	1808	CRG:147
Stewart, Wm.	Alexandria	Tax Charge	1799	Tax PP 1799:39
Stewart, Wm. B., at his house	Arlington	Ordinary	1835	OBL5(np)
Stewart, Wm., nail agent	Alexandria	Housekeeper	1808	1808(2):15A
Stewartt, Wm., shopkeeper	Alexandria	Housekeeper	1808	1808(1):01A
Stidolph, Sarah	Alexandria	Will	1897	WB2:239; LP
Stieber, Michael	Alexandria	Tax Charge	1799	Tax PP 1799:38
Stieber, Michael, Royal St.	Alexandria	Occupant	1790	Tax L 1790:10
Stieber, Michael, Royal St.	Alexandria	Owner	1790	Tax L 1790:10
Stieber, Michael, w1, baker	Alexandria	Head	1796	1796(3):3
Stieber, Michl.	Alexandria	Tax Charge	1796	Tax PP 1796:18
Stieber, Michl., Royal St.	Alexandria	Owner	1795	Tax L 1795:29
Stier, Charles J., w2, merchant	Alexandria	Head	1796	1796(3):1
Stier, Chas. Jno.	Alexandria	Tax Charge	1799	Tax PP 1799:39
Stille, John, of Philadelphia	Alexandria	Deed	1811	CRK:048

NAME OR SUBJECT	LOCATION	TYPE	YEAR	REFERENCE(S)
Stillwell, John	Arlington	Deposition	1806	ACR:030
Stillwell, John	Arlington	Deposition	1806	ACR:034
Stillwell, John	Alexandria	Deposition	1806	CRE:131
Stinly, Theodosius	Alexandria	Tax Charge	1800	Tax PP 1800:39
Stoddard, John	Alexandria	Tithable +16	1788	Tax PP 1788:14
Stohler, Johannes, b. Liestab, Switz.	Arlington	Alien Entry	1825	RA:26/02/25
Stokes, John	Alexandria	Tax Charge	1790	Tax PP 1790:13
Stokes, John, Duke St.	Alexandria	Occupant	1790	Tax L 1790:11
Stone, Charles	Arlington	Defendant	1821	ACO:197
Stone, Charles	Arlington	Inventory	1857	WB7:178; LVA-LP
Stone, Charles	Arlington	Account	1859	WB7:408; LVA-LP
Stone, Charles	Arlington	Guard. Acct.	1859	WB7:409
Stone, Charles	Arlington	Account	1861	WB8:062
Stone, Charles	Arlington	Guard. Acct.	1870	WB9:282
Stone, Charles	Arlington	Guard. Acct.	1870	WB9:255
Stone, Charles S.	Arlington	Will	1875	WB9:372
Stone, Jacob, l.b. baker	Alexandria	Housekeeper	1808	1808(3):20A
Stone, Levi	Alexandria	Tax Charge	1795	Tax PP 1795:29
Stone, Penelope	Arlington	Exor. Bond	1849	EBB(np)
Stone, Penelope	Arlington	Will	1849	WB5:172; File #453A
Stone, Robert	Alexandria	Tax Charge	1796	Tax PP 1796:18
Stone, Samuel	Arlington	Ordinary	1821	OBL3(np)
Stone, Sarah	Arlington	Inventory	1845	AB9:100; LVA-LP
Stone, Sarah	Arlington	Will P.	1845	OCR1842:104, 106
Stone, Sarah	Arlington	Will	1845	WB4:392; File #421A
Stone, Thos.	Alexandria	Boarder	1808	1808(3):18A
Stone, Will.	Alexandria	Tax Charge	1800	Tax PP 1800:39
Stone, William	Alexandria	Tax Charge	1799	Tax PP 1799:37
Stone, William, def.	Alexandria	Suit	1802	CRC:216
Stone, Wm.	Alexandria	Tax Charge	1798	Tax PP 1798:17
Stone, Wm. & wife, shoemaker	Alexandria	Housekeeper	1799	1799(2):14A
Stone, [blank], mariner	Alexandria	Head	1810	1810(1):08A
Stone, [blank], on the wharf	Alexandria	Occupant	1795	Tax L 1795:29
Stonemetz, Casper	Arlington	Ordinary	1803	OBL1(np)
Stonemetz, Casper	Arlington	Ordinary	1804	OBL1(np)
Stonestreet, Charles H., of DC	Alexandria	Will	1896	WB2:331; LP
Stonnell, William	Alexandria	Will	1875	WB1:135; LP
Stoop, Adam S.	Alexandria	Mer. License	1799	Tax PP 1799:52-10r
Stoopes, William	Alexandria	Tax Charge	1796	Tax PP 1796:18
Stoopes, William	Alexandria	Tax Charge	1798	Tax PP 1798:17
Stoopes, William	Alexandria	Tax Charge	1799	Tax PP 1799:38
Stoopes, William, w(1)2, ship carpenter	Alexandria	Head	1795	1796(3):7
Stoopes, Wm.	Alexandria	Tax Charge	1795	Tax PP 1795:28
Stoops, James	Arlington	Apprentice	1828	OCR1822:159a
Stoops, William	Alexandria	Tithable +16	1790	Tax PP 1790:05
Stoops, William	Alexandria	Tax Charge	1800	Tax PP 1800:39
Storke, John, grantee	Arlington	Indenture D.	1828	ID:212
Stout, Alexander C.	Arlington	Inventory	1815	AB2:167a; LVA-LP
Stout, Alexander C.	Arlington	Admin.	1815	WB2:065
Stoutenburgh, Seymour B.	Alexandria	Will	1892	WBC1:062; LP
Stoutenburgh, Tobias A.	Alexandria	Will	1873	WB1:082; LP
Stovin, Charles James	Arlington	Guard.	1827	OCR1822:138
Stovin, Charles James	Arlington	Guard.	1847	WB3:288
Stovin, Henry, Jr.	Alexandria	Tax Charge	1796	Tax PP 1796:18
Stovin, Hy., Sr.	Alexandria	Tax Charge	1796	Tax PP 1796:18
Straas, George F., Estate, plt.	Alexandria	Suit	1815	CRK:389
Straas, George Frederick, plt.	Alexandria	Suit	1800	CRK:209
Stras, George F.	Alexandria	Agreement	1800	CRK:233
Stras, Martha, Exrx. of G.F., Richmond	Alexandria	Agreement	1814	CRK:374
Strayer & Heide, Prince St.	Alexandria	Owner	1790	Tax L 1790:11
Strayer & Heide, Prince St.	Alexandria	Occupant	1790	Tax L 1790:11

NAME OR SUBJECT	LOCATION	TYPE	YEAR	REFERENCE(S)
Strayer, Jacob	Alexandria	Tax Charge	1788	Tax PP 1788:15
Strayer, Jacob	Alexandria	Tax Charge	1789	Tax PP 1789:17
Stribling, Magnus L.	Arlington	Admin.	1842	WB4:308
Stribling, Magnus T.	Arlington	Defendant	1823	ACO:226, 227
Stribling, Magnus T.	Arlington	Admin.	1842	OCR1842:009
Stringfellow, Horace, Rev.	Arlington	Ordination	1850	BB(np)
Stroman, Henry	Alexandria	Tax Charge	1788	Tax PP 1788:15
Stroman, Henry	Alexandria	Tax Charge	1789	Tax PP 1789:16
Stroman, Henry	Alexandria	Tax Charge	1795	Tax PP 1795:27
Stroman, Henry	Alexandria	Tax Charge	1796	Tax LP 1796:26
Stroman, Henry	Alexandria	Tax Charge	1799	Tax PP 1799:38
Stroman, Henry, Royal St.	Alexandria	Owner	1795	Tax L 1795:26
Stroman, Henry, Royal St.	Alexandria	Occupant	1795	Tax L 1795:26
Stroman, Hy.	Alexandria	Tax Charge	1798	Tax PP 1798:17
Stroman, John, c/o Mary E.	Arlington	Apprentice	1803	OCR1801:078
Strong, Andrew	Arlington	Will	1866	WB8:385; File #644A
Stroud, John	Arlington	Ordinary	1802	OBL1(np)
Stroud, Jos. & wife, cooper	Alexandria	Housekeeper	1799	1799(2):01A
Stroud, Joseph	Alexandria	Tax Charge	1799	Tax PP 1799:38
Stroud, Joseph	Arlington	Ordinary	1802	OBL1(np)
Stroud, Joseph, cooper	Alexandria	Housekeeper	1808	1808(2):16A
Stroud, Joseph, cooper	Alexandria	Head	1810	1810(1):12A
Strowman, Henry	Alexandria	Owner	1787	Tax L 1787:23
Strowman, Henry	Alexandria	Tax Charge	1800	Tax PP 1800:39
Strowman, Henry, Royal St.	Alexandria	Occupant	1787	Tax L 1787:23
Strowman, Henry, Royal St.	Alexandria	Owner	1790	Tax L 1790:10
Strowman, Henry, Royal St.	Alexandria	Occupant	1790	Tax L 1790:10
Strowman, John	Alexandria	Boarder	1808	1808(2):11A
Strowman, Mary	Alexandria	Head	1810	1810(2):05A
Strowman, Mary Eliz., sempstress	Alexandria	Housekeeper	1808	1808(2):14A
Struder, Daniel, painter	Alexandria	Housekeeper	1808	1808(1):02A
Stuart, Ann L.	Alexandria	Will	1871	WB1:043; LP
Stuart, Archibald	Alexandria	Deposition	1818	CRL:080
Stuart, Betty	Alexandria	Tax Charge	1787	Tax PP 1787:15
Stuart, Charles E.	Alexandria	Will	1889	WB1:523; LP
Stuart, Elizabeth	Alexandria	Owner	1787	Tax L 1787:23
Stuart, J., Prince St.	Alexandria	Occupant	1787	Tax L 1787:23
Stuart, John	Alexandria	Owner	1787	Tax L 1787:23
Stuart, John	Alexandria	Tax Charge	1787	Tax PP 1787:14
Stuart, John A., def.	Alexandria	Suit	1822	CRL:232
Stuart, Mary, sumpster	Alexandria	Boarder	1800	1800(4):11A
Stuart, Thomas	Alexandria	Tax Charge	1787	Tax PP 1787:14
Stuart, W.B., his house on Union St.	Arlington	Ordinary	1833	OBL5(np)
Stuart, William B.	Arlington	Ordinary	1821	OBL3(np)
Stuart, William B., at his house	Arlington	Ordinary	1832	OBL4(np)
Stuart, William B., in Alexandria Co.	Arlington	Ordinary	1828	OBL4(np)
Studer, Victor, b. Tremback, Switz.	Arlington	Alien Entry	1824	RA:10/12/24
Studor, Catherine	Arlington	Guard.	1838	WB4:175
Stuhl, Lutwady	Alexandria	Tithable +16	1789	Tax PP 1789:17
Stull, Thos., Prince St.	Alexandria	Occupant	1795	Tax L 1795:21
Stutsman, Tho.	Alexandria	Tax Charge	1798	Tax PP 1798:17
Stutson, John	Alexandria	Tax Charge	1790	Tax PP 1790:13
Sudduth, Joseph A.	Alexandria	Will	1892	WB2:031; LP
Sugar	Arlington	Suit	1820	ACO:174, 178
Sugar, brown and logwood	Arlington	Suit	1808	ACR:045
Sugar, logwood and piano fortes	Arlington	Suit	1808	ACO:096, 099
Sugars, Michael	Alexandria	Tithable +16	1789	Tax PP 1789:08
Sugars, Zachariah	Alexandria	Tax Charge	1787	Tax PP 1787:14
Sugars, Zachariah	Alexandria	Tax Charge	1788	Tax PP 1788:15
Sugars, Zachariah	Alexandria	Tax Charge	1789	Tax PP 1789:16
Suits at common law, in clerk's office	Arlington	General Rule	1807	ACO:072

NAME OR SUBJECT	LOCATION	TYPE	YEAR	REFERENCE(S)
Sulilvan, Timothy	Alexandria	Tax Charge	1796	Tax PP 1796:18
Sulivan, Humphrey	Alexandria	Tax Charge	1799	Tax PP 1799:39
Sulivan, Jno.	Alexandria	Tax Charge	1795	Tax PP 1795:29
Sulivan, John	Alexandria	Tax Charge	1796	Tax PP 1796:17
Sulivan, John, labourer	Alexandria	Head	1810	1810(4):04A
Sulivan, John, St. Asaph St.	Alexandria	Owner	1795	Tax L 1795:28
Sulivan, John, St. Asaph St.	Alexandria	Occupant	1795	Tax L 1795:28
Sulivan, John, w(3), bricklayer	Alexandria	Head	1796	1796(3):2
Sulivan, Tim.	Alexandria	Tax Charge	1795	Tax PP 1795:28
Sulivan, Tim., King St.	Alexandria	Occupant	1795	Tax L 1795:17
Sulivan, Timothy, w(1), taylor	Alexandria	Head	1796	1796(3):3
Sullivan, Danl.	Alexandria	Tax Charge	1790	Tax PP 1790:13
Sullivan, Elizabeth, grocer	Alexandria	Housekeeper	1799	1799(2):15A
Sullivan, Humphrey	Alexandria	Tithable +21	1787	Tax PP 1787:06
Sullivan, Humphrey	Alexandria	Tithable +16	1789	Tax PP 1789:08
Sullivan, Humphrey	Alexandria	Tax Charge	1790	Tax PP 1790:13
Sullivan, Humphrey & wife, tailor	Alexandria	Housekeeper	1799	1799(2):03A
Sullivan, James	Alexandria	Tax Charge	1787	Tax PP 1787:13
Sullivan, Jno. & wife, bricklayer	Alexandria	Housekeeper	1799	1799(2):09A
Sullivan, John	Alexandria	Tax Charge	1787	Tax PP 1787:14
Sullivan, John	Alexandria	Tax Charge	1789	Tax PP 1789:16
Sullivan, John	Alexandria	Tax Charge	1790	Tax PP 1790:14
Sullivan, John	Alexandria	Tax Charge	1796	Tax LP 1796:27
Sullivan, John	Arlington	Account	1815	LVA-LP
Sullivan, John, children of	Arlington	Account	1816	LVA-LP
Sullivan, John Holmes	Arlington	Guard. Acct.	1836	LVA-LP
Sullivan, John, Water St.	Alexandria	Owner	1790	Tax L 1790:11
Sullivan, Owen, gardner	Alexandria	Head	1810	1810(4):09A
Sullivan, Roger	Arlington	Apprentice	1826	OCR1822:117
Sullivan, Thomas	Arlington	Apprentice	1824	OCR1822:075
Sullivan, Timothy	Alexandria	Tax Charge	1788	Tax PP 1788:14
Sullivan, Timothy	Alexandria	Tax Charge	1790	Tax PP 1790:13
Sullivan, Timothy	Alexandria	Tax Charge	1796	Tax LP 1796:27
Sullivan, William F.	Alexandria	Will	1894	WB2:076; LP
Sulliven, John, Water St.	Alexandria	Occupant	1790	Tax L 1790:11
Sumby, Lucy, c/o Letty	Arlington	Apprentice	1813	OCR1811:153
Sumby, Sampson	Alexandria	Head	1810	1810(4):08A
Summers, Ann E.	Arlington	Guard. Acct.	1842	AB8:308
Summers, Cath., sempstress	Alexandria	Housekeeper	1808	1808(3):20A
Summers, Catharine E.	Alexandria	Will	1893	WB2:042; LP
Summers, Catharine, seamstress	Alexandria	Head	1810	1810(3):04A
Summers, Charles Y.	Arlington	Guard. Acct.	1842	AB8:308
Summers, Craven	Arlington	Will	1851	WB5:318; File #469A
Summers, Craven, c/o John	Arlington	Guard.	1819	WB2:330
Summers, Danl.	Alexandria	Boarder	1808	1808(1):07A
Summers, Elisha, in jail	Arlington	Insolvent	1827	ID:080
Summers [Somers], Elisha, grantor	Arlington	Indenture D.	1827	ID:082
Summers, Francis	Alexandria	Tax Charge	1799	Tax PP 1799:37
Summers, Francis	Alexandria	Tax Charge	1800	Tax PP 1800:39
Summers, Geo., Washington St.	Alexandria	Owner	1795	Tax L 1795:26
Summers, George	Alexandria	Owner	1787	Tax L 1787:24
Summers, George	Alexandria	Tax Charge	1787	Tax PP 1787:14
Summers, George, assignee	Arlington	Plaintiff	1802	PA:336
Summers, George W., of Brinkley AR	Alexandria	Will	1883	WB1:383, 389; LP
Summers, George, Washington St.	Alexandria	Occupant	1787	Tax L 1787:24
Summers, Henry	Arlington	Guard. Acct.	1842	AB8:308
Summers, Isabella, gentlewoman	Alexandria	Housekeeper	1808	1808(2):14A
Summers, J.	Alexandria	Reference	1808	1808(4):25B
Summers, John	Alexandria	Tax Charge	1796	Tax PP 1796:17
Summers, John	Arlington	Division S.	1818	AB3:271
Summers, John	Arlington	Inventory	1818	AB3:255; LVA-LP

NAME OR SUBJECT	LOCATION	TYPE	YEAR	REFERENCE(S)
Summers, John	Arlington	Admin.	1818	WB2:259
Summers, John	Arlington	Account	1819	AB3:405; LVA-LP
Summers, John	Arlington	Account	1821	AB4:249; LVA-LP
Summers, John	Arlington	Inventory	1826	AB6:233
Summers, John	Arlington	Dower	1826	OCR1822:123
Summers, John	Arlington	Account	1827	AB6:270; LVA-LP
Summers, John	Arlington	Guard. Acct.	1842	AB8:307
Summers, John	Alexandria	Will	1880	WB1:290; LP
Summers, John, age 70 and upwards	Alexandria	Deposition	1768	CRI:280
Summers, John, age over 70	Alexandria	Deposition	1767	CRI:231
Summers, John, c/o John	Arlington	Guard.	1819	WB2:330
Summers, John, w(2), bricklayer	Alexandria	Head	1796	1796(3):2
Summers, Lewis	Alexandria	Tax Charge	1798	Tax PP 1798:16
Summers, Lewis	Alexandria	Tax Charge	1799	Tax PP 1799:37
Summers, Lewis	Alexandria	Tax Charge	1800	Tax PP 1800:39
Summers, Lewis, dcf.	Alexandria	Suit	1804	CRF:067
Summers, Lewis, grantee	Arlington	Indenture D.	1803	ID3:006
Summers, Lewis, grantee	Arlington	Indenture D.	1804	ID3:074
Summers, Lewis, grantee	Arlington	Indenture D.	1804	ID3:056
Summers, Lewis, grantee	Arlington	Indenture D.	1804	ID3:066
Summers, Lucinda, c/o John	Arlington	Guard.	1819	WB2:330
Summers, Margaret	Arlington	Guard.	1820	WB3:252
Summers, Margaret	Arlington	Guard.	1826	OCR1822:121a
Summers, Margaret	Arlington	Guard. Acct.	1839	AB8:031
Summers, Margaret, c/o John	Arlington	Guard.	1819	WB2:330
Summers, Mary M.	Alexandria	Will	1882	WB1:365; LP
Summers, Simon L.	Arlington	Guard. Acct.	1842	AB8:308
Summers, Simon, plt.	Alexandria	Suit	1803	CRD:095
Summers, Wesley	Arlington	Will	1862	WB8:106; File #591A
Summers, Widow	Alexandria	Head	1810	1810(2):05A
Summers, William	Alexandria	Tax Charge	1787	Tax PP 1787:14
Summers, William	Alexandria	Tax Charge	1790	Tax PP 1790:13
Summers, William	Arlington	Account	1800	WBA:008; LVA-LP
Summers, William	Arlington	Account	1807	WBB:505; LVA-LP
Summers, William, Estate	Alexandria	Tax Charge	1799	Tax PP 1799:37
Summers, William, Prince St.	Alexandria	Occupant	1790	Tax L 1790:10
Summers, William, Prince St.	Alexandria	Owner	1790	Tax L 1790:10
Summers, Wm.	Alexandria	Tax Charge	1788	Tax PP 1788:15
Summers, Wm.	Alexandria	Tax Charge	1789	Tax PP 1789:17
Summers, Wm.	Alexandria	Tax Charge	1795	Tax PP 1795:27
Summers, Wm.	Alexandria	Tax Charge	1796	Tax LP 1796:26
Summers, Wm.	Alexandria	Tax Charge	1796	Tax PP 1796:18
Summers, Wm., Estate	Alexandria	Tax Charge	1798	Tax PP 1798:16
Summers, Wm., Estate	Alexandria	Tax Charge	1800	Tax PP 1800:39
Summers, Wm., King St.	Alexandria	Owner	1795	Tax L 1795:26
Summers, Wm., Prince St.	Alexandria	Owner	1795	Tax L 1795:26
Summers, Wm., Princess St.	Alexandria	Owner	1795	Tax L 1795:26
Summers, Wm., Washington St.	Alexandria	Occupant	1795	Tax L 1795:26
Sunday, Jacob	Alexandria	Tax Charge	1800	Tax PP 1800:39
Sunday, Jacob & wife Sarah	Alexandria	Resident	1800	1800(4):09B
Sunday, Jacob, taylor	Alexandria	Head	1800	1800(4):09A
Sunday, John J. & wife, taylor	Alexandria	Housekeeper	1799	1799(2):06A
Supple, John	Alexandria	Tithable +16	1788	Tax PP 1788:15
Supple, John	Alexandria	Tax Charge	1789	Tax PP 1789:18
Suspenders, imported	Arlington	Suit	1803	ACO:013
Suter, Ann Charlotte, c/o John	Arlington	Guard.	1830	WB3:386
Suter, Charlotte, c/o Sarah	Arlington	Defendant	(nd)	LSA:124
Suter, Eudocia, c/o John	Arlington	Guard.	1830	WB3:386
Suter, John	Arlington	Ordinary	1810	OBL2(np)
Suter, John	Arlington	Inventory	1826	AB6:174
Suter, John	Arlington	Admin.	1826	OCR1822:110a

NAME OR SUBJECT	LOCATION	TYPE	YEAR	REFERENCE(S)
Suter, John	Arlington	Admin.	1826	WB3:222
Suter, John	Arlington	Account	1827	AB6:434; LVA-LP
Suter, Rebecca [Myres]	Arlington	Complainant	(nd)	LSA:124
Suter, Sarah Elizabeth, c/o Sarah	Arlington	Defendant	(nd)	LSA:124
Suter, Sarah Elizabeth, c/o John	Arlington	Guard.	1830	WB3:386
Suttles, William	Arlington	Crime	1794	OT:07/11/1794
Sutton, James A.	Arlington	Sale	1806	WBB:234
Sutton, James A.	Arlington	Inventory	1806	WBB:232; LVA-LP
Sutton, James A.	Arlington	Account	1806	WBB:324; LVA-LP
Sutton, James America	Arlington	Account	1810	WBC:387; LVA-LP
Sutton, James D.	Alexandria	Tax Charge	1800	Tax PP 1800:39
Sutton, Jno.	Alexandria	Tax Charge	1798	Tax PP 1798:16
Sutton, John	Alexandria	Owner	1787	Tax L 1787:24
Sutton, John	Alexandria	Tax Charge	1787	Tax PP 1787:13
Sutton, John	Alexandria	Tax Charge	1788	Tax PP 1788:14
Sutton, John	Alexandria	Tax Charge	1789	Tax PP 1789:16
Sutton, John	Alexandria	Tax Charge	1790	Tax PP 1790:13
Sutton, John	Alexandria	Tax Charge	1796	Tax LP 1796:26
Sutton, John	Alexandria	Tax Charge	1796	Tax PP 1796:18
Sutton, John	Alexandria	Tax Charge	1800	Tax PP 1800:39
Sutton, John, & John D.	Alexandria	Tax Charge	1799	Tax PP 1799:37
Sutton, John, citizen	Alexandria	Head	1810	1810(2):05A
Sutton, John D. & John	Alexandria	Tax Charge	1799	Tax PP 1799:37
Sutton, John, def.	Alexandria	Suit	1809	CRH:484
Sutton, John, journeyman, gentleman	Alexandria	Housekeeper	1808	1808(2):15A
Sutton, John, Royal St.	Alexandria	Occupant	1787	Tax L 1787:24
Sutton, John, Royal St.	Alexandria	Owner	1790	Tax L 1790:10
Sutton, John, sea captain	Alexandria	Housekeeper	1808	1808(2):17A
Sutton, Mrs.	Alexandria	Head	1810	1810(2):07A
Swain, Clarke	Alexandria	Boarder	1808	1808(1):01A
Swain, George W.	Alexandria	Will	1896	WB2:162; LP
Swain, Jane A., w/o Julius G.	Arlington	Will	1864	WB8:208; File #615A
Swallow, John Zephaniah	Arlington	Guard.	1817	WB2:184
Swallows, Joseph	Alexandria	Tax Charge	1789	Tax PP 1789:16
Swan & Steiber, Royal St.	Alexandria	Occupant	1787	Tax L 1787:02
Swan, Lawrence	Alexandria	Tax Charge	1796	Tax LP 1796:26
Swan, Lawrence	Alexandria	Tax Charge	1796	Tax PP 1796:17
Swan, Lawrence	Alexandria	Tax Charge	1800	Tax PP 1800:39
Swan, Thomas	Alexandria	Tithable +21	1787	Tax PP 1787:14
Swan, Thos.	Alexandria	Tithable +16	1788	Tax PP 1788:15
Swan, Thos.	Alexandria	Tax Charge	1800	Tax PP 1800:39
Swan, Thos., atty. at law	Alexandria	Head	1810	1810(4):05A
Swann, Frances	Arlington	Will	1856	WB7:126; File #530A
Swann, Frances	Arlington	Inventory	1857	WB7:176; LVA-LP
Swann, Frances, Admx. Wm. T. Swann	Arlington	Defendant	1824	ACO:245, 246
Swann, Frances, Admx. Wm. T. Swann	Arlington	Defendant	1825	ACO:254, 255, 259
Swann, Frances, Admx. Wm. T. Swann	Arlington	Defendant	1826	ACO:262, 265
Swann, Frances, Admx. Wm. T. Swann	Arlington	Defendant	1827	ACO:268, 269, 274
Swann, Frances B.	Arlington	Will	1886	WB10:077; File #725A
Swann, James S.	Arlington	Admin. Bond	1848	ABB(np)
Swann, James S.	Arlington	Account	1851	WB6:006; LVA-LP
Swann, Jane and Mary	Arlington	Report	1860	WB7:563; LVA-LP
Swann, Jane Byrd	Arlington	Admin.	1820	WB2:346
Swann, Jane E.	Arlington	Guard. Acct.	1849	WB5:133; LVA-LP
Swann, Jane E.	Arlington	Account	1860	WB7:557; LVA-LP
Swann, Jane E., c/o Thomas	Arlington	Guard.	1846	LVA-LP (Box 214)
Swann, Jane Elizabeth, c/o Thomas	Arlington	Guard.	1846	OCR1842:171
Swann, Jno.	Alexandria	Boarder	1808	1808(4):24A
Swann, John	Arlington	Apprentice	1803	OCR1801:143
Swann, John C.	Arlington	Admin. Bond	1848	ABB(np)
Swann, John C.	Arlington	Account	1851	WB6:006; LVA-LP

NAME OR SUBJECT	LOCATION	TYPE	YEAR	REFERENCE(S)
Swann, Julia	Arlington	Petition	1846	LVA-LP (Box 214)
Swann, Julia	Arlington	Guard. Acct.	1852	WB6:116; LVA-LP
Swann, Julia	Arlington	Guard. Acct.	1854	WB6:314; LVA-LP
Swann, Julia	Arlington	Guard. Acct.	1855	WB7:014; LVA-LP
Swann, Julia A., c/o Thomas	Arlington	Guard. Acct.	1847	WB5:023, 192; LVA-LP
Swann, Julia A., c/o Thomas	Arlington	Guard. Acct.	1847	WB5:306; LVA-LP
Swann, Julia, c/o Thomas	Arlington	Guard.	1846	OCR1842:166
Swann, Laurance	Alexandria	Tax Charge	1799	Tax PP 1799:38
Swann, Lawrence & wife, baker	Alexandria	Housekeeper	1799	1799(2):10A
Swann, Mary	Arlington	Guard. Acct.	1852	WB6:101; LVA-LP
Swann, Mary	Arlington	Will	1859	WB7:442; File #567A
Swann, Mary	Arlington	Account	1860	WB7:560; LVA-LP
Swann, Mary, c/o Thomas	Arlington	Guard.	1846	LVA-LP (Box 214)
Swann, Mary, c/o Thomas	Arlington	Guard.	1846	OCR1842:171
Swann, Mary M.	Arlington	Will	1872	WB9:345; File #685A
Swann, Mary M.	Arlington	Inventory	1873	WB9:359
Swann, Mary M.	Arlington	Appraisal	1873	WB9:359
Swann, Samuel, plt.	Alexandria	Suit	1801	CRC:001
Swann, Thomas	Alexandria	Deposition	1800	CRE:061
Swann, Thomas	Alexandria	Deed	1800	CRL:030
Swann, Thomas	Alexandria	Deed	1806	CRH:227
Swann, Thomas	Alexandria	Deed	1814	CRK:434
Swann, Thomas	Alexandria	Deposition	1817	CRK:430
Swann, Thomas	Arlington	Will P.	1845	OCR1842:146, 148
Swann, Thomas	Arlington	Will	1845	WB4:408; LVA-LP
Swann, Thomas	Arlington	Inventory	1846	AB9:160; LVA-LP
Swann, Thomas	Arlington	Account	1847	AB9:276; LVA-LP
Swann, Thomas	Arlington	Account	1848	WB5:147
Swann, Thomas	Arlington	Bond	1854	BB(np)
Swann, Thomas	Arlington	Account	1856	WB7:050, 552; LVA-LP
Swann, Thomas	Arlington	Report	1860	WB7:552; LVA-LP
Swann, Thomas, attorney	Arlington	Proof	1803	ACO:019
Swann, Thomas, def.	Alexandria	Suit	1810	CRH:197
Swann, Thomas, def.	Alexandria	Suit	1815	CRK:389
Swann, Thomas, def.	Alexandria	Suit	1819	CRL:024
Swann, Thomas, def.	Alexandria	Suit	1821	CRL:089
Swann, Thomas, def.	Alexandria	Suit	1821	CRL:159
Swann, Thomas, def.	Alexandria	Suit	1822	CRL:389
Swann, Thomas, grantee	Arlington	Indenture D.	1806	ID3:259
Swann, Thomas, Jr.	Arlington	Defendant	1823	ACO:228-231
Swann, Thomas, Jr.	Arlington	Defendant	1824	ACO:236, 250
Swann, Thomas, Jr.	Arlington	Defendant	1825	ACO:253, 254, 258
Swann, Thomas, Jr.	Arlington	Defendant	1826	ACO:261, 264
Swann, Thomas, Jr.	Arlington	Defendant	1827	ACO:268, 274
Swann, Thomas, plt.	Alexandria	Suit	1813	CRI:158
Swann, Thomas W.	Arlington	Will	1895	WB10:296
Swann, Thos.	Alexandria	Tax Charge	1798	Tax PP 1798:17
Swann, Thos.	Alexandria	Tax Charge	1799	Tax PP 1799:39
Swann, Thos.	Alexandria	Boarder	1808	1808(1):04A
Swann, Thos., lawyer	Alexandria	Housekeeper	1808	1808(4):26A
Swann, William T.	Arlington	Inventory	1821	AB4:267; LVA-LP
Swann, William T.	Arlington	Admin.	1821	WB2:420
Swann, William T.	Arlington	Account	1822	AB5:117; LVA-LP
Swann, William T.	Arlington	Account	1822	OCR1822:005a
Swann, William T.	Arlington	Account	1827	LVA-LP
Swann, William T. & wife Fanny, def.	Alexandria	Suit	1820	CRL:175
Swann, William T., assignees of	Arlington	Plaintiffs	1823	ACO:228-231
Swann, William T., of Washington DC	Arlington	Will	1860	WB7:546; File #575A
Swaye, John Henry	Arlington	Apprentice	1826	OCR1822:117
Swayne, Julius G.	Arlington	Apprentice	1828	OCR1822:154a
Sweeney, Felix	Alexandria	Tax Charge	1795	Tax PP 1795:28

NAME OR SUBJECT	LOCATION	TYPE	YEAR	REFERENCE(S)
Sweeney, Geo.	Alexandria	Tax Charge	1795	Tax PP 1795:29
Sweeney, Geo., King St.	Alexandria	Occupant	1795	Tax L 1795:06
Sweeney, Geo., Royal St.	Alexandria	Occupant	1795	Tax L 1795:26
Sweeney, George	Alexandria	Tax Charge	1796	Tax PP 1796:17
Sweeney, Wm.	Alexandria	Boarder	1808	1808(3):21A
Sweeny, Felix & wife, blacksmith	Alexandria	Housekeeper	1799	1799(2):03A
Sweeny, Francis	Alexandria	Boarder	1808	1808(2):16A
Sweeny, Jas.	Alexandria	Boarder	1808	1808(2):12A
Sweeny, Phelix	Alexandria	Tax Charge	1798	Tax PP 1798:16
Sweet, Capt., Royal St.	Alexandria	Occupant	1790	Tax L 1790:01
Sweet, John	Alexandria	Tax Charge	1789	Tax PP 1789:16
Sweet, Margaret	Arlington	Guard.	1809	WBC:221
Swellett, Jno.	Alexandria	Boarder	1808	1808(4):25A
Swift, John	Alexandria	Tax Charge	1790	Tax PP 1790:14
Swift, Johnerthan & wife Ann	Alexandria	Resident	1800	1800(4):12B
Swift, Jona.	Alexandria	Tax Charge	1790	Tax PP 1790:13
Swift, Jonan.	Alexandria	Tax Charge	1798	Tax PP 1798:17
Swift, Jonathan	Alexandria	Owner	1787	Tax L 1787:23
Swift, Jonathan	Alexandria	Tax Charge	1787	Tax PP 1787:14
Swift, Jonathan	Alexandria	Tax Charge	1788	Tax PP 1788:15
Swift, Jonathan	Alexandria	Tax Charge	1789	Tax PP 1789:17
Swift, Jonathan	Alexandria	Tax Charge	1796	Tax PP 1796:17
Swift, Jonathan	Alexandria	Tax Charge	1799	Tax PP 1799:38
Swift, Jonathan	Alexandria	Tax Charge	1800	Tax PP 1800:40
Swift, Jonathan	Arlington	Admin.	1824	WB3:142
Swift, Jonathan	Arlington	Inventory	1825	AB6:035; LVA-LP
Swift, Jonathan	Arlington	Account	1825	AB6:103; LVA-LP
Swift, Jonathan	Arlington	Sale	1825	AB6:037
Swift, Jonathan &wife, merchant	Alexandria	Housekeeper	1799	1799(2):19A
Swift, Jonathan, Fairfax St.	Alexandria	Occupant	1787	Tax L 1787:23
Swift, Jonathan, Fairfax St.	Alexandria	Owner	1790	Tax L 1790:10
Swift, Jonathan, Fairfax St.	Alexandria	Occupant	1790	Tax L 1790:10
Swift, Jonathan, Fairfax St.	Alexandria	Owner	1795	Tax L 1795:28
Swift, Jonathan, Fairfax St.	Alexandria	Occupant	1795	Tax L 1795:28
Swift, Jonathan, gentleman	Alexandria	Housekeeper	1808	1808(3):18A
Swift, Jonathan, gentleman	Alexandria	Head	1810	1810(3):10A
Swift, Jonathan, murchant	Alexandria	Head	1800	1800(4):12A
Swift, Mary D.	Alexandria	Will	1870	WB1:002; LP
Swift, Mary Donaldson	Alexandria	Will	1870	WB1:002
Swift, Tohna.	Alexandria	Tax Charge	1796	Tax LP 1796:27
Swiley, Joseph	Alexandria	Tax Charge	1798	Tax PP 1798:17
Swiley, Joseph	Alexandria	Tax Charge	1799	Tax PP 1799:38
Swiley, Joseph & wife, taylor	Alexandria	Head	1795	1795(4):02
Swillers, Hawke & Binne	Alexandria	Occupant	1790	Tax L 1790:03
Swillivant, John	Alexandria	Tax Charge	1788	Tax PP 1788:15
Swillors, Joseph	Alexandria	Tax Charge	1790	Tax PP 1790:13
Swilor, James, c/o Joseph	Arlington	Apprentice	1805	OCR1801:264
Swisher, George, plt.	Alexandria	Ejectment	1802	CRE:242
Switzer, Phil.	Alexandria	Boarder	1808	1808(2):10A
Swoope, Adam	Alexandria	Tax Charge	1789	Tax PP 1789:17
Swoope, Adam	Alexandria	Tax Charge	1795	Tax PP 1795:29
Swoope, Adam & Jacob	Alexandria	Owner	1787	Tax L 1787:24
Swoope, Adam & Jacob, Prince St.	Alexandria	Occupant	1787	Tax L 1787:24
Swoope, Adam, Prince St.	Alexandria	Owner	1795	Tax L 1795:27
Swoope, Adam, Prince St.	Alexandria	Occupant	1795	Tax L 1795:27
Swoope, Adam S.	Alexandria	Tax Charge	1787	Tax PP 1787:14
Swoope, Adam S.	Alexandria	Tax Charge	1790	Tax PP 1790:13
Swoope, Adam S.	Alexandria	Tax Charge	1796	Tax PP 1796:18
Swoope, Adam S.	Alexandria	Mer. License	1798	Tax PP 1798:20-7
Swoope, Adam S.	Alexandria	Tax Charge	1798	Tax PP 1798:17
Swoope, Adam S.	Alexandria	Tax Charge	1799	Tax PP 1799:38

NAME OR SUBJECT	LOCATION	TYPE	YEAR	REFERENCE(S)
Swoope, Adam S.	Alexandria	Mer. License	1800	Tax PP 1800:54(20)r
Swoope, Adam S.	Alexandria	Tax Charge	1800	Tax PP 1800:39
Swoope, Adam S. & mother, retailer	Alexandria	Housekeeper	1799	1799(2):01A
Swoope, Adam Simon	Arlington	Defendant	1802	PA:253
Swoope, Eve	Arlington	Plaintiff	1802	PA:144
Swoope, Eve, widow, (2)4	Alexandria	Head	1796	1796(3):5
Swoope, Geo.	Alexandria	Tax Charge	1795	Tax PP 1795:29
Swoope, George	Alexandria	Tax Charge	1796	Tax PP 1796:18
Swoope, Jacque	Alexandria	Tax Charge	1788	Tax PP 1788:15
Swope, A.S., Prince St.	Alexandria	Occupant	1790	Tax L 1790:10
Swope, Adam	Alexandria	Tax Charge	1796	Tax LP 1796:27
Swope, Adam	Arlington	Sale	1804	WBB:008; LVA-LP
Swope, Adam	Arlington	Inventory	1804	WBB:003; LVA-LP
Swope, Adam S.	Arlington	Admin.	1804	WBA:315, 324
Swope, Adam S.	Arlington	Account	1807	WBB:486; LVA-LP
Swope, Adam S., Prince St.	Alexandria	Owner	1790	Tax L 1790:10
Swope, Eve Barbara	Arlington	Sale	1804	WBA:258
Swope, Eve Barbara	Arlington	Inventory	1804	WBA:256; LVA-LP
Swope, Eve Barbara	Arlington	Admin.	1804	WBA:238
Swope, Eve Barbara	Arlington	Account	1807	WBB:485
Sword, John [Sarah]	Arlington	Account	1818	LVA-LP
Sword, Sarah	Arlington	Admin.	1812	WB1:175
Sword, Sarah	Arlington	Renounce	1818	LVA-LP
Swyler, Jos. & wife, taylor	Alexandria	Housekeeper	1799	1799(2):16A
Swylers, J.	Alexandria	Tax Charge	1796	Tax PP 1796:17
Swylor, Jane	Alexandria	Resident	1800	1800(4):02B
Swylor, Jane, spinster	Alexandria	Head	1800	1800(4):02A
Swylor, John, c/o Joseph	Arlington	Apprentice	1805	OCR1801:270
Syke, Peter	Arlington	Apprentice	1801	OCR1801:008
Syke, Peter, hatter	Alexandria	Head	1810	1810(1):06A
Symonds, Elizabeth, c/o James	Arlington	Guard.	1826	OCR1822:117
Symonds, Elizabeth, c/o James	Arlington	Guard.	1826	WB3:241
Symonds, James, orphans of	Arlington	Guard.	1826	OCR1822:117
Symonds, Jane, c/o James	Arlington	Guard.	1826	OCR1822:117
Symonds, Jane, c/o James	Arlington	Guard.	1826	WB3:241
Symonds, John, c/o James	Arlington	Guard.	1826	OCR1822:117
Symonds, John, c/o James	Arlington	Guard.	1826	WB3:241
Symonds, Julia Ann, c/o James	Arlington	Guard.	1826	OCR1822:117
Symonds, Julia Ann, c/o James	Arlington	Guard.	1826	WB3:241
Symonds, Samuel	Arlington	Bond	1809	WBC:294
Symonds, Samuel	Arlington	Will	1809	WBC:292; File #044A
Symonds, Samuel	Arlington	Inventory	1809	WBC:299; LVA-LP
Symonds, Samuel	Arlington	Account	1811	LVA-LP
Syphax, Maria	Arlington	Will	1889	WB10:155
Syphax, William	Arlington	Will	1900	WB10:450; File #802A

NAME OR SUBJECT	LOCATION	TYPE	YEAR	REFERENCE(S)
T				
Tabb, Jno.	Alexandria	Tax Charge	1795	Tax PP 1795:30
Tabb, [blank], King St.	Alexandria	Occupant	1795	Tax L 1795:13
Taber, Bradford, sea captain	Alexandria	Housekeeper	1808	1808(1):07A
Tacey, Jefferson	Arlington	Will	1880	WB10:002; File #699A
Tacey, Maud	Alexandria	Will	1886	WB1:442; LP
Talbert, Jessy	Alexandria	Serv./Appr.	1800	1800(4):09B
Talbert, John	Alexandria	Tithable +16	1790	Tax PP 1790:06
Talbert, Levi, Fairfax St.	Alexandria	Occupant	1787	Tax L 1787:09
Talbert, McKinzey	Alexandria	Deposition	1802	CRI:075, 079
Talbert, Osburn, age 43	Alexandria	Deposition	1767	CRI:252
Talbert, William	Alexandria	Tax Charge	1796	Tax PP 1796:19
Talbot, Elisha, tanner	Alexandria	Head	1810	1810(3):06A
Talbot, Eliza	Arlington	Guard.	1826	WB3:264
Talbot, Jesse, druggist	Alexandria	Head	1810	1810(4):01A
Talbot, Levi	Alexandria	Mer. License	1799	Tax PP 1799:52-10r
Talbot, Levi & wife	Alexandria	Housekeeper	1799	1799(2):04A
Talbot, Levi, cooper	Alexandria	Head	1810	1810(2):03A
Talbot, Levi, nr. Royal St.	Alexandria	Occupant	1790	Tax L 1790:06
Talbot, Levi, Water St.	Alexandria	Occupant	1790	Tax L 1790:05
Talbot, Levy	Alexandria	Tax Charge	1790	Tax PP 1790:14
Talbot, Mary	Arlington	Apprentice	1823	OCR1822:051a
Talbot, Mrs., Queen St.	Alexandria	Occupant	1787	Tax L 1787:01
Talbot, Mrs., Queen St.	Alexandria	Occupant	1790	Tax L 1790:01
Talbott, Charles, c/o McKenzie	Arlington	Apprentice	1815	OCR1811:294
Talbott, Daniel, c/o McKenzie	Arlington	Apprentice	1815	OCR1811:248
Talbott, Daniel, c/o McKenzie	Arlington	Apprentice	1818	OCR1811:184
Talbott, Elisha, carpenter	Alexandria	Housekeeper	1808	1808(4):25A
Talbott, Jesse	Alexandria	Boarder	1808	1808(4):25A
Talbott, Levi	Alexandria	Tax Charge	1799	Tax PP 1799:40
Talbott, Levi	Alexandria	Tax Charge	1800	Tax PP 1800:43
Talbott, Levi, cooper	Alexandria	Housekeeper	1808	1808(2):11A
Talbott, Mrs., Queen St.	Alexandria	Occupant	1795	Tax L 1795:01
Talbott, Phill. (C), laborer	Alexandria	Housekeeper	1808	1808(1):05A
Talbott, Thomas	Arlington	Bond	1852	BB(np)
Talbott, Thomas	Arlington	Appraisal	1852	WB6:114; LVA-LP
Talburt, John	Alexandria	Tithable +16	1789	Tax PP 1789:08
Talburt, Levi	Alexandria	Tax Charge	1788	Tax PP 1788:16
Talburt, Levi	Alexandria	Tax Charge	1789	Tax PP 1789:18
Talbutt, George	Arlington	Ordinary	1809	OBL2(np)
Talbutt, Levi, plt.	Alexandria	Suit	1799	CRB:041
Taler, John, w(4), blacksmith	Alexandria	Head	1795	1796(3):7
Tandy, Moses	Alexandria	Tax Charge	1787	Tax PP 1787:15
Tandy, Moses	Alexandria	Tax Charge	1788	Tax PP 1788:16
Tannehill, Wm.	Alexandria	Tax Charge	1799	Tax PP 1799:40
Tanner, Jno.	Alexandria	Tax Charge	1795	Tax PP 1795:30
Tanner, Pierce L.	Arlington	Plaintiff	1802	PA:060
Tannery, Samuel H.	Alexandria	Will	1887	LP
Tarleton, Jas., seaman	Alexandria	Housekeeper	1808	1808(1):08A
Tarleton, Joseph	Alexandria	Tax Charge	1799	Tax PP 1799:40
Tarleton, Richd., waterman	Alexandria	Housekeeper	1808	1808(1):08A
Tarleton, Robt.	Alexandria	Boarder	1808	1808(1):08A
Tarleton, Stephen	Arlington	Will (NP)	1811	File #057A
Tarlton, James	Arlington	Admin.	1815	WB2:090
Tarlton, James	Arlington	Admin.	1815	WB2:090
Tarlton, James, seaman	Alexandria	Head	1810	1810(2):06A
Tarlton, Jeremh., Prince St.	Alexandria	Occupant	1795	Tax L 1795:15
Tarlton, Jeremh., Wales' alley	Alexandria	Occupant	1795	Tax L 1795:29
Tarlton, Jeremiah	Alexandria	Tax Charge	1795	Tax PP 1795:31
Tarlton, Jno., taylor	Alexandria	Boarder	1799	1799(2):03A
Tartanson, Francis	Arlington	Inventory	1812	AB1:184; LVA-LP

NAME OR SUBJECT	LOCATION	TYPE	YEAR	REFERENCE(S)
Tartanson, Francis	Arlington	Admin.	1812	WB1:160
Tartanson, Francis	Arlington	Account	1813	AB1:327; LVA-LP
Tartanson, Francis	Arlington	Settlement	1815	AB2:157; LVA-LP
Tartanson, John Alexander, c/o Francis	Arlington	Guard.	1812	WB1:161
Tartarson, Alexander, grantee	Arlington	Indenture D.	1826	ID:014
Tartespaugh, Elizabeth, washwoman	Alexandria	Housekeeper	1808	1808(4):24A
Tartsabaugh, George	Alexandria	Tax Charge	1799	Tax PP 1799:40
Tartsabaugh, Peter	Alexandria	Tax Charge	1799	Tax PP 1799:40
Tartsepaugh, Henry, s/o Peter	Alexandria	Boarder	1808	1808(4):26A
Tartsepaugh, John, s/o Peter	Alexandria	Boarder	1808	1808(4):26A
Tartsepaugh, Peter, shopkeeper	Alexandria	Housekeeper	1808	1808(4):26A
Tasapaw, Adam & wife Elizebeth	Alexandria	Resident	1800	1800(4):13B
Tasapaw, Adam, carpenter	Alexandria	Head	1800	1800(4):13A
Tate, Harry (C)	Alexandria	Boarder	1808	1808(3):22B
Tate, Jesse, ship carpenter	Alexandria	Housekeeper	1808	1808(1):09A
Tate, Samuel	Arlington	Libellant	1803	ACO:022
Tate, William, c/o Samuel	Arlington	Apprentice	1804	OCR1801:176
Tate, Wm.	Alexandria	Boarder	1808	1808(2):13A
Tatsapau, Peter, Fairfax St.	Alexandria	Occupant	1790	Tax L 1790:11
Tatsapau, Peter, Fairfax St.	Alexandria	Owner	1790	Tax L 1790:11
Tatsapaugh, Adam	Alexandria	Tax Charge	1800	Tax PP 1800:43
Tatsapaugh, John	Arlington	Bond	1855	BB(np)
Tatsapaugh, John	Arlington	Inventory	1855	WB6:430; LVA-LP
Tatsapaugh, John	Arlington	Inventory	1855	WB6:434; LVA-LP
Tatsapaugh, John	Arlington	Account	1856	WB7:072; LVA-LP
Tatsapaugh, John	Arlington	Creditors	1857	WB7:238; LVA-LP
Tatsapaugh, John, c/o Elizabeth	Arlington	Apprentice	1815	OCR1811:255
Tatsapaugh, Peter	Alexandria	Tax Charge	1795	Tax PP 1795:31
Tatsapaugh [Tartsabaugh], Adam	Alexandria	Tax Charge	1799	Tax PP 1799:40
Tatsapaugh [Terdszpaugh], Adam	Alexandria	Tax Charge	1798	Tax PP 1798:18
Tatsapaugh [Terdszpaugh], Peter	Alexandria	Tax Charge	1798	Tax PP 1798:18
Tatsapaw, Adam	Alexandria	Tax Charge	1789	Tax PP 1789:18
Tatsapaw, Adam	Alexandria	Tax Charge	1790	Tax PP 1790:14
Tatsapaw, Peter	Alexandria	Tax Charge	1790	Tax PP 1790:15
Tatsapaw, [blank], Fairfax St.	Alexandria	Occupant	1790	Tax L 1790:07
Tatsbaugh, Adam	Alexandria	Tax Charge	1796	Tax PP 1796:19
Tatsebaugh, Peter	Alexandria	Tax Charge	1787	Tax PP 1787:15
Tatsepaugh, Elizabeth, seamstress	Alexandria	Head	1810	1810(4):09A
Tatspaugh, Adam & wife, carpenter	Alexandria	Housekeeper	1799	1799(2):18A
Tatspaugh, Geo. & wife, carpenter	Alexandria	Housekeeper	1799	1799(2):06A
Tatspaugh, Peter	Alexandria	Tax Charge	1796	Tax PP 1796:19
Tatspaugh, Peter & wife, carpenter	Alexandria	Housekeeper	1799	1799(2):06A
Tatstapaw, Peter	Alexandria	Tax Charge	1789	Tax PP 1789:18
Tattershall, Joseph, gard. f/G. Deneale	Alexandria	Housekeeper	1808	1808(4):28A
Tattershall, Thos., shoemaker	Alexandria	Housekeeper	1808	1808(1):05A
Tattershall, Thos., shoemaker	Alexandria	Head	1810	1810(2):01A
Tatterson, Alexander, grantor	Arlington	Indenture D.	1827	ID:071
Tatterson, Alexander, in jail	Arlington	Insolvent	1827	ID:070
Tatterson, Harriet Mason, children of	Arlington	Guard.	1828	OCR1822:162a
Tattsapaugh, Peter	Alexandria	Tax Charge	1800	Tax PP 1800:43
Tatzapaugh, Adam, Oronoko St.	Alexandria	Occupant	1795	Tax L 1795:04
Tatzapaugh, P., Duke St.	Alexandria	Occupant	1795	Tax L 1795:02
Tatzapaugh, Peter, Fairfax Co.	Alexandria	Occupant	1795	Tax L 1795:14
Tatzepaugh, Peter, cake baker	Alexandria	Head	1810	1810(4):01A
Tatzepaw, Adam & wife, carpenter	Alexandria	Head	1795	1795(4a):09
Tatzpaugh, Adam	Alexandria	Tax Charge	1796	Tax LP 1796:28
Tatzpaugh, Peter	Alexandria	Tax Charge	1796	Tax LP 1796:28
Tavender, Esther, c/o Susanna	Arlington	Apprentice	1802	OCR1801:047
Tayler, James	Arlington	Apprentice	1803	OCR1801:121
Tayloe, John, of *Mt. Airy*	Arlington	Will	1827	CF# *Carter v. Tayloe*
Taylor & Ghequiere, Union St.	Alexandria	Occupant	1795	Tax L 1795:08

NAME OR SUBJECT	LOCATION	TYPE	YEAR	REFERENCE(S)
Taylor & Wattles, merchants	Alexandria	Housekeeper	1808	1808(2):11A
Taylor, Alexander	Alexandria	Tax Charge	1787	Tax PP 1787:15
Taylor, Allen	Arlington	Guard. Acct.	1859	WB7:449; LVA-LP
Taylor, Andrew	Alexandria	Tithable +16	1790	Tax PP 1790:14
Taylor, Andrew	Alexandria	Tax Charge	1796	Tax LP 1796:28
Taylor, Andrew	Alexandria	Tax Charge	1796	Tax PP 1796:19
Taylor, Andrew	Arlington	Will	1806	WBB:358; File #013A
Taylor, Andrew, 3, merchant	Alexandria	Head	1796	1796(3):5
Taylor, Andrew, def.	Alexandria	Suit	1801	CRC:118
Taylor, Andw.	Alexandria	Tithable +16	1788	Tax PP 1788:16
Taylor, Andw.	Alexandria	Tithable +16	1789	Tax PP 1789:18
Taylor, Andw.	Alexandria	Tax Charge	1795	Tax PP 1795:31
Taylor, Andw.	Alexandria	Tax Charge	1799	Tax PP 1799:40
Taylor, Andw., Fairfax St.	Alexandria	Occupant	1795	Tax L 1795:19
Taylor, Ann A.B.	Arlington	Will	1855	WB6:418; File #515A
Taylor, Ann A.B.	Arlington	Account	1856	WB7:087; LVA-LP
Taylor, Anna B.	Arlington	Appraisal	1855	WB6:458; LVA-LP
Taylor, Anne E.V.	Alexandria	Will	1891	WB1:588; LP
Taylor, Anne H.	Arlington	Guard. Acct.	1860	WB8:508
Taylor, Anne H.	Arlington	Guard. Acct.	1860	WB8:003; LVA-LP
Taylor, Archd.	Alexandria	Tax Charge	1795	Tax PP 1795:30
Taylor, Archd.	Alexandria	Tax Charge	1796	Tax LP 1796:28
Taylor, Archd. J.	Alexandria	Tax Charge	1796	Tax PP 1796:19
Taylor, Archibald	Arlington	Admin.	1818	WB2:248
Taylor, Archibald, 1, merchant	Alexandria	Head	1796	1796(3):3
Taylor, Archibald Henderson	Arlington	Guard. Acct.	1859	WB7:451; LVA-LP
Taylor, Archibald Henderson	Arlington	Guard. Acct.	1860	WB8:502
Taylor, Archibald Henderson	Arlington	Guard. Acct.	1860	WB8:001; LVA-LP
Taylor, Archibald I., def.	Alexandria	Suit	1801	CRC:118
Taylor, Archibald J.	Arlington	Inventory	1818	AB3:197; LVA-LP
Taylor, Benjamin	Arlington	Fid. Bond	1859	FBB(np)
Taylor, Benjamin	Arlington	Will (NR)	1859	File #080A
Taylor, Bennet, def.	Alexandria	Suit	1818	CRK:390
Taylor, Charles G.	Arlington	P. of Atty.	1845	OCR1842:108
Taylor, Charles M.	Alexandria	Will	1873	WB1:067; LP
Taylor, Charles W.	Arlington	Will	1887	WB10:093; File #727A
Taylor, Clarence W.	Alexandria	Will	1893	WB2:066; LP
Taylor, Daniel, ship carpenter	Alexandria	Head	1810	1810(1):11A
Taylor, David	Arlington	Apprentice	1802	OCR1801:024
Taylor, Elijah, drayman	Alexandria	Head	1810	1810(3):02A
Taylor, Elisha, cartman	Alexandria	Housekeeper	1808	1808(3):23A
Taylor, Elizabeth	Arlington	Inventory	1845	AB9:099; LVA-LP
Taylor, Elizabeth	Arlington	Admin.	1845	OCR1842:101
Taylor, Elizabeth	Arlington	Account	1846	AB9:192; LVA-LP
Taylor, Elizabeth	Arlington	Division	1846	LVA-LP
Taylor, Elizabeth, at Balls Crossroads	Arlington	Plat	1846	LVA-LP
Taylor, Elizabeth, w/o Jesse, def.	Alexandria	Suit	1801	CRC:118
Taylor, Evan	Alexandria	Boarder	1808	1808(4):27A
Taylor, Evan P.	Arlington	Division	1825	OCR1822:093
Taylor, Geo.	Alexandria	Tax Charge	1795	Tax PP 1795:31
Taylor, Geo.	Alexandria	Tax Charge	1798	Tax PP 1798:18
Taylor, Geo.	Alexandria	License Due	1800	Tax PP 1800:54(24)
Taylor, Geo. & wife, merchant	Alexandria	Housekeeper	1799	1799(2):04A
Taylor, Geo., Fairfax St.	Alexandria	Occupant	1795	Tax L 1795:22
Taylor, George	Alexandria	Tax Charge	1789	Tax PP 1789:18
Taylor, George	Alexandria	Tax Charge	1790	Tax PP 1790:14
Taylor, George	Alexandria	Tax Charge	1796	Tax LP 1796:28
Taylor, George	Alexandria	Tax Charge	1796	Tax PP 1796:19
Taylor, George	Alexandria	Mer. License	1798	Tax PP 1798:20-7
Taylor, George	Alexandria	Tax Charge	1799	Tax PP 1799:40
Taylor, George	Alexandria	Tax Charge	1800	Tax PP 1800:43

NAME OR SUBJECT	LOCATION	TYPE	YEAR	REFERENCE(S)
Taylor, George	Arlington	Juryman	1804	ACO:024, 027
Taylor, George	Arlington	Juryman	1808	ACO:081
Taylor, George, def.	Alexandria	Suit	1822	CRL:389
Taylor, George, merchant	Alexandria	Head	1795	1795(4):05
Taylor, George, plt.	Alexandria	Suit	1813	CRI:158
Taylor, George, plt.	Alexandria	Suit	1813	CRL:438
Taylor, George, Prince St.	Alexandria	Occupant	1790	Tax L 1790:06
Taylor, Harriet C.	Alexandria	Will	1893	WB2:055; LP
Taylor, Harriet C., c/o Robert J.	Arlington	Guard.	1841	WB4:281
Taylor, Henry	Alexandria	Tax Charge	1795	Tax PP 1795:30
Taylor, Henry	Arlington	Will	1863	WB8:145; File #597A
Taylor, Henry Allen, c/o Robert J.	Arlington	Guard.	1841	WB4:281
Taylor, J., Duke St.	Alexandria	Occupant	1787	Tax L 1787:20
Taylor, James	Alexandria	Tax Charge	1787	Tax PP 1787:15
Taylor, James	Alexandria	Tithable +16	1788	Tax PP 1788:08
Taylor, James	Alexandria	Tax Charge	1795	Tax PP 1795:31
Taylor, James, c/o Augustine	Arlington	Apprentice	1846	OCR1842:159
Taylor, James, Pitt St.	Alexandria	Occupant	1795	Tax L 1795:33
Taylor, Jesse	Alexandria	Owner	1787	Tax L 1787:25
Taylor, Jesse	Alexandria	Tax Charge	1787	Tax PP 1787:15
Taylor, Jesse	Alexandria	Tax Charge	1788	Tax PP 1788:16
Taylor, Jesse	Alexandria	Tax Charge	1789	Tax PP 1789:18
Taylor, Jesse	Alexandria	Tax Charge	1790	Tax PP 1790:14
Taylor, Jesse	Alexandria	Tax Charge	1795	Tax PP 1795:30
Taylor, Jesse	Alexandria	Tax Charge	1796	Tax LP 1796:28
Taylor, Jesse	Alexandria	Tax Charge	1796	Tax PP 1796:19
Taylor, Jesse	Alexandria	Tax Charge	1798	Tax PP 1798:18
Taylor, Jesse	Alexandria	Tax Charge	1799	Tax PP 1799:40
Taylor, Jesse	Arlington	Complaint	1800	LVA-LP
Taylor, Jesse	Alexandria	Tax Charge	1800	Tax PP 1800:43
Taylor, Jesse	Arlington	Apprentice	1802	OCR1801:050
Taylor, Jesse	Alexandria	Boarder	1808	1808(1):02A
Taylor, Jesse	Alexandria	Boarder	1808	1808(3):22A
Taylor, Jesse & Co., St. Asaph St.	Alexandria	Occupant	1787	Tax L 1787:03
Taylor, Jesse & others, Pitt & King sts	Alexandria	Occupant	1787	Tax L 1787:25
Taylor, Jesse & wife	Alexandria	Housekeeper	1799	1799(2):05A
Taylor, Jesse A.	Arlington	Deposition	1801	PA:180
Taylor, Jesse, clerk	Alexandria	Boarder	1799	1799(2):02A
Taylor, Jesse, def.	Alexandria	Suit	1801	CRC:118
Taylor, Jesse, Esq., Pitt & King Sts.	Alexandria	Owner	1790	Tax L 1790:11
Taylor, Jesse, Estate, def.	Alexandria	Suit	1801	CRC:054, 058
Taylor, Jesse, Estate, def.	Alexandria	Suit	1801	CRD:034
Taylor, Jesse, Estate, def.	Alexandria	Suit	1802	CRC:280
Taylor, Jesse, Jr.	Alexandria	Tithable +16	1790	Tax PP 1790:14
Taylor, Jesse, King St.	Alexandria	Owner	1795	Tax L 1795:29
Taylor, Jesse, King St.	Alexandria	Occupant	1795	Tax L 1795:29
Taylor, Jesse, on the wharf	Alexandria	Owner	1795	Tax L 1795:29
Taylor, Jesse, Pitt & King Sts.	Alexandria	Occupant	1790	Tax L 1790:11
Taylor, Jesse, w(3)10, merchant	Alexandria	Head	1796	1796(3):2
Taylor, Jno.	Alexandria	Tax Charge	1795	Tax PP 1795:31
Taylor, Jno., clerk	Alexandria	Boarder	1799	1799(2):04A
Taylor, John	Alexandria	Tithable +16	1789	Tax PP 1789:20
Taylor, John	Alexandria	Tithable +16	1790	Tax PP 1790:16
Taylor, John	Alexandria	Tax Charge	1796	Tax LP 1796:28
Taylor, John Charles, s/o Bennet, def.	Alexandria	Suit	(nd)	CRK:430
Taylor, John Henry, c/o Mary Duncan	Arlington	Apprentice	1811	OCR1811:044
Taylor, Joshua	Arlington	Apprentice	1811	OCR1811:041
Taylor, Julian	Arlington	Inventory	1854	WB6:309; LVA-LP
Taylor, Julian	Arlington	Guard. Acct.	1859	WB7:450; LVA-LP
Taylor, Julian	Arlington	Guard. Acct.	1860	WB8:001; LVA-LP
Taylor, Julian	Arlington	Guard. Acct.	1860	WB8:505

NAME OR SUBJECT	LOCATION	TYPE	YEAR	REFERENCE(S)
Taylor, Julian, c/o Robert J.	Arlington	Guard.	1841	WB4:281
Taylor, M. Elizabeth	Arlington	Will	1866	WB8:416; File #648A
Taylor, Mary	Arlington	Admin.	1823	OCR1822:059
Taylor, Mary	Arlington	Admin.	1823	WB3:169
Taylor, Mary	Arlington	Inventory	1824	AB5:230; LVA-LP
Taylor, Mary	Arlington	Sale	1824	AB5:231
Taylor, Mary	Arlington	Account	1825	AB5:378
Taylor, Mary H.	Arlington	Guard. Acct.	1859	WB7:452; LVA-LP
Taylor, Mary H.	Arlington	Guard. Acct.	1860	WB8:002; LVA-LP
Taylor, Mary H.	Arlington	Guard. Acct.	1860	WB8:499
Taylor, Mary Jane	Arlington	Will	1880	WB10:004; File #700A
Taylor, Mary, Mrs.	Alexandria	Tax Charge	1800	Tax PP 1800:43
Taylor, Mary, shopkeeper	Alexandria	Housekeeper	1808	1808(1):01A
Taylor, Mary, shopkeeper	Alexandria	Head	1810	1810(1):01A
Taylor, Mary, shopkeeper	Alexandria	Head	1810	1810(2):04A
Taylor, Mary, shopkeeper	Alexandria	Head	1810	1810(3):04A
Taylor, Mary, washwoman	Alexandria	Housekeeper	1808	1808(1):05A
Taylor, Mary, washwoman	Alexandria	Housekeeper	1808	1808(2):14A
Taylor, Mrs., Water St.	Alexandria	Occupant	1795	Tax L 1795:05
Taylor, Nannie P.	Alexandria	Will	1897	WB2:236; LP
Taylor, Rebecca	Arlington	Will	1856	WB7:065; File #526A
Taylor, Rebecca	Arlington	Appraisal	1857	WB7:221; LVA-LP
Taylor, Rebecca	Arlington	Account	1858	WB7:313; LVA-LP
Taylor, Rebecca	Arlington	Letter	1860	LVA-LP
Taylor, Richard	Arlington	Apprentice	1828	OCR1822:154
Taylor, Robert I.	Alexandria	Deed	1814	CRK:434
Taylor, Robert I.	Alexandria	Deposition	1817	CRK:430
Taylor, Robert I., def.	Alexandria	Suit	1801	CRC:118
Taylor, Robert I., def.	Alexandria	Suit	1801	CRC:054
Taylor, Robert I., def.	Alexandria	Suit	1801	CRD:034
Taylor, Robert I., def.	Alexandria	Suit	1802	CRC:280
Taylor, Robert I., def.	Alexandria	Suit	1803	CRD:093
Taylor, Robert J.	Arlington	Respondent	1812	ACO:122
Taylor, Robert J.	Arlington	Account	1840	LVA-LP
Taylor, Robert J.	Arlington	Will	1840	WB4:263b; File #380A
Taylor, Robert J.	Arlington	Bond	1840	WB4:268
Taylor, Robert J.	Arlington	Account	1842	AB8:265
Taylor, Robert J.	Arlington	Account	1843	AB8:394; LVA-LP
Taylor, Robert J.	Arlington	Account	1845	AB9:080
Taylor, Robert J.	Arlington	Debts Due	1845	AB9:082; LVA-LP
Taylor, Robert J.	Arlington	Account	1846	AB9:320; LVA-LP
Taylor, Robert J.	Arlington	Account	1847	AB9:320
Taylor, Robert J.	Arlington	Account	1848	WB5:092; LVA-LP
Taylor, Robert J.	Arlington	Account	1851	WB5:268; LVA-LP
Taylor, Robert J.	Arlington	Account	1852	WB6:065; LVA-LP
Taylor, Robert J.	Arlington	Appraisal	1856	WB7:061; LVA-LP
Taylor, Robert J.	Arlington	Account	1857	WB7:208; LVA-LP
Taylor, Robert J.	Arlington	Account	1867	WB8:524
Taylor, Robert J., children of	Arlington	Suit	(nd)	LSA:134
Taylor, Robert J., grantee	Arlington	Indenture D.	1806	ID3:136
Taylor, Robert J., grantee	Arlington	Indenture D.	1806	ID3:123
Taylor, Robert J. to Thomas Braddock	Arlington	Deed	1816	LVA-LP (Accts. 1844)
Taylor, Robert J., trustee	Arlington	Respondent	1815	ACO:143
Taylor, Robt. I., atty. at law	Alexandria	Head	1810	1810(4):07A
Taylor, Robt. J., lawyer	Alexandria	Housekeeper	1808	1808(4):25A
Taylor, Saraën Fitch Brainerd, c/o Fitch	Arlington	Guard.	1845	OCR1842:104, 108
Taylor, Sarah Easton Ladd	Arlington	Will P.	1843	OCR1842:034
Taylor, Sarah Easton Ladd	Arlington	Will	1843	WB4:330; File #400A
Taylor, Susan, w/o Bennet, def.	Alexandria	Suit	(nd)	CRK:430
Taylor, Susanna	Arlington	Guard.	1804	WBB:102
Taylor, Theodore A.	Alexandria	Will	1889	WB1:535; LP

NAME OR SUBJECT	LOCATION	TYPE	YEAR	REFERENCE(S)
Taylor, Tho.	Alexandria	Tax Charge	1795	Tax PP 1795:30
Taylor, Thomas	Alexandria	Tax Charge	1796	Tax PP 1796:19
Taylor, Thomas, c/o Ann	Arlington	Apprentice	1802	OCR1801:032
Taylor, Thomas, segar maker	Alexandria	Head	1810	1810(1):04A
Taylor, Thos.	Alexandria	Tax Charge	1798	Tax PP 1798:18
Taylor, Thos.	Alexandria	Tax Charge	1799	Tax PP 1799:40
Taylor, Thos.	Alexandria	Tax Charge	1800	Tax PP 1800:43
Taylor, Thos.	Alexandria	Boarder	1808	1808(4):25A
Taylor, Thos., tobacconist	Alexandria	Housekeeper	1808	1808(1):02A
Taylor, W. Arthur	Alexandria	Will	1884	WB1:405; LP
Taylor, Widow & child	Alexandria	Boarder	1799	1799(2):05A
Taylor, William	Alexandria	Tax Charge	1790	Tax PP 1790:14
Taylor, William	Arlington	Ordinary	1810	OBL2(np)
Taylor, William A., c/o Robert J.	Arlington	Guard.	1841	WB4:281
Taylor, William A., defendant	Arlington	Suit	(nd)	LSA:134
Taylor, William, def.	Alexandria	Suit	1801	CRC:118
Taylor, William, Fairfax St.	Alexandria	Occupant	1790	Tax L 1790:02
Taylor, William P.	Arlington	Appraisal	1866	WB8:405
Taylor, Wm.	Alexandria	Tax Charge	1789	Tax PP 1789:18
Taylor, Wm.	Alexandria	Boarder	1808	1808(1):02A
Taylor, Wm.	Alexandria	Boarder	1808	1808(3):21A
Taylor, Wm., baker	Alexandria	Head	1810	1810(1):03A
Taylor, Wm., journeyman baker	Alexandria	Housekeeper	1808	1808(4):28A
Tayor, Archibald J., grantee	Arlington	Indenture D.	1814	ID2:360
Teachun, John Henry, c/o Mary	Arlington	Apprentice	1804	OCR1801:168
Tebbs, William P., of Botetourt Co.	Alexandria	Deposition	1819	CRL:087
Tenley, Zenos, tanner	Alexandria	Housekeeper	1808	1808(4):24A
Tenly, William	Arlington	Guard.	1818	WB2:247
Tennason, Saml., cooper	Alexandria	Housekeeper	1808	1808(4):27A
Ter<u>ns</u>, Philip	Alexandria	Tax Charge	1790	Tax PP 1790:12
Terry, Fredrick, gunsmith	Alexandria	Housekeeper	1808	1808(2):14A
Terry, Jacob (C)	Alexandria	Boarder	1808	1808(2):14B
Tertzbach, Peter	Alexandria	Tax Charge	1788	Tax PP 1788:16
Tetsibaugh, [blank], Fairfax St.	Alexandria	Occupant	1787	Tax L 1787:05
Theobald, Saml.	Alexandria	Tithable +21	1787	Tax PP 1787:16
Thom, Christopher N.	Arlington	Will	1895	WB10:301, File #700A
Thomas, Benjamin	Arlington	Apprentice	1828	OCR1822:161a
Thomas, Benjamin	Arlington	Inventory	1857	WB7:164; LVA-LP
Thomas, Benjamin	Arlington	Account	1857	WB7:271; LVA-LP
Thomas, David	Arlington	Witness	1794	OT:07/11/1794
Thomas, David, age seventy odd	Alexandria	Deposition	1768	CRI:277
Thomas, David, labourer	Alexandria	Head	1810	1810(3):07A
Thomas Dempsey & Co.	Alexandria	Tax Charge	1799	Tax PP 1799:09
Thomas Dempsey & Co.	Alexandria	Mer. License	1800	Tax PP 1800:54(12)r
Thomas, Edward A.	Arlington	Guard.	1839	WB4:229
Thomas, Edward Augustine, c/o James	Arlington	Guard.	1836	WB4:115
Thomas, Elizabeth, sempstress	Alexandria	Housekeeper	1808	1808(1):01A
Thomas, Emily, c/o James	Arlington	Guard.	1836	WB4:108
Thomas, Geo., labourer	Alexandria	Head	1810	1810(3):08A
Thomas, Henson, house joiner	Alexandria	Head	1810	1810(3):06A
Thomas, J.V.	Alexandria	Mer. License	1799	Tax PP 1799:52-10r
Thomas, James	Arlington	Libellant	1805	ACO:033
Thomas, James	Arlington	Libellant	1805	ACO:042
Thomas, James	Arlington	Libellant	1806	ACO:049
Thomas, James	Arlington	Admin.	1838	WB4:160
Thomas, James	Arlington	Account	1839	AB8:018; LVA-LP
Thomas, James	Arlington	Account	1841	AB8:278; LVA-LP
Thomas, James	Arlington	Account	1842	AB8:278
Thomas Janney & Co.	Arlington	Claim	1812	ACO:124
Thomas, Jno. V., Royal St.	Alexandria	Occupant	1795	Tax L 1795:13
Thomas, Joe (C)	Alexandria	Tax Charge	1800	Tax PP 1800:43

NAME OR SUBJECT	LOCATION	TYPE	YEAR	REFERENCE(S)
Thomas, John	Alexandria	Boarder	1808	1808(2):15A
Thomas, John	Arlington	Admin.	1818	WB2:261
Thomas, John V.	Alexandria	Tax Charge	1796	Tax LP 1796:28
Thomas, John V.	Alexandria	Tax Charge	1795	Tax PP 1795:30
Thomas, John V.	Alexandria	Tax Charge	1796	Tax PP 1796:19
Thomas, John V.	Alexandria	Tax Charge	1798	Tax PP 1798:18
Thomas, John V.	Alexandria	Mer. License	1798	Tax PP 1798:20-7
Thomas, John V.	Alexandria	Tax Charge	1799	Tax PP 1799:40
Thomas, John V.	Alexandria	Tax Charge	1800	Tax PP 1800:43
Thomas, John V.	Arlington	Defendant	1802	PA:277
Thomas, John V.	Arlington	Defendant	1802	PA:274
Thomas, John V.	Arlington	Defendant	1802	PA:300
Thomas, John V., def.	Alexandria	Suit	1802	CRC:238
Thomas, John V., def.	Alexandria	Suit	1802	CRC:262
Thomas, John V., def.	Alexandria	Suit	1802	CRC:213
Thomas, John V., def.	Alexandria	Suit	1802	CRB:224
Thomas, John V., def.	Alexandria	Suit	1802	CRD:059
Thomas, John V., def.	Alexandria	Suit	1803	CRD:084
Thomas, John V., def.	Alexandria	Suit	1804	CRF:067
Thomas, Joseph	Alexandria	Tax Charge	1789	Tax PP 1789:18
Thomas, Joseph	Alexandria	Tax Charge	1790	Tax PP 1790:15
Thomas, Joseph	Arlington	Account	1815	AB2:197; LVA-LP
Thomas, Joseph	Arlington	Sale	1815	AB2:168
Thomas, Joseph	Arlington	Inventory	1815	AB2:092; LVA-LP
Thomas, Joseph	Arlington	Admin.	1815	WB1:345
Thomas, Joseph	Arlington	Account	1816	AB2:319; LVA-LP
Thomas, Joseph	Arlington	Account	1824	AB5:308
Thomas, Joseph	Arlington	Account	1825	LVA-LP
Thomas, Joseph	Arlington	Inventory	1831	LVA-LP
Thomas, Joseph (C), c/o Araminta	Arlington	Apprentice	1822	OCR1822:009a
Thomas, Joseph, baker	Alexandria	Head	1810	1810(2):07A
Thomas, Joseph, orphans of	Arlington	Guard. Acct.	1816	AB2:414; LVA-LP
Thomas, Joseph, orphans of	Arlington	Guard.	1824	OCR1822:069
Thomas, Joseph, Princess St.	Alexandria	Occupant	1790	Tax L 1790:07
Thomas, Josiah (C), laborer	Alexandria	Housekeeper	1808	1808(1):09A
Thomas, Levering	Arlington	Guard. Acct.	1815	AB2:220
Thomas, Levering	Arlington	Guard. Acct.	1817	AB2:414
Thomas, Levering	Arlington	Guard. Acct.	1824	AB5:305
Thomas, Levering	Arlington	Guard. Acct.	1824	AB5:251
Thomas, Levering	Arlington	Admin. Bond	1848	ABB(np)
Thomas, Levering & Sarah	Arlington	Guard. Acct.	1823	LVA-LP
Thomas, Levering, c/o Joseph	Arlington	Guard.	1815	WB2:009
Thomas, Levy	Alexandria	Tax Charge	1790	Tax PP 1790:15
Thomas, Margaret, c/o James	Arlington	Guard.	1836	WB4:115
Thomas, Margaret E.	Arlington	Guard.	1839	WB4:229
Thomas, Margaret Elizabeth	Arlington	Apprentice	1842	OCR1842:001
Thomas, Mary Ann, c/o James	Arlington	Guard.	1836	WB4:108
Thomas, Patty	Alexandria	Head	1810	1810(4):06A
Thomas, Sampson	Alexandria	Boarder	1808	1808(1):01A
Thomas, Sarah	Arlington	Guard. Acct.	1815	AB2:220
Thomas, Sarah	Arlington	Guard. Acct.	1817	AB2:414
Thomas, Sarah	Arlington	Guard. Acct.	1824	AB5:251
Thomas, Sarah	Arlington	Guard. Acct.	1824	AB5:305
Thomas, Sarah	Arlington	Guard. Acct.	1826	LVA-LP
Thomas, Sarah	Arlington	Admin. Bond	1848	ABB(np)
Thomas, Sarah	Arlington	Account	1848	WB5:122
Thomas, Sarah	Arlington	Inventory	1848	WB5:085; LVA-LP
Thomas, Sarah	Arlington	Account	1849	WB5:124; LVA-LP
Thomas, Sarah	Arlington	Account	1851	WB5:211; LVA-LP
Thomas, Sarah	Arlington	Account	1851	WB5:213; LVA-LP
Thomas, Sarah, c/o Joseph	Arlington	Guard.	1815	WB2:009

NAME OR SUBJECT	LOCATION	TYPE	YEAR	REFERENCE(S)
Thomas, Simon, late P. Comr.	Alexandria	Housekeeper	1808	1808(2):15A
Thomas, Simon, old constable	Alexandria	Head	1810	1810(1):04A
Thomas, Skinner	Alexandria	Tax Charge	1796	Tax PP 1796:19
Thomas, Spencer	Alexandria	Tax Charge	1799	Tax PP 1799:40
Thomas, Spencer	Alexandria	Tax Charge	1800	Tax PP 1800:43
Thomas, Spencer & wife, shoemaker	Alexandria	Housekeeper	1799	1799(2):14A
Thomas, Spencer, c/o Spencer	Arlington	Apprentice	1802	OCR1801:020
Thomas, Spencer, plt.	Alexandria	Suit	1801	CRB:342
Thomas, Thomas V., def.	Alexandria	Suit	1803	CRD:086
Thomas, William, at his house	Arlington	Ordinary	1828	OBL4(np)
Thomas, William, at his house	Arlington	Ordinary	1829	OBL4(np)
Thomas, William, at his house	Arlington	Ordinary	1830	OBL4(np)
Thomas, William, at his house	Arlington	Ordinary	1832	OBL4(np)
Thomas, William, at his house	Arlington	Ordinary	1834	OBL5(np)
Thomas, William, at his house	Arlington	Ordinary	1835	OBL5(np)
Thomas, William, at his house	Arlington	Ordinary	1839	OBL5(np)
Thomas, William, at Union Hotel	Arlington	Ordinary	1838	OBL5(np)
Thomas, William, gc/o Spencer	Arlington	Apprentice	1802	OCR1801:030
Thomas, William H., c/o Sophia	Arlington	Apprentice	1822	OCR1822:027
Thomas, William Henry	Arlington	Guard.	1838	WB4:171
Thomas, William, his house in Alexa.	Arlington	Ordinary	1833	OBL5(np)
Thomas, William, in Alexandria Co.	Arlington	Ordinary	1827	OBL4(np)
Thomas, Winney	Alexandria	Head	1810	1810(4):09A
Thomas, Wm., clerk	Alexandria	Boarder	1799	1799(2):18A
Thomison, Sarah, visiter	Alexandria	Boarder	1800	1800(4):13A
Thompson & Veitch	Alexandria	Mer. License	1800	Tax PP 1800:54(21)w
Thompson & Veitch	Alexandria	Tax Charge	1800	Tax PP 1800:43
Thompson & Vietch	Alexandria	Mer. License	1798	Tax PP 1798:20-7
Thompson & Vietch	Alexandria	Tax Charge	1799	Tax PP 1799:40
Thompson & Vietch	Alexandria	Mer. License	1799	Tax PP 1799:52-10w
Thompson, Aaron	Alexandria	Boarder	1808	1808(1):02A
Thompson, Abraham, labourer	Alexandria	Head	1810	1810(2):07A
Thompson, Abram (C), baker	Alexandria	Housekeeper	1808	1808(2):14A
Thompson, Ann, washerwoman	Alexandria	Head	1810	1810(1):08A
Thompson, Catherine Foote	Alexandria	Will	1873	WB1:072; LP
Thompson, Charles	Alexandria	Tax Charge	1795	Tax PP 1795:31
Thompson, Craven, merchant	Alexandria	Housekeeper	1808	1808(1):02A
Thompson, Craven P.	Arlington	Inventory	1831	LVA-LP
Thompson, Craven P.	Arlington	Will	1831	WB4:013; File #303A
Thompson, Craven P.	Arlington	Bond	1831	WB4:014
Thompson, Craven P., def.	Alexandria	Suit	1822	CRL:389
Thompson, David	Arlington	Will	1800	WBA:084; LVA-LP
Thompson, David	Arlington	Renounce	1802	WBA:086
Thompson, David	Arlington	Bond	1802	WBA:087
Thompson, Domingo C.	Alexandria	Will	1880	WB1:292; LP
Thompson, Edward K.	Alexandria	Tax Charge	1787	Tax PP 1787:15
Thompson, Edward K., Prince St.	Alexandria	Owner	1790	Tax L 1790:11
Thompson, Edward K., Prince St.	Alexandria	Occupant	1790	Tax L 1790:11
Thompson, Edwd. K.	Alexandria	Owner	1787	Tax L 1787:25
Thompson, Edwd. K.	Alexandria	Tax Charge	1788	Tax PP 1788:16
Thompson, Edwd. K.	Alexandria	Tax Charge	1789	Tax PP 1789:18
Thompson, Edwd. K.	Alexandria	Tax Charge	1790	Tax PP 1790:14
Thompson, Edwd. K., Prince St.	Alexandria	Occupant	1787	Tax L 1787:25
Thompson, Edwd. K., Water St.	Alexandria	Occupant	1790	Tax L 1790:01
Thompson, Elias (C)	Arlington	Apprentice	1829	OCR1822:173
Thompson, Elizabeth Griffith	Arlington	Admin.	1825	OCR1822:083a
Thompson, Elizabeth Griffith	Arlington	Will P.	1825	OCR1822:083
Thompson, Elizabeth Griffith	Arlington	Will	1825	WB3:153; File #228A
Thompson, Elizabeth Griffith	Arlington	Bond	1825	WB3:155
Thompson, Emeline	Arlington	Appraisal	1855	LVA-LP
Thompson, George	Alexandria	Serv./Appr.	1800	1800(4):11B

NAME OR SUBJECT	LOCATION	TYPE	YEAR	REFERENCE(S)
Thompson, George	Arlington	Admin.	1805	WBB:208
Thompson, George	Arlington	Inventory	1805	WBB:211
Thompson, George, at crossroads, Co.	Arlington	Ordinary	1844	OBL6(np)
Thompson, George, Ball's Tavern, Co.	Arlington	Ordinary	1842	OBL6(np)
Thompson, George D., Alexandria Co.	Arlington	Ordinary	1848	OBL6(np)
Thompson, George, in Alexandria Co.	Arlington	Ordinary	1843	OBL6(np)
Thompson, George, in Alexandria Co.	Arlington	Ordinary	1846	OBL6(np)
Thompson, George, in Alexandria Co.	Arlington	Ordinary	1847	OBL6(np)
Thompson, Isaac, clerk	Alexandria	Boarder	1799	1799(2):04A
Thompson, Israel P., grantee	Arlington	Indenture D.	1811	ID2:052
Thompson, Israel P., grantee	Arlington	Indenture D.	1812	ID2:148
Thompson, Israel P., grantee	Arlington	Indenture D.	1813	ID2:157
Thompson, J., Fairfax St.	Alexandria	Occupant	1787	Tax L 1787:24
Thompson, J., Royal St.	Alexandria	Occupant	1787	Tax L 1787:21
Thompson, James	Alexandria	Tax Charge	1787	Tax PP 1787:15
Thompson, James, Princess St.	Alexandria	Occupant	1787	Tax L 1787:17
Thompson, Jane	Arlington	Will	1864	WB8:183; File #608A
Thompson, Jno. & wife, baker	Alexandria	Housekeeper	1799	1799(2):10A
Thompson, Jno., waterman	Alexandria	Housekeeper	1808	1808(1):08A
Thompson, John	Alexandria	Tax Charge	1796	Tax PP 1796:19
Thompson, John	Alexandria	Tax Charge	1799	Tax PP 1799:40
Thompson, John	Alexandria	Tax Charge	1800	Tax PP 1800:43
Thompson, John	Arlington	Admin.	1815	WB2:008
Thompson, John	Alexandria	Deposition	1822	CRL:471
Thompson, John Ford, c/o Charles	Arlington	Apprentice	1802	OCR1801:060
Thompson, John, ropemaker	Alexandria	Head	1810	1810(3):06A
Thompson, John, ropemaker	Alexandria	Housekeeper	1808	1808(3):18A
Thompson, John, w, baker	Alexandria	Head	1796	1796(3):2
Thompson, Jonah	Alexandria	Tax Charge	1787	Tax PP 1787:15
Thompson, Jonah	Alexandria	Tax Charge	1788	Tax PP 1788:16
Thompson, Jonah	Alexandria	Tax Charge	1789	Tax PP 1789:18
Thompson, Jonah	Alexandria	Tax Charge	1790	Tax PP 1790:14
Thompson, Jonah	Arlington	Witness	1794	OT:03/07/1794
Thompson, Jonah	Alexandria	Tax Charge	1795	Tax PP 1795:31
Thompson, Jonah	Alexandria	Tax Charge	1796	Tax LP 1796:28
Thompson, Jonah	Alexandria	Tax Charge	1796	Tax PP 1796:19
Thompson, Jonah	Alexandria	Tax Charge	1798	Tax PP 1798:18
Thompson, Jonah	Alexandria	Tax Charge	1799	Tax PP 1799:40
Thompson, Jonah	Alexandria	Tax Charge	1800	Tax PP 1800:43
Thompson, Jonah	Alexandria	Deposition	1802	CRI:079
Thompson, Jonah	Arlington	Juryman	1804	ACO:026
Thompson, Jonah	Arlington	Bond	1833	WB4:065
Thompson, Jonah	Arlington	Will	1833	WB4:063; File #324A
Thompson, Jonah	Arlington	Inventory	1834	LVA-LP
Thompson, Jonah	Arlington	Citation	1835	LVA-LP (Box 214)
Thompson, Jonah	Arlington	Account	1836	AB7:234; LVA-LP
Thompson, Jonah	Arlington	Account	1837	AB7:257; LVA-LP
Thompson, Jonah	Arlington	Account	1840	AB8:115; LVA-LP
Thompson, Jonah	Arlington	Account	1842	AB8:311; LVA-LP
Thompson, Jonah	Arlington	Petition	1845	LVA-LP (Box 214)
Thompson, Jonah	Arlington	Admin.	1845	OCR1842:127, 132
Thompson, Jonah	Arlington	Admin.	1845	OCR1842:134
Thompson, Jonah & wife, merchant	Alexandria	Housekeeper	1799	1799(2):02A
Thompson, Jonah, def.	Alexandria	Suit	1814	CRK:136
Thompson, Jonah, Exor. of	Arlington	Suit	1835	LVA-LP (Box 214)
Thompson, Jonah, Fairfax St.	Alexandria	Owner	1795	Tax L 1795:29(2)
Thompson, Jonah, Fairfax St.	Alexandria	Occupant	1795	Tax L 1795:29
Thompson, Jonah, King St.	Alexandria	Occupant	1790	Tax L 1790:01
Thompson, Jonah, merchant	Alexandria	Housekeeper	1808	1808(2):15A
Thompson, Jonah, merchant	Alexandria	Head	1810	1810(2):04A
Thompson, Jonah, plt.	Alexandria	Suit	1802	CRC:019

NAME OR SUBJECT	LOCATION	TYPE	YEAR	REFERENCE(S)
Thompson, Jonah, w(5)7, merchant	Alexandria	Head	1796	1796(3):4
Thompson, Jonah, Water St.	Alexandria	Owner	1795	Tax L 1795:29
Thompson, Joseph	Arlington	Guard.	1819	WB2:308
Thompson, Julia R.	Arlington	Guard.	1835	WB4:085
Thompson, Lucinda Stoddert	Arlington	Will	1856	WB7:125; File #079A
Thompson, Lucy, washwoman	Alexandria	Housekeeper	1808	1808(4):29A
Thompson, Margaret	Arlington	Apprentice	1822	OCR1822:003a
Thompson, Margaret	Arlington	Will	1838	WB4:300; File #071A
Thompson, Margaret	Arlington	Will P.	1845	OCR1842:128
Thompson, Peyton	Alexandria	Boarder	1808	1808(2):15A
Thompson, Richd., wheelright	Alexandria	Head	1810	1810(3):07A
Thompson, Samuel	Arlington	Admin.	1826	OCR1822:122a
Thompson, Samuel	Arlington	Admin.	1826	WB3:253
Thompson, Samuel	Arlington	Inventory	1827	AB6:395; LVA-LP
Thompson, Samuel	Arlington	Account	1831	AB7:027; LVA-LP
Thompson, Samuel P.	Arlington	Guard.	1835	WB4:085
Thompson, Samuel [Emeline]	Arlington	Renounce	1826	OCR1822:122a
Thompson, Thomas	Arlington	Will	1859	WB7:411; File #565A
Thompson, Thomas	Arlington	Appraisal	1859	WB7:414; LVA-LP
Thompson, Thomas, seaman	Arlington	Libellant	1818	ACO:152
Thompson v. Thompson	Arlington	Suit	1835	LVA-LP (Box 214)
Thompson, Veitch & Co., def.	Alexandria	Suit	1810	CRK:164
Thompson, W.S.	Alexandria	Mer. License	1798	Tax PP 1798:20-7
Thompson, William	Alexandria	Tax Charge	1788	Tax PP 1788:16
Thompson, William	Arlington	Apprentice	1804	OCR1801:205
Thompson, William, currier	Alexandria	Head	1810	1810(4):03A
Thompson, William S.	Arlington	Admin.	1804	WBA:313
Thompson, Wm. Henry	Arlington	Bond	1850	BB(np)
Thompson, Wm. S.	Alexandria	Tax Charge	1798	Tax PP 1798:18
Thompson, Wm., tanner	Alexandria	Housekeeper	1808	1808(4):29A
Thomson, Elizabeth G.	Arlington	Inventory	1825	AB5:417; LVA-LP
Thomson, John	Arlington	Inventory	1815	AB2:101; LVA-LP
Thomson, John & wife, baker	Alexandria	Head	1795	1795(4a):03
Thomson, Sarah	Alexandria	Resident	1800	1800(4):13B
Thorn, M., Prince St.	Alexandria	Occupant	1787	Tax L 1787:16
Thorn, Michael	Alexandria	Owner	1787	Tax L 1787:25
Thorn, Michael	Alexandria	Tax Charge	1787	Tax PP 1787:15
Thorn, Michael	Alexandria	Tax Charge	1789	Tax PP 1789:18
Thorn, Michael	Alexandria	Tax Charge	1790	Tax PP 1790:14
Thorn, Michael, nr. Union St.	Alexandria	Owner	1790	Tax L 1790:11(3)
Thorn, Michael, Prince St.	Alexandria	Occupant	1787	Tax L 1787:25
Thorn, Michael, Prince St.	Alexandria	Owner	1790	Tax L 1790:11
Thorn, Michael, Prince St.	Alexandria	Occupant	1790	Tax L 1790:11
Thorn, Michael, Thorn alley	Alexandria	Occupant	1787	Tax L 1787:25
Thorn, Michael, Union St.	Alexandria	Occupant	1787	Tax L 1787:19
Thorn, Michl.	Alexandria	Tax Charge	1788	Tax PP 1788:16
Thorn, Michl.	Alexandria	Tax Charge	1796	Tax LP 1796:28
Thorn, Michl., Wales' alley	Alexandria	Owner	1795	Tax L 1795:29
Thorn, Simon Miller	Arlington	Apprentice	1804	OCR1801:193
Thornton, George A.	Arlington	Inventory	1818	AB3:277, 292; LVA-LP
Thornton, George A.	Arlington	Bond	1818	WB2:268
Thornton, George A.	Arlington	Will	1818	WB2:266; File #156A
Thornton, George A.	Arlington	Account	1820	AB4:120; LVA-LP
Thornton, George A.	Arlington	Account	1825	AB6:150; LVA-LP
Thornton, George A., Dr.	Arlington	Sale	1819	AB3:300
Thornton, George A., Dr.	Arlington	Inventory	1819	LVA-LP
Thornton, George F., def.	Alexandria	Suit	1821	CRL:172
Thornton, Jos.	Alexandria	Tax Charge	1795	Tax PP 1795:30
Thornton, Jos.	Alexandria	License Due	1800	Tax PP 1800:54(24)
Thornton, Jos. & wife, baker	Alexandria	Housekeeper	1799	1799(2):05A
Thornton, Joseph	Alexandria	Tax Charge	1789	Tax PP 1789:18

NAME OR SUBJECT	LOCATION	TYPE	YEAR	REFERENCE(S)
Thornton, Joseph	Alexandria	Tax Charge	1790	Tax PP 1790:14
Thornton, Joseph	Alexandria	Tax Charge	1796	Tax LP 1796:28
Thornton, Joseph	Alexandria	Tax Charge	1796	Tax PP 1796:19
Thornton, Joseph	Alexandria	Mer. License	1798	Tax PP 1798:20-7
Thornton, Joseph	Alexandria	Tax Charge	1798	Tax PP 1798:18
Thornton, Joseph	Alexandria	Tax Charge	1799	Tax PP 1799:40
Thornton, Joseph	Alexandria	Mer. License	1799	Tax PP 1799:52-10r
Thornton, Joseph	Alexandria	Tax Charge	1800	Tax PP 1800:43
Thornton, Joseph, b. baker	Alexandria	Housekeeper	1808	1808(2):11A
Thornton, Joseph, baker	Alexandria	Head	1810	1810(2):01A
Thornton, Joseph, King St.	Alexandria	Occupant	1795	Tax L 1795:29
Thornton, Joseph, King St.	Alexandria	Owner	1795	Tax L 1795:29
Thornton, Joseph, w(1)3, shopkeeper	Alexandria	Head	1796	1796(3):4
Thornton, Joseph, Water St.	Alexandria	Occupant	1790	Tax L 1790:02
Thornton, Nicholas C.	Arlington	Admin.	1829	OCR1822:175a
Thornton, Nicholas C.	Arlington	Admin.	1829	WB3:357
Thornton, Samuel	Alexandria	Will	1870	WB1:010
Thornton, Samuel (C)	Alexandria	Will	1870	WB1:010; LP
Thornton, Thos.	Alexandria	Boarder	1808	1808(1):05A
Thornton, Tim	Alexandria	Boarder	1808	1808(4):24A
Thornton, William	Arlington	Bond	1852	BB(np)
Thornton, William	Arlington	Account	1871	WB9:333
Thornton, William (C)	Arlington	Will	1852	WB6:153; File #487A
Thornton, Wm.	Alexandria	Boarder	1808	1808(1):01A
Thorps, John, shopkeeper	Alexandria	Head	1810	1810(1):01A
Thrift, Ann	Arlington	Guard.	1805	WBB:133
Thrift, James	Arlington	Inventory	1811	AB1:133; LVA-LP
Thrift, James	Arlington	Admin.	1811	WB1:114
Thrift, James	Arlington	Account	1812	AB1:269; LVA-LP
Thrift, James, grantee	Arlington	Indenture D.	1826	ID:039
Thrift, Jas.	Alexandria	Boarder	1808	1808(2):13A
Thrift, Priscilla, shopkeeper	Alexandria	Housekeeper	1808	1808(1):05A
Thrift, Priscilla, spinstress	Alexandria	Head	1810	1810(1):02A
Throckmorton, Matthew, clerk	Alexandria	Boarder	1799	1799(2):03A
Throop, Geo. Hy., c/o Marg. Anderson	Arlington	Apprentice	1822	OCR1822:020a
Throop, Jacob S.	Arlington	Apprentice	1828	OCR1822:166a
Throop, John, house joiner	Alexandria	Head	1810	1810(3):07A
Throop, Mary Ann (Mankin), w/o Thos.	Arlington	Defendant	1841	LSA:070
Throop, Mary Ann, w/o Thomas	Arlington	Defendant	1842	LSA:087
Throop, Pharis, house joiner	Alexandria	Head	1810	1810(4):07A
Throop, Thomas	Arlington	Defendant	1842	LSA:087
Throop, Thomas, removed to AL	Arlington	Defendant	1841	LSA:070, 073
Throop, Thomas S., grantor	Arlington	Indenture D.	1828	ID:212
Throop, Thomas S., in jail	Arlington	Insolvent	1828	ID:210
Throop, Thos., Sr.	Alexandria	Tax Charge	1800	Tax PP 1800:43
Throy, David	Alexandria	Tax Charge	1787	Tax PP 1787:15
Thurber, Charles	Arlington	Inventory	1803	WBA:225; LVA-LP
Thurber, Charles	Arlington	Sale	1803	WBA:228
Thurber, Charles	Arlington	Admin.	1803	WBA:214
Thurber, Charles	Arlington	Account	1806	WBB:264; LVA-LP
Thurber, Charles	Arlington	Account	1808	WBC:166; LVA-LP
Thurber, Charles	Arlington	Account	1812	AB1:197; LVA-LP
Thurman, Elizabeth	Arlington	Guard.	1805	WBB:193
Tibbetts, A.G., on King St.	Arlington	Ordinary	1841	OBL6(np)
Ticer, Lewis	Arlington	Apprentice	1828	OCR1822:165a
Tiding, Richard, labourer	Alexandria	Head	1810	1810(1):07A
Tidler, George	Alexandria	Tax Charge	1790	Tax PP 1790:14
Tierceback, Peter, w(6), carpenter	Alexandria	Head	1796	1796(3):5
Tignell, Major, waterman	Alexandria	Housekeeper	1808	1808(1):08A
Tillett, Catharine	Arlington	Inventory	1819	AB3:380; LVA-LP
Tillett, Catharine	Arlington	Bond	1819	WB2:329

NAME OR SUBJECT	LOCATION	TYPE	YEAR	REFERENCE(S)
Tillett, Catharine	Arlington	Will	1819	WB2:328; File #168A
Tillier, Andrian	Alexandria	Tithable +16	1788	Tax PP 1788:13
Tilton, Thos.	Alexandria	Reference	1808	1808(3):21B
Timberlake & Taliaferro	Arlington	Sale	1852	WB6:046; LVA-LP
Tiney, Mary, labourer	Alexandria	Boarder	1800	1800(4):03A
Tingey, Thomas, Commander	Arlington	Respondent	1808	ACO:084
Tinney, Mary	Alexandria	Resident	1800	1800(4):03B
Tippett, John	Arlington	Apprentice	1829	OCR1822:173
Tippett, John	Arlington	Guard.	1829	OCR1822:173
Toaff, James, w(1), labourer	Alexandria	Head	1796	1796(3):4
Tobey, Linney, labourrer	Alexandria	Boarder	1800	1800(4):05A
Tobey, William J.	Arlington	Inventory	1825	AB6:104a; LVA-LP
Tobey, William J.	Arlington	Will	1825	WB3:189; File #236A
Tobey, William J.	Arlington	Bond	1825	WB3:198
Tobin, J.	Alexandria	Tax Charge	1796	Tax PP 1796:19
Tobin, Jno. & wife, cooper	Alexandria	Housekeeper	1799	1799(2):16A
Tobin, Jno., Water St.	Alexandria	Occupant	1795	Tax L 1795:05
Tobin, John	Alexandria	Tax Charge	1795	Tax PP 1795:31
Tobin, John	Alexandria	Tax Charge	1796	Tax LP 1796:28
Tobin, John	Alexandria	Tax Charge	1799	Tax PP 1799:40
Tobin, John	Arlington	Apprentice	1804	OCR1801:220
Tobin, John, w(2), cooper	Alexandria	Head	1795	1796(3):7
Tobin, Richard, c/o Rachael	Arlington	Apprentice	1802	OCR1801:049
Tobing, Richd.	Alexandria	Serv./Appr.	1800	1800(4):02B
Tobson, James & wife, coppersmith	Alexandria	Head	1795	1795(4):01
Toby, William J., master	Arlington	Libellant	1818	ACO:152
Todd, Henry W.	Alexandria	Tax Charge	1799	Tax PP 1799:40
Todd, Henry W.	Alexandria	Tax Charge	1800	Tax PP 1800:43
Toffler, Peter	Alexandria	Tax Charge	1795	Tax PP 1795:30
Toffler, Peter	Alexandria	Tax Charge	1796	Tax LP 1796:28
Toffler, Peter	Alexandria	Tax Charge	1796	Tax PP 1796:19
Toffler, Peter	Alexandria	Tax Charge	1798	Tax PP 1798:18
Toffler, Peter	Alexandria	Mer. License	1798	Tax PP 1798:20-7
Toffler, Peter	Alexandria	Tax Charge	1800	Tax PP 1800:43
Toffler, Peter, Prince St.	Alexandria	Occupant	1795	Tax L 1795:15
Toffler, Peter, w(3), hatter	Alexandria	Head	1796	1796(3):6
Toffler, PEter	Alexandria	Tax Charge	1799	Tax PP 1799:40
Tofler, Peter	Arlington	Juryman	1804	ACO:024, 027
Tofler, Peter & wife, hatter	Alexandria	Housekeeper	1799	1799(2):01A
Tofler, Peter, hatter	Alexandria	Housekeeper	1808	1808(1):02A
Tofler, Peter, hatter	Alexandria	Head	1810	1810(2):02A
Toll [Tull], Rachel, sempsters	Alexandria	Head	1800	1800(4):09A
Tolson, Anthony, labourer	Alexandria	Head	1810	1810(1):12A
Tomlin, Richard	Alexandria	Tax Charge	1788	Tax PP 1788:16
Tomlin, Robert, at his house	Arlington	Ordinary	1849	OBL6(np)
Tomlin, Robert, on Cameron St.	Arlington	Ordinary	1844	OBL6(np)
Tomlin, Robert, on Cameron St.	Arlington	Ordinary	1845	OBL6(np)
Tomlin, Robert, on Cameron St.	Arlington	Ordinary	1846	OBL6(np)
Tomlin, Robert, on Cameron St.	Arlington	Ordinary	1847	OBL6(np)
Tomlins, Richard	Alexandria	Tax Charge	1787	Tax PP 1787:15
Tomy, Martin	Alexandria	Tithable +21	1787	Tax PP 1787:04
Tonkin & Dublois	Alexandria	Lease	1800	CRB:317
Tonkin & Langdon	Alexandria	Tax Charge	1796	Tax LP 1796:28
Tonkin, William, def.	Alexandria	Suit	1801	CRB:313
Tonkin, William, def.	Alexandria	Suit	1801	CRB:329
Tonkin, Wm.	Alexandria	Tax Charge	1799	Tax PP 1799:40
Toomy, Martin	Alexandria	Tithable +16	1788	Tax PP 1788:04
Torbert, James M.	Arlington	Complainant	1842	LSA:094
Torbert, Mary Eliz. (Peyton), w/o Jas.	Arlington	Complainant	1842	LSA:094
Tounzen, Thophilus, w(1) (C)	Alexandria	Head	1795	1796(3):7
Towers, Edmund	Arlington	Guard. Acct.	1824	AB5:273; LVA-LP

NAME OR SUBJECT	LOCATION	TYPE	YEAR	REFERENCE(S)
Towers, Edward	Arlington	Guard. Acct.	1828	AB6:443
Towers, Edward	Arlington	Guard. Acct.	1833	AB7:327; LVA-LP
Towers, Edward	Arlington	Guard. Acct.	1839	AB7:327
Towers, Edward, c/o Thomas	Arlington	Guard.	1822	WB3:063
Towers, James, c/o Thomas	Arlington	Guard.	1822	WB3:063
Towers, James M.	Arlington	Guard. Acct.	1828	AB6:443
Towers, James M.	Arlington	Guard. Acct.	1835	AB7:162; LVA-LP
Towers, James M.	Arlington	Guard. Acct.	1836	AB7:162
Towers, James Madison	Arlington	Apprentice	1826	OCR1822:117
Towers, John	Alexandria	Tax Charge	1798	Tax PP 1798:18
Towers, John	Alexandria	Mer. License	1799	Tax PP 1799:52-10r
Towers, John	Alexandria	Tax Charge	1799	Tax PP 1799:40
Towers, John	Alexandria	Tax Charge	1800	Tax PP 1800:43
Towers, John, Capt.	Alexandria	Account B.	1797	CRD:162
Towers, John, def.	Alexandria	Suit	1803	CRD:158
Towers, John T.	Arlington	Guard. Acct.	1832	AB7:045; LVA-LP
Towers, John Thomas	Arlington	Guard.	1822	WB3:063
Towers, John Thomas	Arlington	Apprentice	1823	OCR1822:032
Towers, John Thomas	Arlington	Guard. Acct.	1828	AB6:443
Towers, Lemuel	Arlington	Guard. Acct.	1837	AB7:252; LVA-LP
Towers, Lemuel	Arlington	Guard. Acct.	1837	AB7:252
Towers, Lemuel, c/o Thomas	Arlington	Guard.	1822	WB3:063
Towers, Polly G.	Arlington	Ordinary	1810	OBL2(np)
Towers, Samuel	Arlington	Guard. Acct.	1828	AB6:443
Towers, Thomas	Arlington	Inventory	1820	LVA-LP
Towers, Thomas	Arlington	Admin.	1820	WB2:373
Towers, Thomas	Arlington	Debts Due	1821	AB4:285
Towers, Thomas	Arlington	Account	1821	AB4:281
Towers, Thomas	Arlington	Account	1821	AB4:279; LVA-LP
Towers, Thomas	Arlington	Account	1821	AB5:025; LVA-LP
Towers, Thomas	Arlington	Account	1822	AB5:097; LVA-LP
Towers, Thomas	Arlington	Account	1822	AB5:139; LVA-LP
Towers, Thomas	Arlington	Inventory	1822	LVA-LP
Towers, Thomas	Arlington	Account	1823	AB5:177; LVA-LP
Towers, Thomas	Arlington	Guard. Acct.	1824	AB5:274; LVA-LP
Towers, Thomas	Arlington	Account	1824	AB5:229; LVA-LP
Towers, Thomas	Arlington	Account	1824	AB5:319; LVA-LP
Towers, Thomas	Arlington	Account	1825	AB5:383
Towers, Thomas	Arlington	Account	1826	AB6:188; LVA-LP
Towers, Thomas	Arlington	Account	1828	AB6:442; LVA-LP
Towers, Thomas, grantee	Arlington	Indenture D.	1812	ID2:173
Towers, Thomas, orphans of	Arlington	Guard.	1822	OCR1822:021, 023a
Towers, Thomas, orphans of	Arlington	Guard.	1824	OCR1822:068
Towers, Thomas, orphans of	Arlington	Guard. Acct.	1828	OCR1822:155; LVA-LP
Towers, Thos.	Alexandria	Tax Charge	1800	Tax PP 1800:43
Towers, Thos., livery stable keeper	Alexandria	Housekeeper	1808	1808(2):14A
Towers, Thos., livery stable keeper	Alexandria	Head	1810	1810(2):05A
Towers, Tomas	Arlington	Sale	1820	AB4:173, 175
Towers, William	Arlington	Guard. Acct.	1828	AB6:443
Towers, William, c/o Thomas	Arlington	Guard.	1822	WB3:063
Towles, Henry, Estate, plt.	Alexandria	Suit	1801	CRB:279
Towles, Stockley, plt.	Alexandria	Suit	1801	CRB:279
Town of Alexandria, Commerce St. E.	Arlington	Plat	1842	LSA:123
Town of Alexandria, Commerce St.	Arlington	Plat	1842	LSA:121
Town of Alexandria, Duke & Pitt Sts.	Arlington	Plat	1837	LSA:023
Town of Alexandria, King St. Extended	Arlington	Plat	1842	LSA:122
Town of Alexandria, Market Space	Arlington	Plat	1840	LSA:061
Town of Alexandria, Pendleton St.	Arlington	Plat	1839	LSA:046
Town of Alexandria, Queen St.	Arlington	Plat	1835	LSA:014
Town of Alexandria, Upper	Arlington	Plat	1835	LSA:013
Towns, Thomas	Alexandria	Tithable +21	1787	Tax PP 1787:02

NAME OR SUBJECT	LOCATION	TYPE	YEAR	REFERENCE(S)
Tracey, George, c/o Susannah	Arlington	Apprentice	1802	OCR1801:022
Tracey, James Francis, b. Dublin	Arlington	Alien Entry	1822	RA:04/12/22
Tracey, Thomas	Arlington	Inventory	1821	AB4:305
Tracey, Thomas	Arlington	Library	1821	AB4:305
Tracey, Thomas	Arlington	Bond	1821	WB3:012
Tracey, Thomas	Arlington	Will	1821	WB3:012
Tracey, Thomas	Arlington	Account	1823	AB5:147; LVA-LP
Tracey, Thomas	Arlington	Account	1824	AB5:347; LVA-LP
Tracey, Thomas	Arlington	Account	1829	AB6:467; LVA-LP
Tracey, Thomas, c/o Susanna	Arlington	Apprentice	1803	OCR1801:096
Tracy, Geo.	Alexandria	Boarder	1808	1808(1):04A
Tracy, Mrs., schoolmistress	Alexandria	Head	1810	1810(4):01A
Tracy, Susanah, teacher	Alexandria	Housekeeper	1808	1808(4):26A
Tracy, Thomas	Arlington	Account	1828	AB6:467
Tracy, Thos.	Alexandria	Boarder	1808	1808(2):12A
Trammel, Gerrard	Alexandria	Deposition	1768	CRI:278
Trammell, Clara L., c/o Alice T. Wilson	Arlington	Apprentice	1812	OCR1811:120
Trammell, George W., at his house	Arlington	Ordinary	1849	OBL6(np)
Trammell, George W., in Alexandria Co.	Arlington	Ordinary	1850	OBL6(np)
Trammell, George W., on King St.	Arlington	Ordinary	1847	OBL6(np)
Trammell, Gerrard, age 56	Alexandria	Deposition	1767	CRI:238
Transton, John	Alexandria	Tax Charge	1795	Tax PP 1795:30
Travers, Frederick, master	Arlington	Respondent	1808	ACR:045
Travers, Henry W.	Arlington	Will	1887	WB10:133; File #733A
Travers, Isaiah	Alexandria	Tax Charge	1795	Tax PP 1795:30
Travers, John	Arlington	Will	1838	WB4:158; File #353A
Travers, John	Arlington	Bond	1838	WB4:159
Travers, John	Arlington	Account	1839	AB8:114; LVA-LP
Travers, John	Arlington	Account	1840	AB8:114
Travers, Mary, c/o John N.	Arlington	Guard.	1849	GBB(np)
Traverse, Mesheck, def.	Alexandria	Suit	1801	CRC:203
Treat, Samuel, plt.	Alexandria	Suit	1801	CRC:039
Tredle, Fredk.	Alexandria	Tax Charge	1795	Tax PP 1795:30
Tresise, Thos.	Alexandria	Boarder	1799	1799(2):04A
Tresize & May	Alexandria	Tax Charge	1796	Tax PP 1796:19
Tresize & May	Alexandria	Tax Charge	1799	Tax PP 1799:40
Tresler, Lewis & wife, blacksmith	Alexandria	Housekeeper	1799	1799(2):06A
Tresler, Lewis, c/o Catharine	Arlington	Apprentice	1815	OCR1811:295
Tretcher, Thomas	Arlington	Will	1813	WB1:258
Tretcher, Thomas	Arlington	Account	1814	AB2:070; LVA-LP
Tretcher, Thomas	Arlington	Inventory	1814	AB2:049; LVA-LP
Tretcher, Thomas	Arlington	Admin. DBN	1823	WB3:091
Tretheway, William	Arlington	Admin.	1822	WB3:045
Tribbets, Samuel	Alexandria	Tax Charge	1789	Tax PP 1789:18
Tridal, Fredaric	Alexandria	Tax Charge	1800	Tax PP 1800:43
Tridell, Frederick	Arlington	Account	1825	AB5:397
Tridell, Mary	Arlington	Guard.	1826	WB3:234
Tridle, Frederick, a slaughter house	Arlington	Defendant	1802	PA:025
Tridle, Frederick, Washington St.	Alexandria	Owner	1795	Tax L 1795:29
Tridle, Fredk., Washington St.	Alexandria	Occupant	1795	Tax L 1795:29
Trimble, Isaac, plt.	Alexandria	Ejectment	1802	CRE:242
Trip, Ophaniel	Alexandria	Tax Charge	1787	Tax PP 1787:15
Triplet, Cesar, labourer	Alexandria	Head	1810	1810(1):07A
Triplet, Phillip, merchant	Alexandria	Head	1810	1810(3):03A
Triplet, Thos., stage [driver]	Alexandria	Head	1810	1810(2):03A
Triplett, Betty (C), washwoman	Alexandria	Housekeeper	1808	1808(1):06A
Triplett, Charles	Arlington	Apprentice	1826	OCR1822:127a
Triplett, Daniel, assignee, plt.	Alexandria	Suit	1801	CRB:214
Triplett, John	Alexandria	Boarder	1795	1795(4):02
Triplett, John, shopkeeper	Alexandria	Housekeeper	1808	1808(1):01A
Triplett, Margaret	Alexandria	Boarder	1799	1799(2):10A

NAME OR SUBJECT	LOCATION	TYPE	YEAR	REFERENCE(S)
Triplett, Philip, merchant	Alexandria	Housekeeper	1808	1808(3):20A
Triplett, Septr. (C)	Alexandria	Boarder	1808	1808(2):13B
Triplett, Stephen	Arlington	Account	1812	AB1:173; LVA-LP
Triplett, Stephen	Arlington	Will	1812	WB1:153; File #100A
Triplett, Thomas	Arlington	Admin.	1821	WB3:039
Triplett, Thomas	Arlington	Admin.	1824	OCR1822:077a
Triplett, Thomas, def.	Alexandria	Suit	1815	CRK:134
Triplett, Thos.	Alexandria	Tax Charge	1799	Tax PP 1799:40
Triplett, Thos.	Alexandria	Boarder	1808	1808(2):15A
Triplett, Thos., physician	Alexandria	Boarder	1799	1799(2):10A
Triplett, William	Arlington	Plaintiff	1802	PA:265
Triplett, William	Alexandria	Will	1893	WB2:041; LP
Tripp, L., Fairfax St.	Alexandria	Occupant	1787	Tax L 1787:15
Triseler, Lewis	Alexandria	Tax Charge	1799	Tax PP 1799:40
Trisize, Thos.	Alexandria	Tax Charge	1795	Tax PP 1795:30
Trisler, Lewis	Alexandria	Tax Charge	1787	Tax PP 1787:15
Trisler, Lewis	Alexandria	Tithable +16	1788	Tax PP 1788:07
Trisler, Lewis	Alexandria	Tax Charge	1795	Tax PP 1795:30
Trisler, Lewis, def.	Alexandria	Suit	1801	CRB:088
Trisseler, Lewis	Alexandria	Tax Charge	1798	Tax PP 1798:18
Trist, Nicholas P.	Alexandria	Will	1874	WB1:098; LP
Trolle, Andrew	Alexandria	Tax Charge	1790	Tax PP 1790:15
Trope, Thomas & wife Carthren	Alexandria	Resident	1800	1800(4):11B
Trope, Thomas, schoolmaster	Alexandria	Head	1800	1800(4):11A
Trotter, Charles	Arlington	Apprentice	1804	OCR1801:226
Trotter, Charles, c/o Lionel	Arlington	Apprentice	1804	OCR1801:227
Trotter, Lionel	Arlington	Suit	1803	ACO:019
Trotter, Lionel	Arlington	Defendant	1804	ACO:025
Trotter, Lionel	Arlington	Bail	1805	ACO:034, 038, 039
Trotter, Lionel, master Barque *Henry*	Arlington	Suit	1803	ACO:013
Troup, John, carpenter	Alexandria	Housekeeper	1808	1808(3):23A
Troup, Pharis, carpenter	Alexandria	Housekeeper	1808	1808(4):26A
Trout, Jacob	Alexandria	Tax Charge	1795	Tax PP 1795:30
Trout, John	Alexandria	Tithable +16	1788	Tax PP 1788:16
Trout, John	Alexandria	Tithable +16	1789	Tax PP 1789:18
Trout, Paul	Alexandria	Tax Charge	1787	Tax PP 1787:03
Trout, Paul	Alexandria	Tax Charge	1788	Tax PP 1788:16
Trout, Paul	Alexandria	Tax Charge	1789	Tax PP 1789:18
Trout, Paul	Alexandria	Tax Charge	1790	Tax PP 1790:14
Troutwine, Fred.	Alexandria	Tithable +16	1790	Tax PP 1790:05
Troutwine, Frederick	Alexandria	Tithable +16	1788	Tax PP 1788:06
Trueheart, Wilson	Alexandria	Will	1874	WB1:090; LP
Trugan, Edward & wife, shopkeeper	Alexandria	Head	1795	1795(4):06
Trugen, Edwd.	Alexandria	Tax Charge	1795	Tax PP 1795:31
Trugen, Edwd., Fairfax St.	Alexandria	Owner	1795	Tax L 1795:29
Trugen, Edwd., Fairfax St.	Alexandria	Occupant	1795	Tax L 1795:29
Truman, Daniel, waterman	Alexandria	Housekeeper	1808	1808(3):22A
Truman, Samuel, w(2), mariner	Alexandria	Head	1796	1796(3):6
Truman, Thos.	Alexandria	Tax Charge	1798	Tax PP 1798:18
Truscott, William, b. Cornwall	Arlington	Alien Entry	1817	RA:22/12/17
Trusler, Geo., coppersmith	Alexandria	Boarder	1799	1799(2):02A
Trusler, Lewis	Alexandria	Tax Charge	1796	Tax LP 1796:28
Trutton, Lucinda A., teacher	Alexandria	Head	1795	1795(4):02
Trutton, Lucinda, Fairfax St.	Alexandria	Occupant	1795	Tax L 1795:18
Trydle, Frederick	Alexandria	Tax Charge	1796	Tax LP 1796:28
Tubman, James	Arlington	Will	1865	WB8:264; File #633A
Tucker, Edward	Alexandria	Tax Charge	1796	Tax LP 1796:28
Tucker, Edward	Alexandria	Tax Charge	1796	Tax PP 1796:19
Tucker, Edward	Alexandria	Tax Charge	1799	Tax PP 1799:40
Tucker, Edward	Alexandria	Tax Charge	1800	Tax PP 1800:43
Tucker, Edwd.	Alexandria	Tax Charge	1795	Tax PP 1795:30

NAME OR SUBJECT	LOCATION	TYPE	YEAR	REFERENCE(S)
Tucker, Edwd.	Alexandria	Tax Charge	1798	Tax PP 1798:18
Tucker, Francis, b. Bermuda	Arlington	Alien Entry	1801	RA:24/06/01
Tucker, Henry H., Rev.	Arlington	Ordination	1854	BB(np)
Tucker, Henry St. Geo., plt.	Alexandria	Suit	1820	CRL:070
Tucker, James Henry, b. Bermuda	Arlington	Alien Entry	1801	RA:25/06/01
Tucker, John	Alexandria	Tax Charge	1789	Tax PP 1789:18
Tucker, John	Alexandria	Tax Charge	1789	Tax PP 1789:18
Tucker, John	Arlington	Inventory	1822	AB5:129; LVA-LP
Tucker, John	Arlington	Admin.	1822	OCR1822:028
Tucker, John	Arlington	Admin.	1822	WB3:072
Tucker, John	Alexandria	Will	1889	WB1:520; LP
Tucker, John & James H.	Alexandria	Suit	1804	CRE:139
Tucker, John & Jas. H.	Alexandria	Mer. License	1800	Tax PP 1800:54(21)r
Tucker, John, b. Bermuda	Arlington	Alien Entry	1801	RA:24/06/01
Tucker, John, merchant	Alexandria	Housekeeper	1808	1808(4):27A
Tucker, John, merchant	Alexandria	Head	1810	1810(4):07A
Tucker, Maria D., b. Bermuda	Arlington	Alien Entry	1801	RA:24/06/01
Tucker, Robert	Arlington	Libellant	1805	ACO:045
Tucker, Sally E., b. Bermuda	Arlington	Alien Entry	1801	RA:24/06/01
Tucker, Samuel	Arlington	Will	1863	WB8:161; File #601A
Tufts & Brooks, plt.	Alexandria	Suit	1801	CRC:090
Tuley, Thomas C., grantor	Arlington	Indenture D.	1828	ID:200
Tuley, Thomas C., in jail	Arlington	Insolvent	1828	ID:198
Tull, Charlotte, sempster	Alexandria	Boarder	1800	1800(4):09A
Tull, Rachel	Alexandria	Resident	1800	1800(4):09B
Tull, Rachel, sempsters	Alexandria	Head	1800	1800(4):09A
Tull, Rachel, tayloress	Alexandria	Housekeeper	1799	1799(2):15A
Tupper, Nathan	Arlington	Ordinary	1805	OBL1(np)
Turberville, John	Alexandria	Will Extract	(nd)	CRH:422
Turberville, John, Estate, def.	Alexandria	Suit	1810	CRH:404
Turberville, John, Estate, plt.	Alexandria	Suit	1821	CRL:162
Turberville, John, Westmoreland Co.	Alexandria	Tobacco	1793	CRH:419
Turnbaugh, Henry	Alexandria	Owner	1787	Tax L 1787:25
Turnbaugh, Henry	Alexandria	Tax Charge	1787	Tax PP 1787:15
Turnbaugh, Henry, Fairfax St.	Alexandria	Occupant	1787	Tax L 1787:25
Turner, Charles	Alexandria	Tithable +16	1789	Tax PP 1789:05
Turner, Charles	Alexandria	Tax Charge	1796	Tax PP 1796:19
Turner, Charles	Alexandria	Deed	1798	CRF:197
Turner, Charles	Alexandria	Deed	1799	CRI:064
Turner, Charles	Alexandria	Tax Charge	1799	Tax PP 1799:40
Turner, Charles	Alexandria	Tax Charge	1800	Tax PP 1800:43
Turner, Charles	Alexandria	Death	1802	CRE:205
Turner, Charles	Arlington	Defendant	1802	PA:054
Turner, Charles	Arlington	Defendant	1802	PA:144
Turner, Charles	Arlington	Defendant	1802	PA:197
Turner, Charles	Arlington	Apprentice	1842	OCR1842:016
Turner, Charles & wife, sheriff	Alexandria	Head	1795	1795(4):08
Turner, Charles & wife, town sergeant	Alexandria	Housekeeper	1799	1799(2):13A
Turner, Charles & wife Rebeckah	Alexandria	Resident	1800	1800(4):12B
Turner, Charles & wife Rebecca	Alexandria	Removal	1801	CRF:200
Turner, Charles, def.	Alexandria	Suit	1801	CRB:054
Turner, Charles, def.	Alexandria	Suit	1801	CRC:098
Turner, Charles, def.	Alexandria	Suit	1801	CRC:072
Turner, Charles, def.	Alexandria	Suit	1801	CRB:208
Turner, Charles, def.	Alexandria	Suit	1801	CRC:224
Turner, Charles, def.	Alexandria	Suit	1802	CRB:227
Turner, Charles, def.	Alexandria	Suit	1802	CRD:067
Turner, Charles, Estate, def.	Alexandria	Suit	1807	CRF:193
Turner, Charles, late town sergeant	Arlington	Defendant	1802	PA:203
Turner, Charles, plt.	Alexandria	Suit	1801	CRB:076
Turner, Charles, sheriff	Alexandria	Head	1800	1800(4):12A

NAME OR SUBJECT	LOCATION	TYPE	YEAR	REFERENCE(S)
Turner, Charles to Francina West	Alexandria	Marriage	1794	CRE:205
Turner, Charles W.	Arlington	Will P.	1845	OCR1842:123
Turner, Charles W.	Arlington	Will	1845	WB4:397; File #425A
Turner, Chas.	Alexandria	Tax Charge	1795	Tax PP 1795:30
Turner, Chas.	Alexandria	Tax Charge	1798	Tax PP 1798:18
Turner, Chs.	Alexandria	Tax Charge	1796	Tax LP 1796:28
Turner, Dennis	Arlington	Apprentice	1804	OCR1801:149
Turner, Edward	Arlington	Suit Bond	1827	ACO:273
Turner, Edwd., Gretter's alley	Alexandria	Occupant	1795	Tax L 1795:10
Turner, Francina	Arlington	Will	1804	WBB:050; LVA-LP
Turner, Francina	Arlington	Bond	1804	WBB:055
Turner, Francina	Arlington	Inventory	1805	WBB:216
Turner, Francina	Arlington	Sale	1805	WBB:218
Turner, Francina	Arlington	Account	1805	WBB:217; LVA-LP
Turner, Francina, d/o John West	Alexandria	Death	1796	CRE:202
Turner, George (C)	Arlington	Apprentice	1846	OCR1842:190
Turner, James	Alexandria	Resident	1800	1800(4):12B
Turner, James & wife, cooper	Alexandria	Head	1795	1795(4a):04
Turner, James, for playing Faro	Arlington	Defendant	1802	PA:073
Turner, James, sergent	Alexandria	Boarder	1800	1800(4):12A
Turner, Jane W.	Alexandria	Will	1887	WB1:472; LP
Turner, Jas., clerk	Alexandria	Boarder	1799	1799(2):13A
Turner, Jno., merchant	Alexandria	Boarder	1799	1799(2):05A
Turner, John	Alexandria	Tax Charge	1800	Tax PP 1800:43
Turner, John, carpenter	Alexandria	Housekeeper	1808	1808(3):19A
Turner, Joseph	Alexandria	Tax Charge	1787	Tax PP 1787:15
Turner, Joseph	Alexandria	Tax Charge	1788	Tax PP 1788:16
Turner, Joseph	Alexandria	Tax Charge	1789	Tax PP 1789:18
Turner, Joseph	Alexandria	Tax Charge	1790	Tax PP 1790:15
Turner, Joseph	Alexandria	Tax Charge	1795	Tax PP 1795:30
Turner, Joseph	Alexandria	Tax Charge	1796	Tax LP 1796:28
Turner, Joseph	Alexandria	Tax Charge	1796	Tax PP 1796:19
Turner, Joseph, Princess St.	Alexandria	Occupant	1795	Tax L 1795:20
Turner, Lucy L.	Alexandria	Will	1871	WB1:040; LP
Turner, Mary Polly	Arlington	Guard.	1812	WB1:195
Turner, Philip	Alexandria	Tax Charge	1787	Tax PP 1787:15
Turner, Polly	Alexandria	Head	1810	1810(3):06A
Turner, Polly (C)	Alexandria	Boarder	1808	1808(3):22B
Turner, Richd.	Alexandria	Boarder	1808	1808(4):28A
Turner, Samuel, Jr., plt.	Alexandria	Suit	1822	CRL:544
Turner, Walker	Alexandria	Tax Charge	1800	Tax PP 1800:43
Turner, Walker	Arlington	Will P.	1822	OCR1822:028
Turner, Walker	Arlington	Will	1822	WB3:073; File #212A
Turner, Walker & wife Elizebeth	Alexandria	Resident	1800	1800(4):11B
Turner, Walker, ship carpenter	Alexandria	Head	1800	1800(4):11A
Turner, Walker, ship carpenter	Alexandria	Housekeeper	1808	1808(1):07A
Turner, Wm.	Alexandria	Resident	1800	1800(4):12B
Turner, Wm., clerk	Alexandria	Boarder	1799	1799(2):13A
Turner, Wm., sergent	Alexandria	Boarder	1800	1800(4):12A
Turner's Exors. v. White	Arlington	Suit	1834	LVA-LP (Judgments)
Turnpaw, Ann, Fairfax St.	Alexandria	Owner	1795	Tax L 1795:29
Turnpaw, Ann, Fairfax St.	Alexandria	Occupant	1795	Tax L 1795:29
Turnpaw, Mary	Arlington	Admin.	1816	WB2:101
Turnpaw, Nancy	Arlington	Inventory	1817	AB3:013; LVA-LP
Turnpaw, Widow	Alexandria	Tax Charge	1796	Tax LP 1796:28
Tuson, Marshal	Alexandria	Tax Charge	1790	Tax PP 1790:14
Tuttle, Thomas, c/o William	Arlington	Apprentice	1803	OCR1801:128
Tutton, Eliza	Arlington	Guard.	1823	WB3:089
Twyman, Albert	Arlington	Will	1900	WB10:455; File #803A
Tyler, Daniel	Arlington	Libellant	1827	ACO:275
Tyler, George	Arlington	Apprentice	1803	OCR1801:122

NAME OR SUBJECT	LOCATION	TYPE	YEAR	REFERENCE(S)
Tyler, James	Alexandria	Tax Charge	1789	Tax PP 1789:18
Tyler, James	Alexandria	Tax Charge	1796	Tax PP 1796:19
Tyler, James	Alexandria	Tax Charge	1799	Tax PP 1799:40
Tyler, James	Alexandria	Tax Charge	1800	Tax PP 1800:43
Tyler, James	Arlington	Sale	1819	AB3:327
Tyler, James	Arlington	Inventory	1819	AB3:325; LVA-LP
Tyler, James	Arlington	Will	1819	WB2:295; File #162A
Tyler, James	Arlington	Bond	1819	WB2:297
Tyler, James, Jr.	Arlington	Account	1820	AB4:141; LVA-LP
Tyler, Jas.	Alexandria	Tax Charge	1795	Tax PP 1795:31
Tyler, Jas.	Alexandria	Tax Charge	1798	Tax PP 1798:18
Tyler, John, c/o James & Sarah	Arlington	Apprentice	1803	OCR1801:079
Tyler, John C., grantor	Arlington	Indenture D.	1826	ID:049
Tyler, John C., in jail	Arlington	Insolvent	1826	ID:046
Tyler, Littleton	Alexandria	Tax Charge	1790	Tax PP 1790:15
Tyler, Saml.	Alexandria	Boarder	1808	1808(1):04A
Tyler, Saml.	Alexandria	Boarder	1808	1808(4):26A
Tyler, Thomas	Arlington	Apprentice	1805	OCR1801:247
Tyler, William	Alexandria	Tax Charge	1799	Tax PP 1799:40
Tyler, William, c/o Sarah Ann	Arlington	Apprentice	1812	OCR1811:130
Tyler, Wm.	Alexandria	Tax Charge	1795	Tax PP 1795:30
Tyler, Wm.	Alexandria	Tax Charge	1796	Tax LP 1796:28
Tyler, Wm.	Alexandria	Tax Charge	1796	Tax PP 1796:19
Tyler, Wm.	Alexandria	Tax Charge	1798	Tax PP 1798:18
Tyler, Wm., Queen St.	Alexandria	Occupant	1795	Tax L 1795:21
Tylor, William	Alexandria	Tax Charge	1800	Tax PP 1800:43

NAME OR SUBJECT	LOCATION	TYPE	YEAR	REFERENCE(S)
U				
Uhler, Elizabeth	Arlington	Guard.	1806	WBB:365
Uhler, John, c/o Cath. Uhler Simpson	Arlington	Apprentice	1801	OCR1801:012
Uhler, Peter G.	Alexandria	Will	1879	WB1:251; LP
Uhler, Valentine	Alexandria	Tax Charge	1787	Tax PP 1787:15
Uhler, Valentine	Alexandria	Tax Charge	1788	Tax PP 1788:16
Uhler, Valentine	Alexandria	Tax Charge	1789	Tax PP 1789:19
Uhler, Valentine	Alexandria	Tax Charge	1790	Tax PP 1790:15
Uhler, Valentine & wife, sadler	Alexandria	Head	1795	1795(4a):10
Uhler, Valentine, St. Asaph St.	Alexandria	Occupant	1790	Tax L 1790:09
Underwood, Chas.	Alexandria	Tax Charge	1795	Tax PP 1795:31
Underwood, Chas., Jr.	Alexandria	Tax Charge	1796	Tax PP 1796:19
Underwood, John	Alexandria	Tithable +21	1787	Tax PP 1787:01
Underwood, John	Alexandria	Tithable +16	1788	Tax PP 1788:02
Underwood, John	Alexandria	Tax Charge	1788	Tax PP 1788:16
Underwood, John	Arlington	Admin.	1818	WB2:235
Underwood, Mary, sempstress	Alexandria	Housekeeper	1808	1808(1):06A
Underwood, Mary, shopkeeper	Alexandria	Head	1810	1810(1):08A
Union Bank of Alexandria, def.	Alexandria	Suit	1820	CRL:213
Union Bank of Alexandria	Alexandria	Stockholders	1820	CRL:216, 223
Union Bank of George Town, plt.	Alexandria	Suit	1811	CRI:124
Union Bank of George Town, plt.	Alexandria	Suit	1811	CRI:116
Urie, Arthur T.	Arlington	Appraisal	1831	LVA-LP
Urie, Arthur T.	Arlington	Admin.	1831	WB4:036
Urie, Arthur T.	Arlington	Account	1836	AB7:219; LVA-LP
Urie, Arthur T.	Arlington	Account	1836	AB7:215; LVA-LP
Urie, Arthur T.	Arlington	Sale	1836	LVA-LP
Urie, Arthur T.	Arlington	Inventory	1840	AB8:161; LVA-LP
Urie, Arthur T.	Arlington	Petition	1845	LVA-LP (Box 214)
Urie, Arthur T.	Arlington	Citation	1845	OCR1842:147
Urie, Arthur T.	Arlington	Guard. Acct.	1848	WB5:031
Urie, Arthur T.	Arlington	Account	1848	WB5:028; LVA-LP
Urie, Arthur T.	Arlington	Guard. Acct.	1850	WB5:234; LVA-LP
Urie, Arthur T.	Arlington	Guard. Acct.	1851	WB6:029; LVA-LP
Urie, Arthur T.	Arlington	Guard. Acct.	1851	WB5:235; LVA-LP
Urie, Arthur T.	Arlington	Account	1851	WB6:027; LVA-LP
Urie, Arthur T., b. 25 OCT 1830	Arlington	Guard. Acct.	1845	AB9:041; LVA-LP
Urie, Arthur T., c/o Arthur & Eliz.	Arlington	Guard.	1831	WB4:037
Urie, Arthur T., c/o Arthur T.	Arlington	Guard. Acct.	1846	AB9:192; LVA-LP
Urie, Arthur T., children of	Arlington	Guard.	1848	LVA-LP
Urie, Arthur T., heirs of	Arlington	Account	1845	AB9:034; LVA-LP
Urie, James	Arlington	Guard. Acct.	1845	AB9:040; LVA-LP
Urie, Maria L.	Arlington	Guard. Acct.	1851	WB6:029
Urie, Maria L., c/o Arthur T.	Arlington	Guard. Acct.	1846	AB9:192; LVA-LP
Urie, Maria Louisa, b. 13 JAN 1828	Arlington	Guard. Acct.	1845	AB9:040; LVA-LP
Urie, Mariah, c/o Arthur & Eliz.	Arlington	Guard.	1831	WB4:037
Urie, Marie L.	Arlington	Guard. Acct.	1848	WB5:033, 232; LVA-LP
Urie, Martha E.	Arlington	Guard. Acct.	1848	WB5:034, 233; LVA-LP
Urie, Martha E.	Arlington	Guard. Acct.	1851	WB6:028
Urie, Martha E., c/o Arthur & Eliz.	Arlington	Guard.	1831	WB4:037
Urie, Martha E., c/o Arthur T.	Arlington	Guard. Acct.	1846	AB9:192; LVA-LP
Urie, Martha Elizabeth, b. 20 DEC 1826	Arlington	Guard. Acct.	1845	AB9:040; LVA-LP

NAME OR SUBJECT	LOCATION	TYPE	YEAR	REFERENCE(S)
V				
Vaccari, Frederick	Arlington	Will	1858	WB7:350; File #558A
Vaccari, Frederick, at Alexandria	Arlington	Ordinary	1833	OBL5(np)
Vaccari, Frederick, at his house	Arlington	Ordinary	1830	OBL4(np)
Vaccari, Frederick, at his house	Arlington	Ordinary	1832	OBL4(np)
Vaccari, Frederick, at his house	Arlington	Ordinary	1834	OBL5(np)
Vaccari, Frederick, at his house	Arlington	Ordinary	1835	OBL5(np)
Vaccari, Frederick, at his house	Arlington	Ordinary	1837	OBL5(np)(2)
Vaccari, Frederick, b. Leghorn, Italy	Arlington	Alien Entry	1827	RA:29/10/27
Vaccari, Frederick, his house Prince St.	Arlington	Ordinary	1838	OBL5(np)
Vaccari, Frederick, Union btw. King/Pr.	Arlington	Ordinary	1836	OBL5(np)
Vaccari, Frederick [Rose]	Arlington	Executrix	1858	LVA-LP
Vaccari, Rose	Alexandria	Will	1886	WB1:430; LP
Valengen, Charles W.	Arlington	Inventory	1819	AB3:319; LVA-LP
Valengen, Charles W.	Arlington	Will (N)	1819	WB2:287; File #160A
Valengen, Charles W.	Arlington	Bond	1819	WB2:288
Valentine, Caesar	Arlington	Will	1834	File #064A
Valentine, Edward, on Union St.	Arlington	Ordinary	1842	OBL6(np)
Valentine, Jacob	Alexandria	Tax Charge	1788	Tax PP 1788:16
Valentine, Jacob	Alexandria	Tax Charge	1789	Tax PP 1789:19
Valentine, John, c/o Mary	Arlington	Apprentice	1815	OCR1811:290
Valentine, John, cooper	Alexandria	Head	1800	1800(4):06A
Valentine, Joseph, c/o Mary	Arlington	Apprentice	1803	OCR1801:116
Valette, Elie & wife Betty Fleming, def.	Alexandria	Suit	1801	CRC:194
Vallette, Elie	Alexandria	Tithable +16	1788	Tax PP 1788:08
Vallingtine, John & wife Mary	Alexandria	Resident	1800	1800(4):06B
Van Dicklin, Bernd.	Alexandria	Tax Charge	1800	Tax PP 1800:45
Van Havre, Jno. A.	Alexandria	Tax Charge	1800	Tax PP 1800:45
Van Havre, John Mich. Ant., w(2)1, mer.	Alexandria	Head	1796	1796(3):1
Van Reisen, John	Arlington	Inventory	1825	AB5:419; LVA-LP
Van Reisen, John	Arlington	Admin.	1825	OCR1822:082
Van Reisen, John	Arlington	Will P.	1825	OCR1822:082
Van Reisen, John	Arlington	Account	1826	AB6:168; LVA-LP
Van Reisen, John	Arlington	Account	1827	AB6:272; LVA-LP
Van Reisen, John	Arlington	Account	1828	AB6:472; LVA-LP
Van Riesen, John	Arlington	Bond	1825	WB3:150
Van Riesen, John	Arlington	Will	1825	WB3:149; File #227A
Vance, Alexander	Arlington	Apprentice	1803	OCR1801:125
Vandeap, Richard	Alexandria	Tax Charge	1787	Tax PP 1787:15
Vandehider, Matthihas	Alexandria	Tax Charge	1790	Tax PP 1790:15
Vanderwerken, Gilbert	Arlington	Will	1894	WB10:263; File #761A
Vandicklen, Bernard	Alexandria	Tax Charge	1799	Tax PP 1799:43
Vandiver, William	Arlington	Admin.	1810	WBC:488
Vane, Emma	Arlington	Guard. Acct.	1865	WB8:244
Vanhaave & Stier	Alexandria	Tax Charge	1796	Tax PP 1796:19
Vanhaaven & Stier	Alexandria	Tax Charge	1798	Tax PP 1798:19
Vanhaaver, J.A.M.	Alexandria	Tax Charge	1799	Tax PP 1799:43
Vanharver & Stier	Alexandria	Tax Charge	1796	Tax LP 1796:27
Vanhorn, Samuel	Arlington	Respondent	1819	ACO:166
Vanhorne, Jas.	Alexandria	Tax Charge	1796	Tax PP 1796:19
Vanhorne, Samuel, c/o Amelia	Arlington	Apprentice	1803	OCR1801:111
Vaninburgh, Gilbert, cooper	Alexandria	Boarder	1795	1795(4a):02
Vanmeter, Isaac, plt.	Alexandria	Suit	1821	CRL:365
Vanmeter, Joseph, plt.	Alexandria	Suit	1821	CRL:365
Vansant & Rockwell	Arlington	Defendants	1826	ACO:266
Vansant, James	Arlington	Will	1866	WB8:359; File #285A
Vansant, James	Arlington	Inventory	1866	WB8:391
Vansant, James	Arlington	Appraisal	1866	WB8:390
Vansant, James	Arlington	Account	1867	WB8:555
Vanzandt, Nicholas B.	Arlington	Defendant	1827	ACO:272
Vanzemmond, Fredk.	Alexandria	Tithable +16	1789	Tax PP 1789:12

NAME OR SUBJECT	LOCATION	TYPE	YEAR	REFERENCE(S)
Varden, John	Arlington	Guard.	1821	WB3:020
Varden, Joseph	Alexandria	Mer. License	1798	Tax PP 1798:20-8
Varden, Joseph	Alexandria	Tax Charge	1799	Tax PP 1799:43
Varden, Joseph	Alexandria	Mer. License	1799	Tax PP 1799:52-11r
Varden, Joseph	Alexandria	Tax Charge	1800	Tax PP 1800:45
Varden, Joseph	Arlington	Guard.	1821	WB3:014
Varnell, George	Arlington	Apprentice	1827	OCR1822:138
Vasse, Ambrose	Arlington	Admin.	1838	WB4:162
Vasse, Ambrose, merchant	Alexandria	Housekeeper	1808	1808(3):20A
Vasse, Ambrose, merchant	Alexandria	Head	1810	1810(3):02A
Vasse, Ambrose, plt.	Alexandria	Suit	1808	CRG:177
Vasse, Ambrose, s/o Ambrose	Alexandria	Boarder	1808	1808(3):20A
Vasse, Charles, s/o Ambrose	Alexandria	Boarder	1808	1808(3):20A
Vasse, James, c/o Ambrose	Arlington	Apprentice	1805	OCR1801:315
Vasse, Peter, rigger	Alexandria	Head	1810	1810(4):07A
Vassee, Peter, rigger	Alexandria	Housekeeper	1808	1808(4):29A
Vassey, Peter	Alexandria	Tax Charge	1796	Tax LP 1796:29
Vassey, Peter	Alexandria	Tax Charge	1798	Tax PP 1798:19
Vassey, Robert, c/o Peter & Ann	Arlington	Apprentice	1804	OCR1801:214
Vassy, Peter & wife, mariner	Alexandria	Housekeeper	1799	1799(2):11A
Vaugh, Milly (C), washwoman	Alexandria	Housekeeper	1808	1808(4):24A
Vaughn, Robt.	Alexandria	Head	1810	1810(4):08A
Veich, Alexander & wife Babbey	Alexandria	Resident	1800	1800(4):16B
Veich, Alexander, carpenter	Alexandria	Head	1800	1800(4):16A
Veich, Richard, w(1)1, merchant	Alexandria	Head	1796	1796(3):5
Veitch, Alexander	Alexandria	Tax Charge	1799	Tax PP 1799:43
Veitch, Alexander	Alexandria	Tax Charge	1800	Tax PP 1800:45
Veitch, Alexander	Arlington	Account	1810	LVA-LP
Veitch, Alexander, brickmaker	Alexandria	Head	1810	1810(3):02A
Veitch, Alexander, plt.	Alexandria	Suit	1802	CRC:245
Veitch, Alexr.	Alexandria	Reference	1808	1808(4):29B
Veitch, Alexr. & wife, carpenter	Alexandria	Housekeeper	1799	1799(2):19A
Veitch, Alexr., brickmaker	Alexandria	Housekeeper	1808	1808(1):06A
Veitch, Mary M.L.	Arlington	Account	1858	WB7:378; LVA-LP
Veitch, Peter	Arlington	Ordinary	1804	OBL1(np)
Veitch, Peter & Elizabeth his wife, def.	Alexandria	Suit	1801	CRC:016
Veitch, Peter, at Four Mile Run	Arlington	Ordinary	1803	OBL1(np)
Veitch, Peter, ret. liquor w/o license	Arlington	Defendant	1802	PA:313
Veitch, Richard	Alexandria	Tax Charge	1796	Tax PP 1796:19
Veitch, Richard	Alexandria	Tax Charge	1800	Tax PP 1800:45
Veitch, Richard	Arlington	Libellant	1812	ACO:122
Veitch, Richard	Arlington	Libellant	1815	ACO:143
Veitch, Richard	Arlington	Defendant	1823	ACO:209
Veitch, Richard & Co., plt.	Alexandria	Suit	1810	CRK:162
Veitch, Richard, grantee	Arlington	Indenture D.	1816	ID2:386
Veitch, Richd.	Alexandria	Tax Charge	1796	Tax LP 1796:29
Veitch, Richd., & wife, merchant	Alexandria	Housekeeper	1799	1799(2):02A
Veitch, Richd., merchant	Alexandria	Head	1810	1810(4):04A
Veitch, Sarah	Arlington	Will	1892	WB10:239; File #756A
Veitch, William	Alexandria	Tax Charge	1799	Tax PP 1799:43
Veitch, William	Arlington	Defendant	1823	ACO:219, 223
Veitch, William	Arlington	Defendant	1824	ACO:243, 248
Veitch, William	Arlington	Defendant	1826	ACO:261, 264
Veitch, William	Arlington	Defendant	1827	ACO:268, 274
Veitch, William	Arlington	Inventory	1856	WB7:083; LVA-LP
Veitch, William	Arlington	Will	1856	WB7:063; File #525A
Veitch, William	Arlington	Account	1857	WB7:252; LVA-LP
Veitch, William	Arlington	Account	1857	WB7:342; LVA-LP
Veitch, William C.	Arlington	Will	1888	WB10:147; File #739A
Veitch, William C., grantor	Arlington	Indenture D.	1833	ID:407
Veitch, William C., in jail bounds	Arlington	Insolvent	1833	ID:405

NAME OR SUBJECT	LOCATION	TYPE	YEAR	REFERENCE(S)
Veitch, William, house joiner	Alexandria	Head	1810	1810(4):07A
Veitch, William P.	Arlington	Fid. Bond	1856	FBB(np)
Veitch, Wm., carpenter	Alexandria	Boarder	1799	1799(2):19A
Veitch, Wm., carpenter	Alexandria	Housekeeper	1808	1808(4):29A
Vendichler, Bernard	Alexandria	Tax Charge	1796	Tax PP 1796:19
Vendichler, Bernd.	Alexandria	Tax Charge	1798	Tax PP 1798:19
Veniman, Henry, of Pr. Geo. Co. MD	Arlington	Will	1812	WB1:150; File #099A
Verden, Joseph	Alexandria	Tax Charge	1796	Tax PP 1796:20
Vere, Jno.	Alexandria	Tax Charge	1795	Tax PP 1795:31
Vernon, James	Arlington	Apprentice	1843	OCR1842:037
Vernon, Thomas, c/o Nancy Davis	Arlington	Apprentice	1804	OCR1801:221
Verone, Joseph	Alexandria	Tax Charge	1795	Tax PP 1795:31
Verone, Joseph	Alexandria	Tax Charge	1798	Tax PP 1798:19
Verone, Joseph	Alexandria	License Due	1800	Tax PP 1800:54(24)
Veroney, Joseph, Royal St.	Alexandria	Occupant	1795	Tax L 1795:24
Veroni, Joseph	Alexandria	Tax Charge	1796	Tax LP 1796:29
Verony, Joseph	Alexandria	Tax Charge	1787	Tax PP 1787:15
Vervney, Joseph	Alexandria	Tax Charge	1796	Tax PP 1796:20
Vessel *Pickering*, armed	Arlington	Suit	1808	ACO:084
Vewell, Capt.	Alexandria	Tax Charge	1800	Tax PP 1800:45
Vickers, Margaret, of Fauquier Co. VA	Arlington	Will (NR)	1849	File #077A
Vietch, Alexr.	Alexandria	Tax Charge	1798	Tax PP 1798:19
Vietch, Richd.	Alexandria	Tax Charge	1798	Tax PP 1798:19
Vietch, Richd.	Alexandria	Tax Charge	1799	Tax PP 1799:43
Vigilante, Levy, Rev.	Arlington	Ordination	1854	BB(np)
Viley, Ephraim	Alexandria	Tax Charge	1790	Tax PP 1790:15
Vincent, James	Alexandria	Tithable +16	1788	Tax PP 1788:07
Vincent, James	Alexandria	Tithable +16	1789	Tax PP 1789:08
Vincent, James	Alexandria	Tax Charge	1790	Tax PP 1790:15
Vincent, John, waterman	Alexandria	Housekeeper	1808	1808(2):14A
Vincent, Robert	Arlington	Executor	(nd)	LVA-LP
Vincent, Robert	Arlington	Will	1819	WB2:314; File #165A
Vincent, Robert	Arlington	Bond	1819	WB2:315, 316
Vincent, Robert	Arlington	Account	1820	AB4:190; LVA-LP
Vincent, Robert	Arlington	Admin.	1822	OCR1822:017
Vincent, Robert	Arlington	Account	1825	AB5:416
Vincent, Robert	Arlington	Admin.	1826	OCR1822:118
Vincent, William F.	Alexandria	Will	1899	WB2:319; LP
Vineman, Henry	Arlington	Account	1813	AB1:289; LVA-LP
Vinson, Mathew R., retailer	Alexandria	Housekeeper	1808	1808(4):25A
Violet, Jno. & wife, grocer	Alexandria	Housekeeper	1799	1799(2):10A
Violet, John	Alexandria	Tax Charge	1796	Tax LP 1796:29
Violet, John	Alexandria	Tax Charge	1800	Tax PP 1800:45
Violet, John, merchant	Alexandria	Head	1810	1810(3):05A
Violet, William, drayman	Alexandria	Head	1810	1810(2):06A
Violett, Amanda M.	Alexandria	Will	1896	WB2:160; LP
Violett, Ann	Arlington	Will	1836	WB4:121; File #341A
Violett, Ann, seamstress	Alexandria	Head	1810	1810(1):06A
Violett, Ann, sempstress	Alexandria	Housekeeper	1808	1808(1):09A
Violett, Harriet E.	Arlington	Will	1855	WB7:026; File #659A
Violett, Jno.	Alexandria	License Due	1800	Tax PP 1800:54(24)
Violett, John	Alexandria	Tax Charge	1799	Tax PP 1799:43
Violett, John	Arlington	Inventory	1818	AB3:214; LVA-LP
Violett, John	Arlington	Account	1818	AB3:223; LVA-LP
Violett, John	Arlington	Debts Due	1818	AB3:263
Violett, John	Arlington	Sale	1818	AB3:220; LVA-LP
Violett, John	Arlington	Admin.	1818	WB2:248
Violett, John	Arlington	Account	1819	AB3:305; LVA-LP
Violett, John	Arlington	Account	1819	AB3:353; LVA-LP
Violett, John, def.	Alexandria	Suit	1808	CRF:188
Violett, John, merchant	Alexandria	Housekeeper	1808	1808(3):19A

NAME OR SUBJECT	LOCATION	TYPE	YEAR	REFERENCE(S)
Violett, John, ret. liquors w/o license	Arlington	Defendant	1802	PA:017
Violett, Mary	Arlington	Guard.	1817	WB2:206
Violett, Robert G.	Alexandria	Inventory	1870	WB1:005
Violett, Robert G.	Arlington	Will	1870	WB9:237; File #680A
Violett, Thomas	Arlington	Inventory	1805	WBB:135
Violett, Thomas	Arlington	Admin.	1805	WBB:132
Violett, Thomas	Arlington	Account	1806	WBB:326; LVA-LP
Violett, Thomas	Arlington	Debts Due	1815	AB2:205
Violett, Thompson	Arlington	Sale	1815	AB2:215
Violett, Thompson	Arlington	Inventory	1815	AB2:191; LVA-LP
Violett, Thompson	Arlington	Admin.	1815	WB2:074
Violett, Thompson	Arlington	Account	1816	AB2:362; LVA-LP
Violett, Thompson	Arlington	Sale	1816	AB2:278
Violett, Thompson	Arlington	Account	1817	AB3:021; LVA-LP
Violett, Thompson	Arlington	Account	1817	AB3:068; LVA-LP
Violett, Thompson	Arlington	Account	1818	AB3:126; LVA-LP
Violett, Thompson	Arlington	Account	1819	AB3:315; LVA-LP
Violett, Thompson	Arlington	Account	1819	AB3:368; LVA-LP
Violett, Thompson	Arlington	Account	1820	AB4:126; LVA-LP
Violett, Thompson	Arlington	Account	1833	AB7:075; LVA-LP
Violett, William	Arlington	Inventory	1822	AB5:100; LVA-LP
Violett, William	Arlington	Admin.	1822	OCR1822:020a
Violett, William	Arlington	Admin.	1822	WB3:063
Violett, William	Arlington	Account	1823	AB5:177; LVA-LP
Violett, William	Arlington	Apprentice	1828	OCR1822:165a
Violett, Wm., cartman	Alexandria	Housekeeper	1808	1808(3):22A
Violett, Wm., grantee	Arlington	Indenture D.	1813	ID2:198
Vismillar, Jacob	Alexandria	Tithable +16	1788	Tax PP 1788:15
Vivent, Frances	Alexandria	Tax Charge	1796	Tax LP 1796:29
Vivent, Francis	Alexandria	Tax Charge	1796	Tax PP 1796:19
Vivent, Francis, 2, merchant	Alexandria	Head	1796	1796(3):6
Vogelsang, Daniel	Arlington	Appraisal	1863	WB8:180
Vogelsang, Daniel	Arlington	Account	1865	WB8:236
Vollin, Wm. & wife, carpenter	Alexandria	Housekeeper	1799	1799(2):11A
Vorce, Henry N.	Arlington	Will	1888	WB10:146; File #738A
Voss, Nichl., w(1)9, bricklayer	Alexandria	Head	1796	1796(3):5
Voss, Nicho.	Alexandria	Tax Charge	1798	Tax PP 1798:19
Voss, Nicholas	Alexandria	Tax Charge	1799	Tax PP 1799:43
Voss, Nicholas	Alexandria	Tax Charge	1800	Tax PP 1800:45
Voss, Nicholas, def.	Alexandria	Suit	1801	CRB:113
Voss, Nicholas, def.	Alexandria	Suit	1801	CRB:279
Voss, Nicholas, def.	Alexandria	Suit	1803	CRD:090
Vosson, John & wife Ellon	Alexandria	Resident	1800	1800(4):10B
Vosson, John, bricklayer	Alexandria	Head	1800	1800(4):10A
Vowel, Jno. & wife, merchant	Alexandria	Housekeeper	1799	1799(2):17A
Vowel, John, w2, merchant	Alexandria	Head	1796	1796(3):3
Vowel, Thomas, w(1)2, merchant	Alexandria	Head	1796	1796(3):4
Vowel, Thos. & wife, merchant	Alexandria	Housekeeper	1799	1799(2):17A
Vowell, Charlotte	Arlington	Inventory	1846	AB9:167; LVA-LP
Vowell, Charlotte	Arlington	Account	1847	AB9:294
Vowell, Elizabeth	Arlington	Guard.	1805	WBB:165
Vowell, Harriet N.	Arlington	Guard. Acct.	1848	WB5:086; LVA-LP
Vowell, Harriet Newell, c/o Thomas	Arlington	Guard.	1846	OCR1842:170
Vowell, Jas. & Thos.	Alexandria	Tax Charge	1796	Tax PP 1796:19
Vowell, Jno.	Alexandria	Tax Charge	1795	Tax PP 1795:31
Vowell, Jno.	Alexandria	Tax Charge	1800	Tax PP 1800:45
Vowell, Jno. & Thos., King St.	Alexandria	Occupant	1795	Tax L 1795:14
Vowell, Jno. & Thos.	Alexandria	Tax Charge	1798	Tax PP 1798:19
Vowell, Jno. & Thos.	Alexandria	Mer. License	1800	Tax PP 1800:54(21)w
Vowell, Jno. & Thos.	Alexandria	Tax Charge	1800	Tax PP 1800:45
Vowell, John	Alexandria	Tithable +16	1790	Tax PP 1790:15

NAME OR SUBJECT	LOCATION	TYPE	YEAR	REFERENCE(S)
Vowell, John	Alexandria	Tax Charge	1796	Tax LP 1796:29
Vowell, John & Thos., Prince St.	Alexandria	Occupant	1795	Tax L 1795:30
Vowell, John & Thos., Prince St.	Alexandria	Owner	1795	Tax L 1795:30
Vowell, John & Thos., King St.	Alexandria	Owner	1795	Tax L 1795:30
Vowell, John & Thos., King St.	Alexandria	Occupant	1795	Tax L 1795:30
Vowell, John & Thos.	Alexandria	Mer. License	1798	Tax PP 1798:20-8
Vowell, John & Thos.	Alexandria	Tax Charge	1799	Tax PP 1799:43
Vowell, John & wife Margret	Alexandria	Resident	1800	1800(4):07B
Vowell, John C.	Alexandria	Tax Charge	1799	Tax PP 1799:43
Vowell, John C.	Arlington	Bond	1853	BB(np)
Vowell, John C.	Arlington	Account	1853	WB6:439; LVA-LP
Vowell, John C.	Arlington	Inventory	1853	WB6:201; LVA-LP
Vowell, John C.	Arlington	Account	1853	WB6:248; LVA-LP
Vowell, John C.	Arlington	Will	1853	WB6:178; File #489A
Vowell, John C.	Arlington	Account	1859	WB7:434; LVA-LP
Vowell, John C., pur. *Mount Hybla*	Arlington	Sale	1810	AB1:005
Vowell, John, merchant	Alexandria	Head	1810	1810(4):08A
Vowell, John, murchant	Alexandria	Head	1800	1800(4):07A
Vowell, Margaretta, c/o John D.	Arlington	Guard.	1829	WB3:353
Vowell, Marry	Alexandria	Resident	1800	1800(4):09B
Vowell, Mary	Alexandria	Boarder	1800	1800(4):09A
Vowell, Mary, c/o John D.	Arlington	Guard.	1829	WB3:353
Vowell, Sally H., c/o John D.	Arlington	Guard.	1829	WB3:353
Vowell, Saml.	Alexandria	Tithable +16	1790	Tax PP 1790:15
Vowell, Thomas	Alexandria	Tax Charge	1788	Tax PP 1788:16
Vowell, Thomas	Alexandria	Tax Charge	1789	Tax PP 1789:19
Vowell, Thomas	Alexandria	Tax Charge	1790	Tax PP 1790:15
Vowell, Thomas	Alexandria	Tax Charge	1795	Tax PP 1795:31
Vowell, Thomas	Alexandria	Tax Charge	1796	Tax PP 1796:19
Vowell, Thomas	Alexandria	Tax Charge	1798	Tax PP 1798:19
Vowell, Thomas	Arlington	Inventory	1845	AB9:138; LVA-LP
Vowell, Thomas	Arlington	Debts Due	1845	AB9:140
Vowell, Thomas	Arlington	Citation	1845	OCR1842:149
Vowell, Thomas	Arlington	Will P.	1845	OCR1842:148
Vowell, Thomas	Arlington	Admin	1845	OCR1842:153
Vowell, Thomas	Arlington	Will	1845	WB4:410; File #429A
Vowell, Thomas	Arlington	Account	1846	AB9:270; LVA-LP
Vowell, Thomas	Arlington	Two Wives	1846	OCR1842:159
Vowell, Thomas	Arlington	Account	1847	AB9:270; LVA-LP
Vowell, Thomas & wife Mary	Alexandria	Resident	1800	1800(4):07B
Vowell, Thomas, c/o John D.	Arlington	Guard.	1829	WB3:353
Vowell, Thomas, def.	Alexandria	Suit	1808	CRG:086
Vowell, Thomas, Fairfax St.	Alexandria	Occupant	1790	Tax L 1790:12
Vowell, Thomas, Jr.	Alexandria	Deposition	(nd)	CRE:346
Vowell, Thomas, Jr.	Alexandria	Tithable +16	1789	Tax PP 1789:19
Vowell, Thomas, Jr.	Alexandria	Tithable +16	1790	Tax PP 1790:15
Vowell, Thomas, merchant	Alexandria	Head	1810	1810(1):11A
Vowell, Thomas, murchant	Alexandria	Head	1800	1800(4):07A
Vowell, Thomas, plt.	Alexandria	Suit	1822	CRL:232
Vowell, Thomas, Prince St.	Alexandria	Occupant	1790	Tax L 1790:06
Vowell, Thomas [Charlotte]	Arlington	Petition	1846	LVA-LP (Box 214)
Vowell, Thomas [Elizabeth]	Arlington	Renounce	1845	OCR1842:150, 154
Vowell, Thos., merchant	Alexandria	Housekeeper	1808	1808(1):03A
Vowell, Thos., Sr.	Alexandria	Tax Charge	1796	Tax LP 1796:29
Vowell, Thos., Sr., Prince St.	Alexandria	Owner	1795	Tax L 1795:30
Vowell v. Douglas	Arlington	Suit	1846	OCR1842:157
Vowells, John & T.	Alexandria	Tax Charge	1796	Tax LP 1796:29
Vowells, John & Thos.	Alexandria	Mer. License	1799	Tax PP 1799:52-11w

NAME OR SUBJECT	LOCATION	TYPE	YEAR	REFERENCE(S)
W				
Waa [Waugh], William	Alexandria	Head	1810	1810(3):07A
Waddell, William C.H.	Arlington	Deposition	1831	ACR:083
Waddkins, Robt., labourer	Alexandria	Head	1810	1810(2):08A
Wade, John, c/o John (Norwich, Eng.)	Arlington	Apprentice	1805	OCR1801:239
Wade, Julia A.	Alexandria	Will	1897	WB2:221; LP
Wade, Mary A.	Alexandria	Will	1893	WB2:044; LP
Wade, Robt. H.	Alexandria	Tax Charge	1799	Tax PP 1799:45
Wade, Zephaniah S., grantor	Arlington	Indenture D.	1828	ID:168
Wade, Zephaniah S., in jail bounds	Arlington	Insolvent	1828	ID:166
Wadkins, Judy (C), washwoman	Alexandria	Housekeeper	1808	1808(1):05A
Wadsworth & Butler, def.	Alexandria	Suit	1808	CRG:117
Wadsworth, Charles	Arlington	Defendant	1808	ACO:082, 089
Wadsworth, Charles	Arlington	Bond	1809	WBC:263
Wadsworth, Charles	Arlington	Inventory	1809	WBC:264; LVA-LP
Wadsworth, Charles	Arlington	Sale	1809	WBC:285
Wadsworth, Charles	Arlington	Will	1809	WBC:261; File #038A
Wadsworth, Charles	Arlington	Account	1810	WBC:490
Wadsworth, Charles	Arlington	Admin.	1824	OCR1822:072
Wadsworth, Chas., merchant	Alexandria	Housekeeper	1808	1808(1):04A
Wadsworth, Elizabeth	Arlington	Renounce	1809	WBC:262; File #040A
Wadsworth, Jane L.	Arlington	Guard.	1823	OCR1822:041
Waggener & Deneal	Alexandria	Owner	1787	Tax L 1787:27
Wahl, Jas. & wife, mariner	Alexandria	Housekeeper	1799	1799(2):18A
Wailes, John, def.	Alexandria	Suit	1802	CRD:188, 190
Wailes, Leven	Alexandria	Tithable +16	1789	Tax PP 1789:17
Wair, George	Arlington	Will	1816	WB2:164; File #137A
Waite, William, b. Hallwell, Leisc., Eng.	Arlington	Alien Entry	1826	RA:04/07/26
Walcum, John, w(3), merchant	Alexandria	Head	1796	1796(3):6
Walder, Christian	Alexandria	Tax Charge	1789	Tax PP 1789:19
Walder, Jacob	Alexandria	Tithable +16	1790	Tax PP 1790:13
Wales, Andrew	Alexandria	Tax Charge	1788	Tax PP 1788:17
Wales, Andrew	Alexandria	Tax Charge	1789	Tax PP 1789:20
Wales, Andrew	Alexandria	Tax Charge	1790	Tax PP 1790:16
Wales, Andrew	Alexandria	Tax Charge	1796	Tax LP 1796:30
Wales, Andrew	Alexandria	Tax Charge	1796	Tax PP 1796:21
Wales, Andrew	Alexandria	Housekeeper	1799	1799(2):01A
Wales, Andrew	Alexandria	Tax Charge	1799	Tax PP 1799:45
Wales, Andrew	Arlington	Will	1800	CRA:302
Wales, Andrew	Arlington	Sale	1800	WBA:059
Wales, Andrew	Arlington	Account	1805	WBB:110; LVA-LP
Wales, Andrew, Fairfax St.	Alexandria	Owner	1790	Tax L 1790:12(2)
Wales, Andrew, nr. Water St.	Alexandria	Occupant	1790	Tax L 1790:12
Wales, Andrew, nr. Water St.	Alexandria	Owner	1790	Tax L 1790:12
Wales, Andrew, Union St.	Alexandria	Owner	1790	Tax L 1790:12
Wales, Andrew, w2, brewer	Alexandria	Head	1796	1796(3):6
Wales, Andrew, Water St.	Alexandria	Owner	1790	Tax L 1790:12
Wales, Andw.	Alexandria	Tax Charge	1795	Tax PP 1795:32
Wales, Andw.	Alexandria	Tax Charge	1798	Tax PP 1798:19
Wales, Andw., Fairfax St.	Alexandria	Owner	1795	Tax L 1795:31
Wales, Andw., Union St.	Alexandria	Owner	1795	Tax L 1795:31
Wales, Andw., Wales' alley	Alexandria	Occupant	1795	Tax L 1795:34
Wales, Andw., Wales' alley	Alexandria	Owner	1795	Tax L 1795:34
Wales, Daniel (C)	Alexandria	Boarder	1808	1808(3):19B
Wales, John J.	Alexandria	Tax Charge	1800	Tax PP 1800:46
Wales, Wm.	Alexandria	Boarder	1808	1808(3):18A
Walker, A.	Alexandria	Tax Charge	1796	Tax PP 1796:20
Walker, Andrew J., c/o Levin P.	Arlington	Guard. Acct.	1866	WB8:414
Walker, Aradena, c/o Levin P.	Arlington	Guard. Acct.	1866	WB8:414
Walker, Camilla, c/o Levin P.	Arlington	Guard. Acct.	1866	WB8:414
Walker, Emma Catherine, c/o Levin P.	Arlington	Guard. Acct.	1866	WB8:414

NAME OR SUBJECT	LOCATION	TYPE	YEAR	REFERENCE(S)
Walker, Frances, c/o Elizabeth	Arlington	Apprentice	1805	OCR1801:257
Walker, George	Arlington	Apprentice	1804	OCR1801:153
Walker, George W., Constable	Arlington	Appointment	1854	BB(np)
Walker, Henry	Alexandria	Tax Charge	1795	Tax PP 1795:33
Walker, Henry	Alexandria	Tax Charge	1796	Tax LP 1796:30
Walker, Henry	Alexandria	Tax Charge	1796	Tax PP 1796:20
Walker, Henry	Arlington	Defendant	1801	PA:172
Walker, Henry, btw. Fairfax	Alexandria	Occupant	1795	Tax L 1795:19
Walker, Henry, Royal St.	Alexandria	Occupant	1795	Tax L 1795:01
Walker, Henry, St. Asaph St.	Alexandria	Occupant	1790	Tax L 1790:09
Walker, Henry, w(3)1,schoolmaster	Alexandria	Head	1796	1796(3):3
Walker, Jno.	Alexandria	Tax Charge	1795	Tax PP 1795:32
Walker, John Edward, c/o Cath. Glenn	Arlington	Apprentice	1814	OCR1811:216
Walker, Joseph	Alexandria	Tax Charge	1788	Tax PP 1788:17
Walker, Leven, mail carrier	Alexandria	Housekeeper	1808	1808(3):18A
Walker, Levin	Arlington	Inventory	1826	AB6:177
Walker, Levin	Arlington	Admin.	1826	OCR1822:115
Walker, Levin	Arlington	Admin.	1826	WB3:232
Walker, Levin P.	Arlington	Account	1866	WB8:412
Walker, Robert	Alexandria	Tax Charge	1795	Tax PP 1795:33
Walker, Robert	Alexandria	Tax Charge	1798	Tax PP 1798:20
Walker, Robert	Alexandria	Tax Charge	1800	Tax PP 1800:46
Walker, Robert & wife, carpenter	Alexandria	Head	1795	1795(4):01
Walker, Robert & wife Mary	Alexandria	Resident	1800	1800(4):04B
Walker, Robert, c/o Geo., Mathews Co.	Arlington	Apprentice	1815	OCR1811:315
Walker, Robert, house carpenter	Alexandria	Head	1800	1800(4):04A
Walker, Robt. & wife, carpenter	Alexandria	Housekeeper	1799	1799(2):16A
Walker, Robt., Water St.	Alexandria	Occupant	1795	Tax L 1795:18
Walker, Robt., Water St.	Alexandria	Owner	1795	Tax L 1795:34
Walker, Robt., Water St.	Alexandria	Occupant	1795	Tax L 1795:34
Walker, Soln.	Alexandria	Boarder	1808	1808(2):15A
Walker, Statia, washwoman	Alexandria	Housekeeper	1808	1808(2):17A
Walker, Thomas, laborer	Alexandria	Housekeeper	1808	1808(4):26A
Walker, Thos., labourer	Alexandria	Head	1810	1810(4):05A
Walker, William, grantee	Arlington	Indenture D.	1829	ID:221
Walker, Wm.	Alexandria	Boarder	1808	1808(1):04A
Walkom, John & wife, retailer	Alexandria	Housekeeper	1799	1799(2):01A
Wall, John	Alexandria	Tax Charge	1788	Tax PP 1788:17
Wallace, Ann, seamstress	Alexandria	Head	1810	1810(1):05A
Wallace, George	Arlington	Apprentice	1815	OCR1811:277
Wallace, George, c/o Nancy	Arlington	Apprentice	1812	OCR1811:112
Wallace, James	Arlington	Admin.	1814	WB1:305
Wallace, John	Alexandria	Tax Charge	1796	Tax PP 1796:20
Wallace, John	Arlington	Appraisal	1851	WB6:008; LVA-LP
Wallace, John Robert	Arlington	Bond	1851	BB(np)
Wallace, John Robert	Arlington	Will	1851	WB5:329; File #470A
Wallace, John Robert, Genl.	Arlington	Sale	1851	WB6:008; LVA-LP
Wallace, John Robert, Genl.	Arlington	Inventory	1852	WB6:012; LVA-LP
Wallace, John Robert, Genl.	Arlington	Account	1852	WB6:170; LVA-LP
Wallace, Leven, shopkeeper	Alexandria	Housekeeper	1808	1808(1):03A
Wallace, Nancy, washwoman	Alexandria	Housekeeper	1808	1808(4):24A
Wallace, Nathaniel & wife, labourer	Alexandria	Housekeeper	1799	1799(2):07A
Wallace, Nathanl.	Alexandria	Tax Charge	1799	Tax PP 1799:45
Wallace, Polly	Arlington	Will	1891	WB10:193; File #752A
Wallace, Richard, labourer	Alexandria	Head	1810	1810(4):03A
Wallace, Richd., laborer	Alexandria	Housekeeper	1808	1808(4):28A
Wallace, Thomas, bricklayer	Alexandria	Housekeeper	1808	1808(4):28A
Wallace, William, c/o Richard	Arlington	Apprentice	1815	OCR1811:296
Waller, Constance Gardner Cazenove	Alexandria	Will	1884	WB1:420; LP
Waller, Elijah	Arlington	Ordinary	1821	OBL3(np)
Waller, Elijah	Arlington	Ordinary	1823	OBL3(np)

NAME OR SUBJECT	LOCATION	TYPE	YEAR	REFERENCE(S)
Waller, Elijah, at his house	Arlington	Ordinary	1831	OBL4(np)
Waller, Elijah, Fayette/King & Cameron	Arlington	Ordinary	1822	OBL3(np)
Waller, Elijah, in Alexandria Co.	Arlington	Ordinary	1830	OBL4(np)
Walner, Cragy (C)	Alexandria	Housekeeper	1799	1799(2):19A
Walsh, Alice	Arlington	Guard.	1808	WBC:066
Walsh, Catesby Jones	Arlington	Guard.	1808	WBC:066
Walsh, Richard	Arlington	Inventory	1815	AB2:186; LVA-LP
Walsh, Richard	Arlington	Sale	1815	AB2:187
Walsh, Richard	Arlington	Admin.	1815	WB2:069
Walsh, Richard	Arlington	Account	1816	AB2:388; LVA-LP
Walsh, Richard	Arlington	Account	1817	AB3:060; LVA-LP
Walsh, Richard	Arlington	Suit	1828	LVA-LP (Accounts)
Walsh, Richard, brother Fairburne	Arlington	P. of Atty.	1825	LVA-LP (Accounts)
Walsh, Richd.	Alexandria	Boarder	1808	1808(1):05A
Walter, Christian	Alexandria	Tax Charge	1787	Tax PP 1787:15
Walters, Thomas	Arlington	Defendant	1804	ACO:028
Walters, Thomas	Arlington	Defendant	1805	ACO:031
Walton, Eliza	Arlington	Guard.	1843	OCR1842:027
Walton, Eliza, c/o William C.	Arlington	Guard.	1843	WB4:318
Walton, Michael & Richard	Alexandria	Mer. License	1799	Tax PP 1799:52-11w
Walton, Michl. & Richd.	Alexandria	Mer. License	1798	Tax PP 1798:20-8
Walton, Richard	Alexandria	Tax Charge	1799	Tax PP 1799:44
Walton, William C., Rev., Hartford CN	Arlington	Will (NR)	1834	File #065A
Wampler, Jacob	Alexandria	Tithable +16	1788	Tax PP 1788:15
Wannonmaker, Jno.	Alexandria	Tithable +21	1787	Tax PP 1787:06
Wanshear, Martin, plaisterer	Alexandria	Housekeeper	1808	1808(3):22A
Wanton, Phil.	Alexandria	Tax Charge	1795	Tax PP 1795:33
Wanton, Phil.	Alexandria	Tax Charge	1798	Tax PP 1798:20
Wanton, Phil., Fairfax St.	Alexandria	Occupant	1795	Tax L 1795:27
Wanton, Phil., Prince St.	Alexandria	Occupant	1795	Tax L 1795:27
Wanton, Philip	Alexandria	Tax Charge	1796	Tax LP 1796:31
Wanton, Philip	Alexandria	Tax Charge	1796	Tax PP 1796:20
Wanton, Philip	Alexandria	Mer. License	1799	Tax PP 1799:52-11r
Wanton, Philip	Alexandria	Tax Charge	1799	Tax PP 1799:45
Wanton, Philip	Alexandria	Mer. License	1800	Tax PP 1800:54(22)r
Wanton, Philip	Alexandria	Tax Charge	1800	Tax PP 1800:46
Wanton, Philip & wife, merchant	Alexandria	Housekeeper	1799	1799(2):09A
Wanton, Philip, late trader	Alexandria	Housekeeper	1808	1808(4):25A
Wanton, Philip, w(4)2, merchant	Alexandria	Head	1796	1796(3):2
Wanton, Phillip, schoolmaster	Alexandria	Head	1810	1810(4):03A
Ward & Haggerty, Princess & Oronoka	Alexandria	Occupant	1787	Tax L 1787:27
Ward, Andrew, ship carpenter	Alexandria	Head	1810	1810(1):07A
Ward, Cecelia	Alexandria	Tax Charge	1795	Tax PP 1795:32
Ward, Cecelia, Fairfax St.	Alexandria	Occupant	1795	Tax L 1795:25
Ward, Cornelius, consignee	Arlington	Suit	1808	ACR:039
Ward, Elizabeth	Arlington	Guard.	1821	WB2:424
Ward, Enoch, def.	Alexandria	Suit	1801	CRB:048
Ward, George	Alexandria	Tithable +16	1788	Tax PP 1788:01
Ward, George	Alexandria	Tithable +16	1789	Tax PP 1789:10
Ward, George, c/o Josiah	Arlington	Apprentice	1812	OCR1811:189
Ward, James, cabbinet maker	Alexandria	Head	1810	1810(3):03A
Ward, Jas.	Alexandria	Boarder	1808	1808(3):22A
Ward, John	Alexandria	Tithable +16	1789	Tax PP 1789:17
Ward, John	Arlington	Will	1899	WB10:409; File #791A
Ward, Joseus	Alexandria	Tax Charge	1799	Tax PP 1799:44
Ward, Josiah, labourer	Alexandria	Head	1810	1810(1):02A
Ward, Josias & wife, labourer	Alexandria	Housekeeper	1799	1799(2):07A
Ward, Mary E.	Alexandria	Will	1883	WB1:380; LP
Ward, Robert D.	Arlington	Apprentice	1827	OCR1822:148
Ward, Thos.	Alexandria	Boarder	1808	1808(4):24A
Ward, Walter, labourer	Alexandria	Head	1810	1810(1):05A

NAME OR SUBJECT	LOCATION	TYPE	YEAR	REFERENCE(S)
Ward, William	Alexandria	Owner	1787	Tax L 1787:26
Ward, William	Alexandria	Tax Charge	1787	Tax PP 1787:16
Ward, William	Alexandria	Tax Charge	1788	Tax PP 1788:17
Ward, William	Alexandria	Tax Charge	1790	Tax PP 1790:15
Ward, William, Royal St.	Alexandria	Occupant	1790	Tax L 1790:09
Ward, William, Royal St.	Alexandria	Occupant	1790	Tax L 1790:09
Ward, William, Union St.	Alexandria	Occupant	1787	Tax L 1787:01
Ward, William, Union St.	Alexandria	Occupant	1787	Tax L 1787:26
Warden, James	Alexandria	Tax Charge	1796	Tax PP 1796:20
Warden, James	Alexandria	Tax Charge	1798	Tax PP 1798:19
Warden, Joseph	Alexandria	Tax Charge	1798	Tax PP 1798:19
Warden, William	Alexandria	Owner	1787	Tax L 1787:26
Warden, William	Alexandria	Tax Charge	1787	Tax PP 1787:16
Warden, William	Alexandria	Tax Charge	1789	Tax PP 1789:19
Warden, William	Alexandria	Tax Charge	1790	Tax PP 1790:15
Warden, William, Cameron St.	Alexandria	Owner	1790	Tax L 1790:12
Warden, William, Cameron St.	Alexandria	Occupant	1787	Tax L 1787:26
Warden, William, Cameron St.	Alexandria	Occupant	1790	Tax L 1790:12
Warden, Wm.	Alexandria	Tax Charge	1788	Tax PP 1788:17
Warden, Wm.	Alexandria	Tax Charge	1796	Tax LP 1796:31
Warder, John (Philadelphia), King St.	Alexandria	Owner	1790	Tax L 1790:13
Ware, Geo.	Alexandria	Tax Charge	1796	Tax LP 1796:31
Ware, Geo., labourer	Alexandria	Head	1810	1810(4):09A
Ware, George	Alexandria	Tax Charge	1796	Tax LP 1796:24
Ware, James F., in Alexandria Co.	Arlington	Ordinary	1850	OBL6(np)
Ware, James F., in Alexandria Co.	Arlington	Ordinary	1850	OBL6(np)
Ware, Nancy, washwoman	Alexandria	Housekeeper	1808	1808(2):14A
Ware, Sally	Arlington	Apprentice	1812	OCR1811:084
Ware, Sally	Arlington	Guard.	1812	WB1:137
Waring, Arthur V., c/o Arthur	Arlington	Guard.	1850	GBB(np)
Waring, David, c/o Arthur	Arlington	Guard.	1850	GBB(np)
Waring, Julia Ann Eliza (Hepburn)	Arlington	Guard. Acct.	1832	AB7:142; LVA-LP
Waring, Julianna, late Hepburn	Arlington	Guard. Acct.	1835	AB7:142
Waring, William H., c/o Arthur	Arlington	Guard.	1850	GBB(np)
Warnell, Henry	Alexandria	Tax Charge	1788	Tax PP 1788:17
Warnell, Henry	Alexandria	Tax Charge	1789	Tax PP 1789:20
Warner, Alexander	Arlington	Libellant	1811	ACO:119
Warner, Edmund	Alexandria	Tax Charge	1787	Tax PP 1787:16
Warner, Henry	Arlington	Apprentice	1827	OCR1822:130a
Warner, Jack (C), laborer	Alexandria	Housekeeper	1808	1808(1):05A
Warner, James, labourer	Alexandria	Head	1810	1810(4):02A
Warner, Jane	Alexandria	Resident	1800	1800(4):03B
Warner, John, labourer	Alexandria	Head	1810	1810(1):11A
Warner, Leander A., grantor	Arlington	Indenture D.	1827	ID:144
Warner, Leander A., in jail	Arlington	Insolvent	1827	ID:141
Warner, Saml., turner	Alexandria	Housekeeper	1808	1808(1):03A
Warner, Samuel, turner	Alexandria	Head	1810	1810(1):13A
Warner, William (C)	Arlington	Apprentice	1826	OCR1822:112a
Warner, Zebulon	Arlington	Ordinary	1804	OBL1(np)
Warning, Henry	Alexandria	Tax Charge	1790	Tax PP 1790:16
Warrell, Maurice	Alexandria	Tax Charge	1790	Tax PP 1790:16
Warwick, Wm.	Alexandria	Tax Charge	1787	Tax PP 1787:16
Washington, Ann Maria, c/o George	Arlington	Guard.	1852	BB(np)
Washington, Ann R.	Alexandria	Will	1893	WB2:048; LP
Washington, Bayley	Alexandria	Tithable +16	1790	Tax PP 1790:16
Washington, Bushrod	Alexandria	Tax Charge	1789	Tax PP 1789:20
Washington, Bushrod	Alexandria	Tax Charge	1790	Tax PP 1790:16
Washington, Bushrod, Duke St.	Alexandria	Occupant	1790	Tax L 1790:05
Washington, Bushrod, Jr., grantor	Arlington	Indenture D.	1826	ID:004
Washington, Bushrod, the Younger	Arlington	Insolvent	1826	ID:001
Washington, Bushrod, Wolf St.	Alexandria	Owner	1790	Tax L 1790:12

NAME OR SUBJECT	LOCATION	TYPE	YEAR	REFERENCE(S)
Washington, Bushrod, Wolf St.	Alexandria	Occupant	1790	Tax L 1790:12
Washington, Elizabeth	Arlington	Will	1805	WBB:218; File #005A
Washington, Elizabeth	Arlington	Inventory	1806	WBB:270; LVA-LP
Washington, Elizabeth	Arlington	Bond	1806	WBB:227
Washington, Elizabeth	Arlington	Sale	1806	WBB:284
Washington, Frances V., c/o George	Arlington	Guard.	1852	BB(np)
Washington, Genl.	Alexandria	Owner	1787	Tax L 1787:26
Washington, Genl., Cameron St.	Alexandria	Occupant	1787	Tax L 1787:26
Washington, Geo.	Alexandria	Tax Charge	1796	Tax LP 1796:30
Washington, Geo.	Alexandria	Boarder	1799	1799(2):06A
Washington, Geo., Cameron St.	Alexandria	Owner	1795	Tax L 1795:33
Washington, George W., c/o George	Arlington	Guard.	1852	BB(np)
Washington, Harriet	Arlington	Will	1855	WB6:418; File #514A
Washington, Henry	Arlington	Admin.	1812	WB1:199
Washington, John	Alexandria	Tithable +16	1788	Tax PP 1788:13
Washington, John	Alexandria	Tithable +16	1789	Tax PP 1789:09
Washington, John	Arlington	Trustee Acct.	1839	AB8:218; LVA-LP
Washington, John	Arlington	Inventory	1839	AB8:045; LVA-LP
Washington, John	Arlington	Account	1840	AB8:167; LVA-LP
Washington, John	Arlington	Account	1841	AB8:167
Washington, John	Arlington	Account	1841	AB8:218
Washington, John	Arlington	Account	1846	AB9:174; LVA-LP
Washington, John Hill	Arlington	Bond	1839	WB4:213
Washington, John Hill	Arlington	Will	1839	WB4:212; File #371A
Washington, Lund	Alexandria	Account B.	1798	CRC:159
Washington, Lund, def.	Alexandria	Suit	1802	CRC:155
Washington, Lund, def.	Alexandria	Suit	1803	CRD:071
Washington, Maria	Alexandria	Will	1884	WB1:524; LP
Washington, Mary C., c/o George	Arlington	Guard.	1852	BB(np)
Washington, Mrs., Cameron St.	Alexandria	Occupant	1795	Tax L 1795:33
Washington, Mrs., Pitt St.	Alexandria	Owner	1795	Tax L 1795:33
Washington, Nat.	Alexandria	Tax Charge	1796	Tax PP 1796:21
Washington, Nathaniel	Arlington	Defendant	1802	PA:222
Washington, William	Alexandria	Tax Charge	1799	Tax PP 1799:45
Washington, William H.	Arlington	Ordinary	1803	OBL1(np)
Washington, William H.	Arlington	Sale	1804	WBB:020
Washington, William H.	Arlington	Bond	1806	WBB:383
Washington, William Henry	Arlington	Admin.	1803	WBA:168
Washington, William Henry	Arlington	Inventory	1804	WBA:325; LVA-LP
Washington, William Henry	Arlington	Guard.	1806	WBB:247
Washington, William Henry, def.	Alexandria	Suit	1801	CRB:261
Washington, William Henry, def.	Alexandria	Suit	1803	CRD:081
Washington, Wm.	Alexandria	Boarder	1800	1800(4):05A
Washington, Wm.	Alexandria	Resident	1800	1800(4):05B
Washington, Wm.	Alexandria	Boarder	1808	1808(1):08A
Washington, Wm., M.D.	Alexandria	Tax Charge	1800	Tax PP 1800:46
Washington, Wm., physician	Alexandria	Head	1810	1810(1):04A
Washington, Wm., student of medicine	Alexandria	Boarder	1799	1799(2):15A
Wasson, Jno. & wife, bricklayer	Alexandria	Housekeeper	1799	1799(2):13A
Wasson, John	Alexandria	Tax Charge	1799	Tax PP 1799:44
Waterman, Simon	Alexandria	Will	1882	WB1:374; LP
Waters, Ann	Arlington	Guard.	1821	WB2:430
Waters, Benjamin	Arlington	Inventory	1864	WB8:195
Waters, Benjamin	Arlington	Will	1864	WB8:185; File #611A
Waters, Christian	Alexandria	Tax Charge	1788	Tax PP 1788:17
Waters, Eliza	Arlington	Apprentice	1843	OCR1842:027
Waters, Elizabeth	Arlington	Guard.	1817	WB2:194
Waters, Ignatius	Alexandria	Tax Charge	1799	Tax PP 1799:44
Waters, Ignatius	Alexandria	Tax Charge	1800	Tax PP 1800:46
Waters, Ignatius, hatter	Alexandria	Boarder	1799	1799(2):02A
Waters, Jonathan, grantor	Arlington	Indenture D.	1827	ID:132

NAME OR SUBJECT	LOCATION	TYPE	YEAR	REFERENCE(S)
Waters, Jonathan, in jail	Arlington	Insolvent	1827	ID:130
Waters, Sarah	Arlington	Will P.	1846	OCR1842:182
Waters, Theodore D., c/o Kezia	Arlington	Apprentice	1811	OCR1811:044
Waters, Thomas A.	Alexandria	Appraisal	1871	WB1:021
Waters, William	Alexandria	Deed	1803	CRH:220, 223
Watkins, John, w(2), mariner	Alexandria	Head	1796	1796(3):6
Watkins, Thomas	Arlington	Admin.	1820	WB2:350
Watson, Eliza	Arlington	Guard.	1823	OCR1822:055a
Watson, James	Alexandria	Tithable +16	1789	Tax PP 1789:20
Watson, James	Alexandria	Tithable +16	1790	Tax PP 1790:16
Watson, James	Arlington	Defendant	1801	PA:176
Watson, James, w2, merchant	Alexandria	Head	1796	1796(3):4
Watson, Jane	Arlington	Guard.	1820	WB2:341
Watson, Jno., merchant	Alexandria	Boarder	1799	1799(2):02A
Watson, John	Alexandria	Tax Charge	1796	Tax PP 1796:21
Watson, Josia, 2(4)6, merchant	Alexandria	Head	1796	1796(3):4
Watson, Josiah	Alexandria	Owner	1787	Tax L 1787:26
Watson, Josiah	Alexandria	Tax Charge	1787	Tax PP 1787:16
Watson, Josiah	Alexandria	Tax Charge	1788	Tax PP 1788:17
Watson, Josiah	Alexandria	Tax Charge	1789	Tax PP 1789:20
Watson, Josiah	Alexandria	Bond	1790	CRI:393
Watson, Josiah	Alexandria	Tax Charge	1790	Tax PP 1790:16
Watson, Josiah	Alexandria	Tax Charge	1795	Tax PP 1795:33
Watson, Josiah	Alexandria	Tax Charge	1796	Tax LP 1796:30
Watson, Josiah	Alexandria	Tax Charge	1796	Tax PP 1796:21
Watson, Josiah	Alexandria	Tax Charge	1798	Tax PP 1798:20
Watson, Josiah	Alexandria	Tax Charge	1799	Tax PP 1799:44
Watson, Josiah & Co., Union St.	Alexandria	Occupant	1787	Tax L 1787:11
Watson, Josiah & wife, merchant	Alexandria	Housekeeper	1799	1799(2):04A
Watson, Josiah, Fairfax St.	Alexandria	Occupant	1787	Tax L 1787:26
Watson, Josiah, Fairfax St.	Alexandria	Owner	1790	Tax L 1790:12(2)
Watson, Josiah, on wharf	Alexandria	Owner	1795	Tax L 1795:33
Watson, Josiah, Pitt St.	Alexandria	Occupant	1787	Tax L 1787:26
Watson, Josiah, Pitt St.	Alexandria	Owner	1790	Tax L 1790:12(2)
Watson, Josiah, Pitt St.	Alexandria	Occupant	1790	Tax L 1790:12
Watson, Josiah, Pitt St.	Alexandria	Owner	1795	Tax L 1795:33(2)
Watson, Josiah, Prince St.	Alexandria	Owner	1790	Tax L 1790:12
Watson, Josiah, Prince St.	Alexandria	Owner	1795	Tax L 1795:33(3)
Watson, Josiah, Prince St.	Alexandria	Occupant	1795	Tax L 1795:22
Watson, Josiah, Union St.	Alexandria	Occupant	1787	Tax L 1787:26
Watson, Josiah, Union St.	Alexandria	Occupant	1790	Tax L 1790:12
Watson, Josiah, Union St.	Alexandria	Owner	1790	Tax L 1790:12
Watson, Josiah, Union St.	Alexandria	Owner	1795	Tax L 1795:33
Watson, Josiah, Water St.	Alexandria	Owner	1790	Tax L 1790:12
Watson, Josiah, Water St.	Alexandria	Owner	1795	Tax L 1795:33
Watson, Leven	Arlington	Defendant	1802	PA:200
Watson, Leven, grantor	Arlington	Indenture D.	1804	ID3:086
Watson, Leven, seaman	Alexandria	Head	1810	1810(1):08A
Watson, Levin, in jail bounds	Arlington	Insolvent	1804	ID3:077
Watson, Mary	Alexandria	Resident	1800	1800(4):11B
Watson, Mary, labourrer	Alexandria	Boarder	1800	1800(4):11A
Watson, Thomas	Arlington	Inventory	1818	AB3:164; LVA-LP
Watson, Thomas	Arlington	Admin.	1818	WB2:237
Watson, Thomas	Arlington	Admin.	1825	OCR1822:084a
Watson, Thomas (C)	Arlington	Apprentice	1826	OCR1822:111a
Watson, Thos.	Alexandria	Boarder	1808	1808(2):16A
Watters, Ignatius	Alexandria	Tax Charge	1796	Tax PP 1796:20
Watters, Sarah	Arlington	Will	1846	WB4:415
Watters, Sarah (Fairfax)	Arlington	Will P.	1846	OCR1842:156
Wattles, Charles T.	Arlington	Settlement	1824	AB5:232; LVA-LP
Wattles, Charles T.	Arlington	Admin.	1823	OCR1822:039

NAME OR SUBJECT	LOCATION	TYPE	YEAR	REFERENCE(S)
Wattles, Charles T.	Arlington	Admin.	1823	WB3:091
Wattles, Charles W.	Alexandria	Will	1887	WB1:459; LP
Wattles, Ichabod	Alexandria	Boarder	1799	1799(2):09A
Wattles, Nathaniel	Alexandria	Tax Charge	1799	Tax PP 1799:45
Wattles, Nathaniel	Alexandria	Tax Charge	1800	Tax PP 1800:47
Wattles, Nathaniel & wife, sea captain	Alexandria	Housekeeper	1799	1799(2):09A
Wattles, Nathaniel, complt.	Alexandria	Suit	1821	CRL:038
Wattles, Nathaniel, merchant	Alexandria	Housekeeper	1808	1808(1):10A
Wattles, Nathaniel, plt.	Alexandria	Suit	1821	CRL:347
Wattles, Nathl., mariner	Alexandria	Head	1810	1810(1):07A
Wattles, Sarah	Alexandria	Boarder	1799	1799(2):09A
Watts, A., back building	Alexandria	Occupant	1795	Tax L 1795:03
Watts, Adam (C), laborer	Alexandria	Head	1795	1795(4):05
Watts, Adeline, c/o Edward	Arlington	Guard.	1812	WB1:185
Watts, Jno., merchant	Alexandria	Boarder	1799	1799(2):02A
Watts, John	Alexandria	Tax Charge	1795	Tax PP 1795:33
Watts, John	Arlington	Security	1801	ACO:006
Watts, John	Arlington	Plaintiff	1802	PA:065
Watts, John	Arlington	Will	1808	WBC:091; File #036A
Watts, John	Arlington	Inventory	1808	WBC:094; LP
Watts, John	Arlington	Bond	1808	WBC:092
Watts, John	Arlington	Account	1810	WBC:332; LVA-LP
Watts, John	Arlington	Sale	1810	WBC:330; LVA-LP
Watts, John	Arlington	Account	1811	AB1:026; LVA-LP
Watts, John	Arlington	P. of Atty.	1811	LVA-LP
Watts, John	Arlington	Account	1812	AB1:147; LVA-LP
Watts, John	Arlington	Account	1813	AB1:277; LVA-LP
Watts, John	Arlington	Account	1814	AB2:065; LVA-LP
Watts, John	Arlington	Account	1814	AB2:030; LVA-LP
Watts, John	Arlington	Account	1816	AB2:233
Watts, John	Arlington	Account	1820	AB4:180; LVA-LP
Watts, John, Estate, def.	Alexandria	Suit	1814	CRI:363
Watts, John, merchant	Alexandria	Housekeeper	1808	1808(1):04A
Watts, John, plt.	Alexandria	Suit	1801	CRB:063
Watts, John, plt.	Alexandria	Suit	1802	CRC:274
Waugh, Beverly & wife Catherine	Alexandria	Suit	1821	CRL:369
Waugh, Mary (C), washwoman	Alexandria	Housekeeper	1808	1808(3):23A
Waugh, McKenzie (C)	Arlington	Apprentice	1801	OCR1801:013
Waugh [Waa], William	Alexandria	Head	1810	1810(3):07A
Waugthen, Alburn	Arlington	Apprentice	1804	OCR1801:174
Wawson, John	Alexandria	Tax Charge	1800	Tax PP 1800:46
Way, Andrew, Jr.	Arlington	Defendant	1824	ACO:238
Way, Frederick, plaisterer	Alexandria	Boarder	1799	1799(2):19A
Way, Frederick, plaisterer	Alexandria	Housekeeper	1808	1808(4):29A
Way, Frederick, plasterer	Alexandria	Head	1810	1810(4):03A
Waylie, Jno., Jr.	Alexandria	Tax Charge	1799	Tax PP 1799:44
Weaver, Fredk.	Alexandria	Tax Charge	1789	Tax PP 1789:20
Weaver, George	Alexandria	Tax Charge	1787	Tax PP 1787:16
Weaver, Jacob	Alexandria	Tax Charge	1799	Tax PP 1799:44
Weaver, Joanna & a child	Alexandria	Boarder	1799	1799(2):10A
Weaver, John	Alexandria	Tax Charge	1789	Tax PP 1789:20
Weaver, Wm.	Alexandria	Boarder	1799	1799(2):10A
Webb, Chas. F.	Alexandria	Boarder	1808	1808(2):10A
Webb, John	Arlington	Apprentice	1826	OCR1822:127a
Webb, Thomas	Arlington	Inventory	1812	AB1:193; LVA-LP
Webb, Thomas	Arlington	Account	1812	LVA-LP
Webb, Thomas	Arlington	Admin.	1812	WB1:167
Webb, Verlinda	Arlington	Guard.	1827	OCR1822:144a
Webb, Walter	Alexandria	Tax Charge	1799	Tax PP 1799:44
Webb, Walter, taylor	Alexandria	Boarder	1799	1799(2):06A
Webster, Aaron	Alexandria	Tithable +16	1789	Tax PP 1789:03

NAME OR SUBJECT	LOCATION	TYPE	YEAR	REFERENCE(S)
Webster, Adam	Alexandria	Boarder	1808	1808(3):21A
Webster, Araminta, Royal & Princess	Arlington	Ordinary	1823	OBL3(np)
Webster, Araminta, in Alexandria Co.	Arlington	Ordinary	1821	OBL3(np)
Webster, Araminta, Royal & Queen Sts.	Arlington	Ordinary	1822	OBL3(np)
Webster, C.F.	Alexandria	Will	1873	WB1:083; LP
Webster, Ebenezer	Arlington	Seaman	1803	ACO:007
Webster, Geo., plasterer	Alexandria	Head	1810	1810(4):02A
Webster, George	Arlington	Apprentice	1842	OCR1842:003
Webster, George, grantor	Arlington	Indenture D.	1831	ID:290
Webster, George, in jail	Arlington	Insolvent	1831	ID:287
Webster, Henry A., grantor	Arlington	Indenture D.	1827	ID:113
Webster, Henry A., in jail	Arlington	Insolvent	1827	ID:110
Webster, Henry Augustus, c/o Mary	Arlington	Apprentice	1812	OCR1811:122
Webster, John	Alexandria	Tax Charge	1796	Tax LP 1796:30
Webster, John, c/o James	Arlington	Apprentice	1810	OCR1811:010
Webster, Maria	Arlington	Apprentice	1844	OCR1842:092
Webster, Mary	Alexandria	Tax Charge	1799	Tax PP 1799:45
Webster, Philip	Alexandria	Owner	1787	Tax L 1787:27
Webster, Philip	Alexandria	Tax Charge	1787	Tax PP 1787:16
Webster, Philip	Alexandria	Tax Charge	1788	Tax PP 1788:17
Webster, Philip	Alexandria	Tax Charge	1789	Tax PP 1789:19
Webster, Philip	Alexandria	Tax Charge	1790	Tax PP 1790:16
Webster, Philip	Alexandria	Tax Charge	1796	Tax LP 1796:30
Webster, Philip, St. Asaph St.	Alexandria	Occupant	1787	Tax L 1787:27
Webster, Philip, St. Asaph St.	Alexandria	Occupant	1790	Tax L 1790:12
Webster, Philip, St. Asaph St.	Alexandria	Owner	1790	Tax L 1790:12
Webster, Philip, St. Asaph St.	Alexandria	Owner	1795	Tax L 1795:32
Webster, Walter	Arlington	Guard.	1823	WB3:086
Webster, William Warner, c/o Mary	Arlington	Apprentice	1812	OCR1811:123
Webster, Wm.	Alexandria	Boarder	1808	1808(3):21A
Wedderburn, Alexander J., c/o Wm.	Arlington	Guard.	1817	WB2:205
Weech, William T.S.	Alexandria	Will	1895	WB2:124; LP
Weeden, Cornelius	Alexandria	Boarder	1808	1808(2):11A
Weeden, Harry	Alexandria	Tax Charge	1800	Tax PP 1800:47
Weeden, Wm.	Alexandria	Tax Charge	1795	Tax PP 1795:32
Weedon, Nathaniel, def.	Alexandria	Suit	1801	CRC:190
Weeks, Bob (C), waterman	Alexandria	Housekeeper	1808	1808(1):09A
Weeks, Jacob	Alexandria	Tax Charge	1789	Tax PP 1789:20
Weeks, Robt.	Alexandria	Head	1810	1810(4):09A
Weems, Nathaniel	Alexandria	Tax Charge	1799	Tax PP 1799:45
Weems, Nathaniel, student of medicine	Alexandria	Boarder	1799	1799(2):15A
Weidemeyer & Delius	Alexandria	Mer. License	1799	Tax PP 1799:52-11r
Weightman, John	Alexandria	Boarder	1808	1808(1):04A
Weightman, Richard	Alexandria	Owner	1787	Tax L 1787:27
Weightman, Richard	Alexandria	Tax Charge	1787	Tax PP 1787:16
Weightman, Richard	Alexandria	Tax Charge	1788	Tax PP 1788:17
Weightman, Richard	Alexandria	Tax Charge	1789	Tax PP 1789:19
Weightman, Richard	Alexandria	Tax Charge	1790	Tax PP 1790:16
Weightman, Richard	Alexandria	Tax Charge	1796	Tax PP 1796:20
Weightman, Richard	Arlington	Defendant	1802	PA:277
Weightman, Richard	Arlington	Juryman	1804	ACO:026
Weightman, Richard	Arlington	Juryman	1808	ACO:081
Weightman, Richard	Arlington	Will	1812	WB1:157; File #101A
Weightman, Richard	Arlington	Account	1813	AB1:299; LVA-LP
Weightman, Richard	Arlington	Inventory	1813	AB1:296; LVA-LP
Weightman, Richard	Arlington	Account	1820	AB4:148; LVA-LP
Weightman, Richard, Princess St.	Alexandria	Occupant	1787	Tax L 1787:27
Weightman, Richard, Princess St.	Alexandria	Owner	1790	Tax L 1790:12
Weightman, Richard, w(6)3, taylor	Alexandria	Head	1796	1796(3):5
Weightman, Richd.	Alexandria	Tax Charge	1795	Tax PP 1795:33
Weightman, Richd.	Alexandria	Tax Charge	1796	Tax LP 1796:30

NAME OR SUBJECT	LOCATION	TYPE	YEAR	REFERENCE(S)
Weightman, Richd., Fairfax St.	Alexandria	Occupant	1790	Tax L 1790:05
Weightman, Richd., Fairfax St.	Alexandria	Owner	1795	Tax L 1795:30(2)
Weightman, Richd., Prince St.	Alexandria	Owner	1795	Tax L 1795:30(2)
Weightman, Richd., Prince St.	Alexandria	Occupant	1795	Tax L 1795:30
Weightman, Richd., taylor	Alexandria	Housekeeper	1808	1808(1):04A
Weiles, Leven P.	Alexandria	Tithable +16	1788	Tax PP 1788:15
Weiles, William, Jr.	Arlington	Apprentice	1804	OCR1801:228
Weir, Elizabeth, c/o Nancy	Arlington	Apprentice	1813	OCR1811:142
Weisemiller, Jacob	Alexandria	Tax Charge	1790	Tax PP 1790:16
Weismiller, Jacob, St. Asaph St.	Alexandria	Owner	1790	Tax L 1790:13
Weisy, Peter	Alexandria	Tax Charge	1800	Tax PP 1800:47
Welborne, David	Arlington	Will	1827	WB3:289; File #258A
Welby, Richard Earle	Arlington	Account	1835	LVA-LP
Welch, Erasmus	Alexandria	Tax Charge	1787	Tax PP 1787:16
Welch, Harry	Alexandria	Boarder	1808	1808(2):11A
Welch, James	Alexandria	Account B.	1797	CRF:311
Welch, James	Alexandria	Suit	1807	CRG:210
Welch, James	Alexandria	Suit	1807	CRF:298
Welch, James, Estate, plt.	Alexandria	Suit	1816	CRK:276
Welch, James, of Greenbrier Co.	Alexandria	Deed	1799	CRF:322
Welch, James, plt.	Alexandria	Suit	1807	CRG:163
Welch, John, carpenter	Alexandria	Boarder	1799	1799(2):06A
Welch, John, def.	Alexandria	Suit	1807	CRG:104
Welch, Patrick	Arlington	Admin.	1814	WB1:310
Wellinder, Malinda (M)	Arlington	Apprentice	1802	OCR1801:061
Wellinder, Melinder	Arlington	Apprentice	1803	OCR1801:109
Wells, Alice	Arlington	Bond	1851	BB(np)
Wells, Andrew	Alexandria	Owner	1787	Tax L 1787:26
Wells, Andrew	Alexandria	Tax Charge	1787	Tax PP 1787:16
Wells, Andrew, Fairfax St.	Alexandria	Occupant	1787	Tax L 1787:26
Wells, Andrew, Fairfax St.	Alexandria	Occupant	1787	Tax L 1787:26
Wells, Andrew, Gibbon St.	Alexandria	Occupant	1787	Tax L 1787:04
Wells, Andrew, Water St.	Alexandria	Occupant	1787	Tax L 1787:26
Wells, Daniel	Alexandria	Head	1810	1810(4):07A
Wells, John Thomas	Arlington	Apprentice	1846	OCR1842:175
Wells, Joseph Edward	Arlington	Apprentice	1847	OCR1842:202
Wells, Margaret A.	Arlington	Apprentice	1842	OCR1842:015
Wells, Nathl.	Alexandria	Tax Charge	1788	Tax PP 1788:17
Wells, Sarah	Alexandria	Deposition	1814	CRI:502
Wells, William	Arlington	Admin.	1805	WBB:168
Wells, William	Arlington	Inventory	1805	WBB:194
Wells, William	Arlington	Sale	1805	WBB:197
Wells, William	Alexandria	Deposition	1814	CRI:521
Wells, William, grantor	Arlington	Indenture D.	1815	ID2:390
Wells, William Henry, c/o Elizabeth	Arlington	Guard.	1847	OCR1842:202
Wells, William, in jail	Arlington	Insolvent	1815	ID2:388
Welsh, Erasmus	Alexandria	Tax Charge	1788	Tax PP 1788:17
Welsh, Erasmus	Alexandria	Tax Charge	1789	Tax PP 1789:20
Welsh, James	Alexandria	Tax Charge	1796	Tax PP 1796:21
Welsh, James, plt.	Alexandria	Suit	1814	CRK:013
Welsh, Jas.	Alexandria	Tax Charge	1798	Tax PP 1798:20
Welsh, Richard	Alexandria	Tax Charge	1799	Tax PP 1799:44
Wendall, Isaac	Alexandria	Tax Charge	1796	Tax PP 1796:21
Wendall, Isaac	Alexandria	Tax Charge	1800	Tax PP 1800:46
Wenzel, Mary	Alexandria	Will	1898	WB2:270; LP
Wersey, Peter	Alexandria	Tax Charge	1799	Tax PP 1799:45
Wert, Christian	Alexandria	Tax Charge	1799	Tax PP 1799:45
Wescot, James D. & Jno.	Alexandria	Tax Charge	1800	Tax PP 1800:46
Wesenius, John, b. Stockholm, Swe.	Arlington	Alien Entry	1823	RA:23/12/23
Wesley, Richard	Alexandria	Tax Charge	1788	Tax PP 1788:17
West & Peyton	Alexandria	License Due	1800	Tax PP 1800:54(24)

NAME OR SUBJECT	LOCATION	TYPE	YEAR	REFERENCE(S)
West, Alexander	Arlington	Ordinary	1820	OBL3(np)
West, Alexander	Arlington	Ordinary	1822	OBL3(np)
West, Alexander	Arlington	Ordinary	1827	OBL4(np)
West, Alexander, at his house	Arlington	Ordinary	1825	OBL4(np)
West, Alexander, at his house	Arlington	Ordinary	1826	OBL4(np)
West, Alexander, at his house	Arlington	Ordinary	1828	OBL4(np)
West, Alexander, at his house	Arlington	Ordinary	1831	OBL4(np)
West, Alexander, at his house	Arlington	Ordinary	1832	OBL4(np)
West, Alexander, at his house	Arlington	Ordinary	1833	OBL5(np)
West, Alexander, at his house	Arlington	Ordinary	1834	OBL5(np)
West, Alexander, at his house	Arlington	Ordinary	1835	OBL5(np)
West, Alexander, at his house	Arlington	Ordinary	1836	OBL5(np)
West, Alexander, in Alexandria Co.	Arlington	Ordinary	1822	OBL3(np)
West, Alexander, in Alexandria Co.	Arlington	Ordinary	1824	OBL3(np)
West, Alexander, in Alexandria Co.	Arlington	Ordinary	1830	OBL4(np)
West, Ann M., c/o Roger	Arlington	Guard.	1809	WBC:167
West, Benjamin	Alexandria	Tax Charge	1799	Tax PP 1799:44
West, Charles, labourer	Alexandria	Head	1810	1810(1):08A
West, Chas. (C), laborer	Alexandria	Housekeeper	1808	1808(1):08A
West, Fanny (C), washwoman	Alexandria	Housekeeper	1808	1808(2):14A
West, Fanny, washerwoman	Alexandria	Head	1810	1810(2):04A
West, Hugh	Alexandria	Tax Charge	1789	Tax PP 1789:19
West, Hugh	Alexandria	Tax Charge	1795	Tax PP 1795:33
West, Hugh	Alexandria	Tax Charge	1796	Tax LP 1796:30
West, Hugh	Alexandria	Tax Charge	1798	Tax PP 1798:20
West, Hugh	Alexandria	Tax Charge	1799	Tax PP 1799:44
West, Hugh	Alexandria	Tax Charge	1800	Tax PP 1800:46
West, Hugh	Arlington	Inventory	1807	WBB:507; LVA-LP
West, Hugh	Arlington	Admin.	1807	WBB:483
West, Hugh	Arlington	Account	1808	WBC:104; LVA-LP
West, Hugh	Arlington	Sale	1808	WBC:103
West, Hugh	Arlington	Account	1812	AB1:162; LVA-LP
West, Hugh & wife, scrivener	Alexandria	Head	1795	1795(4):07
West, Hugh & wife, officer of customs	Alexandria	Housekeeper	1799	1799(2):19A
West, J. Thomas, Jr.	Arlington	Will	1900	WB10:440; File #800A
West, James C.	Arlington	Admin.	1815	WB2:135
West, James C., c/o Roger	Arlington	Guard.	1809	WBC:167
West, Jas.	Alexandria	Boarder	1808	1808(1):08A
West, John	Alexandria	Boarder	1808	1808(4):27A
West, John	Arlington	Ordinary	1821	OBL3(np)
West, John	Arlington	Plat	1839	LSA:047
West, John	Arlington	Defendant	1839	LSA:039
West, John, at his house	Arlington	Ordinary	1833	OBL5(np)
West, John, on Cameron St.	Arlington	Ordinary	1822	OBL3(np)
West, Margaret, Admx., def.	Alexandria	Suit	1801	CRB:128
West, Mary C., c/o Roger	Arlington	Guard.	1809	WBC:167
West, Rebecca, seamstress	Alexandria	Head	1810	1810(1):07A
West, Roger	Arlington	Guard. Acct.	1812	AB1:242; LVA-LP
West, Roger, c/o Roger	Arlington	Guard.	1809	WBC:167
West, Roger, c/o Roger	Arlington	Guard.	1810	WBC:534
West, Roger, Estate, def.	Alexandria	Suit	1801	CRB:186
West, Sinah	Alexandria	Tax Charge	1790	Tax PP 1790:16
West, Sybel	Alexandria	Owner	1787	Tax L 1787:27
West, Thomas	Alexandria	Owner	1787	Tax L 1787:27
West, Thomas	Alexandria	Tax Charge	1788	Tax PP 1788:17
West, Thomas	Alexandria	Tax Charge	1789	Tax PP 1789:19
West, Thomas	Alexandria	Tax Charge	1790	Tax PP 1790:16
West, Thomas	Alexandria	Account B.	1798	CRB:131
West, Thomas, Estate, def.	Alexandria	Suit	1801	CRB:128
West, Thomas, Prince St.	Alexandria	Occupants	1790	Tax L 1790:13
West, Thomas, Prince St.	Alexandria	Owner	1790	Tax L 1790:13

NAME OR SUBJECT	LOCATION	TYPE	YEAR	REFERENCE(S)
West, Thomas, Princess St.	Alexandria	Owner	1790	Tax L 1790:13
West, Thos.	Alexandria	Boarder	1808	1808(2):10A
Westcott, James D.	Arlington	Defendant	1802	PA:047
Westcott, Jas. D.	Alexandria	Tax Charge	1799	Tax PP 1799:44
Westcott, Jas. D. & wife, printer	Alexandria	Housekeeper	1799	1799(2):04A
Westcott, Jas. T.	Alexandria	Tax Charge	1798	Tax PP 1798:19
Westcott, John	Arlington	Inventory	1813	AB1:348; LVA-LP
Westcott, John	Arlington	Admin.	1813	WB1:267
Westcott, John	Arlington	Dividend	1814	AB2:053
Westcott, John	Arlington	Sale	1814	AB2:020
Westcott, John	Arlington	Account	1814	AB2:052
Westcott, John	Arlington	Account F.	1817	AB3:105; LVA-LP
Westcott, John, retailer	Alexandria	Housekeeper	1808	1808(1):01A
Westcott, John, storekeeper	Alexandria	Head	1810	1810(1):01A
Westcott [Wescott], John	Arlington	Account	1811	AB2:052; LVA-LP
Weston, Ann F.	Arlington	Guard.	1825	OCR1822:090
Weston, Clement	Alexandria	Boarder	1808	1808(3):19A
Weston, John	Alexandria	Boarder	1808	1808(1):04A
Weston, John	Arlington	Bond	1850	BB(np)
Weston, John, c/o Mary	Arlington	Apprentice	1805	OCR1801:265
Weston, Joseph L.	Arlington	Guard. Acct.	1832	LVA-LP
Weston, Joseph L.	Arlington	Guard. Acct.	1837	LVA-LP
Weston, Joseph L.	Arlington	Guard. Acct.	1839	AB8:149; LVA-LP
Weston, Joseph L., c/o William	Arlington	Guard.	1826	OCR1822:106a
Weston, Joseph L., c/o Joseph L.	Arlington	Guard.	1826	WB3:215
Weston, Joseph Lewis	Arlington	Guard. Acct.	1827	AB6:263; LVA-LP
Weston, Joseph Lewis	Arlington	Guard. Acct.	1829	LVA-LP
Weston, Joseph Lewis	Arlington	Guard.	1840	AB8:149; LVA-LP
Weston, Lewis	Alexandria	Tax Charge	1788	Tax PP 1788:17
Weston, Lewis	Alexandria	Tax Charge	1789	Tax PP 1789:20
Weston, Lewis	Alexandria	Tax Charge	1790	Tax PP 1790:15
Weston, Lewis	Arlington	Inventory	1803	WBA:142
Weston, Lewis	Arlington	Account	1803	WBA:144; LVA-LP
Weston, Lewis	Arlington	Admin.	1807	WBB:508
Weston, Lewis	Arlington	Sale	1811	AB1:102
Weston, Lewis	Arlington	Account	1811	AB1:103; LVA-LP
Weston, Lewis	Arlington	Guard. Acct.	1831	LVA-LP
Weston, Lewis, Estate	Alexandria	Tax Charge	1795	Tax PP 1795:33
Weston, Lewis, Estate	Alexandria	Tax Charge	1796	Tax LP 1796:30
Weston, Lewis, Estate	Alexandria	Tax Charge	1796	Tax PP 1796:20
Weston, Lewis, Estate, Water St.	Alexandria	Owner	1795	Tax L 1795:33(2)
Weston, Lewis, Gibbon St.	Alexandria	Occupant	1787	Tax L 1787:04
Weston, Lewis, Water St.	Alexandria	Occupant	1787	Tax L 1787:05
Weston, Lewis, Water St.	Alexandria	Occupant	1790	Tax L 1790:12
Weston, Lewis, Water St.	Alexandria	Owner	1790	Tax L 1790:12(2)
Weston, Lucinda	Arlington	Guard.	1826	OCR1822:108
Weston, Lucinda	Arlington	Guard. Acct.	1830	LVA-LP
Weston, Lucinda, c/o Joseph L.	Arlington	Guard.	1826	WB3:214
Weston, Lucinda R.	Arlington	Guard. Acct.	1827	AB6:266; LVA-LP
Weston, Lucinda R.	Arlington	Guard. Acct.	1827	AB6:428
Weston, Lucinda R.	Arlington	Guard. Acct.	1828	AB6:445; LVA-LP(2)
Weston, Lucinda R.	Arlington	Guard. Acct.	1829	LVA-LP
Weston, Lucinda R.	Arlington	Guard. Acct.	1830	AB6:511; LVA-LP
Weston, Mary	Alexandria	Housekeeper	1799	1799(2):08A
Weston, Mary, Mrs.	Alexandria	Tax Charge	1800	Tax PP 1800:46
Weston, Mary, Water St.	Alexandria	Occupant	1795	Tax L 1795:33
Weston, Mary, widow (4)1	Alexandria	Head	1795	1796(3):7
Weston, Polly	Alexandria	Tax Charge	1798	Tax PP 1798:19
Weston, Saml.	Alexandria	Tithable +16	1790	Tax PP 1790:15
Weston, Washington	Arlington	Guard. Acct.	1827	AB6:268; LVA-LP(2)
Weston, Washington	Arlington	Guard. Acct.	1828	LVA-LP

NAME OR SUBJECT	LOCATION	TYPE	YEAR	REFERENCE(S)
Weston, Washington	Arlington	Guard. Acct.	1831	LVA-LP
Weston, Washington	Arlington	Guard. Acct.	1835	AB7:200; LVA-LP
Weston, Washington A.	Arlington	Guard. Acct.	1829	LVA-LP(2)
Weston, Washington A.	Arlington	Guard. Acct.	1836	AB7:198
Weston, Washington, c/o William	Arlington	Guard.	1826	OCR1822:106a
Weston, Washington, c/o Joseph L.	Arlington	Guard.	1826	WB3:214
Weston, Washington, c/o William	Arlington	Guard.	1827	OCR1822:140
Weston, William	Arlington	Inventory	1824	AB5:279; LVA-LP
Weston, William	Arlington	Will P.	1824	OCR1822:067a
Weston, William	Arlington	Will	1824	WB3:125; File #223A
Weston, William	Arlington	Bond	1824	WB3:126
Weston, William	Arlington	Account	1826	AB6:173; LVA-LP
Weston, William	Arlington	Guard. Acct.	1827	AB6:425
Weston, William	Arlington	Guard. Acct.	1827	AB6:264; LVA-LP
Weston, William	Arlington	Guard.	1827	OCR1822:142, 142a
Weston, William	Arlington	Guard. Acct.	1828	LVA-LP(2)
Weston, William	Arlington	Account	1830	AB7:001a; LVA-LP
Weston, William	Arlington	Guard. Acct.	1830	LVA-LP
Weston, William	Arlington	Account	1832	AB7:345; LVA-LP
Weston, William	Arlington	Guard. Acct.	1835	AB7:196; LVA-LP
Weston, William	Arlington	Account	1836	AB7:196
Weston, William	Arlington	Account	1839	AB7:345
Weston, William	Arlington	Account	1839	AB8:144; LVA-LP
Weston, William, c/o William	Arlington	Guard.	1826	OCR1822:106a
Weston, William, c/o Joseph L.	Arlington	Guard.	1826	WB3:213
Weston, William, c/o William	Arlington	Guard.	1827	OCR1822:140
Weston, William C.	Arlington	Guard. Acct.	1829	LVA-LP(2)
Weston, William C.	Arlington	Guard. Acct.	1832	LVA-LP
Weston, William C.	Arlington	Guard.	1833	AB7:084; LVA-LP
Weston, William, Capt.	Arlington	Account	1825	AB6:072; LVA-LP
Weston, William, Capt.	Arlington	Sale	1825	AB6:043
Weston, William, Master	Arlington	Defendant	1821	ACO:197
Weston, William, orpans of	Arlington	Guard. Acct.	1827	OCR1822:128a, 139
Weston, William, orphans of	Arlington	Petition	1827	OCR1822:140
Weston, William, orphans of	Arlington	Guard. Acct.	1829	OCR1822:167a
Weston, William [Mary]	Arlington	Renounce	1824	OCR1822:066a
Weston, Wm., captain	Alexandria	Head	1810	1810(1):04A
Weston, Wm., sea captain	Alexandria	Housekeeper	1808	1808(1):04A
Weston [Western], Lewis	Alexandria	Tax Charge	1787	Tax PP 1787:16
Weston's Orphans v. Smoot	Arlington	Suit	1827	OCR1822:143, 145a
Wetherley, Jesse, Fairfax St.	Alexandria	Occupant	1787	Tax L 1787:05
Wey, Frederick	Alexandria	Tax Charge	1799	Tax PP 1799:44
Weyley & Langley	Alexandria	Mer. License	1798	Tax PP 1798:20-8
Weylie, Jno., Queen St.	Alexandria	Occupant	1795	Tax L 1795:24
Weyly, Ephraim	Alexandria	Tax Charge	1800	Tax PP 1800:46
Whaland, Dennis	Alexandria	Tax Charge	1789	Tax PP 1789:20
Whaland, Dennis	Alexandria	Tax Charge	1790	Tax PP 1790:16
Whaley, James	Arlington	Apprentice	1827	OCR1822:140
Whann, Adam, plt.	Alexandria	Suit	1801	CRD:178
Wharton, Benjamin, labourer	Alexandria	Head	1810	1810(4):06A
Wharton, Lewis	Arlington	Sale	1849	WB5:187; LVA-LP
Wheat, Benoni	Arlington	Bond	1852	BB(np)
Wheat, Benoni	Arlington	Will	1852	WB6:154; File #486A
Wheat, Benoni	Arlington	Inventory	1853	WB6:204; LVA-LP
Wheat, Benoni	Arlington	Account	1854	WB6:228; LVA-LP
Wheat, Benoni	Arlington	Account	1854	WB6:296; LVA-LP
Wheat, Benoni	Arlington	Account	1854	WB6:450; LVA-LP
Wheat, Benoni	Arlington	Account	1857	WB7:275; LVA-LP
Wheat, Clarence	Alexandria	Will	1889	WB1:528; LP
Wheat, Robert	Arlington	Account	1871	WB9:307
Wheat, Robert W.	Arlington	Account	1868	WB9:056

NAME OR SUBJECT	LOCATION	TYPE	YEAR	REFERENCE(S)
Wheat, Robert W.	Arlington	Account	1869	WB9:173
Wheat, Robert W.	Alexandria	Account	1871	WB1:017
Wheat, Robert W.	Arlington	Account	1871	WB9:321
Wheat, Robert W.	Arlington	Account	1877	WB9:474
Wheat, Robert Wilson	Arlington	Will	1865	WB8:237; File #623A
Wheat, Robert Wilson	Arlington	Appraisal	1865	WB8:238
Wheat, Robert Wilson	Arlington	Account	1866	WB8:419, 561
Wheat, Thomas	Alexandria	Tax Charge	1796	Tax PP 1796:20
Wheating, Henry & wife Sarah	Alexandria	Resident	1800	1800(4):13B
Wheating, Henry, labourrer	Alexandria	Head	1800	1800(4):13A
Wheatley, Ann	Arlington	Guard.	1821	WB2:426
Wheatley, Benedict	Alexandria	Will	1900	WB2:385; LP
Wheatley, Thomas, fishmonger	Alexandria	Head	1810	1810(1):08A
Wheatley, Thos., laborer	Alexandria	Housekeeper	1808	1808(1):08A
Wheatley, William	Arlington	Defendant	1823	ACO:219
Wheatley, William	Arlington	Defendant	1824	ACO:250
Wheatley, William	Arlington	Defendant	1825	ACO:255
Wheatley, William	Arlington	Suit Bond	1827	ACO:273
Wheaton, Catherine	Arlington	Guard.	1822	WB3:055
Wheaton, Jno. R.	Alexandria	Tax Charge	1795	Tax PP 1795:33
Wheaton, Jno., R., Prince St.	Alexandria	Occupant	1795	Tax L 1795:33
Wheaton, John	Alexandria	Tithable +16	1788	Tax PP 1788:11
Wheaton, John	Alexandria	Tithable +16	1790	Tax PP 1790:09
Wheeler, Clement	Alexandria	Tax Charge	1799	Tax PP 1799:45
Wheeler, Clement, nail maker	Alexandria	Boarder	1799	1799(2):09A
Wheeler, Ephraim, c/o Samuel	Arlington	Guard.	1826	WB3:265
Wheeler, Jabez, c/o Samuel	Arlington	Guard.	1826	WB3:265
Wheeler, James Parsons, c/o Samuel	Arlington	Guard.	1826	WB3:265
Wheeler, John, c/o Samuel	Arlington	Guard.	1826	WB3:265
Wheeler, Saml., shoemaker	Alexandria	Head	1810	1810(1):01A
Wheeler, Samuel	Alexandria	Tax Charge	1799	Tax PP 1799:44
Wheeler, Samuel	Alexandria	Tax Charge	1800	Tax PP 1800:46
Wheeler, Samuel, by Sarah Parsons	Arlington	Guard.	1826	OCR1822:126a
Wheeler, Samuel, grantee	Arlington	Indenture D.	1827	ID:079
Wheeler, Samuel, retailer	Alexandria	Housekeeper	1808	1808(1):01A
Wheeler, William	Arlington	Agreement	1839	WB4:294
Wheelwright, John	Arlington	Insolvent	1826	ID:041
Wheelwright, John, def.	Alexandria	Suit	1818	CRK:458
Wheelwright, John, grantor	Arlington	Indenture D.	1826	ID:044
Wheelwright, John, plt.	Alexandria	Suit	1822	CRL:232
Wheeton, Leonard, house joiner	Alexandria	Head	1810	1810(4):08A
Wherrey, Jesse, w(1)2, merchant	Alexandria	Head	1795	1796(3):7
Wherry & Ricketts	Arlington	Defendants	1824	ACO:250
Wherry & Ricketts	Arlington	Defendants	1825	ACO:253, 258
Wherry & Ricketts	Arlington	Defendant	1826	ACO:261, 264
Wherry & Ricketts	Arlington	Defendants	1827	ACO:268, 274
Wherry, Jesse	Alexandria	Tax Charge	1795	Tax PP 1795:32
Wherry, Jesse	Alexandria	Tax Charge	1796	Tax LP 1796:30
Wherry, Jesse	Alexandria	Tax Charge	1796	Tax PP 1796:20
Wherry, Jesse	Arlington	Defendant	1823	ACO:228
Wherry, Jesse	Arlington	Defendant	1823	ACO:211, 212
Wherry, Jesse	Arlington	Defendant	1824	ACO:235
Wherry, Jesse, King St.	Alexandria	Occupant	1795	Tax L 1795:07
Whinler, Mark	Alexandria	Tithable +21	1787	Tax PP 1787:07
Whitacer, Robert	Alexandria	Tax Charge	1787	Tax PP 1787:17
Whitacre, Robert	Alexandria	Owner	1787	Tax L 1787:27
Whitacre, Robert, Gibbon St.	Alexandria	Occupant	1787	Tax L 1787:04
Whitacre, Robert, King St.	Alexandria	Occupant	1787	Tax L 1787:07
Whitcroft, Catharine	Alexandria	Boarder	1799	1799(2):03A
Whitcroft, Henry	Alexandria	Deposition	(nd)	CRK:070
White, Ambrose	Alexandria	Tax Charge	1799	Tax PP 1799:44

NAME OR SUBJECT	LOCATION	TYPE	YEAR	REFERENCE(S)
White, Ambrose	Alexandria	Tax Charge	1800	Tax PP 1800:46
White, Ambrose & wife, bricklayer	Alexandria	Housekeeper	1799	1799(2):09A
White, Ann Sophia	Alexandria	Will	1882	WB1:366; LP
White, B.	Alexandria	Tax Charge	1796	Tax LP 1796:30
White, Bartemius, in jail	Arlington	Insolvent	1803	ID3:001
White, Bartimeus	Alexandria	Tax Charge	1795	Tax PP 1795:33
White, Bartimeus	Alexandria	Tax Charge	1796	Tax PP 1796:20
White, Bartimeus	Alexandria	Tax Charge	1798	Tax PP 1798:20
White, Bartimeus	Alexandria	Boarder	1799	1799(2):08A
White, Bartimeus	Alexandria	Tax Charge	1799	Tax PP 1799:45
White, Bartimeus, grantor	Arlington	Indenture D.	1803	ID3:006
White, Bartimus	Alexandria	Tax Charge	1800	Tax PP 1800:46
White, Bartimus	Arlington	Defendant	1802	PA:186
White, Bartimus	Arlington	Juryman	1804	ACO:024, 025
White, Bartimus, def.	Alexandria	Suit	1801	CRC:090
White, Benj.	Alexandria	Tax Charge	1798	Tax PP 1798:19
White, Benj.	Alexandria	Tax Charge	1799	Tax PP 1799:45
White, Benjn.	Alexandria	Tax Charge	1800	Tax PP 1800:46
White, Christian, w(2), brickmaker	Alexandria	Head	1796	1796(3):1
White, Edgar D.	Arlington	Guard. Acct.	1848	WB5:065, 252; LVA-LP
White, Edgar D.	Arlington	Guard. Acct.	1850	WB3:352; LVA-LP
White, Edgar D.	Arlington	Guard. Acct.	1853	WB6:197
White, Edgar D.	Arlington	Guard. Acct.	1854	WB6:323; LVA-LP
White, Edgar D., c/o Robert L.	Arlington	Guard. Acct.	1846	AB9:200; LVA-LP
White, Edgar D., c/o Robet L.	Arlington	Guard. Acct.	1855	WB7:035; LVA-LP
White, Edgar D., c/o Robert L.	Arlington	Guard. Acct.	1855	WB7:010; LVA-LP
White, Edgar Doddridge, c/o Robert L.	Arlington	Guard.	1845	OCR1842:126
White, Eleanor	Arlington	Guard. Acct.	1821	AB4:206
White, Frank	Alexandria	Will	1899	WB2:314
White, Frederick	Alexandria	Tax Charge	1796	Tax PP 1796:20
White, George, sheriff	Arlington	Appointment	1851	BB(np)
White, George, sheriff	Arlington	Appointment	1852	BB(np)
White, George, w, mariner	Alexandria	Head	1796	1796(3):1
White, Gilbert	Arlington	Admin.	1841	WB4:287
White, James	Alexandria	Tax Charge	1796	Tax PP 1796:20
White, James	Arlington	Guard.	1816	WB2:110
White, James, labourer	Alexandria	Head	1810	1810(1):06A
White, James, n/o Joseph Nevett	Arlington	Apprentice	1827	OCR1822:146
White, Jas.	Alexandria	Tax Charge	1798	Tax PP 1798:20
White, Jno.	Alexandria	Tax Charge	1795	Tax PP 1795:32
White, Jno.	Alexandria	Tax Charge	1798	Tax PP 1798:19
White, Jno. (s. carpenter)	Alexandria	Tax Charge	1800	Tax PP 1800:46
White, Jno. & wife, ship builder	Alexandria	Housekeeper	1799	1799(2):07A
White, Jno., cooper	Alexandria	Boarder	1799	1799(2):01A
White, Jno., Fairfax St.	Alexandria	Occupant	1795	Tax L 1795:01
White, Jno., Fairfax St.	Alexandria	Owner	1795	Tax L 1795:31(2)
White, John	Alexandria	Tithable +21	1787	Tax PP 1787:16
White, John	Alexandria	Tithable +16	1788	Tax PP 1788:17
White, John	Alexandria	Tithable +16	1789	Tax PP 1789:19
White, John	Alexandria	Tax Charge	1790	Tax PP 1790:15
White, John	Alexandria	Tax Charge	1796	Tax LP 1796:30
White, John	Alexandria	Tax Charge	1796	Tax PP 1796:21
White, John	Alexandria	Tax Charge	1799	Tax PP 1799:45
White, John	Alexandria	Resident	1800	1800(4):16B
White, John	Arlington	Guard. Acct.	1821	AB4:208
White, John	Arlington	Guard. Acct.	1822	AB5:069; LVA-LP
White, John	Arlington	Guard. Acct.	1824	AB5:271; LVA-LP
White, John	Arlington	Guard. Acct.	1825	AB5:394
White, John	Arlington	Guard. Acct.	1826	AB6:260
White, John	Arlington	Guard. Acct.	1827	AB6:440
White, John	Arlington	Guard. Acct.	1828	AB6:469; LVA-LP

NAME OR SUBJECT	LOCATION	TYPE	YEAR	REFERENCE(S)
White, John	Arlington	Will (N)	1836	WB4:107
White, John, barber	Alexandria	Housekeeper	1808	1808(2):14A
White, John, cooper	Alexandria	Tax Charge	1800	Tax PP 1800:46
White, John, coopper	Alexandria	Boarder	1800	1800(4):16A
White, John, plt.	Alexandria	Suit	1802	CRC:051
White, John T.	Arlington	Guard.	1834	AB7:118; LVA-LP
White, John, w, sadler	Alexandria	Head	1796	1796(3):2
White, Joseph, c/o Thomas	Arlington	Guard.	1819	WB2:333
White, Joseph H.	Arlington	Guard. Acct.	1821	AB4:202
White, Joseph H.	Arlington	Guard. Acct.	1822	AB5:067; LVA-LP
White, Joseph H.	Arlington	Guard. Acct.	1824	AB5:269
White, Joseph H.	Arlington	Guard. Acct.	1825	AB5:394
White, Margaret	Arlington	Guard.	1816	WB2:110
White, Maria A.	Arlington	Guard. Acct.	1848	WB5:063; LVA-LP
White, Maria A.	Arlington	Guard. Acct.	1851	WB5:247; LVA-LP
White, Maria A.	Arlington	Guard. Acct.	1853	WB6:198
White, Maria A.	Arlington	Guard. Acct.	1854	WB6:323; LVA-LP
White, Maria A., c/o Robert L.	Arlington	Guard. Acct.	1846	AB9:201; LVA-LP
White, Maria A., c/o Robert L.	Arlington	Guard. Acct.	1855	WB7:010, 36; LVA-LP
White, Maria A., c/o Robert L.	Arlington	Guard. Acct.	1855	WB7:188; LVA-LP
White, Maria A., c/o Robert L.	Arlington	Guard. Acct.	1856	WB7:250
White, Maria Antoinette, c/o Robert L.	Arlington	Guard.	1845	OCR1842:126
White, Mary Ann	Arlington	Guard.	1816	WB2:110
White, Mary Ann, seamstress	Alexandria	Head	1810	1810(2):05A
White, Nicholas	Alexandria	Tax Charge	1799	Tax PP 1799:44
White, Nicholas, cooper	Alexandria	Boarder	1799	1799(2):15A
White, Patrick, shoemaker	Alexandria	Housekeeper	1808	1808(3):21A
White, Prudence	Arlington	Guard. Acct.	1821	AB4:206
White, Prudence, c/o Thomas	Arlington	Guard.	1819	WB2:333
White, Prudence M.	Alexandria	Will	1873	WB1:063; LP
White, Richard	Alexandria	Tax Charge	1795	Tax PP 1795:32
White, Richard	Alexandria	Tax Charge	1796	Tax PP 1796:20
White, Richard	Alexandria	Tax Charge	1799	Tax PP 1799:44
White, Richard	Alexandria	Tax Charge	1800	Tax PP 1800:46]
White, Richd.	Alexandria	Tax Charge	1796	Tax LP 1796:30
White, Richd., btw. Union/Water	Alexandria	Occupant	1795	Tax L 1795:01
White, Robert L.	Arlington	Inventory	1845	AB9:102; LVA-LP
White, Robert L.	Arlington	Admin.	1845	OCR1842:111
White, Robert L.	Arlington	Account	1846	AB9:198; LVA-LP
White, Robert L.	Arlington	Account	1846	AB9:196, 202; LVA-LP
White, Robert L.	Arlington	Sale	1846	AB9:206; LVA-LP
White, Robert L.	Arlington	Account	1848	WB5:067, 168, 255
White, Robert L.	Arlington	Account	1851	WB5:287; LVA-LP
White, Robert L.	Arlington	Guard. Acct.	1853	WB6:195; LVA-LP
White, Robert L.	Arlington	Guard. Acct.	1853	WB6:321; LVA-LP
White, Robert L.	Arlington	Report	1857	LVA-LP
White, Robert L., c/o Robert L.	Arlington	Guard. Acct.	1855	WB7:008, 34, 186
White, Robert L., children of	Arlington	Guard. Acct.	1846	AB9:197; LVA-LP
White, Robert L., heirs of	Arlington	Guard. Acct.	1856	WB7:248; LVA-LP
White, Robert, smith	Alexandria	Head	1800	1800(4):05A
White, Thomas	Alexandria	Tax Charge	1790	Tax PP 1790:15
White, Thomas	Alexandria	Tax Charge	1796	Tax PP 1796:21
White, Thomas	Alexandria	Mer. License	1798	Tax PP 1798:20-8
White, Thomas	Alexandria	Mer. License	1799	Tax PP 1799:52-11r
White, Thomas	Alexandria	Mer. License	1800	Tax PP 1800:54(22)r
White, Thomas	Arlington	Deposition	1802	PA:193
White, Thomas	Arlington	Inventory	1819	AB4:001; LVA-LP
White, Thomas	Arlington	Admin.	1819	WB2:331
White, Thomas	Arlington	Guard. Acct.	1821	AB4:204
White, Thomas	Arlington	Account	1821	AB4:199
White, Thomas	Arlington	Account	1822	AB5:063; LVA-LP

NAME OR SUBJECT	LOCATION	TYPE	YEAR	REFERENCE(S)
White, Thomas	Arlington	Guard. Acct.	1822	AB5:067; LVA-LP
White, Thomas	Arlington	Guard. Acct.	1824	AB5:267; LVA-LP
White, Thomas	Arlington	Guard. Acct.	1825	AB5:394, 395
White, Thomas	Arlington	Guard. Acct.	1825	AB6:140; LVA-LP
White, Thomas	Arlington	Account	1826	AB6:258; LVA-LP
White, Thomas	Arlington	Guard. Acct.	1826	AB6:260; LVA-LP
White, Thomas	Arlington	Account	1827	AB6:440
White, Thomas	Arlington	Guard. Acct.	1827	AB6:440; LVA-LP
White, Thomas	Arlington	Guard. Acct.	1828	AB6:470; LVA-LP
White, Thomas	Arlington	Account	1832	AB7:178; LVA-LP
White, Thomas	Arlington	Account	1835	AB7:178
White, Thomas, at the coal yard	Arlington	Inventory	1826	AB6:155
White, Thomas, blacksmith	Alexandria	Head	1810	1810(1):07A
White, Thomas, c/o Thomas	Arlington	Guard.	1819	WB2:333
White, Thomas, Jr.	Arlington	Ordinary	1810	OBL2(np)
White, Thomas, orphans of	Arlington	Guard. Acct.	1826	OCR1822:127
White, Thomas, orphans of	Arlington	Guard. Acct.	1827	OCR1822:129a
White, Thomas, the Younger	Arlington	Guard. Acct.	1824	AB5:272
White, Thos, Jr.	Alexandria	Tax Charge	1800	Tax PP 1800:46
White, Thos.	Alexandria	Tax Charge	1795	Tax PP 1795:32
White, Thos.	Alexandria	Tax Charge	1795	Tax PP 1795:32(2)
White, Thos.	Alexandria	Tax Charge	1796	Tax LP 1796:30
White, Thos.	Alexandria	Tax Charge	1798	Tax PP 1798:19
White, Thos.	Alexandria	Tax Charge	1799	Tax PP 1799:45
White, Thos.	Alexandria	Tax Charge	1800	Tax PP 1800:46
White, Thos. (merchant)	Alexandria	Tax Charge	1799	Tax PP 1799:45
White, Thos., blacksmith	Alexandria	Housekeeper	1808	1808(1):09A
White, Thos., Fairfax St.	Alexandria	Occupant	1790	Tax L 1790:01
White, Thos., Fairfax St.	Alexandria	Occupant	1795	Tax L 1795:01
White, Thos., Fairfax St.	Alexandria	Owner	1795	Tax L 1795:31
White, Thos., merchant	Alexandria	Housekeeper	1808	1808(2):12A
White, Thos., merchant	Alexandria	Head	1810	1810(2):03A
White, Truman W.	Arlington	Will	1898	WB10:358; File #783A
White, Virginia C.	Arlington	Guard. Acct.	1853	WB6:199
White, Walter	Alexandria	Tax Charge	1789	Tax PP 1789:20
White, William	Alexandria	Tax Charge	1800	Tax PP 1800:40
White, William	Arlington	Guard. Acct.	1821	AB4:202
White, William	Arlington	Guard. Acct.	1822	AB5:065
White, William	Arlington	Guard. Acct.	1824	AB5:270; LVA-LP
White, William	Arlington	Guard. Acct.	1825	AB5:394
White, William	Arlington	Guard. Acct.	1826	AB6:260; LVA-LP
White, William	Arlington	Guard. Acct.	1827	AB6:440
White, William	Arlington	Guard. Acct.	1828	AB6:457; LVA-LP
White, William, c/o Thomas	Arlington	Guard.	1819	WB2:333
White, William, of Philadelphia	Alexandria	Deposition	1802	CRC:089
Whitehead, Jas., bricklayer	Alexandria	Boarder	1799	1799(2):20A
Whitehead, Vincent	Alexandria	Tax Charge	1798	Tax PP 1798:19
Whitehead, Vincent	Alexandria	Tax Charge	1799	Tax PP 1799:44
Whitely, Jas.	Alexandria	Boarder	1808	1808(3):18A
Whitemyer, H.M.	Alexandria	Boarder	1799	1799(2):08A
Whiting, Carlisle Fairfax	Arlington	Inventory	1832	LVA-LP
Whiting, Carlyle F.	Arlington	Account	1838	AB7:264; LVA-LP
Whiting, Carlyle Fairfax	Arlington	Bond	1831	WB4:012
Whiting, Carlyle Fairfax	Arlington	Will	1831	WB4:011; File #302A
Whiting, Carlyle Fairfax	Arlington	Account	1834	AB7:123; LVA-LP
Whiting, Charles	Arlington	Will P.	1842	OCR1842:010
Whiting, Charles	Arlington	Will	1842	WB4:309; File #390A
Whiting, Charles Henry, c/o Carlyle F.	Arlington	Complainant	1840	LSA:054
Whiting, Ellen M.	Arlington	Defendant	1840	LSA:054
Whiting, Fairfax	Arlington	Defendant	1840	LSA:054
Whiting, Louisa Tuscan	Arlington	Will	1869	WB9:061; File #661A

NAME OR SUBJECT	LOCATION	TYPE	YEAR	REFERENCE(S)
Whiting, Robert W.	Arlington	Will	1889	WB10:157; File #743A
Whiting, Sarah M.	Arlington	Defendant	1840	LSA:054
Whiting, William W.	Arlington	Defendant	1840	LSA:054
Whitley, Thomas	Alexandria	Tithable +16	1789	Tax PP 1789:19
Whitley, Thomas	Alexandria	Tax Charge	1800	Tax PP 1800:46
Whitlow, Isaac, grantor	Arlington	Indenture D.	1827	ID:136
Whitlow, Isaac, in jail	Arlington	Insolvent	1827	ID:134
Whitman, Frederick	Alexandria	Tithable +21	1787	Tax PP 1787:01
Whitman, Frederick	Alexandria	Tax Charge	1788	Tax PP 1788:17
Whitman, Frederick	Alexandria	Tax Charge	1789	Tax PP 1789:20
Whitman, Sarah	Alexandria	Serv./Appr.	1800	1800(4):13B
Whitmore, Humphry, laborer	Alexandria	Housekeeper	1808	1808(2):17A
Whitmore, John P.	Arlington	Apprentice	1822	OCR1822:017a
Whitmore, Samuel, plt.	Alexandria	Suit	1820	CRL:036
Whitney, Gilbert	Alexandria	Tax Charge	1788	Tax PP 1788:17
Whitney, Gilbert	Alexandria	Tax Charge	1789	Tax PP 1789:19
Whitney, Joshua	Arlington	Will	1873	WB9:350
Whitright, Jacob, def.	Alexandria	Suit	1801	CRB:217
Whitson, Charles	Alexandria	Tax Charge	1796	Tax LP 1796:30
Whitten, Dorcus, washwoman	Alexandria	Housekeeper	1808	1808(1):02A
Whitter, James, c/o Darchus Gooding	Arlington	Apprentice	1812	OCR1811:139
Whitter, William, c/o Darkers Gooding	Arlington	Apprentice	1811	OCR1811:043
Whitticoe, William, labourer	Alexandria	Head	1810	1810(2):06A
Whittington, John, c/o Thomas	Arlington	Apprentice	1815	OCR1811:303
Whittington, Thomas, c/o Thomas	Arlington	Apprentice	1815	OCR1811:347
Whittington, Thomas, Sr., grantor	Arlington	Indenture D.	1827	ID:139
Whittington, Thomas, Sr., in jail	Arlington	Insolvent	1827	ID:137
Whittington, Thos., cartman	Alexandria	Housekeeper	1808	1808(4):29A
Whittington, Thos., drayman	Alexandria	Head	1810	1810(4):05A
Whittle, Edw.	Alexandria	Tax Charge	1795	Tax PP 1795:33
Whittle, Edward	Alexandria	Tax Charge	1799	Tax PP 1799:44
Whittlesey, Luman	Arlington	Will	1868	WB9:018; File #658A
Whorrell, Morris	Alexandria	Tax Charge	1796	Tax LP 1796:30
Wibert, Isaac	Arlington	Will	1875	WB9:373; File #692A
Wibert, Isaac	Arlington	Appraisal	1876	WB9:387
Wicks, Emeline	Arlington	Guard.	1826	WB3:256
Wicks, Mary	Arlington	Guard.	1826	WB3:256
Wicks, William	Arlington	Admin.	1826	WB3:255
Wiggington, Seth B.	Arlington	Admin.	1807	WBB:475
Wiggins, William	Alexandria	Tax Charge	1799	Tax PP 1799:44
Wiggins, William	Alexandria	Tax Charge	1800	Tax PP 1800:46
Wiggins, William, grantor	Arlington	Indenture D.	1806	ID3:269
Wiggins, William, in prison bounds	Arlington	Insolvent	1806	ID3:264
Wigginton, James	Arlington	Ordinary	1811	OBL2(np)
Wiggs, Jacob	Alexandria	Tithable +16	1790	Tax PP 1790:04
Wigham, Thomas	Alexandria	Tax Charge	1799	Tax PP 1799:44
Wilbar, Henry	Alexandria	Boarder	1808	1808(1):01A
Wilbar, Henry	Arlington	Bond	1837	WB4:131
Wilbar, Henry	Arlington	Will	1837	WB4:129; File #345A
Wilbar, Henry & wife, schoolmaster	Alexandria	Head	1795	1795(4a):05
Wilbar, Henry, schoolmaster	Alexandria	Housekeeper	1808	1808(4):27A
Wilcocks, James S.	Arlington	Apprentice	1824	OCR1822:062
Wilcoxen, Walter, c/o Thomas	Arlington	Apprentice	1802	OCR1801:034
Wild, Jno., clerk	Alexandria	Boarder	1799	1799(2):13A
Wild, John	Alexandria	Tax Charge	1800	Tax PP 1800:46
Wilder, Amherst H., of St. Paul MN	Arlington	Will	1895	WB10:270; File #763A
Wildman, C.G.	Arlington	Trustee Acct.	1861	LVA-LP
Wiley, Ephraim	Alexandria	Tax Charge	1796	Tax LP 1796:30
Wiley, Ephraim	Alexandria	Boarder	1808	1808(3):18A
Wiley, Epm.	Alexandria	Tax Charge	1798	Tax PP 1798:20
Wiley, George	Alexandria	Tax Charge	1800	Tax PP 1800:46

NAME OR SUBJECT	LOCATION	TYPE	YEAR	REFERENCE(S)
Wiley, George	Arlington	Apprentice	1825	OCR1822:103
Wiley, Hiram	Arlington	Apprentice	1803	OCR1801:127
Wiley, Jno., chair maker	Alexandria	Boarder	1799	1799(2):08A
Wiley, John	Alexandria	Tax Charge	1796	Tax LP 1796:30
Wiley, John	Arlington	Apprentice	1803	OCR1801:126
Wilis, Abel	Alexandria	Mer. License	1800	Tax PP 1800:54(22)r
Wilk, Peter	Alexandria	Tithable +21	1787	Tax PP 1787:01
Wilk, Peter	Alexandria	Tax Charge	1788	Tax PP 1788:17
Wilkerson, Thomas	Alexandria	Owner	1787	Tax L 1787:27
Wilkerson, Thomas	Alexandria	Tax Charge	1787	Tax PP 1787:17
Wilkes, Barbarah, cake baker	Alexandria	Head	1810	1810(4):06A
Wilkes, Jacob	Alexandria	Tithable +16	1788	Tax PP 1788:17
Wilkes, Michael, c/o Jacob & Catharine	Arlington	Apprentice	1805	OCR1801:284
Wilkes, Peter	Alexandria	Tax Charge	1795	Tax PP 1795:32
Wilkes, Peter	Alexandria	Tax Charge	1796	Tax LP 1796:30
Wilkes, Peter	Alexandria	Tax Charge	1798	Tax PP 1798:19
Wilkes, Peter	Alexandria	Tax Charge	1799	Tax PP 1799:45
Wilkes, Peter & wife, baker	Alexandria	Housekeeper	1799	1799(2):11A
Wilkeson, Thomas, Fairfax St.	Alexandria	Occupant	1787	Tax L 1787:05
Wilkinson, Elizabeth, merchant	Alexandria	Head	1795	1795(4):03
Wilkinson, James	Alexandria	Tax Charge	1799	Tax PP 1799:45
Wilkinson, Jane	Alexandria	Resident	1800	1800(4):05B
Wilkinson, Jane, boarding house	Alexandria	Housekeeper	1799	1799(2):15A
Wilkinson, Jane, boarding house	Alexandria	Head	1800	1800(4):05A
Wilkinson, Jane, Fairfax St.	Alexandria	Occupant	1795	Tax L 1795:34
Wilkinson, Margaret	Alexandria	Will	1883	WB1:393; LP
Wilkinson, Thomas	Alexandria	Tax Charge	1788	Tax PP 1788:17
Wilkinson, Thomas	Alexandria	Tax Charge	1789	Tax PP 1789:20
Wilkinson, Thomas	Alexandria	Tax Charge	1790	Tax PP 1790:16
Wilkinson, Thomas, Fairfax St.	Alexandria	Occupant	1790	Tax L 1790:12
Wilkinson, Thomas, Fairfax St.	Alexandria	Owner	1790	Tax L 1790:12
Wilkinson, Thos., Estate, Fairfax St.	Alexandria	Owner	1795	Tax L 1795:34
Wilkinson, Will. B.	Alexandria	Tax Charge	1800	Tax PP 1800:46
Wilkinson, Wm.	Alexandria	Tax Charge	1796	Tax LP 1796:31
Wilkinson, [blank], hatter	Alexandria	Boarder	1799	1799(2):01A
Wilkison, Jane, shopkeeper	Alexandria	Head	1795	1795(4a):03
Wilkison, Thomas, Fairfax St.	Alexandria	Occupant	1787	Tax L 1787:27
Wilks, Barbara, washwoman	Alexandria	Housekeeper	1808	1808(4):26A
Wilks, Peter	Alexandria	Tax Charge	1789	Tax PP 1789:19
Wilks, Peter	Alexandria	Tax Charge	1800	Tax PP 1800:46
Wilks, Peter, Fairfax St.	Alexandria	Occupant	1795	Tax L 1795:20
Willard, Ehud H.	Arlington	Will	1885	WB10:067; File #718A
Willbar, Henry C., schoolmaster	Alexandria	Head	1810	1810(4):05A
Willender, Melinder	Arlington	Apprentice	1804	OCR1801:172
Willentzki, Ivanoff Stanislaus	Arlington	Will (N)	1864	WB8:226; File #620A
Willey, America	Arlington	Will	1890	WB10:172; File #857A
William Hartshorne & Co., plt.	Alexandria	Suit	1800	CRC:034
William Hartshorne & Sons, plt.	Alexandria	Suit	1801	CRB:349
William Hodgson & Co.	Arlington	Inventory	1819	AB4:084
Williams & Carey	Alexandria	Tax Charge	1796	Tax LP 1796:31
Williams & Carey, Prince St.	Alexandria	Occupant	1795	Tax L 1795:27
Williams, A.C., of Fairfax Co. VA	Arlington	Will	1899	WB10:371; File #087A
Williams, Alex.	Alexandria	Tax Charge	1798	Tax PP 1798:19
Williams, Alexander	Alexandria	Tax Charge	1799	Tax PP 1799:44
Williams, Alexander	Alexandria	Tax Charge	1800	Tax PP 1800:47
Williams, Alexander	Arlington	Inventory	1821	AB4:308; LVA-LP
Williams, Alexander	Arlington	Admin.	1821	WB3:016, 116
Williams, Alexander	Arlington	Inventory	1823	AB5:201; LVA-LP
Williams, Alexander	Arlington	Sale	1823	AB5:217
Williams, Alexander	Arlington	Admin.	1823	OCR1822:055a
Williams, Alexander	Arlington	Account	1825	AB6:112; LVA-LP

NAME OR SUBJECT	LOCATION	TYPE	YEAR	REFERENCE(S)
Williams, Alexr., butcher	Alexandria	Housekeeper	1808	1808(1):02A
Williams, Alexr., capt. of the watch	Alexandria	Head	1810	1810(4):04A
Williams, Alexr., *Towlston* from Fairfax	Alexandria	Lease	(nd)	CRH:553
Williams, Ann, spinster	Alexandria	Boarder	1800	1800(4):14A
Williams, Anthony & wife, labourer	Alexandria	Head	1795	1795(4):06
Williams, Basil, of *Prince Seaton*	Arlington	Will	1855	WB6:415; File #513A
Williams, Bazel	Arlington	Inventory	1855	WB6:419; LVA-LP
Williams, Bazil	Arlington	Sale	1855	WB7:021; LVA-LP
Williams, Bazil	Arlington	Account	1856	WB7:132; LVA-LP
Williams Carey & Co.	Alexandria	Tax Charge	1787	Tax PP 1787:16
Williams, Cary & Co., Fairfax St.	Alexandria	Occupant	1787	Tax L 1787:13
Williams, Charles	Arlington	Guard.	1819	WB2:301
Williams, David	Alexandria	Will	1899	WB2:315
Williams, Edward	Arlington	Crime	1799	OT:22/04/1799
Williams, Elisha, laborer	Alexandria	Housekeeper	1808	1808(2):14A
Williams, Eliza, sempstress	Alexandria	Housekeeper	1808	1808(2):17A
Williams, Eliza, washerwoman	Alexandria	Head	1810	1810(2):07A
Williams, Elizabeth	Alexandria	Housekeeper	1799	1799(2):03A
Williams, Eveline, c/o Fanny	Arlington	Apprentice	1815	OCR1811:276
Williams, Fanny	Alexandria	Will	1889	WB1:544; LP
Williams, Frank & 3 children (C)	Alexandria	Boarder	1799	1799(2):12A
Williams, Frankey	Alexandria	Resident	1800	1800(4):14B
Williams, Frankey, spinster	Alexandria	Head	1800	1800(4):14A
Williams, Franky, washwoman	Alexandria	Housekeeper	1808	1808(4):29A
Williams, Geo.	Alexandria	Boarder	1808	1808(2):14A
Williams, Geo., taylor	Alexandria	Head	1810	1810(3):07A
Williams, George, c/o Elizabeth	Arlington	Apprentice	1815	OCR1811:270
Williams, Henry	Arlington	Defendant	1821	ACO:199, 200, 203
Williams, Henry	Arlington	Apprentice	1827	OCR1822:145
Williams, Henry & wife (C), labourer	Alexandria	Housekeeper	1799	1799(2):15A
Williams, Henry & wife Elner	Alexandria	Resident	1800	1800(4):06B
Williams, Henry, mariner	Alexandria	Head	1810	1810(1):11A
Williams, Henry, ship carpenter	Alexandria	Head	1800	1800(4):06A
Williams, Hiram, c/o Ann	Arlington	Apprentice	1813	OCR1811:194
Williams, James	Alexandria	Tax Charge	1787	Tax PP 1787:17
Williams, James	Arlington	Apprentice	1813	OCR1811:202
Williams, James	Arlington	Apprentice	1823	OCR1822:049
Williams, James H.	Arlington	Apprentice	1822	OCR1822:029
Williams, Joe (C), King St.	Alexandria	Occupant	1795	Tax L 1795:13
Williams, Joe (C), shopkeeper	Alexandria	Housekeeper	1808	1808(1):03A
Williams, John	Alexandria	Tax Charge	1796	Tax LP 1796:30
Williams, John	Alexandria	Tax Charge	1796	Tax PP 1796:21
Williams, John	Arlington	Apprentice	1829	OCR1822:173a
Williams, John S.	Arlington	Defendant	1821	ACO:198
Williams, John, shopkeeper	Alexandria	Housekeeper	1808	1808(2):12A
Williams, John, shopkeeper	Alexandria	Head	1810	1810(2):03A
Williams, John, w(2), watch maker	Alexandria	Head	1796	1796(3):5
Williams, Joseph	Alexandria	Tax Charge	1799	Tax PP 1799:45
Williams, Joseph (C)	Alexandria	Tax Charge	1795	Tax PP 1795:32
Williams, Joseph, a slave	Arlington	Crime	1797	OT:01/08/1797
Williams, Joseph, labourer	Alexandria	Head	1810	1810(1):05A
Williams, Julia Ann	Arlington	Apprentice	1825	OCR1822:085
Williams, L.	Alexandria	Boarder	1799	1799(2):12A
Williams, Lilbourn	Alexandria	Tax Charge	1790	Tax PP 1790:16
Williams, Lilbourn, Wilkes St.	Alexandria	Occupant	1790	Tax L 1790:11
Williams, Lizzey	Arlington	Admin.	1824	OCR1822:064a
Williams, Lizzy	Arlington	Admin.	1824	WB3:124
Williams, Margaret	Arlington	Guard.	1806	WBB:235
Williams, Martha	Arlington	Guard.	1846	LVA-LP (Box 214)
Williams, Martha, c/o Peter	Arlington	Guard.	1846	OCR1842:168
Williams, Mary, c/o Ann Jones	Arlington	Apprentice	1804	OCR1801:187

NAME OR SUBJECT	LOCATION	TYPE	YEAR	REFERENCE(S)
Williams, Mary E., w/o David	Alexandria	Will	1888	WB1:491; LP
Williams, Nancey	Alexandria	Resident	1800	1800(4):07B
Williams, Nancey, laundress	Alexandria	Boarder	1800	1800(4):07A
Williams, Peter	Alexandria	Tax Charge	1787	Tax PP 1787:17
Williams, Peter	Alexandria	Tithable +16	1788	Tax PP 1788:06
Williams, Peter	Alexandria	Tax Charge	1789	Tax PP 1789:20
Williams, Peter	Arlington	Apprentice	1826	OCR1822:119
Williams, Philip, plt.	Alexandria	Suit	1802	CRD:067
Williams, Prince	Alexandria	Boarder	1800	1800(4):04A
Williams, Rennis	Alexandria	Boarder	1799	1799(2):04A
Williams, Sam (C), foreman	Alexandria	Housekeeper	1808	1808(1):06A
Williams, Saml., seaman	Alexandria	Head	1810	1810(1):10A
Williams, Samuel	Alexandria	Will	1873	WB1:060; LP
Williams, Sophia, washerwoman	Alexandria	Head	1810	1810(4):04A
Williams, Sophy Clephane, washwoman	Alexandria	Housekeeper	1808	1808(4):27A
Williams, Sylvina, c/o Ann Jones	Arlington	Apprentice	1805	OCR1801:268
Williams, Thomas	Alexandria	Tithable +21	1787	Tax PP 1787:16
Williams, Thomas	Alexandria	Tax Charge	1788	Tax PP 1788:17
Williams, Thomas	Alexandria	Tax Charge	1789	Tax PP 1789:19
Williams, Thomas	Alexandria	Tax Charge	1790	Tax PP 1790:16
Williams, Thomas	Alexandria	Tax Charge	1796	Tax LP 1796:30
Williams, Thomas	Alexandria	Tax Charge	1796	Tax PP 1796:21
Williams, Thomas	Arlington	Defendant	1802	PA:265
Williams, Thomas	Arlington	Will	1803	WBB:190; File #010A
Williams, Thomas	Arlington	Admin.	1809	WBC:200
Williams, Thomas, c/o Anthony (C)	Arlington	Apprentice	1804	OCR1801:203
Williams, Thomas, c/o William	Arlington	Apprentice	1809	OCR1811:007
Williams, Thomas, def.	Alexandria	Suit	1801	CRB:063
Williams, Thomas, def.	Alexandria	Suit	1802	CRC:047
Williams, Thomas, plt.	Alexandria	Suit	1802	CRB:273
Williams, Thomas, Prince St.	Alexandria	Owner	1790	Tax L 1790:12
Williams, Thomas, Royal St.	Alexandria	Owner	1790	Tax L 1790:12
Williams, Thomas, w(1)5, merchant	Alexandria	Head	1796	1796(3):5
Williams, Thos.	Alexandria	Tax Charge	1795	Tax PP 1795:33
Williams, Thos.	Alexandria	Tax Charge	1798	Tax PP 1798:19
Williams, Thos.	Alexandria	Tax Charge	1799	Tax PP 1799:45
Williams, Thos.	Alexandria	Tax Charge	1800	Tax PP 1800:46
Williams, Thos.	Alexandria	Boarder	1808	1808(2):11A
Williams, Thos. & wife, merchant	Alexandria	Housekeeper	1799	1799(2):02A
Williams, William	Alexandria	Serv./Appr.	1800	1800(4):12B
Williams, William, b. Maryport, Eng.	Arlington	Alien Entry	1825	RA:21/07/25
Williams, William A.	Arlington	Juryman	1824	ACO:237
Williams, William, c/o Eleaner	Arlington	Apprentice	1804	OCR1801:209
Williams, Wm.	Alexandria	Boarder	1808	1808(1):09A
Willing, Thomas M., of Philadelphia	Alexandria	Deed	1811	CRK:048
Willing, Thomas, of Philadelphia	Alexandria	Deed	1811	CRK:045, 048
Willis, Abel	Alexandria	Tax Charge	1796	Tax PP 1796:20
Willis, Abel	Alexandria	Mer. License	1798	Tax PP 1798:20-8
Willis, Abel	Alexandria	Tax Charge	1798	Tax PP 1798:19
Willis, Abel	Alexandria	Mer. License	1799	Tax PP 1799:52-11r
Willis, Abel	Alexandria	Tax Charge	1799	Tax PP 1799:44
Willis, Abel	Alexandria	Tax Charge	1800	Tax PP 1800:46
Willis, Abel	Arlington	Ordinary	1803	OBL1(np)
Willis, Abel	Arlington	Ordinary	1804	OBL1(np)
Willis, Abel	Arlington	Ordinary	1805	OBL1(np)
Willis, Abel	Arlington	Ordinary	1807	OBL2(np)
Willis, Abel	Arlington	Receipt	1816	LVA-LP
Willis, Abel	Arlington	Admin.	1816	WB2:156
Willis, Abel	Arlington	Inventory	1817	AB2:408; LVA-LP
Willis, Abel	Arlington	Account F.	1817	AB3:103; LVA-LP
Willis, Abel & wife, retailer	Alexandria	Housekeeper	1799	1799(2):01A

NAME OR SUBJECT	LOCATION	TYPE	YEAR	REFERENCE(S)
Willis, Abel, Capt.	Arlington	Sale	1817	AB2:426
Willis, Abel, def.	Alexandria	Suit	1802	CRD:051
Willis, Abel, harbour master	Alexandria	Head	1810	1810(1):03A
Willis, Abel, retailer	Alexandria	Housekeeper	1808	1808(1):05A
Willis, Abel, w, mariner	Alexandria	Head	1796	1796(3):3
Willis, Archibald	Arlington	Apprentice	1822	OCR1822:027a
Willis, Betty, c/o Robert	Arlington	Apprentice	1815	OCR1811:263
Willis, John W.T.	Arlington	Apprentice	1812	OCR1811:067
Willis, Nace (C)	Alexandria	Tax Charge	1795	Tax PP 1795:33
Willis, Nancy, washwoman	Alexandria	Housekeeper	1808	1808(4):28A
Willis, Nathan, w (C)	Alexandria	Head	1795	1796(3):7
Willson, James	Alexandria	Tax Charge	1796	Tax LP 1796:30
Willson, James	Alexandria	Mer. License	1799	Tax PP 1799:52-11w
Willson, James	Alexandria	Tax Charge	1800	Tax PP 1800:47
Willson, James, drayman	Alexandria	Head	1810	1810(3):03A
Willson, Lucy	Alexandria	Reference	1808	1808(2):16A
Willson, Oliver, currier	Alexandria	Head	1810	1810(4):03A
Willson, William	Alexandria	Owner	1787	Tax L 1787:27
Willson, William	Alexandria	Mer. License	1799	Tax PP 1799:52-11w
Willson, William, Fairfax St.	Alexandria	Occupant	1787	Tax L 1787:27
Willson, William, Wilks St.	Alexandria	Occupant	1787	Tax L 1787:13
Willson, Wm.	Alexandria	Tax Charge	1796	Tax LP 1796:30
Willson, Wm.	Alexandria	Tax Charge	1796	Tax LP 1796:31
Wilman, Oliver	Alexandria	Tax Charge	1800	Tax PP 1800:46
Wilmer, William H.	Arlington	Will	1828	WB3:312; File #270A
Wilmer, William H.	Arlington	Bond	1828	WB3:324
Wilson & Potts, def.	Alexandria	Suit	1801	CRD:178
Wilson, Albert	Alexandria	Will	1897	WB2:230; LP
Wilson, Allender, washwoman	Alexandria	Housekeeper	1808	1808(1):06A
Wilson, Ann C. & Jane R., c/o Wm.	Arlington	P. of Atty.	1831	LVA-LP (Accounts)
Wilson, Betsy, washwoman	Alexandria	Housekeeper	1808	1808(2):16A
Wilson, Campbell, def.	Alexandria	Suit	1802	CRB:174
Wilson, Charles F.	Alexandria	Will	1882	WB1:346; LP
Wilson, Cumberland, Estate	Alexandria	Account B.	1793	CRH:420
Wilson, Cumberland, Estate, plt.	Alexandria	Suit	1810	CRH:404
Wilson, David	Arlington	Inventory	1825	AB5:403; LVA-LP
Wilson, David	Arlington	Admin.	1825	OCR1822:084
Wilson, David	Arlington	Admin.	1825	WB3:159
Wilson, Eliza	Arlington	Account	1823	AB5:180; LVA-LP
Wilson, Elizabeth	Alexandria	Head	1810	1810(1):01A
Wilson, Elizabeth	Arlington	Inventory	1821	AB5:005; LVA-LP
Wilson, Elizabeth	Arlington	Admin.	1821	WB3:029
Wilson, Elizabeth, gentlewoman	Alexandria	Housekeeper	1808	1808(1):02A
Wilson, Enoch, grantee	Arlington	Indenture D.	1827	ID:082
Wilson, Geo.	Alexandria	Housekeeper	1799	1799(2):11A
Wilson, George	Alexandria	Tax Charge	1788	Tax PP 1788:17
Wilson, George	Alexandria	Tax Charge	1789	Tax PP 1789:19
Wilson, George	Alexandria	Tax Charge	1799	Tax PP 1799:45
Wilson, George	Alexandria	Tax Charge	1800	Tax PP 1800:46
Wilson, George	Arlington	Admin.	1809	WBC:233
Wilson, George	Arlington	Inventory	1810	WBC:344
Wilson, George	Arlington	Sale	1810	WBC:343
Wilson, George, c/o Isaac	Arlington	Guard.	1834	WB4:103
Wilson, George W.	Arlington	Guard.	1838	WB4:173
Wilson, Hannah	Alexandria	Will	1875	WBC1:019; LP
Wilson, Jacob A., at his house	Arlington	Ordinary	1849	OBL6(np)
Wilson, Jacob H., on King St.	Arlington	Ordinary	1847	OBL6(np)
Wilson, James	Alexandria	Tithable +16	1789	Tax PP 1789:20
Wilson, James	Alexandria	Tax Charge	1790	Tax PP 1790:16
Wilson, James	Alexandria	Tax Charge	1796	Tax PP 1796:21
Wilson, James	Alexandria	Mer. License	1798	Tax PP 1798:20-8

NAME OR SUBJECT	LOCATION	TYPE	YEAR	REFERENCE(S)
Wilson, James	Alexandria	Tax Charge	1799	Tax PP 1799:44
Wilson, James	Alexandria	Mer. License	1800	Tax PP 1800:54(22)w
Wilson, James	Arlington	Plaintiff	1801	PA:176
Wilson, James	Arlington	Admin.	1805	WBB:172
Wilson, James	Arlington	Account	1810	WBC:397; LVA-LP
Wilson, James	Arlington	Sale	1810	WBC:373
Wilson, James	Arlington	Debts	1810	WBC:368
Wilson, James	Arlington	Inventory	1810	WBC:359
Wilson, James	Arlington	Account	1812	AB1:210; LVA-LP
Wilson, James (cooper)	Alexandria	Tax Charge	1799	Tax PP 1799:45
Wilson, James & wife Elizabeth, def.	Alexandria	Suit	1801	CRC:118
Wilson, James C.	Arlington	Guard.	1807	WBB:506
Wilson, James C.	Arlington	Defendant	1823	ACO:213, 216
Wilson, James C.	Arlington	Defendant	1825	ACO:259
Wilson, James C.	Arlington	Defendant	1826	ACO:265
Wilson, James C.	Arlington	Defendant	1827	ACO:271
Wilson, James, King St.	Alexandria	Occupant	1790	Tax L 1790:12
Wilson, James, w(3)4, merchant	Alexandria	Head	1796	1796(3):4
Wilson, Jas.	Alexandria	Tax Charge	1798	Tax PP 1798:19
Wilson, Jas. & wife, merchant	Alexandria	Housekeeper	1799	1799(2):02A
Wilson, Jas., cooper	Alexandria	Boarder	1799	1799(2):16A
Wilson, John	Alexandria	Tithable +16	1788	Tax PP 1788:03
Wilson, John	Alexandria	Tax Charge	1789	Tax PP 1789:20
Wilson, John	Arlington	Admin.	1806	WBB:382
Wilson, John	Arlington	Inventory	1807	WBB:430; LVA-LP
Wilson, John	Arlington	Sale	1807	WBB:446
Wilson, John	Arlington	Account	1808	WBC:074; LVA-LP
Wilson, John	Arlington	Settlement	1815	AB2:110; LVA-LP
Wilson, John W., c/o Isaac	Arlington	Guard.	1834	WB4:103
Wilson, Margaret	Arlington	Will	1803	WBA:161; LVA-LP
Wilson, Margaret	Arlington	Bond	1803	WBA:166
Wilson, Margaret	Arlington	Sale	1804	WBA:261
Wilson, Margaret	Arlington	Inventory	1804	WBA:260; LVA-LP
Wilson, Margaret	Arlington	Account	1808	WBC:165
Wilson, Margaret	Arlington	Admin.	1808	WBC:034
Wilson, Margaret, c/o George & Rachel	Arlington	Guard.	1804	WBB:003
Wilson, Margret, blind woman	Alexandria	Housekeeper	1808	1808(1):09A
Wilson, Oliver	Arlington	Bond	1815	WB2:081
Wilson, Oliver	Arlington	Will	1815	WB2:079
Wilson, Oliver	Arlington	Sale	1816	AB2:264
Wilson, Oliver	Arlington	Account	1817	AB3:101; LVA-LP
Wilson, Oliver	Arlington	Inventory	1817	AB3:096; LVA-LP
Wilson, Rachell	Alexandria	Boarder	1795	1795(4a):09
Wilson, Robert J.T.	Alexandria	Will	1877	WB1:219; LP
Wilson, Talbott	Arlington	Inventory	1815	AB2:208
Wilson, Thomas	Alexandria	Serv./Appr.	1800	1800(4):04B
Wilson, Thomas Knox, c/o Isaac	Arlington	Guard.	1834	WB4:103
Wilson, Walter T., c/o Isaac	Arlington	Guard.	1834	WB4:103, 173
Wilson, William	Alexandria	Deposition	(nd)	CRE:347
Wilson, William	Alexandria	Tax Charge	1787	Tax PP 1787:15
Wilson, William	Alexandria	Tax Charge	1789	Tax PP 1789:20
Wilson, William	Alexandria	Tax Charge	1790	Tax PP 1790:16
Wilson, William	Alexandria	Tax Charge	1790	Tax PP 1790:16
Wilson, William	Alexandria	Mer. License	1798	Tax PP 1798:20-8
Wilson, William	Alexandria	Tax Charge	1799	Tax PP 1799:44
Wilson, William	Alexandria	Tax Charge	1799	Tax PP 1799:45
Wilson, William	Alexandria	Tax Charge	1800	Tax PP 1800:46
Wilson, William	Arlington	Defendant	1802	PA:345
Wilson, William	Arlington	Libellant	1803	ACO:022
Wilson, William	Arlington	Libellant	1804	ACO:029, 031
Wilson, William	Arlington	Libellant	1804	ACO:024

NAME OR SUBJECT	LOCATION	TYPE	YEAR	REFERENCE(S)
Wilson, William	Arlington	Juryman	1808	ACO:081
Wilson, William	Arlington	Insolvent	1830	ID:249
Wilson, William	Arlington	Admin.	1841	WB4:286
Wilson, William & wife, carpenter	Alexandria	Head	1795	1795(4):03
Wilson, William, c/o Eleanor	Arlington	Apprentice	1811	OCR1811:038
Wilson, William, carpenter	Arlington	Insolvent	1804	ID3:069
Wilson, William, carpenter, grantor	Arlington	Indenture D.	1804	ID3:074
Wilson, William, def.	Alexandria	Suit	1801	CRB:001, 004
Wilson, William, def.	Alexandria	Suit	1801	CRB:125
Wilson, William, def.	Alexandria	Suit	1801	CRD:178
Wilson, William, def.	Alexandria	Suit	1802	CRB:174
Wilson, William, def.	Alexandria	Suit	1804	CRG:191
Wilson, William, Duke St.	Alexandria	Occupant	1790	Tax L 1790:06
Wilson, William, Fairfax St.	Alexandria	Owner	1795	Tax L 1795:31
Wilson, William, insurance broker	Alexandria	Head	1810	1810(1):01A
Wilson, William, plt.	Alexandria	Suit	1801	CRB:051
Wilson, William, plt.	Alexandria	Suit	1801	CRC:194
Wilson, William, plt.	Alexandria	Suit	1801	CRB:307
Wilson, William, plt.	Alexandria	Suit	1807	CRF:151
Wilson, William, plt.	Alexandria	Suit	1807	CRH:017
Wilson, William R.	Arlington	Account	1807	WBB:468, 525; LVA-LP
Wilson, William R.	Arlington	Account	1812	AB1:201
Wilson, William R.	Arlington	Account F.	1822	OCR1822:004a
Wilson, William Ramsay	Arlington	Admin.	1805	WBB:162
Wilson, William Ramsay	Arlington	Account	1822	AB5:047; LVA-LP
Wilson, William Ramsay, dec.	Arlington	Estate Ref.	1806	ACO:051
Wilson, William Ramsay, dec.	Arlington	Estate Ref.	1805	ACO:042, 046
Wilson, William, wharf	Alexandria	Occupant	1790	Tax L 1790:02
Wilson, Wm.	Alexandria	Tax Charge	1795	Tax PP 1795:33
Wilson, Wm.	Alexandria	Tax Charge	1795	Tax PP 1795:32
Wilson, Wm.	Alexandria	Tax Charge	1796	Tax PP 1796:20
Wilson, Wm.	Alexandria	Tax Charge	1798	Tax PP 1798:19
Wilson, Wm.	Alexandria	Head	1800	1800(4):07A
Wilson, Wm. & wife, carpenter	Alexandria	Housekeeper	1799	1799(2):17A
Wilson, Wm. & wife Ellender	Alexandria	Resident	1800	1800(4):07B
Wilson, Wm., Fairfax St.	Alexandria	Occupant	1790	Tax L 1790:04(2)
Wilson, Wm., Fairfax St.	Alexandria	Occupant	1795	Tax L 1795:13
Wilson, Wm., late merchant	Alexandria	Housekeeper	1808	1808(3):19A
Wilson, Wm., Water St.	Alexandria	Occupant	1795	Tax L 1795:17
Wilson, Wm., wharf	Alexandria	Occupant	1795	Tax L 1795:06
Wilson, Zachariah	Alexandria	Tithable +16	1788	Tax PP 1788:08
Wilson, Zachariah	Alexandria	Tithable +16	1789	Tax PP 1789:08
Wilsons & Maris, plt.	Alexandria	Suit	1801	CRB:066
Wily, Geo.	Alexandria	Tax Charge	1798	Tax PP 1798:19
Wily, George	Alexandria	Tax Charge	1799	Tax PP 1799:44
Wimsatt, Mary H.	Alexandria	Will	1894	WB2:097; LP
Wincett, Pricilla, seamstress	Alexandria	Head	1810	1810(2):01A
Winch, David B., at his house	Arlington	Ordinary	1848	OBL6(np)
Windsor & Mills	Arlington	Defendants	1823	ACO:221, 224
Windsor & Mills	Arlington	Defendants	1824	ACO:241, 243, 248
Windsor & Mills	Arlington	Defendants	1825	ACO:253, 257
Windsor & Mills	Arlington	Defendants	1826	ACO:261, 264
Windsor & Mills	Arlington	Defendants	1827	ACO:274
Windsor & Mills, assignee of	Arlington	Plaintiff	1823	ACO:221
Windsor, David A.	Alexandria	Will	1892	WBC1:058; LP
Windsor, Julia Ann, c/o Winney	Arlington	Apprentice	1815	OCR1811:272
Windsor, Richard	Alexandria	Will	1876	WB1:193; LP
Windsor, Richard, grantee	Arlington	Indenture D.	1832	ID:399
Windsor, Richard, grantee	Arlington	Indenture D.	1832	ID:372
Windsor, Richard W.	Arlington	Defendant	1823	ACO:221, 224
Windsor, Richd.	Alexandria	Boarder	1808	1808(3):19A

NAME OR SUBJECT	LOCATION	TYPE	YEAR	REFERENCE(S)
Windsor, Robert N.	Arlington	Appraisal	1852	WB6:078; LVA-LP
Windsor, Robert N.	Arlington	Account	1854	WB6:348; LVA-LP
Windsor, Robert N.	Arlington	Account	1859	WB7:459; LVA-LP
Windsor, Robt.	Alexandria	Boarder	1808	1808(3):19A
Windsor, Robt., merchant	Alexandria	Head	1810	1810(3):05A
Winset, Henry	Arlington	Apprentice	1802	OCR1801:023
Winset, John, waterman	Alexandria	Housekeeper	1808	1808(2):12A
Winsor, Alney	Alexandria	Tax Charge	1789	Tax PP 1789:20
Winsor, Jas.	Alexandria	Tax Charge	1795	Tax PP 1795:32
Winsor, Nathaniel	Alexandria	Tax Charge	1799	Tax PP 1799:44
Winsor, Olney	Alexandria	Tax Charge	1787	Tax PP 1787:16
Winsor, Olney	Alexandria	Tithable +16	1788	Tax PP 1788:09
Winsor, Olney	Alexandria	Tithable +16	1790	Tax PP 1790:07
Winsor, Olney, King St.	Alexandria	Occupant	1790	Tax L 1790:07
Winstandly, John, c/o Elizabeth Dice	Arlington	Apprentice	1802	OCR1801:021
Winter & Harman, assignees of	Arlington	Libellants	1812	ACO:122
Winter, John	Alexandria	Tithable +16	1789	Tax PP 1789:15
Winter, John, printer	Alexandria	Housekeeper	1808	1808(2):16A
Winter, John W.	Alexandria	Deposition	1814	CRI:522
Winter, Saml.	Alexandria	Tax Charge	1796	Tax LP 1796:30
Winter, Saml.	Alexandria	Tax Charge	1798	Tax PP 1798:19
Winter, Samuel	Alexandria	Tax Charge	1796	Tax PP 1796:20
Winter, Samuel	Alexandria	Tax Charge	1799	Tax PP 1799:45
Winter, Samuel & wife, mariner	Alexandria	Head	1795	1795(4):07
Winterberry, Jno.	Alexandria	Tax Charge	1788	Tax PP 1788:17
Winterberry, Jno.	Alexandria	Tax Charge	1795	Tax PP 1795:33
Winterberry, Jno. & wife, cryer	Alexandria	Housekeeper	1799	1799(2):15A
Winterberry, Jno., Jr.	Alexandria	Tax Charge	1800	Tax PP 1800:46
Winterberry, John	Alexandria	Tax Charge	1787	Tax PP 1787:16
Winterberry, John	Alexandria	Tax Charge	1789	Tax PP 1789:20
Winterberry, John	Alexandria	Tax Charge	1790	Tax PP 1790:16
Winterberry, John & wife, shoemaker	Alexandria	Head	1795	1795(4):02
Winterberry, John, clerk	Alexandria	Head	1810	1810(1):09A
Winterberry, John, Jr	Alexandria	Tax Charge	1796	Tax PP 1796:21
Winterberry, John, Jr., clerk	Alexandria	Boarder	1800	1800(4):06A
Winterberry, John, Sr.	Alexandria	Tax Charge	1796	Tax PP 1796:21
Winterberry, John, Sr.	Alexandria	Tax Charge	1800	Tax PP 1800:47
Winterbery, John & wife Mary	Alexandria	Resident	1800	1800(4):06B
Winterbery, John, Jr.	Alexandria	Resident	1800	1800(4):06B
Winterbery, John, vendue crier	Alexandria	Head	1800	1800(4):06A
Winterbury, Jno.	Alexandria	Tax Charge	1798	Tax PP 1798:19
Winterbury, Jno., Water St.	Alexandria	Occupant	1795	Tax L 1795:09
Winterbury, John	Alexandria	Tax Charge	1796	Tax LP 1796:31
Winterbury, John, Jr.	Alexandria	Tax Charge	1799	Tax PP 1799:45
Winterbury, John, Sr.	Alexandria	Tax Charge	1799	Tax PP 1799:45
Winterbury, John, Water St.	Alexandria	Occupant	1790	Tax L 1790:04
Winters, John, printer	Alexandria	Head	1810	1810(2):07A
Winters, Saml., ship builder	Alexandria	Housekeeper	1799	1799(2):16A
Wirgman, John, grantor	Arlington	Indenture D.	1812	ID2:133
Wirgman [Workman], John, in prison	Arlington	Insolvent	1812	ID2:130
Wirony, Joseph	Alexandria	Tithable +16	1789	Tax PP 1789:19
Wirtenbecker, Jno.	Alexandria	Boarder	1808	1808(4):24A
Wise, Charles J.	Alexandria	Will	1898	WB2:274; LP
Wise, Doctor	Alexandria	Tax Charge	1800	Tax PP 1800:46
Wise, Elizabeth	Alexandria	Head	1810	1810(3):06A
Wise, Geo.	Alexandria	Tax Charge	1795	Tax PP 1795:32
Wise, Geo.	Alexandria	Tax Charge	1798	Tax PP 1798:20
Wise, Geo. K., retailer & tavern lic.	Alexandria	Housekeeper	1808	1808(1):03A
Wise, Geo. K., retailer	Alexandria	Housekeeper	1808	1808(2):15A
Wise, Geo. P., at the City Hotel	Arlington	Ordinary	1836	OBL5(np)
Wise, Geo. P., City Hotel, Royal St.	Arlington	Ordinary	1841	OBL6(np)

NAME OR SUBJECT	LOCATION	TYPE	YEAR	REFERENCE(S)
Wise, George	Alexandria	Tax Charge	1796	Tax LP 1796:30
Wise, George	Alexandria	Tax Charge	1796	Tax PP 1796:20
Wise, George	Arlington	Apprentice	1804	OCR1801:148
Wise, George	Arlington	Will	1856	WB7:069; File #327A
Wise, George K.	Arlington	Defendant	1802	PA:065
Wise, George K.	Arlington	Defendant	1802	PA:060, 061, 064
Wise, George K., taylor	Alexandria	Head	1810	1810(1):01A
Wise, George P., at his house	Arlington	Ordinary	1837	OBL5(np)
Wise, George P., at his house	Arlington	Ordinary	1838	OBL5(np)
Wise, George P., at City Hotel	Arlington	Ordinary	1842	OBL6(np)
Wise, Jno.	Alexandria	Tax Charge	1798	Tax PP 1798:19
Wise, Jno., Royal St.	Alexandria	Occupant	1795	Tax L 1795:31
Wise, John	Alexandria	Owner	1787	Tax L 1787:26
Wise, John	Alexandria	Tax Charge	1787	Tax PP 1787:16
Wise, John	Alexandria	Tax Charge	1788	Tax PP 1788:17
Wise, John	Alexandria	Tax Charge	1789	Tax PP 1789:19
Wise, John	Alexandria	Tax Charge	1790	Tax PP 1790:15
Wise, John	Alexandria	Tax Charge	1795	Tax PP 1795:32
Wise, John	Alexandria	Tax Charge	1796	Tax LP 1796:30
Wise, John	Alexandria	Tax Charge	1796	Tax PP 1796:21
Wise, John	Alexandria	Deposition	1808	CRH:115
Wise, John	Arlington	Will	1815	WB2:085
Wise, John	Arlington	Bond	1815	WB2:103
Wise, John	Arlington	Account	1826	AB6:229; LVA-LP
Wise, John	Arlington	Bond	1826	OCR1822:125a
Wise, John, def.	Alexandria	Suit	1801	CRB:085
Wise, John, def.	Alexandria	Suit	1806	CRE:063
Wise, John, Fairfax St.	Alexandria	Occupant	1787	Tax L 1787:05
Wise, John, Fairfax St.	Alexandria	Occupant	1790	Tax L 1790:05
Wise, John, Fairfax St.	Alexandria	Owner	1790	Tax L 1790:12
Wise, John, gentleman	Alexandria	Housekeeper	1808	1808(3):20A
Wise, John, gentleman	Alexandria	Head	1810	1810(2):03A
Wise, John, Prince St.	Alexandria	Owner	1790	Tax L 1790:12
Wise, John, Royal St.	Alexandria	Occupant	1787	Tax L 1787:26
Wise, John, Royal St.	Alexandria	Owner	1790	Tax L 1790:12(2)
Wise, John, Royal St.	Alexandria	Owner	1795	Tax L 1795:31(2)
Wise, Michael	Alexandria	Tax Charge	1799	Tax PP 1799:45
Wise, Michael & wife, labourer	Alexandria	Head	1795	1795(4a):09
Wise, Michael & wife, labourer	Alexandria	Housekeeper	1799	1799(2):08A
Wise, Michl.	Alexandria	Tax Charge	1795	Tax PP 1795:32
Wise, Michl.	Alexandria	Tax Charge	1796	Tax LP 1796:30
Wise, N.S., grantee	Arlington	Indenture D.	1813	ID2:209
Wise, N.S., grantee	Arlington	Indenture D.	1813	ID2:214
Wise, Nathaniel L., grantee	Arlington	Indenture D.	1812	ID2:110
Wise, Nathaniel S., grantee	Arlington	Indenture D.	1826	ID:004
Wise, Nathaniel S., grantee	Arlington	Indenture D.	1827	ID:068
Wise, Nathl.	Alexandria	Boarder	1808	1808(3):20A
Wise, P., King St.	Alexandria	Occupant	1787	Tax L 1787:26
Wise, Peter	Alexandria	Owner	1787	Tax L 1787:26
Wise, Peter	Alexandria	Tax Charge	1787	Tax PP 1787:15
Wise, Peter	Alexandria	Tax Charge	1788	Tax PP 1788:17
Wise, Peter	Alexandria	Tax Charge	1789	Tax PP 1789:19
Wise, Peter	Alexandria	Tax Charge	1790	Tax PP 1790:16
Wise, Peter	Alexandria	Tax Charge	1795	Tax PP 1795:32
Wise, Peter	Alexandria	Tax Charge	1796	Tax LP 1796:30
Wise, Peter	Alexandria	Tax Charge	1796	Tax PP 1796:20
Wise, Peter	Alexandria	Tax Charge	1798	Tax PP 1798:19
Wise, Peter	Alexandria	Tax Charge	1800	Tax PP 1800:46
Wise, Peter	Arlington	Order	1828	LVA-LP
Wise, Peter	Arlington	Admin.	1828	OCR1822:160a
Wise, Peter	Arlington	Admin.	1828	WB3:233

NAME OR SUBJECT	LOCATION	TYPE	YEAR	REFERENCE(S)
Wise, Peter	Arlington	Account	1829	AB6:486; LVA-LP
Wise, Peter, def.	Alexandria	Suit	1801	CRD:038
Wise, Peter, Fairfax St.	Alexandria	Owner	1790	Tax L 1790:12(2)
Wise, Peter, Jr.	Arlington	Account	1810	AB1:015
Wise, Peter, Jr.	Arlington	Account	1814	AB2:019; LVA-LP
Wise, Peter, Jr.	Arlington	Debts Due	1814	AB2:016; LVA-LP
Wise, Peter, Jr., def.	Alexandria	Suit	1804	CRF:030
Wise, Peter, Jr., def.	Alexandria	Suit	1808	CRF:334
Wise, Peter, Jr., Dr.	Arlington	Admin.	1808	WBC:111
Wise, Peter, Jr., Dr.	Arlington	Inventory	1808	WBC:118
Wise, Peter, Jr., druggist	Alexandria	Housekeeper	1808	1808(1):01A
Wise, Peter, Jr., plt.	Alexandria	Suit	1805	CRF:127
Wise, Peter, King St.	Alexandria	Occupant	1790	Tax L 1790:12
Wise, Peter, King St., tanyard	Alexandria	Owner	1790	Tax L 1790:12(2)
Wise, Peter, King St.	Alexandria	Owner	1790	Tax L 1790:12(5)
Wise, Peter, King St.	Alexandria	Occupant	1795	Tax L 1795:32
Wise, Peter, Sr.	Alexandria	Tax Charge	1799	Tax PP 1799:44
Wise, Peter, Sr. Fairfax St.	Alexandria	Owner	1795	Tax L 1795:32
Wise, Peter, Sr., King St.	Alexandria	Owner	1795	Tax L 1795:32(6)
Wise, Peter, St. Asaph St.	Alexandria	Occupant	1787	Tax L 1787:03
Wiseman, Martin	Alexandria	Tax Charge	1787	Tax PP 1787:16
Wisemiller, Ja. [biscuit baker]	Alexandria	Housekeeper	1808	1808(4):25A
Wisemiller, Jacb.	Alexandria	Tax Charge	1795	Tax PP 1795:33
Wisemiller, Jacob	Arlington	Account	1820	AB4:176; LVA-LP
Wisemiller, Jacob	Arlington	Inventory	1820	AB4:110; LVA-LP
Wisemiller, Jacob	Arlington	Admin.	1820	WB2:348, 349
Wisemiller, Jacob	Arlington	Account	1822	AB5:085; LVA-LP
Wisemiller, Jacob, baker	Alexandria	Boarder	1799	1799(2):10A
Wisemiller, Jacob, def.	Alexandria	Suit	1801	CRD:152
Wisemiller, Jacob, def.	Alexandria	Suit	1809	CRG:345
Wisemiller, Jacob, def.	Alexandria	Suit	1809	CRG:238
Wisenhall, Bernd.	Alexandria	Tithable +16	1788	Tax PP 1788:15
Wismillar, Jacob	Alexandria	Tithable +16	1789	Tax PP 1789:10
Wissendal, Lewis	Alexandria	Tax Charge	1787	Tax PP 1787:16
Withers & Sangster	Alexandria	Boarder	1808	1808(2):10A
Withers, Cave	Alexandria	Boarder	1808	1808(2):10A
Withers, Cave, def.	Alexandria	Suit	1818	CRK:317
Withers, John	Arlington	Will	1861	WB8:165
Withers, John, def.	Alexandria	Suit	1805	CRF:127
Withers, John, grantor	Arlington	Indenture D.	1806	ID3:136
Withers, John, in jail	Arlington	Insolvent	1806	ID3:133
Withers, Reuben	Alexandria	Boarder	1808	1808(3):19A
Witman, Fred.	Alexandria	Tax Charge	1790	Tax PP 1790:16
Witmer, George K. & Brothers	Arlington	Account	1871	WB9:311
Witney, Gilbert	Alexandria	Tax Charge	1790	Tax PP 1790:16
Witson, William (Carp.)	Alexandria	Tax Charge	1800	Tax PP 1800:47
Wm. Oiley & Co.	Alexandria	License Due	1800	Tax PP 1800:54(24)
Wolcott, Oliver, 1801	Arlington	Certificate	1830	ACR:089
Wolcott, Oliver, New York	Alexandria	Deed	1811	CRK:048
Wolf, George, plt.	Alexandria	Ejectment	1802	CRE:242
Wolf, Tobias	Alexandria	Tax Charge	1787	Tax PP 1787:16
Wolfe, William	Alexandria	Will	1891	WB2:001; LP
Wood, Andrew	Alexandria	Tax Charge	1796	Tax PP 1796:21
Wood, Ann	Alexandria	Resident	1800	1800(4):14B
Wood, Ann, sumpster	Alexandria	Head	1800	1800(4):14A
Wood, Araminta	Arlington	Appraisal	1837	LVA-LP
Wood, Araminta	Arlington	Admin.	1857	WB4:157
Wood, Benjamin, clerk	Alexandria	Head	1810	1810(4):01A
Wood, Benjn. C., clerk	Alexandria	Housekeeper	1808	1808(3):18A
Wood, David	Alexandria	Boarder	1795	1795(4a):01
Wood, Elizabeth	Arlington	Admin.	1813	WB1:222

NAME OR SUBJECT	LOCATION	TYPE	YEAR	REFERENCE(S)
Wood, Harriet	Arlington	Guard.	1823	WB3:082
Wood, James	Arlington	Guard.	1826	WB3:211
Wood, James P., c/o William	Arlington	Guard.	1826	OCR1822:108
Wood, John	Alexandria	Serv./Appr.	1800	1800(4):02B
Wood, John	Arlington	Inventory	1815	AB2:184
Wood, John	Arlington	Inventory	1815	AB2:166; LVA-LP
Wood, John	Arlington	Bond	1815	WB2:063
Wood, John	Arlington	Will	1815	WB2:062
Wood, John	Arlington	Account	1870	WB9:232
Wood, John, b/o Richard	Arlington	Apprentice	1815	OCR1811:284
Wood, John, cooper	Alexandria	Head	1810	1810(2):01A
Wood, John P.	Arlington	Apprentice	1828	OCR1822:160
Wood, John, shoemaker	Alexandria	Housekeeper	1808	1808(1):08A
Wood, John, shoemaker	Alexandria	Head	1810	1810(1):12A
Wood, Jonathan	Alexandria	Tax Charge	1787	Tax PP 1787:16
Wood, Joseph	Alexandria	Boarder	1808	1808(2):13A
Wood, Louisa	Arlington	Guard.	1806	WBB:276
Wood, Marian	Arlington	Guard.	1826	WB3:264
Wood, Orlando	Alexandria	Will	1889	WBC1:054
Wood, Richard	Arlington	Apprentice	1802	OCR1801:042
Wood, Richard	Arlington	Juryman	1824	ACO:237
Wood, Richd.	Alexandria	Boarder	1808	1808(2):11A
Wood, Richd., barber	Alexandria	Head	1810	1810(2):03A
Wood, Sarah J.	Alexandria	Will	1890	WB1:569; LP
Wood, William	Alexandria	Tax Charge	1800	Tax PP 1800:46
Wood, William	Arlington	Apprentice	1802	OCR1801:042
Wood, William	Arlington	Sale	1822	AB5:096
Wood, William	Arlington	Inventory	1822	AB5:090; LVA-LP
Wood, William	Arlington	Will P.	1822	OCR1822:017a
Wood, William	Arlington	Bond	1822	WB3:061
Wood, William	Arlington	Will	1822	WB3:060; File #209A
Wood, William	Arlington	Account	1823	AB5:175; LVA-LP
Wood, William	Arlington	Appraisal	1836	LVA-LP
Wood, William	Arlington	Admin.	1836	WB4:109
Wood, William, orphans of	Arlington	Guard.	1826	OCR1822:126a
Wood, William S.	Arlington	Guard.	1826	WB3:264
Wood, Wm., storekeeper	Alexandria	Housekeeper	1808	1808(3):18A
Woodard, Andrew, c/o Thomas	Arlington	Apprentice	1804	OCR1801:156
Woodard, Richard	Arlington	Apprentice	1815	OCR1811:322
Woodcock, Burle	Alexandria	Serv./Appr.	1800	1800(4):11B
Woodcock, Samuel, carpenter	Alexandria	Boarder	1799	1799(2):15A
Woodcock, Wm. & brother	Alexandria	Tax Charge	1799	Tax PP 1799:45
Woodcock, Wm. & wife, carpenter	Alexandria	Housekeeper	1799	1799(2):15A
Woodcock, Wm. & [Bro.]	Alexandria	Tax Charge	1800	Tax PP 1800:46
Woodhouse, John Thos., Liverpool	Alexandria	Suit	1808	CRF:290
Woodhouse, Phil.	Alexandria	Boarder	1808	1808(2):12A
Woodhouse, Thomas	Arlington	Deposition	1806	ACR:014
Woodhouse, Thomas, master	Arlington	Respondent	1805	ACO:042
Woodhouse, Thomas, master	Arlington	Respondent	1805	ACO:033
Woodhouse, Thomas, master	Arlington	Respondent	1806	ACO:049
Woodhouse, Thomas, master	Arlington	Respondent	1808	ACR:039
Woodhouse, Thos.	Alexandria	Boarder	1808	1808(2):12A
Woodman, John, seaman	Arlington	Libellant	1818	ACO:152
Woodrow, Henry	Alexandria	Tax Charge	1798	Tax PP 1798:19
Woodrow, Jno. & wife, carpenter	Alexandria	Housekeeper	1799	1799(2):06A
Woodrow, John	Alexandria	Tax Charge	1796	Tax PP 1796:21
Woodrow, John	Alexandria	Tax Charge	1798	Tax PP 1798:20
Woodrow, John	Alexandria	Tax Charge	1799	Tax PP 1799:44
Woodrow, John	Alexandria	Tax Charge	1800	Tax PP 1800:46
Woodrow, John	Arlington	Sale	1810	WBC:424
Woodrow, John	Arlington	Collection	1810	WBC:390; LVA-LP

NAME OR SUBJECT	LOCATION	TYPE	YEAR	REFERENCE(S)
Woodrow, John, constable	Alexandria	Housekeeper	1808	1808(3):21A
Woodrow, John, def.	Alexandria	Suit	1807	CRF:131
Woodrow, John, w(4), carpenter	Alexandria	Head	1796	1796(3):2
Woodrow, Josh.	Alexandria	Tax Charge	1796	Tax LP 1796:31
Woods & Bemis, assignees, plt.	Alexandria	Suit	1801	CRB:147
Woods & Bemis, plt.	Alexandria	Suit	1805	CRE:058
Woods, D.	Alexandria	Tax Charge	1796	Tax LP 1796:30
Woods, Daniel	Alexandria	Tax Charge	1796	Tax PP 1796:20
Woods, Daniel	Alexandria	Tax Charge	1799	Tax PP 1799:45
Woods, Danl.	Alexandria	Tax Charge	1798	Tax PP 1798:20
Woods, Danl.	Alexandria	Boarder	1799	1799(2):08A
Woods, David, b. Ireland	Arlington	Alien Entry	1801	RA:06/07/01
Woods, Hannah	Arlington	Inventory	1822	AB5:116; LVA-LP
Woods, Hannah	Arlington	Admin.	1822	WB3:068
Woods, John, of Port Tobacco Md.	Alexandria	Deposition	1800	CRE:060
Woodward, Adw.	Alexandria	Boarder	1808	1808(3):21A
Woodward, Capt., Prince St.	Alexandria	Occupant	1787	Tax L 1787:16
Woodward, Hardy	Arlington	Libellant	1813	ACO:137
Woodward, James	Alexandria	Tax Charge	1787	Tax PP 1787:16
Woodward, John	Arlington	Libellant	1813	ACO:137
Woodward, William A., Cameron/Royal	Arlington	Ordinary	1844	OBL6(np)
Woolard, Samuel	Alexandria	Tax Charge	1790	Tax PP 1790:15
Woolls, William	Alexandria	Tax Charge	1789	Tax PP 1789:19
Woolls, William	Alexandria	Mer. License	1798	Tax PP 1798:20-8
Woolls, William	Alexandria	Tax Charge	1800	Tax PP 1800:47
Woolls, William	Arlington	Ordinary	1803	OBL1(np)
Woolls, William	Arlington	Account	1806	WBB:356; LVA-LP
Woolls, William	Alexandria	Will	1874	WB1:101; LP
Woolls, William, def.	Alexandria	Suit	1801	CRC:066
Woolls, Wm.	Alexandria	Tax Charge	1788	Tax PP 1788:17
Woolls, Wm.	Alexandria	Tax Charge	1796	Tax PP 1796:20
Woolls, Wm.	Alexandria	Tax Charge	1798	Tax PP 1798:19
Woolls, Wm.	Alexandria	Tax Charge	1799	Tax PP 1799:45
Woolls, Wm., Princess St.	Alexandria	Occupant	1795	Tax L 1795:12
Wools, William	Alexandria	Tax Charge	1787	Tax PP 1787:17
Wools, William	Alexandria	Tax Charge	1790	Tax PP 1790:15
Wools, William, ret. liquors w/o license	Arlington	Defendant	1802	PA:028
Wools, William, Water St.	Alexandria	Occupant	1790	Tax L 1790:07
Wools, Wm.	Alexandria	Tax Charge	1795	Tax PP 1795:32
Wools, Wm.	Alexandria	Tax Charge	1796	Tax LP 1796:30
Wools, Wm.	Alexandria	Boarder	1808	1808(1):05A
Workman, Catherine	Arlington	Guard.	1816	WB2:120
Worle, Mourice, w1, constable	Alexandria	Head	1796	1796(3):4
Worner, Cragey	Alexandria	Resident	1800	1800(4):08B
Worner, Cragey (C)	Alexandria	Head	1800	1800(4):08A
Worner, Jane, labourer	Alexandria	Boarder	1800	1800(4):03A
Worrel, Morris	Alexandria	Tax Charge	1800	Tax PP 1800:46
Worrell, Elizabeth	Arlington	Will	1820	WB2:363; File #176A
Worrell, Maurice, carpenter	Alexandria	Head	1810	1810(1):02A
Worrell, Morris	Alexandria	Owner	1787	Tax L 1787:27
Worrell, Morris	Alexandria	Tax Charge	1787	Tax PP 1787:17
Worrell, Morris	Alexandria	Tax Charge	1789	Tax PP 1789:19
Worrell, Morris	Alexandria	Tax Charge	1796	Tax PP 1796:20
Worrell, Morris	Alexandria	Tax Charge	1798	Tax PP 1798:20
Worrell, Morris	Alexandria	Tax Charge	1799	Tax PP 1799:44
Worrell, Morris & wife, carpenter	Alexandria	Housekeeper	1799	1799(2):04A
Worrell, Morris, laborer	Alexandria	Housekeeper	1808	1808(1):01A
Worrell, Morris, plt.	Alexandria	Suit	1802	CRC:216
Worrell, Morris, Royal St.	Alexandria	Occupant	1787	Tax L 1787:27
Worrell, Morris, Royal St.	Alexandria	Occupant	1795	Tax L 1795:32
Worrell, Morris, Royal St.	Alexandria	Owner	1795	Tax L 1795:32(2)

NAME OR SUBJECT	LOCATION	TYPE	YEAR	REFERENCE(S)
Worrell, Morriss, nr. Royal St.	Alexandria	Occupant	1790	Tax L 1790:12
Worrell, Morriss, nr. Royal St.	Alexandria	Owner	1790	Tax L 1790:12(2)
Worrill, Morris	Alexandria	Tax Charge	1788	Tax PP 1788:17
Worsley, Joseph	Arlington	Defendant	1815	ACO:142, 144, 147
Wort, Christian & wife, brickmaker	Alexandria	Housekeeper	1799	1799(2):12A
Wray, John	Arlington	Admin.	1820	WB2:382
Wray, Thomas, in prison rules	Arlington	Insolvent	1806	ID3:222
Wray, Thomas, trustee	Arlington	Bond	1805	ID3:111
Wren, Daniel	Alexandria	Tax Charge	1796	Tax PP 1796:21
Wren, Danl.	Alexandria	Tax Charge	1798	Tax PP 1798:20
Wren, Edmund	Arlington	Apprentice	1828	OCR1822:166
Wren, John	Alexandria	Tithable +16	1789	Tax PP 1789:08
Wren, John	Alexandria	Tax Charge	1796	Tax PP 1796:20
Wren, John	Alexandria	Tax Charge	1798	Tax PP 1798:20
Wren, Richard & wife Susanna, plt.	Alexandria	Suit	1810	CRH:197
Wren, Solomon	Arlington	Ordinary	1805	OBL1(np)
Wrenn, Geo.	Alexandria	Boarder	1808	1808(1):01A
Wrenn, James, of Fairfax Co.	Alexandria	Deed	1815	CRL:490
Wrenn, John	Alexandria	Tithable +16	1790	Tax PP 1790:06
Wrenn, Richard	Alexandria	Tithable +21	1787	Tax PP 1787:15
Wrenn, Richard, in Alexandria Co.	Arlington	Ordinary	1822	OBL3(np)
Wrenn, William	Arlington	Appraisal	1875	WB9:382
Wright, Daniel, hatter	Alexandria	Housekeeper	1808	1808(1):05A
Wright, Danl. & wife, hatter	Alexandria	Boarder	1799	1799(2):04A
Wright, Danl. & wife, hatter	Alexandria	Housekeeper	1799	1799(2):18A
Wright, Danl., hatter	Alexandria	Head	1810	1810(1):03A
Wright, Elizabeth	Alexandria	Housekeeper	1808	1808(3):18A
Wright, George	Arlington	Apprentice	1803	OCR1801:117
Wright, Israel	Alexandria	Tax Charge	1788	Tax PP 1788:17
Wright, James	Alexandria	Tax Charge	1790	Tax PP 1790:16
Wright, James, Queen St.	Alexandria	Owner	1790	Tax L 1790:13
Wright, Richard, grantor	Arlington	Indenture D.	1827	ID:102
Wright, Richard, in jail	Arlington	Insolvent	1827	ID:101
Wright, Robert	Alexandria	Tax Charge	1799	Tax PP 1799:45
Wright, Robert	Alexandria	Tax Charge	1800	Tax PP 1800:47
Wright, Robt.	Alexandria	Tax Charge	1798	Tax PP 1798:19
Wright, Robt. & wife, blacksmith	Alexandria	Housekeeper	1799	1799(2):09A
Wright, T.C.	Arlington	Claim	1812	ACO:124
Wright, Thomas C.	Arlington	Defendant	1823	ACO:217
Wright, William	Alexandria	Tax Charge	1787	Tax PP 1787:17
Wright, William	Alexandria	Tax Charge	1788	Tax PP 1788:18
Wright, William	Alexandria	Tax Charge	1789	Tax PP 1789:20
Wright, William	Alexandria	Tax Charge	1790	Tax PP 1790:16
Wright, William	Alexandria	Tax Charge	1800	Tax PP 1800:46
Wright, William & wife, bricklayer	Alexandria	Head	1795	1795(4):04
Wright, William & wife, stone cutter	Alexandria	Head	1795	1795(4a):04
Wright, William, plt.	Alexandria	Suit	1802	CRB:132
Wright, William, Prince St.	Alexandria	Occupant	1787	Tax L 1787:16
Wright, William, Prince St.	Alexandria	Owner	1790	Tax L 1790:13
Wright, William, Wilks St.	Alexandria	Occupant	1787	Tax L 1787:09
Wright, William, Wilks St.	Alexandria	Owner	1790	Tax L 1790:13(2)
Wright, William, Wilks St.	Alexandria	Occupants	1790	Tax L 1790:13
Wright, Wm.	Alexandria	Tax Charge	1795	Tax PP 1795:32
Wright, Wm.	Alexandria	Tax Charge	1796	Tax LP 1796:30
Wright, Wm.	Alexandria	Tax Charge	1796	Tax PP 1796:20
Wright, Wm.	Alexandria	Tax Charge	1798	Tax PP 1798:19
Wright, Wm.	Alexandria	Tax Charge	1799	Tax PP 1799:45
Wright, Wm. & wife, bricklayer	Alexandria	Housekeeper	1799	1799(2):20A
Wright, Wm. & wife Ann	Alexandria	Resident	1800	1800(4):04B
Wright, Wm., mason	Alexandria	Head	1800	1800(4):04A
Wright, Wm., Water St.	Alexandria	Occupant	1795	Tax L 1795:30

NAME OR SUBJECT	LOCATION	TYPE	YEAR	REFERENCE(S)
Wright, Wm., Water St.	Alexandria	Owner	1795	Tax L 1795:30(2)
Wright, Zachariah, at his house	Arlington	Ordinary	1849	OBL6(np)
Wright, Zachariah, at his house	Arlington	Ordinary	1849	OBL6(np)
Wright, Zachariah, in Alexandria Co.	Arlington	Ordinary	1850	OBL6(np)
Wright, Zachariah, on Prince St.	Arlington	Ordinary	1845	OBL6(np)
Wright, Zachariah, on Prince St.	Arlington	Ordinary	1846	OBL6(np)
Wright, Zachariah, on Prince St.	Arlington	Ordinary	1847	OBL6(np)
Wrightman, Richd., taylor	Alexandria	Head	1810	1810(1):04A
Write, Daniel & wife Harriot	Alexandria	Resident	1800	1800(4):09B
Write, Daniel, hatter	Alexandria	Head	1800	1800(4):09A
Write, Robert & wife Sarah	Alexandria	Resident	1800	1800(4):05B
Write, Robert, smith	Alexandria	Head	1800	1800(4):05A
Wroe, Absalom	Alexandria	Tax Charge	1798	Tax PP 1798:19
Wroe, Absalom	Alexandria	Tax Charge	1799	Tax PP 1799:45
Wroe, Absalom	Alexandria	Tax Charge	1800	Tax PP 1800:46
Wroe, Absalom & wife, wharf builder	Alexandria	Housekeeper	1799	1799(2):07A
Wroe, Absalom, surety	Arlington	Bond	1806	ID3:210
Wroe, Absolom	Alexandria	Tax Charge	1790	Tax PP 1790:16
Wroe, Nancy	Arlington	Guard.	1817	WB2:180
Wroe, Richard, c/o Absolum	Arlington	Apprentice	1805	OCR1801:246
Wyld, John	Arlington	Will	1821	WB3:009; File #197A
Wyld, John	Arlington	Bond	1821	WB3:011
Wyld, John, of Liverpool	Arlington	Account	1822	LVA-LP
Wyley, Ephraim	Alexandria	Tax Charge	1795	Tax PP 1795:32
Wyley, Ephraim	Alexandria	Tax Charge	1796	Tax PP 1796:20
Wyley, John	Alexandria	Tax Charge	1796	Tax PP 1796:21
Wylie, Ephraim	Alexandria	Tax Charge	1788	Tax PP 1788:18
Wylie, Ephraim	Alexandria	Tax Charge	1799	Tax PP 1799:44
Wyllie, Ephraim	Alexandria	Tax Charge	1789	Tax PP 1789:20

NAME OR SUBJECT	LOCATION	TYPE	YEAR	REFERENCE(S)
Y				
Yates, Henrietta	Arlington	Will	1881	WB10:027; File #707A
Yates, John L., at his house	Arlington	Ordinary	1849	OBL6(np)
Yates, John L., on Union St.	Arlington	Ordinary	1846	OBL6(np)
Yates, John L., on Union St.	Arlington	Ordinary	1847	OBL6(np)
Yates, Letty	Alexandria	Head	1810	1810(4):08A
Yates, William	Arlington	Inventory	1826	AB6:252
Yates, William	Arlington	Admin. Bond	1849	ABB(np)
Yates, Wm., pump maker	Alexandria	Head	1810	1810(1):11A
Yearby, Francis	Alexandria	Tax Charge	1796	Tax LP 1796:32
Yeateman, Henry E.	Alexandria	Tax Charge	1796	Tax PP 1796:21
Yeates, Letty, washwoman	Alexandria	Housekeeper	1808	1808(4):24A
Yeates, William	Arlington	Admin.	1826	OCR1822:124a
Yeates, William	Arlington	Admin.	1826	WB3:263
Yeates, William	Arlington	Report C.	1852	LVA-LP
Yeates, William J.	Arlington	Apprentice	1827	OCR1822:140
Yeates, Wm., pump maker	Alexandria	Housekeeper	1808	1808(1):06A
Yeates [Yates], William	Arlington	Account	1827	AB6:436; LVA-LP
Yeatman, Hy. E.	Alexandria	Tax Charge	1798	Tax PP 1798:20
Yeatman, P.T.	Alexandria	Will	1897	WB2:211; LP
Yeaton, John	Arlington	Admin.	1808	WBC:031
Yeaton, Joshua	Arlington	Deposition	1806	ACR:011
Yeaton, Joshua	Arlington	Deposition	1806	ACR:029
Yeaton, Joshua	Alexandria	Boarder	1808	1808(3):19A
Yeaton, Joshua	Arlington	Defendant	1808	ACO:085, 087
Yeaton, Joshua	Arlington	Inventory	1834	LVA-LP
Yeaton, Joshua	Arlington	Will	1834	WB4:075; File #328A
Yeaton, Joshua	Arlington	Account	1835	AB7:180; LVA-LP
Yeaton, Joshua	Arlington	Account	1836	AB7:180; LVA-LP
Yeaton, Joshua	Arlington	Account	1840	AB8:261; LVA-LP
Yeaton, Joshua	Arlington	Account	1842	AB8:261
Yeaton, Matthew	Alexandria	Tax Charge	1798	Tax PP 1798:20
Yeaton, Sprague	Alexandria	Tax Charge	1799	Tax PP 1799:52
Yeaton, William	Alexandria	Tax Charge	1799	Tax PP 1799:52
Yeaton, William	Alexandria	Tax Charge	1800	Tax PP 1800:53
Yeaton, William	Alexandria	Deed	1803	CRH:502
Yeaton, William	Arlington	Witness	1806	ACR:002, 013
Yeaton, William	Arlington	Defendant	1807	ACO:073
Yeaton, William	Alexandria	Account B.	1807	CRH:447, 455
Yeaton, William	Arlington	Defendant	1808	ACO:092, 093
Yeaton, William	Arlington	Defendant	1808	ACO:087, 088, 090
Yeaton, William	Arlington	Defendant	1808	ACO:104, 105
Yeaton, William	Arlington	Defendant	1808	ACO:080, 083
Yeaton, William	Arlington	Defendant	1809	ACO:107, 108, 113
Yeaton, William	Arlington	Defendant	1810	ACO:114
Yeaton, William	Arlington	Defendant	1821	ACO:196
Yeaton, William	Arlington	Defendant	1824	ACO:237
Yeaton, William	Arlington	Defendant	1824	ACO:240
Yeaton, William	Arlington	Defendant	1825	ACO:255
Yeaton, William	Arlington	Defendant	1825	ACO:259
Yeaton, William	Arlington	Account	1852	WB6:043
Yeaton, William, applt.	Alexandria	Suit	1806	CRE:086
Yeaton, William C., notary public	Arlington	Appointment	1852	BB(np)
Yeaton, William C., notary public	Arlington	Appointment	1853	BB(np)
Yeaton, William C., notary public	Arlington	Appointment	1854	BB(np)
Yeaton, William, def.	Alexandria	Suit	1806	CRG:037
Yeaton, William, def.	Alexandria	Suit	1807	CRE:145
Yeaton, William, def.	Alexandria	Suit	1811	CRH:438
Yeaton, William, def.	Alexandria	Suit	1811	CRH:496
Yeaton, William, defendant	Arlington	Suit	1841	LSA:152
Yeaton, William, defendant	Arlington	Suit	1842	LSA:149

NAME OR SUBJECT	LOCATION	TYPE	YEAR	REFERENCE(S)
Yeaton, William, grantor	Arlington	Indenture D.	1816	ID2:386
Yeaton, William, in prison	Arlington	Insolvent	1816	ID2:383
Yeaton, William, merchant	Alexandria	Head	1810	1810(3):06A
Yeaton, William, owner	Arlington	Respondent	1806	ACO:053, 056, 063
Yeaton, William, owner	Arlington	Respondent	1806	ACO:065
Yeaton, William, owner	Arlington	Respondent	1806	ACO:070
Yeaton, Wm.	Alexandria	Reference	1808	1808(4):27B
Yeaton, Wm., merchant	Alexandria	Housekeeper	1808	1808(3):19A
Yeiser, E.	Alexandria	Land in Ga.	1799	CRD:134
Yoest, Jno., Jr.	Alexandria	Tax Charge	1795	Tax PP 1795:34
Yoest, Jno., Sr.	Alexandria	Tax Charge	1795	Tax PP 1795:34
Yoest, John	Alexandria	Tax Charge	1798	Tax PP 1798:20
Yoest, John, Fairfax St.	Alexandria	Occupant	1795	Tax L 1795:34
Yoest, John, Fairfax St.	Alexandria	Owner	1795	Tax L 1795:34
Yoest, John, Jr.	Alexandria	Tax Charge	1796	Tax PP 1796:21
Yoest, John, Sr.	Alexandria	Tax Charge	1796	Tax PP 1796:21
Yost, J., Fairfax St.	Alexandria	Occupant	1787	Tax L 1787:25
Yost, James	Arlington	Apprentice	1812	OCR1811:075
Yost, James	Arlington	Apprentice	1813	OCR1811:167
Yost, John	Alexandria	Owner	1787	Tax L 1787:27
Yost, John	Alexandria	Tax Charge	1787	Tax PP 1787:17
Yost, John	Alexandria	Tax Charge	1789	Tax PP 1789:21
Yost, John	Alexandria	Tax Charge	1790	Tax PP 1790:16
Yost, John	Alexandria	Tax Charge	1796	Tax LP 1796:32
Yost, John	Arlington	Account	1806	LVA-LP
Yost, John	Arlington	Inventory	1806	WBB:256
Yost, John	Arlington	Admin.	1806	WBB:245
Yost, John	Arlington	Sale	1806	WBB:252
Yost, John	Arlington	Account	1807	WBB:502; LVA-LP
Yost, John, Fairfax St.	Alexandria	Occupant	1787	Tax L 1787:27
Yost, John, Fairfax St.	Alexandria	Owner	1790	Tax L 1790:13
Yost, John, Fairfax St.	Alexandria	Occupants	1790	Tax L 1790:13
Yost, John, Jr.	Alexandria	Tithable +16	1789	Tax PP 1789:21
Yost, John, Jr.	Alexandria	Tithable +16	1790	Tax PP 1790:16
Yost, Maria, n/o William Simpson	Arlington	Apprentice	1814	OCR1811:237
You, John C., at his house	Arlington	Ordinary	1831	ODL4(np)
Young, Ann	Arlington	Guard.	1809	WBC:315
Young, Barnabas, segar maker	Alexandria	Head	1810	1810(1):08A
Young, Charles	Alexandria	Tithable +16	1790	Tax PP 1790:16
Young, Charles	Alexandria	Tax Charge	1796	Tax LP 1796:32
Young, Chas.	Alexandria	Tax Charge	1798	Tax PP 1798:20
Young, Cornelius	Arlington	Account	1878	WB9:522
Young, David	Alexandria	Owner	1787	Tax L 1787:27
Young, David	Alexandria	Tax Charge	1787	Tax PP 1787:17
Young, David	Alexandria	Tax Charge	1788	Tax PP 1788:18
Young, David	Alexandria	Tax Charge	1789	Tax PP 1789:21
Young, David	Alexandria	Tax Charge	1790	Tax PP 1790:16
Young, David, Capt. of Brig Mary	Alexandria	Deposition	1805	CRF:270
Young, David, Royal St.	Alexandria	Occupant	1787	Tax L 1787:27
Young, David, Royal St.	Alexandria	Occupants	1790	Tax L 1790:13
Young, David, Royal St.	Alexandria	Owner	1790	Tax L 1790:13
Young, Elizabeth	Arlington	Admin.	1812	WB1:197
Young, Elizabeth, c/o Robert	Arlington	Guard.	1822	WB3:052
Young, Elizabeth Mary	Arlington	Guard.	1825	WB3:052, 152
Young, Elizabeth Mary, c/o Robert	Arlington	Guard.	1825	OCR1822:082a
Young, Elizabeth, sempstress	Alexandria	Housekeeper	1808	1808(3):22A
Young, Henry	Alexandria	Tax Charge	1799	Tax PP 1799:52
Young, Henry	Arlington	Apprentice	1822	OCR1822:027
Young, Henry & wife (C), labourer	Alexandria	Housekeeper	1799	1799(2):10A
Young, James	Alexandria	Tax Charge	1787	Tax PP 1787:17
Young, James	Alexandria	Tax Charge	1788	Tax PP 1788:18

NAME OR SUBJECT	LOCATION	TYPE	YEAR	REFERENCE(S)
Young, James	Alexandria	Tax Charge	1789	Tax PP 1789:21
Young, James	Alexandria	Tax Charge	1796	Tax LP 1796:32
Young, James	Alexandria	Tax Charge	1796	Tax PP 1796:21
Young, James	Alexandria	Tax Charge	1798	Tax PP 1798:20
Young, James	Alexandria	Tax Charge	1799	Tax PP 1799:52
Young, James	Alexandria	Tax Charge	1800	Tax PP 1800:53
Young, James	Arlington	Ordinary	1802	OBL1(np)
Young, James	Arlington	Ordinary	1805	OBL1(np)
Young, James	Arlington	Ordinary	1806	OBL2(np)
Young, James	Arlington	Ordinary	1807	OBL2(np)
Young, James	Arlington	Ordinary	1808	OBL2(np)
Young, James	Arlington	Ordinary	1809	OBL2(np)
Young, James	Arlington	Ordinary	1810	OBL2(np)
Young, James	Arlington	Will P.	1822	OCR1822:023a
Young, James	Arlington	Will	1822	WB3:066
Young, James, blacksmith	Alexandria	Head	1810	1810(2):06A
Young, James, def.	Alexandria	Suit	1806	CRE:082
Young, James E.	Arlington	Will	1895	WB10:308; File #768A
Young, James, plt., Brig *Liberty*	Alexandria	Suit	1805	CRF:218
Young, James Robert	Arlington	Guard.	1825	WB3:152
Young, James Robert, c/o Robert	Arlington	Guard.	1825	OCR1822:082a
Young, James, tavern license	Alexandria	Housekeeper	1808	1808(2):16A
Young, Jno., Union St.	Alexandria	Occupant	1787	Tax L 1787:11
Young, John	Alexandria	Tax Charge	1795	Tax PP 1795:34
Young, John	Alexandria	Tax Charge	1796	Tax LP 1796:32
Young, John	Alexandria	Tax Charge	1796	Tax PP 1796:21
Young, John	Alexandria	Tax Charge	1799	Tax PP 1799:52
Young, John	Alexandria	Tax Charge	1800	Tax PP 1800:53
Young, John	Arlington	Defendant	1809	ACO:108
Young, John	Arlington	Defendant	1812	ACO:126
Young, John	Arlington	Defendant	1817	ACO:149
Young, John	Arlington	Admin.	1819	WB2:329
Young, John, b. baker	Alexandria	Housekeeper	1808	1808(2):15A
Young, John, def.	Alexandria	Suit	1811	CRI:116
Young, John, grantor	Arlington	Indenture D.	1813	ID2:209
Young, John, in jail bounds	Arlington	Insolvent	1813	ID2:207
Young, John M.	Arlington	Will	1896	WB10:313; File #769A
Young, John, merchant	Alexandria	Head	1810	1810(2):08A
Young, John T., at his house	Arlington	Ordinary	1849	OBL6(np)
Young, John, w(1), baker	Alexandria	Head	1796	1796(3):6
Young, Josiah	Arlington	Apprentice	1814	OCR1811:217
Young, Nancy, Royal St.	Alexandria	Occupant	1795	Tax L 1795:34
Young, Nancy, Royal St.	Alexandria	Owner	1795	Tax L 1795:34
Young, Nicholas, baker	Alexandria	Head	1810	1810(1):02A
Young, Rebecca	Arlington	Admin.	1819	WB2:302
Young, Robert	Alexandria	Tax Charge	1796	Tax LP 1796:32
Young, Robert	Alexandria	Tax Charge	1796	Tax PP 1796:21
Young, Robert	Arlington	Plaintiff	1802	PA:222
Young, Robert	Alexandria	Deed	1803	CRH:220, 223
Young, Robert	Arlington	Defendant	1807	ACO:073
Young, Robert	Alexandria	Account B.	1807	CRF:347
Young, Robert	Alexandria	Coffee	1807	CRH:461
Young, Robert	Arlington	Defendant	1808	ACO:104, 105
Young, Robert	Arlington	Defendant	1808	ACO:092, 093
Young, Robert	Arlington	Defendant	1808	ACO:080, 083
Young, Robert	Arlington	Defendant	1808	ACO:087, 088, 090
Young, Robert	Arlington	Defendant	1809	ACO:108
Young, Robert	Arlington	Defendant	1810	ACO:114
Young, Robert	Arlington	Commission	1814	WB2:001
Young, Robert	Arlington	Defendant	1821	ACO:196
Young, Robert	Arlington	Will P.	1825	OCR1822:097

NAME OR SUBJECT	LOCATION	TYPE	YEAR	REFERENCE(S)
Young, Robert	Arlington	Will	1825	WB3:187; File #235A
Young, Robert & Co., plt.	Alexandria	Suit	1801	CRB:023
Young, Robert, complt.	Alexandria	Suit	1807	CRF:203, 340
Young, Robert, def.	Alexandria	Suit	1805	CRE:058
Young, Robert, def.	Alexandria	Suit	1807	CRE:149
Young, Robert, def.	Alexandria	Suit	1807	CRG:211
Young, Robert, def.	Alexandria	Suit	1821	CRK:321
Young, Robert, Fairfax St.	Alexandria	Occupant	1795	Tax L 1795:11
Young, Robert, orphans of	Arlington	Guard.	1825	OCR1822:082a
Young, Robert, owner	Arlington	Respondent	1806	ACO:070
Young, Robert, plt.	Alexandria	Suit	1809	CRH:423
Young, Robert, plt.	Alexandria	Suit	1811	CRH:438
Young, Robert, Union St.	Alexandria	Occupant	1795	Tax L 1795:34
Young, Roberta Eugenia	Arlington	Guard.	1825	WB3:152
Young, Roberta Eugenia, c/o Robert	Arlington	Guard.	1825	OCR1822:082a
Young, Robt.	Alexandria	Tax Charge	1795	Tax PP 1795:34
Young, Robt.	Alexandria	Tax Charge	1798	Tax PP 1798:20
Young, Robt.	Alexandria	Tax Charge	1799	Tax PP 1799:52
Young, Robt. & Co., Union St.	Alexandria	Occupant	1795	Tax L 1795:18
Young, Robt., late merchant	Alexandria	Housekeeper	1808	1808(3):20A
Young, Robt., merchant	Alexandria	Head	1810	1810(3):04A
Young, Robt., Union St.	Alexandria	Occupant	1795	Tax L 1795:05
Young, Robt., Union St.	Alexandria	Owner	1795	Tax L 1795:34
Young, Robt., Water St.	Alexandria	Occupant	1795	Tax L 1795:28
Young, Thomas	Alexandria	Owner	1787	Tax L 1787:27
Young, Thomas	Alexandria	Tithable +16	1788	Tax PP 1788:02
Young, Thomas, Fayette Co. Ky.	Alexandria	Plat	1784	CRH:391
Young, William	Alexandria	Tax Charge	1787	Tax PP 1787:17
Young, William	Alexandria	Tax Charge	1788	Tax PP 1788:18
Young, William	Alexandria	Tax Charge	1789	Tax PP 1789:21
Young, William	Alexandria	Tax Charge	1790	Tax PP 1790:16
Young, William	Alexandria	Tax Charge	1790	Tax PP 1790:16
Young, William	Alexandria	Tax Charge	1796	Tax PP 1796:21
Young, William	Arlington	Admin.	1818	WB2:219
Young, William & James	Arlington	P. of Atty.	1822	WB3:096
Young, William, Prince St.	Alexandria	Occupant	1790	Tax L 1790:06
Young, William, Queen St.	Alexandria	Occupant	1790	Tax L 1790:04
Young, William Smith	Arlington	Guard.	1825	WB3:152
Young, William Smith, c/o Robert	Arlington	Guard.	1825	OCR1822:082a
Young, Wm.	Alexandria	Tax Charge	1795	Tax PP 1795:34
Young, Wm.	Alexandria	Tax Charge	1796	Tax LP 1796:32
Young, Wm.	Alexandria	Boarder	1808	1808(2):16A
Young, Wm., Princess St.	Alexandria	Occupant	1795	Tax L 1795:12
Younge, Wm. Thomas, b. Co. Down	Arlington	Alien Entry	1819	RA:16/01/19
Youngs, Geo.	Alexandria	Tax Charge	1796	Tax LP 1796:32
Youngs, Geo.	Alexandria	Boarder	1799	1799(2):15A
Youngs, Geo.	Alexandria	Boarder	1799	1799(2):08A
Youngs, Geo., atty. at law	Alexandria	Head	1810	1810(2):02A
Youngs, Geo., lawyer	Alexandria	Housekeeper	1808	1808(1):01A
Youngs, Geo., lawyer	Alexandria	Housekeeper	1808	1808(2):15A
Youngs, George	Alexandria	Tax Charge	1795	Tax PP 1795:34
Youngs, George	Alexandria	Tax Charge	1796	Tax PP 1796:21
Youngs, George	Alexandria	Tax Charge	1798	Tax PP 1798:20
Youngs, George	Alexandria	Tax Charge	1799	Tax PP 1799:52
Youngs, George	Alexandria	Tax Charge	1800	Tax PP 1800:53
Youngs, George, def.	Alexandria	Suit	1807	CRG:211
Youst, John	Alexandria	Tax Charge	1788	Tax PP 1788:18
Youst, John & wife, blacksmith	Alexandria	Head	1795	1795(4):07
Yundt & Brown, plt.	Alexandria	Suit	1803	CRD:086

NAME OR SUBJECT	LOCATION	TYPE	YEAR	REFERENCE(S)
Z				
Zaeb, Wm., b. Bubach, Wutemberg	Arlington	Alien Entry	1820	RA:11/01/20
Zane, Elisebeth	Alexandria	Serv./Appr.	1800	1800(4):04B
Zane, Elisebeth	Alexandria	Resident	1800	1800(4):04B
Zane, Peter	Alexandria	Serv./Appr.	1800	1800(4):04B
Zane, Peter	Arlington	Apprentice	1803	OCR1801:077
Zane, Samuel	Alexandria	Tax Charge	1787	Tax PP 1787:17
Zane, Simon	Alexandria	Tax Charge	1788	Tax PP 1788:18
Zane, Simon	Alexandria	Tax Charge	1789	Tax PP 1789:21
Zantzinger, William P. (ship)	Arlington	Account	1816	LVA-LP
Zelefro, Andrew & wife, taylor	Alexandria	Housekeeper	1799	1799(2):05A
Zellipo, Andrew	Alexandria	Tax Charge	1796	Tax PP 1796:21
Zellipo, Andrew	Alexandria	Tax Charge	1799	Tax PP 1799:52
Zellipo, Andw.	Alexandria	Tax Charge	1798	Tax PP 1798:20
Zepernick, Maryann	Arlington	Will	1810	WBC:446; File #050A
Zepernick, Maryann	Arlington	Bond	1810	WBC:447
Zillipo, Andw.	Alexandria	Tax Charge	1795	Tax PP 1795:34
Zimmerman, Adam	Arlington	Guard.	1817	WB2:217
Zimmerman, Eliza	Arlington	Guard.	1825	WB3:174
Zimmerman, Henry	Alexandria	Tax Charge	1795	Tax PP 1795:34
Zimmerman, Henry	Alexandria	Tax Charge	1796	Tax LP 1796:32
Zimmerman, Henry	Alexandria	Tax Charge	1796	Tax PP 1796:21
Zimmerman, Henry	Alexandria	Tax Charge	1799	Tax PP 1799:52
Zimmerman, Henry	Arlington	Admin.	1807	WBB:408
Zimmerman, Henry	Arlington	Account	1808	WBC:089, 435; LVA-LP
Zimmerman, Henry	Arlington	Account	1810	LVA-LP
Zimmerman, Henry, a slaughter house	Arlington	Defendant	1802	PA:013
Zimmerman, Henry, Washington St.	Alexandria	Occupant	1795	Tax L 1795:34
Zimmerman, Henry, Washington St.	Alexandria	Owner	1795	Tax L 1795:34
Zimmerman, Hy.	Alexandria	Tax Charge	1798	Tax PP 1798:20
Zimmerman, Jacob	Alexandria	Tax Charge	1796	Tax LP 1796:15
Zimmerman, Mary A.E.	Alexandria	Will	1875	WB1:150; LP
Zimmerman, Reuben	Arlington	Will	1859	WB7:444; File #568A
Zimmerman, Tobias	Alexandria	Tax Charge	1787	Tax PP 1787:17
Zimmerman, Tobias	Alexandria	Tax Charge	1789	Tax PP 1789:21
Zimmerman, Tobias	Alexandria	Tax Charge	1790	Tax PP 1790:16
Zimmerman, Tobias, Princess St.	Alexandria	Occupant	1787	Tax L 1787:09
Zimmerman, Tobs.	Alexandria	Tax Charge	1788	Tax PP 1788:18
Zimmerson, Samuel, b/o John	Arlington	Apprentice	1813	OCR1811:197

NAME OR SUBJECT	LOCATION	TYPE	YEAR	REFERENCE(S)
NO SURNAME				
[ ], Adam (C)	Alexandria	Tax Charge	1800	Tax PP 1800:01
[ ], Alexander (C)	Arlington	Crime	1799	OT:11/12/1799
[ ], Ann	Alexandria	Boarder	1800	1800(4):13A
[ ], Anna (C), washwoman	Alexandria	Housekeeper	1808	1808(1):09A
[ ], Armistead (C)	Arlington	Apprentice	1815	OCR1811:328
[ ], August (French)	Alexandria	Tax Charge	1795	Tax PP 1795:01
[ ], Betty	Alexandria	Serv./Appt.	1800	1800(4):15B
[ ], Betty, labourrer	Alexandria	Boarder	1800	1800(4):07A
[ ], Birster (C)	Alexandria	Tax Charge	1800	Tax PP 1800:02
[ ], Black Betty (C), washwoman	Alexandria	Housekeeper	1808	1808(2):14A
[ ], Bristol (C)	Arlington	Crime	1798	OT:05/03/1799
[ ], Cato (C), laborer	Alexandria	Housekeeper	1808	1808(1):09A
[ ], Cattey Nogrow	Alexandria	Head	1800	1800(4):11A
[ ], Catty Negrow	Alexandria	Resident	1800	1800(4):11B
[ ], Celia (C), washwoman	Alexandria	Housekeeper	1808	1808(4):28A
[ ], Charles	Alexandria	Resident	1800	1800(4):11B
[ ], Charles (C)	Alexandria	Tax Charge	1799	Tax PP 1799:07
[ ], Charles (C), measurrer	Alexandria	Head	1800	1800(4):11A
[ ], Charles, a Frenchman	Alexandria	Boarder	1808	1808(1):01A
[ ], Charlotte	Alexandria	Resident	1800	1800(4):09B
[ ], Daphnee (C), washwoman	Alexandria	Housekeeper	1808	1808(3):18A
[ ], Elizabeth, labourrer	Alexandria	Boarder	1800	1800(4):06A
[ ], Elizabeth, sempster	Alexandria	Boarder	1800	1800(4):09A
[ ], Ellick (C), laborer, of B. Howard	Alexandria	Housekeeper	1808	1808(4):29A
[ ], Frank (C)	Alexandria	Boarder	1808	1808(1):03B
[ ], French Jack (C)	Alexandria	Boarder	1808	1808(1):04B
[ ], George (C)	Arlington	Apprentice	1802	OCR1801:034
[ ], Hannah (C), Pitt St.	Alexandria	Occupant	1790	Tax L 1790:12
[ ], Harris (C)	Alexandria	Boarder	1808	1808(3):23B
[ ], Harry (C)	Alexandria	Boarder	1808	1808(1):06B
[ ], Hetty, labourrer	Alexandria	Boarder	1800	1800(4):13A
[ ], Ishmael, (C) of Dennis Ramsay	Arlington	Crime	1794	OT:16/04/1794
[ ], Israel (C)	Alexandria	Boarder	1808	1808(1):01B
[ ], Israel (C)	Alexandria	Boarder	1808	1808(2):15B
[ ], Janney, (C) of Penelope French	Arlington	Crime	1794	OT:16/04/1794
[ ], Jerry (C)	Alexandria	Boarder	1808	1808(1):03B
[ ], Jesse (M)	Arlington	Apprentice	1804	OCR1801:178
[ ], Joseph, seemen	Alexandria	Head	1800	1800(4):12A
[ ], Katy (C), washwoman	Alexandria	Housekeeper	1808	1808(1):09A
[ ], Kelley, labourer	Alexandria	Boarder	1800	1800(4):13A
[ ], Leonard (C)	Alexandria	Tax Charge	1796	Tax PP 1796:10
[ ], London (C)	Alexandria	Tax Charge	1788	Tax PP 1788:10
[ ], London (C)	Alexandria	Tax Charge	1789	Tax PP 1789:11
[ ], London (C)	Alexandria	Tax Charge	1790	Tax PP 1790:09
[ ], London, a pauper, plt.	Alexandria	Suit	1805	CRF:102
[ ], Lotty (C)	Alexandria	Housekeeper	1808	1808(3):23A
[ ], Lucy, labourrer	Alexandria	Boarder	1800	1800(4):09A
[ ], Lukey (C)	Alexandria	Boarder	1799	1799(2):15A
[ ], Lukey (C)	Alexandria	Boarder	1799	1799(2):15A
[ ], Lydia (C)	Alexandria	Boarder	1799	1799(2):15A
[ ], Mary Ann (C), sempstress	Alexandria	Housekeeper	1808	1808(4):29A
[ ], Mary, labourrer	Alexandria	Boarder	1800	1800(4):09A
[ ], Milly (C), washwoman	Alexandria	Housekeeper	1808	1808(1):07A
[ ], Monaky (C), washwoman	Alexandria	Housekeeper	1808	1808(1):07A
[ ], Nancey, labourrer	Alexandria	Boarder	1800	1800(4):13A
[ ], Negro Cato, inspector	Alexandria	Head	1810	1810(4):06A
[ ], Norris (C)	Arlington	Apprentice	1816	OCR1811:335
[ ], Old Cato, labourer	Alexandria	Head	1810	1810(1):07A

NAME OR SUBJECT	LOCATION	TYPE	YEAR	REFERENCE(S)
[ ], Phebe & Nancy (C)	Alexandria	Boarder	1799	1799(2):17A
[ ], Polly, nr. Fairfax St.	Alexandria	Occupant	1790	Tax L 1790:02
[ ], Rachael (C), washwoman	Alexandria	Housekeeper	1808	1808(2):11A
[ ], Rachel (C), washwoman	Alexandria	Housekeeper	1808	1808(1):09A
[ ], Randall (C), laborer	Alexandria	Housekeeper	1808	1808(3):20A
[ ], Robt. (C)	Alexandria	Boarder	1808	1808(1):08B
[ ], Rose (C), washwoman	Alexandria	Housekeeper	1808	1808(1):09A
[ ], Rosetta, Dr. Stewart's, washwoman	Alexandria	Housekeeper	1808	1808(1):03A
[ ], Sall (C)	Alexandria	Housekeeper	1808	1808(2):17A
[ ], Sam (C)	Alexandria	Boarder	1808	1808(4):25B
[ ], Sarah (C)	Alexandria	Boarder	1799	1799(2):18A
[ ], Sarah (M), washer woman	Alexandria	Housekeeper	1799	1799(2):07A
[ ], Silvey	Alexandria	Resident	1800	1800(4):11B
[ ], Susanah	Alexandria	Resident	1800	1800(4):09B
[ ], Susaner, labourrer	Alexandria	Boarder	1800	1800(4):09A
[ ], Susaner, labourrer	Alexandria	Boarder	1800	1800(4):12A
[ ], Susannah, visiter	Alexandria	Boarder	1800	1800(4):09A
[ ], Sylvia (C)	Alexandria	Housekeeper	1808	1808(1):04A
[ ], Sylvia & Nanny (C)	Alexandria	Housekeeper	1799	1799(2):13A
[ ], Tom (C)	Arlington	Hanged	1797	OT:27/02/1797
[ ], Violet & Hannah (C)	Alexandria	Housekeeper	1799	1799(2):17A
[ ], Violett (C), washwoman	Alexandria	Housekeeper	1808	1808(1):05A
[ ], Walter (C)	Alexandria	Boarder	1808	1808(3):20B
[ ], Wm. (C)	Alexandria	Boarder	1808	1808(3):23B
[ ], [blank] (C), Water St.	Alexandria	Occupant	1795	Tax L 1795:05

Heritage Books by Wesley E. Pippenger:

Alexander Family: Migrations from Maryland

Alexandria (Arlington) County, Virginia Death Records, 1853–1896

Alexandria City and Arlington County, Virginia Records Index: Vol. 1

Alexandria City and Arlington County, Virginia Records Index: Vol. 2

Alexandria County, Virginia Marriage Records, 1853–1895

Alexandria, Virginia Marriage Index, January 10, 1893 to August 31, 1905

Alexandria, Virginia Marriages, 1870–1892

Alexandria, Virginia Town Lots, 1749–1801
Together with the Proceedings of the Board of Trustees, 1749–1780

Alexandria, Virginia Wills, Administrations and Guardianships, 1786–1800

Alexandria, Virginia 1808 Census (Wards 1, 2, 3, and 4)

Alexandria, Virginia Death Records, 1863–1896

Alexandria, Virginia Hustings Court Orders, Volume 1, 1780–1787

Allen-Lewis and Davison-Ridgeway Families: Migrations to Missouri

Connections and Separations: Divorce, Name Change and Other
Genealogical Tidbits from the Acts of the Virginia General Assembly

Daily National Intelligencer *Index to Deaths, 1855–1870*

Daily National Intelligencer, *Washington, District of Columbia*
Marriages and Deaths Notices (January 1, 1851 to December 30, 1854)

Dead People on the Move: Reconstruction of the Georgetown Presbyterian
Burying Ground, Holmead's (Western) Burying Ground, and
Other Removals in the District of Columbia

Death Notices from Richmond, Virginia Newspapers, 1841–1853

District of Columbia Ancestors:
A Guide to Records of the District of Columbia

District of Columbia Death Records:
August 1, 1874–July 31, 1879

District of Columbia Foreign Deaths, 1888–1923

District of Columbia Guardianship Index, 1802–1928

District of Columbia Interments (Index to Deaths)
January 1, 1855 to July 31, 1874

District of Columbia Marriage Licenses, Register 1: 1811–1858

District of Columbia Marriage Licenses, Register 2: 1858–1870

District of Columbia Marriage Records Index
June 28, 1877 to October 19, 1885: Marriage Record Books 11 to 20
Wesley E. Pippenger and Dorothy S. Provine

District of Columbia Marriage Records Index
October 20, 1885 to January 20, 1892: Marriage Record Books 21 to 30

District of Columbia Marriage Records Index
January 20, 1892 to August 30, 1896: Marriage Record Books 31 to 40

District of Columbia Marriage Records Index
August 31, 1896 to December 17, 1900: Marriage Record Books 41 to 65

District of Columbia Probate Records, 1801–1852

District of Columbia: Original Land Owners, 1791–1800

Early Church Records of Alexandria City and Fairfax County, Virginia

Essex County, Virginia Death Records, 1856–1896

Essex County, Virginia Deed Abstracts, 1786–1805, Deed Books 33 to 36

Essex County, Virginia Deed Abstracts, 1805–1819, Deed Books 37 to 39

Essex County, Virginia Guardianship and Orphans Records, 1707–1888:
A Descriptive Index

Essex County, Virginia Buildings in Photographs

Essex County, Virginia Marriage Bonds, 1804–1850, Annotated

Essex County, Virginia Marriage Records, Transcripts of Consents Affidavits,
Minister Returns, and Marriage Licenses, Volume 1: 1850–1872
Suzanne P. Derieux and Wesley E. Pippenger

Essex County, Virginia Marriage Records, Transcripts of Consents Affidavits,
Minister Returns, and Marriage Licenses, Volume 2: 1873–1883
Suzanne P. Derieux and Wesley E. Pippenger

Essex County, Virginia Newspaper Notices, 1738–1938

Essex County, Virginia Newspaper Notices, Vol. 2, 1735–1952

Essex County, Virginia Will Abstracts, 1751–1842
and Estate Records Index, 1751–1799

Georgetown, District of Columbia 1850 Federal Population Census
(Schedule I) and 1853 Directory of Residents of Georgetown

Georgetown, District of Columbia Marriage and Death Notices, 1801–1838

Husbands and Wives Associated with Early Alexandria, Virginia
(and the Surrounding Area), 3rd Edition, Revised

Index to District of Columbia Estates, 1801–1929

Index to District of Columbia Land Records, 1792–1817

Index to Virginia Estates, 1800–1865:
Volumes 4, 5 and 6

John Alexander, a Northern Neck Proprietor, His Family, Friends and Kin

Legislative Petitions of Alexandria, 1778–1861

Marriage and Death Notices from Alexandria, Virginia Newspapers, 1784–1852

Pippenger and Pittenger Families

Proceedings of the Orphan's Court, Washington County,
District of Columbia, 1801–1808

Richmond County, Virginia Marriage Records, 1854–1890, Annotated

Tappahannock and Essex County, Virginia in Early Photographs

The Georgetown Courier *Marriage and Death Notices:*
Georgetown, District of Columbia, November 18, 1865 to May 6, 1876

The Georgetown Directory for the Year 1830: to which is appended,
a Short Description of the Churches, Public Institutions, and the
Original Charter of Georgetown, and Extracts of the Laws
Pertaining to the Chesapeake and Ohio Canal Company

The Virginia Gazette and Alexandria Advertiser:
Volume 1, September 3, 1789 to November 11, 1790

The Virginia Journal and Alexandria Advertiser:
Volume I (February 5, 1784 to January 27, 1785)

Volume II (February 3, 1785 to January 26, 1786)

Volume III (March 2, 1786 to January 25, 1787)

Volume IV (February 8, 1787 to May 21, 1789)

The Washington and Georgetown Directory of 1853

Tombstone Inscriptions of Alexandria, Volumes 1–5

Virginia's Lost Wills: An Index

Westmoreland County, Virginia Marriage Records, 1850–1880, Annotated

www.ingramcontent.com/pod-product-compliance
Lightning Source LLC
LaVergne TN
LVHW020518100826
845148LV00010B/1267

* 9 7 8 1 5 8 5 4 9 7 1 8 8 *